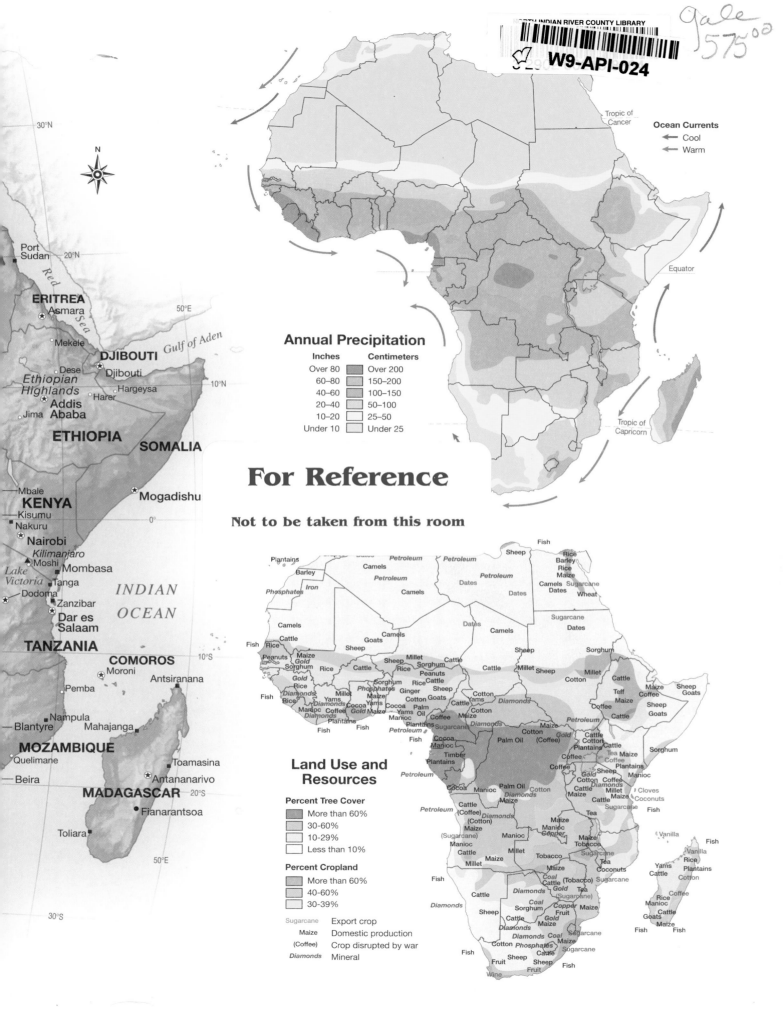

30°N

N

Port
Sudan 20°N

ERITREA
★ Asmara

Mekele
DJIBOUTI
Dese ★ Djibouti

*Ethiopian
Highlands*
★ Addis
Harer
Jima Ababa

ETHIOPIA

SOMALIA

Mbale
KENYA
Kisumu
Nakuru

Nairobi
Kilimanjaro
Moshi ★ Mombasa
*Lake
Victoria* Tanga
Dodoma
Zanzibar
Dar es
Salaam

TANZANIA

COMOROS
Moroni
Antsiranana

Pemba

Nampula
Blantyre Mahajanga

MOZAMBIQUE
Quelimane

Beira

MADAGASCAR
Fianarantsoa

Toliara

30°N
50°E
*Red
Sea*
Gulf of Aden
10°N

0°

*INDIAN
OCEAN*

10°S

Antananarivo
Toamasina

20°S

50°E

30°S

Annual Precipitation

Inches	Centimeters
Over 80	Over 200
60–80	150–200
40–60	100–150
20–40	50–100
10–20	25–50
Under 10	Under 25

Tropic of
Cancer

Ocean Currents
← Cool
← Warm

Equator

Tropic of
Capricorn

For Reference

Not to be taken from this room

Land Use and Resources

Percent Tree Cover
More than 60%
30-60%
10-29%
Less than 10%

Percent Cropland
More than 60%
40-60%
30-39%

Sugarcane	Export crop
Maize	Domestic production
(Coffee)	Crop disrupted by war
Diamonds	Mineral

NEW ENCYCLOPEDIA OF
AFRICA

NEW ENCYCLOPEDIA OF

AFRICA

Volume 1

ʿAbd al-Qādir–Cummings-John

John Middleton

EDITOR IN CHIEF

Joseph C. Miller

EDITOR

CHARLES SCRIBNER'S SONS
An imprint of Thomson Gale, a part of The Thomson Corporation

THOMSON
™
GALE

Detroit • New York • San Francisco • New Haven, Conn. • Waterville, Maine • London

THOMSON

GALE

New Encyclopedia of Africa
John Middleton, Editor in Chief
Joseph C. Miller, Editor

© 2008 The Gale Group

Thomson, Star Logo, and Charles Scribner's Sons are trademarks and Gale is a registered trademark used herein under license.

For more information, contact
Charles Scribner's Sons
An imprint of The Gale Group
27500 Drake Rd.
Farmington Hills, MI 48331-3535
Or you can visit our Internet site at
http://www.gale.com

NEW ENCYCLOPEDIA OF AFRICA

John Middleton, editor in chief ; Joseph C. Miller, editor.
    p. cm.
        Includes bibliographical references and index.
        ISBN 978-0-684-31454-9 (set : alk. paper)
        ISBN 978-0-684-31455-6 (vol. 1 : alk. paper)
        ISBN 978-0-684-31456-3 (vol. 2 : alk. paper)
        ISBN 978-0-684-31457-0 (vol. 3 : alk. paper)
        ISBN 978-0-684-31458-7 (vol. 4 : alk. paper)
        ISBN 978-0-684-31459-4 (vol. 5 : alk. paper)
        Africa—Encyclopedias. Middleton, John, 1921-
    Miller, Joseph Calder.
    Title.

DT2.N48 2008
960.03—dc22

2007021746

ISBN-10:

0-684-31454-1 (set)
0-684-31455-X (vol. 1)
0-684-31456-8 (vol. 2)
0-684-31457-6 (vol. 3)
0-684-31458-4 (vol. 4)
0-684-31459-2 (vol. 5)

This title is also available as an e-book.
ISBN-13: 978-0-684-31557-7; ISBN-10: 0-684-31557-2
Contact your Gale representative for ordering information.

Printed in the United States of America
10 9 8 7 6 5 4 3 2 1

Joseph Harris
Howard University
Historian

Goran Hyden
University of Florida
Political scientist,
East Africa

Ali Mazrui
State University of New York,
Binghamton
Political scientist,
East Africa

Sally Falk Moore
Harvard University
Anthropologist, lawyer, East
Africa

V. Y. Mudimbe
Duke University
Philosopher, novelist, poet,
Central Africa

Roland Oliver
School of Oriental and African
Studies, University of London
Historian

Abdul Sheriff
Zanzibar Indian Ocean Research
Institute
Historian, East Africa

Wim Van Binsbergen
University of Leiden,
Netherlands
Anthropologist, philosopher,
Southern Africa

Jan Vansina
University of Wisconsin
Historian, Central Africa

CONSULTANTS

Kelly Askew
University of Michigan
Anthropologist, musicologist,
East Africa

Karin Barber
University of Birmingham
Historian, West Africa

Julia Clancy-Smith
University of Arizona
Historian, North Africa

Mamadou Diouf
Columbia University
Anthropologist, historian, West
Africa

Toyin Falola
University of Texas, Austin
Historian, West Africa

Richard Fardon
School of Oriental and African
Studies, University of London
Anthropologist, Central Africa

Gillian Feeley-Harnik
University of Michigan
Anthropologist, Madagascar

Peter Geschiere
University of Amsterdam
Anthropologist, Central Africa

Michelle Gilbert
Sarah Lawrence College
Art historian, West Africa

Jane Guyer
Johns Hopkins University
Historian, West Africa

Andrew Hill
Yale University
Paleontologist, East Africa

Michael Lambek
University of Toronto
Anthropologist, East Africa

George Nelson
University of Liverpool
Medicine, East/West Africa

Kimani Njogu
Twaweza Communications,
Nairobi
Director, linguist, East Africa

John Peel
School of Oriental and African
Studies, University of
London
Anthropologist, West Africa

Paul Richards
Wageningen University and
Research Centre,
Netherlands
Geographer, West Africa

Janet Roitman
University of Paris
Anthropologist,
Central Africa

Parker Shipton
Boston University
Anthropologist, East Africa

Thomas Spear
University of Wisconsin
Historian, East Africa

Dorothy Woodson
Yale University
Librarian, Africa

EDITORIAL AND PRODUCTION STAFF

Project Editor
Ken Wachsberger

Contributing Editors
Jaime Lieber, Carol Schwartz

Manuscript Editors and Proofreaders
Paul Greenland, Jessica Hornik-Evans, John Krol, Amy Loerch-Strumolo, Gina
Misiroglu, Sarah O'Mahen, Kathleen Roy, Kathy Wilson

Editorial Support
Kari Bethel, Justine Ciovacco, Katrina Couch, Angela Doolin, Sara Teller,
Jennifer Wisinski

Editorial Technical Support
Mark Drouillard, Joshua Kondek, Paul Lewon, Mark Springer

Translators
Paul Ellis, Alfonso Illingworth-Rico

Indexer
Katharyn Dunham (ParaGraphs)

Page Design
Pamela A. E. Galbreath

Photo Research and Design
Deborah Van Rooyen (DVR Design), Shana Mueller

Imaging
Lezlie Light

Permissions
Margaret A. Chamberlain-Gaston, Barb McNeil, Robyn V. Young

Graphic Art
GGS Information Services, Mapping Specialists, XNR Productions

Composition
Evi Abou-El-Seoud

Manufacturing
Rhonda Dover

Editorial Director
John Fitzpatrick

Vice President and Publisher
Jay Flynn

TABLE OF CONTENTS

In this encyclopedia, page numbers start at 1 for each volume. In the following list, 3:23, for example, means the item appeared in the third volume on page 23.

C

VOLUME 2

D

E

F

VOLUME 3

VOLUME 4

VOLUME 5

LIST OF MAPS, COUNTRY SUMMARIES, TABLES, AND FIGURES

In the lists included in this section, the country maps and country summaries may be found in the entries of the same name under the "Geography and Economy" and "Society and Cultures" subentries respectively. For example, the map of Algeria will be found in Algeria: Geography and Economy; Algeria's country summary will be found in Algeria: Society and Cultures. The entries where thematic maps, tables, and figures may be found are listed in parentheses after the image titles: i.e., Years of decolonization for countries of Africa (Decolonization); 2:36 means that image may be found in the second volume on page 36.

COUNTRY MAPS/SUMMARIES

Algeria

Angola

Bénin

Botswana

Burkina Faso

Burundi

Cameroon

Cape Verde

Central African Republic

Chad

Comoro Islands

Congo, Democratic Republic of the

Congo, Republic of

Côte d'Ivoire

Djibouti

Egypt, Modern

Equatorial Guinea

Eritrea

Ethiopia, Modern

Gabon

Gambia, The

Ghana

Guinea

Guinea-Bissau

Kenya

Lesotho

Liberia

Libya

Madagascar

Malawi

Mali

Mauritania

Mauritius

Morocco

Mozambique

Namibia

Niger

Nigeria

Rwanda

São Tomé e Príncipe

Senegal

Seychelles

THEMATIC MAPS

TABLES AND FIGURES

EDITOR IN CHIEF'S PREFACE

This *New Encyclopedia of Africa* is the successor to the *Encyclopedia of Africa South of the Sahara* that was conceived in 1991 by the late Charles E. Smith of Simon & Schuster and was eventually published by Charles Scribner's Sons of New York in 1997. It became the standard four-volume encyclopedia of Africa: earlier works were either too short, too limited in content, old-fashioned, or out of print. It was obvious that a million and a half words could not include everything known about Africa south of the Sahara, at the time usually referred to as "Black Africa." Information changes continually and classifications alter with amazing speed: our original plans required continual rethinking as to approach, structure, content, length of entries, and choice of authors. But we were able to set out coherently what was at the time generally known and accepted about human endeavor and achievement in Africa south of the Sahara. Today and in future years other definitions, classifications, and interpretations have replaced and will continue to replace both those of 1997 and those of today.

We have now produced a new, larger, and broader encyclopedia, the *New Encyclopedia of Africa*, again under the Charles Scribner's Sons imprint. This encyclopedia includes coverage of northern Africa, and thus the entire continent, in both space and history; is some two million words in length; and has five volumes. The original *Encyclopedia of Africa South of the Sahara* was prepared and published not long after the formal end of the colonial interlude, when colonial overrule and the Cold War were still very much part of the experience of its inhabitants. The *New Encyclopedia of Africa* is prepared and published only ten years later, but Africa and the world around it are very different now from what they were then, and this encyclopedia is very different in intention, viewpoint, and philosophy from its predecessor. Some of the situations and problems of African peoples today are longstanding while others are new; some have been classified as solely "African," others as introduced by external interference or aggressive commercial or military exploitation. In both cases there have been deep and complex changes in the idea of "Africa," of how both Africans and non-Africans have envisaged its peoples and their continent as Africa has become a more central part of the world. In V. Y. Mudimbe's words the "inventions" and "ideas " of "Africa" are different today from what they were a few years ago; the analysis of these differences and of the idioms and ambiguities by which they are expressed form the basis for this new collection of information and the knowledge based upon it.

The earlier encyclopedia described what was even then relatively little known to the world at large, as the unveiling of distant peoples. We continue this process here, as ever more is learned about the continent every year, even every month. Yet even though the veil has been lifted there is still much ignorance. Outside Africa, with the continuing process of modernization, there remains a widely held assumption that the image of a "traditional" Africa has been merely an expression of an "Orientalism" as applied to Africa. Even now many writers still describe African institutions and cultures in the past tense, as though Africa today remains "primitive" and "exotic," unable or unwilling to change. What has often been overlooked and is difficult to appreciate are the strength and the beauty of both the "traditional" and the modern Africas, which together form a single phenomenon and cannot be separated. This "new" encyclopedia does not merely look at the new: it also looks at the traditional cultures, of which so much more is today known than in the past. There is no essential distinction between past and present; there never has been, but many observers have been blind and their viewpoints biased.

We have therefore invited authors to emphasize the powers and the complexities of the societies of Africa as forming an integral part of a single world. Their peoples are no longer distant or exotic but are as central as any others anywhere: there is no longer isolation but instead a conscious commonality. Whereas previously Africa was usually described from the viewpoints of those outside it, it can now also more clearly and vividly be seen from the perspectives of its own peoples. Some writers have suggested that the earlier and largely Eurocentric views should be ignored and superseded by "Afrocentric" ones. We hold that we need both, as together they comprise a single worldview and understanding.

THE STRUCTURE OF THE ENCYCLOPEDIA

An encyclopedia is not a dictionary, a string of articles each concerned to define a single item of information. An encyclopedia has an integrated structure, and an order of articles of which the pieces of information are chosen to fit together so as to form a single coherent body of knowledge. This *New Encyclopedia of Africa* comprises 1,121 articles. Of these, 821 are essays, both long and short, on specific topics, many of them placed in some 86 composite entries on wider topics or in 53 composite entries on all the particular independent countries; 96 of them are on particular towns and cities. There are also 305 biographies, of both present-day and historical figures. We have decided not to include separate articles on selected ethnic groups, as it is not for us to emphasize certain groups merely because they are well known outside Africa; but the larger ones are mentioned in the entries on particular countries and a thousand or so groups are listed in Appendix C. There are over 650 maps, diagrams, portraits, photographs, and tables; three appendices, one on the outline chronology of Africa, one on the periodization of history that we have used in the encyclopedia, and the aforementioned Appendix C; a very detailed general index; and each volume has an eight-page color-insert section on various aspects of African cultures. An encyclopedia's coverage can never be complete enough for every reader, but we have done what can now be done.

Many encyclopedias are produced today by publishers who advertise for voluntary authors. In our case we, as members of the editorial side of the project, comprising the editor in chief, the editor, and the advisers, assistant editors, and consultants, have chosen the authors, basing our choices on our experience and knowledge of their abilities and promise. This careful selection has been a long and difficult task, indeed the most difficult of any leading to the publication of this work. Our end result brings together Africanists whose expertise goes back over sixty years as well as the best minds of the upcoming generation. Some sixty of the major entries have stood the test of time and are reproduced here (with appropriate updating) as superior to anything we could now commission. We have tried to balance female and male authors, and authors from Africa itself, Europe, North America, and the remainder of the world, although their origins are no longer as relevant in today's "global" world as they used to be. Their identities and fields of scholarship reflect the fact that "Africa" is no longer an isolated and disregarded place but instead an integral part of a single world, and that there is but one image of Africa that today comes from those within it as well as from those outside it.

ACKNOWLEDGMENTS

I should like to thank the many people whose help has been crucial to the encyclopedia.

First is Frank Menchaca, who in March 2003 invited me to become editor in chief of this new encyclopedia, and whose imagination, foresight, and encouragement gave the project an inspired start.

I then wish to thank those who have helped so much with the basic editorial planning and work. First, Joseph C. Miller, editor, with me both from our joint work on the earlier *Encyclopedia of Africa South of the Sahara* and from the planning of this new encyclopedia; then associate editors Ann Biersteker, Dale Eickelman, Sandra Greene, Mark Horton, Célestin Monga, Kathleen Sheldon, Aliko Songolo, and Michael Watts, all of whom have suggested authors and who have joined in the often tedious work of checking and reviewing entries as we received them from their authors; the main advisers and consultants, listed on the Editorial Board page, all of whom have maintained contact with us and all distinguished scholars and none mere figureheads; and Nancy Gratton, who revised those biographies and city entries repeated from the 1997 encyclopedia.

I thank the many hundred authors, who have done so much difficult and taxing work, often at inconvenient times in their own programs. They have truly been our partners and colleagues.

I wish also to thank those project editors and others at the publisher's headquarters, especially John Fitzpatrick, an old colleague from Charles Scribner's Sons who supervised the original *Encyclopedia of Africa South of the Sahara* and has continued to advise while we have made this new encyclopedia; Ken Wachsberger, who took over from Nancy Matuszak, our first project editor and has remained with us since, miraculously keeping track of the complex and seemingly never-ending tasks of contacting authors and organizing their writings into the more than one thousand coherent articles that comprise the encyclopedia, and equally miraculously always being at the other end of our continual stream of email messages and telephone calls; Jaime Lieber and Carol Schwartz, who have at times worked with Ken; and finally the immense team of copy editors and researchers, proofreaders, designers, cartographers, indexers, typesetters, and others working behind the scenes and invisible to us as an editorial team.

JOHN MIDDLETON

INVENTION AND IMAGES
OF AFRICA

How can I visualize Africa's images and representations from my present perspective? It is possible to choose at least three ways of circumscribing the continent of Africa. The first would use historical and literary texts, from the Egyptians and the Greeks down to Western writers of the nineteenth century, that explicitly thematized scientifically the "otherness" of Africa. The second would, from the background of present-day social sciences and humanities, examine the grids and paradigms that directly contributed to the extension of Europe outside its borders beginning in the fifteenth century, as well as to the progressive development of anthropology. That discipline is a science dwelling on societies functioning according to "traditionalist motivations" and thus different from those organized and behaving according to "rationalist motivations," which, because of this capacity, are objects of sociology.

But let us be rigorous in conceptualizing the third way—the final panel in our triptych. With British anthropologist E. E. Evans-Pritchard's work on the Azande in 1935, white academia adopted a theoretical relativism that questioned the very deviation between the primitive and the civilized and, thus, between Africa and Europe. On the other hand, French academics, for instance, tended to maintain the dualism. This dualism is present in what anthropologist Jack Goody (in *The Domestication of the Savage Mind*, 1977) has called "the grand dichotomy" by extracting from the oeuvre of anthropologist Claude Lévi-Strauss a series of conceptual pairs opposing the wild to the domesticated: "cold" versus "hot," Neolithic versus modern, the science of the concrete versus the science of the abstract, mythical thought versus scientific thought, magical thought versus scientific knowledge, bricolage versus engineering, intuition/imagination/perception versus abstract thought, atemporality versus history. Jean Poirier's *Histoire de l'ethnologie* (1969) confirms such a distinction between prescriptural civilizations and high preindustrial civilizations, such as Islam or China, and contrasts these two societal types to Western civilization. From this background, one could then understand the metaphysics of a highly respected African thinker like Léopold Sédar Senghor, when he claimed that reason is "Greek" and emotion "Negro," which in actuality translates Jean-Paul Sartre's perception of Africa (the conquered) as feminine versus Europe (the conquering) as masculine. In circumscribing Africa, therefore, one could use the intellectual and political disciplines of the nineteenth and twentieth centuries, and their successive fragmentations, and analyze the concepts that progressively organized an epistemology promoting two types of scientific competencies and discourses. One of these describes "normal" cultural spaces, and the other "abnormal" cultural spaces, with Africa incarnating the latter in an exemplary manner.

PANEL ONE OF THE TRIPTYCH: THE EGYPTIAN AND GREEK KNOWLEDGE OF AFRICA

Historians and philologists refer us to early documents witnessing to a good perception of the continent. Among the most important explorations was that achieved by Pharaoh Necho II in circumnavigating the continent in the sixth century BCE. Another was that of the Persian Sataspes, who between 485 and 463 BCE tried and failed to reproduce the first voyage around Africa. Yet, his journey, reversing Necho's route, nevertheless succeeded, according to reports, in reaching Mount Cameroon. We could add other narratives: the anonymous *Periplus of the Erythraean Sea,* probably published between 130 and 95 BCE, and the voyages of Skylax of Caryanda, Polybius, and Eudoxus of Cyzicus, as rendered by the Roman Pliny and compiled by Karl Muller *(Geographi Graeci Minores,* 1882). But the most vivid representations of the continent were modeled by the Greek historian Herodotus, who visited Egypt and, in a systematic description, established the geography of the northern area of the continent, inventing, on the basis of local narratives, some monstrosities, such as African oxen that walk backward, peoples without individual names, dog-headed humans, headless beings—in brief, as he writes in book 4 of his *Histories,* wild men and women. Despite his otherwise careful ethnographic descriptions of the things and beings he really saw, this negative image imposed itself throughout history and still influences twenty-first-century representations of Africa, notwithstanding our more rigorous anthropological work that has been completed. In contrast to Herodotus, Homer spoke of Africa and Africans with admiration and designated Ethiopia as the locus where the gods go in order to recreate themselves. In Greek mythology, Memnon, a Trojan hero, a black son of Eos and a descendant of Tros and Dardanos, is presented as an ancestor of Ethiopian kings. Heliodoros' novel *Theagenes and Charicleia* (c. third century CE; also known as *Aethiopica)* conveys an amazing idea according to which the Greeks include among their ancestors "Gods, the Sun, Dionysos, Perseus, Andromeda, and Memnon." From the mythical period of Homer to the Alexandrian renaissance, Africa and Africans are portrayed in literature, art, and even philosophy (in Aristotle, for instance) as ordinary human beings.

Indeed, a rereading of these texts has allowed some of our contemporary scholars, such as Cheikh Anta Diop in West Africa and Martin Bernal in the United States, to rewrite the history of the Greek miracle, thus rethinking the very genesis of Western civilization from an African contribution. What this new perspective signifies has been widely misunderstood. What is important, from a strictly theoretical viewpoint, has nothing to do with the pertinence of a possible black genesis of Western culture. What matters instead is that the new thesis posits itself as an antithesis in opposition to an ethnocentric view of human histories.

PANEL TWO OF THE TRIPTYCH: THE EXPANSION OF THE WEST

By the end of the fifteenth century in the West the principle of *terra nullius* had become constitutive; it reduced all of the non-Western world to the Christian project, which perceived itself in both its textuality and significance as the most perfect expression of human culture. During the Baroque period in the seventeenth century, one notes something else: an explicit and radical epistemological reversal magnificently represented in the intellectual explorations of René Descartes and John Locke. They invented nothing new but systematized what was already there. Opposed to the preceding centuries' perceptual behavior, it became obvious that knowledge is about critical examination, the discrimination of beings and things, and the representation and comparison of their virtues and constitutive elements. New sciences organized themselves, such as natural history and theories of wealth. These are sciences of separation and announce in their being the scientific and philosophical practice of racism and the demonization of Africa. They ultimately led, insofar as Africa is concerned, to the constitution of a "colonial library."

Yet, we should note, at the foundation of race-thinking practice, a curious genealogy which arose in France just before the French Revolution. Its proponents were French aristocrats theorizing on "nations." According to Count de Boulainvilliers (1658–1722), the history of France would have been a history of two states: one of Germanic origin, a superior nation by blood; the second, the nation of formerly enslaved and Romanized Gallics. Count Dubuat-Nancay in 1785 went so far as to propose an International Society of Noblemen of German origin. In the late 1780s, Count de Montlosier mocked the Gallics "risen from slavery." Count Arthur de Gobineau's well-known treatise on the inequality of races published in 1853 transformed the legacy of the French theorists by mutating it from race thinking to scientific racism. One should add that, contrary to what may be inscribed in our memories, when all this racial theorizing was going on, Prussian noblemen, at least under Frederick II, seem to have been preoccupied not by matters of race but by the rising of their own bourgeoisie as a class.

This panel of the triptych raises fundamental questions. First, a historical fact that should be noted in reference to what is symbolized in the French and American Revolutions at the end of the eighteenth century, based on the equality of the "We, the People" paradigm, clearly marks a fundamental principle of separation. To use the Marquis de Condorcet's words: "There are people who are more equal than others." Condorcet, a generous man and a militant for the cause of women and other marginals, was merely expressing a critical suspicion in his own mind. It corresponded, unfortunately, to what he hated most: discrimination as a technique for the control of both the processes of production and their links to social relations of production in Europe, and discrimination as a political reference in the hierarchy of nations that Europe was then determining. A second fact, more directly dependent upon the epistemological grid employed by Western scholarship at the end of the eighteenth century and the beginning of the nineteenth century, is the sanctioning of positive or negative qualities of non-Western cultures. For the first time, thanks to the Enlightenment, European sciences established two spaces of knowledge and two types of beings and human experiences: the normal and the abnormal. The new sciences (such as biology, economics, and philology) almost naturally qualified Africa as a paradigm of otherness, a deviation between "us" and "them." And, thus, a colonial library was created. It is both a body of knowledge and a body of techniques for the domestication of what is different, be it a being, a place, or a theory. These bodies complement each other, simultaneously spelling out ways of knowing the otherness incarnated by Africa, with its lack of historicity, and postulating the meaning of that otherness vis-à-vis European or Judeo-Christian achievements. African anthropology, or what modern scholars call African studies, in its best expression—from James G. Frazer (1854–1941) and Edward B. Tylor (1832–1917) to this encyclopedia—deals with the nightmare represented by this colonial library.

PANEL THREE OF THE TRIPTYCH: RECENT EPISTEMOLOGY AND IMAGES OF AFRICA

One could take a different angle and situate African studies and its predicament in the history of the sciences. Here, what we are facing is something that would neutralize the marginality of African studies by inscribing it in the body of what made it both thinkable and possible. French philosopher and historian Michel Foucault suggested *(The Order of Things,* 1971) that the whole of our human and social sciences, its regular crises and discontinuities, could be understood from the evidence of three sets of paired concepts that have organized our perceptual behaviors since the end of the eighteenth century: *function* and/or *norm, conflict* and/or *rules, signification* and/or *system.*

Should we consider Foucault's theory to be intellectually appropriate, we would have to face certain implications. But before deducing them, let us pay attention to what these three paradigmatic pairs indicate.

It is obvious that, if we decide to understand the human being as a being who lives, works, and dies—a definition we have inherited from the Enlightenment—we note also that the Enlightenment designated the constitution of new ways, and three new disciplines for understanding what it means to exist as a human being: biology, economics, and philology. For the sake of clarity, let us say that an epistemology imposes both its normativity and its absolute validity. For instance, in biology and medicine, the basic fact of the matter is that a living human body operates according to specific *functions* of organs, elements, and relations; and these organs, elements, and relations obey or, more exactly, are submitted to, demanding *norms* in terms of balance. In the same way, any social formation survives and develops by negotiating the tension between its social functions and the norms it has chosen for itself. Employing this perspective, one can understand the genesis of philology at the end of the eighteenth century and the beginning of the nineteenth century in Germany: to study languages is to comprehend their constituent elements as functional vis-à-vis specific norms.

The second set of Foucault's conceptual pairs opposes or integrates *conflict* and *rules.* It is easier to understand insofar as it affirms something that is commonsensical: as the human body in its normal miseries has to obey specific rules in order not to destroy itself, so do any culture and any language. And education in all its implications is about how to transmit a body of knowledge and techniques that will allow future generations to negotiate correctly and pertinently between the two opposed elements: *conflict* and *rule.*

Finally, the last conceptual pair stipulates the same exigency: in natural sciences, we learn that any living being in the complexity of its organs and other elements witnesses to a signification that is comprehensible really only if we accept the evidence that it reflects a regulating system. It is exactly the same in economics, if one wants to understand the dialectic between processes of production and social relations of production. It is also the same in languages, if one wishes to understand the revolution represented by Swiss linguist Ferdinand de Saussure, who taught us that the signification conveyed by any speech *(parole)* depends upon a social abstraction—a language, that is to say, an institutional system *(langue)*.

What is fascinating in Foucault's framework is as much what is left unsaid as what is said. Explicitly, we can insist on certain facts that directly contributed to both the invention of Africa (since the end of the fifteenth century) and its reification throughout the slave trade and colonization in the nineteenth century.

Let us be demonstrative and focus on three major issues. First, and concretely, the biological, the economic, and the philological models have successively dominated the practice of our sciences since the Enlightenment: that of natural sciences since Carl Linnaeus; then the economic model from David Ricardo and Karl Marx onward; and, finally, with de Saussure inheriting the great work of German philologists, the linguistic. What these dominating paradigms reveal and actualize are normative spaces of living, working, and speaking, which are European. From this viewpoint, it becomes simpler to understand what, a bit too easily, Foucault considered as a different and radical angle: by emphasizing biology, economics, and linguistics, and by using categories conceptualized by Georges Canguilhem in his landmark 1943 work *On the Normal and the Pathological Function, Conflict, and Signification*—the history of our social and human sciences led to the constitution of two fields for each discipline: one dealing with the normal and the normative, and the second concerned with the abnormal and the diseased. The latter was readily deemed colonizable, so that it could be salvaged. On the other hand, by giving primacy to the other entries—norm, *rule,* and system—it becomes simply nonsensical to diagnose an abnormality; and everyone, everything, and every event can thus be thought of, analyzed, and understood as constituting its own *system* with its own *rules* and *norms.*

Second, the epistemological discontinuity explicit in de Saussure's *langue* and *parole* tension, and actualized differently by Africanists, made possible the originality of our twentieth-century practice of African studies represented in the work of Leo Frobenius in Germany, Wilhelm Schmidt in Austria, Bronislaw Malinowski in England, Melville Herskovits in the United States, Marcel Griaule in France, and Placied Tempels in the Belgian Congo. Their works signify a major rupture in the Western intellectual perception of Africa. Structuralist theory as exemplified by Luc de Heusch, a disciple of both Marcel Griaule and Lévi-Strauss, confirms this radical reversal. And, a maverick, Jan Vansina, challenges the solidity of the very principle of distinction between "cold" or primitive (and ahistorical) societies and "hot" civilized societies by insisting on the simple fact that orality conveys history. In America, the Harlem Renaissance, illustrated by black intellectuals such as Langston Hughes and Zora Neale Hurston, and in France, the negritude movement with Léopold Sédar Senghor (Senegal), Aimé Césaire (Martinique), and Leon-Gontran Damas (Guyana) fleshed out a theme of difference which, politically manipulated, made possible both African independence and the development of a beautiful and, alas often naive, politics of otherness. Even the politically empiricist realism of Kwame

Nkrumah in West Africa or Julius Nyerere in East Africa was predicated upon an apprehension of the African experience as radically different from that of Western civilization. On the other hand, the proclamation that went all over the world in the 1960s, "Black is beautiful," reconceptualized and reenacted a very old statement that the Hebrew Bible indicates in a song of love attributed to Solomon, who would have written it for a Shulamite beloved woman: "I am black and beautiful, O ye daughters of Jerusalem."

This encyclopedia witnesses to a radical reconversion that subsumes a new intellectual configuration. We should be grateful to Editor in Chief John Middleton for having sensed the necessity of its production—that is, the urgency of establishing a new understanding of what the African difference means as a sign.

Third, should we not, also, insist on the fact that this word *sign* could be a key to both a semiological and hermeneutical decoding of this monumental work? By semiology, I simply understand the totality of knowledge that makes us capable of reading social marks in a given social formation, in any culture. By hermeneutics, I mean the totality of knowledge and skills that give us the conceptual tools and the capacity to read and understand meanings. What John Middleton is offering us here, semiologically and hermeneutically, is a fabulous new invention made possible by our twentieth- and twenty-first-century intellectual configuration. I would suggest three possible codes in order to fully understand what is presented in the encyclopedia. First, let us focus on the two complementary concepts of the French and American Revolutions at the end of the eighteenth century: "We, the People," affirming our liberties in a "Nation State." Individuals take nationality and inscribe themselves in a cultural and political construction and progressively the European nations thus constituted themselves. They experimented all over the world, building and fabricating other new nations. Second, almost immediately after the genesis of this invention, a challenge arose. People like Charles Fourier in France and other socialists in Germany and England began to critique the mythology of the nation-state, its hypocrisy, and the so-called democratic principles by which it regulated unequal citizens. They proposed a new horizon dominated by the notion of class, and thus introduced the possibility of conceiving an international proletariat transcending all differences, including those of race and sex. Against the false mirror of a nation-state they imposed a new dogma—that of the Party. If the "We, the People, and Our Nation State" paradigm made comprehensible, for better or for worse, the colonization of Africa and, in terms of knowledge, an explicit constitution of a "colonial library," the Marxist paradigm signified for African cultures and identities an incredible project: the possibility of transcending localities and envisioning oneself in terms of universals. A third and most visible key lies in the well-controlled methodological perspective in the encyclopedia: that is, the best way of decoding rigorously the relationship and tensions between civil society and diverse popular cultures. Such a perspective transcends frontiers, making us all members of the same human condition.

This encyclopedia speaks. Any encyclopedia is a witness to an *episteme,* that is, the intellectual configuration of a period. This one is a reflection of ourselves and will tell the generations to come how, at the beginning of the twenty-first century, we reinvented Africa.

V. Y. MUDIMBE

THE IDEA OF AFRICA IN POLITICAL AND SOCIAL THOUGHT

The African presence in political theory is sometimes *explicit* (as when Hegel or Hugh Trevor-Roper portray Africans as a people without history). But even more often, the African presence in political thought is *implicit* (as when Rousseau hypothesizes about the Noble Savage without mentioning Africa). A third form of African presence in political thought is *comparative*: when a theory exclusively intended for one part of the world is reinterpreted and applied to Africa (as when Edmund Burke's reflections on the French revolution are used to interpret a failed state in postcolonial Africa.

When Aristotle drew a distinction between natural slaves and natural masters, he did not necessarily have different *races* in mind. Even the same family could include one sibling who is a natural slave and another sibling who is born a natural master or leader. Centuries later, the distinction was more explicitly racialized. White Europeans were deemed to be natural masters and Black people were regarded by others as natural slaves. Even such a remarkable sixteenth-century humanitarian as Bartolomé Las Casas (1474–1566), who passionately defended the Indians of the Americas against enslavement, was nevertheless prepared to regard the enslavement of Africans as more legitimate, on Aristotelian grounds.

The American statesman and political theorist, John C. Calhoun (1782–1850), was also among those who combined Aristotelian and Biblical arguments to rationalize and justify both the general institution of slavery and Black eligibility for enslavement. The legacy of Aristotle was synthesized with the racialization of the Biblical Ham.

The idea that some people are born natural slaves withered away with the successes of the abolitionist movement. However, the parallel idea that some people are born natural masters was much more resilient and lasted much longer. The whole imperial ideology of "the White Man's Burden" was one version of the concept of a master race, and Rudyard Kipling immortalized the doctrine in his poem, "The White Man's Burden," published in 1899.

The twin images of "half-devil and half-child" often formed the basis of Western concepts of Africa. The image of Africa as "half-devil" was a process of *heathenizing* African societies; and helped to mobilize Christian missionary response to Africa. The idea of Africa as "half-child" stimulated Western paternalism and a humanitarian response.

Great humanitarians like Albert Schweitzer (1875–1965) illustrated a form of racism which was paradoxically *benevolent*. Schweitzer retrained himself as a medical doctor, and gave up a comfortable alternative career in Western Europe in order to serve rural Africans amidst the mosquito-infested hazards of colonial Gabon.

He made so many sacrifices for Africa precisely because he did not regard Africans as equals. These "natives" aroused in Schweitzer the paternal protectiveness of an adult toward a child. When pressed, Schweitzer conceded that the African was his brother—"but younger brother." Schweitzer's form of racism resulted in benevolence and generosity, very different from the racism of hate and oppression (malevolent racism). Nevertheless, the concept of a Master Race was alive and well in Albert Schweitzer's worldview. He viewed Africans neither as natural slaves nor as half-devils—but in relation to Europeans he did view all Africans as children and fundamentally immature.

While the legacy of Aristotle was dichotomous (natural masters and natural subjects), the legacy of Charles Darwin was evolutionary. Theories about the "survival of the fittest" and "natural selection" had profound consequences, not just in biology, but also in social and political theories for generations after Darwin.

FROM SOCIAL DARWINISM TO THEORIES OF MODERNIZATION

Charles Darwin's *Origin of Species* was published in 1859. It was soon to have long-term repercussions for the "study of man" in almost all its dimensions. Racists could now proceed to demonstrate, by the utilization of the theory of natural selection, that major differences in human capacity and human organization were to be traced to biological distinctions between races. Black Africans were almost always ranked lowest. But to some extent this theory was much older than Darwin. What Darwin added to it was the dynamism of converting mere classification of beings into a *process*. The static version of the theory was *religious* and went back to the ancient idea that God had so organized the world that the universe and creation were arranged in a "Great Chain of Being"—that all creatures could be classified and fit into a hierarchy extending "from man down to the smallest reptile, whose existence can be discovered by the microscope." "Tribal peoples" were deemed particularly close to the natural world.

In other words, it was not just the lower species who were so classified. Even within the highest species created in the Almighty's image, there were, in turn, other divisions. Theories of the Great Chain of Being assumed that the Almighty in His wisdom did not want a big gap between one type of creature and the next. And so there had to be intermediate categories between orangutans and the white man. As early as 1713, naturalists began looking for the "missing link" between men and apes and apparently speculated on the possibility that "Hottentots" in Africa and orangutans might be side by side in the "scale of life," separated only by the fact that orangutans could not speak.

What Darwinism helped to refine into specific theoretical form was the element of *motion* in this process, the idea that the backward people might be on the move toward a higher phase, and those in front further still. *Progress* was activated at last.

The link between racism and ethnocentrism is not difficult to see. Even for the earliest racist theories, there had been no difficulty about deciding where to place the white man in the chain of being. As Phillip D. Curtin puts it in discussing these early biological theorists:

> Since there is no strictly scientific or biological justification for stating that one race is "higher" than another, the criteria of ranking has to come from nonscientific assumptions. All of the biologists ... began by putting the European variety at the top of the scale. This was natural enough if only as an unthinking reflection of cultural chauvinism. It could be held to follow from the assessment of European achievements in art and science ... it was taken for granted that historical achievement was intimately connected with physical form—in short, that race and culture were closely related. (Curtin 1965, pp. 38–39)

The dynamic element in ethnocentric theories of evolution inevitably led to assumptions about white leadership in the whole process of historical change. Progress was social selection, if not natural selection. And within the white races themselves specific leadership was assumed to come from the "tougher" of the European stock. For example, in his inaugural lecture as Regius Professor of Modem History at Oxford in December 1841, Thomas Arnold gave a new lease on life to the ancient idea of a moving center of civilization. Arnold argued that the history of civilization was the history of a series of creative races, each of which made its impact and then sank into oblivion, leaving the heritage of civilization to a greater successor. What the Greeks passed on to the Romans, the Romans bequeathed, in turn, to the Germanic race and of that race the greatest civilizing nation was England. In many cases, this was seen as part of God's Grand Design. Emperors and Kings were God's anointed.

Notions of leadership very often led to notions of the right to rule the less-developed societies of Africa and much of Asia. Even that prophet of liberalism, John Stuart Mill, could still argue that despotism was "a legitimate mode of government in dealing with barbarians, provided the end be their improvement...."

In Mill also there began to emerge the notion that Western democratic institutions constitute the ultimate destination of much of socio-political development. And the capacity to operate democratic institutions was already being regarded as an index of political maturity and institutional stability. Mill even seemed to share some of the reservations held by current modernization theorists about the possibility of operating liberal institutions in multi-ethnic situations. To use Mill's own formulation, "Free institutions are next to impossible in a country made up of different nationalities." Here, then, is the essential assumption of some of the current theories of political integration—a process toward the fusion of nationalities within a single territory into a new entity capable of sustaining the stresses of a more liberal polity. Since the rise of Afro-Asian nationalism, at least one major approach in theorizing about political modernization has rested on what Robert A. Parkenham describes as "the idea that political development is primarily a function of a social system that facilitates popular participation in governmental and political processes at all levels, and the bridging of regional, religious, caste, linguistic, tribal and other cleavages" (Parkenham 1964).

Parkenham goes on to argue that one form which this particular approach has taken today is to assess the social correlates of democracy. Are these the new criteria of the chosen people? These correlates are supposed to include relatively high "scores" on such sociological variables as an open class system, literacy and/or education, high participation in voluntary organizations, urbanization and communication systems. Much of this side of analysis assumes that the highest of modem institutions must inevitably be those which have been devised in the West. The Darwinian evolution toward modernity is evolution toward Western ways. Edward Shils seemed to be expressing as much his own view of the matter as of some members of the Afro-Asian elite when he said, "Modem means being Western without the onus of dependence on the West." And much of the rest of Shils' theorizing on the process of development bears the stamp of ethnocentric preference for "a regime of representative institutions" of the Western kind (Shils 1965). African studies since the 1950s has been replete with democratic assumptions which have been ultimately neo-Darwinian.

There have been models of theorizing about developments which have gone as far as to classify political regimes in the world in terms of, first, the Anglo-American type; secondly, the continental European types; thirdly, totalitarian types; and fourthly, the types that one found in Africa and Asia. The ancient concept of the chosen people of the Old Testament has found a liberal secular guise.

Evidently, this is ethnocentrism which has strong links with older theories of Anglo-Saxon leadership as a focus of a new wave of civilization. Again, theories of *evolutionary* change culminating in the pre-eminence of a single nation had major *philosophers* of the West among their disciples. Not least among these philosophers was Hegel, for whom the entire process of change in the universe had for its ultimate human culmination the emergence of the Prussian state and the Germanic genius. Hegel, too, was, in a sense, a pre-Darwinian social Darwinist, both in his notion of a creative tension between thesis, antithesis, and synthesis and in his notion of a powerful evolution toward the emergence of a high species. To Hegel, the Black people of Africa were prehistory.

More recently, there have been *historians* who have seen human evolution in terms of a progressive rise to the pre-eminence of their own nation or group of nations. William H. McNeill, in our own day—though by no means lacking in humility—had interpreted world history in such a way that he might easily belong to this tradition. McNeill challenges in part the Spenglerian pessimism of a Western decline and the whole conception of history as a collection of separate civilizations, each pursuing an independent career. For McNeill, human cultures have had a basic interrelationship; and their history has been leading to a global pre-eminence of Western civilization.

In the field of sociology, Talcott Parsons has talked about "evolutionary universals" in terms which do indicate a belief that ultimately development is in the direction of greater comparability with the political systems of the Western world. Parsons argues that the existence of a definitive link between popular participation and ultimate control of decision-making is so crucial for building and maintaining support for the political-legal systems as a whole and for its binding rules and decisions that, insofar as large-scale societies are concerned, the "democratic association" is an "evolutionary universal."

A similar prophetic ethnocentrism is evident in the approach of J. Roland Pennock to the study of political development. Pennock enumerates principles like "justice according to law," "the rule of law," and "due process" as among the political goods which are delivered when a society attains a certain degree of political development.

He also refers to other tendencies in the discussion of political development which bear the ethnocentric theme that the history of human evolution is toward the type of institutions and ideals cherished in the Western world. This is a new type of ethnocentric universalism. Pennock does not describe them as Western ideals. There is a tendency to refer to such things as "world culture." But the inclination to discern an upward movement of human evolution toward Westernism is recurrent in social and political theory. In Pennock's theory:

> It is common today to compare or rank states by the degree of party competition, or their adoption and use of the major devices of representative government, or their social mobilization. It is my suggestion that, to see a more nearly complete picture and to make more highly discriminating judgments, anyone who is concerned with political development in any way involving measurement of comparison should take full account of some of the measurable elements of the political goods of security, justice, liberty, and welfare. (Pennock 1966: 424)

After briefly flirting with theories about the one-party state, even African thinkers like Julius K. Nyerere began to tilt back to pluralistic democratic thought. The West was once again the ultimate role model.

Of course, by the time of our current theories of modernization and Fukuyama's "end of history," the racist element in theories of human development had considerably declined, at least within the ranks of scholarship.

In the modem theories of development and modernization, Darwinism has been substantially debiologized. It is no longer pure racial bigotry that is being invoked to explain stages of political growth. What is now invoked is a kind of cultural Darwinism. Fukuyama is almost Hegelian. For Hegel, Prussia was the ultimate synthesis in the dialectic of history. For Fukuyama, the United States is the final stage of human history. Africa continues to be relegated to historical irrelevance.

BETWEEN MULTICULTURALISM AND AFROCENTRICITY

But African thinkers of the twentieth and twenty-first centuries were not all converted to the proposition that the West was the ultimate role model, and cultural Darwinism the process of ultimate progress. In reality, there were two splits. One was a split between those who saw Africa's future as ultimately *multicultural* and those who insisted on an African return to Black authenticity. The multicultural Africanist thinkers included Kwame Anthony Appiah, with his own version of a cultural philosophy of synthesis. The Afrocentric thinkers ranged from negritude philosophers like Léopold Sédar Senghor of Senegal to Nilocentric thinkers like Cheikh Anta Diop, also of Senegal, and Molafe Asante of the United States.

But what are the analytical differences between Afrocentricity (negritude and Asante) and multiculturalism (in the tradition of Appiah)? Firstly, multiculturalism is a *pluralistic* method, seeking to represent diverse cultures: Latino, Asian, African, Native American, women. Therefore multiculturalism is pluralistic in that sense. Afrocentricity is a *dialectical* method, seeking to negate the negation in an almost Hegelian sense, seeking to negate the negative portrayal of the most distorted history in the world, that of the African people.

While multiculturalism is a quest for diversity, Afrocentricity is an antithesis. It is an antithesis to the thesis of Eurocentrism. The antithesis is searching for a synthesis. The thesis ultimately was white history; the antithesis was Africana history. Is there a synthesis? If the thesis is Eurocentrism and the antithesis is Afrocentricity, is the synthesis multiculturalism?

Multiculturalism is also a rainbow coalition representing the colors of different global realities. Afrocentricity is a quest for a reconciliation of opposites, confronting Eurocentrism with its ultimate other: Africanity. It is confronting white focus with its ultimate Other: black focus. Politically, Afrocentricity is a declaration of racial independence; it seeks to promote global Africana, self-reliance.

Urgent questions arise for those of us who are in Africana studies who are ourselves Africans, in that global sense. Should we be inspired by Afrocentricity or should we respond to a quest for multiculturalism? Afrocentricity is predicated on the uniqueness of the African peoples. Multiculturalism is predicated on the universal cultural interdependence of all people. Afrocentricity emphasizes the impact of the African people on world civilization. Multiculturalism sees world civilization as a pooling of the cultural resources of many peoples. What negritude is to the Black poet, Afrocentricity is to the Black scholar. They are a celebration of Africanity. Multiculturalism, on the other hand, is a chorus of diverse legacies.

To return to Afrocentricity as a perspective on world studies. Afrocentricity is not just a method of looking at the history of Africa, but it is a method of looking at the history of the world. Afrocentricity moves the African experience to the middle stage. There is first the concern with the *evolutionary genesis*, the origins of our species. Because on present evidence our human species begins in the African continent, the entire human race becomes a global African Diaspora. Every human being becomes a descendant of Africa. It is in that evolutionary sense that the rest of the world is a massive African Diaspora.

Then there is *the cultural genesis*. If from present evidence our species began in Africa, then our basic institutions also began in Africa: human language, human family. Some of you who saw my television series probably remember my statement, "*WE* invented the family." By that I precisely meant that if the species began in Africa, then Africans must have begun the kinship institutions which crystallized into the human family.

Thirdly, there is the *civilizational genesis*, which is not exactly the same as the cultural genesis. Civilizationally, much of Africana studies has focused especially on the role of ancient Egypt as a grand civilization which shaped not only other parts of Africa, but had a considerable impact on civilizations in the rest of the Mediterranean. Most recently discussion has emphasized its impact on ancient Greece. Martin Bernal's book, *Black Athena*, has generated a new examination of that debate. Bernal's approach to the subject is telling us that these distortions were not made by ancient Greeks. It was not the Greeks who did not acknowledge their debt to ancient Egyptians. It has been modem Europeans who have changed classical history. This massive macroplagiarism of lifting a whole civilization without footnotes was done not by the ancients but in the eighteenth and nineteenth centuries with revisionist European historians of the classics.

Bernal's thesis is that modern Europeans, entering a new era of racism and antisemitism, could not make themselves bear the thought that what they regarded as the pristine origins of their civilization should have had much to do with either Africans or such Semitic peoples as the Phoenicians. Modern Europeans therefore promptly understressed, if not "obliterated," Egypt's contribution to Athens.

Fourthly, there is the *geographical centrality* of Africa. It is almost as if the Almighty in His infinite wisdom had cut Africa into two equal parts. Africa is certainly the only continent that is thus cut almost in half by the equator. Africa is also the only continent that is traversed by both the tropic of Cancer and the tropic of Capricorn. In many ways, therefore, Africa is also the most tropical of all continents by its centrality. The geographical centrality of Africa is therefore clear.

Fifthly, there is the *monotheistic genesis*, the debate as to whether monotheism began in Africa. There is disagreement among Africana scholars whether the Pharaoh Ikhanatan was in fact the first thoroughgoing monotheist in history or not. His years were 1379 to 1362 (BCE) in Egypt. There is the related debate as to whether the Semites, who helped universalize monotheism, were originally African or not, because their distribution has since been on both sides of what is now the Red Sea. After all the Red Sea itself was created by one massive earthquake which also created the Rift Valley. Indeed, was Moses an African? Was he an Egyptian? If he was indeed an Egyptian, did that therefore make him an African? All this is part of the monotheistic debate concerning the origins of Africa in that regard. It is in this sense that Afrocentricity has to be considered in many fundamental ways as a perspective on world history. The forces of world history often have their origins in Africa.

There are two types of Afrocentricity. Gloriana Afrocentricity emphasizes the great and proud accomplishments of people of African ancestry: Africa at its most complex. Africa on a grand scale. The castle builders, those who built the walls of Zimbabwe or the castles of Gondär, or the sunken churches of Lalibäla. Some would argue those who built the pyramids of Egypt. This is Gloriana Afrocentricity.

There is also Proletariana Afrocentricity. This emphasizes the sweat of Africa's brow, the captured African as a co-builder of modern civilization. The enslaved as creator, the slave as innovator. Slave labor building or helping to build the Industrial Revolution in the Western world. Slave labor for better or for worse, helping to fuel the capitalist transformation in the northern hemisphere. The colonized peoples, both as victims and as builders of the industrialized modern world. The resources of Africa, the minerals of Africa, extracted from beneath our feet, have been used for factories which have transformed the nature of the twentieth century. Without those minerals this century would have been vastly different. The primitivist version of negritude celebrates Africa's simplicity rather than Africa's complexity. It salutes the African cattle herder, not the African castle builder. To that extent it is part of Afrocentricity Proletariana.

As for the case for multiculturalism, the argument would go this way. The problem is not merely the demeaning of African culture. It is the threatening hegemonic power of Western culture. Western cultural hegemony in the world cannot be challenged by Africana studies alone. It must be tackled by an alliance of all other cultures threatened by Western hegemony—sometimes even by an alliance which includes dissident elements within Western culture itself.

The present world culture is Eurocentric; the next world culture is unlikely to be Afrocentric, even if that was desirable. The best solution is therefore a more culturally balanced world civilization. That is the burden of the next generation, to attempt to enlist the participation of other civilizations, not to provide an alternative hegemony, but to provide a new balance. Africana studies should do joint projects with groups like Latin American studies, Middle Eastern studies, or studies of other parts of the Third World.

Part of the mission is to reduce the global Eurocentric presence in scholarship, in research, and in education. The problem is not simply that African culture has been demeaned, that is true. African culture will continue to be demeaned, as long as Western culture is hegemonic, and Western culture is so triumphant in the very citadels of Africa. Only an alliance with other groups can even approximate a dent on this ever-expansionist European giant, and its extensions. If Africana is to go multicultural, it must internally go comparative. African studies should include the study of global Africa. Even within Africana studies we need to broaden out.

The history of Africa does not end on Africa's shores. In fact African children in African schools in continental Africa are mistaught. "African history" is assumed to be the history of that piece of land which is bounded by those particular oceans. And yet one must ask, "When did those Africans exported as slaves cease to be part of African history: when they left Cape Coast in Ghana? when they were midway across the Atlantic? when they got to the Western Hemisphere? in the first hundred years? in the first two hundred years? What was the African cutoff point of those captives? When did they cease to be African? When did they walk out of African history?"

ISLAM AND PAN-AFRICANISM

Among Diaspora Africans of the Western hemisphere generally there are, in fact, two spiritual routes toward re-Africanization. One route is through Pan-Islam—the transition chosen by Elijah Muhammad and Malcolm X, or Al-Hajj Malik Al-Shabbazz). The other is directly through Pan-Africanism—the transition chosen by Marcus Garvey and the Rastafari movement. The Pan-Islamic route has been particularly striking in Black America, where conversions to the Muslim faith are still on the ascendant. The direct Pan-African route has often been led by Caribbean Africans, either in the West Indies themselves or in North America.

One question which arises is: why has Islam made much more progress among North American Blacks than among Blacks in Blyden's beloved West Indies? The second question is: why does African traditional religion (or beliefs rooted in sacred Africanity) sometimes appear to be more visible in the new Caribbean after Blyden than among Africans of North America?

One major variable was the tendency of African Americans to equate Brown with Black. No sharp distinction was made in the Black American paradigm between brown Arabs and black Africans. Mazrui's dual ancestry as Afro-Arab would feel at home in this paradigm. Indeed, until the second half of the twentieth century, almost all "Coloured people" in North America—whether they came from Africa or Asia or *elsewhere*—were treated with comparable contempt. When W. E. B. Du Bois (born American, died Ghanaian) argued that it was not Blacks who were a "minority" but whites, he had added up the teeming millions of Asia with the millions of Africans to give the coloured races a massive majority in the *global* population.

If the transition from brown Asian to black African was so smooth in the Black American paradigm, the transition from Africanity to Arabness continues to be even easier. Indeed, of all the religions associated with Asia, the one which is the most *Afro-Asian* is indeed Islam. The oldest surviving Islamic academies are actually located on the African continent, including Al-Azhar University in Cairo and Fez in Morocco. The Muslim academy of Timbuktu in what is today Mali is remembered by many Pan-Africanists with pride.

In Nigeria there are more Muslims than there are Muslims in any Arab country, including the largest Arab country in population, Egypt. In 1981, Nigerian Muslims comprised the largest contingent worldwide making the pilgrimage (Hajj) to Mecca and Medina. On the other hand, there are more Arabs in Africa as a whole than in Asia.. Indeed, demographically, two-thirds of the Arab world lies in the African continent.

Given then the tendency of the Black American paradigm to draw no sharp distinction between being Black and being "coloured," Islam's Africanness was not too diluted by its Arab origins.

Islam in the Caribbean, on the other hand, has been handicapped by two factors. First, race consciousness in the Caribbean does not as readily equate black with brown as it has historically done in the United States. The Caribbean historical experience was based on a racial hierarchy (different shades of stratification) rather than racial dichotomy (a polarized divide between white and "coloured"). Arabs in the Caribbean racial paradigm therefore belonged to a different pecking order from Africans. Indeed, Lebanese and Syrians were more likely to be counted as white rather than black. Because of that, the Arab origins of Islam were sometimes seen as being in conflict with Islam's African credentials. Despite his Caribbean origins, Edward Blyden would have been confused by that.

Moreover, the Caribbean has a highly visible East Indian population, a large proportion of whom are Muslims. In the black population in Guyana and Trinidad, there is a tendency to see Islam neither as *African* nor as *Arab*, but as *Indian*. The result is a much slower pace of Islamic conversions among Caribbean Africans than among African Americans. Most Caribbean Blacks are unlikely to see the Muslim holy city of Mecca as a spiritual port of call on the way back to the cultural womb of Africa. On the contrary, Mecca is more likely to be perceived by the majority as a stage of cultural refueling on the way to the Indian sub-continent.

In contrast, indigenous African religiosity has often prospered more in the post-Blyden Caribbean than in Black America. Why? One reason is that cultural nationalism in Black America is rooted in *romantic gloriana* rather than *romantic primitivism*. Gloriana takes pride in the complex civilizations of ancient Africa; primitivism takes pride in the simplicity of rural African village life. In the words of Aimé Césaire, the Caribbean romantic primitivist of Martinique who coined the word *negritude*:

> Hooray for those who have invented neither powder nor the compass, Those who have tamed neither gas nor electricity, Those who have explored neither the seas nor

the skies, … My negritude [my Blackness] is neither a tower nor a cathedral. It plunges into the red flesh of the soil. (Césaire 1939)

While this idealization of simplicity can capture the Caribbean mind both before and after Blyden, it seldom inspires the imagination of the African American. The dominant North American culture is based on the premise of "bigger, better and more beautiful." African-American rebellion against Anglo-racism therefore seeks to prove that Africa has produced civilizations in the past which were "as big and beautiful" as anything constructed by the white man.

In this cultural atmosphere of gloriana, African indigenous religion appears capable of being mistaken for "primitivism." Indigenous African rituals appear rural and village-derived. While Yoruba religion does have an impressive following in parts of the United States, and its rituals are often rigorously observed, the general predisposition of the African-American paradigm of nationalism is afraid of appearing to be "primitive."

The Islamic option is regarded by African Americans as a worthier rival to the Christianity of the white man. Parts of the Qur'an seem to be an improvement upon the white man's Old Testament. The Islamic civilization once exercised dominion and power over European populations. Historically Islamic culture refined what we now call "Arabic numerals," invented Algebra, developed the zero, pushed forward the frontiers of science, designed and built legendary edifices from Al-Hambra in Spain to the Taj Mahal in India. Black America's paradigm of romantic gloriana is more comfortable with such a record of achievement than with the more subtle dignity of Yoruba, Igbo, or Gikuyu traditional religion.

There is a related difference to bear in mind. Cultural nationalism in Black America often looks once again to ancient Egypt for inspiration, perceiving pharaonic Egypt as a *Black* civilization. Caribbean Black nationalism has shown a tendency to look to Ethiopia. The Egyptian route to Black cultural validation again emphasizes complexity and gloriana. On the other hand, the Ethiopian route to Black cultural validation can be biblical and austere. Thinkers like Nkrumah and Mazrui are caught in between Egyptophilia and Ethiophilia.

The most influential Ethiopic movement in the African Diaspora has become the Rastafari movement, with its Jamaican roots. Named after Haile Selassie's older titled designation, the Jamaican movement evolved a distinctive way of life, often austere. Curiously enough, the movement's original deification of the Emperor of Ethiopia was more Egyptian than Abyssinian. The fusion of Emperor with God-head was almost pharaonic. The ancient kings of Egypt built the pyramids as alternative abodes. The divine monarchs did not really die when they ceased to breathe; they had merely moved to a new address. In this sense the original theology of the Rastafari movement was a fusion of Egyptianism and pre-biblical Ethiopianism. The resulting lifestyle of the Rastas, on the other hand, has been closer to romantic simplicity than to romantic gloriana. In North America the Rasta style is still more likely to appeal to people of Caribbean origin than to long-standing African Americans, with their grander paradigm of cultural pride.

Pan-Africanism and Pan-Islamism are still two alternative routes toward the African heritage. After all, Islam did first arrive in the Americas in chains—for it was brought to the Western hemisphere by West African slaves. In reality the family under slavery was better able to preserve its African pride than to protect its Islamic identity. Slavery damaged both the legacy of African culture and the legacy of Islam among the imported Black captives. But for quite a while Islam in the Diaspora was destroyed more completely than was Africanity.

But now Islamization and Africanization in the Diaspora are perceived as alternative spiritual routes to the cultural bosom of the ancestral continent. It remains to be seen whether the twenty-first century will see a similar equilibrium in Blyden's Caribbean—as the search continues for more authentic cultural and spiritual paradigms to sustain the Global Africa of tomorrow.

It was in his book *Consciencism* that Nkrumah most explicitly addressed the triple heritage of African culture, Islam, and what he called "Euro-Christianity." For Nkrumah the biggest challenge for African philosophy was how to synthesize these three very different traditions of thought. Nkrumah's concept of consciencism was the nearest approximation to Mazrui's concept of "the Triple heritage"—a search for an African synthesis of three distinct civilizations.

Nkrumah groped for a principle of compassionate ecumenicalism. He said:

> With true independence regained . . . a new harmony needs to be forged, a harmony that will allow the combined presence of traditional Africa, Islamic Africa and Euro-Christian Africa, so that this presence is in tune with the original humanist principles underlying African society. Our society is not the old society, but a new development society enlarged by Islamic and Euro-Christian influences. (Nkrumah 1964: 68–70)

Nkrumah urged a new synthesis of these legacies to produce what he called "Philosophical Consciencism":

> The theoretical basis for an ideology whose aim shall be to contain the African experience of Islamic and Euro-Christian presence as well as the experience of traditional African society, and, by gestation, employ them for the harmonious growth and development of that society.

Future generations of Africans may one day say Amen to Nkrumah's vision.

BIBLIOGRAPHY

Césaire, Aimé. *Return to My Native Land*. Paris: Presence Africaine, 1939.

Curtain, Philip. *The Image of Africa*. London: Macmillan, 1965.

Nkrumah, Kwame. *Consciencism: Philosophy and Idealogy for Decolonization*. London: Heinemann, 1964.

Parkenham, Robert A.. "Approaches to the Study of Political Development." *World Politics* 17:1 (1964): 108–120.

Pennock, James Roland. "Political Development, Political Systems, and Political Goods." *World Politics* 18:3 (1966): 415–434.

Shils, Edward. *Political Development in the New States*. The Hague: Mouton, 1965.

ALI A. MAZRUI

AFRICANS: THE PAST IN THE PRESENT

Africa is a bewildering kaleidoscope of different and overlapping societies and cultures. The second largest continent in the world, it includes over fifty countries and nearly every one of these contains separate and overlapping local societies, cultures, and languages, as well as national and regional institutions and languages. Moreover, all of these are changing before our eyes. Hardly any other continent, except perhaps for Asia, appears to be quite as complex as Africa. Hence, to speak of Africans in general seems to be vacuous.

Yet, perceived from another angle, the overall attitudes and reactions of people in tropical Africa and somewhat beyond appear to be similar to each other, and from that approach there is much to say about Africans in general. So how to understand what makes this complex, vibrant, modern Africa tick? One approach is to follow the dynamics of how it came into being, and in doing this one soon finds that present-day Africa is in large part the product of recent developments, but also in large part a legacy of a recent colonial past, and to yet another, rather surprisingly large extent still, the modern outcome of processes that hark back to the distant past.

THE DISTANT PAST

For most of their long history, Africans, similar to other humans everywhere, survived and thrived by constantly adapting to different and rapidly changing natural and human environments. They also used their collective imaginations to invent communal ways to better their living conditions and, in general, to make life more interesting. But fundamental choices once made were never questioned again. A striking case, for example, is a choice Egyptians made over six thousand years ago—namely the decision to tie their whole system of food production to the floods of the Nile, a decision to which they still adhere. With the passage of centuries and even millennia, African communities have thus adapted ever more efficiently to particular surroundings and responded to different imaginative visions, so that their societies and cultures gradually diverged more and more from each other. Yet at the same time different communities found that it was profitable to remain in contact with each other, if only to learn from one another's experiences and to exchange both know-how and the products of their different environments with each other. Over time, repeated borrowings of this sort then made the societies and cultures involved more convergent, that is, more similar to each other, thus counterbalancing the trend toward divergence.

There is enough archaeological and historical evidence in the early twenty-first century to follow these dynamics of divergence and convergence over the centuries and even millennia almost everywhere in Africa. And as people nearly always chose to add additional refinements to further elaborate on choices once made, rather than to abandon them, they built up their societies and cultures to increasingly intricate levels. In doing so, convergence eventually gained the upper hand over divergence in their seesaw dynamic. The result was the emergence of regional cultural traditions. The most famous of these grew ever larger in area along the shores of the Mediterranean, to eventually culminate in the Roman Empire and then the realm of Christianity. Some six centuries later Islam was born within this area and rapidly spread over nearly all of western Asia and the northern half of Africa. Meanwhile, convergence had created a few other cultural traditions elsewhere in the continent, especially during the first millennium and a half of our era. As a result, by about 1200–1500 there were a small but recognizable number of thriving, still growing, and internally fairly complex regional traditions that were linked by webs of trade and communication covering most of the continent and extending well into the two adjacent continents from Spain to India and sometimes even China. Nevertheless, even then a single overarching set of institutions or cultural patterns that affected inhabitants in all the parts of this huge continent still did not exist.

Such integrated development did take place, however, and rather suddenly, too, because it occurred within somewhat less than three generations between the mid-fifteenth century and 1525. It was part of the rise of a new economic world order, centered on Europe, and it signaled the dawn of a new era in Africa. First, Portuguese ships encircled Africa and then Europeans planted scattered mercantile settlements along the coasts of the Atlantic and Indian Oceans to complement others that already existed along the Mediterranean. This train of events is especially significant in African history because it was the first time that Africans from all parts of the continent shared a single common experience. Soon thereafter, Europeans began to export slaves from the coasts of the southern Atlantic to the Americas thus completing a ring of slave trading around the continent, as slaves had already been carried for almost a millennium to the shores of the Mediterranean from points south of the Sahara and from eastern Africa to the Middle East and India. By the eighteenth century, however, the ever-increasing numbers of persons exported by Europeans to the Americas dwarfed all earlier exports. From the early 1600s onward this traffic in humans lowered demographic growth rates in many regions of the continent, and bred insecurity, moral callousness, violence, and war. Additionally, it bolstered class formation as well as more autocratic leadership in many of the affected societies. But perhaps the most durable and most nefarious effect of the slave trade has been to foster worldwide racism against Africans as an outgrowth of the contempt attached to the slave status, a contempt later transferred to that of colonial subject. Meanwhile the Atlantic slave trade also sped up the existing older trends toward sociocultural convergence within the continent. It did so as this trade, abetted by a parallel commerce in other products, increased in spatial reach, volume, and frequency, affected an ever-widening circle of societies and cultures and created diasporic cultures in the Americas. The trend accelerated even further during the industrial age as the continent came to be flooded with hitherto undreamed of quantities of all sorts of old and new commodities.

YESTERDAY: THE COLONIAL PAST

After the encirclement of the continent, the next turn in African history that affected its inhabitants in all parts of the continent almost simultaneously was its military colonization by European powers during the nineteenth and twentieth centuries. Whereas a few colonial outposts (for example, Angola, and Cape Town in South Africa) had been founded well before 1800, the colonial age that followed was wholly different, fueled as it was by the rise of competitive nation–states in Europe and their concern with commodity exports markets. As the century wore on, the creation of colonies was further facilitated by Europe's increasing military superiority. The French conquest of Algeria in 1830 and the British takeover of Sierra Leone in 1808 are early cases of a process that had overrun nearly the whole continent well before 1900. Conversely, when the balance of power in the world shifted away from Europe during World War II, there followed an even more rapid decolonization of the continent that reached its peak in 1960.

So, as Jacob Ajayi once remarked, colonialism was but an episode in the African history. Yet it has been a crucial episode. To begin with, colonialism created the present-day states whose territories form the continent's political skeleton, a skeleton that has changed very little since the late-nineteenth century. Most of the time nearly all colonies were bureaucratic police states whose rule seemed arbitrary to their subjects and who stifled liberty until they mutated into welfare states during their last years and introduced elective local government. Yet in detail each colony was different, and by independence each colony had acquired its own individuality, along with its own particularized nationalist elite, ready to be transformed into a notional nation-state. Just as important has been the reorganization of space according to the new economic and bureaucratic needs through the creation of new urban nodes and the development of some older ones, and the reorientation of spatial patterns of transport and communication. So strong was the pull of the cities that, by independence, up to 40 percent of the population in some countries had become urban.

Urbanization is all the more significant because the city was a place in which most inhabitants were newcomers and hence was also the place in which the people created an innovative mixture of older African sociocultural patterns with European ways of living and working. Moreover, major cities became fountains for fashions, sophistication, and knowledge that were then imitated far and wide. Even in the countryside there was a significant introduction of novel, mostly European, lifestyles and values ranging from new foods or clothes, to languages, education, law, literature, art, Christianity, nationalism, and Pan-Africanism. Colonialism also fostered the expansion of cultural movements and religions that were foreign to Europe. The most significant of these was the rapid turn to Islam, especially in West Africa, an embrace that preceded and was accompanied by a surge of faith and piety among Muslims all over North Africa.

Westernization, in opposition to African tradition, is the usual label given to the influence of metropolitan societies and cultures on the behavior and the minds of the Africans they ruled. By the end of the colonial period, African ways of life and thought in the colonies were usually interpreted as acculturation, that is, as a relatively stable mixture of modern Westernization and tradition. Yet this syncretic view is fatally flawed because neither of the two opposing poles was really homogeneous, nor remained static, and they were not necessarily in opposition. At the Westernization pole, Africans adopted or rejected practices, values, and ideas from the individual colonial nation that ruled them, not often from others, and, despite all these Western ways having much in common, their customs still turned out to be quite different. To cite a seemingly banal example: the Tio, who until the 1880s formed a single society on both sides of Malebo Pool, had adopted wine and baguettes on the French-colonized side of the Pool by the 1950s but favored beer and bread in slices on the side colonized by Belgium. At the other pole, tradition usually referred in a vague fashion to a sum of all the different local societies with their own practices, languages, and culture found within a single colony, and, even though many of these might also have ultimately much in common, they too remained different from one another.

A second fatal flaw is to perceive tradition and Westernization as static entities that could be mixed at leisure over time to produce a stable, new, and blended culture. The world has never known an unchanging cultural tradition, and in the turbulence of colonial conquest and rule individual societies and cultures could and sometimes did react quickly. For instance, so-called urban customary law, a fresh set of rules often with negligible European influence apart from the practice of codifying it, developed rapidly to cope with the new conditions of urban life, whereas on the Western side, different colonizers developed various versions of welfare states and social democracies after 1945, sometimes in sharp contrast to their earlier attitudes of ruthless exploitation.

Change did not occur in terms of choices between two abstract poles. What occurred in practice was the pragmatic adoption of whatever was perceived to be the most desirable solution to each new circumstance that occurred, irrespective of the foreign or local origin of the innovations adopted, and even though such novel features might contradict older practices, values, or beliefs. Yet innovations did not directly clash with each other or with preexisting patterns because they were understood by reference to different elements in the common worldviews. For example, once maternity clinics became an option in the Belgian Congo, expectant mothers often patronized them, but death in childbirth was still attributed to witchcraft, the evil eye, or bad ancestors, rather than to a scientific explanation or by the will of an almighty Western-like God. It did not even occur to these mothers that, by their choices in childbirth, they were setting up a contradiction between different worldviews. The multiplication of such eclectic activities then created a web of heterogeneous sociocultural practices, values, and thoughts that few attempted to coalesce into a single harmonious or balanced, logical whole. Despite this loosely integrated configuration, cultural tensions did build up, partly as the result of unforeseen but inevitable side effects of some innovations, and partly in consequence of an extremely fast pace of change. Different groups within each country and even within each community invented or adopted innovations at different rates or adopted different methods to cope with the same problem, thus creating local stresses by age, by gender, by occupation, and especially strong oppositions between cities and rural regions.

TODAY

As a consequence of further social and cultural transformations brought about by independence, and in particular as a consequence of the increasingly direct and unmediated impact of international political and economic trends in the new countries, African ways of life and aspirations are significantly different in the early twenty-first century from what they were only half a century ago in late colonial times. Despite these changes, however, major social and cultural adaptations are still urgently required in most countries so as to better fit the formal institutions and ideologies of the new nation-states into the present practices, habits, and worldviews of local societies. The most glaring but also superficial difference between late colonial times and the present may well be the frequency of calamities such as famines, wars, and AIDS. Yet, despite these catastrophes, Africa's population has increased between three- and four-fold from the 1950s, and it is still growing faster than that of any other continent. Hence in many ways changes in Africa must have been beneficial, even though the benefits are not all that obvious. One example of subtle gains, for instance, is the successful resolution of huge numbers of conflicts in not always officially acknowledged local courts. Indeed, the present recurring risks of famine are linked to overall success because they stem less from climatic vagaries than from the failure of local food production to keep up with the huge population increase in general and further flight to the cities in particular. But some adaptations have not yet been made: most of the wars, whether between neighbors or within a state, are obviously still an undesirable side effect of independence.

More important than the calamities mentioned has been the overall impact of a shrinking world, to wit the still ongoing revolutions in transportation and communication. The introduction of the jet plane, the transistor radio, television, the container ship, the computer, the Internet, and now mobile phones result in nearly instantaneous flows of communication and information as well as much faster and more efficient systems of transportation. Most Africans now, even far away from major cities, are immeasurably better informed about events and even about some conditions of living elsewhere in the world than ever before, and they are also more influenced by them. More Africans travel to the rest of the world as students or laborers, and to a lesser extent also elsewhere in Africa, and more non-African foreigners, stemming from more countries, such as diplomats, United Nations and other experts, soldiers, foreign aid specialists, businesspeople, and tourists, visit Africa, although most of them now stay for much shorter periods than ever before. The new conditions of transport and information have also generated strong emigration flows and a severe brain drain out of Africa.

Yet, along with more efficient transport and instant communication, economic indicators show that Africa's shares of world trade and financial income is falling further and further behind that of other continents, despite the surge in the development and export of its energy resources and raw materials. Indeed, by most economic indicators Africa is the continent least integrated into the world economy, whereas the block of countries south of the Sahara is now the poorest part of the world. Why this should be so is still not evident, despite the many different tentative explanations that have been offered. The same figures also diagnose a deep social crisis in Africa, not so much because of considerable inequalities of income and living standards between countries and regions within Africa as because of the huge and ever-growing socioeconomic inequalities and the ever more diverging standards and patterns of living within countries. Such inequalities have recruited the combatants for most civil wars and are the ultimate causes of the widespread internal political instability.

Although some inequalities and differences of this sort have always existed, their huge increases in recent years flow directly from the activities of a free market and free enterprise, unfettered capitalism, and unbridled individualism—a trio of practices, attitudes and values that have become the expected norm in international relations, including those between African states. They are accompanied by a secularist, supposedly rationalist worldview based on science and evolution, and by dismissal of all the ethics of social solidarity. The whole package of such practices and thoughts is usually referred to as globalization, or modernity. But apart from a tiny wealthy minority of rulers and economic elites in Africa, these values and practices are bitterly resented and vehemently opposed by most other people. As a result the ruling elite has little or no legitimacy, and practical conditions are adverse to the implantation of new democratic forms of governance, although they too are supposed to be part of the globalization package.

The secularist worldview, however, is only one of three such worldviews that coexist in Africa today. It is the most divergent one, however, because the two others are based on religion. The second worldview, whether Christian or Muslim, is a completely internalized monotheistic worldview often with a tendency toward fundamentalism or toward a mysticism that hankers to withdraw from the profane world. The two religions provide existential security and social solidarity, and they reassure the faithful by proposing a righteous, strict, and detailed code of ethics. This code also provides them with criteria by which to evaluate political legitimacy. Unlike secular rationalism, which thrives only among elite individuals in urban milieus, Christianity and Islam flourish in small local parish or mosque communities in rural as well as in urban surroundings. Their leadership is usually provided by literate and schooled religious professionals.

The third main worldview is also based on religion. It rests on the conviction that ultimate reality includes such unseen entities as local nature spirits, ancestors, power objects, and witches that interact with the living. A strict code of ethics regulates mutual relations between the living and between such entities and the living, and its paramount obligation is to uphold social solidarity within one's community. From this obligation flows among others an unspoken social contract that grants political legitimacy only to those who are seen to act as careful stewards of the community.

Africa today is plagued by severe tensions between the external modern secular worldview and the internal religious worldview. The first one, with a free market economy, capitalism, individualism, and some semblance of democracy attached to it, is the currency of all international relations. The internal religious worldview, based on Islam, Christianity, or local religion, is all about the conditions necessary for health and well-being, about the ethics of equality, about the need for solidarity, and about the evil nature of all selfishness. The contradictions between the rationalist and the believer are most severe at the level of ethics. For the religious, the individual's pursuit of wealth or power is pure evil, whereas for the rationalists, corruption, a misappropriation of wealth to eat (share) with one's social brethren, is also pure evil. For rationalists, political legitimacy flows from elections; for believers, from supernatural approval indicated, for instance, by *baraka* or by magical good fortune. For believers, good government is paternalistic, whereas for rationalists it is a scrupulous observance of the will of a legislative majority. As the forces of globalization emanating from

Europe, North America, and Asia increase, those contradictions spiral into ever-larger internal social rifts and inequalities that create still further political and social instability as Africans continually attempt to defuse such internal tensions by tinkering with their institutions and their ideologies.

JAN VANSINA

GENOCIDAL WARS
OF IDENTITY

Genocide is an extreme level of conflict between racial, ethnic, religious, or cultural identity groups. Although it can be instantaneous and perpetrated within a limited time frame, as happened in Rwanda in 1994, it is more likely to be a lengthy process and an incremental outcome of a protracted conflict. Often, it is easier to identify conflicts as genocidal than it is to prove genocide. The former is the effect, while the latter is calculated intent, provable only in a court of justice, presumably by international law. For the same reason, it is more constructive to aim at preventing, managing, and resolving conflicts than to focus on the legal proof and punishment of those charged with the crime of genocide.

ANATOMY OF GENOCIDE

The 1948 Convention on the Prevention and Punishment of the Crime of Genocide defines genocide in article II as any acts committed with intent to destroy, in whole or in part, a national, ethnic, racial, or religious group. These acts include killing selected and identified members of the group; causing serious bodily or mental harm to members of the group; deliberately inflicting on the group conditions of life calculated to bring about its physical destruction in whole or in significant part; imposing measures to prevent births within the group; and forcefully transferring children of the group to another group.

Article IV of the Convention includes in the category of persons criminally liable rulers, public officials, and private individuals. Proving intent to commit acts of genocide, where large numbers of victims and victimizers are involved, is a formidable and almost impossible task. It is in this context that the criterion of criminal intent comes under scrutiny. Some scholars have argued that intentionality be removed from the definition of genocide, as it is increasingly difficult to locate responsibility on the societal level, given the anonymous and structural forces at work. Although they do not dismiss the importance of individuals, these scholars consider it more productive to probe into the societal structures that are prone to generating or preventing genocide.

As one observer put it, "A genocidal society exists when a government and its citizens persistently pursue policies which they know will lead to the annihilation of the aboriginal inhabitants [or members of other groups] of their country. Intentionality is demonstrated by persistence in such policies whether or not the intent to destroy the . . . groups is verbalized" (Chalk 1997). Admittedly meeting these standards of proof is a formidable task. "In a world that historically has moved from domination based primarily on the will of given individuals. . .to one in which individuals are dominated by anonymous forces such as market mechanisms, bureaucracies, and distant decision making committees and parliaments, the emphasis on intentionality almost appears anachronistic. . . . [I]n the modern age, the issue of intentionality on the societal level is harder to locate because of the anonymous and amorphous forces that dictate the character of our world" (Walliman and Dobkowski 1987).

With these problematic criteria, genocide is usually proven after the crime has been committed and well documented. Although prevention is prominent in the title of the Convention, undertaking preventive measures is inhibited by both the complexities of the definition and lack of clear enforcement mechanisms. It is, of course, in the nature of prevention that it is not easily verifiable. Success essentially means that the prevented crime and the method of preventing it are invisible, unless those responsible for success expose the details of what has happened, which would be distastefully self-serving. Contemporary experience indicates that even when abundant evidence reveals that genocide may be in the making, the record of action to stop it is dismally poor. That, indeed, was the experience of Rwanda when human rights observers warned the world that genocide was in the making.

All these considerations show that genocide is easier to prove when evidence becomes abundant, when, in most cases, it is too late to prevent it, except perhaps to stop its continuation. Even then, establishing criminal liability is bound to be problematic. A few leaders at the top and in command positions on the ground may be identifiable as responsible for genocidal acts in the sense of having authority to promote or prevent actions of subordinates and their intent might be inferred from the pattern of purposeful action that leads to the destruction of a significant part of the targeted group. However, war is generally an intergroup affair, orchestrated and conducted by political and military leaders and carried out by field commanders and rank-and-file, as members of a group against another group or groups. This situation, in essence, is what has been referred to as the anonymous and amorphous process of decision-making and action. The question of who should be held accountable and punished becomes elusive.

There is also the issue of enforcement. One of the criticisms against the Genocide Convention is the absence of an international enforcement mechanism in the form of a criminal tribunal that would punish convicted perpetrators of genocide. Although the newly established (2002) International Criminal Court (ICC) now fills that void, the problem is compounded by the fact that the state—for the most part the primary perpetrator of genocide—is charged with the responsibility to prosecute, which makes the Convention mostly unenforceable. As for the role of the international community, Leo Kuper (1908–1994), who is recognized as having "contributed more to the comparative study of the problem of genocide in the twentieth century than anyone else since Raphael Lemkin [the brain-father of the Genocide Convention]," has observed: "The resistance of the United Nations to charges of genocide is not simply a reaction to the trivializing abuse of the concept. A significant factor is that genocide is usually, though not exclusively, a crime committed by governments or with governments' condonation or complicity.... The United Nations is a professional association of governments which cannot be counted upon to act in any way likely to undermine the authority of—and, by implication, all of–the member regimes" (Chalk 1997). As another scholar observed: "The United Nations, being an international organization composed of sovereign states and committed to the principles of sovereignty and territorial integrity, is hardly the place to generate proceedings against fellow member states. Even if there were provisions for an international penal tribunal, it is highly unlikely that the system would be of much use as long as only governments could take cases to court" (Kuper 1997).

The case of Germany in the aftermath of the Second World War, and, more recently, the cases of former Yugoslavia and Rwanda in the early 1990s indicate that the prosecution of individuals involved in genocide can be more effectively carried out after the overthrow of the genocidal regime. Where governments are still in control and continuing to perpetuate genocidal acts, as is the case in the Sudanese region of Darfur, "the failure of the United Nations to take effective action against genocide," Leo Kuper argues, "renders necessary the search for alternative structures and processes." He looks to the "networks of international organizations that have proliferated in recent years [which may] provide an effective structural base for monitoring UN performance and exerting pressure," and "the extension of domestic jurisdiction to the prevention and punishment of genocide" (Kuper 1997). In this context, the role of civil society, both local and international, becomes a critical factor.

While this pessimistic assessment of the role of the United Nations is understandable in light of experience with international response to genocide, as the ultimate guarantor of global peace and security and the protection of universal human rights, the organization cannot be dispensed with or sidestepped. Neither alternative regional and international organizations nor unilateral action by individual governments or "coalitions of the willing" can be credible substitutes to the United Nations. Ultimately, the solution lies in global partnership in which non-UN actors can support, complement, and provide needed pressure on governments and therefore on the United Nations to take appropriate and effective action.

CONTEXTUALIZING GENOCIDAL ACTS

It has been observed that "domestic genocides are those which arise on the basis of internal divisions within a single society, with its marked divisions between racial, ethnic, and/or religious groups. Plural society theory deals with the relations between these groups, and the conditions promoting peaceful cohabitations, integration or violent polarization leading to genocide" (Kuper 1997).

Although the Genocide Convention has been criticized on several grounds, what is particularly pertinent is the debate between those who place primary emphasis on the roles of individual and collective actors, and those who see genocide as a systemic part of social and political processes. Correlative to these positions would be the attribution of responsibility to identifiable individuals and group actors on the one hand, and approaching the problem structurally and contextually as part of a broader political problem on the other.

Another way of framing the debate would be that the emphasis on actors' responsibility is more legalistic, with an emphasis on conclusive evidence and consequential criminal liability, whereas the systemic approach tends to lean toward addressing the root causes to bring peace, security, and stability to the conflict situation. Although the two are not entirely mutually exclusive, they certainly generate a tension in prioritization. If the explicit goal is to hold those who are personally responsible criminally accountable, whether immediately or in the foreseeable future, those at risk of being held accountable may see no personal interest in promoting peace. The Lord's Resistance Army (LRA) in Uganda, which has inflicted untold atrocities on civilian populations for decades and whose leaders are being sought for prosecution in front of the ICC for those crimes, is a case in point. They have openly declared that unless these indictments are withdrawn, they will not sign a peace agreement with the government of Uganda. To facilitate the peace process, the president of Uganda has pledged to grant the LRA full amnesty for all the crimes they have committed. On the other hand, there is concern that this reprieve would undermine the principles of accountability that are the bedrock of the ICC.

Justice, social cohesion, and political stability require more than formal state institutions. In this context, civil society—which is becoming increasingly involved in nation building, formerly left to the state—has a crucial role to play. As an array of citizen associations independent of the state and driven by shared social, economic, and cultural purposes, civil society has become a vital participant in monitoring genocidal conflicts and mediating processes aimed at promoting peace and national reconciliation. Society also has a part in broadening participation in the shaping and sharing of power, wealth, services, resources, and development opportunities, all of which are essential for sustaining peace, security, and stability.

One of the keys to a functioning democratic political system is a society capable of peacefully channeling needs and demands upward and acting as a check on the power entrusted to political authorities, thereby serving to increase responsiveness and accountability. Political parties have a specific role to play in contesting elections and institutionalizing channels that tie state and society. Other associational groups have distinct roles to play in a functioning democratic system. According to John Harbeson, civil society is the "key to sustained political reform, legitimate states and governments, improved governance, viable state-society and state-economy relationships, and prevention of the kind of political decay that undermined new African governments a generation ago" (Harbeson et al., 1994, pp. 1–2).

THE GENOCIDAL WAR IN DARFUR

Atrocities of genocidal magnitude have been intermittently perpetrated in south Sudan for half a century, going back to a southern uprising in 1955 that triggered a seventeen-year war, and since the mid–1980s when the war resumed, extending into the neighboring regions of the Nuba mountains and southern Blue Nile Province. After the resumption of hostilities in 1983, over two million people have died, over four million have been displaced internally, and half a million have been forced into refuge abroad. The international community generously provided humanitarian assistance to the victims of the war, but the crisis in Darfur, which erupted relatively recently (2003), has engaged intense international attention and generated debate on whether what is occurring there is ethnic cleansing, crimes against humanity, or genocide, thereby implying an increase in magnitude. Although Darfur has a history of conflict between Arab herders and African farmers over scarce resources–which are becoming even scarcer as a result of encroaching desertification–the current conflict is the result of regional rebellion by non-Arab groups against a potential, Arab-centric government authority and the government's brutal counterinsurgency response. The rebellion in Darfur was first attempted in 1992, when some Darfurians, supported by the southern-based Sudan People's Liberation Movement and Army (SPLM/A), staged an attack on the government forces in the region, the objective being liberation from real or perceived marginalization, discrimination, and neglect. Government forces ruthlessly crushed that rebellion, and about one thousand of those involved were killed. In February 2003, two previously unknown movements, the Justice and Equality Movement (JEM) and Sudan Liberation Movement and Army (SLM/A), staged a surprise attack that devastated and almost overwhelmed the government forces in the region. In desperation, the government turned to Arab militias known as *janjaweed*, which they recruited, trained, armed, and unleashed against both the rebels and local African communities assumed to be supportive of the rebels. Backed by the government ground forces and aerial bombardment, the janjaweed waged a scorched-earth campaign of destruction: burning villages, killing, kidnapping, and raping. Since the hostilities erupted, several hundred thousand people have reportedly died, over two million have been displaced internally, and a half million have been forced into refuge in Chad, while additional millions remain at risk within Darfur.

Although the atrocities began in early 2003, it was only in April 2004, during the tenth anniversary of the genocide in Rwanda, that international attention was drawn to the crisis in Darfur. It was then that the UN secretary-general, Kofi Annan, in an unusually strong statement to the Commission of Human Rights, declared that what was happening in Darfur might justify international intervention. By September 2004, the United States Congress and the U.S. Department of State concluded that what had occurred in Darfur, and may still be occurring, was indeed genocide (U.S. State Department 2004). A special commission established by the United Nations to investigate the allegation concluded that, although what was happening in Darfur did not meet the legal definition of genocide, war crimes and crimes against humanity "not less heinous than genocide" had been committed (United Nations 2005). The Commission released a list of some fifty-one individuals who were suspected of having engaged in these crimes and recommended that they should be indicted and brought to justice before the ICC. And yet, the international community, by January 2007, had not intervened in Darfur to stop the alleged genocide or taken any measures against those suspected of having committed equally heinous crimes.

The National Congress Party-dominated government of the Sudan, invoking national sovereignty and resistance to what they claim would be tantamount to a recolonization, has vehemently resisted the involvement of UN forces, compromising on accepting only an African Union (AU) force that has proved to lack the required capacity and that has failed to provide the protection needed. After intense international pressure, Sudan eventually accepted a hybrid force, in which the UN would supplement the AU with forces, equipment training, finance, and logistics. Sudan has also ruled out any prospects for handing over any individual to be tried by the ICC. Meanwhile, the crisis in Darfur, civilian casualties, and humanitarian suffering continue unabated.

SUDAN'S GENOCIDAL WARS IN CONTEXT

Although the crisis in Darfur has generated debate on whether genocide has occurred and may still be occurring in that region, the tragedy of Sudan has been ongoing since the conflict in the south erupted in 1955, with only a ten-year pause from 1972–1982. The atrocities, which have been associated with the civil war, reflect an acute crisis of national identity in which the conflict is perceived as zero-sum and therefore inherently genocidal. Indeed, many observers and human rights and humanitarian organizations have argued for decades that genocide was being committed in the south, the Nuba mountains, and southern Blue Nile regions. It can be argued that it is the guilt over the horrific 1994 genocide in Rwanda, watched by the world on television screens, without any effort to stop it, that accounts for the international outrage over Darfur, though yet with no effective action.

In the end, the most effective way to stop genocide or genocidal acts is ending the conflict by engaging the contexts that produce the conflict. Prevention is therefore the key concept. And prevention can best be achieved through peace. Rather than waste valuable time in the debate over whether or not genocide has occurred or is occurring in Darfur, energies could be more constructively invested in addressing the challenge comprehensively, to bring peace, justice, security, and stability to the whole country. Whatever the nature of the atrocities or crimes being committed, prevention, rather than condemnation or punishment after the fact, is what should be a priority. Although the conflict between punitive justice and the search for reconciliation poses a serious dilemma, the case for accountability and criminal liability has to be weighed against mobilizing all those with a potentially effective role to play in promoting the cause of peace, security, and stability.

BIBLIOGRAPHY

Audreopoulos, George J., ed. *Genocide: Conceptual and Historical Dimensions.* Philadelphia: University of Pennsylvania, 1997.

Chalk, Frank. "Defining Genocide." In *Genocide: Conceptual and Historical Dimensions,* George Audreopoulos, ed. Philadelphia: University of Pennsylvania, 1997.

Harbeson, John W. "Civil Society and Political Renaissance in Africa." In *Civil Society and the State in Africa,* John W. Harbeson, et al., eds. Boulder: Lynne Rienner, 1994.

Kuper, Leo. "Theoretical Issues Relating to Genocide: Uses and Abuses." In *Genocide: Conceptual and Historical Dimensions,* ed. George Audreopoulos. Philadelphia: University of Pennsylvania, 1997.

United States State Department. *Documenting Atrocities in Darfur.* State Department Document 11182, September 2004.

United Nations Human Rights Compilation of International Instruments, Vol. 1 (Second Part). Geneva, Switzerland: United Nations, 1994.

United Nations. *Report of the International Commission of Inquiry on Darfur to the U.N. Secretary-General.* Geneva, Switzerland: United Nations, 2005.

Walliman, Isidor, and Michael Dobkowski, eds. *Genocide and the Modern Age: Etiology and Case Studies of Mass Death.* New York: Greenwood Press, 1987.

FRANCIS M. DENG

A

‘ABD AL-QĀDIR (1808–1883). ‘Abd al-Qādir ibn Muhyi al-Din al-Hasani al-Jazā’irī, to use the fullest form of his name, was born on September 2, 1808, in western Algeria. The appellation al-Hasani indicates his claim of descent from the Prophet Muhammad. Al-Jazā’irī, which means "the Algerian," was a name bestowed on him later in life. His father, Muhyi al-Din, was a spiritual leader in the Qadiriyya religious brotherhood and a political opponent of the former Turkish Regency of Algiers, which was toppled in 1830 by the French.

Two years later, at age twenty-four, ‘Abd al-Qādir became the head of a tribal coalition against the French. He unified and administered western and central Algeria under a peace treaty that prevailed from May 30, 1837, until November 18, 1839, when he became known as amir, or ruler. In the 1840s, however, France continued its conquest of Algeria. ‘Abd al-Qādir finally surrendered to the French in 1847 and was held prisoner in France until 1852, when he was conditionally freed and given a state pension.

He went first to Bursa, in Asia Minor, and then to Damascus, where he arrived in 1855. ‘Abd al-Qādir was widely respected as a notable. When anti-Christian massacres broke out in Damascus in 1860, he helped save many lives. Napoléon III subsequently invited him to act as a local ruler within the Ottoman Empire, under French protection, but ‘Abd al-Qādir declined the offer. He spent 1863 and 1864 in Mecca and Medina, and in 1865 traveled to Europe, where he was highly honored by the French.

‘Abd al-Qādir (1808–1883). The Algerian Islamic scholar and military/political leader is a national hero for his effective use of guerrilla warfare against the French. While living in exile in Damascus, he wrote on philosophy in addition to authoring a book on the Arab horse. © Hulton-Deutsch Collection/Corbis

Afterward, he lived a quiet and spiritual life in Damascus on his pension and income from his estates, acquiring a reputation as a religious scholar, although he also took a certain interest in the nascent Arab nationalist movement. In 1871, after the fall of Napoléon III, he advised Algerians to remain loyal to France. He died in Damascus on May 26, 1883. The Algerian people have always venerated him as the founder of their nation; in the twentieth century he came to be regarded as country's national hero. After the Algeria's independence in 1962, the new Algerian government asked Syria to repatriate his remains; on July 5, 1966, he was buried with great honor in Algiers, among the martyrs of the country's war of liberation.

See also **Algeria: History and Politics.**

BIBLIOGRAPHY

Blunt, Wilfrid. *Abd el-Kader, Hawk of the Desert*. London: Methuen, 1947.

Etienne, Bruno, and François Pouillon. *Abd el-Kader le magnanime*. Paris: Découvertes/Institut du Monde Arabe, 2003.

King, John. *'Abd al-Qādir: An Algerian Life*. London: Hurst, 2007.

JOHN KING

ABEOKUTA. Abeokuta (literally, "under the rocks") is a Yoruba town and capital of Ogun State, Nigeria. Its name is derived from the dominant land feature in its location, a massive granite outcropping called Olumo Rock. The town was founded after the sack of Egba towns in the 1821 Owu war. Abeokuta was settled by four Egba groups—the Ake, Oke-Ona, Owu, and Gbagura. Each group lived in a separate ward and had its own leader. A central council led by a traditional ruler called the *alake* handled issues concerning the town as a whole.

In the late 1830s slaves of Egba descent, liberated by the British anti-slavery naval squadron and taken to Sierra Leone, began to return to Abeokuta, bringing with them Christianity and Western education acquired in Freetown. Abeokuta thus became the center of Western influence in Yorubaland. It was also home to the first newspaper in Nigeria, *Iwe iroyin*, which began publication in 1859. Cotton was the first major industry in the region, and by 1859 there were about 300 cotton ginneries and six presses in Abeokuta.

The returnees also created an Egba United Government, a council centered at Abeokuta, the first adaptation of a Western political institution in the region. It was founded in 1864 in reaction to the British annexation of Lagos (1861). Abeokuta's relationship with Lagos deteriorated over the next several years, culminating in an uprising—the *Ifole*—against European missionaries in 1867.

Britain forced Abeokuta to sign a treaty of friendship and commerce in 1893, signifying the end of Egba independence. In 1915 Britain bombarded Abeokuta, and a protest against taxation was violently suppressed in 1918.

In 2007 Abeokuta is an important market center, with a population of some 530,000 and an additional 170,000 living in the surrounding countryside. Important locally produced items include palm oil, rubber, and timber, as well as yams and kola nuts. The women of Abeokuta are famous for the production of *adire* (indigo-dyed cloth). The town is also home to a museum and a university.

See also **Freetown; Nigeria; Textiles.**

BIBLIOGRAPHY

Ajisafe, Ajayi Kolawole. *History of Abeokuta*. Rev. edition. Abeokuta: Fola Bookshops, 1964.

Gailey, Harry A. *Lugard and the Abeokuta Uprising: The Demise of Egba Independence*. London: F. Cass, 1982.

OLATUNJI OJO

ABI BAKR, MUHAMMAD IBN. *See* **Abu Bakr, Muhammad ibn.**

ABIDJAN. Abidjan was the capital city of Côte d'Ivoire (Ivory Coast), and is situated along the edge of the Ebrié Lagoon on the Gulf of Guinea. The importance of the city increased dramatically in 1950, when the lagoon was opened to maritime shipping by the construction of the Vridi Canal. Abidjan's population skyrocketed from around 60,000 to well over 3.5 million in the early twenty-first century, and it was firmly established as one of the most important seaports in Francophone Africa.

Abidjan's port handles cargo for Côte d'Ivoire, Burkina Faso, Mali, and Niger, forwarded by rail and truck. Principal exports are cocoa, coffee, timber, and petroleum. Abidjan is also a financial center: it is the headquarters of the International Bank of West Africa and of the African Development Bank library. There are numerous educational institutions in the city as well. The national university (Université Nationale de Côte d'Ivoire), archives, museum, and library are all in Abidjan. There is a research center for coffee and cocoa, as well as schools for marine science, communications, and administration. During the 1960s and early 1970s, Abidjan experienced rapid economic growth and prosperity due to the profitability of the country's cocoa and coffee exports. However, these two commodities have been in decline since the early 1980s, and Abidjan serves contemporary economists as an example of the instability of an undiversified economy.

The Krou and Akan are the two major ethnic groups in Abidjan. Both migrated from the east relatively recently: the Krou around the sixteenth century and the Akan in the eighteenth and nineteenth centuries. Little is known about the inhabitants of the distant past. The Portuguese were the first Europeans to arrive, but it was the French who warred through the 1890s to claim the country as their own.

Abidjan is clearly divided into modern and underdeveloped areas. The Hotel Ivoire, a tourist resort equipped with an ice rink, bowling alley, cinema complex, and casino, is one of the city's main attractions. Another landmark is the modern, Italian-designed St. Paul's Cathedral, one of the most elaborate churches in Africa, though the Christian population of the city (around 10%) is far outnumbered by Muslim and animist inhabitants.

The principal airport of the Côte d'Ivoire, Félix Houphouët-Boigny Airport, is on the island of Petit-Bassam, an industrial suburb connected to mainland Abidjan by a bridge. Abidjan is linked to other Ivoirian cities by highway, and to Burkina Faso by railroad.

See also **Colonial Policies and Practices; Côte d'Ivoire; Transportation; Urbanism and Urbanization: Overview.**

BIBLIOGRAPHY

Handloff, Robert E., ed. *Côte d'Ivoire: A Country Study*, 3rd edition. Washington, DC: Federal Research Division, Library of Congress, 1991.

SARAH VALDEZ

ABOLITION OF SLAVERY. *See* **Slave Trades.**

ABOUZEID, LEILA (1950–).

Leila Abouzeid (Leila abu Zayd) was born in the small Moroccan Middle Atlas town of Qsiba. She holds a bachelor of arts degree in English, a diploma in journalism from the London Institute of Journalism, and a diploma in American affairs from the Higher Institute of Journalism in Minnesota. She began work as a journalist and radio broadcaster under a male pseudonym. One of the first women journalists to work on Moroccan television as a newscaster, she also writes for various Moroccan newspapers and British radio. Abouzeid has written short stories and novels, the most famous of which is *Year of the Elephant* (1983), which has been translated into several languages.

In "Two Stories of a House," Abouzeid tells the true story of elderly Moroccan women who fight for survival, and of the strong bond that unites women even in conflict. At the end of the story the younger wife becomes an accomplice of the older. Any solidarity between cowives in some rural Muslim areas is perceived as a strike against male power. Yet here women defy both judges and husbands. The story provides a glimpse into a multilingual society where the use of language has strong social significance. The two women use Moroccan Arabic in a formal setting where only standard Arabic carries force. Standard Arabic is taught at school and hence illiterate women do not have access to it.

Moroccan author and journalist Leila Abouzeid (1950–). Abouzeid is one of the first women journalists to work on Moroccan television as a newscaster. An English translation of her short stories has been published by the American University in Cairo Press. PROF AIDA A. BAMIA

BIBLIOGRAPHY

Abouzeid, Leila. *Ām al-fil* (Year of the elephant), trans. Barbara Parmenter. Austin: University of Texas Press, 1989.

Accad, E. "The Themes of Sexual Oppression in the North African Novel." In *Women in the Muslim World*, ed. Lois Beck and Nikki Keddie. Cambridge, MA: Harvard University Press, 1978.

FATIMA SADIQI

ABU BAKR, MUHAMMAD IBN

(c. 1442–1538). Ruler of Songhay from 1493 to 1528 and founder of the Askiya dynasty, Muhammad ibn Abu Bakr, of probable Soninke descent, was born into a family whose sons traditionally served in the cavalry of the sixteenth-century Songhay state. It is probable as well that he was educated in the Islamic tradition. When he came of age to join the military, he served under the emperor Sunni Ali. In return for this service, he was eventually rewarded with an appointment as a Songhay regional governor. Following the death of Sunni Ali in 1492, Askiya Muhammad defeated Ali's successor, Sunni Barou, and became the new Songhay ruler. He quickly established control over the state and by 1497 was able to embark on a year's journey to perform the pilgrimage to Mecca.

Imbued with Islamic charisma (*baraka*) from this journey, and with the authority of the Abbasid caliph in Cairo, Askiya Muhammad set about expanding the empire, using Islam as the cement to hold it together. He patronized Muslim scholars and secured further legitimization of his rule from the North African scholar al-Maghili.

Tributary territories were added to his empire, including parts of Mali, the Saharan salt pans of Taghaza (an important source of revenue), the uplands of Aïr in the east, and perhaps temporarily some of the Hausa states. A complex system of administration was set up with numerous officeholders: the *kanfari*, the *askiya's* vice-regent for the western provinces; the *hi-koi* (master of the Niger fleet); the *hugu-korei-koi* (master of the royal household); and the *fari-mondio* (inspector of fields). Important provincial governors were located in Dendi (the south), Hombori (facing the Mossi country), Timbuktu, and Jenne. Blind and enfeebled, Askiya Muhammad was deposed by his son Musa in 1528 but lived on in retirement until his death in Gao.

See also **Islam; Sunni 'Ali.**

BIBLIOGRAPHY

Hunwick, John O. "Songhay, Bornu, and the Hausa States, 1450–1600." In *History of West Africa*, Vol. 1, ed. J. F. Ade Ajaji and Michael Crowder. London: Longman, 1985.

Levtzion, Nehemia. *Islam in West Africa: Religion, Society, and Politics to 1800.* Brookfield, VT: Variorum, 1994.

JOHN HUNWICK

ABYSSINIA.   *See* **Eritrea; Ethiopia, Modern; Ethiopia and Vicinity, History of (600 to 1600 CE).**

ACCRA.

The capital of Ghana, Accra is located on the Gulf of Guinea on the Gold Coast. It is the commercial, educational, governmental, and cultural center of Ghana, the hub of its road and rail system, and the site of Kotoka International Airport. The population is around 1.7 million. A village at this site was founded some time in the 1600s, when a group of people known as the Ga settled in the area. Possession of the settlement was contested by other peoples of the region, and the Asante ultimately proved victorious.

The Portuguese were the first Europeans to arrive in the vicinity of Accra in the mid-fifteenth century. They were seeking gold. Slaves, however, proved to be the most profitable industry, and the Portuguese built Elmina Castle as a base from which the trade could be controlled. Dutch and British arrived shortly thereafter. In 1637, the Dutch chased the Portuguese from Elmina Castle. Forts were built along the adjacent coast, two of which—Fort Ussher, built by the Dutch in 1652, and Fort James, built by the British in 1673—expanded into present-day Accra. Due to its relatively dry climate, the British chose Accra as the capital of their Gold Coast colony (which was renamed Ghana in 1957, when the country gained its independence).

Industries in Accra include brewing and distilling, fish and fruit canning, clothing, shoes, and pharmaceuticals. There is a deep-water port used in colonial times, but it has been surpassed in importance by Tema, 17 miles east. There is also a growing tourist industry; Accra offers a host of accommodations in addition to a nightlife unparalleled in Africa. On any given night, there are live music performances and cinemas where international films can be seen. The landscape of Accra is dramatic in its division between skyscrapers and shantytowns, the sectors of the city that have connected economically with the industrialized Western world and sectors that have not.

A suburb of Accra (Legon) is home to the University of Ghana, and the city has schools for communications, science, and technology. It is also the location of the national museum and archives, and the National Theater.

See also **Ghana; Slave Trades; Tourism; Urbanism and Urbanization.**

BIBLIOGRAPHY

Owusu-Ansah, David, and Daniel M. McFarland. *Historical Dictionary of Ghana.* Lanham, MD: Scarecrow Press, 2005.

SARAH VALDEZ

Chinua Achebe (1930–). The Nigerian novelist and poet often wrote about African politics, how Africa and Africans were seen in the West, and the effects of colonialism on African societies. JERRY BAUER

ACHEBE, CHINUA (1930–). Chinua Achebe is a Nigerian novelist and one of Africa's most famous authors. Also known as Albert Chinualumogu Achebe, he was born in Ogidi, Eastern Nigeria, into the family of a devout evangelist who mixed his Christianity with traditional Igbo values. Achebe attended the University College of Ibadan and graduated in 1953 with a bachelor's degree in English. The founding editor of Heinemann's African Writers Series, his work forms the benchmark of African writing in English and he is considered the father of the Anglophone African novel.

Achebe's first and most famous novel, *Things Fall Apart* (1958), has sold more than 10 million copies worldwide. His early novels showcase the complexity of African cultures but also subtly criticize certain ethnic practices. His later novels use satire to criticize corruption and abuse of office, while his short stories and poetry focus mainly on the tragedy of civil conflicts. In his literary essays and scholarship, Achebe discusses the aesthetic and political imperatives of African literature, sometimes strongly condemning Western misperceptions of the continent. *The Trouble with Nigeria* (1983), a collection of political commentaries, is a stringent analysis of the failure of African political leadership. Achebe has also written children's books.

See also **Language; Literature.**

BIBLIOGRAPHY

Carroll, David. *Chinua Achebe: Novelist, Poet, Critic.* Basingstoke, U.K.: Macmillan, 1990.

Ezenwa-Ohaeto. *Chinua Achebe: A Biography.* Bloomington: Indiana University Press, 1997.

Gikandi, Simon. *Reading Chinua Achebe: Language and Ideology in Fiction.* Portsmouth, NH: Heinemann, 1991.

Sallah, Tijan M. *Chinua Achebe, Teacher of Light: A Biography.* Trenton, NJ: Africa World Press, 2003.

EVAN MWANGI

ADAMA, MODIBBO (c. 1771–1848).

Modibbo Adama was emir of one of the most extensive Fulani (Fulbe) emirates of the Sokoto Caliphate (present-day northern Nigeria), which subsequently became known as Adamawa Province. He was a product of Shaikh 'Uthman dan Fodio's jihad. Originally an Islamic scholar, he studied first under Mallam Kyari in Borno and later under 'Uthman. He became a flag bearer in 'Uthman's religious campaigns of conquest among peoples living to the southeast of what would was then becoming the Sokoto Caliphate. With the advent of European colonial rule, the Anglo-German boundary ran through the province, so that part of the territories he controlled fell under German authority in Kamerun (present-day northern Cameroun).

Adama, who came from the small Fulani Ba clan, was challenged by leaders of the more powerful clans, like the Wolarbe and the Jillaga, but the intervention of 'Uthman helped Adama to retain his authority. Adama also faced strong opposition from recalcitrant local residents who did not embrace Islam. He was pragmatic enough to grant such groups some measure of autonomy in return for payment of tribute to him as suzerain, but they continued to trouble his successors.

Adama is reputed to have given out twenty-four flags to local leaders—that is, he authorized them to act as his military agents to ensure the continued vitality of his jihad. He later established Yola as his capital and founded a dynasty that rules as the *lamidos* of Adamawa.

See also 'Uthman dan Fodio.

BIBLIOGRAPHY

Abubakar, Saad. "The Established Caliphate: Sokoto, the Emirates, and the Neighbours." In *Groundwork of Nigerian History*, ed. Ikime Obaro. Ibadan, Nigeria: Heinemann Educational Books, 1980.

Idama, Adamu. *Perspectives on the Industrialization of Adamawa State.* Yola, Nigeria: Paraclete Publishers, 2000.

Kirk-Greene, Anthony H. M. *Adamawa Past and Present.* London: Oxford University Press, 1958.

OLUTAYO ADESINA

ADDIS ABABA.

The capital of the expanding Ethiopian Empire in 1892, Addis Ababa was the home of the Organization of African Unity when it was founded in 1963. It is the largest city in Ethiopia. Situated at 7,800 feet above sea level on a well-watered plateau, Addis Ababa is the seat of the national government; the hub of the country's air, rail, and road network; the center of the trade and financial system; and the base for Ethiopia's radio and television stations.

Empress Taytu, the wife of Emperor Menelik II, founded the city in 1886 while her husband was on a military campaign in Harar. Under Menelik's and Taitu's influence, the town grew outward from around the palace, Saint George's Cathedral, and the central market, an area known collectively as Arada. Outside the center, Addis Ababa grew as a series of military encampments (*safar*) founded by nobles with land grants.

Although Addis Ababa was at the geographic center of the expanded empire, it lacked sufficient firewood to support its growing population. After the populace had rapidly deforested the area, the emperor considered moving his capital—as Amharic rulers before him had done for centuries—but importation of the fast-growing wattle (acacia, or eucalyptus) tree from Australia solved the problem. In addition, Addis Ababa's position as capital was strengthened by the extension and consolidation of Menelik's rule to the south and the east, after his defeat of the invading Italians at Adwa in 1896.

A rail line from Djibouti was completed in 1917, connecting Addis Ababa to the Red Sea and increasing the city's commercial prosperity. The population of the city grew as well, in part due to slave raiding in the southwestern part of the country. In 1912, for example, Prince Iyasu captured 40,000 people and ordered them to the capital; as many as half are said to have died on the way.

When the Italians controlled Ethiopia (1935–1941), they planned to remake Addis Ababa on a European model. Though not all these plans were implemented, they shaped the city as it is today. The town center, Arada, was renamed Piazza and became the commercial district. The indigenous market was moved from there to Mercato, which today is one of the largest open-air markets in Africa, teeming with people and goods from every corner of the country. The Italians also built factories, mills, and roads.

The mid-1990s found Addis Ababa (and Ethiopia) in transition from a Marxist to a free-market economy. In the shadows of the large Soviet-style monuments to the people and the army (erected during Mengistu Haile Mariam's rule), hawkers sold curios, and merchants around the city offered fancy Italian shoes and European clothing for sale. By the year 2000, the number of people living in the city reached 2.3 million.

See also **Colonial Policies and Practices: Italian; Djibouti, Republic of; Ethiopia: Modern; Harar; Menelik II; Mengistu, Haile Mariam; Organization of African Unity; Slave Trades; Taytu, Empress.**

BIBLIOGRAPHY

Zewde, Bahru. *A History of Modern Ethiopia, 1855–1991.* Oxford: James Currey; Athens: Ohio University Press; Addis Ababa: Addis Ababa University Press, 2001.

THOMAS F. McDow

Performer King Sunny Adé (1946–). Adé introduced the pedal steel guitar to Nigerian pop music after hearing it in American country and western songs. JACK VARTOOGIAN

ADÉ, SUNNY (1946–). One of Africa's most famous popular musicians, "King" Sunny Adé is a bandleader, guitarist, and vocalist. He performs *juju* music, a style mainly associated with the Yoruba people of southwest Nigeria. Most of his songs are sung in the Yoruba language, and his lyrics tend to be either praise lyrics, traditional Yoruba aphorisms, or excerpts of Christian hymns and Biblical verse. Adé has been one of Nigeria's top musicians since he began performing in the late 1960s with his first band, the Green Spots. In the early 1980s, he made several well-publicized tours of Europe, American, and Japan with his next band, the African Beats.

Since the late 1990s, his band has been called the Golden Mercury of Africa. Adé owns several recording companies and most of his recordings have been released on his own labels. He is also a successful businessman who holds several non-music related companies, as well. His best known albums include *Challenge Cup '67* (1968), *Ogun* (1970), *Juju Music* (1982), and *Synchro System* (1983). His 1998 album *Odu* was nominated for a Grammy award. Adé has also been a leading figure in the Performing Musicians Association of Nigeria (PMAN).

See also **Music, Modern Popular.**

BIBLIOGRAPHY

Thomas, T. Ajayi. *History of Juju Music.* New York: Thomas, 1992.

Waterman, Christopher. *Juju: A Social History and Ethnography of an African Popular Music.* Chicago: University of Chicago Press, 1990.

MICHAEL VEAL

ADULIS. The port of Adulis, located in present-day Eritrea, was of great significance in ancient times, best known for its role in Aksumite trade during the fourth through seventh centuries CE. It is connected to Aksum in Ethiopia by a tortuous mountain route to Qohaito, then across the plateau to the metropolis itself. Adulis is also listed as a major port of the *Periplus of the Erythraean Sea,* a sailors' handbook of the first century CE. Not only did it offer a good harbor on the route to India, but it was a source for luxuries such as ivory, tortoiseshell, and rhinoceros horn.

The ancient site was first identified by Henry Salt, who visited it in 1810, and noted that it was still called "Azoole." There is little reason to doubt Salt's identification as it accords well with the *Periplus.* It lies in the Gulf of Zula, a deep bay of exactly the correct dimensions (200 stades or 20.5 miles deep), and at the entrance, close to the opposite shore is Dese island, called "Oreinê" in the *Periplus.* The site is about 10 hectares (25 acres) in extent and comprises substantial mounds, some of which have clear indications of walls. Trenches have been dug into a few revealing impressive buildings, but excavation has barely touched the site.

There have always been, however, both chronological and topographical problems with the identification of the site as Adulis. First, the surface pottery is late in date and accords with Aksumitic importance. In addition there are topographic problems. Adulis is referred to as a port, but it is four miles from the sea. At the time of the *Periplus* it was twenty stades (less than two miles) from the coast. There has clearly been major coastal change in the area and the harbor and settlement must always have been at some distance from one another. Furthermore, the *Periplus* refers to an island approached by a causeway, which suggested to some that the site was originally at Massawa, thirty-seven miles km to the north, a town which in the twenty-first century comprises islands connected by causeways.

Christian Topography, a work by Cosmas Indicopleustes written in the sixth century CE, has a map showing Adulis a little way from the coast clearly connected with Aksum. It seems to have been an important place with a throne and inscription which Cosmas recorded. On the shore are two other places, Gabaza and Samidi, which have never been identified. However, three miles to the southeast are the Galala hills, where large quantities of pottery have been discovered. It was suggested by Sundström in 1909 that this could be the site of Gabaza, perhaps even the port of Adulis itself.

Pottery from the Galala hills and structures on them, possibly lookout towers, show that this was almost certainly the site of Gabaza. However, off the seaward end of the hills is a rock that would have been a small island in Roman times; a scattering of first-century CE Roman wine amphorae were found there. The *Periplus* relates that ships used to moor off Diodorus Island, which was connected to the mainland by a causeway, but it became overrun by barbarians and was considered too dangerous, and the anchorage was moved to an island called Oreinê ("hilly"). This can be none other than Dese, the only hilly island in the area.

Field survey on the island has located a fine harbor and a settlement marked by early Roman pottery. The two Roman period harbors mentioned in the *Periplus* have now been located. The remaining site, Samidi, a large mound of schist stones with traces of steps leading up it has also been found four miles north of Adulis. Architectural fragments of Aksumite date and fragments of human bone suggest that this may have been an impressive mausoleum, perhaps the burial place of a king of Adulis.

See also **Aksum; Eritrea: Geography and Economy.**

BIBLIOGRAPHY

Casson, Lionel. "The Location of Adulis." *Periplus Maris Erythraei 4.* In *Coins, Culture, and History in the Ancient World,* ed. Lionel Casson and Martin Price. Detroit: Wayne State University Press, 1981.

Casson, Lionel. *The "Periplus Maris Erythraei."* Princeton, NJ: Princeton University Press, 1989.

Paribeni, R. "Richerche nel luogo dell'antica Adulis." *Monumenti Antichi* 18 (1907).

Sundström, R. "Report on an Expedition to Adulis." *Zeitschrift für Assyriologie* 20 (1907): 171–182.

Wolska-Conus, Wanda. *La topographie chrétienne: Sources chétienne III.* Paris: Presses Universitaires de France, 1968.

DAVID PEACOCK

AFARS ET DES ISSAS, TERRITOIRE DES. *See* **Djibouti, Republic of.**

AFONSO I.   *See* **Mvemba Nzinga.**

AFRICA, HISTORY OF THE NAME.

The toponym "Africa" is first known to have been used by the Romans to designate the core area of the Carthaginian Empire (modern-day Tunisia). When the Romans occupied this area they divided it into a number of provinces, among them *Africa Proconsularis* (northern Tunisia) and *Africa Nova* (much of present-day Algeria, also called Numidia). This usage was continued by the Arabs following their conquest of the area, *Ifrîqiyâ* or *Ifrîqiyyah* referring to the northern part of modern-day Tunisia.

There is no consensus on the original meaning of the term "Africa" and a variety of explanations have been proposed. Some Hellenistic-era authors proposed that Africa was the land of the descendants of "Afer," the offspring of a mythical hero or god. Based on Old Testament genealogy, Isidore of Seville (seventh century) proposed that Afer was one of the sons of Ham, son of Noah. Medieval Christian sources referred to "Affer," a bastard son of Abraham. For al-Ya'qûbî, the grandson of Ham who gave his name to the country was "Fâriq." Al-Kalbî proposed that the mythical ancestor of the Africans (original Berber inhabitants of Tunisia) was *Ifrîqîs*, a legendary Arab hero from Yemen.

Numerous philological explanations of the toponym have also been proposed. The sixteenth-century writer Leo Africanus derived the term from the hypothetical Greek expression *a-phrike*, "without cold" or "without horror." It has also been proposed that the Roman term derived from the Latin *aprica*, "sunny," or "hot," or else that it was a contraction of *Africa terra*, or "land of the Afri." This supposes that the Afri, Afer, or Ifri were a people, possibly a Berber tribe residing in the area of Carthage at the time of Phoenician colonization, but there is no evidence of this ethnonym in the primary sources. Furthermore, it is highly unlikely that there is any relation to the Afar people of modern Djibouti. Others, beginning with al-Bîrûnî, have proposed to derive "Africa" from the Semitic root *f-r-q*, which can connote "apart from," "separate from," but also

"portion of," "division of." In this case the Romans would have adopted an existing Punic term referring to some portion of territory or population. More recently, it has been proposed that the term derives from *ifri*, a Berber word meaning "cave," which could have been used as a name for the cave-dwelling indigenous inhabitants of the area. As with the previous propositions however, there is no evidence for any of these in the primary sources of the Punic or Roman Republican eras.

The use of the toponym "Africa" to designate the entire continent is modern. Prior to the seventeenth century, a number of other names: principally "Libya," "Ethiopia," "Sudan," and "Guinea," were commonly used by European and Muslim geographers. This is because neither the Greek, Roman, nor Arab geographers could conceive of a continent requiring a single designation. For the ancient Greeks, the landmass to the south was called "Libya," a toponym derived from Lebu, or Rebu, an ancient Egyptian ethnonym that designated a people (probably Berber) living in its western desert. "Libya" consisted of the Pentapolis (Cyrenaica), Tripolitania, and "Libya Interior" but did not include Egypt, which was considered a land on its own.

Early Arab geographers maintained this wide definition of Libya. Medieval European geographers, influenced by the Latin texts and by the continued use of the Arabic *Ifrîqiyâ*, used the term in a wider sense to designate North Africa generally. The use of the term to designate the Saharan interior of the continent persisted in Europe until the nineteenth century. Early authors used "Africa" interchangeably with "Barbary" (derived from a Greek ethnonym) to designate what Arab geographers called "the Maghrib," the "setting-place" of the sun. In addition, Arabs called the entire zone south of the Sahara extending from the Senegal River to the Red Sea *Bilad al-Sûdân*, the "land of the blacks," and used *Zanj* to designate the East African landmass accessible from the Indian Ocean.

After the Portuguese rounded the Cape of Good Hope and made contact with the Christian Empire of Abyssinia, the ancient Greek toponym "Ethiopia" was revived. The term was applied loosely to all the tropical parts of the continent, with the south Atlantic being designated as the "Ethiopian Sea." "Guinea," derived from "Ghana," also gained currency in Europe in the early modern period. Usually subdivided into "Upper" and "Lower" Guinea, it designated areas of West Africa accessible from the Gulf of Guinea.

Until the mid-seventeenth century these various designations appeared boldly on European maps and globes. Both "Guinea" and "Ethiopia" were used to designate the interior tropical parts of the continent Europeans knew virtually nothing about, while "Libya" and "Africa" appeared prominently over northern and Saharan latitudes. No single toponym designated the continent as a whole. Eventually, possibly due to the canonical status of classical texts in Latin, "Africa" won out over the others; it is a case of one of the parts giving its name to the whole. Following this transmutation of meaning, North Africa ("Barbary," i.e.,"the Maghrib") was occasionally called "Africa Minor," by analogy with Asia Minor (Anatolia, the original "Asia" of the Greeks), and Africa/*Ifrîqiyâ* stopped being used as a designation for Tunisia, even in Arabic.

See also **History of Africa; Leo Africanus.**

BIBLIOGRAPHY

Fall, Yoro K. *L'Afrique à la naissance de la cartographie moderne: Les cartes majorquines (XIVe–XVe siècles)*. Paris: Editions Karthala, 1982.

Lewis, Martin W., and Kären E. Wigen. *The Myth of Continents: A Critique of Metageography*. Berkeley: University of California Press, 1997.

Talbi, M. "Ifrikiya." In *The Encyclopaedia of Islam*. Leiden: Brill, 2001.

ERIC S. ROSS

AFRICAN AMERICAN RELIGIONS. *See* **Religion and Ritual; Religion and the Study of Africa.**

AFRIKANER REPUBLICS. *See* **Cape Colony and Hinterland, History of (1600 to 1910); South Africa, Republic of.**

AFRIKANERS. *See* **South Africa, Republic of.**

AFRO-ASIATIC LANGUAGES. *See* **Languages: Afro-Asiatic.**

AFROCENTRISM.

Afrocentrism (alternate designation: afrocentricity) is a perspective within African and diaspora studies and historiography that seeks to position Africans and their histories more centrally within world histories. Afrocentrism has marked both English- and French-language scholarship in Africa, North America, and the Caribbean since the 1970s and has analytical elements in common with contemporary trends in postcolonial studies, cultural studies, subaltern studies, and neo-Marxist and postmodern theory.

The roots of the Afrocentric perspective can be traced to thinkers such as W. E. B. Du Bois, Aimé Césaire, and Léopold Sédar Senghor. They postulated a common black heritage across the continent and the diaspora and saw higher education and the writing of history as tools with which to combat racism, oppression, and colonialism.

Two landmark publications in 1954 helped articulate what were to become central issues of Afrocentrism: in *Nations nègres et culture*, Cheikh Anta Diop argued that the civilization of ancient Egypt was essentially black African in character and that this was relevant to the study of contemporary Africa; in *Stolen Legacy*, George G. M. James advanced that Greek philosophy was stolen from the Egyptians. These authors framed their respective arguments in Pan-Africanist and anticolonial terms, seeking to challenge what they saw as a deeply entrenched Eurocentric and racist bias within European and North American scholarship and academia. Further, they argued, these biases affected not only the production of knowledge about Africa and its history, but the construction of white Western identity, as well.

Since then, these theses have been further investigated and the Black Egypt paradigm has come to dominate the corpus, to the point where it is sometimes characterized as Egyptocentric or Nilocentric, rather than Afrocentric. Egypt (usually designated by its ancient indigenous name Kemet in the literature) is central to the Afrocentric perspective for three reasons. First, it is argued that the ancient civilizations of the Nile Valley share a common black African cultural foundation with subsequent African civilizations. Ancient Egypt and the Nile Valley thus serve as civilizational hearth for Africa and the diaspora, just as Ancient Greece does for Europe and its overseas offshoots. Secondly, it is argued that pharaonic civilization exerted a determining influence on classical antiquity: Ancient Greece and the Hellenistic world. Thirdly, pharaonic Egypt is held to have played a determining role in the development of the Abrahamic monotheist faiths, first of Judaism, then of Christianity and Islam. Thus, if ancient Egypt, an African civilization, had such an important role in the development of Greco-Roman, Judeo-Christian civilization, then Africa and Africans are central to world history rather than marginal to it.

The centeredness of Afrocentrism is twofold; it aims to recenter Africa within world history, but also to write African and diaspora history from its own centers, or unique experience, as opposed to the external historiography of the continent and its peoples inherited from colonial-era scholarship. It has thus developed as a strong epistemological critique of African Studies. Colonial-era European scholarship on Africa and Africans, the roots of which lie in the previous era of slavery, served to promote the myth of European (Judeo-Christian, Greco-Roman) cultural and racial superiority. It also celebrated individualism and materialism over more communal and cooperative values. More generally, the epistemological Eurocentrism of Africanist discourse positioned Africa as a foil for Europe in such a way that Africa was always found to be lacking in some essential way.

The view that African history needs to be recentered is shared across the spectrum of Afrocentric thinkers, but there is no agreement on how the Afrocentric project is to be accomplished. At the outset, Cheikh Anta Diop, though cautioning that cultural alienation was an "age-old weapon of domination" (1954, vol. 1: 14), nonetheless called on those who wished to embark upon the project to arm themselves with scientific method, considered the surest means of combating the unscientific falsehoods of Eurocentrism. For some postmodern thinkers, however, science itself is ideological and positivist empiricism, constrained by theory, can only continue to devalue Africa's place in history. An alternative Afrocentric theory and methodology, rooted in African values and philosophies,

has been developed by Molefi Asante (b. 1942). Alternative values such as orality, human perspective, the search for justice, and clear conception of place (centeredness) are required to fill in the interstices caused by the silence of the historically oppressed. These latter arguments for cognitive relativism, grounded in postmodern theory, are among those most severely critiqued by Afrocentrism's detractors.

By the 1970s, the centrality of pharaonic civilization for African history had been recognized by a wide cross section of scholars in Francophone Africa and the Caribbean. Although it is not a hegemonic paradigm, neither is it considered a particularly radical or tendentious perspective; the cultural unity of black Africa, including ancient Egypt, has become a mainstream assumption on the continent. The same is not the case in the United States, where the issue of the scientific validity of Afrocentrism within academia is still debated.

In the United States, the scope of Afrocentrism has expanded far beyond intellectual circles. Since the 1980s it has become a social and cultural movement among African Americans, with a well-developed pop culture dimension expressed in hip-hop and rap for example, and it has impacted curriculums in public schools. Thus, Afrocentricity is now integral to identity politics and wider race relations, and this has become inseparable from the arguments over its scientific validity. Conservative and establishment thinkers have critiqued both the movement and the scholarship for being deliberately polemical and divisive, or separatist. Activist academics, on the other hand, maintain that the teaching of African and African American history must serve a larger social purpose: that of regenerating an African American society whose problems are being perpetuated by the entrenched, exclusionary Canons of academia.

See also **Africa in Political and Social Thought; Césaire, Aimé; Diop, Cheikh Anta; Du Bois, W. E. B; Senghor, Léopold Sédar.**

BIBLIOGRAPHY

Asante, Molefi Kete. *Afrocentricity: The Theory of Social Change.* Chicago: African American Images, 1980.

Asante, Molefi Kete. *The Afrocentric Idea.* Philadelphia: Temple University Press, 1987.

Ben-Jochannan, Yosef. *Africa, Mother of Western Civilization*. Baltimore: Black Classic Press, 1988.

Ben-Jochannan, Yosef. *African Origins of the Major "Western Religions"*. Baltimore: Black Classic Press, 1991.

Bernal, Martin. *Black Athena: The Afroasiatic Roots of Classical Civilization*, Vol. 1: *The Fabrication of Ancient Greece 1785–1985*. New Brunswick, NJ: Rutgers University Press, 1987.

Diop, Cheikh Anta. *Nations nègres et culture: de l'antiquité nègre égyptienne aux problèmes culturels de l'Afrique noire d'aujourd'hui*. 2 vols. Paris: Présence africaine, 1954.

Diop, Cheikh Anta. *The African Origin of Civilization: Myth or Reality*. Chicago: Laurence Hill Books, 1974.

Gray, Chris. *Conceptions of History: Cheikh Anta Diop and Theophile Obenga*. London: Karnak House, 1989.

James, George G. M. *Stolen Legacy: Greek Philosophy is Stolen Egyptian Philosophy*. Trenton, NJ: Africa World Press, 1992.

Lefkowitz, Mary. *Not out of Africa: How Afrocentrism Became an Excuse to Teach Myth as History*. New York: Basic Books, New Republic Publishing, 1996.

Moses, Wilson Jeremiah. *Afrotopia*. New York: Cambridge University Press, 2002.

Ross, Eric S. "Africa in Islam: What the Afrocentric Perspective Can Contribute to the Study of Islam." *International Journal of Islamic and Arabic Studies* 11, no. 2 (1994): 1–36.

Van Sertima, Ivan, ed. *Journal of African Civilizations*. New Brunswick, NJ: Transaction Publishers (first issue 1983).

ERIC S. ROSS

AFTERLIFE.   *See* **Death, Mourning, and Ancestors.**

AFUA KOBI (1815–1900). Historical records and published work on Akan *ahemaa* (queen mothers) reveal them as dynamic women who had a keen sense of history, politics, and responsibility toward the preservation of their societies. Afua Kobi (1815–1900) succeeded her mother Afua Sapon (1790–1859) as *Asantehemaa* (which can also mean queen mother), following a palace coup exiling her mother and brother that Kobi is alleged to have engineered.

After the death of her uncle, Asantehene (king) Kwaku Dua I (d. 1884), Afua Kobi successfully advocated for the enstoolment (accession) of her son Kofi Kakari (d. 1884). Despite Afua Kobi's reputed judicious counseling, the Asantehene's rule was tarnished by his extravagant expenditures and imprudent decisions. The unsuccessful 1873–1874 Asante war against the British, which Afua Kobi ardently opposed, was one such unwise choice.

In spite of her 1872 challenge to the British envoy Henry Plange that "I am only a woman, but would fight the governor with my left hand," Afua Kobi preferred a negotiated solution to the 1873 dispute with the British. Assessing that war with the British would be catastrophic for Asante, Afua Kobi insisted that "I lived before Kwakoo Dooah, and I have now placed my son on the Ashantee throne. . . . I do not wish for our successors to say my son was the cause of the disturbance of the sixty *nkurow* [(towns); i.e. the whole of Asante]" (Aidoo, 70). The Asantehemaa's statement illustrates her insightfulness and, more importantly, sense of her role in history. As *Ohemaa* (queen mother), she was the preeminent counselor of the king, and she held herself accountable for the detrimental effects of his rule on the nation.

Accordingly, Afua Kobi recommended Kofi Kakari's removal from power following Asante's defeat in the war. Motivated by her wish to continue her dynasty, Afua Kobi maneuvered to achieve the enstoolment of her younger son, Mensa Bonsu. Similar to his older brother, the new Asantehene was inept in political management. In a canny repetition of history, Afua Kobi's eldest daughter Yaa Akyaa (1884–1917), ousted her mother from office, sent her into exile with Mensa Bonsu (d. 1896), and installed herself and her son in their place, much in the same way that Afua Kobi had deposed her own mother and brother decades earlier.

See also **Ghana; Queens and Queen Mothers.**

BIBLIOGRAPHY

Aidoo, Agnes Aidoo. "Women in the History and Culture of Ghana" *Research Review* 1, no. 1 (1985): 14–51.

Aidoo, Agnes Akosua. "Asante Queen Mothers in Government and Politics in the Nineteenth Century." In *The Black Woman Cross-Culturally*, ed. Filomena C. Steady. Rochester, Vermont: Schenkan Books, Inc, 1985.

Arhin, Kwame. "The Political and Military Roles of Akan Women." In *Female and Male in West Africa*, ed. Christine Oppong. London: Allen and Unwin, 1983.

Wilks, Ivor. *Forests of Gold: Essays on the Akan and the Kingdom of Asante.* Athens: Ohio University Press, 1993.

TAKYIWAA MANUH

AGAJA (1673–1740). Agaja was the brother of the fourth king of Dahomey, Akaba, and succeeded to the throne in 1708 because Akaba's only son was too young to rule when Akaba died. To avoid later challenges to his rule, he sent Akaba's son into exile.

Upon taking the throne, Agaja began a series of expansionist wars and managed to extend his kingdom of Dahomey, today encompassed by the southern part of Bénin, southward to the western coast. However, the belief that he established and fought with an army of women soldiers, known to the Europeans as Amazons, and with them seized control of the kingdom of Allada in 1724, and then the coastal trading town of Ouidah (Whydah) in 1727, has been shown to be a myth.

Meanwhile, in 1726, the formidable Yoruba kingdom of Oyo, to the northeast of Dahomey, invaded Agaja's kingdom for the first time. They succeeded in burning Dahomey's capital, Abomey, and Agaja and his forces were forced into hiding while the Oyo continued to plunder and ravage. In a series of subsequent invasions occurring in 1728, 1729, and 1730, the Oyo depleted the strength of Dahomey and ultimately forced Agaja to pay tribute as recognition of their superiority.

Presuming the relative stability of his political position, Agaja re-established the capital of Dahomey at Allada, to the south of the former capital, in 1730. Agaja proceeded to consolidate and centralize his government under royal control, and it followed that Agaja's involvement in the slave trade was also subjected to his singular control. Agaja's rule ended in 1732, but some sources suggest that he lived another eight years, dying in 1740.

Agaja was succeeded by Tegbessou, who lost many of the gains in wealth and territory achieved under Agaja's reign. Internal unrest in Dahomey ensued after 1735, because Agaja's policies prohibited subordinate chiefs from owning and selling slaves. To quell this unrest, the slave trade was opened to their participation in 1737. As a result, Dahomey's economic viability was diminished, and in 1739 it was no longer able to pay tribute to the Oyo; Tegbessou was a poor military planner, and during his reign the Oyo invaded Dahomey for the last time, leaving the kingdom much diminished.

See also **Kings and Kingdoms; Kingship.**

BIBLIOGRAPHY

Herskovits, Melville J. *Dahomey: An Ancient West African Kingdom.* Evanston, IL: Northwestern University Press, 1967.

SARAH VALDEZ

AGE AND AGE ORGANIZATION. The indigenous cultures of sub-Saharan Africa are characterized by respect for age, legitimizing the authority claimed by older people. There are, of course, variations on this theme, and it persists into the twenty-first century only to the extent that it has not been outmoded by the drift toward individualism. But typically in agricultural and pastoral areas, and notably where local communities have a certain autonomy, older people are expected to have cultivated a sense of respect, and they claim a right to the respect of others stemming from their seniority and accumulated experience. In this traditional setting, younger people are expected to acquire a stake in this way of thinking, investing in their own futures, even before middle age. It is in this context that terms such as "elder" and "elderhood" are so apt in the literature as translations of vernacular terms. They convey a consciousness of age with a sense of status and respect.

This ideal pervades institutions ranging from the extended family, dominated by the senior generation with control over collective property and marriage for juniors, to ancestor cults in which older people closest to the ancestors hold sway, and most explicitly, to societies organized by male age cohorts. Apart from age, the balance of power between male and female domains varies, as does the extent to which ritual expertise is a specialty that is not necessarily linked to old age as such. Generally, however, the premise of age seniority holds in traditional Africa. In those domains where women have a measure of power, such power increases with age, and where the skill of ritual experts is called upon, this tends to complement the authority of older people rather than detract from it.

RESPECT AND THE ANOMALIES OF OLD AGE

Indirectly associated with the high status of older people is a prevailing notion of population growth as propitious. The larger the family, the greater its security in situations of unexpected crisis. Immortality as a future ancestor—or even simply a vague sense of continuity beyond death—lies in the survival and prosperity of living descendants. The recurrent themes in ethnographic accounts of African societies that cite multiple wives, the propitiation of ancestors, and concern over women's fertility bear on this notion of propitious growth. Polygyny is by no means invariable, but surveys reveal that this practice is very common in traditional Africa and altogether more prevalent than in any other continent. It is this factor especially that colors the authority of older men and retards the rate at which they allow their sons to mature. By delaying the marriages of these younger men for a decade or more, the elders as a body create a surplus of marriageable girls as brides, collectively enhancing their chances of polygyny and of creating large families extending over time.

The way in which widespread polygyny was facilitated by extended bachelorhood among younger men (moran, in the local language) is graphically illustrated in Figure 1 showing the demographic balance by age and sex among Samburu pastoralists in northern Kenya. Even though widows were not allowed to remarry, the polygyny rate still averaged 1.5 wives per married elder, and this is not excessive by traditional African standards. The broad-based profile of this pyramid points to a generally high mortality rate, especially among children. Only the toughest survived to respected and polygynous old age.

A further asset among elders is their control over information and resources. Their claim to be the true custodians of tradition extends to a rapport with supernatural forces. Their accumulated wisdom provides a protection from the brutish forces of nature, placing society at a higher level. It inverts the natural process of aging in a display of hidden power. The wisdom, social networks, and diplomatic skills of elders are community assets that

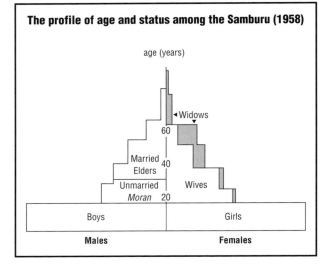

The profile of age and status among the Samburu (1958)

Figure 1.

are cultivated with experience. They are the repositors of the system of beliefs and symbolic superstructure, maintaining power and dignity through their ability to interpret and give meaning to the vagaries of social existence.

There is a charismatic aspect to this authority that older people embed in performance. Survival to old age is not in itself sufficient. Not all older people can display wisdom, especially once their competence diminishes, and their role in ritual is sometimes nominal rather than essential. But even in these circumstances, the premise of age superiority is propped up by younger elders, whose future depends on maintaining respect for age in their community. Elders who retain the ability to overawe from a position of superior age and experience use the symbolic idiom to effect, giving it an immediacy that conveys power. Each ritual event has to be both acted and stage-managed, responding to opportunity. To the extent that it is manipulated with panache, older people are endowed as repositors of symbolic knowledge, and the very fact of old age is imbued with a certain charisma.

The widespread awe of ancestors, whose presence is often invoked and even made visible in ritual, elevates the respect for old age to a higher level. Ancestors are older even than the oldest men, and their survival after death gives them access to hidden cosmic powers and knowledge. Beyond the ancestors, this characteristic is exaggerated further in the various manifestations of the belief in God, widely perceived as a being that precedes all existence and possesses supreme knowledge and omnipotence, evoking a grossly magnified image of old age. This supernatural aspect of respect for old age may be tinged with fear. A grotesque caricature of self-indulgence among older people may be one of greed and envy, associated with witchcraft and sorcery and sometimes with the ancestors themselves. This appears as a perversion of the norm, dissociated from the ideal, but hinting also at the absoluteness of the power of older people.

This orientation toward old age contains the type of anomaly associated with absolute authority. Respect has the appearance of a clear-cut notion, but it does not quite match up to relations between young and old. If older people are characterized as having achieved a sense of respect—a state where they are both respected and respecting—then this implies that younger people have not yet achieved this ideal. To this extent the young do not invariably show respect for elders, and elders do not have respect in every sense of the term; they have a sense of respect, but are not altogether respected in practice, but they cannot altogether respect the disrespectful young. The antithesis of the power of older men is the physical virility of youth, often associated with an alternative lifestyle in "warrior" societies. This differentiation in power poses a contradiction between the moral advantage that lies with older men and the more immediate interests of younger men, who may react against traditional restrictions.

Again, in such societies, women may not always accept their position of subordination to older men. Their collective rituals and dancing frequently are conducted in a spirit of ritualized rebellion, undermining the prestige of their husbands and serving as a warning against the abuse of their power.

In such ways, the ideal of respect is relevant to the rhetoric between different ages and sexes, but ultimately it is flawed. One is therefore led to look more closely at ways in which the ambiguities of aging are handled in various contexts, and particularly with reference to aging among men.

INITIATION AND HIERARCHIES OF POWER

Ambiguities may be identified in both youth and old age, which together mark the anomalous boundaries of active adult life. The first draws attention especially to the process of initiation as a gateway to adulthood, and the second concerns the contradiction between respect for old age and the loss of control and dignity among those who survive to attain it.

Accounts of initiation often emphasize the element of performance that exaggerates age differences, imposing sharp discontinuities on the continuous process of aging. Older men parade their power, overawing the initiates with dramatic revelations and threats, confusing them, exposing their ignorance, emphasizing the termination of their childhood as a prelude to rebirth and renewal. Typically, these demonstrations occur at a time when young initiates are entering their physical prime and those overseeing the performance are visibly aging. A stable moral universe in which frail elderhood reigns is imposed on the transient physical world, and with it arises the prospect of an enhanced elderhood for the initiates in the longer term.

The power of older people on such occasions lies in their control over the system of beliefs. What they are assumed to conceal in the manipulation of knowledge may be more important than the knowledge they in fact hold. This has been vividly demonstrated for societies whose gerontocratic organization is based on a hierarchy of secrecy, extending the induction into full elderhood almost indefinitely. It is through the hiding of secrets rather than sharing knowledge as such that power is displayed, impeding the careers of ambitious younger men.

Among the Kpelle of Liberia, for instance, all ritual knowledge was the possession of one or other of their secret societies: the Poro among men and the Sande among women. The content of the secrets was often insignificant compared with the privileges generated by possessing them. The existence of secrets was paraded by older members, masquerading as spirits, to control their juniors. Youths first had to submit to an extended initiation school with persistent threats of beating, poisoning, or mysterious death if they betrayed the secrets. In learning to honor the code of secrecy, they learned to respect the elders. Higher status within the society involved further initiations, and these were restricted to those who had mastered the secrets at lower levels and could afford the fees.

The assumption of an esoteric knowledge placed the elders in the central arena, and the assumption of ignorance placed the youths on the periphery from where they had to buy their way in. The overall pattern, however, was not one of elders passing on cultural traditions, but of withholding more than they taught in order to retain control over the young and innocent. In the final resort, the content of knowledge was elusively shallow, and paradoxically it was the ritual display mounted around secrecy that underpinned the system, confusing the initiates with misinformation and enhancing rather than detracting from the power of those at the top who ultimately controlled the code of ritual deceit through a fictional display of secrecy.

The widespread practice of group initiations introduces a further theme: the bond of fellowship among peers as the antithesis of the inequalities of age. While there is an element of isolated uniqueness in the mental and physical ordeal that accompanies initiation for each novice, they all share in the prospect and retrospect as a group, lending one another moral support and emerging to share the credit. The notion of communitas (human fellowship) is an especially apt expression for the shared experience of initiation. The participants are exposed to the cosmic mysteries that underlie their existence, in whatever form the forces of gerontocratic repression are expressed. They are drawn together as mere mortals, with a prevailing emphasis on total equality, sharing everything as a group, reduced to a uniform condition that transcends all distinctions of rank, kinship, and wealth.

There is, however, a shift from the notion of communitas developed by Victor Turner, which involved the opposition between the structured inequalities that prevail in daily existence and the antistructure of rituals of transition. On the occasion of initiation—and indeed in Turner's own description of the Ndembu of Zambia—the structure of age inequality prevails and is imposed quite deliberately on the initiates. The boundary is not so much between profane authority and sacred communitas, extending to humanity at large, as between elders masterminding the occasion and youths experiencing the spirit of communitas among themselves. The close fellowship of the peer group would perhaps be a less ambiguous description of this experience, but the point to stress is that, within the peer group, the sense of communitas prevails and persists even into old age.

It is in old age that the further contradiction occurs between respect in principle and loss of authority in practice. This is especially characteristic of the more competitive public domain controlled by men as opposed to the more supportive domestic domain within which women have built up their networks of influence. The demographic profile for the Samburu (as depicted in Figure 1) also indicates the contrasting life trajectories of women who are married young to much older men. Among patrilineal societies, the depressed status of women has to be viewed in relation to their total life-course, that is, as they age. Whereas initiation for a boy is his first step from the obscurity of childhood toward a promising adulthood, the marriage of a girl transforms her from the obscurity of childhood to further obscurity as a young wife and stranger in her new home, with very restricted opportunities. A view of women as the victims of male exploitation is particularly apt at this low point early in their careers, and especially in societies where there is a sharp separation between male and female domains.

An alternative viewpoint portrays women as agents who can manipulate their depressed situation to their own advantage. Their rituals of rebellion display their own exclusive communitas, pitted against a world dominated by men. This interpretation becomes increasingly apt as a woman's life course develops and notably once she surmounts the restrictions of her reproductive years and grows increasingly independent of her aging husband. Women's networks, especially through growing family links, tend to persist throughout life, whereas older men, as they lose the will to compete in the public arena, have to accept a loss of power with dignity in order to retain respect. In this way, the profiles of aging for the two sexes frequently diverge, and women, who were utterly subordinated at the time of their first marriage as girls, continue to gain confidence and status at advancing ages when older men face a loss. Old age is frequently characterized as a general process of irreversible loss, but the losses are especially marked for men in male-dominated societies.

SYSTEMS OF AGE ORGANIZATION

Forms of age organization characterize societies in various parts of Africa. In such systems, those of a similar age are grouped together as an age-set (or age-group), maturing and aging together. Their position at any stage consists of an array of expectations and privileges and may be termed an age grade. In effect, the age-set passes up, rung by rung, an age ladder of successive age grades in a defined progression, like a class of children passing through the grades of school, but over a more extensive period that extends into old age. The left-hand side of the Samburu demographic pyramid illustrates such a society. Each step in this demographic profile broadly represents an age-set, and the successive statuses for married elders could be elaborated to provide a more detailed hierarchy of age grades. In general, age-sets tend to involve males only, but they may also define critical aspects of men's relations with or through women, giving women a distinctive role within the age system. Thus, the position of a woman may be highlighted in relation to the age-set of her husband or father or sons, but women are only rarely grouped together by age, except sometimes during the brief period leading up to their marriages (reflected in the steps on the right-hand side of Figure 1).

The practice of group initiation may be regarded as a microcosm of age organization. In published accounts of age systems in Africa there is a similar contrast between horizontal unity and vertical subordination, and one or other theme tends to predominate according to the thrust of the analysis. But these are complementary features. Within age systems in general, the dominance of those in the more senior age grades evinces the charisma of old age, and the equality of age mates at each level re-invokes the close fellowship or communitas of the peer bonds of their youth, which continues to cut across rivalries in other aspects of their social life.

Historically, the best-known age systems were associated with military organization, mobilizing active young men into successive age cohorts of warriors. The persistence of such systems into more recent times when local warfare has been stemmed, notably among pastoralists in East Africa, raises searching questions concerning their non-military significance. Far from representing an obsolete form of social organization, as is sometimes suggested, the survival and adaptation of age systems has to be viewed in context.

East African age systems display a similar mystique and hierarchy of power as in West African secret societies, where careers are controlled by the ritual authority ascribed to those higher up. However, in East Africa it is as age-sets rather than as individuals that promotion takes place; and to the extent that the pace of these promotions is controlled by older men, they seek to ward off the inevitability of their own aging.

The age organization of the Maasai, for instance, is typical in many ways of this type of system. The survival of the institution of warriorhood among the Maasai, may be seen as more relevant to gerontocratic power over the young men, or moran, than to any threat from enemies. Any attempt to relax marriage restrictions to encourage young men to settle down, for instance, would loosen the monopoly over women held by their seniors. As boys, youths have first to jostle with their seniors to be accepted as the next age-set of moran, and then as moran they are suspended in a limbo somewhere between boyhood and full adulthood for an extended period of adolescence that stretches well into their twenties. They are denied access to deliberations on the affairs of elders, and hence to the knowledge and wisdom of elderhood, because they are held to lack respect. And they are not held in respect because they lack the knowledge and wisdom of elderhood.

The emphasis on ultimate ritual authority among older men creates a power vacuum lower down, and the price that the elders pay for their heavy-handed dominance is a certain loss of control over the delinquencies of younger men. These range from theft and brawls to adulteries with the wives of elders, and they extend to jostling between young men of successive age-sets for the privileges of moranhood. The gerontocratic rule of the elders and the control they claim over the disposal of women is tempered by the extent to which they have only partial control over the disrespect and suppressed anger of young men. When moran eventually manage to marry and settle down, this delayed admission to the company of elders has certain characteristics of a second initiation, faced with the need to adapt their lifestyles. However, this does not diminish their display of loyalty to their age-set peers.

Thus, while Arnold van Gennep considered Maasai initiation and the transition from boyhood to moran-hood as a preeminent example in his analysis of rites of passage, he could have traced his model several steps further. Moran-hood itself may be seen as part of an even more inclusive transition from childhood through to elderhood a decade or so later. The communitas and antistructure of moran-hood involve an extended period of marginality. The age system, in fact, very clearly displays the social construction of adolescence, holding men in their physical prime in a heavily ritualized suspension, imposed by much older men who are playing for time and for wives.

This holistic approach toward age systems leads one to examine the relationship between principles of age organization and aspects of the family. As in other polygynous societies, the delayed marriage of younger men and competition for wives can give rise to tension between generations and to rivalry between brothers. Age systems can serve to diffuse these strains by imposing the restrictions on younger men from beyond the family (Samburu), by creating an alternative and prized niche for younger men (Maasai, Nyakyusa), or by maintaining a disciplined queue toward marriage (Jie, Karimojong). A variation of this general pattern occurs among the Cushitic-speaking peoples in Ethiopia and Kenya, where the age system underpins the privileges of first-born sons within the family. These variations are characterized by rules that introduce generational restrictions as well as age, producing hybrid "age/generation" systems. The rules can be highly elaborate, leading to speculation that they either are spurious or have been misunderstood. However, their implications for the distribution of power and authority with age are very specific, and appreciating the nuances in each instance derives from a wider analysis of relations between old and young within the family and the wider community. The demise of age systems and of respect for older people in the developing areas of Africa is an offshoot of the demise of the corporate family away from its agricultural and pastoral roots.

THE DYNAMICS OF AGE SYSTEMS AND THE SENSE OF TIME

The general premise of this article excludes the larger scales of African political systems where birth in certain privileged lines rather than age was the principal determinant of status; in extreme instances these distinctions by birth entailed certain caste-like qualities. The contrasts and parallels between these two forms of stratification are revealing. As opposed to the total personal immobility in a caste system, where status at birth persists throughout life, age systems guarantee total mobility for the individuals in them: a young man is initiated onto the lowest rung of the age ladder as a member of the most junior age-set, and he is systematically promoted with his age-set from one age grade to the next toward the top. A caste system is eternal, whereas an age system processes through time. At the same time and in practice, both forms of stratification display anomalies at the ends of their social scales and a certain jockeying for position in-between.

It is characteristic of age systems generally that they focus on the course of maturation among younger men, whose careers subsequently tend to merge into elderhood as the popular gaze switches to the initiation of the next age-set. The competition for privilege with age, however, does not necessarily end at that point, and the dynamic character of age systems may extend to the crisis of aging among senior age-sets as older men are forced into premature retirement. Among the Maasai, elders jostle for power within the public domain as successive age-sets rather than as individuals. Younger age-sets are excluded from this arena as too inexperienced, and older age-sets are edged out of it. Those who dominate the arena of elderhood in middle age are in a vulnerable position. Periods of stability, when the authority of one age-set is unquestioned, overlie mounting ambiguities that lead sooner or later to an effective challenge from the next age-set. The collective aim of younger elders is to enter the arena and, in due course, to wrest the initiative from their predecessors. Then, as they too begin to dwindle in number and lose the collective will to assert themselves in some crucial debate, they in their turn find their position of dominance discredited. Young men come, old men go, while the contest for power is an issue that is waged by elders in their political prime, paralleling the contests among younger men in their physical prime. The nuances of each age system relate to the process of promotion, involving certain pressures from below and resistance from above. It is these pressures, arising from the interplay between a concern for status and the physical process of aging, that provide the mainspring for the recurring cycle of promotions and delays, spanning the interval between successive age-sets.

This changing configuration between age-sets has a bearing on the perception of time. With the unfolding sequence from one set of initiations to the next, there is a widely shared awareness of aging and the passage of time, and ultimately of history itself, perceived as a succession of age-sets associated with oral tradition. While this sense of time as a continuum is very explicit in societies with age organization, a discontinuous awareness of time through aging obtains elsewhere. Implicitly, there tends to be a certain disregard of the process of aging during periods when the configuration of relations within the family or community (or age system) remains unchanged, and this results in a timeless sense of stability as the months and years roll by.

This static view is inevitably challenged by the next critical change, whether due to migration, illness, death, or some planned life transition and its accompanying rites. At such points, the involvement of the wider community concerns the irreversible shift in the configuration of power relations, and with this comes an awareness of the competencies of actors in their modified roles. The young have matured to a point and older people have aged. In the new configuration, everyone is manifestly older. From this point of view, all crises that mark changes in relationships may be regarded also as crises of aging in an endless process of renewal. Rites of passage and anxieties over changing relations are also rites and anxieties of aging. Steps in the transition of roles are steps in time. As opposed to the predictable cycles of the natural calendar, when time appears to repeat itself endlessly, the personal awareness of the passage of time with age has a uniquely unrepeatable and discontinuous aspect. It tends to be punctuated by steps between periods of stability. Whereas physical aging is continuous but imperceptible, social aging is perceptible, precisely because of the discontinuities.

The construction of time through human experience, then, can be viewed as an aspect of aging peculiar to each culture, marked by the peaks and troughs of social existence. At the level of semi-autonomous local communities and families the dynamics of power relations between young and old thus create time. This point is highlighted in societies with age systems, who provide just a special case of a more general phenomenon in rural Africa.

Pastoralist societies in East Africa display the most concentrated array of age systems anywhere in the world. It is among pastoralists that differences in wealth tend to be transient, and hence more compatible with the ideal of age-set equality, which is the basis for age organization. It is significant that Islamic pastoralists further north do not have age systems, and instead they tend to have marked social inequalities associated with extensive forms of lineage organization. This seems linked to Muslims' introduction of commercial trade into Africa that has run in parallel with adoption of Islam, bringing with it the development of family interests and more permanent inequalities. This suggests that the expansion of the world market economy into the remoter pastoralist areas of East Africa—with or without Islam—could weaken the surviving systems of age organization; and a local form of society that was once altogether more widespread throughout the world will finally disappear into the larger networks of modern commercial relations.

See also **Initiation; Kinship and Descent; Knowledge: Traditional; Marriage Systems; Masks and Masquerades; Secret Societies; Time Reckoning and Calendars.**

BIBLIOGRAPHY

Baxter, P.T.W., and Almagor U., eds. *Age, Generation and Time: Some Features of East African Age Organizations.* London: Hurst, 1978.

Bernardi, B. *Age Class Systems: Social Institutions and Polities Based on Age.* Cambridge, U.K.: Cambridge University Press, 1985.

Dumont, L. *Homo Hierarchicus: The Caste System and Its Implications.* London: Paladin, 1972.

Foner, N. *Ages in Conflict: A Cross-Cultural Perspective on Inequality between Old and Young.* New York: Columbia University Press, 1984.

Kertzer, D. I, and J. Keith, eds. *Age and Anthropological Theory.* New York: Cornell University Press, 1984.

La Fontaine, J. S. *Initiation: Ritual Drama and Secret Knowledge across the World*. Harmondsworth: Penguin, 1985.

Murphy, W. P. "Secret Knowledge as Property and Power in Kpelle Society: Elders versus Youth." *Africa* 50 (1980): 193–207.

Spencer, Paul. *The Pastoral Continuum: The Marginalization of Tradition in East Africa*. Oxford: Clarendon, 1998.

Spencer, Paul. *Time, Space and the Unknown: Maasai Configurations of Power and Providence*. London: Routledge, 2003.

Spencer, Paul. *The Samburu: A Study of Gerontocracy*. London: Routledge, 2004.

Stewart, F. H. *Fundamentals of Age-Group Systems*. New York: Academic Press, 1977.

Turner, V. W. *The Forest of Symbols: Aspects of Ndembu Ritual*. New York: Cornell University Press, 1967.

Turner, V. W. *The Ritual Process: Structure and Antistructure*. London: Routledge and Kegan Paul, 1969.

Van Gennep, A. *The Rights of Passage*. London: Routledge and Kegan Paul, 1960.

PAUL SPENCER

AGGREY, JAMES (1875–1927).

The educator and missionary James Emman Kwegyir Aggrey was born in Ahambu, Gold Coast (later Ghana), where he attended Wesleyan Methodist mission schools. At age sixteen he began preaching and teaching at Methodist schools in the Cape Coast region. Aggrey believed that African submission to British colonial rule was beneficial because it brought knowledge and Christianity, advancement and deliverance from sin, to Africa. But Aggrey also believed in limits on imperial power: He was recording secretary of the Aborigines' Rights Protection Society, established in 1897 to oppose a bill in Parliament that would have given most of Gold Coast land to the British Crown.

In 1898 Aggrey attended the all-black Livingstone College in Salisbury, North Carolina. After graduating first in his class in 1902, he then joined the college's faculty. In 1905 he married Rosebud Douglass, an African-American woman. Nine years later he became the pastor of two rural black churches near Salisbury. Aggrey was strongly influenced by the famous American black educator Booker T. Washington, who believed that blacks should work within a framework of segregation to advance themselves through hard work and a practical education stressing industrial arts.

Unlike Washington, however, Aggrey believed that the best-qualified Africans and African Americans should also seek higher education. He returned to Africa in 1920 and 1924 as the only black member of the Phelps-Stokes Commission on education in Africa. During both visits he made many hundreds of speeches in both East and West Africa that inspired numerous Africans, including Kwame Nkrumah, to pursue higher learning abroad. He helped found a school in Achimota, Gold Coast (opened in 1927), that was intended to become sub-Saharan Africa's first university.

See also **Education, School; Education: University and College.**

BIBLIOGRAPHY

Howard, Thomas C. "West Africa and the American South: Aggrey and the Idea of a University for West Africa." *Journal of African Studies* 2, no. 4 (Winter 1975–1976): 445–465.

Ofosu-Appiah, L. H. *The Life of Dr. J. E. K. Aggrey*. Accra, Ghana: Waterfield Publishing House, 1975.

MICHAEL L. LEVINE

AGRICULTURE

This entry includes the following articles:
BEGINNINGS AND DEVELOPMENT
PESTS AND PEST CONTROL
WORLD MARKETS

BEGINNINGS AND DEVELOPMENT

Africa is an agricultural continent, and this commitment to cultivation has long been central, culturally as well as economically, to most people living south of the Sahara. Although there exist in places small communities with strong hunting and gathering traditions, and, in rather arid areas or those with fine grasslands, others who subsist partly or largely off cattle or other livestock, these are relatively few in number. In fact most pastoralists interact with cultivators or actively contribute to an integrated agro-pastoral economy. With or without a marked pastoral element, African agricultural practices are extremely varied, much of this variation being explicable, up to a point, by the ecological diversity of the continent with its contrasting terrains and climatic zones. But at the same time agricultural systems and their variety betray deep cultural attachments; certain foods and ways of cultivating and using them are peculiar to particular communities. Within this balance of cultural and environmental factors, the agricultural diversity of Africa can be explained as the result of a long history, with the evolution not only of individual crops and their numerous varieties but equally of the techniques of growing them and overall farming strategies.

VEGETATIVELY PROPAGATED CROPS

Farming in Africa may be typified as belonging to two main crop regimes: the tending of gardens and the cultivation of fields. The regime of gardens belongs to the wetter and naturally forested regions. It comprises largely roots and other planted crops; these are propagated vegetatively; that is, not by sowing seed but by planting a tuber, shoot, or corm, either whole or part, into the ground. Notable in the tuber category are yams (of the genus *Dioscorea*), certain species of which are native to the African forests and their edges. It is not yet known how many thousands of years ago some of these yams were first cultivated in a more or less formal way, nor is it clear just when new "domesticated" varieties developed in the western and central African forested zone. But the exploitation of these plants must be very ancient indeed. The same applies to several distinct tubers, sometimes loosely but inaccurately called "potatoes," in the forests as well as the wooded savannas of eastern and western Africa. Often such crops are planted together with legumes, oil plants, and condiments in clearings around the homesteads in what may strike an outsider as a haphazard arrangement, with domestic and animal refuse enhancing the soil's organic content.

Yams, like most root and tuber carbohydrates, tend to be low in other nutritional qualities. This is not usually a serious disadvantage for a tasty and reliable staple with good storage properties for a warm and humid region, as long as one combines vegetables and other crops to provide a mixed diet with an adequate supply of protein, fat, and vitamins. These latter are not easily supplied by domestic animals because, in the wetter and more forested regions, the lack of pasture as well as the presence of tsetse fly prevents or severely restricts cattle husbandry and dairy production. Instead, livestock here usually comprises a few goats and chickens. Animal protein may be augmented by game and in particular by fish, either fresh or preserved. Also important, for cuisine as well as nutrition, are oil crops, notably types of groundnuts (some indigenous to Africa, others more recently introduced from the New World) and oil-palm. The latter is another African domesticate, native to the forest edges and clearings. Its history of human exploitation and use is presumably as old as that of yams, the two being essentially complementary in southerly parts of western Africa.

Whereas yams themselves are unlikely to survive archaeologically, carbonized oil-palm seeds or their husks are occasionally preserved. At Kintampo in central Ghana they have been recovered from a site about 3,500 years old, although these were not necessarily formally planted and domesticated palms. Evidence of roughly similar date has come to light in excavations in the elevated Cameroon Grassfields and in clearings in the equatorial rainforest to the south. In light of such archaeological evidence, it is natural to wonder if the use of oil-palm seeds was associated with that of yams in that place and at that time.

The other carbohydrate crop of prime importance in the history of the people of the rainforest is the plantain, which constitutes a division of the bananas. Like bananas generally, especially those of the wetter parts of eastern Africa, the plantains of the rainforest have been used mostly for cooking, with some varieties selected for brewing. There is no doubt about the plantain's domesticated status in Africa, since the banana is botanically native to Southeast Asia. Certain basic cultivated varieties were introduced to Africa, presumably through the east coast, long ago, and over time a vast number of secondary varieties have been developed by eastern and central African peoples to suit their various requirements in different environments. To serve as a reliable staple, bananas need rainfall through a large part of the year, as occurs in the equatorial forest zone and around Lake Victoria to its east, and again on the slopes of Kilimanjaro and Rungwe.

The date at which bananas first reached east Africa, and plantain varieties the rainforest further west, has long been a matter of debate; since the banana is essentially a seedless plant, propagated from a shoot or by self-regeneration in established gardens, it leaves no direct archaeological evidence. It has usually been assumed that it was introduced to Africa from India or directly from Southeast Asia with the opening up of trade in the Indian Ocean late in the first millennium CE. However, the time depth indicated by the complex genetic mutations of bananas in eastern Africa, and equally of the plantain group further west in the rainforest, demand, in the view of some crop botanists, a history in Africa of twice that length. Indeed, from an archaeological excavation in Cameroon traces of this plant, in the form of silica phytoliths, have been claimed as early as 500 BCE, although that identification and dating await corroboration. Either way, the mechanisms of the transit of bananas to Africa and of their spread and development in the continent remain unexplained.

There is a wild plant of the banana family in Africa, called enset (*Ensete edulis*) or "false banana." In outward appearance it resembles the banana, although it does not produce an edible bunch of fruit. Different species of enset occur across the continent; the stems are used for fibers and ropes, and the seeds for ornamental, medicinal, and divination purposes in several regions. Only in wet parts of the southwestern Ethiopian Highlands has enset been formally cultivated, with domesticated varieties selected and developed. Here the starchy fibrous stem is used as a carbohydrate; pounded and cooked it serves as the staple of several peoples who have clearly a long and deep cultural as well as subsistence attachment to this crop.

Since the opening of the Atlantic Ocean, other planted crops have been introduced to Africa. These are principally roots and tubers, and their initial adoption doubtless benefited from older acquaintance with yams and other African tubers. Their popularity as supplementary crops is largely due to their different or more versatile growing periods or harvesting seasons. Moreover, the most widespread of these, cassava (manioc), can grow in

a fair range of conditions, with the advantage that it can be left in the ground in wet and dry seasons much longer than most crops. Capable of uprooting almost as required and usually demanding less labor per unit of food yield than yams, it has come to serve as a rural staple in many parts of western, central, and eastern Africa, and as an important drought crop in others—notwithstanding the mild toxicity of certain varieties, especially on the western side, which may need to be purged by extra soaking or boiling. Cassava's advance as a staple in the equatorial rainforest and its southerly edge, in particular at the expense of plantains, began on the Atlantic coast in the eighteenth century and has been continuing up to the present. Similarly, sweet potatoes have become a popular, usually supplementary, food on both sides of the continent, and cocoyams, also of American origin, in the west. A counterpart of cocoyams in eastern Africa, commonly seen growing in damp patches and fringing watercourses, is taro (*Colocasia*), a crop of Southeast Asian origin.

Alongside these carbohydrates, various other food plants have been introduced from the Americas and then "Africanized." These include several types of beans, important since they can be dried and stored and also for their protein content, as well as groundnuts valued for their oil. Here again, older African crops in these groups have been overshadowed or superseded. Noteworthy too is the American contribution during the last half-millennium to the cuisine of much of the Old World, including Africa, in the realm of condiments, from chili peppers to tomatoes.

SEED CROPS

In contrast to those crops propagated by planting root or stem cuttings, grains or cereals require that seeds saved from the previous harvest be sown. This regime is typical of the savanna and medium-rainfall regions of Africa. The fields are prepared by hoe, with the bush or the previous season's trash cleared in time for the rains (which may fall in two main seasons close to the equator or in a single season to the south and north). From hoeing and sowing till harvest and threshing, such fields require laborious attention, in particular weeding when the shoots are young and protection from birds (and often wild pigs and baboons) as the crops ripen. The principal grains of intertropical

Africa are of the millet type. (Wheat and barley of more temperate zones are found only in restricted areas of the Lower Nile Valley and highland Ethiopia, and in recent times, through selection of suitable varieties, have been introduced to parts of the southern and eastern African highlands.) After these cereals are pounded in a mortar and ground on a stone, the flour is used in different ways. The commonest foods are porridges and what is inadequately translated as "stiff porridge" or "boiled dough," which is eaten with meat, fish, vegetable stews, or relishes. Sometimes the flour may be mildly fermented, as with teff in Ethiopia. And commonly grain growers select some of the harvest, or special varieties, for brewing.

The most widespread of African grains—and the most important food in the history of the continent—is sorghum. Its ancestry is African, this crop deriving from a wild grass native to the savanna country adjacent to the Middle Nile. Here archaeological evidence shows that sorghum has been intensively exploited as a food for at least seven thousand years: preserved seeds and impressions of seeds in pottery have been recovered in excavations of settlements which bordered the Nile's floodplain in the Khartoum region. There remains some debate about whether this early sorghum constituted a formally cultivated crop, or whether essentially wild stands succored by the receding flood were being carefully encouraged and harvested. For it is not until considerably later that seeds show the signs of having been formally domesticated and becoming botanically distinct from the wild type. Once sorghum underwent such formal domestication, cultivators were able to spread across the savannas both westward and southward where, in experimenting with different terrains, they selected new strains suited to various environmental conditions and adapted their agricultural strategies accordingly.

In parts of the African middle belt, between the Sahara and the equator, this process would have begun a few millennia ago. Such early grain cultivation was very likely pioneered in close association with stock keeping in some regions. But the main spread and intensification of sorghum cultivation across broader regions of western Africa, and also into eastern and southern Africa, occurred later alongside the rapid development of iron industries around two thousand years ago. Iron tools may not

have been strictly essential for such grain cultivation, especially on light, soft, fertile soils such as those of floodplains. Nevertheless, for efficient clearing of bush and breaking of hard and parched savanna soils, and equally for the constant need to prepare new fields as those of the previous one or two years exhausted their fertility, as well as for weeding, harvesting, and the whole range of domestic and building requirements of agricultural communities, an immeasurable difference was made by hoes, knives, and axes forged from wrought iron and steel which were locally smelted. Thus, though various African food crops have a history of cultivation over several thousand years, the emergence of communities economically dependent on and culturally adjusted to a sustained agricultural life occurred in most parts of sub-Saharan Africa alongside the adoption of iron between 2,500 and 1,500 years ago.

In the African savannas there are several other millets, in the broad sense of that term, which have been used as food. Some of them in west Africa and the Sahel are valued as fallbacks in famine years, for instance *Digitaria*, one species of which is inaccurately called "hungry rice." More important are pearl (or bulrush) millet, of the genus *Pennisetum*, which originated in the western Sahel, and finger millet (*Eleusine*), native to the Ethiopian and east African highlands. The development of cultivated pearl millet has been traced at the archaeological site of Tichit, in present Mauritania. Here this grass was gathered for its seeds on a small scale in the second millennium BCE. But it was in the succeeding millennium that it came to be more intensively exploited and attained a truly cultivated status through wide areas of the west African savanna zone, with domesticated varieties becoming increasingly dependent for their continuity on the farming communities.

This ancient tradition of millet and especially sorghum cultivation across Africa has, rather ironically, facilitated the recent replacement of these crops to a considerable degree by another grain suited to the intertropical zones, namely maize. Maize was brought to the Old World from Central America. Except in certain areas near the west African coast, its cultivation was restricted until the nineteenth century, or indeed the twentieth in most areas. As mechanized methods of grinding became available (and replaced the family grindstone in many areas) and as maize became a more prestigious food, especially in towns or among wage earners, it took over as a staple in many regions, especially within eastern and southern Africa. Intensive maize cultivation has become frequently assisted by artificial fertilizers and mechanized plowing; and even where these are lacking, hoe farmers often find it less laborious than sorghum and other millets (and any surplus more marketable).

Another factor often mentioned for the increasing preference for maize over sorghum is that maize cobs are more compact and are sheathed, making them less vulnerable to birds at ripening stage: with the increase of formal schooling in most regions, child labor for bird scaring has become scarce. Where now one finds small plots of sorghum or finger millet grown, the yield may be for brewing. But in many parts where maize has in the last generation become the dominant crop, the experience of one or two bad harvests may drive farmers back to planting more sorghum, local varieties of which tend to be better attuned to withstand unpredictable weather and more tolerant of either drought or waterlogging. At the same time one hears the virtues of "original" African crops and "traditional" foods being lauded by politicians and journalists with a touch of sentimentality, as much as by agricultural experts and the rural farmers themselves.

Finally, there is one grain that requires wet conditions for its growth. This is rice, of which two species are known in Africa. Common rice, *Oryza sativa*, originated in Southeast Asia and probably reached eastern Africa more than a thousand years ago by the Indian Ocean sea routes. The distinct *Oryza glaberrima*, or Guinea rice, is native to the wet hinterland of the western Guinea coast and the Upper Niger Basin. There its exploitation by farmers has been shown archaeologically to be at least two thousand years old. As a grain that does not require grinding and can be stored and transported relatively easily, rice acquired in certain places—for instance the towns of the Swahili coast in the medieval period—a prestige as a cosmopolitan food, one suitable for serving to travelers and guests, in preference to millets and other local "peasant" foods.

Sorghum and millets, being predominantly crops of medium rainfall and of the savannas in the broad sense, are frequently grown alongside the rearing of livestock. Most grain farmers keep some goats or sheep for meat, and usually cattle

too, the latter raised for milk as much as for meat, provided there is adequate grass free of tsetse fly. Sometimes there is a division of labor between neighboring or interacting communities, with one specializing in pastoralism, the other in cultivation, who then exchange their surplus products. Equally frequent are internal mechanisms of specialization, by age, sex, or even, among certain societies in the interlacustrine region, caste-like distinctions between herders and cultivators.

In areas of dense population or special conditions, the farming and the livestock economies may be essentially integrated, through manuring of fields and the stall-feeding of cattle. Such methods of maintaining fertility may allow more permanent cropping of a chosen area of fertile ground around a settlement. If the site is located in hills, it may be necessary, or worth the effort, to terrace such fields with stone revetments to preserve the soil from erosion, and also to give a more obvious sense of demarcation and permanence than is apparent in the more extensive agricultural systems of the plains. Where population pressure is not too severe, shifting or recurrent techniques of cultivation are the preferred means of maintaining a fertile reserve of potential soil. Selected areas of bush are cleared and sometimes burned to return natural nutrients to the soil and maintain ecological stability. This may be followed up by suitable field techniques of mounding or ridging of the soil by hoe, as different crops may require for tilth, drainage, or aeration, and equally to facilitate weeding.

Old systems of terraced fields are maintained by a number of hill communities in northern Nigeria and Cameroon, in Darfur and the Nuba hills of Sudan, and in the Ethiopian Highlands and certain east African localities. Abandoned examples occur in places, the most extensive and spectacular being in the Nyanga hills of Zimbabwe: these steep terraced slopes and the community which built, cultivated, and depended on them were eventually phased out some two hundred years ago. Occasionally such specialized or intensive practices are combined with artificial irrigation systems, particularly in circumscribed areas with reliable but limited water supplies in the midst of dry uncultivable terrain. Irrigation of varying kinds, some very informal, is employed in many parts of the continent; more formal systems of ingeniously engineered gravity-fed canals, transporting water from mountain streams into grids of leveled fields, occur in select places along the Great Rift Valley escarpments of east Africa.

Some examples lie abandoned as archaeological relics. Especially famous is the site of Engaruka, in what has been more recently Maasai country in a dry and dusty stretch of the northern Tanzanian rift. Here lie two thousand hectares of ancient stone-divided fields intersected by such irrigation channels. This was the work of a community that thrived between three and six centuries ago, but that in the long run became too successful and overspecialized in this restricted situation. Population increase outstripped the circumscribed resources of water and soil despite the community's technical ingenuity, and eventually this community and its wonderfully integrated and engineered agricultural system expired. Certain elements of those irrigation techniques have survived among people living and cultivating by other springs and mountain streams scattered about this region. These examples offer, when correlated with the archaeology of Engaruka, a valuable resource for African agricultural history.

See also **Archaeology and Prehistory; Ecology; Ecosystems; Livestock; Nile River; Plants; Production Strategies.**

BIBLIOGRAPHY

Clark, J. Desmond, and Steven A. Brandt, eds. *From Hunters to Farmers: The Causes and Consequences of Food Production in Africa*. Berkeley: University of California Press, 1984.

Harlan, Jack R.; Jan M. J. de Wet; and Ann B. L. Stemler; eds. *Origins of African Plant Domestication*. The Hague: Mouton, 1976.

Sutton, John E. G., ed. *History of African Agricultural Technology and Field Systems*. Special vol. 24 of *Azania* (1989).

Sutton, John E. G., ed. *The Growth of Farming Communities in Africa from the Equator Southwards*. Nairobi: British Institute in Eastern Africa, printed by English Press, 1996.

Van der Veen, Marijke, ed. *The Exploitation of Plant Resources in Ancient Africa*. New York: Kluwer Academic/Plenum Publishers, 1999.

Widgren, Mats, and John E. G. Sutton, eds. *Islands of Intensive Agriculture in Eastern Africa: Past and Present*. Athens: Ohio University Press, 2004.

JOHN E. G. SUTTON

PESTS AND PEST CONTROL

Most African agriculture takes place in tropical climates, on small landholdings with little access to machinery and agricultural chemicals. These conditions influence the type and severity of crop pest problems, and make pest control in sub-Saharan Africa distinct from pest control in industrialized, temperate regions. Farmers in tropical agroecosystems are challenged with a comparatively rich variety of major and minor pests; and the combination of warm temperatures and abundant rains during the growing seasons support many pest generations per year. Subsistence farmers and small-scale growers with little access to costly farm inputs such as pesticides, herbicides, and synthetic fertilizers must place strategic importance on cultural practices, such as the selection of crop varieties resistant to pests and the use of crop mixtures, to reduce the impact of pests on particular crops.

Average yield losses due to insects attacking crops in the field have been estimated at 9 to 15 percent, with additional losses varying from 10 to 50 percent during storage, processing, and marketing. Targeted research on pests and pest management in Africa has flourished since the late twentieth century. It has become obvious that knowledge derived from studies in the temperate zone—usually on commercial varieties of industrial crops grown in mechanized, chemical-intensive, large, single-crop fields—has limited application to the majority of African growers, 80 to 90 percent of whom are involved in subsistence-crop production. Until the 1980s, research on African pests and pest control focused mainly on the 15 percent of agricultural enterprises devoted to industrial crops, such as coffee, tea, cotton, groundnuts, and tobacco. Technical knowledge is advancing rapidly on pests attacking the major staples (cassava, maize, sorghum, millet, teff, and legumes) and minor food crops (such as sweet potato, plantains, and wheat), which comprise over 80 percent of the agriculture in African countries. Very little has been documented on the pests of the more than two thousand native grains, roots, fruits, and other food plants that are grown traditionally in different regions of Africa.

Common pests of African crops range widely in size, feeding habits, and mobility. Insect pests number in the thousands and include native and introduced species. Common pests native to the African continent range from the large migratory locusts to the minute, solitary bean flies. Migratory locusts are 1.5 to 2 inches long, have a single generation per year, periodically fly in swarms covering 60 to 600 square miles, with up to 50 million insects per square mile, and descend to devour almost all green parts of crops, shrubs, and trees. In contrast, bean flies measure .08 inches long, complete each generation in twenty to thirty days, and feed internally as stem-boring maggots only on plants in the bean family. Introduced species such as the greenbug aphid on cereals, the cassava mealybug, and the sorghum panicle bug were transported accidentally from other parts of the world. These introduced pests often multiply rapidly and cause devastating losses. Arriving in the early 1970s from South America, the newly established cassava mealybug threatened the major staple of more than 200 million people across the African continent.

Insect pests attack every crop in every field in Africa, but vertebrate pests and weeds also cause substantial crop losses. Relatively few species of birds, notably those that form large feeding groups such as weaverbirds, cause crop destruction in the field. Weeds reduce crop yields through competition for light, nutrients, and moisture, with especially devastating effects from parasitic plants such as witchweed, which attaches to the roots of grain legumes and cereal crops. Along with insects, rodents destroy a large proportion of stored food products. Stored-food pests are particularly critical in regions with long dry seasons during which subsistence-based families must rely on these stores until the next harvest. Termites, which live in large, social colonies, can devour not only crops in the field but, with the help of gut bacteria that digest cellulose, they can feed on the structures that house stored food products.

Pest control methods selected for most African crops can be relatively labor intensive and may take advantage of local knowledge, resources, and flexibilities in the design of cropping systems.

Physical, cultural, and biological control methods are the cornerstones of pest management for resource-poor farmers. Examples of physical methods include the use of brushes and tarred paper dragged over crops to crush or remove insects, the use of barriers such as metal sheaths around storage bins to deter termites, and the use of traps with baits or synthetic chemical attractants to capture and destroy pests in large numbers. Storage pests can be killed through the use of dusts that abrade their protective waxy cuticle and allow desiccation, or through airtight containers or high temperatures.

Cultural control methods based on manipulations of crops and land have rich traditional histories. Shifting agriculture, crop rotation, and intercropping are examples of widely practiced cultural controls against the proliferation of insect pests, diseases, and weeds. Additional measures include the destruction of crop residues and alternative hosts of pests as well as the selection of planting and harvest dates to avoid peak pest populations or prevent pest development. The selection of pest-resistant varieties from locally grown seed stock is an effective and common practice in crops grown on small landholdings, and the use of hybrids resistant to pests and disease is practiced for many industrial crops in Africa. Malawian subsistence farmers, for example, routinely incorporate varieties that tolerate attack by bean flies to reduce the risk of crop loss. Farmers who were not familiar with the tiny insects themselves selected the bean varieties that showed fewer symptoms of dried stems (caused by the maggots as they feed on the passageways for water movement up the stem).

Resistant cultivars can also be toxic to pests, such as certain young sorghum plants that are protected from attack by the release of hydrogen cyanide gas when chewed by insects or rodents. Because resistance traits are genetically inherited, farmers develop cultivars that thrive despite attack from local pests. Since the late 1990s new varieties resistant to insect pests and diseases are being developed with advances in biotechnology for use in sub-Saharan Africa. For example, white maize varieties have been developed with genes from a bacterium that produces proteins toxic to certain caterpillars. The proteins protect the crop from damage by susceptible pests. Access to genetically engineered crop varieties such as these may be adopted more frequently by larger-scale producers.

Biological control by naturally occurring beneficial organisms is encouraged through certain cultural methods. For example, farmers may increase the suitability of the crop habitat for herbivores that feed specifically on weeds and predators or parasitic insects that kill crop pests. Pest regulation is also enhanced by introducing beneficial organisms through mass releases into the field or through importation from other geographic areas. The cassava mealybug, which caused losses of 80 percent of the root crop in West Africa, was reduced dramatically after the importation and establishment of a small parasitic wasp from the Americas that kills cassava mealybugs. The wasp deposits its eggs only in the body of this type of mealybug, and the young feed and develop on the internal tissues and vital organs. Biological control through carefully planned introductions of specific natural enemies of appropriate pests is a relatively inexpensive and potentially permanent management tactic for reducing pest outbreaks, but remains an underexploited area of research in many parts of the world. Rapid advances in biological control research, and a number of innovative programs have taken place the growing regions of Africa.

Appropriate cultural and biological pest-control methods often require knowledge of the biological and ecological characteristics of the species. Identifications of insect pests can be relatively accurate and simple, as with the six common species of migratory locusts, or extremely difficult. Several species of bean flies are identical as adults and can be distinguished morphologically only by examining the internal reproductive organs of male flies. Despite their similarity in appearance, bean flies respond differently to management tactics. One species is not sensitive to changes in soil quality, but suffers high death rates from parasitic wasps, which regulate its density. Another species tends to proliferate in beans growing in fertilized soil and is rarely killed by parasitic wasps. These differences are critical knowledge for regulating pest densities at low levels through management practices.

Of all the pest-control methods available to growers in tropical Africa, chemical controls may be least sensitive to specific biological differences among pest species. Most commercial pesticides and herbicides are formulated to have broad-spectrum toxicity effective against a wide range of insect pests, or pathogens, or weeds. Although common synthetic pesticides such as organophosphates and pyrethroids used in response to imminent pest outbreaks are often cost effective in commercial crops, recommendations originating outside tropical Africa are subject generally to climatic and socioeconomic constraints. Problems with relying on imported pesticides for crop protection in Africa include the reduction of persistence and efficacy of pesticides under frequent, heavy rains and elevated temperatures, the scarcity of capital for farmers to purchase and apply pesticides, and the human and environmental health hazards magnified by the costs of protective measures and the labeling of imported materials in foreign languages.

Experts in African pest-management research, policy, and practice promote a range of innovative strategies for reducing yield losses in Sub-Saharan African agriculture. Some favor the importation and adoption of technological advances such as precision sprayers, hybrid seed-fungicide-fertilizer packages, and genetically engineered crop varieties, while others promote the exploration of local farmer knowledge to development strategic farming practices using available materials as the major tools of pest management. Hallmarks of African crop protection research, crop breeding and risk analysis work in recent decades is a multidisciplinary approach including social and natural science expert knowledge within a participatory process involving local growers. The challenges to African growers are diverse and sometimes overwhelming, but these comprehensive and inclusive approaches to finding appropriate solutions are exemplary in world agriculture.

See also **Ecology; Ecosystems; Plants.**

BIBLIOGRAPHY

Abate, T., and J. K. O. Ampofo. "Insect Pest of Beans in Africa: Their Ecology and Management." *Annual Review of Entomology* 41 (1996): 45–73.

Gahukar, R. T. "Role of Extension in Protecting Food Crops of Sub-Saharan Africa." *Outlook on Agriculture* 19 (1990): 119–123.

Greathead, D. J. "Opportunities for Biological Control of Insect Pests in Tropical Africa." *Revue de zoologie africaine* 110 (1986): 85–96.

Herren, H. R., and P. Neuenschwander. "Biological Control of Cassava Pests in Africa." *Annual Review of Entomology* 36 (1991): 257–283.

National Research Council. *Lost Crops of Africa*. Vol. 1, *Grains*. Washington, DC: Author, 1996.

Odhiambo, Thomas R. "International Aspects of Crop Protection: The Needs of Tropical Developing Countries." *Insect Science and Its Application* 5 (1984): 59–67.

Sridhar, M. K. C. "African Researchers on Pesticide Use and Poisoning." *African Environment* 6 (1989): 69–102.

DEBORAH K. LETOURNEAU

WORLD MARKETS

For many sub-Saharan African (SSA) countries, agriculture remains a central part of their economies. It contributes at least 40 percent of exports, 30 percent of gross domestic product (GDP), up to 30 percent of foreign exchange earnings, and 70 to 80 percent of employment. Therefore, accelerating growth in agriculture is critical to sustained growth and poverty reduction. Growth in agriculture will also help combat gender inequality, as women play a major role in African agriculture. However, others argue that agriculture is not important in the liberalized economies of the early twenty-first century because employment in intensive manufacturing and services create comparative linkages as in agriculture The agricultural sectors of many SSA countries still face serious constraints including (1) low productivity in agriculture, (2) private underinvestment in agriculture, (3) weak human capital base, institutions, and policy environment, and (4) non-competitiveness of the agricultural sector due to poor infrastructure and lack access to domestic and international markets. The African countries have been unable to access sufficiently export markets largely because of Organisation for Economic Co-operation and Development (OECD) policies that provide huge subsidies to certain farmers. The producer subsidy and tariff protection measures supported, in particular, by OECD countries (European Union [EU], the United States, and Japan) have significant negative impacts on agricultural production in Africa. The producer and export subsidies that these countries provide to agricultural commodities combined with high import tariffs, particularly on semi-processed or processed foods (also known as escalating tariffs), depress agricultural prices in the world market. This undercuts the potential profitability of African producers in their own markets and simultaneously limits their export opportunities.

The economic losses to developing countries because of OECD policies has been estimated at about US$24 billion per year in lost agricultural production and incomes of farm households, and about US$40 billion per year in lost access to markets in OECD countries. For sub-Saharan Africa, the loss in market access is estimated at US$4 billion per year. An International Food Policy Research Institute (IFPRI) report indicates that net trade (exports minus imports) would increase from about US$7 billion to some US$11 billion if industrialized countries liberalized their agricultural policies. For sub-Saharan Africa, about half of its increase in exports (US$2 billion of about US$4 billion) would result from trade liberalization in the European Union.

Within the agricultural sector, high value-added goods represent the most dynamic growth segment of the market. These goods include products such as meat, fruits, vegetables, cash crops, and nuts. Exports of these goods are growing faster than the sector as a whole. But African countries seeking access to high value-added markets face an array of trade barriers. Tariff escalation, or duties that rise with each step of processing, is a standard feature of industrialized-country protectionism. In the EU, fully processed food products face tariffs almost twice as high as tariffs in the first stage of processing.

Such trade policies create disincentives for investment in African processing and deny producers in Africa opportunities to enter high value-added markets. With the exception of certain commodities that face limited import tariffs because of the EU's African, Caribbean and Pacific Group of States (ACP) agreement, many developing countries, including African countries, wanting to export beef to Europe face tariffs of up to 150 percent, whereas fruit and nut exporters to the United States face tariffs of 200 percent or more. And this is before taking into account non-tariff barriers, including sanitary and phytosanitary (SPS) regulations. Although the supply of safe and high quality food stuff is important, the selective application of health standards is often directed toward protectionist goals.

Serious agricultural policy reforms need to occur. Export subsidies should be removed and domestic producer subsidies reduced. Access to developed countries markets under tariff-rate quotas must be increased and tariff escalation on processed agricultural products removed. But policy reforms in the OECD countries will not be sufficient to improve the well-being of the smallholder farmers in SSA. Smallholder farmers—especially women—often lack access to the land, capital, information, and marketing infrastructure needed to take advantage of export opportunities. In the absence of domestic public policies in African countries to overcome these disadvantages (such as access to credit for producers), export growth can marginalize the poor.

African countries need to take a number of actions. First, they should continue to improve human resources in the provision of health and education, especially for women. Second, they need to improve market infrastructure and institutions so that poor farmers can fully capture the benefits from improved human resources and access to improved technologies. Third, there needs to be more research and development (R&D) investment in agriculture that leads to improved technologies. This could increase agricultural production, provide greater employment opportunities and higher wages, and reduce the vulnerability of the poor to shocks via asset accumulation. Finally, SSA countries need to continue to position themselves and adopt policies that will minimize the negative effects and maximize the positive effects of globalization on the rural poor and food security. They also need to reform their domestic trade policies so as to improve intraregional trade. Enhanced openness to interregional trade would go a long way to improve growth. But the international community will help a great deal by eliminating the constraints on agricultural trade imposed by other countries. Agricultural policy reforms in OECD countries will be necessary to create an enabling environment in which pro-poor domestic reforms in SSA can work.

The views expressed in this entry are those of the author and do not necessarily represent those of the World Bank.

See also **Production Strategies; Trade, National and International Systems.**

BIBLIOGRAPHY

Diao, Xinshen; Eugenio Diaz-Bonilla; Sherman Robinson; and David Orden. "Tell Me Where It Hurts, and I'll Tell You Who to Call: Industrialized Countries' Agricultural Policies and Developing Countries." Markets, Trade and Institute Divisions Discussion Paper No. 84. Washington, DC: International Food Policy Research Institute, Washington, DC, 2005.

Ehui, Simeon; Samuel Benin; Timothy Williams; and Siet Meijer. "Food Security in Sub-Saharan Africa to 2020." Socio-economics and Policy Research Working Paper 49. Nairobi, Kenya: International Livestock Research Institute, 2002.

Hazell, Peter. "The Rural Contribution to Pro-Poor Growth in Low Income Countries." Paper presented at the World Bank Rural Week, Washington, DC, 2005.

Organisation for Economic Co-operation and Development. *Agricultural Policies in OECD Countries: Monitoring and Evaluation.* Paris: Organisation for Economic Co-operation and Development, 2003.

Watkins, Kevin, and Joachim von Braun. *Time to Stop Dumping on the World's Poor. 2002–2003.* International Food Policy Research Institute, Annual Report Essay. Washington, DC, 2003.

Wood, S., et al. 2006. "Food." In *Ecosystems and Human Well-being: Current State and Trends*, Volume 1, ed. Rashid Hassan, Robert Scholes, and Neville Ash. Washington, DC: Island Press, 2006.

SIMEON EHUI

AHIDJO, EL HAJJ AHMADOU

(1924–1989). El Hajj Ahmadou Ahidjo was the prime minister and, later, the president of Cameroon. Born in the northern Cameroon city of Garoua, an Islamic and political center in the French-administered part of the colony, Ahidjo completed his education in 1939 and in 1942 joined the French civil service. In 1947 he won election to the colonial Representative Assembly. By 1958 he had developed a political party, l'Union Camerounaise (UC), and become president of the new Legislative Assembly.

Cameroon political life at that time was dominated by the Union des Populations des Cameroun (UPC), a popular nationalist movement that, under Félix-Roland Moumie, was demanding radical reform and reunification. The organization advocated militant activities to end French colonialism, but Ahidjo favored a continuing political and economic relationship with France. In 1958 the French co-opted the movement by granting independence to the colony (effective 1960) and appointing Ahidjo to head the newly created

Ahmadou Ahidjo (1924–1989), October 1971. Ahidjo is credited with bringing stability to Cameroon, even as he showed dictatorial actions. He became the first president of the United Republic of Cameroon after he created a constitution that ended the autonomy of British Cameroon. KEYSTONE/GETTY IMAGES

government. The former colonial power also provided military force to suppress Ahidjo's rivals in the UPC. Moumie was forced to flee into exile, and was killed in 1960.

Ahidjo remained in power until his resignation on November 4, 1982. He established a stable but highly centralized and authoritarian government by instituting a single-party system (the Cameroon National Union, successor to the UC). He maintained close relations with France while achieving some success in constructing a capitalist economy.

After resigning from office, Ahidjo remained politically involved. He engaged in public confrontations with his successor, Paul Biya, and ultimately attempted to stage a coup to retake the presidency. He was unsuccessful, leading to his exile first in France and then in Senegal. The

Biya administration tried him in absentia and found him guilty of plotting to overthrow the government and sentenced him to death in 1983, although a pardon was issued the following year. Ahidjo died in Dakar in 1989, at the age of sixty-five.

See also **Cameroon: History and Politics.**

BIBLIOGRAPHY

Awasom, N. F. "Politics and Constitution-Making in Francophone Cameroon, 1959–1960." *AfricaToday* 49 (4) (2002): 3–30.

Joseph, Richard, ed. *Gaullist Africa: Cameroon under Ahmadu Ahidjo.* Nigeria: Fourth Dimension Publishers, 1995.

MARK W. DELANCEY

AHMAD, MAHDI MUHAMMAD

(1848–1885). The Sudanese religious leader and founder of the Mahdist movement Muhammad Ahmad ibn 'Abd Allah was born at Darar, a village in the northern Sudanese province of Dongola. His father was a local boat builder who claimed descent from the Prophet Muhammad. After attending a Qur'anic school in Omdurman on the Nile River Muhammad Ahmad moved with his father to Aba Island on the White Nile. Since an early age, Muhammad Ahmad adopted a life of learning and meditation. He later joined the Sammaniyya Muslim brotherhood.

Muhammad Ahmad could not reconcile his religious beliefs with the conditions prevailing in the Sudan under the Turco-Egyptian rule. In 1881 he declared himself the Mahdi (the guided one) and began to call for the overthrow of the Turco-Egyptian government and the establishment of a purified Islamic state. Through the mobilization of disaffected groups in the western parts of the region, Muhammad Ahmad led an armed rebellion, which spread to other parts of the country and eventually led to the downfall of the Turco-Egyptian regime. In 1885 the Mahdist forces took over the city of Khartoum in a battle in which General Charles Gordon, the renowned British officer, was killed. The Mahdi then moved his capital across the river to Omdurman, where he died in June 1885. He was succeeded by the Khalifa (caliph, or successor) 'Abd Allahi, who ruled the Mahdist state until the Anglo-Egyptian conquest of the upper Nile Sudan in 1898.

See also **Gordon, Charles George; Sudan.**

BIBLIOGRAPHY

Holt, P. M. *The Mahdist State in the Sudan, 1881–1898.* Oxford: Clarendon, 1970.

Shaked, Haim. *The Life of the Sudanese Mahdi.* New Brunswick, NJ: Transaction Books, 1978.

AHMAD ALAWAD SIKAINGA

AHMAD GRAN BIN IBRAHIM. *See* Ahmad ibn Ibrahim al-Ghazi (Ahmad Grañ).

AHMAD IBN IBRAHIM AL-GHAZI (AHMAD GRAÑ) (1506–1543). Ahmad ibn Ibrahim al-Ghazi, also known as Ahmad Grañ, meaning "the left-handed," was a Horari Muslim leader who conquered much of the Ethiopian empire in the sixteenth century. He was born in the state of Adal, an emirate in the lowlands east of Shewa. Ahmad allied himself as a young man with the warlord Jarad Abun, who had long opposed the Christian domination of the region and the pacific policy of the Walashma, the established leaders of Adal. Ahmad succeeded Jarad Abun upon his death and promptly defeated and killed the sultan of Adal, Abu Bakr. He refused to assume the secular title of sultan and insisted, instead, upon the Islamic title of imam (religious leader).

Ahmad openly refused to acknowledge the dominance of the region's Christian ruler, the Negus Lebna Dengel, and thus provoked a war that was to last many years. Aiming at the total occupation and conversion of Ethiopia, Ahmad led several successful raids, many of which occurred in the years 1526–1527. His most pivotal victory was at Shembera-Kure in eastern Shewa in 1529. His forces continued on to take Dawaro, south of the Awash River, and Shewa in 1531; Amhara and Lasta fell to him in 1533. In 1534, he simultaneously acquired Bale, Gurage, Hadeya, and the Sidama region, all to the south of Shewa. His 1534 invasion of Tigre in the north incurred previously unknown complications due to the mountainous geography and resilient Tigreans, but the sacred city of Aksum fell nonetheless. Ahmad relentlessly pursued Lebna Dengel until Dengel's death in 1540, at which point the Ethiopian empire seemed irredeemably doomed.

Portuguese ships allied with Lebna Dengel, however, arrived at Massawa, on the Red Sea coast, and gave military help to the faltering Ethiopians. Ahmad met his first defeat in 1542 and quickly sent to the Ottoman pasha of Zabid on the coast of Yemen for reinforcements of troops and arms. With his rehabilitated forces, Ahmad attacked the Portuguese in the valley of Wolfa, and won. He captured Cristóvão da Gama, Vasco da Gama's son, and believing in his infallibility, confidently sent his Turkish mercenaries away. The new Ethiopian emperor, Galawdewos, aided by the Portuguese, prepared to challenge Ahmad when he came out from his fortress in the Zobel Mountains. Ahmad was finally defeated and killed on February 25, 1543, at the battle of Wayna Daga, north of Lake Tana. The Muslim invasion of Ethiopia disintegrated with his death.

See also **Aksum; Galawdewos.**

BIBLIOGRAPHY

Henze, Paul B. *Layers of Time: A History of Ethiopia.* New York: Palgrave Macmillan, 2004.

Oliver, Roland, ed. *The Cambridge History of Africa,* Vol. 3. Cambridge, U.K.: Cambridge University Press, 1977.

SARAH VALDEZ

AID AND DEVELOPMENT

This entry includes the following articles:
OVERVIEW
CONSEQUENCES
STRUCTURAL ADJUSTMENT
BALANCE OF PAYMENTS
ENVIRONMENTAL IMPACT
HUMANITARIAN ASSISTANCE

OVERVIEW

Foreign aid includes public resource transfers to poor countries for developmental purposes. It excludes quasi-commercial transactions such as export credits whose benefits to the lender approximate their cost. It also excludes government transfers for nondevelopmental objectives, such as military assistance and private charity. It is referred to in professional circles as official development assistance (ODA). Foreign aid originated from the disruption of the world economy that followed World War II. The forerunner of aid programs to developing countries was the European Recovery Program, known as the Marshall Plan, which had two main objectives: to restore the economies of Europe and to develop a viable pattern of trade so that further concessional loans would not be needed in the near future.

Since the Marshall Plan, two opposite views have dominated the debate over the rationale for aid and its potential contribution to growth and poverty reduction. On the one side, there have always been aid skeptics. In his critique of that group which he called the "aid dependency school," Paul Collier noted, "Just as the 'old left' believed that trade between poor and rich economies caused immiserising dependency, so the 'new right' currently believes that aid has had this effect" (1999). From Peter Bauer, who argued in 1982 that aid reduced the incentive for recipient governments to adopt good policies, to Ravi Kanbur and colleagues, who in 1999 suggested that large gross flows of project aid overwhelm the management capacity of governments, the aid dependency school has offered sophisticated economic arguments. In fact, just as recent analysis of poor households in developed countries has established reasonable evidence for a dependency syndrome, whereby welfare payments create very high implicit marginal tax rates on incomes earned and so discourage work, trapping recipients into continued need for welfare, aid dependency theorists infer that poor countries are subject to the same trap. Twenty-first-century versions of the same arguments were made by William Easterly in 2001 and 2006 and Raghuram Rajan, who claimed that "there is general agreement among economists is that there is little evidence of a robust unconditional effect of aid on growth" (2005).

On the other end of the spectrum, there is a much more optimistic view held by those who believe that aid has been by and large effective throughout history, as some countries have been able to use external public finance wisely to build infrastructure or to fund social programs that are indispensable to long-term stability. Referring specifically to Africa, those who hold this second, optimistic view even suggest that the current state of affairs is such that economic development cannot take place in the poorest regions of the world without massive injections of official development assistance. A twenty-first-century advocate for this group is Jeffrey Sachs (2005), who sees aid as a key instrument for getting sub-Saharan Africa out of its "poverty trap." Obviously, between these two opposing opinions, there are many others that are more balanced and support the view that aid can be effective only under specific institutional or policy conditions.

The genesis of the charged and often emotional debate on aid effectiveness can be found in Figures 1 and 2. The general trend of aid flows to sub-Saharan Africa has been on the rise, despite some temporary declines in disbursements in the early 1980s and late 1990s. Sub-Saharan Africa (SSA) has been the most aided region of the world since the mid-twentieth century, with foreign aid transfers well over 4 percent of the continent's gross national income (GNI) since the mid-1980s (see Figure 1). In fact, despite a significant decline of aid volumes in the 1990s—following the fall of the Berlin Wall, the end of the Cold War, and the relative depoliticization of aid—foreign assistance to African countries has remained consistently higher than in other developing regions. By comparison, aid has always represented less than 2 percent of GNI in all other regions of the world, except for a couple of brief periods in South Asia.

These relatively large amounts of aid notwithstanding, economic growth in SSA has been lagging compared to other regions of the world (see Figure 2). Because of these contrasting trends, the issue of aid dependency has taken center stage, with the World Bank publishing every year an aid dependency ratio among its World Development Indicators. While some authors like Bauer and more recently Easterly have warned against the dangers of taking high levels of aid flows for granted, others like Carol Lancaster have argued that a dependence on high aid inflows is not necessarily a bad thing. "If aid is used productively to promote social and economic progress, its net effect is likely to be highly positive for development in the country receiving the aid. But where the aid is

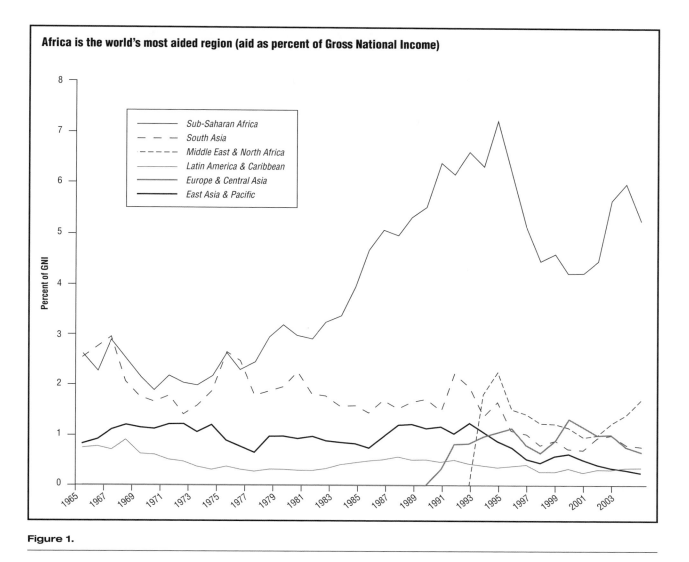

Africa is the world's most aided region (aid as percent of Gross National Income)

Legend:
- Sub-Saharan Africa
- South Asia
- Middle East & North Africa
- Latin America & Caribbean
- Europe & Central Asia
- East Asia & Pacific

Y-axis: Percent of GNI

Figure 1.

ineffective, it is important to consider the potential negative effects of that aid which may outweigh its positive impact and set development back rather than carry it forward" (1999).

Despite the large body of empirical research on the relationship between aid and economic development behind these figures, it is still difficult to rigorously sort out the validity of the arguments on both sides of the debate. First, the very definition of what constitutes foreign aid is often loose, which complicates the interpretation of findings from econometric studies like the data presented in the figures. Second, there are some unresolved methodological difficulties in the way economists analyze the links between aid, growth, and poverty reduction.

DEFINITIONS AND MEASUREMENT

At the Financing for Development conference held in Monterrey in 2002, industrial countries made the commitment to provide more and better aid to developing countries. This decision was based on the agreement on the Millennium Development Goals by the world's heads of state in 2000, a series of indicators that reflect the multidimensional nature of poverty, the need to focus on outcomes and to systematically track progress at the country level. At its recent summit at Gleneagles, Scotland, the group of industrialized countries (G-8) also committed to a doubling of aid to sub-Saharan Africa by 2010 (from about $25 to $50 billion). The donor community's renewed commitment to increased aid flows has also generated greater

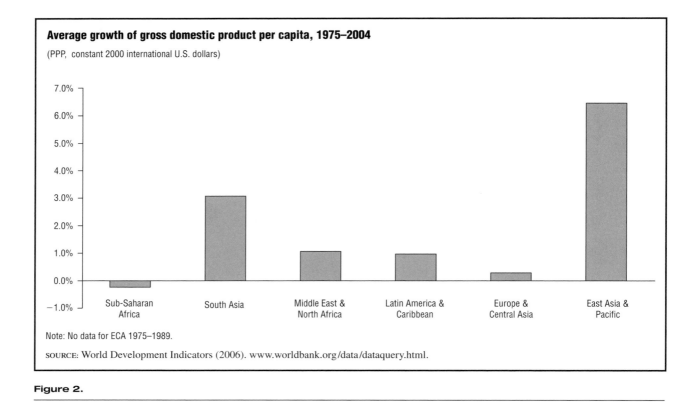

Average growth of gross domestic product per capita, 1975–2004

(PPP, constant 2000 international U.S. dollars)

Note: No data for ECA 1975–1989.

SOURCE: World Development Indicators (2006). www.worldbank.org/data/dataquery.html.

Figure 2.

scrutiny towards the use of funds and debate over ways of making aid more effective.

Despite being the most commonly used indicator, aid as a share of GNI or gross domestic product (GDP) is only one of the three ways often used to measure aid flows. The two others are: Total ODA flows in US dollars (nominal or real terms); and Aid per capita. Each of these measures is useful in in combination with the others but could be misleading if analyzed in isolation. Moreover, they all provide different results when applied to aid recipients in sub-Saharan Africa. From 1960 to 2004, Tanzania, the Democratic Republic of the Congo, and Ethiopia were the top three African recipients of foreign aid as measured by total ODA flows. The islands of Mayotte, Seychelles, and Cape Verde were the top three in terms of aid measured as GDP per capita. São Tomé and Príncipe, Guinea-Bissau and Somalia ranked first when using aid as a percentage of GNI.

METHODOLOGICAL ISSUES

During the Cold War era, the role of ODA in promoting growth and reducing poverty was not at the core of development policy. In fact, the whole

issue of aid effectiveness was not framed in macro-economic terms. It was raised only at the micro (project) level by some of the donors. In recent years—perhaps linked to the end of the Cold War and the emergence of new international security challenges like terrorism, poverty, or epidemics—the focus has been shifting to macro level objectives. This shift has coincided with the work on cross-country analysis launched at the same time by Robert Barro in 1991 and others on the empirics of growth. Yet the quest for clear answers about the relationship between aid, economic growth, and poverty reduction has so far been a vexing empirical issue. Whereas one can point to successful aid recipients, there is at least equal evidence to the contrary, and consistent historical, cross-country answers have proven elusive.

The question remains whether one can rigorously assess the impact of foreign aid using the so-called cross-country regressions; that is, correlations of variables like those discussed here. It is the traditional approach to looking at the relationship between aid and growth, for example. In this sense, it mirrors much of the recent work on understanding the determinants of economic growth, and in particular, assessments of which economic policies influence growth and by how much. Reflecting recent advances in econometric techniques and computational power, the use of cross-country regressions has become something of a growth industry for analyzing the general determinants of growth as well as the impact of aid on growth more specifically.

Identifying clear, indisputable causal relationships between specific transfers of money from one donor to its supposed impact in a recipient country is a major methodological challenge. Aid can foster economic growth, but slow growth may also lead to higher aid levels. Econometricians have tried to control for this aid [endogeneity issue] through the use of instrumental variables—but the validity of these instruments themselves is always a matter of debate. Moreover, by definition, cross-country regressions do not capture the specifics of each country's situation, or the multiple objectives beyond sheer macro-quantitative measures of foreign aid in each country. While there have been some changes in the aid architecture since the end of the Cold War, much aid is still provided primarily for political purpose (support to friendly governments, peace-keeping operations, the fight against terrorism, strategic or commercial interests, and promotion of the donor country's culture or language). Therefore, it would be inappropriate to measure these flows of aid by their growth or poverty reduction impact.

Also, short-term effects of aid may differ sharply from effects in the longer term. In 2004 M. Clemens and colleagues divided aid into three categories: (1) short-term emergency and humanitarian assistance, which is often negatively correlated with longer-term growth because transfers typically occur in desperate country situations; (2) aid to build social capital (education, health, environment, democracy), which affects growth only in the long-term and therefore does not appear in cross-country analyses whose time horizon is often short; and (3) aid that is directed to productive sectors (infrastructure, budget, and balance of payments support). By disaggregating ODA flows among these various categories of assistance, they find that only this third category, which accounts for about half of total aid flows, has a positive causal relationship with growth over a four-year period, with diminishing returns. Unfortunately, both aid optimists and aid skeptics generally do not disentangle all these effects, which are likely to create a lot of interference in the analysis of the relationship between external assistance and economic growth.

Finally, recent advances in growth theory suggest that economic growth is not just a function of how much investment could be obtained with any given amount of aid. At stake, there is also the role of institutions that affect the behavior of all stakeholders involved in the process. The impact of aid on growth logically depends on country characteristics (governance among others) and policies being pursued. Limited statistical degrees of freedom may prevent estimating this complex relationship among larger numbers of variables than the data are sufficient to correlate. It is therefore possible that aid indeed fosters growth in a subsample of countries—and during some subperiods—and not in others. Cross-country regressions reveal only an "average relationship" and distinguish only in a very crude way—and *a priori*—various types of countries. But despite the limitations of these techniques, they can offer useful insights on possible correlation among economic variables. But they must be complemented with analyses and evidence from micro and country-specific studies.

Fortunately, changes in aid policies that started in the 1990s as a result of post–Cold War concerns have also influenced the global aid architecture—its objectives, institutions, and instruments. This change is accompanied by a greater commitment to both measurable results on the ground as well as stronger emphasis on good governance, well-functioning institutions, local ownership of reforms, and an increasing use of budget support for channeling aid rather than project financing. While it is premature to conclude that the new paradigm is generating sustained improvements over past performance, it clearly holds the promise for better research on the relationship between foreign aid and economic development.

See also **Cold War; Debt and Credit; Economic History; International Monetary Fund; Urbanism and Urbanization; World Bank.**

BIBLIOGRAPHY

Alesina, Alberto, and David Dollar. "Who Gives Foreign Aid to Whom and Why?" *Journal of Economic Growth* 5, no. 1 (2000): 33–63.

Barro, Robert J. "Economic Growth in a Cross-Section of Countries." *The Quarterly Journal of Economics* 106, no. 2 (1991): 407–443.

Bauer, Peter. "The Effect of Aid." *Encounter* (1982).

Bourguignon, François, and Danny Leipziger. *Aid, Growth, and Poverty Reduction: Towards a New Paradigm.* Washington, DC: World Bank, 2006.

Chenery, Hollis. "Foreign Aid." In *The New Palgrave: A Dictionary of Economics*, ed. John Eatwell et al. New York: Stockton Press, 1987.

Clemens, M., S. Radelet, and R. Bhavnani. *Counting Chickens When They Hatch: The Short-Term Effect of Aid on Growth.* Working Paper No. 44. Washington, DC: Washington D.C. Center for Global Development, 2004.

Collier, Paul. "Aid 'Dependency': A Critique." *Journal of African Economies* 8, no. 4 (1999): 528–545.

Easterly, William. *The Elusive Quest for Growth: Economists' Adventures and Misadventures in the Tropics.* Cambridge, MA: MIT Press, 2001.

Easterly, William. *The White Man's Burden: Why the West's Efforts to Aid the Rest Have Done So Much Ill and So Little Good.* New York: Penguin Press, 2006.

Kanbur, Ravi, et al. *The Future of Development Assistance: Common Pool and International Public Goods.* Washington, DC: Overseas Development Council, 1999.

Lancaster, Carol. "Aid Effectiveness in Africa: The Unfinished Agenda." *Journal of African Economies* 8, no. 4 (1999): 487–503.

Monga, Célestin. *Aid Addiction in Africa: Symptoms, Side Effects, and Possible Cures.* Policy Research Working Paper. Washington, DC: World Bank, 2006.

Radelet, Steven. *A Primer on Foreign Aid.* Working Paper No. 92. Washington, DC: Center for Global Development, 2006.

Rajan, Raghuram. "Aid and Growth: The Policy Challenge." *Finance and Development* 42, no. 4 (December 2005).

Sachs, Jeffrey. *The End of Poverty: Economic Possibilities for Our Time.* New York: Penguin Press, 2005.

CÉLESTIN MONGA

CONSEQUENCES

In the 1990s international financial institutions and bilateral donors reexamined the purview of economic aid, analyzing the stakes involved, and its quality and effectiveness. An important reason has been the poor economic performance of sub-Saharan Africa, which continued to exhibit slow growth rates in spite of the significant sums of official development assistance that had been disbursed since independence in the 1960s (see Table 1). Developing countries may receive different forms of external finance in order to meet the needs of their economies, in particular foreign direct investment, external borrowing, and official development assistance. Foreign investment in sub-Saharan Africa remains limited and is mostly focused on primary sectors such as oil and minerals. Because of its political economy—especially political instability, poor rule of law, and inadequate protection of property rights—the region is perceived by investors as a place of high risk.

Official development assistance (ODA) refers to heterogeneous phenomena and different types of flows, such as program aid, support for the budgets of recipient countries, project aid (aid flows are earmarked for specific projects), debt relief, technical cooperation, food aid, untied aid, and tied aid, which is conditioned to the purchase of goods from the donor country. ODA is not a gift, as aid flows include both elements of grant and loan. From 1995 to 2003 sub-Saharan Africa has been the region of the world that has received the largest share of total ODA (between 30 and 35 percent). ODA to sub-Saharan Africa represented in 2004 about $23.3 billion in 2003 prices. In 2005 total aid to sub-Saharan Africa was $31.4 billion (excluding Nigeria, total ODA to the region dropped by 2.1%, to $24.9 billion, as Nigeria benefited from special debt relief). Sub-Saharan Africa receives less net aid per capita than other regions, however: in 2003 sub-Saharan Africa received $31 per capita, while Oceania received $218 and Europe $35 per capita. Reflecting the persistence of economic stagnation, the share of aid to sub-Saharan Africa has tended to increase, as shown by the ODA given by the Development Assistance Committee (DAC) of the OECD. The DAC is the forum that coordinates the aid of major bilateral donors, that is, twenty-three developed countries (including the European Union). Sub-Saharan Africa received 35.8 percent of the ODA given by the members of the DAC in fiscal year 1993–1994, and 42 percent in fiscal year 2003–2004.

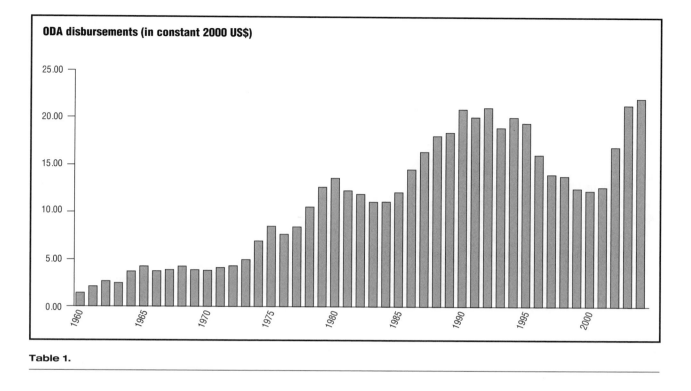

ODA disbursements (in constant 2000 US$)

Table 1.

THE ROLE OF INTERNATIONAL FINANCIAL INSTITUTIONS IN SUB-SAHARAN AFRICA

Types of aid have evolved after independence: the "big push" of the 1960s (support to public investment in infrastructure and industry), then rural development, mainly via project aid, followed by the enhancement of "basic needs." In the 1980s, due to the drop in the prices of tropical commodities, African countries were constrained to implement stabilization (supported by the International Monetary Fund [IMF]) and structural adjustment programs (supported by the World Bank). The loans that are associated with programs (support to budget and balance of payments), as well as with the projects of the IMF and the World Bank, are linked to conditionalities, that is, the implementation of specific economic policies, including stabilization of budgets and balance of payments and structural adjustment programs, which implied a reduction of fiscal deficits, a limitation of state intervention in the economy, liberalization, and privatization.

International financial institutions thus play a leading role in the creation of the conceptual frameworks and the settling of objectives regarding development and aid, because they are the key lenders to low-income countries and devise policy reform programs. Bilateral donors increasingly tend to align their development assistance on them. After the crisis of developing countries in the 1980s (debt crisis and fluctuations in commodity prices) and the drying-up of private flows to low-income countries, especially in Africa, ODA became increasingly multilateral. African countries became heavily dependent on the loans of the IMF and World Bank. African debt also became increasingly public and multilateral. In 1990 private nonguaranteed external debt represented 0.03 percent of total external debt (and 0.07% in 2003). World Bank loans represented 17 percent of public and publicly guaranteed debt in sub-Saharan Africa in 1990, and 27 percent in 2003.

The results of the stabilization and adjustment programs launched in the 1980s have been mixed. As William Easterly emphasized in 2001, the IMF and the World Bank in the late 1990s launched new lending facilities that were more focused on poverty: the Poverty Reduction Strategy Papers (World Bank) and Poverty Reduction and Growth Facility (IMF). These programs, however, have not yet spectacularly improved the growth performance of sub-Saharan African countries. Causes are multiple, such as adverse domestic market structures (commodity dependence) and global conditions (rise in world interest rates, fall in terms of trade, global growth increasingly pushed by a demand in skilled labor). These programs aimed to take better account of the political and social structures of African states and the adhesion of recipient governments to conditionalities and reforms.

As the indebtedness of most sub-Saharan countries had become unsustainable by the end of the 1990s, these programs were associated with an initiative aimed at reducing multilateral debt, the Heavily Indebted Poor Country Initiative. Debt relief is conditional on the implementation of programs focused on poverty reduction, health, and education. It is viewed as aid and may represent a substantial share of it, which has generated debate. Indeed, debt relief does not always add new resources: debt relief represents additional financial resources if the debt is actually being serviced, but it amounts to little if it is not. Since the late 1990s, debt relief has represented a larger share of the increased aid flows to sub-Saharan Africa, and there has been an emphasis on providing budget support to recipient governments, especially in the form of debt relief. For example, according to the DAC, aid levels increased in 2005 and 2006 due to a specific event: major debt relief for Iraq and Nigeria totaling $19 billion in 2005 and $11 billion in 2006, for a total of around $100 billion in each of those years.

THE REFLECTIONS ON AID EFFECTIVENESS IN THE 1990S

During the 1990s the disappointing economic performances of sub-Saharan Africa led donors to deepen their reflection on aid effectiveness. Some donor countries and their public opinions were indeed subject to "aid fatigue" and became reluctant to increase their aid, in particular because of recurrent assessments of the "poor governance" of African governments and the misuse of aid flows. Beyond donors' "fatigue," trends in aid flows are linked to specific situations in both donor and recipient countries. Donors differ in their aid effort: for example, Scandinavian countries are more generous in terms of aid-to-gross domestic product (GDP) ratio than other developed

countries, such as the United States. The development paradigm underlying aid may be different, with some donor countries giving more importance to market solutions while others rely on a philanthropic framework.

On the recipient side, political and economic situations are heterogeneous: countries receive aid according to particular circumstances, for example whether they have strategic natural resources, suffer a civil war, or move to democratic institutions. The efficiency of the instruments of aid were called into question, especially in the United States (the second donor country in terms of amount, after Japan), which restructured its aid toward those countries that seemed to be "playing the game." Many donors attached the conditionality of "good governance" to their aid, which means more accountability and less corruption in civil services. They also recommended more "selectivity" in aid. Given that aid resources are scarce, aid should thereby be preferentially oriented toward countries that deserve it; that is, that implement sound economic policies, build democratic and accountable political institutions, and promote the rule of law. The new paradigm created by the end of the Cold War also reduced the utility of the former client states in the developing world while at the same period most donor countries were subjected to the constraints of tightening their budgets, and in the European Union as well as in the United States. The reflection on aid effectiveness has thus been associated with a stagnation of ODA, with the motto becoming "not more aid, but better aid."

Better effectiveness and the streamlining of global aid have also been emphasized by international financial institutions, especially the World Bank and IMF. After a period of stability (from 1973 to 1992), annual flows of ODA fell sharply in the early 1990s, including toward the poorest countries—and therefore sub-Saharan Africa, which, according to the World Bank, received less aid through the late 1990s, even in nominal terms. The decline has stopped since the beginning of the twenty-first century, with aid increasing again from 2003 onward. This resumption of aid flows may be explained by the emergence of the paradigm of poverty reduction as a primary goal of the donor community: at the turn of the century all donors committed themselves to a set of objectives aimed at reducing poverty and enhancing human development (health, education), coined as the Millennium Development Goals (MDGs). The reverse of the decline is also caused by particular circumstances such as assisting transitions, debt cancellation, and postconflict reconstruction.

THE IMPORTANCE OF HISTORICAL CONTEXTS AND POLITICAL DETERMINANTS

For donor countries the end of the Cold War in 1989 put an end to a series of political rationales that justified aid flows to sub-Saharan Africa, particularly bilateral aid, which stemmed from the East-West competition for influence. The economic motives for aid have not disappeared, however, for example, the easing of access to the resources of recipient countries for private firms from donor countries, and the establishment of privileged trade relationships. Aid is indeed always linked to objectives—political and economic—of foreign policy. Countries that are perceived as strategic tend to receive more aid, which is one of the explanations for the fluctuation of aid flows. The strategic importance of a given country or a resource changes with time. In 2003 the two main recipients of aid in volume from the top donors were thus the Democratic Republic of the Congo and Iraq (debt relief being a substantial part of aid). In 2004 the two main recipients of aid in sub-Saharan Africa were Ethiopia and the Democratic Republic of the Congo. The fact that aid reflects global and national priorities partially explains the resumption of aid toward Africa in the early 2000s in a context of emerging perceptions that poverty and weak states may foster global insecurity. The changes in the objectives of aid manifested themselves in a change in focus from southern to eastern countries and the increase of humanitarian aid due to the management of postconflict reconstruction by donors.

Aid flows sometimes have an indirect relationship with the level of poverty of a recipient country as measured by GDP per capita, which should normally be the basic indicator of aid. These discrepancies, however, vary depending on the donor country. For example, Scandinavian countries (which are among the few countries that comply with the United Nations target of allocating 0.7% of GDP to aid) and the United Kingdom put poverty reduction at the forefront of their agenda. Other donors may focus on the enhancing of growth, trade, or the private sector. These discrepancies were also reduced because of the end of the Cold War and the focus on poverty reduction, which became the key paradigm of the World Bank and the International Monetary Fund in the 1990s. Another important paradigm is sustainable development, which means political and economic stability, free markets, preserving environment, and a stronger private sector.

THE MIXED RESULTS AND THE QUESTIONING OF THE ECONOMIC IMPACT OF AID

In the 1990s questions were raised in academia as well as aid agencies concerning the impact of aid at the macroeconomic and microeconomic levels. Questions were also raised regarding the institutional dimension of aid and the effects of aid on the local institutions of the recipient countries. The first theorists of development economics after World War II justified ODA by models that consider developing countries to be characterized by a series of deficits or "gaps." An increase of available resources therefore helps to trigger virtuous circles of growth. These models justify active intervention by the state—state policies and resources—and external aid as crucial factors of growth acceleration.

The Harrod-Domar model linking growth to investment, which aid agencies still used in the 1990s, and the "take-off" theory of Walt Rostow accorded, in the mid-1950s, a critical role to aid: the rate of investment in a developing country is increased by an injection of foreign capital, which increases domestic savings without reducing consumption; the literature coined this as the "big push" that justified external aid. Following Paul N. Rosenstein-Rodan, Hollis Chenery and Alan M. Strout elaborated the "two gaps" model: besides the gap between savings and investment, aid fills the temporary gap in foreign exchange induced by disequilibria of the trade balance at the first stage of development. The conditions for the transformation of an economy characterized by poverty are the increase in investment and domestic savings. Physical capital, such as infrastructure, and human capital, such as education and health, had to be increased.

Problems with aid became apparent with the disappointing growth performances and the persistence of deficits, which called into question the link between aid and growth. The impact of aid on growth and other economic phenomena has become a matter of intense debate at the beginning of the twenty-first century, which is compounded by the difficulty in assessing causalities with certainty and measuring effects on account of methodological problems (relating to the use of cross-country regressions or country studies). World Bank studies argue that aid is effective in countries that implement sound policies and the appropriate economic and institutional reforms. Reviews of existing studies find that is a broad consensus that "aid works." Many studies, however, have emphasized a negative impact, even within the IMF: In 2005 Raghuram G. Rajan and Arvind Subramanian thus found that aid has a negative relationship with growth, particularly in aid-dependent countries, as it contributes to the overvaluation of the exchange rate and hinders the competitiveness of recipient countries.

Aid may also adversely affect domestic savings and investment by reducing government incentives to conduct developmental policies (what is called its "ownership") and tax effort. Indeed, if states rely on donors for finance, why should they bother to tax their own citizens? Aid provides incentives for reducing the tax effort and lowers the incentives to broaden the tax bases and reduce aid dependency, though the latter also constitute other objectives for the donors. Aid therefore generates contradictory incentives and outcomes. Large aid inflows may also go beyond the recipient country's capacity of absorption and ability to spend the aid within the appropriate time span. Another problem is aid fungibility; that is, the possibility for a government to allocate aid funds to objectives that may differ from the donor's objectives (or the fact it frees public resources, for example, for military spending). Aid flows may also contribute to corruption.

Aid has been viewed as a burden on the civil services of the recipient countries, and even harmful for development. A key problem of aid indeed refers to the multiplicity of donors in a given country and the harmonization of their objectives and procedures, which may have eroded the positive effects of aid. International financial institutions claim to be more efficient and better able to coordinate the great number of bilateral aid agencies and to channel aid toward objectives such as poverty reduction. Given that aid is a dimension of foreign policy, however, bilateral donors are reluctant to entirely follow the recommendations of the World Bank and often do not harmonize their aid—particularly project aid—with the World Bank and other bilateral donors. Lack of coherence and coordination among an excessive number of donors is one of the main reasons for aid failure in low-income countries, in particular when the latter display weak institutions and poor governance, such as in sub-Saharan Africa.

A key problem of aid that emerged in the late 1990s is aid dependency, which affects poor countries and particularly in Africa, whose public budgets depend on very limited resources (for example the taxation of one or two primary commodities): when aid flows are high relative to budgets or the size of the economies, countries may become excessively dependent on external aid. In 2005 according to the IMF, sixteen sub-Saharan African countries had a ratio of aid-to-government expenditure exceeding 50 percent. The World Bank World Development Indicators show that in sub-Saharan Africa aid represented in 1998 4.7 percent of the region's Gross National Income (GNI) and in 2004 5.3 percent. Aid represented in 1998 23.9 percent of the region's gross capital formation, and 26.1 percent in 2004. The calls by the international community for a dramatic rise in aid flows to Africa, and the focus by the IMF and the World Bank on poverty and their new conditionalities (poverty reduction, health, and education), may even have the unexpected effect of increasing aid dependency. Aid dependency creates vicious circles, as African governments have difficulties in gaining autonomy and implementing the "learning-by-doing" processes that are the conditions of sustainable development.

Aid flows are moreover characterized by high volatility, which is due to various causes: for example, to factors internal to donor countries, fads in the development discourse, bureaucratic procedures, and time lags in disbursements. Studies have found that in highly dependent countries aid is even more volatile than fiscal revenues and that unpredictability and volatility have increased since

1975; donors' commitments are also significantly lower than effective aid disbursements. Program aid is also more volatile than project aid, which has reinforced previous problems, as aid has shifted to program aid and budget support since the end of the 1990s. Public budgets that are dependent on flows that cannot be predicted are obviously very difficult to manage. At the institutional level, aid may weaken political institutions: when budgets depend excessively on aid, this may transform the relationship between the state and its citizens: if governments raise their revenues from foreign aid, they are accountable toward external donors, not toward domestic parliaments and constituencies.

THE COMPLEX RELATIONS BETWEEN DONORS AND BENEFICIARIES

The device of conditional lending induces a multiplication of conditions when the conditions initially prescribed by programs are not met, which in a vicious circle tends to increase the resistance from governments: these repeated bargaining games have been coined the "ritual dance" between donors and recipient governments. The donor countries likewise implement numerous projects that impede aid coordination, with bilateral agencies sometimes competing with each other and with the multilateral institutions. For the IMF and World Bank, the main objectives of structural adjustment programs were to help African states with their balance of payments problems and fiscal deficits. Aid coordination is inherently difficult given that bilateral agencies, which tend to promote national interests, do not share the same objectives as international financial institutions. The multitude of aid agencies may nullify the requirements and the credibility of the economic policies recommended by the multilateral financial institutions, thus increasing the inefficiency of aid.

The institution of aid itself may be a problem, because it has often been "top down" rather than "bottom up." In the 1970s aid promoted expensive projects that had poor profitability due to adverse fluctuations in world prices and recurring costs. In the 1980s the IMF and the World Bank emphasized policy reform, then institutional reform, but recipient governments tended to resist the implicit political objectives of "good" governance. For their part, international financial institutions are not equipped for using political conditionalities, as

their mandates forbid them from using political criteria. Reciprocal expectations between donors and recipients built over decades make it difficult to change the rules of the game even if failure is recognized. Reforms are handicapped by the weakness of local institutions. The recommendations by donors for a better "ownership" of aid and local participation are confronted with the donors' focus on disbursements and the recipients' expectations of the continuation of aid, which hampers innovation and erodes the credibility of sanctions from the donors. The political determinants of the formation of postcolonial states and civil services have impeded the learning processes that would have gradually made aid more effective. The weakness of local capacities is also compounded in some countries by the massive intrusion of donors within civil service activities through multiple and non-coordinated projects and monitoring tasks, which induce incoherence. The emphasis by donors on nongovernmental organizations (NGOs) may not strengthen local institutions and aid coordination.

Sub-Saharan African countries are facing uncertain prospects, in both economic terms and in terms of human development. They are confronted with limited foreign investment and a small share in world trade, which moreover may diminish as global trade and growth are pushed by skilled labor and knowledge-based services. This creates a dilemma: it shows the necessity of a continuation or an augmentation of ODA, although the negative effects of aid dependency have come to be better understood. Moreover, the contribution of aid to growth remains subject to debate, as in the case of the growth of East Asian countries and the massive amounts of American aid after World War II. African countries are handicapped by the protectionism of developed countries and the growing competition from emerging Asian countries, as well as a poor domestic political economy and the difficulty of diversifying from the postcolonial economic model. The result is an "aid economy" rather than an economy oriented toward production or development. Aid in itself seems unable to lift countries out of poverty, although without it the situation would have been worse.

See also **Cold War; Debt and Credit; Economic History; Economic Systems; International Monetary Fund; World Bank.**

BIBLIOGRAPHY

Alesina, Alberto, and David Dollar. "Who Gives Foreign Aid to Whom and Why?" *Journal of Economic Growth* 5, no. 1 (2000): 33–63.

Bulir, Ales, and Javier Hamann. *Volatility of Development Aid: From the Frying Pan into the Fire?* Washington, DC: International Monetary Fund, 2006.

Dollar, David, and Lant Pritchett. *Assessing Aid: What Works, What Doesn't, and Why.* Oxford: Oxford University Press for the World Bank, 1998.

Dollar, David, Torgny Holmgren, and Shantayanan Devarajan. *Aid and Reform in Africa.* Washington, DC: The World Bank, 2001.

Easterly, William. *The Elusive Quest for Growth: Economists' Adventures and Misadventures in the Tropics.* Cambridge, MA: MIT Press, 2001.

Easterly, William. *The White Man's Burden: Why the West's Efforts to Aid the Rest Have Done So Much Ill and So Little Good.* New York: Penguin, 2006.

Gupta, Sanjeev; Robert Powell; and Yongzheng Yang. *The Macroeconomic Challenges of Scaling Up Aid to Africa.* Washington, DC: International Monetary Fund, 2005.

Gupta, Sanjeev; Catherine Pattillo; and Smita Wagh. *Are Donor Countries Giving More or Less Aid?* Washington, DC: International Monetary Fund, 2006.

McGillivray, Mark; Simon Feeny; Niels Hermes; and Robert Lensink. *It Works; It Doesn't; It Can, But That Depends...: 50 Years of Controversy over the Macroeconomic Impact of Development Aid.* Helsinki, Finland: United Nations University, World Institute for Development Economics Research, 2005.

Moss, Todd, and Arvind Subramanian. *After the Big Push: The Fiscal Implications of Large Aid Increases.* Washington, DC: Center for Global Development, 2005.

Moss, Todd; Gunilla Pettersson; and Nicolas van de Walle. *A Review Essay on Aid Dependency and State Building in Sub-Saharan Africa: An Aid-Institutions Paradox?* Washington, DC: Center for Global Development, 2006.

Rajan, Raghuram G., and Arvind Subramanian. *Aid and Growth: What Does the Cross-Country Evidence Really Show?* Washington, DC: International Monetary Fund, 2005.

Rajan, Raghuram G., and Arvind Subramanian. *What Undermines Aid's Impact on Growth?* Washington, DC: International Monetary Fund, 2005.

World Bank and International Monetary Fund. *Global Monitoring Report 2006.* Washington, DC: The World Bank and International Monetary Fund, 2006.

ALICE NICOLE SINDZINGRE

STRUCTURAL ADJUSTMENT

The roots of the structural adjustment era of the mid-1980s to the present can be traced to the mid and late 1970s, when many developing countries, including most countries in Africa, incurred large debts to private American, European, and Japanese banks. The Organization of Petroleum Exporting Countries (OPEC) embargo and oil price spikes of the 1970s, together with the recession of the early 1980s, created severe fiscal crises in developing countries that depended heavily on imported oil and exported commodities. With a double-squeeze of increased energy prices and reduced prices for exported primary commodities, most countries in Africa experienced severe current account imbalances. At the same time, international banks were competing to invest large sums of "petrodollars" deposited largely by OPEC members. With a crisis of current account imbalances in many Third World countries and with large amounts of cash on hand, banks relaxed their normal lending criteria and issued large loans to developing countries that would not previously be considered suitable borrowers.

By the early 1980s, the financial wisdom of these loans began to look questionable, as heavy loan burdens, decreasing export earnings, and rising interest rates threatened the capacity of borrower countries to repay their debts. The decline of OPEC as an effective cartel in the early 1980s drove down the price of petroleum and reduced deposits to international banks. At the same time, the United States government under President Ronald Reagan was borrowing large sums on international markets to finance a defense build-up and domestic tax cuts. Together, the decreased supply of OPEC dollars on the international lending markets and the increased demand for money to finance the United States deficit drove interest rates rapidly upward. In addition, the major international recession of the early 1980s drove the prices of primary commodities that many developing countries depended upon for export earnings to historic lows. With rapidly increasing interest rates on variable-rate loans coupled with reduced export earnings, many developing countries faced a serious prospect of default.

As in other regions, indebted nations in Africa turned to the major multilateral lending institutions, the World Bank and the International Monetary Fund, to re-finance their debts. Following the leadership of the United States, these institutions adopted a policy for lending based on the concept of "conditionality": developing nations would receive financing for their external debts on the condition that they adopt economic reforms consistent with neoliberal economic ideology. The World Bank shifted an increasing portion of its lending from traditional project lending to "structural adjustment" lending. To qualify to receive balance-of-payments relief, countries had to agree to the terms of Structural Adjustment Programs (SAPs).

The SAPs were heavily influenced by the Berg Report, published by the World Bank in 1981. This highly influential "neoliberal manifesto" asserted that the disappointing economic performance of most African countries in the period after World War II was primarily a result of heavy-handed interference with the free market by inefficient, top-heavy, corrupt governments. The failures of development in Africa were contrasted to the allegedly more free market-oriented policies of the newly industrialized nations of East Asia (which were, in reality, heavily managed and subsidized by government and international bodies). Structural adjustment programs would, according to neoliberal theory, produce long-term growth in Africa by reducing government regulation, privatizing state-owned industries, and reducing barriers to trade.

The standardized, primarily externally conceived menu of reforms imposed on debt-strapped African countries included "austerity" measures to reduce government spending by cutting subsidies and social services (including education and health care) and increased export production to increase revenue available to repay international debt; elimination of price controls (such as price controls on basic food staples and agricultural inputs such as fertilizer); reduced regulation (including labor and environmental protections); devaluation of domestic currencies to make exports more competitive; reduced restrictions on imports; free entry for foreign firms into domestic markets; and privatization of state-owned enterprises. Little effort was made to take into account the unique circumstances and history of each country—the SAPs were largely a one-size-fits-all solution. By the end of the 1980s, almost every country in Africa had

engaged in some form of this basic structural adjustment "package."

By the beginning of the 1990s, the World Bank and other international financial institutions (IFIs) gradually began to recognize that inequality and human suffering had actually increased in those countries that had implemented SAPs since the 1980s. The IFIs interpreted this result as a temporary, painful-but-necessary part of the transition to long-term stability and growth. According to this interpretation, the primary cause of increased suffering under SAPs was the failure among many African countries to fully implement the SAP policies, and, more generally, an absence of "good governance." Yet, the case for continuing the standard SAP policies seems particularly problematic in Africa where, after more than two decades, much of the continent (unlike Asia and Latin America) continued to stagnate economically, slipping backward in terms of per capita income, infrastructure, education, health care, and other measures of basic human well being. Moreover, IFI advocacy of a stay-the-course commitment to a more open, outward-looking economy and nonintervention in the market appeared hypocritical to many poor countries, since the wealthy industrialized countries had generally practiced strongly interventionist measures (and still do, especially in agriculture, for example) during their own scramble to modernity.

Indeed, the standard prescriptions offered by the SAPs recommended that African states largely withdraw from development at precisely the time when African society and economies most needed them—the egregious behavior of many African governments not withstanding. A growing consensus emerged that African countries need to reform, rather than eviscerate, the state. It has become increasingly clear that the "invisible hand" of the market is not an adequate substitute for thoughtful, locally contextualized, long-term planning and appropriate, effective market intervention. A growing consensus of African and non-African economists and scholars concluded that conventional SAPs fail to address the most fundamental problems underlying African poverty and failures of development. Moreover, continuing the SAP-induced cutbacks in public services that provide food security and public health care appears increasingly unacceptable in an era when chronic and episodic hunger and famine, as well as the pandemic of AIDS, malaria, and other diseases, have reached biblical proportions. They reveal that large sums of public funding have After more than twenty years, the SAP policies appear to many ordinary African people to have done little or nothing for their lives except reduce or eliminate vital government services and raise the cost of food, fertilizer, and other essential goods. For international lenders and businesses, however, debt and SAPs have been an "effective tool" that ensures debt repayment and access to steady supplies of cheap raw materials and labor. This situation seems increasingly open to charges of neocolonialism in the form of globalized debt servitude.

This condition of widespread indebtedness and the resulting diminution of political and economic autonomy in Africa due to the SAPs has drawn particularly severe criticism because much of the existing debt in African countries consists of "odious" debt that was knowingly provided by international lenders to despotic, corrupt regimes that squandered the loans. These loans often provided no benefits to the ordinary African people who are now left to repay the debt in the form of reduced public services, higher food prices, and so on. For example, the Democratic Republic of Congo (formerly Zaire, under the extreme corrupt leadership of Mobutu), Ghana (under numerous military dictatorships), Malawi (under the corrupt "Life President" Kamuzu Banda), Nigeria (with some of the most corrupt military regimes in the world), South Africa (under Apartheid), and Sudan (under oppressive military rule) accrued enormous debts that are still being repaid by ordinary people today, many of whom were not even alive when irresponsible international lenders originally provided the loans to autocratic leaders who are now long gone (though much of this wealth remains in their private overseas bank accounts).

For example, in Nigeria, Sudan, South Africa, Democratic Republic of Congo, Ghana, and Malawi, as much as 100 percent of existing debt in 2004 consisted of "odious" debt, resulting in large *net international transfers of wealth* (namely, aid minus debt repayments) from poor Africans to wealthy industrialized countries and IFIs. According to UNICEF data, by the turn of the twenty-first

century, as many as 5 million children and vulnerable adults had died in Africa as a result of debt incurred before they were born, or from which they never benefited in any way.

Accordingly, in the early twenty-first century, the IFIs have largely replaced the term "structural adjustment programs" with the more benign-sounding "Poverty Reduction Strategy Papers" (PRSPs, also known as "public relations SAPs"). Embattled and lacking their previous sense of supreme confidence in the wisdom of SAPs, the IFIs looked to enhance the "participatory" image of adjustment lending. The International Monetary Fund renamed its structural adjustment program the Poverty Reduction and Growth Facility (PRGF). From 2000, borrowing countries have been required to prepare PRSPs as a condition for receiving loans. The stated intention of this requirement is to use a consultative process to identify individual countries' poverty-reduction needs and strategies. Many humanitarian non-governmental organizations and other critics, however, suggest that PSRP priorities continue to be set primarily by the industrialized western powers that fund the IFIs, and represent very minimal changes from the basic neoliberal model of the original SAPs—old wine in new bottles.

The changing of labels attached to the SAPs coincided with a growing global political movement to eliminate debt and abolish the "poverty trap" widely associated with IFI structural adjustment policies. The most prominent movement of the late twentieth and early twenty-first century was Jubilee 2000, an international coalition of civic and church organizations in more than forty countries that called for the cancellation of unpayable and crippling Third World debts by the year 2000. The name of this movement, whose logo was an iron chain being broken, derived from Leviticus, which requires that in the fiftieth year servants forced by poverty into service of a master be freed, any property sold in distress be restored to the original owner, and all liabilities to creditors be erased. This movement coincided with the Great Jubilee celebration of the year 2000, initiated by Pope John Paul II in 1994, exactly fifty years after the creation of the "Bretton Woods" institutions—the World Bank and International Monetary Fund.

The Jubilee 2000 campaign aimed for the elimination of $90 billion in unpayable debt among the world's poorest countries. Facing fierce political protests from anti-debt and anti-globalization movements across the globe, international lenders pledged in September 2000 to loosen cumbersome Poverty Reduction Strategy requirements and expand debt relief to get closer to their own pledges from the 1999 G7 summit in Cologne for debt relief to 20 heavily indebted poor countries. Pledges reached $17.5 billion—an amount that the Jubilee 2000 organizers described as disappointing and inadequate.

The political, or at least rhetorical, commitment to finally come to grips with poverty and debt relief reached a zenith at the G8 Summit in Gleneagles, Scotland in 2005. As host, British Prime Minister Tony Blair identified debt relief and economic development in Africa as one of two top priorities for the summit (the other was to address global warming). An agreement was reached to cancel the entire $40 billion debt owed by eighteen highly indebted poor countries, most of them in Africa, to the World Bank, IMF, and the African Development Fund. Debt relief advocacy groups responded that the proposal would eliminate only a small proportion of overall Third World debt. The agreed-upon $40 billion in debt cancellation would reduce Third World debt repayments by $1 billion per year—far below the $45.7 billion per year identified by debt-relief advocates as necessary to remove crushing debts and crippling structural adjustment policies in the world's poorest countries. Moreover, countries targeted for relief under the Gleneagles agreement would qualify only by agreeing to further neoliberal "reforms." Nevertheless, groups advocating increased aid and debt relief to Africa acknowledge the value of the first, limited steps taken at Gleneagles. The British development organization Oxfam stated that "Across Africa, lifting the burden of debt is allowing millions of dollars to be directed to fighting poverty instead of repaying rich countries" (Loyn 2006).

Critical questions remain: whether these successes will be replicated in other heavily indebted countries; whether debt relief and freedom from external structural adjustment conditionality will translate into effective investments in poverty reduction; and whether pledges for debt relief will be matched by urgently-needed increases in development assistance. Above all, the question remains whether the international political momentum to assist African countries politically and economically ensnared by debt and SAPs will be sustained. At the 2006 G8 Summit in St. Petersburg, African poverty and debt barely registered on the agenda; and this topic appears to have vanished from discussions in preparation for the 2007 G8 Summit in Berlin.

See also **Apartheid; Banda, Ngwazi Hastings Kamuzu; Debt and Credit; Economic History; International Monetary Fund; Mobutu Sese Seko; World Bank.**

BIBLIOGRAPHY

Dollar, David, and Jakob Svensson. *What Explains the Success or Failure of Structural Adjustment Programs?* Policy Research Paper 1938. Washington, DC: World Bank, 1998.

Dornbusch, Rudiger. "Balance of Payment Issues." In *Open Economy: Tools for Policymakers in Developing Countries*, ed. Rudiger Dornbusch and F. Leslie C. H. Helmers, pp. 37–53. New York: Oxford University Press, 1988.

Guillaumont, Patrick and Syviane, eds. *Adjustment and Development.* Paris: Economica, 1994.

Hadjimichael, M. T., et al. *Adjustment for Growth: The African Experience.* Occasional Paper 143. Washington, DC: IMF, 1996.

Khan, Mohsin S., and Malcolm D. Knight. "Stabilization Programs in Developing Countries: A Formal Framework." *Staff Papers* 28 (March 1981): 1–53.

Killick, Tony. *IMF Programmes in Developing Countries: Design and Impact.* London: Routledge, 1995.

Lipumba, Nguyuru H. I. *Africa beyond Adjustment.* Policy Essay 15, Washington, DC: Overseas Development Corporation, 1994.

Loyn, David. *G8 "Failing to Meet Aid Pledges,"* 9 June 2006 (accessed December 15, 2006). Available from http://news.bbc.co.uk/2/hi/business/5061764.stm.

Monga, Célestin. "Commodities, Mercedes-Benz, and Structural Adjustment: An Episode in West African Economic History." In *Themes in West Africa's Economic History*, ed Emmanuel Akyeampong, pp. 227–264. Oxford: James Currey, 2006.

Mussa, Michael, and Miguel Savastano. *The IMF Approach to Economic Stabilization.* Working Paper WP/99/104. Washington, DC: IMF, 1999.

Tarp, Finn. *Stabilization and Structural Adjustment: Macroeconomic Frameworks for Analyzing the Crisis in Sub-Saharan Africa.* London: Routledge, 1993.

PETER WALKER

BALANCE OF PAYMENTS

The balance of payments is a statistical statement that mirrors economic and financial dealings during a certain period of time between any given country and the rest of the world. It is typically defined as the record of a country's international economic transactions during a period of one year. It is thus an accounting tool for quantifying and measuring the relationship between two flows of payments, one coming in, one going out, in which a country is continuously involved. A country is said to have a positive balance of payments when there is more money flowing into than there is flowing out; if, on the other hand, more money flows out than in, the balance of payments is negative.

In reality, since the balance of payments records all the payments and receipts of the residents of one country in their transactions with residents of other countries, the payments and receipts of each country are, and must be, equal. Any apparent inequality simply leaves one country acquiring assets in the others. For example if Nigeria sells oil to the United States and has no other transaction with the United States, Nigerians will end up holding dollars, which they may hold in the form of bank deposits in the United States or in some other American investment. The payments of Americans to Nigeria for oil are balanced by the payments of Nigerians to American citizens or institutions, including banks, for the acquisition of dollar assets. Put another way, Nigeria sold the United States oil, and the United States sold Nigeria dollars or dollar-denominated assets such as Treasury bills and land acquisitions.

While the sum of all payments and receipts are necessarily equal from each country's perspective, there will be inequalities—excesses of payments or receipts, called deficits or surpluses—in particular categories of transactions. Thus, there can be a deficit or surplus in any of the following: merchandise trade (goods), services, foreign investment income, unilateral transfers (foreign aid), private investment, the flow of gold and money between central banks and treasuries, or any combination of these or other international transactions. Therefore, the statement that a country has a deficit or surplus in its "balance of payments" must refer to some particular class of transactions. That is why the international transactions recorded in the balance of payments are often grouped into two broad categories: first, the goods and services that a country has received from and provided

to the rest of the world, called the *current account*. It includes all transactions involving currently produced goods, or currently rendered services. These transactions can be either "visible" trade of merchandise, or "invisibles" which, broadly, cover payments for services like insurance, shipping, and tourism; transfer of profits and dividends currently earned on assets held abroad; and other transfers such as migrants' remittances and gifts. Second, changes in a country's claims on and liabilities to the rest of the world—referred to as the *capital account*. It includes all payments arising from transfers of capital and extensions of credit. Since all countries have a zero balance of payments, their current account deficits must be balanced by capital account surpluses.

It is difficult to apply the concept of a balance of payments to earlier economic transactions between Africa and the rest of the world. First, these international economic and financial flows were not carefully measured, and the flow proceeded in many commodities and currencies without restriction, clearing being a matter of judgement by individual, private banks. In fact, the methodology for compiling and presenting the balance of payments is still relatively new in macroeconomics: the standard concepts, rules, definitions, guidelines, conventions, and classification scheme to be employed by each country in assembling uniform statistics for a balance of payments statement, as well as the conceptual framework for analysis, have been designed only in the 1960s and 1970s by the International Monetary Fund. Second, the form of presentation of the balance of payments accounts varies between countries, and even between different periods of time for the same country. Moreover, Africa includes a large number of individual countries with very different statistical systems and data gathering capacities.

From a historical perspective, African continental commercial and financial transactions with the rest of the world were initially dominated by the slave trade. Between 1450 and the end of the nineteenth century, slaves were sent from along the west coast of Africa, often with the cooperation of African kings and merchants, who received in return various trade goods including mostly textiles but also beads, cowries (used as money), alcoholic drinks, horses, and guns. Since the Berlin Conference in 1885, it would appear that most African countries have gone through several stages: first, between 1885 and 1945, they were mainly *small creditor colonies* (or territories). Had the balance of payments methodology been available, they would have experienced surpluses in the current account due to large volumes of pre–World War II exports. Their capital accounts would have been in deficit due to high investments by European-based colonial companies. Second, between the end of World War II and the late 1970s, African countries were mostly *small debtor nations.* They recorded current account deficits due to their needs to import capital goods and their inability to maintain high levels of exports. They also had capital account surpluses due to high levels of foreign investment in the areas of manufacturing and services (roads, railroads, telecommunications, etc.). Their external situation worsened in the 1980s and 1990s because of the declining prices of major export commodities like cotton or coffee and the external debt crises.

In the first years of the new century, major oil-producing countries like Nigeria, Angola, and Gabon have enjoyed high price for their exports and positive current account balances. Conversely, oil importers like Senegal, Mali, Malawi, or Ethiopia, have experienced deterioration of their capital accounts, which they have been able to finance mostly through foreign aid. Although the oil-exporting nations have recorded surpluses in their current account balances, their capital account balances are in deficit due to investments and other financial flows deposited in Western countries. The oil importers—a much larger group of African countries—have experienced large (and growing) current account deficits financed by foreign aid and some foreign investment. These current account deficits often reflect various types of external shocks: Recessions in industrial countries tend to create world business cycles that affect African economies, creating current account deficits as they reduce the market for their exports. Changes in commodity prices (notably oil) also are often translated into a deteriorated current account position: an increase in international prices for commodities leads to higher external revenues for exporters, while a decline would be reflected in heavier costs of their importations. Likewise, changes in the exchange rate of the dollar—the currency in which most African exports are sold and revenues

realized—also determine the level of external revenues. Finally, inflation and interest rate levels in industrial countries directly affect debt levels and financial flows in African countries' balances of payments, with higher rates of interest increasing external debts.

Still, economic theory and recent development experience confirm the benefits of outward-looking policies that exploit the potential opportunities of international trade and external capital flows. Therefore, African countries cannot (and should not) isolate themselves from the world economy. In principle, policy options to address current account deficits include three steps: (1) Deciding whether to finance—that is, whether to borrow abroad on the assumption that a current deficit is simply a temporary problem—or to adjust—to increase exports and cut import-on the assumption that a deficit is permanent, or structural; (2) If the path of adjustment is chosen, countries must then decide the appropriate mix of expenditure cuts and expenditure switching (changing spending patterns from foreign to domestic goods); and (3) If the decision is made to switch expenditures, countries must decide whether to devalue their national currency, or to rely on commercial policies like higher tariffs or quotas on imports. In trying to address their balance of payments problems, many African countries have used all these tools clumsily, often aggravating their external situation.

See also **Cold War; Debt and Credit; Economic History; Economic Systems; International Monetary Fund; Slave Trades.**

BIBLIOGRAPHY

Dornbusch, Rudiger. "Balance of Payment Issues." In *The Open Economy: Tools for Policymakers in Developing Countries*, ed. R. Dornbusch and F. Leslie C.H. Helmers. Washington DC: World Bank and Oxford University Press, 1988.

International Monetary Fund. *Balance of Payment Manual*, 4th edition. Washington DC: International Monetary Fund, 1977.

Krugman, Paul. "External Shocks and Domestic Policy Responses." In *The Open Economy: Tools for Policymakers in Developing Countries*, ed. R. Dornbusch and F. Leslie C.H. Helmers. Washington, DC: World Bank and Oxford University Press, 1988.

Lovejoy, Paul E. *Transformations in Slavery.* Cambridge, U.K.: Cambridge University Press, 2000.

Monga, Célestin. "A Currency Reform Index for Western and Central Africa." *The World Economy* 20, no. 1 (1997): 103–121.

CÉLESTIN MONGA

ENVIRONMENTAL IMPACT

The Earth Summit in Rio de Janeiro in 1992 and the World Summit for Sustainable Development in Johannesburg in 2002 both emphasized the importance of sustainable development. High priority was given to linking environmental, social, and economic considerations, recognizing that only a holistic approach to development could ultimately be sustainable. In the aftermath of the Rio Conference, the donor community gave considerable attention to developing different tools, methods, and guidelines to integrate environmental and social components into the planning process and project life cycle. These included environmental impact assessments (EIAs) and strategic environmental assessments (SEAs), as well as other specialized guidelines, such as social impact assessments, cultural heritage safeguards, involuntary resettlement, and protection of indigenous peoples.

The extent to which EIAs are applied and integrated into African government policy provides insight into how well African governments incorporate environmental considerations into their policy "frame of reference."

Since the 1980s, EIAs have been applied to many development projects across Africa, especially those with a perceived major environmental "footprint." Most writers consider EIAs policy and management tools for planning and decision making. Others define them as evaluators of the consequences likely to arise from projects that significantly affect the environment. Critics see EIAs as time-consuming, costly, and a hindrance to the development process. In general, EIAs help identify, predict, and evaluate the environmental consequences of proposed development projects or policy actions.

INSTITUTIONAL, POLITICAL, AND RESOURCE CONSTRAINTS TO EIA IMPLEMENTATION

The following observations highlight the institutional, political, and resource constraints that impede a more systematic use of EIAs in the planning and project cycle:

Many EIA reports are bulky, technical volumes that are not easy to read or understand. Few local citizens are aware of the studies undertaken, as they are generally not well publicized. Other than those who are intimately involved in the process, few people in the region understand the concept of EIA, or appreciate that it is part art and part science, with a variety of definitions and methods. However, even though some Africans are knowledgeable in EIA theory, many lack practical experience, which is in turn reflected in the quality of work undertaken. To make things worse, most of these experts work in the private sector, for foreign entities, or for international organizations based in Africa, leaving governments with limited institutional capacity.

In this connection, the International Association of Impact Assessment (IAIA) organized a conference in Marrakesh in 2003 aimed at strengthening the EIA process in Africa. The conference recommended that donor agencies should continue to support African countries in various training efforts to strengthen the capacity of African professionals in EIA and related fields. There is, however, no easy solution to capacity building in Africa. Long-term support is required to build and strengthen existing capacities and promote sustainable partnerships, both within and between African countries. Ultimately, this burden must be met as a policy priority by African governments themselves. Specifically, they should commit themselves to civil service reforms that reward performance, commitment, and professionalism.

Many African countries have enacted environmental legislation that, if enforced, would strengthen or complement the EIA process, including fisheries, forest, water, and land-use acts. Mauritius, Mozambique, South Africa, Swaziland, and Zambia, and other South African Development Community (SADC) countries have specific EIA legislation. South Africa has a dual system in which EIA and spatial planning operate under different legal bodies, which could lead to confusion, conflict, and ineffectiveness. Scholars such as Jens Staerdahl and colleagues and Alex Weaver have acknowledged, however, that South Africa has successfully integrated the diverse environmental regulations into local EIA practice, which stands up well against the best international standards.

Nonetheless, the EIA process still needs further clarification in most African countries and existing regulatory systems require harmonization to avoid confusion and duplicated effort. In addition, given the shortage of environmental lawyers in Africa, greater emphasis should be given to train more of them. This, in turn, will help not only in publicize existing national environmental legislation but will also help enforce them.

Various EIA case studies and reviews present a mixed record on the extent to which environmental considerations have been incorporated in the African policy planning process. In 1997 Raphael Mwalyosi and Ross Hughes noted that EIA preparation has had very little impact on decision making in Tanzania. A 2001 review of thirteen development projects in Egypt confirmed that most had not had an EIA before implementation, although some were conducted during project implementation. Elsewhere, however, Per Christensen and colleagues concluded in 2005 that EIAs have influenced decision making. If they are to play a critical role in the decision-making process, they must be carried out at the appraisal stage of project planning. This, in turn, will ensure that mitigation measures are built into projects not only to minimize negative effects, but also to maximize benefits. Moreover, further comparative analysis is required to draw lessons on best practices and better understand what common factors, if any, were relevant in giving priority to EIA preparation and its inclusion in the policy and program planning experience.

Public participation in the EIA process is critical, but is also controversial. In 1999, Prasad Modak and Asit Biswas emphasized the importance of effective public participation for successful development projects. However, no there are no clear strategies on how this can be achieved. The lack of public involvement in various EIAs is known to have been costly, and has caused the failure of a number of development projects. Given the low level of literacy in many communities where development projects are sited, one option is for project proponents to use traditional communication structures, such as open forums (e.g., "barazas" in East Africa) to gauge and guide public opinion. Chiefs and elders can call for meetings to discuss important matters affecting their communities and obtain local support. Additionally, greater use might be made of donor agencies and other development partners support civic education programs. In short, public participation calls for the use of awareness-raising. such as radio programs in local languages, theatre programs, newspaper articles, and better-publicized environmental concerns with specific emphasis on EIAs and other related processes.

African governments rarely fund EIAs themselves. Given current revenue constraints, most EIA studies in the region are funded by donors and private sector investors. In many instances, donor agencies are mandated to undertake EIA studies for specific categories of projects and investments. Generally, African governments have no choice but to agree, if they wish to see the project or policy support move forward. Donor agencies and other development partners could help African governments by encouraging greater local ownership of environmental planning and application of EIA-like tools. In addition, African governments must devise ways to finance EIA activities for which they are responsible. As a clear demonstration of ownership of and commitment to the EIA process, other African countries should follow examples of South Africa, Namibia, and Seychelles, and set aside funds specifically for EIA activities.

CONCLUSIONS

If the effective use of EIAs is a barometer for the extent to which African governments give adequate policy priority to environmental considerations, then most African governments still have much more to do. By and large, EIAs in Africa today are still largely donor driven and reflect donor concerns and priorities. This approach has not been particularly successful. The international community and African governments jointly must examine new ways to foster greater collaboration among African governments, local communities, donor agencies, and the private sector to ensure greater attention to environmental policy considerations.

A key component of such a partnership strategy could come through South–South Cooperation. As recommended by the Rio Earth Summit in 1992 and the Durban African Ministerial Meeting in 1995, African countries should identify those developing countries from other regions with a good track record in EIA, so that their best practices can be shared and replicated. For example, the EIA process has been well integrated in development planning in Singapore, and environmental laws and regulations are strictly enforced.

Mainstreaming environmental considerations into policy and program planning is essential to sustainable development and the realization of millennium development goals. Without sound environmental policies, development is likely to fail because unintended and adverse consequences limit economic opportunities. Without development, environmental protection usually fails because society and individuals then lack the means and material to invest in environmental protection.

See also **Johannesburg; Literacy; Marrakesh; Media.**

BIBLIOGRAPHY

Modak, P., and A. K. Biswas. *Conducting Environmental Impact Assessment for Developing Countries.* Tokyo: United Nations University Press, 1999.

Mwalyosi, R., and R. Hughes. *The Performance of EIA in Tanzania: An Assessment.* London: International Institute for Environment and Development and Dar es Salaam: Institute of Resource Assessment, 1998.

Staerdahl, J., et al. "Environmental Impact Assessment in Malaysia, South Africa, Thailand, and Denmark: Background, Layout, Context, Public Participation and Environmental Scopes." *Journal of Transdisciplinary Environmental Studies* 3, no. 1 (2004): p. 46–65.

Weaver, A. "EIA and Sustainable Development: Key Concepts and Tools." In *Environmental Impact Assessment in Southern Africa.* Windhoek: Southern African Institute for Environmental Assessment, 2003.

JOHN O. KAKONGE

HUMANITARIAN ASSISTANCE

Humanitarian assistance is a term that is commonly applied to the delivery of international aid to populations affected by natural disasters and wars. It is sometimes used interchangeably with the term *emergency assistance* (or *emergency aid*). However, the latter is a more narrowly focused concept and does not necessarily incorporate the widely recognized humanitarian principles of impartiality, universality, political neutrality, and protection of vulnerable populations.

The idea of humanitarian assistance has roots in religious beliefs about charity: that is, the notion that things should be given to those in acute need without expectation of recompense (at least in this world). To an extent this altruism is true of all international aid, but humanitarian aid is more overtly associated with philanthropic motivation. The argument that development aid should be given to strategically important political allies or to the governments of countries adhering to certain kinds of political and economic reforms, is explicitly set aside. This political neutrality has been particularly important in regions of Africa, where large numbers of people have been severely affected by armed conflicts, droughts, and other environmental catastrophes, but governments have been unable or unwilling to establish peaceful administration, respect human rights, introduce democratic reforms, or implement structural adjustment programs of interest to prospective donor nations. In these places, aid in the form of medical care, food relief, and water supplies are provided by a host of international agencies.

AGENCIES

Agencies normally providing human assistance include the Red Cross movement, various United Nations (UN) agencies, and a large (and ever growing) number of nongovernmental organizations (NGOs). The Red Cross is made up of the International Committee (which concentrates on the effects of armed conflict), the International Federation (which works primarily in natural disaster situations) and the national Red Cross and Red Crescent societies (which act as local partner agencies). The Red Cross is an international network of organizations, which have a mandate based in the Geneva Conventions (1859–2005, treaties which set agreed limits to the barbarity of war). The United Nations agencies mostly involved in humanitarian assistance include the Office of the United Nations High Commissioner for Refugees (UNHCR), the United Nations Children's Fund (UNICEF), and the World Food Program (WFP). The UN system also aims to assist in the coordination of the humanitarian assistance operations of its own agencies, the Red Cross, and NGOs through the UN Organization for the Coordination of Humanitarian Affairs (OCHA). Certain UN agencies may run their own operations on the ground in some emergencies, but much of the humanitarian assistance funding that pass through UN agencies is channelled to NGOs, which are subcontracted as local implementing partners.

In African emergencies, there are usually scores of international NGOs. Some of these have quite a long history and, like the Red Cross, were established in response to the suffering of people caught up in wars. Save the Children emerged from a campaign to assist people in Germany and Austria-Hungary during World War I, both Oxfam and CARE were products of World War II, and Doctors Without Borders (MSF, Medecins sans Frontières) was founded in response to experiences of French physicians during the Nigerian civil war. Since the founding of MSF in the early 1970s, a large number of others have been established, often in direct response to media coverage of events like the Ethiopian famines and the sudden availability of funding.

FUNDS

Humanitarian assistance funds are partly provided by the philanthropic/charitable donations of individuals, private companies, solidarity groups, and religious organizations. Public concern about a particular event (such as the Asian tsunami in 2005) can result in very large earmarked contributions. However, for the majority of years most humanitarian funds come from official aid programs, such as the United States Agency for International Development (USAID). Official aid programs also run their own relief operations, or jointly finance the emergency programs of multilateral agencies, such as the European Union. It is difficult to give an accurate figure for the total amounts spent on humanitarian assistance. There are a number of reasons for this: (1) charitable donations are not systematically collated; (2) some donors (such as Saudi Arabia) do not report to the Development Assistance Committee of OECD (Organization for Economic Co-operation and Development); and (3) even the reporting of the main official donors is not altogether clear—funding for food aid, for example, is not adequately disaggregated between emergency and nonemergency purposes, and some donors report funding for domestic refugees as part of their humanitarian assistance. According to the data available, in 2005 bilateral donors provided $8.4 billion in humanitarian assistance (about 14% of bilateral official development assistance). The United States is by far the biggest donor, in most years exceeding the combined contributions of all six of the next

largest donors. There are no robust data for private and nonofficial contributions, and they vary widely from year to year. In 2005 they may have been as much as $10 billion.

EFFORTS AND ISSUES

Humanitarian aid agencies and the official programs of the major aid donors generally claim to provide humanitarian aid to the world's most acutely suffering populations. There is no doubt that their activities save lives. Nevertheless, a glance at the amounts of humanitarian assistance deployed to particular places indicates that assertions about concentrating resources on the worst affected regions are more of an aspiration than a reality. Data collated from the amounts of humanitarian aid reported by the major donors during the 1990s show that in the second half of the 1990s, none of the top five recipients of official humanitarian assistance were in Africa. The next five—Rwanda, Sudan, Afghanistan, Angola, and Indonesia—included three nations in Africa: Rwanda, where genocidal conflict had afflicted many and created large refugee populations, Sudan, where civil war and increasing allegations of enslavements prevailed in its southern regions, and Angola, landmine-laden and wracked by a war then twenty years in duration. But the total provided to these countries was less than half that provided to the top five, a group that included Israel.

Moreover, even when humanitarian aid is concentrated on an African emergency, it is common for the worst affected populations to be inaccessible or impossible to protect for logistical and security reasons. These have been huge problems in the Democratic Republic of the Congo (DRC), where the UNHCR lost contact with more people supposedly under its protection in the late 1990s, many of them Rwandan refugees, than the total cumulative total for all situations in which the agency had become involved up to that time, and an estimated 3 to 4 million people have been killed (probably ten times more than the total death toll from the Asian tsunami). Such incapacity is compounded by the constant need for humanitarian organizations to publicize their activities in order to sustain funding. Reporting of the events in the Congo is very poor. In 1994 there were dramatic television images of hundreds of thousands of refugees fleeing into eastern Congo from Rwanda.

These prompted huge amounts of international concern and interest, resulting in a sudden surge of funding. Over 100 aid agencies started operating around Goma, where some 850,000 people were concentrated. However, when large numbers of those who were supposed to have been assisted found themselves under attack a few years later, their plight was largely unreported in the international media and therefore ignored. Relatively less significant emergencies were prioritized, particularly the Mozambique floods of 2000, which could readily be covered by news organizations.

Humanitarian assistance operations can also be adversely affected by short-term concentrations of funds, which have to be spent on particular places. In several African emergencies this has led to severe problems of coordination, compounded by outright competition between agencies to secure funds and spend them as quickly as possible. The relief activities in Goma during 1994 are a good example. The rapid proliferation of agencies made a systematic approach impossible, and the cholera epidemic that broke out among the refugees could not be contained for several weeks. The situation was eventually brought under control by the provision of clean water and with the help of French and U.S. military forces, but not until an estimated 50,000 people had died. In other words, while scores of humanitarian aid agencies were falling over one another to set up projects, the epidemic claimed about the number of lives as might have been expected had there been no assistance at all. It effectively ran a natural course.

Another problem that arises when relatively large amounts of humanitarian aid are deployed in places where state systems are viewed as compromised or inadequate, as they so often are in Africa, is that the effects may undermine existing local structures, because agencies establish separate administrations. Often this failure to utilize existing services is an inevitable consequence of having to provide urgent assistance, but it makes it very difficult to sustain services once the humanitarian assistance funding stops. There was a great deal of discussion in the late twentieth and early twenty first centuries about the lack of a relief-to-development continuum, that is, how to provide relief in ways that lay a basis for future local sustainability and development, and efforts have been made to resolve this further inefficiency. But political realities and the

nature of aid agency financing make it a recurrent issue. In Goma it was compounded by the fact that the members of the militia that had been involved in the Rwandan genocide were present among the refugees, and aid agencies had little choice other than to work with them in order to operate. As an Oxfam report observed: "Having condemned the genocide and demanded that its perpetrators be brought to justice, Oxfam and other agencies have found themselves in the invidious position of delivering aid through structures controlled by the very people responsible for the crimes committed in Rwanda. . . . It is difficult to imagine a graver abuse of international assistance" (Watkins 1995, 52). According to the president of MSF at the time, "The humanitarian intervention, far from representing a bulwark against evil, was in fact one of its appendages" (Rony Brauman, quoted in Prunier 1995, 277).

This paradox highlights what surely is the most serious dilemma facing humanitarian aid agencies on the ground in Africa. In order to operate, they commonly have to negotiate with the very groups and individuals who are causing the suffering that they intend to alleviate. This reality is one reason why existing state structures may be bypassed, but to do so can require bribing government officials and military personnel. In several places, arrangements may be even more problematic, as in Goma, in that the afflicted populations are in territories controlled by nonstate parties. Here the aid agencies may have to find ways of negotiating access with violent organizations, who may not view themselves as constrained by conventions about human rights or the rules of war agreed between sovereign states. Humanitarian assistance in these circumstances can have the effect of supporting the activities of armed groups and may end up becoming integrated into local economies in which war or famine are resource-generating activities. In some circumstances, such as in Nigeria in the late 1960s, Ethiopia in the 1980s, and Sudan in the 1990s, humanitarian assistance has been accused of effectively sustaining the emergencies.

These problems associated with humanitarian assistance have led to scathing critiques, with some analysts going so far as to argue that assistance to better human lives can actually make situations worse. Others have mounted vigorous defence, arguing that to suggest that humanitarian agencies are responsible for suffering is like blaming ambulances for the afflictions of hospital patients. Essentially those who argue in favor of humanitarian assistance adopt one of two positions, which are not easy to reconcile. Either they call for a reinvigoration of the original principles of humanitarianism—notably those associated with the founding of the Red Cross—or they call for a more robust approach that combines an integration of those principles with strong, even forceful "humanitarian intervention" (note that this was the expression used by the president of MSF in the aforementioned quote about Goma).

Humanitarian intervention is conventionally distinguished from humanitarian assistance. Although usages are not always consistent, the former tends to refer to the deployment of military personnel to prevent genocide or comparable atrocities. The idea of a government evoking humanitarian principles to justifying military intervention in a territory beyond its national borders is not something new—for example, the suppression of the slave trade was given as a reason for the Anglo-Egyptian invasion of Sudan in the late nineteenth century. But a problem with such assertions is that military interventions may be viewed as having more self-serving motives too. Also, while governments may sign agreements and conventions about protecting civilians and rules of war, they tend to be hostile to any interventions that threaten their own national sovereignty. This tension is manifested in the United Nations Charter itself.

The founders of the United Nations, still shaken by the appalling events that they had witnessed during the world wars, wanted to establish internationally agreed principles to prevent such events occurring again. Under Chapter VII of the UN Charter the Security Council was empowered to take measures to keep the global peace, including the initiation of military action. Soon after the signing of the UN Charter, other international agreements aimed at strengthening enforcement procedures, notably the Convention on the Prevention and Punishment of the Crime of Genocide (1948) and the Geneva Conventions of 1949. However, Article Two of the UN Charter guaranteed the sovereignty of UN member states, and during the Cold War era, it proved difficult to reach the necessary consensus in the Security Council to activate its powers under Chapter VII, and thereby

provide formal support for humanitarian intervention under international law. It also proved impossible to make use of the Genocide Convention, even when there was widespread acceptance that crimes against humanity were occurring. Reference was made to it when Tanzania invaded Uganda in 1971 to overthrow the brutal regime of Idi Amin, but this rationale was not accepted by the Security Council.

Matters did not begin to accommodate greater UN humanitarian initiatives until the late 1980s, when a demand for military support for humanitarian assistance accompanied the prospect of a more interventionist UN. Although many agencies and individuals involved in humanitarian assistance have resisted the trend, continuing to distance themselves from any enforcement operations, others have openly called for military protection and support, arguing that assertions about political neutrality can be naïve and irresponsible where so-called crimes against humanity are occurring. One of the most prominent advocates for this new interventionist humanitarianism has been Bernard Kouchner, who worked in Nigeria during the civil war (1967–1970) and was one of the founders of MSF. Later he became a minister in the French government and head of the UN operation in Kosovo. He is closely associated with the controversial view that there is, or should be, is a universal duty and a legally binding right to interfere anywhere if human rights are being violated (this is a principle that is generally referred by the French phrase *le droit d'ingérence* (the duty/right/ obligation to intervene/interfere).

During the 1990s, militarized humanitarianism was attempted in several countries, including some in Africa, notably the United States intervention in Somalia in 1992–1993, and similar interventions have continued to occur since the late twentieth century. However their high costs and their very mixed results have meant that the United States and other major powers have become reluctant to support them, unless their strategic and economic interests are directly threatened. Thus, the apparent failure of militarized humanitarianism in Somalia influenced the decision by the United States and the United Kingdom to prevent the UN Security Council accepting that "genocide" was underway in Rwanda during 1994, because it would have required enforcement action to be initiated. Since then, efforts have been made to encourage and support African states to take a more substantial role in monitoring and limiting humanitarian crises, mainly through the African Union. But this approach too has run into serious difficulties, such as in the Darfur region of Sudan.

For humanitarianism in Africa and elsewhere, the fallout of these experiments has been far reaching. World events since the 1980s have had the effect of eroding the distinction between humanitarian assistance and humanitarian intervention, such that in some circumstances it has been impossible to sustain in any meaningful way. One adverse effect is that aid workers are increasingly viewed as legitimate military targets. A further complication is that military personnel are also directly engaged in humanitarian assistance, as with the involvement of the British army in providing emergency aid during the Mozambique floods. The Ministry of Defense received humanitarian assistance funds from the official United Kingdom aid budget.

The blurring of humanitarianisms is a reason why some commentators and organizations have adopted the catch-all term *humanitarian action*, and have tried to establish agreed guidelines that take account of the changing situation and prevent the term *humanitarianism* being used as a gloss for actions motivated by less than magnanimous interests. Two examples are the principles for good practice in humanitarian action, endorsed by most donors in Stockholm in 2003 and the Humanitarian Charter and Minimum Standards in Disaster Response.

See also **Amin Dada, Idi; Disease; Famine; Nongovernmental Organizations; Sudan: Wars; United Nations; Warfare.**

BIBLIOGRAPHY

Allen, T., and D. Styan. "A Right to Interfere? Bernard, Kouchner and the New Humanitarianism." *Journal of International Development* 12, no. 6 (2000): 825–842.

De Waal, Alexander. *Famine Crimes: Politics and the Disaster Relief Industry in Africa.* Bloomington: Indiana University Press, 1997.

Keen, David. *The Benefits of Famine: A Political Economy of Famine and Relief in Southwestern Sudan, 1983–1989.* Princeton, NJ: Princeton University Press, 1994.

ODI Humanitarian Practice Network Reports. London: Overseas Development Institute. 1994–. Available from http://www.odihpn.org/aboutpn.asp.

Prunier, Gerard. *The Rwanda Crisis 1959–1994: History of a Genocide.* London: Hurst, 1995.

Rieff, David. *A Bed for the Night: Humanitarianism in Crisis.* New York: Simon & Schuster, 2002.

Slim, H. "Doing the Right Thing: Relief Agencies, Moral Dilemmas and Moral Responsibility in Political Emergencies and War." *Disasters* 21, no. 3 (1997): 244–257.

Stockton, N. "In Defence of Humanitarianism." *Disasters* 22, no. 4 (1998): 352–360.

Watkins, Kevin. *The Oxfam Poverty Report.* Oxford: Oxfam, 1995.

Wheeler, Nicholas J. *Saving Strangers: Humanitarian Intervention in International Society.* New York: Oxford University Press, 2002.

TIM ALLEN

AIDOO, AMA ATA

(1942–). The novelist and playwright Ama Ata Aidoo was born in central Ghana and completed her bachelor of arts degree at the University of Ghana. Her two first books, *Dilemma of a Ghost* (1965) and *Our Sister Killjoy* (1977), helped position her among the rising African women writers of the time. *Dilemma of a Ghost* was taught in a lot of West African universities because it features an African American woman, Eulalie, coming to Ghana with her husband Ato, who had problems with his Western experience. Aidoo's play *Anowa* (1970), which was about the amnesia of the people who were involved with the slave trade, was published in this period as well. Aidoo wrote several short stories, which she classifies as dilemma stories with orature, including *No Sweetness Here* (1970) and *The Girl Who Can* (1997). Her novel *Changes* (1991), about a family's problems in Ghana, is studied in many U.S. university courses.

Aidoo is one of the most vital and innovative voices that discusses women's roles in her work. As both an author and activist, she truly integrates the personal with the political as she reaches back to inform readers of women's roles throughout West Africa before the colonial era and compels them to envision another place for women. In her writings, Aidoo deals with the patriarchal societies of Europe and the United States.

Ama Ata Aidoo and admirers. Aidoo, a novelist and playwright, poses with author and English professor Gay Wilentz and her East Carolina University students. Aidoo's writing focuses on women's roles in patriarchal societies. PHOTOGRAPH COURTESY OF GAY WILENTZ

In the early 2000s Aidoo does a lot of work in Accra, Ghana. She is the executive director of *Mbaasem*, which translates as "Women's Words, Women's Affairs." Through this organization, Aidoo helps women writers tell their experiences in Ghana. Aidoo is writing books for children, and has published *Birds and Other Poems* (2002).

See also **Literature.**

BIBLIOGRAPHY

Odamtten, Vincent O. *The Art of Ama Ata Aidoo: Polylectics and Reading against Neocolonialism.* Gainesville: University Press of Florida, 1994.

Uzoamaka, Azodo Ada, and Gay Wilentz. *Emerging Perspectives on Ama Ata Aidoo.* Trenton, NJ: Africa World Press, 1999.

GAY WILENTZ

AIDS. *See* **Disease: HIV/AIDS, Medical Aspects; Disease: HIV/AIDS, Social and Political Aspects.**

AKSUM. The Aksumite Empire, which dominated the northern Ethiopian/southern Eritrean highlands during approximately 100–600 CE, was centered upon the modern town of Aksum with other major urban centers at Matara, Qohaito (Koloë), and Adulis (the latter a port city on the Red Sea through which Aksumite international trade was routed). Aksum has been the focus of many archaeological investigations, beginning with the *Deutsche Aksum Expedition* of 1906, with later Italian, French, and most recently joint U.S.-Italian and British excavations, making the town one of the most heavily researched sites in eastern Africa.

It is becoming clear that the Aksumite state did not emerge from the south Arabian-influenced pre-Aksumite phase of the mid-late first millennium BCE with its probable capital at Yeha to the northeast of Aksum. Although epigraphic south Arabian inscriptions, ideological evidence, and certain architectural features seem to point to direct influences from across the Red Sea, many local material culture traits are apparent. The major sites of this period cluster to the northeast of Yeha, and there is only

The southern face of stela three at Aksum. Erected as a pre-Christian grave marker for an elite individual, the decoration (here in carved syenite) recalls the decoration of Aksumite secular architecture. © NIALL FINNERAN

sparse domestic-level settlement at Aksum. A stronger African emphasis is visible in the recently defined proto-Akusmite period (c. 350–150 BCE); excavations by Rodolfo Fattovich and Kathryn Bard on the top of the hill of Beta Giyorgis, Aksum, have yielded evidence of mortuary practices indicative of individual commemoration. The finds include small monoliths (stelae, or grave markers) and imports that imply a stronger link with the Gash Delta region, and even Meroë. It is from this hilltop settlement that Aksum subsequently develops.

During the third century CE, the urban focus shifted to the valley floor; during this period the major decorated stelae of the Central Stela Park are built, reflecting a shift towards lineage-based, dynastic commemoration. The stelae are carved from local igneous syenites and were probably designed as copies of multistoried buildings complete with distinctive door and window frames and horizontal stone courses tied with protruding wooden beams (monkey heads) rendered in stone. The large fallen stela (stela one weighs some 500 tones) is associated with an underground tomb complex: the Mausoleum to the west and a probably unfinished eastern complex. Stela two to the east was moved to Rome during the Italian occupation of the late 1930s and has only been recently returned to await re-erection; stela three is the sole large decorated stela to remain standing and appears to be associated with catacombs.

To the east of the main group, and seemingly not associated with a standing stela is the Tomb of the Brick Arches, again of third-century date. Excavation here yielded fine glasswork, beads and ivory grave goods. These are all clearly graves of the political elite; the earliest mention of Aksum in the first-century *Periplus of the Erythraean Sea* (1912) gives the name of a king: Zoskales. Third-century kings' names are known from monumental inscriptions from southern Arabia, indicating at this stage that Aksum was involved in a colonial venture. With the introduction of a tri-metallic coinage during the reign of Endybis in about 270 CE, a clearer basic royal chronology can be framed.

The Aksumite coinage bears witness to the cosmopolitan nature of the polity; the *Periplus* lists the main exports of Aksum as ivory, gold, and spices. Aksumite coins, based upon the Roman tremissis gold standard, facilitated trade with the eastern Mediterranean. The gold issues bore Greek inscriptions and have been mainly found in Arabia (and some as far as Palestine), and Aksumite pottery has been found in India as well as at ports along the Egyptian Red Sea coasts. Roman amphorae have been excavated at Aksum, and it is possible that some glass and metalwork may have originated from India or the east (a cache of third-century Indian coins was found at the monastery of Debre Damo).

A major event that cemented Aksum's place in the eastern Mediterranean economic world was the adoption in roughly 340 CE of Christianity by King Ezana. He had been converted by a Syrian of Tyre named Frumentius (d. c. 383; he was consecrated Bishop of Aksum at Alexandria, an action that henceforth tied the Ethiopian church to the Copts rather than the west Syrians). The material culture ramifications of the adoption of Christianity are clear; inscriptions and Ge'ez coinage mottoes change; the king was often shown carrying a hand cross, and a small Greek cross replaced the sun-moon motif on the top of the pagan issues. Stelae were no longer erected as grave markers (some anthropologists argue that the massive stela 1, which was never set upright, fell at the period of religious change at Aksum. This might have been taken as a profound omen), and burials tended to take on a more Christianized pattern; the tombs of Kaleb and Genre Masqal are prime examples. Churches were also built; excavated examples show a standard basilican model constructed in the architectural manner of the elite palace buildings, of which Ta'akha Maryam was probably the largest and most extensive.

During the sixth century, Christian Aksum reached its apogee under King Kaleb (b. c. 500) who organized a military expedition into southern Arabia at the behest of the Byzantine emperor. It was during this period that a number of holy men from Syria (the Nine Saints) settled in the region and founded a number of important monastic establishments. The last coinage issues are those of the seventh-century king Armah (b. c. 614) who might be identified in Muslim tradition with King Ashama; the archaeological evidence suggests that Aksum was abandoned at this time, possibly in response to a combination of Islamic disruption of Red Sea trade allied to localized environmental degradation. From then on it retained its status as

the prime ecclesiastical, rather than political, center of Ethiopia when, over the next thousand years, the Christian kingdom looked south rather than toward the sea.

See also **Adulis; Alexandria; Archaeology and Prehistory; Christianity; Ivory; Literature; Urbanism and Urbanization.**

BIBLIOGRAPHY

Fattovich, Rodolfo, et al. *The Aksum Archaeology Area: A Preliminary Assessment.* Naples, Italy: Istituto universitario orientale, 2000.

Munro-Hay, Stuart. *Aksum: An African Civilisation of Late Antiquity.* Edinburgh: Edinburgh University Press, 1991.

Phillipson, David. *Ancient Ethiopia: Aksum, its Antecedents and Successors.* London: British Museum Press, 1998.

Phillipson, David. *Archaeology at Aksum, Ethiopia, 1993-7,* 2 vols. London: British Institute in Eastern Africa, 2000.

Schoff, Wilfred Harvey, trans. *The Periplus of the Erythraean Sea: Travel and Trade in the Indian Ocean, by a Merchant of the First Century.* New York: Longmans, Green, and Co., 1912.

NIALL FINNERAN

ALEXANDRIA.

Alexandria, Egypt's second largest city, lies northwest of the Nile Delta on the Mediterranean. It is named after Alexander the Great, who around 331 BCE ordered the building of a city there, apparently to serve as a connection to the Nile Valley, and beyond, to Persia and India. Alexandria experienced its Golden Age under the first three Ptolemaic rulers (323–221 BCE). It became the major exporter of grain in the ancient world and possibly the world's largest city, as well as the intellectual and artistic capital of the Mediterranean world. Its famous library had 500,000 works.

Alexandria became a Roman city in 30 BCE after Octavian defeated Cleopatra at the Battle of Actium. Some of Christianity's earliest institutions were established there. Over its many centuries under Arab and Turkic rule beginning in 641, the city declined. In 973 Cairo replaced it as Egypt's capital. When Napoleon and his soldiers entered Alexandria in 1798, it was a mere village of 8,000 inhabitants.

The modernizing policies of Ottoman viceroy Muhammad 'Ali (r. 1805–1848) began the revival of Alexandria. He revamped the state's administration and revived the economy, building a new harbor and linking the city to the Nile River by canal. By the end of his rule, the population had grown to 60,000.

Alexandria's population in 2006 was 4.6 million. The country's most cosmopolitan city, it has residents with many Mediterranean backgrounds. Eighty percent of Egyptian exports and imports leave from Alexandria, which is also a center for oil refining and food processing.

See also 'Ali, Muhammad; Egypt, Early; Egypt, Modern; Nile River.

BIBLIOGRAPHY

Hirst, Anthony, and Michael Silk, eds. *Alexandria, Real and Imagined.* Burlington, VT: Ashgate, 2004.

Pollard, Justin, and Howard Reid. *The Rise and Fall of Alexandria: Birthplace of the Modern Mind.* New York: Viking, 2006.

MICHAEL L. LEVINE

ALFONSO I.   *See* Mvemba Nzinga.

ALGERIA

> *This entry includes the following articles:*
> GEOGRAPHY AND ECONOMY
> SOCIETY AND CULTURES
> HISTORY AND POLITICS

GEOGRAPHY AND ECONOMY

Algeria's economy emerged from the export-oriented growth model of the colonial period (1830–1962) to the postcolonial model of import substitution industrialization (ISI), creating major imbalances in the economy. Despite the revolutionary, anticolonialist implication of economic self-sufficiency that was sought through ISI, Algeria relied heavily on the exportation of its primary natural resource, oil, which has dominated public receipts and the economy in general. After the hike in oil prices, an estimated $61 billion of income generated by the exportation of oil will account for about two-thirds of Algeria's national gross national product (GNP) in 2006.

Under French colonial rule, Algeria's economy was dominated by French *colons* who owned most of the arable land. By the early twentieth century, around 18.5 million acres were expropriated from the Algerian native population, and the Algerian economy was transformed into a French-controlled and -owned agricultural export economy, in which most of the consumer goods were imported from the French metropolis. Exported goods included wine, grains, and unprocessed raw materials such as iron ore, and phosphates. Industrialization was not a priority before the war of independence broke out in 1954, when an economic reform program, the Constantine plan, made industrialization an official policy.

Under the French, oil explorations already took place, and the first major discovery occurred in 1956. The French public enterprise *Société Nationale de Recherches Pétrolières en Algérie* conducted most of the exploration, and when independence was achieved in 1962, this meant that the new Algerian state had to negotiate with the French government for further exploration, capital investments, and licenses in the oil sector. Consequently, in the immediate postindependence period, the main ambition was to establish the infrastructure and the expertise in the oil sector so that the oil industry could be nationalized along other sectors by the end of the 1960s.

Oil is primarily located at the Hassi Messouad field nearby Haoud El Hamra, as well as in the area of Zarzaïtine and Endjeleh fields in proximity of the Libyan border. Production was at around 1.2 million barrels per day (b/d) in the early 1980s, to decrease to 700,000 b/d in the 1990s to extend the exploitation of this natural resource beyond an estimated fifty-year period, and to abide by the Organization of the Petroleum Exporting Countries (OPEC) production quota. With higher oil prices and new, foreign investment in production and exploration facilities, oil export increased to reach 1.3 million b/d in 2006. In addition to crude oil, natural gas reserves are abundant at around 3,200 billion cubic meters and are expected to last for at least another sixty years.

Rents acquired in the oil sector have been used to establish massive industrialization plants, whereas

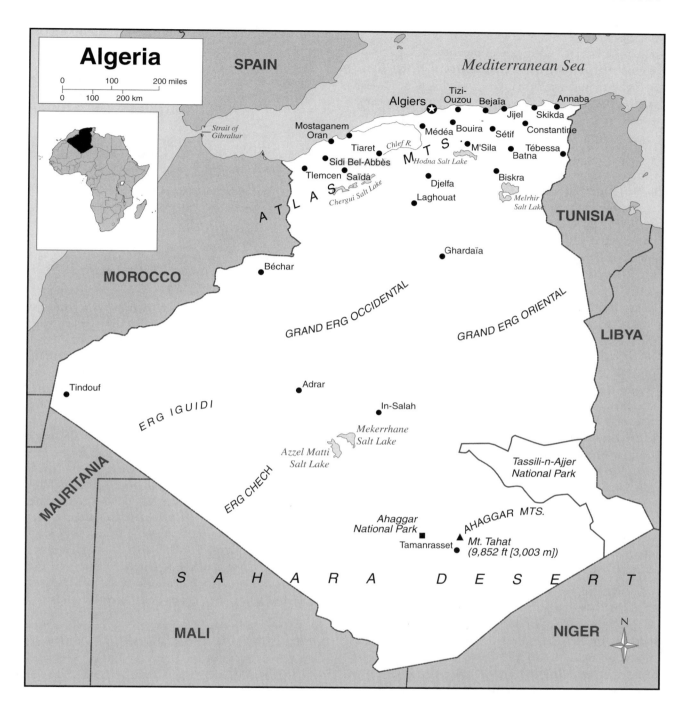

the agricultural sector was put under state control; lands abandoned by the French and lands controlled by larger Algerian landowners were organized in collectives. This had negative consequences for agricultural production, as peasants were told how much to produce and prices were fixed, leading to shortages in agricultural production and ultimately

rural exodus. Therefore, up to the late 1980s, Algeria provided an interesting example of a distorted economy, where money was abundant but markets were empty, because production did not keep up with consumer demands. In industries, this had the consequence that many state-controlled plants never worked at full capacity, as inputs from the agricultural sector, for example, did not follow demands for lack of financial incentives. Bad management and poor factory discipline had the effect that the major iron and steel complex at El Hadjar was only working at 40 percent capacity in the early 1980s, raising costs for end consumers and forfeiting economies of scale.

Apart from these domestic economic problems related to inefficiency of state capitalism, Algeria faced mounting international debts for the borrowing with which it had fueled its economic expansion in the 1970s. The debt crisis occurred when oil prices plummeted. In 1986 the World Bank reported Algerian debt at $15 billion, and the Organization for Economic Cooperation and Development (OECD) figure was at $24. By 1992 the figure was at around $26 billion, which was twice as much as Algeria's total export earnings despite slightly higher oil prices in the aftermath of the 1991 Gulf crisis (Richards and Waterbury, 71, 231). In order to prevent International Monetary Fund (IMF) intervention, in the early 1980s the Algerian leadership under Chadli Benjedid imposed austerity plans, encouraged private investment, broke up the large state-controlled monopolies, and spurred decentralization. However, it refrained from a devaluation of the Algerian dinar, kept interest rates artificially low, and continued to provide important subsidies to state-owned companies. This encouraged inflation, low productivity, and ultimately unemployment, and Algeria continued to rely on external credits. An IMF agreement to reschedule Algeria's external debts followed in 1989.

Algeria's economic recovery since the end of its civil war has depended heavily on stable oil prices. GDP growth rates of 5.4 percent in 2005 and 5.1 percent in 2006 are directly linked to the international oil market. Oil revenues are used to increase domestic spending in infrastructure and public sector wages. New infrastructure in the natural gas sector—the *In Salah* and *In Amenas* gas projects—will increase production, government income, and therefore government spending. The goal is diversification and escape from the economy's heavy dependence on oil export; however, most of the new oil and gas downstream projects such as refineries still depend on the availability of oil. As in other parts of North Africa, economic decisions are closely related to political developments, and increased government spending aims at establishing a constituency for the government to go ahead with and find more support for its peace and reconciliation program.

See also **Colonial Policies and Practices: French North Africa; International Monetary Fund; World Bank.**

BIBLIOGRAPHY

Economist Intelligence Unit Country Reports—Algeria. London: Economist Intelligence Unit, 2006.

Richards, Alan, and John Waterbury. *A Political Economy of the Middle East.* Boulder, CO: Westview Press, 1996.

JAMES SATER

SOCIETY AND CULTURES

Algeria's people are mostly Arabic-speaking descendants of Berber inhabitants. In the medieval and early modern periods, Arabic became the majority language in most of the country, leaving Berber-speaking communities in a number of mountainous areas and in the Sahara. Beginning in the early sixteenth century, Turks, southern Europeans, and significant numbers of immigrants from the formerly Muslim lands of Spain (Andalus), made up important sections of urban society. There was also a small Jewish community (1–2% of total population), formed by both descendants of ancient Jewish communities and refugees from Spain. This population claimed genealogical ties that bound extended groups together for market, land-access, and water-resource rights. Around half the population at the beginning of the French conquest in 1830 lived in settled agricultural villages. Most of the remainder were nomadic; some groups combined both lifestyles, moving with flocks and cultivating crops in different seasons.

Islamic schools, courts, and a cosmopolitan, Andalusian-influenced Mediterranean culture were found in cities. Education and culture in rural areas were expressed through oral tradition, including epic poetry, and through Islam fused with local customs, often centered on saintly lineages and the shrines of their founders. By the nineteenth century, Islam was frequently articulated through local branches of religious brotherhoods or orders (*tariqa*s) spread throughout the Middle East and sub-Saharan Africa. Literacy and religious learning was transmitted through Qur'anic schools, and in pilgrimage and teaching centers led by shaikhs (leaders) of the *tariqa*s, who were frequently also believed to transmit charismatic blessing (*baraka*).

SOCIAL CHANGE IN THE NINETEENTH AND TWENTIETH CENTURIES

Algeria experienced rapid and profound social change in the mid-nineteenth century, as precolonial economic and cultural systems were transformed under French colonial rule (1830–1962), in the war of independence (1954–1962), and by the subsequent development of the independent state.

Colonization and wars of conquest (1830–1870)—with their resultant economic disruption—combined with epidemics, led to a drastic decrease in Algeria's population and the destruction of much existing socioeconomic and cultural infrastructure. Although most Europeans stayed in the coastal cities, colonial settlement in the countryside came to dominate a market economy in which landholdings were increasingly concentrated in French hands; indigenous Algerian agriculture became unsustainable.

As the Algerian population grew and land resources remained scarce, increasingly impoverished people migrated in greater numbers to the cities, where after 1936 Algerians outnumbered Europeans. Algerians were forced into wage labor, seasonal work on European farms, and migration to the cities or to France. A new social stratification emerged, with the proletarianization of the rural poor and the emergence of a new middle class of landlords, entrepreneurs, official functionaries, and liberal professionals.

The war of independence, begun as an armed insurrection by a small number of nationalists, escalated into a massive counterinsurgency campaign by the French authorities, and its effects marked Algerian society deeply. The forced relocation (*regroupement*) of some three million people from rural areas into controlled "strategic hamlets," combined with massive bombings and the destruction of rural settlements, completed the earlier disruption of Algerian agriculture and permanently affected rural life. Atrocities were committed by both the Algerian National Liberation Front (FLN) and the French army; the latter also conducted roundups, internment, torture, and summary executions. This had a profound effect on society, symbolized after independence by the proclamation of "one and a half million martyrs." Later calculations of the actual death toll suggest a figure around 300,000.

At the war's end, resistance to decolonization by ultracolonialist French Algerians led to the rapid departure of almost a million Europeans, depriving Algeria suddenly of most of its technical, managerial, and professional workers. After independence, technical advisers and ready-made industry from Europe became crucial to the national development effort. Societal reconstitution through massive expansion of the state infrastructure, a centrally planned industrializing economy, and free and universal education and health care became important goals, financed by hydrocarbon exports that were first tapped in 1958.

The revolution's promises were unevenly delivered, however. Women, especially, were returned to a subordinate social status officialized by a conservative family law in 1984. Algeria's population increased threefold between the 1960s and the 1990s, and the projected social transformation through planned industrialization failed to keep pace with the demands of population growth. The rapid development of the French economy from the 1950s to the 1970s encouraged increasing numbers of Algerian families to migrate to the former colonial power.

Political changes in the 1980s scaled down the centralized building projects of the 1960s and 1970s, and increased social, cultural, and religious conflicts. In the 1990s, Algerian society experienced an internal war between Islamist insurgents and state military and security forces. The trauma of terrorist and counterinsurgency actions again took their toll on society, and 100,000–200,000 people are thought to have been killed. As the country emerged from this political crisis, the restructured economy and unresolved social and cultural conflicts continued to produce tensions in a society characterized by a growing and very young population. Twenty-nine percent were under fifteen years of age in 2005, and unemployment was around 25 percent.

ALGERIAN CULTURES FROM COLONIALISM TO POSTCOLONIALISM

Throughout the colonial period, Islamic culture continued to provide the basic framework for much of Algerian life. Rural Algeria's cultural infrastructure was severely weakened by the expropriation of property for the maintenance of religious institutions; the functioning of mosques and the exercise of Muslim civil law was controlled by the colonial state, which also established official schools to train judges and other personnel. Nonetheless, the *tariqa*s, which remained important institutions under French rule, were challenged from the 1920s onwards by a modernist movement for the reform of Islam called the Salafiyya. This movement became dominant in defining official religious culture after independence before it was challenged in turn by radical Islamist ideology from the Middle East. Local, popular religious forms were not, however, entirely eliminated, and showed a resurgence after 1990.

The independent state committed itself to a national, revolutionary and scientific culture, and to the reassertion of an Algerian "authenticity" defined by the Arabic language and Islam. Francophone intellectuals, frequently viewed with some suspicion, nonetheless continued to play major roles in the development of Algerian culture after independence. While French Algeria had itself produced significant cultural works—paintings by Pierre Auguste Renoir, the letters and diaries of Isabelle Eberhardt, the novels and plays of Albert Camus—Algerian culture also testified to the colonial experience in French, through novelists like Mouloud Feraoun and Yacine Kateb. Older Algerian cultures were expressed in the colonial period through Kabyle (a Berber people and language native to northeastern Algeria) poets like Shaykh Mohand Ul-Hocine and the singer Marguerite Taos Amrouche, through Arabic writers like Reda Houhou (killed by French troops during the war of independence). After independence, Algerian literature developed both in French, with writers like Rachid Mimouni and Rachid Boudjedra, and in Arabic through the works of novelists like Tahar Ouettar and Abdelhamid Benhadouga.

The plurality of Algerian culture became particularly problematic during the nineteenth century, when European racial theories developed a distinction between lowland, Arabophone, nomadic groups, whom they dubbed "Arabs," and highland, Berberophone, agriculturalists called "Berbers." In the twentieth century, this distinction was reactivated as a basis for cultural and political claims by Algerians, especially in the Berberophone Kabylia region. In 1980, the cancellation by state authorities of a lecture on Berber poetry at Tizi Ouzou, Kabylia's major city, by the writer and linguist Mouloud Mammeri led to widespread protests, eventually spawning a Berber cultural movement that articulated both a general set of political grievances and demands for Berber recognition. This movement has been opposed by the conservative view of Algeria's exclusively Arab-Islamic cultural identity.

Despite these polarizations, an outpouring of music and literature in the period after independence, in French, Arabic, and Berber indicated the multiplicity and richness of Algerian cultures. European writers who remained in independent Algeria, however, often had unhappy fates: the poet Jean Sénac was murdered in Algiers in 1973; the writer Anna Greki faced criticism from the "official" cultural lobby, which did not consider non-Muslims as truly Algerian. Other Algerian Francophone writers expressed the difficulties of writing in the "colonizer's language," or, like Malek Haddad, ceased writing altogether. Many of the bestselling and best-known Algerian writers nonetheless continued to work in French, including novelists Assia Djebbar, Mohamed Dib, and Tahar Djaout (assassinated in 1993); in the 1990s writers schooled entirely in Arabic also began writing in French, notably the novelist Yasmina Khadra, whose accounts of the war in the 1990s became international successes. At the same time, Ahlem Mostaghanemi became the first Algerian woman to become a major internationally successful writer in Arabic.

Algerian music, especially *raï* (opinion) and *sha'bi* (popular) music in Arabic. Neotraditional forms of Kabyle music became internationally popular from the 1980s onward. The film industry, buoyant in the 1970s, produced the first African film to win the Golden Palm at Cannes (Lakhdar-Hamina's epic *Chronicle of the Years of Embers*, 1975) and more realist and intimate films (Allouache's *Omar Gatlato*, 1976). In the early 1990s, personal safety as well as economic incentives and the appeal of a larger, more developed market drove many Algerian cultural producers into exile in France.

See also **Djebar, Assia; Kateb, Yacine; Law: Islamic; Literacy.**

BIBLIOGRAPHY

Amrouche, Jean. *Chants berbères de Kabylie*. Paris: L'Harmattan, 1986.

Armes, Roy. *Postcolonial Images. Studies in North African Film*. Bloomington and Indianapolis: Indiana University Press, 2005.

People's Democratic Republic of Algeria

Population:	33,333,216 (2007 est.)
Area:	2,381,740 sq. km (919,595 sq. mi.)
Official language:	Arabic
Languages:	Arabic, Berber (national language), French
National currency:	Algerian dinar
Principal religions:	Sunni Muslim (state religion) 99%, Christian and Jewish 1%
Capital:	Algiers (est. pop. 2,142,000 in 2005)
Other urban centers:	Oran, Constantine, Annaba
Annual rainfall:	400 mm (16 in.)–670 mm (26 in.) at the coast, as much as 1,000 mm (39 in.) in the north
Principal geographical features:	*Mountains:* Hogar, Atlas *Rivers:* Chelif, Djedi, Medjerda *Other:* Sahara Desert
Economy:	*GDP per capita:* US$7,700 (2006)
Principal products and exports:	*Agricultural:* wheat, barley, oats, grapes, olives, citrus, fruits, sheep, cattle *Manufacturing:* light industries, electrical, petrochemical, food processing *Mining:* petroleum, natural gas
Government:	Independence from France, 1962. Constitution, 1963; revised 1976, 1988, 1989, and 1996. Republic. President elected by popular vote for 5-year term (limit 2 terms). Bicameral Parliament consists of the National People's Assembly (389 seats; members elected by popular vote; 5-year terms) and the Council of Nations (or Senate; 144 seats; one-third appointed by the president, two-thirds elected by indirect vote; 6-year terms). Cabinet of Ministers and prime minister appointed by president. For purposes of local government, there are 48 provinces.
Heads of state since independence:	1962–1963: President Ferhat Abbas 1963–1965: President Ahmed Ben Bella 1965–1978: Colonel Houari Boumediene 1978–1992: Colonel Chadli Benjedid 1992–1994: General Khaled Nezzar 1994–1999: President Lamine Zeroual 1999–: President Abdelaziz Bouteflika
Armed forces:	Armed forces are comprised of the People's National Army (127,500 active duty and 100,000 reserves), a navy, an air force, and the Territorial Air Defense Force. President is commander in chief. Compulsory 18-month service.
Transportation:	*Rail:* 3,973 km (2,469 mi.) *Ports:* Algiers, Annaba, Arzew, Bejaia, Djendjene, Jijel, Mostaganem, Oran, Skikda *Roads:* 108,302 km (67,296 mi.), 70% paved *National airline:* Air Algerie *Airports:* International facilities at Algiers. More than 140 other airports throughout the country. *Heliports:* There is 1 heliport.
Media:	34 newspapers, including *El Khabar, El Moudjahid,* and *Ech Chaab.,* Radio Algerienne is the national radio service. 26 radio stations, 46 television stations.
Literacy and education:	*Total literacy rate:* 70% (2004). Education is compulsory from ages 6–15, and more than 90% of children attend school. Postsecondary education provided by 10 universities and several technical colleges.

Bennoune, Mahfoud. *The Making of Contemporary Algeria, 1830–1987. Colonial Upheavals and Post-Independence Development* Cambridge, U.K: Cambridge University Press, 1988.

Berger, Anne-Emmanuelle, ed. *Algeria in Others' Languages.* Ithaca, NY: Cornell University Press, 2002.

Brett, Michael, and Elizabeth Fentress. *The Berbers.* Oxford: Blackwell, 1996.

Djaout, Tahar. *Last Summer of Reason.* Trans. Marjolijn de Jager. St. Paul, MN: Ruminator Books, 2001.

Djebar, Assia. *L'amour, la fantasia.* Paris: Albin Michel, 1995.

McMurray, David, and Ted Swedenburg. "Rai Tide Rising." *Middle East Report* 169 (March–April 1991): 39–42.

Ruedy, John. *Modern Algeria: The Origins and Development of a Nation,* 2nd edition. Bloomington and Indianapolis: Indiana University Press, 2005.

Ouettar, Tahar. *The Earthquake.* Trans. William Granara. London: Saqi Books, 2000.

JAMES MCDOUGALL

HISTORY AND POLITICS

The history and politics of Algeria since independence in July 1962 is a paradigmatic case for the study of third world politics. The 132 years of French colonial rule in Algeria (1830–1962) witnessed one of the most intensive forms of colonization experienced by any African or Asian people, resulting in some 1 million largely French settlers (*colons*) who called themselves *pieds noirs*, by the 1950s. Algeria's war of independence (1954–1962) was among the most deadly ones in terms of human lives, reaching between 500,000 and 1 million Algerian casualties. After independence, it experienced a socialist-style, single-party rule, and claimed a leading role in third world policies, serving as a model for other recently independent states. It was a rare example among Arab states of a populist single-party state with substantial oil and gas resources and a correspondingly high disposable income.

Algeria also became one of the first Arab states to experiment with serious economic restructuring and democratization and the change from a single-party to a multiparty system in 1988–1989. This opening enabled the large-scale success of the Islamic Salvation Front (FIS), first in municipal then in national elections in 1990–1991, cancelled by a military coup d'état in January 1992.

Much of Algeria's political character derives directly from its colonial experience and the war of independence. Whereas Tunisia's and Morocco's colonial experiences were short-lived in comparison, and resulted in either keeping a traditional oligarchy in power (Morocco) or creating new ones, such as an embryonic middle class (Tunisia), Algeria's traditional elite had been crushed in the nineteenth century. In the twentieth century, a new aspiring political elite had been discredited among ordinary Algerians in the post–World War II context with their strategy of seeking independence by peaceful means through petitions and political activity. It became clear that the French *pieds noirs* would not accept the creation of an Algerian state peacefully, in which they would emerge a numerical minority. Members of established political organizations, such as Messali Hadj, despite their nationalist rhetoric, were seen as co-opted Algerians or *Beni Oui Ouis*, "yes-men" unable to lead the country to independence.

The younger generation of Nationalists in Algeria was radical, populist, and clearly antipolitical and antiparty in its beginning. A handful of self-appointed fighters organized the Front de Libération Nationale (FLN), led the war of independence, and saw themselves as self-sacrificing heroes. The ferocity and violence by both the French and native Algerian communities and the French army, with the violence exported to the French metropole itself, led to the peace treaty between the provisional government of Algeria and Charles de Gaulle in 1962, followed by the exodus of all but a handful of settlers. The result was that experienced civil servants left, paralyzing most state institutions. The economy also collapsed, leaving the country in disarray. The FLN had become the principal organization with which other organizations such as parties and labor unions had to associate. The one exception was Messali, who with his autocratic tendencies mistrusted those who challenged his authority. This gave way to extreme factional violence between clans, resulting in the FLN's dominance and intra-Algerian blood-letting in the immediate postindependence period.

The FLN's internal factionalism led to its concentrating on themes on which all factions could agree. Algerian nationalism focused on populist issues that combined Arabism, Islamism, and anticolonialist struggle. This meant a strong developmentalist agenda that emphasized building a socialist economy, a welfare state, land-reform, and state-led growth through Import Substitution Industrialization (ISI). It also meant a clear neglect of Berber identity, language, and culture, especially as the official language switched from French to Arabic, disadvantaging the Berbers who account for a substantial minority of the population (about 30%).

After a short-lived power struggle, Ahmed Ben Bella, who had been the leader of the Liberation Army, was ousted by Houari Boumediene on June 19, 1965. Elections were held but controlled by secret services and the military, who had become the real powers. Boumediene relied increasingly on the security services and the military, in addition to his own network of support, the so-called Oujda group, named after the Moroccan border town from which the FLN operated during the struggle for independence. On the day of his "rectification," the 1963 constitution was suspended, and Boumediene henceforth ruled through a revolutionary council. Some elections were locally organized to give the single party a blend of pluralism at the popular level.

Under Boumediene, single-party rule was superseded by that of the military. Leading clans continued to vie for power but were held off by the possibility of patronage that emerged through the construction of the modern state. Its revolutionary ideology came into confrontation with conservatism in neighboring Morocco, where border disputes forged Algerian nationalism in the early years of independence. A border war broke out in 1963, blamed on Morocco's irredentist claims to parts of eastern Algeria around the southern oasis of Tindouf. Revolutionary socialism, however, was not the only source of Algeria's ideology, as Islam was proclaimed the state religion.

The 1 million departed French *colons* left substantial amounts of land, private property (flats, villas), industry, and business that the Algerian state used as sources of patronage, allocating some to Algerians who flocked into the cities. Free housing, even if increasingly scarce, became part of the "spoils" of independence. Increasing oil and gas revenues, rising from $4.2 billion in 1972 to about $20.2 billion in 1980 following the price hikes of the 1970s, were invested in heavy industry, comprehensive health care, and education programs. Agriculture was nationalized and collective farms integrated into Algeria's increasingly state-planned economy.

Foreign credits became another major source of national income. With interest running low and inflation high throughout the 1970s, foreign borrowing was regarded a feasible strategy to finance domestic economic development. Algeria entered a major debt crisis in the 1980s as a result with debt servicing reaching 80 percent of income earnings by 1988 (Henry and Springborg, 53). As in other countries of the era, the seemingly efficient technocratic management of development took precedence over accountability and democratic procedures, which finally meant that the state took all responsibility in return for citizen's passivity. This equation was even more pronounced as the Algerian state did not rely on direct taxation of its citizens. It instead first distributed the spoils of

independence and then oil income, becoming what has become known as a distribution, not an extraction, state. The consequence was to create a state-dependent middle class that had more interest in the status quo rather than in asking for more accountability and representation.

The major problem that Algeria faced under Boumediene's successor, Chadli Benjedid (1979–1992), was that this implicit social contract no longer worked. A new generation of Algerians born after independence no longer shared the regime's revolutionary ideology. In addition, the economic consequences of state planning were negative, with shortages in food due to stringent price controls and mismanagement in public enterprises. Liberal reforms to transform Algeria into a market economy meant that entrenched interests in the status quo had to be sidelined, economic and social hardship among the population endured, and a new governing formula to legitimize these negative aspects of economic reforms. This became all the more urgent as Benjedid not only faced intra-regime challengers, but also popular resistance as exemplified in riots that rocked the country in October 1988.

The October 1988 crisis, which saw tanks rolling into Algiers after demonstrations went out of control, was a major event in contemporary Algerian history. It resembled the bread riots in other North African and Middle Eastern countries, protests triggered by the rise in the price of bread after International Monetary Fund (IMF) negotiated structural adjustment programs forced Middle Eastern states to cancel their substantial subsidies of essential foodstuffs (Jordan, Morocco, Egypt, Tunisia). The Algerian October riots may also have been orchestrated by intra-regime and FLN challengers to Benjedid. This is one of the reasons why Chadli Benjedid, and not the state per se, was challenged in slogans such as *Chadli assassin*. The Islamists also showed their political strength in the demonstrations.

Benjedid called on the military to suppress the demonstration and to reestablish order. His ensuing moves to democratize the country aimed at reestablishing his own firm power base. Benjedid and some of his reform-minded allies drafted a new, liberal constitution that allowed for free political association and separation of powers. The military members of the FLN's higher ranks were asked to leave the party. In essence, he intended for a multiparty system to replace single-party rule, the FLN to lose its identification with the state, and free and fair elections to replace the older system of presidential designation and rule by clans emanating from the military. The constitution was passed in a referendum on February 23, 1989.

This reform was ambitious, given the absence of democratic beliefs and culture among those who initiated this program of political liberalization. Later, in 1989, the Islamic party Front Islamique du Salut (FIS) was authorized apparently by Benjedid himself, possibly believing that he could use them against internal regime challengers despite the fact that the law on political parties, passed in the same year, outlawed parties that were exclusively based on religion.

The unfolding drama of the 1990s was a direct result of the contradictions that postindependence state and nation building involved. A top-down liberalization attempt to keep challengers off limits paid little attention to the democratic safeguards needed to prevent a complete Islamization of the country. When first in the municipal elections and later in the national elections the FIS emerged as the victor that aimed not at further democratization but rather Islamization of Algerian society, the military stepped in not to safeguard "democracy," but rather to safeguard a republican ethic that identified the army with the state. In the ensuing civil war between the regime and the FIS and its increasingly uncontrollable military wings, the Armée Islamique du Salut (AIS) and Groupes Islamiques Armés (GIA) religious legitimacy clashed with revolutionary republicanism as embodied by the army. Despite attempts at reconciliation, such as the Rome platform of 1995, the idea that Algeria could return to normalized, electoral politics while excluding the FIS was unacceptable. Both the regime and the Islamists resorted to unprecedented violence—resulting in more than 150,000 mostly civilian victims according to Amnesty International reports. With Bouteflika's "election" as president in 1999— he was the only candidate and proposed by the military—his main success has been to propose a program of peace and reconciliation. Combined with increasing security and military successes in the major cities, Algeria entered a phase of relative calm. In this period, a strong executive, continuing restrictions on the liberty of speech, and an army that seemed less involved in politics coincided with both increasing oil revenues and controversial presidential amnesties of former Islamist activists if they promised to lay down their arms.

See also **Bouteflika, Abdelaziz; Colonial Policies and Practices: French Northern Africa.**

BIBLIOGRAPHY

Bouandel, Youcef. "Bouteflika's Reforms and the Question of Human Rights in Algeria." *Journal of North African Studies* 7, no. 2 (2002): 23–42.

Henry, Clement M., and Robert Springborg. *Globalization and the Politics of Development in the Middle East.* Cambridge, U.K.: Cambridge University Press, 2001.

Korany, Bahgat, and Saad Amrani. "Explosive Civil Society and Democratization from Below Algeria." In *Political Liberalization and Democratization in the Arab World*, Vol. 2, ed. Bahgat Korany. Boulder, CO: Lynne Rienner, 1998.

Quandt, William B. *Between Ballots and Bullets. Algeria's Transition from Authoritarianism.* Washington, DC: The Brookings Institution Press, 1998.

Ruedy, John. *Modern Algeria: The Origins and Development of a Nation*, 2nd edition. Bloomington: Indiana University Press, 2005.

JAMES SATER

ALGIERS. The capital and largest city of Algeria, Algiers (*al-Jaza'ir* in Arabic, *Alger* in French) is located on a bay on the Mediterranean coast. The population of the municipality is estimated at 2.3 million (2006) while that of the urban agglomeration stands at 5.7 million. Algiers is Algeria's principal seaport as well as its main commercial, financial, industrial, educational, cultural, communications, and media center. A port city has existed on the site since Phoenician and Punic times, but Algiers rose to prominence only in the sixteenth century, following the expulsion of Muslims and Jews from Catholic Spain. By 1550 the city was firmly under Ottoman rule, being the seat of a *beylik* (autonomous province). The Ottoman *beys* (governors) actively promoted privateering (the so-called Barbary pirates), aimed principally against Spanish shipping. In 1830 the city fell to the French and became their springboard for colonization. The lower half of the old city, contiguous to the port, was redeveloped as a European city while the upper half, called the casbah, remained primarily Arab in character and population. During the war of independence the casbah suffered greatly from the attempts of French forces to suppress the nationalist movement there (the Battle of Algiers, 1956–1957). Following independence, petrochemical and heavy industrial sectors developed in Algiers. Since the 1980s the city has been the scene of major confrontations between government forces and disenfranchised youth (1988, 2002), Berber nationalists (1995), and Islamist militants (1992–2003).

See also **Algeria.**

BIBLIOGRAPHY

Çelik, Zeynep. *Urban Forms and Colonial Confrontations: Algiers under French Rule.* Berkeley: University of California Press, 1997.

ERIC S. ROSS

'ALI, MOHAMMED DUSE (1886–1945).

The Pan-African journalist and entrepreneur Mohammed Duse 'Ali was born in Egypt, when that country was under Ottoman rule. He lived for many years in Great Britain and the United States, during which time he shared ideas of racial rehabilitation with Winfried Tete-Ansa of Ghana and mentored Marcus Garvey, both of whom were active in the struggle for economic power and independence for the "black race."

After working as a freelance journalist, 'Ali became editor and proprietor of various magazines in London, New York, and Lagos that were published intermittently between 1912 and 1945. All of these publications were dedicated to the promotion of Pan-African business schemes and offered advice and information to black farmers and traders. He was joint editor of the *West African Dictionary and Year Book, 1920–1921* (1921). From 1912 to 1931 he engaged in marketing ventures aimed at improving credit and banking facilities for farmers and produce traders throughout British West Africa.

'Ali was a vice president of the African and Orient Society, formed in 1912 with the aim of encouraging trade among African peoples. By 1923 he was promoting the American-African Oriental Company, to foster cooperation between black peoples across the Atlantic.

'Ali was twice married, to a British woman and to an American woman; there were no children. His last newspaper, *The Comet,* launched at Lagos in 1933, survived 'Ali's death on June 16, 1945.

See also **Garvey, Marcus Mosiah; Media: Book Publishing.**

BIBLIOGRAPHY

Adi, Hakim, and Marika Sherwood. *Pan-African History: Political Figures from Africa and the Diaspora since 1787.* London; New York: Routledge, 2003.

Duffield, Ian. "The Business Activities of Duse Mohammed Ali: An Example of the Economic Dimension of Pan Africanism, 1912–1945." *Journal of the Historical Society of Nigeria* 4, no. 4 (June 1969): 571–600.

Hopkins, A. G. "Economic Aspects of Political Movements in Nigeria and the Gold Coast, 1919–1939." *Journal of African History* (1966): 133–152.

Zachernuk, Philip Serge. *Colonial Subjects: An African Intelligentsia and Atlantic Ideas.* Charlottesville, VA; London: University Press of Virginia, 2000.

S. ADEMOLA AJAYI

'ALI, MUHAMMAD (late 1760s–1849).

Known in Ottoman Turkish as Mehmed 'Ali Pasha, Muhammad 'Ali was appointed Ottoman governor, or *pasha*, of Egypt in 1805, a post he held until 1848. The dynasty that he founded continued to rule Egypt until 1952. Himself illiterate, he nonetheless laid the foundation for modern Egypt, created a Ministry of Education, sent hundreds of Egyptians on educational missions to Europe, created a modern conscript army, and vigorously neutralized or eliminated opponents to his rule. The autonomy of religious scholars (*'ulama*) collapsed when he seized the religious endowments (*waqfs*) that provided them income. Egypt's hereditary military caste, the Mamluks, were slaughtered in 1811 on the eve of the departure of Egyptian troops for the Arabian Peninsula to challenge growing Wahhabi influence and to capture the holy cities of Mecca and Madina for the Ottomans. In consolidating his rule in the 1820s he excavated canals, broke the power of tribal leaders, and became in effect Egypt's sole proprietor, introducing cotton as an export crop. The collapse of world cotton prices in 1836–1837, and increasingly heavy taxes, produced sporadic revolts that Muhammad 'Ali countered by reversing his earlier policy and granting large tracts of land to elites who guaranteed the payment of taxes to the central treasury. Under his leadership, Egypt had become *de facto* independent of Ottoman rule by the late 1830s and the advances of European colonial powers were temporarily checked.

See also **Egypt, Modern; Military Organizations.**

BIBLIOGRAPHY

Marsot, Afaf Lutfi Al-Sayyid. *A History of Egypt: From the Arab Conquest to the Present*, 2nd edition. Cambridge, U.K.: Cambridge University Press, 2007.

Toledano, Ehud R. *State and Society in Mid-Nineteenth Century Egypt*. Cambridge, U.K.: Cambridge University Press 1990.

DALE F. EICKELMAN

ALI, ZINE EL-ABIDINE BIN. *See* **Bin Ali, Zine el-Abidine.**

ALLAL AL-FASSI (1910–1974). Allal al-Fassi was one of the founders and later the president of the Istiqlal party. His profound knowledge of Islamic traditions and his writings made him one of the most respected scholars in the Arab world.

In 1930, he led the protests against France's Berber Decree that was meant to intensify divisions between Berbers and Arabs in Morocco. He was arrested and spent thirteen months in prison. After he was freed, he became the president of the Movement of Moroccan Action, then of the Nationalist party.

In 1946, after nine years of exile in Gabon, he returned to Morocco only to clash with Istiqlal leaders and Sultan Mohammed V (1909–1961). Forced into exile again, he moved to Cairo, where he championed the cause of armed resistance against the French in Morocco.

When France granted Morocco its independence in March 1956, Allal al-Fassi negotiated with rebel leaders who held out against the monarchy and won them over to the Istiqlal party, of which he became president in 1959. In 1962 he was appointed minister of Islamic affairs, and in 1963 he was elected to the parliament, which King Hasan II (b. 1929) dissolved in 1965.

Muhammad Allal al-Fassi (1910–1974). Al-Fassi founded the nationalist Istiqlal party, which pushed for Moroccan independence from French colonial rule.

As a main leader within the loyal opposition, he campaigned against Hasan and demanded constitutional reforms and a parliamentary government. He remained an outspoken proponent of Morocco's territorial claims to the Sahara and Tindouf, until his death on May 19, 1974.

See also **Hasan II of Morocco.**

BIBLIOGRAPHY

Ennaji, Moha. *Multilingualism, Cultural Identity and Education in Morcco.* New York: Springer, 2005.

Halstead, John P. *Rebirth of a Nation: The Origins and Rise of Moroccan Nationalism, 1912–1944.* Cambridge, MA: Distributed for the Center for Middle Eastern Studies of Harvard University by Harvard University, 1967.

Landau, Rom. *Moroccan Drama 1900–1955.* San Francisco: American Academy of Asian Studies, 1956.

Nelson, Harold D., ed. *Morocco: A Country Study*. Washington, DC: U.S. Government Printing Office, 1985.

MOHA ENNAJI

AMERICAS, AFRICAN LINKS WITH. *See* Diasporas.

AMIN DADA, IDI (1925–2003). The Ugandan military leader and president Idi Amin was born in the West Nile district of Arua, in Uganda, in the mid-1920s, and was of Kakwa descent. The exact date of his birth is not known (some sources give 1925, others give 1928). His family was poor, and he received little or no education. As a young man he joined the British colonial army, enlisting in the King's African Rifles in 1946. He served in Kenya during the Mau Mau uprising (1952–1956). He was also the heavyweight boxing champion of Uganda from 1951 to 1960. Amin's rise through the ranks was swift: he was one of the few Ugandans to become an officer before independence in 1962, and he was a major general and the commander of the army and air force by 1968.

Amin was a close ally of Milton Obote, an important political figure and president of independent Uganda at the head of the Ugandan People's Congress, and cemented this alliance by marrying a woman from Obote's clan. Both were accused of smuggling gold, ivory, and coffee out of Uganda in 1965, and in the ensuing controversy, Obote used Amin and his army to defend his position. In 1969 Obote suspended the constitution and declared himself executive president of Uganda, forcing King Mutebi II of Buganda into exile.

Amin's loyalty to Obote did not run deep, however, and Obote soon became suspicious of the ambitions that Amin might be harboring. Amin had developed close ties with Sudanese and Congolese insurgents as the head of army recruitment and, through these contacts, established links with British and Israeli agents. As he grew in

African dictator Idi Amin (1925–2003). The former president of Uganda gestures during an interview in Kampala. His reign of terror lasted from 1971, when he seized power from Milton Obote, to 1979, when Tanzanian soldiers and the Uganda National Liberation army forced him into exile in Saudi Arabia. AFP/GETTY IMAGES

strength and influence, Obote placed him under house arrest in 1970.

In January 1971, while Obote was out of the country, Amin led a coup with the tacit support of Great Britain and Israel. He was welcomed as president at first, but his brutal rule soon turned the Ugandan populace and the international community against him. Fearing disloyalty, he rid the army of soldiers from Obote's home region (Acholi and Lengi, primarily) and replaced them with Kakwa and Nubi. In 1972 Obote supporters tried to invade from Tanzania, and Amin retaliated by killing civilian Acholi and Langi. He also ordered the execution of the chief justice, the chancellor of Makerere College, and the governor of the Bank of Uganda. Later that year, in a self-declared economic war, Amin expelled Asians holding British passports from Uganda, charging that they controlled too many of the nation's businesses. Within a few years, Amin's cronies had looted the businesses and all but destroyed the country's economy.

Amin next repudiated his Western and Israeli supporters, positioning himself as pro-Africa and pro-Palestine. Though only a small portion of Ugandans were Muslim, Amin declared it an Islamic state and received aid from many Arab countries, especially Libya. Tanzania refused to recognize Amin's presidency and rumors of his mistreatment of his citizens became increasingly widespread. Nonetheless, Amin was elected chairman of the Organization of African States in 1975; the gathering was boycotted by Tanzania, Zambia, and Botswana because it was held in Uganda.

In 1976, Palestinian hijackers operating with Amin's support brought a plane full of Israelis to Uganda's Entebbe airport. Israeli commandos stormed the airport and freed the hostages, bringing intense international scrutiny upon the Amin regime. Amin received further international attention in 1977 after an Anglican archbishop and two cabinet ministers were killed under suspicious circumstances and more Acholi and Langi were murdered. No unified opposition arose within Uganda, however, because Amin successfully exploited ethnic divisions within the country. The international community did little either, until Amin invaded and annexed Tanzania's Kagera Salient in 1978.

When Tanzanian forces responded by invading Uganda in early 1979, they served as a rallying point for the various groups who opposed Amin's regime. After the Tanzania People's Defence Force and Ugandan rebels took Kampala (12 April) and defeated Ugandan and Libyan units, Amin fled to Libya, then Iraq, before settling into exile in Saudi Arabia. He tried to return to Uganda in 1989, but failed in the attempt. Amin remained in exile in Saudi Arabia until his death, in August 2003.

See also **Mutebi II; Obote, Milton; Uganda: History and Politics.**

BIBLIOGRAPHY

Jamison, Martin. *Idi Amin and Uganda: An Annotated Bibliography.* Westport, CT: Greenwood Press, 1992.

Kiwanuka, M. S. M. Semakula. *Amin and the Tragedy of Uganda.* Munich: Weltforum Verlag, 1979.

Kleinschmidt, Harald, ed. *Amin Collection: Bibliographical Catalogue of Materials Relevant to the History of Uganda under the Military Government of Idi Amin Dada.* P. Kivouvou-Éditions Bantoues, 1983.

Mittelman, James H. *Ideology and Politics in Uganda: From Obote to Amin.* Ithaca, NY: Cornell University Press, 1975.

Seftel, Adam. *Uganda: The Rise and Fall of Idi Amin: From the Pages of Drum.* Lanseria, South Africa: Bailey's African Photo Archives Production, 1994.

Tripp, Aili M. "The Changing Face of Authoritarianism in Africa: The Case of Uganda." *Africa Today* 50 (3) (2004): 3–26.

THOMAS F. MCDOW

AMINA (c. 1533–1610). Amina, the daughter of a female ruler named Bakwa Turunku (c. 1560–1610), was a queen in the northern Nigerian Hausa state of Zazzau (also known as Zaria). A warrior, Amina was named as her mother's heir apparent around 1550, at age sixteen. She ascended to the throne herself after the death of her uncle (some sources say her brother) Karama, in 1576 and ruled for thirty-four years. Amina was renowned for her efforts in expanding the boundaries of her state and for building the earthworks that surrounded many Hausa city-states, including a well-known wall around Katsina. She was also responsible for expanding Hausa trade along east-west trade routes, and some credit her with the spread of kola nut in trade. A legendary woman, she apparently never married and no heirs followed her, but stories circulated that she had a lover in each town under her jurisdiction, and some versions claimed each was beheaded the next morning. Although she is generally described as ruling in the sixteenth century, some suggest that she was a contemporary of Sarki Dauda (r. 1421–1438), who was active in the early fifteenth century, and that because the Songhay empire already controlled Zaria, Kano, and Katsina by the sixteenth century, it was not likely that Amina would have dominated in Zaria if she ruled in the sixteenth century.

See also **Women: Women in African History.**

BIBLIOGRAPHY

Abubakr, Sa'ad. "Queen Amina of Zaria." In *Nigerian Women in Historical Perspective*, ed. Bolanle Awe. Lagos, Nigeria: Sankore Publishers, 1992.

Ajayi, Jacob Festus A., and Michael Crowder. *History of West Africa*, Vol. 1. New York: Columbia University Press, 1972.

KATHLEEN SHELDON

ANCESTORS.   *See* Death, Mourning, and Ancestors; Kinship and Descent.

ANDRIANAMPOINIMERINA

(c. 1750–1810). Andrianampoinimerina is remembered as a keen military strategist in late eighteenth- and early-nineteenth-century Madagascar, a masterful administrative organizer, and a proponent of ancestral traditions. He had usurped the throne in the microkingdom of Ambohimanga in about 1783. At the time, Ambohimanga suffered from internal divisions as members of the royal line fragmented the territory. During the first fifteen years of his rule Andrianampoinimerina reunified the kingdom while building the economy by participating in the export trade in slaves from central Madagascar to the Mascarene Islands. He redistributed the wealth so generated among leaders across the central highlands of the island (Imerina) in order to increase his network of political supporters. By 1808 Andrianampoinimerina had managed to displace the rulers of competing microkingdoms within Imerina, uniting them all into a single polity that dominated the island until the arrival of French colonialism in the 1880s.

To enhance the cultural cohesiveness of his kingdom, Andrianampoinimerina fostered the development and expansion of a Merina ethnic identity, from whence comes the term "Merina kingdom." Among the cultural innovations he employed in this effort was the building of the large stone tombs in which Merina bury their dead in the early twenty-first century and which serve as foci of Merina ritual.

Andrianampoinimerina is renowned for masterful public speeches (*kabary*), in which he promoted both social justice and hard work. The founder-king

died of old age in 1810, an event attributed in oral traditions to the premature departure of his spirit, sapping the sovereign's body of its life force.

See also **Antananarivo; Slave Trades.**

BIBLIOGRAPHY

Berg, Gerald M. "Sacred Acquisition: Adrianampoinimerina at Ambohimanga, 1777–1790." *Journal of African History* 29, no. 2, 1988: 261–279.

Covell, Maureen. *Madagascar: Politics, Economics, and Society.* New York: Frances Pinter, 1989.

Larson, Pier. *History and Memory in the Age of Enslavement: Becoming Merina in Highland Madagascar, 1770–1882.* Portsmouth: Heinemann, 2000.

PIER M. LARSON

ANGOLA

This entry includes the following articles:
GEOGRAPHY AND ECONOMY
SOCIETY AND CULTURES
HISTORY AND POLITICS

GEOGRAPHY AND ECONOMY

Bordering the Atlantic Ocean for more than 1,994 miles, the Republic of Angola is situated between 5 degrees and 18 degrees south latitude and 12 degrees to 24 degrees east longitude. It is the seventh largest country in Africa, larger than Texas and California combined. Its 481,353 square miles include the enclave of Cabinda, an administratively integral part of Angola separated from the rest of the country by a strip of the Democratic Republic of the Congo (DRC, formerly Zaire). A low coastal plain, cut by river valleys and dotted with natural harbors, is separated from the vast interior plateaus by often dramatic escarpments. Together, these provide a rich variety of tropical environments and abundant repositories of natural resources.

The coastal lowlands vary in width from about 99 miles just south of Luanda to only 14 miles near Benguela. The cold, northward-flowing Benguela Current contributes to both rich ocean fisheries and a coastal climate ranging from semi-arid near Luanda to fully desert near the Namibian border.

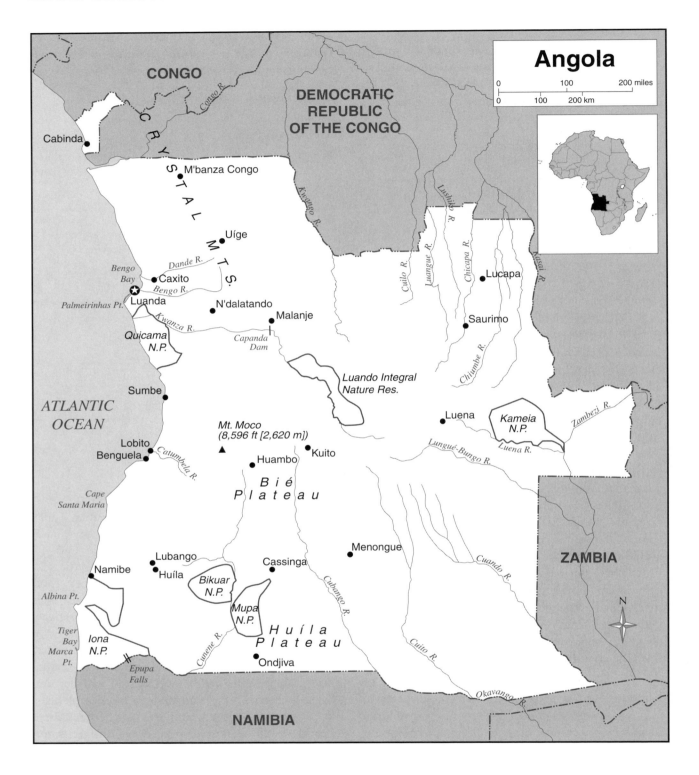

Angola's plateau lands average 3,149 to 4,429 feet above sea level, with some western peaks as high as 8,464 feet. From north to south and from lowest to highest elevation they are the Kongo Highlands, the Malanje Plateau, and the Central Highlands. These western highlands are generally better watered than either the adjacent coast or the extensive plains to the east and south.

A series of westward-flowing rivers cuts through the coastal lowlands. Their fertile valleys have long attracted intensive agricultural settlement. With the exception of the Congo River (formerly Zaire), which borders Angola for about eighty miles in the north, these rivers originate in Angola itself and include the Cuanza (Kwanza) and Cunene (Kunene). Important inland rivers include northward-flowing Congo tributaries, the Cuango (Kwango) and Cassai (Kasai); upper reaches of the Indian Ocean-bound Zambezi with its major regional affluent, the Cuando (Kwando) and the Cubango (Okavango), which flows into the Okavango Swamp in modern Namibia. Only the Congo and the Cuanza are navigable for even modest distances inland.

With the exception of the more temperate Central Highlands, Angola's climates are tropical. Rainfall is distributed in a generally north-south pattern, with higher amounts in the northern and central plains. It falls seasonally, with rainy periods of varying lengths coming between October and May. The drier east and inland south have very sandy soils, a legacy of ancient northward winds carrying the sand of the Kalahari Desert, which now reaches only as far as the southern slopes of the Central Highlands.

NATURAL RESOURCES AND THE ECONOMY

The diverse environments of Angola are best considered by dividing the country's eighteen provinces into six geographic regions: north, Luanda, Central Highlands, coastal lowlands, south, and east.

The north includes Cabinda, Zaire, and Uíge provinces. Forested Cabinda receives the most rainfall, producing such tropical forest products as timber and palm oil, as well as rubber, coffee and cocoa. South of the Congo River tropical woodland savanna predominates, with hilltops ideally suited for coffee, the leading Angolan cash crop in colonial times before 1974. Cocoa, cotton, tobacco, sisal, rice, palm oil, sugar, and timber have also been also grown commercially, though more than a quarter of a century of war (1975–2002) has severely limited production of these commodities. Cassava, the most important staple nationally, is the mainstay here. Yams, sweet potatoes, and bananas are also cultivated. The tsetse fly makes cattle raising uneconomical, but there are sheep, goats, pigs, and poultry.

Mineral resources include phosphates, manganese, copper, and diamonds, as well as the dominant resource, petroleum, mostly from offshore wells in the Atlantic. Cabinda accounts for much of Angola's petroleum production. At more than

1.4 million barrels per day, according to 2005 World Bank statistics, Angola's petroleum output is second only to Nigeria in Africa and oil production and its supporting activities has become the mainstay of the national economy, accounting for 90 percent of government revenues.

Going south, one enters the populous Luanda region, which encompasses coastal and plateau lands between the Dande and Cuanza Rivers, and includes Luanda, Bengo, and Cuanza Norte (Kwanza North) provinces, as well as most of Malanje and northern Cuanza Sul (Kwanza South). The region, home to more than half of all Angolans, centers on Luanda, the administrative and cultural capital of the country, which is also a shipping and manufacturing center.

Cassava and maize are the staple crops. Cash crops in the past included coffee, sisal, bananas, and cotton. Timber is abundant in Bengo and Cuanza Norte. There are manganese deposits in Malanje. A large hydroelectric power project at Cambambe (Cuanza River) supplies power for manufacturing in Luanda, whilst construction on the Capanda Dam (Cuanza River) in Malanje Province was finished in 2004, providing hydro-electric power for Luanda and other large towns and irrigation for farming in the lower Cuanza valley.

The Central Highlands region includes the provinces of Bié, Huambo, Huíla, and part of Cuanza Sul and is subject to intense population pressures. Farming is the principal economic activity, with maize being the main crop for both subsistence and commercial farmers. Other crops of importance are potatoes, cassava, arabica coffee, tobacco, and beans. In the south, rearing livestock (mostly cattle) predominates. Although the Cassinga iron mines have been inactive since 1975, there are proven reserves of more than 1 billion tons of high-grade hematite, and also reserves of copper and feldspar.

The coastal lowlands south of Luanda form a distinctive region of ports, salt pans, and fisheries, which includes most of Benguela and Namibe Provinces. Economic growth here is tied to the flow of exports from the more populous inland regions through the ports of Lobito, Benguela, or Namibe.

Livestock are grazed, while irrigation permits cultivation of sugar, tobacco, and sisal in Benguela province. Salt is produced, and there are reserves of copper. Power for urban industries is produced by two hydroelectric projects on the Catumbela (Katumbela) River.

The south encompasses the basins of the Cubango and Cunene rivers and includes the large provinces of Cunene (Kunene) and Cuando-Cubango (Kwando-Kubango). These extensive arid or semi-arid southern plains are bordered by Namibia in the south and Zambia in the east. Livestock grazing predominates, with some farming in the bottoms of seasonal rivers. These regions were known to the Portuguese colonizers as "the end of the world" and were significant theatres of the lengthy wars following Angola's independence in 1975.

In addition to livestock, the region has significant resources in water power, with a large joint Namibian-Angolan hydroelectric project long under development on the Cunene River. Chronic warfare initially prevented completion of this ambitious project, designed mainly to provide power to Namibia. More recently, concerns over the project's environmental impact and potential displacement of the local Himba cattle herders have put a halt to its development at Epupa Falls.

The vast east encompasses Lunda Norte (Lunda North), Lunda Sul (Lunda South), and Moxico provinces. The land is open, rolling country cut by tributaries of the Congo River that support farming and fishing. Cattle are raised in the Zambezi Basin to the south. The northeast is rich in diamonds, the second most important Angolan export after petroleum. It also has reserves of copper and timber.

Nationally, more than 80 percent of Angola's citizens work in the subsistence agricultural sector, which nonetheless accounts for only 15 percent of the gross domestic product (GDP). A substantial impediment to growing agricultural production in Angola remains the incomplete removal of vast numbers of anti-personnel mines scattered around the countryside since the war, and Angola consequently has to import significant amounts of food. Nevertheless, resettlement of millions of displaced people has translated into an increase in agricultural production. The principal crops grown are cassava, coffee, bananas, sisal, corn and cotton, with cassava being grown widely as the main domestic staple and coffee being the primary export crop.

Principal manufacturing activities include oil refining, food processing, brewing, textiles, and construction materials. The principal exports are petroleum and diamonds. Other exports include fish and fish products, timber, gas, and cotton. Imports include food, vehicles, textiles, clothing, medicines, machinery, and electrical equipment.

Prior to independence in 1975, Angola enjoyed a robust economy, with an expanding manufacturing sector, near self-sufficiency in agriculture, and crop surpluses for export along with petroleum, diamonds, and iron ore. From 1975 to 1988 the MPLA government pursued Marxist-Leninist economic policies. Existing enterprises, many owned by departed Portuguese, were nationalized, as a result of which output fell. Principal trading partners were Soviet and Eastern Bloc allies. Military costs fuelled rapid growth of external debt, most notably to the Soviet Union, which was owed $4 billion by 1993.

In 1987 President José Eduardo dos Santos announced major reforms aimed at reducing reliance on the state sector and increasing productivity, purchasing power, and consumption levels. He also announced that Angola would seek membership in the International Monetary Fund (IMF) in order to take advantage of Western financial assistance. The 1988 reform program included some managerial and financial decentralization of state enterprises, improvements in supply and distribution systems, and more price incentives for smaller enterprises. Joint ventures between Angolan and foreign enterprises were also actively encouraged. In response to these economic liberalization efforts, the IMF admitted Angola to membership in September 1989.

Domestic economic reform accelerated in early 1990 when the MPLA-PT (Workers Party) central committee announced it would reintroduce a market economy, beginning with the return of one hundred companies nationalized after independence to their original owners, and the sale of up to 49 percent of equity in some state-owned enterprises, including the national airline, to private-sector investors.

Further reforms, announced in November 1991, included a 33.3 percent devaluation of the currency, reductions in some personal taxes, abolition of most price ceilings on consumer goods, salary increases for public sector workers, and a higher national minimum wage. The impact of these reforms was overshadowed by the renewal of war, however, which resulted in a negative economic growth rate of minus 25 percent in 1993. In 1995–1996 economic development efforts got back on track, with new fiscal reforms and a substantial influx of both international aid and new investment, mostly in mining, once more disrupted by renewed fighting in 1998, as a result of which hundreds of thousands of rural residents were displaced, mostly flooding into the cities, especially Luanda.

Since the end of the twenty-seven-year civil war in 2002, Angola has slowly begun to rebuild its economy and continued with economic reform, though the magnitude of the economic challenge remains staggering, with much of the country's infrastructure still damaged or underdeveloped as a result of the war. Oil production has driven economic growth, Angola now being one of the fastest growing economies in Africa and in the world. A $2 billion line of credit from China has been used to start rebuilding Angola's public infrastructure, and a number of large-scale projects were scheduled for completion by 2006.

GDP growth reached 20 percent in 2005, according to 2006 World Bank statistics, and inflation has been falling steadily in recent years, largely driven by increased revenues from exports of oil. Despite such promising indicators, Angola remains one of the poorest nations in the world, and human development indicators remain problematic, with no basic services being provided for much of the population and income levels largely at unsustainable levels. Ultimately, Angola's ability to take advantage of its vast natural resources will depend on internal political stability and transparency, as well as the government's ability to finally turn the promise of rich resources into the reality of economic development outside of the petroleum sector and for the vast majority of Angolans.

See also **Benguela; Cabinda, Angola; Congo River; Economic History; Ecosystems; Geography and the Study of Africa; Independence and Freedom, Early African Writers; International Monetary Fund; Kalahari Desert; Livestock; Luanda; Metals and Minerals; World Bank; Zambezi River.**

BIBLIOGRAPHY

Bhagavan, M. R. *Angola's Political Economy: 1975–1985*. Research Report No 75. Uppsala, Sweden: Scandinavian Institute of African Studies, 1986.

Conçalves, José. *Economics and Politics of the Angolan Conflict: The Transition Re-Negotiated*. Bellville, South Africa: Center for Southern African Studies, University of the Western Cape, 1995.

Hart, Keith, and Joanna Lewis, eds. *Why Angola Matters*. London: James Currey Publishers, 1995.

Hodges, Tony. *Angola: From Afro-Stalinism to Petro-Diamond Capitalism*. Bloomington: Indiana University Press, 2001.

Hodges, Tony. *Angola: Anatomy of an Oil State*. Bloomington: Indiana University Press, 2004.

Tvedten, Inge. *Angola: Struggle for Peace and Reconstruction*. Boulder, CO: Westview Press, 1997.

SUSAN HERLIN BROADHEAD
REVISED BY ALEXANDER C. THORNTON

SOCIETY AND CULTURES

Five centuries of interaction with the Portuguese empire, including three centuries of integration into a trans-Atlantic slaving economy, colonization characterized by forced labor and little infrastructure, and an armed independence struggle followed by almost thirty years of civil war are the major processes within and against which Angolans have created their societies and cultures.

Significant and constant exchange of people (via marriage, migration, and slavery), political institutions, cultural practices, and social systems occurred over centuries between the societies that came to constitute Angola's population. The Ovimbundu, Kongo, and Mbundu are the three largest ethnolinguistic groups in Angola in the early twenty-first century but all groups have experienced, and continue to experience, intermixing. Smaller ethnolinguistic groups include the Lunda-Chokwe, Nganguela, Nyaneka-Humbi, Herero, and Ovambo. Between the fifteenth and nineteenth centuries these ethnolinguistic groups were forged from diverse origins in the context of the local environment, trade, and wars that dominated West-Central Africa. Dynamic interactions within and between the groups continued through the colonial period and after independence.

Historically, sociopolitical organization ranged from monarchies (among the Kongo, Mbundu, Lunda-Chokwe, smaller-scale but numerous Ovimbundu state formations, and the nineteenth century Kuanhama—an Ovambo speaking group—kingdom along the southern border) to *soba* and *sekulu* (African leader) headed village size organizations among the Nganguela, Nyaneka-Humbi, and

Herero. Economies were based on various combinations of agricultural production, pastoralism and trade, and societies were primarily organized by way of matrilineal kinship systems. Trade between different communities existed before the Portuguese presence but also shifted and boomed in interaction with the Portuguese and other European traders. The warrior and trading kingdoms that developed in the seventeenth to nineteenth centuries worked with and against Portuguese and Brazilian traders to protect and foster African commercial interests and systems.

The central plateau and the riverine areas (particularly around the Congo River in the north, the Kwango river in the north-central area, the Kwanza river in mid-central Angola, and the Kunene river in the south) have been the areas of greatest population concentration. The temperate climate and rainfall of the central plateau and the rich soils of the river valleys made them propitious for agriculture. Agricultural surplus and the exploitation of local mineral resources (iron and salt) formed the basis of intercommunity trade prior to the development of the trans-Atlantic slave trade and its later replacement by legitimate commerce in goods required by an industrializing Europe (such as rubber, wax, and palm oil). These agricultural regions were dominated by Mbundu and Ovimbundu societies in central and west-central Angola, by Kongo societies in the north, and by Lunda-Chokwe societies in the east. Outside of these areas agriculture was mixed with cattle-herding and hunting, and ranged from more sedentary forms practiced by the Nganguela, to more nomadic forms practiced in Herero and Ovambo societies. With the exception of political capitals such as the Kongo's Mbanza Kongo or the Lunda Empire's Musumba, daily life was organized at the village level around family, age, and gender distinctions.

Coincident with the abolition of the slave trade and shift to legitimate trade by other European powers, and the eventual division of the continent at the Berlin Conference (1884–1885), the Portuguese renewed and intensified expansion in Angola. They expanded the reach and degree of their control, often by force, from the late nineteenth century, either bringing local rulers into the colonial system or doing away with them completely. This wrought further changes in production and the movement of peoples with the introduction of cash crops, a colonial market, state bureaucracy, and industrial mining in the eastern region. The colonial state introduced a system of forced labor (on the heels of the abolition of slavery), of tax collection, and introduced cash crop production (coffee, cotton, and sisal). These new institutions had a profound impact on everyday life and society.

Forced labor, in which Africans were required to work for the government for a certain number of months per year or signed up on unfair contracts to work—often far from their homes and for little compensation—was the basis of colonial economy and rule. This system disrupted everyday life and production by removing able-bodied males from their fields and herds to work on state-run projects (either agricultural or infrastructural) and for private companies. The deleterious economic and social consequences for African families were compounded by land alienation, particularly in the central highlands, in the 1940s when the colonial government subsidized impoverished Portuguese in planned settlements. Ovimbundu societies suffered under this system when their best lands were taken away for settlers, and Ovimbundu men were then forced to work on Portuguese-owned coffee plantations in northern regions. This created tensions between Ovimbundu workers and the local Kongo populations who had been displaced from their farms and coffee production by Portuguese plantations.

In general, the Portuguese government invested little in education (most schools were foreign-financed mission schools) and infrastructure. To unload the costs and work of economic development and colonial administration, the Portuguese government gave concessions to foreign companies that then exploited local resources and administered the surrounding areas. This was the case in the east-central region where a Portuguese company (Cotonang) was given an area and local people were forced to grow cotton and sell it to the company for a low price determined by the government. In the northeastern part of Lunda province, the international consortium Diamang received a concession for diamond mining. The company controlled education, health care, employment, and had its own security service. Forced labor led to both international censure and local rebellions, two of which occurred in 1961 and helped swell nationalist consciousness and forces.

República de Angola (Republic of Angola)

Population:	12,263,596 (2007 est.)
Area:	1,246,700 sq. km (481,353 sq. mi.)
Official language:	Portuguese
Languages:	Portuguese, Kikongo, Kimbundu, Umbundu, Kioko, Ganguela, Fiote
National currency:	kwanza
Principal religions:	Roman Catholic 68%, various Protestant 20%, indigenous 12%
Capital:	Luanda (est. pop. 4,000,000 in 2006)
Other urban centers:	Huambo, Benguela
Annual rainfall:	varies from 0 in southwestern coastal desert to 1,780 mm (70 in.) in extreme north
Principal geographical features:	*Mountains:* Central Highlands, Chela range, Tala Nugongo range, Vissecua range, Mount Elgon, Loviti, Caiculo-Cabaza *Rivers:* Zaire (Congo), Kwanza, Kwango, Kubango, Kwando, Kasai, M'bridge, Loje, Dande, Bengo, Katumbela, Kunene
Economy:	*GDP per capita:* US$4,300 (2006)
Principal products and exports:	*Agricultural:* bananas, sugarcane, coffee, sisal, corn, cotton, manioc, tobacco, vegetables, plantains; livestock; forest products; fisheries products *Manufacturing:* basic metal products, fish processing, food processing, brewing, tobacco products, sugar refining, textiles *Mining:* petroleum products, natural gas, diamonds, iron ore, manganese, copper, phosphates
Government:	Independence from Portugal, 1975. Constitution, 1975. New constitution approved in 1991. President elected by universal suffrage. Elected 220-member Assembleia Nacional. President appoints Council of Ministers, which president and prime minister oversee. The 18 provinces are administered by government-appointed commissioners.
Heads of state since independence:	1975–1979: President Antonio Agostinho Neto 1979–: President José Eduardo dos Santos
Armed forces:	President is commander in chief. Universal draft. *Army:* 130,000 *Navy:* 3,000 *Air force:* 7,000 *Paramilitary:* 40,000
Transportation:	*Rail:* 2,798 km (1,739 mi.) *Ports:* Cabinda, Luanda, Soyo *Roads:* 73,830 km (45,878 mi.), 51% paved *National airline:* Transportes Aéreos de Angola *Airports:* International facility at Luanda, domestic facilities at Benguela, Cabinda, Huambo, Lobito, Namibe
Media:	2 daily newspapers: *Diá rio da República* and *O Jornal de Angola.* Radio Nacional de Angola broadcasts in Portuguese, English, French, and Spanish. Televisão Popular de Angola, a parastatal company, provides television programming.
Literacy and education:	*Total literacy rate:* 42% (2002). Education is free, universal, and compulsory for ages 6–14. Postsecondary education provided through Universidade de Agostinho Neto, Centro Nacional de Investigação Cientifica de Angola, and Instituto de Educação e Servicio Social de Angola.

Colonial society was defined by the disparity between colonizer and colonized. Before the 1930s, social policy was informal and offered assimilation to a few Africans as the way to achieve Portuguese citizenship within the colony. *Assimilados* were those individuals who had acquired so-called European practices (Christianity, Portuguese language, European dress, and a certain degree of education) and occupied military, civil service, or local leadership positions.

In the 1930s, António Salazar's fascist government, seeking to increase metropolitan control over the colonies, codified this social regime. It divided the entire African population in Angola into two groups: *indígenas* (indigenous or natives) and *assimilados* (assimilated). The number of *assimilados* was always less than 1 percent of the African population. *Indígenas* were subject to taxation, forced labor, and were required to carry identification books that denoted their place of employment.

A new wave of Portuguese immigration in the 1940s caused many urban-based *assimilados* to lose their positions and jobs in the colonial bureaucracy or in commerce as settlers escaped to urban areas, especially the capital, Luanda. Colonial society became more racially divided and racist. As a result, by the 1950s some *assimilados* began to identify with the majority of Africans (*indígenas*), with

African cultural practices, and with the Angolan territory. Nationalist movements began to develop in the 1950s, expanding on a sense of *angolanidade* (Angolan-ness or Angolan distinctiveness) that first surged in turn-of-the-century Luanda. Three different movements formed by the mid-1960s (the National Liberation Front Angola, FNLA; the Popular Movement for the Liberation of Angola, MPLA; and the National Union for the Total Independence of Angola, UNITA). The divisions at the basis of the nationalist movements were social, cultural, regional, and political, created by the colony's history and not by a rigid notion of ethnicity.

The armed struggle for independence exploded with three rebellions in 1961 (in the coffee growing region, in the cotton growing area, and in Luanda) and continued until April 1974. All three armed movements waged war from exile in neighboring countries. Thirteen years of anticolonial war created different experiences among those in the guerrilla struggle versus those who stayed behind in urban areas, and those who lived in rural areas (many of whom experienced forced villagization by the Portuguese army or became involved with supplying and supporting the guerrilla forces). It also exacerbated the tensions and differences between the three nationalist movements.

A military coup in Portugal in 1974 toppled the fascist government and set in motion Angola's transition to independence. The groups involved in the three armed movements returned to Angola to become political parties, and unsuccessfully attempted to negotiate joint rule. Shortly after independence was declared on November 11, 1975, a civil war broke out.

The socialist-oriented ruling party, the MPLA, attempted to implement policies that would address the grievances and divisions created by colonial rule. They made some headway in the area of education, particularly for girls, but the intensification of the civil war distracted energy and resources from social services and infrastructure.

The civil war created a new set of exiles, although this time they became part of a growing humanitarian crisis of refugees and internally displaced people (an estimated one-third of the population in 2007) who suffered from the terrors of war, multiple displacements, hunger, and disease.

This war was quickly mired in the geopolitics of the Cold War until the late 1980s, at which time it became a war fueled and funded by the control of scarce and precious resources (oil for the government and diamonds for the rebels). The civil war was eventually referred to as the politicians war, which underscored the growing gap between those with political power (whether the state or rebel leaders) and those without.

The fighting ended in 2002. Postconflict Angolan society is characterized by a sharp division between the haves and have-nots. Whereas the majority of the population survives on less than US$1 a day, a small elite prospers on the revenue of petroleum production and related businesses and investments. The majority of Angolans are still waiting for a peace dividend: improved education, increased employment, land security, the removal of land mines, and political stability.

See also **Bantu, Eastern, Southern, and Western, History of (1000 BCE to 1500 CE); Cold War; Colonial Policies and Practices; Ethnicity; Labor: Conscript and Forced; Socialism and Postsocialisms; Warfare: Civil Wars.**

BIBLIOGRAPHY

Bender, Gerald. *Angola under the Portuguese: The Myth and the Reality.* Berkeley: University of California, 1978.

Castro Henriques, Isabel. *Percursos de Modernaidade Em Angola: Dinâmicas comerciais e tranformações no século XIX.* Lisbon, Portugal: Instituto de Investigação Científica Tropical, 1997.

Heywood, Linda. *Contested Power in Angola: 1840s to the Present.* Rochester, New York: University of Rochester Press, 2000.

Miller, Joseph. "Worlds Apart: Africans' Encounters and Africa's Encounters with the Atlantic in Angola, before 1800." In *The Atlantic Slave Trade—Volume III: Eighteenth Century,* ed. Jeremy Black. Aldershot, England: Ashgate, 2006.

MARISSA J. MOORMAN

HISTORY AND POLITICS

The Republic of Angola is descended from an early Portuguese military *conquista* whose name, Angola, was appropriated from the conquered sixteenth-century Mbundu state known as Ngola. It also has two modern predecessors, the twentieth-century Portuguese colony of Angola and its independent successor, the Marxist-Leninist People's Republic of Angola.

Colonial Angola was small and organized almost entirely around supplying slaves to Brazil from two port towns, Luanda—the larger and seat of the Portuguese military government—and Benguela in the south. By the mid-nineteenth century, with the slave trade ending, it was still a largely coastal, Afro-Portuguese outpost with a network of more or less dependent trading forts stretching inland up the Kwanza River valley, as well as others on the high plateau inland from Benguela.

By 1891 Portugal had succeeded in obtaining European diplomatic recognition of its claims to rule the lands and peoples now constituting the nation of Angola. It was just beginning, however, to extend its administrative authority beyond these earlier coastal centers. The demise of the Atlantic slave trade after 1850 produced dramatic growth in exports of ivory, beeswax, and then rubber from the Kongo regions to the north and the remote areas east of the upper Kwanza and Kunene Rivers thus conceded to Portugal.

The Chokwe hunters and traders of that region, as well as the Kongo, the Mbundu inland from Luanda, and the Ovimbundu of the high plateau responded with generally successful efforts to compete economically. Portuguese investors also established coffee plantations on the hills above the Kwanza and sugar estates in the far southern coastal settlement at Moçamedes. Between 1890 and 1922, more than ninety Portuguese military campaigns were launched to establish control throughout the region. At the same time, English-speaking Protestant missionaries arrived: British Baptists in the Kongo region, American Methodists in Luanda and its hinterland, and Canadian Congregationalists among the Ovimbundu.

By the early twentieth century this extension of military control and a wave of settlers from Portugal were marginalizing the long-established urban, assimilated Africans and Afro-Portuguese of Luanda. Many were squeezed out of the administrative and commercial sectors that they had dominated. One result was the emergence of literary and journalistic circles in Luanda and other coastal cities, dedicated to finding the meaning of an Angola rooted in Africa, rather than in Portugal. They founded newspapers and cultural organizations, a few of which even

moved beyond parochial complaints about their own exclusion to attack forced labor, racism, and other abuses that were widespread throughout the colony as Portuguese authorities attempted to pay for the costs of conquest and administration with violent recruitment of ill-paid workers for settler farms and plantations.

Portugal became a republic in 1910, and after 1932 a fascist dictatorship under António Salazar. Imposition of strong economic and military controls enabled the regime to concentrate on solidifying a colonial hierarchy based on Lusophone culture. The Salazarist New State abolished these early nationalist organizations or forced them to operate as government-approved cultural societies.

Despite tight economic controls and government schemes promoting the settlement of poor Portuguese peasants in the Central Highlands, overall economic development in Angola was slow. Portugal itself did not have adequate resources for colonial development, nor would the xenophobic New State allow foreign investors in the colony. The two major exceptions were concession of the entire northeastern quadrant of the territory to the Belgium-based Companhia dos Diamantes de Angola (DIAMANG), and a railroad linked to the Cecil Rhodes' British South Africa Company, running from Benguela to the copper mines of Northern Rhodesia. Elsewhere, land expropriation, divide and rule tactics, forced labor, and coerced cultivation formed the basis of Portugal's part the colonial economy.

Not surprisingly, discontent in the countryside became endemic. Even the people who did not protest, turning instead to the Christian missions for access to modern schools, medical services, and information, were often considered subversive, especially if they associated with suspect foreign Protestants. During the 1950s, tensions escalated significantly as the nationalist currents sweeping through French, British, and Belgian Africa seeped into Angola, sparking the foundation of modern nationalist movements by elements of the (often Protestant) educated few, who were also influenced by the cultural nationalist underground. In 1951 Angola officially became an overseas province of Portugal, which subjected its people to even more systematic repression enforced by the feared Policia

Internacionale de Defensa do Estado (PIDE), the Portuguese secret government police.

Portugal, remaining impervious to pressures for change, responded by sending more settlers to the colony and enforcing more crackdowns on African political activity, thus provoking a serious anticolonial rebellion in 1961. Mobs attacked the political prison in Luanda, which proved a major historical turning point. From that time forward more and more Angolans were drawn into an intensifying liberation struggle led by three often-competing nationalist movements: the Popular Movement for the Liberation of Angola (MPLA), founded in 1956, based in the Afro-Portuguese and Mbundu region of Luanda and organizer of the 1961 revolt; the National Front for the Liberation of Angola (FNLA), with its roots in the Kongo region, founded in 1962 and essentially operating from exile in the Kongo regions of the newly independent (and formerly Belgian) Democratic Republic of the Congo; and National Union for the Total Independence of Angola (UNITA), founded in 1966, that drew on the Canadian Congregationalist mission network and appealed to an Ovimbundu constituency. By the end of the decade each had set up offices outside the colony (or overseas province, as the Portuguese insisted) and launched guerrilla operations inside it, the FNLA in the north and the MPLA in the east.

The Portuguese government answered with ever-larger military campaigns. By 1970, its army in Angola was sixty-thousand strong. A few minor political concessions did little to mollify the nationalist movements. Portugal, however, did succeed in promoting economic development by finally opening up the colony to international corporations such as the U.S.-based Gulf Oil Company and other European petroleum companies to develop major offshore oil fields.

The April 1974 military coup in Lisbon, which ended fascism in Portugal, led to almost immediate independence in all of the overseas provinces. The new military government moved quickly to terminate its colonial wars and negotiate terms for independence with the nationalist movements there. In Angola, however, fighting continued as the three rival liberation armies contested control of the country. The last eighteen months of the colonial era in 1974–1975 were marked by a series of multiparty agreements which ultimately failed to stop the fighting or prevent increased internationalization of the conflict as each of the movements, reconstituted as political parties, sought outside aid.

THE PEOPLE'S REPUBLIC OF ANGOLA

By November 11, 1975, the day of Angolan independence, the Portuguese had departed, but without formally transferring power to any one of the competing nationalist groups. However, the People's Republic of Angola (RPA), proclaimed in Luanda by the MPLA under the leadership of President Agostinho Neto, with Soviet and Cuban aid gained control of almost all of the country by early March 1976.

The rivalries of the MPLA, FNLA, and UNITA were a prime factor in preventing a peaceful transition to independence in the period 1974–1976. But pressures from outsiders, particularly the Soviet Union (MPLA), South Africa (UNITA), and the United States (FNLA), intensified the conflict and helped the MPLA to triumph. The withdrawal of American aid from the FNLA in December 1975, the discrediting of UNITA once it had solicited a South African army invasion on its behalf, and Soviet and Cuban aid to the MPLA, coupled with the fact that the MPLA was able to hold on to its traditional power base in Luanda, all helped the organization emerge victorious. Within a few months, most African and European countries had recognized the MPLA government. In December 1976 Angola was admitted to the United Nations.

From March 1976 the MPLA began to build a sense of Angolan national identity by implementing its Marxist-Leninist principles. Apart from grappling with new administrative structures, the RPA government in the late 1970s had to rebuild a war-shattered economy further weakened by the departure of virtually the entire corps of Portuguese skilled personnel—some hundreds of thousands of *retornados* to Portugal—who also destroyed the equipment and infrastructure they abandoned. It had to deal with factionalism within its ranks, particularly between the military wing who had fought and died in the bush for more than a decade and the civilian politicians who had worked for independence in relative comfort in the capital cities of Europe. It also had to contend with continuing guerrilla actions mounted by UNITA and its ally, South Africa, all while trying to improve education, health, and transport; create mass political organs; and foster the growth of an authentic Angolan cultural expression.

President Neto could still have been optimistic about achieving these goals at the time that cancer claimed his life in 1979. However, by 1981 his successor, former planning minister José Eduardo dos Santos, faced escalating conflict, again pitting the Cuban-aided MPLA against UNITA and its South African ally in the context of Cold War politics and the struggle for independence in neighboring Namibia, run for more than half a century essentially as a colony of South Africa. At mid-decade the South Africans occupied Angola's southern borderlands, UNITA was receiving aid from the United States, fifty thousand Cubans were performing military and civilian tasks for the MPLA government, and the Angolan army and air force were being built into formidable modern operations. In 1983 the provinces most affected by the conflict were put under military governors.

The war prevented implementation of planned social and economic programs, stymieing efforts to institutionalize the government's key principle of people's power. It also contributed to the evolution of a more centralized, presidentialist form of government. The leadership of the ruling party, now called the MPLA-PT (Workers Party), remained relatively closed and ethnically linked to the Luanda region, despite the success of President dos Santos in adding a few technically trained and less ideologically oriented individuals, similar to himself, to its ranks.

Even as war settled into the fabric of life throughout the country, the government participated in a lengthy international diplomatic process designed to end it. These diplomatic efforts focused on the issue of Namibian independence, with South Africa insisting on linking its withdrawal to the removal of Cuban troops from Angola. In 1981 the United States accepted this linkage, and despite initial Angolan rejection of the principle, a lengthy series of talks involving Angola, Cuba, South Africa, and the United States began. These culminated only in 1988, with agreements both on independence for Namibia and withdrawal of Cuban troops from Angola.

With the regional situation thus stabilized, the Angolan government intensified its drive to improve the national economy and end the internal fighting with UNITA. African heads of state brokered talks

between the parties, which resulted in a short-lived (but prophetic) agreement signed in Gabdolite, Democratic Republic of the Congo, in June 1990.

The MPLA initiated important domestic political and economic changes. Most important, at its Third Party Congress in December 1990, the MPLA-PT voted to turn itself into a social democratic party, institute a multiparty system, and further liberalize the economy.

By the end of 1991 peace finally seemed accessible. A cease-fire was holding; the last Cuban troops had departed Angola under the watchful eyes of a United Nations Verification Mission, or UNAVEM; the Estoril (or Bicess) Peace Agreement had been signed by dos Santos and UNITA leader Jonas Savimbi; and campaigning had begun for multiparty elections that were scheduled for the following September.

THE REPUBLIC OF ANGOLA

Constitutional changes instituting a multiparty democracy took effect in August 1992, and thus the Republic of Angola was born. By this time election campaigning was intense, with no fewer than eighteen registered political parties including UNITA and a renamed MPLA contesting the presidency and seats in a new National Assembly.

Hopes ran high in a war-weary land, but—ominously—progress was very uneven in implementing key provisions of the Estoril accords relating to the integration of the MPLA's Popular Armed Forces for the Liberation of Angola and UNITA's troops into the new, nonpartisan Armed Forces of Angola. The five hundred members of the UN Verification Commission, now known as UNAVEM II, were not equipped to enforce, only to observe.

The election, which UN observers rated free and fair, gave the MPLA 129 seats in the National Assembly and UNITA 70 but required a run-off between dos Santos and Savimbi for the presidency. Following the official announcement of election results, however, fighting broke out in Luanda and Huambo. By the end of the year full-scale war had engulfed most of the country.

In January 1993 peace negotiations resumed under the auspices of the UN and the Organization of African Unity, with Portugal, Russia, and the United States as observers. By mid-year both the United States and South Africa had established full diplomatic relations with Angola, and a new UN special representative to Angola, Alioune Blondin Beye of Mali, had arrived. However, it was only in November 1994 that a new peace agreement, the Lusaka Protocol, was signed in Zambia and the fighting subsided. Again, the issues of demobilization and power sharing were central, as the MPLA and UNITA continued their contest for control of the country. This time, however, oversight of the military demobilization was under a much stronger UN mission, the seven-thousand-member UNAVEM III.

The struggle between Savimbi's UNITA forces and the MPLA government in Luanda resumed, with major battles pitting the well-armed combatants. Growing revenues from Angola's petroleum reserves funded the government, and UNITA financed its struggle by seizing control of the diamondiferous northeast. In efforts to inhibit the opponents' forces, both sides laced the rural areas with land mines in such quantities that the country became the most heavily mined area in the world. Rural populations fled to Luanda, flooding the city—with its colonial-era infrastructure damaged by the departing Portuguese—with crowds of refugees. Half a million people may have died in the fighting.

The tide turned against UNITA and Savimbi in 1997 when the UN imposed sanctions on his movement. The Angolan government launched a massive military assault in 1999 and finally managed to ambush and kill Savimbi in 2002. The movement then declared itself a political party and joined a government of national unity in Luanda, under long-serving President dos Santos. In 2007, after Africa's longest-running war, the country is positioned to apply its considerable returns from its oil and diamond wealth to reconstruction and national reconciliation. Doubters worry that the small MPLA elite in Luanda will find it difficult to share the massive gains they enjoyed during the war and wonder how long the nearly 5 million residents in the city's shantytowns (more than a third of the nation's total population) will wait for the infrastructure and other services they badly need.

The Republic of Angola is a multiparty democracy with a social market economy and a presidential form of government. The president of the republic is directly elected and may serve three five-year terms.

The National Assembly is authorized at 223 seats, but three seats reserved for Angolans living abroad have been left vacant. The assembly is the supreme state legislative body, to which the government is responsible. Its members, elected to four-year terms, convene twice yearly. A Standing Commission of the Assembly assumes power between sessions.

The government comprises the president, vice-presidents, ministers, and secretaries of state. The Council of Ministers, whose members are appointed by the president, is headed by the prime minister and is answerable to the National Assembly.

See also **Benguela; Cold War; Colonial Policies and Practices; Luanda; Neto, Agostinho; Rhodes, Cecil John; Savimbi, Jonas; Socialism and Postsocialisms; United Nations; Warfare: Internal Revolts.**

BIBLIOGRAPHY

Birmingham, David. *Empire in Africa: Angola and its Neighbors* Athens: Ohio University Press, 2006.

Birmingham, David, and Phyllis M. Martin, eds. *History of Central Africa*, 2 vols. New York: Longman, 1983.

Clarence-Smith, W. Gervase. *The Third Portuguese Empire, 1825–1975.* Manchester, U.K.: Manchester University Press, 1985.

James, W. Martin. *A Political History of the Civil War in Angola, 1974–1990.* New Brunswick, NJ: Transaction Publishers, 1992.

James, W. Martin. *Historical Dictionary of Angola.* Lanham, MD: Scarecrow Press, 2004.

Marcum, John. *The Angolan Revolution*, Vol. 1, *The Anatomy of an Explosion, 1950–1962.* Cambridge, MA: M.I.T. Press, 1969.

Marcum, John. *The Angolan Revolution*, Vol. 2, *Exile, Politics, and Guerilla Warfare, 1962–1976.* Cambridge, MA: M.I.T. Press, 1978.

Núñez, Benjamin. *Dictionary of Portuguese-African Civilization.* Vol. 1. London, 1995.

Pearce, Justin. *An Outbreak of Peace: Angola's Situation of Confusion.* Claremont, South Africa: D. Philip, 2005.

Sommerville, Keith. *Angola: Politics, Economics, and Society.* London: F. Pinter Publishers, 1986.

SUSAN HERLIN BROADHEAD
REVISED BY JOSEPH C. MILLER

ANIMALS, DOMESTICATED. *See* Livestock: Domestication.

ANIMALS, WILD. *See* **Wildlife.**

ANNAN, KOFI (1938–). The Ghanaian economist and secretary general of the United Nations (1997–2006), Kofi Annan was born in Kumasi, Ghana, on April 8, 1938. Annan was educated in Cape Coast, Kumasi, and Macalester College, Minnesota (earning a BA in economics in 1961). He moved to Geneva, Switzerland, for graduate studies, and in 1962 he took a position at the World Health Organization, serving in various capacities until 1971. In 1971–1972 Annan earned his master's degree in management at the Massachusetts Institute of Technology in Boston, returned to Ghana to become director of tourism (1974–1976), and then moved back to Switzerland to work with the United Nations (UN) High Commission on Refugees. Annan remained in Geneva throughout the 1980s, then transferred to the UN in New York, carrying out several special assignments for then-Secretary-General Boutros Boutros-Gahli. From 1993 to 1996 he served as under-secretary general of the UN.

In December 1996 Annan was elected secretary-general of the UN and undertook a series of institutional reforms. During this term he was awarded (jointly with the UN) the Nobel Peace Prize, and was unanimously re-elected as secretary-general in 2001. His second term was less successful than the first. His opposition to the United States' war in Iraq weakened U.S.-UN relations, his mishandling of sexual harassment allegations against certain UN staff members diminished his credibility, and he was accused of complicity in kickback schemes involving the UN-administered oil-for-food program in Iraq during the Saddam Hussein regime. Annan was eventually exonerated of any active complicity in the last case, but was deemed guilty of lax oversight of the program. By 2005 the UN-U.S. relationship was in tatters, and there were calls for Annan's resignation, particularly by the United States. Elsewhere in the world, however, there have been strong statements of support. Annan has been married twice and has two children. His second term as secretary-general ended in December 2006.

See also **United Nations: Africa in the United Nations; United Nations: United Nations in Africa.**

BIBLIOGRAPHY

Annan, Kofi. *Global Values: The United Nations and the Rule of Law in the Twenty-First Century.* Singapore: Institute of Southeast Asian Studies, 2000.

Annan, Kofi. *We the Peoples: The Role of the UN in the Twenty-First Century.* New York: United Nations Department of Public Information, 2000.

NANCY E. GRATTON

Former UN secretary general Kofi Annan (1938–) at the United Nations Office in Geneva, November 2006. In his farewell address to world leaders at UN headquarters in New York on September 19, 2006, Annan cited violence in Africa and the Arab-Israeli conflict as two of the major issues that needed immediate attention. FABRICE COFFRINI/AFP/GETTY IMAGES

ANTANANARIVO. The capital of Madagascar, Antananarivo was founded in the early seventeenth century by the Hova king Andrianjaka. The name means "City of a Thousand," a reference to the guard that served to defend the settlement. The early city was situated on hills overlooking the Ikopa and Betsiboka Rivers and wide marshes suitable for rice cultivation. After unifying conquests ended in 1794, Antananarivo became the center of the most important of the Merina kingdoms that came to dominate the island.

During the nineteenth century, Merina rulers restricted foreign access by refusing to build roads into the city and at times banning Westerners entirely. Nonetheless, missionaries, traders, and architects gradually brought European education, fashion, and design to the local elites. The steep-roofed Gothic revival forms of the hillside Manjakamiadana Palace, built in 1839 by Jean Laborde, inspired a vernacular architecture that contributes to the city's unique and traditional beauty.

Antananarivo's population passed 50,000 toward the end of the nineteenth century, half of them slaves emancipated after the French conquest of Madagascar in 1895. Although the last Hova monarch, Queen Ranavalona III, fled into exile the following year, the French conserved the capital's palaces and mausoleums and moved royal bones into the upper city to consolidate ancestral authority in the capital of the new territory.

Under Governor-General Joseph-Simon Gallieni (1896–1905), the administrative, economic, and educational apparatus of the colonial regime was concentrated in the city, now renamed Tananarive. Early projects reshaped the *andohalo* (public gathering place) and the *zoma* (market), widened streets, and developed zoning initiatives to contain plague, malaria, and tuberculosis and to protect areas of "European construction." Roads and rail lines to the coast were completed in 1910, and the city became the center of the island's transportation networks. Urban expansion continued through the early 1930s, at times with forced labor, rebuilding the center while preserving aside the upper city as a historic district. Growth accelerated, with the population reaching 140,000 by 1940 and nearly 250,000 by independence in 1960.

Although subsequent national governments have generally drawn their top political personnel from regions outside the capital, the primacy of Antananarivo (the name was changed back after the 1972 revolution) has not been challenged. Betsileo, Antandroy, and Antaisaka peoples from regions to the south complement the Merina majority in a population that exceeds 5.1 million in the early twenty-first century. The city's main industries process agricultural products (mainly rice, pepper, cloves, and vanilla) and textiles, as well as cement, soap, cigarettes, and beer. The city therefore remains the economic as well as political center

of the island, despite crises that have brought the deterioration of infrastructure and increasing insecurity and homelessness in many quarters. In 1995 the Queen's Palace was destroyed by fire, but royal relics inside were rescued from the flames.

See also **Andrianampoinimerina; Madagascar; Ranavalona, Mada.**

BIBLIOGRAPHY

Bradt, Hilary, comp. *Madagascar*. Santa Barbara, CA: Clio, 1993.

THOMAS F. MCDOW

ANTHROPOLOGY, SOCIAL, AND THE STUDY OF AFRICA.

Sociocultural anthropology has altered its aims and meanings over the past 150 years of its existence. It has directed those concerns over societies in most parts of the world. Yet some of its major achievements and all of its changing concerns are embodied in research and publications on sub-Saharan Africa. Anthropology in Africa was dominated up to World War II by the two major colonial powers, Britain and to a lesser extent France. American anthropological research in Africa, undertaken initially under the inspiration of Melville J. Herskovits in the 1930s, focused on possible links between Africa and black culture in the Americas but had little wider importance for Africa itself until after World War II.

Early anthropological studies in Africa were conducted by colonial administrators such as R. S. Rattray, A. Dale, and C. K. Meek; soldiers such as M. Merker; and missionaries such as Bruno Gutmann, Henry A. Junod, Paul Schebesta, W. C. Willoughby, John Roscoe, and E. W. Smith. Surprisingly, the first fieldwork by a professionally trained, analytically sophisticated anthropologist was not conducted until 1926–1930, by E. E. Evans-Pritchard. Earlier researchers such as the British C. G. Seligman, the German Leo Frobenius, and the Swedish Gerhard Lindblom were self-taught anthropologists or very old-fashioned ethnographers. Seligman's and Frobenius' scholarly contributions lay mainly in the interest their surveys generated for others, both for subsequent fieldwork and in the collection of artifacts. Lindblom, however, wrote one of the first great descriptive African ethnographies based on research among the Kamba of Kenya, carried out from 1910 to 1912. Lindblom's study was probably one of the very first truly comprehensive ethnographies published by a social scientist rather than a colonial servant.

Early-twentieth-century anthropological research in Africa had two complementary aims: to develop and refine social theory and to provide information to assist European colonial powers' rule over Africans. Scholars sought to describe, understand, and compare African ways of life (beliefs and values as well as social organizations and practices) with those of others elsewhere. Initially they fitted such data into an evolutionary scheme, often constructed in terms of material culture or the scale and complexity of political organization. A few researchers even theorized about the diffusion of cultural traits they viewed as sophisticated southward from the Nile Valley, thereby implicitly giving Africans little credit for independent invention of either technology or cultural institutions. Some of the most sympathetic, richest early accounts were by missionaries such as Smith, Junod, and Gutmann, who had long resided among a single people, mastered a local language, and honestly striven to understand a different way of life. Their standards of long residence, linguistic knowledge, and intensive social interaction with local groups were later emulated by the best social anthropologists.

Early studies sought to describe a particular society in all its aspects, producing general, descriptive volumes not focused upon any social theory or single institution. Only with the first of Evans-Pritchard's many books, *Witchcraft, Oracles, and Magic among the Azande* (1937), was there an African anthropological monograph formulated around a basic issue of social theory. That work, the greatest and most influential book ever written in African anthropology, initiated a new era of specialized, theoretically oriented studies. Subsequently, a series of brilliant works by Evans-Pritchard, Meyer Fortes, Max Gluckman, Audrey Richards, Isaac Schapera, Monica Wilson, and their students revolutionized anthropological analysis and reportage in Africa. Evans-Pritchard's initial work provided a persuasive study of how Africans could find a belief in witchcraft to be both plausible and useful. It led the way for a spate of sympathetic studies portraying African systems of belief—among them, a collection edited by Fortes and Germaine Dieterlen, *African Systems of Thought* (1965).

More important, *Witchcraft, Oracles, and Magic among the Azande* used African material to broaden general sociological thinking about the relations between systems of thought, rationality and nonrationality, social motives, and organization. Subsequently, anthropological concerns switched to issues of kinship and social organization (for example, A. R. Radcliffe-Brown and C. Daryll Forde's study from 1950, *African Systems of Kinship and Marriage*); political systems (Fortes and Evans-Pritchard's *African Political Systems*, published in 1940); and legal systems (Max Gluckman's *The Judicial Process Among the Barotse of Northern Rhodesia*, published in 1955). In all these cases, the analyses generated theory which influenced sociological scholarship in many disciplines far beyond Africa. Their more focused concerns encouraged increasingly detailed and specialized field studies. Whereas earlier an African society would have been described in one comprehensive volume, researchers now produced clusters of specialized studies, each focused upon a particular social issue such as family, marriage and kinship, ancestral propitiation, the initiation of adolescents, livestock herding, agriculture, witchcraft and sorcery, kingship, age-sets, or courts and legal procedures.

During the 1940s, 1950s, and 1960s, studies of Africans produced much of the most significant theory in cultural anthropology. At this time French anthropologists, most notably Marcel Griaule and Germaine Dieterlen, were far more concerned with the study of African beliefs as these formed remarkable cosmologies than they were with matters of social organization and economy or even with connecting beliefs to social actions. There were, however, exceptions to those absorbed with traditional life. Georges Balandier in France, for example, Clyde Mitchell in Britain, and the Swedish missionary Bengt Sundkler pioneered in studying life in African towns, modernization, and the ways in which Africans there and in rural areas took over Western systems of thought such as Christianity.

While scholars advocated studies that would illuminate social theory by providing useful comparative data from different societies or which examined some social institution in a more detailed and revealing manner, colonial governments encouraged more practical research with the assumption that such knowledge would facilitate the political administration or economic development of the regions they controlled. Important ethnographic research centers were established in Paris, Brussels (Musée Royale de l'Afrique Centrale), London (International African Institute), faculties of anthropology at Oxford, Cambridge, and Manchester, and also in the colonies themselves at Dakar (Institut français de l'Afrique Noire), and universities with faculties at Léopoldville (now Kinshasa), Ibadan, Cape Town, Kampala, Khartoum, and Livingstone. (The Livingstone center was later moved to Lusaka.) The International African Institute based in London played a special and deeply influential role not only in promoting research and publication but in encouraging an international forum on African studies, prompting exchanges between British and continental European scholars and, after World War II, scholars in the United States and East Asia.

Throughout the colonial era, foreign-based anthropologists held problematic relations with colonialism. While rarely directly promoting colonial policies, they inevitably conducted research that many Africans saw and have continued to see as part of the colonial endeavor to appropriate and dominate the indigenous peoples. Researchers in South Africa such as A. W. Hoernlé, E. J. Krige, and later Godfrey and Monica Wilson, Max Gluckman, Leo and Hilda Kuper, and Isaac Schapera occupied problematical positions in that they developed a valuable local school of anthropological research and analysis but grew to be increasingly at odds with the South African government on account of its repressive policies against Blacks. Some, such as Schapera, Gluckman, and the Kupers, left Africa to teach and write in Britain and the United States.

Two of the most famous social anthropologists of the interwar period, A. R. Radcliffe-Brown and Bronislaw Malinowski, were not Africanists but had great influence on African anthropology. Radcliffe-Brown taught for some years at Cape Town and later promoted many of the early analyses and the publication of research on traditional African social organization. Malinowski, the originator of systematic anthropological field research during World War I in Melanesia, briefly toured Africa and, as a result of what he saw there, worked hard back in Britain to promote an applied anthropology which would relate ethnographic research to practical problems of colonial development.

Since World War II, American researchers, influenced by their British and French predecessors, have made a deep impact on all sectors of African anthropological research. By the late twentieth century anthropology in Africa came to exhibit little difference from comparative sociology in its engagement with contemporary issues of society and cultures. In the early twenty-first century, primary interest is directed toward the study of contrasts and of relations between national and local identities, including ethnicity; urban and rural modes of life; the growth of indigenous popular cultures influenced and promoted by modern Western media; the challenges of economic development; and rising and rapidly growing problems with health, political refugees, overpopulation, and the devastation of the environment. Too, many African intellectuals are deeply concerned with reinterpreting the classic ethnographies of the colonial era in the quest to construct new theories about quintessential aspects of African thought and society (see Kwame Anthony Appiah, *In My Father's House*, 1992). Others, often Americans, have restudied these early works to place them in their historical contexts.

The most significant social anthropological achievements based on African research involve eight key topics:

1. The description of stateless societies held together politically through a web of interrelated corporate groups (lineages) whose members are recruited by patrilineal or matrilineal descent and whose moral continuity is underpinned by propitiation of the ancestral dead. Such lineage-based communities provided political, economic, and social coherence and stability to societies seemingly lacking the conventional, by modern Western definitions, centralized institutions of order. Evans-Pritchard and Fortes pioneered this approach.

2. Indigenous legal practices. Researchers have explored how law and order are enforced through feuds, local moots, and other means outside modern Western conventions. African data and ethnography greatly contributed to the revision of social theories about the nature of law and politics in nonliterate societies. Evans-Pritchard and Gluckman

greatly advanced understanding in this realm of knowledge.

3. The description of kingship and queenship. Scholars have focused on societies that conceive of monarchy in terms of a broad matrix of cosmology and social values. Research on "divine" kingship in Africa deeply influenced historical interpretations of monarchy in Europe and Asia. Evans-Pritchard, Kuper, Gluckman, S. F. Nadel, and Richards led the research on African monarchies.

4. Oral history. The collection of oral history led to the reevaluation of thinking about the many changes that occurred in Africa long before colonialism. Such oral histories contributed to general understanding of how social memory is repeatedly reconstructed to sustain changing social patterns and identities in the present.

5. Kinship and marriage. The comparative study of kinship and marriage, including detailed accounts of matriliny, patriliny, polygyny, bride-wealth payments, the levirate and other forms of widow inheritance, woman-woman and ghost marriages, all profoundly expanded understanding of the many possible types of domestic groups and families.

6. African cosmologies. The exposition of different African cosmologies and the analysis of the ways these fit with values and beliefs about causation, misfortune, and social order revolutionized anthropological thinking about knowledge. In the course of such explication anthropologists developed new and rich analyses of how symbols work and what rituals mean. Few contemporary studies of symbols and ceremonies can afford to ignore comparing their findings to those in the anthropological scholarship on Africa.

7. Local economies. Anthropologists have studied herding, hunting and gathering, and shifting and intensive agriculture and how they have influenced different forms of social organization and beliefs. Studies of pastoralist economies are mainly grounded in African research, and studies of hunters and gatherers such as the "bushmen" and "pygmies" figure in all current theory about social evolution.

8. Colonialism. The richest and most innovative research on colonialism and the politics of modern cross-cultural contacts has been done in Africa, both in terms of the social, political, and economic repercussions of colonialism and in terms of the ways that Christianity and Islam have been adapted by proselytized peoples.

These eight areas of research have had lasting influence on all fields of social studies in Africa and of the sociological and other academic disciplines worldwide. Furthermore, in many ways ethnographic research and analysis carried out in Africa during the period 1940–1960 set the worldwide standard for sophistication and excellence in anthropological research. Africa was at that time seen as generating the cutting edge of social anthropological theory. Some critics even argued that African models had become so influential that they skewed the findings of research done in the Americas, the Pacific, and Asia. No other geographical area in the world between 1940 and 1960 had such profound impact upon anthropological research as Africa.

See also **History and the Study of Africa; Kingship; Kinship and Affinity; Kinship and Descent; Literature: Oral; Marriage Systems; Queens and Queen Mothers; Philosophy and the Study of Africa; Research: Social Sciences; Witchcraft.**

BIBLIOGRAPHY

Balandier, Georges. *Sociologie actuelle de l'Afrique noire.* Paris: PUF, 1971.

Fyfe, Christopher, ed. *African Studies since 1945.* London: Longman, 1977.

Gaillard, Gerald. *The Routledge Dictionary of Anthropologists.* New York: Routledge, 2004.

Goody, J. *The Expansive Moment: The Rise of Social Anthropology in Britain and Africa, 1918–1970.* Cambridge, U.K.: Cambridge University Press, 1995.

Guyer, Jane. *African Studies in the United States: A Perspective.* Atlanta, GA: African Studies Association, 1996.

Moore, S. F. "Changing Perspectives on a Changing Africa: The Work of Anthropology." In *Africa and the Disciplines: The Contribution of Research in Africa to the Social Sciences and Humanities,* ed. R. H. Bates, V. Y. Mudimbe, and J. O'Barr. Chicago: University of Chicago Press, 1993.

Moore, S. F. *Anthropology and Africa: Changing Perspectives on a Changing Scene.* Charlottesville: University Press of Virginia, 1994.

T. O. BEIDELMAN
REVISED BY JOHN MIDDLETON

APARTHEID. In 1948 the National Party, with the assistance of the small Afrikaner Party, which it subsequently absorbed, won a narrow election victory in South Africa and thereafter proceeded to implement the apartheid policy. The party would retain power for the next forty-six years over which time a huge exercise in social engineering was attempted. By the 1980s it was obvious that apartheid had failed, and the National Party looked for various alternatives that would ensure that it retained power. In 1990 President F. W. de Klerk accepted the inevitable and agreed to initiate negotiations for an inclusive, democratic system.

By 1948 South Africa was already a highly segregated society. From the creation of the Union of South Africa in 1910 successive administrations had committed themselves to segregationist policies, but during the 1940s, under the exigencies of a war economy and the concomitant large-scale urbanization of Africans, there were some signs of a reconsideration of aspects of policy. Jan Smuts, leader of the governing United Party and prime minister, said in 1942 that "segregation has fallen on evil days"; and that the townward migration of Africans was unstoppable: "You might as well try to sweep the ocean back with a broom" (Smuts, 10). The opposition National Party, the political arm of Afrikaner nationalism, seized upon these and other signs of flexibility to argue that they were a prelude to "integration" and the engulfment of whites by Africans. It was classic "black peril" electioneering, which had a long and dismal record in the country's politics.

The Nationalists fought the 1948 election principally on the issue of Afrikaner solidarity, but its proposals for apartheid, presented as the traditional policy of Afrikanerdom, accompanied a campaign that was in the worst tradition of "black peril" propaganda. To what extent the apartheid policy was a carefully worked out blueprint or merely an election stratagem remains a disputed issue. Various intellectuals, think tanks (including the secret Afrikaner Broederbond), and an internal party commission had produced broad policy goals, but as it unfolded in the 1950s and 1960s, policy making proceeded in an ad hoc way—always, though, based on the premise of white control:

baasskap ("mastership"), as J[ohn] G. Strijdom, prime minister from 1954 to 1958, termed it.

From the policy's inception in 1948 it was made clear that while apartheid envisaged the maximum separation of whites and nonwhites, total separation, advocated by a few intellectuals, was not possible, due to the economic dependence of the economy on African, Coloured, and Indian labor. Instead, apartheid focused on two interlinked aims: reinforcing racial inequality wherever it was perceived to be breaking down (as in the labor market) and limiting the urbanization of Africans by freezing the number of permanently urbanized people and attempting as far as possible to ensure that migrant labor was used, as had long been the case in the mining industry. Policy also sought to ensure that white workers would be given additional protection in the labor market by means of "job reservation." African labor unions, while not prohibited, were not officially recognized, and strikes by African workers continued to be illegal. Legislation changed this situation, and during the 1980s African labor unions became a critical anti-apartheid force.

Apartheid prescribed total political separation between whites and nonwhites. Provision made in 1946 for limited communal parliamentary representation of Indians by whites (boycotted by the Indian community) was repealed, the rights of qualified Coloured males to vote on the common voters' roll in Cape Province were abolished in 1956 after a protracted constitutional crisis, and in 1959 the limited rights of Africans to parliamentary representation by whites were terminated. The central premise of apartheid was that blacks could enjoy political rights only in institutions created in the "homelands."

The homelands, previously called reserves, were the shrunken, fragmented remnants of land that had been historically occupied by black Africans. Under the terms of legislation passed in 1913 and 1936, they amounted to 13.7 percent of the country. Here, in the vision of apartheid's planners, African "nations," as the ethnolinguistic clusters were called, could enjoy evolving political rights and "develop along their own lines," while the homelands continued to serve their historic function as reservoirs of labor. Traditional chiefs were deemed to be the authentic leaders of the black African peoples, and beginning in the 1950s, energetic steps were taken to establish pyramids of so-called "Bantu Authorities" in the homelands. Policy postulated that Africans in the urban areas must remain linked to these authorities, and accordingly, efforts were made to create urban representatives of homeland chiefs. These, however, proved unsuccessful.

A major focus of apartheid was the effort to gear education of blacks at all levels to the aims of policy. School education had been largely in the hands of missionary bodies under the aegis of provincial authorities. Under the Bantu Education Act of 1953 the central government assumed control, missionary-run schools were taken over, and a new curriculum was instituted. In the words of the legislation's sponsor, Hendrik F. Verwoerd (minister of native affairs, 1950–1958; prime minister, 1958–1966), who was also apartheid's principal planner and theoretician, the "Bantu must be guided to serve his community in all respects. There is no place for him in the European community above the level of certain forms of labor. Within his own community, however, all doors are open" (Pelzer, 53).

Education policy was ideologically inspired. Although the numbers of African children entering primary school rose substantially over time, the education they received was of poor quality. "Bantu Education" became a major political grievance: indeed, it was an educational issue, the attempt to force the teaching of certain subjects in higher grades through the medium of Afrikaans, that sparked the Soweto Uprising in mid-1976.

Apartheid was also enforced at the university level. Separate university colleges were established for Africans, as well as for Coloured and Indian students. These were mediocre institutions of low academic quality, whose students were kept under tight political control.

Vigorous efforts were made to reinvigorate the principle, upheld by successive governments since 1910, that urban Africans were "temporary sojourners." Beginning in the 1950s the pass laws, officially known as influx control, were drastically tightened and permanent rights of urban residence became hard to obtain. In 1960 the system was extended to women. Furthermore, freehold property rights were prohibited, and numerous black

African communities that had enjoyed such rights in urban and rural areas (where they were termed *black spots*) were dispossessed. More than 3.5 million people were affected. Black African-owned businesses in urban areas were placed under severe restrictions that limited their capacity to expand. Deliberate measures were taken to ensure that the availability of family housing was limited, whereas, alternatively, huge hostels were constructed for single, male migrant laborers. The migrant labor system, favored by apartheid's planners because it supposedly limited permanent urbanization, played havoc with family life, breaking down functioning social and economic units in the rural areas and encouraging male migrants in the towns to start second families with urban women.

Prior to 1948 the Coloured and Indian groups (accounting, respectively, for 9% and 3% of the total population in 1992) were intermediate categories in the racial hierarchy; both, but especially the Indians, were discriminated against, particularly as residential segregation in terms of the Group Areas Act of 1950 was enforced. Between 1960 and 1984 an estimated 860,000 people, mostly Coloured and Indian, were forced to relocate if their houses or businesses were in areas zoned for occupation by other groups.

In 1959 a switch of emphasis in the ideological underpinning of apartheid took place. Whereas the maintenance of racial inequality was as rigidly enforced as previously, the National Party under Verwoerd now embarked upon "positive" apartheid, terming it "separate development." Legislation was enacted to give black Africans "full rights" to develop in the homelands, eight of which were designated on an ethnolinguistic basis. Verwoerd emphasized that whites would never cede or share power in the remainder of the country. Originally, policy held that political evolution of these embryonic states would stop short of sovereign independence, but this limitation was dropped after 1959.

By 1960 apartheid and the South African government's continuing control over Namibia had increasingly become the object of international censure. In his "Wind of Change" speech, delivered in Cape Town in 1960, British prime minister Harold Macmillan served notice that apartheid was an unacceptable doctrine. Shortly thereafter, on March 21, 1960, police opened fire on Africans in

Sharpeville who were demonstrating against the pass laws, killing sixty-nine. The ensuing disturbances in different parts of the country were quelled, and the major black African political movements, the African National Congress (ANC) and the Pan-Africanist Congress, were banned. This was a landmark event in the increasing international isolation of the South African government.

After the banning of the ANC and the PAC, both opted to adopt violent methods of resistance. Nelson Mandela, a rising star in the ANC, joined the ANC's armed wing *Umkhonto we Sizwe*. He and eight others were arrested for sabotage and conspiracy to overthrow the government, and convicted in June 1964. All of the accused, but one, were sentenced to life imprisonment.

Verwoerd recognized that racial domination per se could no longer be justified in an increasingly hostile world in which, moreover, decolonization was proceeding apace. He attempted to appease criticism and to divert domestic black militancy by accelerating homeland political evolution. Ultimately four such homelands, Transkei (1976), Bophuthatswana (1977), Venda (1979), and Ciskei (1981), were granted independence, but in no case was it internationally recognized. Citizens of these states (whether they resided in them or not) were deprived of their South African citizenship. None was economically viable, and none, with the qualified exception of Bophuthatswana, succeeded in maintaining a semblance of democratic government. As the showpiece of apartheid they were a failure.

Most of the homelands were fragmented in discrete blocks of territory. For example, KwaZulu, the homeland of the biggest ethnolinguistic group, the Zulu, who made up 22 percent of the African population, consisted of twenty-nine separate blocks; for Bophuthatswana and Ciskei the corresponding figure was nineteen each. Consolidation plans were drawn up, but implementation was slow and expensive. By the early 1980s the government effectively gave up the unequal struggle.

An important component of apartheid was the vigorous use of security legislation to restrict opposition. Apart from proscribing organizations, individual activists were liable to be banned, detained without trial, and deprived of their passports,

without recourse to judicial reviews. More serious breaches of the security laws were tried in the Supreme Court. Although many judges reflected conventional white supremacist attitudes, some did their best to find loopholes in the law that mitigated the consequences of apartheid. In political cases heard in the Supreme Court the accused had the service of defense lawyers, often some of the leading barristers.

During the 1970s and 1980s apartheid unravelled steadily. Predictions made by Verwoerd in the 1960s that by 1978 the townward flow of Africans from the homelands would cease were shown to be hopelessly inaccurate. Apartheid's planners had seriously underestimated the rate of increase of the African population, which between 1946 and 1991 had nearly quadrupled, from 7.7 million to more than 29 million. Influx control was unable to prevent black African urbanization, as economic conditions in the homelands deteriorated. Job reservation by race steadily fell away as the demand for skilled workers increased. Efforts to force industry to make do with less African labor or to decentralize factories to the borders of homelands proved costly failures.

P[ieter] W[illem] Botha (prime minister, 1978–1983; state president, 1983–1989) tried unsuccessfully to reinvigorate what was obviously a failing policy. He permitted black labor unions to participate in statutory industrial relations mechanisms, allowed urban Africans to acquire property in freehold, repealed legislation prohibiting interracial sex and marriage, and in 1986 abolished the pass laws. He acknowledged that the homelands could never support more than 40 percent of the black African population and accepted that those resident in the white-controlled areas would have to be politically accommodated in those areas. In 1986 he announced that a common South African citizenship would be restored to those homeland citizens who had been deprived of theirs. Effectively, this was a nail in apartheid's coffin: Its ideological basis, separate nations, had been abandoned.

Botha tried to co-opt the Coloured and Indian categories by means of the Tricameral Constitution of 1983. It was intended to accord political rights, in separate chambers of Parliament, in such a way as not to threaten or significantly dilute white hegemonic control. The exclusion of Africans, who were still deemed to have alternative channels of political expression, provoked a massive backlash. During 1985–1986 South Africa witnessed serious unrest that was curbed (partially) by the application of stringent emergency regulations. The mass mobilization of millions of people and the growing influence of the ANC persuaded President de Klerk that "South Africa had reached a point in its history that offered an opportunity to break out of the current impasse...." (Cape Town: *Die Burger*, August 21, 1989. Translated from Afrikaans).

Apartheid had palpably failed in all respects, but by 1986 Botha had run out of reformist steam and until mid-1989 he and his party drifted rudderless. De Klerk came to the presidency at that time, and in his historic speech of February 2, 1990, he announced the lifting of the ban against the ANC and other proscribed organizations, the release of Nelson Mandela and other imprisoned leaders, and his intention of negotiating a democratic constitution. In subsequent years he repealed all apartheid legislation, and opened his party membership to all races.

Apartheid has left major scars on South African society in the form of severe inequalities in education, housing, welfare, and income that will not easily be overcome. Nor will it be easy to knit together a society that was forcibly compartmentalized for so long. The legacy of conflict and racial polarization, exacerbated by deepening poverty, make the prospects for democracy questionable.

See also **Cape Town; De Klerk, Frederik Willem; Johannesburg; Labor: Trades Unions and Associations; Mandela, Nelson; Mandela, Winnie; South Africa, Republic of; Verwoerd, Hendrik Frensch.**

BIBLIOGRAPHY

Adam, Heribert. *Modernizing Racial Domination: South Africa's Political Dynamics.* Berkeley: University of California Press, 1971.

Barber, James. *South Africa in the Twentieth Century: A Political History—In Search of a Nation State.* Malden, MA: Blackwell Publishers, 1999.

Giliomee, Hermann. *The Afrikaners: Biography of a People.* London: C. Hurst, 2003.

Kenny, Henry. *Power, Pride and Prejudice: The Years of Afrikaner Nationalist Rule in South Africa.* Johannesburg: J. Ball Publishers, 1991.

Lipton, Merle. *Capitalism and Apartheid: South Africa, 1910–1986.* Aldershot, U.K.: Wildwood House, 1986.

Pelzer, A[driaan] N[icolaas], ed. *Verwoerd Speaks: Speeches 1948-1966.* Johannesburg: APB Publishers, 1966.

Posel, Deborah. *The Marking of Apartheid, 1948–1961: Conflict and Compromise.* Oxford: Clarendon Press, 1991.

Schrire, Robert, ed. *Malan to de Klerk: Leadership in the Apartheid State.* London: Hurst, 1994.

Smuts, Jan Christian. *The Basis of Trusteeship.* Johannesburg: South African Institute of Race Relations, 1942.

DAVID WELSH

ARCHAEOLOGY AND PREHISTORY

This entry includes the following articles:
OVERVIEW
TOOLS AND TECHNOLOGIES
STONE AGE SOCIETIES
HISTORICAL
INDUSTRIAL
MARINE
ISLAMIC
CHRISTIAN

OVERVIEW

Knowledge about the archaeology of Africa for many parts of the continent is comparatively recent, while explorations north of the Sahara, in particular the Nile Valley, and to a lesser extent North Africa, go back to the very beginnings of the discipline. There still remains a divide between these two broad areas in terms of how archaeology is conducted and how archaeologists perceive themselves—whether for example Egyptologists consider themselves to be African archaeologists or part of another community who study Near Eastern civilizations. The evidence can also be very different; from the Nile Valley are historical records and the use of writing systems from 3400 BCE (among the earliest in the world) and from around this time, the beginnings of monumental stone and brick architecture, urban settlements, elaborately furnished graves, art, and complex social organization. In sub-Saharan Africa, complexity was expressed in different ways, which could be much less obvious in the archaeological record. Monumental architecture was more often constructed in mud than stone, urbanism takes on a very different character, while art styles are more difficult to interpret.

However it was in the use of writing systems that sub-Saharan African was seen to lag behind the rest of Eurasia. The earliest examples of indigenous writing systems south of the Sahara are the use of Himyaritic scripts (but probably introduced from Arabia) in temple inscriptions in northern Ethiopia from circa 600 BCE, the Tifinagh scripts (probably based on Phoenician, used by Berber groups) from circa 300 BCE, and Meroitic in the middle and upper Nile, from circa 200 BCE. Elsewhere, writing develops in response to contact with outsiders: Arabic is found along the East Coast, and in the Sahel on inscriptions from the early eleventh century CE, and a little earlier on locally minted coins, while for much of the continent it is introduced by European colonizers between the sixteenth and nineteenth centuries. The absence of writing does not necessarily mean an absence of history, as many African societies transmitted historical information orally or through formally recited chronicles and histories. Like written documents, some survive well, and others have been lost, but there is no reason to believe that the recording and transmission of historical information is necessarily more recent south of the Sahara, than it is north.

THE IDEA OF "PREHISTORIC AFRICA"

Because of this absence of surviving historical records, much of the archaeology of Africa has been classed as prehistoric, and this was given voice in 1947, with the foundation of the Pan African Congress for Prehistory. Here, under the guiding force of Louis Leakey, the congress brought together archaeologists, geologists, and geomorphologists to outline the continent's remoter past. A new generation of fieldworker went out to locate and excavate sites and study collections, mostly relating to the earlier periods of human evolution.

These prehistoric societies were generally defined, as Desmond Clark, one of these pioneers, noted in the earlier edition of this encyclopedia, as those "that antedate the beginning of contemporary written records, local or from elsewhere, of people and their culture." To Clark, African prehistory was like a moving front—where there was contact with the outside world (for example along the Nile Valley, the Sahara, or the East African coast), societies could become protohistoric, and eventually historical. Some African

societies therefore remained "prehistoric" until the nineteenth century when European explorers reached them and could record then in written form. To Clark and others, how one approached these societies depended on their degree of historical evidence; if they were genuinely prehistoric, then virtually everything was learned from archaeology, but for historic societies, archaeology had a different role to play. The agency of outsiders transformed these societies from prehistory (and an implied backwardness) into history and the modern world.

While this may seem a semantic argument, some scholars have used this as an excuse to characterise Africa as a kind of primitive backwater, a cultural museum. Despite the early work of the Pan African Congress to create a scientific rigour to the African past, historians, especially in Europe, remained unconvinced. Hugh Trevor-Roper, the Regius Professor of History at Oxford University, and later master of Peterhouse, Cambridge, in an often-quoted British Broadcasting Company radio talk show in 1963, was able to characterize prehistoric Africa as a place not worthy of study by historians, and as little more than the "unrewarding gyrations of barbarous tribes in picturesque but irrelevant corners of the globe: tribes, whose chief function in history, in my opinion, is to show to the present an image of the past from which, by history, it has escaped" (Trevor-Roper, 9–11).

Some British archaeologists even shared this general view. Sir Grahame Clark (whom Trevor-Roper succeeded as Master of Peterhouse) wrote the first general survey of the prehistory of the world in 1961, and is generally credited with giving the idea of prehistory its academic credibility. In his *World Prehistory*, Clark claimed that in Africa, primitive Lower Palaeolithic cultural traditions continued down to recent times, and that Europe was already, by 30,000 BCE, superior to some modern African societies. By the second edition in 1969, Clark viewed the continent's past in slightly less extreme terms:

> By comparison with the role it played during the earlier stages of prehistory Africa had...already relapsed into provincialism during the late Pleistocene. From this time much of the continent remained a kind of cultural museum in which archaic cultural traditions.... continued to adapt to ecological change and even on occasion to display idiosyncratic variations without contributing to the main course of human progress (Clark, 181).

While, in the twenty-first century, no archaeologist would subscribe to these ideas, there remains the suspicion that the concept of African prehistory was associated with an earlier generation of white archaeologists working within a colonial milieu. Archaeologists, for whom the absence of written documents is of no great concern, should have been uniquely placed to challenge the colonial orthodoxy, that Africa was a primitive backwater, ripe for Western improvement, with their own evidence. But it is only a full generation after many African countries gained independence that a new and radical view of the African past is emerging, based largely on nationalist archaeologies, rather than the neo-evolutionary models still employed by many archaeologists. These do not see Africa as a museum piece, but as a dynamic and innovative continent that made major contributions to the development of the ancient and medieval worlds, and which has important things to say about the human condition. Research by African scholars such as Felix Chami is even turning the classical sources into a powerful re-examination of Africa's role in the ancient world.

AFRICAN ARCHAEOLOGY AND THE THREE-AGE SYSTEM

African archaeologists (who when Clark and Trevor-Roper were writing were almost exclusively European) had already done much to establish the basic cultural sequences of the continent, but still reflected the prejudices of their time. Africa was placed within the Three-Age System, developed in Scandinavia in the eighteenth century to describe the archaeological sequences in prehistoric Europe. While Africa apparently had a Stone Age and an Iron Age, the almost complete absence of an intervening Bronze or Copper Age limited the universal application of this system of humankind's development. However, Stone Age and Iron Age are still employed widely as chronological descriptive terms in African archaeology.

The Old Stone Age in Europe was divided into three, and given the scientific sounding names of Lower, Middle and Upper Palaeolithic, while Africanists retained the more antiquarian, Early (2.6 million–200,000 years ago), Middle (200,000–40,000 years ago) and Late Stone Age 40,000–to recent "ethnographic" past), to broadly correspond to these divisions in Europe. The devisers of this system understood that there was a relationship between Europe and Africa during the Palaeolithic but could not have foreseen that many of the cultural and biological features of modern humans worldwide came from "out of Africa" as a succession of population radiations, beginning about 2 million years and ending about 40,000 years ago, rather than "into Africa" from a more developed Europe. New dating methods that are being employed on African materials show that anatomically modern humans, as well as the features that go with them such as the use of art and decoration, blade technologies, use of bone, broad spectrum economies, and long distance exchange systems extend into the Middle Stone Age, indeed largely define it. As recently as the 1990s these were all thought to be Late Stone Age features.

The second part of the Stone Age, the New Stone Age or Neolithic, has also been applied to Africa with considerable difficulty. Within Europe, the Neolithic was defined through introduction of farming (both the cultivation of crops, and the domestication of animals) to the hunter-gatherer societies (sometimes called Mesolithic), who either adopted agriculture themselves, or were replaced by migrating groups who already had the technology. In Europe, there was virtually no overlap between the hunter-gatherers and the farmers, except in the most extreme and marginal areas. This model does not work in Africa. Hunter-gatherers continued (and in some areas, continue) to live alongside farming societies, and indeed could maintain a very close relationship with them. The adoption of a mixed farming regime (employing both cultivated crops and domesticated animals), common in Europe was unusual in Africa. Domesticated animals, especially cattle in East Africa, or sheep in southern Africa, could be maintained without the need for cultivating crops. Where there is evidence for food processing in these societies, this is as likely using gathered wild grasses rather than cultivated crops. The recognition whether a particular seed, pulse, or animal bone recovered from an excavation was domesticated is often very difficult and frequently misidentified. The labelling of a particular African society as Neolithic is much more difficult than for comparable examples in Eurasia, and many archaeologist avoid using the term altogether.

Similar issues surround the African Iron Age. The smelting of iron ore developed in Anatolia during the second millennium BCE, and the technology spreads across Europe and Asia; like farming, it was either adopted by local societies or introduced through population movements, so that by about 600 BCE iron was in widespread use as weapons and everyday tools. In sub-Saharan Africa, the earliest reliable dates for iron metallurgy are also about 600 BCE, but the major point of controversy is whether it spread from the iron-using Mediterranean region (the Phoenicians living along the North African coast being a possible source) or more likely independently invented in the Sahel, West African forests and/or the interlacustrine area of East Africa. Unlike Europe, the take-up of the new iron technology was very variable within the complex mosaic of African societies during the first millennium BCE; some were able to smelt, others obtained iron through trade, while most continued to use stone, wood and bone as their main materials. The use of Iron Age is therefore normally confined to groups who are using iron on a systematically basis, and in particular with the village-based farming societies, generally thought to be Bantu speaking, that spread through Eastern and Southern Africa from the middle of the first millennium BCE onward.

CLASSIFICATION SYSTEMS
If the use of terms that originated in the European Three Age System appliedto the African past is inappropriate, then some other way of ordering the archaeological material needs to be found. Here systems have been introduced from outside the continent, although not exclusively from Europe. For the Stone Age, classification is largely based upon stone tool typology, as this is often what survives. The basic unit that is used is an *industry*, defined as where a number of similar types of stone tool co-exist in defined strata. They tend to be named after where the industry was first located, or the type-site where the analysis was undertaken. Early workers defined industries in a normative way; now statistical analysis, often involving multivariate tests, is employed. Once defined, industries can be dated through radiometric methods, such as

radiocarbon or uranium-series dating, and their spatial distribution can be plotted. Examples of Stone Age industries might include Howieson's Port or Wilton.

Industries are often grouped together as *technocomplexes*. In the earliest, the Olduvan and the Acheulean, the recognition of individual industries is very difficult, with a large degree of homogeneity across much of the continent—indeed extending over much of the Old World in the case of the Acheulean. It is only with the Middle Stone Age that one sees regional diversification and the emergence of definable industries. It is often unclear whether these classifications are recognizing evolutionary differences, as cognitive abilities improve, or cultural differences, between what later on would be classed as ethnic groups. Alongside these methods, some archaeologists have employed a developmental model, first proposed by Desmond Clark, where tools are seen as becoming more sophisticated, along a series of definable *modes*, ranging from pebble tools, handaxes, to prepared cores (mode 3), long blades (mode 4), and backed microliths (mode 5). This simple system has been widely criticized because of the occurrence of a single artifact type, whereas the assemblage will include many different types.

With the addition of ceramics to the archaeological assemblage from around 9,000 years ago, classification becomes more difficult, not least because different systems tend to be employed for stone tools and pottery. Ceramics are generally more culturally sensitive that stone tools and have more variables to classify. Early attempts to study ceramic-based societies used the concept of cultures—borrowed again from prehistoric Europe—which were thought to define ancient groups that included not just their pottery, but their rituals, art and settlements; the idea of a culture still persists in North and West Africa and the Nile Valley.

In East and southern Africa, most groups are defined by their pottery. Particular distinctive types of pottery were given the term *ware*, a rather ill-defined concept, but included a range of shapes, decoration, and sometimes fabric. In the twenty-first century, most ceramic classification has been statistical, although this is very time consuming. An alternative has been a version of the Mesoamerican type-variety system, which is able to place ceramics into *phases* (groups of types that are contemporary), *facies* (shared spatial distributions) and *traditions* (combining phases and facies). The most developed and intricate ceramic typologies have probably been developed in southern Africa, largely based on this system. Some archaeologists have even grouped several traditions together into much larger groups, like the techno-complexes of the stone tools, but the validity of this has not been widely accepted.

THE INTERDISCIPLINARITY OF AFRICAN ARCHAEOLOGY

This rather narrow discussion of what constitutes an archaeological entity (culture, ware, industry, and techno-complex) is, however, fundamental in the dealing with other disciplines, that also hope to narrate an African past. Most prominent of these has been historical linguistics, which has moved from the modeling of the movement of peoples to the full reconstruction of past diets and technologies. The correlation between the linguistic and the archaeological evidence has often been uncomfortable, often with the suspicion of circular arguments. The often-repeated refrain "how can pots talk" has been used against those who believe that is a one-to-one relationship between language groups and ceramic types. Such debates have flavored discussions of the Bantu migrations and a tendency by some archaeologists to doubt the prevailing orthodoxy. There has been scepticism by archaeologists for many of the dates proposed for early domestication by the linguists, notably Christopher Ehret. His reconstructions are often at odds with the existing archaeological evidence, although this evidence itself is very thin and poorly documented.

In the early years of the discipline in Africa, historians tended to view archaeological data as something to mine at will, to enable them to develop broad syntheses of the past. As the use of oral traditions as literal accounts of the past has been replaced by more nuanced interpretation, archaeological data has become important to enable some external control. However this data has often become too complex for many non-archaeologists to understand and archaeologists are prepared to write their own syntheses and debate existing historical interpretations. Historical archaeology is becoming a major part of the discipline, with archaeological data coming from the nineteenth or even twentieth centuries, where there may well be already a rich historical record. The potential challenge of archaeological evidence to established historical narratives (for examples the slave trade) would be interesting.

Archaeologists also work closely with anthropologists. Indeed biological anthropology and archaeology go back to the very first research, and has been fundamental in telling the story of human origins. The close relationship between human evolution, diet, and behavior can only be understood by linking the fossil record with the site distribution and material culture. Cultural anthropology has also contributed through the study of contemporary hunter-gatherer societies, as has the study of primate behaviors. The sub-discipline of ethnoarchaeology has also been important in contributing to the understanding of taphonomic processes (such as bone distribution on kill sites or predator activity). More generally, ethno-archaeology has been important in understanding iron-working, pottery production, cultural distributions and human activity patterning.

HISTORY OF AFRICAN ARCHAEOLOGY

North of the Sahara, archaeology has been practiced since the early nineteenth century. In Egypt the beginning of scientific investigation is normally attributed to the *savants*, who accompanied Napoleon's invasion (1798–1801) and led to the publication of the monumental *Description d'Egypte* (1809–1813). The decipherment of hieroglyphic writing by Champollion in 1822 enabled historical texts to be placed alongside monuments and tombs, so enabling a scholarly history to be developed. But the fascination in Egypt also led to the removal of many antiquities to private collections and European museums, and controls were only introduced in 1858, with the establishment of the Egyptian Antiquities Organisation. Scientific archaeology dates only from the 1880s, with the arrival of the English archaeologist Flinders Petrie, and a little later the American George Reisner, whose pioneer work in Nubia did much to link Egypt with its African hinterland.

The twentieth century saw a huge expansion in Egyptian archaeology, fueled by public fascination, tourism, and by those public museums whose collections were built up in the nineteenth century. There has been the need for major salvage campaigns required in the 1960s under the supervision of the United Nations Educational, Scientific and Cultural Organization (UNESCO) in the areas to be flooded by the Aswan High Dam in Nubia. The interest in Lower Nubia (by the early 1990s unfortunately largely flooded) stimulated other research beyond the classic sites of ancient Egypt, with work in the desert oases, on the Red Sea coast, in the Delta. Interest has also moved beyond the classic Pharaonic periods, into prehistoric and predynastic Egypt (first studied scientifically by Petrie) as well as the Greco-Roman, Byzantine, and Islamic periods. Modern Egyptology, which for many years was heavily literary-based, has moved into a scientific discipline, reliant upon geophysics, CT scanning, precision radiocarbon dating, and a range of analytical methods on the often well-preserved organic remains.

South of the Sahara, early research was confined to sites that demonstrated signs of "civilization." Ethiopia, for example, was visited by Henry Salt in 1809, and he left detailed records of the Aksumite monuments, but the first systematic recording was undertaken by the Deutsche Aksum Expedition in 1906, and published in 1913. Another area of early interest were the monuments of Great Zimbabwe, "discovered" by Karl Mauch in 1872, and seized upon by Cecil Rhodes as a way of legitimizing his imperial dream by locating a long-lost Phoenician civilization. He and his associates realized that money could also be made by looting sites of their gold, and went to the lengths of setting up the Rhodesian Ancient Ruins Company. Great Zimbabwe was reserved however for scientific investigation, although in practice unsystematically dug over, first by Theodore Bent and then by R. N. Hall in the search for Phoenician artifacts.

The London establishment did not accept Hall's conclusions, and in 1905 sent an experienced Mediterranean archaeologist, David Randall McIver, to investigate the site. He concluded that the site was indigenous and medieval in date, although controversy continued until a remarkable all female expedition was sent out in 1929, led by Gertrude Caton Thompson. The careful use of excavation, the recording of stratigraphy, and placement of monuments within their landscape were all new methods in archaeology, and her conclusions caused a storm at the time, not just among the settlers, but also respected archaeologists such as Raymond Dart.

The first Pan African Congress, held in Nairobi in 1947 was an important moment in the development of African archaeology. The discipline moved, south of the Sahara, from the work of individual pioneers to a formative stage. There were signs before World War II that research needed to be undertaken on a systematic basis, and in 1937 the two great pioneers of African archaeology, Desmond Clark and Thurston Shaw, were in posts that enabled them to undertake some fieldwork. Louis Leakey had begun his research in East Africa in 1926, and had published his *Stone Age Cultures of Kenya Colony* in 1931, followed by *Stone Age Africa* in 1936, and was beginning to establish the claim that Africa was the cradle of humankind.

The 1950s and 1960s saw the steady growth of archaeological activity. While the study of human origins attracted the largest share of worldwide publicity (and research grants), the discipline broadened to establish detailed regional sequences and multiperiod excavations, enhanced by the new technique of radiocarbon dating. Iron Age archaeology and the problem of Bantu origins were one particular focus of research, as was the East African coast, under Neville Chittick (working for the British Institute in Eastern Africa) and James Kirkman. National museums were now being established, and legislation was put in place to preserve sites and antiquities.

With many African countries gaining independence, archaeology and museums were neither high on the legacy "wish list" of projects that colonial powers might leave behind, nor on the development agenda of the new nations. Furthermore, very few local archaeologists had been trained, and some nations relied on expatriates to fill important administrative positions for a number of years. Some universities were able to offer archaeological training within their history departments. Outside South Africa (where there were well-established archaeology departments at Cape Town, Witswaterrand, and Pretoria), the first freestanding departments were in Legon (Ghana) in 1957 and Ibadan (Nigeria) in 1970, followed by Dar es Salaam (Tanzania) in 1982. In the late twentieth century, there were a number of initiatives to train African archaeologists to postdoctoral standard, of which the most notable was that in the 1990s supported by the Swedish government's SAREC program, which enabled twenty-five students to gain their doctorates in East African archaeology, many of whom serve in university posts in the late 2000s.

METHODS AND MODELS

Modern archaeological research in Africa looks very different to that even conducted in the 1990s, when it was described by Clark in the earlier edition to this encyclopedia. During this period, for example, the digital revolution has changed fundamentally how data can be handled and stored. Archaeology recovers huge quantities of data, from individual sherds, stone tools, and ecofacts to site information, and the ready availability of laptops mean that projects are able to undertake data analysis in the field. Consequently, it is possible to undertake increasingly sophisticated statistical analysis, rather than rely upon simple descriptions and crude counting methods.

At the same time, archaeology has moved away from site based excavations into what is broadly termed landscape archaeology. This has been greatly helped by the availability of hand-held GPS devices that provide accurate site location, especially useful where detailed maps are unavailable. The combination of data sets and Geographical Information Systems mean that landscapes can be understood and manipulated in new ways, while the availability of both satellite and air photography assist site location and analysis. Landscape survey can be based upon testable methods, using sampling strategies, linked to shovel and test pits or coring to model for example site density at particular times, or the way different groups or societies used the landscape. It is possible to generate real figures of predicted site density on only 5 to 10 percent of samples. Geophysics is beginning to be used beyond Egypt (where it routinely produces spectacular results), and has the potential to plot the extent and form of pits, postholes, walls and ditches, without the need for excavation.

Scientific analysis is also becoming routine, and laboratories in South Africa have become world leaders in archaeological science. Radiometric dating, in particular radiocarbon, have been applied to African sites since the early 1960s. High precision and AMS dating enables more accurate dates, or dates taken from small samples (such as individual seeds) or very old material. Precision has been greatly enhanced by a southern African radiocarbon calibration curve

available since 1993 and developed at the Pretoria laboratory. Other routinely used methods include potassium argon (K-Ar) dating, uranium-series and obsidian hydration, where dates lie outside the range of radiocarbon, or samples of carbon are unavailable. One of the most exciting new methods, developed at Cape Town University, employs isotopes of carbon and nitrogen to map ancient diet patterns through surviving bone collagen. It has also been possible to trace movement of animals (and potentially humans), through oxygen isotopes preserved in tooth enamel. The recovery of environmental samples from excavations—sometimes using routine floatation methods, but also in the microscopic analysis of soils to locate phytoliths—allow ancient plants remains to be recovered.

THE FUTURE

Archaeology in Africa in 2007 is very much at a crossroads. Security problems have curtailed fieldwork several across parts of the continent of great archaeological interest. Economic collapse has also made research very difficult, with the ethical concerns of undertaking academic research in such conditions. As the amount of European and American sponsored research has declined, it has not really been replaced by local initiatives, even though the number of trained African archaeologists is greater now than at any time in the past.

There is nonetheless a considerable excitement about the future directions. Two examples can be cited. The challenge laid down by global DNA studies, which provide the clearest indication of the "out of Africa" model of human origins, mean that the archaeological evidence for human evolution in Africa is one of the great scientific questions of the age. The year 2007 marks the 200th anniversary of the British abolition of the trade in slaves, and with this renewed global interest in the role Africa played in the supply of unfree human labor, both across the Atlantic, but also in antiquity, and in the Indian Ocean. Historical archaeology has an important part to play to retell this story, especially by those whose left no or few documents behind and often have no voice.

It has been exactly 100 years since the first scientific work south of the Sahara at Aksum and Great Zimbabwe. During the intervening period, African archaeology has been largely in the hands of

European and American trained archaeologists, and the narratives that they have written have perforce given a Eurocentric perspective to an African past. National archaeologies, written by locally trained scholars, will hopefully emerge that are better able to assist in the continent's development, by helping to understand the immense cultural diversity and human achievements over the last 2.5 million years.

See also **Aksum; Anthropology, Social, and the Study of Africa; Ceramics; History of Africa; Human Evolution: Origins of Modern Humans; Leakey, Louis and Mary; Linguistics, Historical; Linguistics and the Study of Africa; Nubia; Rhodes, Cecil John; Slave Trades; Travel and Exploration.**

BIBLIOGRAPHY

Chami, Felix. *The Unity of African Ancient History: 3000 BC to AD 500*. Dar es Salaam: E and D, 2006.

Clark, Grahame. *World Prehistory: A New Outline*. Cambridge, U.K.: Cambridge University Press, 1969.

Clark, J. Desmond. *The Prehistory of Africa*. New York: Praeger, 1970.

Connah, Graham. *African Civilisations, an Archaeological Perspective*, 2nd edition. Cambridge, U.K.: Cambridge University Press, 2001.

Ehret, Christopher. *An African Classical Age Eastern and Southern Africa in World History 1000 BC to AD 400*. Charlottesville: University Press of Virginia, 1998.

Ehret, Christopher. *Civilizations of Africa: A History to 1800*. Charlottesville: University Press of Virginia, 2002.

Hall, Martin. *Archaeology Africa*. Cape Town: David Philip, 1996.

Phillipson, David. *African Archaeology*, 3rd edition. Cambridge, U.K.: Cambridge University Press, 2005.

Robertshaw, Peter, ed. *A History of African Archaeology*. London: James Currey, 1990.

Shaw, Thurston; Paul Sinclair; Bassey Andah; and Alex Okpoko. *The Archaeology of Africa: Food, Metal and Towns*. London: Routledge, 1993.

Stahl, Ann B., ed. *African Archaeology: A Critical Introduction*. Oxford: Blackwell Publishing, 2005.

Trevor-Roper, Hugh. *The Rise of Christian Europe*. London: Thames and Hudson, 1965.

MARK HORTON

TOOLS AND TECHNOLOGIES

Technology, the manufacture and use of tools, is commonly employed by two extant species in Africa: human beings (*Homo sapiens*) and the chimpanzee (*Pan troglodytes*). Technology can be seen generally as learned, culturally transmitted behavior that is key to gaining greater resources from an environment. One makes an investment in one part of that environment—a tool—so as to focus one's energy and amplify one's gains. It may seem surprising that technology is not more widely used by other species, but making and using tools depends on high intelligence, behavioral flexibility, and suitable anatomy. Since the time of a common ancestor, perhaps 8 million years ago, the forebears of both chimpanzees and humans have been characterized by relatively large brains, manipulative hands, and advanced hand-eye coordination. Some of these traits are characteristic of all primates, but they are particularly developed in apes and even more so in hominids. In human ancestors, marked brain enlargement is visible beginning about 2 million years ago.

EARLIEST TOOL USE

Since the chimpanzee is an African species, and since the oldest known hominids also come from the continent, it seems likely that technology has its origins in Africa. The chimpanzee's level of technology may provide some idea of how such behavior may have first been acquired by hominids, although it is far from certain that even the simplest technology goes back to the common ancestor: it may have developed separately in the descendant species. The gorilla is closely related to both hominids and chimpanzees, but only in 2005 was discovered also to use tools. Evidence of chimpanzees suggests that initial technology involved the use of modified plant resources, such as stripped branches and stems, coupled perhaps with stones, the latter used as anvils and hammers. It is common to distinguish between tool-use and tool-making, and chimpanzees have certainly crossed the threshold to the latter, as demonstrated, for example, by the way they prepare stems for fishing termites.

There is no archaeological record of chimpanzee tools (except for recent stone chips made accidentally on a West African site), and so it is extremely unlikely that archaeologists will ever find the earliest hominid products. A key step that would have made early hominid technology potentially visible as an archaeological record was the introduction of flaked stone tools. The development of this technology probably took place between 2.5 and 3 million years ago. Stone tools have not been found at the earliest sites where there is abundant evidence of hominids—Laetoli in Tanzania (3.56–3.77 million years ago) and Hadar in Ethiopia (2.8–3.2 million years ago)—but they have been found in the upper levels at Hadar. Here volcanic ashes labeled BKT2 and BKT3 are probably to be dated in the period 2.4–2.6 million years ago. Stone artifacts have been located in and above these levels.

Other sites nearly as old where some stone tools have been found are in Senga, by the Semliki River in eastern Zaire; on the shores of Lake Turkana (East and West) in Kenya; and perhaps also in Malawi and Israel. Flaked stone tools become more plentiful a little later, as evidenced at Olduvai Gorge Bed I in Tanzania and in the KBS tuff (a principal volcanic ash) at East Turkana; both sites have been dated to 1.8–1.9 million years ago. All these artifacts can be grouped into a variable tradition named the "Oldowan" after Olduvai Gorge ("Olduvan" to some authors). This tradition is characterized by simple but skillful knapping (flaking) of the stone, which yields both core and flake components. In conventional classifications, such as the typology devised by Mary Leakey at Olduvai, the Oldowan includes named tool types such as choppers, discoids, and scrapers.

Early artifacts were made in forms that recur regularly, but researchers do not know their functions, and are not agreed about the extent to which form represents design content. Some scholars believe that the artifacts were intentionally made according to patterns; others, that any regularities result from inevitable common factors of material and function, which induced the early hominids to follow paths of least resistance. More complex shapes, however, are present in varieties of the Developed Oldowan tradition, which appeared in eastern and southern Africa at about 1.6 million years ago. These include the keeled, heavy-duty "scrapers" of the Karari industry found on many sites at East Turkana, and tools from Swartkrans in South Africa. There is near consensus among archaeologists that more complex designs appear during the Acheulean phase, starting about 1.6 million years ago.

All together, the early artifact material is quite informative about early hominid behavior; it also raises numerous questions, including these three basic ones: What advantages did the artifacts offer early hominids? What abilities did crafting and using them require? What social information about the early hominids do the tools record, which otherwise scholars would not have?

ADVANTAGES OF TECHNOLOGY

Experimental work and replication, as much as excavation, help in answering the first question. The early tools provided sharp, robust edges and a component of battering power. They might have been used to allow the early hominid to cut his way rapidly into a carcass, thus gaining meat either ahead of other predators or even after they had taken the main share. These tools would have enabled hominids to process hides and to cut tendons. They may have been even more useful in the processing of plant materials for food, and perhaps also for preparing other artifacts. These may have included digging sticks and possibly containers. Since such materials are perishable, one would expect very little evidence of them to survive. The first direct evidence of wooden tools in Africa comes about 200,000 years ago at Kalambo Falls, in the form of a wooden club and other sticks, preserved in permanently waterlogged deposits. Microscopic wear analysis of stone tools suggests that wood was worked far earlier, as much as 1.5 million years ago, and evidence of the use of wood on other continents reaches to about 800,000 years ago.

SKILLS REQUIRED BY TECHNOLOGY

The abilities required for making the earliest stone tools appear to be greater than those possessed by chimpanzees as seen in the wild, although some scholars argue that the conceptual abilities of chimpanzees and early hominids are on a par. Recent experiments have shown that the pygmy chimpanzee Kanzi (kept in captivity and researched by Nicholas Toth) can strike flakes from stone cobbles. Even so, researchers such as Toth are not convinced that such efforts match those of early hominids: even early artifacts show a pattern of competent knapping, with few basic errors.

Why do chimpanzees, who use simple tools, have no flaked industry comparable to the Oldowan? This is a particularly intriguing question because the environments of chimpanzees overlap with those of early hominids. The large shearing teeth that chimpanzees have may provide a partial answer. Chimpanzees may not have been subject to great enough pressures to develop either the habit of stoneworking or the necessary intelligence. It follows that hominids were subject to such pressures. In evolution it often happens that creatures make an advantageous behavioral change, and this is then followed by genetic selection for the advantage, leading to obvious physical changes in subsequent generations. The record suggests that by the time they adopted stone tools hominids had already evolved bipedalism and lost the large front dentition of apes. Possibly, if confronted with a need or opportunity for a change of environment at that stage, they would have been required to adopt different responses than apes.

SOCIAL INFORMATION IN THE ARCHAEOLOGICAL RECORD

Unfortunately most social information about the earlier hominids is indirect, and it is not known which lineages of hominid made stone tools. The simplest taxonomic view of hominids identifies two main groups: the robust australopithecines and the more gracile species, one of which led to *Homo sapiens*. Eastern and southern Africa provide us with a picture of regional and local diversification. In eastern Africa three lines of *Homo* are recognized in the crucial period of 2.0–1.7 million years ago, but there is no direct evidence as to which made stone tools. Both *Homo habilis* and *Homo erectus* probably engaged in toolmaking. Australopithecines were commonly thought not to be toolmakers, but their developed thumbs may suggest otherwise, as may polished bones at Swartkrans in South Africa. Nevertheless, the robust australopithecines became extinct about 1 million years ago, without any visible impact on toolmaking traditions.

Stone artifacts do provide valuable insights into the use of landscape. Hominids found the best sources of suitable rocks for making tools and sometimes transported the materials for many miles. At East Turkana studies of transport suggest size grading, with smaller pieces being found at the greatest distance from their sources. This indicates that hominids made value decisions. The movement of rocks also suggests size of territories, an aspect important for comparison with apes. The late Glynn Isaac referred to such rocks as Stone Age "visiting cards." In Olduvai Gorge Bed I most pieces have been transported fewer than 3 miles, but movements of approximately 8 miles are known. By 1.0 million years ago many pieces were carried 12 miles, and distances of 62 miles are involved in the transport of rare obsidian tools to the Gadeb site in Ethiopia.

THE GREAT HAND AX TRADITION

The Stone Age record can be followed through the Pleistocene in Africa. A significant step forward came with the introduction of the long-axis artifacts known as bifaces or hand axes. Sites where these are found are far more common than Oldowan sites and are placed in the Acheulean tradition. The Acheulean extended outside Africa but probably began on the continent, since Africa has the oldest sites, including Olduvai and Peninj in Tanzania and Konso-Gardula in Ethiopia, all aged 1.4–1.5 million years. Similar finds of later date are known from hundreds of sites all over Africa, including the Sahara and the west.

Hand axes are the most common bifaces: they are usually between 3 and 10 inches long and roughly walnut-shaped, with a somewhat pointed end. Their use function is uncertain—they are useful for skinning animals but occur in such great concentrations that other uses must be implied, perhaps in plant preparation. Other forms of biface include picks and ax-edged cleavers. These are not the only tools: smaller flakes were as important as ever, and other forms such as scrapers persist. The Acheulean is best known from a number of sites in eastern Africa, such as Kalambo Falls, Olorgesailie, Kilombe, and Isenya, most aged between 1 million and 300,000 years, but also from major South African sites such as Sterkfontein, Amanzi and Montagu Cave.

Numbers of finds suggest that the Acheulean is linked with the hominid species *Homo erectus*. Findspots of human remains include Olduvai, Lake Ndutu, and Konso-Gardula. Later Acheulean sites, however, fall within the time range of *Homo sapiens*. One of the earliest known specimens of this species, from Bodo in Ethiopia, was found close to large numbers of bifaces. The continuity of the stone technology suggests that the species boundary between *erectus* and early *sapiens* may be an artificial one.

Until the 1950s, it was assumed that a line of progress could be drawn through the Acheulean, from primitive beginnings to later sophistication. But an aspect of "variable sameness" has become apparent, with some late sites resembling much earlier ones. Mary Leakey could discern no progress through the Acheulean at Olduvai, which provides the longest site record—over a million years.

Nevertheless, new features of toolmaking do appear from as much as 400,000 years ago. These technological developments roughly parallel the evolution of early modern *Homo sapiens sapiens* from more archaic ancestors. Refinements of technology—allowing greater concentration of power for less effort—may have played some part in the "gracilization" of the human skeleton, which was largely complete by 100,000 years ago. They may be part of a package of "modern behavior." The developments include the Levallois technique, used for creating both biface blanks and other flakes. Examples of this technique are seen in artifacts that date from as far back as 280,000 years ago, discovered at Kapthurin in eastern Africa and at Tabelbalet and Casablanca in the north. The desired tools were achieved by shaping the core through flaking, and then releasing the Levallois piece entire by one final blow.

Some authors now reject the idea of a progression through the Stone Age, but to do so betrays the basic record: there is no doubt that the Oldowan is followed by the Acheulean and the Acheulean by more refined later industries. The best model appears to be one of a "stasis" nevertheless overprinted by a long-term gradient toward more elaborate forms, largely obscured by the "noise" of random variations that can, at best, only partly be explained.

LATER DEVELOPMENTS

Around 150,000 years ago the Acheulean biface forms started to fall into disuse, although their end point cannot be identified exactly. This is partly because of the limits to the precision of dating techniques but also because there is no natural archaeological boundary. Although there is no solid documentation of artifacts such as the spear-thrower or the bow and arrow, hafting of tools is one major development certainly attested. It was present in simplest form 400,000 years ago at Schöningen in Germany. By 100,000 years ago it probably involved skilful use of glue or fixing twine, as evidenced by projectile points rather similar to miniature bifaces which appeared in many areas of Africa. In parts of central and southern Africa rough and heavy bifacial implements were used in the Sangoan and Lupemban traditions. Small crescent tools, as in the Howieson's Poort industry of South Africa, appear to confirm the use of hafting. The emergence of more modern humans and refined technologies around the end of the Acheulean may be seen as the beginning of what some scholars refer to as the "human revolution.". The period generally known as the African Middle Stone Age begins at least 200,000 years ago by many reckonings. In addition to its regional variety, and the delicately flaked points and other small tools of some areas, it is marked by use of bone tools, and first signs of personal decoration, as in pierced shells from Blombos Cave in South Africa. Technology thus developed on many fronts, and its link with the emergence of modern humans is increasingly strong.

See also **Early Human Society, History of (c. 50,000 BP to 19,000 BCE); Leakey, Louis and Mary; Prehistory; Technological Specialization Period, History of (c. 19,000 to 5000 BCE).**

BIBLIOGRAPHY

Chavaillon, Jean. "Africa during the Lower Paleolithic and the First Settlements." In *The History of Humanity*, Vol. 1, ed. S. J. De Laet et al. New York: Routledge/UNESCO, 1994.

Gamble, Clive. *Timewalkers: The Prehistory of Global Colonization.* Stroud: Alan Sutton, 1994.

Gowlett, John A. J. *Ascent to Civilization: The Archaeology of Early Humans*, 2nd edition. New York: McGraw-Hill, 1994.

Isaac, Barbara, ed. *The Archaeology of Human Origins' Papers by Glynn Isaac.* Cambridge, U.K.: Cambridge University Press, 1989.

Isaac, Glynn L. "The Archaeology of Human Origins." In *Advances in World Archaeology*, Vol. 3, ed. Fred Wendorf and Angela Close. London and San Diego, CA: Academic Press, 1984.

Kibunjia, M. "Pliocene Archaeological Occurrences in the Lake Turkana Basin." *Journal of Human Evolution* 27 (1994): 159–171.

Klein R. G. *The Human Career: Human Biological and Cultural Origins*, 2nd edition. Chicago: University of Chicago Press, 1999.

McGrew, W. C. *Chimpanzee Material Culture: Implications for Human Evolution*. Cambridge, U.K.: Cambridge University Press, 1992.

Mitchell, P. *The Archaeology of Southern Africa*. Cambridge, U.K.: Cambridge University Press, 2002.

Schick, Kathy D., and Nicholas Toth. *Making Silent Stones Speak: Human Evolution and the Dawn of Technology*. New York: Simon and Schuster, 1993.

Toth, Nicholas, and Kathy D. Schick. "The First Million Years: The Archaeology of Protohuman Culture." In *Advances in Archaeological Method and Theory*, Vol. 9, ed. Michael B. Schiffer. New York: Academic Press, 1986.

JOHN A. J. GOWLETT

STONE AGE SOCIETIES

Until recently, archaeologists used the term Stone Age to refer to prehistoric hunter-gatherer societies and their evolutionary ancestors who lived before plant and animal domestication. Since the early 1900s, archaeologists have divided the African record into periods defined by changes in stone tool-making techniques because stone is the most enduring of materials used and, as such, provides a record of continuity and human behavioral changes. The Stone Age as a time period, however, encompassed profound changes in human anatomy, cognition, society, and technology, including the development of tools made from bone, wood, and clay—not just stone. Biological and behavioral evolution cannot easily be constrained within arbitrarily defined ages based on stone tool technology alone. Because of this, the term Stone Age is being replaced by frameworks of comparison based on the global sequence of glacial cycles that characterizes the past 1.8 million years of the Pleistocene geological era.

In sub-Saharan Africa, the Stone Age has traditionally been separated into three sequential Ages: the Early, Middle, and Later Stone Ages. In western and northern Africa, a European-derived terminology was applied, also divided into three periods: the Lower, Middle, and Upper Palaeolithic (Palaeolithic = Old Stone Age). The two systems of classification recognized broadly equivalent changes in technology.

The Early Stone Age and Lower Paleolithic both include the first flaked-stone technology called the Oldowan industry, named after the site of Olduvai Gorge, Tanzania, where it was first formally defined and dated. Oldowan tools are sharp flakes of stone created by striking together two blocks of stone so that the angle of blow by the hammer stone detaches a flake from the other block (the core). The core may also be used as a chopping tool. Such apparently simple tools require an understanding of the interplay between the physical properties of stone, the geometry of the core, and the angle and force of the strike needed to detach flakes. These basic abilities are beyond those observed among contemporary chimpanzees that use tools in the wild or in captivity. Early hominins (humans/human ancestors) used flakes and choppers to extract meat and marrow from carcasses—probably scavenged rather than hunted—and perhaps made other tools, such as digging sticks. The Oldowan tools date to between 2.6 and 1.5 million years ago, appearing first in eastern and then in southern Africa; it was also the first technology to be found outside Africa.

The earliest Oldowan tools could have been made by more than one species of hominin, including *Paranthropus boisei*, *Australopithecus garhi*, and more than one species of early *Homo* who all lived in East Africa and whose remains are sometimes found with Oldowan artifacts. There is no undisputed evidence that any of these species hunted game or behaved in ways recognizable to early twenty-first century hunter-gatherers. Around 1.8 million years ago, one species of Homo, *Homo erectus*, is found with Early Stone Age tools, and this species is the first known to have spread outside Africa into Asia and Europe. Homo erectus is also the species that harnessed fire as a tool for warmth, protection, cooking, tool-making, and possibly as a focus of social life around hearths. Early, but disputed, evidence for fire between 1.5–1.0 million years ago comes from Koobi Fora and Chesowanja, Kenya, and from Swartkrans Cave, South Africa.

Oldowan technology continued to be used after 1.5 million years ago, but Homo erectus appeared to have made new, more complex tool forms. The Early Stone Age saw the development of bifaces, elongated cutting tools formed by removing flakes on either side of a single geometric plane. The handaxes and cleavers of the Early Stone Age are characteristic of the Acheulean industry (named after the site of St. Acheul, France). They represent greater dexterity in the shaping of stone and required the maker have a mental image of the final shape. This level of premeditation marks a cognitive advance over the flakes and chopper-cores of the Oldowan tools.

The planning involved in making bifaces may have been learned by observation, or taught by parents to offspring. The deliberate transmission of technological and social information between generations is a feature of human societies, and the regularity of handaxes appearance at archaeological sites may reflect social learning among Homo erectus groups, but the role of language in the process is unknown. Indirect anatomical evidence from the skeleton of a Homo erectus boy found at Nariokotome, Kenya, dated to 1.5 million years ago, suggests this species had limited linguistic ability. However, it was the first hominin to have an extended childhood, suggesting a period of cultural learning. Its tall modern-like physique (males 5'8", females 5'1") suggests it was well adapted to ranging long distances during the heat of daylight hours in search of food and water. It is not known if these hominins behaved like modern hunter-gatherers and shared food with kin, but with males only 20–30 percent larger than females (sexual dimorphism), their societies may have involved more cooperation between males than earlier hominin societies where size differences were greater. The role of hunting and meat in their lives is uncertain, but brain size increased during the time of erectus (1.8–0.5 million years) from 335 cubic inches to 433 cubic inches, suggesting this species was able to meet the high energy and protein demands of this organ, especially during early childhood.

The physical, technological, and social abilities of Homo erectus explain its widespread occurrence across Africa (and Eurasia), except for the Congo Basin. Bifaces continued to be made for more than one million years with some refinements, but the overall longevity and conservatism of this technology distinguishes the Early Stone Age from later

periods that see more rapid rates of technological and behavioral changes.

Between 400,000 and 200,000 years ago, a fundamental change in technology took place. Stone edges, mounted in handles or shafts of wood, bone, ivory, or other organic materials, largely replaced the hand-held tools of the Early Stone Age. The innovation of hafted, or composite, tool technology gave greater killing power to thrown stone-tipped spears, improved food security, and reduced the risk of close encounters with dangerous animals. Hafting was also a more efficient way of using stone, enabling people to develop new types of tools for specific purposes and to colonize areas where stone resources were scarce (such as the Congo Basin). These changes marked the transition from the Early to Middle Stone Age (Lower to Middle Palaeolithic), and were made by *Homo heidelbergensis*, the first species to have a brain in the size range of early twenty-first century humans. (472–551 cubic inches).

The first evidence for the use of symbols, and indirectly for language, occurs in the Middle Stone Age, perhaps with Homo heidelbergensis. Claims have been made for symbol use beginning as early as 300,000 years ago in central Africa, pointing to the use of ochre pigments associated with a new and distinctive type of tool, the Lupemban point. This early evidence remains controversial because ochre could be used for purposes that are not necessarily symbolic. Most archaeologists agree that symbol use and most other behaviors associated with modern hunter-gatherers are present by 77,000 years ago in southern Africa, and perhaps elsewhere across the continent. The strongest evidence for symbol use comes from the site of Blombos Cave, South Africa, where shell beads were found with engraved pieces of ochre and bone (Rock-art paintings on portable slabs or cave walls appeared after 27,000 years ago, and is generally associated with the Later Stone Age).

Elaborations of composite technology are recognized by the term Later Stone Age (Upper Paleolithic in North Africa) that refers to the systematic production of long, thin blade-like inserts used to make a wider range of tools. Later Stone Age blade technologies first appeared in East Africa after 50,000 years ago at the site of Enkapune ya Muto, Kenya, and were found across the continent by 20,000 year ago, perhaps associated with the spread of the bow and arrow. Unlike the earlier two ages, the Later Stone Age may be linked with historic hunter-gatherers in southern Africa, in particular the San speaking peoples of the Kalahari, whose ancestors were widespread across the subcontinent before the arrival of herders and farmers 2000 years ago. The Later Stone Age is associated not just with stone tool technology, but with the broad range of behaviors seen with modern hunter-gatherers, including the use of symbols (art) linked to beliefs, formation of alliance networks, burial rites, and a highly mobile life linked to seasonal variations in the availability of water, plants, and animals. These are all recognizably twenty-first century behaviors that have their roots in the Middle Stone Age. In the past 10,000 years, most Later Stone Age hunter-gatherers developed or adopted farming and herding. For many, the making of stone tools remained a practical use of resources, even alongside iron. Technologically they would be Stone Age peoples, but economically they were dependent on domesticated foods.

See also **Agriculture; Art, Genres and Periods: Rock Art, Eastern Africa; Art, Genres and Periods: Rock Art, Saharan and Northern Africa; Art, Genres and Periods: Rock Art, Southern Africa; Human Evolution: Origins of Modern Humans; Production Strategies; Technological Specialization Period, History of (c. 19,000 to 5000 BCE).**

BIBLIOGRAPHY

Deacon, Hilary J., and Janette Deacon. *Human Beginnings in South Africa: Uncovering the Secrets of the Stone Age.* Lanham, MD: AltaMira Press, 1999.

Klein, Richard G. *The Human Career*, 2nd edition. Chicago: University of Chicago Press, 1999.

Mitchell, Peter. *The Archaeology of Southern Africa.* Cambridge, U.K.: Cambridge University Press, 2002.

Phillipson, David. *African Archaeology*, 3rd edition. Cambridge, U.K.: Cambridge University Press, 2005.

Stringer, Chris, and Peter Andrews. *The Complete World of Human Evolution.* London: Thames and Hudson, 2005.

LAWRENCE S. BARHAM

HISTORICAL

Historical archaeology first emerged as a distinct subfield of the broader discipline in North America during the mid-twentieth century. Initial studies focused on the remains of buildings, artifacts, and settlements associated with European colonization for which documentary sources also survived. Attempts to tie written sources to material traces of civilization and assess them against one another remain primary concerns. Although the field has matured significantly since the mid-twentieth century, there remain considerable variation in definitions, methodologies, and theoretical underpinnings. For many scholars, historical archaeology is concerned primarily with examining the impact of European expansion (c. 1500 onward), through the combined study of archaeological remains and associated historical sources that include oral, cartographic, and photographic materials as well as written texts. For some, this limits their studies to the archaeology of the modern world; others emphasize such themes as the impact of colonialism and/or mercantile and industrial capitalism.

RESEARCH THEMES IN AFRICA

All of these themes have been pursued by archaeologists working on the African continent; investigating the archaeology of European contact has had particular influence on research in southern, and to a lesser degree, West Africa. In other parts of the continent different strategies have been employed. James Kirkman, the first scholar to employ the term "historical archaeology" with reference to African materials, clearly employed the texts of various classical authors (most notably the second-century CE *Periplus of the Erythrean Sea*) and somewhat later Arabic sources to interpret the origins and development of urbanism and transoceanic trade among the Swahili peoples of the eastern Africa littoral.

In North Africa, Arabic texts are emphasized over those in European languages; much of the historical archaeology in this region has studied urbanization during the Islamic period and the extent to which these cities corresponded to the Islamic ideal. Late-twentieth-century studies, however, moved away from text-driven approaches, and sought instead to juxtapose the emergence and transformation of Islamic societies against broader the backgrounds of state formation, discontinuities between rural and urban economies, and European trade with Africa.

Other themes include the archaeology of slavery, the African diaspora, and the influence of Christian missions. Much work on the latter has been influenced by the writings of John and Jean Comaroff, who claim that missionary endeavors changed not only house forms, but spatial organization of settlements, patterns of consumption, and even artifact styles and decorative practices. The various slave trades with their socioeconomic and cultural consequences also offer rich research potential in oral, written, and material records. Although most studies have concentrated on the Atlantic slave trade in West and Southern Africa, new studies in East and northeast Africa have begun to demonstrate that older patterns of cultural interaction and exchange were radically disrupted by the increased demand for slaves in the Arab world during the eighteenth and nineteenth centuries. The transformation of African cultural identities and "creolization" as a consequence of the Atlantic slave trade also feature prominently in studies of the African diaspora throughout the New World, alongside more specific studies of the material dimensions of Maroon culture and the archaeology of race.

ORAL SOURCES AND ALTERNATIVE VOICES

One common distinction often made in Western archaeology—between prehistory and later periods (however defined)—is often avoided by those who work in Africa, usually to counter the negative implication of a lack or absence of history. Such distinctions are further blurred by the rich vein of historical information about Africa's multifaceted past that is found in oral traditions. This information is frequently used among those working on virtually any aspect of the continent's later Holocene archaeology. While archaeological data may be able to verify some oral sources by tying physical evidence to stories of migration or similar claims made about origins common among many African ethnic groups, some scholars view historical sources—oral, documentary, material and/or linguistic—as parallel histories rather than a single narrative.

Recent examples of this latter approach to historical archaeology on the African continent include Richard Helm's 2004 reexamination of Shungwaya traditions concerning the origin of the Mijikenda on the coastal hinterland of Kenya, Johnny van Schalkwyk and Benjamin Smith's 2004 examination of the contrasting accounts and related material evidence concerning the Malebho war of 1894 between the Hananwa and the government of the South African Republic, and Ann Stahl's 2001 appraisal of the multiple histories of Banda and Ghana and changing patterns of consumption beginning in the sixteenth century. In these studies, any bias against different types of evidence were identified, and contemporary and/or historical power relationships that drove particular interpretations of the past teased out, allowing the resultant dissonance between the various sources to be heard. Such strategies are considered essential if archaeologists wish to generate the kind of alternative histories of Africa's pasts as argued for by Bassey Andah, in which the voices of marginal and subaltern groups are heard alongside those of dominant elites and the politically powerful.

See also **Diasporas; Early Human Society, History of (c. 50,000 BP to 19,000 BCE); Prehistory; Research: Historical Resources; Slave Trades; Technological Specialization Period, History of (c. 19,000 to 5000 BCE).**

BIBLIOGRAPHY

Andah, Bassey. "Studying African Societies in Cultural Context." In *Making Alternative Histories*, ed. Peter Schmidt and Thomas Patterson. Santa Fe, NM: School of American Research Advanced Seminar Series, 1995.

Boone, James; Emlen Myers; and Charles Redman. "Archaeological and Historical Approaches to Complex Societies: The Islamic States of Medieval Morocco." *American Anthropologist* 92 (1990): 630–646.

Comaroff, John L., and Jean Comaroff. *Of Revelation and Revolution: Christianity, Colonialism and Consciousness in South Africa.* Chicago: University of Chicago Press, 1991.

DeCorse, Christopher, ed. *West Africa during the Atlantic Slave Trade.* Leicester: University of Leicester Press, 2001.

Funari, Pedro; Martin Hall; and Siân Jones; eds. *Historical Archaeology: Back from the Edge.* London: Routledge, 1999.

Hall, Martin. "The Archaeology of Colonial Settlement in Southern Africa." *Annual Reviews in Anthropology* (1993) 22: 177–200.

Helm, Richard. "Re-Evaluating Traditional Histories on the Coast of Kenya: An Archaeological Perspective."

In *African Historical Archaeologies*, ed. Andrew Reid and Paul Lane. London: Kluwer Academic/Plenum Publishers, 2004.

Kusimba, Chapurukha. "Archaeology of Slavery in East Africa." *African Archaeological Review* 21, no. 2 (2004): 59–88.

Reid, Andrew, and Paul Lane, eds. *African Historical Archaeologies*. London: Kluwer Academic/Plenum Publishers, 2004.

Stahl, Ann. *Making History in Banda: Anthropological Vision's of Africa's Past*. Cambridge, U.K.: Cambridge University Press, 2001.

van Schalkwyk, Johnny, and Benjamin Smith. "Insiders and Outsiders: Sources for Reinterpreting a Historical Event." In *African Historical Archaeologies*, ed. Andrew Reid and Paul Lane. London: Kluwer Academic/Plenum Publishers, 2004.

PAUL LANE

INDUSTRIAL

Industrial archaeology is generally taken to mean the systematic study of the artifacts, structures, sites, and landscapes providing material evidence of past industrial activity, but the boundaries of the discipline are often indistinct. Barrie Trinder, noting that most studies take the "industrial revolution" of the eighteenth century, in Britain and elsewhere, as a starting point, cautions against denying "the enlightening value of studies that bestride the centuries, examining the ways in which humans have kindled fire, woven cloth or fired ceramics" (Trinder 1992, 350), and he might have had the remains of past productive activities in Africa in mind.

DEFINING INDUSTRIAL ARCHAEOLOGY

What sets the modern industrial period apart is the radical socioeconomic transformation wrought by the transfer of people from agrarian to large-scale manufacturing concerns, the development of new prime movers, such as steam and internal combustion engines, and electrical generators, and the improvement of local and international transport and communication systems. Significantly, and far from coincidentally, this period of industrial revolution is contemporaneous with the ravages of European colonial expansion in Africa. This begs the question as to whether the material evidence of slavery, itself a critical link between the exploitation of Africa for resources, human and material, and the development of

industrialized Europe and North America, should be the subject of industrial archaeology. Certainly the discipline has taken credible steps away from its early and narrow focus on machines and technologies toward including the social and cultural impacts of industry, but the material evidence of slavery is more usually the domain of historical archaeologists, who work in the same period, but without the focus on industrial processes and practices.

INDUSTRIAL ARCHAEOLOGY'S UNACCEPTABLE DISCIPLINARY ABSENCE IN AFRICA

As an academic discipline, industrial archaeology has yet to address the material evidence of the development of industry in Africa. This is not to suggest that Africa does not have an industrial history, but archaeologists who have studied earlier African ceramics, iron making, and gold production have not defined their work as industrial archaeology. While many of the raw materials on which the industrialization of the colonial powers was to depend were taken from Africa, and the manufacturing sites and processes for extracting these materials has formed the basis of many industrial archaeology research papers in Europe and North America, the sites of origin for commodities such as cotton, coffee, copper, and rubber have generally been overlooked.

The discipline's minimal engagement with Africa is further evidenced by its absence in the leading journals of the field; even in an article titled "Industrial Archaeology Goes Universal" (Falconer 2005) the entire continent is not mentioned. Not a single UNESCO-designated African World Heritage Site is of an industrial nature.

The Research Unit for the Archaeology of Cape Town, responding to complaints about the lack of attention given to industrial archaeology in South Africa, ran the first and, as of 2007, only industrial archaeology workshop on the continent in 1999, while Cape Town also claims Africa's first book on industrial archaeology, the study of an early-twentieth-century, but short-lived, local glass factory.

THE POTENTIAL FOR INDUSTRIAL ARCHAEOLOGY IN AFRICA

The aforementioned examples notwithstanding, the potential for industrial archaeology in Africa is considerable. Of the primary industries, agriculture is the most widespread and most important economically. While much agricultural activity is at the level of local food production, there also exist cash crop activities such as the production of cocoa beans, coffee beans, and sugar cane, and forestry, the last particularly in areas such as the Democratic Republic of the Congo. Extractive industries are also widespread, with the mining of gold, diamonds, coal, copper, and tin being supplemented by the tapping of natural gas and oil reserves, and salt has long been mined at Taodeni, in Mali. The nineteenth-century origins of South Africa's diamond (Kimberley) and gold (Pilgrim's Rest) mining industries, together with early-twentieth-century tin mining (Jos, Nigeria) and copper mining (the Democratic Republic of the Congo and Zambia) would all be worthy subjects of research in this area.

Of the secondary industries, manufacturing may be usefully split into those industries processing agricultural products and mineral and other natural resources (such as sugar and grain milling; meat, fruit and fish canning; tanning and smelting), and those manufacturing goods to substitute for imports (such as clothing, footwear, soap, soft drinks, and small engineering items). Activities such as these have formed the backbone of industry in Sahelian countries such as Senegal and Maurentania. Transport, utilities (such as electricity, water, and telecommunications), and social infrastructure (such as places related to the provision of health care, education, or entertainment) are also considered secondary industries in this respect. There is great potential for industrial archaeological research into the material evidence of transport systems, such as Kenya's railways, Burundi's important reliance on Lake Tanganyika as an export route, and the use by the Democratic Republic of the Congo and other nations relying on the Congo River for transport. Characteristic of Egypt are the major infrastructural developments related to the Aswan High Dam, which provides flood control for a major irrigation scheme and forms part of Africa's largest hydro-electrical power scheme, and the 102-mile-long Suez Canal, completed in 1869. Libya's Great Man-made River and Sudan's Gezira cotton scheme are further examples of important irrigation schemes.

Research in industrial archaeology is often, though by no means always, followed by conservation of the material evidence of the industrial past. Conservation is, in its turn, frequently followed by commodification as industrial heritage. Economic and social development is often seen to be at odds with conservation, particularly when cultural and historical values asserted by world bodies such as the United Nations Educational, Scientific and Cultural Organization (UNESCO) are privileged over local needs. It is in this context that a 2004 study of the industrial archaeology of South Africa's 1920s grain elevator network addressed the enduring divide between conservation and development by arguing that in developing economies, the conservation of industrial heritage must respond to the wider socioeconomic imperatives of sustainable development.

Given that so little work has been done in this area, it is clear that there is a considerable need for sustained research into the material evidence of Africa's industrial period. This would serve to mitigate a worldview that characterizes Africa as wholly rural and nonindustrialized, and facilitate comparison between continents, particularly among the developing regions. Particular focus needs to be given to understanding how technologies and working practices have been created locally, or modified, in response to local conditions and local and traditional technologies and practices.

Grain elevator at Davel, South Africa. This disused grain elevator, built in 1924 for South African Railway, is one of an extant network of 33 country elevators provided in the maize-growing region to promote exports and the interests of farmers. PHOTOGRAPH BY DAVID WORTH, 2001

See also **Cape Town; Congo River; Metals and Minerals; Prehistory; Production Strategies; Rhodes, Cecil John.**

BIBLIOGRAPHY

Esterhuysen, Peter, ed. *Africa A-Z Continental and Country Profiles.* Pretoria: Africa Institute of South Africa, 1998.

Falconer, K. "Industrial Archaeology Goes Universal." *Industrial Archaeology Review* 27, no. 1 (2005): 23–26.

Hall, M. *Block 11, Cape Town: An Archaeological Assessment.* Cape Town: Department of Archaeology, University of Cape Town, 1989.

Hall, M. "The Industrial Archaeology of Entertainment." In *Industrial Archaeology: Future Directions,* ed. E. Conlin Casella and J. Symonds. New York: Springer Science and Business Media, 2005.

Palmer, Marilyn. "Understanding the Workplace: A Research Framework for Industrial Archaeology in Britain." *Industrial Archaeology Review* 27, no. 1 (2005): 9–17.

Palmer, Marilyn, and Peter Neaverson. *Industrial Archaeology: Principles and Practice.* London: Routledge, 1998.

Plug, I., and J. C. C. Pistorius. "Animal Remains from Industrial Iron Age Communities in Phalaborwa, South Africa." *African Archaeological Review* 16, no. 3 (1999): 155–184.

Saitowitz, S. J., and E. Lastovica. *Rediscovering the Cape Glass Company at Glencairn.* Germiston: Consol Ltd., 1998.

Trinder, B. "Industrial Archaeology." In *The Blackwell Encyclopaedia of Industrial Archaeology.* Oxford: Blackwell Publishers, 1992.

Worth, David. "A Smoke Belching Congestion of Factories: Cape Town's Neglected Industrial Heritage." *Patrimonie de l'Industrie* 2 (1999): 65–72.

Worth, David. "Gas and Grain: The Conservation of Networked Industrial Landscapes." In *Industrial Archaeology: Future Directions,* ed. E. Conlin Casella and J. Symonds. New York: Springer Science and Business Media, 2005.

DAVID WORTH

MARINE

Marine archaeology in an African context is a relatively new area of study. It is a subject that has been traditionally viewed as dealing primarily with shipwrecks and associated waterfront facilities. The emergent nature of the discipline in Africa has been more inclusive and integrated, dealing with coastal landscape and material cultural remains of past settlement, trade, and movement. Marine or maritime archaeology is then applicable to the full chronological spectrum of human presence. Early Middle Stone Age artifacts were found on an emerged reef terrace on the Red Sea coast of Eritrea, which have been dated to the last interglacial period (about 125,000 years ago) while similar discoveries have been made in cave sites such as Blombos in South Africa. These finds demonstrate that early humans occupied coastal areas and exploited near-shore marine food resources by this time, the earliest well-dated evidence for human adaptation to a coastal marine environment. Extensive shell-middens along the South African coastline testify to later intensive hunter gatherer exploitation of these marine resources.

Africa functions within a number of marine systems and has been subject to a wide variety of both internal and external cultural influences. Along North Africa's coast cultural activity was dominated by trade and conquest throughout the east and western Mediterranean regions. Extraordinary finds, including inscribed columns, shipwrecks, and foundations have been made underwater at the Egyptian port of Alexandria where the Pharos lighthouse was built during the Ptolemaic period. Other significant ports included the Phoenician foundation at Carthage in Tunisia and Tripoli in Libya. The Red Sea region was closely related to the Mediterranean system, initially with overland caravan routes north through the desert and up the Nile River and later by sea with the construction of the Suez Canal. This was an important trading and migrant system throughout the historical period as exemplified by the Roman period ports at Berenike and Quseir al-Qadim in Egypt and later medieval ports like Suakin in the Sudan and Adulis in Eritrea. The Ascara Island shipwreck, Eritrea, dated on the basis of ceramic finds to around the seventh century CE testifies to the continued importance of coastal movement in this region whereas the eighteenth-century shipwreck at Sadana Island, Egypt is evidence of the globalized nature of trade with its cargo of coffee, spices, and Chinese export porcelain.

The Indian Ocean system is dominated by the Monsoon, which controls much of its sea-based traffic. There has been a long tradition of coastal archaeology undertaken along the East African coast examining medieval Swahili settlements, towns with architecturally significant stone-built buildings that were engaged in extensive hinterland and foreland trade between the African interior and the broader Indian Ocean. Both European and Arab colonial expansion is visible archaeologically along this coast. Fort Jesus at Mombasa is a significant physical expression of fortification and control of mercantile seaways. The wreck of the *Santo Antonio de Tanna*, sunk in 1696–1697 during the course of an Omani siege of Fort Jesus, represents the well-preserved remains of a Portuguese frigate lying on the seabed beneath the walls of the fort. Similar colonial period architecture dominates sections of the South African coastline where a number of significant state-sponsored coastal and shipwreck surveys and management programs have been initiated. Important waterfront excavations have taken place in Cape Town and on shipwrecks such as the Dutch East Indiaman *Oosterland*, lost in Table Bay in 1697. Other vessels of historic importance include the German warship *Konigsberg* lost in the Rufigi Rufiji Delta during World War II.

The West African seaboard became part of a wider globalized network from the sixteenth century onward when European mercantile and slaving activity worked with a number of regional power bases to systematically exploit both natural and human resources. This coastline experienced little systematic marine archaeological research yet future investigations should ultimately add significantly to scholars' understandings of pre-European contact activity, early exploration, and historical analysis of the emergent Atlantic slave system within the broader Atlantic social world. Underwater investigations have taken place at the former port of Elmina, Ghana, the first European slave-trading post in sub-Saharan Africa, built in 1482. However, as with other parts of Africa a number of commercially led operations have been undertaken along the West coast and at offshore islands like Cape Verde. This type of operation poses a significant risk to the future protection and management of the marine archaeological resources and also sets a negative precedent for other African countries.

See also **Alexandria; Cape Town; Carthage; Ceramics; Nile River; Prehistory; Tripoli.**

BIBLIOGRAPHY

Breen, C., and P. Lane. "Archaeological Approaches to East Africa's Changing Seascapes." *World Archaeology* 33, no. 5 (2003): 469–492.

La Riche, William. *Alexandria: The Sunken City.* London: Weidenfeld and Nicholson, 1997.

Phillipson David W. *African Archaeology.* Cambridge, U.K.: Cambridge University Press, 2005.

COLIN BREEN

ISLAMIC

Since the late twentieth century archaeologists have made a major contribution to the study of Islamic societies in Africa, both north and south of the equator, and Islamic archaeology is well established as an important component of the study of African history. In earlier, colonial discourses, Islam in Africa, especially sub-Saharan Africa, was seen as something foreign, and introduced by settlers from beyond African shores, with the clear implication that the so-called civilization that came with it (literacy, stone and mud architecture, urbanism) was also foreign and non-African. The singular contribution of archaeologists has been to root African Islam within the mainstream cultural traditions of Africa and to show that the civilizations that are associated with Islam are wholly indigenous. Broadly, there have been three categories of research questions, which have been addressed by archaeologists in this reevaluation: conversion, integration, and trade systems.

The process of the Islamic conversion is a subject to which archaeology has made a unique contribution. The main reason for this is the dearth of reliable documentary sources that document the process, especially south of the Sahara. Because Islam is so recognizable in the archaeological record, through mosque building, diet, house construction, burial rites, coining and inscriptions, scholars can be certain of the presence of Islamic communities in dated strata. In eastern Africa, Arabic geographers, such as al-Idrisi and Ibn Said, paint a picture of a largely pagan coast until the twelfth century, but finds of mosques, coins, and burials dating to the late eighth century CE, at Shanga near Lamu, on Zanzibar and Pemba islands, and as far south as Chibuene in Mozambique make it clear that Islam was widespread a full four hundred years earlier.

In the western Sahel, the situation is the reverse. Here the historical sources suggest the activities of Ibadi (Kharijite) traders in the late eighth century, but the first archaeological evidence for Islam in the region dates to the tenth century, in the form of inscriptions and mosques. There are also noteworthy differences in the conversion process between eastern and western Africa. At Shanga, the first timber mosque, dating to circa 780 CE, was found overlying a burnt out tree stump in the middle of the site—possibly the vestige of a sacred grove—suggesting the replacement of traditional practice by Islam. While some have argued that the Shanga evidence is only provision for visiting merchants from the Middle East, its location in the center of the site, the associations of burials of women and children, and the production of local coins, with Arabic inscriptions, but with names often chosen by converts, show that the local community were converted to Islam from very early on. But in West Africa, it has been suggested that there were dual settlements, one for Muslim merchants (by implication from foreign parts), the other for the non-Muslim ruler and his court. One such merchant's town has been partly excavated at Koumbi Salaeh, although the non-Muslim part has never been found, and in fact may never have existed. The supposed evidence at the site for a mass destruction when the kingdom of Ghana was converted to Islam in 1076–1077 is as illusory as the historical evidence for forced conversion by the Almoravids.

The second group of questions concern the degree of integration of Islam within African societies—or, more crudely, how much of African traditions were incorporated into Islamic practice. Randall Pouwels has argued that traditional belief systems were not so incompatible with Islam—for example, ideas of a single supreme being is widespread in both Bantu and Cushitic belief systems, while ideas of spirits and ancestors could readily be incorporated within Islam. More problematical are representations of the person, found in various forms in African art, as well as masks, but as René Bravmann has pointed out, even these can find their way into African Muslim societies. The archaeological contribution takes this debate out of ethnography into the past. Rather than syncretism, these practices should be seen as a distinctive form of African Islam, where spirits and ancestors remain an important and acknowledged part of the belief system. A particularly good example is the site of Pujini, on Pemba island (Tanzania), where within a fifteenth-century palace complex—built by a man who is remembered for his Muslim piety—is a specially constructed spirit cave, with a plaster relief of a horn, the traditional symbol of African kingship. Over much of the continent, the source of conversion did not come from the metropolitan centers such as Cairo or Baghdad, but from the tribal areas of Arabia, by the Ibadis from Uman or the sharifs from the Hadhramaut valley in Yemaen, where Islam was already much closer to African practice.

Third, the main route for the spread of Islam through Africa often followed long-distance trade. Apart from the historically recorded seventh-century military conquests in North Africa and a twelfth-century expedition into Nubia, there is little evidence for forced conversion imposed by jihadist armies. Existing trade routes extended throughout the western half of Sahara, linking the Mediterranean with the Sahel, southward through the Nile corridor, and following the monsoon winds between the Red Sea, western Asia and eastern Africa. In all these regions, the exports were generally high value commodities, principally ivory (both elephant and hippo), gold and slaves, although more bulky items such as timber, salt, and mineral ores were also involved. In return, manufactured goods find their way into the settlements; these include Islamic glazed ceramics, Chinese stoneware and porcelain, glass beads and glass vessels.

Archaeological evidence is largely confined to these durable items, and organic trading goods, such as cloth, survive only in exceptional circumstances. With trade went urbanization, and the construction of monumental structures in either in stone (the general practice in eastern Africa) or the spectacular mud mosques and houses of the western Sahel. In both eastern and western Africa, these are spectacular architectural achievements rooted in local traditions rather than brought from overseas. The archaeological perspective suggests a complex relationship between local building traditions, long distance trade as a factor in urbanization, and the spread of Islam. While Islam followed trade routes, and may have been a contributor to urbanization, there are many examples in sub-Saharan Africa of urbanization and long-distance trade, where Islam is completely absent. Great Zimbabwe and allied sites in southern Africa, the interlacaustrine kingdoms of eastern

Africa, and the forest societies of western Africa are good examples; each lay at the end of a trade route that connected to the Islamic world, but show no evidence of conversion.

See also **Cairo; Ceramics; Islam; Ivory; Nubia; Prehistory; Trade, National and International Systems; Zimbabwe, Great.**

BIBLIOGRAPHY

Bravmann, René A. *African Islam*. Washington, DC: Smithsonian Institution Press, 1983.

Frishman, Martin, and Hasan-Uddin Khan. *The Mosque: History, Architectural Development and Regional Diversity*. London: Thames and Hudson, 1994.

Horton, M. C. *Shanga: The Archaeology of a Muslim Trading Community on the Coast of East Africa*. London: British Institute in Eastern Africa, 1996.

Horton, M. C. "Islam, Archaeology and Swahili Identity." In *Changing Social Identity with the Spread of Islam: Archaeological Perspectives*, ed. Donald Whitcomb. Chicago: Oriental Institute of the University of Chicago, 2004.

Horton, Mark, and John Middleton. *The Swahili: The Social Landscape of a Mercantile Society*. Oxford: Blackwell, 2000.

Insoll, Tim. *Islam, Archaeology and History: Gao Region (Mali) ca. AD 900–1250*. Oxford: Tempus Reparatum, 1996.

Insoll, Tim. *The Archaeology of Islam in Sub-Saharan Africa*. Cambridge, UK: Cambridge University Press, 2003.

LaViolette, Adria. "Report on Excavations at Swahili Site of Pujini, Pemba Island, Tanzania." *Nyame Akume* 46 (1996): 72–83.

Pouwels, Randall L. "The East African Coast, c. 780–1900 CE." In *History of Islam in Africa*, ed. Nehemia Levtzion and Randall L. Pouwels. Athens: Ohio University Press, 2000.

MARK HORTON

CHRISTIAN

The emergence of Christianity within Africa, part of the wider Christianization of the Roman Empire during the first three centuries CE, is remarkably consistent with what is known about this process in Mediterranean Europe and western Asia. The first African Christians were persecuted by the imperial authorities prior to the Edict of Milan in 313 CE, which recognized the legality of Christianity within the empire, leaving little archaeological evidence before this time. Distinctive Christian burials—such as those found in catacombs in Alexandria (Egypt) dating to the second century CE—are often the only archaeological indicators.

In the fourth century the provinces of North Africa and Egypt rapidly became the focus of extensive Christian activity, and Carthage (Tunisia) and Alexandria became hotbeds of a dynamic Christian intellectual culture. This shift is reflected archaeologically in massive well-appointed North African church buildings (basilicas), often richly decorated with some of the best mosaic work found anywhere in the empire; they include those at Carthage (especially Damous el-Karita dating from the fourth century), Haïdra (Tunisia), and eastward into Cyrenaica (Libya). The baptistery building at Djemila (Cuicul, Algeria) is noted for its scale and decoration. The Vandal conquest of northern Africa by Gaiseric in 429 followed by the Byzantines in 533 saw a continuation of Christian material culture, albeit with some degree of reinterpretation according to each empire's artistic and liturgical tastes.

Alexandria during the fourth and fifth centuries saw the triumph of Christianity within the pagan city, as Christian mobs forcibly seized pagan temples and converted them into churches (attested to by excavations at the Serapeum). In the countryside a vigorous monastic movement was taking hold; the first solitary monks (hermits) left little archaeological trace, but later semi-eremitic settlements such as those at Kellia (south of Alexandria) attest to a gradual trend toward monastic life. Archeologists have found many small "living-working" units, walled compounds that include cells, small oratories, and kitchens. The establishment of a fully communal monastic life (attributed to St. Pachome, 292–346 CE) is evidenced by large enclosed monasteries that contained churches, cells, kitchens, refectories, and other working spaces. The best archaeological examples of these types of structures are found at Epiphanius at Thebes, Apa Jeremias at Saqqara, and St Simeon at Aswan. The monasteries of the Wadi Natrun and Red Sea, although most of their present forms date from the eighteenth century, embody a number of much older features, and the site of Abu Menas to the south of Alexandria represents a fine archaeological example of a late antique pilgrimage center. Ceramic flasks, used by pilgrims to carry holy water from the

Aswan, St. Simeon's monastery (more accurately the monastery of Anba Hatre). One of the most important early-Egyptian communal monasteries, showing the central keep (Qasr) used as a place of refuge. The monastery was abandoned in the thirteenth century. PHOTOGRAPH BY NIALL FINNERAN

site, have been found as far north as the Danube frontier, thus attesting to the international importance of the place.

In the three medieval kingdoms of Nubia (Nobatia, Makhuria, and Alwa) south along the Nile River, a distinctive Christian material culture emerged during the sixth century; scholars note the massive cathedral at the capital of Faras, with its distinctive wall paintings and burials of bishops, and the churches at the Makhurian capital of Old Dongola. Southeastward, the Aksumite kingdom of northern Ethiopia was converted by the Syrian Frumentius in the mid-fourth century, introducing changes in elite burial practices, church and monastery construction (the latter from the seventh century onward), and the appearance of Christian iconography on the coinage.

In later periods archaeological models for the Christianization of African material culture include the encounter between the Portuguese and the Kongo kingdom in the sixteenth century and European missions to South Africa during the nineteenth century

See also **Alexandria; Carthage; Christianity; Nile River; Prehistory.**

BIBLIOGRAPHY

Badawy, Alexander. *Coptic Art and Archaeology.* Cambridge, MA: MIT Press, 1978.

Finneran, Niall. *The Archaeology of Christianity in Africa.* Charleston, SC: Tempus, 1992.

Finneran, Niall, and Tania Tribe. "Towards an Archaeology of Kingship and Monasticism in Medieval Ethiopia." In *Belief in the Past: The Proceedings of the Manchester Conference on Archaeology and Religion,* ed. Timothy Insoll. Oxford, U.K.: British Archaeological Reports, International Series 1212, 2004.

Frend, William. *The Archaeology of Early Christianity: An Introduction.* London: Geoffrey Chapman, 1996.

Grossmann, Peter. *Christliche Architektur in Aumlgypten.* Leiden: Brill, 2002.

Mattingley, David. *Tripolitania.* London: Batsford, 1995.

Abu Menas, southwest of Alexandria, one of the most important pilgrimage centers in the late antique world. Pligrims came to venerate the martyr St. Mina, and took home holy water from the site in distinctive clay bottles or ampoullae. PHOTOGRAPH BY NIALL FINNERAN

Raven, Susan. *Rome in Africa*. London: Routledge, 1993.

Welsby, Derek. *The Medieval Kingdoms of Nubia*. London: British Museum Press, 2002.

NIALL FINNERAN

ARCHITECTURE

This entry includes the following articles:
DOMESTIC
COLONIAL
CONTEMPORARY
MONUMENTAL
TOWN PLANNING

DOMESTIC

Domestic architecture in Africa, normally outside Western definitions, includes building forms and types tightly integrated with the natural environment, conceptually and physically. Like all architecture it involves an interdisciplinary approach integrating a wide range of skills and allied arts: building technologies, pottery, wood carving, metalworking and weaving. Despite the dictate of materials, which encourage architectural homogeneity, there is great regional heterogeneity in form, in style, in technology and in aesthetic preference. Factors that militate against its architectural history include impermanent natural building materials, Africa's oral traditions, the scarcity of early European accounts and the sparseness of Islamic records.

THE PHYSICAL ENVIRONMENT

Design diversity, profoundly influenced by natural building materials and a limited tool repertoire, is initially a result of the broad climatic belts that extend across the continent: grassland and woodland savannas are sandwiched in between arid desert zones with a minimal annual rainfall and humid rain forest regions. In regions with heavy rainfall, sloping roofs facilitate water runoff, and multiple openings encourage evaporative cooling. In the hot, dry regions with marked diurnal temperature change and minimal rainfall, thick earthen walls with few openings moderate the heat of the midday sun. Prevailing trade winds and alternating monsoons dictate building orientation and wall reinforcement. In regions of heavy tropical growth, the natural tree cover provides shade from the sun's heat and radiation, while in the desert and savanna regions shade and shadow define daily human activity and movement in space.

BUILDING MATERIALS

The range of local building materials is also a function of the physical environment. In Swahili cities on the East African coast, coral, which hardens on exposure to the air, was used a basic building block. In North African oases, ksars and cities, *pise* (earth packed into wooden slip forms) and sun-dried brick were used for walls and exterior wall decor, and split palm was used structurally for ceiling and roof systems. In West African cities (e.g., Timbuktu) and in the ancient Mauritanian cities (Tichit, Chinguit, and Walāta) limestone, rough or dressed, set in mortar or laid up dry, was used for wall systems and their reinforcing, and for foundations, vaulting and domes. Among sedentary rural populations such as the Dogon, stone continues to be used extensively for housing, granaries, and wall foundations.

In rain forest regions, hardwood timbers are used for wall planking, for ceiling and roof structures, for arches, window frames and doors. Transported to the savanna, sahel, and Saharan regions, they are used selectively for architectural features such as window grilles, in contrast with the split palm tree trunks used for roof framing. In the rain forest, bamboo is used structurally for wattles and rafters; split, it is used as a decorative armature. The roots of the acacia, the most common timber in Africa, are particularly suited for bent wood armatures. Vegetal materials such as palm fronds, grasses, raffia, and creepers, woven or braided into wall and roof mats, are used both structurally and decoratively among sedentary as well as nomadic and pastoralist populations throughout much of the African continent.

Earth is used extensively for both circular and rectangular wall systems and the shape of earthen building units varies from a hand-molded ball of mud, a conical or cylindrical sun-dried clay brick or a rectangular brick cast into a wooden mold (see Figure 1). Exterior wall surfaces are rendered by applying a coat of "stucco" made by mixing ground shell and beanpod juices with cow dung. Architectural pottery, consisting of fired clay pots and potsherds, is selectively used for paving tiles, pinnacle covers, skylights, latrine linings, leaders, gutters, grilles, wall linings, backdrops, hearthstones, and granary stores.

Stone, earth, timber, textiles, and leather are often integrated architecturally and structurally: wattle (light stick armatures) and daub (mud, air-dried) walls, wooden plank ceilings laid over with an earthen roof, structural earthen arches reinforced within with acacia bent wood or corbeled split palm, earthen brick walls reinforced with wooden ties and cross members, and grille work made by bending split bamboo and overlaying it with clayey earth are frequently used in combination. Textiles and leather are also used architecturally in combination for tensile tent structures and tent linings by means of various tying and attachment systems.

BUILDERS AND THE BUILDING PROCESS

Much domestic architecture, both rural and urban, has evolved out of a communal building process, established via long tradition, in which specific building skills and tasks are gender discrete. In both the rural and the urban contexts, house builders are often non-specialized and house building is a communal effort. However, building processes also involve the combined skills of artisan castes such as masons, blacksmiths, woodworkers, weavers, and potters under the direction of the male head of the household. Male blacksmiths-cum-woodworkers, having acquired their skills by apprenticeship in endogamous castes, are often responsible for the cutting and carving of wooden posts, door planks, and window frames and grilles, while their wives manufacture the architectural pottery. The gender division of labor is related: in principle, men construct the earthen walls of housing while wives apply the finish coats of "stucco" or plaster on walls, floors benches, and shelves. Although women normally are responsible for providing the water essential for molding the earth, it is the men who shape, mold and cast the earthen coils or bricks. Among pastoral and/or nomadic populations women, responsible for creating, erecting, dismantling and transporting their mobile residences, have jural rights over them as well.

Ritual frequently envelops the architectural process: building performance is perceived in terms of both structural integrity and the power of sacrificial acts performed prior to, during, and upon completion of a building project in order to guarantee its success and longevity. Among nomadic

Figure 1. Tallensi compound, northern Ghana. The several separate houses of the compound are set in a circle, sharing a central open courtyard. Domestic architecture in Africa includes buildings tightly integrated with the natural environment, from conception to completion. PHOTOGRAPH BY LABELLE PRUSSIN

peoples, the creation of a new tent takes place in the course of the extended marriage ritual, during which the bride, assisted by her female relatives, gradually assembles it.

CULTURAL IDENTITY

The shape, form, structure, ornamentation, and spatial organization of domestic architecture constitute a visual system that defines the cultural identity of particular ethnic groups. In some architectures, the ornamentation is integral with the building; elsewhere, it is applied to the structure. Stone or cast brick is laid up chevron-like or as an openwork grille within the wall system, coral is carved into arabesque patterns while still moist, earthen walls are crowned with earthen pinnacles, timbers and vegetal materials are selectively reinforced and twisted into decorative

features, roof thatch is cut and laid up in contrasting patterns, and intricate patterns are woven into roof and wall mats. Mud, the most commonly applied surface decoration on stone or earthen walls, is hardened into with additives such as ground shells and dung, colored with vegetable extract or kaolin, and carved in bas-relief. Cowrie shells, china or enamel plates, pottery, and ostrich eggshell, embedded in the mud, are applied decoratively.

Ornamentation is applied most frequently on doorways and entrances; around window openings; on exterior facades and interior courtyards; at hearths; on granaries and storerooms; on eaves, roof finials, pinnacles, and parapets; and on the exterior surfaces of community buildings and the residences of elite community members. The patterns of surface design vary from one ethnic

Figure 2. Hausa housefront, Zaria, northern Nigeria. Arabic calligraphy ornamenting Hausa architecture attests to the strong influence of Islam. Islamic religion and culture was first introduced among the Hausa as early as the 1500s. It became a prominent part of their society during the holy war of the early nineteenth century. PHOTOGRAPH BY LABELLE PRUSSIN

Pastoral, hunter-gatherer, and transient populations create a mobile architecture whose components can be easily dismantled, relocated, and reassembled into a precise replica at a new location. The integration of architectural and transport technology into sophisticated tensile structures composed of a woven velum and carved wooden poles or bent wood armatures tied with rawhide thongs and covered with woven mats of diverse vegetal materials results in diverse shapes and sizes. Their architectural form is dictated by spatial orientation, tightly constructed geometries based on balance and symmetry, and interior foci (see Figure 3). In plan, the four quadrants of the tent interior, articulated by the central hearth or tent pole, are specifically defined as public or private space and men's or women's space.

group to another, from one religious affiliation to another, and from one domestic function to another. The Islamic proscription against the depiction of the human form at one time favored geometric, abstract, and arabesque design (see Figure 2), while other populations employ more representational designs.

Human values are expressed formally and spatially via anthropomorphic iconography. The basis for the aesthetic, continuity from the past to the future, is expressed by formal monuments to the ancestral presence rising from the earth itself, and in the multiplicity of architectural elements which symbolize fertility. The ideal of verticality, voiced by and striven for by communal builders and traditional architects alike, belies the limitations of available materials and technologies. Basic colors such as white, red, and black, preferentially used in the architectural context as contrasts with the muted hues of the natural environment, are equally imbued with symbolic meanings. Architectural continuity is achieved by wall resurfacing and the replacement or renewal of building components. The primary criterion for permanence in African domestic architecture is its ongoing human occupancy, validated by genealogies that are reflected in the markers of "ancestral presence," rather than the longevity of the building materials used in construction. Abandoned residences are either left to disintegrate or are stripped of re-usable materials.

Figure 3. Housing construction, northern Kenya. The housing of nomadic pastoralists must be rebuilt at each new settlement site. Here women builders among the Gabra work together to build the shell of a new house. PHOTOGRAPH BY LABELLE PRUSSIN

DOMESTIC SETTLEMENT PATTERNS

In North and West African savanna climates, rural, sedentary agricultural communities, consisting of isolated housing compounds, are composed of a perimeter of earthen walls and/or room units and granaries arranged around an open courtyard in order to accommodate an extended family network, standing alone, surrounded by a cultivated landscape. In the urban context, these same compounds, clustered in close proximity, result in a complex, winding street pattern punctuated by single entry doors into reception antechambers; when reinforced and surrounded by towering protective walls such as the *ksars*, these same compounds are often multi-storied. Characteristically, each housing compound constitutes a visual sociogram consisting of a set of building units, each serving a specific purpose: separate cooking spaces, sleeping spaces and storage spaces frequently accommodating polygynous marriage patterns, spaces for worship, spaces for domestic animals, and sometimes burial spaces. These building units, into which ancestral markers, granaries, cattle kraals, chicken coops, and freestanding walls have been integrated, delineate an open, central courtyard within which daily life unfolds. Among some East and South African pastoral populations, residential units are arranged in circular fashion, either encircling cattle kraals or serving as entrances to them, whereas among other more nomadic, desert populations, house units are arranged lineally with attached camel kraals projecting behind. In the rainforest regions of West Africa, small, single rectangular homestead buildings constructed of timber and vegetal materials, are often arranged in linear fashion, either along both sides of a street or, perched on poles, interfacing with the water's edge. Punctuated at one end by grave markers and on the other by the residence of a village elder, they constitute an open village plan.

MODERNIZATION

Former colonial policies, currently available resources and Western technology, have rapidly changed the nature of domestic architecture in the twentieth century by encouraging the introduction of new building materials, building systems, and building functions.

The introduction of a "bungalow" style by former colonial powers, particularly in West and South Africa, was further encouraged by the importation of prefabricated residential units assembled in-situ, while kiln-fired brick, cement, concrete block and steel reinforcing rods opened up new building options.

Contemporary domestic architecture is remarkable for the ways in which it has integrated the new materials into traditional techniques and influenced aesthetic choice. The widespread preference of imported corrugated iron or aluminum sheets for roofing, walls, doors, and window shutters can in part be explained by their adaptability to traditional building technologies of thatch and palm fronds; the easy substitution of concrete blocks for sun-dried earthen bricks stems from similarities with traditional masonry systems; both accommodate the traditional accumulative character of building materials. Earthen surface ornamentation can be enhanced with cement to achieve a more permanent quality, whereas terrazzo floor finishes easily endow earthen floor paving with a more permanent quality. Poured and reinforced concrete, requiring radical changes in labor relations and building technology, is limited to contemporary domestic urban architecture. Most critical to the development of a new domestic African architecture is the recent involvement by professionally trained African architects, graduates of African schools of architecture and environmental design. Drawing on the architectural resources and imagery embodied in their *own* cultural legacy, they have begun to introduce insights and perspectives that are rapidly becoming precursors for a modern African style.

See also **Art; Ecosystems: Savannas; Symbols and Symbolism; Timbuktu; Urbanism and Urbanization: Housing; Walāta.**

BIBLIOGRAPHY

Andersen, Kaj Blegvad. *African Traditional Architecture.* Nairobi: Oxford University Press, 1978.

Blier, Suzanne Preston. *The Anatomy of Architecture.* Cambridge, U.K.: Cambridge University Press, 1987.

Carver, Norman F. *North African Villages. Morocco, Algeria, Tunisia.* Kalamazoo, MI: Documan Press, 1989.

Denyer, Susan. *African Traditional Architecture.* New York: Africana Publishing Company, 1978.

Frescura, Franco. *Rural Shelter in Southern Africa.* Johannesburg: Ravan Press, 1981.

Oliver, Paul, ed. *Shelter in Africa.* New York: Praeger, 1971.

Prussin, Labelle. *African Nomadic Architecture: Space, Place, and Gender.* Washington, DC: Smithsonian Institution Press, 1995.

Wenzel, Marian. *House Decoration in Nubia.* Toronto: University of Toronto Press, 1972.

LABELLE PRUSSIN

COLONIAL

Colonial architecture, including European-designed government and commercial buildings and the residences of wealthy Africans, was the product of a specific historical moment and reflected the political and economic relations of the colonial period. Colonial architecture was primarily an expression of European political authority and power. Some edifices, however, such as the houses of Afro-Brazilian merchants, were not directly associated with the assertion or symbolic presentation of an imposed foreign authority. Whether constructed by Europeans or by members of local, largely African populations, colonial architecture shared elements of form, style, and scale. At the same time, this architecture addressed the physical needs of peoples living in a subtropical or tropical climate without electricity (until the twentieth century); furthermore, these needs were met by using locally available building materials or, at considerable expense, imported supplies.

Although most colonial buildings were constructed for the use of Europeans, the architecture itself frequently incorporated elements that were indigenous to Africa. The development of colonial architecture reflects cultural contact between Africans and Europeans, and the buildings reflect African as well as European prototypes.

A historical forerunner of colonial architecture may be found in the Portuguese style dwellings built along the Upper Guinea Coast as early as the sixteenth century by both European traders and wealthy African rulers and merchants. Portuguese style architecture reflects mutual, two-way interaction between European and African society; nevertheless, all of the component elements already existed in indigenous West African architecture. In sixteenth- and seventeenth-century sources, the term *à la portugaise* generally implied rectangular houses that were constructed of dried earth or sun-dried bricks, whitewashed on the exterior, and possessed a verandah or vestibule in which to receive visiting traders. In particular the verandah, nearly ubiquitous in tropical and subtropical houses, was an indigenous West African architectural element that was well suited to the local climate. It is likely that verandahs developed independently in several cultures, in Africa, Asia, and Europe.

In all these locations, the buildings were a response both to the exigencies of climate and to the colonial situation. The monumental administrative and government buildings of colonial capitals, in particular, incorporated a desire to express and affirm the power of the colonizers. The scale, the use of durable materials, and a visual rhetoric of power that typify government buildings from Dakar (in present-day Senegal) to Harare (in present-day Zimbabwe) may also be found in the imposing buildings of colonial New Delhi, Hanoi, and Hong Kong.

Saint-Louis (in present-day Senegal), the first colonial capital of French West Africa, provided a prototype for colonial building. Established in 1658, Saint-Louis was home to a community of Creole merchants; their houses, built around an interior courtyard and with a second-floor porch, incorporated several elements that later characterized colonial architecture. Dakar, the capital since 1902, became the site of monumental government buildings, as well as of merchants' homes on whose porches the owners entertained and conducted business.

In Guinea, the establishment of Conakry as capital in 1893 marked the advent of planned urbanization in French West Africa. With geometric city blocks and residential quarters segregated officially by wealth but effectively by race, Conakry experienced rapid construction during the two decades preceding World War I. Administrative buildings provided the city with a panoply of monumental public structures that give concrete expression to the reality of colonial power. The monumental scale of these buildings is also related to architecture in France, recalling the neoclassicism of Parisian government buildings during the Third Republic. It is significant that civil engineers designed these buildings; in Conakry (as in Abidjan), design was not entrusted to architects until the 1920s. After World War II, official buildings in Conakry featured the work of architects from France. Their high-rise constructions transformed the porch/veranda into tiers of balconies. Use of fans and air conditioning eliminated the need for such features of earlier colonial architecture as galleries, aligned windows to set up air currents, and louvered windows. The resulting modern style is less distinctively African. The internationalization or homogenization of the urban skyline was more evident in cities that, even briefly, experienced postwar prosperity, notably Dakar, Abidjan, Lagos, and Nairobi.

The capital of Côte d'Ivoire, established at Grand Bassam in 1893, was twice moved before it settled in Abidjan. Grand Bassam, neglected since the early twentieth century, became a repository of early colonial buildings, their arcaded galleries and sweeping staircases a dilapidated monument to the former grandeur of government buildings.

Abidjan, by contrast, has experienced successive periods of explosive growth. In the years immediately preceding and following independence, the infusion of wealth from agricultural exports made the city a showcase for International style buildings.

In Gold Coast (present-day Ghana), where European traders were established on the coast by 1482 (at the Portuguese fort at Elmina), extensive intercultural contact resulted in the development of a distinctive colonial architecture by the early nineteenth century. In Elmina, wealthy European-African merchants constructed two- and three-story stone houses with arcaded balconies, perhaps inspired by European coastal forts. By the middle of the century, the establishment of missionaries in the southern Gold Coast provided another source of European architectural influence. The mission station, a two-story structure with porch and gallery, would become a model for the colonial style.

The British government came to the work of urban development after the annexation of Asante territory in 1901 in Gold Coast. Post–World War II prosperity enabled the government to finance the design, by architects, of buildings inspired by Walter Gropius (1883–1969) and other proponents of modernism. Maxwell Fry (1899–1987) and Jane Drew (1911–1996) adapted their contemporary designs to the requirements of the local climate.

A generation after the construction of the early nineteenth-century merchants' homes in Elmina, an analogous form of vernacular architecture grew up in the future states of Bénin, Togo, and Nigeria: the distinctive houses of the Afro-Brazilian bourgeoisie. These sumptuous dwellings, with living quarters situated above and the ground floor devoted to business, defined a style much like the Portuguese style houses of earlier Afro-Portuguese traders. Afro-Brazilian houses, with their grand façades embellished by balustrades and curvilinear entablatures and pediments, were ornate monuments to the wealth and opulent taste of their owners. Similar houses were constructed in Bénin (Dahomey) into the twentieth century. This style, combining elements from Africa, Europe, and the Americas, embodies the intercontinental character of nineteenth-century commerce (and architecture) in West Africa.

Urbanization is indigenous to Nigeria. Fifteenth-century Benin City, the northern city-states, and the Yoruba cities such as Abeokuta all predate the colonial period. Lagos, on the other hand, developed as a nineteenth-century trading city with its own Afro-Brazilian traders, a few of whose baroque houses still exist. Early-twentieth-century Lagos, with its administrative and financial buildings, their raised porches and verandas encrusted in Victorian artifice, is the British colonial counterpart of Dakar. The city's recent explosive growth, however, that has made it the largest urban conglomeration in sub-Saharan Africa with an estimated 12 million inhabitants in 2006, has surrounded the colonial core with 12 miles of urban sprawl. After independence in 1960, modernist structures designed by international firms (including Fry and Drew) and by young Nigerian architects transformed the center of Lagos.

The German contribution to colonial architecture was limited to the period before 1914. German government buildings shared the same architectural idiom as prewar French colonial structures. In the 1880s, German authorities experimented with imported prefabricated structures, some of which proved ill-suited to the climate.

Subsequently, in Togo, Cameroon, and Tanganyika, the German colonial style combined the characteristic galleries or continuous exterior verandas and two-story construction featuring raised subbasements and louvered windows with a heavy Wilhelmine façade that reflected the German penchant for dressed stone. In the former German East Africa, Dar es Salaam is distinguished by both the vestiges of German colonial-style buildings and the influence of the stone houses characteristic of Swahili coastal architecture.

In South Africa, the earliest colonial dwellings were the houses of Dutch settlers at the Cape. Cape Dutch houses combined thatched roofs and white stucco walls with ornate gables; this eighteenth-century style derived from a variety of influences, including Dutch, German, and Malay. With the British occupation in 1806, this style was supplanted by Cape Georgian. A century later, Cape Town was adorned with government buildings in an English neoclassical style—for instance, Cape Town's city hall, the massive scale of which bespoke power. British government buildings in South Africa brought neoclassicism to a monstrous scale, as in Durban's town hall, the cupolas and colonnaded façades of which might be termed colonial wedding cake in style.

The East African coast experienced successive colonizations beginning with Islamic settlement by the tenth century CE and followed by the Portuguese (sixteenth century), the Omani Arabs, and the British. The earliest of these waves was accompanied by a distinctive architecture. Mosques and palaces of coral stone, walls decorated with arches and geometric designs in lime mortar and plaster, characterized Swahili architecture of the thirteenth through the eighteenth centuries, whereas the stone houses of wealthy traders dominated the nineteenth-century urban centers of Zanzibar and the mainland coast.

In British East Africa, Nairobi, from the time of its establishment as a way station on the Mombasa-Uganda railroad (1899), grew rapidly and was made the capital of Kenya in 1907. Early colonial-style buildings, some constructed of prefabricated materials and most with corrugated metal roofs, were one or two stories tall with encircling porches. The rows of corrugated roofs dominated urban

thoroughfares such as Bazaar Street before World War I. In the city center, the stately, solid façades of the major buildings three to five stories high—reflecting, perhaps, British architecture in India—were less monumental than government structures in other British African colonies. The more modest scale may have reflected the presence of a significant English settler population; these settlers did not need to be impressed by a monumental architecture symbolizing imperial power.

In Africa, no neat distinction exists between French, German, and British colonial architecture. Rather, there is a common stylistic core. This style is at times articulated in regionally specific variations that reflect local African building traditions as well as local political developments. One important example is the French neo-Sudanese style used in Senegal and Mali and based on the monumental mud architecture of the western Sudan. The common style derives from several factors. Colonial buildings had to meet the demands of the local climate; furthermore, they had to express and enhance either the authority of the European powers or the wealth and prestige of their local owners. In addition, colonial borders did not always limit missionaries, who played a role in the development of early colonial architecture. The Basel Mission, for example, constructed stations in both Cameroon and Gold Coast. Finally, it is likely that each of the European colonial powers was inspired by the architecture developed during the eighteenth century by Europeans living in India and the Caribbean.

Consideration of postcolonial architecture and urbanization in sub-Saharan Africa concludes with reference to Democratic Republic of the Congo and to its major city, Kinshasa. The former capital of the Belgian Congo, situated on the Congo River, had a population of 40,000 in 1940 and of 1.2 million in 1970; by the mid-1990s it had more than 3 million inhabitants. The business quarter (deserted at night) and the residential center of Gombé have wide avenues, fifteen-story office buildings, and apartment blocks (this was, at least, the case before the political and economic catastrophe that began in the last decade of the twentieth century); but the vast majority of Kinshasans inhabit the *cités*. These sprawling and impoverished urban agglomerations, with unpaved, rutted streets and houses built of *banco*, or dried earth, are almost entirely without public services. Five of six families have no ready access to water; six of seven have no electricity. Sanitation services are largely nonexistent. Most inhabitants survive by means of the unofficial economy and by informal cooperation—for example, when constructing new dwellings.

Such postmodern urban environments, increasingly common in Africa, illustrate the inability of governments, with severely limited resources, to control urban growth or to provide fundamental public health services. In this context, architecture becomes an abstract notion, an unattainable luxury. In the words of Roland Pourtier, Kinshasa illustrates the growth of "a double urban culture, that of the rich with their Westernized consumption, and that of the poor ("Le Zaire: L'Immensité des possibles," in Dubresson et al., 251). If colonial architecture embodied the ideology of the European imperial dream, and if the international modernism of the 1960s expressed the optimistic hopes for postindependence economic prosperity, then structures built in Kinshasa's cités bespeak the harsh reality of impoverishment, of inequitable distribution of wealth, and of lost hopes for economic betterment.

See also **Abidjan; Benin City; Cape Town; Colonial Policies and Practices; Colonial Traditions and Inventions; Conakry; Dakar; Dar es Salaam; Elmina; Kinshasa; Lagos; Nairobi; Saint-Louis; Urbanism and Urbanization: Housing.**

BIBLIOGRAPHY

Dubresson, Alain; Jean-Yves Marchal; and Jean Pierre Raison; eds. *Les Afriques au sud du Sahara.* Paris: Belin/Reclus, 1994.

King, Anthony D. *The Bungalow: The Production of a Global Culture.* New York: Oxford University Press, 1995.

Ministère des Affaires Culturelles, Côte d'Ivoire. *Architecture coloniale en Côte d'Ivoire.* Abidjan, Côte d'Ivoire: Ministère des Affaires Culturelles, Côte d'Ivoire: CEDA, 1985.

Sinou, Alain. *Comptoirs et villes coloniales au Sénégal: Saint-Louis, Gorée, Dakar.* Paris: Editions de l'Orstom, 1993.

Soulillou, Jacques, ed. *Rives coloniales: Architectures de Saint-Louis à Douala.* Marseilles, France: Editions Parenthéses, 1993.

Wright, Gwendolyn. *The Politics of Design in French Colonial Urbanism.* Chicago: University of Chicago Press, 1991.

PETER MARK

CONTEMPORARY

The term "contemporary African" architecture can be misleading because it has the tendency to focus on styles and models of architectural practices that have supposedly left behind, "traditional African architectural models—mud houses, grass huts, and buildings that are designed with traditional materials"—in favor of buildings that are designed by trained architects and draftsmen and constructed with "modern" materials. This line of thinking is perpetuated by the misguided notion of development that conflates the construction of structures with materials that are produced in factories like concrete masonry blocks and roofing materials such as zinc, as the evidence of the adoption of "Western" building practices. Reading African architecture from that perspective distorts the real condition of its contemporary practices in favor of an elitist, middle and upper class-inspired concept of architectural development, against the real contemporaneous productions that are happening in the cities, towns, villages, and hamlets around the continent. Two contrasting examples will expand on these points.

First, there is no doubt that throughout the continent, African cities have been privileged in the provision of amenities over villages and rural areas. These advantages begin with advanced planning and the provision of basic utilities such as electricity, running water, paved roads, the removal of waste, and the provision of drainage infrastructure. Such considerations are most visible with the insertion of the Cartesian grid on the African cities' landscapes, as opposed to the less regulated landscapes of the village and the rural settings. In many African countries, the major cities like Cairo, Johannesburg, Cape Town, Abuja, Lagos, Port Harcourt, Nairobi, Dar es Salaam, and Kinshasa, are the centers of economic activities and government bureaucracies. The majority of jobs outside of agriculture and subsistence living in the respective countries can be found in the cities. The result is the large disparity of migration from the rural to the urban areas by able-bodied youths who go to the cities in search of employment. This migration is visible on the contemporary architectural practices of the continent.

The majority of the built projects on the African continent are still the family home. But a new trend is emerging in the manner that the family home is designed in African cities. The most prominent feature that dominates the designs of many middle class homes in cities such as Lagos, Abuja, Cape Town, and Johannesburg, is the fence. The fence traditionally is the instrument for keeping people and things that are not wanted outside the family yard, and for keeping people and things that are wanted safe inside the family yard. However, the fence manifests in contemporary architecture of the middle and upper class family homes in the cities named above as statements of security and as statements of status. The immediate effect is the newly constructed houses in the cities of Africa turn away from the cities' activities.

Unlike the traditional, meandering, labyrinthine plan of traditional cities such as Kano and Zaria where the narrow paths are framed by walls and the compound are intentionally designed to look inwards into the central courtyards, the experience of walking through the contemporary suburbs of Abuja and Johannesburg is disorienting because the insertions of the fences in front of the houses has started to turn the frontage of houses in the cities of Africa to behave like the village setting where the houses are designed to look inwards. Granted, the streets are linear and wider unlike the village alleys. Nevertheless, the cities, the contemporary fencing technique is giving the façades of the houses new looks and functions: the façades of the buildings no longer face the streets and the relationships that existed between the street and the house is now blocked with high electronic and concrete walls. The sidewalk is reduced to strips of lines and the walls push the pedestrian towards the traffic on the street. The resident in the traditional family house no longer maintains visual dialogue with the street and the pedestrian. Instead, he looks inward to the surrounding walls and to the upward view that one can see in the sky. More than anything, the arrangement of the interior spaces into living room, dinning room,

kitchen, bedrooms, and bathrooms in an apartment-like structure is seen as the new civility that contrasts the "modern and the contemporary" African family home from the traditional African compound or homestead settlement. This rearrangement of the entire familial way of life that is closely tied to the social and industrial practices of the urban setting is often articulated with different elements and facades that sometimes borrow from traditional motifs. The abundant use of glass, metal, stone, timber, fiberglass, and other hardware for structural, ornamentation, and aesthetic purposes in such family homes is often seen as signs of modernity and contemproneity.

Second, a large number of contemporary African architecture is being excluded because they do not meet what is called the "standards" of "modern construction." In the ghettos and townships of African cities such as Shomolu Barriga in Lagos, and in lower classes neighborhoods such as Soweto, near Johannesburg, what one sees is a mixture of houses that are constructed with "modern" materials and houses that utilize both "traditional" and "modern" materials such as clay and zinc. In the villages, the houses that are made of clay, grass, and sometimes, products from factories such as glass, louvers, etc, are strategically eliminated from the list of contemporary African architecture. What do these two simple illustration impart?

In the latter part of the twentieth century and in the early part of the twenty-first century, the term "contemporary African" architecture is materially class driven and it does not tell the real story about what is going on in contemporary African architecture. It is an effective tool for defining class distinctions—for proclaiming the values and economic powers of the people who are educated and have good income earning jobs—as opposed to those who do not. As such, if the elitist definition of contemporary African architecture were to be adopted, one can suggest that what is called contemporary African architecture is negligible if placed along side the bulk of the building experiences of the majority of the citizens in different African countries. A true understanding of contemporary African architecture will be achieved when the holistic architectural practices that are going on around the continent are taken into consideration.

See also **Alexandria; Cairo; Cape Town; Dar es Salaam; Harcourt; Hasan II of Morocco; Johannesburg; Kano; Kinshasa; Lagos; Nairobi; Port Harcourt; Urbanism and Urbanization: Housing.**

BIBLIOGRAPHY

Denyer, Susan. *African Traditional Architecture: An Historical and Geographical Perspective.* London: Heinemann, 1978.

Elleh, Nnamdi. *African Architecture: Evolution and Transformation.* New York: McGraw-Hill, 1996.

Judin, Hilton, and Ivan Vladislavic, eds. *Architecture, Apartheid, and After.* New York: Distributed Art Publishers, 1998.

NNAMDI ELLEH

MONUMENTAL

What is monumental architecture in Africa and when did it begin? That depends on whether one is referencing the architectural heritage of indigenous people, Western-influenced, or Islamic-influenced monumental structures.

It is useful to extend Ali Mazrui's concept of a "triple heritage African" culture to the study of monumental architecture of the continent in order to summarize a history that is so geographically, culturally, and temporally expansive. The term "monument" is used here in a limited sense, as memorials—mnemonic structures—for the explicit purpose of remembering the collective experiences of a society or the lonesome handiworks of monarchs and rulers.

Many scholars would suggest that monumental architecture in Africa began in ancient Egypt, Axum, Lalibella, or at Great Zimbabwe, and usually include the well-known African monuments. Such an answer ignores the possibility that Africa has much older prehistoric cultures that predated the ancient Egyptian architectural heritage by more than 3,000 years. Studying monumental architecture in Africa calls for a historiography that takes into consideration the prehistoric art one finds in the Fezzan and Tassili in the Sahara Desert (6000 BCE), and those one finds in the Brandenberg Range in the Kalahari Desert, South Africa. Although the cave paintings do not depict built structures as much as they depict cultural and ritual

memories, one cannot ignore the fact that the interiors of the caves were sacred centers of learning for the communities where such paintings existed. As such they qualify as the most ancient of Africa's monumental architecture and one cannot discourse monumental art and architecture in Africa without taking them into consideration. Labelle Prussin's book *African Nomadic Architecture* (1995) provides an in-depth history of how architecture is part of a cultural memory that is transmitted from one generation to another by the nomadic women of the Sahara from prehistoric times to the present.

Indigenous monumental architectural heritage in Africa ranges from cave settings and huts to monumental structures such as the stone structures of Great Zimbabwe. At Great Zimbabwe, one would find three complexes known as the Hill Complex, the Valley, and the Great Enclosure, each one named after its location within the ensemble and the manner in which it is built. While Great Zimbabwe is one of the well-known monuments in sub-Saharan Africa, there are many sites that include religious edifices and tombs such as the Tomb of the Kabakas in Buganda (now part of Uganda), palaces, and communal environments. Architectural historians often overlook the prehistoric centers of memory transfers and jump to sites such as the stepped pyramid of Zoser (2700 BCE) as one of the major landmarks for the evolution of monumental architecture in Africa. Yet one can understand why architectural historians are fascinated by the Zoser's step pyramid because it demonstrates how the burial tombs that were once made of a single mastaba (inclined freestanding tomb) grew to greater heights by the stacking of multiple mastabas with the largest at the bottom and the smallest at the top, thereby forming a peak. Built during the Third Dynasty at Saqqara, the pyramid of Zoser is also seen as the transitional structure that brought about new methods of construction for the articulation of the king's burial chamber. The structure combined timber, clay, sand, and stone. It paved the way for the construction of the great triad pyramids of Cheops, Chefren, and Mycerinus during the Fourth Dynasty (c. 2530–2470 BCE).

According to Lásló Török (1999, 47), the ancient Nubian capital at Kerma had a walled enclosure of "about 10 meters high" with multiple gates. Török noted that this Kermitic phase of monumental architectural development was contemporaneous "with the Egyptian Middle Kingdom and Second Intermediate Period (2055–1550 BC)" (1999, 47). Such comparative analysis of ancient Egyptian and Nubian histories are problematic because scholars privilege the ancient Egyptian edifices over the Nubian structures and they end up denying the ingenuity of the Nubian people. Moreover, one cannot overlook the great capital of Axum (300 CE), Ethiopia, and the sunken churches of Lalibäla that were built during the thirteenth century. The stone structures of Great Zimbabwe (from about 1000 CE), which has grand walls, multiple gates, and royal chambers, the royal palaces of the Oba of Ife (eleventh–twelfth centuries), and the complex palaces of the Obas of Bénin, whose cities and kingdom were well established by the fifteenth century, are among the well-known monumental indigenous architectural structures in Africa.

Islamic monumental architecture includes structures that followed the spread of Islam from the Arabian Peninsula to the northern parts of the continent from the seventh century CE. Here examples such as the Kairouan Mosque (800 CE), Kairouan, Tunisia, and the Ibin Tulun Mosque (876 CE), in Cairo, Egypt, demonstrate the emergence of new forms of monumental architectural construction that are tied to Islamic religious worship. Geography and cultural technologies facilitated the production of distinct kinds of mosques in sub-Saharan Africa from the kind of mosques that were constructed in Northern Africa. The Djinguere Ber Mosque dates to 1100 CE, and the Great Mosque of Jenné dates to the thirteenth century but was destroyed several times; however the rebuilt one standing on the site today dates to about 1906–1907. The mosque of Jenné differs from the ancient mosque at Futa Jallon, Guinea. Whereas the rectangular Jenné mosque is made up of the adobe structures in what is known as the "Sudanese style," featuring its distinct, symbolic, structural expressions for portals and pillars, the mosque at Futa Jallon is made mostly of thatch materials and it is round in the typical beehive model of tropical Guinea coast construction.

Contemporary examples illustrating the influence of separate heritages are the recently completed library in Alexandria (1989–2000), Egypt, and the 1993 Hassan II Mosque at Casablanca, Morocco. Commentators suggest that the library structure is intended to help Egypt reclaim its place among the nations of the world as a leading center of learning; whereas the mosque claims its origin in the formation of the al-Walid Dynasty from the sixteenth century CE. Imbued with new meanings, one can still find the threads that explain the strong, nostalgic, nationalistic references that Egyptians and Moroccans are making to the ancient library in Alexandria and to the twelfth-century Almohad mosques of Morocco respectively for the purposes of justifying the present constructions.

See also **Archaeology and Prehistory; Art, Genres and Periods; Cairo; Casablanca; Jenné and Jenné-jeno; Kalahari Desert; Prehistory; Sahara Desert; Tunisia; Zimbabwe, Great.**

BIBLIOGRAPHY

Denison, Edward; Ren Guang Yu; and Gebremedhin Naigzy. *Asmara: Africa's Secret Modernist City.* London and New York: Merrell, 2003.

Denyer, Susan. *African Traditional Architecture: An Historical and Geographical Perspective.* New York: Africana Publishing Company, 1978.

De Vere, James Allen, and Thomas H. Wilson. *Swahili Houses and Tombs of the Coast of Kenya.* London: AARP, 1979.

Elleh, Nnamdi. *African Architecture: Evolution and Transformation.* New York: McGraw-Hill, 1997.

Elleh, Nnamdi. *Architecture and Power in Africa.* Westport, CT: Praeger, 2002.

Gardi, Rene. *Indigenous African Architecture*, trans. Siegrid McRae. New York: Van Nostrand Reinhold, 1974.

Garlake, Peter. *The Early Islamic Architecture of the East African Coast.* Nairobi: Oxford University Press, 1966.

Láslo Török, "Ancient Nubia." In *Africa: The Art of a Continent*, ed. Tom Phillips. Munich: Prestel, 1999.

Lawrence, A. W. *Trade Castles and Forts of West Africa.* Stanford, CA: Stanford University Press, 1964.

Mark, Peter. *"Portuguese" Style and Luso-African Identity: Precolonial Senegambia, Sixteenth-Nineteenth Centuries.* Bloomington: Indiana University Press, 2002.

Morris, James, and Suzanne Blier. *Butabu: Adobe Architecture of West Africa.* Princeton, NJ: Princeton Architectural Press, 2004.

Moughton, J. C. *Hausa Architecture.* London: Etbnographica, 1985.

Phillipson, David, ed. *The Monuments of Aksum.* Addis Ababa: Addis Ababa University Press, 1997.

Prussin, Labelle. *Architecture in Northern Ghana: A Study of Forms and Functions.* Berkeley: University of California Press, 1969.

Prussin, Labelle. *Hatumere: Islamic Design in West Africa.* Berkeley: University of California Press, 1986.

Prussin, Labelle. *African Nomadic Architecture: Place, Space, and Gender.* Washington, DC: Smithsonian Institution Press, 1995.

NNAMDI ELLEH

TOWN PLANNING

No urban space is ever truly unplanned. No matter how random or haphazard a site might seem, on further examination one can often discern underlying cultural logics at work. From the earliest times, African settlements have been structured by diverse informal planning principles: land use conventions, religious prescriptions, neighborhood norms, and kinship relations, among others. These indigenous practices are quite distinct from formal town planning, however, which arose in Africa in a colonial context in the late nineteenth century, predicated on the idea of overcoming or radically reordering local urban landscapes.

The development of town planning in Africa was inextricably linked to European ideologies of the so-called civilizing mission—the need to legitimate colonial control by representing it as a form of modernizing improvement. In this sense, town planning often arrived on the scene wrapped in the guise of scientific reform and enlightened rationality. But despite the views of practitioners or officials, the remaking of African urban sites by colonial regimes was always more than simply technical or aesthetic. Across the continent, diverse initiatives were driven by a wide array of motives, but everywhere planning was deeply connected to issues of power.

In certain cases, as with the mining towns of the Copperbelt, new cities were laid out in accord with the demands of colonial economies, extractive nodes in a global imperial order. Throughout central, southern, and eastern Africa, colonial cities were often gendered worlds, as male migrants were allowed temporary residence to support production, while their families (and the costs of social reproduction) were relegated to rural reserves. In other instances, urban designs intersected with ideological goals, as colonial rulers sought to deploy architecture as an assertion of Western superiority and the permanence of its civilization. Colonial cities were also laboratories or experimental terrains where metropolitan powers could try out new technologies of the modern. In North African colonies, for example, the French founded *villes nouvelles* as geometric counterpoints to more organic older sites, labeled as "casbahs" or preserves of native "tradition."

As with "slum" clearances and sanitary intervention in Europe, the ideological and economic aspects of planning were linked to the political imperatives of empire. Various spatial practices emphasized the containment and separation of African "others" in the urban sphere. Especially in the later nineteenth century, segregation became a driving force in colonial city planning, setting European districts or garden suburbs off from native reserves or locations. As Frantz Fanon and others have argued, colonial urbanism was quintessentially defined by dualistic oppositions, as inequalities of race and class were literally inscribed in the built environment. These strategies of enframing or isolation were operative in varying degrees in different contexts, with perhaps the most extreme examples being found in the forms of urban *apartheid* that later developed in South Africa.

As this suggests, colonialism was fundamentally predicated on racial difference and unequal access—to resources, rights, opportunities, and even the space of the city. Officials and planners had multiple motives for seeking to keep Africans in their "proper places." In some cases they were driven by desires for exclusivity or elite status, while European racism, preoccupations with security, and cultural arrogance all played a role. More than anything else, however, sanitary concerns figured centrally in urban planning in colonial Africa. Within Europe itself, nineteenth-century industrial cities had long been seen as dangerous if not morally and socially degenerate. Reformers seized on various strategies to civilize and uplift the lower classes. From its Victorian roots, planning developed with a distinct obsession with health, light, and air, especially apparent in later British garden city movements. Sanitarians advocated clearing out crowded districts as a means of simultaneously "cleaning" them up. Even in Europe, the body politic came to be understood in terms of a new politics of the body, as states sought to intervene in ever more intimate domains, surveying space, monitoring behavior, and managing populations by means of statistics and surveys. In the tropical world, of course, sanitary ideology took on even greater force, informed by a sort of environmental determinism. Especially prior to germ theory, Africans and the spaces in which they lived were seen as potential sources of contagion or miasma, which Europeans sought to avoid or contain by means of green belts or *cordons sanitaires.* Planning, policing, and public health regimes all too often went hand in hand.

Urban planning has always been a capital and resource intensive process, and African colonial landscapes were deeply marked by the legacy of failed, imperfect, or partial schemes. When planning did occur, it was generally both elitist and exclusionary, leaving the needs of the vast majority of urban dwellers unmet. Anticolonial movements had a strong base in urban centers in the postwar period, castigating European imperialists for failing to deliver the goods they promised. When decolonization swept the continent in the 1960s, however, new African states found themselves confronting a huge reserve of unmet needs and high expectations from urban residents. Colonialism had excluded the majority from services and social welfare and left behind a legacy of weak states and uneven economies. Even in the most promising of circumstances, postcolonial regimes—whether socialist or capitalist—would be challenged to overcome these difficulties in the urban milieu.

The postcolonial period produced quite rapid rates of urbanization across the continent, increasing the demands on municipal regimes precisely at a moment when faith in planning and the funds to support it were most in doubt. As cities experienced exponential rates of growth from Cairo to Kinshasa and Cape Town, squatters and informal settlements proliferated, as ordinary Africans responded with enormous creativity and ingenuity to carve out urban spaces for themselves, even in the absence of basic services such as water, waste disposal, and electricity. Informal cultural practices and spatial norms, negotiated and debated against the rhythms of daily life, continue to shape the contours of African cities, even in the most difficult

conditions. At the new millennium, burgeoning sprawl and structural adjustment have coincided with the virtual collapse of planning, producing vast urban conurbations—megacities of almost bewildering complexity that Mike Davis has identified as new African nodes in an emergent "planet of slums."

See also **Apartheid; Cairo; Cape Town; Colonial Policies and Practices; Decolonization; Fanon, Frantz; Kinshasa; Urbanism and Urbanization.**

BIBLIOGRAPHY

Bissell, William Cunningham. "Conservation and the Colonial Past: Colonialism, Space, and Power in Zanzibar." In *Africa's Urban Past,* ed. David M. Anderson and Richard Rathbone. Oxford, U.K. and Portsmouth, N.H.: James Currey and Heinemann, 2000.

Davis, Mike. *Planet of Slums.* London: Verso, 2006.

Home, Robert K. *Of Planting and Planning: The Making of British Colonial Cities.* London: E & FN Spon, 1997.

King, Anthony D. *Urbanism, Colonialism, and the World Economy.* London: Routledge, 1990.

Mabogunje, Akin L. "Urban Planning and the Post-Colonial State in Africa: A Research Overview." *African Studies Review* 33, no. 2 (1990): 121–203.

Murray, Martin J., and Garth Myers, eds. *Cities in Contemporary Africa.* New York: Palgrave MacMillan, 2007.

Wright, Gwendolyn. *The Politics of Design in French Colonial Urbanism.* Chicago: University of Chicago Press, 1991.

WILLIAM CUNNINGHAM BISSELL

ARMAH, AYI KWEI (1939–). Armah was born in Sekondi-Takoradi, the twin harbor city of western Ghana. He underwent his early education at the prestigious Achimota School, then won a scholarship to the Massachusetts Groton School in the United States. Armah earned a first degree in sociology at Harvard University and then worked in Algeria as a translator for the magazine *Révolution Africaine.* Upon his return to Ghana in 1964, he served as a scriptwriter for Ghana Television and taught English in a local school. Back in the United States, he earned a master of fine arts in creative writing at Columbia University in New York. From there he continued his peripatetic existence, serving as editor of the well-known magazine *Jeune Afrique* in Paris, and teaching at universities in Tanzania, Lesotho, and the United States in the 1970s and 1980s. He then settled down in the village of Popenguine in Senegal where he runs a publishing house, Per Ankh. Having lived in all the regions of Africa, Armah is one of the rare intellectuals who can claim firsthand knowledge of the continent as a whole. Armah attained immediate fame with his first novel, *The Beautyful Ones Are Not Yet Born* (1968), one of the first indictments of the postcolonial African state. His subsequent novels, *Fragments* (1970), *Why Are We So Blest?* (1972), *Two Thousand Seasons* (1973), *The Healers* (1979), *Osiris Rising* (1995), and *KTM: In the House of Life* (2002), demonstrate an iconoclastic and visionary commitment to the liberation of African peoples. His essays also insist on the social efficacy of literature.

See also **Literature.**

BIBLIOGRAPHY

Damodar Rao, K. *The Novels of Ayi Kwei Armah.* New Delhi, India: Prestige Books, 1993.

Fraser, Robert. *The Novels of Ayi Kwei Armah: A Study in Polemical Fiction.* London: Heinemann, 1980.

Lazarus, Neil. *Resistance in Postcolonial African Fiction.* New Haven, CT: Yale University Press, 1990.

Ogede, Ode. *Ayi Kwei Armah, Radical Iconoclast: Pitting Imaginary Worlds against the Actual.* Athens: Ohio University Press, 2000.

Wright, Derek. *Critical Perspectives on Ayi Kwei Armah.* Washington, DC: Three Continents Press, 1992.

ALIKO SONGOLO

ARMIES. *See* **Government: Military; Military Organizations; Warfare.**

ART

This entry includes the following articles:
OVERVIEW
MARKETS

OVERVIEW

"African art" as a concept and practice segments and selects from African genres while at the same time imposing a spurious unity on the continent's artistic products. There is no universal category of art in Africa, nor, in a continent inhabited by speakers of four or five unrelated language groups and as many distinct civilizations, any uniform aesthetic. Historic objects now recognized and collected as art are likely to have been made for use in some ritual context; when not in use they would probably have been hidden, not displayed for aesthetic contemplation. In modern times, however, African artists living on the continent and abroad have produced art intended, in the European manner, for display in galleries and museums.

SIGNIFICANCE IN AFRICAN ART

In traditional contexts, African sculptors may be admired for their skill, but their works are not valued primarily as products of a distinctive sensibility that comments on human experience. Very often a carved figure is merely the base for a complex product to be completed by others who add medicines and sacrificial or other materials. The result is something more than an object: It may have a personality of its own, imposing rules of conduct upon people in its vicinity. Its significance is apprehended not in objective isolation but in a context of social excitement and tension, accompanied by music, dancing, and dramatic events. Examples include masquerades of the Igbo in southeastern Nigeria, and *minkisi* (ritually significant objects) formerly made in Kongo, a province in the western Democratic Republic of the Congo. Wyatt MacGaffey has documented the processes by which a *nkisi* (singular) sculpture and its medicines were assembled according to an obligatory process supervised by an appropriate expert. When properly respected, the resulting composite was believed able to confer benefits or to inflict harm at a distance by mysterious means. If its rules were broken, or the medicines hidden in it fall out, it reverted to the status of a mere object, even though its outward appearance might not have changed.

Henry Drewal describes the appearance of a sacred mask, Eyánlá "the great mother," among the Yoruba of southwestern Nigeria. "Preliminary masqueraders prepare the entrance of Eyánlá, who comes in total darkness. While she is abroad, all lights must be extinguished for no one must gaze on the face of the mother." As she moves in a gentle, slow dance, matching her steps with the drum rhythms, the elders of the cult flock around her to limit the audience's view of the headdress, which is carried in an almost horizontal position and largely obscured by a long white cloth. The mask itself is a bold, simple shape, consisting of a head with a long, flat "beard." When the carver has completed it, using a prescribed type of wood obtained from the forest in a prescribed fashion, the elders apply medicines to empower the mask, which otherwise is just a piece of wood. The relatively large size of the mask indicates its importance, the prominence of the forehead suggests that it is swollen with spiritual force, and the long white cloth symbolizes the unity and prosperity of the community.

In this example, the significance of the object lies in what is not seen as much as in what is visible, and in the rule-governed process of production as much as in the product. Even that which is there to be seen may be a disguise: apparently decorative geometrical patterns may have a more profound significance than an anthropomorphic component of the same sculpture. In West Africa a tight zigzag pattern indicates water, earth, or sky, one of the three cosmological domains. In Tabwa art, from the southeastern Democratic Republic of the Congo (DRC), a simple pattern that appears purely decorative conveys a basic cosmological idea that is also the key to a profound philosophy. Called "the rising of the moon," it consists of a row of isosceles triangles arranged in such a way that their bases form two parallel lines. For the Tabwa, according to Allen Roberts, the new moon is a time of renewal and the darkened moon is a time of danger, when witchcraft threatens.

In Kongo the significance of an element in a composition may be its name rather than its appearance. Words are associated with African art forms in varying degrees of intimacy, particularly in the case of textiles. In some areas, weaving itself is regarded as a metaphor for authoritative speech. Names and proverbs may be literally inscribed on cloth, or implicit in the pattern for those who know how to read it. Industrially produced cloths, local or imported, used to make women's costumes,

have names and proverbs attributed to them on account of some association with the pattern; for example, "My husband is a good provider," or, perhaps, "I feel sorry for his mistress." Women buy such cloths for the message they wish to broadcast. This medium is most highly developed in East Africa, where a style of clothing called *kanga* collectively constitutes the equivalent of a community bulletin board, on which all kinds of references and messages can be posted, many having ambiguous and alternative meanings.

EUROPEANS AND AFRICAN ART

In Europe, the first African objects to be preserved were regarded as curios rather than art, although their workmanship was admired and they found their way into prestigious European collections. They include an Ife divination tray from modern Nigeria, raffia textiles from the Kuba kingdom (modern central DRC), and beautifully carved ivory horns from Kongo. The earliest-known African objects of this kind in Europe date from the seventeenth century. In nineteenth-century Europe the development of theories of social evolution and the imperial expansion that accompanied them aroused great interest in African and other exotic objects, collected as evidence of primitiveness, as tokens of barbarism to be overcome, and as trophies of conquest. These objects were not seen at the time as having aesthetic merit.

By the end of the century, every respectable museum had its ethnographic collection; some sailors, traders, and other travelers made a business of supplying this demand. Most of what is now regarded as classical African art results from the conquests and conversions that took place from about 1880 to 1920. These processes were actively creative of "African art," in that collectors chose what interested them, neglected or destroyed other material, damaged or otherwise modified much of it in transit, and placed it in new contexts where it acquired new names and meanings.

The British conquest of the Kingdom of Bénin (in modern Nigeria) in 1897 brought the now-famous Bénin "bronzes" (in fact, brass) to the attention of Europeans, who found them so exceptional that they attributed them to influences from outside Africa. Modern evidence shows that the Bénin bronze tradition, casting what are often very complex images by the lost-wax method, is only one of several distinct bronze traditions in the area, whose forms developed centuries ago from preceding ceramic traditions.

At the turn of the century, such postimpressionist artists as Paul Gauguin, Pablo Picasso, and Amedeo Modigliani found some of the flotsam of empire in the flea markets of Paris and were influenced in their work by the formal transformations of the human face achieved by West African sculptors. However, apart from a few scholarly studies and the continued interest shown by certain European sculptors, African art did not attract much attention as art until the 1950s, when interest still focused mostly on sculptures in wood and bronze conforming approximately to European tastes.

Since the independence of the majority of African states starting in 1960, however, an ever-growing list of African object-genres has come to be recognized as art by collectors, scholars, auction houses, and museums. In Africa itself, museums of art have been established, and a few individuals now build personal collections. In the past a sculpture, having no value in itself, might have been thrown away at the end of the festival for which it was created, or when it was discovered to be no longer effective for its intended purpose.

A hypothetical example (based on a description by Eberhard Fischer) of an object's social career through several identities might be that of a Dan mask in Liberia. The mask was originally a forest spirit that wanted to help, entertain, and teach the village people. The spirit appeared in a dream to a sympathetic person, dictating the appearance in which it should be manifested and sustained, whether static—in the form of a bundle of fur, antelope horns, or a small snail shell filled with various ingredients—or (as in this case) mobile—in the form of a mask, the focal object in a masquerade performance. The mask was not an image, it *was* the spirit; it was believed to be alive, and it expected sacrifices, gifts, and certain observances. In old age this mask was promoted by the elders, becoming a respected sign of chiefly authority and exercising judicial functions. To suit this higher status it was modified, losing some of its pristine beauty and acquiring new features such as a mustache. In its new function it was not worn or danced but merely placed beside the chief; it was itself masked when in public by a white cloth covering it. Later it fell into the hands of a dealer, was deprived of its costume, and became a commodity. Eventually, it was acquired by a museum and ended its days hung on a wall as a piece of African art, for the first time open to inspection by anyone.

The aptness of an African object as art in Europe has traditionally depended on a set of criteria by which "art" (European) is contrasted with "primitive art" (African, Oceanian, and classical), which is sold in specialized stores and exhibited in segregated spaces. Whereas European art objects are individuated as the unique and dated products of named individuals, intended for sale, an object defined as primitive art is thought of as typical of a group; each piece represents a genre that remains unchanging over time and is produced anonymously for ritual use. Aesthetic considerations come into play only after an object has been classified as art, primitive art, or not-art.

Many collectors of African art refuse to accept objects known to be the work of named individuals or to have been produced for sale rather than for use in some ritual context. This attitude is slowly changing as modern studies show that in Africa sculptures have always been commercially produced and that they were exported to other areas, either as blanks to be transformed into ritual instruments by the appropriate specialist or as parts of complete rituals, purchased together with instructions on the dances to be performed and the rules to be observed. Artists have always been sensitive to the demands of the market; masks or pottery used in one area might be produced in another, and new rituals required new artifacts. European taste has long influenced certain sectors of African art; in the seventeenth century, Portuguese visitors to west Africa commissioned exquisite ivory carvings, and it has been shown that much of what is usually known as "traditional Mangbetu art" in northeastern DRC was produced largely in response to European demand from about 1860 onward.

The fact of changing tastes and markets raises the question of how "authenticity" can to be certified to meet the needs of the art market. The Western idea of art as the unique product of a particular hand calls for a connoisseur's skills to distinguish true art from fakes and copies; but with respect to African art, the short answer to the question must be that the criteria of selection and value can only be based on personal taste, at least until the piece has acquired a market history. In Africa itself, both African sculptors and African and European dealers go to great lengths to foster the illusion of intrinsic authenticity, as Christopher Steiner has recently documented.

DISTINCTIONS IN AFRICAN ART

Recent studies have begun to report on the aesthetic tastes of traditional sculptors and their publics. The Yoruba believe that sculptures should look like their subjects, but not to the point of sacrificing ideally beautiful features, which are associated with youth, proportion, delicacy, symmetry. Sheer technical skill is admired; many Yoruba masks and headpieces are marvels of carving and imagination. The Bamana in Mali, according to Patrick McNaughton, value clarity, geometrical stylization, and resemblance to archetypal images, as in the case of Tye Wara, their celebrated antelope sculptures, which are the headpieces of masquerade costumes seen in agricultural festivals. On the other hand, the masks of the secret Komo society among the Bamana deliberately offend against these values; they are made to be as frightening as possible, with large horns and huge teeth, to represent creatures of darkness, of the bush, their shape obscured by increments of powerful knowledge that portray vicious animality. The dance performance of the mask, lasting all night and demanding great skill and strength, is said to be awesome and intimidating. Another Bamana association, however, uses enigmatic objects called *boli* that turn their back on the viewer, so to speak, and are deliberately unreadable.

A useful though not absolute distinction has been made by Malcolm McLeod between art in Africa that makes a statement about facts and principles that deserve respect by the public at large and art that is adapted over time to a series of contingencies. "Statement images" are those meant to represent that which is formal, fixed, and timeless; they are intended to elevate rulers, whether kings or lineal ancestors, to superhuman status. Their function is to deny time, and they communicate that message by their form alone. They include commemorative bronze heads of Bénin kings in Nigeria and the wooden statues of Kuba kings in central DRC, relatively realistic and readable

sculptures which were among the first African objects to be accepted as art in Europe.

"Process images," on the other hand, mediate relations between persons in real time, as in the case of figures used in divination, healing, and conflict resolution, to which sacrificial blood, coloring, and other material may be added on each occasion. Kongo *nkisi* figures accumulated nails, rags, and little bundles during years of use; supposedly, the professional operator of such a device remembered to what each addition referred. Such objects depend for their readability on associated codes and conventions, such as proverbs, invocations, or other verbal utterances, which adapt their significance to the situation at hand.

To these two categories a third may be added—the mask—in which one must include not only the many hundreds found particularly among Niger-Congo-speaking peoples in West and Central Africa, but all objects in which, from the users' point of view, the essential feature is the relationship between the visible outside and the concealed interior. The exterior contains and transforms the interior, which in turn animates and transforms the exterior. In this category fall certain shrines, magical charms, sculptures, masquerades, sacred chiefs, and persons in a state of spirit possession, whose outer appearance is regarded as a mask. Here the task of art is not to represent the actual but to suggest and make real the unseen. Masks are animated not only by medicines but, of course, by the body of the dancer within, which a museum necessarily eliminates. In turn, the dancer is not any volunteer but an individual or member of a group with an assigned right and obligation to dance this mask.

In a fourth category is placed the art of the useful object. Useful objects include east African headrests, carved Somali or Dan spoons, Asante jewelry, Yoruba houseposts, Mangbetu men's dance hats, and Kongo water pots, hairpins, granary doors, canoe prows, and burial cloths. Such objects may include references to mythical themes, moral precepts, and religious secrets but are primarily intended for use in ordinary life (and death). They are made to please the eye and are subject to critique accordingly, by the standards of the genre and the cultural tradition to which they belong. Often they are items of conspicuous consumption reserved to the wealthy. Among the many materials used must be included the human body, grandly painted and displayed among, for example, the Nuba of Kordofan in Sudan.

In the forest areas of western and central Africa, a certain unity of artistic themes can be identified, attributable not to the forest environment as such but to the religious culture of the populations who have adapted to it, all of whom speak related languages and share, in a broad sense, a similar cosmology expressed characteristically in various forms of "mask." In the Sahel or Sudanic areas of western Africa, the forms and meanings of art are considerably different. In Mali, the much-discussed but still enigmatic civilization of the Dogon has produced sculptures that are among the most widely admired of African artworks. Their remarkable cosmogonic theories, reported by Marcel Griaule and his associates beginning in the 1930s, emphasize the process of differentiation of an original cosmic "egg."

Anthropomorphic figures, often androgynous or as male and female pairs, often covered with a heavy patina of sacrificial material, display distinctively abstract and hieratic forms; they have been said to represent the primordial demiurges, often twins, who appeared in Dogon myths. The three principal types of mask are supposed to refer to three different cosmogonic stages; other masks represent historical events. Unfortunately, not much has been reported on the context in which masks are actually used, and recent research has cast doubt on the authenticity of Griaule's understanding of Dogon cosmology. In modern times, among the Dogon and in much of Africa, masquerades are now primarily public entertainments, rehearsed as such. The events are frequently sponsored by secular governments eager both to attract tourists and to neutralize the religious and potentially political significance of the performances.

The many different art forms in eastern and southern Africa, unlike those of western and central Africa, do not usually refer to spirits or exhibit the same preoccupation with secret meaning and hidden content. The speakers of Nilotic languages in southern Sudan and northern Uganda believe in spirits so abstract as to be barely personified at all; they do not use plastic forms to reinforce belief in them or to suggest the presence of the invisible. On the other hand, both men and women may pay great attention to personal adornment and treasure beautifully carved objects of general utility, such as stools, headrests, pipes, and jewelry. The celebrated artistic traditions and inventions of the Mangbetu and their neighbors in northeastern DRC were almost entirely devoted to personal adornment and conspicuous display associated with the aristocracy of the kingdom.

RECENT AFRICAN ART

In the West, as art in the late twentieth century became increasingly preoccupied with its own conventions, much of the appeal of African art lay in its apparent narrative legibility, despite cultural differences. Paradoxically, the success of two generations of scholars and curators in convincing the American (and, to a lesser extent, European) public of the value of "traditional" African art has led, in the expression of Susan Vogel, to its "museumification"; the institutions that once produced the canonical works are in decline on the continent; for example, repression by colonial and postcolonial authorities has reduced the great sculptured *minkisi* of Kongo to little packets carried about the body, and the Mbari cult houses of the Owerri Igbo, filled with clay figures of men and gods, are no longer built.

At the turn of the twenty-first century, however, the field of African art has shown extraordinary dynamism. Although some religious festivals and other activities for which art was produced have died out, artists adapt to new social forms, new personal experiences, and new materials. Individuals reach various compromises: Some Yoruba carvers have adapted traditional themes to Christian purposes. Some painters and sculptors see their work as the product of the same spiritual revelations that have guided artists in the past. Entirely new schools and styles have emerged, such as the Shona stone sculptures in Zimbabwe. Traditional body and house painting designs have been transferred to canvas and glass. A large sculpture industry has developed, especially in southern Ghana, to supply Western living rooms. Among traditionalists, makers of ritual masks may paint them in bright industrial colors and incorporate new themes, such as the automobile or the white man. The dead may now be commemorated by complex cement sculptures, including portraits. In southern Ghana, sculptor Kane Kwei (1922–1992) began carving particularly dramatic coffins shaped like cars, aircraft, or hens.

At all levels and in most genres, art in Africa is expected to inform, guide, and uplift the public. Aesthetic considerations and appreciation for originality, though present, are not uppermost considerations. Recognized themes, such as the Mami Wata water spirits, who usually take the form of a voluptuous mermaid, often compete for attention with other icons of success, such as Arnold Schwarzenegger.

Studio-trained artists producing for markets in Africa or abroad must also negotiate the tense relationship between "tradition" and "modernity," "Africanity" and "universality." Art produced by Africans, many of them living and working on other continents, is regarded as "contemporary" rather than "African." Among the most distinguished works are the ceramic vases of Magdalene Odundo, born in Kenya, and the mechanized sculptures of Sokari Douglas Camp, born in Nigeria but resident in London. Chris Ofili is a British artist whose work incorporates African elements. The monumental clay sculptures of Salah M. Hassan of Sénégal deal with international themes. An artist whose work but has been hailed as world class is the self-taught Malian photographer Seydou Keita, whose portraits, made between 1962 and 1977 but discovered in New York in 1991, promptly became internationally famous and the center of an international tug-of-war over the rights to his negatives and prints. There is now a thriving art photography scene in Mali.

Scholars, critics, and curators continue to argue among themselves about what is considered "art" and how to evaluate it, but also continue to discover hitherto neglected genres. The work of untrained "popular" painters in urban environments, particularly in DRC, began to attract critical attention in the 1980s; their work, initially scorned as "primitive," has begun to command one-man exhibitions at prestigious museums and galleries. In addition, more attention is being paid to pottery and textiles, many of which express complex social and cosmological themes. "Wrapped in Pride," an exhibition of Ghanaian kente that toured the United States in 1999, aroused the admiration of textile specialists as well as artists and the public.

In Africa itself, there are few galleries, virtually no critics, and no regular market; despite these obvious handicaps, the exciting inventiveness and diversity of new art often appeals to a popular rather than an elite audience. Collectible objects, whose function is that of memory, represent and bring closer a scene distant in time or space and provide food for thought. African nations in the early 2000s feel some obligation to collect ancestral art in museums as a sign of both their distinctive cultural traditions and of their modernity. Popular paintings collected by the urban middle class in DRC show generic scenes such as "Land of the Ancestors," may at first sight seem a trite rendition of a stereotypical rural African landscape, but upon closer inspection evoke problematic contrasts between rural and urban, tranquility and disorder, African and European, the past and the present—thus "remembering" the present through the past, as Johannes Fabian puts it, and continuing the ancient tradition that in seeing you do not see unless you are in the know.

See also **Art History and the Study of Africa; Art, Genres and Periods; Arts; Body Adornment and Clothing; Ceramics; Douglas Camp, Sokari; Languages; Mami Wata; Masks and Masquerades; Postcolonialism; Symbols and Symbolism; Textiles.**

BIBLIOGRAPHY

Barley, Nigel. *Smashing Pots: Works of Clay from Africa.* Washington, DC: Smithsonian Institution Press, 1994.

Barnes, Ruth, ed. *Textiles in Indian Ocean Societies.* Oxford: Ashmolean, 2004.

Biebuyck, Daniel. *Lega Culture: Art, Initiation, and Moral Philosophy among a Central African People.* Berkeley: University of California Press, 1973.

Bravmann, René A. *Islam and Tribal Art in West Africa.* New York: Cambridge University Press, 1974.

Cole, Herbert M., and Chike C. Aniakor, eds. *Igbo Arts: Community and Cosmos.* Los Angeles: University of California Press, 1984.

Drewal, Henry. "Art and the Perception of Women in Yoruba Culture," *Cahiers d'études africaines* 68 (1977).

Drewal, Henry John, and John Pemberton III, eds. *Yoruba: Nine Centuries of African Art and Thought.* New York: Center for African Art, 1989.

Fabian, Johannes. *Remembering the Present: Painting and Popular History in Zaire.* Berkeley: University of California. 1996.

Kennedy, Jean. *New Currents, Ancient Rivers: Contemporary African Artists in a Generation of Change.* Washington, DC: Smithsonian Institution Press, 1992.

Lamp, Frederick L., ed. *See the Music, Hear the Dance: Rethinking African Art at the Baltimore Museum of Art.* New York: Prestel, 2004.

MacGaffey, Wyatt. "The Personhood of Ritual Objects: Kongo *Minkisi.*" *Etnofoor* 3, no. 1 (1990): 45–61.

Nooter, Mary H., ed. *Secrecy: African Art that Conceals and Reveals.* New York: Museum for African Art, 1993.

Phillips, Tom, ed. *Africa: The Art of a Continent.* London: Royal Academy of Arts, 1996.

Rips, Michael. "Who Owns Seidu Keita?" *New York Times.* (January 22, 2006).

Roberts, Mary N., and Allen F. Roberts. *Memory: Luba Art and the Making of History.* New York: Museum for African Art, 1996.

Schildkrout, Enid, and Curt Keim, eds. *African Reflections: Art from Northeastern Zaire.* New York: Cambridge University Press, 1990.

Steiner, Christopher B. *African Art in Transit.* New York: Cambridge University Press, 1994.

Thompson, Robert Farris. "Yoruba Artistic Criticism." In *The Traditional Artist in African Societies,* ed. W. L. d'Azevedo. Bloomington: Indiana University Press, 1973.

Visonà, Monica B., et al., eds. *A History of Art in Africa.* New York: Prentice Hall, 2000.

Vogel, Susan M., ed. *Africa Explores: Twentieth Century African Art.* New York: Center for African Art, 1994.

Vogel, Susan M. *Baule: African Art, Western Eyes.* New Haven, CT: Yale University Press, 1997.

Vogel, Susan M. "Whither African Art? Emerging Scholarship at the End of an Age." *African Arts* 38, no. 4 (2005): 12–17.

WYATT MACGAFFEY

MARKETS

In the second half of the nineteenth century, when European powers established colonial rule over most of Africa, the demand for native objects—including African ivory items such as salt cellars, forks and spoons, and animal horn—increased. Viewed as specimens, they arrived in new ethnographic museums at a time when anthropologists and other scientists sought to affirm ideas about human evolution and the diffusion of culture through the study of artifacts. Missionary societies amassed holdings, and military personnel, administrators, and residents in the colonies acquired African objects. As a result of these activities many pieces created for African patrons and embedded in a range of cultural practices became part of exchanges and trade transactions between indigenous sellers and foreign clients. African artists increasingly catered to the foreigners' tastes and desires and created works in traditional forms as well as souvenirs. In Germany, companies such as J.F.G. Umlauff in Hamburg sent agents to collect abroad, and purchased objects from colonials, fellow dealers, and collectors, then offering them to museums. In Great Britain, William O. Oldman and Kenneth Webster, collectors and dealers, pursued similar business strategies.

THE EXPANDING ART MARKET

Western appreciation of African objects shifted at the beginning of the twentieth century and objects previously perceived as artifacts transformed into works of art—a reevaluation promoted by avant-garde artists and intellectuals in Paris and other European metropolises. Parisian galleries began to display African objects, received mostly through colonial conduits, but occasionally also from Africans among them a large contingent of Senegalese who traveled to France. Collectors cum gallery owners and art promoters were instrumental in the nascent African art market in Europe and the United States. Among them were the Hungarian Joseph Brummer (1883–1947) influential both in France and the United States, the Frenchman Paul Guillaume (1893–1934) in Paris, and the American Alfred Stieglitz (1864–1946) in New York. By the 1920s, dealers such as Charles Ratton in Paris, and collectors—among them Helena Rubinstein in New York—were at the forefront of the commodification of African art. Market structures developed in the West, and colonials and Africans stepped up delivery and production of objects on the supply end.

After World War II, African works gained wide acceptance, and the number of collectors grew. When African countries became independent in the early 1960s many new governments encouraged tourism facilitated by the affordability of air travel. Collectors, who had initially acquired their works through middlemen, now visited the African continent to purchase objects. European and American dealers regularly embarked on shopping trips to their African suppliers. In the United

States, several developments favored the expansion of the art market: the founding of the Peace Corps in 1961, which brought thousands young Americans to Africa, some of whom developed an interest in art; the civil rights movement with its emphasis on African heritage; the introduction of African art as a recognized specialization in art history at American universities; and the establishment of commercial galleries in New York, Los Angeles, and other cities, competing with dealers in Paris and Brussels, the second hub of the European trade in African art.

Commercial structures in West and Central Africa, which had been in place since the 1920s and 1930s, became more elaborate. By the 1960s the West African art market was mainly in the hands of Wolof, Mande, and Hausa merchants, members of groups that had conducted trade in West Africa for centuries. They funneled objects through major cities, such as Dakar, Abidjan, and Bamako. Top African dealers traveled to Paris and later New York and supplied gallery owners. Mid-level merchants also ventured to Europe and the United States. These so-called runners were part of the supply chain, beginning with extracting objects in villages and towns or procuring them in workshops, and ending with their arrival on European and American clients' doorsteps. Belgians dominated market in Zaire, the former Belgian Congo and now the Democratic Republic of the Congo, although African middlemen participated in the trade and also appeared in Brussels.

Workshops in production centers—Kumasi (Ghana), Abidjan (Côte d'Ivoire), Foumban (Cameroon); and Mushenge (the Democratic Republic of the Congo)—multiplied as entrepreneurial men discovered new ways to make a living. Most specialized in wooden sculpture, such as figures and masks, favorites with collectors. Carvers, and African and expatriate dealers were well aware of the fact that their clients preferred so-called "authentic" pieces—that is, works produced for Africans and used by them in ceremonies and rituals—and began to rework older objects and age new ones, creating patinas and other signs of wear. Although such practices had occurred before World War II, the sheer quantity of altered pieces, replicas, and outright fakes adversely affected the market.

By the 1980s, collectors deplored that "authentic" objects no longer came out of Africa and preferred purchasing works with provenances reaching back to the beginning of the twentieth century and associated with well-known dealers or collectors, such as Guillaume, Ratton, and Rubinstein. The sales at Sotheby's and Christies, two major auction houses offering non-Western art, reflect the dramatic gains made by such objects, which culminated in the 2006 auction of a collection assembled by the late Parisian art dealer Pierre Verité. It netted more than $55.5 million and the highest ever price for an African work of art paid at auction to date (2007), a Fang Ngil mask that brought about $7.5 million.

During this same time period the market expanded, now embracing objects that earlier belonged into the craft category. Collectors who worried about the authenticity of masks and figures turned to utilitarian wooden objects, such as spoons and vessels, pottery, textiles, dress and adornment, metal and leatherwork, which were novel and not yet tinged by fakery. Headrests, weapons, and beadwork and other types of objects from southern and eastern Africa, regions that lack the rich sculptural traditions of West and Central Africa, also became popular. Most of the wood carvings were made by men, but with this expansion of the market, women's creations—pots, baskets, and beadwork among them—also entered collections.

By the end of the twentieth century, workshops and artists all over the African continent turned out objects for an increasingly global market, while the high-end dealers and collectors struggled with scarcity of "authentic" works and the large number of replicas and fakes. In the early twenty-first century objects made in workshops all over Africa come to Europe and the United States by the container load, are offered on various Internet sites and in large warehouses. Workshops no longer specialize in the arts germane to their areas. Rather, they produce a pan-African repertoire: Kota reliquary figures, Dan masks, and Bamana ci wara antelopes.

AFRICA'S LOSS OF CULTURAL PATRIMONY

The exodus of objects provided African artists, members of workshops, merchants, and middlemen with a livelihood, but also irreparably damaged many countries' cultural heritage. In the late nineteenth and early twentieth centuries participants in colonial military campaigns often forcefully removed treasures for museums and collections. Among the most infamous events is the so-called "sack of Bénin," when a British punitive expedition destroyed the Bénin kingdom in Nigeria in 1897 and sent King Ovonramwen into exile. Photographs of the British conquerors posing with the booty—bronze plaques, bronze heads of rulers, and works in ivory—are among the most dramatic depictions of plunder of cultural property. The objects, in the early 2000s worth millions of U.S. dollars, ended up in private collections and in major museums, among them the British Museum, and the museums of ethnography in Berlin and Vienna. Similar campaigns in 1874 and 1896 against the Asante kingdom in Ghana yielded regalia, and the subjugation of the Kingdom of Kom in Cameroon helped German military to seize several magnificent royal portrait figures, now in Berlin and in the Museum of World Cultures in Frankfurt, Germany.

Other damaging ways of procuring objects were common. Missionary societies made windfalls confiscating ritual objects and paraphernalia in their effort to eradicate perceived paganism. As the prices for African works increased, so did theft. From the 1960s onward, objects disappeared on a regular basis from some of the newly founded national museums in several West and Central African countries and from palaces of kingdoms or village shrines, only to reemerge on the art market. Political unrest often led to the illegal removal of works. The Biafra War in Nigeria (1967–1970), for example, allowed local middlemen and foreign art dealers to procure many works from this region, some of which are in major museums in the West in the early 2000s.

The collectors' interest in ancient terra-cotta items led to the systematic pillaging of archaeological sites. In the Jenné region of the Inland Niger Delta in Mali and in other areas throughout West Africa local farmers excavated objects and sold them to middlemen for much needed small amounts of cash. Top pieces with scientific dating and other, often forged, official paperwork reached galleries and collections through shady channels and now are valued in the hundreds of thousands of U.S. dollars. In Ghana, there has been an exodus of Koma terra-cotta items, in Nigeria works from the Ife kingdom and the Nok and Bura areas are in high demand, and the

ancient Sao culture on Lake Chad in Cameroon has been another target of these illegal activities.

National and international efforts to protect the cultural patrimony of African nations encountered mixed success. Many countries have implemented strict antiquities legislation (Mali in 1973, Ghana in 1969, Nigeria in 1979, and Cameroon in 1963, to name just a few), and require export permits for objects of cultural significance. Yet the structures to enforce such regulations are often lacking. In addition, African countries signed the 1970 United Nations Educational, Scientific and Cultural Organization (UNESCO) Convention on Prohibiting and Preventing Illicit Import, Export and Transfer of Ownership of Cultural Property, which the United States finally ratified through the Convention on Cultural Property Implementation Act in 1983. Another United Nations effort, the International Institute for the Unification of Private Law (UNIDROIT)Convention on Stolen or Illegally Exported Cultural Objects, followed in 1995. The International Council of Museums (ICOM) has worked with African countries to protect their national heritage and created a Red List of endangered works posted on its web site. In a precedent-setting 1993 bilateral accord, Mali and the United States entered into a partnership to suppress the illegal trade of Malian antiquities. While some dealers, collectors, and auction houses still blatantly disregard issues of cultural patrimony, many museums have implemented stringent acquisition policies banning purchasing or accepting as gifts illegally acquired works of art. Scholars hope that these new governmental and institutional policies will curtail the damaging activities that have been part of the African art market.

See also **Abidjan; Ceramics; Dakar; Heritage, Cultural; Ivory; Jenné and Jenné-jeno; Kumasi; Masks and Masquerades.**

BIBLIOGRAPHY

Bassani, Ezio, and William B. Fagg. *Africa and the Renaissance: Art in Ivory.* New York and Munich: The Center for African Art and Prestel Verlag, 1988.

Corbey, Raymond. *Tribal Art Traffic: A Chronicle of Taste, Trade and Desire in Colonial and Post-Colonial Times.* Amsterdam: Royal Tropical Institute, 2000.

Geary, Christraud M., and Stéphanie Xatart. *Material Journeys: Collecting African and Oceanic Art, 1945–2000:*

Selections from the Geneviève McMillan Collection. Boston: MFA Publications, 2007.

Paudrat, Jean-Louis. "The Arrival of Tribal Objects in the West: From Africa." In *Primitivism in 20th Century Art: Affinity of the Tribal and the Modern*, Vol. 1, ed. William Rubin. New York: Museum of Modern Art and New York Graphic Society Books, 1984.

Schmidt, Peter R., and Roderick McIntosh, eds. *Plundering Africa's Past.* Bloomington: Indiana University Press, 1996.

Steiner, Christopher. *African Art in Transit.* Cambridge, U.K.: Cambridge University Press, 1994.

CHRISTRAUD M. GEARY

ART, GENRES AND PERIODS

This entry includes the following articles:
TOURIST
CONTEMPORARY
ROCK ART, EASTERN AFRICA
ROCK ART, SAHARAN AND NORTHERN AFRICA
ROCK ART, SOUTHERN AFRICA

TOURIST

"Tourist art" usually refers to local artisanal products such as cloth, basketry, and wood or ivory carvings sold to tourists and locals alike, or to new genres invented explicitly as souvenirs. In the Nile Valley, for example, mummified human and animal remains are an additional tourist genre that has spawned its own industry. Souvenirs are often sold to travelers in hotels, airports (hence "airport art," a term introduced by Frank McEwen in the 1950s) and craft markets, from Cairo to the Cape. The most venerable of these is surely the Khan el-Khalili bazaar in Cairo where foreigners have shopped for everything from carpets and books to silks, gold, silver, and brass souvenirs since the fourteenth century.

Egypt has had such travelers at least since the Alexandrian conquest in 330 BCE, when Egypt became renowned as a venerable center of civilization. Early visitors, including Plato and Herodotus, were usually scholars rather than adventurers in search of novelty. But they were followed in later centuries by wealthy collectors such as Pietro della Valle (1586–1652) whose digging in Egypt for mummified relics in 1615 helped establish the idea of the souvenir as a "marvel." The romance attached to souvenirs has had great resilience over time and throughout the continent, persisting into and exemplified in the twenty-first century by African objects as diverse as spears, nomadic jewelry, cloth, and wood or soapstone carvings, each an object of memory representing a fictionalized moment of contact with a culturally distant other.

At the same time that the notion of the personal souvenir of African travel was spreading, a parallel interest in the scholarly study of Africa was also taking hold. While the two have evolved into separate phenomena, the distinction between the amateur and the scientific traveler-collector was often blurred in past centuries. For example, medieval Arab writers such as Ibn Battuta (1304–1368?) extended the coverage of written travelers' accounts beyond the Nile Valley with descriptions of local cultural practice in both East (c. 1331) and West Africa (c. 1352). A century later, the Portuguese initiated exploration and trade, returning with artifacts to grace the tables and drawing rooms of royalty. These included the exquisite carved ivory saltcellars, tusks, and ornaments attributed to Sherbro and Edo sculptors in West Africa, as well as the ivory side-blown royal trumpet presented to Vasco da Gama in 1498 by the Swahili ruler of Malindi on the Indian Ocean. The ivory trumpets were an indigenous court form, given as a gift to the Portuguese navigator, but the saltcellars depicting Portuguese as exotic others were something newly invented, and therefore qualify to be called souvenirs. From that time on, trade, war, exploration, and diplomacy brought more African artifacts to Europe, stimulating the formation of royal collections and *Wunderkammer*, the special rooms in which they were displayed.

But it was not until the decades following the publication of the English naturalist Charles Darwin's *On the Origin of Species* in 1859 that the concept of the scientific natural history museum developed, replacing the "cabinets of curiosities" with public galleries, and the solitary travelers with Royal Geographical Society–sponsored exploring and collecting expeditions. The Berlin Conference of 1884–1885 and the subsequent partition of Africa into European colonies created innumerable sources for museum specimens, both biological and cultural. The recognition quickly developed among colonizers that African artifacts had commodity potential beyond their role as specimens.

The issue of commodification is therefore tied historically to the ruptures in artisanal practice brought about through wider systems of exchange, due first to long distance trade and later to colonization. Some artifacts, such as cloth, were commodified early in the trans-Saharan trade, while others such as the Afro-Portuguese ivories were stimulated by trade with Europe. The commodification of masks and shrine figures came with the collection of objects for early natural history museums such as the Musée Trocadero in Paris and after 1900, with the development of an admiration among European collectors for "the primitive." Early-twentieth-century art critics such as Carl Einstein (1915) and Vladimir Markov (1913) defined the primitive as pristine, authentic cultural expression, free of modern influence. Ironically, the quest for "authentic" artifacts initiated by cultural outsiders ensured that they could no longer be authentic, in the literal sense of unchanged. For example, the Kuba *ndop* (king figure) presented by King Kwete in 1913 to a Danish mercenary is clearly different from the classic examples of the genre, the rules surrounding their ownership having been transformed by European intervention.

At the same time as these former sacra became commodities, colonial administrators and expatriates introduced art workshops in such places as Benin City in Nigeria, which built upon an older artisanal practice but introduced new forms and materials (such as ebony) intended for nontraditional consumers. The result, after World War II, was the continuation of the production of older forms for both local use and export abroad, mainly in West Africa and the Congo, augmented by workshop productions of new genres, some of which were aimed at the local and tourist souvenir market and others at that amorphous new category loosely called the international art market. An example of the first or souvenir genre would be the Kamba carving cooperatives in Kenya and of the second or international genre would be a cluster of expatriate-run painting or graphics workshops such as those of Ulli and Georgina Beier in Oshogbo, Nigeria or Frank McEwen's National Gallery sculpture workshop in Salisbury, Rhodesia (later Harare, Zimbabwe). A half-century later, the art produced in those workshops has acquired an

Yoruba tourist art. Yoruba offering bowl in the style of Olowe of Ise (Nigeria, early twentieth century), for sale in a Nairobi tourist shop, Kenya, 1994. PHOTOGRAPH BY SIDNEY KASFIR

army of imitators in their respective countries, effectively creating another genre of tourist art.

In the twenty-first century both souvenir (or tourist) art and the historical (or precolonial) genres of African art have become globalized forms due to tourism and the international art market. The distinction between them is based less upon any objective characteristics than upon the consumer for whom an artwork is intended. Problems arise because frequently the labels are used as if there were also corresponding distinctions among the artists who produce these forms, but here the boundaries become blurred. The same Yoruba (Nigeria), Senufo (Côte d'Ivoire) or Makonde (Tanzania/Mozambique) carving workshop may produce certain types of artifacts for the local community and others (or even the same ones) for sale to traders and middlemen. In the first instance they may be ritual objects such as masks, which function as inalienable possessions, and in the second, they are straightforward commodities. In large ateliers such as those of the Kulebele caste of Senufo carvers at Korhogo, Dolores Richter has shown that objects intended for ritual use are more likely to be commissioned from a master carver, while the more strictly touristic versions are often the work of less accomplished artists. Whether in a large cooperative or a small family-run workshop, the experienced master carver enjoys a high status and works on commission only, though it may be for a local regulatory society or for a powerful trader with foreign connections.

Another problem with its accepted connotation of "art for foreigners" is that "tourist art" is often purchased by Africans themselves to decorate their homes and offices, even further eroding the descriptive usefulness of the term. In this sense tourist art is one variant of what is more often termed popular or urban art, which also shares a patronage system bifurcated between foreigners and locals. Artifacts made originally as souvenirs may be appropriated by local elites as a sign of upward mobility, as in the case of Makonde and Kamba carvings in East Africa. Conversely, objects made initially for a local audience may be "discovered" by outsiders and subsequently promoted from local merchandise to art status. One example of this is floursack painting in Kinshasa and Lubumbashi, originally made for the urban worker class to express an emerging national cultural identity. Since the 1970s the genre also has been collected and written about by several Africanist scholars, which has had the unintended effect of elevating the whole category of Congolese (Zairean) commercial street painting to a new normative category sought eagerly by collectors of contemporary African art.

The most easily commodifiable forms have not been carvings or paintings but textiles, which have served as precolonial currencies and important goods in the trans-Saharan as well as European trade. Since 1960 both tourists and foreign consumers abroad have increased the demand for African cloth such as *kente* from Ghana and *bogolan* from Mali, both of which enjoy wide popularity in African diaspora communities where they connote a generic African identity. Such cultural reappropriations carry quite different meanings for different groups of consumers, further underscoring the

need to move beyond the current undifferentiated notion of "tourist art" in Africa.

There is a strong tendency in writings on African culture to valorize popular theater, art, music, and fashions that are "by the people and for the people," and therefore genuine cultural expressions, as opposed to those which are "by the people" but intended for strangers, and therefore supposedly less genuine. It is widely assumed by both art professionals and the collecting public that African art made to be sold to foreigners could not possibly express the real cultural values of its makers. Such an assumption is based in the belief that when a small-scale society comes into contact with a highly commodified system of production and consumption such as Western capitalism, its values will be obliterated. Commodification, in this argument, is assumed to be incompatible with the expression of authentic African cultural values. But in reality this viewpoint is partly the remnant of the old notion of a pure but fragile "primitive art" destroyed by external contact, first coined in the early 1900s in Europe, and partly the related assumption that Africans are unable to defend themselves against the onslaught of globalization. The subject of exchange remains a major area demanding serious study in the field of African art.

See also **Arts: Basketry and Mat Making; Arts: Sculpture; Benin City; Cairo; Gama, Vasco da; Harare; Ibn Battuta, Muhammad ibn Abdullah; Kinshasa; Lubumbashi; Textiles; Tourism; Travel and Exploration.**

BIBLIOGRAPHY

Ben-Amos, Paula Girshick. "*A la recherche du temps perdu*: On Being an Ebony Carver in Benin." In *Ethnic and Tourist Arts*, ed. Nelson Graburn. Berkeley: University of California Press, 1976.

El Daly, Okasha. "What Do Tourists Learn of Egypt?" In *Consuming Ancient Egypt*, ed. Sally McDonald and Michael Rice. London: UCL Press, 2003.

Hassan, Fekri A. "Selling Egypt: Encounters at Khan el-Khalili." In *Consuming Ancient Egypt*, ed. Sally McDonald and Michael Rice. London: UCL Press, 2003.

Jules-Rosette, Bennetta. "Aesthetics and Market Demand: The Structure of the Tourist Art Market in Three African Settings." *African Studies Review* 29 (1986): 41–59.

Kasfir, Sidney Littlefield. "Patronage and Maconde Carvers." *African Arts* 13, no. 3 (1980): 67–70, 91.

Lega wood carver. The Lega carver Mushaba Isa specializes in carved chairs for the tourist and local elite market. He emigrated from the Democratic Republic of the Congo to Kampala, Uganda, where his workshop is located. PHOTOGRAPH BY SIDNEY KASFIR

Kasfir, Sidney Littlefield. "African Art and Authenticity: A Text with a Shadow." *African Arts* 25, no. 2 (1992): 40–53, 96–97.

Richter, Dolores. *Art, Economics, and Change: The Kulebele of Northern Ivory Coast.* La Jolla, CA: Psych/Graphic Publishers, 1980.

Steiner, Christopher. *African Art in Transit.* Cambridge, U.K.: Cambridge University Press, 1994.

SIDNEY LITTLEFIELD KASFIR

CONTEMPORARY

Few categories of visual practice in Africa have undergone such rapid transformation and attained such international focus as that of contemporary arts. A series of high-profile exhibitions in Europe, the United States, and Africa have brought the works of a select number of Africa's artists to the forefront of the contemporary art world. These exhibitions, informed by critical theory and emphasizing the links between aesthetics and postcolonial subjectivity, stand in marked contrast to more familiar museum offerings that celebrate the carving, masquerading, metalworking, weaving, or potting traditions found throughout the continent. Perhaps this increased interest in contemporary artistry is a long overdue recognition of the continent's engagement with both modernist and postmodernist histories and serves, at least in part, to question the artificially erected temporal and spatial parameters that separate African cultural achievements from those of the Euro-American sphere.

The category of contemporary African art is inadequate because it fails to address the diversity and complexity of visual expressions practiced within an exceedingly large, culturally varied continent, and within important global diasporas. Under its rubric, scholars, curators, and critics place not only a dizzying array of practices—everything from textile production, fashion design, coffin-carving, and barbershop signs to video art, mixed media, printmaking, sculpture, photography, and performance arts—but also collapse a disparate set of patronage structures, educational histories, audiences, and markets. These latter structures vary according to differing local histories of modernism, experiences of colonialism, and contemporary sociocultural, economic, and political conditions.

Early scholarly literature about contemporary practices either saw them as disturbing, bastardized forms of earlier, more authentic, and known traditions—reflecting the detrimental effects of global market forces (tourism in particular)—or as unreflective mimicry of colonial influence. If on occasion they were celebrated as innovative, they were still deemed less important and certainly less valuable on the market than classical African arts. Contemporary arts' mere existence disturbed the temporal and spatial formulae the field employed to measure authenticity and value within the global marketplace.

In general, scholars, collectors, and critics often described contemporary practice as a radical break from traditional models and modes, and curators made manifest this perceived rupture by situating these arts in modernist white cube spaces, in stark contrast to the dark and intimate spaces reserved for traditional works of art. Indeed, it was not until the last two decades of the twentieth century that important thinkers in the field, such as John Picton and Sidney Kasfir, began to suggest more modulated approaches to understanding traditions, seeing them as changing through time and space rather than operating as essentially stagnant constructs. This scholarship led to more nuanced understandings of the negotiations involved when contemporary artists engage with these ongoing practices.

In global art world usage, the term contemporary refers to postwar artistic practices that engage with and often challenge the histories of modernism—the break is at once about shifts in conceptual approaches, in chosen media, and in techniques. When applied to African art, the same term is often used carelessly to refer to works that may represent particular modernist approaches, practices or genres, and to those that are made in the early twenty-first century in a variety of new media. In many parts of Africa, painting or printmaking, not video or digital work, remain the most common choices of medium for contemporary artists. Yet in the global art world, these forms are often associated with either old-fashioned modernisms or modernist revivals. Furthermore, many African contemporary artists work within local communities of patronage and are trained within workshops, regardless of how informed they may be of practices elsewhere. It is thus impossible to regard contemporary practices as somehow divorced from a variety of ongoing traditions such as masquerades, textile production, sculpting, metalworking, pottery, or basketry. These artistic worlds and their visual vocabularies make for a remarkably sophisticated and multilayered landscape in which all artists work.

Scholars such as Arjun Appadurai (1996), Okwui Enwezor (2001), Geeta Kapur (2000), and Timothy Mitchell (2000) have all shown in different contexts that modernism needs to be viewed as a global phenomenon with many local variations, often tied to emergent nationalisms in the immediate postcolonial period. However, defining the field by time alone is tricky. In the colonial period, which corresponded to the early modern period in Europe, numerous African artists appropriated and experimented with forms (such as painting) and technologies (especially photography) in a self-reflexive manner that mirrored that of the European modernists. In this same period, one sees the emergence of hybrid cultural forms such as the *colon* figures, sculptures with colonial dress or attributes, studied perhaps most sensitively by Phillip Ravenhill in his work on Baule spirit spouses (1996).

So when was modernism in Africa? This question is not as easy to answer as one might imagine, and its answer determines the parameters of when the contemporary started. Many would argue that the modernist periods in many African nations date to the era of decolonization and liberation movements. For most African countries, the time for emergent nationalisms and accompanying aesthetic programs and postcolonial freedoms and sensitivities dated from the 1960s. A notable variation is in the former Portuguese colonies and South Africa in which modernisms struggled to survive under oppressive regimes, often taking the form of protest or resistance arts, and from which diasporic and exilic artists emerged as major voices.

Some of the great modernist schools, movements, and manifestos throughout the African continent date to this postcolonial period—a time that saw the waning of modernism, the rise of postmodernism, and the labeling of contemporary practice in North America and Europe. Art academies and schools of modernism developed throughout the continent, most notably in Senegal, Sudan, Ethiopia, Nigeria, Zaire (present-day Democratic Republic of the Congo), Ghana, and Uganda. Many early painters, printmakers, textile designers, and sculptors trained abroad within the colonial metropoles, to return later to take teaching positions in their nations. In these contexts artists were often concerned with finding a synthesis between recognizably indigenous iconographies and new, modern expressions—Uche Okeke's (b. 1933) Natural Synthesis, Ulism or Onaism in Nigeria, the Ecole de Dakar in Senegal, Ethiopian plays with Ge'ez script painted in abstract forms, or Sudanese meditations on calligraphic forms are just some examples of these early synthetic practices. Some of these reclamations and negotiations of postcolonial identities took place within diasporic or exilic communities, in particular those from Sudan, Ethiopia, or Algeria.

A whole variety of informal and formal workshops operated alongside these more formal academies; the best-known or most successful ones were situated at Oshogbo and in Mbari Clubs in Nigeria, or at Rorke's Drift in South Africa. European mentors ran many of these workshops. Of course, early academies and workshops in South Africa and their subsequent inheritance stood in clear distinction from other areas on the continent because of the tyrannical politics of the apartheid era.

Contemporary practice cannot be seen as merely a continuation of indigenous traditions, nor can it be dismissed as a direct importation of techniques and concepts resulting from colonialism. It must be understood as heir to a complex layering of histories of practice, patronage, and cultural changes. In this age of transnationalism, the contemporary artists from Africa most evident within the global art scene appear in large art fairs such as the biennales that have now proliferated throughout the world. Access to these venues is varied and may occur simply through a chance meeting with a curator. They may also come about via the opportunities afforded through local institutions that are vestiges of colonial or postwar politics such as the French Cultural Center, the British Council, the Goethe Institutes, or American Cultural Centers.

Artists operating within this realm often work in highly conceptual modes that mirror those of their counterparts selling in the galleries of New York, London, and Paris. Yet, similar to their modernist predecessors, these artists, whether based on the continent or living and working permanently within the global diasporas, often create artworks that are insightful commentaries on their postcolonial subjectivity. Theirs is a subjectivity that has been informed by multiple histories of modernism, critical discourses on aesthetics and the role of art in contemporary societies, and the continuing importance of inhabiting and laying claim to one's identity within a charged political, cosmopolitan environment.

See also **Art; Arts; Postcolonialism.**

BIBLIOGRAPHY

Deliss, Clementine, ed. *Seven Stories about Modern Art in Africa: An Exhibition.* Paris: Flammarion, 1995.

Enwezor, Okwui, ed. *The Short Century: Independence and Liberation Movements in Africa, 1945–1994.* New York: Prestel, 2001.

Kasfir, Littlefield Sidney. *Contemporary African Art.* London: Thames and Hudson, 1999.

Tawardos, Gilane. *Fault Lines: Contemporary African Art and Shifting Landscapes.* London: Iniva and the Forum for African Arts and the Prince Klaus Fund, 2003.

Vogel, Susan. *Africa Explores: African Art in the 20th Century.* New York: Center for African Art, 1991.

ELIZABETH HARNEY

ROCK ART, EASTERN AFRICA

The rock art of eastern Africa can be discussed under five geographical areas: the Horn (Eritrea, Djibouti, Ethiopia, and Somalia), southern Sudan, Kenya, the lacustrine (Uganda and parts of Tanzania), and Tanzania. No evidence of rock art exists for the offshore islands of the Seychelles, the Comoro Islands, Madagascar, and Réunion.

THE HORN

Most historical knowledge about the rock art of the Horn comes from the sites of Karora and the Akkele Guzai region sites of Ad Teclesan, Sollum Ba'atti, Zeban Cabessa, Ba'atti Sollum, Ba'atti Focada, Gobon Abaha, and Hulum Bareto in Eritrea; the petroglyphs at El Goran, Bur Dahir, and Chabbé and the rock paintings of the Harar region sites such as Yavello, Harar, Laga Oda, Porc-Epic, Saka Sharifa, Bake Khallo, Genda-Biftou, Errer Kimiet, and Laga Gafra in Ethiopia; and the sites of Bur Eibe, Jid Banan, Karin Heganah, Tug Khaboba, Tug Gerbakele, and Dombosleh in Somalia.

Overall, Ethiopia and Eritrea contain the most impressive and important record of rock art in the Horn. The naturalistic and seminaturalistic pastoral subject matter includes humpless and long-horned cattle in the early phase of rock art, fat-tailed sheep and zebu or humped cattle in the late phase, a few wild animals such as elephants, buffalo, jackal, and ostrich, and schematized humans associated with cattle. The style can be described as representational naturalism executed in shades of red, brown, black, yellow, and white.

Unlike the hunters' art of central Tanzania and southern Africa, the art of the Horn is associated with cattle herding and as such the subject matter is dominated by cattle and cattle brands and tribal signs. Therefore, the images may have had little or no symbolic or metaphoric significance.

SOUTHERN SUDAN AND KENYA

Rock art has been found south of Torit near the Uganda border. The paintings, which are all schematic, are executed in coarse and thick white paint. The subject matter includes humped cattle in black and many twentieth-century graffiti.

Rock painting sites exist on the slopes of Mount Elgon, where the dominant motif is the long-horned humpless cattle, executed in red, white, and bichrome. There are also crude paintings of wild animals. With one exception in Zambia, the Mount Elgon sites are considered the southernmost examples of cattle in rock art before South Africa. The Stone Age pastoralists of Kenya and northern Tanzania do not seem to have practiced rock art like their northern neighbors of the countries of the Horn.

In addition to the few paintings, there are reports of cupules or cup marks (depressions scooped from the rock) at Kebaroti Hills in southern Nyanza. Petroglyphs of a variety of wild animals, humans, and geometric designs are found in Lake Turkana basin at the Mount Porr site. Additional petroglyphs dominated by geometric motifs such as circles, spirals, and crossed circles have been reported from Kangetet, in western Kenya. These occur on a complex of rocks surrounding graves whose burials have been carbon-14 dated to 300

BCE. The geometric designs are said to resemble cattle brands used by the Turkana.

THE LACUSTRINE REGION

The areas surrounding Lake Victoria, especially on the Tanzania and Uganda sides, Lake Kyoga, and northeastern Uganda abound with rock painting sites. The style is unique in that the subject matter is highly stylized and almost exclusively executed in white. Examples can be found at a cluster of sites in the Bukoba or Bwanja-Bugombe area and Mwanza Gulf in Tanzania; Teso Bukedi; and isolated sites at Lolui Island, Nfangano, Nyero, Nyapedha Hill, Loteleleit, and Magosi in Uganda. The art at Lukuba Island just off Musoma in Tanzania differs, however, in that the paintings are representational.

Cattle and occasional anthropomorphs dominate the rather restricted repertoire of subject matter. Depictions consist of linear amorphous geometric designs such as circles, concentric circles, and dots, executed in various shades of red, white, and yellow. There are also numerous dots in circles, ovals, gridirons, and other configurations. Human figures, except in extremely schematized forms and handprints, are absent. A distinctive motif is what has been interpreted as schematized representations of cattle.

Of particular interest is the depiction of known historical or ethnographical objects, such as the canoes at Nyero and the hoes at Nyangoma. Aside from the paintings there are also petroglyphs that, besides the cup marks sometimes arranged in two rows reminiscent of the *bao* or *mancala* board game played throughout sub-Saharan Africa, also include geometric motifs.

TANZANIA

Central Tanzania, especially Kondoa, Singida, Iramba, and to some extent the Mbulu Dodoma and Tabora districts, is by far the most richly endowed in rock art in the whole of eastern Africa. Isolated sites have also been reported from southeast of Tanzania, where the tradition may be connected with the Malawian Nyau cult paintings.

Generally, Tanzania's art is dominated by rock paintings, but there are also a few petroglyphs. It is basically a hunters' art in which animals such as giraffe, eland, kudu, antelope, and elephants are portrayed naturalistically, almost exclusively in monochrome shades of ocherous red. The dominant styles include silhouettes, outlines filled in with lines or shading, and outlines without shading. In most cases, only a side view is shown, although instances of foreshortening can also be found. Animals are sometimes depicted running away, having fallen down, or with lines drawn from the mouth, a feature which on the basis of ethnographical knowledge from southern Africa would be interpreted as bleeding from the nose as experienced by shamans when in trance.

Associated human figures and theriomorphs are highly stylized and executed in the same monochrome shades of red. Sometimes they are depicted holding hands, squatting, dancing, or armed with bows. Geometrics are very rare. These animals and humans constitute the earliest phase.

Distinctive from the naturalistic portrayals are seminaturalistic animals and humans executed in shades of thick white paint. The animal subject matter is dominated by giraffes and reptilian fauna such as lizards. Silhouettes and shading with dots and lines are the dominant style. In addition there is a variety of symbols such as handprints, circles, concentrics, spirals, ladders, circles, and rays, and a plethora of enigmatic configurations.

The motifs and the extant people who have claimed authorship of some of the rock art in Tanzania suggest a connection, however tenuous, with the better-known San paintings of southern Africa. The possibility has therefore led some scholars to ascribe a motivation having to do with the trance hypothesis, which attempts to explain some of the art as a reproduction of the visions that shamans perceive when in trance. Be that as it may, most of the rock art has ritualistic meaning. Indeed, some rock art sites are still being used for occult ceremonial purposes.

DATING

While some of the sites abound with stratified archaeological deposits, dating the rock art by archaeological association has not been possible. Neither do the sheep and cattle associated with the rock art in the Horn shed much light on the age of the art. Although sheep are assumed to derive from Arabia, the time of their introduction into the countries of the Horn is uncertain. Petroglyphs of such sheep have been dated to between 3000 and 1000 BCE in central Asia. A tentative relative chronology would begin at 2000 BCE for the earliest phase of rock art, 300 BCE for the zebu cattle and sheep phase, followed by a period of degenerated art (with fewer anatomical details), inscriptions, and tribal marks.

The same problems exist with dating of the rock art in Kenya. However, judging by the light patination in some of the petroglyphs and a representation of camel, some of the rock art may not be of great age. The earliest evidence for domestic cattle in Kenya is around 400 BCE, a date that would seem to tie in with the earlier dates from the Horn if one can assume, as it is sometimes claimed, that pastoralism was introduced from Ethiopia in the north. Dating the art is less problematic with some of the lacustrine paintings, for as it has already been pointed out there are depictions of objects such as the canoe with lateen sail rigging, the knowledge of which could not have reached the shores of Lake Victoria before the arrival of the Arab and Swahili merchants from the eastern African coast in the middle of the nineteenth century.

With the exception of the Sandawe people in central Tanzania, extant local peoples disclaim knowledge of the artists. However, this has not made the dating of the central Tanzania rock art any easier. On the basis of stylistic similarities, one analyst has suggested they may be as much as twenty thousand years old, but the seminaturalistic silhouettes and geometric designs are later; perhaps as late as the Iron Age. Sophisticated methods of dating such as racemization and cation ratio have not yet been applied in the region.

POSSIBLE SIGNIFICANCE OF THE ART

Unlike the hunters' art of central Tanzania and southern Africa, the art of the Horn is associated with cattle herding and as such the subject matter is dominated by cattle and cattle brands and tribal signs. The images may have had little or no metaphoric significance. Similarly, in the absence of representational or naturalistic art in the lacustrine subregion, sympathetic magic as a motive of the artists can be ruled out, but the purpose that schematization may have served for the communities has not been identified. Conceivably it was taboo to represent the most important source of wealth—cattle—naturalistically lest the herd be made vulnerable to

people who would harm it. As for the more naturalistic hunters' art of central Tanzania, claims of sympathetic magic have been reported from the Sandawe people, some of whom have also claimed authorship of the paintings. On the basis of broadly comparable motifs, some of the art of central Tanzania may be related to trance and shamanism as has been reported from southern Africa.

CONCLUSION

Generally, in sub-Saharan rock art, human figures are less naturalistically portrayed than animals, a feature which has been invoked to support the theory of sympathetic magic, although some authorities especially in southern Africa have criticized this theory in preference to the trance hypothesis supported by ethnographic study. The theory of sympathetic magic holds that animals were painted naturalistically so that they would be drawn to the hunters; as humans were never hunted, there was no need for them to be portrayed naturalistically. Conceivably, the art served other purposes for the community, such as ritual uses, pleasure, or as mnemonic devices, while some of the tectiforms (entoptics) may have been tallies of some sort. Obviously, the questions of meaning and dating will have to be resolved before the significance of rock art can be fully appreciated.

See also **Archaeology and Prehistory: Historical; Art; Art History and the Study of Africa; Art, Regional Styles: Eastern Africa; Symbols and Symbolism.**

BIBLIOGRAPHY

Chaplin, J. H. "The Prehistoric Rock Art of the Lake Victoria Region." *Azania* 9 (1974): 1–50.

Clark, J. Desmond. *The Prehistoric Cultures of the Horn of Africa.* Cambridge, U.K.: Cambridge University Press, 1954.

Graziosi, Paolo. "New Discoveries of Rock Paintings in Ethiopia." *Antiquity* 38 (1964): 91–98; 187–190.

Leakey, Mary D. *Africa's Vanishing Art: The Rock Paintings of Tanzania.* Garden City, NY: Doubleday, 1983.

Masao, Fidelis T. *The Later Stone Age and the Rock Paintings of Central Tanzania.* Wiesbaden, Germany: Steiner, 1979.

Willcox, A. R. *The Rock Art of Africa.* New York: Holmes & Meier Publishers, 1984.

FIDELIS T. MASAO

ROCK ART, SAHARAN AND NORTHERN AFRICA

Tens of thousands of rock images have been found in northern Africa, especially in the massifs and high plateaus of the central Sahara (Ahaggar, Tassili n'Ajjer, Fezzan, Djado), eastern Sahara (Tibesti, Jebel Uweinat, Ennedi), southern Sahara (Aïr, Adrar des Iforas), western Sahara (Dhar Adrar, Dhar Tichitt), and the Atlas Mountains of the Maghreb (see Figure 1). Most of them created during the last humid phases of this desert area, they reflect a story of climatic, ecological, and cultural change, as well as of historical events throughout the Holocene (the last 10,000 years). The oldest images may have even been created in the late Pleistocene. Although methods for the direct dating of images in general are not yet available, they are under development; techniques for direct dating of the patina seem especially promising. In some cases, dates by which the images must have been created have been established by means of the excavation of layers in which their fragments were found. The images have been frequently covered up; these events have been used, along with typological comparison, to assign relative dates and specific periods of development.

During the years from 1994 to 1997 a new species of rock art was discovered in the central Sahara which has to be dated, on account of geomorphological circumstances, to the late Pleistocene. The very rough and simple engravings of this group show mostly human beings, often social groups (see Figure 2). Some of them are superimposed by paintings of the later Round Head period, another indication for their high age. There is even some

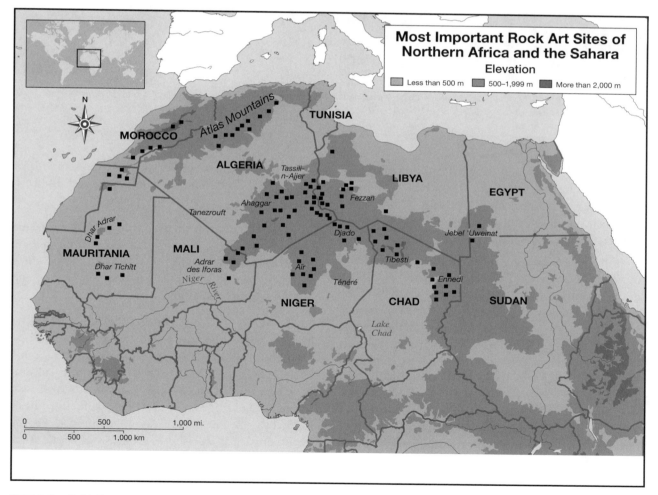

Figure 1. © K. H. STRIEDTER

Figure 2. Rock engraving found in the Algerian Tadrart, probably the most ancient representation of a human couple (male = 22 cm). Tens of thousands of rock images have been found in northern Africa, most of which reflect a story of climatic ecological and cultural change. © K. H. STRIEDTER

evidence that these engravings and the paintings of the beginning phase of the Round Head period, sharing largely the regions of distribution, show formal relationship, so that the roots of the Round Heads may also go back to the Late Pleistocene.

The great Saharan rock art tradition however came into being with the beginning of the Neolithic, in the eighth or seventh millennium BCE. There are rock engravings, with lines carved deep in the stone, and often later polished smooth. They represent the world of the hunter. Animals, which are for the most part large and undomesticated—such as elephants, rhinoceroses, hippopotamuses, giraffes, wild cattle, and antelope—are represented in a naturalistic manner, and not infrequently in full size, on the rock walls of the valleys. Hunting scenes are extremely rare. Where humans are shown together with animals, they are, as a rule, comparatively small and depicted very schematically. Humanlike shapes appear together with hunted or killed animals, and they carry animal masks, mostly reminiscent of the

jackal heads with which Egyptian deities would later be depicted. The weapons in use include clubs, axes, and bows.

The second great theme of the hunting era seems to have been human reproduction, as indicated by representations of scenes of coitus and male figures with abnormally enlarged penises. Here also, the human figures wear animal masks.

A series of rock images testifies that the hunters also attempted to tame wild animals. Domestication of cattle in the Sahara thus seems likely. The centers of the rock art of this cultural epoch lie in Fezzan (Messak), and northern Tassili n'Ajjer (Oued Djerat). In these sites, but more frequently in the Sahara-Atlas (Maghreb), appear depictions of a species of large wild cattle that had already become extinct in prehistoric times, the *Homoïoceras (Bubalus) antiquus*, which gave its name to this period of rock art, the Bubalus period. The careful engravings, often with polished inner surfaces, of rams with disk-shaped objects on their heads (sun rams) are unique to this region and reminiscent of the much more recent Egyptian deity Amon Ra. The "hunter," or Bubalus, period, whose representatives were, at least in part, light skinned, probably ended in the sixth millennium BCE.

The Round Head period is named after a striking stylistic feature, dated from around the seventh to the sixth millennium BCE and leaving traces essentially only in Tassili n'Ajjer and its neighborhood. Its representatives were also probably hunter-gatherers. They created the first rock paintings of the Sahara, some with monumental dimensions, which appear coarse and crude in contrast to the engravings. Group representations of humans are predominant. The content of these images is difficult to interpret; perhaps they represent ritual scenes. Several paintings suggest that they were created by a dark-skinned artist; the principal pigment for the paintings was ochre in its different tones, predominantly redbrown. A proteinaceous substance, such as milk or blood, probably served as the binding medium.

From the beginning of the sixth millennium BCE onward, the hunter cultures were increasingly penetrated by pastoralist cultures. These latter cultures have left behind numerous engravings and paintings throughout northern Africa and the Sahara. However, the artistic zenith of rock art production can be identified in Tassili n'Ajjer, where thousands of rock paintings remain under protective rock overhangs (abris). The painters used monochromatic and polychromatic palettes—the favorite colors being red-brown and white—and represented their subjects realistically, usually on a small scale. Only occasionally were they shown in full size. Although the still-existing fauna of the hunter period continue to appear, the preferred subject is humans with their herds of cattle. The images mostly represent everyday scenes: humans with their herds and dwellings; in their storage areas; in conversation; and so on. Their richness of detail not only allows the weapons (bows and arrows), clothing, and hairstyles to be identified but also allows the representatives of this pastoralist culture to be identified as including both light- and dark-skinned peoples. In the fifth and fourth millennia BCE, the pastoralist culture must have had its heyday. With the increasing desiccation of the Sahara, however, it lost its foundation and collapsed.

From the middle of the second millennium BCE when foreign populations with horses and chariots advanced into the central Sahara, they encountered only the remains of the pastoralist culture. The rock images of the horse period still show cattle, but the leading motif of this epoch is the chariot with horses at a flying gallop. These often occur next to depictions of battles, or occasionally hunting scenes, where the prey is almost always small wild sheep. The hunters are armed with spears and shields. The mostly monochromatic red-brown paintings frequently show expressive dynamics and reveal a clear tendency toward schematization. Many authors connect the horse period with the Garamantes, said by Herodotus to use horses and chariots to attack dark-skinned people. The paintings from this epoch contain the first inscriptions in Tifinar, the writing of the Tuareg, who therefore can also be considered successors of the prehistoric invaders who conquered the native population of the central Sahara. The horse could not last in the long run, but numerous rock images in Aïr testify that in the southern Sahara of this era it was used predominantly for riding. Pictures of chariots, though engraved schematically and without animals pulling them, were also known beyond the Maghreb and the western Sahara; their relationship to the corresponding rock images of the central Sahara remains unclear.

The rock images of the camel period, which opens at the start of the Common Era and continues through the present day, document the penetration of the dromedary into the now fully arid Sahara. The rock art tradition of the previous epochs was carried on and taken further but ended rapidly with their decline. The sketches, paintings, and engravings seem mostly formulaic and rigid. Next to dromedaries and humans armed with spears and shields, or swords, appear animals that still live in the Sahara, as well as occasional depictions of dwellings and palms; these mark the beginning of the oasis culture.

Completely outside this framework are rock carvings in the high Atlas region of Morocco. They show predominantly abstract and geometric forms, as well as weapons. These rock images presumably occur in the context of a Mediterranean bronze age, which left no traces behind elsewhere in Africa.

The rock images of the old epochs (hunter and cattle-herder periods) are often of high aesthetic quality, while in more recent epochs a tendency toward simplification and schematization of the drawings predominates. No conclusive statement can be made on the significance and function of the rock images. Some of them may be related to magic or religious concepts. Most images of the cattle-herder period and the more recent epochs, however, depict everyday scenes and seem to fulfill an aesthetic need on the part of their creators.

The preservation of the rock images is essentially dependent upon local circumstances. In places protected from weathering, they are often remarkably well preserved.

See also **Archaeology and Prehistory; Art; Art History and the Study of Africa; Art, Regional Styles: Northern Africa.**

BIBLIOGRAPHY

Mori, Fabrizio: *The Great Civilisations of the Ancient Sahara. Neolithisation and the Earliest Evidence of Anthropomorphic Religions.* Roma: "L'Erma" di Bretschneider, 1998.

Ritchie, Carson I. A. *Rock Art of Africa.* Philadelphia: Art Alliance Press, 1979.

Wilcox, A. R. *The Rock Art of Africa.* London: Croom Helm, 1984.

KARL HEINZ STRIEDTER

ROCK ART, SOUTHERN AFRICA

Rock art south of the Zambezi and lower Kunene Rivers comprises three traditions. They are the widespread hunter-gatherer San art and two other less well studied traditions: images made by pastoral Khoekoe communities, and those produced by agricultural Bantu-speaking peoples largely in the course of puberty rituals and political protest. This article concerns the abundant and now-famous San rock art, the so-called Bushman paintings and rock engravings of southern Africa.

Approximately 14,000 San sites are known and many more await discovery; in number, they far exceed the total of pastoral and agricultural sites together. The painted images are astonishingly delicate, animated, and detailed, some features being no more than a pinhead in size. The variety of the art

Shaded polychrome eland from a rock shelter site in the southern Drakensberg mountains, South Africa. The eland was a polysemic symbol in San thought. It referred to boys' first-kill rituals, the girls' puberty Eland Bull Dance, marriage, and the supernatural potency that San shamans activate when they enter trance. PHOTOGRAPH BY AZIZO DA FONSECA

and the complexity of the information that the images encode are characteristics that make the sites windows on to San hunter-gatherer life and belief.

The age of individual images is hard to determine, whether paintings (found in rock shelters and on some portable stones) or engravings (found on exposed rock surfaces, largely in the interior of the subcontinent). Various techniques have, however, combined to show that San rock art, still being made at the end of the nineteenth century, was an extraordinarily long tradition. If the tradition is assumed to be unbroken and the geometrically engraved pieces of ochre found together with shell beads in the Blombos shelter on the southern coast of South Africa are accepted as art, it reaches back at least as far as 70,000 BP—the longest art tradition in the world. Researchers have not yet been able to determine distinct periods of art.

The Western explorers and settlers who first encountered the images tended to dismiss them as "idle playthings" or a simple record of daily hunter-gatherer life or, at best, naïve art for art's sake. No serious researchers still entertain views of this kind. During the second half of the twentieth century writers published more sophisticated understandings rooted in San beliefs and practices. This shift to ethnographically founded accounts was facilitated by nineteenth- and twentieth-century records of San beliefs, myths, rituals and daily life, the most comprehensive and valuable of which is the more than 12,000 verbatim manuscript pages that Wilhelm Bleek and Lucy Lloyd compiled in the 1870s. Using this ethnography, researchers are able to form a reliable idea of San cosmology, the beings that inhabited the spirit realm, the activities of ritual specialists who were believed to traverse the cosmos, rites of passage, personal histories, the travails and joys of ordinary life, and even to some extent the actual making of rock art images.

Nineteenth-century /Xam San ritual specialists were known as !gi:ten (sing. !gi:xa) people who were "full of" a supernatural potency known as !gi:, //ke:n, or /ko:ode. By activating this potency they were believed to have the ability to leave their bodies and travel to the spirit world where they pleaded for the sick, captured and killed a "rain-animal" in order to cause rain to fall, saw and fought off malign spirits of the dead who were believed to shoot "arrows of sickness" into people, interacted with mythical

Two human figures. One has his hand raised to his nose in a commonly painted gesture. The nose was closely associated with trance experience. San shamans frequently bled from the nose. PHOTOGRAPH BY AZIZO DA FONSECA.

beings (though there is no evidence that the San painted mythical narratives), and obtained information about spiritual affairs. They thus performed the tasks that shamans around the world tackle.

Potency was activated principally at healing dances, during which women sang and clapped the rhythm of "medicine songs" believed to contain this "energy." Those who had mastered the techniques entered a state of trance and sometimes fell to the ground cataleptic. As far as is known, they did not employ psychoactive substances. These dances are clearly depicted in the art: images show ritual specialists in distinctive dancing postures, bleeding from the nose (a physical response to trance well attested in the nineteenth-century records) and sometimes with potency or sickness (invisible to ordinary people) entering and leaving their bodies.

The animal believed to possess the most !gi: and that was the trickster-deity's favorite creature was the eland antelope (*Taurotragus oryx*). It is also the most frequently depicted creature in many, but not all, regions of southern Africa. In some regions, especially to the north of the Limpopo River in Zimbabwe and immediately to the south of the Limpopo, other animals, such as the giraffe and kudu, are the most frequently painted and engraved. The beliefs of the modern San who live in the Kalahari Desert show that all these animals were believed to have much potency.

In the south, there is evidence that the San used eland blood in the manufacture of some paints. The !gi: of the animal thus went into the paint and then

A transformed San shaman. He is in the kneeling posture that San shamans often adopt when they fall into a trance. The line of dots emanating from the back of his neck (the n/au spot) probably represents the expulsion of sickness of which San shamans speak. PHOTOGRAPH BY AZIZO DA FONSECA

into the painting, which became a reservoir of potency on which people could subsequently draw. Many of the images depict what San shamans, activating this potency, saw and experienced in the spirit realm. This does not mean that the San made images while in a state of altered consciousness, nor that every image was the outcome of a vision, nor that every image-maker was a ritual specialist.

In the early twenty-first century San rock art is now accorded much more attention than was the case under the South African apartheid regime. A number of sites have been well prepared for public viewing and are now tourist attractions that funnel money into poor local communities. A national museum of rock art, the Origins Center, has been established as an arm of the Rock Art Research Institute at the University of the Witwatersrand in Johannesburg. Fine rock art displays are also to be found in other museums around the country.

The recognition now being accorded to South African rock art is reflected in the post-apartheid national coat of arms and motto. There is a rock art image in the center of the coat of arms and the motto is in the now-extinct /Xam San language: *!Ke e: /xarra //ke*, "People who are different come together." San rock art, so long undervalued, is becoming a unifying national symbol.

See also Archaeology and Prehistory; Art; Art, Regional Styles: Southern Africa; Art History and the Study of Africa; Dance: Social Meaning; Kalahari Desert; Spirit Possession; Symbols and Symbolism; Travel and Exploration.

BIBLIOGRAPHY

Bleek, W. H. I., and L. C. Lloyd *Specimens of Bushman Folklore*. London: George Allen, 1911.

Blundell, G. *Nqabayo's Nomansland: San Rock Art and the Somatic Past*. Uppsala: Uppsala University Press, 2004.

Henshilwood, C. S. et al. "Emergence of Modern Human Behavior: Middle Stone Age Engravings from South Africa." *Science* 28 (2002): 1278–1280.

Hollmann, J. C., ed. *Customs and Beliefs of the /Xam Bushmen*. Johannesburg: University of the Witwatersrand Press, 2004.

Lewis-Williams, J. D. *Stories That Float from Afar: Ancestral Folklore of the San of Southern Africa*. Cape Town: David Philip, 2002.

Lewis-Williams, J. D. *Images of Mystery: Rock Art of the Drakensberg*. Cape Town: Double Storey, 2003.

Lewis-Williams, J. D., and D. G. Pearce. *San Spirituality: Roots Expressions and Social Consequences*. Walnut Creek, CA: Altamira Press, 2004.

Marshall, L. J. *Nyae Nyae !Kung: Beliefs and Rites*. Cambridge, MA: Harvard University Press, 1999.

Pager, H. *The Rock Paintings of the Upper Brandberg*. 5 vols. Cologne: Heinrich Barth Institute, 1989–2000.

Smith, B. W., and S. Ouzman. "Taking Stock: Identifying Khoekhoen Herder Rock Art in Southern Africa." *Current Anthropology* 45 (2004): 499–526.

Van Schalkwyk, J. A., and B. W. Smith. "Insiders and Outsiders: Sources for Re-Interpreting a Historical Event." In *African Historical Archaeologies*, ed. A. Reid and P.J. Lane. New York: Kluwer Academic and Plenum Publishers, 2004.

Walker, N. *The Painted Hills: Rock Art of the Matopos*. Gweru, Zimbabwe: Mambo Press, 1996.

DAVID LEWIS-WILLIAMS

ART, REGIONAL STYLES

This entry includes the following articles:
CENTRAL AFRICA
EASTERN AFRICA
NORTHERN AFRICA
SOUTHERN AFRICA
WESTERN AFRICA
EGYPT
ETHIOPIA

CENTRAL AFRICA

Central Africa can be defined as the area between the Atlantic coast and the Western Rift Valley and corresponds to the modern nations of the Democratic Republic of the Congo (Congo-Kinshasa), Republic of the Congo (Congo-Brazzaville), Cabinda, Angola, and Zambia. Traditional art in Central Africa can be associated with three distinct spheres: politics, ritual, and the home; namely, figurative sculpture, masks, ceremonial stools, staffs, and weapons that are used by leaders, ritual specialists, diviners, and healers, whereas the domestic environment is the context for decorated everyday artifacts.

The earliest human artifacts date before 60,000 BCE, the Upper Acheulian Period. Post-Acheulian archaeological contexts reveal handaxes, cleavers, picks, and leaf-shaped projectile points. Later artifacts—tanged arrowheads and polished axes—demonstrate great care and selection of stone. Proto-bushmen and proto-Bantu-speaking peoples were probably the carriers of this Neolithic culture. Early Iron Age culture becomes apparent in the Great Lakes region by about 200 CE, and in the extreme southeast examples of globe-like pottery with the slight dimple at its base and rather short neck is commonly found in graves containing hoes, knives, and iron spearheads. The oldest example of wood sculpture dates from the eighth century CE. It was found in gravel banks along the Liavela River in Central Angola and represents an animal image. From the tenth century CE in the vicinity of Lake Kisale to the southeast, grave goods distinctive of leadership include ceremonial axes studded with nails, cylindrical iron anvils, copper bangles, anklets, belts, necklaces, bracelets, rings, and copper cross-ingots.

Central African rock art is rare due to the limited number of exposed surfaces suitable for decoration. In the southwest of this region, silhouettes of wild animals and a few human representations are found in rock paintings that are regarded as the work of Neolithic hunter-gatherers, whereas Early Iron Age peoples presented petroglyphs that were schematic rather than representational and consisted of concentric and linked circles, chevrons, grids, or ladder-like designs. In the lower Congo River area, rock shelters present only zigzag engravings and black and ochre paintings that are thought to date from the sixteenth century.

Ethnic art—so-called tribal styles—includes figures and masks, sculptured decoration of scepters, staffs, ceremonial spears, adzes, knives, hairpins, pipes, cups, neckrests, ladles, caryatid stools, ritual implements, musical instruments, and various decorative items for buildings. The principal medium is wood, although metal, stone, and clay are occasionally used. Abstract designs are found in textiles, pottery, and basketwork. The styles of artwork are generally categorized by ethnic names, although recent field studies assert that a given style is not necessarily uniform within a given ethnic unit: borrowings of art objects between different groups appear, as well as unexpected forms of stylistic synthesis. Moreover, a style can be linked with ritual institutions that overlap ethnic groupings and thus are effectively transethnic. Much of the literature on Central African art centers on broad regional and local stylistic classifications that are based upon the morphological study of carved statuettes. The classic 1946 work by Frans Olbrechts (1899–1958) established the framework of classification for subsequent researchers. It recognized five stylistic regions, each with several styles and substyles: the Lower Congo or southwest; Kuba-Kasai or south-center; Luba or southeast; the northwest; and the northeast.

FIGURATIVE SCULPTURE

Freestanding figurative sculpture from the Lower Congo stylistic region, bordering the Atlantic Ocean on the west, is termed the coastal style. It consists of Kongo (Kakongo, Solongo, Yombe, Woyo, Sundi, Bwendi, and Vili peoples), the Teke style to the north, and the Kwango style to the east. Within the Kongo style, figurative sculpture is noted for asymmetry and diversity in posture, with the head rendered in a naturalistic manner. Eyes are commonly kaolin or mirror fragments inserted into the sculpture. Mother-and-child themes, together with magical assemblages attached to the head or torso, are distinctive. Items attached to figures include metal rings, seed pods, inserted blades, nails and wrapped screws, tied packets, suspended containers, or tufts of various materials, all of which offer sculptural qualities in an accumulative aesthetic mode. Research has identified independent style groups of the Bwende, Bemebe, Mboma, and Sundi, but often simply designates given objects by the various Kongo ethnic components.

The Teke-style subdivision includes sculpture of the Lari, Mfinu, and Wuum. Figures are shown in a stiff standing posture with striated faces, square beards and on the head either a sagital crest or bun-like hairstyle. Back-to-back double statuettes are common. Usually the magical load—diverse substances of metaphorical reference—surrounds the torso and is enclosed in a resin adhesive, occasionally reinforced by cloth or skin. Thus arms are often omitted and sexual organs rarely shown. Related imagery appears among the northern Mbala, Yansi, Buma, Sakata, and Npepe.

The Kwango-style subgroup includes sculptures of the Yaka, Mbala, and Pende, consisting of figures shown in a standing or squatting posture, with hands held up to the chest or chin. Highly expressive eyes, noses, eyebrows, facial framing, and the elaboration of headgear are richly developed, with the spectrum of creativity ranging from simplified naturalism to grotesque caricature. The attached materials and textures that alter the sculptural form include antelope horns, packets, sticks, skins, bones, encrustations of camwood, and other ingredients suspended, wrapped, or otherwise attached to the statuettes. Further breakdown designates styles of the Suku, Nkanu, Hungaan, Holo, southern Yaka, Tsotso, Kwese, Soonde, Lula, Dikidiki, and Mbeko.

The Kasai, or south-center, stylistic group centers on Bushoong court statues of the Kuba, in which sovereigns are shown seated cross-legged with symbolic attributes carved on the plinth. Rounded treatment of the face and forehead, an angled hairline, and annulated neck are shared to varying degrees with the Ndengese, Biombo, northern Kete, Mbanagani, and Salampasu, although figure sculpture may include a diversity of polychrome patterns painted on the figure's face.

The southeast, or Luba, stylistic cluster, stretching from Katanga to the eastern Kasai, presents a smooth naturalism in human forms; with domed forehead, lowered eyes, and pursed lips highlighted by an elaborate, tiered hairdress that may cascade or end in a cross configuration. Hands and feet may be elongated and simplified but more attention is given to body scarification. Characteristic are depictions of the young female with hands to breast or holding a bowl, or as a caryatid supporting a seat. Males appear either holding regalia or sanding with arms flanking a protruding stomach. Substyles of Luba Shankadi, Luba Upemba, Luba Kasai, Hemba, eastern Luba, Zela, Kanyok, Tabwa, Tumbwe, Holoholo, Bangubangu, Bemba, Sikasingo, Bembe, and Boyo have been distinguished. The Songye substyle is differentiated by geometric treatment of the human face and body forms, which are segmented into distinct volumes. Apart from the figure eight-shaped mouth, prominent chin, and large flat hands and feet, there is the characteristic collage aspect with attachment of copper sheeting, blades, tacks, feathers, and cowry shells, together with the power packet enclosed in a protruding abdomen or inserted into a horn projecting vertically from the figure's head.

The Angolan plateau stylistic group, originally designated by Olbrechts as a Luba substyle, centers on the Chokwe. Broad shoulders and slender torsos with arms thrown back in a dynamic stance are distinctive. Attention is given to flaring headgear and body details down to fingernails and toes. Almond-shaped eyes may be recessed in deep sockets, and the beard projects laterally or is formed of fiber or human hair. Other attachments are usually limited to a proliferation of brass tacks. As with the Kuba and Luba, Chokwe styles overflow into many forms of minor arts with decoration of pipes, combs, staffs, musical instruments, and furniture. Substyles among the Mbunda, Lwena, Songo, Ovimbundu, and Ngangela present variations on scarification designs and headdresses but also add new subjects, such as a figure mounted on an ox.

In the northeastern equatorial stylistic region, various rudimentary human forms are produced in bone, ivory, and wood. Diagnostic are the half figures, double-faced, double-headed, or fully double figures with superimposed faces, heads, or bodies placed in opposition or linked together, many without arms, with one arm, or with short stumps for arms. Relatively small, heart-shaped faces are distinctive, with arched eyebrows forming a single unit, and with a narrow ridge or flat triangular nose. Best-known is the imagery of the Lega, although similar figurines in human form are found among the Yela, Lengola, Mitoko, Bembe, Pere, Komo, Nyanga, Kwami, Nyindu, Songola, and Zimba.

North-central and northwestern stylistic groups are less uniform categories that include the Mangbetu, Zande, and Boa on the one hand, and Ngbaka and Ngbandi farther to the west on the other. Figurative sculpture for the Mangbetu and Zande are more often decorated everyday objects, rather than a prolific tradition in statuary. Delicate female figures decorate the bridges of harps covered with reptile skin. Their highly embellished realism shows distinct cranial deformation and expanding cylindrical headdresses. Zande styles of freestanding sculpture range from rounded forms to great abstracted figures with zigzag or stump-like legs and underdeveloped arms, a characteristic shared with Ngbaka and Ngbandi. Additives to such figures include multiple metal rings and strings of beads embedded in resin. Ngbandi and Ngbaka sculpture is equally rare; it is characterized by large spherical heads, often with heart-shaped faces and brows lined with ridges of scars that also bisect the forehead vertically. Flipper-like arms commonly hang freely at the side, and in highly abstract varieties human figures are barely recognizable.

MASKS

The system for classifying masks, similar to that of freestanding figures, is by ethnic unit, stressing the uniqueness of a chosen mask type. Similarities in size or form are apparent both in contiguous ethnic groups and in isolated pockets within Central Africa. Masks range from miniatures to face coverings, from cap and helmet varieties that surround the wearer's head to massive creations that completely engulf the person beneath. Although the facial portion may be formed of woven materials, bark cloth, or carefully carved and painted wood, masks are found decorated with strips of metal, tacks, shells, calabash segments, beads, feathers, fur, or animal horns and commonly include either a knitted hood or a free-flowing fiber fringe. Representations include humans, animals, and composite creatures made up of elements of both.

Miniature masks, small enough to be held in the palm of the hand, appear in the northeast among the Lega, Nyindu, and Kwami, where they are carved of bone and ivory. In the southwest amid the Pende, southern Suku, Holo, and Chokwe, such masks are made of wood, ivory, seed-pits, lead, and other materials. In the southwest among the Songye, Luba-

Hemba, and northernmost Luba, they appear in wood as miniature white-faced masks with striated markings.

Giant masks are defined as masks measuring 35 inches or more in any direction. They are reported across the southern savanna and the Angolan plateau made of woven materials, bark cloth, or carved from wood, often featuring a face with bloated cheeks or a horned animal. The massive fiber masks of the western or Kwilu Pende called *gikuku mingangi* are the largest recorded in Central Africa: during the dance five or six other masked personages emerge from the mask's flowing fringe skirt.

The white, heart-shaped face is characteristic of mask imagery across the equatorial forest region among Bantu-speaking peoples, including the Mbole, Komo, Tembo, Lega, Bembe, Jonga, and Ngbaka, and into Gabon, where the form dominates. The heart-shaped face can also be found in isolated contexts on the southern savanna amid the Kwese and easternmost Kasai Pende, and indeed whiteness in faces and white areas around the eyes of masks are prevalent throughout Central Africa. Contrasts between the schematization or abstract reductions in mask imagery of the equatorial forest and examples of naturalism among the Vili, Suku, Pende, Chokwe, and Luba are readily apparent. Yet within the savanna belt alone, fantastic exaggerations distantly removed from human facial physiognomy occur in masks of the Yaka, Pende, Kwete, Luluwa, Lwalwa, Dongye, Chokwe, and Hemba.

South of the Congo Basin two macrostyles encompass the diverse ethnic expressions in masking: an upper zone of predominantly wooden helmet-shaped masks, found among populations living near the northern edge of the savanna and nearby forests (such as with the Suku, Kasai Pende, Kwese, Kete, Kuba, Binji, Kanyok, and Luba), and a secondary tier of predominantly resin-and-fabric masks made by peoples across the savanna to the south (including the Chokwe, Lwena, Lunda, Soonde, Yaka, and Nkanu). Moreover, the towering projections, miter-like elements, discs, and painted decoration imply a transtribal interaction of styles. The principal context for both resin-and-fabric masks and wooden helmet-shaped masks across southern Central Africa is that of *Mukanda*, an institution involving collective circumcision and initiation to manhood with widespread similarities in terminology, sequence of events, and use of mask at crucial moments of initiation and coming-out festivities. In the northeastern Congo-Kinshasa, use of the white, heart-shaped face in masks of the Lega and their neighbors is associated with an age-graded association known variously as Bwami, Bukota, Lilwa, or Nsubi. Masks in these contexts serve as mnemonic devices that aid in learning an enormous number of proverbs and ritual actions, secrets reserved to members alone. Other transethnic examples in masking style may be observed in the oblong or oval masks with patterns of incised facial striations among the Songye, Kalebwe, and Luba-Hemba, which are associated with a secret organization known as *Kifwebe*. A still broader view might include diverse peoples using fiber masks and body coverings made of palm leaves and occasionally decorated with other materials. They generally signify bush monsters that terrorize the uninitiated; they are widespread and are the likely source from which more elaborate mask making derives.

TEXTILES AND CERAMICS

In the artistic production of textiles, outsiders have admired Central African cut-pile embroidery, called Kasai velvets, since its first discovery. The oldest examples came to Europe between 1666 and 1674 from the mouth of the Congo River and Angola. Since the late nineteenth century, production has been limited to Kuba-related peoples of the Kasai region, and it continues in the twentieth century among the Shoowa and Ngombe of the Sankuru. The various rectilinear and abstract patterns are assigned individual names by their makers, although patterns bearing the same name are not necessarily identical. The classification of patterns is paralleled by distinctive social meanings of its use. Some were worn by women, others by men; some appeared in ceremonies only, others were in everyday use and distinguished the social position of the wearer. Early accounts further describe a variety of uses: as blankets, in adornment of stools (thrones), as shrouds, and as currency.

Pottery exists primarily as domestic ware. Forms range from jars with long, bottle-shaped necks made in the coastal region to the spherical forms made in the east that bear short necks and a small mouth. Decoration of surfaces with bands of incised crosshatchings and zigzags are common, as are impressions made with cords and other objects. Painting the vessels with mineral or vegetable pigments, as well as use of glazes, often enhances them. Noteworthy is the marbled or mottled effect achieved by splashing oil on the newly fired surface in Kongo and Teke wares. Although rare, figurative decoration on lids takes the form of birds, dogs, or humans among the Kongo, whereas a few ceramic heads and busts used as containers appear among certain groups of the Kwango and Kasai Rivers and the Mangbetu to the north. The influence of woven design is reflected in ceramic decorations, particularly in the Kasai region.

ARCHITECTURE

The most common traditional structure has a square or rectangular plan with walls of palm fronds and a hipped roof of thatch or palm leaf. Distinctive variations appear among Kuba-related peoples, who embellish this basic framework with interwoven materials and mats. The Manbetu in the nineteenth century amplified it into a vast rectangular assembly hall some 49 feet high. Roof structure and thatching could achieve a convex profile, found in structures from the Holo and southern Suku to the Luba, or the pyramidal roof of leaves in the north among the Ngelima and Nalya. Granaries could be elevated versions of the pitched roof structure, or miniature versions of cylindrical buildings with conical roofs, as found among the Chokwe and related peoples in Angola. Carved posts, panels, or figures embellished the domestic dwellings of dignitaries, especially among the Kongo, Chokwe, and Pende. Dressed wooden doorframes were made by the southern Suku and Holo, and the Mangbetu elaborately painted pillars and walls.

EUROPEAN INFLUENCE

Both stylistic diversity and traditional conservatism, apparent in the early twentieth-century art of the region, were products of past isolation as well as of steady intergroup contacts, intermixing, and political emulation or domination. Since then, the disruption of traditional structures of authority, religious proselytizing, the establishment of mission and government schools and rural projects, and the external economic pressures of a cash economy have dramatically changed the traditional setting of art. In some areas a wholesale rejection of traditional ritual and accompanying paraphernalia has resulted. In others, masking in the context of initiations survived or has been revived, both in a quest for cultural authenticity and as a source of local revenue. Retention of the original significance or regulation of art works by traditional leadership is rare at the beginning of the twenty-first century.

The earliest influence of European imagery in Central Africa dates from the beginning of the sixteenth century, following the arrival of Catholic missionaries. The Kongo king Alfonso I (r. 1509–1541) gave the crucifix to clan chiefs and judges presiding over tribunals both in the Mbanza capital and outlying provinces. Later the crucifix became a standard item for the investiture of Kongo chiefs and was incorporated into a syncretic belief system. Cast by the lost-wax or open-mould methods, all brass *nkangi kiditu* (attached Christ) are based on fourteenth to sixteenth century European examples, although African-like features illustrate indigenous adaptation. Wooden crucifixes and freestanding statuary of the Virgin Mary and St. Anthony of Padua were also produced. Within the southwestern region, Christian religious influence into the twentieth century is equally apparent in the *ntadi*stone funerary monuments of the Mboma, and in the Holo framed figures and some Chokwe woodcarving.

CONTEMPORARY DEVELOPMENTS

Art from urban centers derives from some measure of European intervention, not only in the materials, techniques, and format such as easel painting, but also in that the more distinguished artists have had the opportunity to study, train, or visit abroad. The *Academie des Beaux-Arts* in Kinshasa founded in 1943 by Frere Marc-Stanislas, originally named *Ecole St. Luc*, adhered to Belgian educational methods and taught classical European art. Better-known painters from this institution in Kinshasa include Mongita, Domba, Nkusu Felelo, Mavinga, Kamba Luesa (b. 1944), Konde Bila, and Nduku a Nzambi. Two institutes established in 1951 included the *Academie des Beaux-Arts et de Metiers d'Art* in Lubumbashi run by Laurent Moonens, a Belgian artist, and *Centre d'Art Africaine*, also known as the Poto-Poto School, was founded in Brazzaville by Pierre Lods. Lods attempted to foster an African approach, but much of the resulting art became highly decorative and repetitive although the style

took hold as a fad that sold widely. Themes used by Poto-Poto artists initiated the genre of painted tourist art:—the mask, drumming, dance scenes, the hunt, maternity, and the fetisher that continues to the present. In 1953 the Belgian artist Pierre Romain-Desfosses (d. 1954) established the *Atelier d'Art "Le Hangar"* in colonial Elisabethville (Lubumbashi), Democratic Republic of the Congo, producing artists such as PiliPili Malongoy (b. 1914), Msenze, Bella, and Kebala, whose works are in early modernist styles yet depict indigenous African subjects.

In the 1970s a genre of painting emerged painted on cloth recycled from flour sacks in street-side workshops that illustrated the values, conflicts, and concerns of Congolese postcolonial society. Emerging painters include Tshibumba Kanda Mutulu (1947–1980) of Lubumbashi, who chronicled Democratic Republic of the Congo history from the great Lunda and Luba empires through the attempted Katanga secession and murder of Patrice Lumumba, and Chéri Samba of Kinshasa (b. 1956), whose satirical paintings comment on the moral and social crises. Other artists following Chéri Samba include: Moke, Bodo, Bodys Isek Kingelez (b. 1948), Cheik Ledy (1962–1997), Moké, Syms, Vuza Ntoko (b. 1954), and Cheri Cherin (b. 1955).

In the late 1980s and throughout the 1990s, African contemporary artists showed at major exhibitions at the *Centre Georges Pompidou*, Paris; the Center for African Art, New York; Whitechapel Art Gallery in London; the Ikon Gallery in Birmingham, London; in Johannesburg at the first biennial exhibit, and at the Carnegie International in Pittsburgh.

See also **Architecture; Arts; Ceramics; Geometries; Lumumba, Patrice; Masks and Masquerades; Religion and Ritual; Textiles.**

BIBLIOGRAPHY

Biebuyck, Daniel. *The Arts of Zaire*, 2 vols. Berkeley: University of California Press, 1985.

Biebuyck, Daniel. *The Arts of Central Africa: An Annotated Bibliography.* Boston: G.K. Hall, 1987.

Cornet, Joseph. *Art d'Afrique noire au pays du fleuve Zaire.* Brussels: Arcade, 1971. Translated into English as *Art of Africa: Treasures from the Congo.* London: Phaidon Press, 1971.

de Spousberghe, Leon. *L'Art Pende*. Brussels: Beaux-Arts, 1958.

Felix, Mark L. *100 Peoples of Zaire and their Neighbors: The Handbook*. Brussels: Zaire Basin Art History Research Foundation, 1987.

Herreman, F. and C. Petridis, eds. *Face of the Spirits, Masks from the Zaire Basin*. Antwerp: Martial and Snoeck, 1994.

Koloss, H-J. *Art of Central Africa: Masterpieces from the Berlin Museum fur Volkerkunde*. New York: H.N. Abrams, 1990.

Maesen, Albert. "Un Art traditionnel au Congo Belge: La Sculpture." In *Les Arts au Congo Belge et au Ruanda-Urundi, Centre d'information et de documentation du Congo belge*, pp. 9–33. Brussels, 1950.

Olbrechts, Franz M. *Plastiek van Kongo*. Antwerp: N.V. Standaard, 1946.

Verswijver, G., et al., eds. *Treasures from the Africa-Museum, Tervuren*. Tervuren: Royal Museum for Central Africa, 1995.

Visona, Monica B., et al. *A History of Art in Africa*. Upper Saddle River, N.J.: Prentice Hall, 2001.

ARTHUR P. BOURGEOIS

EASTERN AFRICA

Eastern Africa is taken here to comprise the Horn of Africa and east Africa with its offshore islands. It thus encompasses the area occupied in the twenty-first century by Eritrea, Somalia, Djibouti, Kenya, Tanzania, Uganda, and Madagascar; Ethiopia, however, is treated separately. As the borders of modern nation-states are not congruent with cultural areas, mention is also made of the visual traditions of peoples living in adjacent areas of neighboring countries. In particular, the visual traditions of the peoples of Southern Sudan are discussed here.

The region is vast and has a complex history, thus attempts to generalize about its visual traditions serve little point. There is little of interest one could say that would apply equally to the visual traditions of the Khoe-, Cushitic-, Nilotic-, and Bantu-speaking peoples of the region, let alone to the Islamic-influenced traditions of the Swahili people of the east African coast or the Southeast Asian–associated traditions of the peoples of Madagascar. Moreover, the region has not been cut off from the rest of the world; for example, the visual traditions of the east African coast are linked to those of the Persian Gulf and the Indian Ocean.

In addition, it is now better appreciated how mobile both people and their material products have been throughout the history of eastern Africa—before, during, and after the colonial period—and thus how much research needs to be done to uncover and explore the complex historical relationships and influences within the region. For example, it is known that stone bowls and other items were traded from Madagascar to east Africa, but the extent, influence and importance of this trade has yet to be thoroughly investigated. Similarly, information on the trade routes within east Africa itself is often minimal. Moreover, little art-historical research has been carried out and the information that is available tends to relate only to particular historical moments and is in any case partial. For example, scholarly work on the visual traditions of the kingdoms of Uganda has been scarce in recent years, and thus knowledge about them is limited. In contrast, new information on many of the sculptural traditions of Tanzania has been made available only recently and has yet to be assimilated into overviews of the visual traditions of the region.

What it is possible to say in a brief summary is always limited by the information that is available and accessible. For eastern Africa the problem is compounded by the fact that for many years influential scholars regarded much of the region as being "without art." Such a view was limited in two ways. First, it assumed that "art" refers only to certain types of sculpture and painting; and second, it ignored the evidence contained in early publications and museum collections of the existence of a large number of sculptural and graphic traditions.

This neglect may now perhaps be seen as at least partially benign, for it has had a number of distinct benefits for the study of the visual traditions of eastern Africa. First, it has led to relatively greater attention being paid to the supposedly "lesser" arts. Thus a number of recent publications have included information on pots, decorated gourds, snuff containers, tobacco pipebowls, staffs, tools, implements, and utensils of various types. Secondly, the rich traditions of body arts have received greater attention than they might have otherwise, attention that has led to a greater appreciation of African body arts in general. Similarly, greater attention has also been given to the intense aesthetic appreciation of cattle that characterizes the cultural life of many of the Nilotic-speaking pastoralists of the region. The relative lack of visual art objects among such peoples has made a focus on the local aesthetic appreciation of cattle a necessity for scholars interested in their visual culture. New traditions, both popular and academic, have also received greater attention than might otherwise have been the case. Thus, it is relatively easy to find accessible studies of modern Kamba and Makonde carving, as well as surveys of contemporary sculpture and painting in east Africa. For this reason, these new traditions are given relatively little attention here.

BODY ARTS

Arguably, the human body is the prime medium for aesthetic expression in eastern Africa. This is especially so for the pastoralist peoples of the region, for whom the scarred, painted, ornamented, and dressed bodies of young men and women are the epitome of glamorous beauty. As well as providing a medium for aesthetic expression, however, the human body also provides a public vehicle for marking changes in social status and passage through the lifecycle.

Bodies are marked in various ways, both permanently and temporarily. For example, among the Nuer, Dinka, and other Nilotic-speaking cattle-keepers of southern Sudan the foreheads of young men and women are marked at initiation with deep cuts, the healing of which is retarded so that raised scars (or cicatrices) are formed. These scars are of great significance as they both mark the individual's transition from childhood to young adulthood and physically identify him or her as a member of the group. Among the neighboring Mandari, more decorative scars are also found. The tradition here remains unstudied, at least partly because the designs focus on women's navels, which in public tend to remain hidden, but it seems that, as elsewhere in the region, such marks are valued more for their erotic tactile qualities (which will be experienced by the bearer's sexual partners) than for their visual qualities.

Cicatrization is also practiced by many of the Bantu-speaking peoples of the region. For example, the elaborate traditions found in northern Zambia and the Democratic Republic of Congo are also found in western Tanzania. Here the natural symmetry of the body as a whole is emphasized rather than specific parts of it. The scarification patterns are often articulated around a central axis running down the body from the forehead, through the tip of the nose, the neck, and the navel to the genitalia. No full understanding of such traditions will be possible until more is known of the local symbolism of the body, but it seems that for at least some of these peoples, designs that focus on the navel may have connections with birth and transitions, while those that focus on the forehead may have to do with wisdom, dreams, and visions. Cicatrization has been practiced elsewhere in the region. For example, Makonde migrants from Mozambique in Tanzania were, in the past at least, distinguishable by the cicatrized patterns on their faces, while in Madagascar cicatrized marks were once commonly applied to the face, as well as to the shoulders and arms. Rich traditions of both cicatrization and body painting have also been recorded in detail for some groups in the Nuba Mountains, Kordofan, Sudan, on the northern edge of the region.

The traditions of dress and adornment in the region are extraordinarily diverse. Indeed, generally speaking, it is by their distinctive modes of dress and adornment that many of the peoples of eastern Africa are known. Moreover, as styles of dress, adornment, and coiffure are regularly reproduced in figure sculpture, it has often been by these characteristics, rather than by sculptural style as such, that scholars have provenanced many of the works from the region held in museum and private collections.

Among the Nilotic-speaking peoples both men and women use an almost infinitely wide variety of materials to decorate their bodies. For example, mud is a major component of male decoration among the Karamojong of Uganda and their Kenyan neighbors the Turkana and Pokot. It is used particularly at the back of the head where successive layers are built up by pressing mud into the hair. Once the structure has dried to form a hard and smooth surface it is painted. It may then

Figure 1. Young Turkana man, northern Kenya, 1961, with characteristically dressed hair and ornaments. PITT RIVERS MUSEUM, UNIVERSITY OF OXFORD

Figure 2. Young Samburu men, northern Kenya, 1979. Men style one another's hair in elaborate braids. PITT RIVERS MUSEUM, UNIVERSITY OF OXFORD

also be adorned with feathers, beads and other colorful or shiny items (see Figure 1).

Among the neighboring Samburu young men pay great attention to the hair. Indeed, it is not unusual for a man to spend twelve or more hours braiding and dressing his hair. There are a number of styles into which the hair may be made and fashions change over time, but the braiding itself appears to be a continuing and central feature. In the late 1970s it was common to divide the hair into "back" and "forehead" sections, the latter being arranged into one of two general styles. It was either twisted into dozens of thin strands which were then gathered together under a button placed in the center of the forehead, or if it was long enough it was twisted and shaped over a piece of leather or other stiff but flexible material into the form of a visor (see Figure 2). To protect the

elaborate headdress from being crushed, almost every man among these peoples carries with him a small headrest, more accurately neckrest, placed under the neck when lying down.

Hair receives great attention throughout the region. The way it is grown, dressed, or indeed shaved off is often a prime marker of social status or position. For example, coiffure was traditionally very important in Madagascar with styles, which were locally named, varying between the genders as well as with social status and from region to region. Among the Merina there were nine or more distinct styles of female coiffure, ranging from complex plaited styles to the untressed style used as a sign of mourning.

While the head is perhaps the prime focus for young men in northern Kenya, a number of other ornaments may also commonly be worn. For example, young Turkana men wear a variety of ornaments including bead necklaces, metal wristlets, and hide armlets, while young Samburu men may wear beaded chokers and bracelets, animal-hide wristlets, ivory earplugs, and finger rings. Generally speaking, however, it is the head that is emphasized, or parts of it.

Among the same peoples female decoration also focuses on the head. Among women, however, decoration does not seek to alter or emphasize the natural features of the head and face but to separate them visually from the rest of the body. Among east African peoples it is Maasai artists who have exploited the potential of ornamental beadwork to its greatest extent. Maasai women wear the most elaborate beadwork sets, and again the neck is an important point of concentration. Rigid discoid collars of brightly colored beads are often worn in sets. These in turn may be complemented by being worn in conjunction with beaded headpieces, earrings, chokers, and bandoliers, in what might be seen as a form of kinetic sculpture. Beads are also worn on the upper arms and wrists, around the waist and in bands around the thigh, calf, and ankle. Such beadwork is made by women, who develop their own styles within established conventions of form, pattern, and color, which are in turn based on notions of contrast and complementarity. Scholars are also beginning to document changes in form and color over time so that an art history of Maasai beadwork can be said to have begun. It is not only Maasai who wear complex beadwork structures, and further understanding of the beadwork traditions of the region would benefit from comparative studies of the traditions of the Maasai and those of other peoples of Kenya and Tanzania.

Body painting is also practiced in many parts of the region. It is particularly well known among some groups in the Nuba Mountains at the northern edge of the region, but it is also practiced on occasion by young Maasai men and women, and by many of the other Nilotic-speaking peoples.

Traditionally, for both men and women among many of these peoples clothing was minimal, though often decorated. Among the Turkana, for example, women wore animal skins embellished with areas of beadwork. The most elaborate examples of such beadwork-decorated dress, however,

Figure 3. Iraqw beaded hid skirt, from Mbulu, Tanzania; pre-1940. PITT RIVERS MUSEUM, UNIVERSITY OF OXFORD

were found among the Cushitic-speaking Iraqw of northwest Tanzania. Here special skirts consisting of hide panels sewn together were decorated with thousands of glass beads (see Figure 3). Until the 1940s or so, they were made by young girls, to their own designs, during their initiation into Marmo, the Iraqw women's society. Few such skirts have yet been studied, but it seems that, traditionally at least, white, red, and black (or dark blue) beads were predominant. As yet, no reliable information has been published on the significance of the various motifs or the colors used, though the predominance of white beads may be connected with the significance of the color white, *awaak*, in Iraqw culture, where it is associated with light, clarity, health, well-being, healing, curing, and purification. A full aesthetic appreciation of such skirts, however, has to take account of the fact that they were worn by young girls whose bodies were oiled and adorned with various ornaments, and that they were made to be seen in movement, the swish of the skirt being emphasized by the swaying of the fringe; moreover, the weight of the skirt constrained the movements of the girls as they walked and danced.

Rich traditions of dress are found among many other peoples of the region. The regalia of the royal kingdoms of Uganda, for example, deserve greater attention than they have received to date. Such regalia were most prominent at coronations and burial ceremonies. For example, at his coronation the king of Toro wore robes of barkcloth fringed with beads and elephant hair as well as beads around his ankles and a necklace of lions' claws. All these objects were

Figure 4. Beaded bandolier, from Madagascar; pre-1884. Beadwork is separated by nine sets of silver containers representing crocodile teeth. PITT RIVERS MUSEUM, UNIVERSITY OF OXFORD

symbolic of wealth, power, and courage. In Madagascar, charms were traditionally an important component of dress. These took a number of forms, important among which was that of crocodile teeth. These were often worn as charms in their own right, but they were also incorporated into more complex forms, such as beaded bandoliers, where they were sometimes reproduced in the form of hollow, lidded silver containers (see Figure 4).

In the Horn and among the Swahili of the East African coast, women wear elaborate jewelry—necklaces, bracelets, earrings and armlets—especially at weddings and on other important public occasions. Amuletic necklaces consisting of boxes containing Qur'anic inscriptions are often made of silver or gold. In Lamu and elsewhere along the coast earplugs of silver and gold were also made, while in the early twentieth century earplugs made of rolled paper decorated with sequins and other shiny materials were also produced.

DECORATIVE, DOMESTIC, AND OTHER ARTS

There have been and continue to be innumerable traditions of decorative and domestic arts throughout eastern Africa. Only a very few examples of such arts can be dealt with here.

The carved wooden headrests of the Nilotic-speaking peoples of Sudan, Kenya, and Uganda have often been presented as the stereotypical art object of eastern Africa. They have been produced in a vast range of styles and forms, ranging from the virtually "found art" forms of the Dinka and Nuer to the more formal, geometric shapes produced by the Pokot and other peoples of Kenya and Uganda. Typically, the three- or four-legged stools-cum-headrests of the Dinka and Nuer are produced by pruning a found branch to the required shape. Almost all such headrests seem to have zoomorphic features, at least implicitly, and these are often "brought out" by having spots, stripes, or other features pyroengraved or otherwise marked on the surface (see Figure 5). Among the Pokot, Turkana, and other peoples of northern Kenya, headrests are usually single-footed and have a curved top. Most examples are plain, but some are elaborately decorated with beads and other materials. Recent work suggests that a variety of forms are found in any particular area, partly as a result of cultural "borrowing" but also as a result of trade and exchange networks. Thus, "Pokot" and "Turkana" style headrests from Kenya are found in the Karamojong area in Uganda, and vice versa.

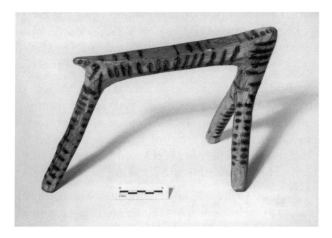

Figure 5. Nuer headrest of carved wood, from Southern Sudan; collected in the 1930s. PITT RIVERS MUSEUM, UNIVERSITY OF OXFORD

Probably the most elaborate items of furniture in the region are the "chairs of power" produced by Swahili artists. These are large, angular constructions with footrests and detachable backs. Highbacked chairs were also produced by the Nyamwezi and neighboring peoples in Tanzania, often incorporating sculptured figures. Other items of furniture include the decoratively carved wooden chests and boxes with brass fittings of the Swahili. Finely worked mats continue to be made by Swahili women up to the present day. Mat making has also been important in parts of Madagascar.

Eastern Africa is not well known for the production of textiles. Some of the peoples of Madagascar, however, produce colorful cloths with elaborate designs. Among the Merina, for example, in the nineteenth century textiles were woven from silk. They were warp-striped with bands of color, the range of which increased with the introduction of commercial dyes. Geometric designs were often applied to the fringes of the cloth as floating weft patterns, though small metal beads were also used. Cotton, raffia, bark, and wool were woven in various parts of the island. Among the Sakalava ikat-dyed raffia cloths were used as mosquito nets and as burial cloths. Decorated barkcloth has also been produced in the region, particularly in Uganda. Since the 1960s, textile production has been developed in many parts of the region, including notably in craft cooperatives in urban areas in Kenya. Some Ugandan and Tanzanian artists have also worked in the medium of batik.

Among the best-known objects from the region are the shields of the Maasai of Kenya and Tanzania (now ostensibly produced only for tourists). A wooden backbone supports an oval of buffalo hide, which is painted with geometric designs. More visually elaborate are the arm shields of the Gikuyu of Kenya (see Figure 6). These were worn by young men on the upper arms during initiation dances. The shields themselves were carved from wood (or bark) by a specialist and used a number of times over the years as they were passed from older to younger relatives. The designs to be painted on them in red, white, and black were agreed in advance of the initiation ceremony and, as they changed through time, were scraped off and replaced.

Figure 6. Gikuyu dance shield, made of wood, soot, paint, and earth. From Murang'a, Kenya, c. 1930. PITT RIVERS MUSEUM, UNIVERSITY OF OXFORD

SCULPTURE AND GRAPHIC ARTS

Distinguishing figurative from nonfigurative traditions is to impose a distinction that may be of little significance in much of eastern Africa itself. Given the way in which the visual traditions of the region have been approached to date, however, it is useful to survey here those traditions that approximate most closely what is conventionally regarded as art in the West. So long as the arbitrary nature of the distinction is kept in mind, little misunderstanding need arise. Nonfigurative traditions are also dealt with here, though the emphasis is on the figurative.

Historically, figurative painting has been a relative rarity in the region, though examples of what may be ancient rock-art traditions survive. In central Tanzania in particular, but also elsewhere in the region, there are a number of rock paintings and petroglyphs in caves and other sheltered places. The forms range from schematic designs to naturalistic representations of animals and human figures. As yet these works remain relatively unstudied and dating them has proved difficult, though it is thought that depictions at Mount Elgon on the Kenya-Uganda border of longhorn cattle not found anywhere in the area may date to the first millennium BCE. (Rock art continues to be produced in Kenya and Tanzania, as during their initiation ceremonies young men of the pastoralist groups make symbolic marks on rock surfaces.) There is little evidence of ancient figurative sculpture from the region, though a terra-cotta head and torso, which may possibly be from the same figure, found in 1929 at Luzira Hill near Lake Victoria in Uganda may be ancient (though equally, given the lack of any dateable associated evidence, it may be no more than two hundred years old).

Two-dimensional figurative traditions are found throughout the region, though rarely in areas where Islam has been influential. Decorated gourds with pyroengraved figures of people and animals are known from the Anuak of Sudan, for example, while young Dinka and Nuer men sketch pictures of cattle and people on hut walls. Among the Sukuma of Tanzania the interior walls of the lodges of the snake charmers society are painted with images of humans, snakes, and mythological figures. Among the Luo of western Kenya fishing boats were traditionally painted with geometric designs. In recent years, the paintings have incorporated the Kenyan national flag and portraits of the boats' owners. Among the Mahafaly of Madagascar it has become common for the sides of tombs (previously left as dressed stone) to be cemented over and painted with figurative scenes (the Antandroy of Madagascar also paint the sides of tombs, but with nonfigurative designs). A number of other figurative painting traditions are known. Generally speaking, however, such traditions have received little anthropological or art-historical attention and thus information about them is limited.

The dominant sculptural form in much of the region is the pole, variously decorated and more or less anthropomorphized. Such sculptures are known to have been produced by the Central Sudanic-speaking Bongo of the southern Sudan, by the Giriama and other Mijikenda-speaking peoples of Kenya, and by numerous other peoples down to the Zaramo and Zagura in Tanzania. Such sculptures tend to be associated with the dead, often with their graves, or with entrances to villages.

The memorial posts of the Giriama have rounded and naturalistic or flat, disc-shaped heads. The pole-like bodies tend to be flat and are characteristically ornamented with incised triangles or other geometric designs. The triangles and other motifs, which are arranged in a variety of patterns, are painted with red, white, and black pigments.

In south and southwest Madagascar, sculpture is also predominantly associated with the dead. There is a vast variety of forms, varying from group to group and from context to context. Sculptures are often placed on tombs but may also be erected away from burial places as ancestral shrines or cenotaphs. The tombs of the Mahafaly elite are huge box-like stone structures erected in isolation in the countryside. They are topped with a miniature forest of wooden sculptures (as many as thirty have been recorded on a single tomb). As with all sculptural traditions, the forms given to these sculptures have varied through time, but there are general principles that underlie all known examples. Each sculpture is carved from a single piece of wood and stands approximately 6.5 feet high. The base may be plain but may also consist of a standing figure. Above this is a pole carved and pierced with geometric forms, often crescents and circles that are said to represent half and full moons. On top of the pole are carved more figures, in the past generally birds and humped cattle, though in the twentieth century figural groups, cyclists, buses, and airplanes were also represented. Sakalava-Vezo tomb sculpture, in contrast, features pairs of naked human figures (sometimes posed sexually) in conjunction with figures of birds and double-headed pots.

The sculptures of the Bongo, the Giriama, and the peoples of Madagascar are often grouped together as if they comprise a set of variations on a theme. Apart from their very general pole-like form, however, and their general association with the dead they have little in common; although the chip-carved ornamentation of some Giriama and some Madagascan posts is intriguingly similar it may well have resulted from separate Swahili influence, rather than from direct contact or a common origin. Further understanding of these traditions may be better served by focusing on internal variations—especially through time—rather than by continually lumping together very different traditions.

Other traditions of figure sculpture are known from elsewhere in the region. In many cases, detailed study of them may be said to be only just beginning. One of the better-known traditions is that of the Nyamwezi of north-central Tanzania, a large, loosely organized group of diverse origins, a number of whom were involved in the caravan trade between the Indian Ocean and the Congo in the late nineteenth century. The most distinctively Nyamwezi works are high-backed wooden stools and human figures. In Tanzania, there is a widespread tradition (also found in Zambia) of using pottery figurines in initiation ceremonies and other rituals. Such figurines have yet to receive significant art-historical attention. Many of the amulets and charms produced in Madagascar were also figurative, incorporating figures of human heads, oxen, and crocodiles. Spoons were also decorated with human and zoomorphic forms. From the early nineteenth century the side panels of wooden beds were carved with elaborate scenes in low relief.

Elaborate traditions of masking are found only among some of the Bantu-speaking peoples of the region; though a few masks from other peoples are attested, they remain poorly studied. The best-known masking tradition of the region is that of the Makonde people of southern Tanzania, whose distinctive face masks should not be confused with the more naturalistic helmet masks of the culturally related but distinct people of northern Mozambique who happen to share a name. The Makonde also used body masks in the past. Our knowledge of other masking traditions in the region is extremely limited, being based in the main on poorly documented museum collections, though the Nyau masking traditions of the Chewa of Malawi are becoming better known.

Of the new figurative traditions that have been developed in the twentieth century, the best known are the sculptural traditions of the Kamba and the Makonde and the painting tradition known as Tingatinga. The development of these traditions has depended on the growth of nonindigenous markets among expatriate colonial administrators, missionaries, and settlers, and tourists. Export

markets have also been developed. In both the Kamba and Makonde cases ethnic labels have been used to refer to a wide range of products, from curios mass-produced for the tourist trade through unique sculptures by self-aware artists with little ostensible concern for the market.

The modern tradition of Kamba sculpture was originated by Mutisya Munge (c. 1892–1928), who was in part inspired by the work of Zaramo carvers that he saw while doing military service in what was then Tanganyika during World War I. On returning home he took up carving full-time, producing small figures of people and animals. The practice was soon taken up by other Kamba men, until it had become a thriving industry. Intense demand, especially after World War II, led to the establishment of a production-line style industry producing simple, standardized figures, letter openers, and salad servers. By the late 1980s some ten thousand people belonged to cooperatives producing Kamba-style carvings.

Modern Makonde sculpture also developed in the years after World War I, and in particular, after World War II, when a number of Makonde left the Makonde plateau in northeastern Mozambique to work on the sisal plantations in Tanzania. Through the talent of individual artists and the enthusiasm of a few non-Makonde dealers various styles of carving were developed. The earliest works were figures of characters from traditional village life. Later, elaborate group figures in pole form were produced, as well as more or less abstracted, open-work "spirit" carvings. Demand increased to such an extent that many non-Makonde took up the making of Makonde art. The label is now applied to everything produced in the Makonde style—from ashtrays to unique expressions of individual creativity by such established artists as John Fundi (1939–1991), whose work was included in the exhibition *Magiciens de la terre* at the Centre Georges Pompidou in Paris in 1989.

Tingatinga painting was originated by Edward Saidi Tingatinga (1937–1972). He drew on modern Makonde sculpture and contemporary painting from the Congo to create a new art form consisting of an invented and stylized imagery of animals and plants, which he painted on hardboard squares using brightly colored house paints. As with the modern Kamba and Makonde traditions, Tingatinga painting proved very successful commercially and was taken up by many people.

The most important institution in the history of modern art in east Africa has been the Margaret Trowell School of Fine Arts at Makerere University in Kampala, Uganda. The institution has its origins in classes taught by Margaret Trowell at Makerere College in the mid-1930s. From the beginning students came from Kenya and Tanzania as well as Uganda, and it quickly gained an international reputation.

This international aspect is also marked in the careers of individual artists. A good example is provided by Elimo Njau, who was born in Marangu, Tanzania, in 1932. From 1952 to 1957 he attended Makerere as a student and from 1962 to 1963 he taught there. From 1965 to 1969 he taught at the University of Dar es Salaam, Tanzania. Between 1961 and 1972 he founded a number of galleries in Tanzania and Kenya. Later he became a freelance artist and a lecturer at Kenyatta University in Nairobi. The careers of many other leading East African artists have followed similar patterns. The work of such artists is as diverse as that of the artists of any other region of the world. Among the dominant themes, however, are traditional life and local narrative and commentary, the political content of which has occasionally brought artists into conflict with the authorities.

In Madagascar a number of sculptors have risen to prominence in the twentieth century, both in Madagascar itself and internationally. For example, the painted funerary sculptures made by the Mahafaly sculptor Efiaimbelo (b. 1925) have been included in such international art exhibitions as the touring show *Africa Now* (1991).

ARCHITECTURE

The most-studied and therefore best-known architectural traditions of eastern Africa are those of the Swahili towns of the Indian Ocean coast and offshore islands. From the late fourteenth to the sixteenth century tombs and mausoleums were built for the Swahili elite from plastered coral rag. Generally, they had a surrounding wall, sometimes with panels and niches, and a superstructure, often with finials decorated with ceramic bowls from China and Persia. Variations include domed superstructures and steps or wings rising from the walls.

Some were mounted by a pillar approximately 16 feet high.

The characteristic features of the buildings of Swahili towns are the use of coral blocks and mangrove poles as basic building materials and their decoration with ornate plasterwork on the inside and carved wooden doors on the outside. The interior walls of eighteenth- and nineteenth-century mosques and private houses are decorated with ornate plasterwork carved in situ with curves, spirals, rosettes, chains, zigzags, and other motifs. The jambs, lintels, and centerposts of the double-paneled wooden doors of the houses of the elite were also intricately carved with similar motifs, though in Zanzibar, and perhaps elsewhere, fish, date palms, and other natural objects were also represented. Such doors were often the only external feature of an otherwise plain, whitewashed building. Generally speaking, before the nineteenth century such doors had rectangular lintels and geometric carving. In the nineteenth century, arched lintels and more curvilinear motifs became common as a result of the influence of Indian traditions. The tradition of ornately carved doors was most developed in Zanzibar Town, where there are more than five hundred such doors, often also decorated with brass studs (see Figure 7), but the tradition also existed in Kenya, especially in Lamu, Malindi, and Mombasa. Swahili carved doors are also found in Oman, whence they were exported in finished form. The stone town of Zanzibar, with its multistory houses, elaborate wooden balconies, and famous doors, was restored in the 1980s.

The Arab quarters of Mogadishu in Somalia were once walled and contained one- and two-story stone houses. Stone-built towns also flourished in northwestern Somalia in the fifteenth and sixteenth centuries. The stone houses of the coastal regions of Somalia often have wooden windows, doors, and lintels, carved with floral motifs.

In rural areas of the region, traditional architecture is characterized by the use of whatever materials—wood, grass, clay, sun-dried mud, stone, cow dung, mats, and skins—are locally available. These deceptively simple materials have been combined in innumerable ways to produce a range of temporary and semipermanent buildings for humans, animals, and the storage of foodstuffs. The forms these structures take are often referred to as "beehive" or

Figure 7. Carved wooden door decorated with brass studs, Zanzibar, Tanzania, 1963. PITT RIVERS MUSEUM, UNIVERSITY OF OXFORD

"cone-and-cylinder," but there is in fact a vast range of forms, architectural details, methods of construction, and materials. For example, among the nomadic Somali, women construct a small dome-shaped portable hut from a framework of branches covered with mats or skins. In contrast among the Chagga of Tanzania round huts are built with grass roofs that reach to the ground. Each Chagga family's homestead is surrounded by a banana grove and a dry-stone wall or low hedge, larger hedges or earth banks being used to demarcate clan areas. Such an arrangement of buildings is only one of the many settlement plans found throughout the region. Another distinctive arrangement is that of the Maasai *manyatta*, constructed by women for their sons' circumcision and initiation ceremonies, in which a hundred or more low, oblong cow dung-plastered huts are arranged in a circle with their

doorways opening on to a large open area. Strikingly, no African-style round houses are found in Madagascar; buildings there are strictly rectilinear—as in Asia.

Throughout the region great attention is paid to decorating, maintaining, and cleaning and tidying homesteads, such work amounting to competition between households in some areas of Uganda and elsewhere. The aesthetic aspects of such daily activity have yet to be studied in great depth, perhaps because it is everyday, women's work. Greater attention has been paid to house and hut decoration. Generally, the arrangement of grass thatching on roofs and walls and the shaping and finishing of the surfaces of mud walls and floors are the subject of much careful labor. In addition, both exterior and interior walls are often painted. For example, the Hima of southwestern Uganda paint the entrances and interior walls of houses with bold geometric black-and-white designs. At the very edge of the region in Kordofan in Sudan, many Nuba decorate their wet-brick huts and granaries with paintings and with sculptural additions in mud. Special buildings often receive special attention. Among the Nuer and Dinka of southern Sudan, for example, large mounds and huge cattle byres have been constructed at important shrines.

New and imported styles of building were introduced in the twentieth century. Many of the cities of the region—for example, Nairobi in Kenya and the city of Djibouti—were founded or developed during colonial times and have many characteristic colonial-style street-plans and buildings. Many of the colonial buildings are neoclassical in style, while mosques and Hindu and Sikh temples draw on Middle Eastern and Oriental traditions. More recently many buildings have been built in International Style. A good example is the Kenyatta Conference Centre (1979) in Nairobi, designed by K. K. Nøstrik. Its conical roof—visible from many points throughout the city—echoes the form of traditional rural dwellings, while the rural dwellings themselves—in Kenya and elsewhere—increasingly incorporate the materials previously associated with urban areas, such as cement blocks and corrugated metal sheets for roofing.

See also **Aksum; Architecture; Art, Genres and Periods: Rock Art, Eastern Africa; Arts; Body Adornment and Clothing; Languages; Symbols and Symbolism: Animal; World War I; World War II.**

BIBLIOGRAPHY

Agthe, Johanna. *Wegzeichen: Kunst aus Ostafrika 1974–89/ Signs: Art from East Africa 1974–89*. Frankfurt am Main: Museum für Völkerkunde, 1990.

Andersen, Kaj Blegvad. *African Traditional Architecture: A Study of the Housing and Settlement Patterns of Rural Kenya*. Nairobi and New York: Oxford University Press, 1977.

Arero, Hassan, and Zachary Kingdon, eds. *East African Contours: Reviewing Creativity and Visual Culture*. London: The Horniman Museum and Gardens, 2005.

Barbour, Jane, and Simiyu Wandibba. *Kenyan Pots and Potters*. Nairobi: Oxford University Press, 1989.

Best, Gunther. *Markwet and Turkana: New Perspectives on the Material Culture of East African Societies*. Frankfurt am Main: Museum für Völkerkunde, 1993.

Burt, Eugene C. *An Annotated Bibliography of the Visual Arts of East Africa*. Bloomington: Indiana University Press, 1980.

Carey, Margret. *Beads and Beadwork of East and South Africa*. Aylesbury, U.K.: Shire Publications, 1986.

Coote, Jeremy. "'Marvels of Everyday Vision': The Anthropology of Aesthetics and the Cattle-Keeping Nilotes." In *Anthropology, Art, and Aesthetics*, eds. Jeremy Coote and Anthony Shelton. New York: Oxford University Press, 1992.

Deliss, Clémentine, ed. *Seven Stories about Modern Art in Africa*. London: Whitechapel Art Gallery, 1995.

Ewel, Manfred, and Anne Outwater, eds. *From Ritual to Modern Art: Tradition and Modernity in Tanzanian Sculpture*. Dar es Salaam: Mkuki na Nyota, 2001.

Faris, James C. *Nuba Personal Art*. London: Duckworth, 1972.

Felix, Mark, et al. *Tanzania: Meisterwerke afrikanischer Skulptur*. Munich: Fred Jahn, 1994.

Garlake, Peter S. *The Early Islamic Architecture of the East African Coast*. Nairobi: Oxford University Press, 1966.

Kingdon, Zachary. *A Host of Devils: The History and Context of the Making of Makonde Spirit Sculpture*. London and New York: Routledge, 2002.

Kreamer, Christine Mullen, and Sarah Fee, eds. *Objects as Envoys: Cloth, Imagery, and Diplomacy in Madagascar*. Washington, DC: Smithsonian Institution Press, 2002.

Lagat, Kiprop, and Julie Hudson, eds. *Hazina: Traditions, Trade and Transitions in Eastern Africa*. Nairobi: National Museums of Kenya, 2006.

Leakey, Mary. *Africa's Vanishing Past: The Rock Paintings of Tanzania*. Garden City, NY: Hamish Hamilton/ Rainbird, 1983.

Loughran, Katherine S.; John H. Loughran; John William Johnson; and Said Sheikh Samatar; eds. *Somalia in Word and Image*. Washington, DC: Foundation for Cross Cultural Understanding, 1986.

Mack, John. *Madagascar: Island of the Ancestors*. London: British Museum Press, 1986.

Prussin, Labelle. *African Nomadic Architecture: Space, Place, and Gender*. Washington, DC: Smithsonian Institution Press, 1995.

Somjee, Sultan. *Material Culture of Kenya*. Nairobi: East African Educational Publishers, 1993.

JEREMY COOTE

NORTHERN AFRICA

Across the Maghrib the arts share greater commonality than differencs. Arts of daily life, ranging from textiles to ceramics to architectural decoration, constitute the primary historical art forms of Morocco, Algeria, Tunisia, and Libya. While artisans continue to play important roles in the twenty-first century, paintings, sculpture, multimedia installations, and photographic imagery destined for international exhibition are equally important.

PREHISTORY

Painted and incised rock art in the southern reaches of the Maghrib, from the western Sahara to Libya, are among the earliest known artworks in North Africa. Their content and style relate to rock art of other African locations, and likely developed independent of European examples. Tassili-n-Ajjer, in south Algeria, is one of the world's most significant rock art sites.

Animals and human figures, the primary subjects of rock art, accompany abstract pattern and decoration that may add symbolic levels of meaning. Hunting scenes are considered the earliest forms, with depictions of herd animals more recent. The oldest are believed to date from at least 4,500 years BCE, though some estimate their origins closer to 10,000 years BCE. Assessing dates is difficult, because it relies on assumptions about climate change and the introduction of agropastoral economies. Many sites show continued usage from prehistoric to modern times, revealing a continuous artistic tradition characterized by simplified of forms and an elegance linked to clear observation of the natural world.

ANTIQUITY

Figurative representations or inscriptions in the indigenous Libico-Berber (Punic) alphabet adorn ancient incised stones and votive stele. Limited remains attest to the local production of pottery across the Maghrib in antiquity. Earthenware, made primarily for local use (and occasionally for broader trade), is generally characterized by minimal decoration. By the fourth century BCE, strong metalworking traditions flourished, especially in the region of Carthage (Tunisia). Silver and gold jewelry from Carthage, subsequently dispersed across the Mediterranean basin, demonstrate the lively trade in everyday and luxury art objects that increased with Roman colonization.

Extensive ruins attest to the flowering of Roman art, including architecture, urban planning, wall painting, mosaics, sculpture, jewelry, and pottery. North African Roman art compares with that produced in Roman colonial outposts elsewhere. Some variation exists, due to local craftsmen working in the Roman style, to the introduction of local themes and deities, and to regional variations in the needs of daily life. Styles of oil lamps made of metal and clay during the Roman period continued to be elaborated in later times, incorporating symbolic decoration for specific Jewish, Christian, and Muslim populations.

In Roman North Africa, the arts contributed to commercial, political, and religious aspects of individual and community life. Local artistic traditions absorbed Roman styles and practices, adapting the successful industrial workshop models that continued in later Islamic and colonial times. From antiquity to the present, Amazigh and nomadic arts remained largely independent of Roman and Islamic arts.

AMAZIGH AND NOMADIC ARTS

Descendants of the indigenous people of North Africa reject the name "Berber," preferring *Imazighen*, which means "the free people." *Amazigh* (the adjectival form) arts share tendencies toward abstract patterning and bilateral symmetry that characterize other nomadic arts. Like nomads elsewhere, their art is portable, including body art (tattooing, clothing, jewelry), textiles (rugs, carpets, other weavings, embroidery), pottery, and work in leather, wood, metal, or stone. With the exception of the latter, which are likely to be worked by men, the arts are, traditionally, the domain of women in the North African Amazigh communities.

Amizagh woven carpets distinguish themselves from the knotted carpets made in urban centers with bold patterns and colors. The textiles' symmetrical geometric patterns are similar to designs found on other Amazigh arts: zigzags, diamonds, triangles, and X shapes, frequently with hatchmark patterns. Although these repeated patterns do not have standardized names, they evoke the natural world metaphorically, sometimes functioning as visual riddles. Related patterns characterize the blue-black tattooing applied to young women at the onset of puberty, though this form of body modification seems to have decreased since the 1970s.

Amazigh metalwork has long been recognized for its excellence. Jewelry made of gold, silver, brass, and other metals beautifies the wearer while performing a practical function, as do the fibulae used to hold or pin robes. One distinctive fibula with triangular adornment has become a symbol of Amazigh culture. Similarly, distinctive cross-form jewelry like the Agadez cross has come to represent the Tuareg (nomadic Imazighen who range from the Maghrib to sub-Saharan Africa). That these have become symbols of tourism signals the degree to which Amazigh metalwork is recognizable, prized for marking identity, and the vitality of art as an element of everyday life. This is also a reminder that tourist markets for all the arts of North Africa have long played a powerful role in promoting art.

COLONIALISM AND THE ARTS

When colonial occupation of North Africa began, in 1830, art was made in urban regions by artisans who worked variations on Islamic or Hispano-Mauresque styles. A reorganization of traditional family and guild workshops followed the rise of the first museums in the Maghrib (beginning with the Musée National des Antiquités Algeriennes et d'Art Musulman in Algiers in 1897). After observing artisanal education in Algeria and Tunisia, Prosper Ricard adapted the Académie des Beaux-Arts curriculum from Paris to the creation of Morocco's museums and the education of artisans. Using the Beaux-Arts ideal of study rooted in the copying of museum pieces, Ricard established museums in Rabat, Fez, and Meknes that served as study centers for the training of artisans in the Service des Arts Indigènes. Ricard's example, influential across the Maghrib, emphasized historical preservation of noteworthy objects and formed the basis of a history of the region's arts. The service enforced quality standards meant to promote tourist and export trade in art objects, especially textiles; without the service's official stamp, rugs could not be exported or sold in the artisanal centers that appealed to colonists and tourists.

Artisanal education was segregated, primarily separating female textile production from the male dominance of other artisanal areas. This perpetuated urban-rural gender distinctions within the arts, as seen in the example of pottery. In rural (primarily Amazigh) communities, women made and decorated pottery by hand, whereas men used wheels to throw and glaze ceramics in urban centers.

While Ricard emphasized region-specific traditions of style and fabrication in his scholarly work, educational training through copying led to the proliferation of a pan-Islamic style that competed with, and sometimes supplanted, local traditions. During the colonial period, the few North Africans who achieved name recognition worked primarily in painting, such as Algerians Azouaou Mammeri and Mohammed Racim, who both exhibited figurative compositions internationally. Algerian ceramicist Boujemââ Lamali, who trained at the Musée National de la Céramique at Sèvres in France, was recruited to establish a new ceramics industry in Safi, Morocco. Lamali's ceramics, heralded in his lifetime for a bold inventiveness anchored in historical techniques, figure prominently in the history of twentieth-century North African art.

CONTEMPORARY ART IN NORTH AFRICA

By the time of independence, increasing numbers of young artists had established connections with European art schools, galleries, and museums. In style and technique, as well as in their relationship to cultural and social institutions, contemporary artists have depended on such international contexts to develop their art and careers. Mohamed Serghini is the artist/educator largely responsible for the blossoming of the visual arts after independence. After completing his studies in Madrid, Spain, Serghini returned to the Escuela Preparatoria de Bellas Artes,

in Tétouan, Morocco, and became the director of the school where his artistic education began.

Figurative art propelled the artists of the Tunis School, founded by Pierre Bacherle late in the 1940s. Artists such as Hatem el-Mekki and Amar Farhat joined Bacherle in reviving earlier pan-Islamic traditions of miniature painting. Abstraction, the primary language of international art after independence, appealed to many, like the self-taught Algerian artist Muhammad Khadda and the European-trained Moroccan Ahmed Cherkaoui, whose paintings incorporated the abstract formal language of Berber patterning. In a similar dialogue with international art movements, the Casablanca Group—Farid Belkahia, Mohammed Melehi, and Mohamed Chebaa, all teachers at the Casablanca École des Beaux-Arts—infused contemporary art with traditional local materials and Arabic calligraphy. From the 1950s through the 1990s, Maghribi artists successful internationally thus engaged the mainstream traditions of abstraction, assemblage, and *art informel* or, alternately, adopted a self-consciously naïve style of figuration.

Growing numbers of North African artists emerged in the early twenty-first century, thanks to increasing efforts to develop audiences and support networks for the visual arts. Alternative exhibition spaces remain essential for the growth of new arts, ranging from the 1969 outdoor exhibition on the Jamaa al-fna in Marrakesh to Abdellah Karroum's 2002 establishment of l'appartement 22 in Rabat, Morocco. Pioneers like Kamel Dridi (Tunisia) bridged photojournalism and the gallery, while the color photography of Omar D. (Daoud) (Algeria) and Yto Barrada (Morocco/France) and the multimedia installations of Mohamed el Baz (Morocco), celebrated in international exhibitions, mark these artists among the next wave to be recognized in the Maghrib and beyond.

See also **Architecture; Art; Arts; Carthage; Ceramics; Fez; Geometries; Metals and Minerals; Prehistory; Rabat and Salé; Textiles.**

BIBLIOGRAPHY

Becker, Cynthia. *Amazigh Arts in Morocco: Women Shaping Berber Identity.* Austin: University of Texas Press, 2006.

Boele, Vincent, ed. *Morocco: 5,000 Years of Culture.* Aldershot, U.K.: Lund Humphries, 2005.

Housefield, James. "Moroccan Ceramics and the Geography of Invented Traditions." *Geographical Review* 87, no. 3 (1997): 401–407.

Institut du Monde Arabe, Paris. *L'Algérie en heritage: Art et histoire.* Paris: Institut du Monde Arabe/Actes Sud, 2003.

JAMES HOUSEFIELD

SOUTHERN AFRICA

Writing on the art of sub-Saharan Africa has, since the 1980s, begun to redress the previous neglect of contributions by southern African artists. Because there was little evidence in southern Africa of sculptural traditions similar to those of western and central Africa, few scholars included this region in surveys of African art. Increased research, however, and a reexamination of the premises on which African art history is based, have shown that there were a number of different sculptural as well as other artistic traditions of considerable longevity in the south. Simultaneously, the trade in southern African artifacts has increased, and, since 1994 awareness of this important heritage material has grown.

Since sculpture was generally made by men, a shift to include women in artistic traditions has blurred the distinction between art and craft. Stylistic classifications based on linguistic and ethnic boundaries have also been challenged, while oral traditions and anthropological and archival research have been used to reconstruct histories. The classification of art forms by technology and functional type is followed here, although language groups are used to distinguish styles. Ethnic or linguistic labels are nevertheless used with discretion since artists of one group often worked for patrons of another.

KHOESAN ROCK ART

The oldest pictorial tradition in southern Africa is that of the Khoesan. These artists painted images on rock shelters, boulders, and overhangs in the mountain ranges and engraved on rocky outcrops across the region. Rock paintings have also been found in archaeological deposits as old as 20,000 BCE. Paintings are found concentrated in the Drakensberg Mountains in the east and in the Twyfelfontein and Brandberg ranges in Namibia.

Earth pigments mixed with albumin binders were used to create paintings, often executed in shaded polychrome. Many consist of only one or a few images in a rock shelter, but in many sites, successive layers of images form large panoramas. Human figures are often more stylized than animal forms, particularly the large mammals. Animals are often represented in scenes with humans. Some paintings include images of other population groups who migrated into the traditional hunting grounds of the Khoesan, particularly the Bantu-speaking peoples of the eastern seaboard and the Boer commandos. Some rock paintings appear to have been made by Bantu-speakers.

Interpreting these paintings and engravings is controversial. Most individual images are recognizable as particular species, but some combine animal and human features. The paintings may reflect Khoesan social organization and their belief that humans could be transformed into spiritual beings. The images may instead record practices in which Khoesan healers went into trance states. This explanation, however, does not account for the modes of visualization of the subject matter and thus cannot explain the meanings generated by style, composition, and context. The function of these paintings remains obscure: Many painted sites were not inhabited, but may have had ritual or social importance for the artists. With the social upheavals of the nineteenth century, the Khoesan were pushed out of their mountain habitats in southern Africa and ceased to produce paintings.

POTTERY

From 200 CE onward, Khoesan- and Bantu-speaking peoples used clay to create vessels and figurative works of art. Women made this pottery and were responsible for gathering the clay and making and firing the objects. Pottery vessels dating from 400 CE have been found in archaeological sites all over southern Africa. These are most commonly round-bottomed spherical pots made by coiling and pulling. Decoration, created by stamping and rolling occurs most frequently on the pot's shoulders. Designs are nonfigurative and geometric, dominated by chevrons and triangles, patterns that occur in other, more recent women's arts, such as wall painting.

Figurative sculpture in clay is known from a number of archaeological sites. The oldest known examples were excavated near the town of Lydenburg and have been dated to 400–600 CE. These sculptures represent cylindrical "heads," some of which have exclusively human features, while others combine human and animal features. The sculptures were made by coiling and pulling, with identical decorative patterns on the necks. Their archaeological context does not offer many clues for interpretation, but they may have been used in initiation rites, as is the case with much of the other figurative sculpture produced in the region.

Smaller figurative clay sculpture, including sculptures of small human, animal, and hybrid figures dating from 900 CE, is known from sites in Zimbabwe and the Limpopo provinces. The simplified style is similar to that of the clay figures made by women for female initiations among Venda and North Sotho peoples well into the twentieth century. Noria Mabasa, a contemporary Venda artist, has developed this tradition into large-scale sculptures of modern subjects for sale in cities.

ARCHITECTURAL DECORATION
Since women worked with clay, building earth walls and decorating the homestead was one of the most significant spaces for expression. Clay relief sculptures were recorded by nineteenth-century travelers among Tswana peoples, and there appears to have been a thousand-year tradition of finger-traced nonfigurative patterns among many of the high veld peoples, particularly on the floors of courtyards and dwellings. Among many of the east coast peoples such as the Tembu, Xhosa, Hlubi, and Zulu in the nineteenth century, men transformed beehive dwellings into woven artworks. Courtyard walls among the high veld peoples were, until the early twentieth century, built of reeds by men. In most areas, mud-walled dwellings with grass or tin roofs were commonly built from the 1920s on, and new forms of decoration emerged.

The emergence of these new forms inspired debate about "traditional" art and about the authenticity of new styles. Most debated is the status of the large murals painted by Ndebele women in the Transvaal (now Mpumalanga and Gauteng)

from the 1930s to the 1980s. Originally, paintings were executed in earth colors using simple, bold geometric shapes in symmetrical arrangements on the outer walls of dwellings and courtyards. By the 1950s, earth pigments were replaced by commercial paints, and designs became more complex, with figurative elements such as light bulbs, houses and lettering interspersed in the abstract designs. These developments were stimulated by the establishment of Ndebele tourist villages where women were supplied with paint. Paintings were both signs of a woman's position as housekeeper within the family unit and as ethnic markers for Ndebele-speakers who had been scattered over the Transvaal high veld after the Mapogga War (also known as "Mapoch's War") of 1882–1883. These people started to regroup in the 1930s, when consciousness of a separate ethnic identity was fostered by both government policies and by traditionalists among Ndebele speakers. Once they had regrouped in a consolidated area in the 1980s under apartheid, few women continued painting since the need to mark their ethnic identity had dissipated.

At the height of apartheid (1960–1988), Tsonga, Venda, and North Sotho speakers, as well as other groups were also resettled according to linguistic classifications. Many of these peoples started painting wall decorations, arguably as a response to unfamiliar circumstances. Among the Pedi of Sekhukhuneland and the Ntwane (both North Sotho speaking), wall paintings were recorded on dwelling walls in the 1930s, but by the early 1980s had expanded across the inner walls of homestead courtyards, with subtle designs in earth pigments consisting of triangles and chevrons.

Using the same materials, Venda women in the 1970s and 1980s molded wall reliefs of playing-card motifs copied from maize-meal sacks, while Tsonga-speakers' murals were composed with earth pigments using geometric patterns. In Botswana in recent years there has also been an increase in wall paintings using older mural designs and new motifs. In the 1950s and 1960s South Sotho women throughout the eastern Orange Free State decorated the walls of their homesteads, especially those close to major roads, often drawing motifs from the packaging of commercial products. More recently they have painted large murals of striking intensity, using floral images constructed from geometric shapes in bright enamel paints. In the eastern Cape, Xhosa women similarly drew on plant motifs but in a nongeometric style, with earth colors creating muted designs. Most of these traditions have survived only through being driven by tourist imperatives since 1994 and many have disappeared as new housing developments alter peoples' living environments.

WOODCARVING

In southern Africa woodcarving was an exclusively male occupation, producing a variety of objects that were aesthetically elaborate. Since these objects were largely functional, their status as art has been debated, but they have been established as authentic and traditional forms in major public collections since 1994. Conversely, whether or not new forms are authentic is a question that forms part of an ongoing debate about changes in production and patronage of art in southern Africa over the past two hundred years.

Wooden headrests in various styles were carved by peoples across the whole region. As personal objects, headrests were often elaborately carved, decorated, and treasured. Some were used in rituals, some buried with their owners, and some handed down from one generation to the next. Others were commissioned by colonists as examples of local industry and often displayed innovative forms. Tsonga and Shona headrests belong to a single stylistic group that uses lobed bases, various supports and separate rest sections. Among peoples of the eastern seaboard, heavier headrests without bases, but with multiple supports, were common. Zulu and Swazi headrests, particularly, followed this pattern, with two, four or more rectangular or hornlike legs supporting a horizontal rest. Other wooden objects commonly given aesthetic emphasis, such as meat plates, milk pails and staffs, are found particularly among the east coast peoples, the Tsonga, Swazi, Zulu, and Xhosa. Staffs often include figurative forms such as snakes, human figures, or heads. In Venda chiefdoms, wooden doors and divining bowls were carved for the courts of chiefs, and on the high veld drums were usually aesthetically elaborate.

In Limpopo Province, figurative sculpture in wood was confined to men's initiation institutions, except among Venda groups where they were used in female initiations. Different styles of carving are known from Sotho, Tsonga, and Venda groups in this area. The figures are all stylistically simple, possibly because this made them easily recognizable in their didactic contexts. Some Tsonga figures are tall and pole-like; others are more squat but similarly stylized. Older Venda figures are smaller and include a greater variety of subjects, from animal to human, but more recent examples are quite large. Among both the Tsonga and the Venda, figures were clothed in actual beads and cloth. Among Pedi groups, human figures were carved in rotund style with clothes and other details rendered sculpturally as integral parts of the figures. Tsonga carvers worked for Venda, North Sotho, and Tsonga chiefs, but they also made figures and staffs for European buyers in the late nineteenth century that show significant deviance in form from those made for indigenous consumption.

It is becoming increasingly apparent that African carvers across southern Africa were commissioned to work for European patrons from the 1850s onward. This variance in patterns of patronage has fueled the debate about ethnically defined styles, about canons of authenticity and the value of "tourist" arts. Animal figures were used throughout Botswana and Sotho territories of South Africa as decorative elements on spoons, staffs, and knife handles made of ivory as well as wood, many of which were sold to colonials and are now surfacing on the art markets.

Some carving traditions have survived into the early twenty-first century in rural areas and formed the basis for a resurgence of production beginning in 1980. Many artists make woodcarvings for sale through urban galleries. Some—like Nelson Mukhuba, Johannes Maswanganyi, and Johannes Mashego Segogela—produce sculptures whose simplified naturalism and inherent humor is enhanced by the use of enamel paint and ready-made elements. Jackson Hlungwane created large, expressively stylized sculptures based on his personal religious experience of Christian and indigenous beliefs. Since 1994 many of these artists have fallen out of favor with the high art market, Mukhuba died in 1987 and Hlungwane has ceased to produce sculptures of note. Samson Mudzunga has reinvented himself as a performance artist, drawing extensively on Venda traditions. Other woodcarvers now make sculptures for sale on the art market, especially those from workshop initiatives in KwaZulu-Natal.

BEADWORK AND THE ART OF THE PERSON

Beadwork has been part of personal adornment in southern Africa since very early times. Among the Khoesan, ostrich eggshell beads were strung and attached to leather clothing. Decoration of clothing was expanded by Khoesan pastoralists with the addition of metal beads obtained from Europeans at the Cape from the fifteenth century onward.

The importation of small numbers of metal and glass beads through trade with peoples on the east coast—whose contact with Islamic traders predated European exploration (from 1400 CE)—supplemented the few beads supplied by the indigenously mined gold and copper of the northern Limpopo province. From the 1830s onward, the importation of large quantities of European glass beads allowed the east coast peoples to create beadwork of increasingly complex designs. Beadwork techniques spread to inland groups in the late nineteenth century. Of these, only Ndebele beadwork achieved an intricacy of design that rivals that of the Tsonga, Zulu, Mfengu, Mpondo, and Xhosa. From strings of beads in white and black interspersed with a few red and pink beads, designs emerged with strings of beads wound around grass coils, and sewn onto cloth and leather backings and into bead fabrics. Recent studies have traced the geometrical principles underlying many of these designs as creative and subtle twists within continually developing stylistic conventions. Innovations also occurred in the inclusion of other materials, from brass and pearl buttons in the nineteenth century to safety pins and medicine vials in the twentieth.

While beadwork must be regarded as a major art form, it has been only recently taken its place in African art studies, possibly because it has been produced by women. Ndebele, Tsonga, Sotho, and Zulu women made beaded figures, largely for use in marriage contexts. These figures varied from one group to the next but were all abstract in design. They have developed in recent times as sculptures, with greater reference to human anatomy. Among the Herero and Himba, leather garments were worn by women, and their headgear was shaped in the form of animal heads and ears. Doll forms made for sale to outsiders followed

both these indigenous patterns of dress as well as those introduced by German missionaries in the nineteenth century. Some artists such as Bronwyn Findlay and Daina Mabunda work with beads as their materials of choice within Western art genres, challenging the primacy of traditionally male media.

CONTEMPORARY ART

Artists of European descent have been producing easel painting and sculpture in southern Africa since at least 1800, and art schools have been operating in the Western and Eastern Cape since the late 1800s. Most settler art was concerned with the land and landscape painting was the dominant genre in the late nineteenth and early twentieth centuries. In spite of the legislated denial of equal education for black people under apartheid, or the simple paucity of opportunity under colonial rule, a number of black artists from across the Southern African region were trained in missions between 1930 and 1979, as well as by independent artists in community arts centers, to produce art in a twentieth-century idiom for sale in galleries.

John Koenakeefe Mohl (b. Namibia) and Gerard Sekoto started painting scenes of the black townships in the 1930s and were followed by others such as Durant Sihlali, who laid claim to the townscape genre, and Dumile Feni and Julian Motau, whose expressive drawings emphasized social issues in urban life. Many of these artists spent a significant amount of time in exile, most never returning to South Africa and major exhibitions are helping to rescue their histories. In the 1950s, 1960s, and 1970s, black artists trained at Thaba Nchu under Frans Claerhout; at the Polly Street Art Centre in Johannesburg under Cecil Skotnes and Sydney Kumalo and its offshoot, the Jubilee Art centre under Esrom Legae; at the Evangelical Lutheran Centre at Rorke's Drift; at the Johannesburg Art Foundation under Bill Ainslie; and at community art centers. Most were trained in a modernist mode as sculptors or printmakers; famous graduates from Rorke's Drift; include Cyprian Shilakoe, Dan Rakgoathe, John Muafangejo (of Namibia), Azaria Mbatha, and later Bongi Dhlomo. One of the few women of this generation to have succeeded as a professional painter is Helen Mmakgoba Sebidi, who produces large, expressive, figurative works. David Koloane and others rejected the figurative tradition advocated by supporters of a Black Consciousness philosophy, favoring instead abstraction as an appropriate form for African artists.

Since the late 1980s a larger number of academically trained artists have begun to show their works in galleries and they have increasingly been invited onto international exhibitions. These include artists such as Churchill Madikida and Tembinkosi Goniwe, who work with imagery centered on initiation; and Berni Searle, Tracey Rose, and Senzeni Marasela, who interrogate elements of apartheid history from the perspective of black women. However, there has been a shift away from art as a polemic or tool of the struggle, common in the 1970s and 1980s, to art as an expression of the individual, modern subject, concerned with issues of gender and identity and a postcolonial dispensation.

Artists of European descent, such as Walter Battiss, Cecil Skotnes (both born in South Africa), and Edoardo Villa, actively strove in the 1960s and 1970s to create an African ethos in their works. Artists of the younger generations—such as Karel Nel, Andries Botha, Joachim Schonfeldt, Walter Oltmann, William Bester, Deborah Bell, Peter Schutz, Jeremy Wafer, and Pippa Skotnes—have consciously sought an African base through reference to African traditions. With the training of all artists in the same institutions, distinctions between black and white artists, that is, the old racial distinctions are becoming difficult to draw, undesirable and therefore largely contested. Many artists reject the need to find an African identity, seeing themselves rather as contemporary and South African or Zimbabwean. Artists such as William Kentridge, Penny Siopis, Pat Mautloa, Sam Nhlengethwa, and Steven Cohen work in Western genres as do Sandile Zulu, Josephine Ghesa, and Nicholas Mukomberanwa whose work is grounded in traditional media. Biennales and major art competitions have, since the 1970s, served to advance the understanding of contemporary art in southern Africa, and many corporations now regularly commission artists for work and have their own art collections. National and civic art museums collect the work of southern African artists and there is a thriving gallery circuit dealing in avant-garde and historical arts in the major cities.

See also **Art; Art, Genres and Periods: Rock Art, Southern Africa; Arts; Body Adornment and Clothing; Ceramics; Prehistory; Symbols and Symbolism.**

BIBLIOGRAPHY

Berman, Esme. *Art and Artists of South Africa: An Illustrated Biographical Dictionary and Historical Survey of Painters and Graphic Artists Since 1875.* Cape Town: Balkema, 1987.

Hammond-Tooke, David, and Anitra Nettleton, eds. *Catalogue: Ten Years of Collecting (1979–1989): Standard Bank Foundation Collection of African Art, University Art Galleries' Collection of African Art and Selected Works from the University Ethnological Museum Collection.* Johannesburg: University of the Witwatersrand, Johannesburg Art Galleries, 1989.

Hooper, Lindsay. "Some Nguni Crafts. Part 3: Woodcarving." *Annals of the South African Museum* (1981).

Johannesburg Art Gallery. *Art and Ambiguity: Perspectives on the Brenthurst Collection of Southern African Art.* Johannesburg: Author, 1991.

Lewis-Williams, J. David. *Believing and Seeing: Symbolic Meanings in Southern San Rock Paintings.* New York: Academic Press, 1981.

Lewis-Williams, J. David, and Thomas Dowson. *Images of Power: Understanding Bushman Rock Art.* Johannesburg: Southern Book Publishers, 1989.

Manaka, Matsemela. *Echoes of African Art: A Century of Art in South Africa.* Braamfontein, South Africa: Skotaville, 1987.

Miles, Elza. *Land and Lives: A Story of Early Black Artists.* Johannesburg: Johannesburg Art Gallery and Cape Town: Human and Rousseau, 1997.

Morris, Jean, with Eleanor Preston-Whyte. *Speaking with Beads: Zulu Arts from Southern Africa.* New York: Thames and Hudson, 1994.

Nel, Karel, and Nessa Leibhammer. *Evocations of the Child: Fertility Figures of the Southern African Region.* Cape Town: Human and Rousseau, 1998.

Nettleton, Anitra, and David Hammond-Tooke, eds. *African Art in Southern Africa: From Tradition to Township.* Johannesburg: A.D. Donker, 1989.

Nettleton, Anitra; Julia Charlton; and Fiona Rankin-Smith. *Engaging Modernities: Transformations of the Commonplace.* Johannesburg: University of the Witwatersrand Art Galleries, 2003.

Perryer, Sophie, ed. *10 Years, 100 Artists: Art in a Democratic South Africa.* Cape Town: Bell-Roberts and Struik, 2004.

Rankin, Elizabeth. *Images of Wood: Aspects of the History of Sculpture in Twentieth-Century South Africa*. Johannesburg: Johannesburg Art Gallery, 1989.

Sack, Steven. *The Neglected Tradition: Towards a New History of South African Art (1930–1988)*. Johannesburg: Johannesburg Art Gallery, 1988.

Schofield, J. F. *Primitive Pottery: An Introduction to South African Ceramics, Prehistoric and Protohistoric*. Cape Town: South African Archaeological Society, 1948.

South African National Gallery. *Ezakwantu: Beadwork from the Eastern Cape*. Cape Town: Author, 1993.

Van Wyck, Gary. *African Painted Houses: Basotho Dwellings of Southern Africa*. New York: Harry N. Abrams, 1988.

Williamson, Sue. *Resistance Art in South Africa*. Cape Town: David Phillip, 1989.

Williamson, Sue, and Ashraf Jamal. *Art in South Africa: The Future Present*. Cape Town: David Phillip, 1996.

ANITRA CATHERINE ELIZABETH NETTLETON

WESTERN AFRICA

The art forms produced by the peoples of western Africa are more diverse than the peoples themselves, for each people creates art in a variety of media, using any of several materials, to produce objects intended to overcome the many afflictions and obstacles people must confront in the course of daily life in the region. Art is made by both men and women, who carve, cast, and model figures and masks; model and mold pottery; build private and public structures of clay, wood, hides, concrete, and other materials; weave textiles and baskets; and tan, cut, dye, and sew leather. Art creation is usually gender-based—that is, men carve masks and figures and forge iron, while women make pottery and some textiles. Art is made of wood, iron, clay, cotton, silk, rayon, brass, leather, straw, recycled tin and plastic, and other materials. Any particular people may make figures and masks to be used by men and women in the context of initiation, fertility, healing, governance, death, and to represent the spiritual beings that play an active and essential role in the course of their lives. Old art forms are constantly being abandoned as particular needs disappear and as people are converted to new religions, and new art forms are constantly being created as people confront afflictions such as HIV/AIDS or personal and political strife, or deal with changing economic, political, social, and educational systems.

While it is very much possible in some areas of western Africa to attend traditional performances in rural agricultural villages where art objects are being used that are indistinguishable from those collected in the nineteenth century and housed in the Musée de l'Homme, the British Museum, the American Museum of Natural History, and Germany's Museen für Völkerkunde, it is also quite possible to discover totally new art forms that have been invented in the past century, decade, or year. Art is vital and constantly changing. Many who have not traveled, worked, or lived in Africa have been misled by popular literature, both print and electronic, into believing that Africa is a continent characterized by poverty, disease, ethnic and political conflict, superstition, underdevelopment, and resistance to change. In reality Africa is a continent of constant, dynamic, and often very rapid change. In the first century CE, the Roman historian Pliny wrote in *Historia naturalis*: "Semper ex africa aliquid novi" ("There is always something new out of Africa"). This is probably the only component of Africa that has not changed in the past two thousand years, and among the many new traditions Africans have invented are impressive, effective, functional, and beautiful forms of art.

STYLE

It is important to understand the styles of art in western Africa if one is to understand which people are responsible for any particular work of art. Attribution continues to be a problem because scholars continue to discover new art forms in Africa, and to discover that many old art forms stored in museums were mislabeled by catalogers. Many African art works were, and still are, collected by art dealers and professional collectors who have little knowledge of the people whose art they are buying, and often care very little for details of attribution, use, or meaning. The result is that one may assign dubious meanings or functions to objects because one does not know with certainty who made the objects.

It is also important to recognize the styles of particular peoples so that one can recognize where there has been contact and influence from one to the other. In the absence of written documents, art has served as an important primary source, along with oral histories, in reconstructing the past. If one were to study a group of Senufo figures from the south, central, and northern Senufo areas, one would see a very clear shift in style from Baule influence in the south to Bamana influence in the north. In the case of the Mossi people of Burkina Faso, the several styles of masks made in different regions are clear and eloquent documents of the ancient history of Dogon, Gurunsi, and Kurumba occupation of Mossi country before the founding of the Mossi states in 1500. Art is in fact the only evidence humankind has of where these pre-Mossi peoples lived before 1500.

Finally, one must be able to recognize and understand nuances of style if one is to distinguish the objects that have been made by Africans for Africans from those made by Africans for the Western consumer.

Western Sudan. It is difficult to generalize about the style even of one group of people because art production in Africa is characterized by its diversity. Nevertheless, there are certain stylistic features that can indicate whether an object was made by a people living on the dry, open savannas of the western or central Sudan or in the forests or dense woodlands of the Guinea Coast. The two largest style groupings in the western Sudan can be labeled by their language families. The Mande-speaking peoples, who include the Bamana, Malinke, and Bobo, carve masks and figures of wood that are composed of broad flat planes that make up the cheeks, shoulders, and sometimes the back of the figures. The torso, arms, and legs are cylinders, and the breasts are cones that intersect the planes of the body and face to form long straight lines and sharp angles. The nose is often a large vertical slab that forms a T where it joins the brows, and the eyes are close to the intersection of nose and brow. Scarification patterns tend to be burned into the surfaces with a hot iron blade, so that they appear to be incised. Scarification patterns are also made up of large geometric shapes. The colors of the wood are dark browns and black (see Figure 1).

To the southwest of the Mande-speaking peoples are the Voltaic peoples, including the Dogon, Senufo, Bwa, Mossi, Gurunsi, and others in northern Ghana, Togo, and Bénin. The style of these peoples is marked by the use of geometric patterns carved in such a way that they are raised above the surface and are painted red, white, and black.

Figure 1. Bamana wood sculpture, Mali. A Bamana wood sculpture of a female figure includes scarification patterns that have been burned into the wood with a hot iron blade. The cylindrical torso, arms, and legs are among the features common to Bamana wood sculpture. THE STANLEY COLLECTION, UNIVERSITY OF IOWA MUSEUM OF ART, IOWA CITY, IA x1986.575

Among the most common are black-and-white checkerboards and concentric circles in red, white, and black. These graphic patterns are not carved as decoration but serve as symbols in a visual language that communicate important ideas about the moral and ethical conduct of life (see Figure 2).

Almost all African art is accumulative. As an object is used, the signs of its use begin to alter

Figure 2. Dogon sculpture of female musician, Mali. Raised geometric patterns mark sculptures by the Dogon of Mali. Here, a female musician has been crafted from wood and metal. THE STANLEY COLLECTION, UNIVERSITY OF IOWA MUSEUM OF ART, IOWA CITY, IA x1986.590

its surface. These changes may be as subtle as the buildup of a patina from frequent handling or as overt as the sudden, obvious, and dramatic alterations from the addition of millet porridge and chicken blood as prayer offerings and the accumulation of materials that give the object supernatural power. The result is that an object that has been used, handled, or worn for decades may look very different from the object created by the original artist. Unfortunately, Western dealers and collectors have often removed this evidence of use and meaning to force the object to conform to their own Western aesthetic sensibilities.

Guinea Coast. There is at least as much variety in the styles of the Guinea Coast as there is in the western Sudan. A style survey of the area is complicated by the fact that there are significant numbers of Mande-speaking peoples such as the Dan, Mende, and Guro who have penetrated the area from the north, and some features of their art are

more typical of the Mande heartland. In contrast to the geometric and angular shapes of the western Sudan, sculpture from the Guinea Coast tends to much more soft, fluid, sensuous, rounded forms. Arms, legs, torsos, and breasts are rounded and smooth and most often are a deep, rich, lustrous black. Scarification patterns are carved to stand up from the surrounding surfaces and are rounded, giving a beautiful texture to the surface. Great care is taken in the carving of details of scarification, sometimes of clothing and jewelry, and especially of hairstyles. The most notable characteristic that appears in figure sculpture all the way from the Mende in the west to the Yoruba in the east is the representation of rings around the neck, which are identified with prosperity and well-being (see Figure 3). Masks from such people as the Baule and the Yaure in Côte d'Ivoire are characterized by very fine, elaborate patterns of lines, either incised or raised, that define beards, hairlines, jewelry, and scars (see Figure 4).

Masks and figures from the Yoruba tend to have large, protuberant eyes and corners of the mouth that end rather abruptly where they join the cheeks (see Figure 5). Figures are both representational and stylized, with the head much larger in proportion to the rest of the body because of its importance as the dwelling place of the spirit (see Figure 6). While many objects were collected in Africa in the twentieth century because they are a rich glossy black and therefore appeal to Western tastes in sculpture, many objects from the entire area were, in the contexts for which they were created, painted with bright, colorful pigments and were worn in performances with elaborate costumes of colorful textiles of raffia and palm fiber.

FUNCTION

African art is a living art. Very few objects are made to decorate people's homes, and almost none were made in the past to be placed in museum collections. Instead, objects are made to solve the problems of life, to overcome adversity, to express the most fundamental beliefs Africans hold about themselves and the world in which they live. It can be said that Africans have not created art for art's sake, but make art for life's sake. Art is created to appear at important moments throughout people's lives, from birth to death, to mark transitions

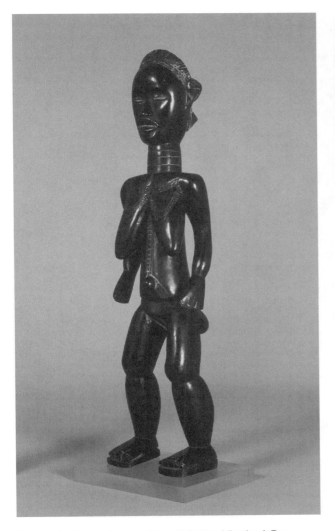

Figure 3. Dan sculpture of female figure, Liberia. A Dan sculpture of a female figure in wood and pigment shows the people's usual style of soft, rounded forms that include details such as hairstyles. THE STANLEY COLLECTION, UNIVERSITY OF IOWA MUSEUM OF ART, IOWA CITY, IA x1986.346

Figure 4. Yaure mask, Côte d'Ivoire. Yaure wooden masks feature elaborate patterns of fine lines that define scars, hair, and other patterns. THE STANLEY COLLECTION, UNIVERSITY OF IOWA MUSEUM OF ART, IOWA CITY, IA x1986.482

from one state of being to another, from one age to the next. African art looks the way it does because it meets these needs. Objects that represent nature spirits are abstract because the beings they represent are abstract. Art that represents living kings is naturalistic because it is necessary to recognize the king's features or his sacred regalia of rule for the art to be effective. Given that all African art has a function to serve, and that the function dictates how the objects appear, it is necessary to understand the functions of these objects if one is to appreciate fully why these objects look as they do, and why they appeal to people as collectors, scholars, or visitors to museums. For the peoples across western Africa, art objects serve important functions during key moments in life.

Birth. The principal concern of Africans and of people all over the world is for their children to grow into healthy adults and guarantee the continuity of the family and clan. On a continent where people face so many endemic diseases and where infant mortality is high, it is especially important that women bear many children, and that those children survive the diseases of childhood to carry on the generations. In countries where there is rarely any state system of social security, a large family can care for aged parents long after they have ceased to be able to work in

Figure 5. Yoruba Gelede mask, Nigeria. Large eyes and a disproportionately big head mark many Yoruba masks, such as this one created from wood and pigment. The large features represent the dwelling place of the spirit. THE STANLEY COLLECTION, UNIVERSITY OF IOWA MUSEUM OF ART, IOWA CITY, IA x1986.341

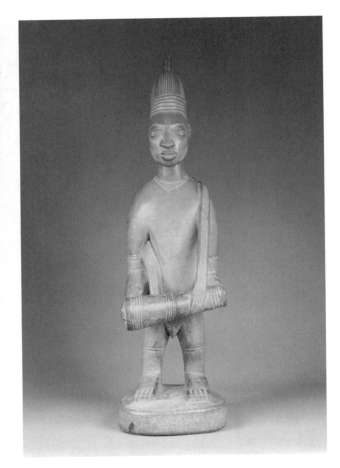

Figure 6. Yoruba shrine figure, Nigeria. Fine lines mark a wooden Shrine figure of *bata* drummer. THE STANLEY COLLECTION, UNIVERSITY OF IOWA MUSEUM OF ART, IOWA CITY, IA x1986.504

the fields. Most traditional rural western African villages have shrines where the men and women of the community can offer prayers to God to provide children. These shrines often include figures that embody the ideal of successful motherhood, most frequently a mother nursing an infant, an icon of fertility.

The Asante people of Ghana tell of a young woman named Akua who, after some months of marriage, had failed to conceive her first infant. Her pastor told her to have a small figure carved that would resemble the child she prayed for. She did as she was told and tucked the carved figure in the waistband of her skirt when she went to market. Her friends in the neighborhood saw her and called out, "Look, see Akua's child [*Akua ba*]," and so these small dolls are called *Akua ba* (pl. *Akua ma*) (see Figure 7).

The Yoruba people of Nigeria pray to the god Shango, who punishes evildoers with lightning and

who may answer prayers for children by giving a woman twins. The Yoruba have the highest rate of twinning in the world, and twins are considered to be good luck and to bring their parents well-being. However, twins are more fragile at birth than are single infants, and often one or both twins dies. In the case of the death of a twin, the mother may commission a small wooden figure that represents the deceased child, which she cares for with food, expensive clothing, and gifts of money and jewelry until the surviving twin is old enough to care for the figure. These "images of twins" (*ere Ibeji*) can be seen in Nigeria and in museum collections with evidence of the loving care that has been lavished on them. Their hair has been dyed a rich blue-black, and there are remains of a red oil cosmetic that is rubbed on the skin to soften and beautify it.

Figure 7. Asante figure (Akuaba), Ghana. The Asante of Ghana carve dolls, sometimes decorated with beads, that are left in shrines to encourage God to help young couples to conceive. THE STANLEY COLLECTION, UNIVERSITY OF IOWA MUSEUM OF ART, IOWA CITY, IA x1986.244

Education. The process by which young men and women acquire the skills they need to prosper in adult society is called education all around the world. Scholars have used another word—initiation—to describe this same process for Africans, who may be subjected to difficult physical tests and may be sworn to secrecy and taught the passwords and special knowledge of the history of the group. Art is often an essential element of the transitions from childhood to adulthood at the end of the initiation period. Among the Bamana of Mali men and women alike are members of the Chi Wara association, dedicated to the spiritual being who taught them how to farm. During the time that the fields are cleared for planting, members wear very dramatic and abstract crests in the form of male and female antelopes.

Among the Igbo (Ibo) people of Nigeria, masks of two types are worn to mark this same transition. Dark, coarse male masks called *okoroshi* represent the powerful, male, prosperous, impure, and crude, while delicate white masks called *mmuo* represent the weak, female, poor, pure, and beautiful in skits that emphasize these major contrasts in the life of the community.

Among the Mende people of Sierra Leone a special initiation is held for young women during which they are taught the use of magical medicine from the wilderness and the skills and responsibilities of mothers and wives. When they return to the community as women ready to marry, they are accompanied by elaborate black helmet masks that represent all of the Mende ideals of feminine beauty. These masks embody a spirit that watches over the young women during initiation, and over older women during the rest of their lives. They are commissioned and worn exclusively by the women who organize the initiation camp.

Spirits. Although many Africans have become Christian or Muslim in the past few centuries, significant numbers also believe that the world is given life by spiritual beings that inhabit natural objects—trees, rocks, clouds, rivers, fields, and especially forests and the untamed, uncut, unfarmed wilderness. These spiritual beings act as intermediaries between the creator god and humankind, and if they are honored they can provide their blessings, or if neglected bring disasters of all kinds. These spirits are normally invisible, though their presence may be felt and their power experienced. Africans are able to communicate with these spirits through the use of art, which makes the spirit world visible. Figures placed on shrines may have extra limbs or even be double faced as a reminder that they represent abstract spiritual beings. Masks can embody the spirits and bring them to life, so that they can perform and interact with the people of the community. The performances are always carefully choreographed and tightly controlled, for they are intended to tell of the sacred encounters between spiritual beings and the human ancestors at the time of creation, or at least at the founding of the village.

Among the Baule, a man or woman who has failed to fill his or her gender role, such as a man who does not marry or hold a good job or a woman who cannot conceive children, is believed to be afflicted by the spirit spouse he or she left behind in the spirit world at birth. In this instance, a spirit spouse is commissioned from an artist, a figure so beautiful, with such careful carving of hairstyle, dress, and jewelry, that the spirit spouse will take up residence in it and can be honored, cared for, and loved, and so bring success and well-being to its human spouse.

When an Igbo community has experienced a series of disasters, when children sicken, crops wither, or trading ventures fail, the elders consult a diviner who may advise them to restore the balance of spiritual forces by offering a prayer called *mbari* to honor an offended god. *Mbari* is a structure designed by an itinerant architect and made of clay by a group of workers who come from all of the families of the community. *Mbari* may consist of a large, single-story structure decorated with a large number of modeled clay figures that depict the gods, humans, animals, and spirits of all kinds. The human characters are often shown going about their daily affairs in scenes that comment on the changes the Igbo have experienced, on the characters of members of the community, and generally on human virtues and vices. When the group of workers has finished construction they return to their families, the village comes to see *mbari*, and the structure is abandoned to the forest, for once the prayer has been offered in the building of the structure, the building itself is of little value. As Herbert M. Cole, the principal scholar of the Igbo, has noted, "art is verb in Igboland."

When a family or community must solve a problem, they may turn to a diviner who is able to communicate with the supernatural world and make known the wishes of the gods. Among the Yoruba this middleman between humankind and the spirit world is called a *babalawo*, or "father of secrets." The Yoruba diviner uses a wooden tray (*opon Ifa*) covered with wood dust, and sixteen palm nuts, which he tosses in his hands. He makes sixteen marks in the dust on the tray and stores the nuts in a beautifully carved bowl. To call the attention of the gods he taps a carved ivory stick against the edge of the tray. The top of the tray, placed facing the diviner, represents Eshu, the messenger of the gods, and the trickster, the god without whom all the other gods would go hungry.

Rule. Europeans who needed to justify the slave trade in the seventeenth to nineteenth centuries wrote that Africans were without centralized political systems above the level of the local chief. In truth, West Africa has been a land of great kings and empires whose illustrious histories stretch back in time to long before the first European contact. Like peoples all over the world, Africans have created political art that validates rule, identifies kings, and represents the wealth and military power of the royal family.

Among the Asante people of Ghana, who formed a mighty military and political confederacy in the seventeenth century, swords and staffs of iron with handles of gold-covered wood served as symbols of leadership, held against the palanquin in which the king was carried in procession in such a way that the handles were always within the king's reach. Much Asante leadership art consists of carved representations of sayings about the use and abuse of political power; a staff with its finial carved in the form of a man holding an egg reminds all who see it that power is like an egg, if you hold it too firmly you crush it, but if you hold it too loosely it slips from your grasp and falls to the ground.

Among some people in both the Guinea Coast and the Sudan, power is held not by a king or chief, but by a council of senior village elders. Sometimes these elders represent all of the families in the community; sometimes membership is open only to those who have achieved significant status and are able to purchase membership. Here political art may take the form of masks, such as those used among the Ibibio people in southern Nigeria, which are responsible for spreading the news of important decisions made by the elders or executing judgments against those who have committed serious offenses. The masks give anonymity to the man who is delegated to carry out the sentence, just as a police officer's uniform identifies the wearer as a public servant, subjugating his or her individual identity.

Death. The final passage of life is from the world of the living to the world of the ancestors. Much West African art is used in the context of death, funerals, and the departure of the spirits of the deceased to the land of the ancestors. Among the Dogon of Mali, in particular, men wearing masks appear at the *dama*, or celebrations that mark the end of the period of mourning. They perform on the roof of the dead elder's house or before his or her threshold to break the lifelong ties that bind the dead to the living, and honor the dead, sending their souls on the long road to the spirit world. Following mock battles and hunts a dead man's tools and weapons are smashed on his doorstep, and a woman's cooking pots are broken by her friends because she will no longer use them in this world.

In very much the same way, the Yoruba honor their ancestors once a year with elaborate performances in which masks called *egungun*, made up of colorful and expensive textiles and a small carved wooden head, spin and twirl in spectacular displays that are evidence of the expense the family will go to honor their dead.

In the easternmost area of West Africa, in the grasslands of Cameroon on the Nigeria/Cameroon border, masks that represent both human and animal characters appear at the funerals of important elders, including and especially of kings, to serve as testimony to the status and prestige of the deceased. The masks that each elder had acquired the right to wear appear at a celebration called a cry-die, which is a final summing up of all of the dead person's accomplishments in life.

In some cases art associated with death and ancestors serves as a physical representation of the dead—as a portrait. The Anyi people of the lagoon area of southern Côte d'Ivoire, as well as their Akan-speaking neighbors, make modeled clay heads called *mma* that are portraits of the deceased that are displayed at memorial services and then are discarded in a field of pots called the *mmaso*. The heads are very lifelike, but the identity of the individual is recognized not by the facial features but by patterns of scars, marks of rank, jewelry and costume, and especially hairstyle. The tradition of memorial heads is found among other important peoples along the Guinea Coast, including the Yoruba at Ife and the court of Bénin.

Africans think of the course of life as a circle. Men and women die so that their souls may be reborn in the next generation. Life leads to death and to rebirth and new life in a never-ending cycle like that of the seasons. And so the next chapter following death and the ancestors is birth and the continuity of the generations. At every stage, art plays an essential role, helping Africans express their ideas about themselves and their world and serving as tools in meeting and overcoming life's difficulties.

See also **Art; Arts; Body Adornment and Clothing: Cosmetics and Body Painting; Ceramics; Death, Mourning, and Ancestors; Initiation; Masks and Masquerades; Slave Trades; Textiles.**

BIBLIOGRAPHY

Phillips, Tom, ed. *Africa: The Art of a Continent.* New York: Prestel, 1995.

Turner, Jane, ed. *The Dictionary of Art.* New York: Grove's Dictionaries, 1996.

CHRISTOPHER D. ROY

EGYPT

Africans, African Americans, Europeans, and Middle Easterners all claim as their heritage the glorious tradition of Egyptian art. Ancient Egyptians called their country *Kemet*, meaning the black land, in reference to the fertile soil produced by the overflowing of the Nile River. Art historians have severed Egypt from its geographical context, excluding it from general studies of African art and rarely comparing it to artistic traditions of other regions on the continent. In the past, scholars focused instead upon the important impact the art of this African civilization has had upon the art of Greece, and hence its role in the development of art in the West. Nevertheless, Egypt is and has always been at the crossroads of African, Near Eastern, and Mediterranean cultures, and its art reflects this.

PERIODS

With an artistic production spanning six thousand years, Egypt is known for its highly developed aesthetics as well as for its conservatism. Many of the fundamentals of Egyptian art were established at the beginning of Egyptian history and changed little until the Byzantine period. Still, this long history has been marked by innovation and evolution. Although scholars continue to debate exact periodization, it should be safe to say that the divisions are accepted even if there is disagreement about the dates. The following timeline is proposed: The Predynastic Period (5000–2920 BCE), the Early Dynastic Period (2920–2649 BCE), followed by the Old Kingdom (2649–2134 BCE). The Middle

Bust of Queen Nefertiti Akhenaton. The 3,300-year old bust sits on display in the Kulturforum (The Old Museum), Berlin. The painted limestone statue will be permanently relocated to the New Museum once it is reopened in 2009 after undergoing major renovations following its destruction in World War II. © AP IMAGES

Islamic period (from 639 CE), Egypt continued as a major artistic center, especially during the Fatamid, Mameluk, and Ottoman periods. European domination began with the Napoleonic expedition in 1798 and continued with the British occupation and Protectorate (1882–1922). Modern Egyptian art began around 1910. Each of the major periods of Egyptian art (the art of Kemet, generally known as the Pharaonic era, Coptic art, Islamic art, Modern art and Contemporary art) are studied by specialists who rarely cross disciplinary boundaries—no single art historical text has as its subject the last five thousand years of art in Egypt.

ANCIENT EGYPTIAN ART

Ancient Egyptian art served almost exclusively to link the natural and supernatural worlds. Images, whether written into the pictographs called hieroglyphics, or painted onto walls, or carved into three dimensions, were believed to transmit prayers or incantations, or to be the receptacles of spiritual forces. As in many African cultures, the people of Kemet believed that the soul of a deceased elder could travel to the afterlife. Depending upon the time period, wealthy Egyptians sought to increase their chances for survival during this perilous journey by having their bodies mummified and by filling their tombs with art works. One Egyptian word for sculptor was "He-who-keeps-alive." As in other African cultures, the ancestors played an important role in the everyday life of the ancient Egyptians.

Egyptian art's harmony and aesthetic elegance are the result of careful planning and strict conventions regulating subject matter, sizes, proportions and colors. Because images were created to communicate with supernatural beings, they followed a clear grammatical structure. Within that structure, during certain periods, artists could experiment with naturalism or even realism. Artists worked from a grid to mark out mathematically derived proportions. This helped even the gigantic monuments and sculptures look graceful. Characteristic of graphic composition is the "hierarchical scale" in which the heroic size of the Pharaoh reflects his divine status; his inferiors are represented in smaller stature. This feature is also common in art from elsewhere on the continent. Also characteristic of ancient Egyptian art is the "law of frontality." Because images were meant to assure life after death, they needed to present as full a picture as

Kingdom (2040–1640 BCE) is known for mortuary complexes and tombs with exquisite relief carvings, and for royal statues reflecting a new concept of kingship. The New Kingdom (1550–1070 BCE), an exceptional period of wealth and creativity that has been dubbed the Golden Empire, was the time during which artists produced many of the masterpieces famous in the early twenty-first century, such as the bust of Nefertiti and the mask of Tutankhamen.

The Late Period (712–332 BCE) saw the introduction of new forms of art as Kemet fell under the rule of Nubians, Libyans, and Persians. The Greeks of the Ptolemaic Dynasty (304–30 BCE) were followed by the Roman (30 BCE–395 CE) and Byzantine periods (395–642 CE). During the possible. Human figures were drawn with the head in profile but with both shoulders, arms, legs and feet visible.

As in much of African art, materials were carefully chosen by Egyptian artists for their supernatural qualities. Clay (whether used to build a wall around a temple or dried in an image of the god Osiris) was associated with the life-giving waters of the Nile. The vitreous paste often called "faience" produced a shiny blue color when fired, and was linked to the sky and to water. Stone was eternal, and was used for monuments and images that needed to endure until the end of time. This emphasis on durability and scale distinguishes the Egyptians from all other African peoples, and was greatly admired by the Greeks and Romans.

Egyptian temples, pyramids and statues are famous for their impressive size; Egyptologists' works resound with the terms "massive" and "colossal." The Temple of Karnak remains the largest religious complex on earth. The pyramids, Egypt's most recognizable symbol, are also among the world's largest human-made constructions. There are more than one hundred pyramids in Egypt. Built as tombs, the pyramids' construction was a remarkable feat mobilizing religious belief, mathematical skill, and a huge labor force in support of political power. The Great Pyramid at Giza, built for Cheops (ruled 2551–2528 BC), was constructed of more than two million stone blocks averaging 2.5 tons each. Its base covers thirteen acres and the structure originally measured 146 meters high. It is the oldest and only remaining of the Seven Wonders of the Ancient World. Also prominent in architecture were *tekhen* (obelisks), tall, thin tapering monuments with a pyramidal top; they are important for their solar symbolism within the temple setting.

The Mask of King Tutankhamen (who reigned 1347–1337 BC) was among the treasures unearthed

The colossal pyramids of Giza, Egypt, just before sunset. The three pyramids—the Pyramid of Menkaure (Mycerinus), the Pyramid of Khafre (Chephren), and the Great Pyramid of Khufu (Cheops)—were built for the fourth dynasty of kings, Khufu, Khafre, and Menkaure, who ruled from 2589 to 2504 BCE. © ROGER RESSMEYER/CORBIS

Funeral mask of King Tutankhamen. The mask, in gold inlaid with semi-precious stones and glass-paste, c. 1323 BCE, was in the tomb of the pharaoh Tutankhamen, which was discovered in the Valley of the Kings, Thebes, Egypt. ROBERT HARDING/GETTY IMAGES

Statue of King Menkaure and Queen Kha-merer-nebty II. This famed sculpture of King Menkaure and his wife is believed to have been created between 2490 and 2472 BCE. It shows her to be equal in height to him, which shows her importance. Yet, her positioning depicts her supporting role to the king. © ARCHIVO ICONOGRAFICO, SA/CORBIS

in 1922 in the only pharaonic tomb discovered in modern times with all of its contents intact. The painted limestone Bust of Queen Nefertiti has been the object of controversy related to the "race" of ancient Egyptians. Conversely, the portrait of Nubian Queen Tiye, wife and mother of pharaohs, constitutes an example of a powerful black woman in Egyptian society. The sculpture of King Menkaure and Queen Kha-merer-nebty II depicts the queen as being of almost equal stature, reflecting her high status, but her position suggests she played a supporting role. Low relief sculpture is common and often found on temple walls. The Palette of Narmer (c. 3000–2920 BCE) tells the story of the unification of Upper and Lower Egypt and exemplifies this style.

Egyptians used paint to decorate sculptures, furniture, everyday objects, and tomb walls. Scenes depicted deities and animals, but especially humans in engaged in everyday activities, battles,

and ceremonies. The Books of the Dead, painted papyrus scrolls placed in mummy cases, contained charms and spells to protect the soul on its journey to the afterlife. The Rosetta Stone (203 BCE) is a slab of granite, the remains of a stele inscribed in hieroglyphic, Egyptian demotic, and ancient Greek scripts.

Ancient Egyptian art and architecture significantly influenced the civilizations of Greece, Rome, and Europe in the Renaissance and Napoleonic eras. Waves of "Egyptomania" sparked new architectural styles and decorative fashions. Art inspired proponents of Afrocentrism who argued for the African origins and nature of Egyptian civilization. The books of Molefi Kete Asante and Cheikh Anta Diop are illustrated with Egyptian images. Clinton Crawford's *Recasting Ancient Egypt in the African Context* (1996) investigates art. Celenko's *Egypt in*

Africa (1996) and Visonà's chapter on Egyptian, Nubian and Ethiopian art (2001) examine ancient Egyptian art in its relation to Africa.

ROMAN, BYZANTINE, AND ISLAMIC PERIODS

Egyptian art and architecture of the Roman and Byzantine periods owes a debt to the ancient Egyptian funerary tradition, but its techniques and styles mainly resemble Greek and Roman art. The term Copt, derived from the Greek word for Egypt, came to designate Egyptian Christians. Coptic art designates works from the second to the twelfth centuries. The most recognizable of these are the Faiyum portraits.

Egyptian art flourished during the Islamic period. The Fatimid dynasty (969–1171) is known for the luxury of its court and its new capital in Cairo. During the Mamluk dynasty (1250–1517), Cairo became the spiritual and political center of the Islamic world. Trade in luxury goods between China and the West helped stimulate artists' creativity. Fine examples of brass vessels, calligraphy, ceramics, and architecture (palaces, mosques, *madrasas*) date from this period. The Ottoman period also influenced Egyptian art.

Throughout the ages, Egyptians have produced a diversity of decorative arts in elegant forms. These include textiles, ceramic vessels, alabaster lamps, gold and stone jewelry, faïence animal figurines, glass bottles, headrests, staffs, fans, musical instruments, mirror cases, combs, spoons, metal objects, and furniture.

MODERN EGYPTIAN ART

Scholars of modern Egyptian art characterize it as a layering of Western styles and techniques over pharaonic and Islamic artistic traditions. Art historians rarely link it to contemporary arts from other parts of Africa. Egyptian artists themselves generally disregard the connections as well. From the time of Napoleon's 1798 expedition, European art wielded a major influence in Egypt.

Foreign artists visited the country, and Egyptian leaders commissioned European works of art; Egyptians were sent to study in Paris, London, or Berlin. Europeans were the first teachers in the School of Fine Arts that opened in 1908, although by 1928 all its faculty members were of Egyptian descent. From the first generation, modern Egyptian

artists strove to ground their work in the local environment and promoted a renewed appreciation for national patrimony. In the early twentieth century they sought inspiration in folk arts, rural life, and regional architecture. Artists explored pharaonic traditions. By the late 1960s the movement to revive the aesthetics of Islamic art, focusing on geometric abstraction and calligraphic art, was in full force. Some artists, intrigued by internationalism, followed Western styles. Although architecture, sculpture and painting enjoy continued popularity, in the early twenty-first century artists are experimenting with newer media, including installations, photography, and video. They are also reviving the ancient art of papermaking and are experimenting with fiber arts. Tradition versus modernity debates give way to discussions about internationalism and specificity.

Art theoreticians, art societies, and art education helped foster modern Egyptian creation. Influential teachers include Habib Gorgui (1892–1965) and Hussein Youssef Amin (1904–1984). Official patronage plays an important role. Since the 1920s, government support of and control over art institutions has been praised for allowing art to flourish and cursed for creating a stagnant official culture. Abstract artist Farouk Hosni (b. 1938) served nearly twenty years as minister of culture (1987–2005). Egypt boasts numerous museums, including the Museum of Islamic Art (1880s), the Greco-Roman Museum (1892), the Egyptian Museum (1902), the Museum of Modern Art (1931), and the Grand Museum of Egypt located between the pyramids and Cairo. Foreign cultural centers and private and state-owned galleries provide exhibition venues.

Ramses Wissa Wassef (1911–1975) and Hasan Fathi (1902–1989) were great modern architects. Fathi worked to revive sustainable traditional architecture; Abdel Halim Ibrahim (1929–1977) designed a prizewinning Cultural Park for Children (1982–1991) in Cairo. Sculptors Mahmoud Mokhtar (1891–1934) and Adam Henein (b. 1929) drew inspiration from ancient Egypt and modern Paris. Mokhtar, the father of modern Arab sculpture, was the first to exemplify a national artistic identity. His *Egypt Awakening* epitomizes the neopharaonic style. Henein theorized Egyptian art and initiated the Aswan International Sculpture Symposium. Mona Marzouk (b. 1968) also creates reconfigured archetypes that command a revision of the heritage of the past. Painters Raghib Ayyad (1892–1982), Mahmoud Said (1897–1964) and Abdel-Hadi el Gazzar (1925–1965) depicted local Egyptians peasants and street scenes, and played on symbolism. Effat Nagui (1910–1994) showed a similar preoccupation with folklore and the sacred. Egyptian feminists Inji Aflatun (1924–1989) and Gazbia Sirry (b. 1925) linked the political to the personal. Sirry's *The Two Wives* comments on the condition of women as mothers and wives in a polygamous society.

The late 1960s witnessed an Islamic art revival that showed up in abstraction, geometry, calligraphy, and political art. Ramzi Moustafa (b. 1926), Mohamed Taha Hussein (b. 1932), Sami Rafei (b. 1932), and Ahmad Moustafa (b. 1943) are associated with this movement.

In the work of Fathi Hassan (b. 1957), invented forms allude to koufic calligraphy. Karnouk considers Hassan's art "an inquiry into his identity as Nubian, which he assumes freely in all its complexity as African, Arab, Italian, or simply a global nomad. [. . . He] emigrated to Italy, but instead of redirecting his gaze toward the East, Hassan kept looking South" (Karnouk 2005). Egypt's importance on the global art scene is growing. The Cairo International Biennale is the largest international exhibition in the Arab world. In 2003, artists represented around sixty nations, but only Mauritius and Sudan represented sub-Saharan Africa. Unlike Hassan, most contemporary Egyptian artists—and their administrators, historians, and critics—have not turned south.

See also **Architecture; Art, Genres and Periods; Ceramics; Egypt, Early; Nile River; Symbols and Symbolism; Tourism; Travel and Exploration.**

BIBLIOGRAPHY

Blackmun Visonà, Monica. "Lands of the Nile: Egypt, Nubia and Ethiopia." In *A History of Art in Africa*, ed. Monica Blackmun Visonà, Robin Poynor, Herbert M. Cole, and Michael D. Harris. New York: Harry N. Abrams, 2001.

Blair, Sheila S., and Jonathan Bloom. *The Art and Architecture of Islam 1250–1850.* New Haven, CT: Yale University Press, 1994.

Celenko, Theodore, ed. *Egypt in Africa.* Bloomington: Indiana University Press, 1996.

Crawford, Clinton. *Recasting Ancient Egypt in the African Context: Toward a Model Curriculum Using Art and Language.* Trenton, NJ: Africa World Press, 1996.

Ettinghausen, Richard; Oleg Grabar; and Marilyn Jenkins-Madina. *The Art and Architecture of Islam, 650–1250.* New Haven, CT: Yale University Press, 2001.

Hunt, Lucy-Anne. "Coptic Art." In *Dictionary of the Middle Ages*, Vol. 3, ed. Joseph R. Strayer. New York: Scribners, 1983.

Karnouk, Liliane. *Modern Egyptian Art: 1910–2003.* New York: American University in Cairo Press, 2005.

Malek, Jaromir. *Egypt: 4000 Years of Art.* London: Phaidon, 2003.

Robins, Gay. *The Art of Ancient Egypt.* Cambridge, MA: Harvard University Press, 2000.

MARY VOGL

ETHIOPIA

The area of northeast Africa defined by the borders of the modern nation of Ethiopia has been a major crossroads of cultural tradition—a place where the peoples of Africa, the Middle East, and the Mediterranean world have been meeting for thousands of years. The area's cultural diversity is revealed in the rich and varied art and architectures of its peoples, though by the early twenty-first century only a handful of traditions had received much attention from scholars.

The earliest evidence of artistic activity in Ethiopia is revealed in the 4,000-year-old rock paintings of cattle, antelopes, and hyenas found in the eastern part of the country near the towns of Dire Dawa and Harar. Little is known about the people who produced these paintings, but the subject matter suggests that herding cattle and hunting wild game were important activities for the early inhabitants of this region.

The best-known and best-studied architectural and artistic traditions are associated with the peoples, particularly the Tigre and Amhara, of the northern highlands. Many of these traditions, especially those associated with religious life and secular authority in this region, originated with the meeting of the indigenous Agaw (a Cushitic people) and Semitic peoples from southern Arabia, which took place during the first millennium BCE. Evidence of this interaction may be seen in the vestiges of palaces and temples, as well as stone sculpture, pottery, and metal objects, from sites such as Yeha, Hawelti, and Melazo. The state of Aksum emerged at the beginning of the first millennium CE, reaching its zenith during the third to the sixth centuries and bringing the peoples of the region under the rule of a single king. Today at the town of Aksum one encounters the architectural remains of this great state: multistoried stone palaces built on raised platforms, royal tombs lined with dressed stone, and magnificent stone stelae that marked the tombs of Aksum's ruling elite.

Christianity was first introduced in Ethiopia at Aksum during the fourth century. The foundation of the first church, built on a basilican plan and dedicated to Saint Mary of Zion, may still be seen. Ethiopia's most famous churches, located 174 miles to the south of Aksum in the province of Welo at the ceremonial center of Roha (commonly known as Lalibäla), were built roughly eight hundred years later under the patronage of the kings of the Zagwe dynasty (1137–1270). These churches, cut from "living" rock, house the oldest extant examples of Ethiopian religious painting.

It is very likely that soon after Christianity's introduction in Ethiopia, paintings on church walls, on wood panels as icons, and in religious texts began serving as important vehicles for teaching and sustaining the faith, as they do today. The history of Ethiopian church painting is generally divided into two periods. The first dates from the time of Christianity's introduction in Ethiopia up until the fifteenth century, and is heavily rooted in Byzantine and Middle Eastern tradition. Indeed, stylistically, Ethiopian painting is readily recognizable as a manifestation of an Eastern Orthodox canon. The fifteenth century marks the beginning of the second phase, during which western European religious art became the primary source. Similarly, the distinctive style of monumental architecture associated with the seventeenth and eighteenth centuries, found at and around the city of Gondär to the north of Lake Tana, such as the buildings built under the patronage of Emperor Fasiladas (r. 1632–1667), bespeak close ties with Europeans, especially the Portuguese.

External contacts certainly had an impact on the Ethiopian priests and monks who produced religious paintings over the centuries, but it is also apparent that many of the religious themes depicted in these paintings were interpreted through Ethiopian eyes. Subjects are often set in Ethiopian contexts, and figures are depicted with the distinctive accoutrements of highland Ethiopian society. In addition, the distinctive religious and social values of the northern highlands of Ethiopia are reflected in the popularity of specific themes such as the Virgin Mary and Saints Giyorgis (George) and Gebre Menfas Qiddus. In the realm of architecture, churches built on a circular plan represent another Ethiopian interpretation of an imported ideology.

Though the depiction of important historical events may date back several centuries and appears to be an outgrowth of the religious painting tradition, it was not until the nineteenth century that nonreligious painting came into its own. Since the early twentieth century, painters, often originally trained within the context of the church and working primarily in urban centers, have been producing paintings on cloth depicting a variety of secular subjects—historical, genre, and allegorical—as well as religious themes, often for foreign patrons. Some of the most popular subjects have included the battle of Adwa, the life of the Queen of Sheba, and St. George Slaying the Dragon.

Most people living in Ethiopia are not Christian and do not possess the artistic traditions (painting and monumental church architecture) associated with the Semitic peoples of the northern highlands. Though the aesthetic traditions of peoples living in the eastern, southern, and southwestern parts of the country have received little scholarly attention, one must acknowledge that, viewed within their respective social and cultural contexts, they are just as important as those of the Ethiopian Orthodox church. In the context of this brief essay, a glimpse at a few of these traditions must suffice.

The art of the Muslim peoples of eastern Ethiopia, in places such as Harar, is similar to that of their neighbors in Somalia and on the Arabian peninsula. Harari jewelry, for instance, is often difficult to distinguish from that produced by Bedouin and Yemeni silversmiths. A magnificent array of multicolored baskets, made by the women of the house, often hang on the walls of meeting rooms in Harari homes. In addition to their function as containers and covers, their designs and places on the wall tell much about their owners' past, as well as their current social and economic status. Baskets are also important among the pastoral Boran (Oromo) people of southern Ethiopia; their designs and functions also reflect close cultural ties with neighbors to the east (in Somalia) and south (in Kenya). As in Harar, all Boran women learn to make baskets, which in addition to serving as containers for milk, butter, and water are associated with female identity in Boran society. One of Ethiopia's few figurative sculpture traditions is found among the Konso, who live to the west of the Boran. Here stylized wood figures referred to as *waga* are carved to commemorate deceased leaders of the community.

Moving farther west to the Omo River region near the Sudan border, the human body becomes a primary vehicle for artistic expression. Distinctive coiffures, body painting, scarification, and dress make both aesthetic and social statements among the Hamer, Nyangatom, and Karimojon peoples.

The Gamu of the southern highlands are known for their finely woven cotton textiles. Here women grow the cotton and spin thread, but men weave the cloth. Perhaps the most distinctive artistic traditions associated with this area are "basketry" houses—conical structures constructed of woven bamboo strips and thatched with either barley, wheat straw, or the stem sheaths of bamboo that can be 20 to 30 feet high. To the north, and in the region west of Addis Ababa, the Gurage produce some of Ethiopia's finest woodworking. In fact, most of the beautifully incised and painted domestic utensils and furniture used by the Gurage are produced by the Fuga, a group of ritual and occupational specialists who live among—but are socially isolated from—the majority population. This separation is a common feature of many highland Ethiopian societies, where there is a social and sometimes a religious stigma attached to certain creative activities. Metalworkers, especially blacksmiths, are typical of artists or artisans whose products are vital to the farmers among whom they live, yet who are ostracized from the rest of society. Depending upon the people, these attitudes may also pertain to leatherworkers, potters, weavers, woodworkers, and goldsmiths and silversmiths, and perhaps reflect the ambivalent position that creative people often hold in many African cultures. Perhaps the best-known group to occupy this status are the Beta Israel (Falasha) who live around the northern city of Gondär.

Academic art has flourished in Addis Ababa since the middle of the twentieth century, with its nucleus at the School of Fine Arts. Founded in 1957, it has trained most of Ethiopia's contemporary artists. In 2000, the school was incorporated into Addis Ababa University and renamed the School of Fine Arts and Design. The 1960s and early 1970s produced a number of exceptional artists including Gebre Kristos Desta (1932–1981), Afewerk Tekle (b. 1932), Skunder Boghossian (1937–2003), Zerihun Yetmgeta (b. 1941), and Wosene Kosrof (b. 1950). Drawing on Ethiopian culture and history as well as abstract expressionism, their work reveals a dynamic synthesis of local and global tradition, with found in museum and private collections throughout the world.

Much of the creative energy of this period was suppressed in 1974 when the Derg regime came to power and some of Ethiopia's finest artists were forced to leave the country. The government's overthrow in 1991 began a revival of the contemporary art scene in Addis Ababa. A host of galleries and artist collectives regularly display the works of a thriving artistic community. Among the many talented young artists working in Addis in 2005, Engdaget Legesse's (b. 1971) "magic pillar" sculptures and his oil paintings are sought after by collectors, as are Behailu Bezabih's (b. 1960) collage-style paintings. Bisrat Shibabaw (b. 1965) is one of a small number of women artists whose abstract collages have received local recognition. Tesfahun Kibru (b. 1978), Tamrat Gezahegn (b. 1977), Assefa Gebrekidan (b. 1964), and Elias Sime (b. 1960) are innovative young artists who use found objects to produce three-dimensional works. The inclusion of Engdaget in the 2001 Venice Biennale and Assefa and Elias in the 2004 Dakar Biennale signals that the localized renaissance in Ethiopian contemporary art is beginning to find an international audience.

See also **Addis Ababa; Aksum; Architecture; Art; Arts; Christianity; Gondär; Harar; Islam; Lalibäla; Prehistory.**

BIBLIOGRAPHY

Anfray, Francis. *Les anciens éthiopiens: Siècles d'histoire.* Paris: Armand Colin, Éditeur, 1990.

Biasio, Elisabeth. *Die verborgene Wirklichkeit: Drei äthiopische Maler der Gegenwart* (The hidden reality: Three contemporary Ethiopian artists). Zurich: Völkerkunde-museum der Universität Zürich, 1989.

Fisseha, Girma and Walter Raunig. *Mensch und Geschichte in Äthiopiens Volksmalerei.* Innsbruck, Austria: Pinguin-Verlag, 1985.

Heldman, Marilyn, with Stuart C. Munro-Hay et al. *African Zion: The Sacred Art of Ethiopia.* New Haven, CT: Yale University Press, 1993.

Holbert, Kelly M., Getachew Haile, et al. *Ethiopian Art. The Walters Art Museum.* Baltimore: The Walters Art Museum, 2001.

Mekonnen, Geta. "[Ethiopia] Currents of Change." *Revue Noire,* no. 24 (1997): 36–75.

Mercier, Jacques. *L'Arche ethiopienne. Art chrétien d'Ethiopie.* Paris: Pavillon des Arts, 2000.

Phillipson, David. *Ancient Ethiopia, Aksum: Its Antecedents and Successors.* London: British Museum Press, 1998.

Silverman, Raymond, ed. *Ethiopia: Traditions of Creativity.* Seattle: University of Washington Press, 1999.

Stappen, Xavier Van der, ed. *Æthiopia: Pays, histoire, populations, croyances, art and artisanat.* Waterloo, Belgium: Cultures and Communications, 1996.

RAYMOND A. SILVERMAN

ART HISTORY AND THE STUDY OF AFRICA.

At the most basic level, art refers to the skillfulness needed to bring something into existence that was not already there; and this would apply as much to the extant ruins of Great Zimbabwe as it would to the earliest chipped stone pebbles that, more than anything else, mark the earliest appearance of human species. Any artifact is made to be used, owned, given as a gift, inherited, and so forth, and acquires a context of ideas and values. This is a field of study in which anthropology and art history coincide; for material artifacts are "chains along which social relationships run" (Evans-Pritchard, 89).

The earliest evidence for a skillfulness that is more than tool-making are the pieces of red ochre, one with a pattern incised on one side from Blombos cave on the southern coast of South Africa some 77,000 years BP. The art here is not just the pattern, the purpose of which one simply cannot know: is it mere doodling, a map, a mark of ownership, a mark related to divination procedures,

an attempt to document the entoptic phenomena associated with trance . . . ? All this and more has been documented in research since the mid-twentieth century, but the very fact that it is red ochre that is so marked alerts scholars to the uses of the substance itself in rock painting, body marking, murals and the painting of sculpture and other artifacts. Pictorial art, as preserved on rock surfaces, seems to appear in several parts of the world (Africa, Europe, Australasia) from around 30,000 years BP onward and marks the certain presence of modern humans. The earliest firmly dated example from Africa remains the painted fragments from the Apollo 11 cave in Namibia (27,000 BP). Painting thus has a very long prehistory in Africa.

DESPERATELY SEEKING AFRICA

Art historians know much less about art in Africa than in other parts of the world. There is plenty of art, but the documentation crucial to the study of art elsewhere is lacking. All too often the only dates are those of acquisition by museums; and there are no detailed accounts of metaphysics or ritual prior to the late nineteenth century. Historians do have a wealth of coincidental documentation largely contingent upon European contacts with Africa, colonial and missionary archives, as well as (in more recent years) twentieth-century collections of oral narrative. Artifacts might or might not be mentioned in passing, and though the oral narratives might or might not reveal local theories about the significances of artworks the references are highly generic. None of this provides a substitute for absent documentation. Explaining art is rarely their purpose; but they can indicate other questions that might be asked art-historically. For example, ethnography and oral tradition may point towards the manner in which the identities and life histories of individuals and communities are structured and constituted in terms of the practice and performance of art. In this context the invention of "primitivism" by artists in Paris and elsewhere in Europe is an irrelevance.

TRACING THE LINES

Nevertheless, sometimes there is evidence for changes in art that can be seen in a specific historical and social context. For example, from the late fifteenth century, beginning with the Portuguese as they came around the coast of West Africa looking for direct access to Malian gold and Indian pepper. In 1485 they visited Benin City establishing a monopoly of the trade that lasted until the 1530s; and European trade provided its casters with new sources of imagery and brass. Moreover, in Sierra Leone, Bénin, and Kongo, the Portuguese commissioned the ivory sculptures that were the first African art works known to have entered European collections.

In the region Europeans called the Gold Coast they had initiated a competition over access to both trans-Saharan and coastal demands for gold; and towards the close of the seventeenth century a few small Akan states joined forces under the leadership of the king of Kumasi to win their freedom from the kingdom of Denkyira. This led to the institution of the Asante nation, marked by the descent of the Golden Stool from the sky on a Friday. Here too, as in Benin City, the visual arts are elaborated in support of the state, and also record impact of the European trading presence; yet the visual character of the arts of the Asante confederacy, with an emphasis on gold and silk, could hardly be more different than Bénin brass, ivory, and red cloth.

Between the Gold Coast and the lower Niger for more than two hundred years the kingdom of Oyo controlled the region from the middle Niger to the coast, and thereby access to both trans-Saharan and coastal trade. Oyo established its authority by means of the effective use of cavalry until the advent of the Fulani jihad in the early nineteenth century, also dependent upon cavalry. These rival cavalries provided the source material for sculptures of mythic heroes, and conceptual images of possession by a deity. The fall of Oyo resulted in a series of wars out of which came a modern sense of Yoruba ethnic identity and a focus upon Ife as the "cradle" of Yoruba civilization, a city now known for its corpus of naturalistic sculpture prior to European coastal contact. Moreover, in the northeast of what is now "the Yoruba-speaking region" it has sometimes been possible to assemble a corpus of sculpture and data about artists and schools that signals a cultural revival in the immediate aftermath of the Fulani jihad.

In 1483 the Portuguese had already encountered the kingdom of Kongo; and a contrast between royal authority and *minkisi* ("fetishes," power figures) as instruments of individual achievement was noted. With the destruction of the kingdom in 1665 consequent upon the expansion of the Atlantic trade, *minkisi* assumed greater prominence. Elsewhere, at the southern margin of savanna and forest, by the beginning of the seventeenth century, the hero, Shyaam a-Mbul a-Ngoong, had established the dominance of the Bushoong as the ruling group within the region (still known by the alien term *Kuba*). Among other things he introduced from Kongo the cut-pile embroidery of raffia cloth. Portrait statues commemorate Bushoong kings, and masquerades dramatize the origins of and matrilineal succession to kingship.

Islam and Christianity are as much African religions as the cults of local deities, ancestors and spirit forces. Yet the identification of an Islamic art for sub-Saharan Africa is not straightforward. Is it the art of people who are Muslim, or the art of populations some of whom are Muslim, or art forms that are part of the liturgical practice and theological perceptions of Islam, or art forms that draw upon Islamic source material, or what? These questions can be explored through architecture and the decorative arts in Mauritania, Mali, the Hausa-Fulani emirates of northern Nigeria, the Sudan, and Somalia and coastal northeast and east Africa. However, many of the well-known monumental buildings of Mali were in fact reconstructed within a French colonial rule that, like the British in northern Nigeria, privileged Islam. In contrast, however, the ongoing reconstruction of housing in the Hausa-Fulani city of Zaria that marks the development of families indicates that the current perceptions of conformity to Islamic ideals is largely a twentieth-century phenomenon. Likewise the rebuilding of houses in Nubia, and the consequent emergence of new styles of decorative art, was contingent upon the wealth generated by twentieth-century migrant laborers. In Somalia and East Africa, the distinctive forms of architecture and design developed in response to Islam and the Indian Ocean trade.

There is also the relationship, invariably complex and often heterodox, between Islam and local tradition, especially as documented in Mali. The same applies to discussion of the development of Christianity, especially in Ethiopia where traditions in art and architecture developed within a local Coptic Christianity transmitted along the Nile valley, but with later influences from Catholic imagery through the Portuguese. The other source of African Christianity, nineteenth-century missionary activity, has been manifestly successful elsewhere through the sub-Saharan region, and from the mid-twentieth century onward has sometimes provided patronage for the emerging modernisms in art.

However, while each of these examples allows one to understand relationships developing through specific time periods between political authority, trade, art, religion, and technology, in their concentration upon kingdoms and states there is the danger of overlooking other kinds of art history. First, the works themselves have histories. Secondly, in a number of documented masquerade traditions in West and Central Africa (for example: Mende, Sierra Leone; Yoruba and Ebira, Nigeria; Chewa, Zambia; Pende, Congo/Zaire) there are temporal dimension embedded within performance. It is not just a matter of mythic references but rather that, imploded within a current format of performance, one can distinguish successive layers of incorporation. In other words, one sometimes finds in performance the traces of a history specific to that performance. Third, the life histories of communities and individuals are invariably configured through successive performances. Artifacts may be made to encode the memories of events (Luba memory boards in Zaire/Congo, or the use of sculpture in the didactic context of southern African initiations to adulthood). The passage of time is marked, for example, or new sets of elders are created, or the physiological and social standing of women are marked. Lines of development can thus be traced in several dimensions of historical understanding.

MAKING ONE'S MARK

Through art people hold things in common. People place things in the world and place themselves (in relation to one another) thereby. The world is rendered social by the marks people make. Buildings and the layout of communities are cases in point. So too are the boundaries between the tracts of land belonging to different communities; or the terracing of farmland by hillside peoples; or the yam heaps of a Tiv farmer, Nigeria, carefully shaped to give aesthetic satisfaction. By means of selective breeding, castration and other techniques the prize ox, the supreme object of aesthetic

devotion for Nuer and Dinka pastoralists was manufactured. By various means the human body is socialized through marking, cutting, reshaping, oiling, painting, dressing, shaving, and so forth. Whether these markings-out are primarily the exercise of a concern with form as if for its own sake, or whether they have connotations of other kinds can only be discerned through particular case-study detail. There are some obvious contrasts: forms that signify protection from the evil eye (Berber tattooing and decorative arts), forms that simply look good (Tiv scarification, S E Nuba male body paint), forms that signify changes in physiological (Nuba female scarification), social (East African pastoralists), and political (Giriama) status. All of these examples show that it is possible to identify in them aesthetic fields in which the perception, assessment, and evaluation of forms are matters of local interest. It is also relevant that artifacts themselves (Somalia, for example) can provide the stimulus for the invention of poetic form.

In this context the comment of the Nigerian printmaker, Bruce Onobrakpeya, is particularly relevant: "body marking is a corner-stone in all African art" (Onobrakpeya, 139). There are many parts of Africa where decorating the body, socializing it by one means or another, constitutes the entire visual field of aesthetic practice. Yet, in those areas of sub-Saharan Africa where sculpture is a major art form, one of its most obvious features is the way it can provide a catalog, internal to the social environment concerned, of the forms of body art, often documenting elements that continue to exist only through the medium of sculpture. Moreover, it is possible to argue that African sculpture never shows a naked body, but the person already socialized through an art prior to sculpture.

MASKS AND IDENTITIES

Bodily transformations through the personal arts inevitably lead to masquerade. They are very far from being the same kinds of activity, however. In personal art the socialized body is constituted. In masquerade, that socially constituted person is redefined, although exactly how that is achieved, and the nature and significance of that redefinition is far from simple; and there are exceptions, as when social identity is heightened rather than denied in virtue of masked performance (Yoruba *efe/gelede* is a case in point). Part of the problem is that *mask* is a word with complex histories within a European history of ideas. Using "mask" to speak of works of art in Africa cannot be straightforward; and sometimes it is simply confusing. So what does happen when someone puts on a mask? With what are the mask its performer identified? Nothing can be taken for granted. Yet two of the most striking things about masquerade are its utility in addressing almost every aspect of social life, and in dramatizing issues of social change. Some masked performance traditions focus upon concerns with play, gender, and power (metaphysical energy, political strategy, legitimation, authority). Moreover, through the use of masks, the identities, variously, of communities, kings, elders, descent groups, age sets, trading corporations, and so on, are enacted.

It is also characteristic of masquerade throughout Africa, with rare exceptions, that women are in some sense placed socially by their exclusion, more or less, from performance. The Sande/Bondo complex in Sierra Leone and adjacent regions is the great exception. Senior Mende women are the spouses of the aboriginal spirit inhabitants, embodied in the masks women control, of the forests colonized in the sixteenth century. Finally, masquerade is by no means a static property. In Mali, Dogon people perform in masks for the tourists that depict a "traditionalism" as expected by their audience, as well as performances on other occasions for themselves that respond to local social change. Masquerade is both the trace and the representation of local history.

IMAGE AND FORM
Several published cases studies look at the relationship between visual and verbal imagery, and wider contexts of ritual and political institutions. For example, Kalabari sculpture has been presented as a "language of signs" for the benefit of the spirits of the Niger delta (other than which, this analogy is highly problematic). In contrast, the ritual and paraphernalia of the Yoruba thunder god, ancestor of the kings of Oyo, has been explored in the complete absence of verbal explanation by looking at the wider significances of colors and dance movements. The art of Benin City has been studied

for the way it participates in the constitution of authority. However, although this is an art made through five or six centuries, the published accounts of it depend upon twentieth-century ethnography and local historical writing in a context of reconstruction following the destruction of the city and the removal of its art by British forces in 1897. The differing ways in which this art is thus now seen as bearing the complex traces of a heroic past, and the use of twentieth-century data in the interpretation of artworks made through the several centuries, can hardly be considered unproblematic.

In Europe one is, of course, habituated to see pictures with captions and have them explained in catalogs, whereas for many African traditions the relationship between the visual and the verbal is far from as obvious. Indeed as in the case of the paraphernalia of the Yoruba thunder god it was absent. Yet there are two examples, Lega and Asante, in which artifacts work as mnemonic referrals to proverbs and aphorisms, which is perhaps closer to "Western" habits than one might have expected.

The work of visual metaphors in art obviously deserve attention as providing access to local interpretations of visual imagery. One must also consider how visual metaphors differ from the metaphorical connotations of the ingredients of magical medicine, often found in conjunction with visual images, also revealing an imaginative perception of things. Kongo and Kuba usages indeed suggest that while visual metaphors are concerned with defining what people know, the preparation of magical medicines entails the use of metaphors capable of actualization as energy. Blier's 1995 study of Dahomean magical statuary supports this interpretation. Moreover, the distinctions that can be identified between metaphor and synechdoche in the interpretation of art and the making of magical medicine provides intriguing insight into the "mechanisms" of the intellectual, imaginative and poetic processes materialized in art.

TECHNOLOGY, TRADITION, AND LUREX
Woven, dyed, and printed textiles, especially from the eighteenth century onward, allow scholars to assess many questions about form and aesthetics, tradition and innovation, agency, and identity. This assessment must also pay attention to the technical

means at textile artists' disposal: the loom types, weave structures, raw materials (whether local or imported, including, of course, the laminated plastic fibers marketed as lurex), and so forth. The formation and success of Asante promoted the demand for patterned textiles, and in the 1730s European traders observed local textile artists unravelling imported silk and woollen cloths in order to reweave the yarn with locally hand-spun cotton. Indeed, the responses to novel yarns, colors, design interests, and consumer demands can be noted in many parts of West Africa. Among Hausa embroiderers the sewing machine has generated a set of patterns quite distinct from the hand embroidered tradition. The Kuba embroidered raffia cloth, display an obsession of pattern that has given rise to a dynamic of pattern exploration; and yet in contrast this tradition seems to have been particularly resistant to change.

Other well-documented aspects of textile design include Yoruba traditions of resist-dyeing, Asante printing, and Fante applique. These fabrics illustrate design interests as well as local perceptions of social change; and they are among the local bases for the late-nineteenth-century reception and popularity of industrially produced yet exotic fabrics based upon Indonesian wax batiks and the consequent inception of a new field of textile interest. In East Africa a tradition of hand-block printing from India has given rise to a quite separate industrial design tradition.

TRADITION AND THE TWENTIETH CENTURY
Neither the diversity of local traditions that are among the resources used by artists in the developments in art of the present century, nor the shared experiences of colonial rule, while promoting distinct ethnic and national identities, can be reduced to a common narrative or aesthetic. Ideas about spirit doubles, familiars and spouses, about the healing energies of masks, mythic heroes and magical medicines, are widespread alongside Islam and Christianity. Coincidentally, the twentieth-century European interest in African art together with the development of a local middle class have sometimes brought more work to local artists than in the past. It will be evident that a sense of tradition is fundamental to many aspects of art, but this does not imply stasis, for the word refers to a process of

handing over from one person/region/generation/etc to another that is both social and temporal. This provides for the occasions and possibilities of change such that tradition is not a brake working against creativity or innovation but the framework within which these are possible. An evolving tradition can be the agent of other forms of development as well as their representation.

However, if one limits one's attention only to those traditions inherited from the past one is guilty of inventing an "African art" that bears only little resemblance to the diversity of extant and contemporary practice. In Liberia and Sierra Leone from the 1850s an African-American photographer was active, while Europeans also arrived with photographic equipment and West Africans travelling to Europe, usually to take higher degrees, brought photographic skills back with them. From the 1850s onward one can see photography as a developing African visual practice, with portraiture emerging as a local interest in the new medium. By the beginning of the twentieth century a young man in Lagos, Aina Onabolu, initiated local interest in easel painting and art education, which led to developments within the colonial education system in several countries throughout Africa; and these developments were almost invariably taken up in the context of reiterating local and national identities in opposition to colonial rule. Senegal, Ghana, Nigeria, Uganda, Sudan and South Africa were the pioneers (though in the latter case one has also to take account of apartheid).

In Nigeria in the late 1950s a group of students set about reforming their teaching program to give attention to the indigenous art traditions of the country. They believed then, as indeed they do still, that these differing traditions could enrich a modern Nigerian art and promote a sense of national identity and that a synthesis was possible between modern art techniques and indigenous forms. In contrast, in Senegal its first president, Léopold Sédar Senghor, continued to promote his philosophy and aesthetic of Négritude, originally formulated in 1930s Paris in consequence of the unexpected experience of racism. In Ghana, local culture was celebrated with all the visual realism of advertising.

In Uganda, existing local resources were less adaptable and students were encouraged to look more widely at the art of the continent. In the Sudan, a synthesis was achieved between the forms of Islamic calligraphy and local design. In South Africa, art education was forbidden to black South Africans within the education permitted under apartheid, with the result that overt and cover projects were initiated to enable all South Africans access to the forms and technologies of the twentieth century. Art making was thus inevitably part of the strategies of opposition to apartheid. In conclusion, it can be said that not only is art alive and well in Africa, and flourishing in many guises, but that its continued florescence is the current manifestation of a history of art of greater antiquity than in any other continent of the world.

See also **Art; Arts; Fetish and Fetishism; Masks and Masquerades; Senghor, Léopold Sédar.**

BIBLIOGRAPHY

Abiodun, Rowland, Henry John Drewal, and John Pemberton III, eds. *The Yoruba Artist*. Washington, DC: Smithsonian Institution, 1994.

Agthe, Johanna. *Wegzeichen—Signs: Art from East Africa*. Frankfort am Main: Museum fur Volkerkunde, 1990.

Anthology of African and Indian Ocean Photography. Paris: Revue Noire, 1999.

Arnoldi, Mary Jo. *Playing with Time*. Washington, DC: Smithsonian Institution, 1995.

Barley, Nigel. *Foreheads of the Dead*. Washington, DC: Smithsonian Institution, 1988.

Bassani, Ezio, and William Fagg. *Africa and the Renaissance*. New York: The Center for African Art, 1988.

Biebuyck, Daniel. *Lega Culture*. Berkeley: University of California, 1973.

Bradbury, R. E. *Benin Studies*. New York: Oxford University Press, 1973.

Cole, Herbert M. *Mbari: Art and Life among the Owerri Igbo*. Bloomington: Indiana University Press, 1982.

Colleyn, Jean-Paul, ed. *Bamana*. New York: Museum for African Art, 2001.

Deliss, Clementine, et al. *Seven Stories about Modern Art in Africa*. London: Whitechapel Art Gallery, 1995.

Elliot, David, et al. *Art from South Africa*. Oxford: Museum of Modern Art, 1990.

Evans-Pritchard, E. E. *The Nuer*. Oxford: Oxford University Press, 1940.

Fall, N'Gone, and Jean-Loup Pivin, eds. *Anthologie de l'art Afrique du XXe siecle*. Paris: Revue Noire, 2001.

Fosu, Kojo. *20th Century Art of Africa*, rev. edition. Accra: Artists Alliance, 1993.

Fund, Prince Claus, ed. *The Art of African Fashion*. Trenton, NJ: Africa World Press, 1998.

Gardi, Bernard, et al. *Boubou − c'est chic*. Basel: Christoph Merian Verlag, 2000.

Garlake, Peter. *Early Art and Architecture of Africa*. New York: Oxford University Press, 2002.

Girshick Ben-Amos, Paula. *The Art of Benin*, 2nd edition. London: British Museum, 1995.

Glaze, Anita. *Art and Death in a Senufo Village*. Bloomington: Indiana University Press, 1981.

Harney, Elizabeth. *Ethiopian Passages: Contemporary Art from the Diaspora*. Washington, DC: National Museum of African Art, 2003.

Harney, Elizabeth. *In Senghor's Shadow: Art, Politics and the Avant-Garde in Senegal, 1960–1995*. Durham, NC: Duke University Press, 2004.

Hassan, Salah, et al. *Authentic/Ex-Centric: Conceptualism in Contemporary African Art*. Ithaca, NY: Forum for African Arts, 2001.

Heldman, Marilyn, et al. *African Zion: The Sacred Arts of Ethiopia*. New Haven, CT: Yale University Press, 1993.

Herreman, Frank, ed. *Liberated Voices: Contemporary Art from South Africa*. New York: The Museum for African Art, 1999.

Horton, Robin. *Kalabari Sculpture*. Lagos: Nigerian Museum, 1967.

Kwami, Atta, "Ghanaian Art in a Time of Change." In *Ghana, Yesterday and Today*, ed. Christiane Falgayrettes-Leveau and Christiane Owusu-Sarpong. Paris: Musee Dapper, 2003.

Kwami, Atta, et al. *Kumasi Junction*. Llandudno, Wales: Oriel Mostyn Gallery, 2002.

Lawal, Babatunde. *The Gelede Spectacle*. Seattle: University of Washington, 1996.

Loughran, Katheryne S., et al., eds. *Somalia in Word and Image*. Washington, DC: The Foundation for Cross Cultural Understanding in Cooperation with Indiana University Press, Bloomington, 1986.

MacGaffey, Wyatt, and Michael Harris. *Astonishment and Power*. Washington, DC: Smithsonian Institution, 1995.

Mack, John. *Emil Torday and the Art of the Congo*. London: British Museum, 1990.

Magnin, Andre, ed. *Seydou Keita*. Zurich: First Scalo Edition, 1997.

Magubane, Peter, and Sandra Klopper. *African Renaissance*. London: Struik, 2000.

McLeod, Malcolm. *The Asante*, London: British Museum, 1981.

Miles, Elza. *Polly Street: The Story of an Art Centre*. Pretoria: Ampersand Foundation, 2004.

Murray, Barbara, and John Picton, eds. *Transitions: Botswana, Namibia, Mozambique, Zambia, Zimbabwe, 1960–2004*. London: Africa Centre, 2005.

Oguibe, Olu, and Okwui Enwezor, eds. *Reading the Contemporary: African Art from Theory to the Marketplace*. Cambridge, MA: MIT Press, 1999.

Oliver, Paul, ed. *Shelter in Africa*. London: Barrie and Jenkins, 1971.

Onobrakpeya, Bruce. *The Spirit in Ascent*. Lagos: Ovuomaroro Gallery, 1992.

Ottenberg, Simon. *Masked Rituals of Afikpo*. Seattle: University of Washington, 1975.

Ottenberg, Simon. *New Traditions from Nigeria*. Washington, DC: Smithsonian Institution, 1997.

Phillips, Ruth. *Representing Woman*. Los Angeles: University of California, 1995.

Phillips, Tom, ed. *Africa: The Art of a Continent*. London: Royal Academy of Arts, 1995.

Picton, John, and John Mack. *African Textiles*. London: British Museum, 1989.

Picton, John, et al. *The Art of African Textiles: Technology, Tradition and Lurex*. London: Barbican Art Gallery, 1999.

Picton, John, et al., eds. *Action and Vision: Painting and Sculpture in Ethiopia, Kenya and Uganda from 1980*. London: Triangle Arts Trust, 2002.

Preston Blier, Suzanne. *The Anatomy of Architecture: Ontology and Metaphor in Batammaliba Architectural Expression*. Cambridge, U.K.: Cambridge University Press, 1987.

Preston Blier, Suzanne. *African Vodun*. Chicago: University of Chicago, 1995.

Ravenhill, Philip L. *Dreams and Reverie: Images of Otherworld Mates among the Baule, West Africa*. Washington, DC: Smithsonian Institution, 1996.

Richards, Polly. "Imina Sangan, or 'Masques a la mode.'" In *Re-Visions: New Perspectives on the African Collections in the Horniman Museum*, ed. Karel Arnaut. London: Horniman Museum and Gardens; [Coimbra, Portugal]: Museu Antropológico da Universidade de Coimbra, 2000.

Roberts, Alan, and Mary Nooter Roberts. *A Saint in the City: Sufi Arts of Urban Senegal*. Los Angeles: University of California, 2003.

Ross, Doran H. *Wrapped in Pride*. Los Angeles: University of California, 1998.

Rubin, Arnold, ed. *The Marks of Civilization*. Los Angeles: University of California, 1998.

Sack, Steven. *The Neglected Tradition*. Johannesburg: Johannesburg Art Gallery, 1988.

Secretan, Thierry. *Going into Darkness*. London: Thames and Hudson, 1995.

Siroto, Leon. "Gon: A Mask Used in Competition for Leadership." In *African Art and Leadership*, ed. Douglas Fraser and Herbert Cole. Madison: University of Wisconsin Press, 1972.

Strother, Zoe. *Inventing Masks*. Chicago: University of Chicago, 1998.

Walker, Roslyn. *Olowe of Ise: A Yoruba Sculptor to Kings*. Washington, DC: Smithsonian Institute, 1998.

Wenzel, Marian. *House Decoration in Nubia*. Toronto: University of Toronto Press, 1972.

Wescott, Joan, and Peter Morton Williams. "The Symbolism and Ritual Context of The Yoruba Laba Shango." *Journal of the Royal Anthropological Institute* (1962).

Willett, Frank. *African Art*. London: Thames and Hudson, 2002.

Williamson, Sue. *Resistance Art in South Africa*. Cape Town: David Philip, 1998.

Williamson, Sue, and Jamal Ashraf. *Art in South Africa: The Future Present*. Cape Town: David Philip, 1996.

Younge, Gavin. *Art of the South African Townships*. London: Thames & Hudson, 1988.

JOHN PICTON

ARTS

This entry includes the following articles:
BASKETRY AND MAT MAKING
BEADS
SCULPTURE

BASKETRY AND MAT MAKING

Both men and women make a wide range of utensils and artifacts in basketry and matting. Vegetable materials are used primarily; other types include wood, palm leaves, reeds, grasses, and roots, which are usually available locally. Decorative effects come from texture, such as the alternation of shiny and matte surfaces; and varying plaiting and stitching techniques; or from the use of color, such as combining natural with black or dyed colors in patterns. Sometimes leather is applied to reinforce the base or rim, often ornamentally.

TOOLS OF BASKETRY AND MAT MAKING

The tools of basketry are simple, and may include a sharp knife, an awl, a mallet, or a needle, and a bowl of water in which to soak the elements. There are two primary basketmaking techniques. The first is plaiting (often called weaving, although since weaving should involve a loom, this is not strictly correct). Plaited baskets may be composed of plain over-and-under plaits; they may be variously twilled or twined in different patterns. The second, sewn basketry—often called coil-sewn—involves a thin continuous foundation, usually of grass, sewn spirally on itself, using split palm leaf, raffia, or similar fiber. Some baskets are so tightly sewn that they become watertight when the fibers have swelled. Other sewn basketry may have the foundation elements plaited or lying in parallel rows, sewn together, and then sewn to the rest of the basket.

BASKETS

Most baskets are used as containers to store food and trinkets, carry goods, and serve food. Basketry techniques are also used in the framework for thatched roofs and in wattle-and-daub walling. Fish weirs, combined with conical valve traps, are a form of basketry widely used in Congo and surrounding areas, as are finger-stall traps to catch small animals. Large storage pots may be reinforced with a basketwork casing. In food preparation, winnowing utensils and flour strainers are made of baskets, often decoratively patterned, as among the Mbundu of Zambia.

In beer making, funnel-shaped beer strainers, drinking straws with a sieve at the end, and strainer spoons are used. Basketry techniques are used in clothing, especially hats, which come in a variety of forms, colors, and plaits, ornamented with fiber tufts, feathers, fur, and leather. Beaded crowns among the Yoruba of Nigeria and older-style beaded headdresses have a basketry foundation. Over much of eastern Africa, from the Horn southward, ornamental baskets embellished with cowries, beads, dyed leather, and metal dangles, finely made in a range of colors, may form part of a bride's trousseau and wedding decorations or may be presented as an honorific gift. Some dance masks are made of basketry or of barkcloth on a wicker frame as among the Cokwe of Angola and Zambia.

MATS

Mats differ from baskets in that they are flat. They are made as ground coverings on which to sleep or sit, or for use as a surface to catch flour as it is ground. Flexible mats tied to a hooped framework form roof coverings among the nomadic Somali. Rigid mats, decoratively patterned in black on natural pale-yellow background, form house walls in the Congo basin area. Several techniques are used in mat making, including finger plaiting over a large surface, joining aligned split reeds with needle and twine, and plaiting a long, narrow strip of split palm leaf and then sewing the butted edges to make a broad mat.

THE ART OF TWILLING

Twilling consists of the interweaving of two elements of equal thickness and flexibility, whereby at least some strands pass over or under two or more strands in the opposite direction. Twilling is used in various African cultures to produce rectangular mats, circular basket trays, and cylinders and cones.

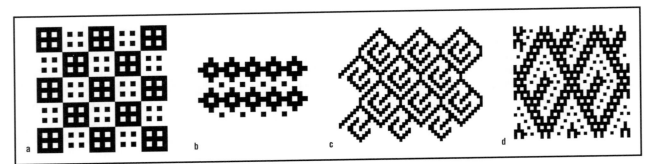

Figure 1. Examples of Yombe patterns, each with a different symmetry structure. COURTESY OF PAULUS GERDES

Rectangular Mats. Rectangular mats may be plaited in two ways; either the strands are parallel to the sides of the mat or they make angles of 45 degrees with the sides. In his 2004 article "Symmetries on Mats Woven by Yombe Women from the Lower Congo Area," Paulus Gerdes analyzes symmetries on sleeping and sitting mats of the first type, plaited by Yombe women from the lower Congo at the end of the nineteenth and beginning of the twentieth centuries. The decorative designs, called *mabuinu*, represent elements of the human body, animals, plants, or aspects of Yombe ethics and social order. A design motif may be repeated to form patterns. Figure 1 displays examples of Yombe patterns, each with a different symmetry structure.

Makhuwa artisans in northeastern Mozambique make mats whose strands form 45 degree angles with the plaited sides. They use the same technique to produce bands to decorate, for example, hats. Similar bands are woven in Tanzania and Uganda (see Figure 2). As the strands are "reflected" in the sides of the band, a particular class of designs and strip patterns is produced.

Circular Basket Trays. Circular basket trays have been produced in several African countries, from Guinea and Senegal (e.g., among the Bedik and Bassari) in West Africa to Angola on the Atlantic coast and countries on the eastern shore. Schematically circular basket trays are made in the following way: a square plaited mat is fastened to a circular rim, then the outstanding strands are either cut off or interlaced with the rim. It may be easier to fasten the square mat to the rim if its midlines are visible.

Among the Changana in southern Mozambique men make them and they are called *rihlèlò* (plural: *tinhlèlò*). Most *tinhlèlò* are used daily both in the household (for instance, for winnowing maize) and for exhibiting agricultural products for sale such as bananas, cashews, and peanuts. They are woven plainly, "over two, under two" (2/2), without introducing any particular design. A few exceptionally talented artisan-artists break the regular plain weave to introduce designs, often accented with plant strips colored before interlacing. Often the design has two axes of symmetry, making it easier to fasten the initially square plaited mat to the circular wooden rim.

Ipadge trays among the Makhuwa of northeastern Mozambique employ a spiral structure where the center of the spiral structure coincides with the center of the tray, displaying a rotational symmetry. Makhuwa basket weavers also produce a type of container, called *nivuku* (plural: *mavuku*), used to keep and transport food or valuable objects like jewelry. The container consists of two circular

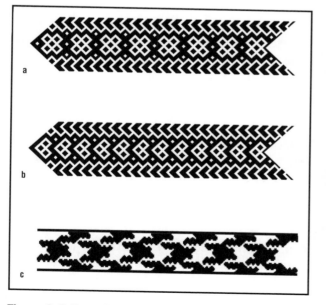

Figure 2. Patterns for woven hat bands from Tanzania and Uganda. COURTESY OF PAULUS GERDES

Figure 3. Nivuku (plural: mavuku), used to keep and transport food or valuable objects like jewelry. The container consists of two circular trays, one being the lid and the other the base of the container. COURTESY OF PAULUS GERDES

trays, being the lid and the other the base of the container (see Figure 3), made by the old basket weaver Mulaliha. In the twenty-first century, only a very few basket weavers produce *mavuku*.

Gerdes's book *The Circle and the Square* (2000) presents a comparative analysis of the production of circular basket trays. Various chapters of Gerdes's *Basketry, Geometry, and Symmetry in Africa and the Americas* (2004a) deal with circular basket trays from Mozambique and Angola.

Cylinders and Cones. Plaited cylinders or cones appear in baskets, handbags, and hats. Frequently strip patterns or plane patterns may be observed.

See also **Architecture: Domestic; Art; Body Adornment and Clothing; Masks and Masquerades.**

BIBLIOGRAPHY

Gerdes, Paulus. *Geometry from Africa: Mathematical and Educational Explorations.* Washington, DC: The Mathematical Association of America, 1999.

Gerdes, Paulus. *Le cercle et le carré: Créativité géométrique, artistique, et symbolique de vannières et vanniers d'Afrique, d'Amérique, d'Asie et d'Océanie* (The circle and the square). Paris: L'Harmattan, 2000.

Gerdes, Paulus. *Sipatsi: Cestaria e Geometria na Cultura Tonga de Inhambane.* (Sipatsi: basketry and geometry in the Tonga culture of Inhambane). Maputo: Moçambique Editora, 2003.

Gerdes, Paulus. *Basketry, Geometry, and Symmetry in Africa and the Americas.* Belgrade: Visual Mathematics, 2004. Available at http://www.mi.sanu.ac.yu/vismath.

Gerdes, Paulus. "Symmetries on Mats Woven by Yombe Women from the Lower Congo Area: On the Interplay between Cultural Values and Mathematical-Technical Possibilities." In *Symmetry Comes of Age: The Role of Pattern in Culture,* ed. Dorothy K. Washburn and Donald W. Crowe, 81–99. Seattle: University of Washington Press, 2004.

Locke, Marjorie. *The Dove's Footprints. Basketry Patterns in Matabeleland.* Harare: Baobab Books, 1994.

Shaw, E. Margaret. "The Basketwork of Southern Africa." *Annals of the South African Museum* 100, no. 2 (1992): 53–248; 102, no. 8 (1993): 273–301.

Sieber, Roy. *African Furniture and Household Objects.* Bloomington: Indiana University Press, 1980.

MARGRET CAREY
REVISED BY PAULUS GERDES

BEADS

A bead is not a bead unless there is a perforation for threading. Piercing a hole in the selected object makes a perforation, the first essential step in making a bead. Archaeologists believe the earliest hand tool used to make the hole was a sharp thorn. Later on, a sharpened iron bit was used with a bow-drill. In Ilorin, Nigeria, a small mallet was used with a series of sharp needle-like drills of increasing length to pierce jasper beads up to two inches long, working from both ends of the bead. Beads pierced in this way often have a crooked perforation, the ends of which are wider at the mouth than in the center; this method of piercing was applied to beads made from stone, large pieces of shell, coral, bone, or amber.

MATERIALS

Beads are made of many different materials. Among natural materials, there are the perishable ones such as vegetable stems and fibers; shaped wood; dried clay; scented pastes, roots, and tubers; nuts, seeds, and seedpods. Animal products include elephant ivory, teeth, lion and leopard claws, and porcupine quills. Bones range from pieces of large bones or smaller ones such as lengths of bird bone and snake vertebrae. The oldest known African beads are shell beads from Blombos Cave, South Africa, estimated to be 75,000 years old. Some are made from discs of ostrich eggshell, or the large land snail. Marine shells of all sorts are also used: Cowrie shells from the Indian Ocean and olivella shells are in beadmaking and as currency. Coral is important in the court of Great Bénin, Nigeria, and is also worn among the Kalabari of the Niger Delta region. Pearls seem only to occur among the Arabs of the Swahili coast of eastern Africa. Amber, a fossilized resin, and copal, a semifossilized resin, are used to make chunky beads that are highly valued among the peoples of the Sahara region.

Stone beads come mostly from western Africa, where specialist workers make jasper, cornelian, amazonite, bauxite, and granite beads. Metal is also widely used: gold from such regions as Ghana and its adjacent areas, while the Tuareg in the Sahara region use silver, and silversmiths of Jewish, Indian, or Yemeni origin operate in the Swahili coast region of eastern Africa. Otherwise, the most widely used metals are brass, bronze, copper, iron, and aluminum.

Another group of bead materials could be called "found materials." This diverse group includes metal and plastic washers, ballpoint pen caps, metal cartridges, plastic or mother of pearl buttons, and safety pins.

Glass comes first to mind when discussing African beads, because of the prevalence of imported glass seed beads, most of which were exported by Venice (Murano) from the late fifteenth century onward; later, seed beads came from Bohemia (Gablonz) and the Netherlands (Amsterdam). In the late twentieth and the early twenty-first century, India became a prime exporter.

The earliest imported glass beads date from the eighth century, and came from southeastern Asia, entering Africa south of Madagascar. Later, bead imports came via Arab traders using the monsoon winds to make landfall on the eastern African coast. Many beads came in overland from the Mediterranean coast or from Egypt and Sudan, but the real influx of glass beads occurred from the late fifteenth century onward, and came from Europe.

Plastic beads are popular in modern southern Africa, primarily because they are cheaper and lighter than glass. At the start of the twenty-first century a new industry—melting down broken plastic bowls and other goods, and winding the viscous plastic onto metal rods to make colorful beads—emerged in Ghana.

TECHNIQUES

Ostrich eggshell, snail shell, coconut shell, and stiff plastic were shaped into blanks, which were then pierced and threaded on a cord. These were ground down on a stone to make discs, to be worn as a long strand. In Ghana, thick red disc beads of bauxite, an aluminum ore, were made by threading the shaped and pierced blanks onto something rigid, such as a bicycle spoke, then grinding and polishing. Hammering, grinding, and polishing were used to shape hard stone beads. Bead design choices and styles were and are governed by available materials.

At Nupe, in northern Nigeria, waste glass (cullet) is collected and melted down in glass furnaces where groups of five men make beads and bracelets in a manner that has hardly changed since it was first recorded in the early twentieth century.

Imported glass beads were modified in a great variety of ways. Even as early as circa 1000 CE, seed beads from southeast Asia that had entered the country by the southern route were fused together in a mold to make the much larger garden-roller beads found at Mapungubwe and other sites in southern Zimbabwe. In West Africa, modifying beads became a fine art. At Ife, Nigeria, excavations showed that beads were melted down and reformed in the eleventh and twelfth centuries. Thomas Bowdich, writing in 1819, described how the Asante of present-day Ghana ground down and reshaped imported European beads to suit their taste. Other beads were boiled to modify their shape, texture, and color.

Powder-glass beads are most often made in western Africa, and are the most inventive in variety of design, especially in Ghana. Their manufacture is simple but labor intensive, calling for experience and skill. Whole families are involved in collecting, sorting, and grading scrap glass, which is then pounded into a fine powder and fed into molds of various shapes and sizes. Short lengths of cassava stem are inserted into molds before firing to make the perforations. After firing, the sintered glass beads are ground and polished. Colors are determined by the scrap glass used, also from powdered imported beads, and commercial dyes. Designs come from layering different colors of powder-glass, twisting the sintered glass before it has fully set, or applying designs after firing, in a technique similar to enameling. Beads made by the wet-glass firing technique come from Mauritania, in the Kiffa region. There, women mix the powdered glass into a paste with saliva or gum arabic mixed with water; the beads are molded, decorated with powdered glass in colors, and fired.

Metal beads are made out of gold, silver, copper, brass, iron, and aluminum. In Ghana and Côte d'Ivoire, the lost-wax process is used to make gold beads. Many silver, copper, brass, and iron beads are made from short strips that are hammered and bent into a ring form. In Kenya, aluminum, a soft metal gathered from recycled cooking pans, is hammered into a rectangular rod, which is then chopped into bead-sized pieces, and pierced with a nail; the eight corners are then hammered to make distinctive cornerless-cube beads. The material for brass beads comes from melted-down cartridge cases or telegraph wire.

Beads made of metal are always made by men, such as those made in the Nupe kilns. While the dry powder-glass beads are the product of a family team, the design work is carried out by one or more of the men, while women and children do the finishing, threading, and marketing. Exceptionally in the Kiffa area of Mauritania, women are the bead makers.

USES

Beads are used to adorn the person or to decorate objects. Certain beads are worn as status markers; sometimes the sheer number and weight of beads used is significant. Beads can indicate how a baby has grown, that a girl is of marriageable age; that a woman has had her first child, or how her children are progressing through life. A widow might wear no beads at all. Beads can decorate ornaments for the marriage room and adorn religious figures and insignia. Some beads are awarded to brave warriors and hunters. Among the Yoruba of Nigeria, chiefs wear heavy robes and slippers covered in beadwork; there, and in neighboring Cameroon, royal thrones and regalia are likewise covered in seed beads strung in decorative designs. In southern Africa, seed bead dress ornaments show the local and social identity of the wearer.

Royal necklet from Bemba of Zambia (pre-1900). The necklet is made with glass trade beads and triangular ivory beads to imitate the rare *conus* shell from the Indian Ocean. Note: The circular base of the *conus* shell was halved, pierced, and ground into a triangle. Registration number A.1906 from the Adam Purves Collection. COURTESY OF TRUSTEES, NATIONAL MUSEUMS OF SCOTLAND, EDINBURGH. PHOTOGRAPH BY MARGRET CAREY

VALUES

Beads become valuable if made of scarce materials. To begin with, glass beads were valuable imports and the right to wear them was controlled by the local king. In Benin City, Nigeria, the use of coral beads from the Mediterranean was restricted to members of the royal family and court, and had to be recharged in an annual ceremony. In central Africa, beads made from *conus* shells, which were transported over hundreds of miles from the eastern coast, were reserved for important people, as were cowrie shells. Apart from beads made of especially significant materials such as elephant ivory (reserved for royalty), wearing beads in quantity was a major status marker, since they cost money. Thus a chief wearing regalia heavy with beads, or a young South African man with numerous beaded ornaments made for him by young women who hope to attract him as a suitor, show how beads can enhance personal image.

See also **Art; Body Adornment and Clothing; Masks and Masquerades.**

BIBLIOGRAPHY

Carey, Margret. *Beads and Beadwork of East and South Africa.* Princes Risborough, U.K.: Shire Books, 1986.

Carey, Margret. *Beads and Beadwork of West and Central Africa.* Princes Risborough, U.K.: Shire Books, 1991.

Fisher, Angela. *Africa Adorned.* London: Collins, 1984.

Hodge, Alison. *Nigeria's Traditional Crafts.* London: Ethnographica, 1982.

MARGRET CAREY

SCULPTURE

Carving, which shapes a solid by cutting, is the act or art of sculpture, especially in wood or ivory. The term also covers modeling in clay, cast metals, and engraving. In Africa, carving is traditionally men's work, for it is widely believed that a woman's fertility would suffer if she were to make something representational. Many carved masks are kept hidden, as the sight of them is believed to be dangerous to women and children.

In sub-Saharan Africa, carving produces more than sculpture and art. Many utilitarian objects that are mass produced in Western society are individually made to a customer's requirements, and a number of these items are carved. Tool handles for axes, adzes, and hoes; dugout boats; stools and headrests in a variety of forms; containers for food and liquids; mortars and pestles; spoons; knives and their sheaths are some examples. Most are plainly made; others are finely embellished for use by royalty, for ceremonial use, or for special occasions such as wedding feasts. Sculptural carvings include figures, masks, drums, containers, stools, and staffs with figures; they may be embellished with fur, feathers, metal, or beads.

Carving tools are simple. An axe to fell trees or cut off branches has the an edge sharpened on both faces, and a blade set along a line parallel to the handle. An adze has the blade set at right angles to the handle, and the cutting edge is sharpened on one face, like a chisel. Sometimes an axe head is hafted transversely to make an improvised adze. Adzes are used for most of the shaping and fine finishing of a carving. A gouge, formed of a knife blade curved into a near-circle and set in a long handle, is used to hollow out mortars, drums, dugouts, and the inner or back cavities of masks. A knife, normally sharpened on both edges, or a chisel, with an oblique cutting edge at one end, may be used for further shaping. If the carver wants a really smooth effect, a rough-surfaced leaf is used like sandpaper.

The type of ornament used distinguishes "quality" artifacts from purely utilitarian varies. The simplest is pyrogravure—blackening the wood surface with a hot iron blade in broad areas or in fine lines combined with incised patterns. The outsides of calabashes are often decorated with a combination of burned and incised linear patterns. Incised pattern (chip) carving can be used to artistic effect on headrests, snuff bottles, spoon handles, and knife sheaths. Stools and headrests belonging to important people tend to be ornamented in the regional style, whether by chip carving over the surface or by incorporating a carved animal or human figure as a support.

These articles are usually made of wood, which is generally cut as needed, whether just a branch or a whole tree. If a tree is felled, the wood carver may make a propitiatory offering to that tree's spirit. Easily carved, straight-grained woods are preferred for tool handles, spoons, or stools, while hard, termite-resistant wood is selected for carved house posts in prestigious dwellings.

Basic carving, such as axe handles, requires no specialized ability. Often the local blacksmith combines ironworking with woodworking and will fit a handle to the metal tool he has just made. He will also make food vessels, stools, and drums on commission. On a higher level, there may be one man in an area who is known for his good craftsmanship; he might spend most of his time carving. A master carver may travel to his clients or have a workshop with apprentices. His work may be found over a wide area. African carving is now even more widely dispersed due to the spread of "airport art" made for tourists; Kamba "Maasai" salad servers from Kenya and polished ebony Makonde carvings from Tanzania are typical.

In carving, the usual practice is to block out the form in stages, from the basic shape to the finished product. In Yoruba country, in Nigeria, Father Kevin Carroll recorded how the carver first blocks out the main form with an axe or adze; then goes over the same surface and breaks it down into smaller areas, such as the ears and eyes, using an adze or chisel. He will then smooth these surfaces over with chisel or knife, finishing off with the small sharp details of hair and pattern work. Different carvers approach a similar carving in their own way. A master carver teaches his apprentices by giving them an original to copy and by allowing them to carve small pieces on their own, progressing to more important work as their skills improve. Just as in the context of Western art, it is possible to recognize the work of an individual carver, that of his pupils, or work from a specific area.

Since the elephant is often linked with royalty or chiefdom, the use of ivory tends to be restricted. In West Africa, some carvings belong to a sixteenth- to seventeenth-century group known as Afro-Portuguese ivories, believed to be by carvers from Sherbro Island, Sierra Leone, or southern Nigeria, or from the Loango region around the mouth of the Congo River. They include exquisitely carved spoons, bracelets, saltcellars, and end-blown oliphants (horns) and are the earliest known examples of African carvings made for the European market.

Benin City, in southern Nigeria, had a guild of ivory carvers whose work goes back to the early sixteenth century. The earliest examples of their work include beautiful hip masks and intricately carved armlets inlaid with bronze. Entire carved tusks, scepters, fly whisk handles, and handheld gongs were made until the eighteenth century. Some Yoruba ivory carvings in the Owo style were also found in Benin City, but because elephants were slaughtered of for the ivory trade, few ivory carvings from western Africa have been made since the eighteenth century.

Side-blown oliphants made of whole tusks come from many parts of Africa, from Sierra Leone through the western African coast and the Congo basin area. The Lega of the Democratic Republic of the Congo (DRC) make masks and figures of elephant ivory and bone associated with their secret-society system. In eastern and southern Africa, ivory is most usually made into bracelets or armlets in various forms.

Hippopotamus ivory is used in the Congo basin area to make small amulets, especially among the Luba; they can be recognized by the distinctive form that follows the curve of the tusk. The Pende, also of the DRC, use elephant and hippopotamus ivory, bone, and wood to make miniature masks worn as pendants.

The southern Bantu carve bone into snuff spoons and hairpins. Rhinoceros horn is carved into long-handled clubs, and also into snuff bottles, in southeastern Africa. Buffalo horn is made into ceremonial drinking horns in the grassland region of Cameroon and among the Kuba of the DRC; the great thickness of the horn base allows for deeply carved ornament. Cattle horn is sometimes heated and steamed into shape as well as carved, making snuffboxes on the ends of long hairpins, crafted and used in southern Africa. The southern Sotho made bone and horn knife handles and sheaths in a distinctive style.

There are several groups of brass, iron, or alloy objects that may be thought of as engraved—and therefore carved. These include the large forged and incised anklets worn by Igbo (Ibo) women of south Nigeria, repoussé brass trays or jugs made among the Nupe of northern Nigeria, and brass collars and bracelets with incised ornament from the Congo basin.

Stone is carved wherever suitable outcrops of soft stone, usually steatite (soapstone) are found. The ancestor heads and small figures locally called *nomoli* or *pomdo* from Mende or Kissi country in Sierra Leone may date to the sixteenth century. A large number of soapstone heads and figures come from the Yoruba town of Esie in northern Yoruba-land, in Nigeria. The figures called *mintadi* by the Kongo of western DRC may represent former kings. The Kisii of Kenya make soapstone bowls for the tourist market; soapstone pipe bowls were made in southern Africa. Newly quarried soapstone is soft enough to be carved with an adze or knife and smoothed down with sand or rough leaves. The porous white coral found off the eastern African coast and in the Red Sea was much quarried to build mosques, palaces, and other permanent buildings along the Swahili coast.

Clay is also carved. Many smoking-pipe bowls are made by modeling the form as a rough block around a stem, allowing it to dry "leather hard," then carving it with a sharp knife and polishing it. Many are fired, while others harden through use. Most of these bowls are plain and functional, but the Asante of Ghana, several of the Cameroon groups such as the Bamun and Bamessing, the Shilluk of Sudan, and the Ila and Tonga of Zambia use this technique to make pipe bowls in various animal forms, which are then fired. In Cameroon, some large ceremonial pipe bowls are up to 10 inches long and elaborately carved.

See also **Art; Body Adornment and Clothing; Masks and Masquerades; Secret Societies.**

BIBLIOGRAPHY

Eyo, Ekpo, and Frank Willett. *Treasures of Ancient Nigeria.* London: Royal Academy of Arts/Collins, 1982.

Fischer, Eberhard, and Hans Himmelheber. *The Arts of the Dan in West Africa.* Zurich: Rietberg Museum, 1984.

Gillon, Werner. *A Short History of African Art.* New York: Viking, 1984.

Ginsberg, Marc. *African Forms.* New York: Skira, 2000.

Sieber, Roy. *African Furniture and Household Objects.* Bloomington: Indiana University Press, 1980.

Willett, Frank. *African Art*, rev. edition. New York: Thames and Hudson, 1993.

MARGRET CAREY

ASANTEWA, YAA (c. 1832–1921). Yaa Asantewa was Queen *Ohemaa* of the Asante town of Edweso in present-day Ghana. In April 1900,

Yaa Asantewa led a three-month siege of the British garrison in the Asante capital of Kumasi. The British had occupied Kumasi in 1896 in their effort to extend military control into the Gold Coast interior. They imposed a heavy indemnity on Asante, and King Prempeh I and a number of his chiefs and elders were deported, first to Sierra Leone and later to the Seychelles. Yaa Asantewa's grandson, Kwasi Afrane II of the Edweso stool (throne), was said to have been among those exiled. During the conflict, the sacred Asante Golden Stool was hidden from the British. In 1900, British governor Sir Frederick Hodgson arrived in Kumasi to demand payment of the indemnity and surrender of the Golden Stool. It was in response to such demands, especially with regard to the sacred stool, that notables of Kumasi and the outlying towns including Edweso rose in rebellion against the British.

Yaa Asantewa led the uprising. The three-month siege caused great hardships to the British garrison in Kumasi. Following the successful pacification of the Asante capital, Yaa Asantewa was also exiled in May 1901 to the Seychelles, where she died twenty-one years later.

See also **Prempeh, Agyeman; Queens and Queen Mothers.**

BIBLIOGRAPHY

Boahen, Adu A. "A Nation in Exile: The Asante on Seychelles Island, 1900–24." In *The Golden Stool: Studies of the Asante Center and Periphery*, ed. Enid Schildkrout. New York: American Museum of Natural History, 1987.

Boahen, A. Adu. *Yaa Asantewaa and the Asante-British War of 1900–1*. Accra, Ghana: Sub-Saharan Publishers; Oxford: J. Currey, 2003.

Lewin, Thomas J. *Asante before the British: The Prempean Years, 1875–1900*. Lawrence: Regent's Press of Kansas, 1978.

Sweetman, David. *Women Leaders in African History*. London: Heinemann, 1984.

DAVID OWUSU-ANSAH

ASMARA. Now the capital of Eritrea, Asmara was originally a minor Tigre village located in the Eritrean highlands southwest of Massawa, an ancient port on the Red Sea coast. It began to assume importance in the region during the latter half of the nineteenth century when Emperor Yohannes IV of Ethiopia made it the headquarters for his army. Menelik, who succeeded Yohannes IV to the Ethiopian throne, ceded Asmara and several other towns to Italy in 1889, in return for Italian recognition of his imperial status. During the late 1800s, Italy expanded its territorial presence in the region, and by 1890 Asmara became the capital of Italy's colony of Eritrea. By 1925 the population of the town had reached approximately 10,000.

Asmara's period of greatest growth occurred in the early 1930s, when the Italians built up the city center. In 1935, the city served as the principal point from which Italy launched its attack on Ethiopia in an effort to expand Italian colonial holdings in the region. In 1941 the city fell under British administration, which continued until 1952, when a United Nations resolution federated Ethiopia and Eritrea. At the time of federation, Asmara became the capital of Ethiopia's Eritrea Province. With Eritrean independence in 1993, Asmara reassumed the status of national capital.

Asmara's population was estimated at around 430,000 in the early 1990s, but that figure declined to about 400,000 in 2004. The majority of Asmara's population are Tigre speakers and members of the Ethiopian Orthodox Church. There is, as well, a large Muslim community and a sizable contingent of Italian residents.

See also **Eritrea; Menelik II.**

BIBLIOGRAPHY

Hill, Justin. *Ciao Asmara: A Classic Account of Contemporary Africa*. London: Abacus, 2002.

NANCY E. GRATTON

ASMA'U, NANA (1793–1864). Asma'u bint Usman dan Fodiyo was a female West African Sufi scholar, poet, and teacher. Widely known by her honorific, Nana, Asma'u was a Sunni Muslim of the Qadiriyya order, born in the northwest region of the country in present-day Nigeria. As a daughter of Shehu 'Uthman dan Fodio, leader of the Sokoto jihad (1804–1830), Asma'u was from her youth keenly aware of the social welfare needs created by jihad warfare. She spent much of her energy negotiating help for the widowed and orphaned, according to Qur'anic precepts. The Fodiyo clan was actively intellectual; both Asma'u's father and her brother, Caliph Bello, wrote treatises and poetry. Like both men and women of the family, Asma'u was taught by her mother and grandmothers. She was literate in Arabic, Fulfulde, and Hausa at a young age, and was also fluent in Tamchek.

Asma'u memorized the Qur'an in her youth, and produced a wide range of poetic verse that was instrumental in educating female teachers of jihad refugees who needed to be resocialized in the newly reformed Islamic state. Her scholarly reputation extended well beyond the region into the scholarly circles of the Maghreb. Asma'u remains an inspiration to both men and women in the region more than a century after her death. Her tomb in Sokoto is a place of pilgrimage.

See also **Bello, Muhammad; Islam; 'Uthman dan Fodio.**

BIBLIOGRAPHY

Boyd, Jean. *The Caliph's Sister: Nana Asma'u 1793–1865, Teacher, Poet and Islamic Leader.* London: Frank Cass, 1989.

Boyd, Jean, and Beverly Mack. *The Collected Works of Nana Asma'u, bint Usman dan Fodiyo 1793–1864.* East Lansing: Michigan State University Press, 1997.

Mack, Beverly, and Jean Boyd. *One Woman's Jihad: Nana Asma'u, Scholar and Scribe.* Bloomington: Indiana University Press, 2000.

BEVERLY B. MACK

A page from Nana Asma'u's 1822 poetic work in Fulfulde. The text reads, "Fa'ina ma'a al 'usrin yusra"—So verily with every difficulty there is relief [Sura 94: 5]. COURTESY OF BEVERLY MACK AND JEAN BOYD

ASTRONOMIES.

People of African descent have a long history of observing the sky. They show their knowledge about the sky and the importance of the sky to them in a variety of ways. Africans create images of celestial bodies, build structures aligned to celestial bodies, and some worship celestial bodies in the twenty-first century, as many did in the past.

Archaeoastronomy research focuses on discovering alignments between human-made structures and celestial bodies. Africans align their homes, temples, villages, and cities to the rising and setting positions of celestial bodies and the cardinal directions. In southern Egypt lies one of the oldest archaeological sites that include standing stones aligned to celestial bodies: Nabta Playa. Dated at 4800 BCE, the inhabitants created a small ring of stones with openings aligned to North and the Sun's solstice positions. This ring can be used as a calendar and a navigation device. This is the oldest solar calendar in existence. Other countries in Africa that have structures aligned to celestial bodies or along cosmological concepts are Bénin, Ethiopia, Kenya, Mali, Nigeria, Togo, South Africa, and Zimbabwe.

Ancient drawings and etching of celestial bodies are preserved in rock art sites in East, West, and southern Africa. There are paintings of comets in rock art sites in southern Africa, drawn by ancient people who were most likely the ancestors of the San people. All over Africa people have artistic symbols for the Sun. These Sun symbols are in rock art in Tanzania and Kenya, decorating houses in Uganda, Togo, and Bénin, in body decoration found in pre-twentieth-century Nigeria and Tanzania, and on fabrics such as the mudcloth found throughout West Africa and the colorful cotton cloth sold continent wide. The Bamana of Mali provide an example of how sky observations emerge in art. They watch the Sun and how it moves over the course of a year. The Sun only rises due East on the equinoxes, the rest of the time it rises either to the north or south of East. The Sun rises the furthest south on the winter solstice, December 21, and rises progressively more northward until the summer solstice, and back. The time it takes for the Sun to travel back to its original position is about one year, making a good calendar. The Bamana symbolize this back and forth motion as a zigzag, and zigzag designs are on Bamana masks and other artwork.

During the dynastic eras, the Egyptians worshipped deities that are part of the sky. Osiris is the constellation Orion. Isis is the bright star Sirius. The Goddess Nut is the starry night itself. Egypt's Mediterranean neighbors such as the Greeks also worshipped deified celestial bodies as shown in the names of the planets. Though few do so in the twenty-first century, during the colonial period many African communities still worshiped celestial bodies. Africans have a rich tradition of observing the sky, and these traditions are still present in some parts of Africa.

In the early twenty-first century, there are many living examples of people observing the sky in Africa. The Dogon of Mali are perhaps the best known because of their detailed knowledge of the Sirius star system. An accurate calendar is necessary for agricultural or ceremonial purposes for most people around the world. Mesoamerican Aztec and Mayan cultures have calendars based on Venus. Most African calendars rely on observations of the Sun and the Moon, but one of the Dogon calendars depends on observing the planet Venus, making it unique for Africa. Africans observe and record temporary celestial events such as eclipses and meteor showers in their oral histories. The 1800s saw seven bright comets. Comets are slow phenomena visible for many months in the night

sky. So many comets in the sky, along with social and cultural upheavals, affected the cosmology of the Tabwe people of the Democratic Republic of Congo. They equate comets with impending change and with the death of chiefs. Their burial rituals include preparing and laying out the body in a way that symbolically represents a comet. The traditions of observing the sky are not limited to Africa; Africans that became slaves in the United States also had knowledge of the night sky.

African slaves in the United States ran away to Canada using the stars for navigation. The Big Dipper can be used to find Polaris, the star that marks North. Contrary to popular belief, Polaris is not a bright star and it is hard to locate. But it is almost directly over the North Pole and over the course of the night it does not move while other stars rise, set, or rotate around Polaris. The song "Follow the Drinking Gourd" refers to the constellation that looks like a drinking gourd: the Big Dipper. The song is a map outlining a safe route for escaping slaves. There is also an example of a meteor shower depicted by freed slave Harriet Powers. In a quilt now owned by the Smithsonian Institute, she recorded the 1833 Leonid meteor shower that happened when she was four years old. This meteor shower was spectacular and recorded and remarked on by people around the world but only found in one quilt: Powers's.

African Americans count Benjamin Banneker as their first astronomer, though he had no formal academic training. The first African American to achieve a Ph.D. in astronomy did so nearly a century after emancipation: Harvey Washington Banks received his degree in 1961 from Georgetown University. The first African-American woman to receive an astronomy degree was Barbara A. Williams, twenty years later in 1981, from the University of Maryland, College Park. Despite a long history of observing the sky in Africa and the importance of stars to escaping slaves, few African Americans are choosing to study astronomy so far in this new century.

In Africa, studying astronomy is slowly gaining in popularity. The first astronomical observatory established in Africa was at the Cape of Good Hope (South Africa) in 1820. In the early twenty-first century, world-class observatories are the South African Astronomical Observatory and Hartebeesthoek Radio Astronomy Observatory, both in South Africa, and the High Energy Stereoscopic System for observing gamma-rays in Namibia. The largest telescope in the Southern Hemisphere is in South Africa. Most African Ph.D.s in astronomy received their degrees from programs outside Africa. Nigeria has graduated many astronomers, but most collected their astronomy data from the observatories in South Africa. A recent milestone is that the first three African South African astronomers all graduated with their Ph.D.s in 2003. In the United States, African-American scientists were not able to find university positions outside of historically black colleges until after the civil rights movement during the 1960s. Fortunately, African astronomers have not experienced the same barriers and work in astronomy and physics departments in Africa. The African astronomers embody the astronomy traditions of Africa and modern astronomy. Many choose to study both and teach both to make astronomy more accessible to students and to illuminate the long history of the astronomy of Africa.

See also **Time Reckoning and Calendars.**

BIBLIOGRAPHY

Fikes, Robert. "Careers of African Americans in Academic Astronomy." *The Journal of Blacks in Higher Education* 29 (Autumn 2000): 132–134.

Finch, Charles, III. *The Star of Deep Beginnings: The Genesis of African Science and Technology.* Decatur, GA: Kheat, 1998.

Griaule, Marcel, and Germaine Dieterlen. *Le Renard Pâle.* Paris: Institut d'ethnologie, 1965.

Malville, J. McKim; Fred Wendorf; Ali A. Mazar; and Romauld Schild. "Megaliths and Neolithic Astronomy in Southern Egypt." *Nature* 392, no. 6675 (1998): 488–491.

Roberts, Allen F. "Comets Importing Change of Times and States—Ephemerae and Process among the Tabwa of Zaire." *American Ethnologist* 9, no. 4 (1982): 712–729.

JARITA HOLBROOK

AUGUSTINE OF HIPPO, SAINT (354
–430). Augustine of Hippo was a saint and Christian theologian. A Roman citizen, born at Tagaste (Souk Ahras, Algeria) to Monnica, a devout Christian, and her landowner husband, he was educated

Depiction of Saint Augustine of Hippo (354–430). Saint Augustine's feast day is August 28, which is the day he died. He is the patron saint of sore eyes, printers, brewers, theologians, and many cities and dioceses. GETTY IMAGES

at Madaura and Carthage, and taught Latin rhetoric at Rome and Milan before renouncing his career in 386 for a celibate life of prayer and Bible study. Returning to Africa, he became priest of the seaport Hippo (Annaba) from 391 to 395 and then its bishop until his death.

He was a brilliant preacher and writer, and his works greatly influenced Western Christian theology. In his experience (*Confessions*, 397) only God's grace frees humankind from the compulsions of inherited ("original") sin; he later concluded that God chooses ("predestines") only some people to receive grace. He argued (*City of God*, 412–426) that God alone knows who belongs to the eternal community of all who love God; in this world, Christians cannot isolate themselves from the temporary social and political systems required to maintain an imperfect peace. "Just war" theory develops his reflections on using authorized force to protect people from themselves and from others. The Order of Saint Augustine still follows his rule for community living.

See also **Christianity.**

BIBLIOGRAPHY

Brown, Peter. *Augustine of Hippo: A Biography*, rev. edition. Berkeley: University of California Press, 2000.

GILLIAN CLARK

AUMA, ALICE. *See* **Lakwena, Alice.**

AUSTRALOPITHECUS. *See* **Prehistory.**

AWOLOWO, OBAFEMI (1909–1987).

The Nigerian author, attorney, businessman, politician, and statesman Obafemi Awolowo was born in Ikenne in western Nigeria. Awolowo participated in politics from 1934, when he joined the Nigerian Youth Movement, until his death. He was a founding member of the Egbe Omo Oduduwa, a cultural organization formed in London in 1945 to promote Yoruba unity; it became the nucleus of the Action Group, a political party that he led during the nationalist decade of the 1950s.

Awolowo held major political offices and acquired many chieftaincy titles and honorary doctorates. He was named the first premier of the Western Region in 1954, during a period of prosperity and good government. In 1958 he became opposition leader in the late colonial federal parliament. After independence in 1960 he was jailed by political opponents in 1962; he was released by the army to become vice chairman of the Federal Executive Council and served as finance minister from 1967 to 1971, during the civil war. In 1979 and 1983, he was an unsuccessful presidential candidate.

Awolowo was a federalist, nationalist, and reformer, a liberal who believed in a welfare state. To his critics, he was both a tribalist and an arrogant man. To his admirers, he was a charismatic hero, gifted with foresight and energy, honest, and committed to uplifting the poor through education. His memory endures in actions and philosophy, as well as in streets, public buildings, and a university that bear his name.

Obafemi Awolowo (1909–1987). Awolowo was a Nigerian political leader who founded numerous organizations, including the Egbe Omo Oduduwa, a cultural organization formed in London in 1945 to promote Yoruba unity. "Chief Awolowo," as he was known, was named the first premier of the Western Region in 1954.

See also **Nigeria.**

BIBLIOGRAPHY

Awolowo, Obafemi. *Awo: The Autobiography of Chief Obafemi Awolowo.* Cambridge, U.K.: Cambridge University Press, 1960.

Falola, Toyin; Sope Oyelaran; Mokwugo Okoye; and Adewale Thompson; eds. *Obafemi Awolowo: The End of an Era?* Ile-Ife, Nigeria: Obafemi Awolowo University Press, 1988.

Ogunmodede, F. I. *Chief Obafemi Awolowo's Socio-Political Philosophy: A Critical Interpretation.* Rome: Pontificia Universitas Urbaniana, 1986.

TOYIN FALOLA

AXUM. *See* **Aksum.**

AZANIA. The principal component or root of the toponym "Azania" forms the first or root element in the name of Zanzibar Island and town; it is also the second element in the name of the modern country of Tanzania, formed by the political union of Zanzibar with Tanganyika in 1964. The decision recalled a history of some two millennia.

Strabo (d. after 23 CE), writing in Greek, and other pre-Islamic writers use the form Azania; Pliny (d. 79 CE), writing in Latin, places Azania north of Adulis on the Ethiopian coast, and refers to a people called Zangenae, of uncertain location. The anonymous Alexandrine *Periplus of the Erythraean Sea* (c. 50 CE) describes Azania as the coastal area from Ras Hafun in modern Somalia to Rhapta, a trading station of greatly disputed location. Ptolemy, whose present text on eastern Africa was probably edited about 400 CE, places Rhapta on a river, possibly the Rufiji.

The only exception among Greek authors is Cosmas Indicopleustes, an Alexandrian merchant who traveled down the Red Sea in 524, and wrote his account in a monastery in 547. He calls the area Zingion and speaks of Cape Zingis. These forms seem transitional to the form used by Arab and Swahili authors. These writers call the area Bilad al-Zanj, and the people Zunuj, cognate with the Swahili Unguja, still used for Zanzibar and for the ancient deserted capital of Unguja Kuu. It is first attested by the poet Jarir ibn Atiyah (d. 729?), and by the belles-lettres author al-Jahiz (d. 869), who may have been born in Pemba.

Buzurg ibn Shahriyar of Ramhormuz (c. 953) speaks of trading visits to Zanj; the traveler al-Masudi (d. 956) visited it in 916, and gives an account of its government and trade. It was known to the geographers Ibn Hawqal (c. 988) and al-Idrisi (1154), and to Yaqut ibn Abdallah al-Hamawi, whose geographical dictionary was completed at Aleppo in 1228. Marco Polo's *Travels* describe Zanzibar on the basis of gossip he may have heard in India about 1295; it is an island 2,000 miles round, a reference to the coastal area

rather than to the island. The poet Ibn al-Baytar (c. 1190–1248) was the first to say that black rhubarb is called *zanji* for its color and not for its provenance, thus prompting Bernhard Krumm and some other European writers to define *zanj* as black, without serious justification. Likewise the use of "Azania" by some southern African political movements has been anomalous.

See also **Travel and Exploration.**

BIBLIOGRAPHY

Buzurg ibn Shahriyar. *The Book of the Wonders of India: Mainland, Sea, and Islands*, ed. and trans. Greville S. P. Freeman-Grenville. London: East-West Publications, 1981.

Chittick, H. Neville, and Robert I. Rotberg, eds. *East Africa and the Orient*. New York: Africana Publishing Co., 1975.

Freeman-Grenville, Greville S. P. "Tanzania, Problems of a Toponym." In *The Swahili Coast: Second to Nineteenth Centuries*. London: Variorum Reprints, 1988.

Krumm, Bernhard. *Words of Oriental Origin in Swahili*. London: The Sheldon Press, 1940.

The Periplus Maris Erythraei, trans. Lionel Casson. Princeton, NJ: Princeton University Press, 1989.

GREVILLE S. P. FREEMAN-GRENVILLE

AZIKIWE, BENJAMIN NNAMDI (1904–1996). The nationalist leader and president of Nigeria Benjamin Nnamdi Azikiwe was born in Zungeru, northern Nigeria. Azikiwe studied in the United States (1925–1934), obtaining a master's degree in political science from Lincoln University and a master's in anthropology from the University of Pennsylvania. After working in Accra, Ghana, as editor of the *African Morning Post* from 1935 to 1938, he returned to Nigeria in 1938 and started the *West African Pilot*. With Herbert Macaulay, the founder of Nigeria's first political party, in 1944 Azikiwe organized the National Council of Nigeria and the Cameroons (later renamed National Convention of Nigerian Citizens), becoming the leader of this party in 1946.

Azikiwe served as premier of Eastern Nigeria from 1954 to 1959 and as governor-general of

Nnamdi Azikiwe (1904–1996). Azikiwe is considered the founder of modern Nigerian nationalism and he was the first president of Nigeria. His political motto was, "Talk, I listen. You listen, I talk."

Nigeria from 1960 to 1963. In 1963, he became the first president of the Federal Republic of Nigeria, a post he held until 1966, when military rule ended party politics. When the military lifted the ban on politics in 1978, Azikiwe joined the Nigerian People's Party, in which he was active until his retirement from politics in 1986. Azikiwe was widely respected as a patriot, political strategist, and humanist. His publications include *My Odyssey: An Autobiography* (1970); *Zik: A Selection from the Speeches of Nnamdi Azikiwe* (1961); *Political Blueprint of Nigeria* (1944); *Renascent Africa* (1937); and *Liberia in World Politics* (1934).

See also **Macaulay, Herbert Samuel Heelas; Nigeria.**

BIBLIOGRAPHY

Glauke, Claris Obiageli. *Zik's Kingdom: Dr. Nnamdi Azikiwe, Nigerian Politics, 1960–1996.* Berlin: Wissenschaft und Technik Verlag, 1997.

Igwe, Agbafor. *Nnamdi Azikiwe: The Philosopher of Our Time.* Enugu, Nigeria: Fourth Dimension, 1992.

Oyewole, Anthony. *Historical Dictionary of Nigeria.* Metuchen, NJ: Scarecrow Press, 1987.

Sklar, Richard. "Nnamdi Azikiwe and the Political Economy of Freedom (1994)." *African Politics in Postimperial Times: The Essays of Richard L. Sklar,* ed. Toyin Falola. Trenton, NJ: Africa World Press, 2002.

BABATUNDE LAWAL

B

BÂ, MARIAMA (1929–1981).

The Senegalese teacher, writer, and feminist Mariama Bâ was born in Dakar, Senegal, into a well-to-do and well-connected Muslim family. She received her elementary education in a French-language school while also attending a Qur'anic school. Her maternal grandparents, who raised her after her mother died, believed that a woman should not get any further education. But Bâ went to a teacher training school in the vicinity of Dakar. After graduating in 1947, she became a primary school teacher. She married Obèye Diop, a Senegalese politician. After divorcing him, she raised their nine children. Suffering from bad health, she ended her teaching career in 1959 and became a school inspector.

Bâ joined women's organizations and advocated for their rights in speeches and newspaper articles. Describing herself as "a modern Muslim woman," she protested women's subordination in both traditional African cultures and Islamic practice. In particular, she stressed the oppression of women in marriage and the institution of polygamy. These themes appeared in her first published novel, *Une si longue lettre* (1980; A very long letter), which won the first Noma Award for Publishing in Africa in 1981. After twenty-five years of marriage, the husband of the novel's protagonist marries a second, younger woman and then ignores his first wife. The plot allows Bâ to express her belief that men act by sexual instinct and women by sexual self-restraint and reason. The novel gained Bâ worldwide renown.

Two years later, just after her death, Bâ's second novel was published. In *Un chant écarlate* (1981; Scarlet song), a Senegalese man marries a French woman. Living in Senegal, they feel the societal pressures imposed on an interracial couple. The woman is unable to bear the constrictiveness of her new life, especially when her husband takes another wife.

See also **Literature: Women Writers, Northern Africa; Literature: Women Writers, Sub-Saharan Africa.**

BIBLIOGRAPHY

Kempen, Laura Charlotte. *Mariama Bâ, Rigoberta Menchú, and Postcolonial Feminism.* New York: P. Lang, 2001.

Sarvan, Charles Ponnuthurai. "Feminism and African Fiction: The Novels of Mariama Bâ." *Modern Fiction Studies* 34, no. 3 (1988): 453–464.

MICHAEL L. LEVINE

BAARTMAN, SARA (mid-1770s–1815)

Sara Baartman was born in the mid-1770s in the present-day Eastern Cape, South Africa. She came from the KhoeKhoe society of the Gonaqua, whose lands were colonized by Dutch settlers. Her father was a cattle driver who made frequent trips to Cape Town. Colonists called her Saartjie, the diminutive of her name that indicated her servile status on a settler's farm. In about 1795, Baartman moved to Cape Town in a wagon caravan owned by butcher Jan Elzer and managed by Pieter Cesars. She worked for Elzer in Cape Town, but on his death seems to have been sold to Pieter Cesars for whom she worked in conditions of slavery as a wet nurse.

In the early 1800s, she was again transferred, to Pieter's brother Hendrik Cesars. Cape racial taxonomies designated the Cesars family as free Black, an indication that they were of acknowledged slave descent. Baartman worked for the Cesars as a washerwoman and nursemaid until 1810. They lived in Papendorp, a working-class suburb near the military hospital in Cape Town. While in Cape Town, Baartman had at least two children, both of whom died in infancy.

Alexander Dunlop, a ship's surgeon who also served as doctor in the slave lodge in Cape Town, got to know Hendrik Cesars and thus Baartman. Dunlop forced Cesars, who was in deep debt, to accompany Baartman on a trip to London. From September 1810 through at least 1812 the Hottentot Venus became the rage of London and then the provinces.

Inspired by the earlier travel writings by authors such as Peter Kolbe and Francois Le Vaillant, the European public was fascinated by accounts of the indigenous Khoesan of the Cape who covered their bodies with grease to protect them from the sun, and who wore few clothes compared to Europeans. Dunlop initially clothed Baartman in very tight clothing that suggested nudity and revealed her bottom and her hips. The exhibit was very popular with the London public and with royalty.

In October and November 1810, the African Institution, an antislavery lobbying group closely connected with the Clapham Sect, lobbied the King's Bench, the highest civil court in the land, to investigate whether Baartman was being held as a slave. Court investigators questioned Baartman, but in the presence of Dunlop. His presence created a coercive context for the interview, making it highly unlikely that Baartman would say something negative about her experiences. Baartman said she enjoyed being in London although she was a bit cold. The court dropped the investigation and Baartman returned to being the Hottentot Venus and, increasingly, the subject of satirical prints and songs.

Baartman was baptized Sara Bartmann and married in Manchester Cathedral in December 1811. Historians do not know why her name was changed. They also do not know why she was in Manchester, as there are no records of her being displayed in that city. Thereafter, she appeared in Limerick, Ireland, in April 1812 and at a local pleasure fair in Suffolk in October 1812.

In September 1814 she arrived in France and was sold to an animal trainer, Reaux, who displayed her at the Palais Royal as the Hottentot Venus. The French public found that icon as fascinating as had their English peers. A vaudeville opera was written about the Hottentot Venus; satirical prints and posters appeared.

In March 1815 French physiologist George Cuvier asked that he be able to examine Baartman at the Jardin des Plantes. Cuvier also employed artists to render her from every angle. After this ignominious experience, Baartman continued to be displayed. She died at the end of 1815, of unknown and disputed causes. No autopsy was conducted to determine the cause of her death.

Instead, Cuvier dissected her body to again explore his interest in comparative anatomy. Cuvier's publications on his study of Baartman as the Hottentot Venus became the foundation for a racial science that remained hugely influential into the twentieth century. He pondered whether "Hottentots" were the missing link between humans and the animal kingdom, and focused especially on the labia of Sara Baartman as being an indicator of the atavistic sexuality of the Hottentot woman. Cuvier put her brains and genitals in jars (his own brain had a similar fate) and displayed her skeleton alongside a plaster cast of her nude body at the Museum of Man. These were on display until at least 1974.

The fame of the Hottentot Venus survived Baartman's death. References to the Hottentot Venus appear in various major works of literature including that of Charles Dickens. A huge picture of the Hottentot Venus graced the entry to the 1889 centenary festival of the French Revolution. In the 1940s and 1950s, Scottish ethnomusicologist Percival Kirby, while teaching in South Africa, saw Baartman's skeleton in Paris and investigated her history.

Kirby's various academic articles on the Hottentot Venus became the basis for a renewed interest in the icon among academics such as Richard Altick and Stephen Jay Gould. Since the 1990s, scholars and activists such as Anne Fausto Sterling, Zoe Strother and Denean Sharply-Whiting,

Burial ceremony for Saratjie (Sara) Baartman (mid-1770s–1815), Gamtoos river valley, 2002. Sara Baartman was a Khoesan slave woman with unusual physical features who became an unwilling participant in European scientists' investigation of black female sexuality. She became known across the country as "The Hottentot Venus." © REUTERS/CORBIS

Suzan-Lori Parks, and Diane Ferrus have begun to explore the life of Baartman through fiction, art, and creative nonfiction.

In 2002, after many years of activism on the part of different South African groups, the French government agreed to relinquish Baartman's remains. She was reburied in August 2002 at a national ceremony attended by Thabo Mbeki, the president of South Africa. Her grave, surrounded by iron bars to keep away devotees and vandals, graces a hill in Hankey, in the Eastern Cape where she was born.

See also **Cape Town; Colonialism and Imperialism; Mbeki, Thabo; Women: Women and Slavery.**

BIBLIOGRAPHY

Crais, Clifton, and Pamela Scully. *Sara Baartman and the Hottentot Venus: A Ghost Story and Biography.* Princeton, NJ: Princeton University Press, 2008.

Kirby, Percival R. "The Hottentot Venus." *Africana Notes and News* 6, no. 3 (1949): 55–61.

Kirby, Percival R. "More about the Hottentot Venus." *Africana Notes and News* 10, no. 4 (1953): 124–133.

Kirby, Percival R. "The 'Hottentot Venus' of the Musee de L'Homme, Paris." *South African Journal of Science* 50, no. 12 (1954): 319–322.

Kirby, Percival R. "A Further Note on the 'Hottentot Venus.'" *Africana Notes and News* 11, no. 5 (1955): 165–166.

The Life and Times of Sara Baartman: "The Hottentot Venus." Directed by Zola Maseko. First Run/Icarus Films, 1998.

Strother, Zoe. "Display of the Body Hottentot." In *Africans on Stage: Studies in Ethnological Showbusiness,* ed. Bernth Lindfors. Bloomington: Indiana University Press, 1999.

PAMELA SCULLY

BABA, AHMAD (c. 1556–1627). The scholar Ahmad Baba was born in the western Sahara Desert into the Aqit clan of the Sanhaja, which had furnished the *qadis* (judges) of Timbuktu in the sixteenth century and was himself a likely candidate for the office. He became head of the University of Sankore (founded as a part of the Sankore Mosque in 989), but his career was interrupted by the Moroccan conquest of the Songhay empire in 1591. Ahmad Baba was deported to Marrakesh, where he was detained until 1608.

During Ahmad Baba's time of exile, Timbuktu became the headquarters of the administration imposed by Morocco. Ahmad Baba spent the time teaching and became celebrated for his judicial opinions. Upon his return to Timbuktu he returned to his post at Sankore and promptly complained that much of the library there had been damaged or destroyed by the Moroccan occupiers.

Ahmad Baba wrote more than fifty works, the best known of which is his *Nayl al-ibtihaj* (1596), a biographical dictionary of scholars of the Maliki law school. His other works deal with the fields of jurisprudence, theology, and Arabic grammar. A number of them have been published in Morocco and Egypt, while others remain in manuscript in North and West African libraries.

See also **Law; Marrakesh; Timbuktu.**

BIBLIOGRAPHY

"Fihris-makhtutat-Markaz-Ahmad-Baba-lil-tawhthiq-wal-buhuth-al-tarikhiyya-bi-Timbuktu—Handlist of manuscripts in the Centre de Documentation et de Recherches Historiques Ahmad Baba, Timbuktu, vol 2." *Bulletin of the School of Oriental and African Studies–University of London* 61 (1998): 207.

Lovejoy, Paul E. "The Context of Enslavement in West Africa: Ahmad Baba and the Ethics of Slavery." In *Slaves, Subjects, and Subversives: Blacks in Colonial Latin America*, ed. Jane G. Landers and Barry M. Robinson, Albuquerque: University of New Mexico Press, 2006.

Zouber, Mahmoud. *Ahmad Baba de Tombouctou (1556–1627): Sa vie et son oeuvre.* Paris: G.-P. Maisonneuve et Larose, 1977.

JOHN HUNWICK

BABANGIDA, IBRAHIM GBADAMOSI

(1941–). Ibrahim Gbadamosi Babangida was the president of Nigeria from 1985 to 1993. A northern Muslim, he was educated at the Nigerian military college and commissioned and sent to India in 1964. He attended the English Royal Armor School in 1966. Decorated for valor in the 1967–1970 Nigerian civil war, he was promoted to colonel and commander of the armed forces in 1975. He successfully led the resistance to a 1976 coup attempt against the government, in which the head of state, General Murtala Muhammad, was killed.

In 1983 Babangida became major general and rapidly built public support. He led a coup against the government of Shehu Shagari that same year and picked Muhammadu Buhari as the new head of state; Babangida became chief of staff. After Buhari's economic program met with failure, Babangida became president in 1985, introducing an austerity plan that saw moderate success. He formed a six-nation task force in 1990 to intervene in Liberia's civil war, backing the interim government of Dr. Amos Sawyer. Babangida emphasized a return to civilian rule and created both parties of a two-party system. Elections were postponed until the system was instituted in 1987. He banned all those who had previously held public office, including himself. Elections were held in 1993, and Moshood Abiola was the victor. Babangida nullified the elections with disastrous results. Three months later he was ousted in a coup led by General Sani Abacha.

See also **Nigeria.**

RICHARD R. MARCUS

BALEWA, ABUBAKAR TAFAWA. *See* Tafawa Balewa, Abubakar.

BAMAKO.

Bamako is located on the left bank of the Niger River in southern Mali and is the capital of the country. Presumably settled by the followers of an early Mande leader, the settlement grew to become a prominent center of Islamic learning during Mali's medieval period (twelfth to fourteenth centuries). As the Malian empires faded, however, Bamako also fell on hard times. It was occupied in the eighteenth century by a warrior group, the Bambara. By 1797, when the Scottish explorer Mungo Park arrived, it had dwindled to little more than a hamlet. In the later nineteenth century the town fell under the suzerainty of Samori Touré, one of the great Muslim empire-builders of the era.

After a protracted struggle for mastery in the area, the French defeated Touré and established a fort at Bamako in 1883. By that time there were only about 1,000 people in the town itself, with a few thousand more scattered around the nearby countryside. The French, however, established a commercial base in Bamako, and the town began to grow again. With completion of a railway line from the Atlantic coast in Senegal in 1904, Bamako became a regional hub, and in 1908 the French made it the capital of their colonial holdings in French Soudan. When Mali achieved independence in 1960, Bamako became the national capital.

Bamako has since blossomed as an administrative and commercial center. Gold is brought in from the west, and kola nuts and rice come in from the south and east. Among the main industries are textiles, ceramics, pharmaceuticals, and generation of electricity. Bamako has a large market, a zoo, an airport, and several scientific research institutes. The population in 2004 was close to 1.2 million.

See also **Mali; Niger River; Touré, Samori.**

BIBLIOGRAPHY

Perinbam, B. Marie. *Family, Identity, and the State in the Bamako Kafu, c. 1800–c. 1900.* Boulder, CO: Westview Press, 1997.

C. OGBOGBO

Hastings K. Banda (1906–1997). Banda was the nationalist leader of the anti-federation movement. Two years before becoming the first president of Malawi, he chose the country's name. He had seen the words *Lake Maravi* on an old French map and played with the name until he liked the sound and spelling. TERRENCE SPENCER/TIME LIFE PICTURES/GETTY IMAGES

BANDA, NGWAZI HASTINGS KAMUZU (1906–1997). The nationalist leader Ngwazi Hastings Kamuzu Banda was the president of Malawi from 1966 to 1994. Born near Kasungu, the then-British colony of Nyasaland, Banda traveled to South Africa at the age of seventeen to pursue his education. He continued to the United States to study first at Wilberforce Academy, in Ohio, and then at Indiana University. He then studied medicine at Meharry Medical College in Nashville, Tennessee, qualifying as a doctor in 1937. He did not return to the country of his birth until 1958, at the age of sixty.

The practice of medicine took Banda to Great Britain and then to Ghana. At the behest of the Nyasaland National Congress, Banda returned to Malawi from Ghana on July 6, 1958. Within months of his arrival, his fiery nationalist rhetoric landed him in detention. He became the first prime minister of Nyasaland in 1961 and continued in this capacity when the country became independent and changed its name to Malawi. A new constitution created the office of president in 1966, and Banda was elected to the post.

Banda proclaimed himself President-for-Life in 1971 and outlawed all political parties except his own, the Malawian Congress Party (MCP). His regime soon became notorious for its harsh repression of political opposition. His conservative foreign policy was both pro-Western and anticommunist, and he was the first black African leader to visit South Africa under apartheid. In the 1980s, Banda earned the disfavor of other African leaders for his support of Renamo (Resistência Nacional Moçambicana) rebels in the Mozambican conflict and for his support of the apartheid government of South Africa. Domestically, Banda enforced a strict Victorian social code while seeking to modernize Malawi's infrastructure.

In 1991 Banda's human rights abuses were condemned by religious leaders, and in 1992 antigovernment rioting forced him to permit the formation of rival political parties. Multiparty elections were eventually held in May 1994, and Banda lost the race to Bakili Muluzi. In 1995 Banda was put on trial on charges that he had ordered the murders of four political rivals but was acquitted. He died in Johannesburg, South Africa, in November 1997.

See also **Human Rights; Malawi; Political Systems.**

BIBLIOGRAPHY

Chiume, M. W. Kanyama. *Banda's Malawi, Africa's Tragedy.* Lusaka, Zambia: Multimedia Publications, 1992.

Kadri, Sadakat. "Prosecuting Hastings Banda in Malawi." In *Justice for Crimes against Humanity,* ed. Mark Lattimer and Philippe Sands. Oxford; Portland OR: Hart, 2003.

ROBERT UTTARO

BANGUI. The capital of the Central African Republic, Bangui had a population estimated at just under 700,000 in 2004. The name of the city means "the rapids," reflecting its situation on the first of the great rapids on the Ubangi-Shari (Chari) River. Archaeological evidence suggests that the area was populated as long ago as the seventh century. A variety of peoples have contested for regional control. The area was subject to much unrest, which was only intensified by the region's long history as a reservoir of slaves who were sold both north across the Sahara and, later, west into the Atlantic trade.

Bangui was well-situated to profit from the riverine trade. The last slave-raiding warlord in the region was Rabih bin Fadlallah. The arrival of European explorers and military personnel challenged his rule in the 1880s and by 1887, the French took control of the region. In 1889 they established a military outpost in the town. It took another sixteen years for the French to consolidate their hold of the region by finally defeating Rabah in 1903.

In the early twenty-first century, Bangui is primarily an administrative and commercial center, but it also hosts some small industries, such as soap manufacturing and breweries. Connected by river, railway, and roadways to the Atlantic coast, Cameroon, Chad, Sudan, and the Congo, Bangui derives its greatest economic importance from its role as the shipping center for the Central African Republic's cotton, timber, coffee, and sisal. The University of Bangui, the Boganda Museum (named after a one-time president of the nation), the National School of Arts, and several research institutes contribute to making Bangui the country's center for artistic and intellectual expression.

See also **Central African Republic; Rabih bin Fadlallah; Travel and Exploration.**

BIBLIOGRAPHY

Villien, François, et al. *Bangui, capital d'un pays enclavé d'Afrique Centrale.* Talence, France: 1990.

JESSE A. DIZARD

BANJUL. The capital and only city in the Gambia, Banjul is located on an island of the same name, at the mouth of the Gambia River. The island is separated from the mainland by a small creek. Portuguese explorers visited the Gambia River in the fifteenth century, and British traders came a century later. The river was a significant source of slaves for the British in the eighteenth century, made (inaccurately) famous by Alex Haley's *Roots* saga of his ancestor Kunta Kinte, who came from upriver and might well have passed through the slaving base on the island. Following the prohibition of slave trading in 1807, the British attempted to control the so-called "legitimate trade" in commodities on the Gambia River by establishing a port, which they named Bathurst, at its mouth in 1816. The government of independent Gambia changed the name of this port and administrative capital to Banjul in 1973.

Wolof, Fulani (Fulbe), and Mandinka are the predominant ethnic groups in the area; about 10 percent of the population has immigrated from Senegal, which surrounds the Gambia on its three noncoastal sides. As of 1994 (the latest date for which there are census figures), the population of the city was just over 49,000; the figure doubles if the suburbs of Bakau and Serrekunda are included.

The economy of Banjul, and of the Gambia, is primarily agricultural. Peanuts are the principal export of the Banjul port and account for two-thirds of its cargo. There is some tourism (mainly from Scandinavia) and some light industry, of which the most important is the processing of fish. Filigree jewelry and textiles are also produced for the tourist trade, but the income generated within the city still does not pay for its imports. Banjul has two radio stations, one of which is government-owned and broadcasts local music; there is also a commercial station that plays popular Western music. In the mid-1900s, nationwide television service was initiated.

There is a small international airport at Banjul, out of which the national airline, Air Gambia, operates. A well-paved road runs along the south side of the river from Banjul to Basse Santa Su and was extended to Senegal in the 1990s. Otherwise, the Gambia River is the main transportation artery serving Banjul.

See also **Gambia, The; Slave Trades.**

BIBLIOGRAPHY

Buckley, Liam Mark. "Studio Photography and the Aesthetics of Postcolonialism in the Gambia, West Africa." Ph.D. diss. University of Virginia, 2003.

Mwakikagile, Godfrey. *Military Coups in West Africa since the Sixties.* Huntington, NY: Nova Science Publishers, 2001.

Uwechue, Ralph, ed. *Africa Today*, 3rd edition. Surrey, U.K., 1996.

Wright, Donald R. *The World and a Very Small Place in Africa: A History of Globalization in Niumi, the Gambia*, 2nd edition. Armonk, NY: M. E. Sharpe, 2004.

SARAH VALDEZ

BANTU, EASTERN, SOUTHERN, AND WESTERN, HISTORY OF (1000 BCE TO 1500 CE).

The term "Bantu" refers to a family of 500 to 600 modern languages spoken in the early twenty-first century by some 240 million Africans (one out of every three Africans), spread out over the subcontinent south of a line from the Cameroon grasslands in the west to southern Somalia in the east. All the Bantu languages stem from a single ancient ancestral language, dubbed proto-Bantu. This shared linguistic descent was proven a century ago by the regularity of the sound correspondences between the phonemes of the contemporary languages, and a common grammar was reconstructed. The Bantu family itself belongs to the Niger-Congo super-family and is a subset of Bantoid, itself a subset of Benue-Congo, itself a subset of Volta-Congo. Most of these languages are very closely related by African, or world, standards of linguistic diversity.

Bantu speakers first divided in two groups: Wide and Narrow Bantu. The modern languages of the first are spoken only on and around the Cameroon grasslands, while all the other Bantu languages belong to the second. Therefore in practice "Bantu" usually refers to Narrow Bantu. Narrow proto-Bantu emerged from Wide Bantu in the Sanaga valley just south of the grasslands of western Cameroon. The people who came to speak its daughters spread from there over nearly the whole subcontinent. Until recent times this huge expansion was believed to have been brought about by a single vast human migration, and hence it seemed that once the genealogy of the languages of the Bantu family had been unraveled one could easily trace the routes taken by the "migrants" who invented them.

It proved however to be exceedingly difficult to establish the genetic subdivisions of Narrow Bantu that such a migration would have produced, mainly because the daughter languages have borrowed so much from each other and otherwise changed over the past millennia that much of the evidence for their exact genetic relationships has been erased. This phenomenon is known as linguistic convergence. Given the large number of languages involved, linguists have attempted to establish a first approximation of the very premise of lexicostatistics, namely that "basic" words are not as easily borrowed as any others. Yet they found that they had been borrowed nearly as freely as any other. Hence no single branching lexicostatistical tree can be accepted as wholly valid. This exceptional degree of convergence among Narrow Bantu languages also impedes the application of the classical method of comparing the phonologies, morphologies, and syntax of Bantu languages. Different groups of linguists continue to actively tackle the issue, but a full genetic classification of Bantu remains in flux.

Hence linguistic consensus about the process that generated the distribution of modern Bantu languages remains fragmentary. Some eighty different low-level, or relatively recent, genetic groups and about twenty-five intermediate level groups (that is, broad stages in the earlier divisions) of Bantu have been identified. Most of the low-level groups are among obviously closely related languages and accepted as valid, but only about half of the hypothesized intermediate groupings of more distantly related ones are. The largest among the latter are Southeastern Bantu, which includes Makua north of the lower Zambezi and all the languages south of that river with the exception of the Venda-Shona group, and Southwestern Bantu (also labeled "Njila") although linguists still disagree about the latter's composition. At an earlier level, only one coherent unit has been fully validated by the comparative method, namely Northeastern Savanna, a group that includes nearly all East African Bantu languages north of central and southern Tanzania. At a still earlier level a single East Bantu or Eastern Savanna unit appears in all lexicostatistic trees and was accepted by most scholars long ago. Yet in the first decade of the 2000s it is not validated by the comparative method, and some linguists question whether it really constitutes a genuine genetic unit. On the other hand the comparative method provides some evidence for the existence of a Forest Bantu in the rainforests from Gabon to the eastern Democratic Republic of the Congo as a major subdivision of Narrow Bantu itself.

Given the uncertain state of the question one can say at this juncture only that Narrow Bantu spread first from Cameroon into the rainforests and later into the savannas to their east and south. Eastern Bantu, if it exists, or otherwise Northeastern

Savanna Bantu, was one of the first savanna groups to emerge. After several further southward dispersals from this base, the expansion concluded with the emergence of the southernmost: Southeastern and Southwestern Bantu.

The dates of all these geographical movements can be estimated only broadly. All linguists, but not all historians, reject the validity of glottochronology in any precise way. This is a method of attempting to date language splits that relies on an assumed fixed rate of replacement of the "basic words" in any language. This rejection means that the chronology of the Bantu dispersion cannot be dated by internal linguistic evidence and so must rely entirely on archaeological data presumed associated with identifiable language communities in the past. Much of the ancestral Narrow Bantu language has been reconstructed by the comparative method, including a sizeable Proto-Bantu lexicon that yields information about the ancestral society and its culture that can be detected archaeologically. Thus Proto-Narrow Bantu speakers lived in relatively stable villages, made and used ceramics, farmed root crops, tree crops, and legumes, and also foraged, fished, and navigated by canoe. But they did not practice any metallurgy nor use any metals.

Because the earliest archaeological evidence for agriculture in the Wide Bantu region emerges at Shum Laka in Western Cameroon some time after 3000 BCE, Wide Proto-Bantu must have begun after that date. Sites south of the Sanaga river (Obobogo) in Cameroon, where Narrow Proto-Bantu took shape, indicate that this its speakers probably happened settled there around or after 2000 BCE. The initial dispersal of Narrow Bantu languages into and somewhat beyond the forests was completed before ca. 450 BCE, the earliest *certain* date for metal working sites in southern Cameroon as well as in the rather distant southern Great Lakes region. In similar ways scholars also know that speakers of Bantu tongues reached their southernmost locales in Angola around the first century CE and in northernmost Natal a few centuries later.

HOW THE BANTU LANGUAGES SEPARATED

It is obvious in the early twenty-first century that to attribute the modern wide dispersion of the

Narrow Bantu languages to a single migration is to collapse into a single event a process that in fact lasted several millennia. Such a vast (hypothetical) migration would require impossibly large numbers of migrants and instantaneous adaptations to the host of natural environments, ranging from giant swamps to semi-deserts, where modern speakers of Bantu languages live. Hence the spreading of these languages was not a single continuing process but the outcome of a host of smaller dispersals over many centuries, triggered by different causes, constrained by the requirements of different environments, and produced by different mechanisms of movement and resettlement. Migrations by their speakers are only one of the two main ways in which all languages spread, the other being language shift–the adoption of entire populations of new languages–over long periods of time. In addition many different sorts of migrations are involved, and we mention only the ones most commonly proposed in relation to one or another of the innumerable small historical movements of Bantu speakers. Some population drifts resulted from shifting sites of cultivation in slowly growing agricultural populations. These slow advances occurred along frontiers of settlement when farmers established new villages every five or ten years to gain access to new fields. Some migrations occurred when settlements split as they became too large for shifting agriculture or experienced challenges to existing leadership. Others resulted from deliberate searches for better environments, such as richer soils for farmers, new ecotones (often forest-savanna borders) for farmer/foragers, or more productive stretches of river or coasts for fishermen.

There were also different ways to leave and settle elsewhere. Villages might move a few miles at a time, and their inhabitants carried their belongings and sometimes even their prefabricated houses to new sites, or they might move further away but then with fewer belongings, in order to leapfrog existing settlements between them and an unoccupied frontier area. Fishermen could travel rapidly along rivers or coasts by canoe, carrying all their goods with them, and cover substantial distances at every move. At least three known sizable language expansions must have been carried by "water people," namely one along the coasts of Cameroon and northern Gabon, one within the inner Congo Basin, and one along the East coast from Tanzania to northern

Natal. Once some Bantu speakers in East Africa had become agro-pastoralists, they could also easily rapidly cover large distances with their herds, but only within well-defined ecological niches suited to cattle. Every type of migration thus left its own spatial signature. These range from solid broad frontiers, to continuous or punctuated ribbon like-patterns along waterways (later also along trade routes), to scattered archipelagoes of settlement in particularly favorable environments.

During the initial stages of the dispersal of Bantu languages language shifts over time must have occurred at least as frequently as migration, as earlier populations of hunters and gatherers learned the languages of the newcomers. More and more of these original inhabitants adopted Bantu languages as their own (even though Bantu tongues had no intrinsic technical advantage over any other language). Nor was the way of life of early Bantu speakers somehow more successful than that of the people they met, especially since their farming at first rendered most local environments less sanitary and probably increased mortality. Yet sedentary Bantu-speaking farmers did enjoy one demographic advantage over their foraging neighbors. They lived in villages that usually contained larger numbers of inhabitants than any of the mobile camps of the original inhabitants who surrounded them, and their villagers were linked with others into regional social units that seem to have been more substantial than those of the dispersed bands of original inhabitants. To some extent archaeology (especially regional styles of pottery) documents these networks, while such a scenario also jibes well with the exceptionally high linguistic convergence, owing to intensive contact and hence word-borrowing over long distances, that characterizes the Bantu language family.

Hence the sociodemographic scale of Bantu speakers was usually larger than that of the original inhabitants. By analogy with the recent past one may suggest that under such circumstances, a village becomes a center of attraction for its diverse surrounding populations, and its language tends to become the *lingua franca* for that area. More nomads became bilingual than villagers and they gradually abandoned their own tongues in favor of the Bantu over several generations. Moreover the subsistence economies of both the Bantu speakers and the surrounding foragers took part in renewed further expansion. Such a scenario seems to be the most obvious way to account for the varied ecological adaptations of Bantu speakers as well as for the demographic growth that made the repeated expansions of Bantu languages possible.

After the initial dispersal of the Bantu languages over much of the subcontinent there still remained both small and large enclaves where other than Bantu languages still flourished for some centuries. Except for portions of East Africa, all of these enclaves then disappeared, probably in the millennium between circa 500 and 1500 CE, when more intensive communications over very long distances among Bantu-speaking societies spread one of their languages as a *lingua france* over the intermediary regions. For after about 500 CE larger and more stable villages as well as patches of higher population densities appeared in favored environments, and new larger-scale sociopolitical societies developed as a result. Such places then became nodes for long distance trading routes. From the middle or later centuries of the first millennium CE onward such links are found all over the savannas of central and southeastern Africa, in the southern parts of east Africa, and along the web of rivers in the inner Congo basin. Traders, metal workers, famous diviners, and medicine men traveled along them, and the languages they spoke acquired great prestige. Their widespread usefulness led foragers to abandon or subordinate their ways of life, and languages, to the dominant economies and societies. The same widespread communications also intensified the pace of convergence between Bantu languages and made it more difficult for modern linguists to trace their genetic connections.

CONCLUSIONS
The area covered around 1900 by Bantu languages is the outcome of both successive small scale migrations and countless language shifts, even though shifts did not invariably turn non-Bantu into Bantu speakers. The reverse is known or suspected in several cases from Namibia and Botswana in the southwestern (Kalahari Desert) fringes of the Bantu dispersal and in the Uele-Ituri forests of the eastern Democratic Republic of the Congo and western Kenya. Indeed a given single population cluster may have undergone several successive language shifts, as seems to have happened to some communities in Uele-Ituri who shifted from Bantu to Central Sudanic and back to a Bantu tongue. Moreover people often abandoned one Bantu language for another, or a halfway shift between Bantu languages led to the emergence of a creole, which later turned into a new language.

Although we will never document all the complex processes that contributed to the eventual modern distribution of the Bantu languages, we should not ignore that they occurred, nor should we aggregate them into single migratory movement with a preordained outcome, triggered by a single cause. Even the spread of farming by speakers of Bantu languages cannot be accepted as such a uniform cause, since Bantu languages spread into and beyond the Great Lakes region into an area already occupied by cereal farmers speaking Central Sudanic languages, who then taught the incoming Bantu speakers how to cultivate these grains. One factor though that may have been involved in nearly all these processes may well have been be the larger size of the sociopolitical organizations adopted by most Bantu speakers compared to the smaller communities of the people they met.

In recent decades beliefs about the dispersal of Bantu languages through a single migrating wave have given rise to a pernicious myth based on the equation of an imagined superior language, culture, and people. According to this myth, present-day Bantu-speaking populations are the descendants and heirs of the original triumphal Bantu speaking pioneers, who—in a single epic migration—brought their superior civilization to a benighted subcontinent, easily subjugating or ousting whomever they met. Political leaders in several countries with linguistically mixed citizenries have invoked this myth of linguistic genius in order to mobilize Bantu-speaking populations against those of different linguistic heritages. Hence one must stress that their views of language and of history are false: there never was a vast single migration, most Bantu speakers are probably the physical descendants of autochtHon populations, and later populations owe just as much if not more of their cultures to the local late stone age autochtHons than to anyone whose ancestors had come from that distant Bantu cradle in Cameroon.

See also **Languages; Linguistics and the Study of Africa.**

BIBLIOGRAPHY

Bastin, Yvonne; Andre Coupez; and Michael Mann. *Continuity and Divergence in the Bantu Languages: Perspectives from a Lexicostatistic Study.* Tervuren: 1999.

Mohlig, Wilhelm J. G. "Stratification in the History of the Bantu Languages." *Sprach e and Geschichte in Afrika* 3 (1981): 251–316.

Nurse, Derek, and Gerard Philippson, eds. *The Bantu Languages.* New York: Routledge, 2003.

Vansina, Jan. "New Linguistic Evidence and the 'Bantu expansion.'" *Journal of African History* 36 (1995): 173–195.

JAN VANSINA

BANTU LANGUAGES. *See* Languages: Niger-Congo.

BARGHASH IBN SA'ID (1833–1888).

Barghash ibn Sa'id was one of several sons of Seyyid Sa'id, Sultan of Oman (1804–1846) at the mouth of the Persian Gulf. Seyyid made Zanzibar the Omani capital in 1832, and upon his death in 1846, a dispute arose among his sons for the right of succession. The British government, which had strong commercial and strategic interests in the region, intervened to settle the dispute by dividing the Omani Sultanate into two parts, giving the eldest son, Thuwain, the rule of Oman and its environs, while allocating Zanzibar and other Omani possessions in East Africa to another son, Majid. Barghash, however, disputed the decision. To ease tensions, Britain again intervened, and sent the younger man to Bombay, ostensibly to further his education.

Majid died in 1870, and Barghash returned to Zanzibar to succeed him as sultan. He began his reign in 1870 by trying to assert his autonomy and reform the corrupt administration of his predecessor. In 1870 he signed a treaty with Britain to prohibit the slave trade on Zanzibar and closed down its major slave market in Mkunazini. However, when a hurricane wiped out the clove economy of the island in 1872, he broke the provisions of the treaty in order to import labor from the African mainland to rebuild the clove plantations. He expanded Zanzibar's commercial sector by establishing a fleet of steamships, quickly tripling state revenues. The sultan then embarked on an ambitious program of public works, building many palaces and modernizing the capital's water and power supplies.

To reinforce Zanzibari autonomy, Barghash tried to transform his father's commercial empire into a political realm by creating a modern army, but he was ultimately forced to acquiesce to growing German colonial claims to the mainland. His realm was reduced to the offshore islands and a ten-mile strip of coastal territory, but these, too, eventually fell under European control. His reign ended in 1888, and he died that year.

See also **Colonial Policies and Practices: British East Africa; Colonialism and Imperialism: Overview; Slave Trades.**

BIBLIOGRAPHY

Bennett, Norman R. *A History of the Arab State of Zanzibar.* London: Methuen, 1978.

Coupland, Sir Reginald. *The Exploitation of East Africa, 1856–1890: The Slave Trade and the Scramble,* 2nd edition. London: Faber, 1968.

Schneppen, H. "Saayid Khalid ibn Barghash: Sultan for Three Days—Exile for Thirty Years (Zanzibar)." *Islam-Zeitschrift fur Geschichte und Kultur des Islamischen Orients* 76 (2) (1999): 299–312.

Sheriff, Abdul. *Slaves, Spices, and Ivory in Zanzibar: Integration of an East African Commercial Empire into the World Economy, 1770–1873.* Athens: Ohio University Press, 1987.

A. SHERIFF

BARTH, HEINRICH (1821–1865). Hein-

rich Barth, born in Hamburg, Germany, ranks as one of the most perceptive and empathetic of the nineteenth-century European travelers to Africa. His magisterial 3,500-page, five-volume *Travels and Discoveries in North and Central Africa* (1857–1858) is more an encyclopedia of the central Sudan than a narrative, and it is recognized as a standard reference and sourcebook.

Barth inherited from his father, a self-made businessman, a capacity for immense hard work and a passion for orderliness and from his mother a stern self-reliance bordering at times on the

German explorer Heinrich Barth (1821–1865). After traveling through West Africa, Barth wrote *Travels and Discoveries in North and Central Africa* (1857–1858), a five-volume set that has been cited by Charles Darwin and many African historians.

introspective. He interrupted his education at the University of Berlin with a year in Italy in 1840, and on his return he entered law school. He completed his Ph.D. in 1844 and then went to London to perfect his Arabic (he already spoke five modern languages) before embarking on what he called his *Studienreise*, a grand tour (1845–1847) along the North African littoral from Morocco to Egypt. Finally taken on as a university lecturer in Berlin's Department of Archaeology, he found his lectures so poorly attended that he quickly accepted an offer manipulated by the Prussian ambassador to London, the scholar Christian Bunsen, to join the British government's expedition into what was then called Central Africa, under the leadership of James Richardson.

The expedition lasted from 1850 to 1855. Following Richardson's death in 1851 in Bornu, Barth assumed leadership of the expedition, and it penetrated as far south as present-day Chad, Cameroon, Nigeria, Niger, and Mali. He made sustained sojourns in such principal cities of the Sokoto Caliphate as Sokoto, Gwandu, Kano, and Yola, as well as in rival Kukawa (Bornu) and Timbuktu.

Barth returned to Europe in 1855 and resided in London while he wrote up his journals. The three volumes of the *Travels* were published in German, French, and Dutch as well as in English and were enhanced by sixty lithographs after J. M. Bernatz. The book was not received with any enthusiasm, aside from the recognition of its undisputed authoritativeness.

Barth's last ten years brought him little happiness. Proud and prickly, he quarreled with both the Royal Geographical Society of England and the British government. Following his return to Germany in 1859, he was piqued by his failure to achieve the public recognition he felt to be his due. He did not obtain the consulships in Constantinople or Siam that he had hoped for; he was not elected to full membership of the Royal Academy of Sciences; and he was not nominated to succeed his mentor, Karl Ritter, as professor of geography in Berlin. Instead, he had to be content—and then not until 1863—with a temporary appointment. The supernumerary post gave him time to resume his traveling, and he spent several months each year in Europe and the Balkans. Apart from his accounts of further journeys in Asia Minor, his most significant scholarship was reserved for work on his Central African vocabularies, published as *Collection of Vocabularies of Central-African Languages* (3 vols., 1862). Barth died on November 25, 1865, after two days' illness. He was buried in the Jerusalem Cemetery in Berlin.

See also **Colonial Policies and Practices; Kano; Sudan; Travel and Exploration: European (Since 1800).**

BIBLIOGRAPHY

Boahen, A. Adu. *Britain, the Sahara, and the Western Sudan, 1788–1861.* Oxford: Clarendon Press, 1964.

Bovill, E. W. "Henry Barth." *The Journal of the African Society* 25 (1926): 311–320.

Italiaander, Rolf. *Im Sattel durch Nord- und Zentralafrika Reisen und Entdeckungen in den Jahren 1849–1855* [1967]. Wiesbaden: Brockhaus, 1980.

Kirk-Greene, Anthony H. M. *Barth's Travels in Nigeria: Extracts from the Journal of Heinrich Barth.* London: Oxford University Press, 1962.

Prothero, R. Mansell. "Heinrich Barth and the Western Sudan." *Geographical Journal* 124, pt. 3 (1958): 326–339.

Prothero, R. Mansell. *Heinrich Barth, ein Forscher in Afrika: Leben, Werk, Leistung.* Wiesbaden, Germany: Steiner, 1967.

ANTHONY KIRK-GREENE

BASHIR, OMAR AHMED EL- (1944–).

Born in Hosh Bonnaga, a village 93 miles north of Khartoum, the capital of Sudan, Omar Ahmed el-Bashir came from a family of rural workers. Trained in military schools, he rose quickly in the army. In 1973 he was sent to Egypt to serve in that nation's army against Israel in the 1973 Mideast War.

During the 1980s, el-Bashir fought against the insurgent Sudanese People's Liberation Army in the nation's civil war, a conflict pitting the mostly Arab and Muslim north, which controlled the government, against the rebellious south, populated mostly by black Christians and animists. In 1989, el-Bashir led a military coup that overthrew a democratically elected government. The constitution, the parliament, and the free press were eliminated; although official restorations of these institutions were made in some form from time to time, in reality el-Bashir remained a military dictator.

At the start of his regime, el-Bashir allied himself with Hasan al-Turabi, the leading radical Islamist in Sudan. Their intensification of previous efforts to impose *shari'a* (Islamic) law upon the country heightened the civil war. As that conflict raged in the 1990s, el-Bashir's regime was frequently accused of genocide against the south. Meanwhile, black southerners were sometimes seized by the army

President of Sudan Omar el-Bashir sits at the beginning of a mini Africa Union summit. The summit, which focused on the Darfur crisis, was held in Tripoli, October 17, 2004. It included heads of state from Libya, Nigeria, Egypt, Sudan, and Chad. JOHN MACDOUGALL/AFP/GETTY IMAGES

and sold into slavery in the north. In 1999, el-Bashir dismissed al-Turabi from the government on the grounds that he was plotting a coup. Two years later al-Turabi was arrested for his involvement in a plot to overthrow el-Bashir.

Since 2003, el-Bashir has placed increasing emphasis on employing Arab militias, or Jinjaweed, to crush the insurgency in the south. They are generally believed to be guilty of committing genocide against black southerners. The militias have been especially active in the Darfur region in western Sudan, and their actions have created an international uproar.

See also **Turabi, Hasan 'Abd Allah al-; Warfare: Civil Wars.**

BIBLIOGRAPHY

Idris, Amir H. *Conflict and Politics of Identity in Sudan.* New York: Palgrave Macmillan, 2005.

Petterson, Donald. *Inside Sudan: Political Islam, Conflict, and Catastrophe*, rev. edition. Boulder, CO: Westview Press, 2003.

MICHAEL LEVINE

BASKETRY AND MAT-MAKING.
See **Arts: Basketry and Mat Making.**

BASUTOLAND. *See* **Lesotho.**

BEADS. *See* **Arts: Beads.**

BEATRIZ, DONA. *See* **Kimpa Vita, Dona Beatriz.**

BECHUANALAND. *See* **Botswana.**

BELGIAN CONGO. *See* **Colonial Policies and Practices: Belgian; Congo, Republic of.**

BELLO, AHMADU (1910–1966). In both the political and physical sense, Alhaji Ahmadu Bello was a "giant" among Nigeria's nationalist leaders in the 1950s. As the first premier of northern Nigeria, he was active in uniting the northern region and helping it to achieve dominance within the federal system. He preferred to be premier of the north rather than be prime minister of the country as a whole. In fact, Bello set his sights upon eventually becoming the sultan of Sokoto, the spiritual leader of northern Nigeria's dominant Muslim population. In this role, Bello would have been able to combine political power with supreme religious authority. In the end, however, an assassin rendered all such ambitions futile.

Bello was a direct descendant of Shehu 'Uthman dan Fodio (1754–1817), founder of the Fulani empire, or Sokoto Caliphate. Like most of the Westernizing elite of northern Nigeria between the world wars, he trained as a teacher and joined the Sokoto Native Administration. Through this agency

Sir Ahmadu Bello (1910–1966). Bello served as the first premier of the Northern Nigeria region. He was assassinated during a military coup.

he became a district head and earned the traditional title of *sardauna* (war leader) before he was thirty years old.

Bello was prominent in transforming the Northern People's Congress (NPC) from a cultural organization to a political party in 1951–1952. By the time Nigeria became independent in 1960, the NPC had, under Bello's leadership, assumed unquestioned dominance in the federal government. Because he was of royal descent and a patron of Islam, Bello persuaded the North's traditional rulers, who were predominantly Muslim, to support him in his modernizing reforms. Arguably his greatest achievement, and ultimately his greatest influence on Nigeria, was to galvanize the socio-educational advance of northerners into positions of power in the postindependence federal institutions. Able, ambitious, and aristocratic, Bello was controversial throughout his life. He was murdered by the military on January 15, 1966, in an uprising that was aimed at overthrowing the corrupt civilian government of Nigeria and purging its leadership.

See also **Nigeria: History and Politics, Northern Nigeria; 'Uthman dan Fodio.**

BIBLIOGRAPHY

Bello, Ahmadu. *My Life*. Cambridge, U.K.: Cambridge University Press, 1962.

Kirk-Greene, A. H. M. "Ahmadu Bello." In *Political Leaders of Contemporary Africa South of the Sahara*, ed. Harvey Glickman. New York: Greenwood Press, 1992.

Paden, John N. *Ahmadu Bello, Sardauna of Sokoto: Values and Leadership in Nigeria*. London: Hodder and Stoughton, 1986.

Whitaker, C. Sylvester, Jr. *The Politics of Tradition: Continuity and Change in Northern Nigeria, 1946–1966*. Princeton, NJ: Princeton University Press, 1970.

A. H. M. KIRK-GREENE

BELLO, MUHAMMAD (1781–1837).

The soldier and statesman Muhammad Bello played both a military and an administrative role in the jihad against the Hausa states led by his father, 'Uthman dan Fodio, in the period 1804–1808. Following the triumph of the jihadist forces, Bello took charge of planning the new state's capital at Sokoto (now the capital of one of Nigeria's constituent states).

In 1812 Bello was given overall responsibility for the eastern emirates of the caliphate, while his uncle Abdullahi was given charge of the western ones. On his father's death in 1817, he became Commander of the Faithful in his place and consolidated the new Islamic state while laying the foundations of its bureaucracy with the help of his vizier, Gidado dan Laima. However, his reign was punctuated by internal revolts and external attacks, in particular by those of the defeated Hausa sultans of Gobir and Katsina. To counter these he built a number of fortresses on the Islamic model of the *ribat* (fortified retreat) and in a spirit of compromise revived a number of older (pre-caliphate) political offices.

Bello wrote more than one hundred scholarly works and more than sixty poems. They range over the Islamic sciences but also contain much on government, administration, and Sufi themes. He also wrote several short works on medicine and, in 1812, an important account of his father's movement, set in the context of regional history, titled *Infaq al-maysur*.

See also **Asma'u, Nana; Islam; 'Uthman dan Fodio.**

BIBLIOGRAPHY

Crowder, Michael. *The Story of Nigeria*, 3rd edition. London: Faber, 1978.

JOHN HUNWICK

BEN BARKA, MEHDI (1920–1965).

Mehdi Ben Barka *(al-Mahdi bin al-Barka)* was one of the few Moroccans to receive a secondary school *(lycée)* diploma under French rule (1912–1956). A brilliant mathematician, he received his diploma in 1950 and taught Hasan II, later to become Morocco's king (r. 1961–1999), at the palace school. One of the youngest leaders of Morocco's nationalist Istiqlal party, after independence he became chairman of the country's Consultative Assembly (1956–1959). In 1959 Ben Barka broke with the Istiqlal party to found the leftist National Union of Popular Forces (UNFP).

Remembrance march for Ben Barka (1920–1965). A Moroccan woman takes part in a remembrance march held in Rabat, Morocco, on October 29, 2006, the forty-first anniversary of the disappearance and suspected murder of Mehdi Ben Barka. ABDELHAK SENNA/AFP/GETTY IMAGES

Hasan II saw the left as a serious threat to his regime and accused Ben Barka of subversion, forcing him into exile in France, where he emerged as a major leader of the third world's anticolonial movement. After Ben Barka criticized Morocco's 1963 invasion of Algeria, he was condemned to death *in absentia*.

On October 29, 1965, two French security officers kidnapped Ben Barka outside a café in central Paris; he was never seen again. They received prison sentences in 1967, although the judge ruled that Muhammad Oufkir, then Morocco's minister of the interior, was complicit in his torture and presumed murder. In 2001 a retired Moroccan intelligence officer published a graphic account of the operation, the French declassified some documents related to the case, and French court proceedings were reopened, but remain inconclusive.

See also **Hasan II of Morocco.**

BIBLIOGRAPHY

Boukhari, Ahmed. *Le Secret: Ben Barka et le Maroc: Un ancien agent des services spéciaux parle.* (The secret: Ben Barka and Morocco: A former special services agent speaks). Neuilly-sur-Seine: Lafon, 2002.

Daoud, Zakya, and Maâti Monjib. *Ben Barka.* Paris: Michalon, 1996.

DALE F. EICKELMAN

BENGA, OTA (c. 1883–1916). Ota Benga was exhibited, along with other African Pygmies—as well as Apaches (including Geronimo, 1829–1909), Zulus, Eskimos, and hundreds of other indigenous people—at the World's Fair in St. Louis in 1904. In September 1906, Ota Benga made headlines when displayed at New York's Zoological

Park (the Bronx Zoo) in the same cage as Dohong the orangutan.

Ota Benga first came to the United States in June 1904, with Samuel Phillips Verner (1873–1943), an ex-missionary hired to bring African Pygmies to the Anthropology Department of the 1904 World's Fair. Benga agreed to go with Verner because his own people had been slaughtered by agents of King Leopold II of Belgium (1835–1909), ruler of what was called the Congo Free State.

After the World's Fair, Ota traveled with Verner through the Congo as the latter tried to make his fortune. In 1906, Ota opted to return with Verner to the United States. He resided, for a time, at the American Museum of Natural History, before Bronx Zoo director William T. Hornaday (1854–1937) put him on display. Protests by black clergymen led to Ota's release from the zoo and to sojourns in Brooklyn and Long Island. In 1910, Ota Benga moved to Lynchburg, Virginia, where he was partially assimilated into the black community and became a friend and guide to many of its children.

In March 1916, Ota Benga, trapped between two worlds, performed a tribal dance and shot himself with a stolen pistol. Verner wrote for *The New York Times* that Ota had been "a brave, shrewd little man who preferred to match himself against civilization rather than be a slave . . . All honor to him, even though he died in the attempt!"

Ota Benga, to be sure, was a victim of racism in raw form but was also an enormously resourceful individual. In the early twenty-first century, artists increasingly honor him. An art collective named Otabenga Jones, for example, exhibited at the 2006 Whitney Biennial. And Africans have seen him as a source of inspiration in the struggle for human rights. The Congolese activists and scholars Jacques Depelchin and Wamba dia Wamba have founded The Ota Benga International Alliance for Peace in the DR Congo, based in Kinshasa.

See also **Human Rights.**

BIBLIOGRAPHY

Bradford, Phillips Verner, and Blume, Harvey. *Ota Benga: The Pygmy in the Zoo.* New York: St. Martin's Press, 1992.

Majavu, Mandisi. "The Failure of an African Political Leadership: An Interview with Professor Wamba dia Wamba." *Znet*, July 18, 2003. Available from http://www.zmag.org/content/showarticle.cfm?SectionID=2&ItemID=3927.

HARVEY BLUME

BENGUELA. The first Portuguese attempt to establish a commercial outpost to develop slaving at this open bay on the southwestern coast of Africa took place in the first half of the seventeenth century. However, for most of that century the settlement there remained largely peripheral in the Atlantic economy, and the Portuguese royal bureaucracy was barely present. By the end of the seventeenth century, following military expeditions into the high plateau inland that led to creation of an outpost in Kakonda, the town was integrated into Atlantic commercial circuits as a provider of slaves for Luanda. Ships sailing from Benguela called into Luanda to pay taxes on the slaves they transported across the Atlantic. The direct slave trade from Benguela to Brazil began in the 1730s, turning the town into a major slave port. Most of the funding for slaving at Benguela originated from Brazil, with Rio de Janeiro standing out as the town's merchants' primary commercial partner. Local society was characterized by a mix of individuals of African, Euro-African, Portuguese, and Brazilian backgrounds. After Brazil became independent of Portugal in 1822, Benguela remained tightly linked to Rio de Janeiro, and secondarily to Salvador in northeast Brazil.

By the mid-nineteenth century, slaves were still shipped from the city, but as the slave trade died out Benguela continued providing forced labor for cocoa plantations on the island of São Tomé and prospered on short-lived succeeding booms in exports of ivory, beeswax, and red (wild) rubber from the eastern regions that also supplied slaves. In the twentieth century, although retaining its standing as a district administrative seat, the economic initiative in the region passed to the bay at Lobito, just to the north, which became Angola's largest port as the terminus of the Benguela Railway, traversing the old slave-, ivory-, wax-, and rubber-producing territories on the route to the large copper-mining complex in the Belgian Congo.

See also **Slave Trades.**

BIBLIOGRAPHY

Miller, Joseph. *Way of Death: Merchant Capitalism and the Angolan Slave Trade, 1730–1830.* Madison: University of Wisconsin Press, 1988.

ROQUINALDO FERREIRA

BÉNIN

This entry includes the following articles:
GEOGRAPHY AND ECONOMY
SOCIETY AND CULTURES
HISTORY AND POLITICS

GEOGRAPHY AND ECONOMY

The Republic of Bénin lies on West Africa's Guinea coast. Bénin can be subdivided into five geographical regions. Moving from south to north, these are: (1) coastal zone, (2) *terre de barre* (a French adaptation of the Portuguese *barro*, or "clay"), (3) Precambrian socket, (4) Atakora mountains in the northwest, and (5) northern plains. There is a marked difference in population density between the north and the south: 12 inhabitants per square kilometer in the northern province of Borgou, and 284 per square kilometer in the southern Atlantique province.

GEOGRAPHY

The seventy-five-mile-wide coastal zone has mangrove vegetation and is rich in lagoons and swamps. North of the coastal zone lies a zone of *terre de barre*, which reaches beyond the city of Abomey. Mostly sandy and lateritic, the soil of this densely populated region is rather poor from an agricultural point of view. An exception may be found in the rich black soils of the Lama depression, where thick layers of alluvial sediment cover a water table between 50 and almost 500 feet underground. Until the early twenty-first century creeks and the rivers Kouffo, Zou, Oueme, and Mono—all of which run from north to south—were the major sources of fresh water. Although the south has two rainy seasons per year, total precipitation is rather low—from thirty-six inches in the southwest to fifty-eight inches in the southeast, compared to other countries of the same

geographical zone. This break in the coastal belt of high precipitation, a phenomenon known as the "Bénin window," may be due to the intensive agriculture in the south, which has destroyed almost all the rain forest and reduced convection rains.

The central part of Bénin is characterized by a plain of the Precambrian socket and granite monadnocks, dry forests, and dry savanna, building the southern verge of the Sudanic vegetation zone. In the northwest lies the Atakora chain, the foothills from the Togo Mountains, with a height seldom over 2,000 feet, occasional plateaus, and poor soil. Some gold is washed from alluvial deposits. The poor infrastructure, limited to one 360-mile-long narrow-gauge railway line from Cotonou to Parakou, and two tarmac roads—one running from east to west along the coast, the other from the coast to Malanville on the frontier to Niger in the north—hinder further prospecting for metal ores such as chrome, uranium, and manganese.

The northern plains west of the Atakora are dominated by short, dry savannas. The precipitation ranges from fifty-six inches west of Djougou to thirty at the Bénin's most northern point, where there is a Sahelian (semiarid) climate, prone to drought. Intensive agriculture has eroded mountain slopes and lateritized soil in the plains. The region's one rainy season per year further limits agricultural potential.

ECONOMY

Bénin's economy has four essential components: agriculture, informal trade (smuggling), foreign aid, and a less important industrial sector.

Agriculture. The lagoons support fishing and related industries, while floodlands are used for intensive agriculture and fish farming. Only one-quarter of the land, mostly in the north, is fit for plow agriculture; for ecological reasons, the rest can only be worked with a hoe. "Forests" are semideciduous savanna, and illegal cutting has depleted much of the state-managed *forêt classée*. The officially classified "residual" or unused land is mostly used as pasture and as a source of wild resources such as shea nuts.

Approximately 70 percent of the population lives and works in the rural sector. Any distinction between food and cash crops make little sense in the

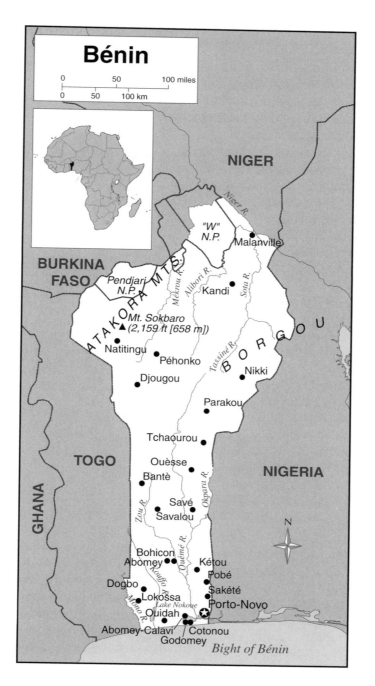

case of Bénin, because a part of all food production is intended for both local and export markets. The most important crops in the south are corn, cassava, palm oil, and coconut trees. Small-scale animal husbandry is limited to pigs, goats, and poultry.

Only in the north is there substantial cattle raising by the Fulbe. All annual crops are grown in the center of the country. Here and in the north, yam is the most important tuber. After corn, sorghum and millet are the most important cereals consumed in the country and are staple foods in the north.

Cotton earns three-quarters of the country's import income, but this is also the biggest weakness in the country's economy; due to falling world market prices, it must be heavily subsidized. According to 2005 statistics, only 36 percent of the gross domestic product (GDP) comes from agricultural production.

Informal Trade. One of the most important pillars of Bénin's economy is the informal trade of staple foods and the reexportation of consumer goods with its neighbor Nigeria. In 2003 Nigeria refused to tolerate this illegal trade any further and began to close the border periodically for few days at a time. This had an immediate and negative effect on Bénin's economy. Some consumer goods produced in Nigeria, especially oil, enter Bénin the same way. In addition, drugs from South America come from Nigeria through Bénin en route to Western Europe.

Transnational Trade and Industry. Bénin's major official trading partners are the countries of the European Union, the United States, China, and Thailand. Trade with African countries, other than Côte d'Ivoire and Nigeria, is hindered by a lack of infrastructure (particularly railways) and illegally imposed customs fees. The small industrial sector, 14 percent of the GDP according to 2005 statistics, produces mainly consumer goods or processes agricultural products. Only the cement industry, with three production sites, and, since 1982, the development of offshore oil production, have successfully reduced Bénin's imports. Despite this improvement, Bénin's trade balance is chronically negative.

Bénin's transformation to a market economy, which started with the end of the socialist era, is not yet complete. However, the privatization of some industries and not-yet-completed government reforms have at least stabilized the economy, which grew between 4 and 6 percent from 2001 to 2005.

Developmental Aid. In 2005 net official development assistance amounted to $240 million, or 35 percent of the national budget. With external aid flowing into infrastructure, health, and agriculture, the state has been able to concentrate on other activities. The number of persons employed in the public service increased fivefold between 1972 and 1991. A similar increase occurred within state-owned businesses. Developmental aid has not always been used effectively. Some has been spent on misguided development projects, such as

repeated, failed efforts to introduce the ox-drawn plow in the south, where it is not ecologically suitable. Other funds have been spent to construct prestigious buildings for politicians. Much developmental aid has gone to pay government salaries, which constitute 75 percent of the national budget during years of economic crisis.

See also **Climate; Ecosystems.**

BIBLIOGRAPHY

Bierschenk, Thomas, Georg Elwert, and Dirk Kohnert. "The Long-Term Effects of Development Aid: Empirical Studies in Rural West Africa." *Economics* 47 (1993): 83–111.

d'Almeida-Topor, Hélène. *Histoire économique du Dahomey.* 2 vols. Paris: L'Harmattan, 1995.

Elwert, Georg, and Lazare Séhouéto. "Local Knowledge and the Improvement of Food Production: A Case Study in Bénin." In *Food Security and Nutrition: The Global Challenge*, ed. Uwe Kracht and Manfred Schulz. New York: St. Martin's, 1999.

Floquet, Anne Niko; von der Lühe; and Hans-Joachim Preuss. *Paysans, vulgarisateurs et chercheurs au sud du Bénin: le trio déconnecté.* Münster: Lit, 1996.

KAROLA ELWERT-KRETSCHMER

SOCIETY AND CULTURES

Bénin has long been portrayed ethnically as being the sum of three major influences: the kingdom of Dahomey in the center, the former French-protected kingdom of Porto Novo in the southwest, and the people in the north. A closer look, however, reveals a much more fluid picture. The types of identity groups that existed in the precolonial period, and that were taken as the reference for the colonial construction of ethnic groups, generally allowed for multiple identification; then, as now, people could produce different ethnic references according to context.

Ethnic identification can be based on any of several elements, including language, ancestry, and religious affiliation. French attributions of ethnicity, following European usage, tended to equate linguistic and ethnic boundaries, but language is only one point of ethnic reference. For example, the ethnic label *Bariba* in the Borgu (northeastern Bénin and northwestern Nigeria), used primarily for all Baatonum speakers, is a term the French had invented for the Baatombu, the major ethnic group in the region. In a broader sense, however, the term identified those people who were ruled by the *wasangari* (precolonial Borgu warlords). Bariba included smaller ethnic groups, such as the Yoruba-speaking Mokole, the Mande-speaking Boko, or even the Fulani in the region.

Linguistic identification was strengthened by the *sous-commissions linguistiques* that were established under the Kérékou regime in 1974. Two villages in Togo on the frontier to Bénin, however, declared themselves to be Bariba and to speak Bariba, although they speak the language of the neighboring city Basila. They identified themselves as Bariba because some of their mixed ancestry includes the Wasangari, who fled from the province of Borgu. Such genealogical claims are also legitimate in Béninese eyes and may also be useful as a reference for the creation of political links. Statisticians and politicians try to reduce this complexity and bring groups under one heading. Based on categories of the censuses of 1966, 1979, and 1992, the sum of these groupings, with estimated figures for 1992, may be seen as follows:

Fon (including Maxi): 1,310,000
Gun and the Western Toli: 620,000
Yoruba-Nago (including Ketu, Chabe, and Idacha): 590,000
Adja and Wachi: 520,000
Batombu (of Gur language and Boko: 420,000
Northern Gur (Betammaribe, Berba, Yoabu, etc.): 320,000
Fulani (including Gando): 270,000
Ayizo, Xweda, Eastern Toli, and Tofin: 240,000
Mina and Xwla: 180,000
Southern Gur (Yom, Anii, etc.): 150,000
Dendi of the Borgu province: 110,000

Some 120,000 people remain unaccounted for, among them the speakers of Fodo, a Guang language of Séméré, and about 1,000 French speakers (most of them of African origin).

These statistics do not provide the many options people have. They may choose to identify with their father's origin (most common because these groups are patrilineal or bilateral), their mother's origin (common if one opts to stay with maternal kin), or their locality and its main language (equally common, and typical in the large cities).

Outside observers customarily reduce the complexity of the multiple ethnic options by creating

large clusters according to the former ruling apparatus of the Fon and the Gun, the Yoruba kingdoms of Save and Ketu, the Wasangari raiders of Paraku, Nikki, and other places of the Borgu. They then add a residual category, called Somba, to include the many segmentary groups around the Atakora Mountains who are otherwise impossible to identify.

That Fongbe, the Fon language, is the main language in the southern part of the country suggests to outsiders that the Fon comprise the dominant group of the country. But this involves a fundamental error, as one cannot deduce sociostructural similarity and political affinity from linguistic kinship.

The Fon exercised power in the precolonial period mainly on behalf of the economy of slave raiding. They incorporated some of their slaves into their elite troops and households, so the slaves also became Fon. The other troops, the military serfs, served only under coercion and refrained from identifying with their masters. One of the populations that had to send serfs to serve in the army every year were the Ayizo, people who probably descended from the plateau of Agbome, the Fon kingdom's capital. Their language, Ayizogbe, is a close dialect of Fongbe. But in their local communities—that are endogamous and closed against alliances with the feared Fon—they chose a different style of culture.

Not just the Fon based their culture and society on the slave trade. Slave raids were also the business of the Wasangari, the Ketu-Yoruba, and the Xweda. This history of slave raids is a clue to understanding the political structure and self-identification of some of the Yoruba groups on the country's western border. These include the Holli, Adja groups in the southeastern borderland of Bénin and Togo, and most of the forty self-identifying scattered groups in the Atakora province in the northwest, called Somba by their former raiding opponents. Some of them were segmentary groups of predatory expansion, such as the Betammaribe. The young warriors held social power, and each group of young men could integrate foreigners—such as refugees from other regions—through their initiation rituals, thus swelling the Betammaribe's ranks.

The word *Berba*, used as an ethnic name for Gur-speaking people north of the Atakora, still means for many people nothing other than membership of a group of males who underwent an initiation together. Those identified by others as Berba see themselves as refugees from political pressure or conflict who sought haven in the open savanna territory north of the Atakora ridge. Their only shared cultural trait is a common initiation ritual.

In contrast to the segmentary lineage systems organizing the aforementioned groups, there are villages—especially in the south of the Atakora province—wherein the main reference was not a construction of common ancestry or an initiation, but a highly organized community of defense. The citizens of Basila, such as the Baseda, remember the different regions from which they arrived and act more as a republic. They base their cohesion, however, on their shared defense, expressed through a yearly ritual involving a general debate concerning possible changes of prices and social norms and, most important, about obedience to their leaders.

The institution of chieftancy exists where it was recognized or invented by the colonial authority (with the *chef de canton* as the hierarchically highest position). In only a few cases in the postcolonial period have new chiefdoms been created after the colonial model. The succession of chiefs following death or, rarely, after deposition, is implemented according to rules established in the colonial era: filial inheritance, rotation of office among established lineages, or selection by chosen voters. Few chiefs may claim that their offices existed in the precolonial era. It is well remembered that, in colonial times, some of them (re-)created authority by privately recruiting troops or relying on the gendarmes.

A central issue making chieftancy an important institution is the right to land. Almost no farmland is owned in a form that could be the basis for a legal claim because there are almost no land registers outside the cities. More than 95 percent of peasant holdings are still administered as *terre domaniale*, given to peasants only as usufruct. Where land is not readily available, it is essential to have a strong and positive link to the chief. Crucial parameters of conflict are: whether a strip of land is defined as belonging to this or to that village (in other words, to this or to that chief's jurisdiction); whether the chief is closely related to the person requesting land; whether one can

split one community into two, or merge two into one, in order to have a chief "of one's own people"; and whether one is defined as a member or an outsider.

A stranger may be a person with whom one is well acquainted but who is devoid of any basic land rights and of any chiefly connection to appeal to. Consequently, there is a demand for pseudo-historical research to define the legitimacy of people's claims to land. Where the value of land increases, the demand for ethnicity increases as well, and chiefs are asked to intervene more often. The colonial administration inadvertently created a territorialization of ethnicity, but people of different origins who actively kept their distinctions lived, and still live, together. A division of labor, occupations of different ecological niches (herders, fishermen, and cultivators), and various histories of flight and domination created a rather mixed settlement pattern that is impossible to render by one-color, one-tribe maps. The territorialization of ethnicity has nonetheless simplified such patterns so that one, and only one, customary authority grants land rights.

Population density in Bénin is currently around ninety-six persons per square mile, but varies largely between North and South. It goes up to 1,532 people per square mile in peri-urban surroundings of the economic capital Cotonou, where a fifth of the total population lives on only 1 percent of the national territory. In the central and northern parts of the country, however, population density does not exceed 113 people per square mile. The city of Cotonou itself has the highest population density in Bénin with approximately 13,548 people per square mile. Furthermore, the entire southern part of Bénin is densely populated: Nearly two-thirds of the population concentrate here on approximately 20 percent of the national territory. Because few possibilities exist to earn money outside the agricultural sector, one may speak of Asiatic conditions of southern Bénin's agriculture in respect to its demographic situation. These conditions refer to non-sustainable forms of land use, a continuous reduction of the area of cultivable land available per capita, as well as increasing landlessness and land tenure conflicts. In Central and northern Bénin however, population density throughout is fewer than 113 people per square mile, except for Parakou.

République du Bénin (Republic of Benin, formerly Dahomey)

Population:	8,078,314 (2007 est.)
Area:	112,622 sq. km (43,483 sq. mi.)
Official language:	French
National currency:	CFA franc
Principal religions:	indigenous (animist) 50%, Christian 30%, Muslim 20%
Capital:	Porto Novo (est. pop. 295,000 in 2006)
Other urban centers:	Cotonou, Abomey, Ouidah, Parakou, Natitingou
Annual rainfall:	varies from 1,500 mm (58 in.) in southeast to 770 mm (30 in.) in extreme north
Principal geographical features:	*Rivers:* Mono, Kuffo, Zou, Ouémé, Sota *Lakes:* Lake Ahémè *Mountains:* Atakora Mountains *Lagoons:* Cotonou, Ouidah, Grand Popo, Porto Novo, Avlékété, Nokwé
Economy:	*GDP per capita:* US$1,100 (2005)
Principal products and exports:	*Agricultural:* corn, sorghum, cassava, tapioca, yams, beans, rice, cotton, palm oil, cocoa, peanuts, poultry, and livestock *Manufacturing:* textiles, cigarettes, food and beverages, construction materials *Mining:* petroleum, iron ore, limestone, chromium ore, gold, phosphates, diamonds
Government:	Independence from France, 1960. Total of six constitutions since independence. Under 1990 constitution president elected for 5-year term by universal suffrage and may serve 2 terms. 83-seat Assemblée Nationale elected for 4-year terms by universal suffrage. President nominates cabinet. For purposes of local government there are 6 provinces, 78 districts.
Heads of state since independence:	1960–1963: President Hubert Coutoucou Maga 1963–1964: Lieutenant-Colonel Christophe Soglo 1964–1965: President Sourou-Migan Apithy 1965: Tahirou Congacou 1965–1967: General Christophe Soglo 1967–1968: Lieutenant-Colonel Alphonse Amadou Alley 1968–1969: President Émile-Derlin Zinsou 1969–1970: Presidential Council (Paul Émile de Souza, Benoît Sinzogan, Maurice Kouandete) 1970–1972: Presidential Council (Hubert C. Maga, Sourou-Migan Apithy, Justin Tometin Ahomadegbe) 1972–1991: Major (later Lieutenant-General) Mathieu Kérékou 1991–1996: President Nicéphore Soglo 1996–2006: President Mathieu Kérékou 2006–: President Yayi Boni
Armed forces:	President is commander in chief. Voluntary enlistment. *Army:* 4,500 *Navy:* 150 *Air force:* 150 *Paramilitary:* 4,000–4,500
Transportation:	*Rail:* 580 km (360 mi.). Railway system is jointly operated by Bénin and Niger (with Bénin holding the controlling interest). *Roads:* 7,500 km (4,660 mi.) *Airports:* Airline is state controlled. International facility at Cotonou, smaller airports in the interior.
Media:	*La Nation* (official government paper), *Le Matin.* 12 periodicals. Principal book publisher: Office National de la Presse et d'Imprimerie. Broadcasting: Office de Radiodiffusion et Télévision du Bénin (RTB).
Literacy and education:	*Total literacy rate:* 33.6% (2002). Education is free, universal, and compulsory from ages 5–11. The Université Nationale du Bénin is 70% subsidized by France. In addition there are 3 polytechnics.

The population density differentials are due to the depopulation of the North by slave raids in the precolonial period; variations in agricultural potential; the effects of economic growth, largely concentrated around Cotonou; and differences in child mortality rates. The only large city in the country, with the only port and international airport, Cotonou became the administrative capital and de facto seat of government in spite of the formal position of Porto Novo. Including the unregistered population and that of the almost integrated city of Godomey, Cotonou's population is, as of the early twenty-first century, probably around 850,000. In 2002, 40 percent of the population were living in cities and towns, and 47 percent of the population were younger than fifteen.

According to Bénin's 2002 census, the country had a total population of 6,750,000 inhabitants.

Since 1992, the annual demographic growth rate averages out at 3.25 percent and thus slightly increased compared to only 2.8 percent between the population censuses of 1979 and 1992. The fertility rate, though in slight decline since 1982, is currently still high at 6.3. Fertility rates are decreasing more significantly in the cities than in rural areas, a phenomenon that is also known in the rest of sub-Saharan Africa. The high birth rates correspond to the age structure (dominated by the under-fifteen-year-olds who constitute nearly half of the total population). The average national demographic growth rate of 3.25 percent however, has to be qualified by the high spatial disparities of demographic growth.

In the densely populated South, the population grows below average, a trend that has already been recorded in 1992 and that is confirmed by early twenty-first century data. This applies to most of the southern communes, except for Abomey-Calavi and Sèmè-Kpodji. These administrative districts bordering Cotonou are Béninise dormitory towns that have an increasing commuter population. Due to lower lease and land prices, these urbanized communes attract and absorb large portions of the population migrating toward Cotonou. This results in high growth rates reaching 6 percent in Sèmè-Kpodji, and the national peak of 9.5 percent in Abomey-Calavi.

Besides the Cotonou agglomeration, some parts of Central and northern Bénin show the highest demographic growth rates, such as the communes Ouèsse, Bantè, Tchaourou, and Bassila in Central Bénin, and Péhonko and Ségbana in the North. In Tchaourou, the commune that had the lowest population density until the 1970s, the growth rates were consistently high for the next three decades, reaching 4.9 percent. Contrary to this, in Bassila the increase in population growth started later. Here, the demographic growth has doubled since the 1980s to 4.8 percent in 2002. Parakou is by far the largest town in the North. Its demographic growth is slower than during the two decades after independence when impressive rates of around 8 percent were common for the major urban centers. But unlike Cotonou, Parakou continues to grow dynamically with rates around 3.8 percent.

See also **Agriculture: Beginnings and Development; Climate; Colonialism and Imperialism: Overview; Geography and the Study of Africa; Porto Novo.**

BIBLIOGRAPHY

Alber, Erdmute. *Im Gewand von Herrschaft Modalitäten der Macht bei den Baatombu (1895–1995).* Studien zur Kulturkunde Band 116. Cologne: Rüdiger Köppe Verlag, 2000.

Bierschenk, Thomas Bierschenk, and Pierre-Yves Le Meur, eds. *Trajectoires peules au Bénin.* Paris: Karthala, 1997.

Elwert, Georg. *Bauern und Staat in Westafrika.* Frankfurt: Campus Verlag, 1983.

Herskovits, Melville. *Dahomey, an Ancient West African Kingdom.* 2 vols. Evanston, IL: Northwestern University Press, 1967.

Lombard, Jacques. *Structures de type féodale en Afrique noir.* Paris: Mouton, 1965.

Manning, Patrick. *Slavery, Colonialism and Economic Growth in Dahomey, 1640–1960.* Cambridge, U.K.: Cambridge University Press, 1982.

Mondjannagni, Alfred. *Campagnes et villes au sud de la République Populaire du Bénin.* Paris: Mouton, 1977.

ERDMUTE ALBER

HISTORY AND POLITICS

The present-day Republic of Bénin was known, until 1975, as the Republic of Dahomey. It emerged as an independent state from the French colony of the same name, built around the old kingdom of Dahomey, a name familiar to scholars and students of the transatlantic slave trade and African diaspora. This famous Aja kingdom, with its capital at Abomey a hundred miles or so from the coast, was the epicenter of the notorious Slave Coast of West Africa between the seventeenth and nineteenth centuries. Some historians estimate that over 1 million Africans were shipped from Ouidah (Whydah), its principal outlet to Atlantic trade, to the North, Central, and South America as well as the West Indies. In the first half of the nineteenth century, the trade, despite its official abolition in 1815, continued to be patronized until 1848 by both the French and notorious Brazilian slave trader Francisco Félix de Souza, ally and friend of king Gezo.

The political and economic history of modern Bénin, heir of precolonial and colonial Dahomey, cannot therefore be properly grasped without taking into account the legacy of this long involvement in the Atlantic trade. This legacy is still visible in many aspects of the country's political, socioeconomic, and cultural life, even though most local studies hardly acknowledge its significance, preferring to focus on the various political crises the country has endured since its independence in 1960. Political instability, characterized by a series of coups d'état, unusual institutions—such as a two-year rotating presidency shared between three rival political leaders—Marxism, and finally democratization, have turned Bénin into a postcolonial African case study.

FRENCH COLONIAL CONQUEST AND ADMINISTRATION, 1892–1960

French presence in precolonial Dahomey dates to the seventeenth-century transatlantic slave trade. Until it was destroyed in 1908, the French slave fort was the most important European commercial building in Ouidah (along with the Portuguese and English establishments); it also served as a consulate until the late nineteenth century. It was also used from the 1840s onward by the Régis family as a center for the lucrative palm oil trade, arousing the suspicion of illegal slave trading from the British naval squadron that policed the area.

Anglo-French rivalry provided the framework for the development of European influence in the Bight of Bénin and the subsequent delimitation of the frontiers of the colony of Dahomey. Military conquest of Dahomey, however, was met with fierce resistance from King Behanzin (1844–1906) and his army. In addition to a superior force, the French benefited from the complicity of areas, such as Ketu, which were raided regularly by government as a major supply source for the slave trade; the inhabitants of these areas saw the French as their liberators.

The fall of Abomey was the starting point of the new colony, with coastal Porto Novo, capital of a kingdom under the French protectorate since the mid-nineteenth century, as its headquarters. To prevent both the Germans in neighboring Togo and the British in Nigeria from stopping their progression to the west, east, and north, protectorate treaties were hurriedly signed with various local authorities. By 1898, border agreements between the major colonial powers in the region had been drawn.

If the French governor in Porto Novo were the head of the colony, the real kingpins of the colonial administration were the *commandants de cercle* (district officers), assisted by influential *chefs de canton* (local representatives of the commandants de cercle), reminiscent of village heads of the precolonial era. The colonial state also enjoyed the civil service of an early local elite living in Ouidah and elsewhere on the coast, made up of returnees from Brazil and products of missionary and state schools. The growing strength and influence of this elite transcended the colony's borders. Dahomean citizens were undoubtedly the most widely represented in the administrative services of French West Africa. Members of this elite played a leading role in the nationalist movement and the post–World War II decolonization of Dahomey (and other French territories) in sub-Saharan Africa.

The road to independence was paved with political and electoral coalitions around three leaders with distinct regional bases: Sourou Migan Apithy and Justin Ahomadégbé in the south, Hubert Maga in the north. Conflicts within and between political parties left no room for unchallenged leadership or implementation of long-term policy. It was during this unstable period, further aggravated by the 1958 expulsion of thousands of Dahomeans from Côte d'Ivoire after the breakup of AOF, that the French colony became an independent state on August 1, 1960. Unfortunately, the new government was hardly able to respond to the urgent need for a coherent economic policy. Political maneuvers began again as soon as independence celebrations were over. To get rid of Ahomadégbé, Maga and Apithy allied to found the *Parti Dahoméen de l'Unité* (Dahomean Unity Party, or PDU). The seeds of a long period of political instability were thus sown.

THE ERA OF COUPS D'ÉTAT, 1960–1972

As to be expected, these political gyrations only worsened the challenging socioeconomic problems facing the new nation. In October 1963, the PDU-led government of Maga and Apithy collapsed in the face of protests by civil servants agitating for better work conditions and decent salaries. Maga was eliminated from the political game by a new alliance of Apithy and Ahomadégbé, who together founded yet another political party. Two years later, the commander of the national army (and a southerner), General Soglo, attempted the first of five coups d'état. Unprecedented solutions to the country's seemingly endless political crises were (unsuccessfully) attempted, including, between 1970 and 1972, a *Conseil Présidentiel* (presidential council), by which the three political leaders were to alternatively head the government for two years at a time. This era of political instability culminated in the revolution of October 26, 1972, and the leadership of Mathieu Kérékou who ruled until 1991, and then again from 1996 to 2006, when age and term limits prevented him from running again.

THE "REVOLUTIONARY" ERA, 1972–1990

The October 26, 1972, coup that brought Kérékou to power proclaimed itself a "revolution"; in 1975 the government adopted Marxism-Leninism as the state ideology. Kérékou instituted a single party system, the *Parti de la Révolution Populaire du Bénin* (People's Revolutionary Party of Bénin, or PRPB), modeled after the Soviet-bloc communist parties. Trade unions and youth organizations were unified along the same lines. All who dared to challenge the government were dubbed "reactionary elements," arrested, and put in jail. Many spent years in prison, particularly in Ségbana in the north. Traditional and religious authorities, whether *vodún* or Christian, were targeted in a ruthless official "campaign against feudalism." At the economic level, collective farms and state enterprises were created, and many private enterprises were nationalized. The ever-expanding state led to an uncontrolled expansion of public employment. Education was also affected, as private schools were taken over by the state and Marxist ideology became compulsory at all grade levels.

Until the early 1980s, the economy seemed to improve. Unfortunately, its apparent health was due not to the revolutionary regime but rather to the petroleum-fueled economic boom in neighboring Nigeria. When the bottom fell out of the oil market in the mid-1980s, the "informal trade" between the two countries was affected adversely. Mismanaged state-owned banks went bankrupt. Salaries were no longer paid regularly. In 1989 Kérékou's government was forced to accept stiff terms for aid and economic recovery from the International Monetary Fund. In addition, rising political opposition to the PRPB and its human rights abuses was fueled by the rapidly deteriorating socioeconomic climate.

The whole country became paralyzed by an unlimited strike by all categories of the working class. To get out of the deadlock, Kérékou called a national conference in February 1990. Presided over by Monsignor Isidore de Souza, Catholic Archbishop of Cotonou, the largest city in the country, the conference adopted far-reaching decisions and inaugurated the era of *renouveau démocratique* (democratic revival).

THE ERA OF DEMOCRATIC REVIVAL, 1990–2005

Kérékou's resolutely secular-materialist regime was doomed. The conference rejected its Marxist ideology, reestablished a multiparty system, returned private enterprises and schools taken over by the state to their former owners, allowed political exiles to return home, and released political detainees. Nicéphore Dieudonné Soglo, a former World Bank administrator, was elected prime minister of a provisional government until free and fair elections could be held. In the meantime, Kérékou continued as head of state without his former authority. Tensions cooled, and the country was saved from a potentially explosive social upheaval. The unprecedented acceptance of the radical changes introduced by the conference marked Bénin as a model in the democratization process.

However, after fifteen years of "democratic renewal," a critical evaluation in early 2006 showed that the performance had fallen far below 1990's optimistic expectations. Soglo, elected president in 1991, disappointed a large portion of his electorate by failing to improve the country's dismal economy, and ignoring government corruption, regionalism, and nepotism. In fact, the "Renaissance du Bénin" political party he founded after his election turned out to be a family affair, with his wife as the leading member.

This made it possible for Kérékou to regain power through elections in 1996 and 2001. Multiparty politics gave rise to innumerable and inconsistent, often idiosyncratically personal political organizations without any clear orientation or program. Widespread corruption poisoned the entire system. Although Kérékou attempted unsuccessfully to change the constitution to allow him to run for a third term, the opposition against him was too great, and he stepped down on April 1, 2006, when Yayi Boni succeeded him as president.

See also **Decolonization; Diasporas; International Monetary Fund; Ouidah; Porto Novo; Slave Trades; World Bank.**

BIBLIOGRAPHY

Garcia, Luc. *Le royaume du Dahomé face à la pénétration coloniale (1875–1894)*. Paris: Karthala, 1988.

Law, Robin. *Ouidah. The Social History of a West African Slaving "Port," 1727–1892*. Athens: Ohio University Press, 2004.

Manning, Patrick. *Slavery, Colonialism, and Economic Growth in Dahomey, 1640–1960*. Cambridge, U.K.: Cambridge University Press, 1982.

Mêtinhoué, Pierre G. *Les gouvernements du Dahomey et du Bénin, 1957–2005*. Porto Novo: Centre National de Production de Manuels Scolaires, 2005.

Schnapper, Bernard. *La politique et le commerce Français dans le Golfe de Guinée de 1838 à 1871*. Paris: La Haye, Mouton & Co., 1961.

ELISÉE SOUMONNI

BENIN CITY.

Benin City is the capital of the ancient kingdom of Bénin in southeastern Nigeria (and quite unrelated to the newly named nation of Bénin, formerly Dahomey, to the west of Nigeria). The city is the seat of the king, or *oba*, whose great palace, which dates from its original foundation in the fifteenth century, is in the center of the crowded city. The city was an early center for trade with Portugal and other European powers and became a place of great wealth and political power. Besides the palace itself it was the center for many guilds, including those of craftsmen in wood, brass, bronze, and ivory, who made the palace one of famous artistic richness and beauty. The palace was sacked and largely destroyed by the British in their invasion of 1897, and most of the royal regalia and palace ornaments were looted, taken to Europe and sold or otherwise dispersed.

The city in 2007 has a population of some 200,000 and is economically dependent upon rubber production and processing, the export of palm oil and kernels, wood and furniture, and is an important trade center for southeastern Nigeria. It is the seat of both Catholic and Anglican bishops. Its people, and those of most of the present kingdom, are known as Edo or Bini.

See also **Bénin; Ivory; Nigeria.**

BIBLIOGRAPHY

Bradbury, R.E. *Benin Studies*. London and New York, Oxford University Press. 1973.

Dark, P.J.C. *An Introduction to Benin: Arts and Technology*. Oxford, Clarendon Press, 1973.

JOHN MIDDLETON

BETI, MONGO

(1932–2001). Mongo Beti long held the distinction of being Cameroon's most significant novelist, even though many of his books were (and remain) banned in the country of his birth. His writing, ranging from satire and farce to full-blown tragedy, subtly explores the incompatibility of European and African values as established on colonial terms and confronts the horrors of despotism as established on postcolonial terms. He was strongly committed to the political novel and derided the "sophisticated uselessness" of some Western fiction as much as he deplored the "folkloric" vision of writers such as Camara Laye. From 1966 to 1994, Beti lived in Rouen, France, where he taught French and classical literature. Even in France, his works were often highly controversial. For instance, *Main basse sur le Cameroun: Autopsie d'une décolonisation* (1972) was banned at the request of a Cameroonian government representative, and its publication and sale was permitted only after a protracted lawsuit.

In 1991, Mongo Beti made a visit to his homeland for the first time in more than two decades. Three years later he retired from his professorship in Rouen and settled permanently in the village of his birth, Akometam. There he became an outspoken activist in civic affairs. He also maintained a presence in the Cameroonian capital of Yaoundé, where he founded the *Librairie des Peuples Noirs* (Library of the Black Peoples). His activism frequently led to confrontation with police, to which he responded as he had throughout his life when faced with injustice: he wrote more novels. In October 2001 he became gravely ill and was hospitalized in Yaoundé, where he was diagnosed with acute kidney failure and placed on dialysis. He was sent to Douala for further treatment, but the disease was too advanced. He died in Douala on October 8, 2001.

Beti remains best known for novels published in the 1950s, in which his characters become slowly and painfully conscious of the injustice they must help bring to an end. In a first book, *Ville cruelle* (1954, published under the pseudonym Eza Boto), a peasant farmer goes to sell his cocoa in the city, where he suffers at the hands of corrupt colonial officials. *Le pauvre Christ de Bomba* (1956), perhaps his most famous work, relates the failure of a missionary (le père Drumont) to convert the people of a small village. Drumont is as committed and well meaning as he is unthinking. As his cook explains, the people come to listen to him only in order to grasp the secret of French power, "the power of your planes, your trains... and instead you set about speaking of God, of the soul, of eternal life.... Do you think they didn't know all this before your arrival?" Drumont is forced to realize that Africa has no need of his "spiritual help." Narrated by his skeptical though devoted cook, the naively objective tone of the novel only confirms the fundamental violence, injustice, and absurdity of the colonial situation. *Mission terminée* (1957) and *Le roi miraculé* (1958) provide further variants on the theme. In the first, a French-educated student returns to his village only to discover the gap that separates him from his family and friends. In the second, a missionary's efforts to force the village chief to renounce polygamy violate the traditional balance of power and lead to open revolt and his own departure.

A second series of novels followed the publication in 1972 of *Main basse sur le Cameroun*, a vehement critique of the post-independence regime. *Remember Ruben* (1974), *Perpétue et l'habitude du malheur* (1974), and *La ruine presque cocasse d'un polichinelle* (1979) all confront fear, violence, and repression in the new despotic state. *L'histoire du fou* (1994) abandons the realism of his earlier work to present a still more pessimistic vision of corruption and deceit through a disjointed narrative driven by repetition and populated with flat, two-dimensional characters. After years of unjust imprisonment, the hero, Zoétéleu, returns to his village only to slip into a world limited by ancestry and procreation, powerless to alter events that affect his life and destroy his family.

See also **Camara Laye; Literature; Literature and the Study of Africa.**

BIBLIOGRAPHY

Bouaka, Charles-Lucien. *Mongo Beti, par le sublime: L'orateur religieux dans l'oeuvre romanesque.* Paris: L'Harmattan, 2005.

Dramé, Kandioura. *The Novel as Transformation Myth: A Study of the Novels of Mongo Beti and Ngugi Wa Thiong'o.* Syracuse, NY: Syracuse University Press, 1990.

Mouralis, Bernard. *Comprendre l'oeuvre de Mongo Beti.* Issy les Moulineaux: Classiques Africaines, 1981.

PETER HALLWARD

BIJAGOS. *See* **Guinea-Bissau.**

BIKO, STEVE (1946–1977). Steve Biko was born in Kingwilliamstown, in eastern Cape Province, South Africa. After graduating from Marianhill in Natal, he studied medicine at the University of Natal from 1966 to 1972.

Throughout the late 1960s and early 1970s, Biko was the chief proponent of "black consciousness," a movement influenced by black liberation movements in the United States. In South Africa the movement was based on two main principles. First, as Biko wrote in "White Racism and Black Consciousness," the institutional divisions between blacks and whites in South Africa were so great that blacks could not rely on whites, not even reform-minded liberals, to end apartheid: "Total identification with an oppressed group in a system that forces one group to enjoy privilege and to live on the sweat of another, is impossible" (1972, 195). Second, Biko insisted that blacks must form separate political structures and change the way they understood their own identities. This included awareness of and renewed pride in black culture, religion, and ethical systems.

To this end, Biko helped establish several all-black associations, such as the South African Students Organization (1969) and the Black People's Convention (1972), a coalition of black organizations. In 1973, as a result of his political activities, the government restricted Biko's movements and forbade him to speak or write publicly. Thereafter the police repeatedly detained him.

South African anti-apartheid activist Steve Biko (1946–1977). Biko's slogan was "Black is beautiful." Although he is considered a nonviolent activist, Biko said he believed that the fight to restore African consciousness had two stages: one psychological and one physical. AP IMAGES

In August 1977, police arrested him for violating his travel ban and held him without trial. In early September, soon after being tortured by the police, he died of a brain hemorrhage. Biko's death became a rallying cry for opponents of apartheid, and he has been commemorated around the world in popular music, drama, and cinema.

See also **Apartheid.**

BIBLIOGRAPHY

Biko, Steve. "White Racism and Black Consciousness." In *Student Perspectives on South Africa*, ed. Hendrik W. Van der Merwe and David Welsh. Cape Town: Philip Publisher, 1972.

Biko, Steve. *I Write What I Like; A Selection of His Writings*, ed. with a personal memoir by Aelred Stubbs; preface by Archbishop Desmond Tutu; with a new introduction by Malusi and Thoko Mpumlwana. London: Bowerdean Press, 1996, 1978.

Biko, Steve. *The Essential Steve Biko.* Compiled by Robin Malan. Cape Town: David Philip Publishers, 1997.

Sanders, Mark. *Complicities: The Intellectual and Apartheid.* Durham: Duke University Press, 2002.

Woods, Donald. *Biko*, rev. edition. New York: Henry Holt, 1991.

JOHN N. JONES

BIN ALI, ZINE EL-ABIDINE (1936–).

Zine el-Abidine Bin Ali assumed Tunisia's presidency on November 7, 1987, the same day that he had his predecessor, Habib Bourguiba (1903–2000), declared medically unfit for office. Bin Ali was subsequently reelected as president in 1989, 1994, 1999, and 2004, once with an official electoral majority of 99.96 percent. He received military training in France and the United States, and assumed intelligence responsibilities in the Ministry of Defense from 1964 until 1974. In 1977 he was appointed director-general of national security in the Ministry of the Interior. Many cases of torture and the disappearances of regime opponents were reported to human rights organizations during his tenure in this post. On October 1, 1987, Bourguiba appointed Bin Ali as prime minister and his constitutional successor, a post that he held for five weeks before assuming the presidency himself in a carefully orchestrated move.

Bin Ali has been staunchly pro-Western in foreign policy, and has supported privatization, liberalization of the investment code to attract foreign capital, reduction of the trade deficit, and improved government efficiency. At the same time, his regime has never tolerated political dissent. Press criticism is actively discouraged and the Internet is carefully regulated.

See also **Bourguiba, Habib bin 'Ali; Human Rights; Tunisia.**

BIBLIOGRAPHY

Beau, Nicolas, and Jean-Pierre Tuquoi. *Notre ami Ben Ali: L'envers du "miracle Tunisien."* Paris: Éditions la Découverte, 1999.

DALE F. EICKELMAN

BIN SHAYKH, TAWHIDA (1909–).

Tawhida bin Shaykh was the first North African Muslim woman to earn a medical degree from the Faculty of Medicine in Paris in 1936, while her native country of Tunisia was still under French colonial rule. After being awarded her medical diploma in France, bin Shaykh returned to Tunis where she opened a private clinic, often providing free medical services for poor women. She served as the vice president of the Red Crescent (Islamic Red Cross) and was active as a doctor in the nationalist movement until Tunisia won independence from France in 1956. From 1963 on, bin Shaykh was instrumental in creating family planning services at the Charles Nicolle hospital; due to her efforts, the first clinic in Tunis devoted solely to women's reproductive medicine opened in 1970. When asked how she came to study in Paris, bin Shaykh noted that her widowed mother played a pivotal role in her education, as did Dr. Étienne Burnet, a French physician who resided in Tunis, and his Russian wife; they helped her gain admission to a French medical school. In 2000 bin Shaykh was awarded the prestigious prix Didon by the Tunisian state in recognition of her contributions.

See also **Islam.**

BIBLIOGRAPHY

Clancy-Smith, Julia. "Envisioning Knowledge: Educating the Muslim Woman in Colonial North Africa, c. 1850–1918." In *Iran and Beyond: Essays in Middle Eastern History in Honor of Nikki R. Keddie*, ed. Beth Baron and Rudi Matthee. Los Angeles: Mazda Press, 2000.

Huston, Perdita. *Motherhood by Choice: Pioneers in Women's Health and Family Planning.* New York: The Feminist Press, 1992.

JULIA CLANCY-SMITH

BIOKO. *See* **Equatorial Guinea.**

BIRTH. *See* **Childbearing; Children and Childhood: Infancy and Early Development.**

BISSAU.

The capital of Guinea-Bissau is situated on the right bank of the mouth of the Geba River in Pepel territory, an area where one of the country's twenty ethnic groups resides. Bissau was officially claimed by the Portuguese government as a commercial and administrative center in 1696. The city thrived on the exchange of gold and slaves, and the African hinterland provided iron bars, gunpowder, arms, kola nuts, and salt. In 1774 Bissau became the main Portuguese stronghold on the Guinea coast with construction of a stone fort, overtaking its rival Cacheu. Bissau first became capital of Portuguese Guinea in 1835 until 1879 when Bolama took its place, then regained its capital status in 1941. The first municipal council, dominated by traders, was formed in 1855. At the time, the walled town counted about 2,000 inhabitants (including over a thousand slaves). Modern urban development began in the 1920s with the town's population growing to 17,000 in 1950. The war of independence (1963–1974) triggered urban migration, which accelerated after independence. The city's population is, in 2006, estimated at almost 400,000 residents—one-third of the country's population—and the city reflects the country's great social and cultural diversity. Bissau harbors the country's main political institutions and is also its economic capital and principal port.

See also **Colonial Policies and Practices; Guinea-Bissau; Slave Trades.**

BIBLIOGRAPHY

Forrest, Joshua B. *Guinea Bissau: Power, Conflict and Renewal in a West African Nation.* Boulder, CO: Westview Press, 1992.

PHILIP HAVIK

BLANTYRE.

Blantyre is the commercial and industrial capital of Malawi and is located in the southern part of the country. Blantyre's growth can be traced to Scottish missionaries who opened a church in the shire highlands as early as 1876. By 1900 commercial interest had developed, and a consulate and an administration were therefore established. This city initially comprised two separate cores—Blantyre and Limbe—but was amalgamated in 1956 to become one municipality and at independence in 1964 was declared the City of Blantyre. The influence of Blantyre declined with the declaration of Lilongwe as national capital in 1975 and of Mzuzu as a city in 1985. In spite of this, Blantyre has remained the biggest city and main industrial and commercial center for Malawi. The population was estimated at 597,619 in 2003 and constituted about 34 percent of Malawi's total urban population. The proportion of men is very high in this population, suggesting a significant rural-urban migration of men seeking jobs and other opportunities. Blantyre has a heterogeneous culture due to intertribal marriages and immigration. The major language is Nyanja but other minor languages are also spoken. The city is an autonomous body governed by the City Assembly, composed of councilors from different political parties. Politically, a mayor heads it, however, administratively the chief executive and the technical and administrative staff manage day-to-day work.

See also **Malawi.**

BIBLIOGRAPHY

Blantyre City Assembly. *Blantyre City Assembly: Blantyre Environmental Profile*, 2000.

Manda, M. A. Z., ed. "Urbanisation and Urban Housing in Malawi: The Case of Blantyre City in Molomo." *Population and Sustainable Development Research Papers.* United Nations Population Fund, 1998.

National Statistical Office. *1998 Malawi Population and Housing Census: Report of the Final Census Results.* Zomba, Malawi: National Statistical Office, 2000.

LUCY CHIPETA

BLYDEN, EDWARD WILMOT (1832–1912).

The Liberian author, political scientist, and pioneer of the Pan-African movement Edward Blyden, was born at Charlotte Amalie on the then Danish Caribbean island of Saint Thomas. Of African descent, in 1850 he was brought to the United States by a Dutch Reformed minister, John P. Knox, to be educated at Rutgers Theological College, but he was denied admission on account of his color. In 1851 he emigrated to Liberia, the settlement of former North American slaves in far western Africa, where he worked as a teacher, a newspaper editor, and a Presbyterian minister.

Blyden also held appointments in the Liberian government service, was twice appointed Liberian ambassador to Great Britain (1877–1878, 1892), and was president of Liberia College (1880–1884).

Blyden ran for president of Liberia in 1885 but failed to be elected. Personal reasons took him from Liberia to Freetown, Sierra Leone, where, having grown increasingly interested in Islam, he held the post of director of Mohammedan education (1901–1906). He died in Freetown in 1912.

A prolific writer of pamphlets and articles, some of them collected in *Christianity, Islam, and the Negro Race* (1887), Blyden's political writings are full of inconsistencies. His ideas, however, are rooted in a sociology of race and present a consistent doctrine of pride and self-assertion for the "Negro race." His emphasis on the strength of the Negro character had immense influence among twentieth-century African and African American leaders and

Professor and politician Edward Wilmot Blyden (1832–1912). Blyden's work, *Christianity, Islam, and the Negro Race* (1887), played a major role in reviving Islam among African Americans in the twentieth century.

intellectuals. Blyden coined the phrase "African personality," and is recognized as one of the forerunners in the development of Pan-Africanism, Négritude, and the Black Personality movements.

See also **Freetown; Liberia: History and Politics; Sierra Leone: History and Politics.**

BIBLIOGRAPHY

Blake, C. "An African Nationalist Ideology Framed in Diaspora and the Development Quagmire—Any Hope for a Renaissance?" *Journal of Black Studies* 35, no. 5 (2005): 573–596.

Johnson, Robert, Jr., J.D. *Returning Home: A Century of African-American Repatriation*. Trenton, NJ: Africa World Press, 2005.

Lynch, Hollis R. *Edward Wilmot Blyden: Pan-Negro Patriot, 1832–1912*. London and New York: Oxford University Press, 1967.

Lynch, Hollis R., ed. *Selected Letters of Edward Wilmot Blyden*. Millwood, NY: KTO Press, 1978.

Mudimbe, Valentin Y. *The Invention of Africa: Gnosis, Philosophy, and the Order of Knowledge*. Bloomington: Indiana University Press, 1988.

CHRISTOPHER FYFE

BODY ADORNMENT AND CLOTHING

This entry includes the following articles:
OVERVIEW
COSMETICS AND BODY PAINTING
FASHION
TRADE

OVERVIEW

In Africa, the human body has been a focus for creative adornment with textiles, cosmetics, scars, coiffures, jewelry, and various accessories. Dress, in Africa as elsewhere, is a system of communication that involves both direct and complex ideas. Sometimes there is simple and immediate recognition of age, gender, occupation, ethnic group, or region based on the symbolism of a single item or the total ensemble. At other times, symbolic nuances of dress are apparent only to those who share specialized knowledge about a complex set of items. Each culture evolves its own patterns of dress and associated symbolic system, and these may change through time. Individual members of a society may also, for various reasons, select distinctive dress patterns. Particular types of clothing and body adornment are often connected with rituals or celebrations.

The earliest written material on African dress and adornment is found in ancient Egyptian, Greek and Roman references, Arabic accounts from the fourteenth century, and European reports of the sixteenth century. These documents provide a significant historical dimension. The systematic study of African dress, which began in the mid-1960s, has included analytical as well as descriptive work by scholars in a number of disciplines, especially textiles and clothing, anthropology, and art history.

BODY DECORATION

Scarification and cicatrization are common types of permanent, irreversible body adornment found throughout the continent. The meanings of such marks are extremely varied. They can be indicators of group membership, emblems of status or accomplishment, magical or protective devices, or expressions of physical beauty. These marks are usually found on the face, torso, thigh, or upper arm. *Ichi* scarification on the forehead of males from the Igbo (Ibo) area of Nigeria is an indicator of high rank within the *ozo* title-taking society. Although overall facial scarification has come to be considered to be characteristic of the so-called Frafra groups of northeastern Ghana, particularly by their non-Frafra neighbors, for the Frafra themselves, facial scarification has always been a matter of individual embellishment. The Tiv of Nigeria believe that to be beautiful or handsome, a person must be scarred. Complex patterns, covering much of the body and often done in different stages that relate to an initiation cycle, are found among the Ganda of Nigeria and the Hemba of the Congo. The aesthetics and forms of scarification are frequently similar to other areas of material culture, especially sculpture and pottery.

African peoples have embellished themselves with paint or pigment in a variety of ways. The earliest reason was probably for decoration or protection. In the Sudan, the use of ocher (an iron ore) as a cosmetic dates back to at least 4000 BCE. In ancient Egypt, malachite and copper ore were

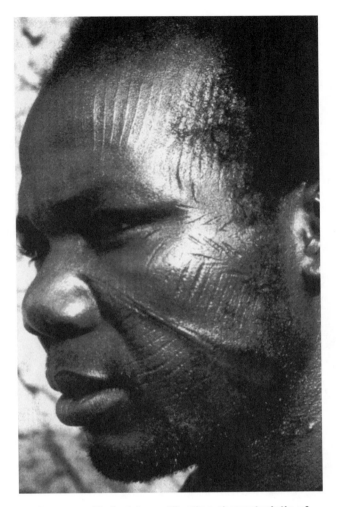

Frafra man with facial scarification characteristic of the Gurensi, a Frafra subgroup in Ghana. The scarification is done by specialists to reflect both ethnic identity and individual preferences of the man. PHOTOGRAPH BY FRED T. SMITH

during puberty ceremonies. Painting is also part of men's initiation in Liberia, Côte d'Ivoire, and Democratic Republic of the Congo.

African women wear a wide variety of coiffures consisting of braids, crests, tufts, cascades, and chignons, which can then be decorated with a medley of items such as beads, pins, combs, pieces of silver, or metal rings. These elaborate coiffures serve many functions such as identifying status or marking participation in a particular ceremony. Among pastoralist men in eastern Africa, elaborate labor-intensive hairdos declare their owner's age, gender, rank, or status, and are often embellished and/or empowered by accouterments and charms of a magio-religious nature. During the training period for warrior status, Maasai boys of Kenya grow their hair into a long pigtail, the distinctive symbol of a warrior (*moran*). Compared to the elaborate hairstyles of men, those of pastoralist women in eastern Africa are relatively simple.

CLOTHING

Skins, woven grass and raffia, leaves, and bark cloth were once used throughout Africa for clothing. Today such materials are regularly worn in only a few locations or during certain ceremonies. Among the Frafra, women traditionally wore woven grass waistbands with small, forked branches of leaves attached to the front and rear, and men wore the skins of sheep, goat, cow, and antelope; one skin was worn over the back and another skin was worn around the waist, covering the genital area. Skins worn by Frafra men symbolized their herding and hunting prowess, just as women's clothing reflected their special relationship to crops and vegetation. Among the Zulu of South Africa, both men and women wore skins. In the past, raffia cloth was woven by many groups in central Africa. The Kuba still produce embroidered raffia skirts with elaborate geometric decoration for both men and women. According to early accounts, these were worn for a number of ritual and public events.

Men in Africa wear a wide range of tailored smocks and robes, usually made of woven cotton. A fourteenth-century Arabic account provides one of the earliest descriptions of men's tailored gowns, still worn in western Africa by Muslim men. In much of the interior of west Africa, smocks made of narrow-band weave are worn. Among the Frafra

ground on stone palettes to produce an eye cosmetic. Among the Kuba and related groups in the Congo, powdered camwood mixed with palm oil is rubbed on the skin to increase its beauty. This mixture is also applied to a corpse before burial. Turkana men of Kenya cake their hair with clay and red color to celebrate a successful hunt or the end of planting. Igbo women paint curvilinear designs, called *uli*, on their faces and torsos to demonstrate their importance and beauty. Body painting can also reflect societal status or position. The use of white clay or kaolin chalk to announce spirituality is widespread. Rites of passage often involve body painting. Young Dan women from Côte d'Ivoire decorate themselves, especially their faces, with bold geometric patterns of northeastern Ghana, the cut and size of the smock reflect status and social importance. A special type of smock is worn by the Bamana of Mali and other Mande-speaking groups. This is the hunter's shirt, which begins quite simply as a tailored garment of woven cloth strips, usually white. It resembles the shirts that Bamana farmers customarily wear, but the hunter's shirt requires more cloth and is decorated with leather-covered amulets, horns, claws, strips of rawhide and fur. Smocks of this type have diffused to other groups in west Africa.

For the Hausa-Fulani of northern Nigeria, a large, elaborately embroidered gown (*riga*) is worn by important men as an outer garment. Designs on the central front and rear portions of the garment are status references. A similar type of robe is found among the Nupe and northern Yoruba, who were influenced by their Hausa neighbors to the north. Hausa, Nupe, and, since the nineteenth century, many Yoruba men wear voluminous drawstring trousers with a wide waist and narrow legs. These trousers, which are often decorated with colorful embroidered patterns, are effectively displayed when worn by horsemen.

Many types of untailored apparel are also worn by men in Africa. Nomadic Fulani (Fulbe) men of Mali weave wool blankets with elaborate geometric designs to be worn during the dry season, when the temperature drops dramatically at night. In the Akan area of Ghana and Côte d'Ivoire, men wear a large, rectangular piece of cloth, either *kente* or *adinkra*, wrapped around the body and draped over the left shoulder like a toga. *Kente* is a spectacular type of woven silk and cotton narrow-band cloth, often colored in blue and gold to symbolize power, and traditionally restricted to royalty and court officials. *Adinkra* is a white commercial cloth that was traditionally dyed red, russet, or black but now is often dyed blue, green, yellow, and purple. Stamped with motifs, *adinkra* was traditionally worn for funerals. In the early twenty-first century, both are commonly worn on various ceremonial occasions and at times for special dress. The decorative patterns of both *kente* and *adinkra* normally allude to proverbs or sayings. The display or manipulation of clothing plays a role in men's funerary ceremonies among various peoples of Africa such as the Frafra, the Kalabari of Nigeria, and the Sakalava of Madagascar.

Hausa-Fulani man from Nigeria wearing a voluminous embroidered gown (riga) as a reflection of status. His white turban is wrapped in such a way as to indicate that he has made his required pilgrimage to Mecca. PHOTOGRAPH BY JUDITH PERANI

The cotton wrapper, a large, rectangular piece of cloth, is a common women's dress form in much of Africa. Women often wear a single wrapper tucked and twisted under the arms when working within their household, but add additional cloths when appearing in public. The specifics of dress ensembles vary considerably from group to group. The costume of a Yoruba woman, for example, includes a wrapper tucked at the waist; a smaller cloth, worn over the first wrapper or over the left shoulder; a tailored, long-sleeved blouse; and a

Asante man from Ghana wearing *adinkra* cloth. Every *adinkra* cloth combines individual motifs that taken together create a message that the wearer wishes to communicate. Formerly this type of stamped cloth was used to express mourning and was worn during funerals. PHOTOGRAPH BY FRED T. SMITH

wrapper is covered by a loose-fitting tunic with seams on either side and sleeves made from another, more exquisite material. Embroidered designs represent popular symbols of luck such as stars, birds, fish and crescents. Today this type of outfit is used only for weddings or festivals with each region having its own specific patterns and colors.

Many new styles of clothing have been introduced into Africa during the past few decades. A recent vogue in Yoruba fashion is a modern form of handwoven cloth made of glistening lurex thread. This cloth, called *shine-shine*, is visually striking and usually worn for special occasions. Commercially printed textiles are now used by women all over Africa, with colors and designs reflecting local preference. In many parts of West Africa, these factory cloths are given a name based on a proverb, local event, or political issue. Many are purchased and worn specifically because of their message. In some cases, especially for a commemorative event, a group of people will express their sense of mutual identity by dressing alike.

ACCESSORIES

Dress in Africa is additive, involving the assemblage of numerous items. At times, it is the accessories, rather than apparel, that better reflect meaning or message. Leaders or individuals with special status sometimes have a monopoly on certain kinds of regalia or accessories made of valued materials, such as ivory, bronze, gold, or particular kinds of beads. The costume of the *oba* (king) of Bénin in Nigeria is extremely elaborate and heavy. In addition to a coral-beaded gown or smock, it consists of a coral-bead crown, coral pendants and necklaces, cloths tied around the waist, ivory pendants, and ivory armlets. Coral and ivory symbolize different aspects of royal power. The red color of coral is viewed as threatening and dangerous, while the white of ivory symbolizes spiritual purity.

Military chiefs in Bénin wear a necklace of leopard teeth and a real or imitation leopard pelt. Among the Zulu of South Africa, the king wears a necklace of leopard claws; lesser chiefs wear one of bone carved in the shape of leopard claws. Conical beaded crowns decorated with designs of birds and human faces and with a beaded fringe are restricted to certain Yoruba kings in Nigeria. To symbolize their position, rulers of the Asante and other Akan

head tie. In the past, the head tie was relatively modest, but since the mid-twentieth century, fashionable women have added more and more cloth to create an elaborate headdresses.

Among the Kalabari of Nigeria's Niger Delta area, the basic female ensemble includes a knee-length wrapper worn over an ankle-length one, an imported lace or eyelet blouse, and a head tie. The traditional dress for a Tunisian woman, characteristic of northwestern Africa, consists of a shawl, wrapper, and tunic. Rectangular shawls of various sizes may be draped over the upper part of the body. These are often decorated with broad bands or intricately patterned with a variety of geometric motifs. Generally, a woman will put on a shawl when leaving the house. A silk, cotton, or wool wrapper draped around the body is attached on the chest with one or two fibulae (pins) and then gathered at the waist with a sash. The

Ozo title holder from the northern Igbo wearing and holding materials reflective of his status. Of particular significance are the gown, red hat with white eagle feather, twisted white fiber anklet, yam knife, and iron staff. The circular stool is also an indicator of high status within Ozo. Nigeria. PHOTOGRAPH BY FRED T. SMITH

Western-oriented rulers often carry them during public appearances. In many areas, the handle material and type of animal hair used determine the whisk's importance. For the Frafra, horsehair carries the highest prestige; for the Asante, elephant tail hair is associated with kings or chiefs of the greatest importance. Various styles of brass, stone, bone, or ivory bracelets and armlets can denote status, success, gender, religious affiliation, or protection. Beaded ornaments have a wide range of use in southern and eastern Africa. Among the Zulu, Swazi, and related peoples, beaded head ornaments, loin dresses, belts, and necklaces were originally the prerogative of women. Beaded necklaces with rectangular or square pendants convey symbolic messages, including expressions of love for a suitor. Beadwork has been incorporated into the attire of men for dances and other festive occasions.

African clothing and accessories enhance an individual, reflect fashion, and attract notice, but, most importantly, also communicate a wide range of messages related to both an individual's public persona and a society's values and sense of identity. Individuals who have achieved special social status or wealth usually draw attention to themselves by means of elaborate apparel. In addition, Africans have for centuries absorbed new ideas, techniques, and materials from neighboring groups or from other parts of the world. Dress ensembles must therefore be viewed as expressions of constantly changing patterns of taste and preference.

See also **Arts: Beads; Initiation; Symbols and Symbolism; Textiles.**

BIBLIOGRAPHY

Darish, Patricia. "Dressing for the Next Life: Raffia Textile Production and Use among the Kuba of Zaire." In *Cloth and Human Experience*, ed. Arnette B. Weiner and Jane Schneider. Washington, DC: Smithsonian Institution Press, 1989.

Domowitz, Susan. "Wearing Proverbs: Anyi Names for Printed Factory Cloth." *African Arts* 25, no. 3 (1992): 82–87.

Eicher, Joanne B, ed. *Dress and Ethnicity: Change across Space and Time*. New York: Berg, 1995.

McNaughton, Patrick. "The Shirts That Mande Hunters Wear." *African Arts* 15, no. 3 (1982): 54–58.

Perani, Judith, and Fred T. Smith. *The Visual Art of Africa*. Upper Saddle River, NJ: Prentice Hall, 1998.

groups wear many gold items, such as necklaces, anklets, large armlets, and rings. Many also wear geometrically shaped Islamic amulets, consisting of leather containers covered in gold leaf, to ensure good health and success in war. Some type of jewelry is worn at all times by women among the Berber-speaking Tuareg of western Africa. Pendants enhanced with incised or repoussé geometric motifs are either worn individually or as part of a necklace. The two most common pendant forms are a pyramid-shaped structure and the Agadez cross, consisting of an upper oval shape above an open lozenge with knobs on each end.

Fly whisks have come to represent leadership throughout the continent. Both traditional and

Perani, Judith, and Norma H. Wolff. *Cloth, Dress and Art Patronage in Africa.* New York: Berg, 1999.

Picton, John, and John Mack. *African Textiles: Looms, Weaving, and Design.* London: British Museum, 1979.

Pokornowski, Ila; Joanne Eicher; M. Harris; and O. Theime. *African Dress II.* East Lansing: Michigan State University Press, 1985.

Rubin, Arnold, ed. *Marks of Civilization: Artistic Transformations of the Human Body.* Los Angeles: UCLA Museum of Cultural History, 1985.

Sieber, Roy, and Frank Herreman, eds. *Hair in African Art and Culture.* New York: Museum for African Art, 2000.

Smith, Fred T. "Frafra Dress." *African Arts* 15, no. 3 (1982): 36–42.

Smith, Fred T., and Joanne B. Eicher. "The Systematic Study of African Dress" *African Arts* 15, no. 3 (1982): 28.

Spring, Christopher, and Julie Hudson. "Urban Textile Traditions of Tunisia." *African Arts* 37, no. 3 (2004): 24–41, 90.

FRED T. SMITH

COSMETICS AND BODY PAINTING

Cosmetics and body painting are used throughout Africa to communicate information about the wearer, including his or her marital status, occupation, lifecycle stage, socioeconomic position, religious and political affiliations, and culture. They may also be used to elicit a particular response in the viewer. For example, a young Mende woman undergoing initiation into the Sande society in Sierra Leone will anoint her body with white kaolin to look unattractive and to signal her unapproachable status. An Ari youth in southwest Ethiopia will apply dabs of white and yellow clay to his face on market day to attract girlfriends. How and what cosmetics and body painting communicate is dependent on the circumstances in which they are worn and their relationship to the other personal art forms, such as clothing, jewelry, and hairstyle, that accompany them. Cosmetics and painting function as signs within the aesthetic system of the body and, therefore, should be viewed as one part of a person's cumulative dress.

Throughout Africa, the skin is used as a portable canvas for the application of body paint, henna designs, scarification patterns, tattoos, and commercial cosmetics. Body arts are particularly common in pastoralist societies. Unlike more sedentary communities where artworks play an important role in social and ceremonial activities, nomadic and seminomadic groups rely heavily on the body as the central mode of cultural expression.

PAINT

Paint is one of the most common ways to accentuate the face and body. The Wodaabe, a subgroup of the Fulani, travel with their camels and cattle in small bands throughout Niger, northern Nigeria, and northeast Cameroon. During the rainy season, when the land can sustain large herds, families come together to participate in the Geerewol festival. It is during this festival that young male Wodaabe herders take part in the *yaake* dance. They spend many hours preparing their face paint and costumes to conform to the Wodaabe ideal of beauty. Their face is typically painted yellow with a

Young woman wearing face mask, Madagascar. Paint and hair dressing are often used to distinguish life cycle stages. RAPHAEL VAN BUTSELE/PHOTOGRAPHER'S CHOICE/GETTY IMAGES

vertical stripe down the nose and chin, partitioning the face into two halves and visually lengthening the face. Dancers also use turbans topped with ostrich feathers and long strings of beads at the sides of their faces and tunics to create height. White circles are cast on the cheeks, forehead, and chin. Performers also paint black lines around their eyes and lips, and continuously roll their eyes and reveal their teeth in order to accentuate the whites of the eyes and the teeth.

The peoples of Nuba Mountains in Sudan use paint and hair dressing to designate their lifecycle stage. A newborn baby is anointed with red or yellow ochre to be initiated into this world. When a man is in his prime, patterning the body with color is essential to looking attractive. Age mates (peers with whom one grows up and is initiated) historically painted each other's skin in bright or white pigments before mirrors were readily available. In the early twenty-first century, the Sudanese government discourages the displaying of the unclothed, painted body. However, the vast dissemination of this practice in the Western world through popular photographs has motivated some Nuba men to paint for the financial incentive of tourism.

HENNA
Henna is a green or brown paste made of leaves of the *Lasonia inermis* mixed with water or oil. Henna was used to adorn the skin in ancient Egypt but today is popular in Islamic centers throughout Africa where female artists commonly apply it to the inner and outer hands and sides of the feet of women. Henna is also applied to women's hair and men's beards to redden, condition, and perfume the hair. On the body, henna paste stains the skin a dark brown or red and fades after a week or two. In recent years henna artists have begun experimenting with longer lasting, darker pigments by mixing henna with permanent black hair dye. Throughout Muslim Africa, henna is used to beautify and soften the skin and hair during coming of age and marriage ceremonies. In countries such as Morocco and Sudan, henna designs are also used as talismans to protect against the evil eye.

COSMETICS
In the last fifty years, there has been a shift in many urban centers away from traditional materials to fashionable commodities of foreign manufacture. The application of Western-made cosmetics to the face has become increasingly popular among urban female elite. Women like cosmetics for its impermanence, its color variety, and its prestige. Whereas permanent scars and tattoos fade and shift over time, face makeup can be applied quickly and painlessly, removed, and reapplied again. Dabs of color on the face allow a young woman creative space to articulate individual style that might catch the attention of a potential suitor, show her fashion consciousness, and exhibit her familial wealth.

In the realm of cosmetics, skin whitening creams must also be mentioned. Although bleaching lotions were most popular in the 1970s and 1980s in African urban centers, the practice of lightening the skin has diminished due to its damaging effects. These include the disfiguring effects of ochronosis, an accumulation of dye in cartilage and connective tissue common with phenol poisoning. In 1983 South Africa restricted the amount of chemicals in certain bleaching creams to lower incidents of the disease.

SCARIFICATION AND TATTOOING
Whereas pigment and cosmetics are temporary alterations, permanent body markings are achieved through the art of scarification and tattooing in Africa. Scars are incised with a sharp thorn or razor that lacerates the first few layers of skin; scars heal in either a raised bump or a recessive valley. Tattoos are created when dark pigment is inserted underneath the skin.

These two practices are most common among peoples with lighter skin tone where dark colors are clearly visible. The Oromo in eastern Ethiopia practice both scarring and tattooing. Cuts above the eyebrow, along the bridge of the nose, and on the cheeks are made at the onset of puberty. Cuts above the eye are intended to keep the eye free of disease. Marks along the nose and cheeks are believed to make the wearer more attractive. Often these scars are enhanced with tattoos, in which a green-black mixture made of soot and plant extract is applied with thorns that are pricked under the skin. The process of scarification and tattooing among the Oromo is usually discussed as a feature-enhancing cosmetic. However, marks

REINVENTING TRADITIONS

Docks at Cape Town. A dockworker sits on a mooring post at a Cape Town wharf. This fog-shrouded image of the city that visitors know for its dramatic Table Mountain, capacious bays, and sun-drenched beaches may come closer to the perspective of many of its 3.5 million residents as they confront the challenges of newly integrated nationhood. © DAVID AND PETER TURNLEY/ CORBIS

La maladie du sommeil étudiée sur les singes

TOP LEFT: Medical clinic in Congo, 2005. Women's health was especially impacted by rape and sexually transmitted diseases among residents and refugees in the war-torn eastern Democratic Republic of the Congo. Doctors Without Borders is among the international organizations bringing medical care to these and other victims of a paralyzing wave of conflict stemming from the 1993–1994 genocide in neighboring Rwanda and Burundi. Ron Haviv/VII/AP Images

BOTTOM LEFT: Sleeping sickness research. This 1907 illustration from *La Croix Illustrée* depicts the benefits of European medical science—without acknowledging colonialism's contributions to the spread of disease. Twenty-first century critics claim that pharmaceutical profiteering dumps unsafe medicines onto the African market. © Stefano Bianchetti/Corbis

TOP RIGHT: Imperial coronation. The independent nations of Africa inherited authoritarian colonial models of political leadership and have struggled to replace them since the late 1960s. Jean-Bédel Bokassa, who had himself coronated as ruler of a Central African empire in 1977, was reportedly one of the most extreme examples. He was deposed and a republic declared in 1979. AP Images

BOTTOM RIGHT: Maasai voters, Kenya, 2005. Although democracy has been difficult to implement where infrastructure is sparse and colonial-style authoritarian military rule endures, citizens even in remote regions have flocked to polling places with a return to democratic processes since the 1990s. AP Images

RIGHT: Lagos newsroom. Reporters for *This Day* employ the same communications technology as journalists throughout the world to bring Nigerians' own perspectives to bear on current events. © James Marshall/Corbis

BOTTOM LEFT: Nubian musician in Nairobi nightclub. Like emigrant communities everywhere, political exiles and refugee communities in many African countries gather in cultural festivals that combine old traditions with modern sensibilities and technologies, as at this 2006 benefit performance. AP Images

BOTTOM RIGHT: Telecommunications worker in Senegal. Improved education levels and infrastructure have facilitated the creation of call centers in West Africa to serve the Francophone world. Africans are now connected via mobile telephones in higher proportions than many other parts of the world. AP Images

TOP LEFT: Congress Palace in Cotonou, Bénin. African governments have sought both traditional architectural grandeur and modernist novelty to express their aspirations. Here the three towers of a new palace symbolize the branches of government on the European model. © ATLANTIDE PHOTOTRAVEL/CORBIS

BOTTOM LEFT: Nomads in Mali. Caravans have connected traders and miners with markets to the north and south of the Sahara for over 1,500 years. African consciousness can readily assimilate a new technology like this global positioning system while sustaining older modes of thought as well. © KAREN KASMAUSKI/CORBIS

TOP RIGHT: Funeral of Ousmane Sembène. In 2007 the world-renowned "father of African cinema" was laid to rest in a traditional Islamic shroud. The filmmaker was praised for addressing the continent's problems in a new medium while staying true to his African voice and language. AP IMAGES

BOTTOM RIGHT: Mahafaly grave markers, Madagascar. Horns of sacrificed zebu cows and carved scenes from the lives of the deceased adorn the *aloalo* towers. Many Africans consider their ancestors as defining figures in present and future as well as past. © GIDEON MENDEL/CORBIS

RIGHT: Graphic protest art. Comic book art has become an effective mode of mass communication and social criticism, as in this dramatic ink and watercolor protest against genital mutilation. Artwork by the Senegalese artist Cissé Samba Ndar. Courtesy, Africa e Mediterraneo and the Artist

BELOW: Ndebele mural. The wall art of the Ndebele of southeastern Africa addresses contemporary subject matter as readily as the objects of daily life in the past. © Lindsay Hebberd/Corbis

around the eyes are also meant to divert the gaze of strangers who could potentially inflict harm through attack with the evil eye.

See also **Arts: Beads; Arts: Jewelry; Tourism.**

BIBLIOGRAPHY

Ebin, Victoria. *The Body Decorated.* New York: Thames and Hudson, 1979.

Faris, James. *Nuba Personal Art.* London: Duckworth, 1972.

Plas, Els van der, and Marlous Willemsen, eds. *The Art of African Fashion.* Red Sea Press and Africa World Press with Prince Claus Fund Library, 1998.

Thevoz, Michel. *The Painted Body.* New York: Rizzoli, 1984.

PERI M. KLEMM

FASHION

Dress and body adornment play a critical role in African social life. Individuals express identities and affiliations through clothing and jewelry (dress) as well as grooming, coiffure, tattooing, and scarification (adornment). These distinguish them by age, gender, ethnicity, religious belief, economic status, and political rank. For example, in South Africa, both women and men use dress to emphasize a particular ethnic identity and history, by wearing *sesotho* dress (reflecting the Sotho culture of southern Africa) or *sekgowa* (European) dress. European dress is associated with Lutheranism and men who are migrant laborers. Women in rural areas continue to wear *sesotho* dress in initiation dances, although leather garments have been replaced with pleated cotton smocks.

Dress and adornment as a marker of political rank and economic status is evident in the large robes, *babban riga*, worn by members of the Hausa-Fulani political elite in Northern Nigeria. Made with quantities of expensive handwoven or imported cotton fabric that is elaborately embroidered, either by hand or by machine, these robes literally accentuate the wearer's political "bigness" and wealth. In addition, caps wrapped with lengths of cloth, known as *rawani* (turbans), are worn by emirs and titled officials.

GROUP AND INDIVIDUAL IDENTITY

Dress and adornment can also simultaneously represent group unity and distinguish individuals within

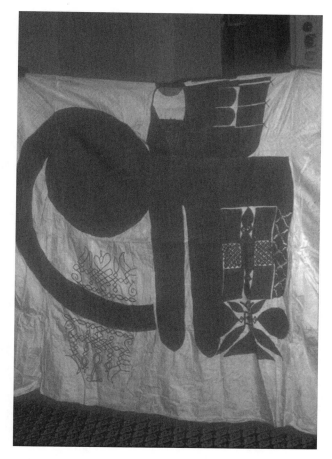

Babban riga. Babban riga owned by the late Magajin Gari Zazzau, Alhaji Nuhu Bamalli, aska biyu design. PHOTOGRAPH BY ELISHA P. RENNE

groups. Specific forms of clothing, head coverings, hair treatments, and body markings may be used to represent a group uniformity. Yet within these groups, individuals may distinguish themselves through different styles of dress and adornment. Pokot men in Kenya, for example, wear mud-plastered coiffures in particular styles according to age; individuals often embellish their hair with feathers and laundry blueing. These two concerns—group uniformity and individual distinction—represent a primary dynamic of fashion in African dress and adornment.

The dual quest for social unity and individual distinction through dress and adornment is seen in the Zanzibari women's initiation ritual known as *mkinda*, which was created after the abolition of slavery in 1897. Many Zanzabari women perform a type of *mkinda* dance known as *kunguiya*. Wearing printed cotton wrappers known as *kanga*, with identical named designs, they emphasize the unity and equality of Zanzabari women with different African and Arab backgrounds. This dance is followed by the *ndege* dance, in which women wear versions of fancy dress formerly worn only by the Arab aristocracy, consisting of expensive embroidered garments, special frilled pants known as *mirenda*, and gold jewelry. During the *ndege* dance, women (and their families) compete to distinguish themselves through the display of individual wealth. Furthermore, the imagined traditions of Arab dress worn in the *ndege* dance are juxtaposed with the latest *kanga* cloths worn in *kunguiya* dances.

FASHION AND CHANGE

Zanzibari women's continual search for new *kanga* cloths underscores the element of change associated with fashion. The unending cycle of fashion may be seen in contemporary capital city of Bamako, where Malian designers produce new clothing and accessories for fashionable customers. By using traditionally patterned mud cloth (*bogalan*) materials in modern fashions, designers such as Alou Traoré confound the dichotomy between traditional dress and adornment, seen as timeless, and modern dress, seen as up-to-date. Traoré uses stencils along with resist-dyeing techniques to produce new *bògòlanfini* designs—both abstract geometric and figurative—or *boubous*, the voluminous robes worn by a local clientele.

The industry associated with international high-fashion designers, models, media, and fashion shows are recent phenomena in Africa. In Mali, the pioneering fashion designer Chris Seydou also uses traditional *bògòlanfini* mud cloth to create garments, although his fitted gowns, blouse, and miniskirts are associated with Western dress styles. In Dakar, Senegal, designers use a range of local and imported materials to create garments, jewelry, and hairstyles, which they display at fashion shows such as the annual Semaine Internationale de la Mode de Dakar. Oumou Sy, who designs lavishly embroidered *boubous* sold through her atelier in Dakar, has shown her work elsewhere in Africa, as well as in Europe and the United States. Her haute couture ensembles serve as models for Senegalese tailors and their clients who, using less costly materials, are able to dress in *sanse* (fancy dress) styles.

Maria Ogunsi. The Nigerian fashion designer, known as Mya, graduated with honors from the London College of Fashion and also won first prize in the 2003 Nigerian Fashion show. This dress, made from damask and appliquéd wax-print fabrics, was one of her entries. PHOTOGRAPH BY FOLLY BROWN FOTOS

African women and men also use fashion to assert individual primacy in the midst of globalization, which has often undermined them economically. In the late 1960s and early 1970s in Brazzaville, the capital of the Republic of Congo, young men and women joined the movement known as the Société des ambianceurs et des personnes elégantes, known as SAPE. Youthful adherents, known as *sapeurs* (from the French verb *se saper*, meaning "to dress oneself up"), in both Brazzaville and Kinshasa in the Democratic Republic of Congo wear garments and accessories made by international haute couture fashion designers, asserting a distinctive individual style and transnational identity.

Nonetheless, not all Africans are able to afford the designer label clothes and SAPE lifestyle. Indeed, many *sapeurs* cannot afford such clothes and may borrow them from one another or wear secondhand garments, preferably those with *la griffe*—a designer label. By the mid-1980s in Zambia, many women and men were buying secondhand clothing from Western countries—known by the Bemba word, *salaula*—to wear clothes that were fashionable yet still affordable. For unmarried young men who worked as traders in Lusaka, their search in *salaula* stalls for items that contribute to "the big look" is underwritten by the desire to appear distinctively fashionable.

AFRICA AND GLOBAL FASHIONS

As African fashion designers have expanded into international markets, African dress and adornment are now available to Western consumers. African Americans, wanting to express their connection with Africa, may wear jackets made with Malian *bògòlanfini* mud cloth or wear shirts with Ghanaian *kente* cloth trim. While some African traders have taken advantage of this demand by supplying African clothing and accessories to Western markets, not all Ghanaian weavers and fashion designers approve of this situation. Rather, they see their cultural property—the design work that goes into weaving *kente* cloth and constructing garments—being taken over by print imitations and garments produced in factories in Pakistan and India. Through legislation in Ghana and through a campaign to inform consumers about African-made clothing and adornment, artisans hope that African creativity and labor will not only be appreciated but will also be appropriately recompensed.

See also **Arts: Beads; Arts: Jewelry; Dance: Social Meaning.**

BIBLIOGRAPHY

Arnoldi, Mary Jo, and Christine Mullen Kreamer. *Crowning Achievement: African Arts of Dressing the Head.* Los Angeles: Fowler Museum of Cultural History, UCLA, 1995.

Boateng, Boatema. "African Textiles and the Politics of Diasporic Identity-Making." In *Fashioning Nations: Clothing, Politics, and African Identities in the Twentieth Century,* ed. Jean Allman. Bloomington: Indiana University Press, 2004.

Fair, Laura. "Remaking Fashion in the Paris of the Indian Ocean: Dress, Performance, and the Cultural Construction of a Cosmopolitan Zanzibari Identity." In *Fashioning Nations: Clothing, Politics, and African Identities in the Twentieth Century,* ed. Jean Allman. Bloomington: Indiana University Press, 2004.

Hansen, Karen. *Salaula: The World of Secondhand Clothing in Zambia.* Chicago: University of Chicago Press, 2000.

James, Deborah. "'I Dress in This Fashion': Transformations in Sotho Dress and Women's Lives in a Sekhukhuneland Village, South Africa." In *Clothing and Difference: Embodied Identities in Colonial and Post-Colonial Africa,* ed. Hildi Hendrickson. Durham, NC: Duke University Press, 1996.

MacGaffey, Janet, and Rémy Bazenguissa-Ganga. *Congo-Paris: International Traders on the Margins of the Law.* Bloomington: Indiana University Press, 2000.

Mustafa, Hudita. "Sartorial Ecumenes: African Styles in a Social and Economic Context." In *The Art of African Fashion,* ed. Els van der Plas and Marlous Willemsen. Trenton, NJ: Africa World Press, 1998.

Perani, Judith, and Norma Wolff. *Cloth, Dress and Art Patronage in Africa.* Oxford: Berg Press, 1999.

Rovine, Victoria. "Fashionable Traditions: The Globalization of an African Textile." In *Fashioning Nations: Clothing, Politics, and African Identities in the Twentieth Century,* ed. Jean Allman. Bloomington: Indiana University Press, 2004.

ELISHA RENNE

TRADE

Dress in Africa is highly complex, incorporating a vast array of natural and factory-made materials that are sometimes locally produced but also imported from all over the world. Clothing and body adornments are a critical part of the economy in many countries, used by men, women, and children for artistic expression as well as to communicate identities and desires. Like the finest pieces of *kente* cloth, originally made from silk threads unraveled from Asian textiles brought to West Africa by European traders, many items of dress display a rich history of connections to the outside world.

For rituals such as masquerades, initiations, weddings, and funerals, items of dress and often whole ensembles have historically been made by hand. Body paints, used by groups such as the Suri of Ethiopia and Nuba of Sudan, are made from ochre (an iron ore), clay, and chalk. For a courtship ritual in West Africa, Woodabe Fulani men use a mixture of plant pigments and modern cosmetics to paint their faces. In North and East Africa women use henna to make elaborate orange or black patterns on their hands and feet.

Although dance masks are generally made of wood and costumes are constructed with strips of fiber from palm leaves, other natural objects such as amber beads (from the Baltic Sea) and cowry shells—which come from the Indian Ocean and were used at one time in West Africa as a type of currency—were first obtained through trade with Arabs after their conquest of North Africa in the eighth century. These beads and shells have been circulating in marketplaces and family collections for centuries. Some Akan groups in Ghana and the Côte d'Ivoire, long known for trading gold, wear gold jewelry and display wooden objects such as scepters and stools that are covered with gold leaf. The Mangbetu of Central Africa, who were well known for trading ivory, wear elegant bracelets and hairpins of that material. The Kalabari of Nigeria, proud of their history as traders going back to contacts with Portuguese sailors in the 1400s, incorporate many foreign objects into their outfits for ritual masquerades: t-shirts, lace, and printed cotton cloth from Europe, madras and embroidered velvet wrappers from India, glass beads from Venice, coral from the Mediterranean, and even novelties like mirrors and glass Christmas ornaments.

In ancient cities such as Kano (Nigeria), Jenné (Mali), and Harar (Ethiopia), artisans have become known for their specialized skills in hand-weaving and hand-dyeing with natural pigments such as mud and indigo. The Tuareg, for example, live in the Sahara desert but travel to Kano to have their turbans and clothing dyed a deep shade of indigo blue. Because the indigo rubs off onto their faces, the Tuareg are known as the "blue men of the desert." In Mali, Bamana families traditionally commissioned hand-woven wrappers dyed with mud (bògòlanfini) for important events such as circumcisions and weddings. This was done only by women who had special knowledge of the materials and symbols that were used. In Mali, by the 1990s mud cloth had become a symbol of national pride as well as a fashion statement. Artists paint strip cloth "canvases" with mud and tailors use both handmade and factory-made versions for everything from shirts and vests to backpacks and school uniforms.

Factory cloth for the African market is made in a wide variety of countries both on and off the continent. In West Africa, the most expensive and prestigious "wax" prints (colorful batik imitations printed on fine cotton cloth) are from the Netherlands. Less costly versions are also produced in Côte d'Ivoire and by numerous factories in Nigeria where imported fabrics have often been banned by the government. "Fancy" prints (imitations of "wax") are made in Nigeria, Ghana, Sénégal, and Mali, but face increasing competition from China, where the patterns are carefully copied. In East Africa, two-yard panels of cotton cloth with Swahili proverbs are referred to as kanga. Most of the fabric is made in India, but there are also factories in Tanzania.

In the Horn of Africa, Somali women wear colorful cotton and synthetic fabrics imported from India and Japan for a three-piece ensemble referred to as dirac (dress), garbasaar (shoulder cloth), and gorgorad (petticoat). These are made specifically for sale to Somalis and are not worn in the places where the factories are located. In southern Africa, women wear skirts and blouses made of cotton print cloth (called chitenge suits in Zambia) that were inspired by garments worn in West and Central Africa. These are popular outfits for going to church or working in an office, but the market faces competition from used clothing that is imported from Europe and North America.

Secondhand, or salaula (meaning "to pick"), clothing is plentiful and affordable, giving men and women in Zambia the chance to be fashionable and creative. The trade in used clothing from Europe has become extremely large and profitable for specialized dealers. In the Congo (and for Congolese living in Europe), expensive brands such as Yves Saint Laurent are highly sought after as a display not only of wealth but of the connections and cultural competence needed to migrate between Africa and Europe. Similar attitudes exist among young people in many of the former French colonies, where students have been educated to revere French history and culture but find it nearly impossible to obtain a French visa.

In North Africa, but also in countries with a large Muslim population such as Sénégal, Niger, and Somalia, people are rethinking their connections to Europe and drawing closer to the Islamic world. In the past, a headwrap was a sign of marriage; in the early twenty-first century increasing numbers of young women are choosing to wear head coverings (*hijab*) to show Islamic religious devotion and make a statement against Western values. Petrodollars and opportunities to work as professionals and migrant laborers in the Middle East have also made these connections economically and politically important for many families and countries. As in any other part of the world, dress in Africa will continue to change as alliances, trade patterns and methods of production come and go.

See also **Harar; Jenné and Jenné-jeno; Kano; Masks and Masquerades; Religion and Ritual.**

BIBLIOGRAPHY

Akou, Heather Marie. "Macrocultures, Migration, and Somali Malls: A Social History of Somali Dress and Aesthetics." Ph.D. diss. University of Minnesota, 2004.

Allman, Jean, ed. *Fashioning Africa: Power and the Politics of Dress.* Bloomington: Indiana University Press, 2004.

Beckwith, Carol, and Angela Fisher. *African Ceremonies.* New York: Abrams, 1999.

Clarke, Duncan. *The Art of African Textiles.* San Diego, CA: Thunder Bay Press, 1997.

Eicher, Joanne B. *Textile Trade and Masquerade among the Kalabari of Nigeria.* Minneapolis: University of Minnesota Media Resources, 1994.

Eicher, Joanne B. "Dress." In *Routledge International Encyclopedia of Women: Global Women's Issues and Knowledge*, ed. Cheris Kramarae and Dale Spender. New York: Routledge, 2000.

Fisher, Angela. *Africa Adorned.* New York: Abrams, 1984.

Gondola, Didier. "Dream and Drama: The Search for Elegance among Congolese Youth." *African Studies Review* 42, no. 1 (April 1999): 23–49.

Murphy, Robert. "Social Distance and the Veil." *American Anthropologist* 66 (1964): 1257–1274.

Picton, John. *The Art of African Textiles: Technology, Tradition and Lurex.* London: Barbican Art Gallery, 1995.

Ross, Doran H., ed. *Wrapped in Pride: Ghanaian Kente and African American Identity.* Los Angeles: UCLA Fowler Museum of Cultural History, 1998.

Ross, Doran H. *Gold of the Akan from the Glassell Collection.* Houston: Museum of Fine Arts, 2002.

Rovine, Victoria. *Bogolan: Shaping Culture through Cloth in Contemporary Mali.* Washington, DC: Smithsonian Institution Press, 2001.

Tranberg-Hansen, Karen. *Salaula: The World of Secondhand Clothing and Zambia.* Chicago: University of Chicago Press, 2000.

Tranberg-Hansen, Karen. "From Thrift to Fashion: Materiality and Aesthetics in Dress Practices in Zambia." In *Clothing as Material Culture*, ed. Daniel Miller and Suzanne Küchler. Oxford: Berg Publishers, 2005.

van der Plas, Els, and Marlous Willemsen, eds. *The Art of African Fashion.* The Hague: Prince Claus Fund, 1998.

HEATHER MARIE AKOU

BOER WAR. *See* **Cape Colony and Hinterland, History of (1600 to 1910); South Africa, Republic of.**

BOKASSA, JEAN-BÉDEL (1921–1996). Bokassa was born at Bobangui in the French Equatorial African colony of Oubangui (present-day Central African Republic) on February 22, 1921, and joined the French army in 1939, fought in Indochina, and was promoted to captain in 1961. Following the colony's independence as the Central African Republic in 1960, he became chief of staff of the armed forces in 1964 and in 1966 led a coup against his cousin, President David Dacko. He took over the presidency, but that title was not enough to assuage his ambitions. He abolished the constitution and began to rule by fiat. After a coup attempt was made against him in 1968, he further strengthened the autocracy of his rule.

In March 1972, Bokassa proclaimed himself president for life. Two years later there was another attempted coup, and he survived an assassination attempt in 1976. In that same year he converted to Islam. On December 4, 1977, Bokassa crowned himself emperor of the Central African Empire, renounced Islam, and returned to Christianity. The international community declined to recognize his claim to imperial status and equated him with the other notorious African dictator of the era, Idi Amin.

Bokassa's true downfall began in early 1979, when riots against his rule erupted in Bangui after he ordered all schoolchildren to wear uniforms purchased in government-owned stores. In response to the unrest, Bokassa ordered his security forces to shoot the demonstrators. Approximately four hundred people were killed. Strikes led by teachers, students, and civil servants ensued. In April 1979,

Jean-Bédel Bokassa (1921–1996). The self-proclaimed emperor of the Central African Empire from 1976 to 1979 looks pensive after crowning himself in Bangui. Bokassa was overthrown by a French-ordered coup and forced into exile until his return in 1987. PIERRE GUILLAUD/AFP/GETTY IMAGES

scores of children were arrested, tortured, and killed. An international inquiry confirmed that the emperor had personally participated in the massacres.

While in office, Bokassa physically assaulted two Western journalists and once tried to strike an envoy of President Valéry Giscard d'Estaing, causing much embarrassment to France, which had supported the dictator. Bokassa's management of the economy worsened the political situation. Hoping to receive assistance from the Eastern European bloc, he temporarily declared himself a Marxist in 1970. When Bokassa visited Tripoli in September 1979, French troops reinstalled Dacko as president. Claiming French citizenship, Bokassa flew to Paris and requested asylum but was refused. He was ultimately given

asylum in Abidjan, Côte d'Ivoire. On October 23, 1986, he returned to Bangui, where he was arrested, tried on fourteen counts of murder, embezzlement, and cannibalism, and sentenced to death on June 12, 1987. General André Kolingba commuted his sentence and freed Bokassa in 1993. Bokassa remained in the Central African Republic after his pardon but was banned from participating in elections after his release from prison. He died of a heart attack on November 3, 1996.

See also **Amin Dada, Imin; Central African Republic: History and Politics.**

BIBLIOGRAPHY

Decalo, Samuel. *Psychosis of Power: African Personal Dictatorships.* Boulder, CO: Westview Press, 1989.

Kalck, Pierre. *Historical Dictionary of the Central African Republic*, trans. Xavier-Samuel Kalck. Lanham, MD: Scarecrow Press, 2005.

Rosberg, Robert H., and Carl G. Rosberg. *Personal Rule in Black Africa: Prince, Autocrat, Prophet, Tyrant.* Berkeley: University of California Press, 1982.

MARIO J. AZEVEDO

BONDAGE, DEBT. *See* **Debt and Credit: Entrustment.**

BOOK PUBLISHING. *See* **Media: Book Publishing.**

BOTSWANA

This entry includes the following articles:
GEOGRAPHY AND ECONOMY
SOCIETY AND CULTURES
HISTORY AND POLITICS

GEOGRAPHY AND ECONOMY

Botswana lies at the center of southern Africa. It is bounded on the north by Zimbabwe, Zambia, and the Caprivi Strip of Namibia; on the west by Namibia; and on the east and south by South Africa. Botswana has a dry continental climate, and most

of the country is arid or semiarid. Annual rainfall ranges from 3.9 inches in the west to nearly 17.5 inches in the east. Rainfall is not only meager but also highly unreliable, and consequently drought is a permanent feature of this climate. The two dominant physiographic features in Botswana are the Kalahari Desert, which occupies the western two-thirds of the country, and the Okavango Delta in the northwest.

The Okavango Delta and river system contain nearly 95 percent of the country's surface water. Other rivers include the Zambezi, which forms part of the northern border, and the Limpopo, which forms part of the eastern border with South Africa. The vegetation in the west is mainly desert grass; dry savanna grass and acacia bushes cover the eastern and northeastern parts of the country.

Botswana has been the world's fastest-growing economy since 1970, with an average annual growth rate that has sometimes exceeded 10 percent, although annual growth declined to about 2.5 percent in the early years of the twenty-first century. Average per capita income increased from $80 in 1966 to about $3,080 in 2002, making Botswana a middle-income country.

Botswana's government has engineered this phenomenal expansion since it became independent in 1966, when the former British colony counted cattle and the remittances from migrant laborers as its main sources of income. The discovery and sound exploitation of diamond mines transformed the country, allowing the government to use the vast revenues from diamond exports to build a modest but functional urban and economic infrastructure. Botswana, unlike many mineral-based economies, has managed its development in such a way that it escaped the boom-and-bust ills frequently associated with such economies. Consequently, with a population of only about 1.8 million people (expected to decline to 1.3 million by 2015), it has one of the largest foreign exchange reserves among the developing countries, more than $5 billion.

Botswana has also been able to manage its economy well because of the unity of its ruling class, the quality of its leadership, and the absence of a viable political opposition. The elite, with the support of skilled foreigners and aid donors, developed effective and accountable public institutions. The government of Botswana played a key role in directing the market to create and expand nontraditional sectors such as industry and commerce. This strategy has been partially successful; employment in sectors other than agriculture and mining has grown significantly since 1975. Despite these important initiatives, Botswana remains dependent on South Africa for most of its industrial needs. Moreover, nearly 50 percent of the country's population lives in rural areas and depends on livestock and farming.

The World Bank and other institutions consider Botswana's economy, its public-management system, and its liberal democratic political order a model of success. Transparency International identifies Botswana as one of the least corrupt countries in the developing world. Severe inequality and South African economic dominance are two critical issues that are often overlooked in the analysis. Botswana's "radical inequality" is among the worst in the world, and South Africa's economic hegemony has frustrated its attempts to diversify its economy. Unfortunately, this remarkable African success story has been tarnished by the HIV/AIDS pandemic that has reduced life expectancy by nearly twenty years.

See also **Ecosystems; Kalahari Desert; Metals and Minerals; World Bank.**

BIBLIOGRAPHY

Curry, Robert. "Poverty and Mass Unemployment in Mineral-Rich Botswana." *American Journal of Economics and Sociology* 46, no. 1 (1987): 71–87.

Good, Kenneth. "At the Ends of the Ladder: Radical Inequalities in Botswana." *Journal of Modern African Studies* 31, no. 2 (1993): 203–230.

Harvey, Charles, and Stephen R. Lewis, Jr. *Policy Choice and Development Performance in Botswana.* London: Macmillan, 1990.

Samatar, Abdi Ismail. *An African Miracle: State and Class Leadership and Colonial Legacy in Botswana Development.* Portsmouth, NH: Heinemann, 1999.

Silitshena, R. M. K., and G. McLeod. *Botswana: A Physical, Social, and Economic Geography.* Gaborone, Botswana: Longman Botswana, 1992.

Werbner, Richard. *Reasonable Radicals and Citizenship in Botswana.* Bloomington: Indiana University Press, 2004.

ABDI ISMAIL SAMATAR

SOCIETY AND CULTURES

The population of Botswana includes members of Bantu- and Khoesan-speaking groups. The Bantu speakers include the Tswana; the closely related Kgalagadi; and the Kalanga, Mbukushu, Herero, Mbanderu, and other groups. Khoesan speakers include members of numerous San or Bushman groups, together with a small number of Khoekhoe (formerly called by the derogatory term "Hottentots").

THE TSWANA

By far the largest population group is the Tswana, who along with the Kgalagadi, the southern Sotho of Lesotho, and some smaller South African groups make up the Sotho branch of the southern Bantu language group. There are more than 1 million Tswana living in Botswana, some 79 percent of the population. They are divided into smaller locally based political and totemic units, including the Ngwato, Kwena, Tawana, Ngwaketse, Kgatla, Malete, Rolong, and Tlokwa. Each group has its own chief, usually the first-born male of the previous chief's first wife; most are still associated with the territorial units that comprise the modern districts—the former reserves of the colonial period. Their migration into the present area of Botswana dates from around 1800, when previously unstable political alliances became solidified into the local groups represented in Botswana and parts of South Africa since then.

In the twentieth century, it was not uncommon for a Tswana family to maintain three or more homes: one in a village, which was divided into kin-based wards where there were facilities such as schools and shops; another, generally occupied by men and boys, being a cattle post; and the third, often mainly occupied by women, on the lands where crops are were grown. Increasing urbanization is rendering this pattern less common since independence in 1966, but many still hold it as an ideal and the traditional pattern is maintained in several areas.

Tswana value cattle, which are used in payments such as bridewealth and legal damages, as well as a form of culturally defined wealth. Another important feature of Tswana life is the *kgotla*, or meeting place, where although much in Tswana life is socially stratified, village matters are discussed democratically. This is also a place where, for example, government officials can hold discussions to reach decisions on local matters.

Traditional Tswana religion is monotheistic, but believes in the spirits of the dead, rainmaking and divination rites, and totemic associations of groups and species of animals that symbolically represent them. At least 15 percent of Botswana's Tswana are Christian, but many hold traditional beliefs as well, as do the remaining 85 percent of the Tswana population.

OTHER GROUPS
Herero and Mbanderu are closely related, cattle-keeping peoples of central African origin, though their arrival in Botswana in large numbers dates from a migration from present-day Namibia around

1905. Unlike the Tswana, they have a system of double descent and distinguish between sacred cattle, which are inherited within the patrilineages, and ordinary cattle, which are inherited within the matrilineages. (Herero and Mbanderu each belong to one patrilineal group and one matrilineal one.) The Mbukushu are also of central African origin but are culturally very different. They live in the Okavango area in the northern part of Botswana, and their economy depends on fishing and horticulture. The Kalanga live mainly around Francistown near the border with Zimbabwe, and represent some 11 percent of the country's population. Traditionally herders, they are related to groups from Zimbabwe and from further north.

The Khoesan peoples of Botswana include members of the northern, central, and southern language groups. Although relatively small in population, less than 3 percent, they are linguistically and culturally diverse. Those who have until recently been mainly hunter-gatherers are in Botswana generally called by the Tswana word (Ba-)Sarwa. The speakers of northern languages are most widely known as !Kung, or more properly Juc'hoansi or Ju/'hoansi. The speakers of Central languages include a great many groups, the best known being the Gcui (or G/wi), who until their forced resettlement by the government in the late 1990s and early 2000s lived in the Central Kalahari Game Reserve; and the Naro (or Nharo) of the Ghanzi farms. The groups in the Central District (east of the reserve) have to a large extent adopted Tswana customs. Many are herders, either in their own right or as the clients of wealthier Tswana pastoralists, for whom they are often still in a position of serfdom to members of the dominant group. Southern Khoesan groups include notably the Qho (or !Xõ) of the Kgalagadi District, who live a relatively isolated existence. The Khoekhoe, who speak a Central Khoesan language related to Gcui and Naro, are cattle, sheep and goat herders and live mainly near the Namibian border.

Since the nineteenth century, Botswana has become the home of a substantial white population, about 7 percent of the total, including Afrikaans and English speakers. Many are ranchers who have settled either along the South African border or in the relatively remote Ghanzi District

République du Botswana (Republic of Botswana)

Population:	1,815,508 (2007 est.)
Area:	582,000 sq. km (224,710 sq. mi.)
Official language:	English
National currency:	pula
Principal religions:	Christian 70%, none 20%, indigenous 6%, other 4%
Capital:	Gaborone (est. pop. 186,007 in 2001)
Other urban centers:	Francistown, Selebi-Phikwe, Molepolole, Kanye, Serowe, Mahalapye, Lobatse, Maun, Mochudi
Principal geographical features:	*Rivers:* Zambezi, Limpopo, Chobe, Okavango, Boteti, Boro, Shashe, Motloutse *Lakes:* Ngami (seasonal), Xau *Other:* Kalahari Desert, Makgadikgadi depression, Okavango Delta
Economy:	*GDP per capita:* US$5,336 (2005)
Principal products and exports:	*Agricultural:* livestock, sorghum, white maize, millet, cowpeas, beans *Manufacturing:* textiles, construction, beef processing, chemical products production, food and beverage production *Mining:* diamonds, copper, nickel, coal
Government:	Independence from Great Britain, 1966. President elected by National Assembly. National Assembly elected by universal adult suffrage. House of Chiefs serves in a consultative capacity. For purposes of local government there are 9 districts that conform closely to ethnic divisions.
Heads of state since independence:	1966–1980: President Seretse Khama 1980–1998: President Quett Ketumile Joni Masire 1998–: President Festus G. Mogae
Armed forces:	First permanent defense force established in 1977. President is commander in chief. *Army:* 7,000 *Air force:* 500 *Paramilitary:* 1,000
Transportation:	*Rail:* 712 km (441 mi.). Railroads run by Botswana Railways Corporation. *Roads:* 11,514 km (7,139 mi.) *National airline:* Air Botswana. *Airports:* Seretse Khama International Airport at Gaborone. International facilities at Kasane. Airports at Francistown, Maun, Ghanzi, Selibi-Phikwe.
Media:	1 daily newspaper: *Botswana Daily News* (government-controlled). 4 weekly or biweekly independent publications. 20 periodicals. Small publishing industry. One television broadcast station.
Literacy and education:	*Total literacy rate:* 81% (2006). Education is free, universal, and compulsory for 7 years. Postsecondary education provided at the University of Botswana.

in the central-western Kalahari. Others have settled in towns, especially Gaborone, the capital.

See also **Gaborone; Urbanism and Urbanization.**

BIBLIOGRAPHY

Barnard, Alan. *Hunters and Herders of Southern Africa: A Comparative Ethnography of the Khoisan Peoples.* Cambridge, U.K.: Cambridge University Press, 1992.

Gibson, Gordon D.; Thomas J. Larson; and Cecilia R. McGurk. *The Kavango Peoples.* Wiesbaden, Germany: Franz Steiner Verlag, 1981.

Griffiths, Anne M. O. *In the Shadow of Marriage: Gender and Justice in an African Community.* Chicago: University of Chicago Press, 1997.

Gulbrandsen, Ørnulf. *Poverty in the Midst of Plenty: Socioeconomic Marginalization, Ecological Deterioration and Political Stability in a Tswana Society.* Bergen: Norse Publications, 1996.

Kuper, Adam. *Kalahari Village Politics: An African Democracy.* Cambridge, U.K.: Cambridge University Press, 1970.

Schapera, I. *The Tswana.* London: International African Institute, rev. edition. London: International African Institute, 1984.

ALAN BARNARD

HISTORY AND POLITICS

After sixty-three years as a British colonial labor reserve for the mines, farms, and factories of South Africa, two unrelated events in 1948 began the process of transforming the Bechuanaland Protectorate into the Republic of Botswana: the heir to the

Ngwato chieftaincy, Seretse Khama—then a student in England—married a white woman, Ruth Williams, and in South Africa the National Party won a narrow electoral victory on the platform of apartheid. The British government reacted to Khama's marriage and the creation of the racist apartheid system in South Africa by banning Khama from the protectorate in 1950, thus placating the government of South Africa.

By 1956 support for Khama and his marriage and Britain's inability to influence the apartheid system led to the acceptance of constitutional change for Bechuanaland. Khama returned to Bechuanaland and a period of rapid political change began. Constitutional steps in 1960 provoked the formation of the Bechuanaland (Botswana) Peoples' Party (BPP) by Kgaleman Motsete, Philip G. Matante, and Motsomai Mpho. Under their leadership the BPP mobilized a newly urban migrant-worker constituency along the north-south rail line and held demonstrations demanding immediate independence and a socialist transformation. The BPP, however, split in 1962 when Mpho left to form the Botswana Independence Party (BIP) and again in 1964 when Matante and Motsete led respective factions into the 1965 elections. The BPP's effectiveness declined as a result.

Perceiving a radical threat in the BPP, Khama joined elements of a cattle-owning, rural-based, royalty-related leadership elite with a growing number of education-based elites, such as Quett Masire, to form the Bechuanaland (Botswana) Democratic Party (BDP) in 1962. The BDP mobilized a rural constituency where households relied mainly on a combination of subsistence agriculture and remittances of wages from a family member employed in South Africa. Household subsistence depended on access to the use of oxen. Because most households did not directly own oxen, access depended upon a relationship to those who did. The cattle owners tended to have inherited political position and to be BDP leaders, particularly in places where its support was greatest. The BDP was therefore a relatively moderate, even conservative, movement desiring independence but not a radical transformation in existing political and labor relations.

In the first national elections in 1965, the BDP won twenty-eight of thirty-one seats in the legislative assembly and 80.4 percent of the votes cast. Local government elections, won by the BDP, were held in 1966, by which time the political party

that was to become the most successful opposition party, the Botswana National Front (BNF) founded by Kenneth Koma, was organized.

The pace of constitutional change was both breathtaking and peaceful. Independence was achieved on September 30, 1966, with a constitution adapted from the British Westminster model. The National Assembly, originally composed of thirty-one directly elected seats (and had increased to fifty-seven by 2004), constitutes the key legislative body. A president is elected indirectly by elected members of the assembly. Together, the president and National Assembly wield sovereign authority. The High Court sits at the pinnacle of the judicial system, which includes regional circuit courts and local-level magistrates.

Local governments exist under statutory law. There are nine elected district councils, three town councils (Selibi-Phikwe, Lobatse, and Jwaneng), and two city councils (Gaborone, the capital city, and Francistown). Councils vary in size depending upon geographic area and population, and provide a limited number of mandated local services; all depend on the national government for financial resources.

Alongside this hierarchy of elected governance is a hierarchy of traditional legitimacy and representation. The House of Chiefs is a constitutional advisory second chamber, the membership of which is primarily the inherited chiefs of the eight principal Tswana tribes. The chiefs supervise a hierarchy of subchiefs and headmen performing both political and judicial functions under customary law. A public assembly, known as a *kgotla*, maintains a connection between the chiefs and the people. While subordinate to the will of the parliament, this hierarchy of traditional authority continues to be accorded legitimacy by many people.

The postcolonial political history of these institutions is on many counts remarkable. Competitive multiparty elections were held every five years beginning in 1969. In 2004 a total of seven political parties nominated candidates for national assembly seats in an electoral process that maintained an openness and transparency unusual in postcolonial Africa. One reason for the lack of corruption in the political space was the electoral hegemony of the BDP, which won commanding majorities in every

National Assembly election including forty-four of fifty-seven seats in October 2004.

This electoral triumph rested partly on the success of its economic policies. Beginning in the 1970s the discovery and exploitation of minerals, particularly diamonds, generated substantial revenue. A fifty-fifty partnership between the government of Botswana and the De Beers Diamond Mining Company resulted in very substantial royalty, tax, and profit-sharing revenue for the government. The government of Botswana also achieved a significant shareholding in and seats on the board of directors of the De Beers Company itself.

The resulting revenue was spent on building an infrastructure and providing public services such as roads, schools, and health facilities. The quality of life improved and a large number of employment opportunities were created. This reduced, then eliminated, direct dependence upon migratory labor for employment in South Africa, the hallmark of Bechuanaland's colonial life. Botswana rose from the ranks of one of the twenty-five poorest countries in the world to achieve the status of a "middle-income" country. This economic success promoted political success for the incumbent party.

The persistent majority of seats won by the BDP, however, masked growing electoral disaffection, political debate, and dissent around several issues, including economic and gender inequalities, the oligarchical tendencies of the BDP leadership, and the government's handling of the HIV/AIDS crisis that threatened economic and social progress. Although the BDP won only 50.6 percent of the total vote in 2004, single-member district plurality elections allowed the party to win seats in twelve constituencies with less than a majority of votes against a divided opposition.

As a result, BDP leadership became more complex and factional. The original wealthy cattle-owning rural-based leadership was joined by some who had careers in the public service and the professions. Festus Mogae, Botswana's president in 2005, was permanent secretary of the ministry of finance and development planning, and then became governor of the Bank of Botswana before joining politics. Ian Khama, the vice president in 2005 and son of Seretse Khama, had a career in the Botswana Defense Force. In addition, new entrants from the professions and private sector created a less homogeneous and more factional BDP leadership than before. In 2005 open debate within the party revolved around the issue of automatic presidential success and whether Mogae's likely retirement before the 2009 elections should automatically catapult Ian Khama to the presidency.

Rural "push" and urban "pull" factors led to rapid urbanization and widening economic inequalities. For example, the population of the capital city, Gaborone, increased from 25,000 in 1973 to more than 186,000 in 2001. A large proportion of this urban population worked for low wages, were unemployed, or worked in the "informal" economy. Diversification seemed as yet unable to provide opportunities equitably across the population. Growing support for opposition parties reflected this situation. In addition, despite steady gains, the economic and political empowerment of women, more than half the population, continued to be a significant issue.

A national challenge to social and economic progress in 2005 was an extremely high rate of HIV infection and AIDS-related illnesses. Despite a wide range of treatment and prevention programs, the scourge of HIV/AIDS had drastically reduced general life expectancy and led to negative population growth.

Opposition parties attracted support based on these and other long-term regional issues in the northwest and southeast. The BNF, for example, won National Assembly seats in Gaborone, the capital, and majority control of the capital's city council as well as the town councils in Lobatse and the mining town of Jwaneng. But, opposition parties individually and jointly were unable to capture national support. And, therefore, with an overwhelming majority of seats and a fragmented opposition, the BDP had no reason to directly suppress the opposing parties.

Finally, these currents and trends in the domestic political economy were embedded in a world and regional context. About 80 percent of Botswana's revenue derived from mining, particularly from diamond sales. The national economy was sensitive to any fluctuation in the market for diamonds. Moreover, Botswana's small economy and its proximity to South Africa limited the ability to diversify the economy. As a result, Botswana played an active part in the Southern African Development

Community, which offered hope for regionalizing production and marketing in which Botswana's location and human resources could be assets. The internal politics of economic and social policy were played out under the umbrella of this overarching regional and world context.

Since 1966 the Bechuanaland Protectorate has changed from a backwater labor reserve of the British Empire to a developing liberal democratic market system based on diamond mining. By not squandering newfound wealth on wasteful monuments or debilitating corruption, a complex politics of market development occupies the political stage in the early twenty-first century. Whether the BDP will retain its majority position through open electoral means remains to be seen.

See also **Apartheid; Disease: HIV/AIDS, Social and Political Aspects; Dow, Unity; Gabarone; Khama, Seretse; Political Systems; Postcolonialism.**

BIBLIOGRAPHY

Briscoe, Andrew, and H.C.L. (Quill) Hermans. *Combating Corruption in Botswana: A Review of the Relevant Policies, Laws and Institutional Capacity to Combat Corruption in Botswana.* Gaborone, Botswana: Frederich Ebert Foundation, 2001.

Crowder, Michael. *The Flogging of Phinehas McIntosh: A Tale of Colonial Folly and Injustice, Bechuanaland 1933.* New Haven, CT: Yale University Press, 1988.

Edge, W. A., and Mogopodi Lekorwe, eds. *Botswana: Politics and Society.* Pretoria, South Africa: Van Schaik, 1998.

Harvey, Charles, and Stephen R. Lewis, Jr. *Policy Choice and Development Performance in Botswana.* London: Macmillan, 1990.

Holm, John D., and Patrick P. Molutsi, eds. *Democracy in Botswana.* Gaborone, Botswana: Macmillan, 1990.

Parson, Jack. *Botswana: Liberal Democracy and the Labor Reserve in Southern Africa.* Boulder, CO: Westview Press, 1984.

Parson, Jack, ed. *Succession to High Office in Botswana: Three Case Studies.* Athens: Ohio University Press, 1990.

Parsons, Neil, Willie Henderson, and Thomas Tlou. *Seretse Khama: 1921–1980.* Braamfontein, Johannesburg, South Africa: Macmillan, 1995.

Presidential Task Group on a Long Term Vision for Botswana. *Vision 2016: A Long Term Vision for Botswana.* Gaborone, Botswana: Presidential Task Group, 1997.

Samatar, Abdi. *An African Miracle: State and Class Leadership and Colonial Legacy in Botswana Development.* Portsmouth, NH: Heinemann, 1999.

Stedman, Stephen J., ed. *Botswana: The Political Economy of Democratic Development.* Boulder, CO: Lynne Rienner, 1993.

Tlou, Thomas, and Alec Campbell. *History of Botswana,* 2nd edition. Gaborone, Botswana: Macmillan, 1997.

Werbner, Richard. *Reasonable Radicals and Citizenship in Botswana: The Public Anthropology of Kalanga Elites.* Bloomington: Indiana University Press, 2004.

JACK PARSON

BOUABID, ABDERRAHIM

BOUABID, ABDERRAHIM (1922– 1992). Abderrahim Bouabid was one of the founders of the Moroccan independence movement, a great political activist, and leader of the Morocco's socialist party until 1991.

In 1944 Bouabid was the youngest of the nationalists who signed the petition for independence. After leading a nationalist demonstration in Salé, the French imprisoned Bouabid in Rabat until 1945.

In 1955 Bouabid participated in the Aix-Les-Bains negotiations, which led to Morocco's independence on November 18, 1956. He held many positions in the early independent Moroccan governments (1956–1960), including minister in charge of negotiations, Moroccan ambassador to Paris, and minister of economic and financial affairs.

On September 9, 1959, Bouabid joined the newly created Union Nationale des Forces Populaires following a split in the ranks of the Istiqlal in January of that year. In 1962 Bouabid opposed the project of the constitution proposed by King Hasan II (b. 1929) and the rigged 1963 communal elections, which cost him one year in prison.

Bouabid was again imprisoned for a year in September 1981, following his reservations about Hasan II's idea of a referendum on the Sahara. After his liberation in 1982, he resumed his political activities in the socialist party and continued his struggle for the rule of law, democracy, and human rights.

See also **Hasan II of Morocco; Human Rights.**

BIBLIOGRAPHY

Agnouche, Abdelatif. *Histoire Politique du Maroc.* Casablanca, Morocco: Afrique Orient, 1987.

Elmandjra, Mehdi. *La décolonisation culturelle: Défi Majeur du 21eme siècle.* Marrakesh, Morocco: Walili, 1996.

Pennell, C. R. *Morocco since 1830: A History.* New York: New York University Press, 2000.

Zartman, I. William, ed. *Man, State and Society in the Contemporary Maghrib.* New York: Praeger; London: Pall Mall Press, 1973.

MOHA ENNAJI

BOUHIRED, DJAMILA (1935–). A member of the Algerian National Liberation Front, Djamila Bouhired was a leading figure in Algeria's war of liberation (1954–1962) and in the movement for women's rights. Born in Algiers, Bouhired came from a middle-class Arab Muslim family and was educated in a European-type school. After the French colonial regime ignored Algerian demands for political and civil rights, armed conflict erupted in 1954. By 1956, when the National Liberation Front (Front de Libération Nationale, or FLN) military strategy shifted to the cities, Bouhired and other young women played a critical role. She assisted FLN leader Saadi Yacef in recruiting young Muslim women from Algiers who could pass as Europeans. Dressed as French women, Bouhired and two other female militants placed concealed bombs in European neighborhoods. Two bombs exploded, causing civilian casualties, but Bouhired's failed to detonate. This event and others unleashed the Battle of Algiers—open warfare between the FLN and the government. In April 1957, Bouhired was arrested, imprisoned, and subjected to torture; in July she was sentenced to death by guillotine after a trial that many observers deemed a travesty of justice. Because Bouhired became a cause célèbre with international media coverage of the French army's systematic use of torture, she was eventually released. In the early twenty-first century, Bouhired, a grandmother, advocated for fundamental transformations in the legal, political, and social status of Algeria's women.

See also **Algeria: History and Politics; Women: Women and the Law.**

BIBLIOGRAPHY

Amrane, Djamila. *Les femmes algériennes dans la guerre.* Paris: Plon, 1991.

Lazreg, Marnia. *The Eloquence of Silence: Algerian Women in Question.* New York: Routledge Press, 1994.

JULIA CLANCY-SMITH

BOUNDARIES, COLONIAL AND MODERN. In precolonial Africa, boundaries were significant factors marking the territories of diverse ethnic groups. They were, however, substantially different from colonial boundaries. Precolonial African boundaries were not fixed in space, were flexible over time, loosely defined between the societies at any given moment, and did not delimit all the space, leaving some areas unclaimed or as neutral zones between ethnic groups. As in other parts of the world, a fundamental concern with land use shaped much of the dynamic of Africa's precolonial history. Ethnic groups fought, migrated, coalesced, or cooperated in a highly movable geography.

The coming of the colonial era changed all this. In the precolonial era, a territory was defined by the society that occupied it. In the colonial era, a society was defined by the territory it occupied. Moving from a social definition of territory to a territorial definition of society is a central point in understanding the transformation from indigenous to colonial rule.

THE COLONIAL SCRAMBLE FOR AFRICA

In the second half of the nineteenth century, European powers began to compete aggressively for rights to territory in Africa. Prior to this, European interest had largely focused on establishing ports that served as trading centers linked to the interior. This period saw an awakening interest in Africa's interior and the possibilities that might lie therein. This attention stemmed in part from a noted series of expeditions of discovery and exploration: names like David Livingstone, Richard Burton, John Speke, Henry Stanley, and Pierre de Brazza became associated not just with exploration but with claimed territorial "rights" from discovery.

Belgium's King Léopold II played a central role in the emerging European definition of space in

Africa. In 1876 he sponsored a geographical conference on Africa at Brussels that hosted distinguished African explorers. The conference called for European cooperation to coordinate the work of exploration, with Belgium playing the contrived role of a benign, neutral power. The publicized motive for this cooperation was to facilitate bringing the "three Cs" to sub-Saharan Africa: commerce, civilization, and Christianity. Trade and compassion, not violence, would liberate Africa. In truth, under the guise of morally based cooperation, the groundwork was being laid for an intense competition for African territory.

Following the conference, the European powers set about staking bounded claims to territories they barely knew. Treaties with African chiefs were produced by Stanley working for Belgium, Brazza for France, Verney Cameron and Edward Hewett for England, and Karl Peters and Gustav Nachtigal for Germany. The African chiefs had no experience with treaties and little understanding of European concepts of space. Treaties with native chiefs had been used in the earlier colonial competition for North America and had been given the stamp of legitimacy by the court of world opinion. Blank treaty forms and national flags became required gear for explorers.

The Germans arrived late in the colonial game but soon took a lead role. Prince Otto von Bismarck hosted a congress at Berlin in 1878 that featured the leading statesmen of the day playing for high territorial stakes—the remnants of the Ottoman Empire, including North Africa. In 1884, another Berlin Congress, seemingly a less ambitious one, was called to deal with western Africa. Several months earlier, Bismarck had ordered Nachtigal to raise the German flag over the Cameroons and seize Togo and South-West Africa (present-day Namibia). The French and the British countered with their own aggressive territorial acquisition. The "Scramble" for Africa was on.

The 1884–1885 Berlin Congress laid the groundwork for how Europe would divide Africa, but it by no means diminished the competition for African territory, which continued unabated through the turn of the century. Indeed, Africa's interior was still largely terra incognita, but many Europeans had the feeling that it might contain unknown rewards (witness North America) and

believed that their countries should not miss out on the grab for potential future resources.

The amount of territory actually colonized was very much a function of the power relations in Europe at the time. Emerging powers like Germany and Italy gained territory while claims were still vague. Declining powers, such as the Netherlands, Scandinavia, and Spain, received little or no territory. The weakened Portuguese received much less territory than that for which they had some degree of initial exploratory claim. The rules were that coastal footholds gave powers claims to the interior, exploration added to those claims, actual settlement took precedent, and treaties enhanced claims.

With so little information about the interior, how were European boundary claims specified? The tidiness of the straight line was clearly a convenient artifice. Yet water had a clear appeal where it was present. Rivers and lakes were targets of exploration and tended to be noticeable features on otherwise blank maps. Examples abound. Britain, Germany, and France insisted that their territories—Nigeria, the Cameroons, and French Equatorial Africa (People's Republic of the Congo) and French West Africa—should extend to Lake Chad. Germany demanded that its eastern African colonies have boundaries on the Great Rift Valley lakes. The British negotiated that the boundary of Nyasaland (Malawi) would extend south to the Shire River. In a strange geographical anomaly, the Germans insisted that South-West Africa's eastern boundary reach the Zambezi River—the resulting Caprivi Strip extends through swamplands to reach the Zambezi along a largely unnavigable stretch. The Congo, Senegal, Limpopo, Orange, and Zambezi Rivers, among others, also divided claims. The claim for the Gambia was based entirely on a river. In other notable cases, the largely unknown drainage basins of the Nile and the Congo provided the geographical limits. Strangely shaped, often illogical geographical entities resulted.

The attempt to unify territories was another clear strategy in the "Scramble." The British had long dreamed of "Cape to Cairo" but were stymied by the German push in Tanganyika. The Portuguese hoped to unify Angola and Mozambique, areas facing opposing oceans, and the Germans hoped to unify their east African holdings and South-West

Africa, also across the entire continent; both were thwarted by Britain's Cecil Rhodes driving north from the Cape of Good Hope in the hope of reaching Cairo. The French were highly successful in uniting their western and central African territories.

After World War I, German territories in Africa were redistributed to the winners as "mandated" guardians. Togo and the Cameroons were split between the British and the French. Boundaries were muted as the British administered their parts of these territories through their neighboring colonies (Ghana and Nigeria, respectively), while the French maintained their shares as separate territories. Italy argued for new units of territory, and boundaries were redrawn so that the Italian colony of Libya was ceded desert sections of Egypt and Sudan, and Italian Somaliland (Somalia) was granted the area from south of the Juba River to the current Kenyan boundary. In all of Africa, only Ethiopia managed to avoid colonization, though it was occupied by Italy prior to and during World War II. (This does not include Liberia, which had been established by the United States prior to the colonial scramble as a "free" home for repatriated slaves and was therefore not claimed by Europeans.)

POSTCOLONIAL RELATIVE STABILITY

The wave of political independence that swept through sub-Saharan Africa from the late 1950s on resulted in very few changes to the colonial boundaries. The African Union (formerly the Organization of African Unity) stands firm on the issue that African borders, however imperfectly created, should remain as they are. That said, the current international borders are often highly permeable; people and goods flow across borders legally and illegally. Near border posts it is not unusual to find motor scooters, camels, or canoes that circumvent the actual border post and associated customs and immigration offices. Though important for commerce, border permeability can also result in the spread of ethnic conflict and disease.

The imposed colonial boundaries resulted in two major problems that would plague postcolonial Africa: ethnic groups were often divided between territories, and ethnic groups with a history of hostility were combined into the same territory. In some cases, colonization created or exacerbated formerly minimal ethnic divisions, the violent repercussions of which have continued after independence. The most tragic example is the Rwandan genocide of 1994, in which nearly 1 million Tutsis and moderate Hutus were killed by Hutu extremists.

Boundaries are still causes of conflict; though Ethiopia's protracted civil war led to the recreation of Eritrea in 1993, a border war followed in 1998. Conflict in Africa often transcends borders instead of being confined within them, however, with ethnic alliances, geopolitical strategizing, and war profiteering by corrupt regimes resulting in regional destabilization. Notable examples are the intertwined conflicts of Sierra Leone, Côte d'Ivoire and Liberia in West Africa; Congo, Uganda, Burundi and Rwanda in central Africa; and the independence wars of southern Africa; for specifics see the articles for each of these countries.

Refugee flows crossing borders to find sanctuary from shifts in economic and political fortunes have greatly increased since the 1960s. Millions of Mozambicans sought refuge and work in Zimbabwe and South Africa during Mozambique's civil war. In the early twenty-first century, Mozambique and South Africa are host to large numbers of people from Zimbabwe who are fleeing that country's crisis. Relative stability in Rwanda and Burundi has resulted in the return of refugees who fled in droves in the mid-1990s, and are fleeing ethnic conflict in eastern Congo.

Initially in the independence period, there were heady talks among strong African leaders like Ghana's Kwame Nkrumah and Tanzania's Julius Nyerere about the possibilities of pan-Africanism, which would diminish the significance of international boundaries to create something akin to a United States of Africa. Although these dreams are unlikely to be realized, a different rhetoric of pan-Africanism has emerged in the rise of the transboundary conservation movement.

The boundaries of conservation areas in Africa are a significant feature; protected areas constitute more than 10 percent of the continent's land surface, and parks and reserves frequently abut international borders. With support from international environmental organizations and development agencies alike, transboundary resource management initiatives are being explored as a means to link ecosystems that were "artificially" divided—along with the human and animal populations they contain—by colonial borders. In spite of skepticism and vigorous debate over the potential for these approaches to improve human livelihoods through ecotourism and regional development, particularly in southern Africa the number of proposed transboundary conservation areas is steadily growing.

In spite of these efforts at increased regional cooperation and an increasingly assertive African Union, the problems presented by the borders between African nations remain significant. Though their creation may have been largely arbitrary, the boundaries drawn by former colonial powers in Africa have proved remarkably persistent because they have proved useful in so many ways to independence-era politicians.

See also **Amin Dada, Idi; Brazza, Pierre Paul François Camille Savorgnan de; Colonial Policies and Practices; Ethnicity; Frontiers; Geography and the Study of Africa; Livingstone, David; Nkrumah, Francis Nwia Kofi; Nyerere, Julius Kambarage; Postcolonialism; Stanley, Henry Morton; Travel and Exploration.**

BIBLIOGRAPHY

Bohannan, Paul, and Philip Curtin. *Africa and Africans*, 4th edition. Prospect Heights, IL: Waveland Press, 1995.

Hodgson, Robert D., and Elvyn A. Stoneman. *The Changing Map of Africa*. Princeton, NJ: Van Nostrand Reinhold, 1963.

Pakenham, Thomas. *The Scramble for Africa, 1876–1912*. London: Abacus, 1991.

Stock, Robert. *Africa South of the Sahara: A Geographical Interpretation*, 2nd edition. London: Guilford Press, 2004.

Van der Linde, Harry; Judy Oglethorpe; Trevor Sandwith; Deborah Snelson; Yemeserach Tessema; et al. *Beyond Boundaries: Transboundary Natural Resource Management in Sub-Saharan Africa*. Washington, DC: Biodiversity Support Program, 2001.

GARY L. GAILE
REVISED BY BENSON FUNK WILDER

BOURGUIBA, HABIB BIN 'ALI (1903–2000). Habib bin 'Ali Bourguiba was the first president of the Republic of Tunisia (1957–1987). Born in Monastir, Tunisia, Bourguiba trained as a lawyer before joining the Tunisian independence movement. He was arrested for sedition by the French in the 1930s and imprisoned in France for eleven years. He was released by the Germans during their World War II occupation of France, but was recaptured after the war and returned to prison. He was released in 1955, when Tunisia achieved independence from France.

Bourguiba's reputation during the independence struggles won him enough public support so that, when the Tunisian constitutional monarchy was overthrown in 1957, he became president of the new republic. He enacted pro-Western reforms, promoted secularism, and advanced women's rights, but never legalized opposition political parties or held democratic elections. In 1975 he declared himself president for life.

Bourguiba never fully allied himself with either of the major Cold War powers, nor with their competing

Habib Bourguiba (1903–2000). Education and women's rights were important to Bourguiba. As the first president of the Republic of Tunisia, he legalized divorce and raised girls' marrying age to 17.

ideologies. His efforts at development were an uneasy blend of urban modernization and rural collectivism. By 1977 the failures of his administration were apparent when Tunisians rioted to demand multiparty elections. By the 1980s rumors that he had become senile prompted his designated successor, Prime Minister Zine el Abidine bin Ali, to invoke the constitution and declare Bourguiba unfit for office. On November 7, 1987, Bourguiba was forced to step down. He lived out his remaining days in Monastir. The reminders of his cult of personality—posters and statues scattered throughout Tunisia—disappeared, but he was accorded respectful treatment until his death.

See also **Bin Ali, Zine el-Abdine; Cold War; Tunisia: History and Politics.**

BIBLIOGRAPHY

Bourguiba, Habib bin 'Ali. *My Life, My Ideas, My Struggle.* Tunis: Ministry of Information, 1979.

Hopwood, Derek. *Habib Bourguiba of Tunisia: The Tragedy of Longevity.* New York: St. Martin's Press, 1992.

NANCY E. GRATTON

President of Algeria Abdelaziz Bouteflika (1937–). Despite the fact that Bouteflika was born in Morocco, Algeria's relations with the country remain tense due to issues surrounding Western Sahara. LANDOV LLC

BOUTEFLIKA, ABDELAZIZ (1937–).

Abdelaziz Bouteflika was born in Oudja, Morocco, near the Algerian border; he grew up and went to school in Morocco. In 1956 he entered the movement for Algerian independence from France by joining the Front de Libération Nationale (FLN; National Liberation Front).

In 1961 Bouteflika was a member of a secret Algerian delegation to Aulnoy, France, to talk to more senior leaders of the independence struggle, who were being detained there by the French. When Algeria became independent the following year, he was selected to serve as minister of youth, sport, and tourism. In 1963 Bouteflika began a sixteen-year tenure as foreign minister; in that post he became a leader of the movement of nonaligned nations because of his work in consolidating and strengthening third world organizations, among other things. In 1979 he expected to succeed Hourari Boumédiène (1938–1978) as president but was passed over. Soon after, a court found Bouteflika guilty of having embezzled funds from

Algerian embassies while he was foreign minister, but he received a pardon from the president.

Because of his conviction, Bouteflika went into exile in 1981. He returned in 1987 in what was seen as part of an attempt to enhance unity within the FLN.

In 1999 he ran for president and won with nearly 74 percent of the vote after the other six candidates quit the race amid claims of fraud. A few months after taking office, Bouteflika offered a pardon to Islamist rebels who had embroiled Algeria in civil war from 1992; a decline in violence followed. His introduction of an economic plan was followed by increased annual growth rates.

In 2004 Bouteflika won a second five-year term with 85 percent of the vote; this time observers declared that the election was free and fair. Again, he offered Islamists an amnesty, which further reduced civil strife. He introduced a plan to cut foreign debt by more than 40 percent. In 2006 Bouteflika's prime minister said he would seek to amend the constitution to end the two-term limit for the president.

See also **Warfare: Civil Wars.**

BIBLIOGRAPHY

Aghrout, Ahmed, ed. *Algeria in Transition: Reforms and Development Prospects.* London: RoutledgeCurzon, 2004.

Amnesty International USA. "Unrestrained Powers: Torture by Algeria's Military Security." 2006. Available from http://www.amnestyusa.org.

MICHAEL LEVINE

BRAIDE, GARRICK SOKARI (1882–1918).

Garrick Sokari Braide was born in the village of Obonoma in Kalabar, in the Niger Delta. Obonoma was a stronghold of traditional religious worship, being a center of pilgrimage to the titular deity, Ogu. Some accounts speak of the young Braide being initiated into the Ogun cult at Obonoma by his mother.

Braide grew up in Bakana, where his father had settled. His parents were too poor to send him to school; consequently, he came of age somewhat on the periphery of Christianity, which missionaries had introduced in the area. However, Christianity would become familiar to him from the practice of open-air meetings that were held in Bakana from about 1886 onward. Such public meetings seem to have had an influence on him; in the 1890s he had become an Anglican inquirer and had joined the St. Andrew's Sunday School in Bakana. While there he came under the instruction of the Reverend Moses Kemmer of Brass. All the instruction was in the Igbo (Ibo) language, which Braide undertook to learn. It was a long apprenticeship; he finally completed his catechetical course and was baptized on January 23, 1910, at age twenty-eight. In 1912, at age thirty, he was confirmed by the eminent Yoruba clergyman Bishop James Johnson.

Braide's mature years increased his sense of personal urgency about the role he would play in his newly adopted religion. He embarked on intense religious exercises at this time, slipping into St. Andrew's Church on weekdays for personal devotions. These devotions focused on prayers for forgiveness of sin and attention to the personal mediation of Jesus.

Braide soon became a prominent figure in the Niger Delta Pastorate Church presided over by Bishop James Johnson, noted for his charismatic gifts of prayer, prophecy, and healing. He used these gifts to advance his claim to authority. Thus, on one occasion he is reputed to have caused a heavy storm as punishment for those who defied his orders to observe Sunday as a day of total rest and prayer. On another occasion he successfully prayed for rain to spoil plans for a local dance that he deemed offensive to religion. Braide also launched a campaign against the symbols of African religion, demanding that devotees abandon their charms, confess their sins, and make trust in God their supreme rule in life. His reputation for thaumaturgy was gaining widespread recognition, which makes it difficult to say which was the more powerful motivator for him—Ogun or Christianity.

Braide was as effective in preaching against alcohol consumption as he had been in his campaign against indigenous gods. Drunkenness and alcoholism had wreaked havoc on the populations of the Delta towns and villages. Some 3 million gallons of gin and rum were consumed there every year, a level of consumption that filled the coffers of the colonial administration with dues from the excise tax. Consequently, Braide's temperance drive threatened the excise revenue and turned him into a major threat to the British regime. By 1916, at the height of Braide's prohibitionist movement, the government was showing a massive loss of revenue, some £576,000 in excise taxes. Tensions among the new colonial regimes ran high as World War I touched western Africa.

Meanwhile, the French in Côte d'Ivoire had at about the same time been closely watching the actions of another charismatic figure, Prophet William Wadé Harris, which prompted the British to take up a similar surveillance of Braide's activities. As a self-declared prophet, Braide had become a lightning rod for local discontent, and he could not be ignored. Braide was arrested in March 1916 and tried for economic sabotage and false teaching. He was found guilty and sent to prison. He died in an "accident" in November 1918, some months after his release.

Two general consequences of Braide's life and work may be considered in conclusion. His preaching had a burgeoning effect on the membership rolls of the churches in the Niger Delta, Protestant, Catholic, and Independent alike. In 1909, when Braide began preaching, there were only 900 baptized Christians on the membership rolls of all the churches. By 1918 that number had increased to some 11,700. The increase for Catholics in the period between 1912 and 1917 was 500 percent, and this growth was due largely to Braide's work.

Such numbers could not be contained within the historic mission churches, and so a large group of followers constituted themselves as a separate body in 1916, taking the name Christ Army Church. The church in effect became a rival to the Niger Delta Pastorate Church. In 1917 the Christ Army Church applied for affiliation to the World Evangelical Alliance in London, a necessary insurance policy for an indigenous movement without much educated leadership and caught in the web of global forces.

The second general consequence was Braide's adoption by early nationalist opinion as an agent of African autonomy. The *Lagos Weekly Standard* espoused his cause in editorials and other leader articles. The *Standard* claimed that Braide was anointed by "the God of the Negro" as an instrument to achieve the liberation of Africa. Braide was defended against the attacks of Bishop James Johnson and other leaders of the Niger Delta Pastorate Church. The *Standard* applauded Braide's career as demonstrating that colonial and episcopal structures and hierarchies were irrelevant to the special conditions of Africa, affirming that he should be endorsed by all genuine patriots. Braide, according to this opinion, had offered an African cultural alternative to the Western forms of Christianity and had relied on people at the grass roots to lead in the church. His accomplishment revealed Africa's potential for independence.

See also **Christianity; Harris, William Wadé; Prophetic Movements: Central Africa.**

BIBLIOGRAPHY

Banfield, A. W. "A Prophet in Iboland." *The Bible in the World* 12 (1916).

Tasie, G. O. M. "The Prophetic Calling: Garrick Sokari Braide of Bakana." In *Varieties of Christian Experience in Nigeria*, ed. Elizabeth Isichei. London: Macmillan, 1982.

LAMIN SANNEH

BRAZZA, PIERRE PAUL FRANÇOIS CAMILLE SAVORGNAN DE (1852–1905).

Brazza was born Pietro Paulo Savorgnan de Brazza near Rome to an Italian noble family, inheriting the title of count. In 1874 he became a citizen of France and joined the French navy as an officer, at which time he adopted the French form of his name. In the navy he accompanied a French expedition (1875–1878) to explore Africa's western coast in the region now known as Gabon, traveling up the Ogowe River to seek its source.

Acting on behalf of France in its competition with other European nations for territories in Africa, Brazza tried to hinder Henry Morton Stanley's annexation of the Congo for King Léopold II of Belgium, mounting an expedition in the region in 1879. He succeeded in laying French claim to a large swath of territory on the right bank of the Congo River, the core of the future Afrique Equatoriale Française, although Stanley and Léopold succeeded in establishing the Congo Independent State on the other side of the river as well.

In 1891 Brazza returned to the new French colony as a representative of the French government, and during this trip he signed the treaties that ultimately established the colony of French Congo. On a subsequent trip (1883) he founded the river port city of Brazzaville at the base of the main navigable channel of the river, which became the capital of French Equatorial Africa. He served for a time as commissioner general of the French administration in the region but was recalled to France in 1898.

In the early 1900s, charges of cruelty and exploitation on the part of the private companies chartered to exploit the resources of the region prompted the French government to send Brazza back again to head an investigation of the charges. On his return to Africa in 1905 he died at Dakar, Senegal, without ever returning to the scene of the

Franco-Italian explorer Pierre Paul Brazza (1852–1905). Born in Italy and later becoming a French citizen, Brazza opened the areas that eventually led to French colonies in Central Africa. In 1886, he became governor-general of the French Congo. THE GRANGER COLLECTION, LTD.

alleged crimes, which turned out to have been considerable.

See also **Brazzaville; Colonial Policies and Practices: French North Africa; Stanley, Henry Morton; Travel and Exploration.**

BIBLIOGRAPHY

Decalo, Samuel; Virginia Thompson; and Richard Adloff. *Historical Dictionary of Congo.* Lanham, MD: Scarecrow Press, 1996.

GARY THOULOUIS

BRAZZAVILLE. In 1880 the Italian-born French explorer Pierre Paul François Camille Savorgnan de Brazza (1852–1905) signed a treaty with the Teke *makol'co* (king) that gave France its critical foothold in the Congo region. The town where this treaty was signed was Ncuna, on the west bank of the Malebo Pool, which forms a part of the Congo River. Three years later, Ncuna was renamed Brazzaville and subsequently played a pivotal role in the development of the French colonial empire.

A key part of the Ncuna treaty gave France control over the Malebo Pool—the gateway to the heart of Africa along the vast navigable basin of the Congo River system. In 1903 it became the administrative headquarters for all French holdings in equatorial Africa, later designated Afrique Équatoriale Française (AEF). The Congo-Océan railroad, built at enormous cost in Africans' lives to compete with the Belgian railroad on the south bank of the lower Congo, made the city a strategic center for French colonialism in central Africa. When Charles de Gaulle's Free French assumed control of AEF in 1940, with Germany's occupation of France at the onset of World War II, Brazzaville became the African center for the resistance. Since independence in 1960, Brazzaville has been the capital of the Republic of Congo.

In the early twenty-first century Brazzaville is one of three industrial centers in the country. The others are Pointe-Noire on the Atlantic coast, the main seaport in the Congo and Brazzaville's marine contact with the world, and N'Kayi, a transit point on the railway linking Brazzaville and Ponte-Noire. The leading industries in Brazzaville are textiles, food processing, and leather goods. As the chief river port in the Congo, Brazzaville is a crucial transshipment point for cargo from the Central African Republic as well as from the interior of the country. Since completion of the Congo-Ocean Railway in 1934, goods have typically been transported from Brazzaville to Pointe-Noire by train. But goods and people also travel between the two cities by motor vehicles and by air: one of the nation's two international airports is located at Brazzaville.

The World Health Organization has its African headquarters in Brazzaville. So does the Pan-African Union of Science and Technology, which promotes research in a wide variety of areas, including agriculture, traditional African medicine, and industrial development. The African Petroleum Producers' Association is also located in Brazzaville. The city is a center for institutions of higher education—among them are the Université Marien Ngouabi; the Poto-Poto School of African Art; and the Institut Africain Monyondzi (which is devoted to the study of living African languages). There are also several technical schools in Brazzaville: the Collège Technique, Commercial et Industriel de Brazzaville; the Centre d'Études Administratives et Techniques Supérieures; and the École Supérieure Africaine des Cadres des Chemins de Fer (a school for railway engineers). A teacher's college—the Institut Supérieur des Sciences d'Education—established in 1962 with a special grant from the United Nations, trains students from Chad, Gabon, and the Central African Republic, as well as the Congo.

A substantial proportion of all Congolese live in Brazzaville: just over 1.1 million, according to a 2005 estimate, out of a total population of about 3.4 million. During the postcolonial period—a time of significant political instability in the Congo—Brazzaville has been the site of violent battles between political factions that have become identified with ethnic groups (especially the M'Bochi, the Pool Lari, and the Nibolek). In addition, there have been tensions between the Congolese and Zairian immigrants, many of whom fled violence in their own capital, Kinshasa, immediately across Malebo Pool, in the fall of 1991, only to be forcibly expelled from Brazzaville months later. Paradoxically, the city has also served as a meeting place for the resolution of some international conflicts. Brazzaville is also home to the African Anti-Apartheid Committee, an agency of the Organization of African Unity that seeks to coordinate antiapartheid movements outside as well as inside Africa.

See also **Brazza, Pierre Paul François Camille Savorgnan de; Congo, Republic of; Congo River; Kinshasa; Textiles.**

BIBLIOGRAPHY

Balandier, Georges. *Sociologie des Brazzavilles noires*. 2e éd. augm. / accompagnée d'un texte et de bibliographies de Jean Copans. Paris: Presses de la Fondation nationale des sciences politiques, 1985.

Ndinga-Mbo, Abraham. *Pour une histoire du Congo-Brazzaville: méthodologie et réflexions*. Paris: L'Harmattan, 2003.

Nwoye, Rosaline Eredapa. *The Public Image of Pierre Savorgnan de Brazza and the Establishment of French Imperialism in the Congo, 1875–1885*. Aberdeen: Aberdeen University, African Studies Group. 1981.

Ollandet, Jérôme. *Brazzaville, capitale de la France libre: histoire de la résistance française en Afrique (1940–1944)* Brazzaville: Editions de la savane, 1980.

Paravano, Patricia. *Working for the Future: Elite Women's Strategies in Brazzaville*. Leiden, The Netherlands: African Studies Centre, 1997.

MARGARET ALISON SABIN

BRIDEWEALTH. *See* **Family; Kinship and Affinity; Marriage Systems.**

BRITISH COLONIES. *See* **Colonial Policies and Practices: British Central Africa; Colonial Policies and Practices: British East Africa; Colonial Policies and Practices: British West Africa.**

BUJUMBURA. The capital of Burundi, Bujumbura (also known as Usumbura) was founded in 1899 by European missionaries and traders. Initially a fishing village, the Germans made it the site of their colonial administration; the town became the seat of Belgium's succeeding colonial administration during World War I. It is now the economic and political hub of Burundi. Its population in 2004 was roughly 340,000, of whom approximately 67 percent are Christian (62% Roman Catholic, 5% Protestant); the rest practice traditional African beliefs, except for a few Muslims. Prior to the late 1990s its ethnic composition was 85 percent Hutu, 14 percent Tutsi, and 1 percent Twa. The Tutsi elite were concentrated in the city proper, whereas the Hutu were predominantly agriculturalists and lived in the surrounding countryside.

In the late 1990s ethnic violence convulsed Bujumbura due to ongoing conflicts between the minority Tutsi, who for centuries had ruled like feudal lords and continued to hold most of Burundi's wealth, and the majority Hutu, who wanted a greater share of the country's riches. In July 1996 a Tutsi, Major Buyoya, staged a coup, ousting the elected Hutu president. In the following years, Hutu guerrilla fighters belonging to the

FNL (Forces for National Liberation) came into the area from the south, recruiting support from among their local political allies.

The FNL did not limit its recruitment efforts to mere persuasion, however: when Hutu did not cooperate willingly, they often forced them to do so. Violence in the region escalated, and the Burundi Tutsi-dominated government in 1999 began a policy of forcibly displacing the Hutu who lived in the area immediately around the city, with the stated intent of reducing FNL rebel influence. The displaced persons were taken away to camps, often with nothing but the clothes on their backs. In spite of this intervention, the area around Bujumbura remained violent well into 2003, with the first negotiations between rebels and government officials occurring only in November of that year. The following December, FNL leader Alain Mugabarabona moved away from violence to negotiation by claiming political party status for his organization.

The University of Burundi is in Bujumbura, and industrial production is concentrated there. Agricultural processing (including soft drink production, sugar refining, and beer brewing) dominates the economic sector. The two official languages are Kirundi and French. Bujumbura is also the hub for regional humanitarian relief efforts.

See also **Burundi; Colonial Policies and Practices.**

BIBLIOGRAPHY

Chrétien, Jean-Pierre. *Great Lakes of Africa: Two Thousand Years of History,* trans. Scott Strauss. New York: Zone Books, 2003.

IAN WATTS

BULAWAYO.

BULAWAYO. Bulawayo (City of Kings), Zimbabwe's second-largest city (population of one million), is situated in southwestern Zimbabwe on the Matshamhlope River at an elevation of 4,449 feet. Bulawayo is the administrative, commercial, and industrial capital of Matabeleland North and South provinces, and remains the cultural capital for the Ndebele people. In 1868 Lobengula, the last Matabele king, chose Bulawayo's site for his capital (then called Gubulawayo). Later in 1894 the British

South Africa Company established Bulawayo as a frontier town and railway station, later ruled by a British colony (1923–1964) and a white minority government (1965–1979) before independence in 1980. The city serves as a transport center, the location of National Railway of Zimbabwe's headquarters, a key service center for regional mining and agriculture, a major hub of engineering industry, and host to the annual Zimbabwe International Trade Fair. Bulawayo has colonial city characteristics: wide avenues, verdant parks, colonial architecture, and distant high-density African suburbs that house the majority of the population. With a national economic crisis characterized by more than 1,200 percent inflation, shortages of fuel, basic commodities, and foreign currency, and the national HIV/AIDS pandemic—with at least 3,000 deaths weekly—Bulawayo has been devastated. Due to high levels of government and nongovernment indebtedness, the city council struggles to provide basic services. Bulawayo is home to the opposition Movement for Democratic Change (MDC) party and recent protest rallies have been marked by police brutality.

See also **Lobengula; Zimbabwe.**

BIBLIOGRAPHY

Berens, Denis, ed. *A Concise Encyclopedia of Zimbabwe.* Gweru, Zimbabwe: Mambo Press, 1988.

City Town Clerk. *Masiye Pambili: Bulawayo—A Century of Development.* Bulawayo, Zimbabwe: Bulawayo City Council, 1994.

MIRIAM GRANT

BURKINA FASO

This entry includes the following articles:
GEOGRAPHY AND ECONOMY
SOCIETY AND CULTURES
HISTORY AND POLITICS

GEOGRAPHY AND ECONOMY

Burkina lies close to the center of West Africa in a region known historically as the Niger bend. It borders on Mali to the north and west, on Côte d'Ivoire, Ghana, and Togo to the south, and on Bénin and Niger to the east. The capital, Ouagadougou, lies

about 500 miles from the Atlantic Ocean. The country consists of an extensive plateau tilting slightly downward to the south. Its former name, Upper Volta, was derived from three rivers that cross the country: the Mouhoun (Black Volta), the Nakambé (White Volta), and the Nazinon (Red Volta). Rainfall is highly variable, ranging from the semiarid northern Sahel where only transhumant (nomadic) pastoralism of cattle, sheep, and camel herds is possible, to the tropical savanna in the south where peasants with very little modern technology farm cereal crops of sorghum, millet, maize, and peanuts. Several small lakes are found,

mainly in the southwest. Water shortages are frequent, especially in the north.

Burkina ranks among the poorest countries in Africa. Most of its population of more than 14 million is concentrated in the center and south, with densities sometimes exceeding 125 people per square mile. In 1998 a major Sahel drought forced 1 million people in Burkina, roughly 10 percent of the population, to turn to international agencies for emergency assistance.

With less than 20 percent of its population living in urban settings, Burkina's economy relies on subsistence agriculture, exports of cotton and livestock, some mining, and, most importantly, remittances from labor migration. Minerals, especially gold and manganese, have from time to time raised hopes for this impoverished nation. Gold mines at Poura, southwest of Koudougou, were reopened in 1984 with reserves at between 59,500 and 77,000 pounds. Smaller gold mines in the north provide decent returns. The manganese deposits at Tambao in the far north are one of the world's richest sources of this mineral but potential is diminished by the excessive costs of extraction and especially of transport to world markets.

While still remaining desperately poor, Burkina's economic indicators have improved since the mid-1990s. The International Monetary Fund notes that the gross domestic product (GDP) growth rate has been more than 6 percent since the mid-1990s, and inflation has been contained. Much of this success came from the expansion of cotton production, which accounts for two-thirds of the country's total exports. In 2004 the account deficit exceeded 10 percent of GDP, but the country's deficit is fully financed, with grants accounting for over half of the deficit financing. Fluctuating oil prices, however, have further hurt Burkina's economy.

Education and health indicators are among the world's worst. Only 30 percent of Burkina's primary children receive a basic education, and few ever reach either the University of Ouagadougou or the Polytechnical University in Bobo-Dioulasso. Overall literacy rates are just under 27 percent, with female rates at an even lower 16 percent.

Gastrointestinal diseases and malaria are the main causes of death, and HIV/AIDS rates are growing. River blindness, sleeping sickness, and schistosomiasis are also endemic. All health indicators established by the World Health Organization fall below 1995 targets. Life expectancy at birth is under fifty; infant mortality is 116 per 1,000; under-five mortality is 150 per 1,000; and 21 percent of babies are born with low birth weights. Sanitation and safe drinking water are inadequate.

The global pandemic of HIV/AIDS reached Burkina Faso in the 1990s, exacerbated by the large numbers of males who depart each year to heavily infected Côte d'Ivoire in search of work. In 2005 an estimated 700,000 Burkinabe were infected; 100,000 of these patients were critically ill and in need of treatment with antiretroviral drugs (ARVs). Burkina is one of three countries in Africa (with Ghana and Mozambique) that were chosen in March 2005 to be part of a new treatment acceleration project (TAP) to provide free ARVs for three years as part of a pilot program that will treat an estimated 7,000 people.

Despite the burdens of poor health and limited resources, cultural life thrives in one domain: African cinema. Ouagadougou draws large numbers of visitors to the biennial Pan-African Film Festival (Fespaco). A burgeoning Burkinabe film industry provides opportunities for local directors, writers, and actors.

See also **Disease; Ecosystems; International Monetary Fund; Metals and Minerals.**

BIBLIOGRAPHY

Baxter, Joan, and Keith Somerville. "Burkina Faso." In *Benin, the Congo, Burkina Faso: Economics, Politics and Society*, ed. Christopher Allen. New York: Printer, 1988.

Pallier, Ginette. *Géographie générale de la Haute-Volta*. Limoges: L'U.E.R. des Lettres et Sciences Humaines de Limoges, 1978.

Peron, Yves, and Victoire Zalcain, eds. *Atlas de la Haute-Volta*. Paris: Editions Jeune-Afrique, 1975.

Walque, Damien D. *Who Gets AIDS and How? The Determinants of HIV Infection and Sexual Behaviors in Burkina Faso, Cameroon, Ghana, Kenya, and Tanzania*. Washington, DC: World Bank, Development Research Group, Public Services Team, 2006.

MYRON ECHENBERG

SOCIETY AND CULTURES

The population of Burkina Faso—over 14 million according to 2007 statistics—covers some sixty ethnic groups that can be aggregated into three language families: (1) the Voltaic or Gur family, to which belong Bwa, Dagara, Gurmance, Gurunsi, Lobi, Mossi, and Senufo; (2) the Mande family, including Marka, Bisa, Bobo, Dafing, Dogon, Dyula, Ouara, Samo, and Sembla; and (3) the West Atlantic family, which has the Fulani as a single member. The composed name of the country, adopted in 1984, alludes to the multitude of ethnicities from which one nation was formed: *Burkina* means "men of dignity" in Moré, the language of the Mossi, *Faso* means "house," "village," or "country" in the vocabulary of the Western Dyula. The people are called Burkinabe, the suffix *bè* meaning "inhabitants" in Fulfulde, the language of the northern Fulani.

ETHNIC GROUPS

The Mossi people comprise 50.2 percent of the total population and mainly occupy the central plateau area. As an ethnic group they are difficult to categorize: they have colonized, integrated, and/or assimilated many groups (e.g., Nioniosse, Ninsi, Yarse, Marense, Zaose, Kurumba, and Dogon), offering shelter to some and marrying into others. Ethnic distinction, however, is based more on language than on culture, so it is actually more appropriate to state that about half of Burkina's population speak Moré. Although French administrators admired the rigid hierarchical structure and well-defined sociopolitical organization that characterized Mossi society, many present-day chieftaincies were created only recently, during the colonial period. The Gurmance, eastern neighbors of the Mossi, have a relatively similar political system.

In the southeast (around Garango and Zabré) live the Bisa, while the southwest, the region between the Black and the Red Volta (present-day Mouhoun and Nazinon), is occupied by Gurunsi (a pejorative collective name for a number of smaller groups like Lela, Kasena, Nuna, Kusase, Ko, and Sisala). Bisa and Gurunsi were considered representative of a type of village-based society in apparent transition to a state-like organization.

The most ethnic diversity is found in the west, where numerous groups live without central authority. Among the Mande-Dyula, Dagara, Dyan, Lobi, and Birifor, a subbranch of the Lobi, authority belongs to the elder within each lineage, whereas the Bobo and Bwa of the west and the Samo, Marka, and Senufo in the northwest are organized in so-called village-societies. Each village, some of them composed of up to 1,000 inhabitants, is a completely autonomous and self-centered unit under gerontocratic leadership.

The Fulani, a formerly nomadic people who have become mostly sedentary since colonization, are found throughout the country, but are dominant in the dry north (Jelgodi) while in the northeast (Oudalan) live some Tuareg who speak a Berberian language. As in all Sudanic countries, many groups were further subdivided into socio-professional castes (blacksmiths, weavers, dyers, musicians, etc.).

Despite the multitude of ethnic identities there are no major conflicts. Some hold the opinion that *joking relationship*, a verbal wordplay alluding to stereotypes attributed to the "others," which is practiced among members of various groups (e.g. among Samo and Mossi, Gurunsi and Bisa, Fulani and Bobo), is a way to diminish underlying tensions between members of a multiethnic society. The strict interdiction of bloodshed, which is considered a transgression that can rupture the social pact, seems to have prevented conflict and helped consolidate a national identity.

ECONOMY

Burkina Faso has few resources and is one of the poorest countries in the world—90 percent of the population live in a rural environment and make their living through subsistence farming. Cotton is the main cash crop; other mainstays are cereal (predominantely different varieties of millet and rice) and/or fishing. The country's limited industrial activity is mainly focused on the processing of primary commodities. Poor soil, droughts, desertification, and a high population pressure in the south and on the central plateau (125 persons per square mile) led many Mossi to move to less densely populated parts of the country; this may contribute to ethnic tensions in the future.

Commerce is largely controlled by Dyula and Yarse traders, with men dominating large-scale trades and women present in small-scale enterprises. Cattle, which in most regions are bred by the Fulani, are exported to the neighboring countries such as Togo, Ghana, and Côte d'Ivoire. As in other sub-Saharan countries, the relationship between the Fulani herdsmen—who settle where they find pastures and wells—and the sedentary population contains the potential for conflict.

Since 1980 the population has grown at a 2.6 percent annually, while life expectancy hovers around forty-eight years. The percentage of people living with HIV/AIDS is increasing; UNICEF estimates that at the end of 2005, 2 percent of the Burkinabe population fifteen and older was infected with the virus. The urban population (19%), specifically, is marked

Wives of a village chief with their youngest sons in front of their homestead, Boulgou Province. In the Boulgou Province many village chiefs have more than one wife. Usually the number depends on age, wealth, and social recognition. Women's customary role is to serve men, mainly by increasing their husbands' offspring. Attempts to change the structure of social and sexual relations have been met by the rural population with reluctance and hostility. PHOTOGRAPH COURTESY OF UTE RITZ-MÜLLER

by rapid growth: Ouagadougou has grown from 700,000 in 1995 to more than 1 million inhabitants.

Beside the rural-urban migration a large number of men migrate to work on plantations in Ghana and Côte d'Ivoire. Until 1999 the Burkinabe diaspora in Côte d'Ivoire counted approximately 3 million people. Because they have regularly been the target of ethnic attacks, approximately 250,000 returned to Burkina, many without any chances of making a better life. More recent destinations of migrants are Nigeria, North Africa (Lybia), France, Italy, and (mainly for students) Canada and the United States.

Traditionally men did not only hold most political and religious offices but largely controlled the economy and made all important decisions. In urban areas the economic role of women is substantial in markets and in the informal sector where they manage to reach some level of independence. Because modern marriage is monogamous, women have to consent if the husband wants to take a second wife. But in the rural areas, where women are estimated to be responsible for 60 to 80% of all

agricultural work, polygamy is still widespread, especially among wealthy old men and chiefs (a term that is commonly used for all political office holders), and their social status remains relatively low.

Women's submission, especially in Mossi society, is mainly based on two institutions: (1) forced or arranged marriages for women (*pog-siure*), and (2) female circumcision, which was practiced by most ethnic groups. Twenty-first-century law forbids and punishes the surgical removal of women's genitalia, but female mutilation continues to be practiced widely and in secret: A nonexcised woman, at least outside the main urban centers and among the less educated, will find it difficult to secure a husband.

RELIGION

Adherents of traditional African religions (estimates range from 38% to more than 50% of the population) are most prevalent in the east (among the Gurmance), within the southwest (around Gaoua) and, to a lesser extent, on the central Mossi plateau and in the Bobo-Banfora region. At the core of traditional religion lies the faith in and the veneration

Wives of Naba Saaga of Tenkodogo, the capital of the province, carrying baskets with paraphernalia for sacrifice. Sacrifices, especially if addressed to the ancestors, are important to maintain general welfare. All proper sacrifices include dolo, the popular sorghum beer that is exclusively made by women. Naba Saaga succeeded his father Naba Tigré (1957–2001), at times one of the country's most influential chiefs, who had about 60 wives. PHOTOGRAPH COURTESY OF UTE RITZ-MÜLLER

of ancestors, who act as mediators between the different worlds, and whose benevolence is sought to ensure the well-being of the living and their adherence to legal norms. The existence of a supreme, but distant (sky) god is generally recognized, and shrines for the goddess of the earth (*tenga*) are found among most groups. In some societies (e.g., Bwa, Nuna, Senufo, Nioniosse, Kurumba) representatives of different masks or secret societies perform at their members' burials.

Islam, which spread in the Mossi Plateau between the sixteenth and nineteenth centuries among the merchant communities of Mande origin that were located on the gold, kola, and slave routes, still prevails at more than 80 percent among the Fulani, Songhay, and Tuareg in the north. It is also widespread around Ouagadougou and Dedougou. Sunni Muslims make up 44 to 50 percent of the population. Because many of them prefer Qur'anic to Western-style education, they are still poorly represented in politics and public administration; however, they control substantial sectors of the economy, mostly commerce, transport, and construction.

Christians, mostly Catholics, make up between 10 and 18 percent of the population. Although they have the fastest rate of growth, they are not the majority in any part of Burkina Faso. Their highest concentration is in Ouagadougou and the regions around Koupéla where White Fathers (*Pères Blancs*) erected the first missionary station in 1900.

Many Burkinabe profess more than one religion and frequently change congregations. As different beliefs are common, not only within one group but also among members of the same family, there is much mutual tolerance. This climate of religious peace is favored by most chiefs, who will go to church on Christian holidays, celebrate Muslim festivals (*tabaski*), and practice traditional religion according to their ceremonial and ritual functions.

Burkina Faso is celebrated for its many forms of art, and indigenous cinema is well known in both West Africa and France.

See also **Art, Regional Styles: Western Africa; Death, Mourning and Ancestors; Disease; Film and Cinema; Initiation; Language; Marriage Systems.**

BIBLIOGRAPHY

Englebert, Pierre. *Burkina Faso: Unsteady Statehood in West Africa*. Boulder, CO: Westview Press, 1996.

Izard, Michel. Moogo: *L'émergence d'un espace étatique ouest-africain au XVIeme siècle*. Paris: Éditions Karthala, 2003.

Kambou-Ferrand, Jeanne-Marie. *Peuples voltaïques et conquête coloniale, 1885–1914*. Paris: L'Harmattan, 1993.

Savonnet-Guyot, Claudette. *Etat et sociétés au Burkina: Essai sur la politique africaine*. Paris: Éditions Karthala, 1986.

Sissao, Alain Joseph. *Alliances et parentés à plaisanterie au Burkina Faso: Mécanismes de fonctionnement et avenir*. Ouagadougou: Sankofa and Gurli Éditions, 2002.

UTE RITZ-MÜLLER

HISTORY AND POLITICS

Burkina Faso, formerly known as Upper Volta, is a landlocked West African nation that was the seat of the Mossi empire, which began in the fifteenth century. The Mossi and other Voltaic- and Mande-speaking peoples mounted an unsuccessful resistance to French military conquest in the mid-1890s, and although the region was also coveted by British and German imperialists, the French gained formal control by 1898. In 1919 the country became the separate colony of Upper Volta (Haute-Volta); it was partitioned in 1932 as an economy measure, and then reconstituted in 1947, when the Mossi were granted their request for separate territorial status. In 1956, as part of the basic law (*loi cadre*) reform of July 23, Upper Volta, along with other territories in French West Africa, was granted a degree of self-government and its own national assembly within the French colonial union. Upper Volta became an autonomous republic in the French community on December 11, 1958, and was granted full independence on August 5, 1960. Nevertheless, a series of bilateral agreements with the former mother country assured significant French economic, political, and military influence in the country.

The first president was Maurice Yaméogo, leader of the Voltaic Democratic Union (UDV), and a staunch ally of President Felix Houphouët-Boigny of Côte d'Ivoire. Yaméogo quickly banned all political parties save his own. After a 1965 election in which UDV officially polled 99 percent of the vote, an opposition coalition of students, trade unionists, and civil servants took to the streets of the capital of Ouagadougou in protest. Mass demonstrations continued the following year and led directly to a military coup, the first of several in the country, in January 1966. Yaméogo fled into exile in France and Lieutenant-Colonel Sangoulé Lamizana took over as president. For the next fifteen years, Lamizana reigned but did not rule over the country. An old noncommissioned warhorse in the *Tirailleurs Sénégalais* (France's colonial army) and a man of limited education, Lamizana relied upon both a younger generation of officers and advice from the French ambassador to run the country. His regime retained power until it was overthrown in 1980 in a coup inspired by protests from workers, teachers, and civil servants.

By 1983 a radical National Revolutionary Council (CNR) gained hegemony. At its head was Captain Thomas Sankara, a thirty-four-year-old junior army officer whose father had served France during World War II as a *Tirailleur Sénégalais*, one of thousands of Burkinabe men who had been conscripted or who had volunteered for military service. In 1984, his power consolidated, Sankara renamed the country Burkina Faso, meaning "land of incorruptible people," and ordered all officials, himself included, to open their bank accounts to public scrutiny.

Dubbed the "Robin Hood of the Sahel," Sankara garnered considerable international attention with his radical policies and flamboyant style. Personally modest, he rode to office each day on a bicycle, sang and played the guitar on variety shows, and often read the evening news on television. His revolutionary program attacked corruption and sought to improve agriculture, education, and the status of women. His rule brought extended vaccination and housing campaigns, tree planting to hold back the Sahel, the promotion of women's rights, and salary cuts for civil servants. He sold off the government fleet of Mercedes cars and made the modest Renault 5 the official vehicle for ministers. His decision to bring a significant number of women into his cabinet was unprecedented in his country and in Africa generally. Sankara banned female circumcision, condemned polygamy, and promoted contraception and family planning. His government removed many of the powers held by traditional chiefs such as their entitlements to tribute payments and to compulsory labor.

République Démocratique du Burkina Faso (Burkina Faso)

Population:	14,326,203 (2007 est.)
Area:	274,200 sq. km (106,000 sq. mi.)
Official language:	French
Languages:	French, Mossi, Dyula
National currency:	CFA franc
Principal religions:	Muslim, traditional, Christian
Capital:	Ouagadougou (est. pop. 1,000,000 in 2006)
Other urban centers:	Bobo-Dioulasso, Koudougou.
Principal geographical features:	*Mountains:* Renankourou *Rivers:* Mouhoun (Black Volta), Nakimbé (White Volta), Nazinon (Red Volta) *Lakes:* Bam Dèm, Mare d'Oursi
Economy:	*GDP per capita:* US$424 (2006)
Principal products and exports:	*Agricultural:* cotton, peanuts, shea nuts, sesame, sorghum, millet, corn, rice; livestock *Manufacturing:* cotton lint, beverages, agricultural processing, soap, cigarettes, textiles *Mining:* gold, manganese, bauxite, lead
Government:	Independence from France, 1960. Constitution, 1960. New constitutions approved in 1970 and 1977, suspended in 1980. New constitution adopted in 1991. President elected for 7-year term by universal suffrage. Bicameral national legislature: 107-member Assemblée des Députées du Peuple elected for 5-year terms by universal suffrage; 178-seat Chambre des Représentants whose members are nominated. President appoints prime minister; prime minister appoints Council of Ministers. For purposes of local government, there are 30 provinces divided into 250 departments, further divided into communes administered by mayors and municipal councils.
Heads of state since independence:	1960–1966: President Maurice Yaméogo 1966–1980: President Sangoulé Lamizana 1980–1982: Colonel Saye Zerbo 1982–1983: Surgeon-Major Jean-Baptiste Ouédraogo 1983–1987: Captain Thomas Sankara 1987–: President Captain Blaise Compaoré
Armed forces:	President is commander in chief. Compulsory 18-month service. *Army:* 5,600 *Air force:* 200 *Paramilitary:* 4,200 *People's Militia:* 45,000
Transportation:	*Rail:* 622 km (386 mi.). Railway links Ouagadougou to Abidjan (in Côte d'Ivoire). *Roads:* 15,272 km (9,484 mi.), 31% paved *National airline:* Air Burkina *Airports:* International facilities at Ouagadougou and Bobo-Dioulasso
Media:	Dailies include *Bulletin quotidien d'information, Jamaa Sidwaya, Le pays, Le journal de soir,* and *L'observateur Paalga.* 14 non-dailies. Radio stations include La Voix de Renouveau. Télévision Nationale du Burkina broadcasts television programming only in Ouagadougou and Bobo-Dioulasso.
Literacy and education:	*Total literacy rate:* 27% (2006). Education is theoretically compulsory from ages 7–13. Schools are overcrowded, and many students drop out when they are unable to pay school fees. Postsecondary education provided at Université de Ouagadougou and Centre d'Études Économiques et Sociales d'Afrique Occidentale. The Polytechnical University in Bobo-Dioulasso opened in 1995.

While Sankara enjoyed good relations with his military counterpart in Ghana, relations with northwestern neighbor Mali deteriorated. A dispute over the allegedly mineral-rich Agacher strip erupted in a five-day border war in December 1985 that produced roughly one hundred casualties, most of them Burkinabe civilians killed in a Malian bombing raid on the town of Ouahigouya in northern Burkina. The dispute was settled in the International Court in The Hague a year later to both parties' satisfaction.

This decision provided a model to many third world countries on how the International Court could render impartial judgments.

Sankara's populist and charismatic rule, along with his speeches and writings on what he called the Burkina Faso Revolution, earned him wide support, especially among students in Burkina and elsewhere in Africa. But tensions began to mount when the government formed village-level groupings, the Committees for the Defense of the Revolution

(CDRs), ostensibly to develop neglected rural areas. In some districts, however, the CDRs behaved like armed thugs. Disgruntled traditional leaders who had lost power joined with the small but powerful middle class to oppose his reforms. By 1987, urban dwellers and a segment of the peasantry complained about poorly devised development schemes. The left accused the government of softening its anti-imperialist stance to secure foreign aid. In spite of initial tensions with the United States because of close links between Sankara and Libya's Colonel Muammar Qadhdhafi, the United States replaced France as Burkina's main aid donor. Relations with established political parties and trade unions broke down. On October 15, 1987, one of his fellow officers and former supporters, Captain Blaise Compaoré, seized control at the head of the Popular Front (FP), and has remained in power in the early twenty-first century.

Compaoré, also a career army officer, quickly abandoned Sankara's radical populism in favor of liberal economics. He complied with International Monetary Fund pressures to privatize and to initiate austerity measures within the civil service. These structural adjustment policies were also accompanied by halting steps towards democratization. Compaoré's new constitution, unveiled in June 1991, established a parliament with two chambers that can be dissolved by the president of the republic, who is elected for a renewable term of seven years. In 2000, an amendment reduced this term to five years as of 2005. In the election of 1998, Compaoré won an easy victory as president when the opposition parties boycotted the poll. The election results were declared fair by local and international observers.

Compaoré has governed with a heavy hand. Shortly after he began his second term as president his government was rocked by what became known as the Zongo affair, the suspicious circumstances surrounding the death of the Burkinabe journalist Norbert Zongo and three of his companions on December 13, 1998. Zongo was an independent-minded journalist, novelist, and publisher who never disguised his opposition to the Compaoré regime. The case was taken up by Reporters without Borders, and the government established a commission of inquiry. Although foul play was suspected, it could not be proved, even though Zongo's life had been threatened previously on several occasions. In the wake of his

death, police broke up a massive student demonstration at the headquarters of Compaoré's ruling party, the Congress for Democracy and Progress (CDP). The next day, 15,000 attended Zongo's funeral.

Since the mid-twentieth century, several hundred thousand Burkinabe have migrated south seasonally (and sometimes for longer periods) to Côte d'Ivoire and Ghana. An estimated 3 million Burkinabe live in Côte d'Ivoire without status as citizens. Tensions in the destination countries have provoked civil disturbances. Struggling with political instability since 2003, Côte d'Ivoire returned 300,000 migrants, depriving Burkina of their substantial remittances and diminishing the economy's limited ability to absorb them. The country accused Burkina Faso of backing northern rebels, a charge which the Compaoré government denied. Another West African controversy alleged that Burkina facilitated the civil war in Sierra Leone by allowing its territory to serve as a transit for smuggled blood diamonds and military hardware.

In the presidential election of November 2005 Compaoré easily won a third term over a badly fragmented opposition, garnering 80 percent of the vote. Among the eleven other candidates was Hermann Yaméogo, son of the country's first president.

See also **Colonial Policies and Practices; Government; Houphouët-Boigny, Félix; Initiation; International Monetary Fund; Postcolonialism; Qadhdhafi, Muammar.**

BIBLIOGRAPHY

Cordell, Dennis D.; Joel W. Gregory; and Victor Piché. *Hoe and Wage: A Social History of a Circular Migration System in West Africa.* Boulder, CO: Westview Press, 1996.

Decalo, Samuel, comp. *World Bibliographical Series*, vol. 169: *Burkina Faso.* Santa Barbara, CA: ABC Clio, 1994.

Echenberg, Myron. *Colonial Conscripts: The Tirailleurs Sénégalais in French West Africa, 1857–1960.* Portsmouth, NH: Heinemann, 1991.

Jaffré, Bruno. *Burkina Faso: Les années Sankara.* Paris: L'Harmattan, 2000.

McFarland, Daniel Miles. *Historical Dictionary of Upper Volta (Haute Volta).* Metuchen, NJ: Scarecrow Press, 1978.

Skinner, Elliot P. *African Urban Life: The Transformation of Ouagadougou.* Princeton, NJ: Princeton University Press, 1974.

MYRON ECHENBERG

BURUNDI

This entry includes the following articles:
GEOGRAPHY AND ECONOMY
SOCIETY AND CULTURES
HISTORY AND POLITICS

GEOGRAPHY AND ECONOMY

Burundi is located in the southern hemisphere between 2°20' and 4°27' south latitude. With a surface of 10,742 square miles, the natural borders, made up of rivers and lakes, form a wedge-shaped territory at the sources of the Nile and Congo Rivers. The administrative divisions of Provinces, Communes, and *Collines* are the heritage of precolonial structures that were adapted under colonization.

Burundi is a country of mountains and thousands of densely populated hills. The relief divides, from west to east, into four main regions: the western lowlands of the Great Rift Valley; the Congo Nile peak, rising to 8,809 feet; central plateaus covering the major part of the country, thousands of hills; and the small eastern depressions and northeastern areas of *Kumoso* and *Bugesera*.

In the western plain, tropical heat is attenuated by the mountains and the southern and eastern breezes of Lake Tanganyika that lower the annual average temperature to 73 degrees Fahrenheit. In the Congo Nile peak the annual average falls to 57 degrees Fahrenheit. It goes up to 60.8 degrees Fahrenheit in most of the country. The effect of altitude, combined with the country's topography, refreshes the temperatures and makes them more pleasant. The equatorial character remains nevertheless in the thermal extremes: 34 degrees in Teza, on the Congo Nile peak, and 39 degrees in Bujumbura, in the Great Rift Valley. The equatorial mode has two wet seasons and two dry seasons. The circulation of the masses of air and the elevations of the land's surface introduce variations into the seasons.

The population density exceeds 400 inhabitants per square mile for a country of seven million inhabitants. Some hills of Burundi have very high densities: 1,613 to 2,419 inhabitants per square mile. Several factors contribute to this: the healthiness of the natural environment, the strong precolonial political and social organizations (e.g., military territorial

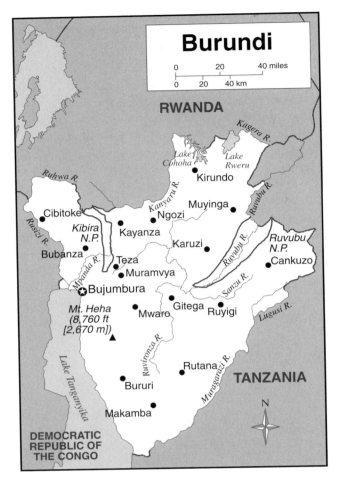

security organizations), and the progress of medical care from the 1950s onward.

Slightly industrialized and urbanized, Burundi's economic activity is still more than 90 percent rural. At the crossroads of the cultures of five continents, with nearly twenty varieties of plants, Burundi developed a diversified agriculture according to the ecological conditions of the territory. In many areas, people breed livestock in order to increase their agricultural outputs, whereas fishing is actively practiced on Lake Tanganyika. Agricultural activities and the countryside underwent significant changes following the assassination of Burundi's first democratically elected president and ensuing civil war in 1993.

The commercial cultures dominated by the coffee (up to 90%), tea, and cotton exports that provided currency for the country saw their importance declining, and even disappearing. Food products and traditionally noncommercial cultures have begun to assume more and more importance thanks to the extension of the urban and regional markets: dealing with sugar, palm oil, and other fresh products.

The consumption of imported hydrocarbons increases regularly and is expensive for the country. Industry, concentrated in the capital, accounts for only 5 percent of gross domestic product and deals primarily with agricultural produce, food, and chemical products. The latter is handicapped by Burundi's geographic isolation, monetary inflation, and the rise in the prices of raw materials, among other factors.

The urbanization of the country relates mainly to Bujumbura, the capital and the administrative, communications, and economic center of the country. The majority of the urbanized population live in Bujumbura.

Classified among the poorest countries in the world, Burundi's major economic problem is that it is a landlocked country. In the early twenty-first century, the country is making efforts at regional integration with the East Africa community or the countries of Comesa.

Because of the civil war, foreign trade was disturbed and Burundians have lived on humanitarian aid since 1993. The goals of restarting of the national economy return with the early twenty-first century policies of the ending of war, and social, political, and economic rebuilding.

See also **Aid and Development; Ecosystems.**

BIBLIOGRAPHY

Bidou, Jacques E. (Jean Etienne); Sylvestre Ndayirukiye; Jean-Pierre Ndayishimiye; and Pierre Sirven. *Géographie du Burundi*. Paris: Hatier, 1991.

Ndayirukiye; Sylvestre. *Bujumbura Centenaire 1897–1997, croissance et défis*. Paris: Harmattan, 2002.

SYLVESTRE NDAYIRUKIYE

SOCIETY AND CULTURES

Despite the prevailing notion that the ethnic identities existing in Burundi in the early twenty-first century, as well as the Burundian polity itself, extend back into the past for centuries, in fact as recently as the early twentieth century the peoples, the identities, and even the polities existing within the contemporary Burundian nation-state were quite different—more particular and more numerous—than in the present day. The dominant process taking place since colonial troops came to the region intending to exert their control, circa 1896, has been consolidation: first territorial, as autonomous and semi-independent regions were forcefully brought under the control of the Burundian kingdom; and then social, as colonial and postcolonial authorities have restructured social relations, causing old identities to merge and coalesce, new identities to form, and existing identities to develop new social and political meanings.

As the result of these processes, Burundi's contemporary population consists of two highly politicized and polarized ethnic groups: Hutu and Tutsi, and a smattering of others, including Twa, the modern descendants of those who formerly dwelled in the great tropical forests that once dominated the region's landscape. There are also significant populations of Europeans, South Asians, Afro-Arabs and Arabs, and immigrants, including refugees, from other African countries. Some members of the latter groups have no legal nationality.

The processes that have transformed Burundi from diversity to what is essentially polarity have been profoundly violent. Particularly since the 1960s, many hundreds of thousands of citizens have lost their lives to political violence cynically manipulated by postcolonial elites on the basis of Hutu-Tutsi ethnicity. Indeed, some analysts have remarked that especially since the 1990s violence itself has become the "language" of politics; that is to say that the killing of ordinary civilians has become the way in which political rivals compete with each other (Human Rights Watch 1998). In this context, many Burundians, riven by grief, loss, fear, and distrust, have come to ask themselves what holds them together as a nation. But undeniably Burundians do share certain outlooks that derive from similar—though not homogeneous—precolonial regional culture, a shared, if unequal, colonial experience, and a modern national infrastructure. As much as Burundians distrust each other—and legitimately so, given their modern history—they do not identify with any other nation, and they do not imagine themselves living in separate Hutu and Tutsi nation-states.

PEOPLE AND POLITIES

Historians often claim that Burundi is one of the few modern African nation-states whose contemporary territorial boundaries correspond to a coherent precolonial kingdom. Therefore, it is said to be surprising that Burundi has remained so continuously embroiled in conflict since its independence in 1962. In fact, Burundi, as defined by its modern boundaries, was not a unified kingdom prior to its colonial experience.

Colonial occupation came to Burundi in 1896 with the building of a German military post on the northeastern shore of Lake Tanganyika near present-day Bujumbura. But the Burundi—or, Urundi, as it was called at the time—that the Germans encountered was one comprised of several culturally and politically distinct regions, and numerous autonomous leaders. One of these was Mwezi Gisabo, the king or *mwami* of a polity in the eastern-central highlands near present-day Muramvya. The royal group that governed this kingdom was the aristocratic Ganwa (or *Baganwa*) dynasty. The territory over which the Ganwa dynasty claimed dominance expanded and shrank over time according to its fortunes. The reign of Mwezi Gisabo (since c. 1850) had been marked more by entropy and regional autonomy than by consolidation. Despite claims to the contrary, the royal court's hold extended little beyond Burundi's central plateau. The political culture, identities, and social institutions that characterized life at the royal court in central Burundi were not replicated in the hinterland, even in the districts where the kingdom claimed authority.

Outlying regions maintained their own distinctiveness, particularly at the grassroots level. In regions such as Imbo lake plain, the Rusizi river plain and the Mumirwa slopes to the west, Bugesera and Bweru in the north, Kumosso and Bunyambo in the east, and Buragane, Bukurira, and Buvugalimwe in the south, residents retained distinctive regional characteristics, such as linguistic traits, spiritual ideas, social institutions, cultural practices, and local identities.

The people of Imbo lake-plain, for example, were actively engaged in a broad lacustrine community composed of the peoples living along the rim of Lake Tanganyika. They were fishermen and traders. They constructed canoes, and transported goods along the lake. They shared with other lake-dwellers certain spiritual beliefs and oral traditions centering on the lake that they did not hold in common with resident of the Burundi highlands. They were attuned to, and engaged in, economic changes wrought by the arrival of Afro-Arab traders of ivory and slaves along the lake's coastline to the south whilst the aristocrats living in the Burundian highlands responded to these changes with considerable resistance.

GERMAN COLONIAL IMPACT

During colonialism, considerable force was applied to pull disparate regions together into a kingdom that could correspond to the territory designated as "Urundi" on European maps.

German policy with regard to what it regarded as the Urundi District of German East Africa vacillated between exploiting and "repairing" the kingdom's weak or nonexistent hold beyond the central plateau. To "conquer" the *mwami*, Germans partnered with his internal and external rivals. Once conquered, from 1903, German policy shifted toward propping up "the traditional sultan" Mwezi Gisabo. The death of the aged king in 1908, which ignited latent rivalries in the kingdom's heartland, and growing German awareness that the royal court simply did not control many of the regions subsumed under the label "Urundi" on European maps, led to the decision in 1911 to divide the district into separate administrative zones. Just as this strategy was being put into effect came the start of World War I, and with it, the demise of German colonial rule. As late as 1916 when the Germans fled Urundi, much of the south, east, northeast, and northwest of the district had still not been fully brought under Ganwa or German rule.

BELGIAN COLONIAL IMPACT

In 1916, Belgians invading from the Congo seized control of Urundi and placed it under interim military rule. Meanwhile, the Ganwa royal court experienced its own version of interim rule when Mwezi Gisabo's young successor, Mutaga Mbikije (1908–1915) failed to consolidate his hold on the royal court and died mysteriously in 1915. Urundi remained in a state of flux—neither royal nor colonial rule was securely established, and many regions either remained or fell back into the old pattern of autonomy. Regional and local identities remained dominant. The majority of Burundians regarded themselves as members of a particular family, residents of a particular hill, skillful practitioners of a certain occupation or livelihood (such as arrow-making or blacksmithing), connected through family oral traditions to a particular historical "clan," and linked through socioeconomic relations to particular wealthy men or "patrons." Identity was not at all constructed in terms of "Hutu" and "Tutsi."

In the early 1920s, with the concomitant establishment of Belgian administration (granted by the League of Nations) and a new set of aristocrats centered on Mutaga's successor, young King Mwambutsa Bangiricenge (1915–1966), a working partnership formed between royal court and the Belgian authorities. As this partnership developed, so too did new political identities.

King Mwambutsa was only a child at his coronation in December 1915. The adult regents who guided him were his uncle Ntarugera, his stepgrandmother Ririkumutima who had been a favored wife of deceased King Mwezi Gisabo, and Ririkumutima's two favorite sons, Nduwumwe and Karabona. This was a complicated group, each pursuing his or her own interests to the extreme—in fact, Ririkumutima was said to have ordered the murder Mwambutsa's real mother so that she could play the role of his political surrogate mother. In 1925, with only two regents still living, the regent system was transformed into a royal advisory council—first the Kingdom Council, 1925–1930, and then the King's Council, 1939–1952. These councils, unlike the original group of regents, were fully colonial institutions, meaning that their role was to "advise" rather than to govern as the regent had done.

This shift from the actual exercise of power by regents to primarily consultative advisory council in 1925, and then the disappearance of an advisory council altogether by 1939, correspond to a sweeping reorganization of Urundi's African administration which began soon after the League of Nations gave Belgium full legal responsibility for the colony. After a systematic survey in 1929, changes came at a swift and relentless pace. The reorganization transformed not only the territorial administration, but the nature of power itself as well as who had access to it.

Prior to the reorganization, local-level authority had derived from local processes. Initially, Belgians had worked with whomever they encountered exercising authority. As long as a local authority collected taxes, carried out orders, and went when called to the colonial post, he or she was normally regarded as viable. This meant that the first generation of local "subchiefs" and "chiefs" under Belgian rule constituted a diverse group. They included both men and women, and members of families that would be later categorized as Ganwa, Tutsi, and Hutu. With the reorganization, this diversity ended. Overwhelmingly the new power structure favored men from one branch of the royal family, known as the Batare. It also gave preference to Ganwa in general, and to Tutsi courtesans from the kingdom's central plateau.

The reorganization represented a crucial step toward new kinds of identities, and new meanings for preexisting identities. For example, local leaders of formerly autonomous regions became integrated into Urundi as ordinary, even poor, subjects living in peripheral districts. Self-sufficient farmers and artisans were transformed by the colonial system as subjects (or servants: *hutu*) of the state who were forced to pay taxes and could be pressed into labor *corvées*. They collectively became known as Hutus.

By contrast, cattle owners and their kin, who were considered wealthy or at least of higher status, became incorporated into colonial Urundi society as Tutsis who could, at times, leverage their status to obtain exemptions from the more onerous colonial obligations, and occasionally benefit from certain advantages, such as access to education or employment. Nevertheless, not all Tutsis received similar preferential treatment. Those who came from the courtesan families of the Urundi heartland were, in general, better placed to benefit from the new system than Tutsis elsewhere.

Resentment grew and festered among the better- and lesser-connected Tutsis, as well as among the more privileged Ganwa, the Batare, and their rivals, the Bezi. Hutus experienced resentment too, but as a group they harbored fewer expectations that the colonial system would deliver advantages to them.

In fact, the Belgian colonial system delivered fewer advantages to Urundi than to its neighbor Ruanda, which Belgians regarded as the more elaborate or "culturally refined" kingdom and the greater prize. The Urundi elite's apparent lack of refinement,

République du Burundi (Republic of Burundi)

Population:	8,390,505 (2007 est.)
Area:	27,822 sq. km (10,742 sq. mi.)
Official languages:	French and Kirundi
Languages:	French, Kirundi, Swahili
National currency:	Burundi franc
Principal religions:	Christian 67% (mostly Roman Catholic), indigenous 23%, Muslim 10%
Capital:	Bujumbura (est. pop. 300,000 in 2006)
Other urban centers:	Cibitoke, Muyinga, Ngozi, Bubanza, Gitega, Bururi
Annual rainfall:	ranges from 1,194 mm (47 in.) on the plateaus to 762 mm (30 in.) in lower areas
Principal geographical features:	*Mountains:* Mount Giziki *Rivers:* Ruvubu, Kagera, Akagera, Rusizi, Lua, Nyamagana, Kaburantwa, Mpanda, Ndahangwa, Doma *Lakes:* Tanganyika, Rugwero, Tsohoha *Other:* Great Rift Valley
Economy:	*GDP per capita:* US$700 (2006)
Principal products and exports:	*Agricultural:* coffee, cotton, tea, corn, sorghum, sweet potatoes, bananas, manioc (tapioca), beef, milk, hides *Manufacturing:* beverage production, coffee and tea processing, cigarette production, sugar refining, pharmaceuticals, light food processing, textiles, chemicals (insecticides), public works construction, consumer goods, assembly of imported components, light consumer goods such as blankets, shoes, soap *Mining:* alluvial gold, nickel, phosphates, rare earth, vanadium, and other; peat mini
Government:	Originally within German sphere of interest, then became a Belgian colony. Independence gained in 1962. Parliamentary democracy under military tutelage. Monarchy (under traditional Tutsi ruler) at independence. Republic declared in 1966. President was elected in 1993 under the terms of the 1992 constitution but was assassinated after 100 days in office, resulting in years of conflict. In 2005 a new constitution and a majority Hutu government were established, and in 2006 the new government signed a ceasefire with the last rebel group. A Council of Ministers is appointed by the president, who is elected by popular vote to a 5-year term. For purposes of local government, there are 17 provinces, further divided into 117 communes.
Heads of state since independence:	1962–1966: King Mwambutsa IV 1966: King Ntare V 1966–1976: President Michel Micombero 1976–1987: President Jean-Baptiste Bagaza 1987–1993: President Pierre Buyoya 1993: President Melchior Ndadaye 1993–1994: Interim rule by the government of Prime Minister Sylvie Kinigi 1994: President Cyprien Ntaryamira 1994–1996: President Sylvestre Ntibantunganya 1996–2003: President Major Pierre Buyoya 2003–2005: President Domitien Ndayizeye 2005–: President Pierre Nkurunziza
Armed forces:	President is commander in chief. Voluntary and compulsory enlistment. *Army:* 701,367 fit for service (2000 est.)
Transportation:	*Ports:* Bujumbura on Lake Tanganyika *Roads:* 12,322 km (7,652 mi.), 10% paved *National airline:* Société des Transports Aeriens du Burundi *Airport:* Bujumbura Airport
Media:	1 national general-interest newspaper, *Kiriumba.* 1 national radio network, La Radio-Television Nationale du Burundi. Other main publications: *Burundi chrétien, Ubumwe, le Burundi en images, Culture et sociétés, Bulletin économique et financier, Au coeur de l'Afrique.* Limited publishing.
Literacy and education:	*Total literacy rate:* 52% (2006). Language of instruction in primary schools is Kirundi; in secondary schools it is French. Postsecondary education provided by Université, du Burundi, Institut des Sciences Agronomiques du Burundi, Lycée Technique, Centre Social et Educatif.

however, translated politically into great *rapprochement* at the onset of decolonization. Unlike Ruandans, whose interpretation of democracy included violent ethnic retribution, Urundians, led by the dynamic Prince Rwagasore, formed a multiethnic coalition.

The success of Rwagasore's coalition struck a nerve among the Ganwa. Rwagasore was identified with the Bezi faction. Therefore, although his party appealed to a broad spectrum of Hutus and Tutsis, in the political calculus of the Ganwa, it was regarded as a Bezi party. By contrast, the party that constituted its strongest opponent was led by Batare. From a Ganwa perspective, Rwagasore's Parti de l'Union et du Progrès National (UPRONA) and the Batare-led Parti Démocrate Chrétien (PDC) were not simple political contenders for governing the state, they were deadly enemies fighting to *be* the state.

In the rounds of elections that ensued, the political playing field was by no means level. Belgian colonial officials backed the PDC and used state mechanisms to obstruct Rwagasore, such as arresting him and detaining hundreds of his supporters. When even these tactics failed to thwart Rwagasore's coalition from winning the September 1961 legislative elections, his PDC rivals arranged Rwagasore's assassination.

Prince Rwagasore's death in October 1961 not only created a leadership void, it opened a chasm in civil society. It dissolved the delicate interethnic trust that Rwagasore's supporters had worked so carefully to create. It also destroyed the balance between party politics and the monarchy, leading to the overthrow of the monarchy in 1966. Within party politics, the killing of Rwagasore demonstrated that coalition, so intensely slow and difficult to form, could be ripped apart in an instant by sheer force of violence. It propagated the cynical message that violence was the easy road to political dominance. But what appeared "easy" to ambitious politicians produced harsh results for Burundian society. It led, politically, to the rupture of cooperation between Tutsi and Hutu, and even schism and political rivalry among Tutsi groups. The unraveling of civil society opened an abyss into which politicians could push their rivals, and in turn be pushed, but from which no leader or solution could emerge. Taking advantage of this, the army took power, bringing a political culture of opaqueness, secrecy, violence and impunity. Inside the army rivalry and factionalism continued to occur, but to most members of civil society, this was rarely outwardly visible.

Since the 1960s, the opacity and exclusivity of Burundian military-based political culture endured despite challenges and resistance. Civilian uprisings, such as in 1972 and 1988, have been met with massive reprisals by the Tutsi-dominated army; the one of 1972 is regarded by many as a genocide against Hutus. International pressure for multiparty democracy, circa 1990, led to a period in which Hutu-led civilian governments found themselves obstructed from governing by the threat of violence of the Tutsi-dominated military, a threat based on the tragic reality of the 1993 military-perpetrated assassination of the first democratically elected Hutu president. This assassination marked the beginning of a drawn-out civil war that has slowly destroyed Burundian society. Not only has the war taken an enormous toll in lives on all sides, but it has also shattered Burundi's infrastructure, including its political infrastructure, leading to a splintering of ethnic blocks into a multitude of highly particular factions claiming to be political parties. By 2006, after more than a decade of continuous war, these factions had signed on to a peace agreement upon which many were looking with hope. But way in which Burundian citizens relate their political and their social identities, and the manner in which they approach the arduous task of building trust and translating that into coalition-building and power-sharing will determine if peace can prevail.

See also **Colonial Policies and Practices.**

BIBLIOGRAPHY

Chrétien, Jean-Pierre. *Burundi: L'histoire retrouvée.* Paris: Karthala, 1993.

Chrétien, Jean-Pierre. *The Great Lakes of Africa.* New York: Zone Books, 2003.

Gahama, Joseph. *Le Burundi sous administration belge.* Paris: Karthala, 1983.

Human Rights Watch. *Proxy Targets: Civilians in the War in Burundi.* New York: Human Rights Watch, 1998.

Lemarchand, René. *Rwanda and Burundi.* London: Pall Mall Press, 1970.

Lemarchand, René. *Burundi: Ethnocide as Discourse and Practice.* Washington, DC: Woodrow Wilson Institute, 1994.

Louis, William Roger. *Ruanda-Urundi 1884–1919.* Westport, CT: Greenwood Press, 1979.

Malkki, Liisa H. *Purity and Exile.* Chicago: University of Chicago, 1995.

Mworoha, Émile. *Histoire du Burundi.* Paris: Hatier, 1987.

Ould-Abdallah, Ahmedou. *Burundi on the Brink.* Washington, DC: U.S. Institute of Peace, 2000.

Reyntjens, Filip. *L'Afrique des grands lacs en crise.* Paris: Karthala, 1994.

Trouwborst, Albert. "Kinship and Geographical Mobility in Burundi." *International Journal of Comparative Sociology* 6, no. 1 (1965): 166–182.

Vansina, Jan. *La légende du passé.* Tervuren, Belgium: Musée Royale de l'Afrique Centrale, 1972.

MICHELE D. WAGNER

HISTORY AND POLITICS

A land-locked country of Lilliputian dimensions (10,742 square miles) and high population density (415 per square mile), Burundi lies atop the Nile-Congo crest, two degrees below the equator, in the Great Rift Valley of the African Great Lakes region. It is a land of rolling hills and lakes, giving way to spectacular escarpments in the northeast, and to grasslands in the southwest. Tempered by altitudes ranging from 9,000 feet in the central region to 3,000 feet along the shores of Lake Tanganyika, the climate is pleasantly cool throughout the year, with temperatures averaging 73.4 degrees Fahrenheit in the capital (Bujumbura). The physical beauty of the country, evocative of pastoral scenes, is in stark contrast with its tragic history. Since 1965, when thousands perished in what turned out to be a prelude to even greater horrors, Burundi has been torn by ethnic conflicts of unprecedented scale in its long history. More than 100,000 people, mostly Hutu, died at the hands of the monoethnic Tutsi army in 1972, in a genocide only surpassed in scale by the 1994 massacre in Rwanda. The latest carnage in 1993, triggered by the attempted seizure of power by the army on October 21, 1993, dealt a devastating blow to a democratic transition that only four months earlier had been characterized as exemplary.

Extreme poverty combined with growing population pressure on the land are key ingredients in the background of the Hutu-Tutsi conflict. The Hutu, accounting for approximately 85 percent of a population of over eight million, are essentially engaged in subsistence agriculture, as is the case for a number of Tutsi. Despite the advent of a functional multi-party system and the 1993 democratic elections that challenged Tutsi hegemony, the modern sector of the economy remains predominantly in Tutsi hands although the Tutsi account for only 14 percent of the population (and the remaining 1% is Twa). Coffee accounts for 90 percent of the country's export earnings, averaging 35,000 tons per year, but production has decreased substantially because of political and societal instability. The effect of social dislocations on food production has been equally severe, with famine conditions threatening many parts of the country.

Similar to Rwanda, its neighbor to the north, Burundi has a long pedigree as an archaic kingdom. Its emergence as a national entity in the early nineteenth century preceded that of many European states. Once part of the German colony of East Africa and later a League of Nations mandate and a UN Trust Territory under Belgian administration until its accession to independence in 1962, Burundi seemed better equipped than most other African states to cope with crises of legitimacy and identity. Just as political legitimacy inhered in the monarchy, the latter, in turn, served as the central focus of loyalty for Tutsi, Hutu, and Twa.

Burundi differs from most other African states in the vertical structuring of ethnic differentiation. Whether Hutu, Tutsi, or Twa, the people of Burundi (collectively known as Barundi or Burundians, and sharing the same native language, Kirundi) are profoundly aware of the social rankings inscribed in ethnic or clan identities. In the traditional hierarchy, the pygmoid Twa, representing 1 percent of the population, were clearly at the bottom, with princely families at the top. Between these two extremes stood the vast mass of Hutu agriculturalists and Tutsi pastoralists, although occupational ties did not inevitably correlate with social ranking. Family and clan ties were the key to prestige and privilege among both Hutu and Tutsi. Thus, within the Tutsi group, now accounting for about 14 percent of the population, significant social differentiation distinguished the low caste Tutsi-Hima from the Tutsi-Banyaruguru. The real power holders were neither Hutu nor Tutsi, but the descendants of princely families, or *ganwa*. The Burundian ethnic and social landscape was and continues to be complicated by the lingering legacy of racist and divisive colonial policies and practices to this day, over four decades after independence.

With the advent of independence, many scions of princely families were catapulted into positions of authority. The appointment of Prince Louis Rwagasore (1932–1961), eldest son of King (Mwami) Mwambutsa (1912–1977), to the post of prime minister-designate in 1961 is as much a commentary on the prestige of the monarchy on the eve of independence as it is a reflection of the enormous popularity enjoyed by Rwagasore as leader of the Parti de l'Union et du Progrès National (UPRONA), a party that enjoyed the solid support of both Hutu and Tutsi. Rwagasore's untimely assassination on October 13, 1961, by an individual of Greek origin considered a member of the Baranyanka clan, a rival princely faction, left a political void that has proved difficult to fill.

The crystallization of Hutu-Tutsi antagonisms is traceable to the demonstration effect of the Rwandan revolution (1959–1962). Few other events have had a more decisive impact on the hardening of ethnic lines in Burundi than the capture of power by Hutu elements in Rwanda. For many Tutsi, the Rwanda upheaval was the premonitory sign of a nightmare to be avoided at all costs; for the Hutu, it stood as a crucially important reference point for defining their future aspirations. Democracy meant majority rule, and majority rule meant Hutu rule.

That the Rwandan revolution happened to coincide with a major struggle for the leadership of the UPRONA greatly magnified its divisive implications. The turning point came shortly after the landslide victory of the Hutu wing of the UPRONA in the 1965 legislative elections when the Crown refused to appoint a Hutu as prime minister and instead turned to a princely candidate. The crunch came on October 18, 1965, when a group of Hutu gendarmerie and army officers unsuccessfully tried to overthrow the monarchy, yet came close enough to realizing their objective to cause the panic-stricken Mwambutsa to flee the country. The army and gendarmerie were thereafter virtually purged of Hutu elements, and scores of Hutu politicians and intellectuals were rounded up and executed by the army. With the formal overthrow of the monarchy in November 1966 and the proclamation of the First Republic by Colonel (later self-appointed President) Michel Micombero (1940–1983), the last obstacle in the path of Tutsi hegemony was removed.

From then on Burundi politics tended to revolve around factional struggles within the Tutsi minority (Hima versus Banyaruguru), unfolding against a background of repeated threats of Hutu insurrection. Intra-Tutsi struggles inside the army led to the overthrow of the Micombero regime in 1976 and the coming to power of President Jean-

Baptiste Bagaza (b. 1946). In 1987 it was Bagaza's turn to be displaced from office by a rival faction, headed by Major Pierre Buyoya (b. 1949), who served as president of the republic from 1987 to 1993. Antiregime violence erupted on a major scale in 1972 and 1988, each time triggering massive retribution. Both insurrections were instigated by Hutu elements; both were the expression of desperate attempts to evade Tutsi oppression; and both were followed by extraordinarily brutal repressions. An estimated 100,000 (some say 200,000) Hutu were executed by the all-Tutsi army between April and September 1972; the 1988 insurgency, limited to the northern provinces of Ntega and Marangara, took an estimated 15,000 lives, mostly Hutu.

The bloodbaths of 1972 and 1988 were critical watersheds in the history of the Hutu-Tutsi conflict, the first because it crystallized the collective self-awareness of the Hutu people as a martyred community, the second because it occurred at a moment in history when international public opinion could no longer remain indifferent to massive human rights violations.

International pressures played a decisive role in setting in motion the train of reforms that led to the June 1993 elections. Before 1988 drew to a close, and for the first time in twenty-three years, a government was appointed consisting of an equal number of Hutu and Tutsi, with a Hutu as prime minister (Adrien Sibomana, b. 1953); in March of the following year a Charter of National Unity was adopted that formally proclaimed the advent of a new era, dedicated to the construction of a society free of prejudice and discrimination; finally, a new constitution was approved by way of a referendum that spelled out the conditions of multiparty democracy and enshrined the sanctity of basic human rights.

With Buyoya's move toward liberalization, new parties emerged to challenge the rule of the UPRONA, such as the Rassemblement du Peuple Burundais (RPB), the Parti du Peuple (PP), the Parti Libéral (PL), and the Front Démocratique du Burundi (FRODEBU). Of these, the last quickly asserted itself as the most promising vehicle of Hutu aspirations. Led by Melchior Ndadaye (1953–1993), a Hutu civilian, the FRODEBU was bitterly criticized by the UPRONA for its ethnic chauvinism. Although both the FRODEBU and the UPRONA claimed a mixed following, they each came to be identified by their opponents with ethnic constituencies, the FRODEBU with the Hutu and the UPRONA with the Tutsi.

Presidential and legislative elections were held on June 1 and 29, 1993, respectively. Despite its ethnic overtones, the race for the presidency was really a test of popularity between the FRODEBU and UPRONA leaders, between Melchior Ndadaye and Pierre Buyoya. The landslide victory of the FRODEBU candidate (64.75% of the vote) bore testimony to his enormous popularity among Hutu and scores of Tutsi, a phenomenon that received further confirmation in the legislative elections. FRODEBU received 71.40 percent of the popular vote, compared to 21.43 percent for the UPRONA. With the formal investiture of Ndadaye as president of the republic on July 10, 1993, and the appointment of a cabinet that was one-third Tutsi and two-thirds Hutu, nearly three decades of Tutsi hegemony came to an end. Burundi's transition to multiparty democracy came to a dramatic halt on October 21, 1993, when units of the Tutsi-dominated army stormed the presidential palace. They took into custody and killed President Ndadaye and two of his closest collaborators, Pontien Karibwami and Gilles Bimazubute, respectively president and vice president of the National Assembly.

As the news of Ndadaye's assassination reached the hills, FRODEBU militants were suddenly seized by a collective rage that transformed every Tutsi in sight, and some Hutu supporters of the UPRONA, into a potential target of ethnic cleansing. Tens of thousands of innocent Tutsi civilians were hacked to pieces or burned alive. No less horrific was the repression. In a reenactment of the 1972 and 1988 massacres, as many as 30,000 Hutu may have died at the hands of the army, causing a huge exodus (800,000) of refugees to neighboring countries. Overall, 50,000 people lost their lives in the wake of the October coup.

With chaos and violence spreading through the countryside, and in the face of their immediate and universal condemnation by the international community, it became increasingly clear to the coup makers that their enterprise was doomed. Some fled to Democratic Republic of the Congo and Uganda; others (such as Colonel Bikomagu) denied having had anything to do with the attempted takeover.

Meanwhile, what was left of the government moved to the French embassy for protection. Not until the swearing-in of a new president—Cyprien Ntaryamira (1955–1994), one of the more moderate FRODEBU leaders—on January 22, 1994, was an uneasy calm restored to the country.

Ntaryamira's term of office came to a premature end on April 6, 1994 when the plane that he and the Rwandan president, Juvenal Habyarimana (1937–1994), were traveling in was hit by rockets as it was about to land in Kigali. Surprisingly, announcement of his death caused little commotion in Burundi. In Rwanda, by contrast, the death of Juvenal Habyarimana—widely perceived among Hutu as the work of Belgian mercenaries acting hand-in-hand with elements of the Tutsi-dominated Rwandese Patriotic Front (RPF)—precipitated a systematic massacre of Tutsis and moderate Hutus, by the Presidential Guard. In an unprecedented orgy of violence, an estimated 800,000 people are reported to have been killed within 100 days following the plane crash. Meanwhile, anticipating a retribution in kind from the RPF, hundreds of thousands of Hutu fled Rwanda. In less than forty-eight hours, beginning on April 28, some 250,000 refugees (mostly Hutu) poured across the border into Tanzania, transforming the Benaco refugee camp into Tanzania's second largest city.

Immediately following the announcement of Ntaryamira's death, Sylvestre Ntibantunganya (b. 1956), a moderate FRODEBU leader of Hutu origin, was named interim president on April 6, 1994. He was later deposed in a military coup led by former president Pierre Buyoya. Buyoya subsequently reappointed himself president of Burundi on July 25, 1996. The continued civil war and the economic sanctions imposed by the international community forced Buyoya to create an ethnically inclusive government. He was then forced to hand over power to his Hutu vice president, Domitien Ndayizeye (b. 1953) on April 30, 2003. Following the democratic elections held in June and July 2005, Pierre Nkurunziza, a Hutu, chairman of the National Council for the Defense of Democracy–Forces for the Defense of Democracy (CNDD-FDD) and former University of Burundi assistant professor, became president of Burundi on August 26, 2005.

Nkurunziza's coalition-style government has ushered in a democratic political dispensation after twelve years of civil war in which some 300,000 Burundians (mostly Hutu) have been killed and hundreds of thousands displaced. Decades of inter-ethnic conflict and violence, rendered even more complex by intra-ethnic struggles among both Hutu and Tutsi, have left most Burundians scrambling for survival as the societal and economic infrastructures have been severely weakened. Since his investiture, President Nkurunziza has enacted policies that will significantly improve access to formal education and health care, and will improve national security. However, the success of these promising reforms will depend upon the articulation and implementation of an inclusive vision of national societal reconstruction that transcends the pursuit of individual—at times even egotistical—gains and benefits, and that is grounded in an affirming quest for justice, equity, and the common good.

See also **Colonial Policies and Practices.**

BIBLIOGRAPHY

Chrétien, Jean-Pierre. *The Great Lakes of Africa: Two Thousand Years of History.* New York: Zone Books, 2003.

Chrétien, Jean-Pierre; André Guichaoua; and Gabriel Le Jeune. *La Crise d'août 1988 au Burundi.* Paris: Karthala, 1989.

Lemarchand, René. *Rwanda and Burundi.* New York: Pall Mall Press, 1970.

Lemarchand, René. *Burundi: Ethnocide as Discourse and Practice.* New York: Woodrow Wilson Center Press, 1994.

Makoba, Johnson W., and Elavie Ndura. "The Roots of Contemporary Ethnic Conflict and Violence in Burundi." In *Perspectives on Contemporary Ethnic Conflict: Primal Violence or the Politics of Conviction?* ed. Santosh Saha. Lanham, Maryland: Lexington Books, 2006.

Malkki, Liisa. *Purity and Exile: Violence, Memory, and National Cosmology among Hutu Refugees in Tanzania.* Chicago: University of Chicago Press, 1995.

Manirakiza, Marc. *Burundi: De la révolution au régionalisme, 1966–1976.* Brussels, Belgium: Le Mat de Misaine, 1992.

Melady, Thomas Patrick. *Burundi: The Tragic Years.* New York: Orbis Books, 1974.

Ndura, Elavie. "Peaceful Conflict Resolution: A Prerequisite for Social Reconstruction in Burundi, Africa." In *Conflict Resolution and Peace Education in Africa,* ed. Ernest E. Uwazie. Lanham, MD: Lexington Books, 2003.

Ndura, Elavie. "Western Education and African Cultural Identity in the Great Lakes Region of Africa: A Case of Failed Globalization." *Peace and Change* 31, no. 1 (2006): 90–101.

Ndura, Elavie. "Transcending the Majority Rights and Minority Protection Dichotomy through Multicultural Reflective Citizenship in the African Great Lakes Region." *Intercultural Education* 17, no. 2 (2006): 195–205.

Reyntjens, Filip. *L'afrique des grands lacs en crise: Rwanda, Burundi, 1988–1994.* Paris: Karthala, 1994.

Reyntjens, Filip. *Burundi: Breaking the Cycle of Violence.* Manchester, U.K.: Minority Rights Group, 1995.

Scherrer, Christian P. *Genocide and Crisis in Central Africa: Conflict Roots, Mass Violence and Regional War.* London: Praeger, 2002.

RENÉ LEMARCHAND
REVISED BY ELAVIE NDURA

BUSHIRI IBN SALIM (??–1889).

Germany's arrival in Eastern Africa, in the region that came to be known as Tanzania, was marked with great brutality. The forced requisition of houses gave great offense to the local peoples. Worse, in Tanga, German-owned dogs entered the Friday mosque services during Ramadan. In Pangani, Emil von Zelewski, the German leader, took down the Zanzibar flag, replacing it with the banner of the German East African Company. Bushiri ibn Salim, from an Arab family that had intrigued against the Busaidi rulers of Zanzibar for more than a century, was a natural leader for the opposition to the German presence. He rallied public indignation in a united voice.

Rebellion soon spread up and down the coast. In Zanzibar, General Lloyd Matthews claimed that "the feeling is against all Europeans." In fact, Bushiri showed particular friendship to both British and French missionaries. On January 25, 1889, the Germans defeated Bushiri decisively when he attempted to seize their coastal garrison at Dar es Salaam. In the south, however, at Mikindani and Lindi, the Germans were forced to evacuate. Bushiri set up headquarters near Bagamoyo. He was again defeated in May and October 1889. The last time, thoroughly routed, he lost public support. Captured, starving, and half naked, he was taken to Pangani, where he was hanged on December 15, 1889. His desperate heroism is commemorated in a

Swahili poem by Hemedi bin Abdallah bin Sa'id al-Buhriy, *The Epic of the War against the German Conquest of the Coast.*

See also **Colonial Policies and Practices: German; Dar es Salaam; Tanzania: History and Politics.**

BIBLIOGRAPHY

Freeman-Grenville, G. S. P. *Chronology of African History.* London: Oxford University Press, 1973.

Freeman-Grenville, G. S. P. *The New Atlas of African History.* Basingstoke, U.K.: Macmillan, 1991.

G. S. P. FREEMAN-GRENVILLE

Kofi Busia (1913–1978). After he fled Ghana because his life was threatened, the former prime minister became a professor of sociology and culture at the University of Leiden in the Hague, Netherlands.

BUSIA, KOFI A. (1913–1978). Kofi A. Busia was born in Wenchi in the center of the Asante region of the Gold Coast colony, a member of the Asante royal family, and was educated in Kumasi and Cape Coast. In 1936 he joined the staff of the Prince of Wales College at Achimota. At Oxford he studied philosophy, politics, and economics and returned to the Gold Coast (Ghana's colonial name) in 1942 as one of the first two Africans to be appointed district commissioners. Returning to Oxford he received a Ph.D. for his thesis *The Position of the Chief in the Modern Political System of Ashanti*, published in London in 1951. In 1947 he wrote a manuscript published as *Report on a Social Survey of Sekondi-Takoradi* (1950). His later works include *Self-government: Education for Citizenship* (1955); *The Challenge of Africa* (1962); *Urban Churches in Britain* (1966); and *Africa in Search of Democracy* (1967).

In 1949 Busia was appointed lecturer in African studies at the University College of the Gold Coast (Legon), in 1954 he became that university's first professor of sociology. In 1951 he returned to the legislative assembly as one of the members for the Asante and led the Ghana Congress Party (GCP) after its formation in 1952 to context the elections scheduled in anticipation of eventual independence. In the 1954 election he was the GCP's only successful candidate and, after that party joined the National Liberation Movement (NLM) in opposition to Kwame Nkrumah's Convention People's Party government, Busia became the NLM leader in 1956. He left Ghana in 1959, only two years after

independence, for fear that he would be arrested under the Preventive Detention Act imposed by the country's first president, Nkrumah.

Busia held academic appointments in Holland and Britain until the 1966 coup d'etat in Ghana, when he returned to join the military regime's political advisory committee. In the elections of 1969 he led the winning Progress Party and became Ghana's prime minister. Clashes with the trade unions, the military, and the judiciary, economic downturn, and the expulsion of "aliens" (non-Ghanaian West Africans, mostly Nigerians) marked an unhappy period in office which was ended by a bloodless military coup in January 1972. He returned to Britain and died in Oxfordshire in 1978.

See also **Ghana: History and Politics; Nkrumah, Francis Nwia Kofi.**

BIBLIOGRAPHY

Austin, Dennis. *Politics in Ghana, 1946–1960.* London: Oxford University Press, 1964.

Rathbone, Richard, ed. *Ghana.* 2 vols. London: HMSO, 1992.

RICHARD RATHBONE

BUTHELEZI, MANGOSUTHU (1928–).

Born in Mahlabathini, KwaZulu, Natal, on August 27, 1928, Mangosuthu Buthelezi was the son of Mathole Buthelezi, then the Zulu chief. He attended the University of Fort Hare, where he joined the African National Congress (ANC) and was expelled for political activism. In 1954, Buthelezi inherited the Zulu chiefship from his father, and worked within the system to secure benefits for his people. For this, some called him a collaborator with apartheid. In 1964 he had a brief moment of fame as a film actor, appearing in the movie *Zulu* in the role of Zulu chief Cetshwayo.

Buthelezi's political choices brought some political advantage for the Zulu, who in 1971 were accorded a *bantustan* (a semi-independent black township). In 1975 he founded the Inkatha Freedom Party (IFP), and in 1976 he was given governorship of the KwaZulu bantustan. In 1980 the IFP split with its ally, the ANC, over differences in policy and strategy.

In 1982 the South African government decided to strip KwaZulu of territory for cession to Swaziland. Buthelezi fought the decision in the courts and ultimately won. Although a member of the ANC in his youth, Buthelezi came to see Nelson Mandela and the ANC as political competitors, a position that initially led him to refuse participation in the first post-apartheid elections of 1994. He relented at the last minute, when he realized that his own party threatened to break apart over the decision. He won his own election for governor of KwaZulu, and in May 1994 was also appointed to the national office of minister of home affairs. During the period 1994 to 1999 he also served as acting president of South Africa several times during Mandela's presidency. In 2004, with the election of Thabo Mbeki (ANC) as president, continued policy disputes led to his dismissal as minister of home affairs.

Mangosuthu Buthelezi (1928–). The South African Zulu leader from 1972 to 1994 attends former British Prime Minister Margaret Thatcher's eightieth birthday party, October 13, 2005, at the Mandarin Oriental Hotel in London, England. Buthelezi founded the Inkatha Freedom party in 1975. TIM GRAHAM/GETTY IMAGES

See also **Apartheid; Cetshwayo; Mandela, Nelson; Mbeki, Thabo.**

BIBLIOGRAPHY

Temkin, Ben. *Buthelezi: A Biography.* Portland, OR: Frank Cass, 2003.

NANCY E. GRATTON

CABINDA, ANGOLA. The enclave of Cabinda is a province of Angola, separated from that country by a narrow strip of the Democratic Republic of the Congo territory and the Congo River estuary. Cabinda is a region of some 4,500 square miles; its coastline was frequented from the sixteenth century on by Portuguese and other European traders buying copper, ivory, and slaves. When Africa was partitioned in the late nineteenth century, Cabinda fell under Portuguese rule. Aware of the separatist tendencies of some elements in the population, Portugal made the port city of Cabinda the capital of the Congo district of northern Angola from 1887 to 1917. After that, Cabinda remained a province of Angola, although local leaders claimed a direct "special relationship" with Portugal by virtue of the Treaty of Simulambuco, concluded by their ancestors and the Portuguese in 1885.

The enclave's status has been formally contested since 1963, when three splinter groups supporting secession from Angola united to form the Frente para a Libertação de Enclave de Cabinda (FLEC). Since 1974 FLEC has conducted a guerrilla struggle in the enclave, at times using bases in neighboring Democratic Republic of the Congo and Congo province. The movement has suffered from factionalism and rivalries among its leaders, however.

Although the Angolan civil war between the Movimento Popular de Libertação de Angola (MPLA)—the government's ruling party—and the rebel force of União Nacional para a Independência Total de Angola (UNITA) ostensibly ended in early 2002, violence continued to erupt in Cabinda. After Angolan military were sent to the region in late 2002, widespread civilian human rights abuses were reported. Attempted negotiations in 2003 foundered, and fighting continues. Significantly, a broad-based coalition of civil and church groups has pressed for a peace process. It is difficult to ascertain the size of the Cabinda population due to the high level of mobility in the late twentieth century and the coming and going of refugees. At the start of the twenty-first century estimates are between 200,000 and 300,000.

The importance of the enclave to both the Angolan government and the secessionist movement rests mainly on its rich resources. Timber, cocoa, and palm products were among the commodities exported during the colonial period. The discovery of offshore petroleum transformed the enclave from a colonial backwater to a key resource for the Angolan government. In 1967, the American Cabinda Gulf Oil Company, a subsidiary of Chevron, started production from its base at Malongo on the coast just north of Cabinda city. As the Angolan economy collapsed in the wars that followed independence, Cabinda oil production continued, protected by a cordon of government forces (including Cuban allies) around the Malongo installation. Indeed, revenues from Cabinda oil were essential to the financing of the MPLA's war effort against UNITA. Cabinda oil amounts to 60 percent of Angola's petroleum production. The Angolan government continues to oppose secession, as does the now-opposition party UNITA, for precisely this reason. Indeed, no Luanda government could afford it. At the same time, the desire to benefit more fully from the rich resources of their homeland has spurred local populations in Cabinda, and Cabindan communities in the Congo and Democratic Republic of the Congo, to support FLEC, which continues to be riddled with factionalism and largely ineffective.

See also **Angola; Colonial Policies and Practices.**

BIBLIOGRAPHY

Martin, Phyllis M. "The Cabinda Connection: An Historical Perspective." *African Affairs* 76 (January 1977): 47–59.

Martin, Phyllis M. "Family Strategies in Nineteenth-Century Cabinda." *Journal of African History* 28, no. 1 (1987): 65–86.

PHYLLIS M. MARTIN
REVISED BY MARISSA J. MOORMAN

CABO VERDE. *See* Cape Verde.

CABRAL, AMÍLCAR LOPES (1924–1973).

The political thinker and revolutionary strategist Amílcar Lopes Cabral was born at Bafata in Portuguese Guinea (later, Guinea-Bissau) to Juvenal Cabral, a nationalist intellectual, and Evora Pinhel, both of Santiago Island in the Cape Verde archipelago. Cabral was able to attend the University of Lisbon because of his Portuguese citizenship, which was generally accorded Cape Verdeans, and his brilliant intellectual capacity. Upon graduation he became an anticolonial leader of sustained intelligence and courage. His political thought, which embraced revolutionary action, reflected the rise of anti-imperialism after World War II. In 1956 he founded the Partido Africano da Independência da Guiné e Cabo Verde (PAIGC), which was dedicated to armed struggle against the Portuguese Empire. His leadership of this underground anticolonial movement led to outright military and political victories in 1974, although Cabral himself was assassinated by agents of the Portuguese dictatorship in January 1973.

Amílcar Lopes Cabral (1924–1973). Cape Verde's main international airport in Sal is named for Cabral, who led the African nationalism movements in Cape Verde and Guinea-Bissau. GETTY IMAGES

Cabral possessed two dominant convictions. One was that those who accept the moral obligation to resist oppression must commit themselves to active participation. His second conviction, deriving from the first, was that this process of self-transformation must grow from the personal realm into a larger vision of social and moral renewal. These convictions enabled him to win a wide range of support both within the country and internationally.

See also **Colonialism and Imperialism.**

BIBLIOGRAPHY

Andrade, Mario de. *Amílcar Cabral: Essai de biographie politique.* Paris: F. Maspero, 1980.

Chabel, Patrick. *Amílcar Cabral: Revolutionary Leadership and People's War.* Cambridge, U.K.: Cambridge University Press, 1983.

Davidson, Basil. *The Liberation of Guiné.* Harmondsworth, U.K.: Penguin, 1969.

BASIL DAVIDSON

CAIRO. Cairo is the dominant city of Egypt and the largest city in the Arab world or Africa. It is located at the apex of the Nile Delta, where the single stream of the river branches out into multiple streams. Deserts lie east and west of the river. Estimating the population of Cairo is hazardous because of uncertainty about boundaries and shaky census figures, but probably 20 million is a good estimate. The urban area of Cairo has spread into three governorates and so complete figures should include all this.

The exact location and function of the delta apex city have varied. The earliest sites of a city were to the north (On or Heliopolis) or south (Memphis) of the present location. By the time of the Muslim conquest in the seventh century CE the present situation had emerged. In the following centuries the city was rebuilt and restarted several times, frequently as an armed camp next to the existing settlement. The religious significance of the early city was enhanced by the construction of two mosques that continue to exist today: the mosque of Amr ibn al-As near the preexisting city, and the mosque of Ibn Tulun on slightly higher ground to the east.

The recognized date for the creation of "al-Qahira" ("The Victorious" or Cairo) dates to the Fatimid conquest in the tenth century. The Fatimids were Ismaili Shi'a who came from their base in Tunisia to conquer Egypt. Like their predecessors they organized the city around its principal mosque, known as "al-Azhar," and which was the seat of learning. But the city was also a political center and an organizing point for trade between Upper and Lower Egypt, and between Egypt and other countries. In this it benefited from its location on the Nile, easily used for transport, and from its relative proximity to the Mediterranean and Red Seas.

In the twelfth century the Fatimid polity gave way to the one founded by Salah al-Din el-Ayyubi, who however added to the existing urban settlement rather than displacing the capital to yet another site. Salah al-Din began the construction of the Citadel that dominates the central city from its rock outcropping, and which henceforth symbolized the concentration of political power. The Ayyubid dynasty was followed by a succession of Mamluk rulers, beginning in the thirteenth century. The Mamluks were derived from slaves brought from the Caucasus and elsewhere and trained as soldiers; eventually this foreign caste became an enduring social group. They in turn were supplanted by the Ottomans, who came from Anatolia and conquered Egypt in 1517, and who ruled Egypt through appointed governors but still with the support of this military caste.

Mamluk-Ottoman power was broken first of all by the French invasion of 1798 led by Napoleon and which led to French rule of Egypt for three years. The chaos the French left behind created an opening for an Ottoman officer, Muhammad 'Ali, to establish himself as ruler in 1805. The descendants of Muhammad 'Ali were the titular rulers of Egypt until 1952. However, European power eventually became predominant, first French, and then British after the occupation of 1882. In 1952 the monarchy was overthrown and a republic was established that has continued under Gamal Abdel Nasser, Anwar Sadat, and Husni Mubarak.

This recitation of a succession of rulers does not convey the flavor of a cosmopolitan capital that continued and maintained its role as the intellectual and commercial center of the country. At various times, Cairo-based merchants were trading around the Mediterranean and across the Red Sea to Arabia and south Asia, and acted as key middlemen in the spice trade between south Asia and Europe. Trade routes also extended across the Sahara to West Africa and up the Nile as far as political conditions would allow. The city continued to be a center for both religious and secular intellectual life.

The modern city began to take shape in the second half of the nineteenth century. The city outgrew its medieval walls, notably in the direction of the Nile where improved control of water levels in the Nile made urbanization of the riverbanks possible. Bridges were built over the Nile, thus bringing the west bank of the river within the urban area. Downtown Cairo was laid out on a grid pattern, and several upscale residential areas with many foreign residents were developed. The pattern of extensive migration into the city accelerated. Modern amenities such as trams and other

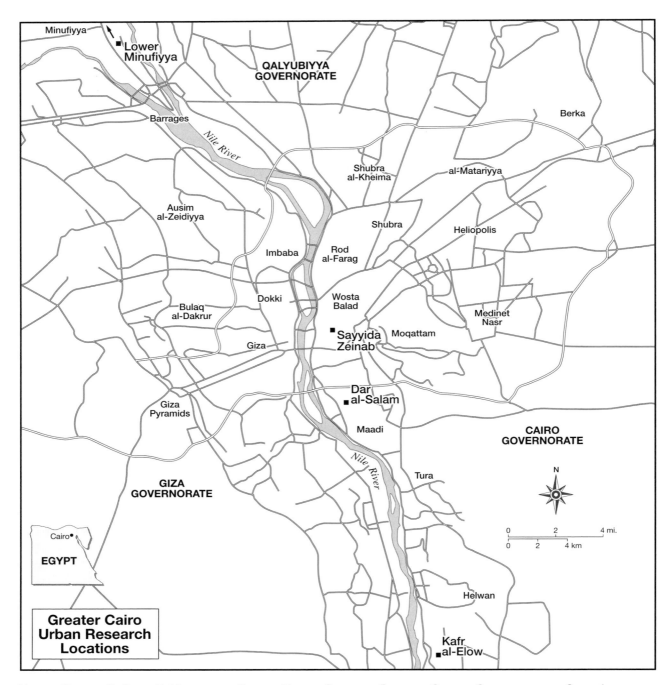

public transport, electricity, water and sewage systems, and telephones were introduced, often not much later than they were in many European cities.

The trend continued in the late twentieth and early twenty-first centuries, except that the foreign elements in the population were vastly reduced after 1952. By the early twenty-first century, amenities included widespread air conditioning, cell phones, DSL connections, and an underground metro system. Television, including satellite broadcasting, and the automobile were ubiquitous. The infrastructure of the city often appeared quite overburdened, most visibly with respect to public utilities, roads, and schools. Vehicle exhaust, industrial waste, and overcrowding have led to serious problems with air, water, and noise pollution.

Enormous population growth and public policy have caused the city to expand outward, and residential areas are segregated by class. Self-built or informal housing for the poor eats up agricultural land as it reproduces the same crowded conditions as in the older areas, but the outlying areas often lack the same utilities, transport, and other amenities. Planned urbanization has focused on extending into the desert areas to the east and west of Cairo. Here the density is low, but the urban area is immense. Some areas are given over to gated communities aimed at the new Egyptian elite. Officials discuss decentralizing the capital by moving offices and services to the outside, notably to desert areas, and a new ring road should facilitate that. Cairo remains the center not only for politics, religion, and education, but also for entertainment, medical care, and paper work.

See also 'Ali, Muhammad; Egypt, Early; Egypt: Modern; Mubarak, Husni; Nasser, Gamal Abdel; Sadat, Anwar al-.

BIBLIOGRAPHY

Golia, Maria. *Cairo: City of Sand*. Cairo: American University in Cairo Press, 2004.

Hopkins, Nicholas S.; Sohair R. Mehanna; and Salah el-Haggar. *People and Pollution: Cultural Constructions and Social Action in Egypt*. Cairo: American University in Cairo Press, 2001.

Rodenbeck, Max. *Cairo: The City Victorious*. London: Picador/Macmillan, 1998.

Singerman, Diane, and Paul Amar, eds. *Cairo Cosmopolitan: Politics, Culture, and Urban Space in the New Globalized Middle East*. Cairo: American University in Cairo Press, 2006.

NICHOLAS S. HOPKINS

CALABAR. Calabar is a port city located in the left flank of the Niger Delta and the principal town of the Efik people and capital of the Cross River State of Nigeria. The original settlement at the site was established by fishing peoples who were eager to exploit the rich resources of the river delta. By the fifteenth century, the population had exploded to some 50,000 people, largely due to the arrival of Europeans and massive expansion of trading opportunities that came with them. Calabar (known as New Calabar, distinguished from the "Old Calabar" on the Cross River to the east) became an important center for the region's participation in the Atlantic slave trade and was populated largely by people captured inland. Control over the other trading towns of the delta, including Duke, Creek, Henshaw, and Obutong, rested with the ruler of Calabar.

In the nineteenth century, when the slave trade was abolished, the region' economy shifted from slaves to palm oil and kernels. With the arrival of the Presbyterian mission in 1846, Calabar became one of the early centers of Christian evangelization and Western education in Nigeria. In 1884 it became a British protectorate and served as capital of the Oil Rivers Protectorate from 1885 to 1893, of the Niger Coast Protectorate between 1893 and 1900, and of Southern Nigeria from 1900 to 1906.

Calabar's population in 2004 was estimated at more than 450,000, putting it among the twenty largest cities in Nigeria. The city has many schools, including Hope Waddell College and a university. There is also a regional airport.

See also Nigeria.

BIBLIOGRAPHY

Ikime, Obaro, ed. *Groundwork of Nigerian History*. Ibadan, Nigeria: Heinemann Educational Books, 1980.

C. OGBOGBO

CALENDARS. *See* Time Reckoning and Calendars.

CAMARA LAYE (1928–1980). The celebrated Guinean Francophone writer Camara Laye was of Mande descent, born to Muslim parents in the Upper Guinean town of Kouroussa. He was given a European education, while simultaneously being initiated into the culture and traditions of his Mande forebears. In 1947 he traveled to France to study automobile mechanics and worked for a time at an automobile plant in Paris. During this period (in 1953) he married Marie Lorifo, whom he had met years earlier in Conakry. He continued with further studies and in 1956 was awarded a diploma in engineering, after which he returned to Africa, settling at first in Ghana but returning to Guinea after the country attained independence in 1958. He served for a time as Guinea's ambassador to Ghana and in other ministries of the government until he had a falling out with Ahmed Sékou Touré, then president of Guinea.

Camara Laye's first novel, *L'enfant noir* (*The Dark Child*, 1953), tells the story of his childhood in Kouroussa, in terms that are accessible and appealing to a wide variety of readers. That lyrical novel is enriched by its double perspective: on the one hand, Camara gives an insider's account of Mande culture, including the secrets of its initiation rites; on the other, the narrator speaks from a position of exile in France, with a tone of nostalgia for the world he has left behind. A second novel bearing Camara's name, *Le regard du roi* (*The Radiance of the King*, 1954) is a surreal allegory of relations between the West and Africa. But shortly before his death, Camara confirmed suspicions that the novel had been written by someone else (see Blachére, 167–168). *Dramouss* (1966) is an autobiographical account of Camara's disillusionment with Ahmed Sékou Touré's postcolonial Guinea; Touré's tyranny drove Camara into exile in Senegal, where he died of kidney disease. His final work is a novelized version of the principal Mande epic, the story of Emperor Sunjata, *Le maître de la parole* (*The Guardian of the Word*, 1954). Camara transcribed, translated, and reinvented the oral performance of the epic by the griot Babou Condé.

See also **Literatures in Eurupean Languages; Touré, Sékou.**

BIBLIOGRAPHY

Blachère, Jean-Claude. *Négritures: Les écrivains d'Afrique noire et la langue française.* Paris: L'Harmattan, 1993.

Camara Laye. *L'enfant noir.* Paris: Plon, 1953. Translated by James Kirkup and Ernest Jones as *The Dark Child* (New York: Farrar, Straus and Giroux, 1954).

Camara Laye. *Dramouss.* Paris: Plon, 1966. Translated by James Kirkup as *Dramouss* (London: Fontana, 1968).

Camara Laye. *Le maître de la parole.* Paris: Plon, 1978. Translated by James Kirkup as *The Guardian of the Word.* New York: Vintage Books, 1984.

Lee, Sonia. *Camara Laye.* Boston: Twayne, 1984.

CHRISTOPHER L. MILLER

CAMEROON

This entry includes the following articles:
GEOGRAPHY AND ECONOMY
SOCIETY AND CULTURES
HISTORY AND POLITICS

GEOGRAPHY AND ECONOMY

GEOGRAPHY

A country that is roughly triangular in shape, the Republic of Cameroon stretches 766 miles north to south and extends 447 miles east to west. Its political borders drawn, for the most part artificially, in the nineteenth-century Scramble for Africa, are still unsettled as shown by disputes. The International Court of Justice has resolved some issues, such as the contested claim between Nigeria and Cameroon over the oil-rich Bakassi, in favor of Cameroon. Its present surface area is 183,520 square miles and growing. Straddling many of Africa's ecological regions, it has been dubbed Africa in miniature.

To the north, the country has a small opening on Lake Chad. To the west, its neighbor is Nigeria, the frontier between them running south by southwest to the Gulf of Guinea. It shares a jagged boundary on the east with Chad and the Central African Republic. On the south, the Peoples Republic of the Congo, Gabon, and Equatorial Guinea border Cameroon. The country has an indented coastline of some 186 miles.

Largely a hilly and mountainous country, its highest point is the volcanic Mount Cameroon (13,435 feet). Its altitude ranges from an average of 295 feet along the coastal lowlands to about 9,843 feet in the central and western highlands. The coastal plain is densely forested with mangroves, marshes, creeks, and sandbars close to the sea that impede the creation of good harbors. The western plateau is composed of granite overlain by basaltic rock, some of the country's highest volcanic peaks, and rich volcanic lakes such as Nyos and Monoum. Farther north is the Adamawa Plateau (3,609 feet high), primarily granite covered by basaltic rock, and the Chad Plain. The Adamawa Plateau serves as the main watershed of the country, drained by rivers that flow into four basins: the Atlantic, Congo, Niger, and Chad basins. Rapids and falls break up most of these rivers. Some of

Cameroon

NIGER

Lake
Chad
Chari R.

Kousséri

*Waza
N.P.*

CHAD

Mokolo

Maroua

NIGERIA

MANDARA MTS.

Logone R.

Garoua

*Lagdo
Reservoir*

*Bouba
Ndjidah
N.P.*

*Bénoué
N.P.*

*Faro
Reserve*

Bénoué R.

M B A N G   M T S.

*GANGDABA
MTS.*

Vina R.

Ngaoundéré

Djerem R.

Wum

*Lake
Bamendjing*

*Mbakaou
Reservoir*

Bamenda

Bali

Bafoussam

*Korup
N.P.*

Bafang

A D A M A W A

P L A T E A U

Mbam R.

Lom R.

Nkongsamba

Kumba

*Mt. Cameroon
(13,435 ft [4,095 m])*

Buea

Douala

Sanaga R.

Bertoua

CENTRAL
AFRICAN
REPUBLIC

*Debundscha
Cape*

Bight of Bonny

Limbe

Yaoundé ✪

Nyong R.

Edéa

*Bioko I.
(EQ GUINEA)*

Mbalmayo

Boumba R.

Kribi

Ebolowa

Dja R.

*Gulf of
Guinea*

Ngoko R.

EQUATORIAL
GUINEA

GABON

REPUBLIC OF
THE CONGO

N

0   50   100 miles
0   50   100 km

these falls have been exploited for power generation, such as those on the Sanaga River, where two hydroelectric power stations are found. Four of the rivers, the Benue, Logone, Chari, and Wouri, are navigable.

CLIMATE AND VEGETATION

Given its geographic variation, Cameroon has a varied climate ranging from equatorial in the south, to tropical above 8 degrees north latitude, to Sahelian in the north. The country is correspondingly hot, with temperatures between 68 and 82 degrees Fahrenheit. The temperatures generally increase to the north. There are two major seasons, a wet and a dry. At the coast the wet season runs roughly from May to October and the dry from November to April, although on the coast rain will fall even during the dry season. Rainfall declines as one moves away from the ocean. Similarly, the dry season lasts from four months in the coastal region to seven months in the Sahelian and semiarid plains.

The vegetation also varies with region and is subject to local diversity. There are two major vegetation zones, which may be further subdivided. These are the equatorial forest and the tropical savannas or grasslands zones, both of which are in flux as forests are cleared and savannas replace them. As one moves north away from the sea, swampy mangrove forest gives way to dense equatorial rain forest. In the far north one finds Sahelian savanna, semidesert with little or no conspicuous vegetation in the dry season but grass and shrubs during the wet season.

THE ECONOMY

Cameroon is richly endowed in natural resources, notably timber, oil, hydroelectric power, natural gas, cobalt, and nickel. It also has a vibrant agricultural sector that produces cash crops (coffee, cocoa, rubber, bananas, tea, palm oil) and food crops. Cameroon's economic performance has been determined as its capability to withstand international shocks. Decline set in after a steady period of the growth, averaging 7 percent per annum between 1977 and 1985. Its GDP was US$11.8 billion in 2004. Sectoral distribution of GDP between agriculture, industry, and services is 44.8 percent, 17 percent, and 38.2 percent, respectively. Real per capita GDP decreased by more than 60 percent between 1984 and 1994. And a household consumption survey in 1996 showed that 51 percent of the households in the country were living below the poverty line and 23 percent were living in extreme poverty.

To stimulate the economy in the early postcolonial state, the state acted as a locomotive. It adopted certain benchmarks that had to be attained in year 2000, notably self-sufficiency in food, health for all Cameroonians, adequate human resource development, balanced development between rural and urban areas, and an average annual increase in per capita income of at least 4 percent. These goals were intrinsic to its economic philosophy that placed planned liberalism, balanced development, self-reliant development, and social justice in the foreground. This required that its role not be limited to providing an enabling environment but that the state also be an entrepreneur. Despite incentives, private investments in terms of value hovered around 25 percent of GDP in the 1980s.

Industry and services employ 13 and 17 percent of the population, respectively. Small family holdings accounted for 80 percent of the country's agricultural production, and agro-industrial complexes dotted throughout the country make up the rest. To increase its earnings from these crops, some were processed before exportation. Deepening, however, proved to be counterproductive, leading to the building of white elephants. Inefficiencies in other state-owned enterprises were also commonplace. Agriculture was still emphasized even after oil production started in 1975. Cameroon, just as other countries of the Central African Economic and Monetary Community (CEMAC) to which it belongs, is a member of the African Financial Community (CFA) that uses the franc CFA as its currency. Initially pegged to the French franc and now the euro, the fixed nominal exchange rate helped to curb inflation. Annual inflation, which reached 32.5 percent prior to the devaluation of francs in 1994, hovered around 2 percent in 2005.

Generally, cautious economic management guaranteed decades of relatively steady economic growth until the mid-1980s when the economy slumped. Against this backdrop, Cameroon signed a Structural Adjustment Program (SAP) with the World Bank in 1987. Cameroonians, having lost confidence in the economy, resorted to the informal economy that has become the net creator of jobs. Some 85 percent of the total labor force, estimated at 4.2 million people in 1996, was employed by this sector. Important shifts have also occurred in the economy, notably a shift from producing cash crops to food crops that have a better rate of return.

Cameroon struggled to implement reforms with mixed results. Privatization stalled, even if other structural reforms such as the introduction of a value-added tax in the 1990s both increased receipts and transparency of non-oil revenues. Tax yield in the early twenty-first century hovered around 5 percent of the GDP. But opacity remained a trademark of the economy and corruption is endemic. Not surprisingly, therefore, Cameroon was named the most corrupt country in the world in 1998 and 1999 by Transparency International. Despite the government's failure to meet the conditionalities in the first four IMF programs, the IMF approved an Enhanced Structural Adjustment Facility (ESAF) for the country in 2000 with a view to reducing poverty and improving social services. Successful implementation of ESAF was a prerequisite for Cameroon to benefit from debt relief among countries in the Heavily Indebted Poor Countries Initiative (HIPC). Cameroon finally reached HIPC's completion point in May 2006 and therefore qualified for relief in debt payments of about US$4.9 billion over the next few decades.

Enforcing legal rights, including contract and property claims through the Cameroonian judicial system, is a slow and arduous process, fraught with administrative and legal bottlenecks. On the average, there are 51 procedures for enforcing contracts, from the moment a plaintiff files a lawsuit to until the moment of payment, and this may take 401 days. Further increasing the risk factor is the tendency of the justice system to collude with unscrupulous individuals, or what is known in Cameroon speak as *feymen*, and corrupt lawyers to sequester bank deposits. These contribute to high transactions costs in the economy while also decreasing its competitiveness in the global economy. Reversing this path with a view to creating an investment friendly environment is imperative to launch the economy growth path. Measures that have been taken to this end include the 1998

creation of the Organisation pour l'Harmonisation du Droit des Affaires en Afrique (OHADA), a treaty between the fifteen states of the CFA plus Guinea, which seeks to promote the birth of an African community, institute a common business policy, and the guarantee of judicial security and compatibility within the community.

See also **Climate; Ecosystems; Geography and the Study of Africa; Metals and Minerals; Plants; World Bank.**

BIBLIOGRAPHY

Amin, Aloysius A. *An Examination of the Sources of Economic Growth in Cameroon.* Nairobi, Kenya: African Economic Research Consortium, 2002.

Baye, Francis M. "Globalisation, Institutional Arrangements and Poverty in Rural Cameroon." *Africa Development* 28, nos. 3 and 4 (2003): 112–141.

Geschiere Peter, and Piet Konings, eds. *Proceedings: Conference on the Political Economy of Cameron: Historical Perspectives.* Leiden, the Netherlands: African Studies Centre, 1989.

Jua, Nantang. *Economic Management in Neo-Colonial States: The Case of Cameroon.* Leiden, the Netherlands: African Studies Centre, 1990.

Manga, Ekema. *The African Economic Dilemma: The Case of Cameroon.* Lanham, MD: University Press of America, 1998.

Roitman, Janet L. *Fiscal Disobedience: An Anthropology of Economic Regulation in Central Africa.* Princeton, NJ: Princeton University Press, 2005.

Schatzberg, Michael G., and I. William Zartman, eds. *The Political Economy of Cameroon.* New York: Praeger, 1986.

Van de Walle, Nicolas. "The Politics of Public Sector Enterprise Reform in Cameroon." In *State-Owned Enterprises in Africa*, eds. Barbara Grosh and Rwekaza Mukandala. Boulder, CO: Lynne Rienner, 1994.

NANTANG JUA

SOCIETY AND CULTURES

Cameroon is one of the more culturally diverse countries in Africa. Its population, which numbered over 18 million in 2007, is divided into some 250–300 ethnic groups speaking upward of three hundred languages. This cultural diversity corresponds to Cameroon's geographical diversity, which ranges from rain forests and mangrove swamps on the Atlantic coast to arid plains of the Sahelian zone adjacent to Lake Chad.

The coastal and inland forest zones of southern Cameroon are home to peoples who engage in swidden agriculture, fishing, and hunting—the Duala, Bakweri, Banyangi, Bakosi, Mbo, Bassa, Bafia, Ewondo, Bulu, Fang, Ngumba, Maka, Mkako, Djem, Badjwe, and Mezime, among others. There are also numerous pygmy hunter-gatherers in southeastern Cameroon, the Baka constituting the largest group. These hunter-gatherers live a mobile existence for at least part of the year, although most also practice agriculture.

The economies of the forest peoples are based on the production of maize, plantains, bananas, groundnuts, and root crops, as well as cocoa, oil palm, and coffee grown on small plantations. Their small, nucleated rural villages are organized around one or more dominant patrilineal descent groups or extended families under the leadership of a headman or council of elders. During precolonial times, most of these forest societies had weakly institutionalized leadership; present-day chieftaincies were created principally during the colonial period. The societies of southern Cameroon near the Atlantic coast experienced the earliest and most intensive European colonial contact, resulting in widespread conversion to Christianity as well as high rates of formal education. In contrast, the more remote forested interior of southeastern Cameroon has been subject evangelized by Christian missionaries for a shorter period, and formal education is less widespread.

To the west and northwest of the forest zone are high grassy plateaus—the Bamileke and Grassfields regions. Whereas the rural forested zones are not densely populated, between 5 and 75 persons per square mile being the normal range, the plateau regions have densities between 200 and 500 persons per square mile. Political structure there has been highly centralized since the precolonial period, with dynasties supported by administrative and ritual associations of nobles and commoners. The numerous chiefdoms referred to by the collective ethnic label Bamileke, a term that became popular only in the colonial period, vary greatly in size from a few to many tens of thousands of people; Bafang, Bafoussam, Bandjun, Bangangte, and Bangwa are some of the larger and better known Bamileke chiefdoms. In the Grassfields, major polities include Nsaw, Kom, Mankon, Bali, Wum, and Bamum.

Christianity has been prevalent in all these Bamileke and Grassfields chiefdoms, except Bamum, from the early colonial period. The ruling stratum of Bamum was converted to Islam in the nineteenth century following contacts with Fulani (Fulbe) invaders and Hausa traders. The powerful rulers of the larger Grassfields chiefdoms have continued to play prominent roles in national political life up to the present.

The commercial dynamism of the plateau peoples is noteworthy. Systems of commercialized craft production and market trade have long been a feature of the plateau zone, supplementing agricultural systems based on maize and cocoyam (taro) for local consumption, and coffee grown as a cash crop. The region is well known for its wide variety of plastic arts, especially wood carving, much of which is utilized by chiefs and their titled associations. Labor out-migration has long been a feature of this densely populated area.

Southern and western Cameroon today are the most urbanized regions in the country. Douala, the largest city, is the business capital and main port, while Yaoundé is the political capital; both cities had populations of over a million in 2003. Other important urban centers in the south and west include Bafoussam, Bamenda, Nkongsamba, Kumba, Limbe, Buea, Edea, Ebolowa, Mbalmayo, and Kribi. The populations of all these cities are a complex multi-ethnic mix, reflecting the high rate of urban migration in recent decades throughout the country.

The center and north of Cameroon are savannas and open woodland, interspersed with mountainous outcrops, stretching all the way to the shores of Lake Chad. The landscape of north-central Cameroon is dominated by the seasonally well-watered grasslands of the Adamawa Plateau, a lightly populated zone that is particularly favorable for cattle husbandry. Moving northward from the Adamawa Plateau, the climate becomes progressively drier, with a short wet season of some five months followed by a long and rigorous dry season.

During the nineteenth century, many of the peoples of the north were conquered by invading Muslim groups such as the Fulani, Mandara, and Bornu. The Fulani in particular established several dozen conquest states—including Ngaoundere, Rei Bouba, Maroua, Garoua, Banyo, and Tibati—following a holy war. Many of the non-Muslim peoples, often referred to collectively by the pejorative terms Kirdi or Haabe, were incorporated into these new states as servile or subject peoples. Warrior and ritual chiefdoms of the plains, such as the Wute, Mbum, Guidar, Musgum, Kotoko, and Guiziga, were especially affected by these incursions. Other peoples, including the Dowayo, Fali, Mafa, Kapsiki, and Mofu, managed to resist from mountainous areas less vulnerable to mounted attacks. There they retained their independence as congeries of patrilineal clans, while developing systems of intensive, terraced agriculture to feed their dense populations. Still others, such as the Gbaya, Massa, Tupuri, and Mundang, remained relatively independent on the margins of the Muslim states.

The society of northern Cameroon is still heavily influenced by Fulani culture and language, although the Fulani comprise only about 35 percent of the region's population. Fulfulde, the Fulani language, is the lingua franca throughout northern Cameroon. Several urban centers, including Garoua, Ngaoundere, and Maroua, have grown rapidly in recent decades, drawing large numbers of rural migrants within the cultural influence of the Fulani. Islam is widespread in northern Cameroon, but many members of the non-Muslim groups have been converted by Christian missions, and others continue to adhere to their ancestral cults. Rates of Western-style education in the north are well below the national average, especially among Muslims where Qur'anic education remains popular.

The rural economy of northern Cameroon is oriented toward rainy season subsistence farming of sorghum, millet, and maize, with cotton and groundnuts raised as cash crops. During the dry season, farmers practice extensive flood-retreat and irrigated cultivation in the plains surrounding Lake Chad and its in-flowing rivers; artisanal fishing is also widespread. Cattle herding is a major occupation for certain groups, especially among the nomadic Mbororo Fulani and Choa Arabs. Northern Cameroon is also known for its well developed system of marketplaces and active networks of long distance trade. Several Muslim ethnic groups, notably the Hausa and Kanuri, have long specialized in trading cattle, cloth, kola nuts, salt, and other commodities throughout the region.

While the many and diverse ethnic groups that make up Cameroon society clearly have their cultural roots in the precolonial past, the composition of these groups and people's perceptions of the ethnic identities of themselves and others are subject to ongoing processes of change arising from political, economic, and religious influences. The assimilation of substantial numbers of non-Fulani into the socially dominant and increasingly heterogeneous Muslim Fulani category in northern Cameroon has already been mentioned, and the creation during the colonial period of an overarching Bamileke identity in western Cameroon is another example of ethnic redefinition. The numerically small ethnic groups inhabiting the coastal region, including the Duala, Bakweri, Batanga, and Ngolo, have also sought to increase their influence in national life by emphasizing their purported common origins and collectively using the Sawa ethnic label.

Constitutional changes in the 1990s that distinguished between native-born and immigrant persons have accentuated tendencies toward either ethnic fusion or ethnic tension in various parts of the country. In addition, the distinction between Anglophone and Francophone Cameroonians, which has its origins in the division of the territory between British and French colonial administrations, has also become a prominent basis for both collective mobilization and exclusion in various domains of present-day life.

See also **Art and Architecture; Arts: Sculpture; Christianity; Ecosystems; Kinship and Descent; Lake Chad Societies; Production Strategies.**

BIBLIOGRAPHY

Ardener, Edwin. *Kingdom on Mount Cameroon: Studies in the History of the Cameroon Coast, 1500–1700.* Providence, RI: Berghahn Books, 1996.

Boutrais, Jean, et al. *Le nord du Cameroun: Des hommes, une région.* Paris: Editions de l'Office de la recherche scientifique et technique outre-mer, 1984.

Fowler, Ian, and David Zeitlyn, eds. *African Crossroads: Intersections between History and Anthropology in Cameroon.* Providence, RI: Berghahn Books, 1996.

Takougang, Joseph, and Milton Krieger. *African State and Society in the 1990s: Cameroon's Political Crossroads.* Boulder, CO: Westview Press, 1998.

Tardits, Claude, ed. *Contribution de la recherche ethnologique à l'histoire des civilisations du Cameroun.* (The Contribution of Ethnological Research to the History of Cameroon Cultures.) 2 vols. Paris: Editions du Centre national de la recherche scientifique, 1981.

PHILIP BURNHAM

République du Cameroun (Republic of Cameroon)

Population:	18,060,382 (2007 est.)
Area:	475,315 sq. km (183,520 sq. mi.)
Official languages:	French and English
Languages:	Bali, Bamileke, Bassa, Duala, English, Ewondo, French, Fulani, Hausa
National currency:	CFA franc
Principal religions:	Christian 53%, Muslim 22%, indigenous African 25%
Capital:	Yaoundé (est. pop. 1,111,641 in 2003)
Other urban centers:	Douala, Garoua, Maroua, Bafoussam, Bamenda, Nkongsamba, Ngaoundere
Annual rainfall:	varies by region: 600 mm (23 in.) in extreme north to 10,000 mm (390 in.) at the coast
Principal geographical features:	*Mountains:* Mount Cameroon, Mandara Mountains, Adamaoua Plateau, Bamenda Plateau *Lakes:* Lake Chad, Lac de Mbakaou, Lac de Lagdo, Lac de Bamendjing *Rivers:* Sanaga, Wouri, Nyong, Ngoko, Benue, Logone, Chari, Mbam, Ntem, Mbere, Ngoko
Economy:	*GDP per capita:* US$2,400 (2006)
Principal products and exports:	*Agricultural:* timber, coffee, tea, bananas, cocoa, rubber, palm oil, pineapples, cotton *Manufacturing:* aluminum production, food processing, light consumer goods, textiles, lumber, ship repair *Mining:* petroleum, some tin, unexploited reserves of bauxite, uranium, rutile, iron ore
Government:	German colony until 1916, then divided as League of Nations mandated territory between France and England. French portion declared independence in 1960. English portion voted in 1961 to split, with part joining Nigeria, remainder joining Cameroon. Constitution ratified in 1972, amended in 1975. Multiparty democracy. President and Assemblée Nationale elected for 5-year renewable terms by universal suffrage. President appoints prime minister and Council of Ministers. For purposes of local government there are 10 provinces headed by governors, broken down into departments, subdivisions, and districts.
Heads of state since independence:	1960–1982: President Ahmadou Ahidjo 1982–: President Paul Biya
Armed forces:	President is commander in chief. Voluntary enlistment. *Army:* 13,000 *Navy:* 1,300 *Air force:* 300 *Paramilitary:* 9,000
Transportation:	*Rail:* 1,104 km (686 mi.) *Waterways:* 2,090 km (1,295 mi.), confined to the Benue River *Ports:* Douala, Bonaberi, Tiko, Garoua, Limbe, Kribi *Roads:* 64,626 km (40,156 mi.), 4% paved *National airline:* Cameroon Airlines (75% government-owned, 25% share held by France) *Airports:* International facilities at Douala, Yaoundé, Garoua. Smaller fields at Ngaoundere, Foumban, Maroua. In total 47 airports throughout the country.
Media:	1 daily newspaper: *Cameroon Tribune;* 25 non-daily newspapers, 54 periodicals. There are 9 publishing houses. There is a virtual monopoly of radio and television by the state-owned broadcaster, the Cameroon Radio-Television Corporation. The 15 private radio stations and 1 private television station have limited coverage.
Literacy and education:	*Total literacy rate:* 75% (2006). Education is free, universal, and compulsory for ages 6–11. Postsecondary education provided by Université de Yaoundé and numerous technical schools.

HISTORY AND POLITICS

Often referred to as "Africa in miniature," Cameroon covers an area of 183,520 square miles, straddles all of Africa's ecological regions, and shares borders with Chad, the Central African Republic, Gabon, Equatorial Guinea, and Nigeria. Its highest point is Mount Cameroon, which was sighted by the Carthaginian explorer Hanno in circa 500 BCE. Portuguese explorers, lead by Fernando Po, were the first Europeans to reach the territory in 1472 after sailing up the Wouri River to Douala. Because of the overabundance of prawns in the river, they named it *Rios de Camarões* (River of Prawns), a term from which the country eventually derived its name. Originally, the several indigenous groups comprising the new nation were independent. They saw others, even those from contiguous areas, as foreigners. Relations between groups were convivial as well as conflictual.

THE COLONIAL STATE

During the precolonial era, prisoners of war were fodder for the slave trade, especially by coastal chiefs who were the middlemen for Portuguese, Dutch, French, and British traders. Large numbers of slaves came from the Cameroon area.

Following the abolition of slavery, the London Baptist Missionary Society created a Christian colony in Victoria for freed slaves from Jamaica, Ghana, and Liberia as well as local converts. European trade with the territory now shifted to natural resources such as ivory, palm oil, and gold. In 1858 Alfred Saker founded the first European settlement in Victoria, which he unsuccessfully implored England to declare a Crown colony. The Germans claimed the territory, which they named Kamerun, in 1884 and ruled until the end of World War I.

After the war, it was partitioned between the French and the British in March 1916 into French Cameroun and British Cameroons (Northern and Southern) respectively. In 1922, the areas became League of Nations mandates mutating into trusteeships of the United Nations following World War II, though still administered under the auspices of Britain and France. Britain ruled largely from Nigeria; the French sphere was administered in association with French Equatorial Africa. Social communication, not developed under the Germans in this territory, was further inhibited by this division. The administering powers reacted differently to the growth of political consciousness in the territories. Britain granted Southern Cameroon semiregional and full regional status within Nigeria in 1954 and 1959 respectively. In French Cameroon, the French banned the Union des Populations du Cameroun.

EARLY POSTCOLONIAL CAMEROON

As United Nations (UN) trusteeships, however, these territories were on a path to independence. French Cameroun gained independence on January 1, 1960. A lack of consensus in British Cameroons led to UN-organized plebiscites in which North Cameroons voted to join Nigeria and Southern Cameroons acceded to independence as part of the Republic of Cameroon. Reunification took place in October 1961. According to the Foumban Talks, Cameroon was to be a federated state comprised of French-speaking East Cameroon and English-speaking West Cameroon. El Hajj Ahmadou Ahidjo became the first president of this bilingual state; the new leader was faced with the twin challenges of fostering a national image and enabling economic development.

Ahidjo continued the police state introduced by the French, and made Cameroon a one-party state under the Cameroon National Union (CNU) in September 1966. In May 1972, following a referendum, the country was renamed the United Republic of Cameroon. The nation's economy managed to grow by 8.5 percent annually between 1975 and 1984, but it depended wholly on the export of cash crops (coffee, cocoa, bananas, and palm kernels) until oil became the main export in the early 1980s. Unfortunately, lack of accountability and transparency fueled tremendous corruption, and the government continued to rule by fear.

BAD GOVERNANCE AND THE STRUGGLE FOR POLITICAL PLURALISM

Ahidjo resigned from power in November 1982, designating Paul Biya as his successor. Biya, who had never held elective office, promised Cameroonians social justice and ethical government, as well as greater individual and political freedoms. Despite his rhetoric, official corruption took center stage and ethnic tendencies tension became the hallmark of his regime. Northern officers in the army attempted a failed coup d'état in April 1984, prompting Biya to call a presidential election in which he was the sole candidate. He won.

Mistaking this vote as political mandate, he summarily changed the name of the country from United Republic of Cameroon to the Republic of Cameroon in 1984. Because this was the Francophone name Cameroon had adopted at independence, it gave renewed urgency to the Anglophone problem.

In 1986, the CNU became the Cameroon People's Democratic Party (CPDM), and another one-man presidential election was organized in 1988. Though these measures were designed to legitimize the government, the erosion trust by bad governance continued unabated. By 1987, the insolvent state was forced to sign a structural adjustment program (SAP) with the World Bank.

Against this backdrop Bamenda launched an opposition party, the Social Democratic Front

(SDF), in May 1990. Six people were killed by government forces in the process. But as opposition continued to spread, Biya signed the so-called Liberty Laws of December 1990. Unsatisfied, opposition parties called for a national conference, then launched a series protests designed to deny the government needed funds. In the face of this impasse, the state called the Tripartite Talks in November 1991, during which it agreed to organize legislative elections and set up a committee to create a new electoral code and a draft constitution.

THE NEW POLITICAL LANDSCAPE

Elections were held in February 1992, although SDF, supposedly the most popular party, boycotted the election. In coalition with other parties, it participated in the October 1992 presidential election that was neither free nor fair. Though most observers thought that Fru Ndi, the leader of this coalition won, Biya was declared the winner. Protests following this declaration caused the regime to declare a state of emergency in the northwest province, and the resultant economic freefall only exacerbated Biya's problems.

The regime drafted a constitution that was adopted only by the assembly, not by a general referendum. Since it was supposed to be phased in, the old constitution remained in force. The regime has used this proviso to selectively apply only articles that were favorable to it. Articles in the 1996 Constitution that do not require any enabling legislation have not been implemented. Notable is Article 66, which requires that officials in public office declare their assets upon entering and leaving office.

Using this legal chaos to its advantage, the regime subverted the will of the people following the January 1997 municipal election by naming government delegates to some important councils the CPDM had lost. In the May 1997 legislative election, the SDF participated and won seats. But with Biya firmly in control, only government bills were adopted. Despite his earlier promise to make Cameroon a democracy, Transparency International named it the most corrupt country in world in 1998 and 1999—unable to meet the conditions prescribed in the first four IMF programs. To help arrest poverty and declining social conditions, the government signed an enhanced structural adjustment facility (ESAF) program with the IMF in 2000 and adopted a poverty reduction strategy paper (PRSP) in 2003. Cameroon struggled to qualify for the heavily indebted poor countries (HIPC) initiative that opens the window of debt relief for its beneficiaries. It finally qualified in April 2006.

In October 2004 the regime held another presidential election, and Biya won again, placing his new administration under a promise of "great ambitions." Achieving this would require a politics of inclusiveness instead of the divisive policies that destroyed people's confidence in the system, as well as an effective separation of powers and the rule of law. All would help usher in democratic culture and free and fair elections.

Over the course of Cameroon's postcolonial history, it has moved from strict nonalignment under Ahidjo to Biya's "politics of presence," evidenced by his decision to join both Francophonie and the Commonwealth. At the subregional level, however, its influence continues to regress, though it harbored more than 60,000 refugees in 2004 from neighboring war-torn countries. Social conflict and a poor economy continue to keep Cameroon a country at risk.

See also **Ahidjo, El Hajj Ahmadou; Aid and Development; Colonial Policies and Practices; United Nations; World War II.**

BIBLIOGRAPHY

Bayart, J.-F. *L'état au Cameroun.* Paris: Presses de la Foundation National de Sciences Politiques, 1979.

Geschiere, P., and F. Nyamnjoh. "Autochthony as an Alternative to Citizenship: New Modes in the Politics of Belonging in Postcolonial Africa." In *Rewriting Africa: Toward Renaissance or Collapse?*, ed. Eisie Kurimoto. JCAS Symposium Series 14. Osaka, Japan: The Japan Center for Area Studies (JCAS) National Museum of Ethnology, 2001.

Jackson, Robert H., and Carl G. Rosberg. *Personal Rule in Black Africa: Prince, Autocrat, Prophet, Tyrant.* Berkeley: University of California Press, 1982.

Joseph, R. *Radical Nationalism in Cameroon: Social Origins of the UPC Rebellion.* London: Oxford University Press, 1978.

Jua, Nantang. "Cameroon: Jumpstarting an Economic Crisis." In *Corruption and the Crisis of Institutional Reform in Africa*, ed. J. M. Mbaku. Lewiston, New York: The Edwin Mellen Press, 1998.

Jua, Nantang. "Democracy and the Construction of Allogeny/Autochthony in Postcolonial Cameroon." *African Issues* 29, nos. 1 and 2 (2001): 37–42.

Kofele-Kale, Ndiva. "Ethnicity, Regionalism, and Political Power: A Post-Mortem of Ahidjo's Cameroon." In *The Political Economy of Cameroon*, ed. Michael Schatzberg and William Zartman. New York: Praeger, 1986.

Konings Piet, and Francis B. Nyamnjoh. *Negotiating an Anglophone Identity: A Study of the Politics of Recognition and Representation in Cameroon*. Leiden: Brill, 2003.

Le Vine, Victor T. *The Cameroon Federal Republic*. Ithaca, NY: Cornell University Press, 1977.

Mbembe, J.-A. *La naissance du maquis dans le Sud du Cameroun, 1920–1960: Histoire des usages de la raison en colonie*. Paris: Karthala, 1996.

Takougang, Joseph, and Milton Krieger. *African State and Society in the 1990s: Cameroon's Political Crossroads*. Boulder. CO: Westview, 1998.

Zakaria, F. "The Rise of Illiberal Democracy." *Foreign Affairs* 76, no. 6 (1997): 22–43.

NANTANG JUA

CANARY ISLANDS.

Between 1474 and 1504, the seven islands called the Canaries by geographers and seafaring nations were finally seized, populated, and incorporated by the kingdom of Castile during Isabella of Castile's reign. The islands were initially populated by natives called *Guanches*, probably from northern Africa, who were subdued by previous European settlers.

As Iberians settled the Canaries during the sixteenth century, the surviving native population adopted Iberian culture and traditions. The islands became part of the Castilian kingdom and were later considered Spanish territory. The Canaries had two main functions: easing Spain's maritime communication with American territories and holding firm against their Islamic antagonists who were settled for centuries in the nearby Maghreb (northwestern Africa).

After the Spanish fascist dictator Generalissimo Franco died in 1975 and constitutional monarchy was reinstated in Spain, the Canaries became one of two Spanish autonomous districts, the other being the Balearic archipelago—Majorca and Minorca, in the Mediterranean—within the new Estado (español) de las Autonomías. The Canaries are located at 28 degrees latitude north, about the same as central Florida, with a population of nearly 2 million inhabitants. Most people live on the two largest and wealthiest islands, Teneriffe and Grand Canary. The islands are a popular winter resort for northern and central European tourists. Its economic (primarily fishing) relationship with northwestern African countries such as Morocco and Mauritania is troubled due to the unending conflict affecting the land and waters of Western Sahara. The Canaries archipelago maintains commercial relationships with Sénégal and Nigeria, however. Recent influxes of immigrants in search of better living conditions are becoming the first social challenge for the local authorities and for Canarian society.

See also **Colonial Policies and Practices: Spanish; Western Sahara.**

BIBLIOGRAPHY

Béthencourt Massieu, Antonio de, et al., eds. *Historia de Canarias*. Las Palmas de Gran Canaria: Ediciones del Cabildo Insular de Gran Canaria, 1995.

Clancy-Smith, Julia, ed. "North Africa, Islam, and the Mediterranean World." Special edition of *Journal of North African Studies* 6, no. 1 (Spring 2001).

Fernández-Armesto, Felipe. *The Canary Islands after the Conquest: The Making of a Colonial Society in the Early Sixteenth Century*. Oxford: Clarendon, 1982.

Hess, Andrew C. *The Forgotten Frontier: A History of the Sixteenth Century Ibero-African Frontier*. Chicago: University of Chicago Press, 1978.

Morales Lezcano, Víctor. "Canarias" and "Ceuta y Melilla." In *España: Autonomías*, ed. Juan Pablo Fusi. Madrid: Espasa-Calpe, S.A., 1989.

VÍCTOR MORALES LEZCANO

CANDACE.

Candace, often interpreted to be a proper name, is more generally associated with queens in ancient times, and derived from the title *Kandake* or *kdke*. In the Kingdom of Meroe this title was used for a number of queens who ruled both with a king and independently. These Candaces are identifiable from archeological remains including reliefs on temples and stelae, from statuary, and from written sources. For example the regalia and activities, including a crowning ceremony depicting Candace Amanitore (c. 1–20 CE) suggest she ruled equally with King Natakamani. Similarly identifiable Candaces include the earliest known, Shanakdakhete (c. 175–155 BCE) and the late first-century Amanishakheto. Pliny the Elder (23–79) in his *Naturalis Historia* (VI, 35) records a Queen Candace, presumed to be Amanarinas, who led a fierce resistance to the Roman occupation of Meroe. In 24 BCE she led her generals in an attack on Syene (Aswan) to which the Romans under Petronius responded by sacking her capital at Napata in 22 BCE. From the sixth through ninth centuries, during Nubia's Christian period, queens and queenmothers remained active in government and were carried the title *Kandake*.

In the New Testament, Candace is the name of the queen of the Ethiopians whose Ethiopian eunuch, who was in charge of all her treasure, was baptized by Philip. This only reference to Ethiopia in the New Testament is of considerable importance to Ethiopians, suggesting one means by which Christianity may have come to Ethiopia. However, whether the Ethiopia over which this Queen Candace reigned is the same as the Ethiopia of the early twenty-first century is inconclusive. The Greek geographer Strabo (c. 63 BCE–c. 24 CE) in his *Geographica* divided Ethiopia into three parts, one of which was the Kingdom of Candace, and in the time of Pliny Ethiopia was used for the southern most parts of the known world, and not always restricted to only Africa.

See also **Queens and Queen Mothers.**

BIBLIOGRAPHY

Belaynesh, Michael, et al, eds. *The Dictionary of Ethiopian Biography*, vol. 1. Addis Ababa, Ethiopia: Institute of Ethiopian Studies, 1975.

Fleuhr-Lobban, Carolyn. "Nubian Queens in the Nile Valley and Afro-Asiatic Cultural History." Ninth International Conference for Nubian Studies. Boston, August 1998.

Sergew, Hable Sellassie. *Ancient and Medieval Ethiopian History to 1270.* Addis Ababa, Ethiopia: United Printers,1972.

Welsby, Derek A. *The Kingdom of Kush: The Napatan and Meroitic Empires.* London: The British Museum Press, 1996.

NEAL W. SOBANIA

CAPE COAST.

Cape Coast is one of the oldest coastal towns of the central region of Ghana and serves as the regional capital. The town is known locally as Oguaa. The Portuguese named the area Cabo Corso (Short Coast), but it is by its English name of Cape Coast that the town is widely known. The city is located at about 105 miles west of the national capital of Accra. Of the almost 1.6 million people recorded in the 2000 census that live in the central region, only some 82,291 persons reside in Cape Coast. For an African urban center, the rise of the city's population from 57,224 in 1984 to its 2000 figures, though high in percentage rise, is moderate. The reason for this slow rate of growth is that Cape Coast is not an industrial town; rather it remains a fishing port, a center of education, and a tourist location.

The city's most important attraction is the historic British Cape Coast Castle from where the colonial government administered the Gold Coast Colony until the national capital was moved to Accra in 1877. In the early twenty-first century the Danish Castle at Osu (Accra), which the British purchased in 1850; the Dutch Elmina Castle, also purchased by the British in the early 1870s; and the Cape Coast Castle are all UNESCO Heritage Trusts, hence their importance to the nation's tourism industry.

Cape Coast features prominently in the history of Ghana as center of education. The earliest schools began at the Castle to educate European children of African women in the town. By the nineteenth century, when mission organizations became aggressive in the establishment of schools in the colony, Cape Coast was already one of the most attractive centers, and all the leading Christian denominations operated educational programs in the city. This European merchant/ Christian missionary impact generated for the city some of the country's early entrepreneurs, such as J. P. Brown, who invested in gold mining at Obuase in the 1920s. But the formal educational institutions at Cape Coast had the most significant impact on national history. For example, the Gold Coast's first Rights' Society of the second part of the nineteenth century had several of its leading members educated at Cape Coast. Newspapers

Front shot of Cape Coast Castle. The top left floor is the governor's residence, the first floor, also to the left, contains the church, and under the church floor are the underground cells that held male slaves. DAVID OWUSU-ANSAH, 2004

owned by local businessmen and religious groups gave voice to nationalist concerns. It was therefore not surprising that local personalities/families represented by such names as Brown, Casely-Hayford, Sarbah, Brew, and many others featured in the nationalist history of the country. In fact, the establishment in 1962 of the nation's third university at Cape Coast was a belated affirmation of Cape Coast's prominence in Ghana's national history.

See also **Accra; Casely-Hayford, Joseph Ephraim; Colonial Policies and Practices; Elmina; Ghana; Mensah, E. T; Tourism.**

BIBLIOGRAPHY

Duah, Francis Boakye. "Ghana Museums and History: The Cape Coast Castle Museum." In *Museum and History in West Africa*, ed. Claude Ardouin and Emmanuel Arinze. Washington, DC: Smithsonian Institution Press, 2000.

Owusu-Ansah, David. *Historical Dictionary of Ghana.* Lanham, MD: Scarecrow Press, 2005.

DAVID OWUSU-ANSAH

CAPE COLONY AND HINTERLAND, HISTORY OF (1600 TO 1910).

The Cape Colony was founded at the southwest tip of Africa by the Dutch East India Company in 1652, primarily to provide a harbor, food, and drinking water for its fleet of ships that rounded Africa every year on the journey between the Netherlands and, mainly, Indonesia. The Colony, greatly expanded from its original settlement, remained in the hands of the Company until 1795, when it was taken over by the British during the French Revolutionary wars. After a brief interlude (1803–1806) when it was returned to the Netherlands, it remained a British colony until 1910, when it was absorbed into the newly formed Union of South Africa. By this time the borders of the Colony had reached the Gariep (formerly Orange) River (and in some areas far to the north), and the east had incorporated all of the Transkei, up to the borders with Natal.

Within a few years after 1652, Europeans were allowed to settle outside of the Dutch East India Company's service, eventually creating a colony at the Cape. This initial expansion came after the expropriation of land held by the Khoekhoe (Khoikhoi) in the region around Cape Town, which was the administrative capital and long the only nonagricultural settlement of any size. It proved impossible for the Dutch to acquire all they needed, particularly agricultural produce from the pastoralist Khoekhoe, and moreover European cattle trade so weakened Khoekhoe society that it was easy to reduce them to laborers for the Europeans.

Nevertheless, the Dutch found it necessary to import slaves to form a labor force. During the century and a half of the slave trade, approximately 60,000 to 70,000 slaves were imported from Indonesia, India, Madagascar, and the East Coast of Africa, in approximately equal numbers. Some worked in Cape Town, where in addition to completing menial tasks like fetching water and firewood, a number became artisans. Their presence also introduced Islam into South Africa, brought by Indonesian men exiled to the Cape for resistance to the Dutch. Others worked the wine and wheat farms in the immediate hinterland of Cape Town, where a prosperous gentry had established itself.

Beyond the mountains of the Cape Fold belt, which formed the limit of commercial agriculture, and in the arid regions to the north, the descendants of Dutch immigrants maintained themselves by producing mutton and beef for the Cape market and selling oxen to farms. The result was a very rapid expansion of the colony, a process made possible by repeated bloody expeditions against the San, nomadic Cape hunter-gatherers, and Khoekhoe who had lost cattle, and often had been in the service of the Europeans. Many Khoekhoe, however, fought on the colonial side.

By the end of the eighteenth century colonial settlement had reached the Gariep River, and indeed the Griquas, of partial Khoi descent but assimilated to colonial ways, began to establish settlements to the north of the river. In the east, colonial settlement was extending to the Xhosa. In the clashes that this produced, however, the Europeans's firearms and horses could not yet overmaster the numbers of the Xhosa.

The incorporation of Cape Colony into the British Empire in 1806 led to the abolition of the slave trade (but not slavery itself) in 1807. The Cape also became the area of Africa with the highest density of Protestant missions, introduced during the last years of Dutch East India Company rule. The missions made a substantial number of converts among the Khoekhoe, who were seeking new explanations of the world after the collapse of their society and their subsequent transformation into laborers. In 1828 the colonial authorities issued a decree known as Ordinance 50 that outlawed all discrimination on the basis of race, followed in 1834 by the abolition of slavery throughout the empire. These changes allowed the development through the nineteenth century of a small "Cape Coloured" elite, but the vast majority of ex-slaves and Khoesan remained as oppressed laborers, especially on western and southern Cape farms.

The arrival of the British greatly expanded commerce throughout the colony, signalled by the founding of numerous small towns and farming in a much wider area. Merino sheep were introduced, replacing the hairy, fat-tailed sheep that the colonists had taken over from the Khoekhoe and providing yet another export product of major significance. British merchants generally maintained good relations with the Dutch agricultural elite. A group of British settlers who arrived in 1820 took up land in the eastern Cape around Grahamstown became the core of Cape conservatism and of English ethnicity in South Africa. The Cape parliament was established in 1854, followed by and ministerial government in 1872. Suffrage was granted without regard to race, and large numbers of "coloureds" and eventually Africans were able to meet the income requirements to vote. None were elected to the Cape parliament, although some who were known to be of partially "coloured" descent were seen as "white" if they achieved political or economic prominence.

The nineteenth century saw the conquest of the relatively densely populated areas of Southern Africa. This began in the eastern Cape with a long series of wars, driven by colonial hunger for land and labor, between British forces and the Xhosa. In 1848 a lasting British colonial administration was imposed on a functioning African society for the first time. However, two years later war broke out again in the Mlanjeni War (1850–1853). The conflict, the longest and bloodiest conflict in the British conquest of Africa with the exception of the Boer War (1899–1902), culminated in the massive defeat of the Xhosa.

Already devastated by this military disaster and an outbreak of cattle lung sickness that struck the Cape in the mid-1850s, the final blow came when a Xhosa prophet predicted that Europeans would be expelled and a new era of greatness would dawn for the Xhosa if all cattle were killed and crops destroyed. Known as the Great Xhosa Cattle Killing, this catastrophe caused as many as 100,000 deaths from famine; most remaining Xhosa were forced to seek work on colonial farms. Thereafter, British dominance was assured, and over the next half-century the Cape steadily incorporated the territories to the East, known as the Transkei, until by the 1890s there were no independent African polities remaining in the area.

Colonial expansion to the north, which had begun with Griquas, of Khoekhoe descent, followed by trekboers who crossed the Gariep in search of pasture, was consolidated with the large-scale exodus of Dutch-speaking farmers in the 1830s, during what became known as the Great Trek. The communities that resulted, though commercially tied to the Cape, were recognized as politically independent, and their populations came to think of themselves as Afrikaner, not British. The region north of the Gariep known as the Orange Free State became a major center for the production of wool.

In 1869, however, diamonds were discovered in very great numbers around what was to become the city of Kimberley. As a result, the Cape Colony annexed both the diamond fields and the lands to the north, up to what was to become Botswana. The later discovery of gold—found well outside what might possibly be considered the Cape Colony—further shifted the balance of South Africa's economic and political power away agriculture and commerce toward the new mining centers. Tensions between British and Afrikaners led to the outbreak of the South African (Boer) War in 1899. British victory in 1902 merged the Cape Colony with Natal and the two former Afrikaner republics to form the new Union of South Africa in 1910.

See also **Colonial Policies and Practices; Nongqawuse; Southeastern Africa, History of; Southern Africa, History of (1000 BCE to 1600 CE).**

BIBLIOGRAPHY

Elphick, Richard, and Hermann Giliomee, eds. *The Shaping of South African Society, 1652–1842,* 2nd edition. Cape Town: Longman, 1989.

Nasson, Bill. *Abraham Esau's War: A Black South African War in the Cape, 1899–1902.* Cambridge, U.K.: Cambridge University Press, 1991.

Peires, J. B. *The House of Phalo; A History of the Xhosa People in the Days of Their Independence.* Johannesburg: Ravan, 1981.

Ross, Robert. *Status and Respectability in the Cape Colony, 1750–1870: A Tragedy of Manners.* Cambridge, U.K.: Cambridge University Press, 1999.

ROBERT ROSS

CAPE TOWN. Established in 1652 on the shores of Table Bay, beneath Table Mountain on land used by Khoikhoi pastoralists, Cape Town was at first a refreshment station for the Dutch East India Company fleets en route to and from the East. By the time the town was taken over by the British in 1795, it had a population of some 15,000, the majority slaves. In form it resembled a Dutch city, which was then overlaid with British architectural styles. It remained the most important port in South Africa well into the twentieth century, and a major administrative and educational center, the seat of the Cape, then from 1910 the Union of South Africa parliament.

There were relatively few black African residents until the twentieth century, but many mixed-race Coloureds lived interspersed with whites in much of the city. As more Africans arrived from the Eastern Cape, they found that they had to live on the outskirts of the city; from 1901 onwards black Africans were forced out of the central city. After the passage of the Group Areas Act of 1950 Coloureds too were forced out of the city itself into separate townships on the windswept Cape Flats. These areas were also settled by large numbers of people, Coloured and African, who could not find houses. They lived in squatter settlements, which mushroomed from the 1970s and constituted some of South Africa's worst slums.

For many whites, especially the Afrikaners who settled in the northern suburbs, Cape Town

Harbor of Cape Town, South Africa. Famous for its natural beauty, including the harbor and the Table Mountains, Cape Town is the economic center of the Western Cape. It is the third most populous city in South Africa. © HERBERT SPICHTINGER/ZEFA/CORBIS

remained "the mother city," but many Africans saw it as too European. Its very cosmopolitanism, along with its spectacular scenery, attracted a large tourist traffic, especially after the advent of a democratic order in 1994. By then the population approached 2 million, with whites in a minority and the Coloured majority falling with the ever-increasing movement of Africans to the city.

See also **Apartheid; Education, University and College: Southern Africa; Mandela Nelson; South Africa, Republic of: Society and Cultures; Van Riebeeck, Jan.**

BIBLIOGRAPHY

Bickford-Smith, Vivian. *Cape Town in the Twentieth Century: An Illustrated Social History.* Cape Town: David Philip Publishers, 1999.

Worden, Nigel, et al. *Cape Town: The Making of a City.* Cape Town: David Philip Publishers, 1998.

CHRIS SAUNDERS

CAPE VERDE

This entry includes the following articles:
GEOGRAPHY AND ECONOMY
SOCIETY AND CULTURES
HISTORY AND POLITICS

GEOGRAPHY AND ECONOMY

Cape Verde, an uninhabited archipelago discovered around 1460 with an arid climate and scarce natural resources, was settled by the Portuguese because of its strategic location: about 311 miles west of Senegal. The islands served as a support base for passing ships and as an intermediary in the intercontinental slave trade. The first island to be settled, Santiago, is also the largest and home to the capital, Praia. It is part of the leeward (southern) group of islands that includes Brava, Fogo, and Maio. The windward (northern) islands are São Vicente, Santo Antão, Santa Luzia, São Nicolau,

Sal, and Boa Vista. Most of the islands are mountainous and are greatly scarred by erosion.

Despite the initial divisions between European settlers and African slaves in early Cape Verdean society, a Creole population eventually emerged from the intermingling of the two populations. Nevertheless, following the legal abolition of slavery in 1878, the shortage of arable land locked former slaves into exploitative relations with their landlords. Population growth, the lack of access to land, and frequent drought-related famines caused poor Cape Verdeans to emigrate in increasingly large numbers, in particular to the United States and to Europe. The 2007 population of Cape Verde, estimated at 423,613, was smaller than the number of Cape Verdeans resident abroad.

On July 5, 1975, Cape Verde became independent. The liberation struggle against Portuguese colonial rule, led by Amílcar Cabral, had been fought on the mainland in conjunction with Guinea-Bissau. The African Party for the Independence of Guinea-Bissau and Cape Verde (PAIGC) governed both countries until 1980, when a coup in Guinea-Bissau marked the end of their political union. Cape Verde established a one-party state governed by the African Party for the Independence of Cape Verde (PAICV). In 1991 it was voted out of office in the country's first multiparty elections, giving place to the Movement for Democracy (MPD), which remained in power for a decade until it was defeated by the PAICV in the 2001 and 2006 elections.

Despite its political independence, Cape Verde continues to be economically dependent on the outside world. With only 10 percent of its surface area (1,557 square miles) potentially arable, coupled with a short and irregular rainy season, the country imports more than 80 percent of its food requirements. It has a large trade deficit because imports, which also include fuel and manufactured goods, are much greater than exports (textiles, footwear, bananas, and tinned tuna). Most of Cape Verde's gross national income (GNI) is made up of remittances from Cape Verdeans living abroad and from foreign aid, with Portugal the main donor. Nevertheless, tourism and other services have also contributed toward the growth (5% in 2004 and 6.5% in 2005) of the economy. The percentage of the population living in poverty has diminished over the years (from 49% in 1989 to 37% in 2002).

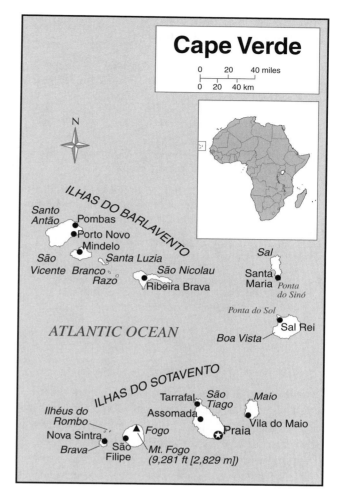

Although in 2006 donors still classify Cape Verde as a Least Developed Country, its GNI per capita (US$1,770 in 2004, among the highest in Africa) corresponds to that of a middle-income country. The United Nations has scheduled Cape Verde's reclassification for 2008. This progress will accelerate current reductions in aid, even though economic growth has been accompanied by an increase in the disparities in income distribution. Despite the permanent threat of drought, agriculture—maize and beans on rain-fed land, and banana and sugarcane on irrigated land—constitutes the major source of income for the rural population (estimated at 204,994 for 2006). The rate of unemployment is rising (up from 17.3% in a 2000 census to 24.4% in a 2005 study), and those most affected are young people and women. Efforts to improve farming conditions include the promotion of drip irrigation schemes and the building of the country's first dam, on Santiago Island, inaugurated in 2006.

See also **Cabral, Amílcar Lopes; Climate; Creoles; Famine; Production Strategies: Agriculture; Slave Trades; United Nations.**

BIBLIOGRAPHY

Chabal, Patrick, et al. *A History of Postcolonial Lusophone Africa.* London: Hurst and Company, 2002.

Instituto de Emprego e Formação Profissional. "Inquérito ao Emprego 2005: Apresentação dos Principais Resultados." Available from http://www.iefp.cv.

Instituto Nacional de Estatística. "Census (2000, 2004)." Available from http://www.ine.cv.

Organisation for Economic Cooperation and Development (OECD) "Development Assistance Committee (DAC) Database." Available from http://www.oecd.org.

ELIZABETH CHALLINOR

SOCIETY AND CULTURES

A volcanic archipelago of ten islands, located off the coast of Senegal, Cape Verde has served as a strategic depot between Africa, Europe, and the Americas since the time of its discovery by the Portuguese in 1460. During the era of the Atlantic slave trade, Cape Verde served as a transhipment point for slaves traveling from the African coast to the Americas and a base for stocking and protecting ships. And although uninhabited before Portuguese settlement in the fifteenth century, the islands since that time became populated by the mixed descendants of African slaves and white Christian and Jewish settlers from Portugal and circum-Mediterranean areas. Cape Verde has a relatively homogenous Mestiço population with a distinctive Creole culture.

Beginning in the late nineteenth century, Cape Verdeans were recruited by their colonial overlords, the Portuguese, to administer its colonies in West and Central Africa, since the Cape Verdeans had better access to education and were culturally and racially closer to Portugal than the mainland communities of Guinea (Bissau) or Angola. From 1959 Cape Verdeans also participated actively in the struggle for independence in Guinea-Bissau in which the Partido Africano da Independência da Guiné e Cabo Verde (PAIGC) sought joint liberation of the two countries.

In addition to their overseas activities as Portuguese civil servants and as freedom fighters, Cape Verdeans have also emigrated in large numbers to different countries in Europe, Africa, and the Americas in response to environmental conditions on Cape Verde. Tree cover, arable land, and water are scarce; drinking water is largely dependent upon conversion of seawater in desalinization plants and droughts are recurrent. The island, in fact, receives so little rainfall that it would be almost pointless to attempt to distinguish a rainy and dry season.

One of the social consequences of these conditions is that emigration, primarily a male path to prosperity, has created a situation in which more than 55 percent of the adult active population is female and 34.2 percent of all households (according to 2005 statistics) are headed by women, many of them single mothers. These female-headed households experience difficulties in obtaining access to education and in maintaining school attendance. Lack of educational opportunity is particularly debilitating given its importance to success in emigration and employment in government administration and economic service sectors.

Historically, Cape Verdeans have been almost exclusively Catholic, albeit with some mixture of African traditional religions. In the early twenty-first century, a mosaic of other mostly Christian religions is forming and attracts almost 10 percent of the population. Predominant among these are the Church of the Nazarene, Jehovah's Witnesses, Seventh-Day Adventists, the Church of Jesus Christ of Latter-Day Saints, Assemblies of God, Bahai, and the Igreja Universal do Reino de Deus (Kingdom of God Universal Church). Catholic influence and Creole culture continue to be dramatically displayed in pre-Lenten carnivals that occur on many of the islands.

Migration, however, has been an important source of innovations in Cape Verde's *crioulo* language, Afro-Caribbean style music and dance, and rituals, themselves originally hybrids of African, Portuguese, Jewish, and other stock. It is this hybridity that has led Cape Verdeans to feel a certain ambivalence about their status as "Africans." Their religion, language, music, and tastes for maize and *aguardente* or cane alcohol make Cape Verde culturally closer to Portugal than to the Muslims of mainland Sahelian West Africa.

República de Cabo Verde (Republic of Cape Verde)

Population:	423,613 (2007 est.)
Area:	4,033 sq. km (1,557 sq. mi.)
Official language:	Portuguese
Languages:	Crioulo, Portuguese
National currency:	Cabo Verde escudo
Principal religion:	Roman Catholic, Protestant
Capital:	Praia (est. pop. 106,052 in 2006)
Other urban centers:	Mindelo
Main islands:	Santiago, São Vicente, Santo Antão, Fogo, São Nicolau
Annual rainfall:	ranges from 127 mm (5 in.) in north to 305 mm (12 in.) in south
Principal geographical features:	*Mountain:* Pico do Cano on Fogo
Economy:	*GDP per capita:* US$6,000 (2006)
Principal products and exports:	*Agricultural:* bananas, corn, beans, sweet potatoes, sugarcane, coffee, peanuts; fish *Manufacturing:* food and beverages, fish processing, shoes and garments *Mining:* salt, pozzolana (volcanic ash used to make cement) *Services:* ship repair, construction
Government:	Independence from Portugal, 1975. Single-party government prior to 1990. Multiparty democracy under the 1992 constitution, revised in 1999. President elected for 5-year term by universal suffrage. 72-member Assembleia Nacional Popular elected for 5-year terms by universal suffrage: 66 deputies elected domestically according to proportional representation, 6 elected by Cape Verdeans living abroad. Assembleia Nacional nominates prime minister, whom president appoints. Prime minister appoints Council of Ministers from among members of Assembleia Nacional. For purposes of local government there are 14 districts divided into 31 parishes.
Heads of state since independence:	1975–1991: President Aristides Pereira 1991–2001: President António Mascarenhas 2001–: President Pedro Verona Pires Monteiro
Armed forces:	Prime minister is responsible for defense. *Army:* 1,000 *Navy:* 50 *Air force:* 100
Transportation:	Primary means of transport: coastal craft *Ports:* Mindelo, Praia, Tarrafal The islands serve as a fueling stop for ships traveling between Europe and Latin America. *Roads:* 2,250 km (1,395 mi.), 29% paved *National airline:* Transportes Aéreos de Cabo Verde *Airports:* Amílcar Cabral International Airport serves as a refueling stop for airlines serving Africa. Praia-Mendes is also an international airport. There are small airports on other main islands.
Media:	Weekly newspapers: *Boletim Informativo, Boletim Oficial, Terra Nova, Uidade e Luta, Agaviva, Economica, Contacto, Novo Jornal Cabo Verde, A Semana, Raizes.* 7 radio stations, 1 television station.
Literacy and education:	*Total literacy rate:* 76% (2004). Education is free, universal, and compulsory for ages 7–13. Teacher training, industrial, and commercial schools. No university.

See also **Colonial Policies and Practices; Creoles; Ecosystems; Household and Domestic Groups; Slave Trades.**

BIBLIOGRAPHY

Carreira, António. *The People of the Cape Verde Islands: Exploitation and Emigration.* Hamden, CT: Archon Books, 1982.

Foy, Colm. *Cape Verde: Politics, Economics, and Society.* London: Pinter, 1988.

Langworthy, Mark, and Timothy Finan. *Waiting for Rain: Agricultural and Ecological Imbalance.* Boulder, CO: Lynne Rienner Publishers, 1997.

Lobban, Richard. *Cape Verde: Crioulo Colony to Independent Nation.* Boulder, CO: Westview Press, 2001.

Lobban, Richard, and Marlene L. Lopes. *Historical Dictionary of the Republic of Cape Verde*, 3rd edition. Metuchen, NJ: Scarecrow Press, 1995.

EVE L. CROWLEY
REVISED BY EVE L. CROWLEY, ZELINDA MARIA SILVA COHEN CORREIA E SILVA, AND ANTONIO CORREIA E SILVA

HISTORY AND POLITICS

The Republic of Cape Verde is a small West African country consisting of ten volcanic islands and five islets 300 miles west of the westernmost point of Africa. Of the islands' estimated 423,613 inhabitants, the majority is of European and African descent. Independence was declared in 1975 after 500 years of Portuguese colonial rule, and a one-party socialist state was established and maintained until multiparty elections were held in 1990. In the early twenty-first century, despite economic hardship due to poor natural resources and impending drought conditions, Cape Verde exhibits one of Africa's most stable and democratic governments.

Between 1455 and 1462 Portuguese and Genoese navigators sailing for Portugal reached the uninhabited archipelago. In 1495 the islands were declared a Crown possession of Portugal and subsequently began importing slaves from western Africa. With expansion of the slave trade in the sixteenth century Cape Verde became a key commercial interface between Africa, Europe, and America, after the failure of early efforts to develop plantation agriculture. Further, the Portuguese Crown established a feudal system known as the *companhia* system. The feudal social structure included *capitãos* (captains), *fidalgos* (noblemen), *cavaleiro-fidalgos* (noble-knights), *almoxarites* (tax collectors), *degradados* (convicts), *exterminados* (exiles), and *lançados* (outcasts). Slaves occupied the bottom of the feudal social structure and were classified as *escravos novos* or *boçales* (raw slaves), *escravos naturais* (Cape Verdean born slaves), and *ladinos* (baptized or "civilized" slaves). In the end, the *companhia* system was abandoned for the *morgado* system of land ownership, a process that transmitted land under the principle of primogeniture. In 1863 the *morgado* system was abolished and land reforms took place, redistribution beyond the historically select circle of "county whites."

As the trans-Atlantic slave trade was reluctantly abandoned in the 1860s, Cape Verde once again became an important commercial center during the late nineteenth century. Despite renewed interests in the islands, the people of Cape Verde suffered from drought, famine, and Portuguese maladministration. While most Cape Verdeans worked as tenant farmers and sharecroppers, tens of thousands sought employment abroad in Brazil and the United States.

Following the Berlin Congress (1884–1885), Portugal's claim to Cape Verde remained intact,

despite losing areas of influence on the Guinea coast. In 1908, both the king and crown prince of Portugal were assassinated, which ushered in a brief period of democratic republicanism in 1910. However, the republic brought little substantive change to Cape Verde. As a result, opposition to Portuguese colonial rule grew in Cape Verde and neighboring Guinea-Bissau. In 1926, fascists, led by António Salazar, took control of the government in Portugal and later added a colonial policy (i.e., the Colonial Act of 1933) to the constitution, which placed severe limitations on civil liberties by expanding the powers of an extremely authoritarian internal police system known as the Police Internacional e de Defesa do Estado (PIDE). Consequently, anticolonialist movements grew in Cape Verde and Guinea-Bissau. Initial nationalist sentiments were expressed in the literary *Claridade* movement, founded by Baltasar Lopes and others in 1936.

In 1951 Portugal changed Cape Verde's status to that of an "overseas province" in an attempt to avert growing nationalism with constitutional standing equal to the provinces in the home country. Despite this action, nationalists responded by founding the clandestine Partido Africano da Independência da Guiné e Cabo Verde (PAIGC), a party established in 1956 by Amílcar Cabral and others in Guinea-Bissau. Influenced by the writings of political theorists Karl Marx, Vladimir Lenin, and others, the PAIGC created a political strategy of national liberation and pan-Africanism; its main goal was to liberate both Guinea-Bissau and Cape Verde from Portuguese colonial authority. In 1958, the PAIGC initiated a series of general strikes but later concluded that the violence practiced by the Portuguese could be defeated only by armed struggle. With the support of the Soviet Union, Cuba, and other socialist/communist countries, the PAIGC abandoned peaceful means of protest in favor of a war of national liberation. They began the armed struggle in 1963, with fighting concentrating in Guinea-Bissau. Due to the logistical difficulties of maintaining forces on the relatively open islands and supplying them by sea, the PAIGC refrained from attacks in Cape Verde.

By 1972, the PAIGC controlled the majority of Guinea-Bissau. On January 20, 1973, Amílcar Cabral was assassinated, but the PAIGC quickly intensified its attacks against the weakened Portuguese military and declared independence on September 24, 1973. Following this declaration, the fascist Portuguese government in Lisbon was toppled in 1974, prompting the new Portuguese government to reconsider Salazarian determination to control the African "overseas provinces" at all costs. Eventually, the revolutionary government in Portugal and the PAIGC agreed to a transitional regime, and full independence was achieved in Guinea-Bissau by September 24, 1974, and in Cape Verde by July 5, 1975. Aristides Pereira became the first president of the Republic of Cape Verde, and Pedro Pires became the first prime minister. Although the original constitution envisioned political unification with Guinea-Bissau, a military coup there in November 1980 strained the relations between the two countries, and the displaced civilian president Luís Cabral fled to Cape Verde. Shortly thereafter, Pedro Pires founded the Partido Africano da Independência de Cabo Verde (PAICV), abandoning the hope for unity with Guinea-Bissau. The PAICV established a one-party system and ruled Cape Verde from independence until 1990.

In 1991 the first multiparty elections took place with the internationally open *Movimento para Democracia* (MPD) replacing the PAICV. António Mascarenas Monteiro replaced Pereira as president, and Carlos Veiga replaced Pires. Under the leadership of the MPD the economy became increasingly privatized. The collapse of the world communist movement had also permitted a broader range of diplomatic choices for the MPD than had formerly been available to the PAICV. On the domestic front, the MPD continued the earlier policies of improving educational and social services, which resulted in assuring the party's parliamentary victory in the second multiparty elections in 1995. Shortly thereafter, Monteiro was reelected to the presidency, while Veiga retained his post as prime minister. Under a growing democracy the economy expanded under the neo-liberal orientation of the MPD, but the prosperous private sector economy benefited relatively few ordinary citizens.

Wanting change, the citizens of Cape Verde returned the PAICV to legislative power in 2001 with José Maria Pereira Neves appointed prime minister and former PAICV stalwart Pedro Pires elected

president. The 2006 legislative and presidential elections resulted in the continuation of a PAICV legislative majority and the reelection of Pires and reappointment of Neves. Under the newly oriented PAICV—which has slowly unhinged itself from an earlier socialist and pan-African orientation—Cape Verde has made major developmental and economic accomplishments. Since 2001, the government has implemented a series of programs supported by Cape Verde's international aid donors to improve the infrastructures fundamental to the development and sustainability of the archipelago. The programs have included public investment in infrastructure; private investment in fisheries, services, and export processing; an increase in agricultural output; and increased services to international air and maritime transport. Further, tourism is now the major industry sector targeted by the government.

As a result of nearly two decades of free and fair democratic elections, good governance, and by extension strengthened political and economic ties with donor states, access to health services and education have greatly increased, making Cape Verde one of Africa's most developed countries; the archipelago recently increased its position on the United Nations (UN) human development index from "least developed country" to a "middle income country."

Ironically, it has been under the PAICV, the political descendent of the pro-African PAIGC, that Cape Verde has moved substantially closer to Europe and away from Africa, expressing greater interest in closer, more intimate ties with the European Union (EU) than with the African Union (AU). In 2002 Prime Minister Neves lobbied the EU for the similar association status accorded to Cape Verde's sister islands in the central and eastern Atlantic, the Azores, Madeira, and the Canary Islands. Given the republic's geographical location, its historical ties to Portugal, good management, and economic interest by European private capital, influential Portuguese and Cape Verdeans have called for Cape Verde to become a member of the EU. In 2005 former Portuguese President Mário Soares submitted a proposal pressing the EU to start formal membership talks with the republic. To this end, despite belonging to the African Union (AU) and the Economic Community of West African States (ECOWAS), the republic's African connections seem more symbolic than substantial. Although many Cape Verdeans in influential positions are in favor of expanding ties with Europe, some are very much opposed and annoyed by the exigencies of the situation that erodes the hard won struggle for their economic sovereignty and cultural independence.

Cape Verde is known throughout Africa and the world for its democratic governance and developmental growth in the early twenty-first century. The Republic is a member of the UN and its various specializing agencies like the United Nations Educational, Scientific and Cultural Organization (UNESCO) and the United Nations Industrial Development Organization (UNIDO). It also has working relationships with the African Development Bank and the International Monetary Fund, and is currently working to become an active member of the World Trade Organization. Cape Verde follows a policy of nonalignment and seeks cooperative relations with all states such as Brazil, China, France, Germany, Portugal, the United States, and various African countries.

See also **Cabral, Amílcar Lopes; Colonial Policies and Practices; Guinea-Bissau; International Monetary Fund; Nationalism; Pereira, Aristides Maria; Slavery and Servile Institutions; Socialism and Postsocialisms; United Nations.**

BIBLIOGRAPHY

Chabal, Patrick; David Birmingham; Joshua Forrest; and Malyn Newitt. *A History of Postcolonial Lusophone Africa*. Bloomington: Indiana University Press, 2002.

Foy, Colm. *Cape Verde: Politics, Economics and Society*. London: Pinter Publishers, 1988.

Lobban, Richard. *Cape Verde: Crioulo Colony to Independent Nation*. Boulder, CO: Westview Press, 1995.

Lobban, Richard, and Paul Khalil Saucier. *Historical Dictionary of the Republic of Cape Verde*, 4th edition. Lanham, MD: Scarecrow Press, 2007.

McQueen, Norrie. *The Decolonization of Portuguese Africa: Metropolitan Revolution and the Dissolution of Empire*. London: Longman, 1997.

PAUL KHALIL SAUCIER

CAPITALISM AND COMMERCIALIZATION

This entry includes the following articles:
OVERVIEW
PRIVATIZATION
EMPLOYMENT AND UNEMPLOYMENT

OVERVIEW

Few concepts are more fraught than "capitalism" and "commercialization" with reference to Africa. They are among those long most invoked in a modern world riding these seeming economic miracles to global triumph to underscore the radical alterity attributed to Africa. In popular culture, at least, they are virtually synonymous with "economics" itself, a modern social science claiming universality in its emphasis on human calculated optimization of individual welfare, but in fact describing only values and interactions particular to a growing, but far from pervasive, sector of economic interactions predominant primarily in Europe since the eighteenth century, though also earlier in parts of the Indian Ocean world and the South China Sea.

Marx perceptively differentiated among "commercial capitalism" in which investment centers on inventories and transportation and storage facilities, "industrial capitalism" in which investment flows primarily into productive equipment, and "finance capitalism" in which liens and other claims on the returns from both commercial and industrial assets become principal forms of investment. Europe (and North America) alone developed widespread industrial capitalism in the nineteenth century, closely integrated with investments in military technology. Scattered other parts of the world moved into industrial development in the twentieth, while the United States and Europe—and recently also parts of southern and eastern Asia—moved on into the realm of finance. The twenty-first century may be the threshold of a further move into investment in, and leading returns from, information technology, retrieval, and management.

AFRICAN DEFINITIONS OF CAPITAL

Africans, by these exceedingly narrow standards, were seen as "non-economic men," mired in mindless repetition of "traditional" or customary behaviors, heedless of the cash incentives of the market, satisfied with whatever they had, rather than ambitiously striving. This exclusion of Africans from the modern world of capitalism very conveniently served the intensely optimizing interests of European colonial regimes in Africa, as it relieved them of responsibility for providing the cash or other incentives that their own neo-liberal economic theory predicted would stimulate the returns that metropolitan governments demanded of their rather costly African possessions. Rather, this mythical African "non-economic man" seemed to make clear, colonial authorities might better apply force to coerce the required effort. Colonial regimes were thus, in a dangerously self-fulfilling prophecy, themselves responsible for bringing about the unresponsiveness of their African subjects that they anticipated.

In fact, Africans' embrace of competitive capitalistic accumulation is as old as the history of humanity. But ambitious African entrepreneurs pursued these early capitalistic strategies in contexts that did not presume the autonomous individuals of modern economic theory, each one calculating personal advantage in monetized, or monetizable, terms in a great anonymous imaginary realm termed "the market." In that market, the independent preferences of these abstracted individuals mysteriously (because collectively) stimulated aggregate supplies of desired products from well-informed and alert producers focused on accumulating the currency that buyers were willing to give up to get what they wanted. In such commercial economies general currencies effectively mediated among producers and consumers entirely unknown to one another. Thus, as families all too often discovered when siblings loaned money to one another or, riskier yet, to brothers-in-law or other affines, or heirs found themselves divided bitterly over distribution of the assets of a deceased parent, they presumed a cold-blooded calculus of individual optimization that was at odds with personal relationships and, in the more extreme—but recurrent—examples of capitalist accumulation, also with the welfare of the society (or the nation) as a whole.

Africans instead optimized human relationships, in numbers, in diversity, and in accessibility. They invested in efficacious communities of kin and clients and wives and other dependents who collectively offered ranges of abilities that would enable the groups they thus assembled to preserve themselves against threats expectable and unanticipated alike, as well as—but in practice secondarily—to seize maximum advantage from opportunities that might appear. Thus, rather than following the risk-taking maxims of capitalist ideology (which selectively emphasizes the small percentage of successful risks taken, while obscuring the more common failures or ascribing them to personal deficiencies of the risk-taker), they accumulated human potential, personnel whom they held in reserve against eventual possible need. This long-term African investment strategy in human resources contrasts radically with the shorter-term focus of investment strategies in economies built around market exchange. Holding human knowledge in reserve anticipates and avoids risk, while its commercial counterpart, "insurance," compensates for the inevitable losses of taking risks after the fact.

Africa's characteristic political economy of people (and characteristic also of most of the rest of the world) contrasts further (still today) with commercial/exchange economies in distributing material wealth to affines in return for women as wives and to clients and other dependents in return for services or sheer availability upon command. The parents (or other relatives) of young women eligible for marriage receive a "brideprice" in compensation for the labors (and in some cases also children) of the women that husbands and their relatives will receive from her as a wife. Or they will return what is, in effect, an investment of a loaned reproductive female by giving the lenders a woman of their own in a future generation. In pastoralist economies, where properly managed herds of cattle multiply faster than humans reproduce and livestock thus bring living bovine interest on investments, wealthy individuals obscure their assets by entrusting them to clients to manage and by paying animals out ostentatiously through marriages to their daughters to create allies; this distributive (rather than accumulative) strategy also lessens risk by spreading it over many small, dispersed herds.

Political economic strategies nearly everywhere in Africa also focus primarily on knowledge, since in non-literate cultures the know-how necessary to maintain the community does not reside externally in books that one might buy or on Internet services or with hired consultants but rather exists only in the minds of people available and willing to contribute to the group what they think. Transfers of material product, that is, of cultivated or processed or fabricated or aesthetically elaborated results of human ability and effort, establish connections between makers and takers that obligate returns in these intellectual forms. The reciprocating services may also involve effort, but the effort is informed, knowledgeable, and not generic but specifically directed, offered to a known beneficiary. The initial "gift" effectively incorporates its recipient in a materialized extension of its creator—cultivator, processor, fabricator, or artist, and the return in "loyalty" or "respect" confirms the linkage established. In commercial economies, in striking contrasts, payment of currency obliterates any potential obligation of seller to buyer, or buyer to seller, both of whom "settle up" and move on, separately. That is, African economic optimization and hence strategies of investment focus on human capital (expertise) and relationships to mobilize it rather than on individual hoarding of commodified material or financial values, which individuals hoard to buy their ways out of trouble, by themselves. An aphorism attributed to the Inuit of northern Canada puts the point concisely: "The best place to store your fish is in someone else's stomach." Africans say "People are wealth; people are power."

Human beings are always scarce relative to such tokens. Herds of cattle increase in numbers faster than human beings reproduce, or one may similarly exceed the rates of reproduction of one's retinue by fabricating (or importing) tokens of relationships, like the misnamed "currency"—like copper crosses spread throughout central Africa since the beginnings of Bantu-speaking settlements in the area, or gold jewelry (but significantly as human adornment rather than for exchange) in parts of western Africa, or even coins minted in the images of Muslim rulers in the cities of the Swahili Coast. Such tokens, in turn, tend to deflate in value against the relationships in which they are invested, creating insatiable demands for more.

Specialized knowledge, always secretive, functions as an asset of the same sort, with the investment coming in the years of always-incomplete training that possessors of it require of their disciples, to penetrate depths ever more arcane. In Islam, blessedness is a principal discourse of mystical awareness in its Sufi versions, and scholarship functions similarly for clerics. In other cultures diviners, iron smelters, healers, and other technical specialists, not to mention priests, wrap themselves in similar mystiques. But since the values offered are

markers of personal connections rather than general (anonymous) tokens of material exchange, distinctiveness—in design, elaboration, style, and so on—is emphasized to identify their wealthy and powerful maker or distributor, who is then marked as someone who can command such skills. Competition among ambitious African investors in relationality creates an infinite demand for novelty, not for more of the same but rather for whatever identifies distributive success by being new, different and not capable of being imitated, that is, counterfeited.

This sort of aggressive, competitive accumulation meets any viably general definition of "capitalism," as investment (at the expense of immediate consumption) of wealth (knowledge, women, livestock, and distinctive materials—in that order) in the expectation of future returns. Such investment strategies operated within communities of people engaged with one another in multiple ongoing relationships, a quality partially identified (but unfortunately contrasted with, rather than demonstrated as parallel to, commercial capitalism) as "substantive economics" by the economist Karl Polanyi by the middle of the twentieth century.

STRATEGIES OF COMMERCIALIZATION IN AFRICA

Commercial relationships in Africa, though ones not facilitated by general-purpose currencies ("money"), had histories of lesser—but still significant—depth. They are distinct in enabling strangers to conduct transactions, substituting currency settlements for enduring relationships of givers and getters. In parts of the continent where rivers or other means of easy transport enabled people not otherwise engaged to establish regular contacts, commercialized guilds or networks (sometimes termed "diaspora") of traders developed soon after the definition of communities sufficiently differentiated to provide one another with exotic commodities or distinctive fabrications that local buyers could then distribute to mark the people in the retinues they led.

Archaeological evidence from the vicinity of the middle and upper Niger River in the last millennium BCE reveals extensive commercialized networks of this sort, capable of moving significant volumes of materials. Ethnographic and linguistic sources from the Congo (Zaire) River basin show the same sort of commercialization there from the first millennium CE. Their merchant-creators, however, maintained the characteristically African underlying prioritization of human relationships over material hoarding. In the vicinity of the Upper Niger, diverse specialized producers integrated balanced networks of face-to-face exchanges among co-resident ethnicized communities; in the more individualized networks of the Congo River, leading men absorbed the personal wealth of successful entrepreneurs into "secret societies," which in turn invested their intake in participatory activities (frequently featuring anonymously masked performers) that consolidated the communities around them.

EARLY SOURCES OF EXTERNAL COMMERCIAL CAPITAL IN AFRICA

Commercial investment from external mercantile sources undermined Africa's communally oriented economies for two reasons. Merchants from afar, particularly itinerant ones, introduced material wealth in quantities that exceeded the productive capacities of the communities, and—having no personal relationships with their suppliers—they generally sought primarily uniform commodities, not decorative distinctiveness. Secondly, African communities muted individual internal authority but centralized responsibility for representing the collectivity to outsiders, so that unrelated merchants dealt not with groups but with individuals, who—being human—frequently took advantage of the opportunity to promote personal rather than community interests. From the first known contacts of more than occasional frequency, well-capitalized foreign traders in search of commodifiable products set off inflationary competition that turned violent, which intensified to the point of turning into systematic slaving.

Asian (Jewish and Christian) merchant communities in the first two or three centuries CE invested their substantial commercial capital into Africa only in the Ethiopian highlands above the Red Sea; their sustaining interest, beyond obtaining such tropical exotica as scents, dyestuffs, ivory, rhinoceros horn, and animal pelts, lay in buying gold. The African suppliers of these commodifiers at Aksum invested their gains primarily in the military capabilities and monumental construction that in the circum-Mediterranean region expressed success; they also used them to integrate local

connections capable of extracting both gold and captives that eventually extended west to the upper Nile River.

Presumably the pattern evident in all Africans' later contacts with the maritime commercial economies surrounding the continent both provoked and financed this extravagant "imperialism." Wealthy commercial economies vested trade goods, on credit (or, as the English later termed it, "trust"), in the hands of African would-be suppliers, who in turn invested in networks of dispersed small-scale suppliers of the gold or other commodities demanded in payment of the commercial loan. Foreign creditors did not invest in production, and so the transaction was not in capital formation. Suppliers, therefore, tended to extract the commodities demanded—e.g. hunting elephant or rhinoceros, or panning gold during the low stream flows of the dry season, when agricultural effort was not needed—rather than diverting their investments in human skills from basic production of food necessary to sustain their communities. Such extraction involved little to no investment in productive facilities (other than human skills) and so tended to exhaust reserves of the commodities supplied. Suppliers, who were indebted to merchant patrons, were then forced to cover what they owed with dependents or other people, in effect sold as slaves. Commercial credit in trade goods extended to obtain commodities thus recurrently tended to shift toward supplemental partial payments in people.

Gold resources in far western sub-Saharan Africa and, by the twelfth century or so, also down the continent's Indian Ocean coast to Zimbabwe in southeastern Africa, attracted early Muslim commercial interest. In western Africa, commercial credit from northern African merchants financed ethnicized commercial sectors, diaspora of traders claiming common remote origins who settled in villages adjacent to, and then intermarried with, local agricultural and other productive communities as far south as the forests. The traders took on Islamic identities as a way of distinguishing themselves, in effect brand-naming themselves in the ethnicized style of designating specialized producers (rather than their products) already ancient in the region, and also to regularize their financial relationships with Muslim traders from the desert by positioning themselves within the mechanisms of Muslim commercial law. On the supply side, the affinal "landlord-stranger" relationships they built with their suppliers effectively insulated the African political economy of people from the more commercially oriented diaspora of traders.

Commercial competition in the latitudes south of the desert turned violent in the eleventh century in the midst of distress from a desiccating climate. The Saharan merchants bred and sold horses from north of the desert into the arms race that ensued there, through the present day. Cavalry forces were extremely expensive to maintain south of the Sahara, and the exports of gold and paid for the original imports of horses soon failed to cover the escalating costs of widespread militarization, leading to use of the horses to capture people, whom the captors then sold to cover the negative balances of their trade with the arms-dealers from the desert. Trans-Saharan exports of captives as slaves ensued, and the captors kept others to staff their growing military establishments. Violence, as Marx famously remarked about what he called "primitive accumulation," always facilitates the initial stages of capital formation, or marks the entry of new entrants forced to steal from established sectors. In Africa, "wealth in people" translated this universal process of capital formation into slaving.

In southeastern Africa, horses could not be maintained and so similar high-investment militarization never became an issue. African suppliers of gold there instead invested in cattle, which evidently multiplied fast enough to maintain workable networks of suppliers without resorting to unaffordable violence, and turned their profits from trading with Muslim merchants at the Indian Ocean coast into the monumental stone structures at what is now Great Zimbabwe.

EUROPEAN COMMERCIAL CAPITAL IN ATLANTIC AFRICA

On the Atlantic side of the continent, the Portuguese brought few capital resources to the encounter in the fifteenth century, but reached western Africa at a moment of escalating violence. Until 1700 in western Africa, they and later other Europeans, including much better-financed Dutch and English, spent more in buying gold than they spent on slaves. The slaves they acquired they obtained largely from the significant and very effective existing commercial communities. In central Africa, however, in the Kongo region just south of the mouth of the Congo River the Portuguese encountered outliers of the integrated commercial networks of the river's vast interior basin. Growing demand for labor on the nearby island of São Tomé to grow sugar, which they supplied with the collaboration of Kongo authorities' military expeditions against neighbors, forced major mobilizations throughout adjacent regions in self-defense throughout the sixteenth century. Without horses to deliver enormous military force against remote populations, the region slipped into a pervasive mobilization of manpower. A severe drought then collapsed the region into pervasive conflict, coincidentally at the very moment that Portuguese ships arrived prepared to carry off all the captives and refugees that they could acquire to Spain's wealthy silver-mining colonies in the New World. Slaving, or investment in human capital acquired through violence, thus came to predominate in the areas of Atlantic Africa lacking gold or other commodities through a combination of fortuitous circumstances. These enabled European traders to move American economies toward operations based on enslaved workers from Africa with relatively little commercial investment.

American silver (and eventually also Brazilian gold) underwrote the ensuing massive development of European commercial capitalism in the Atlantic, centered on the production of sugar with enslaved labor from Africa. Dutch beneficiaries of investments in sugar in northeastern Brazil introduced commercial credit to central Africa by the middle of the seventeenth century, hoping to attract slaves away from the Portuguese in Angola, who were still operating militarily off the aftershocks of the drought of the preceding decades. The English crown chartered the Royal Africa Company in 1672 to divert west African gold from the Dutch, by then buying gold at Elmina on the Gold Coast, but required it also to provide slaves to finance the initial investments in plantation sugar in Barbados.

By the early eighteenth century, the French had joined in the growing competition among European monarchies to staff the sugar boom in the Caribbean islands by flooding Atlantic Africa with commercial credit in the form of Asian textiles, European copper, and other manufactures. Africans bought the copper as means of displaying the growing personal wealth to be gained from exchanges with the Atlantic; copper and its alloys, bronze and brass, not gold, had long been the prestige metal throughout Africa, elaborately worked to distinguish its bearers and to display their power. The cloth, and many other components of their complex demand for imports, they distributed to adorn the retinues of women and other followers they assembled as profits from the trade in colors that identified themselves as patrons.

This unprecedented cornucopia of imports, which competition on the European side made increasingly available to buyers in Africa of marginal—even very dubious—local standing, financed inflationary investments in people. The trade grew much faster than the populations available to African investors in people through conventional means of marriage and clientage. It spilled over, in particular, into a growing demand for women acquired by other means, including kidnapping and capture by men fearing loss of their prospects for adult respectability through exercising the mature responsibilities of marriage and siring children. Violence grew in all the regions stimulated by European commercial capital by the end of the seventeenth century.

The eighteenth century was the period in which defensive measures against the spreading disorder matured in the form of the famous "slaving states" of that period, Segu, Asante, Dahomey, Lunda, and others (but not the cavalry forces of Oyo, who represented the last frontier of sudanic militarization at that time but provided captives for Atlantic buyers rather than sending them north into the Sahara). These costly military regimes absorbed major portions of the investment of gains from exchanges with the Europeans. The remainder of the African investment went into people, as previously, and principally women to reproduce and feed the populations assembled. Europeans were investing their corresponding gains from African exchanges in commercial capacity and the early stages of industrialized productivity.

With the uneasy peace within the protected domains of the large military states, African investment strategies also shifted into building new commercial sectors oriented toward the Atlantic.

They filled coastal towns with slaves employed in brokering the transactions between passing European ships and African buyers, distributors, and ultimately consumers, who paid with slaves whom transporters carried or drove down to the coasts. In areas with riverine transport, these commercial sectors took the form of fleets of large trading canoes; in areas where goods overland, the transporters assembled large caravans of porters and support personnel. These commercial sectors tended to be built through the transfers of people characteristic of the African domestic economies, and so male captives often ended up as enslaved members of these transportation units described in the prevailing language of community as quasi-households.

From the financial perspective of returns on the complementing European and African investments in people, the 12 million or more captives (mostly men) sold to Europeans brought returns in trade goods that allowed Africans, particularly older males, to invest in women, to dispose of younger men who might have challenged their monopoly on female reproductivity, and to work the men and women they retained in Africa harder to support the commercial infrastructure they were building. Though no one will ever know the exact proportions, they probably displaced, reassembled, and retained more individuals in Africa than they sold. The avidity with which African investors bought up distinctive imported wares and their ability to demand higher prices (in the quantity terms generated by African economic thinking, beyond the increased cash costs of slaves to Europeans) translates in economic terms into capital formation through exchanges, always tinged with violence, and profitable in these terms for the small minority involved.

These internal African processes of investment in commercialization complement, not reverse, the usual perspective on exchanges that are usually viewed externally as "the Atlantic slave trade" and do not differentiate African interests in terms of capital formation and the people formed as capital. The same process followed also from the Saharan and Indian Ocean trades, though on more violent terms stemming from the smaller-scale investments provided to the slavers in Africa by North African and western Indian merchants. A vast literature has treated these exchanges as "unequal," in which undifferentiated "Africans" unaccountably (at least as economic optimizers) gave up the continent's life-blood for flimsy, cheap consumer goods; the most sophisticated work in this style, by the late Walter Rodney, grasped the increased differentiation between the wealthy few in Africa, increasingly in positions of political power, and others displaced and vulnerable. The pervasive threat of sale to "cannibal" Europeans surely inspired effort and obedience among the weak and isolated. Viewed in terms of African capitalism and commercialization, investors in Africa were violently accumulating more dependents in circumstances of greater vulnerability, at rates parallel to European expropriation of all-but-free land in the Americas and the concentration of low-cost silver and gold in capitalist financial capability in Europe.

In the nineteenth century, the British gradually drove all European nations out of the business of slaving, but Ottoman-linked and Indian investors backed other violent initial phases of slaving in and around the basin of the upper Nile and in much of eastern Africa. With exports of slaves ending on the Atlantic side, African capitalists there moved into investments in production, again in tandem with, but ultimately less expansive than, the fossil-fuel-driven industrial revolution in Europe and North America. The more commercially developed portions of western Africa intensified slaving to mobilize labor for production of vegetable oils—peanuts, palm oil—demanded in Europe for illumination of cities and lubrication of the wheels of industrial capital. In central Africa, where previous African investments had flowed almost exclusively into building commercial networks, and where the weak Portuguese economy provided less external commercial credit, traders replaced slaves with extracted (rather than produced, from capital investments and improvements) commodities: beeswax, ivory, then wild ("red") rubber, with investments in women to process the wax and rubber and boys and men to transport them to the coast. The displacements and widespread destruction of this intense "robber baron" capitalism again coincided with parallel phases of industrialization and heavy militarization in northwestern Europe and North America.

EUROPEAN INDUSTRIAL CAPITAL AND COLONIALISM IN AFRICA

Industrialization in the North Atlantic matured demands there for strategic resources every part of the globe, moving in Africa from vegetable oils to wild rubber to minerals like copper. The strong—if not leading—military aspect of this process eventuated in medical and communication technologies capable of keeping European troops alive and operative on the ground in Africa. Modern weaponry, first repeating rifles and then Gatling (machine) guns by the 1870s, then led directly to European military conquest of the continent in the 1880s and 1890s. The wealthier trading nations, like England, secured the richest sources of African commodities (e.g. the Gold Coast and Nigeria), leaving the French to move militarily into unpromising drier latitudes on the southern fringes of the Sahara. The Portuguese settle for the otherwise unclaimed residues of their longstanding claims to all of central Africa.

Glittering discoveries of diamonds at Kimberly in southern Africa in the 1870s, and then revelation of a massive stratum of gold-bearing rock beneath the Witwatersrand in the 1880s, fueled a flush of enthusiasm inspired in Europe, at a precarious moment in the initial formation of financial capitalist strategies, growing international rivalries, and utter ignorance of Africa in Europe. A classic "boom" ensued. High-level European finance regarded African investments as highly speculative opportunities, second-rate at best, with the exception of the diamonds and the gold. Investors had little interest in Africa without government support and subsidization; hence the colonial military conquest. Ensuring colonial government investment concentrated on basic transport infrastructure—ports, railroads, secondarily roads for vehicular transport—that immediately put the canoes and caravans of the African commercial sectors out of business. Because the colonial regimes needed African production, they moved more slowly against African investments in personnel and therefore seldom acted on their highly publicized commitments to emancipate the enslaved there, who—in some of the most productive regions—accounted for more than half of the population.

European financial—not industrial—capitalism then swept over Africa in the form of highly speculative private corporations with capitalizations just sufficient to print glowing reports of the prospects of the "tropical treasure trove" they claimed in Africa, to raise more capital from naïve new investors. They operated minimally, and even at that low level only by hiring thugs from all over the world as to act as "company police," who extended the violence and displacements of the preceding era of African slaving to force people driven to desperation by droughts and epidemics, beyond the coercion, to exhaust rubber and the other available extractive resources.

King Léopold (of the small nation of Belgium, otherwise excluded from Africa) attracted private capital to his Congo Independent State (1885-1908) only by giving away mining and other concessions that gave what were in effect corporate warlords all-but-untouchable fiefdoms; the inhabitants of the regions suffered notoriously. The Portuguese, the "weak man of Europe," resorted to similar concessions, which produced similar abuses. France, focused on it colonies in western Africa, also sold its central African possessions to private concessionaires, and their African residents suffered and died accordingly. The Germans were left with territories of distinctly secondary potential, and so they substituted direct government military force for capital investment to attempt to wring some returns from these holdings. Colonial rule brought the violence of primitive accumulation of capital to Africa, and the returns of previous investment of capital in finance and technology flowed into lower-risk and higher-return opportunities in Europe.

Where colonies prospered in Africa they did so not from European investment but rather from the entrepreneurship of Africans left sufficiently alone to mobilize their own assets: cattle herders in southern Angola and elsewhere, cocoa planters in Nigeria and the Gold Coast, peasant farmers growing corn and other supplies for the mines in southern Africa, and sufi leaders (marabouts) in the peanut-producing areas of Senegal. The European powers fought skirmishes of World War I in eastern and southern Africa but left little infrastructure to show for these exertions; instead they drew manpower unproductively away from agricultural economies. Occasional significant investments in idealistic and grandiose schemes of "modernization" during the interwar years, usually intended to lure African cultivators to produce cotton or

other strategic resources, produced enormous suffering among the people recruited to work on them and failed nonetheless. Governments also invested in subsidies (and coercion of African labor) to support European plantation agriculture in Algeria, Kenya, Nyasaland, Southern Rhodesia, and a few other colonies, but these strategies never escaped subsidization.

Only the diamonds and gold of southern Africa, and also copper in central Africa, profited, owing to artificially maintained global cartels or, in the case of copper, from temporary demand owing to widespread mid-twentieth-century electrification around the world. In essence, capitalist Europe, in order to concentrate profits and capital for further investment at home, in Africa turned to the historic African strategy of increasing productivity by coercing human effort, not by investments in industry. European capital reached Africa primarily in the commercial sectors of transportation and consumption.

FINANCE CAPITALISM IN INDEPENDENT AFRICA

World War II brought further investments in African production of militarily strategic commodities but minimal development of further infrastructure. When the smoke of the fires of nationalism in the 1950s cleared away in the 1960s, the new politically independent governments of Africa, popularly elected in impeccably democratic styles, found themselves accountable to their constituents for what amounted to long-deferred maintenance of basic infrastructure, from schooling to train human resources to consumer-goods industries to electrification to adequate supplies of water to drink.

The former colonial powers, quietly relieved to have sold off a longstanding loser as an investment, made minimal efforts to provide further funding. The independent national governments then turned to the multinational corporations, many of them with bases in the United States, that had attained global proportions in the 1950s. African governments welcomed these new investors in a renewed round of grandiose and idealistic schemes, mostly focused on minerals and agricultural commodities. As had been the case in militarily blocking out eventually unremunerative colonial claims, it proved cheaper to build a factory or open a mine than to maintain and operate it profitably. Though some potential investors surely recognized the costs they would have to bear to supply absent modern infrastructure, those who naively ended up trying to operate in Africa found the costs overwhelming.

When world commodity prices nosedived in the 1970s, the first-generation democratic governments failed, yielding to authoritarian regimes of many stripes, with the United States and the USSR investing mostly in meddling in internal affairs in the international chessboard of the Cold War era and in military training and equipment. Even the minimal infrastructure of the 1960s rusted and was abandoned, and most Africans fell back on their own resources in human relationships to survive. Governments nonetheless fell deeply into debt to the Cold War protagonists, which lavished military assistance on military regimes, and to the relatively neutral international sources of credit, the World Bank and the International Monetary Fund (IMF). In the Republic of South Africa, very high costs of containing unrest, and international financial and commercial isolation imposed in abhorrence of the *apartheid* regime there, absorbed even the revenues of ongoing production of gold and diamonds.

By the 1980s, the continent was bankrupt, with debts to the consolidating capitalist world economy far beyond any means that it might generate within the foreseeable future even to begin to repay. Most people lived in "informal economies" that functioned on very small spheres of mutual personal support, largely in the sector of "petty commerce," on the basis of day-to-day or hour-to-hour working capital. A few salaried employees invested what they could save in local real estate, again on a pay-as-you-go basis, and marking the skylines of Africa's burgeoning cities with the skeletons of half-built residential construction awaiting further funding to take the next small step toward finishing them.

In the 1990s, the IMF and the World Bank, backed by foreign government lenders, took advantage of the lowering military costs in the wake of the end of the Cold War to force a beginning of a process of recovery. They imposed varying combinations of outright forgiveness of bad debts, holding governments accountable to their citizens

in the hope of encouraging investment of their private resources, and strict repayment programs. Governments were compelled to abandon subsidies of food on which their citizens had depended, to shrink health programs, and to postpone educational initiatives. Citizens thus abandoned by their governments turned to the only means of survival remaining to them: crime, theft, violence, and seizures of the assets of others, sometimes culminating in genocidal eradication of potential competitors.

Dealing in illegal drugs became a prominent, and dangerously highly remunerative, source of capital. War lords, supplied by a growing international network of arms dealers, returned to violence to pay for highly lethal assault weaponry by seizing control of the only marketable resources of the continent: petroleum was the leading potential source of funding for violence, and so it remained largely in the hands of recognized governments, except in the ungovernable southern Sudan. Diamonds financed the non-government side (UNITA, led by war lord Jonas Savimbi) of a thirty-years struggle in Angola. The diamonds and gold of the remote parts of Sierra Leone and Liberia produced particularly brutal disasters along these same lines. Similar resources in northeastern Zaire (subsequently the Democratic Republic of Congo) funded militias of comparably violent propensities.

SURVIVING THE GLOBAL CAPITALIST ECONOMY

Only strategies of capital investment in people, and in some cases in livestock, enabled Africans to survive this onslaught of insufficiency of European capital in a global economy built on it. Networks of family and community support, often in ethnicized forms, enabled the down-and-out to live at least another day and linked town to country. A new wave of emigrants washed up, this time voluntarily, in Europe and the United States, initiated largely by educated professionals, who were followed by sons of desperately impoverished families seeking wage or salaried employment that would allow them to send remittances back home. The same strategy had long sustained the overcrowded and eroding "Bantustans" deliberately impoverished in and around the Republic of South Africa; their populations served as labor reserves, paid little but living frugally enough to support their families at home, for white South African industry and domestic services. In the colonial era, women from rural areas had similarly performed a particularly self-sacrificing filial duty by serving the men in the cities as prostitutes, and girls from Africa are now prominent among the sex workers in the cities of southern Europe.

Commercial capitalism, which essentially thrives on concentrating resources from elsewhere in highly productive combinations, has failed in Africa for two millennia. Economies built on material sufficiency for accumulating and sustaining people repeatedly overheated under the stimulus of external commercial credit, exploded in violence, and paid in people, their principal form of wealth, for the costs of militarization and defense they had borrowed to create. The growing differential between Europe and the rest of the world in commercial, military, and industrial capacity overwhelmed a commercial sector thriving in Africa beyond the high costs of militarization, though at the expense of the people uprooted and overworked as slaves in all of Africa's expanding economic sectors, leaving the continent weakened by the violence of the process of primitive accumulation. Even at this moment of weakness in the nineteenth century, European military and financial capacities barely sufficed to implement the costly terms of "effective occupation" in the famous colonial partition of 1884-1885. European capital investment never began to cover the costs of integrating Africa viably into the modern commercial economy. The nations of the continent attained independence insufficiently invested to function in the rapidly growing global economy of the second half of the twentieth century. The citizens of the resulting bankrupt nations have either withdrawn from the ruinous repayments of debts accumulated over millennia, increased to the point of bankruptcy after 1970, or emigrated in a new diaspora to tap the illegal, despised but often remunerative underbellies of the wealthy nations of the world. However, though exploited all along the way by investors in their misfortunes, unlike their enslaved predecessors, they are working for themselves, and for their families.

See also **Aid and Development; Aksum; Cold War; Colonial Policies and Practices; Congo River; Debt and Credit; Economic History; Economic Systems; Ethnicity; International Monetary Fund; Ivory; Ja Ja, King; Kinship and Affinity; Kinship and Descent; Labor: Conscript and Forced; Lobengula; Metals and Minerals; Nationalism; Niger River; Nile River; Savimbi, Jonas; Secret Societies; Slave Trades; Socialism and Postsocialisms; Transportation; Travel and Exploration: European (1500 to 1800); World Bank; World War I; World War II; Zimbabwe, Great.**

BIBLIOGRAPHY

Austen, Ralph A. *African Economic History: Internal Development and External Dependency.* London: J. Currey; Portsmouth, NH: Heinemann, 1987.

Blackburn, Robin. *The Making of New World Slavery: From the Baroque to the Modern.* London, New York: Verso, 1996/97.

Brooks, George E. *Landlords and Strangers: Ecology, Society, and Trade in Western Africa, 1000–1630.* Boulder, CO: Westview Press, 1993.

Curtin, Philip D. *Economic Change in Precolonial Africa: Senegambia in the Era of the Slave Trade.* Madison: University of Wisconsin Press, 1975.

Curtin, Philip D. *Disease and Empire: The Health of European Troops in the Conquest of Africa.* Cambridge U.K.; New York: Cambridge University Press, 1998.

Dalton, George, ed. *Primitive Archaic and Modern Economies: Essays of Karl Polanyi.* Boston: Beacon Press, 1971.

Eltis, David. *Economic Growth and the Ending of the Transatlantic Slave Trade.* New York: Oxford University Press, 1987.

Gide, André. *Travels in the Congo,* trans. from the French by Dorothy Bussy. New York: Modern Age Books, 1937.

Herbert, Eugenia W. *Red Gold of Africa: Copper in Precolonial History and Culture.* Madison: University of Wisconsin Press, 1984.

Liesegang, Gerhart; Helma Pasch; and Adam Jones; eds. *Figuring African Trade,* Berlin: Dietrich Reimer Verlag, 1986.

Lovejoy, Paul E., and David Richardson. "Trust, Pawnship, and Atlantic History: The Institutional Foundations of the Old Calabar Slave Trade," *American Historical Review* 104, no. 2 (1999): 333–355.

Lovejoy, Paul E., and David Richardson. "The Business of Slaving: Pawnship in Western Africa, c. 1600-1810." *Journal of African History* 42, no. 1 (2001): 67–89.

MacGaffey, Wyatt. "Am I Myself? Identities in Zaire, Then and Now." *Transactions of the Royal Historical Society,* 6th series, 8 (1998): 291–307.

McIntosh, Roderick J. *Ancient Middle Niger: Urbanism and the Self-Organizing Landscape.* New York: Cambridge University Press, 2005.

Meillassoux, Claude. *Maidens, Meal, and Money: Capitalism and the Domestic Community.* Cambridge U.K.; New York: Cambridge University Press, 1981. (Translation of *Femmes, greniers et capitaux*, Paris: F. Maspéro, 1975.)

Meillassoux, Claude. *The Anthropology of Slavery: The Womb of Iron and Gold,* trans. by Alide Dasnois. Chicago: University of Chicago Press, 1991. (Translation of *Anthropologie de l'esclavage: le ventre de fer et d'argent.* Paris: Presses Universitaires de France, 1986.)

Middleton, John. "Merchants: An Essay in Historical Ethnography." *Journal of the Royal Anthropological Institute* 9, no. 3 (2003): 509–526.

Northrup, David. *Trade without Rulers: Pre-Colonial Economic Development in South-Eastern Nigeria.* Oxford: Clarendon Press, 1978.

Polanyi, Karl; C. H. Arensberg; and H. W. Pearson; eds. *Trade and Market in the Early Empires: Economies in History and Theory,* Glencoe, IL: The Free Press, 1957.

Rodney, Walter. *How Europe Underdeveloped Africa.* London: Bogle-L'Ouverture Publications, 1972.

Shipton, Parker MacDonald. *The Nature of Entrustment: Intimacy, Exchange, and the Sacred in Africa.* New Haven, CT: Yale University Press, 2007.

Vansina, Jan. *Paths in the Rainforests: Toward a History of Political Tradition in Equatorial Africa.* Madison: University of Wisconsin Press, 1990.

JOSEPH C. MILLER

PRIVATIZATION

SOCIALISM

From the 1960s through the early 1980s, many African leaders advocated a socialist (which in reality was statist) approach to development—emphasizing state planning and government intervention in peasant price setting—that contributed to increased rural poverty. African socialism overstressed the state while neglecting the class differences that existed. Although indigenous income discrepancies were de-emphasized during the anticolonial struggle, the differences increased in independent states. President Julius Nyerere, whose 1967 Arusha Declaration committed Tanzania to socialism and egalitarianism, admitted in 1977 that national average incomes were lower than in 1967, and that inequality was higher.

Although socialist governments proclaimed eliminating class privilege, nearly all were dominated by a political and bureaucratic class that was antagonistic to workers. Moreover, although elites lacked centralized planning control, they had the power of life and death over enterprises through taxes, subsidies, and access to inputs and foreign currency. Class differences and inequality varied little between capitalism and African socialism.

PRIVATIZATION AND ADJUSTMENT

Elites changed strategies in the 1980s following a decade of slow growth, rising borrowing costs, reduced aid, and mounting international deficits. The International Monetary Fund (IMF), the lender of last resort, and the World Bank set conditions for loans to reduce external deficits: macroeconomic stabilization and structural adjustment, including trade liberalization, price decontrol, deregulation, and privatization.

Privatization includes changing an enterprise's ownership from public to private; liberalizing entry into sectors previously restricted to state-owned enterprises (SOEs), typically defined as enterprises principally owned by and their chief executive officer appointed by the state; and contracting services or leasing assets to private firms. Privatization was a response to a growing economic liberalism of the IMF's major shareholders and the failure of SOEs to match expectations, especially under a soft budget constraint, and an absence of financial penalties for enterprise failure. Frequently, governments provided subsidies to SOEs expected to produce investible surpluses.

The World Bank and other creditors relied on the IMF's seal of approval, usually contingent on borrower austerity and privatization, before approving aid, loans, or debt rescheduling. IMF Managing Director Jacques de Larosière asserted in 1987 that adjustment was virtually universal in Africa.

STRATEGIES UNDER PRIVATIZATION

Liberalization and privatization provided rising classes chances for challenging the existing elites and threatening their positions, but also contributed to their increased rent seeking, that is, unproductive activity to obtain private benefits from public action and resources. Most African elites eventually supported liberalization, as privatization (requiring access to credit) and restructuring offered new opportunities to expand wealth. Moreover, the elites, by controlling restructuring, protected their enterprises from competition.

PUBLIC AND PRIVATE ENTERPRISES

Public goods, including national defense, sewerage, lighthouses, environmental protection, and others that the market fails to produce, generate externalities, benefits that spill over to society generally rather than to the investor. Surveys indicate that the key factor determining the efficiency of an enterprise is not whether it is publicly or privately owned, but how it is managed. However, the variation in efficiency is greater among SOEs as they are more likely to choose an excessive scale of operations. Furthermore, SOEs have greater access to state financing and face pressure for allocating jobs to elites' clients. Corruption, mismanagement, and limited economic infrastructure contribute to SOEs' low productivity and chronic deficits (or negative savings).

The World Bank, the IMF, and bilateral lenders pressured several African countries to privatize. In the 1980s, Ghana, Mozambique, Tanzania, and Zambia undertook enterprise restructuring, and South Africa, Côte d'Ivoire, and Senegal, because of SOE fiscal drain, restructured and privatized in the 1990s. Still because of public hostility, the state retains control over most infrastructure, industry, and manufacturing. Not surprisingly, many African privatizations lacked adequate preparation, design, and transparency.

In South Africa, the Congress of South African Trade Unions (COSATU), a leader in the anti-apartheid struggle and a traditional ally of the African National Congress, led a two-day antiprivatization strike in 2001. COSATU finally agreed to SOE restructuring and broadening participation in privatization for historically disadvantaged groups, such as blacks, mixed races, Indians, and women.

PROBLEMS OF PRIVATIZATION

In Africa, since laid-off workers have few options, forcing inefficient firms to close is generally unacceptable. Moreover, SOEs may create spillovers that private firms overlook. Nigeria's abolition of the Cocoa Marketing Board and the Board's marketing licenses in 1987 resulted in such poor quality control and fraudulent trading that the government reintroduced inspection and licenses in 1989.

A BRIEF EVALUATION

Africa grew faster in 1960–1973 than in 1973–2000; real income per capita was lower in the 1990s than in the late 1960s. Former World Bank chief economist Joseph Stiglitz (b. 1943) opposed the IMF shift in 1980 from employment expansion and combating market failure to lending conditioned on externally led adjustment and macroeconomic stabilization. Both early and late, Africa's growth was obstructed because of patrimonialism rewarding rent-seeking by political insiders, acquiescence in state misappropriation and nonpayment of taxes, the distribution of jobs to clients, and capricious and unpredictable policies. For economic takeoff, Africa needs transparency, dispersed power, the rule of law, and goals for economic decisions set by indigenous policy makers.

See also **Economic Systems; International Monetary Fund; Labor: Trades Unions and Associations; Nyerere, Julius Kambarage; Socialism and Postsocialism; World Bank.**

BIBLIOGRAPHY

Cook, Paul, and Colin Kirkpatrick, eds. *Privatisation in Less Developed Countries*. Sussex, U.K.: Wheatsheaf, 1988.

Nafziger, E. Wayne. *Economic Development*, 4th edition. New York: Cambridge University Press, 2006.

Nellis, John. "Privatization in Africa: What Has Happened? What Is to Be Done?" Washington, DC: Center for Global Development Working Paper 25, 2003.

Nkrumah, Kwame. *Class Struggle in Africa*. New York: Zed Books, 1970.

Sandbrook, Richard, and Jay Oelbaum. "Reforming Dysfunctional Institutions through Democratization? Reflections on Ghana." *Journal of Modern African Studies* 35, No. 4 (1997): 603-646.

Stiglitz, Joseph. *Globalization and its Discontents*. New York: Norton, 2002.

E. Wayne Nafziger

EMPLOYMENT AND UNEMPLOYMENT

Africa suffers from having been induced to adopt concepts and statistical practices developed for application in rich industrialized countries, notably the United States and western Europe. This applies to how work and labor patterns are perceived. Numerous reports give alarming figures on unemployment and elaborate figures on levels and trends in employment (Economic Commission for Africa 2005), when actually there is a dearth of up-to-date statistics and those that do exist are often flawed conceptually and statistically.

Certain stylized facts are clear. Most economic activity in Africa is still informal in character, and as such is not employment in the standard sense, that is, involving a wage or salary. Many people survive by combining activities in what are best described as *livelihood strategies*. Many countries measure employment and unemployment by using sample surveys in which respondents are asked to identify themselves by their *main* activity in some recent reference period. Close observers of African working patterns understand the distinction between "main" and "secondary" is often arbitrary. Some people think of main as the activity that takes up more of their time than anything else, some think of main as the activity they regard as most important or that yields most income, some identify it as what they would like to be doing. This is important, particularly in Africa where so many people are only able to survive by combining several types of activity.

The standard techniques developed in the United States and western Europe for measuring employment and unemployment are woefully inappropriate in an African setting. To give a real example: If there is an increase in wage employment, it might signal an improvement in employment and production, whereas in reality the shift could have been linked to abandonment of other activities and a disruption to the survival strategies of whole households or communities. Another factor is that data are gathered from household surveys, in which many activities undertaken by the poor are unrecorded. Indeed, because so many people are surviving in the streets or by moving around, they are often omitted from any notion of household, and a result is such people tend to be omitted in sample surveys.

Similar difficulties surround the emotive issue of unemployment. The common understanding is that this relates to being without paid employment and available for such employment, and having sought paid employment in some recent reference period, such as the past week. These criteria are hard to apply objectively in most of Africa. Why seek employment when there are no prospects of finding it? If a person wants a wage job and is having to do some survival activity while waiting or looking, is the person likely to call himself or herself "unemployed" or "working"?

So, Africa poses special problems when coming to monitoring labor developments. And there are other problems. For instance, far more than in other parts of the world, there are enormous numbers of undocumented workers, without passports or permits, living somewhere in fear of identification. Due to the high prevalence of civil wars, the number of refugees and internally displaced persons is huge. And on top of that there are nomads and pastoralists who rarely fit into conventional notions of households.

The sensible answer to these and related dilemmas is to move away from what is called the labor force approach to a measurement of economic activity. Regrettably, much of what passes as knowledge of African work is based on the available data. In the following, this article will summarize the conventional picture of the situation, drawing attention to unresolved dilemmas of interpretation.

AFRICAN EMPLOYMENT AND UNEMPLOYMENT IN GLOBAL PERSPECTIVE

The conventional picture is that Africa has a low level of employment by comparison with the rest of the world. Part of the story, which tells more about the statistical deficiencies than anything, is that in many countries the measured labor force participation rates are low, particularly for women and particularly in predominantly Moslem areas. In a few countries, such participation rates are extremely high, as in Burundi, Rwanda, Tanzania, Burkina Faso, Ethiopia and Ghana. Overall participation rates are measured by the number of employed within the age group defined as labor force age (usually 16 to 64) plus the number of unemployed in that age range divided by the total number of people within that age range. The biggest problem with that measure is that it tends to exclude people in rural areas, and in urban slum areas, doing petty activities in combination with so-called domestic work, such as tending a small plot of land or child-caring or looking after elderly or sick relatives.

With commercialization and urbanization, Africans have become less able or inclined to rely on traditional activities yielding some output but little money, such as smallholder production of staple commodities. Needing cash, more have been shifted into the unemployment category because they have been forced to seek wage labour.

The latest International Labor Organization (ILO) estimates are that over 14 percent of all African adults are unemployed. In South Africa, the official figure is about 30 percent, and in several others it is over 20 percent (e.g., Algeria, Botswana, Nigeria). For methodological and statistical reasons mentioned above, these figures should be treated with extreme caution and are almost certainly an exaggeration. For what it is worth, Africa emerges as a high-unemployment region of the world. But comparisons can be very misleading, given the structural differences between the various regions of the world.

RURAL-URBAN CONNECTIONS
Most African countries remain predominantly rural, and in most agricultural work accounts for most economic activity; in a few, agriculture accounts for over 90 percent of the total (e.g., Burkina Faso and Rwanda). However, it is crucial to analyze changing patterns of labor and work in Africa by taking account of the diverse types of area and region. At least three types should be considered— rural traditional, rural commercial, and urban.

In rural traditional areas, tribal and other networks ensure some division of labor, according to crops, land structure and available resources. Typically, all able-bodied people work to some extent, including children and the elderly. Since the 1980s, such areas have been blighted by such pandemics as tuberculosis, malaria and, most dramatically, HIV/AIDS, which has reduced the capacity of whole communities to reproduce their economic processes, for several reasons, including the loss of prime-age men and the need for women to care for rising numbers of orphans.

In rural commercial areas, open unemployment is more common. This is due to land consolidation and activities by landowners and commercial farms to induce workers to supply labor, using indebtedness and cost-raising measures to induce them to do so.

In urban areas, open unemployment tends to be much higher than elsewhere. In part, this reflects the influx of rural migrants seeking labor, in part it reflects a relative shortage of non-wage income-earning activities that could allow more to be in some sort of visible underemployment. Even so, such underemployment is particularly high in urban areas of Africa. Indeed, numerous alarming reports of the number of working poor have been produced in recent years.

Interpreting area differences in levels of employment and unemployment is made harder by the extensive anecdotal evidence that much urban activity is in the shadow economy, often blurring into illegal production, such as unregistered beer or other alcohol, drugs, prostitution and dealing in contraband. To these should be added the various forms of flexible labor that have been spreading, by which formal enterprises contract out some of their labor in order to bypass labor regulations or tax or insurance obligations. Undocumented labor may serve the interests of both employer and worker, since they can split the economic gain. Of course, such activity is chronically underrecorded. But one may speculate that it is very extensive, if only because of the incentives, if not necessity, to indulge in it and because of the lack of administrative capacity to police it.

YOUTH UNEMPLOYMENT
If there is one stylized fact that excites more attention than any other when considering African employment and unemployment it is that youth unemployment is huge, in absolute terms and relative to the rest of the world. In some countries, more than half the age group fifteen to twenty-four are said to be unemployed. In Ghana, it is claimed that over 80 percent of that age group is unemployed, in Zambia it is over 60 percent.

Readers should view such figures with skepticism. But there is little doubt that many youths are forced to drift around by a lack of work opportunities. Many drift into social illnesses, lose a sense of dignity and end up in abject poverty.

Various explanations have competed for policymakers' attention. One is that there simply are not enough new jobs emerging, so that youths are forced to wait until openings become available. Another is that many migrate into urban areas, and thus are less likely to be recorded as doing some petty economic activity such as smallholding on family farms. Another is that large numbers of young people are voluntarily unemployed, and as such do not merit priority concern. The claim is that as a disproportionate number of the unemployed are more educated than those in jobs and/or come from families that are not among the poorest, they must be voluntarily idle. This claim has not been supported empirically, and it has become generally realized that the positive correlation between probability of unemployment and schooling is due to the fact that successive generations tend to have higher schooling levels on average.

In general, there is some truth in all the explanations, which is why selective policies based on the presumption that one explanation holds may be inequitable and inefficient. For instance, if many of the openly unemployed are the offspring of relatively well-off parents, then policies to give them jobs rather than improve the livelihoods of poorer families would be inequitable and, possibly, inefficient. If, by contrast, the young unemployed have high education and potentially high productivity, it may benefit the economy if preference in job allocation were given to them.

Policymakers worry about youth unemployment in part because discontent can spill over into violence and political opposition. Consequently, they are desperate to be seen to be doing something about it. Public works and food-for-work programs, launched with large amounts of public money or foreign aid, are often targeted on youth. This may not mean that such targeting makes sense economically or socially.

WOMEN'S ECONOMIC ACTIVITY

Traditionally, women were the backbone of African agriculture and have played a vital role in trading activities. It is generally accepted that commercialization led to men taking many of the higher-paying jobs (Boserup 1970). But, as in other parts of the world, since the late twentieth century women have been taking a growing proportion of the emerging jobs due to a feminization of the labor market, that is, a tendency for the types of job to emerge to correspond to the precarious nature of labor in which women have predominated (Standing 1989, 1999). Above all, women have taken a very high proportion of jobs in export processing zones and in relatively successful enclave economic areas, such as Mauritius. No country of Africa has managed rapid development without an impressive mobilisation of women as productive workers. Regrettably, that does not mean that their poverty

and labor precariousness have not remained greater than men's.

AGING IN AFRICA

An almost unnoticed phenomenon in Africa has been the growing number of elderly persons, in their sixties and above. This is paradoxical, since life expectancy remains low in most countries. The reasons for that are that infant and child mortality remain high, while HIV/AIDS, malaria and tuberculosis account for a high incidence of deaths among prime-age adults. The result in some countries is an almost U-shaped age distribution of the population.

Accordingly, many elderly people have no adult offspring to support them in old age. They have to find some activity or retain land to farm. Many cannot do so, and suffer deprivation as a result. Many older people have retained their landholding, and this has been one factor for the surge in rural-urban migration by young people, sometimes to the detriment to productivity on the farmlands.

In several southern African countries, notably Namibia and South Africa, almost universal social pensions for those aged over sixty have enabled elderly citizens to have enough on which to survive and to help pay for the schooling of grandchildren, thus reducing the incidence of child labor and youth unemployment. These pensions have helped some rural communities to maintain family smallholdings and family production systems, while strengthening intergenerational reciprocities. The aged continue to play a significant social and economic role.

PUBLIC SECTOR: FROM ELITE TO MORAL HAZARD

For many years, during the colonial period and perhaps more so afterward, those employed in the public sector, particularly in national civil services and public administration, had much better pay and employment conditions than the vast majority of workers in their respective countries.

This has changed dramatically, particularly as the squeeze was placed on public spending under structural adjustment programs. A consequence was that many civil servants drifted into the habit of petty corruption and into a pattern of moonlighting, doing other economic activity while nominally being employed full time as civil servants.

These traits became a scourge of government efficiency in many, if not most, African countries. In many of them, pay and conditions in public service employment have deteriorated to very low levels, resulting in a deterioration of the quality of service and the calibre of people going into public employment. This is so even though public employment still comprises a high proportion of total wage labor, strikingly so in such countries as Nigeria, Bénin, and Botswana. Public sector employment certainly no longer sets the pattern for working conditions and pay that it did until the 1970s.

INFORMALIZATION

Africa is where social scientists first documented the existence of what was, rather inaccurately, called the informal sector. Initially, anthropological research established its prevalence in west Africa; later it was analyzed for east Africa, beginning with a famous and influential ILO report on Kenya produced in 1972.

The notion of a sector was always inappropriate, in that types of work encompassed by the term "informal" proved to exist in most industries and forms of production, while many registered firms employ casual and subcontracted labor that is informal in character.

What has surprised many observers is that the extent of informal labor has risen steadily since the late twentieth century, rather than declined, as was expected in the course of development. Much of it is counted as self-employment, although it is done on contract with larger enterprises, in part to avoid relatively fixed non-wage labor costs. Countries with particularly high levels of informal activity include Bénin, Congo, the Democratic Republic of Congo, Nigeria and Ghana. By contrast, recorded informal activity is rather low in Mauritius, South Africa and Tunisia, all of which have relatively developed export-oriented modern production. Some observers attribute the re-growth of informality to government "red tape" and regulations. But in most of Africa enterprises can bypass regulations with impunity. Surveys suggest that the informality reflects more the chronic uncertainty and volatility of economic life in much of Africa, in which employers try to give themselves as much flexibility as is feasible.

For workers, informal labor is usually relatively insecure. But it should not be presumed that it is always inferior to available formal labor. Indeed, it would be better to have an image of a continuum, from highly informal (without contracts or sources of social protection) to very formal, with most Africans falling in the lower end of the spectrum.

SOCIAL PROTECTION AND LABOR

One should not analyze patterns of work without taking into consideration the system of social protection. In Africa, tribal and other kinship-based systems of mutual support have been disrupted by commercialization and the development of postcolonial states. For some years, it was expected that welfare systems along lines developed in industrialized countries would emerge as modernization proceeded. The reality has been very different.

Most relevantly, standard insurance-type benefits for unemployment, sickness, maternity, disability and old age have scarcely taken shape. In sub-Saharan Africa, only South Africa and Mauritius have had unemployment benefits; in North Africa, only Algeria, Egypt and Tunisia have them; in those only a small minority of the unemployed have qualified for them. Some modern companies and the public services have supplied a core of their workforce with such benefits, but increasingly coverage has been restricted rather than extended. Meanwhile, the state has found it difficult to fund proper schemes, often being directed by structural adjustment programs and pressure from international financial agencies to cut back on schemes they had set up or had planned to introduce. In some countries, notably in North Africa (Algeria, Egypt, Morocco, and Tunisia), laws exist along the lines of those in rich countries, particularly for work injuries. But they are often inapplicable or poorly implemented. Indeed, the percentage of the workforce covered by state social protection has declined in much of the continent.

Among the consequences of not having unemployment and sickness benefits, for instance, is that when someone falls sick or becomes unemployed, they have difficulty in surviving or in functioning in a way that could secure alternative work or labor. Soon, they die or become ill to the point of being unemployable. But possibly as common is the situation where someone losing a job takes a lower-paying, lower-status activity, and nevertheless calls him- or herself unemployed. This is not to belittle their plight. It is to highlight the inappropriateness of the conventional measures.

Social protection schemes in Africa have varied extraordinarily, making the continent a laboratory for experimental schemes. Most have been selective, directed by the notion of targeting the most needy. Many have been attempts to generate jobs while providing poverty relief. The literature is huge and readers should consult one or more of the several reviews (ILO 2004). A difficulty is that food-for-work and public works tend to generate only low-productivity, short-term jobs, often with high administrative costs. There are growing movements to promote more universalistic schemes, such as the basic income grant.

LABOR AND SOCIOECONOMIC SECURITY

Africa has been the continent where it is generally recognized that many countries have been losers in the early phase of globalization and economic liberalization. The trouble is that many of the countries are small and suffered from a legacy of poor policies and undeveloped institutions. A consequence was that they have been prone to capital flight, indebtedness and volatile economic growth. These structural disadvantages fed into the labor process, leading to low wages, precarious employment and ineffectual systems of labor regulation and social protection.

Finally, it is worth noting that by world standards, most African countries are ranked by the ILO (2005) as having low levels of labor market security, that is, low levels of job opportunities and low employment protection security. Exceptions with regard to employment security are Mauritius and Botswana. Both of these countries have opted for social policies to reduce inequality and the social suffering of their people. These have lessened social tensions, which in turn has contributed to the creation of a stable economic climate conducive to high rates of foreign and domestic investment. As such, they offer hopeful models for emulation by other countries.

There is much to be done to improve the level and quality of African employment. One of the most important tasks will be to find ways of providing basic income security for all groups, for only then will the spirit of ubuntu flourish again, the sense of social solidarity in which enriching livelihoods can flourish.

See also **Disease; Economic Systems; Economics and the Study of Africa; Labor; Warfare: Civil Wars; Women; Youth.**

BIBLIOGRAPHY

Boserup, E. *Women's Role in Economic Development.* New York: St. Martin's Press, 1970.

Economic Commission for Africa. *Economic Report on Africa 2005: Meeting the Challenge of Unemployment and Poverty in Africa.* Addis Ababa: Economic Commission for Africa, 2005.

International Labor Organization. *Employment, Incomes and Equality: A Strategy for Increasing Productive Employment in Kenya.* Geneva: International Labor Organization, 1972.

International Labor Organization Socioeconomic Security Program. *Economic Security for a Better World.* Geneva: International Labor Organization, 2004; reprinted and amended 2005.

Paratian, Raj, and Sukti Dasgupta, eds. *Confronting Economic Insecurity in Africa.* Geneva: International Labor Organization, 2005.

Samson, Michael, and Guy Standing, eds. *The Basic Income Grant for South Africa.* Cape Town: University of Cape Town Press, 2003.

Standing, Guy. "Global Feminisation through Flexible Labour." *World Development* 17, no. 7 (July 1989): 1077–1095.

Standing, Guy. "Global Feminisation through Flexible Labour: A Theme Revisited." *World Development* 27, no. 3 (1999) 583–602.

Standing, Guy; John Sender; and John Weeks. *The South African Challenge: Restructuring the Labor Market.* Geneva and Cape Town: International Labor Organization, 1996.

GUY STANDING

CARNIVALS. *See* **Festivals and Carnivals.**

CARTHAGE. Carthage, located next to the modern city of Tunis, was an important city in ancient times. It was founded as a Phoenician trading colony in the ninth century BCE. Its advantageous location at the juncture of the eastern and western basins of the Mediterranean allowed it to emerge as a major port and trading emporium by the early fifth century BCE. As a city-state, Carthage ruled a commercial empire, which extended across the western Mediterranean and into the Atlantic. The city, located on a fertile promontory, and its complex of ports were heavily fortified. At its apogee early in the second century BCE, Carthage probably had a population of several hundred thousand inhabitants, with some estimates of up to half a million or more. The written language was Punic (derived from Phoenician) but the population would have had an important local Berber component.

Carthage fell to the Roman army in 146 BCE, at the close of the Third Punic War. The Romans destroyed the city but a century later reestablished it as a *colonia*. Roman Carthage became the second-largest city in the western half of the empire, after Rome itself, with up to 300,000 inhabitants circa 400 CE, and it was an important center for the early Christian church. It was capital of the Vandal kingdom (439–533) and then served as the main African outpost of the Byzantine Empire until it fell to the Arab army in 698. In the first decade of the 2000s the archaeological site lies in the municipality of al-Marsâ, an affluent suburb of Tunis, and it has given its name to an annual theater, cinema, and music festival.

See also **Tunis.**

BIBLIOGRAPHY

Lancel, Serge. *Carthage: A History*, trans. Antonia Nevill. Cambridge, MA: Blackwell Publishers, 1997.

ERIC S. ROSS

CARTOGRAPHY.

Cartography, the act of making and studying maps, serves as a powerful example of the way in which notions of representation and image are used and expressed over time. The earliest references to African cartography date back to precolonial Africa. African cartography can be said to start from the twelfth century BCE in greater Egypt, then continued by the Phoenicians as maps were a prime source for their supposed circumnavigation of Africa as early as 600 BCE. By the middle of the second century CE, Ptolemy, working on the mapping of Ethiopia, the Sahara, and the Great Lakes, was already heir to a long geographical tradition. Maps also played a crucial role in the expansion of Arab trade routes and aided in the extensive penetration of Islam through North Africa and across the Sahara by the twelfth century CE. These examples of the cartography of antiquity defined the science as an exploration of the interior of the African continent and the accumulation of its knowledge for future penetration.

The most recent substantial historical shift in the notion of cartography began during the Renaissance, with Europeans following on Ottoman Empire cartographic work. During the Renaissance cartography was established as a formal discipline, bringing together the two forms of earlier mapping; that language of representation from within, and the demarcation and assertion of control over the land. Late in the seventeenth century Dutch cartography, at that time prominent in the fields of navigation and cartography, reflected this huge transition that unified the two representational languages into one multifunctional and assorted language. Though linked together as one language, the second initial form would prove the stronger one within that union, as modern European cartography increasingly imposed its labels and borders designed to conquer the unknown.

Tom Conley, in *The Self Made Map* (1996), argues that from the sixteenth century, the growth of cartography as a discipline can be explained through five important factors. First, is the discovery of the manuscripts and folios of Ptolemy and the innovations in woodcutting, copper engraving, and movable type. These discoveries and developments provided both a historical foundation and the modern means to easily produce new maps. Second, is the increase during the scientific revolution of quantification and measurement of the human body and the geography of nature. The heightened need to understand the world in terms of numbers and measurements spurred the effort to classify and represent external space through maps. Third, these changes were accompanied by the development and refinement of the visual arts, a shift that added aesthetic demands and goals, such as perspective, to existing scientific forms of mapping. Fourth is the development of the notion of private property and state planning, both of which encouraged landowners to commission surveys of their estates and led to the mapping of national possessions abroad. Finally, related to the previous point, the political unification of states and the establishment of nations was constructed upon a system of defense of their national borders, and the borders of colonial possessions, as demarcated on maps.

Conley asserts that cartography as a discipline is closest in nature to literature due to its capacity for imagination. The creation of a map, as much as that of literature, involves the creation of new forms of narrative for a new subject or a new subjectivity (understanding of the self). Cartography, ancient and modern, particularly in the African continent, has been used to imagine, control, and both demystify and exoticize that which lies outside of the dominant culture. In *The Self Made Map*, Conley speaks to the power of cartography to "both foster and to discredit the mystical relation with the unknown." Similarly, maps have been described as scientific abstractions of reality, representing something that already exists objectively. A map anticipated spatial reality. It was a model for, rather than a model of, what it purported to represent, and had become a real instrument to concretize projections on the earth's surface.

The act of mapping formed a network of domination and control over both the Africans who were being mapped, and in relation to the other powers likewise seeking to know and own the world. Maps and modes of navigation played a determining role in the relative stature and wealth of European nations from the fifteenth to the nineteenth centuries, a role that further demonstrates their power to define and order.

A general map of Africa from the year 1595 provides an example of the manner in which the Europeans tried to document the physical space of the African continent, and demonstrates the impossibility of truly representing the cultural complexities that exist beyond the map. This initial representation of African space on the part of the European cultures served primarily to appropriate the space of an Other and demarcate the boundaries of their new possessions.

With its representational language, this map of the African continent is close to contemporary maps of Africa. The notion of representation in this first moment is within the realistic and formal canons that have defined cartographic style. The synonym of reality is related to the mathematical precision of the coordinates and geographic locations that are represented in the plan (map). The map represents in this case the geographic reality of Africa as that which could be represented in a photograph of the continent taken from a satellite. The two mediums (cartographic and photographic) are representing the same object within a convention of reality that humans have catalogued as reality or made realistic by their objective conventions that accord value to perception and not conceptualization. This map contains three types of messages: first, a linguistic code for the utilization of verbal supplements for a better explanation of the map as a document for orientation and navigation; second, iconic messages such as the stamp (illuminated symbol in the left side) that represents the European country that developed this project and ordered the geographic forms represented in the space; and last, the map as a document that is an object of a political and historical moment that represents a view and a form of reality and a conceptualization of the world from the occidental perspective.

The initial European representation of African space served primarily to imagine the exotic continent as they saw fit, appropriate the space of an "other," and to demarcate the boundaries of the Europeans' new possessions. The following map contains detailed images that serve to remind how the navigation of outsiders through the flowing artistic currents of Africa resulted in an influence of one culture on another that continues to this day.

A close reading of a detailed map of an African town—Lwangu (Loango)—drawn by the Dutch artist Olfert Dapper (1635–1689) in the year 1668 specifically illustrates this phenomenon. This map provides an example, at the microlevel, of the manner in which the Europeans tried to document the physical space of the African continent, mainly from the outside with little understanding of the internal structure and definitions. It was an effort that demonstrates the impossibility of truly representing the cultural complexities that exist beyond the map, yet succeeds in providing a window into the traditions of the land and its people.

The contradictions of the view of the city and the culture of its people as portrayed in the map are more complex than the fact that its creator was never actually in the town during the period in which it is represented. Dapper composed his view similar to a puzzle, or rather, designed it by amalgamating various scenes of the city created by other artists, thus creating a physical truth regarding actuality. This map, and its illustration of a foreign locale through such a system of external perception, aids those that argue its critical role in the formation of the Western understanding of the Other.

As Dapper brought together numerous snapshots of life in the town of Lwangu, the most appropriate manner in which to understand his work and learn about the culture he aims to represent is to examine these snapshots as maps themselves, frozen portrayals of a living, active culture.

Ontologically, occidental art theory has defined the notion of production of artwork as important from the Renaissance to the present. Precisely in the moment when the European metropolis needed a new medium for the representation of other space, artistic cartography emerged as a strategy of symbolic domination. The Dutch (and to a large extent, the rest of the European colonial powers) developed an artistic medium that has the function of representing this first moment of recognition and meeting the Other that was that outside the borders of modernity.

In addition to the artistic representations of control over the other, this period saw a transformation of notions of domination and order from theoretical forms expressed through mapping to the literal European occupation and rule throughout the continent. Africa had been an imagined space and desired territory of the Europeans since they first learned of it, though their initial conquest was impeded for various reasons including the military technology of the African civilization, geographic factors such as the climate and disease, and internal conflicts between the diverse ethnocultural groups reins, empires, and civilizations (such as Yoruba Kongo, Akan, and Mande) that dominated the first moments of two centuries (sixteenth and seventeenth). But by the mid-nineteenth century, African space was nearly completely appropriated by foreign powers, ushering in a period of colonial subjugation and exploitation.

Meyer Schapiro (1904–1996), in defining what he termed symbolic national schemes, classified them into two types: that which is defined by characterization of determined social classes, local identities, or marks pertaining to a select group, society or political group; and that which is defined as the

legally and geographically defined character of a nation (country). In general, the first is a symptom of the capitalistic appetite of the European societies, and the second an example of the imposed portrayal of a culture that is expressed beyond the limitations of the medium and the contradictions of the forms of European domination. The maps examined above represent aspects of cultures that maintain these trails and that parallel them in the contemporary culture of the region.

As the production of natural language requires two parts—a mode of call and response—the production of pieces of art, including maps, comes from the interaction between a maker, or artist, and an object that becomes the representation. Dapper, as both a mapmaker and an artist, created a map that has a powerful legacy, and implications for anthropology, art history, and other disciplines examining cultures, expressive forms, and modes of communication and control in Africa.

With the map's double role—that of purveyor of the European ideological and theoretical framework, and that of a window into the barest aspects of Kongo life–it creates an avenue by which to understand not only the cultural values and traditions displayed within it, but the act of mapping the African continent. Though Benedict Anderson (1991) refers to the slew of maps created in the nineteenth century, his comments on their narrative role is relevant here: "Historical maps [are] designed to demonstrate, in the new cartographic discourse, the antiquity of specific, tightly bounded territorial units. Through chronologically arranged sequences of such maps, a sort of political-biographical narrative of the realm came into being, sometimes with vast historical depth." The Lwangu map, with its extensive historical detail, creates a clear narrative that cannot help but be both political and sociobiographical in nature.

It is also valuable to note future avenues for exploration of this map. Primary among these is an investigation of the manner in which an African urban center is designed, experienced, and portrayed. Within this theme one can consider the artist's use of inside and outside, the drawing of boundaries, and the creation of ordered space inside the city walls whereas traditional activities remain outside. The spatial organization of the image is interesting, with easily represented activities of the

Other dominant in the foreground and the calm, gridlike, almost modern town lies in the background. A decision was clearly made as to what was a more accurate picture of this civilization, one can only wonder on what grounds. On a more literal level, the map holds important, detailed information as to the architectural style of Kongo civilization at this point in history, and with a closer look, can help scholars to understand Kongo urban design, building techniques, and town activities.

Cartography as a discipline shows people part of the history of the culture, the nations, possessions, and conquests. But it also shows a peculiar form of communication. The theory of cartography demonstrates the impossibility of summarizing and generalizing about a discipline that is formed by a diversity of styles and forms with their own historical, political, and cultural demands, and a long history and historiography. In the case of Africa, cartography has the challenge of putting into practice all of the history of the earlier cartography, as well as creating new forms of understanding of mapmaking as a language. Finally, cartography could be, in the case of Africa, a medium of intercommunication between Europe and Africa, a back and forth between the politics, the desire to represent the Other in its differences through art.

The cartographic representation is halfway between painting, engraving, and drawing. It is a representational language that teaches us a form of cultural history of peoples as a portrait of the domination of the colonizer over the colonized, between that which is represented and that which represents, and finally, between nature and the cartographic representation of itself as a discipline.

See also **Egypt, Early; Geography and the Study of Africa; History of Africa; Travel and Exploration; Urbanism and Urbanization: Historic.**

BIBLIOGRAPHY

Anderson, Benedict. *Imagined Communities*. London: Verso, 1991.

Balandier, Georges. *Daily Life in the Kingdom of the Kongo*. New York: Pantheon Books, 1968.

Bockie, Simon. *Death and Invisible Power*. Bloomington: Indiana University Press, 1993.

Bozal, Valeriano. *Los orígenes de la estetica Moderna*. Madrid: La balsa de la Medusa. 1996.

Bunseki Fu-Kiau, K. K. *Self-Healing Power and Therapy: Old Teachings from Africa*. New York: Vantage, 1991.

Cavazzi, Giovani Antonio da Montecuccolo. *Istorica descrizione de' tre regni Congo: Matamba ed Angola*. Bologna, Italy: Giacomo Monti, 1687.

Chernoff, John Miller. *African Rhythm and African Sensibility*. Chicago: University of Chicago Press, 1981.

Childers, Joseph, and Gary Hentzi. *The Columbia Dictionary of Modern Literary and Cultural Criticism*. New York: Columbia University Press, 1995.

Conley, Tom. *The Self-Made Map: Cartographic Writing in Early Modern France*. Minneapolis: University of Minnesota Press, 1997.

Curtin, Philip. *The Atlantic Slave Trade: A Census*. Madison: University of Wisconsin Press, 1969.

Dapper, Olfert. *Description de L'Afrique, contenant les noms, situations et confirns de toutes les parties*. Amsterdam, 1685.

Faïk-Nzuji, Clementina M. *Tracing Memory*. Quebec: Canadian Museum of Civilization, 1996.

Glassie, Henry. *Folk Housing in Middle Virginia*. Knoxville: University of Tennessee Press, 1975.

Goodman, Nelson: *Languages of Art. Languages of Art: An Approach to a Theory of Symbols*. Indianapolis, IN: Bobbs-Merrill, 1968.

Hawkes, Terence. *Structuralism & Semiotics*. Berkeley: University of California Press, 1977.

Innis, Robert E. *Semiotics: An Introductory Anthology*. Bloomington: Indiana University Press, 1985.

Kubik, Gerhard. "African Graphic Systems." *Muntu* January, no. 4–5 (1986): 71–137.

Laman, Eduart Karl. *Dictioinnaire Kikongo-Francails*. Brusells, Belgium: Academie Royale des Sciences D' Outre-Mer, 1936.

Laman, Eduart Karl. *The Kongo*, 4 vols. Stockholm: Victor Pettersons, 1953.

MacGaffey, Wyatt. *Religion and Society in Central Africa: The Bakongo of Lower Zaire*. Chicago: University of Chicago Press, 1986.

MacGaffey, Wyatt. *Astonishment & Power*. Washington: Smithsonian Institution Press, 1993.

Mantuba-Ngoma, Mabiala. *Frauen, Kunsthandwerk und Kultur bei den Yombe in Zaïre*. Göttingen, Germany: Edition Re, 1989.

Masolo, D. A. *African Philosophy in Search of Identity*. Bloomington: Indiana University Press, 1994.

McCracken, Grant. *Culture & Consumption*. Bloomington: Indiana University Press, 1988.

Merlet, Annie. *Autour du Loango, XIVe-XIXe siècle: histoire des peuples du sud-ouest du Gabon au temps du Royaume de Loango et du "Congo français."* Libreville, Gabon: Centre culturel français Saint-Exupéry-Sépia, 1991.

Mitchel, W. J. Thomas. *Iconology: Image, Text, Ideology.* Chicago: University Chicago Press, 1986.

Mudimbe, Vumbi Y. *The Invention of Africa: Gnosis, Philosophy and the Order of Knowledge.* Bloomington: Indiana University Press, 1988.

Mudimbe, Vumbi Y. *The Idea of Africa.* Bloomington: Indiana University Press, 1994.

Stone, C. Jeffrey. *A Short History of the Cartography of Africa.* Lewiston, New York: Edwin Mellen Press, 1995.

Thompson, Robert Farris. *African Art in Motion: Icon and Act.* Berkeley: University of California Press, 1974.

Thompson, Robert Farris. *Flash of the Spirit: Afro-American, Art & Philosophy.* New York: Vintage, 1984.

Thompson, Robert Farris. *Dancing between Two Worlds: Kongo-Angola Culture and the Americas.* New York: Caribbean Cultural Center, 1991.

Wilden, Anthony. *System and Structure.* London: Tavistock Publications, 1972.

BARBARO MARTINEZ-RUIZ

CARVING. *See* Arts: Sculpture.

CASABLANCA.

Casablanca (in Arabic, *al-Dar al-Bayda*), with a population of 3.5 million in 2004, is Morocco's main port and largest city. Situated on the Atlantic Ocean, Morocco's road and rail networks radiate from the city. Casablanca began to assume economic importance in the nineteenth century when it became a major supplier of wool to Britain's growing textile industry. At the beginning of the twentieth century its population grew to 20,000. Riots broke out in 1907 when the French built a rail line through a graveyard; this gave the French the excuse they needed to assume direct control of the city prior to the onset of formal French colonial rule (1912–1956). By 1936 Casablanca's population had grown to 260,000; one-third of its inhabitants were European. By 1963 the city had more than 1 million residents, although its European population had dropped to less than 10 percent and has fallen ever

since. Brutally suppressed political protests during the 1960s and 1970s, a major demonstration for women's rights that drew 40,000 in 2000 (quickly followed by a counter-demonstration of half a million women), and terrorist attacks on May 16, 2003, indicate the city's continuing importance as a barometer of Moroccan politics and society. Casablanca remains a magnet for rural immigrants because of its continuing economic growth and a center of modern cultural life.

See also **Morocco.**

BIBLIOGRAPHY

Adam, André. *Casablanca: Essai sue la transformation de la société marocaine au contact de l'Occident.* Paris: Éditions du Centre National de la Recherche Scientifique, 1972.

Ossman, Susan. *Picturing Casablanca: Portraits of Power in a Modern City.* Berkeley: University of California Press, 1972.

DALE F. EICKELMAN

CASELY-HAYFORD, JOSEPH EPHRAIM

(1866–1930). Joseph Ephraim Casely-Hayford, originally named Ekra Agyiman, spent most of his life fighting for African political representation in British West Africa while fostering the Africanization of education and improved social standards for Africans. He was born at Cape Coast (in the Gold Coast, present-day Ghana) into the Fante nation on September 28, 1866. His father was the Reverend Joseph de Graft Hayford.

From November 1885 to December 1887 he assisted his uncle, James Hutton Brew, known as Prince Brew of Dunkwa, in producing a Cape Coast periodical, *Western Echo.* He then ran the *Gold Coast Echo* from 1888 to 1889 and later on managed the *Gold Coast Leader*, published from 1902 to 1934. Educated at Wesleyan Boys High School at Cape Coast, Fourah Bay College in Sierra Leone, and at Cambridge University, he became a lawyer in 1896. In England he married a woman from the Gold Coast, Beatrice Madeline Pinnock, who died in 1902. In 1903, although still mourning the loss of his first wife, he wed Adelaide Smith, of Freetown, Sierra Leone. Together they had a daughter, Gladys. The marriage ended in divorce in 1914.

Casely-Hayford was a member of the Gold Coast's legislative council from 1916 to 1926, a municipal member of the council from Sekondi (1927–1930), and a principal at the Wesleyan Boys High School in Accra. He also founded the Aborigines' Rights Protection Society and the Gold Coast National Research Center in Sekondi with the goal of eliminating a strictly white perspective from the African experience.

Casely-Hayford was a prolific writer, and many of his works focused on the institutions and beliefs of West Africa's indigenous peoples. His work was dedicated to eradicating the European misconception of Africa as a land of "savages," and replacing it with an accurate image of peoples who possessed sophisticated cultural traditions fully compatible with "modernity." Among his writings are *Gold Coast Native Institutions* (1903), *Ethiopia Unbound* (1911), and *United West Africa* (1919).

See also **Colonial Policies and Practices.**

BIBLIOGRAPHY

Cromwell, Adelaide M. *An African Victorian Feminist: The Life and Times of Adelaide Smith Casely Hayford 1868–1960.* London: Cass, 1986.

Ofosu-Appiah, L. H. *Joseph Ephraim Casely-Hayford: The Man of Vision and Faith.* Accra-Tema: Ghana Publishing Corporation for the Ghana Academy of Arts and Science, 1975.

GARY THOULOUIS

CASTE SYSTEMS. *See* **Stratification, Social.**

CENTRAL AFRICAN FEDERATION. *See* **Colonial Policies and Practices: British Central Africa; Malawi; Zambia; Zimbabwe.**

CENTRAL AFRICAN REPUBLIC

This entry includes the following articles:
GEOGRAPHY AND ECONOMY
SOCIETY AND CULTURES
HISTORY AND POLITICS

GEOGRAPHY AND ECONOMY

The Central African Republic boasts great ecological diversity, from deserts to rainforests. However, the country's economy has suffered from transport problems, French domination during the colonial era between 1890 and 1960, and financially irresponsibile authoritarian governments since independence.

GEOGRAPHY

With an area of 240,324 square miles, the Central African Republic boasts of some of the most diverse ecological zones in a single country on the entire continent. Much of the region is part of the larger Benue River ecological zone, a topography of undulating hills that average between 2,000 and 2,500 feet above sea level. Lush rainforests grow near the Ubangi and Mbomou Rivers on the country's southern borders. Sudano-Sahelian regions, such as the Adamawa Plateau in the far western part of the country and the Bongo massif in the remote northeast, make a mountainous contrast to the woodlands and wooded savannas in much of the country. The Salamat marshes along the Chadian-Central African border and much of the northern savannas have an arid, Sahelian climate. The Shari (Chari) River and its affluents in the north, along with the Ubangi and Mbomou Rivers that pass through the southern forests, have served as major commercial routes for centuries.

Rainfall varies from very slight amounts in the far north to very wet conditions in the south. Many rivers in the north are part of the Lake Chad River basin, while the Ubangi and its affluents are part of the Congo River basin. The rainy season lasts from April to October. Although rains in northern CAR often are less than 20 inches per year, the south (including Bangui) annually receives over 80 on average. Temperatures in the north average in the 70s during the dry season; during the rainy season they climb to over 100 in the north and hover in the 90s in the south. The region has abundant natural resources, including salt and ebony, which promoted trade between different parts of the region in the precolonial era.

When French authorities entered central Africa in the 1890s, the region was divided. Yakoma,

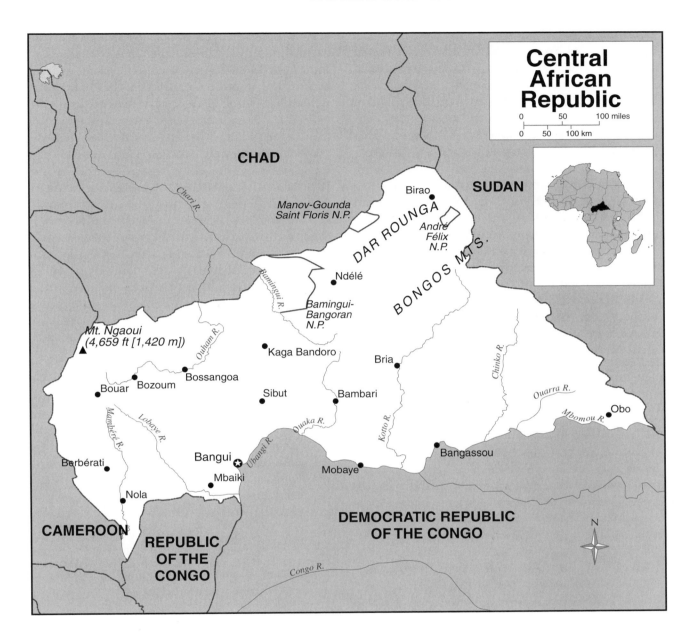

Banziri, and other river communities had ties with communities farther south, while the Zande and Nzakara warlords along the Mbomou had longstanding routes that connected them to the Sudan. To the north, Chadian and Sudanese slave raiders followed paths that linked them to much of the western and northern grasslands.

The French campaign to build roads in the early 1900s proved a heavy burden on the local communities that were expected to provide the manpower. French officials and privately owned companies used troops to collect villagers for extended forced labor details through 1946. The road network that resulted, however, became the envy of other colonies in French Equatorial Africa by the 1920s; in addition to improving transportation, it also spread Sango as the country's lingua franca. However, the colossal mismanagement of public funds under Presidents David Dacko, Jean-Bédel Bokassa, André Kolingba, and Ange-Félix Patassé from the early 1960s to 2003 left many roads in ruins. The country's regions have become increasingly isolated as a result.

ECONOMY

On the eve of French colonial occupation in the 1890s, Central Africans relied on farming, fishing (especially along the rivers), hunting, and slave trading as central parts of their economy. Slave raiding led to widespread dislocation and violence throughout the region, as did French efforts to defeat both anticolonial guerrilla movements and the northern sultanate of Dar el-Kuti. French colonial authorities allowed poorly financed concessionary companies to form large fiefdoms throughout the colony between 1900 and the late 1930s. These companies relied on extortion and intimidation to obtain ivory and other natural resources. Administrators seeking cheap labor to build the Congo-Océan railroad in French Congo forced thousands of Central Africans into labor details; disease and poor treatment killed thousands in the 1920s. The 1928 Kongo Wara revolt in the western part of Central Africa, the largest rebellion in French colonial history in Africa, was brought on by the harsh economy policies set by the government.

French authorities decided to make Central Africa a major exporter of cotton in 1924. This program also relied on force, as the government set an artificially low price on cotton throughout the colony and employed African agents to compel villages to grow the crop. Much as in Portuguese Mozambique, cotton became synonymous with exploitation and tyranny among Central Africans. Cotton remained the biggest crop in the colony through independence in 1960, but state authorities gradually abandoned supporting its cultivation by the 1970s. Southern forests along the Ubangi River along with scattered sisal coffee plantations never challenged cotton's harsh reign.

Diamonds became the one rival to cotton that eventually overtook the crop in economic importance, although timber concessions in the south have continued to produce wood for export. In the thinly populated plains of the eastern Central African Republic near the town of Bria, a French prospector discovered diamond deposits in 1913. French companies began to mine these diamond deposits in earnest in the early 1940s, and a rural mining economy developed and produced 150,000 carats annually by the mid-1950s. Diamonds became the most lucrative export in the postcolonial period. Jean-Bédel Bokassa, who ruled from 1965 to 1981, enriched himself largely through diamond profits.

Unfortunately, the rest of the country's economy remained sluggish throughout the postcolonial period, especially due to corruption and the willingness of foreign (especially French) backers to fund Bokassa and other dictators. Central Africa is among the poorest countries in the world. The unrest that engulfed Central Africa between 1996 and 2004, along with incursions by armed groups from Congo and Chad, further weakened the country's economy. According to 2005 World Bank statistics, the GDP of the Central African Republic is 1.2 billion. Economic growth in 2005 was 1.3 percent, as opposed to a 7.3 percent decline in 2004. Agriculture makes up 53.9 percent of GDP, followed by 24.8 percent in services and 21.4 percent in industries (especially diamonds). Since diamond, gold, and ivory smuggling are common, these statistics may not reflect accurately the value of Central African exports. Thirty-eight percent of the population lives in poverty, and the country's foreign debt is 926 million dollars.

See also **Bokassa, Jean-Bédel; Colonial Policies and Practices; Slave Trades; World Bank.**

BIBLIOGRAPHY

Coquery-Vidrovitch, Catherine. *Le Congo aux temps des grandes compagnies concessionaires, 1898–1930*. Paris: Plon, 1972.

Kalck, Pierre. *Histoire de la République Centrafricaine*. Paris: Berger-Levrault, 1974.

M'Bokolo, Elikia. "Comparisons and Contrasts in Equatorial Africa: Gabon, Congo, and the Central African Republic." In *History of Central Africa: The Contemporary Years*, ed. David Birmingham and Phyllis Martin. New York: Longman, 1998.

O'Toole, Thomas. *The Central African Republic: The Continent Hidden Heart*. Boulder, CO: Westview, 1986.

World Bank Group. Central African Data Profile. Available at http://devdata.worldbank.org/external/CPProfile.asp?CCODE=CAF&PTYPE=CP.

JEREMY RICH

SOCIETY AND CULTURES

The Central African Republic (CAR) has long been a crucible for multiple cultural and economic forces within Africa. Anthropological work has perhaps been most complete concerning the cultural ecology and changing music of Pygmy (Ba Mbenga or Aka, population about 20,000). Historical work, on the other hand, chronicles Bantu speakers' and then Europeans' expansion into the region. Only now are crosscutting studies emerging that can chronicle the vibrant and widely varying exchange relations among and across different peoples in the CAR, where groups have retained their own languages and identities as distinct from their neighbors while becoming interdependent for their diverse economic livelihoods. This is true not only for southern foragers and farmers, but also for seminomadic pastoralists such as the dispersed Fulbe (or Mbororo, population about 17,000), who trade with horticulturalists and hunters such as the Gbaya (population about 350,000) in the northwest. Other major ethnolinguistic groups include the Banda (400,000) in the central and eastern areas, Mbum or Mboum (80,000) in the north, Zande (20,000) of the southeast, and Islamized Hausa traders throughout the country (10,000). The smaller but politically influential groups that live along the Oubangui River and forged early and enduring relationships with European colonizers include the Yakoma, Banziri, Sango, Bobangui, Buraka, and Mbaka.

To name the hundreds of specific different ethnic groups that inhabit the CAR would be impossible. It is worth noting that the variations among them, along with the country's geographical location at all sorts of African crossroads, have generated cultural traditions of remarkable richness and variety. These traditions reflect and express strong rural economies that mix horticulture, hunting, gathering, seminomadic pastoralism, animal husbandry, beekeeping, fishing, and commerce. These practices function across Muslim, Christian, and Animist faiths, through complex systems dominated by structures of clan, kinship, and intergroup accommodation. Musically, they are almost all characterized by a contrast between social music, sung by large groups or even the entire community, and individual songs that emphasize particular expression of form, thought, and feeling accompanied by instruments such as small harps. There are few specialized musicians in these traditions, and this bears out the emphasis in many of the CAR's culture groups on highly fluid and subtle social structures that eschew permanent political hierarchies in favor of contextual emergence of leadership by individuals and the attendant fission and fusion of groups.

These internal and intergroup dynamics, punctuated by ritual warfare with its own complement of musical and oratorical performances, have since at least the seventh century been confronted with the expansion of overlapping empires from the northern regions of Lake Chad, Darfur, and Baguirmi. As northern sultanates extended their reach into this heart of Africa (*Be Afrika*, in the national language, is the vernacular name of the country), the Atlantic slave trade also intensified. Their unfortunate intersection in the mid- to late-1800s in the current territory of the CAR caused fighting, flight, and fear among inhabitants. It also entailed the arrival of new migrants into the area, including many groups from farther south who were, in turn, fleeing slavery or the forced labor brought on by early French colonial trade and expansion. Many Central Africans call this period in their history *bira*; it is recounted in oral histories as well as in the national literature, as in novelist Étienne Goyémidé's (1942–1997) 1985 account of the ravages of slave trading: *Le dernier survivant de la caravane*, or *The Last Survivor of the Caravan*.

The brief period of colonial rule in the 1900s was marked by simmering revolts against French rule, the most significant of which—the Kongo Wara rebellions—represented a significant and historically neglected challenge to the consolidation of colonial rule. By the mid-1900s, however, a concession-based economy based on a combination of agricultural plantations, rubber harvesting and planting operations, and the production of commodities such as cotton and tobacco, had taken hold.

Jean-Bédel Bokassa, a young man from the southwest, saw his own father die at the hands of concession company managers, and subsequently lost his mother as well. He became a soldier, decorated for his service to France in Indochina, and became close to several key French political elites, notably Valéry Giscard D'Estaing (b. 1926). By late 1976, Bokassa had crowned himself emperor of the CAR. His tyrannical reign is a powerful and problematic example of the CAR residents' struggles to make meaning for the nation from the violence of colonialism, and from the combined symbolic repertoires of Europe and Africa. The resultant cultural forms include the novels of Goyemide, paintings by artists such as Clément Marie Biazin (1924–1981), and the vital tradition of theatrical

République Centrafricaine (Central African Republic)

Population:	4,369,038 (2007 est.)
Area:	622,436 sq. km (240,324 sq. mi.)
Official language:	Sangho
Languages:	French, Arabic, Hunsa, Swahili
National currency:	CFA franc
Principal religions:	Protestant 25%, Roman Catholic 25%, Muslim 15%, indigenous beliefs 35%
Capital:	Bangui (est. pop. 690,000 in 2006)
Other urban centers:	Berberati, Bouar, Bambari, Bangassou, Bossangoa, Mbaiki, Carnot
Annual rainfall:	varies from 1,900 mm (75 in.) in the south to 50 mm (2 in.) in extreme northeast
Principal geographical features:	*Mountains:* Mount Ngaoui, Yade Massif, Bongo Massif *Rivers:* Chinko, Mbari, Kotto, Ouaka, Lobaye, Mambere, Kadai, Ouham, Bamingui, Sangha, Ubangi, Mbomou
Economy:	*GDP per capita:* US$1,100 (2006)
Principal products and exports:	*Agricultural:* cotton, coffee, tobacco, manioc (tapioca), yams, millet, corn, bananas, timber *Manufacturing:* brewing, textiles, footwear, assembly of bicycles and motorcycles *Mining:* diamonds, uranium, gold
Government:	Independence from France, 1960. Constitution adopted, 1981. New constitution adopted in 1986, another passed in 1994 then suspended by decree in 2003. New constitution passed by referendum 2004. Multiparty republic. President is elected for a 6-year term by universal suffrage. 85-seat unicameral Assemblée Nationale elected for 5-year terms by universal suffrage. President appoints prime minister and Council of Ministers. For purposes of local government there are 16 subprefectures headed by subprefecture councils, and 174 rural communes headed by municipal councils.
Heads of state since independence:	1959–1966: President David Dacko 1966–1967: Colonel (later General, then Field Marshall) Jean-Bédel Bokassa, Chairman of the Revolutionary Council 1967–1976: President Jean-Bédel Bokassa 1976–1979: Emperor Bokassa I 1979–1981: President David Dacko 1981–1985: General André Kolingba, Chairman of the Military Committee for National Recovery 1985–1993: President André Kolingba 1993–2003: President Ange-Félix Patassé 2003–: President Francois Bozize
Armed forces:	President is commander in chief. Voluntary enlistment. *Army:* 2,500 *Air force:* 150 *Paramilitary:* 2,300 *Foreign forces (French):* 1,300. France is obligated by a 1960 treaty to provide defense against external threats.
Transportation:	*River ports:* Bangui, Ouango, Salo, Nola *Roads:* 23,738 km (14,750 mi.), 2% paved *National airline:* Inter-RCA. The Central African Republic has a 6% share in Air Afrique. *Airports:* Bangui International Airport. In total, 50 airports throughout the country.
Media:	Five daily private newspapers and 1 state-owned biweekly. No significant book publishing. State-controlled Radiodiffusion Télévision Centrafrique provides both radio and television broadcasting services.
Literacy and education:	*Total literacy rate:* 50% (2006). Education is free, universal, and compulsory for ages 6–14. Postsecondary education provided at the Université de Bangui and numerous technical schools.

forms for entertainment and social commentary in Bangui and beyond. These forms combine oral and written elements of expression, and create powerful emotional impressions that range from lamentation to celebration of the colonial past. Much such work also evidences powerful contradictions, for instance subversive mimicry of French conventions.

But postcolonial cultural production has suffered the fate of many African states in the wake of international policies of structural adjustment. The 1980s were a period of relative peace and stability for the CAR, under General Kolingba's single-party system. Its motto was *maboko oko a mu siri na li ti zo pepe*, or, a single hand cannot delouse a head. The regime's discontents gained little political traction due to widespread residual fear that tyranny could again take hold. In the meantime, the country earned revenues from renting large military bases in the northwestern city of Bouar and in Bangui to the

French armed forces, and by exporting a few and poorly controlled key resources such as alluvial diamonds, timber, and gum arabic. Civil servants were often unpaid, and the country's formal educational system struggled with several *annee blanche scolaires*, or missed school years, for lack of funds. As a result, time-honored practices of informal education and initiation that had been curtailed during colonialism have endured in many rural sectors.

In the early twenty-first century, the social makeup of the CAR is under considerable strain from the proliferation in transnational trades in small arms, mineral wealth, and wildlife that tear at the fabric of family life by requiring migration on various scale, and fostering a disturbing trend toward violent banditry in rural areas. Against a backdrop of geopolitical intrigue and international humanitarian failure, much of the mostly rural CAR remains a crucible for historically rooted traditions that incorporate and contribute to transnational economies and cultures in their own particular ways. Economic and political arrangements among identity groups who increasingly compete for resources such as land and water continue to be forged, often across vast and increasingly militarized spaces. Such practices enable the country, though desperately poor, to be well provisioned in a wide variety of foodstuffs including fruits, vegetables, cereals, honey, game meat, cattle, and significant insect proteins that are gathered seasonally, even in Bangui, and prepared in traditional recipes with seed meats and spices. In summary, the resilient and productive societies and cultures of the CAR remain dramatically under-studied, but may be crucial to the CAR's avoidance, until now, of the sorts of large-scale conflicts so common in neighboring countries.

See also **Bokassa, Jean-Bédel; Colonial Policies and Practices; Popular Culture; Slave Trades.**

BIBLIOGRAPHY

Arom, Simha. Liner notes to the recording *Central African Republic: Music of the Dendi, Nzakara, Banda-Linda, Gbaya, Banda-Dakpa, Ngbaka, Aka.* Paris: United Nations Educational, Scientific and Cultural Organization, 1989.

Bahuchet, Serge. *Les pygmees aka et la foret centrafricaine: ethnologie ecologique.* Paris: Selaf, 1985.

Cantournet, Jean. *Des affaires et des hommes: noirs et blancs, commerçants et fonctionnaires dans loOubangui du début du siècle.* Paris: Société d'ethnologie, 1991.

Giles-Vernick, Tamara. *Cutting the Vines of the Past: Environmental Histories of the Central African Rain Forest.* Charlottesville: University Press of Virginia, 2002.

Goyemidé, Etienne. *Le silence de la foret.* Paris: Hatier, 1984.

Goyemidé, Etienne. *Le dernier survivant de la caravane.* Paris: Hatier, 1985.

Kisliuk, Michelle. *Seize the Dance!: BaAka Musical Life and the Ethnography of Performance.* Oxford: Oxford University Press, 1998.

Laude, Jean. *Clement Marie Biazin: Esquisses pour une encyclopedie Biazine.* Paris: Museum des Arts d'Afrique et d'Oceanie, et Cooperation Française, 1994.

Vidal, Pierre. *Garcons et filles: le passage a l'age d'homme chez les Gbaya Kara.* Paris: Labethno (Recherches Oubanguiennes), 1976.

REBECCA HARDIN

HISTORY AND POLITICS

Economists agree that the Central African Republic (CAR) could be one of the wealthiest countries on the continent. However, its estimated annual economic growth rate was only 0.5 percent in 2004. Much of its soil is suited to agriculture, and its mostly untapped mineral and forest resources are vast. Its animal kingdom could enhance tourism and provide for a meat industry. However, the problems are many, and include mismanagement of resources, unnecessary projects such as the US$20 million inauguration of Jean-Bédel Bokassa as emperor in 1977, the country's failed centralized five-year plans, and the weak infrastructure inherited from the colonial past. There is, for example, no railroad in the country. The number of salaried and wage earners is a little over 140,000, of whom some 80,000 are employed in the public sector and 35,000 are industrial workers. The country's per capita income is estimated at US$226. France plays a major role in the economic sector—providing investment, budget subsidies, mineral extraction, and technical assistance. During the early years of the new century, for example, France provided some US$73 million in aid annually.

AGRICULTURE, LIVESTOCK, FORESTRY, AND MINING

About 75 percent of Central Africans are engaged in subsistence agriculture. While the north cultivates sorghum and millet, the south produces corn, peanuts, rice, cassava, yams, bananas, cotton, and coffee. Agriculture accounts for 55 percent of the gross domestic product (GDP). Cotton (since the 1920s) and coffee (concentrated in the southwest) are the major export crops. Cotton, the Central African Republic's largest crop, engages 280,000 farmers. Both crops are grown both by French expatriates and by individual African farmers and account for 35–60 percent of the country's exports. Recent memories of forced cultivation of these low-priced cash crops explain the scant enthusiasm they generate among farmers. Tobacco is also grown in certain regions of the country and accounts for 5 percent of total export earnings. In the tsetse-free areas, Central Africans raise cattle, sheep, goats, and pigs.

The Central African Republic is endowed with vast amounts of hardwood (35.8 million hectares of tropical rain forest), which could easily become the most important export item. Timber contributes 30 percent to export-earned revenue. Gold has been extracted since the 1950s, while diamond mining employs some 50,000 people and accounts for as much as 54 percent of exports. The Central African Republic is also rich in uranium, copper, iron, limestone, manganese, chalk, peat, coal, and mercury. Overall, mining contributes about 3.6 percent to the country's GDP.

INDUSTRY, TRADE, AND SERVICE

The Central African Republic has no heavy industry but only light industry that is dominated by food, sugar, and fiber processing plants, breweries, textiles, leather and shoe factories, and paint, brick, and household utensil plants. The industrial sector accounts for 20 percent of the GDP. Exports of coffee, cotton, diamond, and timber are not enough to offset the heavy imports of foodstuffs, durable goods, and petroleum. The service sector accounts for 25 percent of the country's GDP. The major trading partners are Belgium, Italy, Spain, Indonesia, France, the United States, and the four members of the Central African Customs and Economic Union (UDEAC), who share a central bank and a currency. Since its devaluation in 1994, 100 CFA francs exchange for a fixed rate of one French franc. The Central African Republic is a member of the Organisation Commune Africaine et Malgache (OCAM) and the Communauté Économique des États de l'Afrique Centrale (CEEAC).

What are the future prospects? Austerity measures, careful exploration of natural and human resources, and a reduction of the international debt (which rose from $185 million in 1980 to $901 million in 1992; and to almost $1 billion in 2005, with a budget of $226 million in 2002). The transportation system (which consists mainly of a few airstrips including the international airport at Bangui and a 14,750-mile road network) also needs accelerated improvement. The Structural Adjustment Program which CAR has accepted from the International Monetary Fund and the World Bank has done very little to improve the people's standard of living.

HEALTH AND EDUCATION

The country's population growth rate (1.1% annually) is tempered by a weak health care program, which receives less than 10 percent of the GDP. There is only one major hospital in the country, located in Bangui, while tropical diseases are endemic and often epidemic. Education, which is compulsory and free for ages six to fourteen, gets less than 15 percent of the annual national budget. Thus the school record is unimpressive (according to the 1998 figures, the most recent one provided by the government): 284,398 children in 930 primary schools taught by 3,125 teachers. The 20 secondary schools, taught by 1,317 teachers, enroll only 49,147 students, while the University of Bangui (with a staff of 300) had some 6,229 students. The Central African Republic's literacy rate for those fifteen years of age and above is 43 percent, even though sources differ on this number.

HISTORY

The Central African Republic is a former French African colony known, until independence on August 13, 1960, as Oubangui-Chari. Prior to the French colonization, which began during the 1880s, this area was devastated by slave raids carried out by powerful Sahelian Islamic states. From the first millennium to the late nineteenth century, Oubangui-Chari remained a crossroads of cultures and lifestyles. Paul Crampel's 1891 expedition and the work of French military adventurers imposed treaties of submission on the African chiefs and sultans. After creating the Oubangui post in 1889, the French proclaimed Oubangui-Chari a colony in 1894.

As was common practice among the colonial powers, in 1899 the French introduced concessionary companies in Equatorial Africa. Under the system, the infamous Sangha-Oubangui Society held a monopoly over the exploitation of rubber, timber, and minerals. The use of the corvée beginning in the 1890s, the introduction of taxation in 1902, the forcible recruitment of workers who were poorly paid if paid at all, military conscription, the obligation to grow cash crops such as cotton, and the abuses perpetrated by company agents and the *commandants de cercle* sparked a cycle of revolts among the indigenous peoples, most notably the Baya and the Mandja, in 1909–1911 and during the 1928–1945 period.

The statutes that abolished the *système d'indigénat* in 1946 and proclaimed all Africans French citizens, allowing them to form political parties and establish a territorial assembly, were welcome. These reforms and the *loi-cadre* (enabling law) of 1956, which eliminated the dual electoral college, bred new life into the colony's politics reflected in the parties that sprang up, including the Union Oubanguienne (UO), the Mouvement d'Évolution Sociale de l'Afrique Noire (MESAN) of Catholic priest Barthélemy Boganda, and others. In November 1946, Oubanguians sent their first African representative to the French National Assembly, Boganda, who also became the colony's first prime minister in 1959.

After Boganda's death in an airplane crash in 1959, David Dacko, his cousin, assumed the presidency of the new country, proclaimed the Central African Republic (CAR) in 1958. Dacko introduced a single-party system in 1962, but he was overthrown in 1966 by his cousin Captain Jean-Bédel Bokassa, who presided over one of the most brutal, corrupt, and wasteful regimes in Africa. In 1977, Bokassa crowned himself emperor of the Central African Empire. Discontent with the regime culminated with riots in Bangui in 1979, sparked by the president's participation in the massacres of schoolchildren whose parents had refused to buy school uniforms from the president's private store. On September 20–21, French troops occupied the national airport and the city of Bangui and reinstated Dacko as president. Popular pressure, following the failed presidential elections of March 15, 1981, forced Dacko to hand over power to

General André Dieudonné Kolingba on September 1, 1981. Kolingba suspended the constitution. An attempted coup by military supporters of Bokassa's former prime minister, Ange Patassé, on March 3, 1982, led Kolingba to institute more repressive measures. Under a November 21, 1986, constitution, Kolingba, supported by his Rassemblement Démocratique Centrafricain (RDC), was elected president for a six-year term.

Under Kolingba the economy had deteriorated, and conditions attached to several loans from the World Bank and the International Monetary Fund (IMF) during the early 1980s and 1990s exacerbated the situation. (In 1994, for example, the IMF provided the CAR with US$23 million.) Austerity measures, arrears in civil servants' salaries, and a return to oppressive politics caused riots and strikes led by the Union Syndicale des Travailleurs de la Centrafrique (USTC). In response to the unrest, Kolingba convened a National Debate Conference in August 1992, which eventually resulted in Supreme Court-annulled multiparty presidential elections that had pitted candidates David Dacko, Ange-Félix Patassé, Abel Goumba, and Enoch Durant Lakoue against Kolingba.

In August 1993, monitored presidential and legislative elections finally took place: 37.3 percent of the votes cast went to Patassé, 21.7 percent to Goumba, 20.1 percent to Dacko, and only 12.1 percent to Kolingba. Kolingba (as well as Dacko at first) attempted to challenge the results, but the French demanded that he accept the popular verdict. The second round, or the runoff elections, held on September 19, 1993, gave Patassé, the new president, 52.5 percent of the vote and Goumba 45.6 percent. On the other hand, the second round of the legislative contest resulted in thirty-four seats going to the Mouvement pour la Libération du Peuple Centrafricain (MLPC), led by Patassé; thirteen to the Rassemblement Démocratique Centrafricain (RDC) of André Kolingba; seven to the Front Patriotique pour le Progrès (FPP) of Abel Goumba; seven to the Parti Libéral-Démocrate (PLD), led by Nestor Kombo-Naguemon; six to David Dacko's Mouvement pour la Démocratie et le Développement (MDD); six to the Alliance pour la Démocratie et le Progrès (ADP); and twelve to the remaining seven small parties.

Kolingba had freed Bokassa on September 1, 1993. Bokassa had been tried and condemned to death for murder, a sentence that Kolingba commuted to forced labor. As a result, Patassé appointed a commission to look into Kolingba's abuses as head of state. Kolingba was stripped of his military rank in March 1994.

Patassé's tenure was soon challenged by the several chronic problems he had promised but was unable to resolve, including salary arrears for government employees, better labor conditions, and ethnic discrimination in the Armed Forces. As a result, during 1996 and 1997, protests, violence, and mutinies erupted in Bangui, forcing the President to call for French military assistance. The move was successful and the UN entrusted the mission of peacekeeping to African troops who occupied Bangui until 1998. As soon as they left, however, violence erupted once again and continued until 2001. Gen. Kolingba attempted a coup in May 2001 but Libyan forces and troops from the rebel Movement for the Liberation of the Congo (MLC), joining the loyal troops, crushed the insurgency.

At this juncture, the government had dismissed the chief of staff of the Armed Forces, François Bozize, who was able to seek refuge in Chad, the northern neighboring country. His escape led to intermittent skirmishes between government troops and those loyal to Bozize. Bozize succeeded in overthrowing the government while Patassé was aboard, and declared himself President in March 2003. Bozize suspended the constitution, dissolved the National Assembly, and established a National Transition Committee that would lead to a constitutional referendum on December 5, 2004 (to be adopted December 24, 2004), and to presidential and legislative elections on March 13, 2005. There were eleven presidential candidates, including Gen. Bozize. No one got the absolute majority and a run-off election was scheduled for May 2005. The same applied to the legislative elections. Bozize won the run-off election and he and his government were subsequently installed.

GOVERNMENT
The Central African Republic's 1992 constitution provided for a presidential system, with an independent judiciary and a congress. The president, elected by an absolute majority through direct universal suffrage for a five-year term, is also commander in chief of the 3,000-man armed forces. The president may dissolve the legislature and call for new elections. He also appoints a prime minister who presides over the Council of Ministers (there were twenty-four ministries in 2005). The legislature comprises the National Assembly, whose 109 delegates are elected by universal suffrage for five-year terms, and the advisory Economic and Regional Council. Half of the council members are appointed by the president and half by the National Assembly. Administratively, the Central African Republic is divided into sixteen prefectures. Bangui is administered separately

The judiciary is made up of a supreme court, a court of appeals, a criminal court, sixteen Tribunals of High "Instance," thirty-seven Tribunals of "Instance," six labor courts, a permanent military tribunal, and a high court for crimes against the state. Politically, Dacko declared the MESAN the only legal party in 1962. In 1981, a multiparty constitution was approved but Kolingba scrapped all democratic initiatives, although opposition parties, such as Goumba's Front Patriotique Oubanguien-Parti du Travail (FPO-PT) and Patassé's Mouvemerit pour la Libération du Peuple Centrafricain (MLPC), did not disappear. After 1987, the Central African Republic came under Kolingba's Rassemblement Démocratique Centrafricain (RDC). In 1991, the country reverted to a multiparty system, as noted above. The government controls the country's Radiodiffusion-Télévision Centrafrique and the daily *E Le Songo.*

See also **Agriculture; Bokassa, Jean-Bédel; Ecosystems; International Monetary Fund; World Bank.**

BIBLIOGRAPHY

Coquéry-Vidrovitch, Cathérine. *Le Congo au temps des grandes compagnies concessionnaires, 1898–1930.* Paris: Karthala, 1972.

Decalo, Samuel. *Psychoses of Power: African Personal Dictatorships.* Boulder, CO: Westview Press, 1989.

Englebert, Pierre. "Recent History [Central African Republic]." In *Africa: South of the Sahara.* London: Europa Publishers, 2005.

Gide, André *My Travels in the Congo.* Berkeley: University of California Press, 1927.

Hubbard, Diana. "Economy [Central African Republic]." In *Africa: South of the Sahara*, 265–268. London: Europa Publishers, 1995.

Kalck, Pierre. *Central African Republic.* New York: Praeger, 1971.

Kalck, Pierre. *Historical Dictionary of the Central African Republic.* Metuchen, NJ: Scarecrow Press, 2005.

O'Toole, Thomas. *The Central African Republic: The Continent's Hidden Heart.* Boulder, CO: Westview Press, 1986.

Thompson, Virginia, and Richard Adloff. *The Emerging States of French Equatorial Africa.* Stanford, CA: Stanford University Press, 1960.

MARIO J. AZEVEDO

CERAMICS. Pottery is among the oldest arts of Africa. In Kenya it is documented from the Upper Paleolithic era and in Saharan sites from as far back as the eighth millennium BCE. Its prevalence is in part accounted for by the wide availability of clay across Africa, where it is a very versatile material. Apart from its use in the manufacture of vessels for cooking, storing, and measuring bulk items, clay in various forms is also used to make jewelry, wigs, furniture, paint, coffins, beehives, toys, essential elements of architecture, sieves, grindstones, musical instruments—even rattraps. At the other end of its career, pottery has value in its broken form as gaming chips, floor tiles, spindle weights, roundels, and grog (powdered terra-cotta to temper clay) for making new pots.

Although molds may nowadays be used in industrial production, sub-Saharan pottery has traditionally been handmade without the use of the wheel. The technical simplicity of African pottery has made possible the existence of itinerant potters. Modern analyses have tended to stress the distinctiveness of traditional pottery styles rather than the ways in which they overlap and interrelate. Common traditional techniques include coiling, pulling, and beating (where a depression in the ground or an old pot may be used as a form for new pots.) Such techniques, while extremely simple, require great manual skill and produce pottery more quickly, inexpensively, and of greater strength than is possible on a wheel. Baking may be done over an open bonfire or in fires using retaining walls or pits, or in simple kilns.

Decorative finishes come from burnishing, incised patterning, roulettes, colored slips, and vegetable infusions. African pottery combines total utility and great beauty.

Those west African cultures studied by art historians—Jenné, Sao, Igbo-Ukwu, Nok, and Ife—are known among other things for their terra-cotta works, which show great continuity with contemporary pots. Igbo-Ukwu pottery of the ninth and tenth centuries, for example, shows strong stylistic similarities with modern Igbo forms.

The West normally divides clay objects into the figurative (art) and the functional (craft). The distinction coincides approximately with one often made in Africa between figurative forms, which are largely made by men, and functional vessels made by women. It is a widely held belief in Africa that making images of animals or men in clay endangers female procreative powers. Domestic pots are overwhelmingly made by women and the physical skills involved—kneading, grinding, plastering—are often those gained elsewhere in female life. Potting in Africa has few of the genteel associations it has in the West. It is demanding physical labor, and pots must often be transported for long distances before sale. Yet the male/female distinction is far from hard and fast and in terms of local gender definitions, postmenopausal or politically and ritually powerful women may well be classed as male. Since such women are allowed to make images, much early ethnography becomes difficult to interpret; to understand the rules of pottery production, age as well as sex must be known.

In eastern Africa, women may model images but only in unbaked clay, as among the Cewa. It is clear that in contemporary Africa, traditional divisions between male and female modeling have had to be stretched to cope with the successful introduction of cement sculpture. To determine which gender makes it, a decision must be made about whether it is pottery or sculpture, and different cultures come to different conclusions. Moreover, there are areas, such as Grasslands Cameroon, where both genders pot but use different techniques. Women may form clay while men carve it. Since earliest contacts, however, Europeans have found that the most publicly important pots tend to be made exclusively by a few old women and have wrongly taken this as firm evidence that pottery in Africa is an art form about to disappear.

A potter in Morocco throws a pot in the traditional way. Today, molds are often used in mass production of pottery. Yet, traditional pottery that wasn't created with a wheel or mold tends to be stronger. © Martin Harvey/Corbis

As in the West, vessels classify contents, users, and events. Palm wine is not drunk out of the bowl that sauce is cooked in. A widow might well have to use a vessel formally distinct from that of a married man or a child, so different classes of pots lend themselves to the marking off of different classes of people. Thus, the Sirak use a vegetable pot to bury the placenta of a baby girl but a meat pot for that of a boy, while a fertile mother may have her tomb marked by a flour storage bowl. While he is in an urban beer hall a Zulu man might drink out of a jam jar or plastic cup, but on formal occasions he would use a burnished clay bowl with an ornate cover (*imbenge*) and demonstrate great care for the etiquette of precedence. Nowadays that cover might well be woven from multicolored telephone wire, but the patterns would be traditional. In the everyday grammar of use, African pottery competes with wooden, basketry, and calabash vessels as well as china, aluminum, and enamelware. While in some

parts of the continent pottery is being displaced by expensive imports and increasingly restricted to a ritual role, in others it is staging something of a comeback in elegant urban settings and even moving into the "art" category. The status of pottery differs across contemporary sub-Saharan Africa.

Pots are not only commodities in the African marketplace but instruments of patron-client relations. There is a widespread convention that the price of a pot is the grain that it can contain. Since their price is not subject to negotiation, pots have a special place in exchange relationships, being outside the commercial sphere.

A factor tending to complicate neat Western distinctions is that, at the village level, African pottery often moves quite easily between "ritual" and "everyday" uses. Potted vessels may act as containers of all sorts of spiritual forces, transforming domestic utensils into articles of spiritual significance. A pot that has served for years for the hauling of water may overnight become the dwelling place of a dead woman's spirit (*dowayo*), and the rough handling of a Shona woman's quite ordinary kitchen pots by her husband may be seen as the most explicit of formal insults in a complex language of female sexuality.

It is often said glibly that the West uses the models of natural science to talk about society whereas Africa uses social models to talk about nature. Yet the technology of pottery is widely used in African social thought to inform ideas of the body, life, disease, death, and female powers. It is a common basis for myths of creation but acts much more widely as what George Lakoff has termed a "scenario"—that is, a basic experience used to structure other experiences. A frequent model in west Africa is a woman who is both potter and midwife while her husband is smith and undertaker. The marginal, caste-like position of such artisanal groups—which are often endogamous, live apart, and have strongly regulated contact with outsiders—has long been something of an obsession with Western researchers. Many different arrangements for the production of pots have been documented, from individual women working alone or in groups to rigid guild-like arrangements.

The ritual importance of pottery has been almost totally obscured by a Western preoccupation with metalworking as an epoch-making male activity, the potter being seen as a mere domestic adjunct of her husband. Pottery, however, is just as likely to enter into rituals of transformation and the "thermodynamic philosophies" of cool and hot as are male metalworking skills. To generalize enormously, very broad themes can be traced across sub-Saharan cultures whereby the childbearing powers of women are seen as analogous to the potting process. Parts of bodies (especially women's) are regularly equated with pottery forms, so that death involves the breaking of old pots while marriage involves the making of new ones. Pottery, however, is a versatile idiom. Grinding down a shard from an old vessel and recasting it as part of a new one is a powerful way of creating identity through time, while the molding of new pots over old among the Senufo offers a culturally acceptable vision of the relations between successive generations.

Inevitably, this involves questions of power. Among the northern Sudanese villagers studied by

Janice Boddy, gestation is equated with the preparation of dough in a special leakproof vessel, different from the porous jar used for storing water. Miscarried fetuses are buried in such a watertight pot inside the house. In this culture of pharaonic circumcision, marriage of close kin, and inward-focused architecture, pottery reflects social boundaries and the control of female apertures.

The decoration of sub-Saharan African pottery raises fundamental questions of interpretation. Given the frequent linkage made between pots and the human form in Africa, it is hardly surprising that many of the patterns on pots are the same as those on bodies. Cicatrization is among body arts of sub-Saharan Africa most neglected by scholars, being simultaneously under attack from Islam and secular modernism. Sub-Saharan pottery similarly stresses incised or embossed differences of texture rather than color and warns us that in both pottery and the arts of the body, one may be dealing with an African aesthetic very unlike that dominant in the West, one of touch rather than vision, of the hand rather than the eye.

See also **Art; Geometries; Ife (Ile-Ife); Jenné and Jenné-jeno; Symbols and Symbolism.**

BIBLIOGRAPHY

Aschwanden, Hans. *Symbols of Life*. Zimbabwe: Mambo Press, 1982.

Barley, Nigel. *Smashing Pots: Feats of Clay from Africa*. London: British Museum Press, 1994.

Boddy, Janice. "Womb as Oasis: The Symbolic Context of Pharaonic Circumcision in Rural Northern Sudan." *American Ethnologist* 9, no. 4 (1982): 682–698.

Cline, Walter. *Mining and Metallurgy in Negro Africa*. Menasha, WI: George Banta Publishing Co., 1937.

Heusch, Luc de. "Heat, Physiology, and Cosmogeny: *Rites de Passage* among the Thonga." In *Explorations in African Systems of Thought*, ed. Ivan Karp and Charles S. Bird. Bloomington: Indiana University Press, 1980.

Lakoff, George. *Women, Fire, and Dangerous Things: What Categories Reveal about the Mind*. Chicago: University of Chicago Press, 1987.

Leith-Ross, Sylvia. *Nigerian Pottery: A Catalogue*. Ibadan, Nigeria: Ibadan University Press for the Dept. of Antiquities, 1970.

Rubin, Arnold, ed. *Marks of Civilization: Artistic Transformations of the Human Body*. Los Angeles: Museum of Cultural History, University of California, Los Angeles, 1988.

Sterner, Judy. "Who is Signaling Whom? Ceramic Style, Ethnicity, and Taphonomy among the Sirak Bulahay." *Antiquity* 63 (September 1989): 451–459.

Stössel, Arnulf. *Afrikanische Keramik: Südlich der Sahara.* Munich: Hirmer, 1984.

Yoshida, Kenji. "Masks and Transformation among the Chewa of Eastern Zambia." *Senri Ethnological Studies,* no. 31 (1992): 203–274.

NIGEL BARLEY

CÉSAIRE, AIMÉ (1913–). Born in Basse-Pointe, Aimé Césaire studied at École Normale Supérieure in Paris where he encountered bold new ideas in Marxism and surrealism. It was also here that he discovered Africa through his association with other young black intellectuals from North America, the Caribbean, and Africa, notably the Senegalese Léopold Senghor. Together with Léon Damas (1912–1978) of French Guiana, they created the movement of *Négritude*, a word Césaire coined and Senghor theorized to signify the quest to recover their lost African identity through cultural awareness and political action. Best known for *Cahier d'un retour au pays natal* (1939, 1947), arguably the foundational text of *Négritude*, and *Discours sur le colonialisme* (1955), a sharp analysis and rebuke of colonialism, Césaire also published much hermetic poetry under the influence of surrealism: *Les armes miraculeuses* (1946), *Soleil cou-coupé* (1948), and *Corps perdu* (1950). His later poetry, *Ferrements* (1960), *Cadastre* (1961), and *Moi laminaire* (1982), celebrated African independence and landscapes and heroes of the African world.

He turned to the theatre of decolonization with *Et les chiens se taisaient* (1956), *La tragédie du roi Christophe* (1963), *Une saison au Congo* (1966), and *Une tempête* (1969). Lesser known is his politico-historical essay, *Toussaint Louverture*

Aimé Césaire (1913–) with French prime minister Dominique de Villepin, Fort-de-France, October 2006. Césaire was elected mayor of Fort-de-France in 1945 and became deputy in the Constituent Assembly on the French Communist Party ticket until his resignation in 1956. OLIVIER LABAN-MATTEI/AFP/GETTY IMAGES

(1961) that links Haitian independence to the French Revolution. In 1945 Césaire was elected on the ticket of the French Communist Party as mayor of Fort-de-France and, simultaneously, as representative of Martinique to the French National Assembly. His political legacy includes his fiery *Lettre à Maurice Thorez* (1956) when he resigned from the French Communist Party for failing to condemn the Soviet Union's invasion of Hungary, and his controversial vote in 1946 to transform Martinique, Guadeloupe, and Guiana from colonies to overseas *départements*, that is, provinces of France.

See also **Decolonization; Literature: Modern Poetry; Literatures in European Languages; Senghor, Léopold Sédar.**

BIBLIOGRAPHY

Arnold, James. *Modernism and Negritude: The Poetry and Poetics of Aimé Césaire.* Cambridge, MA: Harvard University Press, 1981.

Cailler, Bernadette. *Proposition poétique: une lecture de l'œuvre d'Aimé Césaire.* Ivry-sur-Seine, France: Editions Nouvelles du Sud, 1994.

Césaire, Aimé, and Françoise Vergès. *Nègre je suis, Nègre je resterai.* Paris: Albin Michel, 2005.

Confiant, Raphaël. *Aimé Césaire. Une traversée paradoxale du siècle.* Paris: Stock, 1993.

Scharfman, Ronnie L. *Engagement and the Language of the Subject in the Poetry of Aimé Césaire.* Gainesville: University of Florida Press, 1987.

Songolo, Aliko. *Aimé Césaire: une poétique de la découverte.* Paris: L'Harmattan, 1985.

ALIKO SONGOLO

CETSHWAYO

CETSHWAYO (c. 1826–1884). Cetshwayo kaMpande was born in about 1826 to Mpande, brother of the then-ruling Zulu king, Dingane. To eliminate rivals, Dingane had had all but one of his brothers killed but, being childless and needing to ensure an heir to the throne, allowed Cetshwayo's father to survive and produce sons. Cetshwayo was thus in line for royal succession. However, Dingane's concern for the future proved to be his undoing, for Mpande seized the throne in 1840. As Cetshwayo grew up, Mpande became concerned about his eldest son's growing influence among the Zulu council of elders and instigated rivalry between Cetshwayo and one of his brothers, Mbuyazi.

In 1856 this rivalry broke into civil war between Cetshwayo and Mbuyazi. Cetshwayo proved the better warrior, and Mpande was forced to recognize him as his heir. Although Mpande retained the title of king for a while longer, in 1857 Cetshwayo assumed effective authority over the Zulu nation, and upon Mpande's death in 1872 was recognized as the new king.

Throughout his reign, Cetshwayo strove with skill and courage against irresistible colonial forces to maintain the integrity and independence of his kingdom. His policy of friendship with the neighboring British colony of Natal was designed to gain its support in his border dispute with the Transvaal. But in 1877 the British annexed the Transvaal as part of an effort to establish a confederation in

Cetshwayo (c. 1826–1884). The last independent king of the Zulus allied himself with the British until they demanded that he disband his army. His troops defeated a British detachment at Isandlwhana in 1878 but were themselves defeated at Ulundi later that year. HENRY GUTTMANN/GETTY IMAGES

southern Africa, and Cetshwayo found himself at odds with his former allies.

Cetshwayo's defiance of the confederation plan led to the Anglo-Zulu war of 1879. Although Cetshwayo fought entirely on the defensive, the British initially suffered severe losses. Opposition in Britain precluded the postwar annexation of Zululand, but Cetshwayo was sent into exile in Cape Town. He visited Britain in 1882 and convinced the new Liberal government that he was not the aggressive tyrant depicted by the local colonial officials who had insisted on going to war with him. The postwar settlement in Zululand had broken down; so, in 1883 the British government restored Cetshwayo to the Zulu throne. Colonial officials were hostile to his restoration and ensured that much of Zululand remained in the hands of his Zulu enemies, a cause of great dissatisfaction to Cetshwayo and his supporters. Civil war followed; Cetshwayo was defeated and died a refugee in Eshowe, in a part of Zululand under the control of the Natal government.

See also **Colenso, John William; Colonial Policies and Practices; Southeastern Africa, History of (1600 to 1910).**

BIBLIOGRAPHY

Cope, R. L. "Written in Characters of Blood? The Reign of King Cetshwayo ka Mpande, 1872–1879." *Journal of African History* 36, no. 1 (1995).

Guy, Jeff. *The Destruction of the Zulu Kingdom: The Civil War in Zululand, 1879–1884.* London: Longman, 1979.

R. L. COPE

CHAD

This entry includes the following articles:
GEOGRAPHY AND ECONOMY
SOCIETY AND CULTURES
HISTORY AND POLITICS

GEOGRAPHY AND ECONOMY

A former French colony, occupying a surface area of 496,000 square miles, the Republic of Chad is about three times the size of California and is the fifth largest country in Africa. Located in North-Central Africa, Chad's neighbors include Libya in the north, Central African Republic in the south, Sudan in the east, and Niger, Nigeria, and Cameroon in the west and south.

Chad's climate is diverse, with two distinct seasons (rainy, from June to October; and dry, from November to May) and four climatic zones. The humid tropical zone borders east Cameroon and Central African Republic and receives between 35 and 47 inches of rain per year. Here, the rains last from six to nine months, and the area comprises the former Prefectures of Mayo-Kebbi, Logone, and Moyen-Chari, which actually constitute a transition zone between the equatorial and tropical zones. The Sudanese, or tropical zone, receives an annual rainfall of 20–35 inches. This area also has a relatively long dry season that lasts between six and nine months on the average, with the amount of rainfall increasing as one moves northwards. The Sahelian zone appears above the Sudanese, comprising Middle Chad, has an average rainfall of 8–20 inches that is uneven from year to year, and higher average temperatures. This zone is the transition between the tropical and the desert climates. Finally, farther north lies the desert climate of the Sahara, receiving only about eight inches of rain annually, and with temperatures that vary greatly between night and day.

These climatic conditions make Chad a difficult living environment and have had a constraining impact on the country's economic conditions, contributing to poverty and an underdeveloped social and physical infrastructure. Chad consists of tropical lowlands in the south, dry mountains in the northwest, broad arid plains in the center, and hot, dry, dusty desert in the north. Both the center and north suffer from the dusty Harmattan winds, with periodic droughts, locust, and plagues. Chad's dryness is somewhat tempered by Lake Chad, at one time the second largest in Africa, but in the early twenty-first century, only 10 percent of its centuries-old pristine size. It varies from 3,861 to 9,653 square miles, depending on rainfall and the level of swelling of the Logone and Chari rivers that flow from the Sudanese zone where rainfall is as much as 36 inches a year. Before they dump their waters into the Lake, the Logone and Chari rivers pass through N'Djamena, the capital. Lake Fitri, shallow and reed-filled, is located in the south-central zone,

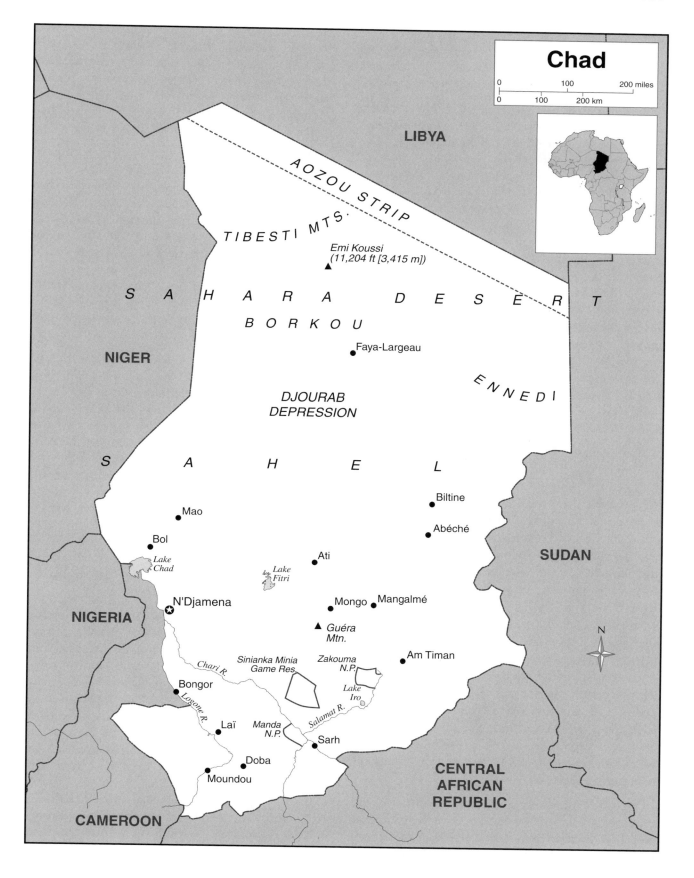

Chad

| 0 | 100 | 200 miles |
| 0 | 100 | 200 km |

LIBYA

AOZOU STRIP

TIBESTI MTS.

Emi Koussi
(11,204 ft [3,415 m])
▲

S A H A R A   D E S E R T

B O R K O U

Faya-Largeau

NIGER

E N N E D I

DJOURAB
DEPRESSION

S A H E L

Biltine

Mao

Abéché

Bol

Lake
Chad

Ati

Lake
Fitri

SUDAN

N'Djamena

Mongo   Mangalmé

▲ Guéra
Mtn.

NIGERIA

Am Timan

Chari R.

Sinianka Minia
Game Res.

Zakouma
N.P.

Bongor

Logone R.

Lake
Iro

Salamat R.

Laï   Manda
N.P.

Sarh

Doba

CENTRAL
AFRICAN
REPUBLIC

Moundou

N

CAMEROON

25 miles south of Ati; northwest and west of Fitri important water tables are found, namely, Batha, Kanem, and Chari-Bagirmi. Eastern Chad consists of a high relief, granitic soil, and has no water tables.

The annual southern rainfall, which literally submerges the region, makes the area almost impassable by vehicle between June and July. The northern zone's surface has hardly any running water except during certain periods of the year, accounting for the transhumant, pastoral, and nomadic lifestyle of its population. Here and there are permanent oases, such as in Borkou. Traveling from the country's center to the northwest, one encounters high plateaus tempered only by the low lying Chad Basin, about 850 feet above sea level, the lowest point being the Djiouraba Depression. The north and the east are essentially high plateaus, with some of the highest peaks in Africa, whereas the Ennedy and Wassai mountains reach 3,000 feet in height. The Chad's highest elevation is in the volcanic Tibesti massif in the north, which reaches 11,204 feet at Emi Koussi. In the southwest are the Mandara and Adamawa mountains that straddle the border with Cameroon.

In general, Chad's soil is either sandy (desert-like) or rocky (in the mountainous regions), both unsuited to farming. Around Lake Chad, the soil is clayish and reddish-brown in the south, where agriculture is practiced. Wet soils are found around the seasonally flooded areas along the Logone, Chari, and Salamat rivers, which can only sustain a farming lifestyle. The tropical wet and dry region is forest and savanna, covered with thick and tall trees, which turns into savanna as one moves north, where abundant animal life is found. The Sahel, or the fringes of the Sahara Desert, is savanna, becoming gradually an area covered with thorn brushes and open grassland, what some geographers have termed a grassy carpet, interspersed with dunes and plateaus and occasional oases. The northeast is mostly desert steppe and arid barren land, also dotted with oases and oasis vegetation, where grains, dates, sheep, goats, donkeys, and camels provide daily livelihood to the area's residents.

As a result of overgrazing, periodic drought, soil erosion, the Harmattan winds, environmental misuse and abuse (such as burn-slash practices), and the natural southward advance of the Sahara Desert—some scientists claiming a six-mile advance annually—Chad suffers from chronic desertification that will require drastic measures to reverse. The average day temperature in the country hovers around 80 degrees Fahrenheit, but the Desert and the Lake areas experience temperatures above 110 degrees Fahrenheit during the day, tempering down during night time.

In Chad, only those in the southern portion of the country can pursue farming for livelihood, cultivating such crops as corn, cotton, millet, cassava, peanuts (groundnuts), yams, rice, sorghum, and gum arabic. Thus, whereas the south has always had the potential for becoming self-sufficient in food production, the north is absolutely unable to survive on its own economically, the reason why the northern leadership, which has controlled the country since 1979, will never entertain the idea of a secession advocated by some southern radical leaders.

In the distant past, the region now called Chad was a major commercial and religious entrepot. Strategically located, straddling east and west, north and south, at the trans-Saharan crossroad, the area attracted merchants, Islamic proselytizers, pilgrims on their way to Mecca, scholars, and people from all walks of life. This region that once comprised the three now famous kingdoms or sultanates of Kanem-Bornu, Bagirmi, and Waddai, flourished from the active trade of slaves, horses, camels, donkeys, dried fish, salt, gold, and other such metals as iron and copper, gun powder and guns, and ostrich feathers, back and forth and as far as Egypt, Libya, Sudan, Ghana, Mali, Songhay, and the Middle Eastern empires.

French colonial policy left the north virtually intact politically, socially, and economically, as long the inhabitants paid taxes on their livestock and did not interfere with the movement of the colonizers in the region, making the south, especially the area where the Sara lived or *le Tchad utile* (useful Chad), the centerpiece of modern capitalist economic activity. Here, since the 1890s, concessionaire companies were given monopolies or concessions over a number of natural resources such as timber, just as King Léopold I (1640–1705) of the Congo Free State had done since 1876. In 1928, France made cotton the mainstay of Chad's industrial output, an activity that was later entrusted to CottonChad. Manpower for agricultural production, road construction and other necessary infrastructure, and military conscription, was acquired through the system of a destructive forced labor policy or corvee.

When the French left Chad at independence in August 1960, the country remained the poorest of the French Equatorial and West African colonies. It was often labeled the Cinderella of the French Empire, where the economy was dominated by low wages, unskilled labor, lack of effective taxation, de-emphasis of capital formation, and the absence of gainful employment. The civil service sector and CottonChad were exceptions, benefiting only a small semi-educated southern class. This situation was exacerbated by civil unrest that began in 1965 and lasted until the early 1990s. The disturbances adversely affected the regimes of François Tombalbaye (1960–1975), Félix Malloum (1975–1979), Goukouni Weddei (1979–1982), Hisseine Habre (1982–1990), and Idris Déby (1990–present). In the early twenty-first century. Chad enjoys only a semblance of peace made more precarious by the Darfur refugee situation of the early 2000s. Throughout this period of extreme unrest, Chad survived only through financial handouts, especially from France, which covered government essential programs and the salary of civil servants.

Chad's economic activity has relied heavily on subsistence agriculture and a light industry that has been based on the manufacture of cigarettes, matches, beer, soap, and cotton derivatives, cattle exports, and the assembly of bicycles and radios. The banking industry has never prospered and has remained virtually the same since the 1960s, the best known institutions being the *Banque des Etats de l'Afrique Centrale* (BEAC), *Banque de Developpement du Tchad* (BDT), *Banque Internationale pour le Commerce et l'Industrie* (BICIT), and *Banque Tchadienne de Credit et Depots* (BTCD).

Chad still imports goods such as fuel (despite a new oil pipeline), and foodstuffs, with the major partners being France (21.5%), Cameroon (16.4%), the United States (12.3%), Belgium (5.6%), Portugal (4.7%), the Netherlands (4.5%), and Saudi Arabia (4.0%). A careful assessment of Chad's economic indicators does not augur a bright developmental future, a situation made more difficult to predict given that the statistical data are generally

contradictory and unreliable. Unemployment still hovers between 60 and 70 percent. About 80 percent of the population, mostly subsistent farmers, fishermen, herders, and hunters, live below the poverty line (make less than US$1.00 per day), representing a per capita income of less than US$200 a year. These statistics are notwithstanding a gross national product (GDP) of $12,723 billion, growing at an estimated rate of 6 percent per year due mainly to the oil boom (being pumped at the rate of 225,000 barrels daily), that would represent US$1,600 per capita. In 2005, revenues amounted to US$1.131 billion, whereas the deficit was US$602 million, and the rate of inflation oscillated between 4 and 8 percent.

Chad's agriculture contributes 30 percent to the country's economy, light industry 26 percent, and the service sector 41 percent. Some sources indicate that industrial growth reached 5 percent in 2005. The export sector, estimated at only US$261 million in 2005, has been extremely weak, with 12 percent coming from the sale of livestock and meat and 40 percent from cotton. For the same period, external aid seems to have totaled US$238.3 billion, which demonstrates Chad's reliance on foreign assistance. As a result of International Monetary Fund (IMF) requirements, the state has nearly privatized all state-owned or operated enterprises in the country. Chad continues to be one of the most heavily indebted poor countries (HIPC) in the world with its external debt, estimated at $1.5 billion in 2003, to be totally forgiven under the qualified debt relief initiative of the IMF and other international financial institutions.

When oil began to be pumped by ExxonMobil, Chevron, and Petronas from the environs of Doba in 2003, the international political and economic circles following world events hailed the project and its agreement as a model for all future agreements governing oil-producing countries. Under this agreement, ExxonMobil was slated to receive 40 percent of the oil proceeds, with Petronas (a Malaysian subsidiary) and U.S. Chevron receiving lesser amounts, and the Chadian government only 12.5 percent. The initial investment by the oil companies has been quoted as having amounted to US$4 billion, with the IMF and the World Bank loaning Chad some US$2 billion for the project. According to the original agreement with the World Bank and the IMF,

80 percent of Chad's portion of the oil proceeds would go to infrastructure development; 12 percent was to be deposited in a bank in Britain, the funds earmarked for future generations of Chadians; and the remainder would be allocated to cover the day-to-day government expenditures. All oil transactions and proceeds expenditures were to be transparent and that the government would be held accountable for any irregularities. In addition, to ensure compliance, a joint government-civil society committee (COLLSGE) was empowered to monitor government conduct. However, there was no provision for specific sanctions were the government to violate the terms of the agreement.

As a result of the ambiguities, a few months into the first flow of oil through the 659-mile pipeline, Chad's president Déby diverted millions of dollars to purchase weaponry and accused the oil companies of siphoning Chad of its precious resource. Subsequently, he asked the IMF and the World Bank to change the agreed formula so that Chad would be able to utilize more of the oil revenues for its immediate needs. Chad eventually managed to get its wish honored. In August 2006, the oil companies' enormous quick rate of return was announced, totaling US$5 billion, whereas Chad's share was a mere US$588 million. Déby was outraged and ordered the expulsion of Chevron and Petronas from Chad on August 26, 2006, accusing the two conglomerates of refusing to pay corporate state taxes. He gave them only 24 hours to leave the country, vowing that, with assistance from ExxonMobil and China, with which Chad had just established diplomatic relations after severing its ties with Taiwan, he would create a national oil company.

As a result of Déby's action, experts have called the oil agreement a mirage and not the miracle it was supposed to be, trampled with corrupt and shady governmental practices. Thus, Chad's development strategies continue to be uncertain and ineffective, as demonstrated by other indicators of development: Infant mortality in the country has remained high and is estimated at 91.45/1000 live births; life expectancy at birth is still 47.5 years; the literacy rate has reached only 47.5 percent of the population; and demographic growth stands at 2.93 percent of the country's present population of nearly 10 million, with the fertility rate at 6.25 children born per women. Chad has only one television channel, and only 60,000 Chadians have access to the Internet. Since the 1960s, the country has had only 166 miles of paved roads, and less than 25 percent of the Chadian population has access to clean water, sanitation, and electricity.

It is clear that Chad has a long way to go in its march toward providing the minimum standards of living to its people. Corruption is rampant in government circles, and disparities based on geography and ethnicity prevail with the northern leadership that installed itself in 1990, whereas capital formation and self-reliance have never constituted the country's major strategic goals.

See also **Climate; Colonial Policies and Practices; Déby Itno, Idriss; Ethnicity; International Monetary Fund; N'Djamena; Sahara Desert; Warfare; World Bank.**

BIBLIOGRAPHY

Africa: South of the Sahara. London: Europa Publishers, 2006.

Azevedo, Mario J. *Roots of Violence: A History of War in Chad.* Langhorn, PA: Gordon and Breach, 1998.

Azevedo, Mario, and Emmanuel Nnadozie. *Chad: A Nation in Search of its Future.* Boulder, CO: Westview Press, 1998.

Burr, J. Millard. *Africa's Thirty Years' War: Chad, Libya, and the Sudan, 1963–1999.* Boulder, CO: Westview Press, 1999.

Decalo, Samuel. *Historical Dictionary of Chad.* Lanham, MD: Scarecrow Press, 1999.

International Monetary Fund. *World Economic Outlook: A Survey by the Staff of the IMF.* September 2006.

MARIO J. AZEVEDO

SOCIETY AND CULTURES

Chad has been described as the meeting place between Arab and Muslim North Africa and black and Christian Southern Africa. Although this description reflects a demographic reality, it fails to capture the complex social and cultural life of the country. In fact, Chad's population of more than nine million includes members of at least 200 different ethnic groups who speak approximately 110 different languages or dialects. Some have suggested that other categorization schemes or ways of making sense of Chad may have equal analytic validity. For instance, Chad can be divided into three geographical or ecological zones—the Saharan, the Sahel, and the more tropical Soudanian zone in the south of the country. These ecological zones capture and shape some of the major differences in social and cultural life in the country.

The southern Soudanian zone is home to the Sara, who are the country's largest ethnic group. The Sara are an agglomeration of at least twelve subgroups, including the Sara Madjingaye, Sara Kaba, Pen, Ngambaye, Mbaye, and Ngama. Although the cultural cohesion of the Sara can be overstated, there are similarities between these ethnic subgroups in culture, language, and social organization. The Sara are agriculturalists who make their living from cotton, peanut, and millet farming, and to a much lesser extent from fishing and hunting. During the colonial period concerted efforts were made to enforce mandatory cotton production throughout the south, dubbed *le Tchad utile*, or useful Chad, by the French. This resulted in the dramatic alteration of many of the Sara's social institutions. For instance, lineage groups were reorganized into villages and new structures of governance and authority were imposed on populations.

Sara society is patrilineal; marriages are generally arranged with women from outside the lineage group; and residence patterns are patrilocal. Sara women have among the highest fertility rates on the continent; recent surveys indicate that the total fertility rate in southern Chad ranges from 6.6 to 7.3 children per woman. Male initiation ceremonies, purportedly copied from the Mbaye subgroup, were widespread but have begun to diminish both in frequency and duration. Female initiation ceremonies are less common. Among some Sara subgroups, including the Sara Kaba, female circumcision has been recently introduced and in some villages is a first generation phenomenon. Christianity is the dominant imported religious influence in the region, and both Catholic and Protestant missionaries settled in southern Chad in the 1920s and built schools and health clinics before the colonial government did. It is not uncommon to find a Catholic church and multiple Protestant churches representing different denominations even in small villages. However, religious practice is syncretic and includes sacrifices and other forms of ancestor worship.

A recent shock to social and culture life in southern Chad is a major oil and pipeline project

that has been underway since 2000. The project has spurred massive in-migration, particularly of young men looking for employment, and has involved the expropriation of large tracts of the Sara's agricultural land. This is forcing many farmers to diversify their sources of income or to shift from agricultural production to wage labor. The pipeline project is likely to have dramatic consequences in the south of Chad over the course of the early twenty-first century.

Chad's Sahelian zone, the country's middle ecological belt, is the most ethnically and linguistically diverse. Residing here are ethnic groups that retain allegiances to the historically powerful kingdoms or sultanates, including the Kanembu in the Kanem-Borno regions, the Barma in the Chari-Baguirmi, and the Maba in the Wadai. Since the colonial period, these sultanates have lost much of their political and military power though they have managed to retain the structure of many of their social institutions. The Moundang, Toupouri, Massa, and Kera populations are found in the western Mayo-Kebbi region of the Chadian Sahel, and the Hajerai in the mountainous central region of Guera. Arabs make up only about 10 percent of the country's population. Most live in the Sahelian region, though their commercial trade and migration routes span all three geographic zones. Chadian Arabs can be subdivided into the Juhayna (or Juhaina), the Hassuna, and the Awlad Sulayman groups, each of which trace their lineage to a common ancestor. The Awlad Sulayman group (the smallest and most dispersed of the Arab groups) maintains strong ties with Libya, which they view as their homeland.

As commercial traders and seminomadic herders, Chadian Arabs are highly mobile. The degree of mobility of Arabs and other Sahelian groups that rely on a combination of animal husbandry and agricultural production for their living becomes more pronounced as one moves from the west to the east. Herders, for instance, migrate to the southern Soudanian zone during the dry season to allow their cattle to graze on dormant agricultural fields. Following the droughts of the early 1970s and the mid-1980s that devastated many herds, Chadian Arabs have increasingly settled at the southern edges of their traditional migratory routes. Conflicts over access to land between southern farmers and Arab and other Sahelian herders have been exacerbated by

République du Tchad (Republic of Chad)

Population:	9,885,661 (2007 est.)
Area:	1,284,634 sq. km (496,000 sq. mi.)
Official languages:	French and Arabic
Languages:	Arabic, French, Sara
National currency:	CFA franc
Principal religions:	Muslim 51%, Christian 35%, animist 7%, other indigenous beliefs 7%
Capital:	N'Djamena (formerly Fort-Lamy, est. pop. 1,000,000 in 2006)
Other urban centers:	Moundou, Abeche, Sarh
Annual rainfall:	variable, from 900–1,200 mm (35–47 in.) in subtropical zone to 20–500 mm (8–20 in.) in Saharan zone
Principal geographical features:	*Mountains:* Guera Massif, Tibesti Mountains, Wadai Plateau, Emi Koussi *Lakes:* Chad, Fitri, Iro *Rivers:* Chari, Logone, Bahr Aouk, Bahr Keita, Bahr Salamat, Bahr Kameur
Economy:	*GDP per capita:* US$1,600 (2006)
Principal products and exports:	*Agricultural:* cotton, sorghum, millet, peanuts, rice, potatoes, manioc (tapioca), cattle, sheep, goats, camels *Manufacturing:* cotton textiles, meatpacking, beer brewing, soap, cigarettes, construction materials *Mining:* oil, natron, uranium, kaolin
Government:	Independence from France, 1960. Constitution adopted in 1962, suspended in 1975. New constitution approved in 1989, suspended in 1990. Transition charter, 1993–1996. New constitution adopted in 1996 by referendum. President elected by universal suffrage. National Assembly deputies elected by universal suffrage for 4-year terms. Prime minister appointed by president. For administrative purposes, there are 14 prefectures.
Heads of state since independence:	1960–1975: President Francois Tombalbaye 1975–1979: General Felix Malloum, chairman of the Supreme Military Council 1979: President Lol Mahamat Chaoua 1979–1982: President Goukouni Weddei 1982–1990: President Hisseine Habre 1990–: President Lieutenant General Idris Déby
Armed forces:	*Army:* 25,000 *Air force:* 350 *Paramilitary:* 5,000
Transportation:	*Roads:* 33,400 km (20,754 mi.), 1% paved *National airline:* Air Tchad *Airports:* International facility at N'Djamena. 51 other airports and airstrips throughout the country.
Media:	*Info-Tchad* is government-produced, mimeographed daily. Two small publishing houses produce booklets and pamphlets. Some independent newspapers, the most important being the weekly *Tchad-Hebdo.* Radiodiffusion Nationale Tchadienne is owned by the government. 6 radio stations, 1 television station.
Literacy and education:	*Total literacy rate:* 48% (2003). Education is free, universal, and compulsory for ages 8–14. Postsecondary education provided by Université du Tchad and several technical and professional schools.

increased competition over land, but also by the introduction of new regimes of land tenure introduced by the oil and pipeline project.

The sparsely populated Saharan zone in the far north of Chad is home to the non-Arab Toubou and Daza ethnic groups who are sometimes collectively referred to as Goranes. They are largely nomadic peoples who circulate through the vast Bourkou, Ennedi, and Tibesti (or BET) regions. They rely heavily on their livestock for food and other needs, but cultivate dates and some cereals on the oases (or *wadis*) in the desert. The Toubou,

of which the Teda are the largest subgroup, and the Daza, including the Kreda and the Daza, live in relatively small, lineage-based settlements. Although these societies are patrilineal, what is most often noted is the extreme fluidity of Toubou and Daza kinship groups and of alliances among segments and subgroups. Terms such as anarchy are frequently used to describe the social organization, or apparent lack thereof, among these groups. Biosocial theories see these forms of social organization as adaptive responses to the harsh and inhospitable environment of the Sahara desert.

See also **Colonial Policies and Practices; Labor.**

BIBLIOGRAPHY

Decalo, Samuel, ed. *Historical Dictionary of Chad*, 2nd edition. Metuchen, NJ: Scarecrow Press, Inc., 1987.

Lemarchand, Rene. "The Politics of Sara Ethnicity: A Note on the Origins of the Civil War in Chad." *Cahiers d'Etudes Africaines* 20 (1980): 449–471.

Lemarchand, Rene. "Chad: The Misadventures of the North-South Dialectic." *African Studies Review* 29 (1986): 27–41.

Leonard, Lori. "We Did It for Pleasure Only: Hearing Alternative Tales of Female Circumcision." *Qualitative Inquiry* 6, no. 2 (2000): 212–228.

Leonard, Lori. "Possible Illnesses: Assessing the Health Impacts of the Chad Pipeline Project." *Bulletin of the World Health Organization* 81, no. 6 (2003): 427–433.

Magnant, Jean-Pierre. *Terre Sara terre Tchadienne*. Paris: L'Harmattan, 1986.

Ouagadjio, Bandoumal., et al. *Demographic and Health Survey Chad, 2004.* Calverton, MD: Institut National de la Statistique, des Etudes Economiques et Demographiques and ORC Macro, 2004.

LORI LEONARD

HISTORY AND POLITICS

Chad has not been fortunate in its governments, and those seeking to govern Chad have rarely been able to muster the resources and determination required for sustained, effective statecraft in a difficult environment. Stretching from the long-contested border in the Libyan desert down to the forests of the Central African Republic and across the center of the continent from Niger to Sudan's Darfur region, Chad has borders with six neighbors, none of them stable and none averse to adding more complications to the factional struggles of N'Djamena and its vast hinterland. Chad's nine million people are variously catalogued in 72 to 110 ethnolinguistic groups. Each of these groups are then divided into clans, subclans, and families, none of them necessarily solidaristic. The French colonial administration effectively divided Chad into useful Chad and useless Chad. The former, inhabitants of the well-watered south, included the Sara, Toupouri, and Ngambaye. Their utility was evidenced by their submission to the forced cultivation of cotton for the French market. As a result, most

of the scant colonial economic and social development expenditures went south.

The country's midsection, home to mixed herding, fishing, and agriculture, includes the Bagirmi, the Hadjerai, and various Arab groups. The Saharan north, counting for over half the area but no more than 7 percent of the population, received minimal attention from the colonial regime. However, the French military had high regard for the military prowess of the natural warriors from the north, such as the Tubu, the Daza (or Goranes), and the Zaghawa, many of whose clans straddled the border with Sudan's Darfur region.

In the years running up to independence in 1960, François Ngarta Tombalbaye, a southerner, emerged as the most successful political maneuverer, and like most African leaders of the time, he quickly installed a single-party authoritarian regime. Since the bulk of schooling resources had gone to the south, it was no surprise that most government posts and other rewards went to Tombalbaye's fellow southerners. Five years after independence a peasant revolt against high-handed administration broke out in the Hadjerai town of Mangalmé. The troubles quickly spread to the north where a loosely organized National Liberation Front of Chad (FROLINAT) took up arms against government installations. To compound his troubles, Tombalbaye forced government employees, whatever their ethnicity, to undergo humiliating—and sometimes lethal—bush school initiation rites, which were particularly offensive to Muslims. On April 13, 1975, the army seized power under General Felix Malloum (b. 1932), who brought the Daza faction leader, Hissène Habré (b. 1942), into the government as prime minister. Habré, one of the few northerners with a university education, then broke with Malloum and formed the FROLINAT's Second Army, soon baptized the Forces Armées du Nord (FAN). Malloum's forces were unable to contain the northern dissidents. His government collapsed in 1969 under heavy attacks by the FAN partly because of the heavy weaponry provided by Libya to Habré's lieutenant, Goukouni Oueddei (b. 1944). Libya's interest was piqued by the unsettled status of the narrow strip of land along the Chad-Libya border. This Aouzou Strip was rumored to contain fabulous, if unproven, mineral wealth.

None of the northern factions were able to control or win over the southerners, many of whom, led by Wadal Kader Kamougué, sought to split the south from the rest of the country. Habré and Goukouni soon fell out, notably over Goukouni's acquiescence to Libya's taking control over much of northern Chad, including the Aouzou Strip. Efforts of the Nigerians to broker a peace, and of the Organization of African Unity to organize a peacekeeping force, were overwhelmed by the intensity of the factional warfare. Finally, Habré was forced to flee with his men across the eastern border to Darfur, where President Nimeiri provided sanctuary and an opportunity to recruit and refit. This effort was aided clandestinely by the United States, as the Reagan administration saw in Habré an ally in America's campaign against Muammar Qadhdhafi's destabilizing regional policies.

With help from friends and neutrality from the small French garrison in Chad, Habré's FAN launched an attack from his Darfur sanctuary. Qadhdhafi, meanwhile, gave priority to his attempt to be chosen chairman of the Organization of African Unity and pulled his troops out of most of Chad, hoping thereby to legitimize his claim to be a man of peace who respected his neighbors' territorial integrity. Without Libyan armor, Goukouni's men were quickly routed, and on June 7, 1982, Habré entered N'Djamena and claimed himself the ruler of all that remained of Chad.

Habré began to reestablish the structures of a state and to extend its reach throughout the national territory. The public face of the regime was dominated by the sole political party, the Union Nationale pour l'Indépendance et la Révolution (UNIR), but real power lay with Habré and a core of comrades-at-arms, mostly northerners who had made the long march to and from Sudan. Within four years, through a combination of military pressure and political and financial enticements, Habré put down the southern attempts at secession and persuaded most faction leaders that it was to their advantage to cut a deal and rally to the national cause. That left most of the Saharan north still under the control of the Libyans and their more or less loyal Chadian factions. Habré's forces prepared well, with significant help from France and the United States. In the first of Africa's Toyota wars, Chadian forces under the field commander Hassane Djamouss outmaneuvered the

Libyan tanks and, in the first half of 1987, drove the Libyan forces out of nearly all of Chad, capturing vast amounts of Soviet-made heavy armaments and significant numbers of Libyan prisoners. By mid-1987, Habré's rule looked to be a success, crowned by state visits to Washington and Paris. His rule had turned a faction-riddled field of battle into an unremarkably poor and routinely authoritarian African state.

Habré's success, however, carried the seeds of failure. The comrades at arms and the newly rallied factions fell to quarrelling over the spoils, particularly the profits from the international sale of captured Libyan arms. First, a group of Hadjerai soldiers turned their guns on their Tubu commanders then abandoned their posts. Habré, fearful of a broader conspiracy, arrested Hassan Djamouss and other leading Zaghawa, just missing Djamouss's successor, Idriss Déby, who fled into exile. With quiet support from Libya, Déby began a tour of African states to raise money and diplomatic support. Déby set up headquarters in Darfur, with the backing of the military regime that had earlier toppled Nimeiri. In a few months of fighting, during which both France and the United States remained studiously neutral, Déby's forces pushed Habré's dispirited army back to N'Djamena, which they had looted before on November 30, 1990, fleeing across the border to Cameroon. Habré himself made off with US$23 million, enough to set himself up comfortably in Dakar.

The Mouvement Patriotique du Salut (MPS) dominates formal politics and, since 2002, has controlled 111 of 155 seats in parliament No one doubts its ability to be declared winner of an election, whether or not opposition parties refuse to participate. Real power lies with the president who in May 2006 was elected to a third term, after having the constitution changed to obviate the two-term limit. Many Chadians perceived the first few years of Déby's rule as a Zaghawa ascendancy, in which Déby's senior military comrades took lucrative positions (in the customs service, for example). Ordinary *combattants* were given license to requisition vehicles and motorcycles, most of which vanished into trading circuits across the Sudanese border. Despite the democratic façade, Déby's government differed little from its predecessor, except on the important matter that, so far as is known, the scale of human rights abuses is much diminished.

Two sets of events had major impact on Chadian politics. The first, in July 2003, was the much awaited coming on stream of petroleum production from the southern oilfields of the Doba region, from which the oil travels by pipeline 621 miles to the Cameroonian coast at Kribi. Along with the principal operating consortium of ExxonMobil, Chevron, and Petronas of Malaysia, the World Bank played a major role in arranging the financing of the US$4.2 billion project. Cognizant of the resource curse and economic distortions that have so afflicted African petroleum exporters, the World Bank insisted that Chad agree to set aside a significant part of its royalties to protect the environment, to build a fund for the future when the oil would run out, and to alleviate poverty, disease, and illiteracy. The set-asides were to be supervised by a control commission with significant participation by leaders of civil society. The first government purchases with its newfound wealth were two assault helicopters The Bank protested; Déby retorted that protecting the people was a priority. A visit to N'Djamena by the Bank's president, Paul Wolfowitz (b. 1943), produced an agreement in July 2006, but it has shown little evidence of narrowing Déby's definition of priority spending, nor of giving the Control Commission any effective power. Meanwhile, Chad has acquired a reputation as one of the most corrupt countries in Africa.

The second set of events is the increasing entanglement of Chadian domestic politics with broader regional conflicts. Concerned with southern rebels operating across the border and threatening petroleum extraction, Déby sent some 4,000 men to the Central African Republic in support of General Bozizé's (b. 1946) contested rule. Chad then became deeply involved in the genocidal violence in Darfur. Zaghawa were among the victims of the Arab Janjaweed depredations, though some Zaghawa clans joined with the Sudanese government forces as a way of settling local quarrels. An April 2006 coup attempt was beaten back with the help of French airpower. With the government distracted, new armed opposition movements formed in both the south and the north. By the end of 2006, Chad seemed to be undergoing yet another period of violence amid fears that the state structure might once again collapse.

See also **Dakar; Déby Itno, Idriss; N'Djamena; Organization of African Unity; Qadhdhafi, Muammar; Tombalbaye, François-Ngarta; Warfare; World Bank.**

BIBLIOGRAPHY

Buijtenhuijs, Robert. *Le frolinat et les guerres civiles du Tchad (1977–1984): La révolution introuvaable.* Paris: Karthala, 1991.

Foltz, William J. "Reconstructing the Chadian State." In *Collapsed States: The Disintegration and Restoration of Legitimate Authority,* ed William Zartman. Boulder, CO: Lynne Rienner, 1995.

Nolutshungu, Sam. *Limits of Anarchy: Intervention and State Formation in Chad.* Charlottesville: University Press of Virginia, 1996.

WILLIAM J. FOLTZ

CHARISMATIC CHURCHES. *See* Christianity: African Instituted Churches.

CHILDBEARING.

Africa has 12 percent of the world's population of 5.6 billion. Each year 21 percent of the live births, 40 percent of the maternal deaths, and nearly 33 percent of the perinatal deaths occur there (see Tables 1 and 2). Motherhood is therefore unsafe, fetal wastage is high, and population growth remains largely uncontrolled. This article explores some of these reproductive patterns and their surrounding circumstances.

MAJOR FACTORS INFLUENCING REPRODUCTION

The social complexity of Africa's population, with its varied ethnic groups, religious beliefs, and traditional forms of health care, has a major impact on reproduction. Nevertheless, poverty, inadequate orthodox health care, illiteracy, and poor nutrition remain the fundamental issues.

Poverty. Spending enough on formal education, basic health, nutrition, and infrastructure is important for successful childbearing and reproduction.

African regional estimates of maternal mortality, lifetime risk, and number of maternal deaths: 1990

	Maternal deaths	Maternal mortality ratio	Lifetime risk of maternal death (1 in x)
World	586,000	430	60
Developed countries	4,000	27	1,800
Less-developed countries	582,000	480	48
Africa	234,600	870	16
Eastern	97,000	1,060	12
Central	31,000	950	14
Northern	16,000	340	55
Southern	3,600	260	75
Western	87,000	1,020	12

SOURCE: World Health Organization and UNICEF, 1996.

Table 1.

African regional estimates of live births, perinatal mortality rates, and number of perinatal deaths

	Number of live births (thousands)	Number of perinatal deaths (thousands)	Perinatal mortality rate
World	140,736	7,635	53
Developed countries	14,359	155	11
Less-developed countries	126,377	7,480	57
Africa	30,729	2,404	75
Eastern	10,593	845	76
Central	3,894	337	82
Northern	4,887	216	43
Southern	1,517	89	57
Western	9,838	917	88

SOURCE: World Health Organization, 1996.

Table 2.

Sub-Saharan Africa with its debt burden and pitifully low income levels cannot do this. In the early twenty-first century the medical infrastructure relevant to reproductive health care is woefully inadequate—indeed, nonexistent in some areas. The World Bank's estimate of the cost of basic primary health care, including reproductive health care, is US$12 per head per year; most governments in sub-Saharan Africa spend just US$2–3 per head per year. User fees are being charged to provide the extra money the hospitals need. The arrangement drives the poor majority to self-treatment, quackery, and harmful or ineffective traditional medicine. Meanwhile, the situation takes other nasty turns, especially for women. They find great difficulty in meeting very basic financial commitments, including feeding their families, and thus are being forced into prostitution, an important factor in the rapid spread of heterosexual HIV/AIDS.

Education and Literacy. At present, adult literacy rates in sub-Saharan Africa are 59 percent for men and 36 percent for women. Little wonder, then, that negative development exists in much of the region. Education makes equality of the genders possible, and it helps to meet women's basic needs and avoid patterns of reproduction known to be bad for motherhood. Education persuades people to use birth control. Moreover, female education is an investment: on the average, in developing countries, each additional year of schooling increases women's earning capacity by 10–20 percent. This economic advantage and knowledge

gained, combined with fewer children in the family, lead to better nutrition, improved domestic hygiene, and better use of health services, with salutary effects on child development and survival.

Improved reproductive health through formal education extends beyond family circumstances. Mass education is a prerequisite for technological progress, which allows for the control of infectious diseases, a stable food supply, and infrastructure construction and maintenance. Political stability and good governance are heavily dependent on it. However, schooling for one or two years (e.g., through adult literacy classes) does not reduce harmful reproductive health patterns to the extent that formal education up to the secondary level does. Thus, there cannot be progress when only 18 percent of eligible females are in secondary schools in sub-Saharan Africa.

Nutrition. In the mid-1990s, 40 percent of Africa's population was undernourished, due mainly to poor food distribution and lack of access. Starvation is ripping through the region. When severe, its effects on reproduction are serious: menstruation becomes irregular; ovulation may cease; and those who get pregnant have very small babies. When women are malnourished but not actually starving, menstruation is not disturbed but fetal growth is, and excessive physical work and food taboos (both common in Africa) aggravate the situation.

A major result of poor nutrition is anemia, defined as a hemoglobin level of less than 3.5 ounces per quart in the peripheral blood. It is estimated that more than half of all pregnant women in Africa are anemic, compared with fewer than one in five in developed countries. Poor nutrition and malaria are the principal causes. Micronutrient supplementation, in this case iron and folic acid, combined with antimalarial medication during pregnancy, constitutes a highly effective preventive regimen.

Whether a woman is fully grown or not greatly influences reproductive outcome. For any individual the optimum stature or height is hereditary. Attainment of this optimum size depends on a favorable environment and the state of nutrition during intrauterine life, childhood, and adolescence. Where socioeconomic circumstances are good, adults grow to their full potential. Conversely, in an environment where disease and poor nutrition are widespread, the growth of most adults will be stunted. In such environments (very common in sub-Saharan Africa), the shortest women bear the lightest babies and, compared with tall women, they experience more difficulties in labor. In each community there is a critical height below which the risk of cesarean section increases, so that maternal height becomes a marker for difficult labor. This critical height ranges between 58 and 60 inches in eastern and western Africa.

Age and Number of Previous Births.

Forty percent of sub-Saharan African women aged nineteen years and under are married, median age at first birth seldom exceeds twenty years except in southern Africa, and the average number of births per woman is more than six. Basically, the pattern of early marriage–early teenage pregnancy–high fertility results from poverty. Once it is established, the pattern increases poverty. Literacy and adequate education break the cycle.

The orthodox view is that girls aged under sixteen years and women aged thirty-five years and over with five or more previous births have more difficult pregnancies. However, living conditions exert a strong confounding effect on these vulnerable groups. Pregnancy is safe for adolescent girls brought up in good circumstances. Although growth of the bony pelvis is incomplete, the deficit is small, so that delivery is usually easy; the only common complication is preeclampsia. By contrast, pregnancy is extremely hazardous in underprivileged girls lacking good obstetric care. Deaths result from severe anemia, preeclampsia, eclampsia, and malaria (in regions where it is endemic). A greater threat is from obstructed labor due to contracted pelvis, the result of stunted growth compounding physical immaturity. In neglected cases, advanced obstruction leads to high rates of unsafe operative deliveries, vesicovaginal fistula (VVF), and fetal and maternal death. But it is not all gloom. A Nigerian study showed that during pregnancy the antianemia measures earlier described caused growth spurts in height and ensured safe childbirth for immature girls. Thus, among Africa's vulnerable teenage pregnant population, VVF prevention through nutritional intervention in pregnancy is possible. However, the bad news is that adolescent girls everywhere wanting to rid themselves of unwanted pregnancies often resort to illegal abortion, with dire consequences.

High parity is not dangerous among the well-to-do and among those of the poor who have an excellent survival record for all previous births. The situation is dangerous when high parity, high child mortality, and extreme socioeconomic and educational backwardness are combined. Death results from the major pregnancy complications listed below. Taken together with the fact that in rich societies, high parity is not risky, it is clear that poverty and ignorance through poor education are the real killers, not high parity per se.

COMMON LIFE-THREATENING PREGNANCY COMPLICATIONS AND ASSOCIATED DISEASES

The most frequent life-endangering pregnancy complications are anemia, postdelivery infections, and conditions requiring operative treatment (e.g., complications of abortion, eclampsia, hemorrhage, and obstructed labor); together they account for 80 percent of maternal deaths. The rest are mostly coincidental diseases, especially malaria, AIDS, tuberculosis, sickle cell disease, heart disease, viral hepatitis, and diarrheal diseases.

Malaria is special in terms of the sheer size of the population involved and the scale of the damage caused. Nearly half of the world's population is exposed to it, and 90 percent of those actually infected are in Africa, the poorest region, indicating that it is a disease of poverty. In areas where it is highly endemic, the most serious consequence of malaria in pregnancy is the indirect effect of maternal anemia, from which huge numbers of mothers and their babies die. In addition, the parasites infect the placenta and impede the growth of the fetus, resulting in a tremendous excess of low-birth-weight babies. These malaria-related complications are much more pronounced in early teenage mothers than in older mothers (presumably because the older women have developed protective immunity), and more in primigravidas (individuals pregnant for the first time) than in multiparous women (those who have produced several offspring). In areas where it is less endemic, malaria deaths commonly result from complications involving the brain, kidneys, and lungs.

MATERNAL MORTALITY

Maternal mortality is the death of a woman at any time during pregnancy and up to forty-two days after its termination. The maternal mortality ratio is the number of maternal deaths for every 100,000 deliveries. Maternal mortality as a health and socio-economic indicator is of special interest because it gives the widest disparity between developed and developing countries. Singapore, with gross national product (GNP) per person of US$16,500, has a maternal mortality ratio of 10 per 100,000 births and a lifetime risk of dying during pregnancy and childbirth of 1 in 4,900; the equivalent figures for Mali in western Africa are US$265, 1,200 per 100,000, and 1 in 10. Hence, a 60-fold difference in GNP per person shows up as a 120-fold difference in maternal mortality ratio, and an almost 500-fold difference in lifetime risk.

Related to the killer diseases already mentioned are the usual factors inimical to good reproductive health and safe childbirth. Poverty, illiteracy, bad housing, poor sanitation, and poor nutrition are of socioeconomic relevance. Damaging gender-discriminatory practices against females in need constitute the cultural and religious determinants. Logistic determinants consist of poor physical infrastructure and transport and telecommunication inadequacies. Of the biological determinants—young age and high parity—the latter plays a minor role, because poverty is the real killer. It must not be forgotten that bureaucratic impediments can undermine the best of efforts.

Unbooked Emergencies. Central to the issue of maternal mortality in Africa are the unbooked emergencies. The term refers to pregnant women who fail to receive prenatal care, develop complications at home, use traditional techniques, and, when these fail, finally go to hospital for care, desperately ill. Often, the major operative interference required has to take place when the women are already poor risks for anesthesia and surgery, hence the high maternal mortality rates. Table 3, constructed from data from Zaria, Nigeria, compares maternal deaths among three groups of hospital-delivered women: those who received prenatal care and remained healthy throughout pregnancy but not necessarily in labor; those who, despite receiving prenatal care, developed pregnancy complications; and the unbooked emergencies. The huge number of fatalities and serious injuries among the unbooked emergencies is very striking. While the death rate in the booked-healthy group is as good as that in many developed countries, the death rate in the unbooked emergencies is the same as the death rate in England in the sixteenth and seventeenth centuries, indicating just how wide the disparity is between the present-day "haves" and "have-nots."

Delay in seeking, and sometimes in giving, medical care is always marked in unbooked emergencies. This is because the unfavorable social, logistical, and institutional factors already mentioned operate widely, and the impetus for change is absent. In parts of eastern and western Africa, controversial evangelical Protestant churches are adding immensely to the problem because the activities of these churches drive women away from orthodox maternity care. Of cultural and religious restrictions that operate at critical moments, two stand out: the refusal by women and their families of lifesaving operations and blood transfusions, and the exclusion of women from decision making. Another restriction is that without male consent, transfer to hospital cannot take place, resulting in denial of lifesaving treatment.

Recognizing this background to unbooked emergencies is important because it provides insight into the inappropriateness of the use of traditional birth attendants and casts doubt on the promotion of cesarean sections by nonphysicians as a management option to improve reproductive outcomes.

Maternal and fetal outcome in booked healthy women, booked women with prenatal complications, and unbooked emergencies; Zaria, Nigeria, 1976–1979

	Booked healthy	Booked with prenatal complications	Unbooked emergencies
Maternal results			
Number of women	11,261	3,759	7,707
Uterine rupture (number)	0	26	164
Obstetric fistula (number)	2	1	62
% blood transfusion	2	10	25
Maternal deaths (number)	5	14	219
Maternal deaths/1,000 deliveries	0.4	3.7	28.4
Fetal results			
Number singleton births	10,896	3,296	5,518
Perinatal deaths (number)	240	243	1,375
Perinatal deaths/1,000 births	22	74	249

SOURCE: Harrison, Kelsey A., and C. T. John, *Lancet* 347 (1996): 400.

Table 3.

THE ROLE OF TRADITIONAL BIRTH ATTENDANTS

Sub-Saharan Africa is the region of the world most deprived of orthodox health care. There is 1 physician for 19,000 persons, compared with a ratio of 1 for 500 in developed countries. Traditional birth attendants (TBAs) are available, and the notion that they hold the key to better maternal and child health in Africa runs deep. However, it has become obvious that the enhancement of their activities cannot reduce maternal mortality and morbidity. Reduction of high maternal mortality requires the effective treatment and eventual elimination of unbooked emergencies, the major high-risk group. Coping effectively with lifesaving management required by the unbooked emergencies is beyond TBAs because they lack the requisite knowledge and skill, and they are usually too old and too set in their ways to adapt to new challenges successfully. Elimination of unbooked emergencies requires that tough decisions involving the underlying political, socioeconomic, cultural, religious, and health causes be taken at the national level and implemented. TBAs' unsuitability for any part of this mammoth task is obvious: being female, being illiterate, and being of low status are all against them. Recordkeeping in the conventional manner is impossible for TBAs, and without reliable records and periodic audit, progress is impossible.

Moreover, the worldwide trend is for births attended by TBAs to fall as illiteracy levels fall, leading to reduction in maternal morality. Therefore, if moves to reduce maternal mortality are to succeed, they must at the same time weaken the hold illiteracy has on the society. Strengthening the position of illiterate TBAs runs counter to this development, and indeed may turn out to be a way of blocking female literacy, which is totally unacceptable. TBAs' involvement is fundamentally flawed; work toward their replacement by midwives should be the priority.

ABDOMINAL DELIVERIES AND LAPAROTOMIES BY NONPHYSICIANS

Another development on Africa's maternal health scene is the concept of cesarean section performed by nonphysicians. Proponents believe that it satisfies a felt need where physicians are scarce and women with major obstetric complications that require emergency operative treatment are not getting it. Opponents accept that short-term results may be good, but they see adverse effects on future health, administrative, and educational development. Increase in quackery, disputes over career structure and payment systems for physicians versus nonphysicians who operate, and weakening of conventional medical education to the point of causing delay in the emergence of top-quality indigenous medical leadership are possible long-term, highly damaging effects. Caution and careful appraisal are essential.

MATERNAL MORBIDITY

For each maternal death there are an estimated fifteen women made miserable for the rest of their lives by injuries sustained during childbirth. The most distressing of these injuries is VVF. Unrelieved obstructed labor is the commonest cause. The fistula involves the urinary bladder, urethra, and sometimes the rectum. Apart from urinary incontinence and fetal death, the picture may be complicated by pressure sores, foot drop from nerve injuries, and cessation of menstruation. Among the Hausa and Fulani (Fulbe) of northern Nigeria, *gishiri* cut adds enormously to the problem. This is a traditional form of surgery, practiced by old women, in which an unsterile razor blade is used to cut the vagina as treatment for many complaints, including prolonged and difficult labor. Rendered incontinent and childless, the victims suffer rejection and, later, destitution. The treatment involves surgical repair, social rehabilitation, and physical therapy. This condition is highly prevalent in areas of deep poverty and extreme female suppression. In Addis Ababa, Ethiopa, since the 1960s, seven hundred repair operations are performed annually, but the situation continues. In northern Nigeria, the scale is even greater; despite an increasing number of treated cases, the waiting lists run to the thousands.

Infertility is another important morbidity. For an African woman, infertility means loss of her security and prestige in society, divorce, lifelong loneliness and unhappiness. Infertility most commonly results from sexually transmitted diseases and infections complicating abortion and childbirth. It also results from tuberculosis. There are accompanying pelvic pain and troublesome menstrual disorders. Ectopic pregnancy—a rapidly fatal condition in the absence of emergency operative treatment—may follow. The areas around Lake Chad and Lake Victoria have the highest rate of infertility.

Despite much international concern, female genital mutilation continues. This writer's view is that it will eventually cease through the spread of development and formal education, just as traditional facial and body markings in Nigeria are fast disappearing. Forcing the pace through legislation is hopeless: strongly held traditional customs do not die through such means.

Other reproductive morbidities unrelated to pregnancy also occur. Special to Africa is severe scarring of the vagina following female circumcision or insertion of caustic substances into the vagina. Coital difficulties occur in severe cases. Treatment requires reconstructive surgery.

PERINATAL MORTALITY AND LOW FETAL BIRTH WEIGHT

Perinatal mortality includes stillbirths and early neonatal deaths that occur during the first seven days of life. The perinatal mortality rate is the number of stillbirths and early neonatal deaths per 1,000 total births. The same factors that kill the mother lead to the baby's death. An important additional factor is low birth weight, defined as less than 5.5. pounds, which results either because the baby is born too soon or because its growth was retarded during intrauterine life. Currently, the proportion of low-birth-weight babies approaches 40 percent in rural Africa, compared with an overall estimate of 16 percent in the region and around 6 percent in developed countries. The reasons for the differences are the varying living conditions and health standards. The high twinning rate in Africa is an important contributory factor; twin babies are smaller at birth.

Low-birth-weight babies are greatly disadvantaged. Apart from the huge numbers of deaths involved, the survivors suffer damage on a large scale, their growth being stunted in adulthood. There is another dimension to the issue of fetal damage before and after birth that the poorer parts of Africa probably face. There, many adult women also have stunted growth, most births are unsupervised, and prolonged labor is frequent, resulting in injury and damage to fully grown babies. Thus, whether of good size or small, in the prevailing bad living conditions the damaged babies grow up to become damaged adults who in turn produce damaged babies: the process becomes a nasty cycle. If it is to be broken, merely saving the lives of mothers and babies is not enough. Instead, the answer is to produce a generation of well-grown fetuses and infants who will then pass on the advantage to succeeding generations. Political intervention and social change are the essential requirements, not fire-brigade action in hospital.

FAMILY PLANNING AND BREAST-FEEDING

Contraception acceptance and usage are heavily dependent on raising women's low status through education and on achieving better child survival through the combined effects of good nutrition, effective health care, and increasing prosperity. Progress is slow on these fronts, hence the strength of the resistance to contraception despite increasing promotion. In addition, Muslim and Catholic teachings are not helpful. Overall, contraceptive use averages less than 10 percent in sub-Saharan Africa.

Breast-feeding in the absence of clean water protects children from fatal diseases, especially diarrhea and pneumonia; postpones pregnancy; and saves mothers the high cost of bottle feeding. Unfortunately, breast-feeding is declining, but action is being taken by United Nations (UN) agencies to reverse this dangerous trend.

SEXUALLY TRANSMITTED DISEASES

The increasing prevalance of sexually transmitted diseases (STDs) among adolescents and the HIV-AIDS epidemic are key issues in international health. An estimated 250 million adults worldwide have STDs, 24 percent of them in Africa. The bulk of STD cases are gonorrhea, chlamydia, syphilis, chancroid, and trichomoniasis. For each, drug treatment is highly effective.

AIDS was first recognized in the early 1980s and already, worldwide, more than 20 million adults are infected with HIV; 65 percent of them are in sub-Saharan Africa, and more than half of those are women. Three modes of transmission—sexual, perinatal, and parenteral—occur; heterosexual HIV predominates in Africa. Parenteral transmission is by exposure to infected blood and blood products. Intravenous drug users and workers in health-care facilities are at considerable risk. Babies are infected in utero, during delivery, and postnatally through breast-feeding. The highest concentration of HIV is in the urban areas of eastern and central Africa, in some of whose cities up to 10 percent of the population and up to 35 percent of pregnant women have acquired it. AIDS-related deaths are increasing fast; the victims are young adults and children, a serious situation in terms of future socioeconomic development. Hopes of holding the epidemic in check rest not on the use of antiviral agents but on increased condom use and on improved diagnosis and treatment of coincidental STDs. Because of poverty, the essential infrastructure for STD management is lacking or poorly used, thus facilitating the spread of HIV.

INTERNATIONAL ASSISTANCE

The Safe Motherhood Initiative (1987), "baby friendly" hospitals (1990), and the "mother baby package" (1995), all launched by UN agencies with support from nongovernmental agencies, raise public awareness, support research, and mount projects that map out strategies to reduce mortality and morbidity, strengthen child-survival efforts, popularize family planning, and check harmful infant feeding practices. These initiatives have added to our knowledge but have yet to make the desired impact because the underlying extreme poverty and grotesque inequalities have not been addressed.

CONCLUSION

Better reproductive health for Africa is a matter of rigorous application of what is already known. Among poor countries China, Cuba, Costa Rica, Sri Lanka, and the Indian state of Kerala have done so with dazzling results. In each of these places the political will to act is present; the right priorities are created; literacy and contraceptive use are widespread; and equity in health-care usage, including antenatal and intrapartum care, takes place. The challenge is to see these things happen in sub-Saharan Africa, and it is not impossible with international support. True, an educated society cannot emerge overnight, but at least basic health care during pregnancy and delivery can be provided free of charge.

See also **Demography: Fertility and Infertility; Demography: Population Data and Surveys; Disease; Education: School; Healing and Health Care: African Theories and Therapies; Initiation; Lake Chad Societies; Literacy; Nongovernmental Organizations; United Nations: United Nations in Africa; Women; World Bank.**

BIBLIOGRAPHY

Arkutu, A. "Family Planning in Sub-Saharan Africa: Present Status and Future Strategies." *International Journal of Gynecology and Obstetrics* 50, Supp. 2 (1995): S27–S34.

Ekwempu, C. C., et al. "Structural Adjustment and Health in Africa." *Lancet* 336 (July 7, 1990): 56–57.

Fleming, Alan F. "Anaemia in Pregnancy in Tropical Africa." *Transactions of the Royal Society of Tropical Medicine and Hygiene* 83 (1989): 441–448.

Harrison, Kelsey A. "Commentary. Obstetric Fistula: One Social Calamity Too Many." *British Journal of Obstetrics and Gynaecology* 90 (May 1983): 385–386.

Harrison, Kelsey A. "Editorial: Macroeconomics and the African Mother." *Journal of the Royal Society of Medicine* 89, no. 7 (July 1996): 361–362.

Harrison, Kelsey A. "Poverty, Deprivation, and Maternal Health. The 1995 William Meredith Fletcher Shaw Memorial Lecture." In *Yearbook of the Royal College of Obstetricians and Gynaecologists*, ed. John Studd. London: Royal College, 1996.

Harrison, Kelsey A. "The Importance of the Educated Healthy Woman in Africa." *Lancet* 349 (March 1, 1997): 644–647.

Kulczycki, Andrzej; Malcolm Potts; and Allan Rosenfield. "Abortion and Fertility Regulation." *Lancet* 347 (June 15, 1996): 1663–1668.

Lankinen, K. S.; S. Bergstrom; P. H. Makela; and M. Peltomaa; eds. *Health and Disease in Developing Countries*. London: Macmillan, 1994.

Lawson, John B. "Vesico-Vaginal Fistula—A Tropical Disease." *Transactions of the Royal Society of Tropical Medicine and Hygiene* 83 (1989): 454–456.

Pereira, C., et al. "Comparative Study of Caesarean Deliveries by Assistant Medical Officers and Obstetricians in Mozambique." *British Journal of Obstetrics and Gynaecology* 103 (1996): 508–512.

Quinn, T. C. "Global Burden of the HIV Pandemic." *Lancet* 348 (July 13, 1996): 99–106.

Summers, Lawrence. "The Most Influential Investment." *Scientific American* (August 1992): 108.

KELSEY A. HARRISON

CHILDREN AND CHILDHOOD

This entry includes the following articles:
INFANCY AND EARLY DEVELOPMENT
STATUS AND ROLES
SOLDIERS

INFANCY AND EARLY DEVELOPMENT

Infancy and early childhood in sub-Saharan Africa can only be understood in terms of the ecological, social, and cultural contexts into which children are born and in which they are raised. These contexts varied in form and content from one people to another even before the major changes and disruptions of the late twentieth century. The foragers of the Kalahari Desert and Central African tropical rain forests, for example, were sharply distinguished from the agricultural majority in sub-Saharan Africa by their reliance on hunting and gathering for subsistence, but they also differed widely among themselves in the environments they provided for infants and young children: Among the Kung San of the Kalahari (Botswana), mothers carried babies in a sling and cared for them without much help from others; among the Efe of the Ituri Forest (the Democratic Republic of the Congo), women of a camp breast-fed and cared for each other's babies; and among the Aka net hunters of the Central African Republic, fathers played an important role in infant care. Similarly, in those agricultural societies where several married women lived within a walled compound and shared a hearth (largely in West Africa), they often shared the care of their infants, while in those populations (largely in East Africa) where each married woman lived in a separate house on her own land, she depended primarily on her own children to help her with infant care. These examples indicate how variations in domestic patterns of work and cooperation create differing interpersonal environments for social development in infancy and early childhood.

SOME COMMON FEATURES

There were region-wide conditions that characterized the agricultural societies and even, to some extent, the foragers, in Africa: First, infants and young children were being raised in an environment high in risk from infectious diseases (malaria, diarrheal diseases, and acute respiratory infections), as indicated by high rates of infant and child mortality. This was particularly true until the 1950s, when public health measures and access to modern medicine began to reduce mortality rates, which continued to decline until the 1980s, when the spread of HIV/AIDS, hepatitis B, and drug-resistant malaria began to push them up again. Second, long birth intervals were typical of populations in the region, with breast-feeding lasting twenty-four to thirty-six months and (especially in West and Central Africa) a norm of three years' postpartum sexual abstinence that extended the birth interval beyond the contraceptive effect of lactation. Extended birth intervals afford protection for both mother and infants, leading to higher child survival rates than are possible with shorter intervals—a long-standing belief in many African societies that was confirmed by epidemiological research. (As modern medical care became available, the duration of breast-feeding and birth intervals tended to decrease, particularly where cow's milk was available for the post-weaning diet.) Thus in the mid-twentieth century a large proportion of African children reached the age of two as the mother's only baby, without having experienced the birth of a younger sibling. African parents at that time believed that that was the way it ought to be.

Finally, in most agricultural and pastoral societies of the sub-Saharan region, polygyny (a man having several wives) was considered the ideal family arrangement, and men strove to gain the wealth necessary to marry a second wife and if possible more. There are many socioeconomic implications and possible functions of polygyny in African societies, but it can also be seen as a social support for the long birth interval, in that the husband has more than one legitimate sexual partner at home and is less likely to violate the extended postpartum abstinence norm. Thus the polygynous family constitutes another element of the child's early social experience: one father, several co-mothers, and numerous half-siblings.

Polygyny takes varying forms across the African continent, in terms of the institutionalized relations among co-wives and their children. There is nonetheless a universal potential for competition among the co-wives, for the favor of the husband and for the property to be transferred to their children. In some societies, this potential is minimized by the ranking of co-wives and other measures that control competition and foster cooperation; in others, competition is translated into conflict that makes enemies of the several co-wives and their children. In either case, the child grows up knowing from a very early age that the home is partitioned by multiple marriages that diversify the interests of family members and that a potential for conflict exists. Thus the polygynous family, along with the extended birth intervals and serious

health risks, are common aspects of the environments into which African children were born in the twentieth century.

SOCIAL EXPERIENCES OF AFRICAN INFANTS
During the lengthy period between his birth and that of his "follower," the suckling infant in an agricultural society has unique claims on the mother's attention, sleeping next to her at night, being carried on her back in the daytime, and being fed on demand—altogether, the primary focus of mother's nurturant and protective activities, although other women and child nurses may assist in caregiving during the daytime when she is working in the fields or at the market.

The socialization of an African child can be said to begin in infancy in two respects: the building of relationships within the domestic group and the shaping of early communications. In societies with extended family compounds, mothers of the same compound tend to cooperate in infant care, and babies form attachments to a number of adult women; this is particularly widespread in western Africa but it can be found elsewhere, like the Kenya coast. Where mothers live separately in their own houses functioning autonomously within a wider domestic group, as in much of eastern Africa, the mother often relies on her own children for supplementary infant care, and then the youngest becomes part of a sibling group at an early age. These early relationships—with grandmothers or other closely related adult women or with a sister five to ten years old who carries the baby on her back—constitute the child's introduction to the kinship system. In some East African societies, the girl who carried her younger brother as an infant has a privileged relationship with him in adulthood, while among some peoples of the Sahel, such as the Hausa-speaking Fulani of northwestern Nigeria, it is considered desirable for the children of such siblings to marry each other.

African children typically learn important lessons about communicating appropriately even while they are still at the breast. Mothers and other caregivers soothe the crying infant rapidly, reducing the frequency of crying and preventing its development as an expression of rage and other emotions. The infant is quietly present at most domestic occasions, rarely the center of attention but able to observe the activities of others. Mothers do not treat their infants as conversational partners or playmates, and they use warnings and commands freely to keep their babies safe and introduce them to the local code of respect for authority that prevails in most rural African communities. By the time a child is two to three years old he or she has learned this code as enacted in the hierarchical world of the domestic group. Although there are variations in gender differentiation among African peoples, they tend to treat male and female infants equally, particularly by comparison with other world regions such as southern Asia and Latin America.

TODDLERS

The child who has been weaned from the breast is expected in many African societies to join the group of siblings and other related children in the home and eventually the neighborhood. Mothers tend to wean when they are pregnant, and once the new child is born, the older one is likely to experience a diminution in maternal attention. The recently weaned toddler has an increased risk of malnutrition, disease, and injury in many African settings, but the speculation that weaning from the breast is traumatic in emotional terms has not been supported by observational studies. Most frequently the weaned child finds its place in the sibling group after a brief period of distress. The actual experience of the child during this period depends in part on the age of weaning, for an eighteen-month-old child is less competent in language, locomotion, and interpersonal management than a child six months older. As the age of weaning decreased in the course of the twentieth century, from close to three years old or more to less than two, the risks of inadequate feeding and other problems probably increased.

Even children two to four years of age may help their elders with household tasks and with the herding of sheep, goats, and cattle. Their older siblings take daytime responsibility for their care and supervise their learning and work activities. Early childhood, roughly equivalent to what are called the preschool years in the West, is a period in which African children, as apprentices, rapidly acquire knowledge of the adult culture represented in their domestic environment: its norms of speech, social conduct, and emotional expression; the relationships among kin, men and women, and children in differing positions in the domestic hierarchy; and the routines of work, play, and ceremonial activity. With a degree of access to the adult world that is unknown in modern urban societies, rural African children—however quiet and peripheral they may seem when adults are present—master a great deal of their culture by the time they are five years old. Yet they have also learned to be compliant and responsible within the domestic hierarchy of the domestic group.

Parents and other adults organized the lives of children so that from infancy they began to acquire the competence in work tasks and interpersonal communication expected of all members of the community. Their early education reflected the labor demands of their rural economies, the socially organized relationships of their domestic groups, and the culturally defined virtues of their local communities.

LATE-TWENTIETH-CENTURY SITUATION

The stability presumed by this portrait of infancy and early childhood among the agricultural peoples of Africa was gradually undermined by social change during the last three decades of the twentieth century. As children increasingly attended school, mothers could no longer count on them to take care of infants. Among the Gusii of Kenya, for example, the seven- or eight-year-old girl who formerly had full-time responsibility for her infant sibling was replaced by a variety of siblings, some in their teens, who did short stints of infant care after school. Mothers had less need for sibling care or child labor in general, as population density increased, agriculture declined, and wells provided water to the home. Some families moved to the city; others stayed home but lived on remittances from fathers working outside. As African rural economies declined, so did the moral order into which young children had been socialized. Parents were often confused about child rearing, attempting to balance traditional values with the new demands of schooling, but their focus had to be on managing to survive amidst the increasing poverty of the 1980s.

In the late 1980s and 1990s, communities in some parts of Africa were severely disrupted by civil wars (creating refugees with malnourished children), the AIDS epidemic (creating orphans on an unprecedented scale), and the spread of other infections that killed infants and young children: drug-resistant malaria and hepatitis B. Child survival was once again at risk, and the local communities that had once nurtured young children could no longer do so. It is estimated that 61 percent of children under five in sub-Saharan Africa are disadvantaged (as measured by poverty and malnutrition), the highest of any region in the world. It is now up to African governments and international agencies to restore the stability and resources of environments for the rearing of infants and young children.

See also **Disease: HIV/AIDS, Social and Political Aspects; Healing and Health Care; Kalahari Desert; Kinship and Descent.**

BIBLIOGRAPHY

Ainsworth, Mary. *Infancy in Uganda.* Baltimore: Johns Hopkins University Press, 1967.

Gottlieb, Alma. *Afterlife Is Where We Come From: The Culture of Infancy in West Africa.* Chicago: University of Chicago Press, 2004.

Grantham-McGregor, S., et al. "Developmental Potential in the First Five Years for Children in Developing Countries." *The Lancet* 369 (2007): 60–70.

Hewlett, Barry S. *Intimate Fathers: The Nature and Context of Aka Pygmy Paternal Infant Care.* Ann Arbor: University of Michigan Press, 1991.

Hewlett, Barry and Michael Lamb, eds. *Hunter-Gatherer Childhoods.* Hawthorne, NY: Aldine de Gruyter, 2005.

LeVine, Robert A., Suzanne Dixon, Sarah LeVine, Amy Richman, P. Herbert Leiderman, Constance H. Keefer and T. Berry Brazelton. *Child Care and Culture: Lessons from Africa.* New York: Cambridge University Press, 1994.

Super, Charles M. and Sara Harkness. "Infant's Niche in Rural Kenya and Metropolitan America." In *Cross-Cultural Research at Issue,* ed. L. L. Adler. New York: Academic Press, 1985.

ROBERT LEVINE

STATUS AND ROLES

Historically, African children have been critical to the domestic economies of their societies. Far from being little helpers in their labor-intensive economies, similar to adults, they have been farmers, herders, fishers, hunters, miners, toolmakers, cooks, child-minders, and soldiers. In such demand was child labor that controllers of labor—largely male heads of households, but also women, as the main food producers—have sought to recruit such labor by means beyond marriage and procreation: captivity and incorporation through raids and wars; tribute from weak states to centrally organized states; pawning or debt servitude; apprenticeship; and fostering. Pawning and fostering are cases in point.

Before colonial rule, family heads who fell on hard times due to natural disaster, political instability, personal misfortune, or other financial need could pawn, or lend, a child (preferably a girl) to wealthier members of their community in exchange for grain or money. The pawn's labor paid the interest on the loan, not the principal, and the pawn could remain in this situation her entire life. A girl pawn could be married to her creditor or his kin, her children taking on the status of pawn as well. In the early decades of colonial rule, pawning increased rather than decreased. The demand for legitimate commerce—the export of raw materials instead of slaves—increased the need for labor in farming, mining, commerce, and transportation. Large-scale cash-crop farmers in need of labor for growing and transporting crops acquired pawns from poorer peasants. Cash-crop farmers in need of loans to purchase land or to make up for low market prices also pawned their female dependents. After various colonial governments outlawed pawning, pawns were disguised as child brides and adoptees. Pawns were acquired increasingly to work as domestic servants in the growing urban areas and as market-stall assistants to (largely female) traders. Fathers also pawned their daughters to raise money to pay the school fees of their sons or to take expensive titles.

Pawning began to decline during the interwar period as parents and creditors were faced with resistance by the pawns themselves: increasingly, children fled this potentially lifelong form of servitude for the anonymity and freedom of town. Moreover, other forms of collateral began to take the place of pawns: land, jewelry, cloth, and access to credit union and bank loans. Nevertheless, pawning, particularly of girls, persists into the early twenty-first century as rural poverty grows and the demand for child labor in both rural and urban areas increases in order to replace the death of adults killed by AIDS.

The fostering of children—the movement of children from their birth parents' home to the home of a kinsman or a stranger—is also widespread in Africa and possibly increasing. According to Isiugo-Abanihe, fostering falls into several categories that are not necessarily discrete: fostering within the kin group; fostering that results from crises; fostering that is designed to forge or solidify alliances or provide apprentices; fostering that provides wealthier families with domestic servants; and fostering to provide an education for children of poor kin or non-kin. The form that most resembles pawning—and possibly grew out of the legal prohibitions on pawning introduced during the colonial period—involves the placement of a child in the home of a near or distant kin member or stranger for the specific purpose of work. The parents receive financial consideration in the form of an up-front lump sum of cash, or periodic payments from the foster parent. Girls were and continue to be fostered to work as domestic servants in the homes of better-off kin or non-kin, particularly in town. Boys are often fostered out in this way to serve as apprentices to artisans. A common form of fostering that emerged early on during the colonial period involves the placement of a child (usually but not always a boy) with wealthier relatives or strangers who promise to send the child to school. He is expected to work for the foster parents and is likely to receive an education that is inferior to that received by the foster parents' own children. Girls are placed with wealthier and educated relatives or strangers with the hope that they will receive training in the ways of Westernized domestic life and thereby acquire a wealthy and educated husband. Children were and are fostered to childless couples. As with pawning, the HIV/AIDS pandemic is likely to see the rise of forms of fostering that are exploitative of fostered children, and an increase in child labor.

See also **Colonial Policies and Practices; Labor: Child; Labor: Domestic; Slavery and Servile Institutions; Women: Women and Slavery.**

BIBLIOGRAPHY

Bass, Loretta E. *Child Labor in Sub-Saharan Africa.* Boulder, CO: Lynne Rienner, 2004.

Grier, Beverly. *Invisible Hands: Child Labor and the State in Colonial Zimbabwe.* Portsmouth, NH: Heinemann, 2005.

Isiugo-Abanihe, Uche C. "Child Fosterage in West Africa." *Population and Development Review* 11, no. 1 (1985): 53–73.

Kielland, Anne, and Maurizia Tovo. *Children at Work: Child Labor Practices in Africa.* Boulder, CO: Lynne Rienner, 2006.

Lovejoy, Paul E., and Toyin Falola, eds. *Pawnship, Slavery, and Colonialism in Africa.* Trenton, NJ: Africa World Press, 2003.

BEVERLY GRIER

SOLDIERS

In recent decades, children and youths feature centrally as both the targets and the perpetrators of violence. In nearly every war and civil conflict, children are among the principal victims. However, the involvement of young people in warfare is not a recent phenomenon; it is deeply rooted in the history of European and American as well as Asian and African civilizations. During the Middle Ages in Europe, for example, upper-class boys who hoped to become knights would serve as squires and were taught skills related to the duties and responsibilities of knighthood. Italians called the young soldiers who followed knights into battle on foot *infante*, which literally means child, and collectively these children made up the *infanteria*, or infantry.

Young people have been at the forefront of warfare and political conflict in many parts of the world. However, the scale and magnitude of the problem today is unprecedented, both in the numbers of young people involved and in the degree of their participation. It is estimated that in Africa, about 100,000 children under the age of eighteen in 2004 were involved in armed conflicts as soldiers in places such as Burundi, Democratic Republic of the Congo, Côte d'Ivoire, Sudan, and Uganda. In past conflicts in Angola, Eritrea, Ethiopia, Liberia, Mozambique, Sierra Leone and Zimbabwe, children also featured as combatants. Children get caught up in armed conflict in a whole host of ways from participation in direct combat to serving as spies, carriers of ammunition, guards, cooks, and servants in military camps. Girls are sometimes involved in combat but usually are subject to sexual abuse, rape, enslavement, and other tribulations during war.

Some children and young people volunteer to fight, either in response to the killing of a family member or because they genuinely want to fight against the denial of jobs and education. But most recruitment into armed groups is predominately through coercion, and the boundaries between forced and voluntary recruitment is blurred, given the limited choices many of the youth face. Once in the armed groups, young people are initiated into violence through a deliberate process of terror. Terrified themselves, they are prepared to inflict terror on others. These are not two separate phases in which child soldiers were first brutalized by soldiers and then forced to brutalize civilians. Rather, the infliction of suffering on others is part of their own initiation into violence.

Child soldiers exist not simply because of a shortage of fighters but because they can be formed into good soldiers. The initiation of the young into violence constitutes a carefully orchestrated process of identity reconfiguration, transforming them into merciless killers. Having started out as victims, many of them are converted into perpetrators of the most violent and atrocious deeds.

Profound changes in the nature of warfare have contributed to the increasing involvement of children in warfare. These changes arise not only from the way wars are fought but also from new military technologies. The new civil wars in which young people are active participants do not resemble the old wars that shaped the Geneva Conventions of 1949. Recent civil wars tend to obliterate distinctions between civilians and belligerents in ways hardly witnessed before. In these new wars, the separation between the battlefield and the home front becomes blurred as civilians are forced to perform military tasks. Also, whereas in the past heavy and unwieldy weapons limited children's usefulness on the frontlines, today's arms' technology has developed in such a way that small boys and girls can handle weapons such as M16 and AK-47 assault rifles. The uncontrolled proliferation of small arms and light weapons adds to this.

The magnitude of children's involvement in war led the international community to establish a legal and normative framework of protection. The 1977 First Protocol Additional to the Geneva Conventions already provided that states shall take "all feasible measures in order that children who have not attained the age of fifteen years do not take a direct part in hostilities and . . . they shall refrain from recruiting them into their armed forces" (United Nations 1977). The 1989 Convention on the Rights of the Child, article 38(2), and the 1990 African Charter on the Rights and Welfare of the Child, article 22(2), both reinforce the provisions of the First Protocol by emphasizing that states must ensure the protection of children under the age of fifteen from taking direct part in hostilities. The Optional Protocol to the Convention on the Rights of the Child on the Involvement of Children in Armed Conflicts, adopted 2000, raises the minimum age for military recruitment to eighteen years of age. Although states are increasingly ratifying these normative instruments, there is still much to be done to prevent child soldering.

Demobilization programs intended to assist former soldiers in the transition home are more immediately designed to contain, disarm, and demobilize armed groups. These programs often exclude soldiers under the legal age for military recruitment and focused exclusively on males, leaving out girls and young women. Postwar healing and reintegration of war-affected children and youth is a major concern, for these young people constitute the next generation, the producers, the parents, and the leaders of tomorrow. Those who welcome them back to local communities seek to ensure that they are fully rehabilitated and prepared to assume their adult social roles. Community-based cleansing and healing rituals seem to be effective in dealing with the emotional and social problems of war-affected children, helping them to come to terms with their war experiences and facilitating their reintegration into family and community life. Studies conducted in Mozambique, Uganda, Sierra Leone and Angola attest to this.

In the aftermath of the war, many demobilized youth continue to be as vulnerable as they were before joining the military; they still have no access to education, employment, and other forms of livelihood. In many cases their socioeconomic situation worsened; as the war brought not only displacement but also a massive destruction of social and economic infrastructure.

Therefore, beyond psychosocial healing in the immediate aftermath of war, lasting results will only be achieved if the world is committed to address the structural causes of this problem, by improving the conditions of the poor through economic development and facilitating political participation and social stability.

See also **Initiation; Warfare; Youth: Soldiers.**

BIBLIOGRAPHY

Boyden, Jo, and Joanna de Berry. *Children and Youth on the Frontline: Ethnography, Armed Conflict and Displacement.* New York: Berghahn Books, 2004.

Brett, Rachel, and Irma Specht. *Young Soldiers: Why They Choose to Fight.* Boulder: Lynne Rienner, 2004.

Graça, Machel. *The Impact of War on Children: A Review since the 1996 United Nations Report on the Impact of Armed Conflict on Children.* New York: Palgrave, 2001.

Honwana, Alcinda. *Child Soldiers in Africa.* Philadelphia: University of Pennsylvania Press, 2006.

Singer, Peter W. *Children at War.* New York: Pantheon Books, 2005.

United Nations. "Article 77 (2)." *Protocol Additional to the Geneva Conventions of 12 August 1949, and Relating to the Protection of Victims of International Armed Conflicts (Protocol 1).* Geneva: Office of the United Nations High Commissioner for Human Rights, 1977.

ALCINDA HONWANA

Reverend John Chilembwe (1871–1915). Chilembwe is considered a hero of independence. A holiday named in his honor is celebrated each year on January 15 in Malawi.

CHILEMBWE, JOHN (c. 1871–1915).
Born Nkologo Chilembwe at Sangano, eastern Chiradzulu in the nascent British colony of Nyasaland (today Malawi), Chilembwe attended the Presbyterian mission in Blantyre, Malawi. He broke with this denomination in 1892 to join Joseph Booth (1851–1932), the radical Baptist missionary who popularized the concept "Africa for the Africans" in central Africa. In 1897 Booth took Chilembwe to America, where his militancy was increased at the Lynchburg, Virginia, black Baptist seminary. Returning home in 1900, Chilembwe, with African American helpers, established the Providence Industrial Mission in Chiradzulu. Chilembwe's independent spirit, church building, and Western-style education and dress soon clashed with the prejudices of local European estate holders. He criticized their domineering attitudes and the abuses of their labor system. By the eve of World War I, he had become bitterly critical of colonialism as well.

On November 26, 1914, Chilembwe published a letter in the *Nyasaland Times,* "The Voice of African Natives in the Present War," which has since become a classic document of African nationalism. Chilembwe secretly organized a millenarian uprising against colonial rule, with the aim of setting up an independent African state or dying in the attempt. The rebellion broke out on January 23, 1915, and ended on February 3, 1915, when Chilembwe was shot escaping into Mozambique. There were few casualties on either side.

The colonial government attempted to stifle discussion of the Chilembwe Rising; nevertheless Chilembwe's reputation grew among central African nationalists. The memory of Chilembwe's anticolonial movement was a factor in the destruction of the Central African Federation (1953–1963) and an inspiration to the establishment of the independent state of Malawi.

See also **Christianity; Malawi: History and Politics.**

BIBLIOGRAPHY

Mwase, George Simeon. *Strike a Blow and Die: A Narrative of Race Relations in Colonial Africa*, ed. Robert I. Rotberg. Cambridge, MA: Harvard University Press, 1967.

Phiri, D. D. *Malawians to Remember: John Chilembwe.* Lilongwe, Malawi: Longman (Malawi), 1976.

Shepperson, George, and Thomas Price. *Independent African: John Chilembwe and the Origins, Setting, and Significance of the Nyasaland Native Rising of 1915.* Blantyre: Christian Literature Association in Malawi, 2000.

GEORGE SHEPPERSON

CHINA IN AFRICAN HISTORY.

Contemporary diplomatic relations between African countries and the People's Republic of China (PRC) officially began following the Bandung Conference, a summit of leaders from African and Asian states that was convened in Indonesia in 1955. The participants at the Bandung meeting came together to forge an international alliance that could become an alternative to the existing diplomatic alignments of late colonialism and the Cold War. Bandung therefore represented an important initial step in the development of subsequent movements of Afro-Asian, third world, and nonaligned solidarity. Yet although the Bandung period (1955–1959) was a time of much diplomatic activity between China and Africa, China's relationship with the African continent had a much deeper history, a history whose significance was often remembered in the speeches and diplomatic exchanges of the mid-twentieth century.

China and Africa had a long record of contacts and trading relationships that extended over a period of several centuries before Bandung. Scholars disagree over the time and place of the first direct communications between China and Africa, but some argue that envoys from the Han Dynasty who were sent west over 2,100 years ago reached Egypt. A Chinese officer described in his travel diary the visit he made to a place called Molin on the East African coast in the middle of the eighth century. The archaeological record shows that Chinese goods, especially porcelain and coins, were circulating in African trade networks from well before the Common Era. A Chinese map of Africa drawn in 1315 showed that Chinese cartographers had an accurate understanding of the shape and geographical position of the African continent, most likely gained through extensive trading contacts in the Indian Ocean region.

The most famous Chinese emissary to East Africa, Admiral Zheng He (1371–1433), made a total of seven sea voyages in the Indian Ocean between 1405 and 1433, stopping on the coasts of present-day Somalia and Kenya, including Mogadishu, Brava, Juba, and Malindi. African ambassadors from these towns and cities also visited China, taking with them gifts that were viewed as exotic in China, for example wild animals. Following Zheng He's visits, direct contacts between China and Africa dropped off, due to internal policy shifts within China and to Portuguese (and later Omani) dominance over the trade of the western Indian Ocean after 1505. China's presence in Africa remained limited during the periods of European imperialism and colonization, with the exception of Chinese indentured laborers. In the nineteenth century Chinese workers were brought to the sugar plantations of the Mascarene Islands, and in the early twentieth century Chinese indentured laborers worked in the gold mines of South Africa's Transvaal following the South African War (1903–1907).

The Bandung Conference of 1955 thus marked a historical turning point for Africa-China relations. Following Bandung, President Gamal Abdel Nasser of Egypt was the first African leader to recognize the PRC in 1956. Sudan followed in 1958, and in subsequent years other independent African state leaders also began to recognize China, including Kwame Nkrumah, the first president of Ghana, who visited Beijing in 1961, and Modibo Keita, the first president of Mali. By 1965, China had established diplomatic relations with nineteen African states.

China's political emphasis at this time was to support those countries sympathetic to socialism, while supporting dissident factions in those that were strongly pro-Western. After 1959, China's relationship with Africa's leaders was deeply affected by the developing rift between China and the Soviet Union. The Sino-Soviet split caused destabilizing policies that encouraged disunity among political factions. As a result, many African leaders became disillusioned with China's political strategy.

From 1963–1964, Zhou En-lai (1898–1976) toured Africa to introduce a new approach to China-Africa relations. During his visits he unveiled the five principles of Chinese political relations and eight principles of Chinese development assistance. Among the most important of these was China's commitment to interest-free or low-interest loans; transfer of technical knowledge rather than reliance on expatriates; and the simple comportment of Chinese project staff. During his tour, Zhou En-lai emphasized that China's role would be that of a true friend and would encourage self-reliance, peace, cooperation, and economic development. The many African leaders who visited China at this time were impressed by China's achievements in literacy and agrarian change, and believed that this development experience held promise for their own countries. By 1975, China had more development programs in Africa than the United States, and by the 1990s had given assistance to forty-seven African countries.

The eight principles of economic aid could be clearly seen in such practical assistance projects as agricultural schemes (especially rice irrigation projects), light industry, roads and infrastructure, educational scholarships, and medical assistance. China's most famous economic development project in Africa was the TAZARA or Great Freedom Railway, built to link the copper mines of Zambia to the Tanzanian port of Dar es Salaam, when rail routes to the south were still controlled by Rhodesia and South Africa. Constructed between 1968 and 1975, the railway has served both as a hauler of heavy goods and as a critical transport link for rural travelers and small-scale traders.

After 1978, economic and political reforms in China caused aid policies to shift again. Economic liberalization and structural adjustment policies adopted by African countries after the mid-1980s have also encouraged market-oriented investment programs in addition to development assistance. In the early twenty-first century, China has continued to articulate an approach to African development that emphasizes political and economic cooperation that is win-win for both sides. Once again, China has emphasized the differences between its approach to development assistance in Africa and that of Western countries that impose conditions on aid.

See also **Aid and Development; Cartography; Cold War; Immigration and Immigrant Groups: Chinese; Literacy; Nasser, Gamal Abdel; Nkrumah, Francis Nwia Kofi; Travel and Exploration: Chinese.**

BIBLIOGRAPHY

Brautigam, Deborah. *Chinese Aid and African Development: Exporting Green Revolution.* New York: St. Martin's Press, 1998.

Hutchison, Alan. *China's African Revolution.* London: Hutchinson, 1975.

Larkin, Bruce. *China and Africa, 1949–1970: The Foreign Policy of the People's Republic of China.* Berkeley: University of California Press, 1971.

Snow, Philip. *The Star Raft: China's Encounter with Africa.* London: Weidenfeld and Nicolson, 1988.

Taylor, Ian. *China and Africa: Engagement and Compromise.* Oxford: Routledge, 2006.

Yu, George. *China's Africa Policy: A Study of Tanzania.* New York: Praeger, 1975.

JAMIE MONSON

CHINGULIA, DOM JERÓNIMO

(1607–c. 1640). Chingulia, the seventeenth-century king of Mombasa, was known before his conversion to Christianity as Yusuf ibn al-Hasan. When the then ruler of the Mombasa city-state died about 1592, Yusuf's father, king of Malindi, moved to Mombasa as his successor. He had frequent episodes of friction with the Portuguese, then intruding everywhere along the Swahili coast, which culminated in his assassination in 1614. Yusuf, aged seven at the time, was put in his father's place, then sent to the Portuguese post in western India, Goa, to be educated. He was pressured to become Christian and was baptized in 1616.

About 1626 he was crowned king of Mombasa in Goa, after marriage to a Portuguese noblewoman. Following service in the Portuguese navy, he returned to Mombasa around 1629. For two years Chingulia complained of the insults and injustice of the Portuguese governor, whom he personally assassinated on August 15, 1631. At the same time he resumed his Muslim name and ordered the Augustinian missionaries, who had educated him, and their Christian parishioners to accept Islam. Almost all refused, and first the clergy, then the men, then women and children were put to death. The incident is best understood as revenge for the assassination of his father, for there was no popular uprising in Mombasa at the time that would otherwise motivate such a slaughter. In 1632 a Portuguese fleet was sent to Mombasa to restore order. Yusuf took up a life of piracy in the Indian Ocean, disappearing from history after 1637.

The fullest details about Chingulia's life were discovered in the Archives of the Postulature of the Augustinian Generalate in Rome in 1964 and have been published in the original and in translation. They are contained in a *processus martyrii*, the ecclesiastical inquiry into whether the victims should be canonized as saints.

See also **Christianity; Mambasa.**

BIBLIOGRAPHY

Alonso, Carlos. *Los Agustinos en la Costa Suahili, 1598–1698*. Valladolid, Spain: Estudio Agustiniano, 1988.

Freeman-Grenville, G. S. P. *The Mombasa Rising against the Portuguese, 1631, from Sworn Evidence*. London: Oxford University Press, 1980.

Freeman-Grenville, G. S. P., comp. *The East African Coast: Select Documents from the First to the Earlier Nineteenth Century*, 2nd edition. London: Collings, 1975.

Mbuia-João, Tomé Nhamitambo. "The Revolt of Dom Jeronimo Chingulia of Mombasa, 1590–1637: An African Episode in the Portuguese Century of Decline. Ph.D. thesis. Catholic University of America, 1990.

Strandes, Justus. *The Portuguese Period in East Africa*, trans. J. F. Wallwork and ed. J. S. Kirkman. Nairobi: East African Literature Bureau, 1968.

G. S. P. Freeman-Grenville

CHITAPANKWA, MUTALE MUTAKA

(??–1883). A cunning and ambitious warrior in what is now northeastern Zambia in the mid-nineteenth century, Mutale Mutaka Chitapankwa had tried in vain to defeat King Chileshye of the Bemba confederation with the aid of the *tafuna* (chief) of the neighboring Lungu people. He returned to the Bemba, feigning conciliation, and Chileshye gave his daughter, Kafula, and a village on the Mabula stream to Chitapankwa as a peace offering. After Chileshye died in about 1860, Chitapankwa saw himself as the rightful successor. He tricked Bwenbya, the designated heir, by inviting him to a feast and then having his followers steal the royal spear and bow (which represented power) while Bwenbya was watching a ceremonial dance. Chitapankwa's brother, Sampa, also had a claim to the title of ruler, and Chitapankwa had to first defeat his brother before confirming his position as king.

As soon as Chitapankwa achieved sovereignty he bullied or killed most neighboring chiefs, obtaining their allegiance or replacing them with kinsmen of his own. He successfully traded with the British for guns, though he did not allow the Bemba people to use these weapons. Instead he enlisted small traders to engage in the frontal attack upon his enemies. Chitapankwa was very successful at war and succeeded in consolidating and greatly extending the Bemba sphere of influence. His greatest achievement was the defeat of the Ngoni nation, militarily powerful intruders from southeastern Africa, then otherwise spreading throughout the region.

Under Chitapankwa the Bemba people greatly increased their profits from slave trading and were able to dictate trade laws designed to enrich the Bemba's connection to important east coast traders such as Tippu Tip. Although the Bemba became militarily dominant in the region, unity was superficial and there was little cooperation among the chiefs. The Bemba raiders and Chitapankwa were feared but never respected. Other nations considered them to be untrustworthy warriors. When the British eventually stopped selling guns to the Bemba their dominance diminished.

See also **Tippu Tip; Zambia: History and Politics.**

BIBLIOGRAPHY

Roberts, Andrew D. *A History of the Bemba: Political Growth and Change in Northeastern Zambia before 1900*. Madison: University of Wisconsin Press, 1973.

Gary Thoulouis

CHRISTIANITY

This entry includes the following articles:
OVERVIEW
AFRICA AND WORLD CHRISTIANITY
AFRICAN INSTITUTED CHURCHES
MISSIONARY ENTERPRISE
COPTIC CHURCH AND SOCIETY
ETHIOPIAN CHURCH

OVERVIEW

"Awake and Sing the Song of Moses and the Lamb"—such was the hymn chanted in 1792 by a group of African Americans as they came ashore at Freetown in Sierra Leone, in what can be seen as the beginning of modern Christian history in sub-Saharan Africa. They were blacks who had fought on the British side in the American Revolution and who had subsequently been resettled in Nova Scotia. Now they had been offered a free passage back to Africa, and more than a thousand came. David George, a Baptist preacher, led one group; Luke Jordan, a Methodist, another; William Ash and Cato Perkins, preachers in the Countess of Huntingdon's Connection, piloted the group that burst into the Exodus homecoming hymn of Moses and the Lamb. There were no missionaries here, only a British governor none too happy with these exuberant sects but unable to control them. Thus Freetown began, the entry point of institutionalized Protestant Christianity into the African continent north of the Cape of Good Hope.

The plan to people Freetown with Nova Scotians seems to have come from Ottobah Cugoano, a freed slave of Fante (Gold Coast) origins with the English name of John Stuart. In 1787 he had published in London a powerful indictment of the slave trade, *Thoughts and Sentiments on the Evil and Wicked Traffic of the Slavery and Commerce of the Human Species Humbly Submitted to the Inhabitants of Great Britain.* Two years later a friend of his, another former slave but of Igbo background, published another book, his autobiography, *The Interesting Narrative of the Life of Olaudah Equiano or Gustavus Vassa, the African.* Equiano had been carried off in childhood from his home, and is seen looking back on it when he reads the Bible, "wistfully surprised" to find "the laws and rules" of the one written "almost exactly" in the other—an alliance detected between traditional Africa and the Bible which missionaries were seldom willing to recognize but to which modern African theologians would often return, only too enthusiastically.

Equiano's high view of his own non-Christian Africa did not imply that he was not a good Evangelical too. The frontispiece of his *Interesting Narrative* portrays him holding the New Testament open at the page in the Acts of the Apostles that brought about his spiritual conversion. His offer to the bishop of London to return home to (modern) Nigeria as an ordained Protestant missionary was not accepted. He was no less a missionary by intent, though the mission that he actually busied himself with was one of persuading the British people of the evil of slavery. But in Equiano, Cugoano, and the preachers who led the returning exiles to Freetown in the 1790s can be discerned already a large part of the Christian Africa they were about to found: a many-churches community of English-speaking Protestants, flourishing upon Bible and hymnbook, strong on liberation from slavery but strong too on the continuities between old Africa and its new gospel.

NINETEENTH CENTURY

In 1807 the British Parliament declared the slave trade illegal. As a consequence, in the following years cargoes of slaves intercepted by British frigates were landed at Freetown. None of these people—known as "recaptives"—had any previous acquaintance with Christianity, but divided as they were among themselves in ethnicity and language and mostly quite young, they could hardly do other than enter into a willing identification with the black community that had become their host and new home. They quickly outnumbered the original Nova Scotian inhabitants, and Freetown, together with its surrounding villages, became a center of African-born Christians. Many of them were Yoruba from the area inland from Lagos, and despite being educated in the schools which the Church Missionary Society (CMS) was beginning to provide, they had by no means lost a sense of belonging to their original homelands farther along the coast. Freetown thus became a bridge for a vigorous Protestantism about to disseminate itself farther afield to Lagos and other Yoruba communities at Abeokuta and Onitsha. Among the many young people landed at Freetown was a Yoruba boy named Ajayi, who arrived in 1822, entered school, and was soon baptized with the name Samuel Crowther. His long and distinguished life as missionary and pastor to his ancestral people would come to symbolize nineteenth-century West African Christianity uniquely well.

Move, however, more to the south, to São Salvador, near the mouth of the Zaire River, the ancient capital of the Kongo kingdom. When Ajayi was baptized, Garcia V had been reigning here for some twenty years. Kongo had been an emphatically Christian kingdom by its own understanding for three hundred years. It had admittedly declined in power and size and, in place of the regular Capuchin and other Catholic ministrations of the past, it now hardly ever saw a priest. Garcia had been king since 1803 but had to wait until 1814 for a Capuchin monk to come from Luanda to crown him in state and solemnize his marriage—ritual crucial for sanctioning the monarchy. Twenty-five thousand of his subjects were baptized at the same time. In such circumstances Garcia, like many of his predecessors, sought the ordination of some Kongo, and his son Pedro became a priest in 1824. Here then is a very different portrait of African Christianity: Catholic, ritualistic, Portuguese-speaking, and ancient, where the face of Freetown was Protestant, hymn-singing, English-speaking, and young. The Kongo face had barely managed to survive at all, and in the course of the nineteenth century it would become almost, though never quite, extinct. But somewhat similar patterns, royal and ritualist, would later spring up elsewhere.

Go south again. The only black Christian communities of any size extant in South Africa by 1820 were of the Khoe, either absorbed within the community of strong Dutch Calvinists at the Cape Colony and clustered together in missions like Bethelsdorp or surviving, still half-independent, as mini-societies on its edges. The largest of these was that of the Griquas, whose elected leader around 1820 was Andries Waterboer, a former mission-school teacher who continued to preach regularly in church and whose praises were sung in later years by David Livingstone. Waterboer, not wholly unlike Garcia V, represented what would in due course be a numerous and significant type of Christian leader, the catechist who becomes local spokesperson and even political power holder.

Now turn to the east. It was probably in 1815 that Ntsikana, an orator and counselor of the Xhosa king Ngquika beyond the Drakensberg Mountains on the coasts above the Indian Ocean, had a vision and heard an inner voice compelling him to baptize himself by plunging into the Ggorha River, washing away the ornamental red ochre of Xhosa tradition, and then to alter his way of life fundamentally. It seems probable that Ntsikana had at some earlier moment heard a passing missionary preach, but here again the decisive step was taken without any missionary presence. Ntsikana was the first major African Christian prophet of modern times. Unbaptized in any way that a missionary would recognize, he became, nevertheless, the most powerful single spiritual influence upon the development of Christianity in southern Africa. "This thing which has entered me says 'Let there be prayer! Let everything bow the knee!'"

The disciples who gathered around Ntsikana learned a simple message concerning the sovereignty of God, the importance of daily prayer, the holiness of Sunday, the rejection of red ochre (the usual bodily adornment of the Xhosa people), the call of pacifism, and—very especially—the hymns for which he became famous. Ntsikana's "Great Hymn" was quickly taken into missionary hymnals, being printed already in the 1820s, but it was treasured above all by the group which came to be known as the Congregation of the God of Ntsikana. This sect was institutionally absorbed within Xhosa Protestantism as it came to develop, but the primacy in the African Christian experience of the spiritual insight of this prophet, who never knew anything of a European language, is here very clear.

Equiano, the Freetown pioneers, Garcia V, Andries Waterboer, and Ntsikana represent a wide range of faces for early nineteenth-century African Christianity: from the Londoner with his fluent command of written English to the illiterate visionary. One point about them is that not one owes much to a missionary, though all showed every intention of adhering to Christianity, as it had existed in one or another of its historic forms outside Africa. Most important, they demonstrate, well before any major wave of missionary activity, the multiplicity of ways in which Christianity could be experienced by Africans, and allow that much-discussed concept, "the Africanization of Christianity," to be understood.

In the 1820s the real European Christian missionary invasion of Africa was just about to begin. It would grow almost unceasingly over the next hundred years, moving in from the coast on every side of the continent until—especially after the completion of Europe's political scramble for the continent around 1890—one could find in almost every part of the continent a network of mission stations, Catholic and Protestant. The effect of this invasion on the spread of what had been a fairly tenuous African Christianity in the early years of the century is striking. In some places, such as the area of the Great Lakes from the late 1870s, the missionary arrival brought an almost completely new start to African church life. Very often, nevertheless, while it was a new start for the missionaries, it was not so on the African side. The Livingstonia missionaries by Lake Nyasa in the 1870s, for instance, had come straight from Scotland, but their assistant, William Koyi, who was really the person who achieved the breakthrough with the Ngoni, was a Xhosa Christian steeped in the tradition of Ntsikana.

In the case of the Anglican mission in Nigeria the missionary and African sides of Christianity were indeed, to a large extent, formally one. While it was certainly a CMS mission, its recruiting base was not Britain but Sierra Leone. When Samuel Crowther was ordained a priest in 1843 and sent back to preach the gospel, first in his native town of Abeokuta and then along the Niger, of which he became bishop in 1864 at the insistence of Henry Venn, the CMS general secretary, a very different principle was in fact being followed than the one Venn is famed for affirming. Venn had formulated the task of the foreign mission as the establishment of "a Native Church under Native Pastors and a Native Episcopate" which was to be followed by the "euthanasia" of the mission or, instead, its relocation to "the regions beyond." It is generally taken for granted that Venn began to carry out this plan with the establishment of Crowther's Niger diocese. It was not so. No "Native Church" had as yet been established in those parts. Crowther went to the Niger as a missionary bishop but was no less an African for that. His appointment was in truth the

recognition of a very different principle—that the conversion of Africa would be achieved by Africans, not by foreigners.

While Crowther's episcopate was exceptional and judged by whites to be a promotion too far, the point that needs stressing is that application of the identical principle at a more local level was regular missionary strategy, but the African evangelization of Africa went far beyond that. In many a case the evangelists acted quite without authorization by their missionary nominal superiors. They moved forward as traders or migrants looking for employment or land to cultivate but were no less keen to share at the same time the Christian beliefs and practices they had learned at home. This sort of informal evangelization across half a continent was far too low-key and disorganized to be adequately documented, but it and not the well-documented activities of the large mission stations constituted the cutting edge of the Christianization process. The comment of R. A. Coker, the Anglican Yoruba priest who presided over the Ijebu conversion movement of the 1890s, is widely true of every part of the continent: "We often have pleasant surprises of adherents in many places we little dreamed of. Again, as the converts are all traders, they go as preachers of the Word taking with them their Bibles and prayerbooks."

Religious conversion, whether of an individual or a group, is something notoriously difficult to analyze. Its takeoff point seems often superficial, materially self-seeking, or just the interpretation of some specific incident in terms of an ultimate meaning which appears to be, to the noninvolved, inadequate to bear so great a weight. Yet once a personal or group process of spiritual change has been set moving, it follows a deeper logic of its own as it becomes receptive to that of the faith it is set upon embracing. However, for this process to gain momentum there generally needs to be some perceptible crumbling in the credibility of that from which one moves. People found their way to Christianity (or, for that matter, to Islam) in Africa in the early modern period within societies whose traditional structures of meaning seemed suddenly shattered either by the impact of colonialism itself or simply by the enlargement of scale, intellectual and commercial, produced in the experience of life by some facet of the Western impact on familiar habits. To non-literate societies the power of writing, of the Book, could seem spectacularly impressive. The most characteristic and effective achievement of the nineteenth-century missionary had been to translate the scriptures, hymnbooks, and catechisms into a great number of Africans' languages. In many of them almost nothing else was ever printed. Literacy meant a near-exclusive exposure to the core writings of the Christian tradition. The power of a single vernacular booklet containing the Gospel of Mark or a collection of hymns could be explosive. It worked in its own terms, combining the modernity of writing with entry into a religious world of angels, miracles, and a very simple lifestyle which might well make far more sense to a nineteenth-century African than to most Victorian Europeans.

TWENTIETH CENTURY

Plenty of African societies all the same responded only marginally to the Christian message. It is far from easy to explain why some did and others did not, but from the viewpoint of Christian history what proved decisively important were the dozen or so ethnic groups where, at some point in the decades after 1890, hitherto marginalized converts suddenly found themselves enthusiastically communicating a message which thousands of their compatriots were anxious to embrace. The Ganda (modern Uganda), Ijebu, Igbo (both southern Nigeria), and Ebrie (Côte d'Ivoire) were some of the early examples. In Buganda the conversion of a handful of young men around the royal court in the early 1880s led across martyrdom and civil war to a snowballing mass movement that not only made Buganda a publicly Christian country by 1900 but had flowed out upon all the neighboring societies. In the Christian conversion of these lacustrian Bantu, people by people, through to the 1930s there was, unquestionably, a measure of Ganda imperialism and linguistic aggression. But it was far more than that, and it included examples of extraordinary apostolic commitment.

Yohana Kitigana was a subchief with five wives when he converted to Catholicism in 1896. He abandoned all five, living henceforth a wholly celibate life, and then left also his chieftainship and possessions. In 1901 he set off as a missionary to peoples other than his own, becoming the apostle first of the kingdom of Bunyaruguru, and then of Kigezi (southwestern Uganda), where only twenty years later did the White Fathers establish a station. A continually peregrinatory figure, dressed except for Sundays only in an animal skin and armed with staff and rosary, Kitigana decisively altered the permanent religious character of Kigezi.

It is remarkable how closely the core of Kitigana's teaching resembled that of the greatest of the West African "prophets," William Wadé Harris, whose most successful missionary journey across the southern Côte d'Ivoire and Gold Coast took place from 1913 to 1915, at just the time Kitigana was making his greatest impact in Kigezi. A stress upon the absolute sovereignty of God and the correlative destruction of the fetishes of every other spirit, coupled with a practical concern for elementary hygiene, was common to both men.

Harris was a Grebo from Liberia disillusioned with its black American-descended rulers and the missionaries who had employed him as a teacher in the Episcopal Church. Empowered by an angelic vision, he rejected the shoes he had been proud of and the westernizing ways that went with them, but felt sure that he had now been commissioned by God to preach the gospel in a far more evidently African way. While he became by good repute a miracle worker, healing was a very secondary part of his activity; preaching and baptizing were primary. Armed with cross, calabash, and Bible, Harris converted and baptized tens of thousands of people, whose villages ever after retained their Christian character. He had no intention of setting up a church of his own and regularly directed his converts to Catholicism or Methodism but, almost inevitably, especially where no mission existed, a Harris church of its own did emerge in numerous Ebrie and Dida villages in the Côte d'Ivoire.

Although Kitigana, the Catholic catechist, and Harris, the prophet, thus had much in common, in terms of the wider history of African Christianity they are just two particularly outstanding examples of something going on at the time in scores of other places: a shift in the primary explicit religious allegiance of large groups of people to one form or another of Christianity. This shift always included a greater affirmation of the unity and sovereignty of God (but God significantly still named in almost all languages by a traditional, pre-Christian term such as Nzambi, Leza, Mulungu, or Katonda) and a commitment to the Bible, the value of reading,

Evangelist Bill John Chigwenembe addresses the Mutare for Jesus Rally, Sakubva Stadium, Mutare, Zimbabwe, October 1995. Preachers such as the late Chigwenembe are able to draw large crowds. Such meetings are used to encourage and build local assemblies. © DAVID MAXWELL

the keeping of Sunday, the singing of hymns mostly of a Christocentric nature, and to certain basic moral norms such as the interdiction of twin-killing (the practice among some, though by no means all, peoples in both eastern and western Africa of putting to death, generally by exposure, one or both of a pair of twins immediately after their birth). All this fervency did not, however, exclude (despite the sharp symbolism of rejection contained in the initial fetish-burning by Harris and many another prophet and catechist) continued belief in large chunks of the spiritual cosmology of former beliefs, to which family and kinship custom remained intimately linked.

The characteristic and central figure of the village Christianity springing up all across the continent was the catechist. If anyone bore the burden of Africa's church, it was he. Often unpaid, frequently almost untrained, the catechist was all the same the village minister, responsible for its local thatched church and primary school, a preacher, a leader of prayers and hymns, someone whose very considerable authority, ecclesiastical and even, in practice, civil, depended upon a minimum of literacy and occasional attendance at a central

mission to report on his work and receive instruction. In worship, in education, in modernity, he led the way.

African clergy were far from numerous until well after World War II; in many parts of the continent they did not exist at all. The catechists, in their place, ensured the survival and growth of the church and its functioning on a day-to-day basis. They did so in an inevitably traditionalist way. That was indeed part of their strength. Through their mediation, a new tradition, a selective appropriation by village society of the instructions of missionaries, quickly became part of the familiar local traditions of the countryside. Portrayed again and again in fiction and in the autobiographies of others, the catechist of the first half of the century, poor but self-assured, was often the father or the grandfather of the politician, priest, and academic of the second half of the century.

At the same time, but especially from the 1920s on, far more professional missionary schooling was developing. If the missionary's most important nineteenth-century contribution to African history was that of Bible translation, printing, and distribution, the most significant twentieth-century contribution was in secondary education. One does indeed find this training beginning far earlier in a few places, especially in the Scottish missions—Calabar (Nigeria), Lovedale (South Africa), and Livingstonia (Nyasaland, now Malawi), for example—and their impact was already great.

Nevertheless it is from the 1920s that this became general and that Catholics began to emulate Protestants in opening well-staffed secondary schools. It was a matter of forming an elite on educational principles almost unchanged from those of Europe, but these graduates proved to be the elite who would take over the government and wider direction of their countries around 1960. Without the best mission schools, such as Mfantsipin in Ghana, Alliance in Kenya, or Budo in Uganda, it is difficult to see from where the new universities of the 1950s would have drawn their students, or the new governments of the 1960s their cabinet members and civil servants. The size of the missionary contribution to secondary education in this period could easily lead to the conclusion that the churches were essentially progressive, though elitist. Yet this prominent, often urban side of their life in the mid-twentieth century, central as it could seem to the observer, has always to be balanced against the much wider, and already deeply conservative, phenomenon of the rural church. It was the strength of African Christianity in many countries that it included both.

For most rural adults, however, schools of any sort did less to meet the needs of daily life than did the provision of hospitals. Health had always been a central concern of local religions, and though missions did provide many well-used hospitals and clinics, they did not and could not meet the health needs of the great majority of the community. Moreover, their increasingly modern and scientific biomedical approach to sickness often responded very poorly to the far more psychological and social expectations of ordinary people.

It is hardly surprising if a growing multitude of prophets and independent churches focused upon healing rather than upon schooling. Harris had been on occasion a healer. His prophetic contemporary in the Belgian Congo, Simon Kimbangu, was less of a preacher and far more of a healer. African prophets tend to be divisible into these two categories—apostles of the Harris model on the one hand, healers in the Kimbangu mold on the other. The healers have outnumbered the apostles. While the latter need to be peripatetic, the former tend to be stationary, and around them a church-clinic develops and out of it a holy city: the Nkamba of Kimbangu (in spite of its banning by Belgian authorities in the 1920s), the Ekuphakemeni of Isaiah Shembe in Natal, the Mount Moria of Samuel Mutende in Zimbabwe. There are many such holy cities in western, eastern, and southern Africa. They constitute the point at which prophetic Christianity becomes permanently visible, the place where, around a healer's work, a complex liturgy develops. In course of time it becomes still holier because the prophet is buried there. Each is a New Jerusalem in which the gift of salvation has been made manifest on African soil, a replica, even replacement, of the original Jerusalem in Palestine.

Even within a single movement like Aladura in western Nigeria one can find both forms of prophet. In the Church of the Lord (Aladura) of Josiah Oshitelu the concentration is upon the centrality of its holy city, Oshitelu's home at Ogere. In the larger, more outgoing, form of Aladura called the Christ

Apostolic Church, led originally by the remarkably powerful preacher Joseph Babalola, a steamroller driver converted in 1928 on the road from Akure to Ilesha, no need is felt for any such thing. Apostolic prophetism seems more deeply at ease within the secular world than the healing prophetism that creates instead a ritualized world of its own. Prophetic religion has not, then, a single form—and a developed church like the Kimbanguist, led from its legalization in 1957 by the prophet's sons, can straddle the two. If Nkamba has remained its New Jerusalem, looked after by one of the sons, Dialungana, the actual headquarters of the church is not there but in Kinshasa where its *chef spirituel*, Diangienda, lived and worked. Thus, a church which began with prophetic healing and a single sacred place has moved with the years toward a more apostolic and even educational form, coming to look not so different from many another Protestant body. Any contrast between the Christianity of "Independency" and the Christianity of erstwhile mission churches should not be overplayed.

Since national independence in the 1960s the increase in Christian adherence has been phenomenal, and its local forms have grown increasingly varied. Whereas the total number of African Christians stood at approximately 75 million in 1965, by 2000 it had risen to approximately 351 million, of an estimated total population of 840 million (or nearly 42%). Social and demographic change means that the township and the middle-class suburb now complement the village as sites of Christian activity. Enhanced communication and social mobility has increased the ranks of proselytizers from labor migrants, catechists and Bible women to include nurses and teachers and civil servants on placement, returning students, often accompanied by their Christian Union or Scripture Union brethren, and urban churches on "crusade" to rural areas. Added to this day-to-day, face-to-face form of evangelism is church planting by the enormous transnational traffic in refugees across so many parts of the continent.

The widely publicized call for a missionary moratorium mooted by leading African Christian thinkers in the early 1970s never happened. Throughout the post colonial period the Catholic Church witnessed remarkable growth, expanding into new regions well beyond former French, Belgian, and Portuguese colonies. Traditional fields

Evangelist Paul Saungweme (left) and translator address a tented crusade, Chisipite, Harare, January 1996. Many young Zimbabweans perceive English speaking to be a sign of sophistication, so many evangelistic events have translators from Chi-Shona or Sindebele. © DAVID MAXWELL

of missionary Catholic recruitment such as Ireland, France, or Holland declined, but more than 1,000 new missionaries from Poland filled the gap. There was also a new Protestant missionary impetus, for the most part driven by North Americans. It was predominantly a movement of Born-Again missionaries, Evangelicals, Charismatics, and Pentecostals, reflecting denominational shifts in American Christianity. Most remarkably the African missionary impulse

has extended beyond the continent. High-flying African Born-Again executives such as the Zimbabwean, Ezekiel Guti, or the Zambian, Nevers Mumba, travel the U.S. and European preaching and healing circuits, often visiting "international" branches of their movements founded by their diaspora. And pastors and priests from the historic churches participate in western mission through diocesan twinning programs.

Delegates pray to receive the Holy Spirit at the 1995 Annual Deeper Life Conference of Zimbabwe Assemblies of God Africa (ZAOGA), Harare, Zimbabwe. The conference draws delegates from across Southern and Central Africa, reflecting the transnational reach of the movement. The size of the auditorium and numbers attending the meeting indicate the success of movements like ZOAGA. © DAVID MAXWELL

The most striking change has been the growth of the African Born-Again movement. Its love affair with the electronic media, global aspirations and character, and adoption of the prosperity gospel means that it fits well with neo-liberalism. But there is a danger in overemphasizing its break with what has gone before. Continuities in membership and religious practice show that contemporary African Pentecostalism lies in colonial- and early national-era independency's shadow. In Pentecostalism African Christian leaders encountered a biblical justification for healing and exorcism that their parents had already experienced in the prophetic churches. Moreover, as they evolve, some of the older Pentecostal churches such as the Zimbabwe Assemblies of God, have also come to look increasingly like the historic mission churches they originally broke away from. The historic churches remain enormously important in their provision of health care, education, and development, taking on increasing significance as African states decline. Prayer rather than politics or development remains the primary focus of all African churches.

Huge tabernacles, chapels, and cathedrals dominate the skylines of many African cities, and Christian music, film, and radio fill their airways, transforming popular culture in the process. Christian ideas have captured the African imagination, providing a potent set of values upon which leaders could draw. Nkrumah's version of African socialism, drawing from Marxism-Leninism, found little sympathy in Ghana, but his use of Christian imagery—"Seek ye first the political kingdom"— resonated widely among friend and foe alike. But these values are also shared with citizens and as such provide a yardstick by which politicians can be judged. This yardstick became particularly important in Africa's second Democratic Revolution at the end of the 1980s, when conferences of Catholic bishops and Protestant Church Councils helped coaxed one-party states toward multiparty democracy. Archbishop Tutu's special role in the transition to black majority rule in South Africa was again possible only because of the degree to which Christianity has become the common religion of South Africans, black and white. Missionaries

A woman receives prayer for deliverance from her ancestor spirits at a Pentecostal crusade, Charter, Zimbabwe, October 1995. Ancestors are understood to be "spirits of poverty," responsible for waste and misfortune. Exorcism and physical separation from "unsaved" kin free Pentecostals to accumulate and build nuclear families. © DAVID MAXWELL

of a hundred years ago could hardly have expected so much, but it is simply a fact of late-twentieth- and early-twenty-first-century African history that Christianity has moved in a large southern half of the continent from marginality to centrality. Without it modern Africa would be quite other than it is.

See also **Crowther, Samuel Ajayi; Education, School; Equiano, Olandah; Freetown; Harris, William Wadé; Kimbangu, Simon; Livingstone, David; Oshitelu, Joseph; Prophetic Movements; Religion and Ritual; Shembe, Isaiah; Tutu, Desmond Mpilo.**

BIBLIOGRAPHY

Agbeti, J. Kofi. *West African Church History.* 2 vols. Leiden: E.J. Brill, 1986, 1991.

Ajayi, J. F. Ade. *Christian Missions in Nigeria, 1841–1891: The Making of a New Elite.* Evanston, IL: Northwestern University Press, 1965.

Baëta, C. G., ed. *Christianity in Tropical Africa.* London: Oxford University Press, 1968.

Brandel-Syrier, Mia. *Black Woman in Search of God.* London: Lutterworth Press, 1962.

Daneel, M. L. *Old and New in Southern Shona Independent Churches.* 3 vols. The Hague: Mouton, 1971, 1974, 1988.

Fasholé-Luke, Edward, et al., eds. *Christianity in Independent Africa.* London: R. Collings, 1978.

Gifford, Paul. *African Christianity: Its Public Role.* London: Hurst, 1998.

Gray, Richard. *Black Christians and White Missionaries.* New Haven, CT: Yale University Press, 1990.

Hastings, Adrian. *A History of African Christianity, 1950–1975.* Cambridge, U.K.: Cambridge University Press, 1979.

Hastings, Adrian. *African Catholicism: Essays in Discovery.* Philadelphia: Trinity Press, 1989.

Hastings, Adrian. *The Church in Africa: 1450–1950*. New York: Oxford University Press, 1994.

Jules-Rosette, Bennetta, ed. *The New Religions of Africa*. Norwood, NJ: Ablex, 1979.

Maxwell, David. *African Gifts of the Spirit: Pentecostalism and the Rise of a Zimbabwean Transnational Religious Movement*. Athens: Ohio University Press, 2006.

Pauw, Berthold A. *Religion in a Tswana Chiefdom*. New York: Oxford University Press, 1960.

Peel, John D. Y. *Aladura: A Religious Movement among the Yoruba*. London: Oxford University Press, 1968.

Ranger, Terence O., and John C. Weller, eds. *Themes in the Christian History of Central Africa*. Berkeley: University of California Press, 1975.

Sanneh, Lamin O. *West African Christianity: The Religious Impact*. Maryknoll, NY: Orbis, 1983.

Schapera, Isaac. "Christianity and the Tswana." *Journal of the Royal Anthropological Institute* 83 (1958): 1–9.

Shepperson, George A., and Thomas Price. *Independent African: John Chilembwe and the Origins, Setting, and Significance of the Nyasaland Native Rising of 1915*. Edinburgh: The University Press, 1987.

Strayer, Robert W. *The Making of Mission Communities in East Africa: Anglicans and Africans in Colonial Kenya, 1875–1935*. London: Heinemann, 1978.

Sundkler, Bengt. *Bantu Prophets in South Africa*, 2nd edition. New York: Oxford University Press, 1961.

Sundkler, Bengt. *Zulu Zion and Some Swazi Zionists*. New York: Oxford University Press, 1976.

Sundkler, Bengt. *Bara Bukoba: Church and Community in Tanzania*. London: C. Hurst, 1980.

Taylor, John V. *The Growth of the Church in Buganda: An Attempt at Understanding*. Westport, CT: Greenwood Press, 1979.

Turner, Harold. *History of an African Independent Church*. 2 vols. Oxford: Clarendon Press, 1967.

ADRIAN HASTINGS
REVISED BY DAVID MAXWELL

AFRICA AND WORLD CHRISTIANITY

At independence in the 1960s, beyond denominational structures, virtually the only Christian institutions in Africa were missionary councils. Christian institutions have proliferated enormously since then. The missionary councils mutated into national Christian Councils. These have subsequently formed regional groupings like the Fellowship of Christian Councils of Eastern and Southern Africa (FOCCESA), up to the continent-wide All Africa Conference of Churches (AACC). Catholics have formed similar groupings: national Episcopal Conferences, ten regional associations of these like the Francophone Association of Episcopal Conferences of Central Africa (ECEAC), and the continent-wide Symposium of Episcopal Conferences of Africa and Madagascar (SECAM). Even those strands of Christianity less given to associating, the evangelicals and independents, have formed similar groupings, up to (respectively) the Association of Evangelicals of Africa (AEA) and the Organisation of African Instituted Churches (OAIC), both based in Nairobi.

There is no need to exaggerate the significance or effectiveness of these bodies; they are subject to all the difficulties of coordinating African regional associations generally. There are other pressures too. For example, the Catholic SECAM seems deliberately to limit its ambitions; its Latin American equivalent CELAM (*Consejo Episcopal Latinoamericano* [Latin American Episcopal Conference]) incurred the wrath of Rome for promoting liberation theology, and SECAM has no wish to run such a risk. Nevertheless, some of these institutions have been key players in their fields. The South African Council of Churches (SACC) (driven by the likes of Anglican Archbishop Desmond Tutu, Dutch Reformed Church clergyman Allan Boesak, SACC General Secretary Beyers Naudé, 1915–2004) was possibly the most important opposition body inside South Africa in the final years of apartheid, as was the New Sudan Council of Churches in southern Sudan during most of the civil war years. Likewise, in the democratic push of the early 1990s some councils (as in Madagascar) almost carried the democratic movement.

Probably even more obvious through the 1980s and 1990s was the proliferation of Christian nongovernmental organizations (NGOs). Some of these, like World Vision, the Lutheran World Federation, and Catholic Relief Services, are major international players, but there are countless smaller, often local, bodies. In fact, in several African countries the majority of NGOs are Christian-related. In places, their significance cannot be ignored: in Liberia for example, before its implosion, the Christian Health Association of Liberia (CHAL) coordinated Christian hospitals and clinics and provided health care unmatched by the government. The years of proliferation of

Christian NGOs have been the years of Africa's economic marginalization, and most of these organizations function through access to outside resources. Many, like the Salvation Army World Service Organization (SAWSO), have been created as autonomous subsidiaries of their parent denominations precisely so they can access USAID and other funds not accessible to churches. Hence the paradox: though African in personnel and focus, they remain very dependent on resources from outside.

Since the liberalization of government controls from the mid-1990s, increasingly ubiquitous are Christian media, like FM stations and television channels. Especially in the case of television, the economic dependencies previously alluded to recur. Of necessity, both resources and programming come from outside, particularly the United States. At the turn of the millennium, increasingly prominent are Christian universities. In a place like Kenya, the majority of the institutions seeking charters as universities are Christian, usually upgraded seminaries or Bible colleges. It is too soon to assess their impact. All these institutions parallel those of other continents but are far more salient in the otherwise limited educational environment of Africa.

Africans have assumed their rightful places in Christianity's international bodies. Africans sit in the Roman Curia (in the papal election after the death of Pope John Paul II, the Nigerian Cardinal Arinze was often named a contender), the Kenyan Samuel Kobia heads the World Council of Churches (WCC) in Geneva, the Ghanaian Setri Nyoni heads the World Association of Reformed Churches (WARC), likewise in Geneva. In the first decade of the 2000s the African church leaders are prominent in restructuring the worldwide Anglican communion over the issue of homosexuality.

Africa is not known internationally for a particular academic theology, as Latin America might be for liberation theology, or Asia for a theology of religious pluralism. Nevertheless, South African theologians (influenced both by Latin America and North American Black theology) developed their own "contextual theology" in opposition to apartheid, receiving definitive expression in the 1985 Kairos Document. Since apartheid's fall, some South African theologians have elaborated a "theology of reconstruction" for the new challenges of recovery from the racialized divisions of the past. In the rest of sub-Saharan Africa, the theological

Cardinal Francis Arinze (1932–). Arinze is a Nigerian prelate of the Roman Catholic Church. He was one of the advisers to former pope John Paul II and had been a contender for the coveted position when John Paul II passed away in 2005. Arinze is among numerous prominent African figures in Christianity. CATHOLIC NEWS SERVICE

focus has been mainly on issues of culture, culminating in the thoroughgoing (particularly Catholic) project of inculturation, that is the integration of externally sourced theological precepts with local cultural expressions.

Although a great deal has been written on this long-standing challenge, a surprisingly large amount is exhortatory and programmatic (e.g., along the lines of, "Let us incorporate our culture into our Christianity"); much less has been offered as finished product. Indeed, profound and unresolved tensions seem to lie at the root of the whole project (not least, who decides what is genuine inculturation as opposed to unacceptable corruption by "syncretism"?). There exist bodies across the continent like the Ecumenical Symposium of Eastern Africa

Theologians (ESEAT) given to promoting academic theological reflection (in which inculturation features increasingly); probably the most impressive has been the Circle of Concerned African Women Theologians whose continent-wide effort (inspired by the Ghanaian Mercy Amba Oduyoye) is essentially to empower local women from a liberationist perspective attentive to African realities.

However, it has been often said that in Africa the real theology is not written but rather prayed, sung, danced, dreamed—in a word, lived. Hence Africa's theologians best known internationally—Jean-Marc Ela (*African Cry*, 1986), Bénézet Bujo (*The Ethical Dimensions of Community*, 1998), John Pobee (*Towards an African Theology*, 1979), and John Mbiti (*African Religions and Philosophy*, 1969)—may be rather unrepresentative (indeed, some have academic jobs in the West, writing for the West). The booming Pentecostal-like churches have a theology stressing health, prosperity, and deliverance from spirits blocking such blessings. No doubt this theology relates closely to the traditional religious imagination, in which religion is closely associated with flocks, crops, abundance, and longevity, and for which spiritual forces are pervasive.

Paradoxically, though, even here a Western element is not totally absent. For example, David Oyedepo, the founder of the Nigerian transnational Winners' Chapel (in 38 African countries by 2000), who might be taken to embody this theology, openly acknowledges his debt to Kenneth Hagin and other propounders of the American prosperity gospel. These flourishing Pentecostal-like churches positively repudiate any inculturation, tending to see African traditions as demonic (although through their very denunciation preserving that religious mindset). African academic theologians have received some if inadequate attention in the mapping of contemporary world Christianity; the lived theology of the masses remains largely unstudied.

See also **Apartheid; Diogo, Luísa Dias; Diop, Alioune; Media: Religion; Religion and the Study of Africa; Tutu, Desmond Mpilo.**

BIBLIOGRAPHY

Magesa, Laurenti. *Anatomy of Inculturation: Transforming the Church in Africa.* Maryknoll, NY: Orbis Books, 2004.

Oduyoye, Mercy Amba. *Introducing African Women's Theology.* Cleveland, OH: Pilgrim Press, 2001.

PAUL GIFFORD

AFRICAN INSTITUTED CHURCHES

As a category of analysis, the term "African Instituted Churches (AICs)" is problematic. It is intended to describe a broad spectrum of Christian movements that have an exclusively African membership and appear to be free from external control. The category was meant to replace and improve upon African Independent Churches. This earlier label represented an attempt to describe a sequence of churches that had broken away from missionary control during the colonial era, roughly the first half of the twentieth century.

But the notion of independence became increasingly meaningless in postcolonial Africa as former mission churches came under local African leadership. The term "African Instituted" (or "African Initiated," which is often substituted) was preferred because it emphasised the African founders of these Christian movements. However, this emphasis on agency has proved equally problematic because the social history of African Christianity has come to show how mission Christianity was also founded by Africans. Missionaries did important work in health and education, translation and ethnography, but African catechists, evangelists, pastors, teachers, and Bible women conducted most of the evangelism. The term African Indigenous Churches is also unhelpful because mission Christianity could be just as indigenous as the AICs in, for instance, its reliance on African agents, its sacralization of the landscape, and its connection with local concepts of illness and healing. Terms such as syncretic or schismatic churches are even more unsatisfactory, as these missionary derived terms suggest that AICs are not properly Christian.

In practice the term African Instituted Churches has been used to describe three separate but related categories of Christian movements. First, there are "Ethiopian" or Separatist churches that broke away from mission churches in the late nineteenth and early twentieth centuries over issues of leadership and authority rather than theology or rites. Second, there are "Zionist" or Aladura churches. These movements of healing and exorcism, usually founded by individuals hailed as prophets, began to appear in the late 1920s and early 1930s. Finally, since the 1980s there are expressions of Pentecostalism. African-led Pentecostal churches first emerged in the 1950s but they gained substantial momentum and followings in the 1980s and 1990s. On closer inspection many AICs are not as indigenous or independent as they first appear, and scholars have come to situate them more closely within a spectrum of African Christianities alongside the historic mission churches.

THE MISSIONARY SOURCES OF AICS

Three major sets of ideological sources explain the emergence of AICs: first, a combination of mission Christianities and ideas from African traditional religions; second, selected elements from within mission Christianities resulting in a different emphasis; third, counterestablishment Christian movements in Europe and America, particularly Pentecostalism. Initially, scholars placed emphasis on the first explanation, arguing that AICs were syncretistic in a pejorative sense—the pollution of a notionally pure tradition by symbols and meanings taken from alien religions. Missiologists and theologians who had a stake in defending religious boundaries often advanced this explanation. However, anthropologists and social historians have increasingly discredited the idea of essential, untainted religious traditions and instead explored the processes by which they were invented or imagined. More recent research has revealed the very considerable connections AICs made with missionary ideas and practices.

The initial categorization of AICs recognized that "Ethiopian" or Separatist churches did not just select doctrine and symbols but rather took wholesale from the mission churches from which they seceded. The name "Ethiopian" symbolized the ancient African tradition of Christianity and its independence from the West and looked to the promise of the psalmist, "Ethiopia shall stretch out her hands to God" (Psalm 68:31). The Native Baptist Church founded in Lagos in 1888, or the South African–based Zulu Congregational Church and African Presbyterian Church founded in 1896 and 1896 respectively, did not challenge the doctrine, theology, or organizational structures of their mission church antecedents. Indeed, they often clung to them with great loyalty. Their separation was

more of a protest against missionary racism, which had hardened in the imperialist age, and consequent exclusion of African personnel from positions of responsibility. African clerics such as Mangane Mokone, who founded the Wesleyan-derived Ethiopian Church in Pretoria in 1892, railed against a white paternalism that sanctioned a vast differential in salary and working conditions between blacks and whites.

Perennially short of resources, even if they did connect with African-American churches, these Separatist movements remained a minority option led by politically minded, articulate black clergy. Although some South African separatists were involved in the 1906 Bambata Rebellion in Zululand (Natal), the movements' political significance lay more in the organizational support they provided in local struggles over land, education, and housing than on larger national political issues. Overall, African elites preferred to stay in mission churches, where better provision for education enhanced their chances of social mobility.

The second major type of AICs, "Zionist" and Aladura churches, also selected from mission Christianities. The Zimbabwean Apostolic movements founded by the Shona prophets Johana Maranke and Johana Masowe in the 1930s drew on Dutch Reform and Wesleyan Methodist models of church government, sabbatarianism inspired by the Seventh Day Adventist Church, and exotic-looking white robes and staffs derived from Catholic and Anglican sources. The robe-wearing Aladuras of West Africa likewise drew much from the Church Missionary Society/Anglican background.

The third source of AICs was counterestablishment movements of Non-Conformity and Radical Evangelism in the West. This wave of evangelical mission activity had its social sources in late nineteenth-century north America and Europe and reflected the aspirations of those who had been who had been marginalized by industrial capitalism. The movements emerged in religious form as a protest against the privilege, priestly supremacy, and secularisation encountered in Establishment churches and often made common cause with African Christians seeking to escape white missionary paternalism. South African Separatist churches connected with the American African Methodist Episcopal Church but quickly discovered that their new black patrons could be just as paternalistic as their white predecessors.

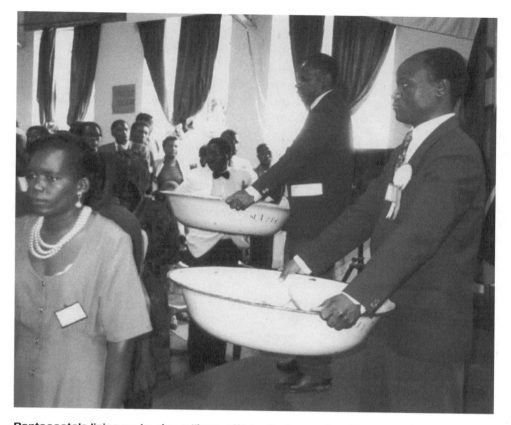

Pentecostals lining up to give a "love-offering" at a service, Harare, October 1995.
Tithing and other forms of giving are enormously important in maintaining African instituted churches. This local giving often far exceeds donations from abroad and helps these movements retain autonomy. © DAVID MAXWELL

Most counterestablishment Christian movements were premillennial, believing in the imminent return of Christ and the commencement of a thousand years of peace and justice. The urgency of this adventist message gave the movements a strong missionary impulse. Missionaries from the Chicago-based Christian Catholic Apostolic Church in Zion arrived in South Africa in 1904 soon after its beginning to proclaim their distinctive message of salvation and divine healing. A host of southern African Zionist movements rapidly followed.

The most vital strand of counterestablishment Christianity was Pentecostalism, which appeared at the turn of the twentieth century. Its apostolic message of adventism, divine healing, and emancipation by the Holy Spirit combined with mainline missionary revivalism to animate South African Zionism and apostolic Christianity in Southern Rhodesia (present-day Zimbabwe). Similar appropriations of

international Pentecostalism led to the rise of AICs in West Africa. In Nigeria the Aladura Movement began in 1922 when Yoruba Anglicans made contact with Faith Tabernacle, a small faith healing church in Philadelphia, and subsequently with the British Apostolic Church.

At first glance it is not difficult to grasp how missionaries came to view Zionist and Aldadura movements as syncretistic. Some of the Pentecostal practices such as hand-clapping, ecstatic dancing, purity laws, charismatic leadership, and polygamy were congruent with traditional religions. Nevertheless, those features that some scholars interpret as typically African were in fact the most Christian aspects of these churches. An openness to dreams and visions, glossolalia ("speaking in tongues"), divine healing, taboos on pork and tobacco, even the wearing of white robes were all prominent in radical Evangelism in North America and Europe.

One of the attractions of these prophetic movements for Africans was that, unlike most missionaries (excepting Pentecostals), their leaders accepted the ontological reality of witchcraft and evil spirits as the Christian devil and as demons and offered protection from them. This appeal however rests upon a disjuncture with African traditional religion. AICs may borrow from traditional beliefs and practices but the content is recoded within a Christian system of ideas, taking on new forms and significance. AICs thus compete for the same metaphysical domain as traditional religion but are at odds with non-Christian belief and practice in pronouncing it demonic. They pit the Holy Spirit against alien and ancestral spirits, and conversion is immediately followed by total-immersion baptism symbolizing rebirth, often accompanied by the destruction of traditional charms and fetishes. Witchcraft and sorcery are also collapsed into the category of the demonic. Witches are divined through prayer and exorcised through the laying on of hands.

THE AFRICAN CONTEXT OF AICS

The causes and motivations for AICs are as diverse as their ideological sources. First, the movements are overwhelmingly Protestant. Contemporary Pentecostal movements are fiercely so, while the earlier movements had little appeal in Catholic or Islamic areas. Separation on the grounds of truth was a defining feature of Protestantism, and once Africans had their own vernacular versions of scripture they found ample authority in them for contesting the missionary message and arriving at their own interpretations of the Christian faith. In Zimbabwe, the Apostolic movements of Maranke and Masowe, characterized by their eschatological (millenialist) biblicism, grew in the fertile soil of popular Methodism with its strong emphasis on equipping the believer with the translated word. Biblical stories of Zion and Bethesda, sacred cities and streams, and holy mountains provided the basis of a new African hymnology and the imaginative material to re-sacralize local landscapes in Christian fashion. In scripture they also read of dreams and visions, exorcism and healing, and notions of provision and personal security absent from the teachings of many missionaries. It is no surprise that the Grebo prophet William Wadé Harris had been an Espicopalian school teacher and the great Congolese prophet, Simon Kimbangu, a Baptist catechist.

The only significant Catholic AIC, Maria Legio, can also be interpreted as a theological protest, but this time a movement seeking to restore orthodoxy. Founded in Kenya in 1963 with its own bishops, cardinals, and pope and using Latin phrases in the Mass, the movement emerged at exactly the same time as Rome abandoned Latin in favor of the vernacular. This top-down program of inculturation was met with scorn from the unimpressed recipients who had come to find meaning and value in pre–Vatican II Catholicism.

The second major contextual factor was existential pressure from African traditional religion. AICs did not so much adopt aspects of African traditional religion as much as compete with it, engaging with the same material and existential issues in the search for healing, purity, and protection from evil. Pioneer missionaries had spent much time with the sick, their quirky medical practices not too dissimilar from those of traditional healers. As missionary medicine professionalized and secularized in mission hospitals, so African Christian prophets such as Simon Kimbangu in the Belgian Congo instituted movements of healing in the villages.

Finally, AICs must be integrated into the spectrum of popular Christianities. Missionaries were always overstretched, preoccupied with building, administration, and Bible translation. They often left evangelization to African catechists and preachers. In the early decades of the twentieth century, mass conversions moved at such a rapid pace that even missionary supervision was not possible. It was at this juncture that the Christian prophet often took on the missionaries' task. Some of these African leaders such as the Grebo (Côte d'Ivoire) Episcopalian, William Wadé Harris, did not view their mission as schismatic. Many of Harris's converts initially joined the Catholic Church in the Côte d'Ivoire and the Methodist Church in the Gold Coast. The Harris Church emerged only later as an independent body. It is noteworthy how prophetic movements took strong root during the Great Depression of the 1930s, when Africans lost faith in mission Christianity's modernizing promise. Their educational and health services contracted, and missionaries withdrew. Africans seeking modernity and material gain through Christianity realized that they might advance further through association with Prophetic movements, which preached withdrawal from the failing migrant labor economy and emphasised a self-reliant life of artisanship or cooperative farming.

SECOND GENERATION AICS AND AFRICAN-LED PENTECOSTALISM

AICs continued to multiply throughout the 1940s and 1950s, aided by growing literacy, scriptures available in the vernacular, and the slow Africanization of leadership within the historic mission churches. These new churches were generally small local congregations, often born out of schism from larger movements. The last major movement was the Lumpa Church of Alice Lenshina founded in Zambia, one of the last colonies to be thoroughly missionized, in the late 1950s.

For the major movements such as the Kimbanguists in Zaire, the Harrisists in West Africa and the Zion Christian Church (ZCC) in southern Africa the 1950s were more important for institutionalization. Such movements "aged" quickly, and under a second generation of leaders more formally educated but less charismatic than their founders they bureaucratized, standardizing and modernizing rules and practices. In time, they came to look more and more like the historic mission churches their founders had criticized a generation earlier. Under Zairian president Joseph Mobutu the Kimbaguist Church found great favor, becoming one of the three official religious bodies in Zaire in 1971, along with the Roman Catholic Church and the Church of Christ. Two years earlier it had been admitted to the World Council of Churches. Moreover movements such as Fambizano ChiShona (cooperation), the ecumenical organization of AICs in Zimbabwe, embraced development and participated in educational and agricultural work. Such organizations often played up supposed authentic credentials to appeal to western donors keen to protect indigenous cultures.

Also new in the 1950s was a sequence of African departures from missionary Pentecostalism, which took a modernizing trajectory different from the theological emphasis of the Prophetic movements. African-led Pentecostalism embraced education, biomedicine, and bureaucracy, where earlier AICs had initially shunned them. They also looked beyond Africa for ideological and material resources, particularly to North America. Prime examples were Nicholas Bhengu's South African Assemblies of God,

Samuel Kobia (1947–). The Kenyan Kobia is the general secretary of the World Council of Churches (WCC) in Geneva, an international Christian ecumenical organization. Kobia is known for his involvement in various social causes, including reorganizing the Zimbabwe Christian Council after independence in 1980. WORLD COUNCIL OF CHURCHES

Ezekiel Guti's Assemblies of God African, based in Southern Rhodesia (present-day Zimbabwe), and the Nigerian Benson Idahosa's Church of God Mission International. These movements were catalyzed and maintained by the restorationist impulse within U.S. Pentecostalism. This reassertion of the millennial urgency and simplicity of first generation Pentecostalism against a growing bureaucratisation of the movement had stimulated a renewed emphasis on proclamation and spiritual gifts that led to salvation/healing revival characterized by crusades, especially overseas.

THE TAKEOFF OF NEO-PENTECOSTALISM IN THE 1980S AND 1990S

Since the 1980s Pentecostalism has grown in prominence throughout sub-Saharan Africa. Huge air-conditioned tabernacles and chapels mark its growing visibility in towns and cities. Pentecostal music, film, and radio fill the airwaves, and Pentecostal leaders wield their enormous followings to influence governments to remoralize politics. In the early twenty-first century Pentecostalism is as mainstream as Anglican or Catholic Christianity. In part, the growth of the Pentecostal movement in Africa can be situated within the steadily increasing missionary input from the older Pentecostal denominations, such as the American and British Assemblies of God. Some African pastors and evangelists such as Ezekiel Guti broke away from these missionary movements to found their own churches,

Young girl singing at a Zimbabwe Assemblies of God Africa (ZAOGA) service, Baines Avenue Assembly, Harare, Zimbabwe, c. 1996. Gospel music and choirs are a great draw to young people, and the born-again music scene is a thriving industry in many African states. © DAVID MAXWELL

retaining part of the original name in their new organizations. The meteoric growth can also be traced to broader interdenominational evangelical ministries such as Scripture Union, Campus Crusade, and the Navigators, which targeted African students in rapidly expanding institutions of secondary and higher education. These African future elites, joined by others with a similar Christian experience of higher education in the West, began ministries in cities amongst the educated middle classes, forming movements such as the Redeemed Christian Church in Nigeria.

The growing momentum of Pentecostalism caused others to leave mainline churches to found new movements of their own, as was the case with Mensa Otabil, who left the Anglican Church to found the Ghana-based International Central Gospel Church in 1984. The growth of these new movements also coincided with a renewed missionary impulse in American Christianity. By 1989, 65 percent of all Protestant missionaries in Africa were North American, and most of these were evangelicals willing to train and fund African Pentecostals, or send their own missionaries to work alongside them.

External funding coupled with enormous local resources generated through tithing and phenomenal growth in membership brought about a new era of neo-Pentecostal ecclesiology and theology in African Pentecostalism. Neo-Pentecostalism's first characteristic is its strong reliance on the electronic media. Audio and video tapes produced locally and internationally supplement printed gospel tracts, Bible study guides, and Christian monthlies as tools of teaching and proselytization. Their use of electronic media contributes to two other markers of new Pentecostalism: its supposedly global, homogenous character and its interdenominationalism. African Pentecostal leaders regularly appear at Born Again conventions in Europe, Asia, and the United States, and participate via printed and electronic media in the global exchange of teachings. African Pentecostal convention centers are decked out in the flags of other nations, and many have their diaspora branches in Western cities. Thus AIC has also come to mean African International Church.

The fourth characteristic of contemporary Pentecostalism is its embrace of the Faith Gospel. African Pentecostalism has drawn from American television evangelists to argue that material success is a sign both of faith and of God's blessing. African neo-Pentecostalism's final marker is its tendency, like its North American inspirations, to produce oligarchic leaders who retain power for decades before bequeathing it to immediate kin.

In some respects, the Faith Gospel facilitates and legitimates the material accumulation of young, upwardly mobile middle class Pentecostals and their leaders in a time of general economic decline. But most African Pentecostals are poor, living in townships and rural locations rather than in suburbs, and bare survival remains their primary concern. As African states retreat in the face of demographic pressure on resources and the demands of Structural Adjustment Programmes, so Pentecostals have taken on provision of welfare, providing education and heath care. Moreover, the Pentecostal community replaces the extended family or politicized and therefore divisive ethnic community, helping believers with access to jobs and accommodation and serving in times of bereavement as a burial society. Pentecostalism also engenders a Puritan ethic of sobriety and industry that makes believers socially mobile, or at least prevents them falling over the edge into poverty.

African Pentecostalism draws its force by delicately balancing two great, but not always congruent, traditions of religious innovation. The first is an internal tradition, best documented in Central Africa but present also in West and Southern Africa, of collective movements of personal security, whose adherents have pursued "good life"—fertility of women; a successful hunt; abundant harvests; material wealth and prosperity; salvation; protection against evil, sorcery or witchcraft—through harmony. This internal dynamic has collided and conflated with an externally derived Protestant tradition, from which Africans have drawn the personal spiritual resources of biblical Christianity, especially Protestantism. These two cycles have come together to form the back-cloth to the great prophetic movements of twentieth-century Africa: Zionist and Aladura Christianity, the movements of Simon Kimbangu and William Wadé Harris.

Contemporary Pentecostalism extends this trajectory. Given African Pentecostals' desire to associate themselves with modernity and to cast themselves as international, they play down their links with the earlier prophetic movements. Like the "Ethiopian" churches they make external connections for resources to do what missionaries do, while seeking to maintain their autonomy from their patrons. Pentecostal notions of the good life have evolved to include exam success, correct emigration papers, and the latest commodities alongside more fundamental material and existential concerns. Witchcraft eradication has been Christianized further within the prophetic movements. But continuities in terms of membership and practice show that contemporary African Pentecostalism stands firmly in the shadow of the prophetic movements. Pentecostalism legitimated the practices of Zionist, Apostolic, and Aladura churches, and in it adherents found a Biblical justification for the healing and exorcism already experienced in the prophetic movements.

See also **Harris, William Wadé; Kimbangu, Simon; Lenshina, Alice; Maranke, John; Witchcraft.**

BIBLIOGRAPHY

Campbell, James, T. *Songs of Zion: The African Methodist Episcopal Church in the United States and South Africa.* New York: Oxford University Press, 1995.

Comaroff, Jean. *Body of Power, Spirit of Resistance: The Culture and History of a South African People.* Chicago: University of Chicago Press, 1985.

Gifford, Paul. *African Christianity: Its Public Role.* London: Hurst and Company, 1998.

Hastings, Adrian. *The Church in Africa 1450–1950.* Oxford: Clarendon, 1994.

Iliffe, John. *Modern History of Tanganyika.* Cambridge, U.K.: Cambridge University Press, 1979.

Kalu, Ogbu, and U. Power. *Poverty and Prayer: The Challenges of Poverty and Pluralism in African Christianity, 1960–1999.* Frankfurt: Peter Lang, 2000.

MacGaffey, Wyatt. *Modern Kongo Prophets: Religion in a Plural Society.* Bloomington: Indiana University Press, 1983.

Maxwell, David. *African Gifts of the Spirit: Pentecostalism and the Rise of a Zimbabwean Transnational Religious Movement.* Oxford: James Currey, 2006.

Peel, John, D. Y. *Aladura: A Religious Movement among the Yoruba.* London: Oxford University Press, 1968.

Sundkler, Bengt. *Zulu Zion and Some Swazi Zionists.* London: Oxford University Press, 1976.

DAVID MAXWELL

MISSIONARY ENTERPRISE

According to biblical tradition, Africa's connection with Christianity goes back to the origins of the religion itself. In the Gospel of Matthew, the parents of Jesus flee to Egypt with the child when they are warned that Herod, the Roman district governor, is seeking to kill the child. Matthew also states that on the way to the Crucifixion, Simon, a native of Cyrene, Libya, was made to carry the cross on which Jesus was executed. Two Africans, Lucius of Cyrene and Simeon, a black man, possibly from the Ethiopic countries, were said to be part of the gathering at Antioch at Pentecost, when the mission to the Gentile world was launched.

As the mission of early Christianity developed there were reports of the apostles making contact with significant African leaders. One such contact, described in the Acts of the Apostles, involved the apostle Philip, who met an Ethiopian government official described as a palace chancellor in the service of Queen Candace. According to Eusebius, the Palestinian bishop of Caesarea (c. 263–c. 340) who is regarded as the father of ecclesiastical history, this Ethiopian official's name was Judich. After ascertaining that Judich was familiar with the Jewish Scriptures and a sincere seeker, Philip baptized him in the first recorded incident of the African mission of the young church. Africa was part of the original mission of Christianity, even before Europe.

The mission in Africa represents Christianity's growth from a sub-apostolate of the Jewish diaspora to a Gentile mission, a change that allowed non-Jews in their preponderance to flock to the church, giving Christianity its non-chosen-people identity. Much controversy accompanied that epochal move and produced a serious, three-century-long split with Judaizers in the Church, who finally lost out to the pro-Gentile party. The apostle Paul was the greatest exponent of this victorious Gentile view. Reared in Rabbinic Judaism and trained to defend the tenets of the Mosaic code against its compromisers, Paul took responsibility for the mission to the Gentiles, describing with fervor his newfound missionary role: on the road to Damascus, where he planned to continue his persecution of the new Christian converts, he was knocked off his stride by the spirit of Christ (Acts 9; Phil. 3:12) and converted on the spot. He described his career as that of being "called as an apostle to the Gentiles" (Rom. 1:1–15; Gal. 1:13ff.), and in that cause he traveled extensively to win Gentile converts, to establish churches, and to encourage, admonish, scrutinize, instruct, sanction, and confirm believers (Rom. 15:17–24; Gal. 2).

The growth of the Gentile church brought on persecution, as converts were caught between the Jewish backlash and Roman imperial opposition. Mission was a consequence of this persecution, offering believers a route of escape from local hostility, though missionary growth also fueled the hostility of mission opponents. Paul became a target of the opposition, as a result of which he was taken prisoner to Rome sometime between 62 and 63 CE, with tradition maintaining that he died in the persecutions of the emperor Nero in about 65 CE. Eusebius follows this Gentile expansion and grasps Christianity's missionary impulse by observing that the scattering of the apostles and disciples led to the planting of the seed of the church in numerous places, including Ethiopia under the apostle Matthew. Persecution energized Christians, as Eusebius indicates and as is testified to by Origen (c. 185–c. 254) of Alexandria in Egypt, who spoke about how Christians left no stone unturned to spread the faith in all parts of the world, with believers visiting cities and villages and country cottages to make "others pious toward God," as he put it. They sought converts not from motives of wealth or gain, he said, for they would not accept money even for the necessities of life. From the point of view of mission, Christianity did as well from negative circumstances as from positive ones.

Thus the positive stimulus of the Roman imperial infrastructure, its exceptional facilities and admirable roads, its blending of states, nations, and nationalities, its cosmopolitanism and the international communication system that effectively promoted it, as well as its heritage of jurisprudence and its liberal philosophical outlook, helped to accelerate the forward missionary thrust of Christianity. Saint Thomas Aquinas (1225–1274) even pointed out the great advantage that accrued to the church fathers and early apologists from the fact that they had been pagans in the Roman Empire. Similarly, the disarray resulting from the collapse of the empire in the fourth century, the irruption into Rome of the northern Germanic hordes, and their utter rout of the citadels of culture and learning, resulted in the invaders being exposed to Christian teaching. A contemporary Christian witness commented that as a consequence of the barbarians occupying the Roman Empire, the churches came to be full of Huns, Suevi, Vandals, Burgundians, and other innumerable believers, so that out of the ruin of Rome arose a new Christian orbit.

From such dispersal, both planned and unplanned, Christianity from the fourth century onward penetrated south into Africa beyond the boundaries of the Roman Empire into Upper Egypt, Meroë, and Aksum, and by the sixth century into Ethiopia.

The classical period of Christian history in North Africa and Ethiopia was also the period of the fiercest theological controversies, but there were, too, vigorous movements in scholarship, philosophical thought, and organizational development. Clement of Alexandria (c. 150–215), Origen (c. 182–251), Tertullian (155–230), and Augustine of Hippo (354–430), all born in Africa, were central voices of African Christianity as well as being recognized authorities of the European church. And it was in Egypt under Anthony and Pachomius that the monastic tradition was first developed as a missionary institution and as such carried into Europe, where monasteries, later reformed by the Cistercians, became the main carriers of the Christian missionary impulse. In spite of its Egyptian roots, monastic Christianity would not reach sub-Saharan Africa until after its long gestation and transformation on European soil, where it became entangled with the machinery of European maritime exploration and commercial expansion.

Aware of the impetus that fifteenth-century Portuguese maritime explorations in the Atlantic had given to the expanding frontiers of Christianity beyond Europe, the papacy became active in pursuing the missionary path in Africa. Yet there would be obstacles to overcome, chiefly the reality of the rising mercantile power of Portugal. In earlier eras Ethiopia had sent embassies to Rome to appeal for contact with the Holy See, but these embassies had returned empty-handed. Even the offer of expensive and rare gifts failed to move the papacy. One such embassy in 1402 brought four leopards fit for the part. The Ethiopians pressed with their appeals, attending for that purpose the Council of Constance (1414–1418) that recognized Martin V. Still yet, Ethiopian representatives carried their appeal to the Council of Florence in 1443, a significant event that led to the Portuguese interest in Africa. Pope Nicholas V in 1451 authorized the sending of a messenger to Ethiopia.

From those early contacts developed real historical knowledge about Ethiopia, knowledge that replaced earlier fanciful concoctions about distant and exotic cultures. Ethiopia attracted the personal interest of Ignatius Loyola himself (1491–1556) who asked to be sent there. The ensuing short-lived Jesuit embassy to Ethiopia in 1554 contained the largest group of Jesuits until then to sail for the mission field anywhere. The popes responded to Ethiopia's entreaties by establishing a hospice for Ethiopian visitors to Rome attached to the church of S. Stefano Maggiore close to St. Peter's.

The situation changed with the establishment abroad of Portugal's trading factories. Portugal became the first European sea-based power to colonize extensively in Africa. Portugal was a small and devoutly Christian monarchy that had arisen during the twelfth-century Christian crusade against the Moors in the Iberian Peninsula. Fortified by Crusader indulgences granted by the pope and seeking gold and slaves, and perhaps the fabled Christian kingdom of Prester John (associated with Ethiopia), fifteenth-century Portuguese kings sent many expeditions to sail ever further southwards along the western African coast and beyond. Although mercantile interests eventually swamped the tide of missionary awakening, the

Portuguese maritime expeditions brought with them priests, many of whom viewed the explorations as part of the Christian crusades.

In the early fifteenth century, Portuguese expeditions reached the Canaries, which were placed under Spanish jurisdiction, Madeira and the Azores, and, in 1460, the Cape Verde Islands where a bishop was based from 1532. These islands provided the base for Portuguese expansion into the gold-yielding African mainland, the real focus of commercial interest. In 1482 Ghana was explored with the landing of a party at Elmina, a promising outpost of the gold trail, which was given the name of São Jorge da Mina. However, it was only in 1572 that four Augustinian priests arrived in Elmina to cultivate a "fortress Christianity" that, in being restricted to castle life, was a stony meadow for missionary prospects. Thus the trading castles provided missionary range, but they also made it possible to afford putting off evangelizing local populations. It is a recurrent theme in the history of the missionary movement that facility of travel brought with it accessibility but also the ability to choose when, where, and how to go. Cultural curiosity ceased to be a motivation, and unfamiliarity became a deterrent.

In the scheme of things, with the discovery of São Tomé in 1470, the Portuguese secured a platform for penetrating the African mainland. São Tomé was the missionary base for the whole of the Guinea coastline as far south as Angola along which the Portuguese were active. It was from São Tomé that Portuguese reached the kingdom of the Kongo, a sophisticated African state along the River Zaire, roughly in the area of present day Angola. Missionaries arrived there in 1491 and received a warm welcome that culminated with the baptism of the ruler, Nzinga Mbemba, as Afonso, and of the ruler of the nearby Soyo kingdom and of hundreds of their subjects. Called the "apostle of the Kongo" and a "new Constantine," Afonso gained the Kongolese throne as a Christian convert in 1506 and reigned until 1543. His was one of the longest reigns in the continent's recorded history.

Establishing a Christian monarchy, creating a new Christian capital called São Salvador, learning Portuguese, building churches, promoting missions, and indeed sending his son, Henry, to Portugal to be educated and commissioned for missionary service in the Kongo, the indomitable King Afonso inaugurated a particularly brilliant epoch of Christianity in Africa. His interest in the religion appeared deep and sincere, as he states in his letters. He did battle with the old Kongo cults, and, in an ironic twist, with corrupt emissaries of Christianity; he accepted the conversion of an old enemy who had led an army against him rather than executing him, and appointed him, as Dom Pedro, guardian of the baptismal waters in the church; three times he sent him as ambassador to Lisbon. In a symbolic move, he built a church dedicated to "Our Savior" on the site of the old shrines and preached after mass. He was tireless in calling for priests to come and serve his people.

The priests who arrived led anything but exemplary lives. Abandoning their vows, the priests broke away from their religious communities and lived in separate houses that they filled with slave girls, to the scandal of new believers and to the disdain of local skeptics. The people mocked the king, saying the priests showed that Christianity was a lie. Stung by the remarks, the king pleaded with Portugal: "In this kingdom the faith is still as fragile as glass on account of the bad examples of those who came to teach it. Today our Lord is crucified anew by the very ministers of his body and blood. We would have preferred not to be born than to see how our innocent children run into perdition on account of these bad examples."

Some semblance of order was restored in later centuries. The Jesuits arrived in the mid-sixteenth century and formed Christian villages. In 1596 the Papacy established the diocese of São Salvador for the Kongo kingdom and the neighboring territory of Angola. The Jesuits established a college at São Salvador in 1624; the first rector, Friar Cardoso, translated the standard Portuguese catechism into the kiKongo language and distributed hundreds of copies. These kiKongo catechisms were used by lay catechists, the *maestri*, who handed on the teachings in the villages from generation to generation, much of the time without clerical presence.

In 1645 the Capuchins, including Italian and Spanish friars, began a mission in the Kongo kingdom, as part of a larger initiative of the Propaganda Fide in Rome to promote mission activity in West Africa. In what marked the beginning of nearly two centuries of Capuchin involvement in the Kongo; the Capuchins established schools in São Salvador and Soyo, learned kiKongo, and began systematic evangelization in the rural districts. They established confraternities among the Africans, among them the Confraternity of Our Lady of the Rosary, which was formed in Luanda in 1658 and which became a forum for promoting African rights. Between 1672 and 1700, thirty-seven Capuchin fathers recorded a total of 341,000 baptisms. Other Capuchin missions were established on the Guinea Coast and Sierra Leone in 1644, in Bénin in 1647, and in the small state of Warri in the 1650s.

Queen Nzinga of Matamba, in eastern Angola, embraced Christianity through the influence of a captured Capuchin priest. She had received baptism in 1622, and then succeeded her brother as ruler of the kingdom of Ndongo in Angola in 1627. Thereafter, she promptly lapsed from the faith. After years of bruising conflict with the Portuguese, however, she received a message from an oracle that if she accepted to return to the faith the Portuguese would stop making war with her and peace and prosperity would return to her kingdom. In 1656 she relented and she and a great number of her troops were received into the faith by the Capuchin priest she had captured. She sought to create a Christian state, personally carrying stones for the building of the church of Our Lady of Matamba, which was completed in 1665, the year of her death. She was a distinguished example of women pioneers of Christianity in the ancient church.

After the Portuguese rounded the Cape of Good Hope in 1498, they set up colonies in east Africa, including fortified trading cities along the coast. The island of Mozambique became the main administrative center of Portuguese East Africa, and the city had an estimated 2,000 Christians by 1586. The Mutapa Empire in Zimbabwe came under Dominican influence in the seventeenth century, and its kings accepted baptism. In the Zambezi valley, the Portuguese crown made large grants of land (*prazos*) to settlers. Jesuits and Dominicans from Portugal accompanied the colonists, and in some cases the fathers owned *prazos*. According to a Portuguese Jesuit in 1667, there were sixteen places of worship pursuing missionary work in the lower Zambezi valley—six conducted by the Jesuits, nine by the Dominicans and one by a secular priest. The Jesuits in 1697 established a college at the small Zambezi River town Sena for the children of both the Portuguese and African elites.

For a time in the early to mid-seventeenth century, there was a real prospect of the large-scale spread of the Catholic faith in Africa, maintained by a network of African kings and the other members of the ruling elite, and pushed forward by a number of remarkable priests and friars. Christianity's close ties with Portugal's imperial ambition, however, became a barrier for mission. Still, while many Africans embraced Christianity to please their Portuguese overlords, many others did so out of genuine faith and commitment.

A graphic example bears this out. In 1631 the city of Mombasa was retaken by the Muslims led by Sultán Yúsúf bin Hasan. Earlier Yúsúf had been adopted as a protégé by the Portuguese after his father was treacherously murdered by a renegade Portuguese captain. He was baptized as Jeronimo Chingulia and educated in Goa, where he was made a knight of the Crusader Order of Christ. On his return to Mombasa Yúsúf suffered ill treatment at the hands of the captain of the fort, and that experience gnawed at his resolve as a convert. In an act of vengeance, Yúsúf had the captain and his guards murdered and followed up this assault with a full-scale attack on the Christians, whom he offered a choice of accepting Islam or death. That seventy-two African men and women, known as the Martyrs of Mombasa, should willingly accept death along with their fellow Christian Portuguese rather than renounce their faith testifies to their genuine commitment to Catholicism. Four hundred other Africans were taken as slaves to Arabia in exchange for ammunition.

By the early eighteenth century, however, the prospects for Christianity in Africa had dimmed markedly. The Christian Kongo kingdom was shattered by civil war, and the power and authority of the kings irreparably compromised. The capital of São Salvador was sacked by a warring faction in 1678 and then was deserted for a quarter century. Reoccupied in the early eighteenth century, its twelve churches were in ruins, and only a single priest, Estavo Botelho, remained in the capital, by which time he had become a slave-trader who lived openly with concubines. Of the several provinces of the kingdom, only the coastal province of Soyo retained a significant Christian population. The forlorn Capuchin mission in the Kongo survived with only two or three friars.

By 1750 responsibility for the Kongo mission fell to one Capuchin missionary, the remarkable Friar Cherubina da Savona, who bravely carried on traversing the country from 1758 to 1774, baptising some 700,000 during his lonely mission of twenty-seven years. Although later Capuchins attempted to carry on the mission, the last regular Capuchin priest withdrew in 1795. In some rural villages, the *maestri* continued to convey Christian teachings, and the people observed Christian rituals and chanted canticles. French missionaries discovered one such village north of the Zaire River in 1773, its Christian identity proclaimed by a great cross.

However, without a regular priesthood empowered to baptize, such communities in time lapsed from their Christian faith. Despite periodic but short-lived missions in Warri and other countries in West Africa, Christianity struggled to survive. In East Africa, the religious orders and secular priests increasingly restricted their ministry to the Portuguese ruling class, and by 1712, missions to Africans continued only in Zambezia. Soon these also died out. In subsequent eras with the onset of colonial suzerainty, Christianity became a mere appendage of the imperial system, and the clergy chaplains to the colonizers and to their apprentices.

There were a number of reasons for this decline of the Catholic missions. After his conversion to Christianity in 1506 King Afonso I of Kongo gradually but inescapably came to the realization that while the slave trade enabled him to hold power and to enlarge and strengthen his kingdom, it also made him dependent on the Portuguese traders for arms and supplies which he needed to avert enslavement in turn for his subjects—such being the cruel logic of the slave trade and of dynastic survival. Afonso called on the help of Portugal and of Rome to save his people and his kingdom. He pleaded with Portugal, saying so great was the calamity caused by Portuguese factors that order was threatened, and with it the cause of the Gospel. "And we cannot reckon how great the damage is, since the mentioned merchants are taking every day our natives, sons of the land and the sons of our noblemen and vassals and our relatives . . . so great

is the corruption and licentiousness that our country is being completely depopulated."

The tripartite alliance of Christianity with commerce and European "civilization" in premodern Africa was turning out to be a deadly combination, Afonso I was discovering the European connection to be a mixed blessing at best. Infiltrated by agents from Lisbon, the Kongo kingdom found all alternative channels of contact with Rome blocked or compromised, and so the kingdom dangled from a noose of isolation. The interest the kingdom aroused in Rome led to the decision by the papal curia to shift control of Catholic missions from Portugal and to create an indigenous priesthood. The Propaganda Fide was set up in Rome in 1622 to return control of missions to the curia. But it was only under the pontificate of Gregory XVI with the appointment of Capellari to run Propaganda Fide from 1826 to 1831 that the papacy succeeded in regaining such control.

The waning power of Portugal in the seventeenth century reduced its ability to recruit and to maintain missionaries, while at the same time increasing its suspicion of missionaries of other nationalities. Moreover, Rome experienced a declining interest in world missions during the eighteenth century, and, accordingly, the supply of missionaries gradually fell. There were never enough priests for the African mission field, and while many of the missionary priests were exemplary in their piety and commitment, others were appreciably less so. Often isolated and lacking regular episcopal supervision or encouragement, many grew discouraged, took concubines or became slavers, bringing scandal and disrepute to their Church and to their calling.

Missionaries succumbed in great numbers to the unfamiliar African disease environment. Of 438 known Capuchin fathers active in the mission to the Kongo between 1645 and 1835, 229 died after a few years in the mission field, while others returned home in poor health. That is well over a 52 percent mortality rate. Portugal's decision to expel the Jesuits from its colonial territories in 1759 further reduced the number of missionaries, especially in Zambesia. Efforts to recruit and to educate an African priesthood produced meagre results, and with the paucity of African priests went a decline in Catholic faith. To compound the problem, Capuchin priests, moreover, were suspicious of the lay *maestri* and often failed to give them the necessary support. These problems and a failure of vision created a setback for the cause.

In spite of early promise, the Catholic involvement in the Ethiopian church hit a rock of stumbling. When in 1622 the Jesuit Pedro Páez succeeded in persuading the emperor Susenyos (1607–1632) to join the Roman Catholic Church, everyone concerned believed that a new era had arrived for Christianity in Ethiopia. But it was not long before those hopes were dashed by the willful and divisive policies of Páez's successor, Alfonso Mendez, who arrived in 1626. He moved promptly to pursue the logic of the counter-reformation by trying to make Roman Catholicism the national faith of Ethiopia, but the implications of foreign domination in such a move antagonized Abyssinian Christians. Mendez adopted a collision course when he rammed through a thoroughgoing purge of the church by suppressing local customs, re-baptizing believers as if they were pagans, having their priests reordained, their churches reconsecrated, and introducing graven images and the Latin rite and calendar. Deeply rooted customs like circumcision, Sabbath observance, and lunar rites, for so long revered marks of Ethiopian Christian identity, were proscribed.

These reforms met with popular insurrection, and a fierce conflict erupted against the Catholic latinization of Abyssinian Christianity. The bitter memories of foreign imposition left a century earlier by the jihad of Ahmad ibn Ibrahim al-Ghazi, the Harari sultan and warleader, nicknamed Grañ, "the left-handed" (1506–1543), were revived by the antagonism sparked by the Catholic attacks on the Abyssinian church. Many Christian chiefs declared that they would prefer a Muslim ruler rather than submit to domination by Catholic Portuguese. The Muslim comparison must be appreciated for its rhetorical posture rather than taken literally. It was an attack on the Catholic purge of local customs by way of the analogy of Islamic extremism. It is doubtful that Ahmad's jihad, which called on the intervention of the Ottomans to counterbalance the rising power of Portugal, would in reality be preferable even to a meddlesome Catholicism. In any case, Susenyos had no choice but to back down, and so he issued a proclamation reinstating the old faith. "We

restore to you the faith of your forefathers. Let the former clergy return to the churches, let them put in their tabots, let them say their own liturgy; and do you rejoice."

Fasilidas (r. 1632–1667), Susenyos's successor, declared that the concessions to make peace with Roman Catholicism were, however, too little too late, "for which reason all further colloquies and disputes will be in vain." He expelled the Jesuits, with Mendez transferring to India after sending a petition to the King of Spain calling for the conversion of Ethiopia and saying the only means for achieving that was military occupation of the country. Such ideas about the forcible conversion of Christian Ethiopia, it turns out, occurred also to Muslims nearer home, and in their case regional jealousies among Christians suggested that Christians, too, had an unsettling premonition of that. The following period of rival regional sovereigns, called the *zamana masáfent*, lasted from 1769 to 1855, and was shaped profoundly by the haunting specter of a surging Islam. One witness expressed in 1840 a sentiment that preserved much older attitudes: a widespread feeling prevailed that the nominally Christian Wallo in the northern part of the country passed their time in the repetition of prayers, while in the meantime a proverb and general belief circulated among them that their country could never be conquered by those who were not followers of the Prophet Muhammad.

It made an impression on Gibbon that for many centuries Ethiopia was shrouded in a haze of obscurity. Gibbon wrote that having slept for a near thousand years Ethiopia became forgetful of the world by which it was in turn forgotten. Yet under the shroud of mystery and far from the prying eyes of hostile neighbors Ethiopia created from the second half of the twelfth century enduring monuments to its Christian heritage, such as the thirteen rock-hewn churches at the monastic settlement of Lalibäla, set at an altitude of some 8,858 feet. Still a place of pilgrimage, Lalibäla's architectural achievement is celebrated in legend as the place that angels built. The deep subterranean trenches, the open quarried caves, and the complex labyrinth of tunnels, narrow passageways with interconnecting grottoes, crypts and galleries, all shrouded in a soft and solicitous holy silence that is filtered with the faint echoes of monks and priests at prayer, justifies Lalibäla's steadfast reputation as a historical wonder.

The real force behind the modern impetus of Christianity in nineteenth-century Africa was the intercontinental antislavery movement. The British evangelical movement that played such a prominent role in the abolition campaign calculated that moral sentiments alone would not be enough to take on the powerful proslavery planter interest in Parliament and society at large, so it looked to empirical evidence and hands-on experience to undermine market-based arguments in favor of slavery. One strategy was to recruit Africans who themselves had been enslaved but were subsequently emancipated and whose voices would add an authentic, concrete dimension to the struggle for abolition.

There had been Africans in earlier periods who wrote and campaigned against slavery and traveled abroad in that cause, among them Laurenço da Silva, an Afro-Brazilian whose lineage went back to Congo and Angola. He single-handedly nudged the Roman Curia toward an antislavery stand in 1686. However, never before had a global movement arisen in which representative Africans could play roles so natural to their experience and circumstances and so effective to the purpose, and their success would have enormous, and as yet unforeseen and unsettling implications for the colonialism that would soon emerge. Thus a straight historical line can be traced from the antislavery campaigns of emancipated slaves like Olaudah Equiano, Ottobah Cugoano (John Stuart), Philip Quaque, Paul Cuffe, and David George, to patriotic and nationalist champions like Samuel Ajayi Crowther, James "Holy" Johnson, and Herbert Macaulay.

These so-called recaptive Africans, Westernized and Christianized, would form a crucial buffer between Western colonial intrusion and an African continent much depleted by slaving, more brokers and mediators than collaborators of the chiefly type. Their example of hard work, productive labor, personal sobriety, integrity, and diligence, and their sense of social responsibility and mutual succor, would distinguish the new society in Africa. In that new society a special place would be reserved for equality, for the rule of law, and for individual enterprise. Social structure, conceived in the image of the chief and embedded in political genealogy, would be scrambled, its place taken by those trampled underfoot and now reinstated. It is that indigenous restoration, rather than foreign missionary suzerainty, that would assure the future of Africa. Similarly, the Catholic missionary impulse was reawakened in response to the slave trade, and, later, to the antislavery movements of the nineteenth century.

It was only in the nineteenth century that a sustained missionary drive was launched, leading to the founding of new missionary orders and congregations: in 1817 the Marist Fathers and Brothers were created; in 1835 the Pallottines of Italy; in 1868 the Society of African Missions was founded in Lyons, and the Society for Missionaries in Africa, or White Fathers, in Algeria; in 1860 the Belgian Sheut Fathers; in 1866 the Mill Hill Fathers, partly British and partly Dutch, in London; and in 1875 the Society of the Divine Word in Germany. Many of these Catholic missions played major roles in Africa, and so did the members of the Catholic Mission to Central Africa (1842–1881), noted for their scientific explorations of the White Nile, their efforts to suppress the slave trade, and their work in Sudanese linguistics and on Dinka society, religion, and government.

In time the Xaverian missionaries also entered West Africa, establishing a base in hinterland Sierra Leone. The major effort to reform Catholic missions came, too, during this period and culminated in the reorganization of the Propaganda Fide in 1817. It fell to Cardinal Mauro Cappellari as prefect of the Propaganda between 1826 and 1831, and later as Pope Gregory XVI (1831–1846), to produce a new missionary doctrine in which responsibility was vested in each missionary institution rather than in a central organ. Furthermore, Gregory XVI acted decisively to move Catholic teaching into line with antislavery, issuing a set of briefs in 1839 condemning the slave trade and slavery, much to the scoffing of the colonial clergy and their unrepentant flocks. Gregory's apostolic briefs were expanded in 1845 in a new instruction he issued, called *Neminem profecto*, whose essential feature was setting the course for mission territories becoming dioceses with Episcopal responsibility for training indigenous clergy and founding seminaries for the purpose. Pope Pius IX (1846–1878) followed in his predecessor's footsteps, though at the

First Vatican Council (1869), which he convened the missionary accent was somewhat muted.

In fact the missionary bishops and vicars apostolic, over eight hundred in total, were all Europeans, and the council's schema on missions disappointed the attending missionary clergy. A word is advisable here about the French missionary architect, Charles Lavigerie of Nancy, where he was bishop. He later moved to Algiers, which Gregory XVI had established as a see in 1838, where he was appointed bishop in 1867. He dreamed of the evangelization of all of Africa. In 1868 he founded the Society of African Missions, otherwise known as the White Fathers (the White Sisters followed in 1869). He worked among the Berbers of the Sahara and later sent some of his missionaries farther south to the Great Lakes region of east and central Africa. He sought to rekindle "memories of a hallowed nature" regarding North Africa's illustrious Christian past, and to press beyond into regions where slavery and the slave trade held sway in order "to wage against them a relentless and unceasing warfare." He emphasized in his missionary method that a church would emerge in Africa only through Africans themselves, with missionaries in the meantime constrained to adopt African manners and customs in language, dress, food, and lodging. "To succeed in the transformation of Africa … the first requirement is to train Africans chosen by us in conditions which from the material point of view leave them truly Africans," he wrote (Comby, 133). He commended cordial relations with Protestant missionaries. He was created a cardinal in 1882 and took the title of archbishop of Carthage and primate of Africa.

At about the same time, Protestant missionary statesmen were charting a fresh and bold course for the missionary enterprise. Rufus Anderson of the American Board of Commissioners for Foreign Missions (founded in 1810), Henry Venn of the Church Missionary Society (founded in 1799 but active only after 1803), and Gustaf Warneck of Germany stressed what they called a "three-self" strategy under which missions would make way for autonomous native pastorates. Many serving missionaries, however, having tasted power and autonomy at a safe distance from the home board, flinched. When in 1895 the conference of Foreign Mission Boards of the United States sent a notice to the missionaries working among the Zulu with the request to encourage the idea of a self-supporting church there, the notice was disregarded. But when the circular was translated into Zulu, the words for self-support (*ukuzondla*) and self-government (*ukuziphatha*) completely changed the dynamics on the ground. Reading the Zulu circular, the African leaders promptly concluded "that the missionaries were withholding from them the rights of Congregational Churches," that is the right to form independent, self-propagating congregations (Sundkler, 30). Such is the potency of translation that in 1896 the Zulu Congregationalist Church was formed as a result.

Missionaries had cause to wonder whether they had created a Frankenstein with their vernacular translation projects. Africans for their turn wondered whether the West had rendered Christianity so nearly unrecognizable from its apostolic source that it would be reasonable to conclude that the religion in their hands was for those for whom it was primarily intended. A new breed of charismatic prophets stepped forward to contend that the God, whom the West claimed, had in fulfillment of the Scriptures spoken in sundry and diverse ways to the tribes of Africa and confirmed it with signs and wonders and with diverse miracles. Christianity's Western dressing had served a necessary purpose for Europeans, but for the Africans facing the fact of Western political subjugation, that Western dressing obscured not only the real intentions of missionaries, but also the religion's resonance with local ideas.

The claim of the early apostles, that Christianity was destined for the world in spite of every attempt by the Roman Empire to stamp out the religion, made it reasonable for Africans in their turn to insist that they should not be made an exception by the modern European imperial sponsorship being required of them. Christianity was born in exile, and in Africa and elsewhere it found a homecoming compatible with its exile origins. In 1851, Venn, responsive to that African urge, spoke about "the euthanasia of mission" as the proper way for missions to go, their place taken by self-supporting, self-governing, and self-propagating churches. True to that ideal, Venn in 1861 transferred to the Native Church Pastorate in Sierra Leone's nine parishes, with the process expanded in 1878 with the transfer of more mission-controlled churches.

This period also coincided with the formative Niger Mission (1841–1891) in Nigeria, which was headed by the first African bishop, Samuel Ajayi Crowther (c. 1806–1891), assisted by fellow Africans. Crowther's leadership was momentous for African Christianity: his translation of the Yoruba Bible was the first translation of the Scriptures into an African language. In addition to Yoruba, Crowther wrote on the Igbo (Ibo), Hausa, and Nupe languages. On his visit to London in 1851 at the instigation of Venn, Crowther had interviews with Queen Victoria and Prince Albert, and such was the effect of his meetings that he was able to move a reluctant British government to intervene against the continuing slave trade in Nigeria. Crowther's linguistic work is part of a larger theme of missionary interest in African languages, including the creation of vernacular alphabets, dictionaries, grammars, and lexicographies. The effects on the affected cultures of such linguistic work cannot be exaggerated. The grammars and dictionaries, for example, sparked wide-ranging cultural and social movements, encouraging Africans to become authorities of their own history.

Missionary translation work offered people a unique opportunity to grasp the native point of view, as the English missionary Bishop John Colenso of Durban, South Africa, astutely put it. Or as another missionary linguist, Johann Christaller of Ghana, affirmed (1879), language contains the sparks of truth with which a culture accedes to its true potential, and no barrier of taboo, stigma, or unfamiliarity should be allowed to stand in the way. Diedrich Westermann, the German missionary linguist, summed up the case in 1925, when he said that the vernacular is not the gift of the white man to the African but God's gift, and is as such the vessel in which is contained the whole national life and through which it finds expression.

One English missionary in South Africa, James Green, challenged other missionaries to accept the only conclusion that is natural to draw from the teeming linguistic and cultural evidence, namely, that "the law which holds the earth in its orbit and regulates the fall of a pin, is the same law which has directed the Greek to call God theos [and] has guided the Zulu to speak of Him as Unkulunkulu. And that law we must accept with its consequences." The successful development of African languages in Bible translation and in worship, prayer, and study repeated the pattern first established at Pentecost, where the assembled company was said to hear "each one in his own language. And they were amazed and wondered, saying, 'Are not all these who are speaking Galileans? And how is it that we hear, each of us in his own native language? . . . We hear them telling in our own tongues the mighty works of God'" (Acts 2:6–8, 11).

Thus destigmatized, African languages were primed to kindle the indigenous cause. The Niger Mission that Crowther led until 1891 carried this African charge by redirecting the focus from European leadership, finance, and scholarship to African agency and local support. Africans not only planned, directed, and implemented missionary policy, they also went on to observe, research, document, and reflect in original ways about doing mission in the African context, producing linguistic materials, ethnographic surveys, historical studies, and religious accounts. Europeans at the time found this African achievement difficult to accept or acknowledge, resulting in a perplexing silence in many standard Western works on the chief African architects.

Yet the Niger Mission, and the native pastorate it produced in Sierra Leone and elsewhere, places us firmly on the path that Africans blazed in the antislavery movement in the eighteenth and nineteenth centuries. In the period since 1945 there have been dramatic changes in Africa. At the beginning of that period, the colonial powers were still more or less ensconced on the continent, assuming that recovery in war-torn Europe would lead to the strengthening of missionary ties in the dominions, Africa included. However, wartime military conscription and the subsequent demobilization stirred the nationalist impulse, which political suppression only served to inflame further. With an upsurge in nationalist sentiment went a corresponding desire to renounce missionary control and domination.

This drive for political independence eventually achieved its most notable results in the 1950s and 1960s, but its religious sources can be traced to the very beginning of Christian missions. After the outbreak of the American Revolution in 1776, a number of African American religious leaders demanded emancipation and resettlement as the price for their participation in the war. Thus was founded the Christian colony in Freetown in 1792. Again, following the Emancipation Proclamation issued during the American Civil War in 1863, African Christian leaders in Nigeria declared that the war that had achieved freedom for blacks in the United States had also helped advance the cause of self-reliance in Christian Africa, this à propos of the fact that African churches had learned to get on without the American missionaries who were recalled during the Civil War.

In another example, when Ethiopia repulsed Italy's military drive to reduce it to an Italian colony at Massawa in 1896, it produced widespread reaction in Africa, a reaction that crystallized into Christian Ethiopianism. In 1935 Benito Mussolini's forces invaded Ethiopia, with the bishop of Cremona consecrating the regimental flags and sending them off with the blessing of the Catholic Church. He found support for his action from Cardinal Schuster of Milan, who hailed the invading Italian army as the force destined to achieve the triumph of the Cross in opening the gates of Abyssinia to the Catholic faith and civilization. However, such religiously motivated encroachments on Africa's oldest surviving Christian kingdom excited sympathy for Ethiopia throughout the continent and in the African diaspora in the Caribbean, where it produced the Rastafarian movement.

Two final themes must conclude this rapid survey. One is the effect of the Second Vatican Council (1962–1965) on missions in Africa. Two particular documents of the Council are relevant, one being on missionary activity, Ad Gentes, which addressed mission as a special activity of the church rather than subsuming it under an all-purpose church function. Mission is constitutive of the church, Ad Gentes stated, based in a Trinitarian affirmation, with the bishops taking joint responsibility for it. The second document, Lumen Gentium, followed up the ideas of Ad Gentes with a discussion about mission bearing fruit in the establishment of local churches which in turn assume responsibility for further missions.

The convening of the African Synod, first at Rome in May 1994 and finally at Yaoundé, Cameroon, in September 1995, a milestone in the evolution of missions and Christianity in Africa, was a major step in taking up the statements of Vatican II

and refocusing them on Africa. The African Synod was convened under the apostolic leadership of Pope John Paul II, who traveled to Cameroon in September 1995 to preside over its substantive deliberations. The synod's detailed and extensive pronouncements, contained in the Propositions and introduced with a list of protocols describing the nature, scope, tasks, hopes, goals, and future direction of the work, marked a decisive step in the church's understanding of mission in Africa, a far cry from the jingoist effusions from Cremona and Milan.

The synod in effect conceived the church as a radical indigenously led missionary movement, committed to engagement with Africa's critical development priorities. For that purpose the synod placed special emphasis on the continent's immense human potential and what that can contribute to global solidarity for peace, justice, and opportunity. If Vatican II was in part an attempt by the church to come to terms with the modern world, as one of its documents states, then another equally important dimension was its coming to terms with the implications of the missionary success of the church, and this required that the younger churches of Asia and Africa not be absorbed into preexisting European structures and ideas, and that the church reinvent itself to respond to changes in the former mission fields.

The vernacular Mass that Vatican II had instituted opened the way for the kind of fundamental rethinking required, but it took the African Synod to draw out in a timely, concrete way the new paths to be followed in Africa. The second of our final themes concerns what might be called the signature tune of African Christianity, namely, the rise and proliferation of African Independent Churches led by charismatic religious figures noted for their appeal to dreams, prayer, and healing. Both Harris and Braide were such indigenous religious pioneers. Independency, as the phenomenon is known, was the African response to Christianity, first to its excessive European political and cultural baggage, and second to its creative transformation in the African crucible. In its political temper, Independency splintered off into varieties of "Ethiopianism," that is, into forms of protest and resistance defined by racial and political concerns. In its essentially religious temper, however, Independency assumed the tones and color of Zionism, that is, charismatic and revivalist expressions that show considerable continuity and overlap with African religions, a process that radically transformed Christianity into an Africanized religion. Here, too, we see Christianity profiting from positive as well as negative circumstances, with colonial repression exciting millenarian Ethiopianism, and independence removing the brakes on spontaneous indigenous development, as the charismatic renewal and expansion prove. It was a process that would produce World Christianity and a new anthropology, that is, Christianity as a truly world religion increasingly defined by the values and idioms of non-Western cultures and languages.

In conclusion, the decisive identity question for Christian Africa, turns on the nature of the transition from a territorial, scholastic church of the medieval period to evangelical, voluntarist forms of the religion, from the concordat approach to mission to independency and personal lay agency, and from metropolitan assimilados to vernacular translation and rural empowerment. What subsequently distinguished African Christianity was its being invested with the idiom of mother-tongue translation, and its emerging from its indigenous transformation as a mass movement, fluent in the native Scriptures, untrammeled by Western borrowing, and able to respond to local life and values with inborn confidence.

See also **Ahmad ibn Ibrahim al-Ghazi (Ahmad Grañ); Braide, Garrick Sokari; Colonial Policies and Practices; Crowther, Samuel Ajayi; Egypt, Early; Fasilidas; Harris, William Wadé; History of Africa; Lalibäla; Macaulay, Herbert Samuel Heelas; Slavery and Servile Institutions.**

BIBLIOGRAPHY

Anstey, Roger. *The Atlantic Slave Trade and British Abolition: 1760–1810.* London: Macmillan, 1975.

Baur, John. *2000 Years of Christianity in Africa: An African History 62–1992.* Nairobi, Kenya: Paulines, 1994.

Cuffee, Paul. *Paul Cuffe's Logs and Letters: 1808–1817: A Black Quaker's "Voice from within the Veil,"* ed. Rosalind Cobb Wiggins. Washington, DC: Howard University Press, 1996.

Du Bois, W. E. B. *The Suppression of the African Slave Trade to the United States of America: 1638–1870* [1898]. New York: Russell and Russell, 1965.

Du Plessis, Johannes. *A History of Christian Missions in South Africa* [1911]. Cape Town: C. Struik [1965.]

Fiddles, Edward. "Lord Mansfield and the Sommersett Case." *Law Quarterly Review* 200 (October 1934).

Flint, John E., ed. *Cambridge History of Africa*, Vol. 5: *c. 1790–c. 1870.* Cambridge, U.K.: Cambridge University Press, 1976.

Fyfe, Christopher. *A History of Sierra Leone.* New York: Oxford University Press, 1962.

Hancock, David Leslie. *Citizens of the World: London Merchants and the Integration of the British Atlantic Community: 1735–1785.* Cambridge, U.K.: Cambridge University Press, 1995.

Hastings, Adrian. *The Church in Africa, 1450–1950.* Oxford: Clarendon Press, 1994.

Latourette, Kenneth Scott. *The History of the Expansion of Christianity*, Vol. 5: *The Great Century in the Americas, Australasia, and Africa, 1800–1914* and Vol. 6: *The Great Century in Northern Africa and Asia, 1800–1914.* Grand Rapids, MI: Zondervan.

Sanneh, Lamin. *Abolitionists Abroad: American Blacks and the Making of Modern West Africa.* Cambridge, MA: Harvard University Press, 1999.

Sherwood, Henry Noble. "Paul Cuffe." *Journal of Negro History* 8 (April 1923).

Sundkler, Bengt, and Christopher Steed. *A History of the Church in Africa.* Cambridge, U.K.: Cambridge University Press, 2000.

LAMIN SANNEH

COPTIC CHURCH AND SOCIETY

The Copts are the present-day descendents of the aboriginal people of Egypt. The phonemes of the word *Copt* are (1) cognates of the phonemes of the name of the creator god *Ptah*, of the pantheon of Memphis; and (2) a transliteration of the second syllable of the word *Egypt*. Beginning in the first century CE, large numbers of Copts converted to Christianity, and virtually all present-day Egyptians who designate themselves as Copts also claim a religious identity as Christians. Their numbers are difficult to estimate due to the highly charged politics of the counting of minorities in a national census. By most estimates they would seem to comprise fewer than 10 percent of the Egyptian population, numbering around 6 million people. Since the late twentieth century, hundreds of thousands of Copts have emigrated to Western nations, and their overall birthrate in Egypt is lower than the birthrate of the Islamic majority.

POLITICAL SETTING

In Upper (southern) Egypt, the concentration of Copts is greater than in Lower Egypt, and one may find certain districts where Copts comprise the majority of the population. The Copts speak Arabic as their first language, although, for ritual purposes, the Coptic Orthodox Church retains the use of the indigenous Coptic language, which is linearly descended from Pharaonic Egyptian. The strongest unifying force of Coptic identity is the Coptic Orthodox Church. As is the case in the Roman Catholic Church, the head of the Coptic Church is a bishop of patriarchal dignity who is designated as "pope," that is, "papa" or "dear father." The Coptic pope personally governs the entire church, with the assistance of bishops who govern individual dioceses. Each diocesan bishop, in turn, governs his diocese with the assistance of priests who preside over the particular congregations of the faithful within it. Beginning in the nineteenth century, both Protestant and Roman Catholic missionaries established enclaves of their respective Western ecclesiastical communities among the Coptic population of Egypt. The success of these missionaries has resulted in the weakening of the solidarity of the Christian Coptic minority relative to the Islamic Arab majority.

In the twenty-first century Copts are represented in every economic class within Egypt. Large numbers of Egypt's farmers, especially in Upper Egypt, have traditionally been Copts. Significant numbers of Copts are also to be found in the sprawling cities of contemporary Lower Egypt. The Copts were traditionally overrepresented in trades and professions that Muslims eschewed— the production and retailing of alcoholic beverages and gold jewelry, the treatment of infectious disease, the conducting of trade with Western nations, and the lending of money at interest. Since many of these professions are relatively lucrative, Coptic brewers, goldsmiths, jewelers, doctors, pharmacists, merchants, and bankers have been able to become relatively prosperous on the whole. Economic prosperity, however, is also a social disadvantage for a religious minority in an otherwise relatively poor Muslim society.

The Copts are certainly underrepresented in the political life of Egypt. Few Copts are elected to the national legislative body, and fewer still are appointed to the presidential cabinet. However, perhaps because of a general Egyptian sense that Copts are better able to gain a diplomatic advantage for Egypt in its dealings with supposedly Christian Western nations, Egypt's foreign ministers have sometimes been Copts. Butros Butros Ghali is one example of this phenomenon. A member of a prosperous and venerable Coptic family, Butros Ghali not only became Egypt's foreign minister (minister of state for foreign affairs, 1977– 1991), but also became the general secretary of the United Nations (1992–1996).

The Copts have no political party that they may call their own. Any explicitly Coptic Christian political party could not enjoy any success in most districts. As a rule, the Copts tend to vote for parties that do not insist on a theological basis for national law and do not promote a foreign policy organized around the principle of pan-Arab unity, first promoted by twentieth-century Egypt's revolutionary founder, President Gamal Abdel Nasser (1954–1970). As a predominantly Muslim nation, Egypt's subsequent national leadership has been in the forefront of Arab nations in the push for pan-Arab identity. Furthermore, Egyptian Muslims in general have been encouraged by a variety of religious movements (the Moslem Brotherhood was founded in Egypt) to base their larger collective identity neither on the geography of the region, nor on Arab language, but rather on the unifying cosmology of Islam. Because of the great extent to which these efforts have succeeded, the political marginalization of the Copts has taken a more dramatic turn.

HISTORICAL SETTING

Egypt was one of the first great acquisitions of the Arab armies that took North Africa in the decades following the death of Mohammed in 632 CE. As farmers in the "bread basket" or wheat granary for the Mediterranean world, the Copts were already disadvantaged by the imperial colonial policies, first of Rome, and then of Constantinople, which had left them Christians by the seventh century. As an exploited indigenous population, these Coptic Christians might have hoped for relief from oppressive foreign bureaucracies, thanks to the coming to power of an idealistic new local regime that promised religious tolerance. Harmonious relations between the then Coptic majority and their new Islamic rulers were, in fact, frequently, though not always, evident. The assessment of the so-called *dhimmi* tax on non-Muslims who were recipients of Muslim government services, however, slowly led to large numbers of Coptic conversions to Islam. These conversions, furthermore, were increased by way of active Muslim proselytizing efforts among Copts. Even so, Copts probably remained the Christian majority of Egypt's population well into the fourteenth century. Throughout the fourteenth century, however, Egypt's Coptic population was so completely decimated by waves of Bubonic plague that the Arabic language and the Muslim religion achieved lasting ascendancy.

RELIGIOUS SETTING

After the armies of Islam occupied Egypt in the seventh century CE, the Copts were largely cut off from the rest of the Christian world. The Coptic Church is well known in academic circles for its early intellectual contributions to Christianity, beginning in the second century CE with the founding of the Catechetical School of Alexandria that was organized around the great figures of Clement and Origen. The patriarchs of the episcopal see of Alexandria played major roles in the resolution of the Trinitarian and Christological controversies that threatened the unity of the Christian Church in the fourth and fifth centuries CE. These same patriarchs often exerted more influence than did the patriarchs of Rome, Constantinople, Antioch, and Jerusalem.

It was within the Coptic Church, furthermore, that Christian monasticism first emerged in the desert retreats of the neighboring Sahara. The spirituality of the "Desert Fathers" of Christian Egypt, in fact, remains a mainstay in contemporary Western Christian spirituality. These facts, are least, are remembered within Western Christian circles. Nonetheless, even many otherwise well-educated academics, Christian as well as non-Christian, are scarcely aware that Coptic ecclesiastical, monastic, and cultural life survives in Egypt until the present day. Both the "Euro-centric" academy and the Islamist school, for reasons peculiar to each, tend to see the Copts as relics of the distant past rather than as participants in the living present.

In the third and early fourth centuries CE, Coptic Christian martyrdom was at one with provincial Egyptian insurrection, and the losses were estimated to be so numerous that the Copts took

to basing their own calendar on the worst year of the Roman persecution. Once the Roman Empire itself embraced Christianity after the Edict of Milan (313 CE), however, Christian Egypt might have hoped for more just treatment as part of a Christian empire that had come to share its God and ethos. When better treatment did not result, some kind of ideological differentiation from the Roman Empire's new Byzantine branch on the part of the Copts was bound to occur. Constantinople's apostolic dignity and pedigree were far less established than was that of Alexandria, however, and so Constantinople itself was motivated further to subordinate the Coptic Church to itself.

Thus, although the Alexandrian patriarchs Athanasius and Cyril were central figures in the ecumenical councils of Nicaea (325 CE) and Ephesus (431 CE), the Alexandrian patriarch Dioscorus found himself deposed by the Council of Chalecedon (451 CE). Dioscorus was deposed for having told the Byzantine emperor, "You have nothing to do with the Church." His deposition, however, was officially justified theologically because he was alleged not to assent to the teaching of Chalcedon with respect to the manner in which the divine Person of Jesus Christ is fully human as well as fully divine. Undoubtedly, the question of the relationship of the divine and human natures of Jesus is of central importance to Christianity, and only on the basis of such an essential question could the universal Church seek to depose the venerable patriarchal bishop of Alexandria. Whether the allegation against Dioscorus was justified, however, is a different question. In fact, Popes Shenouda of the Coptic Church and John Paul II were able to come to an agreement on a functional christological formula that would be equally acceptable both to Copts and to Roman Catholics.

In any event, the deposition of their patriarch succeeded only in alienating the Coptic Church from its sister Churches of East and West, Constantinople and Rome. For the next two centuries, the Copts struggled to replace the foreign patriarchs imposed upon them with Coptic patriarchs elected according to the local tradition of the Coptic Church itself. Because the Coptic community was thus beset with religious division and its attendant political cynicism, the Arab armies were more easily able to take the city of Alexandria in 691 CE, putting the much larger and better supplied forces of the Byzantine Christians to rapid flight in the process.

From that day until the present, Egypt remained by and large under external rule (Arab, Persian, Turk, Mameluk, French, and English). Under all of these regimes, the Copts were able to survive and, sometimes, even able to flourish. The Coptic Church remains, jurisdictionally and sacramentally, independent both of the Catholic Church of Rome and the Orthodox Church of Constantinople. The Copts, however, do maintain ecclesiastical communion with a handful of Eastern churches. The most important of these is the Ethiopian Orthodox Church, which numbers many millions of members. The Ethiopian Orthodox Church was juridically subordinate to the Coptic patriarch of Alexandria as recently as the early twentieth century. In the mid-twentieth century CE, however, under Emperor Haile Selaissie, the bishop of Addis Ababa became the autonomous patriarch of the Ethiopian Orthodox Church.

THE MODERN COPTS

The Coptic Orthodox Church is, in a certain sense, the "soul" of Coptic culture. This religious core of Coptic identity accords with the common African pattern of the superimposition of cult and culture, religion and society, and, in fact, universally evident cross-culturally. The Copts vigorously uphold their special identity in Egypt. Coptic churches are full, and the charities and devotions of the Church are well maintained. The patriarch since the mid-1970s, Pope Shenouda III, powerfully anchors the entire Church and remains a vigorous promoter of Coptic welfare. Many Coptic monasteries have numerous young vocations, with the monastic impulse remaining a vigorous component of Coptic cultural life, even as the Copts lament the sporadic sectarian violence within Egypt of which they especially are the victims.

The advent of French and English political influence in Egypt in the nineteenth and twentieth centuries did not advantage the Copts in any way. Indeed, in order to gain the cooperation of Muslims, the French and English colonial rulers often further marginalized the Copts. When Egypt became ostensibly independent in the 1950s under General Nasser, the Copts found themselves under a government that stressed Arab solidarity over Egyptian identity. As non-Arabs, the Copts thus suffered yet further marginalization. Nasser's successor, President Anwar Sadat (1970–1981), compromised with fundamentalist Islamist movements in order to unify Egypt sufficiently to oust the Soviet forces brought in by Nasser. Sadat's compromise, however, cost him his life at the hands of the Islamist forces he strengthened.

The expanding influence of Islamist organizations in Egypt under President Husni Mubarak (since 1981) contributed to the steady stream of Coptic emigration to Europe, Australia, and North America. It is possible that the Coptic Christian community of Egypt may eventually disappear. The Jewish communities present throughout North Africa for millennia have vanished due to analogous pressures.

On the other hand, historically the Copts evidence a special kind of resilience that may yet help them to maintain themselves in Egypt. Coptic cosmology's embrace of sacrificial symbols (the Cross and the "Desert Father") enables Copts to transform social and political reversals into occasions of symbolic cultural reinforcement.

See also **Egypt, Early; Egypt, Modern; Haile Selassie I; Islam; Mubarak, Husni; Nasser, Gamal Abdel; Sadat, Anwar al-.**

BIBLIOGRAPHY

Atiya, Aziz S., ed. *The Coptic Encyclopedia.* 8 vols. New York: Macmillan, 1991.

Chitty, Derwas J. *The Desert a City: An Introduction to the Study of Egyptian and Palestinian Monasticism under the Christian Empire.* Oxford: Basil Blackwell, 1966.

Doorn-Harder, Pieternella van. *Contemporary Coptic Nuns.* Columbia: University of South Carolina Press, 1995.

Gruber, Mark. *Journey Back to Eden: My Life and Times among the Desert Fathers.* Maryknoll, NY: Orbis Books, 2002.

Gruber, Mark. *Sacrifice in the Desert: A Study of an Egyptian Minority through the Prism of Coptic Monasticism.* Lanham, NY: University of America Press, 2003.

Kepel, Gilles. *Muslim Extremism in Egypt: The Prophet and the Pharaoh,* trans. Jon Rothschild. Berkeley: University of California Press, 1985.

Meinardus, Otta F. A. *Christian Egypt, Ancient and Modern.* Cairo: Cahiers d'Histoire Égyptienne, 1965.

Wakin, Edward. *A Lonely Minority: The Modern Story of Egypt's Copts.* New York: William Morrow, 1963.

MARK GRUBER

ETHIOPIAN CHURCH

The Ethiopian Orthodox Church, in the Horn of Africa, calls itself and its dogma täwaḥḥədo, meaning "unity" or "union," to distinguish itself from the other Eastern Orthodox churches. The emphasis on "union" refers to the theological "oneness" of God, termed monophysite, in contrast to the Trinitarian doctrine of the other principal branches of Christianity. The Ethiopian Orthodox Church also distinguishes itself from the western, or Latin Catholic, church, as among the Oriental Orthodox churches, which also include the Coptic Orthodox Church of Alexandria (Egypt), the Syrian Orthodox Church of Antioch (Syria), the Armenian Orthodox Church of Etch-miadzin (Armenia, present-day Turkey), and the Indian Orthodox Church of Malabar or Malankara (India). This branch of Christian churches started in 451 CE when a group of delegates from these regions at the Council of Chalcedon rejected the formula of faith on the manner of the union of the human and divine natures in Christ.

Scholars of early Ethiopian Orthodox Church history still debate the question of when Christianity was introduced into the Horn of Africa. They are also keenly interested in the local cultures into which the new faith was received. Because Ethiopia is so close to the Christian Holy Land, it is unlikely that many years elapsed between the apostolic era and the time people in the region of modern Ethiopia heard of the teachings of Christ. Three of the first followers of Christ—Matthew, Bartholomew, and Andrew—are alleged to have visited "Ethiopia." Possibly during the first century CE there were already Christian communities, composed of merchants from Judea, in the big cities of the region. Such merchants are known to have traveled near and far to engage in commercial transactions with other nations and also to have lived among the people with whom they traded.

The commonly accepted history is that Saint Frumentius, the fourth-century Apostle of Ethiopia, used such communities of Christians of Jewish background to spread the faith. The "ruler" of the central political and economic city of Aksum, Ezana, reputedly publicly embraced Christianity in 345 CE. The writings of the monastic fathers mention that Gə'əz, Təgrä (Christian Ethiopian) literature had begun to flourish during the reign of a Patriarch Timothy of Alexandria sometime between 384 and 538 CE. These and other historical sources indicate that the Church was a significant institution in the Ethiopian region by the early sixth century.

CONNECTIONS WITH THE CHRISTIAN HOLY LAND

One can also mention in connection with Judaic communities in the area that Ethiopian Christians strictly observe the Old Testament dietary laws, the rules of circumcision, and celebrate the Lord's day on Saturday. The tradition that the state religion before Christianity was Judaism is related, of course, to the central, but unverified, story attributing the origin of the Ethiopian Orthodox Church to a love affair between the Queen of Sheba, known to Ethiopians as Queen Makədda of Ethiopia, and King Solomon of Israel, probably in the seventh century BCE, partially reported in both the Old and New Testaments and elaborated in the Ethiopian national saga, the *Kəbrä Nägäst* or "Glory of Kings." The languages (Gə'əz, Təgrä, and several other languages of Ethiopia) used in and around Aksum belong to the Semitic family, which includes Hebrew (as well as Arabic). It was not difficult to accommodate the Bible to the local Gə'əz language, especially the Old Testament, which was originally written in Semitic languages. The Hebrew Torah and its Gə'əz version show similarities in sentence structure, even though Gə'əz received it through the intermediary of the Greek of the Septuagint.

Bishops, or metropolitans, of the Ethiopian Church were appointed from Egypt by the patriarch of the Coptic Orthodox Church of Alexandria, a convention which started with the fourth-century apostle, Frumentius, and continued until 1951, when the Ethiopian church became autocephalic under a native patriarch, Baswəyos. Through these connections, the Ethiopian church remained well informed about the other, and especially the sister orthodox, churches and their literatures.

Christian Aksum militarily controlled the non-Christian kingdoms in the plateau of the Ethiopian highland region until the ninth century. The power of its Christian rulers over such a large territory came basically from the belief that the dynasty at Aksum and the Christian nation they ruled were the chosen people of God, succeeding Israel in this favored capacity. The *Kəbrä Nägäst*, whose place in the mind of Ethiopian Christians is not much inferior to that of the Bible, records this divine election. According to this source, Queen Makədda conceived a son, Mənilək I, by Solomon when she went to Jerusalem to visit the latter and listen to his wisdom. Mənilək, when it was his turn to visit his father, abducted the Ark of the Covenant, the source of Israel's identity as the chosen people of God, with the help of the Jewish clergy, who moved to Ethiopia with the young king. The fact that the Ethiopian nation accepted Christ while Israel rejected him has been taken as irrefutable proof of complete and perfect divine ordination.

A MONASTIC CHURCH

Ethiopian Christianity can be characterized as a monastic religion. Ascetic monasticism is perceived to be the highest stage of the Christian life and an ideal to be attained by all rather than restricted to a class of devotees. Although the Church does not teach that one need to be clothed in the monastic garb to become a perfect Christian, it is, nevertheless, the aspiration of all Ethiopian Christians to end their lives as monks or nuns, the human saints of the church, whose stories one hears at almost every visit to an Ethiopian church.

The common practice is to join one of the monastic communities as a virgin. The monastic ritual includes a section for small children, often those born to formerly barren parents who had vowed to give any child they conceived to a monastery. But many married people, with children and grandchildren, take the monastic vow at advanced ages and live at home with whatever comforts their homes provide. Ethiopians probably view Christianity in this light because the religion was spread in the country from the beginning mainly by monks, who preached what they practiced.

As there was, until 1951, only one metropolitan or bishop at a given time for the whole of Ethiopia, the country was divided into monastic regions, not dioceses or bishoprics. The large cenobitic (or communitarian) monasteries (the *adbarat*) owned estates and daughter monasteries and churches. Until 1974 these had their own courts to judge disputes among the people who lived in their territories.

Adherents to other type of Ethiopian monasticism—anchoritism, according to the tradition of solitude established by Saint Anthony (d. 356)—live

according to two rules: the *gəhusan*, or "separated ones," and the *bahətawiyan*, or "loners." The *gəhusan* (plural of *gəhus*) are recluses, living in cells attached to monasteries. Younger monks attend them without seeing or talking to them; once a day they put their meals at the doors of their cells and leave. The attendants would know that the recluses are alive if they find the food consumed when they return. The *bahətawiyan* (plural of *bahətawi*) live in the forests with the wild beasts. They are met occasionally by hunters and herdsmen. They live on what the forests offer—wild fruits, leaves, and roots. It is not uncommon for human remains to be found in the wildernesses with crosses and other Christian artifacts near them. The *bahətawiyan* sometimes "go to the world" to admonish Christians and warn the "generation of vipers . . . to flee from the wrath to come" (Matt. 3:7). The nation's political and spiritual leaders consider this class of anchorites archvipers. Several of the *bahətawiyan* have recently been arrested and imprisoned for alleged offenses.

THE ZAGWE DYNASTY

For reasons still unknown, the Aksumite (Solomonic) dynasty lost its power in the ninth century. The succeeding House of Zagwe in the highlands to the south was no less pious than the rulers in the Aksumite palace. Most of the famous rock-hewn monolithic churches of Lalibäla were built in the twelfth and thirteenth Christian centuries during their reign. These churches are, to this day, centers of annual pilgrimage for Ethiopian Christians. Four of the kings of the Zagwe dynasty, including Saint Lalibela, who sold his son when he had no money to give alms to the poor, are among the most celebrated native saints of Ethiopia. Their rule ended in 1270 CE.

RESTORATION OF THE SOLOMONIC DYNASTY

In 1270 CE, a rebel, Yəkunno Amlak or "May God be with Him," who claimed to be the descendant of the ruling family of Aksum, gained the support of the cenobitic monastic leaders to overthrow the Zagwe dynasty. The Church had no reason to regret the help it extended to Yəkunno Amlak, as it expanded and developed its modern identity under the later claimants to the "Solomonic" succession, which continued to the death of Haile Selassie in 1974. Around 1340 CE, monks, especially those of the monastery of Däbrä Asbo (later called Däbrä Libanos) in Šäwa

(Shewa), moved out to Christianize the pagan and Islamic regions to the south and west. Most of Gəʿəz literature, including the rituals and the collections of canon law, is the product of the 330-year period from 1270 to c. 1600. A system of musical notation, unknown in the sister churches, was invented between 1540 and 1559 CE.

Emperor Zärʾa Yaʿəqob (r. 1434–1468) deserves a special place in the history of the Ethiopian Orthodox Church. His contribution, as a prolific writer, a reformer and ruthless suppressor of dissension from the accepted faith, has no equal. He wrote several books aimed at reforming the church order on the basis of the so-called Apostolic Constitution. Unfortunately he had little or no tolerance for differing views and eliminated any who refused to accept his theological positions. In 1445 he led the army personally to defend the Christian kingdom against Islamic assault from the east. He divided northern Ethiopia (present-day Eritrea) among the monasteries in the region and commanded the monks there to evangelize the local populations.

Although the Christian kingdom did not interfere in the internal affairs of the non-Christian principalities it conquered, the *imams* of the Islamic regions to the east never accepted Christian overlordship. In 1527, at a moment of weak leadership in the Christian highlands, the *Imam* Ahmad ibn Ibrahim al-Ghazi (Grañ), revolted. The king of the time, Ləbnä Dəngəl (Wänag Säggäd, r. 1508–1540), oblivious of the fact that his Muslim subjects had received modern arms from the Ottoman Turks, sent a punitive expedition to the region and was defeated. The *Imam*, emboldened by his success in routing the expeditionary army, led his well-armed troops systematically into the Christian highlands. There he destroyed churches whose interiors were plated with pure gold, looted their treasures, and burned the their libraries and other outbuildings. The clergy tried to save their sacred texts by burying them in the ground. Only people who survived the fifteen years of the onslaught were able to recover the literary treasures they had hidden. Of the rest, some were disinterred only recently in this century by farmers stumbling on them with their plows. Christians in the conquered regions were forced to choose between death by the sword or conversion to Islam.

Whatever was left of the national heritage was saved when a small Portuguese contingent of fellow Christians, led by Cristóvão da Gama, son of Vasco da Gama, arrived with modern weapons to match those that the Turks had supplied to the *Imam*. The *Imam*'s army disintegrated in 1543 when he was fatally wounded. However, the *Imam*'s nephew, whom the *Imam*'s wife had refused to marry unless he avenged her husband, led his army into highland Ethiopia and brought back to her Gälawdewos's head.

A NEW CENTER FOR THE STATE AND CHURCH

After Gälawdewos' death, the palace was forced to move far away from the Muslim east—to Dämbiya in the west, where the ruling House of Gondär was founded in the second half of the sixteenth century. The Gondärite kings encouraged the production of Christian literature by highly educated church scholars of the kingdom who had followed them there. But the respite that the Christian community obtained in the west did not last very long. First came invasion by the nomadic pastoralist Oromo from the south, then the attempt by subsequent Jesuit Catholic missionaries to overthrow the Orthodox ruling house, and finally further Muslim encroachment from the Nile River valley.

To the Oromo, the churches and other buildings housing rich works of art meant nothing. As a consequence, the Church's dream of recovering its previous glory remained just unfulfilled. The Christian kingdom's only alternative, after a protracted and futile resistance to the Oromo invasion, was to attempt to Christianize the victorious invaders. But Islam, with its readily intelligible beliefs and rituals as compared to the theological complexities of high Ethiopian Christianity and the personal demands of monastic asceticism spread much faster among the Oromo than Christianity.

In the late nineteenth century, the upper Nile Valley to the west of the remnant Christian highland areas was controlled by the Derwishes under the leadership of Muhammad Ahmad b. Abdallah. Abdallah had declared himself the Mahdi, the prophet/leader who, according to Muslim teaching, was expected to appear on earth to reveal the true path of Islam to righteous believers. Abdallah's successor, the Khalifa, subsequently turned the Mahdist movement into a form of Islamic nationalism that reverberated throughout Ethiopia. The Khalifa called on Ethiopia's Christian king to embrace Islam and, at his refusal, invaded the city of Gondär, set the churches on fire and took thousands as his captives. The challenge of Islam for the Christian Church remains in modern Ethiopia.

CHRISTIAN LIFE

The Church recognizes the sacraments of baptism, penance, Eucharist, matrimony, unction of the sick, and holy order. Funeral (a rite not performed for those who commit suicide or who die during Lent) is also a requirement. Circumcision for both boys and girls has religious meaning for Ethiopian Christians as the chosen people of God, the children of Abraham.

The most difficult practices of Ethiopian Christianity are fasting and observance of the holy days. The greater part of the days of the year is days of fasting, including Fridays and Wednesdays, Lent, the Apostle's Fast, Nativity, Assumption, and Nineveh). Fasting is observed by skipping breakfast and consuming only vegetables and plant products during the rest of the day. Eating fish is allowed during most fast days, but not all; fish is not a common meal.

The Church demands that its followers attend services and refrain from doing any manual work during many monthly and annual holy days in addition to Saturdays and Sundays. Almost every family has a patron saint whose day they observe annually with a great feast. The two conspicuous feasts that characterize the Ethiopian Orthodox Church are Mäsqäl, the day on which Saint Helena found the true cross, on Mäskäräm 16–17 (September 27–28), and Ṭəmqät, or Epiphany, the day on which Christ was baptized at the hand of John the Baptist, on Ṭərr 12 (January 17).

Church services for the faithful start at about 6:00 AM on average days and last for about three hours. In large churches and monasteries these are daily services; otherwise they are performed on certain days of the week (Sundays and other holy days that fall on non-fast days). On fast days, service starts at noon; on Christmas eve it begins at midnight; on Easter the service is continuous from Friday to midnight Sunday. There are no pews or chairs in the church, for one is not supposed to sit before the Lord. The hours feel even longer for the overwhelming majority of churchgoers who do not understand Gəʿəz, the language in which the services are conducted.

Each church is centered around a *tabot*, supposed to be a replica of the Ark of the Covenant confided by Solomon to the Ethiopian Church. The church is a holy place only if the tabot, ritually sanctified by a bishop, is in it, placed on the altar housed in the third (inner) sanctuary, the holy of holies. The tabot serves as a slate placed on the altar on which the Eucharistic bread is broken.

Memorializing the dead is also demanding. It is done on the third, seventh, and fortieth days, on the sixth month, and annually up to the seventh year, with food and beer prepared for the clergy, the poor, and relatives and friends. Some thoughtful people free their survivors of this tradition by putting in their wills that they should do no more than give some alms on those days.

THE CHURCH'S PRESENT CHALLENGES

The modern Ethiopian Orthodox Church faces the immediate challenge of achieving financial and administrative independence of the post-1974 secular government. Until the overthrow of the monarchy in that year, it was a national church, financially supported by the government. The military and Marxist government established in 1974 revoked that status and nationalized church properties. The present government, from 1991, pursues the intrusive policy of the previous socialist regime toward the church, appointing its own candidates to high church offices but giving them no financial support. It is doubtful if the present church leaders would want to be abandoned by a government that has appointed them without the consent, or against the will, of the faithful.

Another dilemma is how to modernize the services of the church. The church lacks modern theological seminaries to produce educated teachers and priests and is not even sure whether these truly ancient practices should be modernized. In the past, education was the church's monopoly, and students received theological educations not because they wanted them to join the clergy but only because that was the only education they were able to get. Employment was available for them in the church, whether or not they felt the call to serve. That is why so many lay scholars serve the church dressed as clergy. Now that education is available also through government schools, the church may not have as many applicants if it opens theological seminaries alongside liberal arts or technical colleges.

The independence of Eritrea in 1991 confronted the church with loss of its northernmost province. The Eritrean political leaders, to complete their country's independence, put pressure on the Eritrean clergy to form an Eritrean Orthodox Church, independent of the Ethiopian Orthodox Church. As soon as the secessionists separated Eritrea from Ethiopia, they sent local monks to Egypt seeking ordination, and the Coptic Patriarch ordained them as Eritrean bishops of the Red Sea Territory (of Alexandrian Church jurisdiction). Unhappy with this separation, the Ethiopian Church leaders sent a letter of protest to the Coptic Patriarch, and the political leaders of Ethiopia immediately replaced them with clergy who expressed no objection to the division.

Ever since the church became autocephalic (governed by its own national synod) in 1951, the political leaders have interfered in the choice of the Ethiopian Patriarch. The faithful feared to express their disapproval of this secular intrusion on religious affairs openly. But they did so with outrage when the regime appointed Patriarch Abunä Paulos in 1993, believing that the choice was based on ethnic grounds. The faithful in the diaspora (especially in Europe and the United States), where there is no fear of retaliation by the Ethiopian government, expressed their anger more forthrightly. Encouraged by several archbishops who had fled the country since the establishment of the present government, Ethiopian Christians abroad have declared their independence administratively and are apparently in the process of organizing themselves as an independent *täwaḥɔdo* church in the diaspora. The archbishop sent to the Americas by Patriarch Paulos has been rejected everywhere by all but the few who are ethnically related to him. Patriarch Paulos himself was not received by Ethiopians as their spiritual father when he visited the United States and England in 1993. The Ethiopian church in the diaspora will face formidable difficulties if its leaders declare its independence, because, however angry with current politics the faithful may be, they are reluctant to sever ties to the ancient and eternal mother church in Ethiopia.

See also **Ahmad ibn Ibrahim al-Ghazi (Ahmad Grañ); Aksum; Death, Mourning, and Ancestors; Galawdewos; Gama, Vasco da; Haile Selassie I; Initiation; Judaism in Africa; Lalibäla; Queens and Queen Mothers; Religion and Ritual; Zara Ya'iqob.**

BIBLIOGRAPHY

Note: *CSCO = Corpus Scriptorum Christianorum Orientalium.* Louvain, Belgium.

Arras, Victor, ed. and trans. *Collection Monastica.* CSCO Scriptores Aethiopici (text) 238/45, (trans.) 239/46 (1963).

Arras, Victor, ed. and trans. *Patericon Aethiopice.* CSCO Scriptores Aethiopici (text). 277/53, (trans.) 278/54 (1967).

Arras, Victor, ed. and trans. *Quadraginta Historiae Monachorum* CSCO Scriptores Aethiopici (text) 505/85, (trans.) 506/86 (1988).

Beckingham, Charles Fraser, ed. and trans. *Some Records of Ethiopia, 1593–1646; Being Extracts from the History of High Ethiopia or Abassia, by Manoel de Almeida, Together with Bahrey's History of the Galla.* London: The Hakluyt Society, 1954.

Bezold, Carl, ed. and trans. *Kebra Nagast: Die Herrlichkeit der Könige: Abhandlungen der Philosophisch-Philologischen Klasse der königlich bayerischen Akademie der Wissenschaften.* Munich: Verlag der K. B. Akademie der Wissenschaften in Kommission des G. Franz'schen Verlags (J. Both), 1909.

Bonk, Jon. *An Annotated and Classified Bibliography of English Literature Pertaining to the Ethiopian Orthodox Church.* Metuchen, NJ: Scarecrow Press, 1984.

Budge, E. A. Wallis, trans. *The Queen of Sheba and Her Only Son Menylek. A Complete Translation of the Kebra Nagast.* London: The Medici Society Limited, 1922.

Budge, E. A. Wallis, trans. *The Book of the Saints of the Ethiopian Church.* 4 vols. Cambridge, U.K. Cambridge University Press, 1928.

Colin, Gérard, ed. and trans. *Vie de Georges de Sagla.* CSCO Scriptores Aethiopici (text) 492/81, (trans.) 493/83 (1987).

Crummey, Donald. *Priests and Politicians: Protestant and Catholic Missions in Orthodox Ethiopia 1830–1868.* New York: Oxford University Press, 1972.

Daoud, Marcos, and Marsie Hazen, trans. *The Liturgy of the Ethiopian Church,* 2nd edition. Cairo: The Egyptian Book Press, 1959.

Gerster, George. *Churches in Rock: Early Christian Art in Ethiopia.* London: Phaidon Press, 1970.

Getatchew Haile, ed. and trans. "The Homily in Honour of St. Frumentius, Bishop of Axum." *Analecta Bollandiana* 97 (1979): 309–318.

Getatchew, Haile. "The Forty-Nine Hour Sabbath of the Ethiopian Church." *Journal of Semitic Studies* 33, no. 2 (1988): 233–254.

Getatchew, Haile, ed. and trans. "The Homily of Abba Eləyas, Bishop of Aksum, on Mätta." *Analecta Bollandiana* 108 (1990): 29–47.

Getatchew, Haile, ed. and trans. *The Faith of the Unctionists: CSCO* Scriptores Aethiopici (text) 517/91, (trans.) 518/92 (1990).

Heldman, Marilyn Eiseman. *African Zion: The Sacred Art of Ethiopia*, ed. Roderick Grierson. New Haven, CT: Yale University Press, 1993.

Kaplan, Steven. *The Monastic Holy Man and the Christianization of Early Solomonic Ethiopia.* Wiesbaden: Franz Steiner Verlag, 1984.

Kur, S., ed. and trans. *Actes de Iyasus Mo'a, abbé du convent de St-Étienne de ayq.* CSCO Scriptores Aethiopici (text) 259/49, (trans.) 260/50 (1965).

Littmann, Enno, ed and trans. *The Legend of the Queen of Sheba in the Tradition of Axum.* Princeton, NJ: Princeton University Press, 1904.

Ricci, Lanfranco, ed. *Vita di Walatta Pietros.* CSCO Scriptores Aethiopici (trans.) 316/61 (1970).

Szymusiak, Jan M., ed. *Athanase d'Alexandrie: Apologie à l'Empereur Constance: Apologie pour sa fuite.* Paris: Les Éditions du Cerf, 1958.

Taddesse, Tamrat. *Church and State in Ethiopia 1270–1527.* New York: Oxford University Press, 1972.

Ullendorff, Edward. *The Ethiopians: An Introduction to Country and People.* New York: Oxford University Press, 1960.

Ullendorff, Edward. *Ethiopia and the Bible.* New York: Oxford University Press, 1968.

GETATCHEW HAILE

CHRONOLOGIES. *See* **King Lists and Chronologies.**

CHURCHES. *See* **Christianity; Prophetic Movements.**

CICATRIZATION. *See* **Arts; Body Adornment and Clothing.**

CINEMA. *See* **Film and Cinema; Media: Cinema.**

CIRCUMCISION. *See* **Initiation.**

CITIES. *See* **Urbanism and Urbanization.**

CIVIL RIGHTS. *See* **Human Rights.**

CIVIL SOCIETY

This entry includes the following articles:
FORMS OF CIVIL SOCIETY
POLITICAL ACCOUNTABILITY

FORMS OF CIVIL SOCIETY

Civil society is a concept with a long pedigree in Western political theory and practice. It emerged as an integral part of the demands for democratization in Europe and North America in the nineteenth century. Among many who have contributed to an understanding of the concept are John Locke (1632–1704), the British philosopher of the late seventeenth century, Alexis de Tocqueville (1805–1859), the nineteenth-century French political scientist who wrote *Democracy in America*, and Antonio Gramsci (1891–1937), the Italian Marxist who wrote his most important pieces while imprisoned for revolutionary activities in the early twentieth century. Like the ideas of "state" and "market," civil society is a core concept in the study of politics and development.

The concept has experienced a renaissance in conjunction with the wave of democratization that began in Latin America in the 1980s and later spread to Eastern Europe, the former Soviet Union, and Africa. It is popular among academic analysts, development advisers, social activists, and political practitioners alike. It has become standard fare in the governance discourse of the international development community.

The definition of civil society is generally clear: voluntarily organized activities with a political intent outside the state but within the public realm. Users typically exclude economic and productive activities and confine it to advocacy work. Thus, for instance, a private company is not part of civil society, but a trade union made up of persons working in that company is.

There is an important difference in the way that people apply this concept. Most use it in a purely functional manner, treating civil society as a "black box" into which all organized activities, whether for good or bad purposes, are grouped. Community-based organizations, vigilante groups, nongovernmental organizations (NGOs), like Catholic Relief Services, even terrorist gangs, are included in this functionalist use of civil society. It simply is the realm of all freely organized activities whether or not they contribute to democratic forms of governance.

Others apply the concept more restrictively. They emphasize the word "civil." By so doing they insist on a more normative application, according to which only those activities that truly contribute to democratization are included. For instance, organizations that empower women, advocate human rights, or assist the poor are cases in point. It is precisely these kinds of civil society organizations that are of special interest to African countries.

Before discussing civil society in its contemporary African context, it may be worth mentioning a little about its past. In colonial Africa, voluntary organizations first became politically significant in urban areas. People who lived and worked in cities came together for a variety of reasons: some because they shared an ethnic origin and spoke the same language, others because they worked in the same industry, yet others because they went to the same church. Some were registered with the colonial authorities, others were not. Regardless, as the British historian Thomas Hodgkin showed in the 1950s, these urban-based voluntary organizations contributed significantly to the growth of nationalism and demands for political independence. Civil society flourished because of the widespread dislike of colonialism.

Once African countries gained their independence, however, civil society turned from hero to villain. New nationalist leaders in government wanted everyone to support their agendas. They wanted all voluntary organizations to join the political movement charged with responsibility for national development. As a result, civil society organizations were co-opted into single political movements or banned outright. Most African countries lost the organizational vibrancy that had characterized the decolonization period. Mahmood Mamdani, professor of government and anthropology at Columbia University, attributes this decline to an absence of civic consciousness outside a relatively small circle of urban-based activists. Other factors include an independently wealthy but weak African middle class, and a poor understanding of the line that distinguishes public from private matters. In short, the conditions that existed in Western countries when civil society emerged simply did not exist in postindependence Africa.

Do those conditions exist in twenty-first-century Africa? Most observers and analysts doubt it, citing the need to create an environment in which civil society organizations become more important governance actors. Social and political activists, however, would ignore the question, believing that their work helps create the conditions for a civil society to emerge. A survey of academic literature conveys the impression that African civil society has become more significant politically, but it is weaker than in Latin America, Eastern Europe, and much of Asia.

In Africa, civil society organizations play a prominent role in service delivery, handling development funding of several billion U.S. dollars annually. They are much less effective, however, in advocacy on behalf of the poor or other underprivileged groups, affecting official policy, and holding governments accountable. In short, they are more important for development than governance in most African countries.

African civil society organizations face several problems: Organized cooperative activities may still be a prominent feature in many villages, but these tend to be small-scale and local. Rural people in Africa typically do not organize outside their own community boundaries, focusing instead on issues that affect their own circumstances. Civil society organizations arise when issues transcend local ties and people group together around policy issues that affect them all. Such organizations are rare in rural Africa; they are largely urban phenomena run by persons who can best be described as members of the elite.

A related problem is that there is no civic public realm in which political actors compete for influence over specific policy agendas. As Peter Ekeh, a Nigerian sociologist, has emphasized, loyalty among Africans lies not with civic institutions but with local communities. State-run institutions become sources of patronage that the political elite shares with their followers. In Africa, using public funds for private interests is an integral part of social and political practice—it is fundamental to the way political systems in these countries function. A lack of loyalty to state-run civic public institutions, therefore, means that the space for people to engage in collective action on specific policy issues is very limited.

Because politics are centered on patronage rather than policy, there are few incentives for collective action—it is much easier to contact a "big man" who can help deliver a good or solve a problem. This is part of the African patriarchal tradition in which men and women alike pay tribute to senior male figures. People relate to each other not in organized hierarchies but in personalized relationships.

This does not mean that African societies are stagnant. Social dynamics exist and the attributes of modern, cosmopolitan society are present in varying degrees, but they do not necessarily produce the type of civic values associated with civil society. Although the legacy of apartheid is still present in South Africa, its cosmopolitan society reflects its close interaction, both social and economic, with the rest of the world. Not surprisingly, civil society organizations are quite strong in that country.

In most other African nations, including the those where a tie to France keeps a measure of cosmopolitan culture alive, the elite that supports and lives according these values is small, made up primarily of academic, professional, and business groups. They often compete against heavy economic and political odds when trying to promote civic values.

Another problem is economic: People in Africa are willing to make significant personal contributions toward the payment of private events like weddings and funerals, collecting money and arranging the events in a manner that shows Africans do not lack organizational skills. There is no tradition, however, of contributing time or money for public causes. Such organizations are typically confined to small communities. Those based in urban areas, with the exception of savings and credit societies, usually exist on paper only. More often than not, people fail to pay their fees, and the organizations founder. For this reason civil society organizations in Africa depend on grants from outside sources.

International donors that support civil society organizations have contributed several billion U.S. dollars to African programs since the early 1990s. Most, like the U.S. Agency for International Development (USAID), support specific projects, but money goes to meet operational costs as well. Critics, especially skeptical politicians, have accused civil society leaders of being in the pockets of these donor agencies, often because political leaders feel that successful civil society organizations steal the public limelight from them.

Civil society is an accepted and integral part of governance in African countries. Although support is lukewarm in some cases, most officials accept the role that civil society plays in both development and the promotion of democracy. As an institution, civil society remains weak in most countries and misappropriation and other shortcomings continue in many organizations. Nonetheless, most civil society organizations improve life for the masses, both rural and urban, and Africa would suffer without the network of NGOs that now make up the core of civil society there.

See also **Aid and Development; Labor: Trades Unions and Associations; Nationalism; Postcolonialism.**

BIBLIOGRAPHY

Ekeh, Peter. "Colonialism and the Two Publics in Africa: A Theoretical Statement." *Comparative Studies in Society and History* 17, no. 1 (1975): 91–112.

Harbeson, John; Donald Rothchild; and Naomi Chazan; eds. *Civil Society and the State in Africa.* Boulder, CO: Lynne Rienner, 1994.

Hodgkin, Thomas. *Nationalism in Colonial Africa.* London: Frederick Muller, 1956.

Mamdani, Mahmood. *Citizen and Subject: Contemporary Africa and the Legacy of Late Colonialism.* Princeton, NJ: Princeton University Press, 1996.

Monga, Célestin. *The Anthropology of Anger: Civil Society and Democracy in Africa*. Boulder, CO: Lynne Rienner, 1998.

Trager, Lillian. *Yoruba Hometowns: Community, Identity, and Development in Nigeria*. Boulder, CO: Lynne Rienner, 2001.

GORAN HYDEN

POLITICAL ACCOUNTABILITY

The sociopolitical situation in most of the African countries since the famous National Conference, which ended an autocratic regime in Bénin, and Nelson Mandela's release from prison (both events occurring almost at the same time in February 1990) features the emergence of new social mechanisms and the discovery of what one might call public opinion. People are becoming more and more aware of belonging to specific groups defined in relation to their standings in the modern nations of the continent and increasingly express the desire to create interest groups in both civil and political arenas. From human rights activists to small businesspeople, from unemployed youths of the suburbs to the intellectual and religious elites, there is hardly a social group that has not felt the need for its members to communally articulate their daily concerns.

For example, in both public and private companies the void due to the absence of structures of collective organization—notably, unions, works committees, employers associations—is being filled by a multiplicity of increasingly dynamic informal groupings, even if these are often established along Weberian lines of sex, age, kinship, and religion. For Africans, these groupings are a way of reclaiming the right of self-expression, long confiscated by the official institutions of power. In establishing their members as full participants in the political game, these groups expand the arena of association, stealthily influencing the ongoing multifaceted transformation. By blurring the rules of the game, they represent a disruptive force in the sociopolitical environment.

After decades of neglect, this dynamic African civil society has become a major topic of study in the social sciences. Landmark publications have been released in since the late twentieth century, and various powerful international and academic institutions have established formal links with civil society organizations. Kofi Annan, the former United Nations (UN) Secretary General (1997–2006), famously noted that its organization "once dealt only with Governments. By now, we know that peace and prosperity cannot be achieved without partnerships involving Governments, international organizations, the business community and civil society. In today's world, we depend on each other." The UN's Department of Public Information has a special section for the contemporary issues of civil society.

Arguing that "the growth of civil society has been one of the most significant trends in international development," the World Bank has also created a special Website that provides information on its evolving relationship with civil society organizations around the world. Many academic institutions have done the same thing. Pioneering institutions in this domain are the Johns Hopkins University Center for Civil Society and the London School of Economics Center for Civil Society, which seeks to improve understanding and the effective functioning of not-for-profit, philanthropic, or civil society organizations throughout the world in order to enhance the contribution these organizations can make to democracy and the quality of human life. Despite the evident success of civil society, there is little consensus among researchers on what it actually constitutes. In fact, because the reasons for the renewed interest in civil society are many, researchers tend to define it in different ways. This makes the challenges of using civil society to build political accountability in the African context even more complex.

CHALLENGES OF DEFINING CIVIL SOCIETY

Concern about civil society is not relevant only to developing world. In fact, the term *civil society* was in vogue in the eighteenth and nineteenth centuries in Western Europe and generally referred to all institutions, formal and informal, between the family and the state. After World War I and the victory of the Russian Communist Party, Antonio Gramsci popularized the idea of civil society to analyze the specificity of the communist parties of Western Europe. The European Commission initiated in the 1990s a "civil dialogue," which was a first attempt by the European Union to give the institutions of society—and not only governments and businesses—voices at the policy-making tables in Brussels. In recent years, civil society has often referred to voluntary and nonprofit organizations of many different kinds, philanthropic institutions, social and political movements, other forms of social participation and engagement and the values and cultural patterns associated with them.

The London School of Economics' Center for Civil Society offers the following definition to guide research activities and teaching but stresses that it is by no means to be interpreted as a rigid statement:

> Civil society refers to the arena of uncoerced collective action around shared interests, purposes and values. In theory, its institutional forms are distinct from those of the state, family and market, though in practice, the boundaries between state, civil society, family and market are often complex, blurred and negotiated. Civil society commonly embraces a diversity of spaces, actors and institutional forms, varying in their degree of formality, autonomy and power. Civil societies are often populated by organizations such as registered charities, development non-governmental organizations, community groups, women's organizations, faith-based organizations, professional associations, trades unions, self-help groups, social movements, business associations, coalitions and advocacy group.

One of the first problems with the term *civil society* in the African context is determining exactly how Africans implement what it means. Although there is evidently a need to define the nature and sphere of political parties' activities in Africa, any attempt to define the forces hastily grouped under the label *civil society* appears problematic and doomed to failure. This difficulty is principally due to the diversity of political situations and the inherent inadequacy of using tools designed for understanding the workings of Western democracies to analyze the situation elsewhere in the world, which raises the general problem arising from the transfer of sociological concepts across space and time beyond the modern, Western contexts they were developed to describe.

Any definition of civil society will be different on the opposite sides of the Sahara, since from a political point of view, the problems are not identical. Sociologists in the Maghreb, for example, include only "the parties and associations that, despite their divergences of opinion on many issues, share the same values of human rights and individual freedoms" (Zghal 1991). Such a definition excludes

movements laying claim to fundamentalist Islam, even if they have a dominant role in the sociopolitical plan. South of the Sahara, things are different. The mullahs do not, at least for the moment, have determining roles on the course of events, although this statement needs qualifying. The mobilizing potential of religious communities is clear in Nigeria, where the smallest clash between members of different faiths may result in hundreds of deaths. The chaotic and violent history of the building of a mosque in Cameroon revealed a well-established "Muslim force" in the capital. In Senegal, the chief of the Mouride community has for many years dominated the country's business affairs. Nevertheless, religious organizations capable of influencing politics as much as the Islamic movements do in Algeria, Tunisia, Egypt, or Morocco do not yet exist in the largely Muslim countries south of the Sahara—Senegal, Mali, Burkina Faso, Niger or Cameroon—though civil society appears to be evolving in that direction in the northern states of Nigeria, where religious conflicts among Muslim and non-Muslim populations in recent years have resulted in large casualties.

That is why the traditional definition of civil society south of the Sahara usually incorporates the churches and other religious movements that, until the twenty-first century, have contributed in their own way to the birth of democratic power. It includes all organizations and individuals whose actions have helped amplify people's voluntary affirmations of social identity and the rights of citizenship, often in opposition to those in power, whose natural tendency is to repress such identities and claims. It obviously does not exclude the interactions among the state, the political parties, and leading personalities. In a nutshell, civil society in Africa is formed by all those who are able to manage and steer collective anger. While such a definition does not escape the criticism of those who reject the notion of civil society in states that are not democratic in the Western sense, it has the advantage of clearly emphasizing the historicity and the capacity of African societies to evolve within their own unique trajectories.

CHALLENGES OF CONCEPTUALIZING CIVIL SOCIETY

There seems to be broad consensus on the important role played by civil society organizations across the continent in bringing down some of Africa's most authoritarian regimes. But there is also a lot of debate about what should be their proper role during the transition toward and the consolidation of democracy. In fact, identifying clear mechanisms through which civil society can help strengthen political accountability remains a major challenge. First, there are many difficulties associated with applying democratic principles in countries where major political change has taken place. The problem starts with the various interpretations of the word *democracy*. The very principle of the rule (*kratos*) of the people (*demos*) opens up an infinite number of questions that are generally ignored but nevertheless explain the heart of the debate among various schools of political thought. As David Held pointed out with respect to the notion of *rule* alone:

> Definitional problems emerge with each element of the phrase: "rule"?—"rule by"?—"the people"? To begin with "the people": who are to be considered "the people"? What kind of participation is envisaged for them? What conditions are assumed to be conducive to participation? Can the disincentives and incentives, or costs and benefits, of participation be equal? The idea of "rule" evokes a plethora of issues: how broadly or narrowly is the scope of rule to be construed? Or, what is the appropriate field of democratic activity? If "rule" is to cover "the political" what is meant by this? Does it cover (a) law and order? (b) relations between states? (c) the economy? (d) the domestic or private sphere? Does "rule by" entail the obligation to obey? Must the rules of "the people" be obeyed? What is the place of obligation and dissent? What mechanisms are created for those who are avowedly and actively "non-participants"? Under what circumstances, if any, are democracies entitled to resort to coercion against some of their own people or against those outside the sphere of legitimate rule? (Held 1987, 2–3)

The definition of *the people*, the other component of the word *democracy*, raises at least as many questions, and each carries with it important implications. Far from being a purely philosophical discussion, an interrogation of the idea of democracy must include philosophical, theoretical, and practical dimensions. The upsurge of civil society groups in that debate has the potential to overturn not just the existing political order but also the surrounding moral order—assuming that such a thing exists. The emergence of such dominant "Their" presence means that the social game has become even more complex. Are civil society groups centrifugal forces that will stimulate and enhance the construction of the state, or will they be swept into the state's centralization and squabble over the remains of the ruined state? Do they aim to embody the earnest proclamations of democracy or to establish alternative values in the spiritual realm and impose radically different modes of social exclusion and violence? Does their tendency to refer to "tradition" reflect any substantive legacy from the past or commitment by its heirs?

Despite these much debated questions, there is broad consensus among social scientists that the viability of democratic consolidation depends in large part on the strength and effectiveness of underlying forces that shape and structure the polity. As Robert Putnam put it, "Social context and history profoundly condition the effectiveness of institutions. Where the regional soil is fertile, the regions draw sustenance from traditions, but where the soil is poor, the new institutions are stunted. Effective and responsive institutions depend, in the language of civic humanism, on republican virtues and practices. Tocqueville was right: Democratic government is strengthened, not weakened, when it faces a vigorous civil society" (1993, 182).

Another dimension in the debate is the assertion by some economists that a strong social capital (defined by Putnam as "features of social organization, such as trust, norms, and networks, that can improve the efficiency of society by facilitating coordinated actions") is an important factor in the process of wealth creation, as it brings large segments of the labor market into the efficient production of goods and services. Social capital reflects the strength of civil society, that is the willingness of individuals from all social groups to adhere to networks where they can equip themselves with the skills needed to improve their productivity.

CHALLENGES OF STRENGTHENING POLITICAL ACCOUNTABILITY

Whereas the debate over which specific organizations of society should be considered civil society in the context of national politics is likely to remain open-ended, most researchers agree that its role in the consolidation of a democratic political system should be encouraged. The question again is what institutional mechanisms should be in place to facilitate this process. In 1994 Larry Diamond suggested an interesting framework for assessing what he enumerated as the ten democratic functions of civil society. The theoretical considerations emphasized in his analysis include the educational virtues of a dynamic civil society, the numerous advantages of social mobilization and participation, the adoption of transparent rules in the political game, and the recognition and institutionalization of lobbies, which means the emergence of a new type of political culture focusing on cooperation, bargaining, and accommodation rather than on conflict and violence.

However, in order to comprehend fully the significance and implications of the rediscovery of civil society in Africa, one must also acknowledge a number of disturbing developments to the contrary. The first is the cult of nihilism and cynicism that is a feature of many religious and civic groups; indeed, in countries whose protagonists are primarily animated with revenge and anger, the dissemination of despair and violence seems to be the main feature of informal political markets. In Senegal, Mali, and Cameroon, for example, some of the most popular slogans used by the new social leaders have to do with organizing public trials of those who were in charge of the country since independence—in other words they are promoting retaliation, punishment, and witch hunts; in effect, vigilantism. Such discourse sets a negative tone for political debate, not least by limiting the types of issues that are brought to the forefront.

The second major threat stems from the extreme informalization of African political markets. Indeed, it is clear that some of the most vocal trade unionists and civil rights activists in Africa have taken advantage of the relative freedom that they have as social leaders to engage in subtle strategies of political entrepreneurship. Given the inflexible structures of government and administration in most of these countries, as well as the fact that political parties are increasingly mistrusted by the general public, many mysterious associations have been created by people who are really running for office. These leaders simply argue that they have found a way of circumventing the current renewal of authoritarianism, since those in power are much less willing to crack down on an amorphous "human rights league" than on a registered political party.

A third issue concerns the political role assigned to international nongovernmental organizations (NGOs). In many countries, they have become so politically powerful and so influential in the design and implementation of public policies that one cannot dismiss the need for scrutiny, regardless of their commitment to ethics. Their strength raises the issues of the legitimacy and responsibilities of those who make decisions in the conduct of public affairs—whether directly or indirectly—which are still much debated among social scientists.

See also **Annan, Kofi; Labor: Trades Unions and Associations; Mandela, Nelson; Nongovernmental Organization; United Nations; World Bank.**

BIBLIOGRAPHY

Annan, Kofi. Speech at the World Summit on the Information Society, November 16–18, 2005. Tunis. Available from http://www.un.org/issues/civilsociety/.

Diamond, Larry. "Rethinking Civil Society: Towards Democratic Consolidation." *Journal of Democracy* 5, no. 3 (1994): 4–17.

Fergusson, Adam. *An Essay on the History of Civil Society* [1767]. Cambridge, U.K.: Cambridge University Press, 1996.

Held, David. *Models of Democracy.* Stanford, CA: Stanford University Press, 1987.

Huntington, Samuel P. *The Third Wave: Democratization in the Late Twentieth Century.* Norman: University of Oklahoma Press, 1993.

Loury, Glenn C. "Social Exclusion and Ethnic Groups: The Challenge to Economics." In *Proceedings of the 1999 Annual World Bank Conference on Development Economics,* ed. B. Pleskovic and J. Stiglitz. Washington, DC: 2000.

Loury, Glenn C. "A Dynamic Theory of Racial Income Differences." In *Women, Minorities and Employment Discrimination,* ed. Phyllis A. Wallace and Annette Lamond. Lexington, MA: Lexington Books, 1977.

Magassouba, Moriba. *L'islam au Sénégal: demain les mullahs?* Paris: Karthala, 1985.

Monga, Célestin. *The Anthropology of Anger: Civil Society and Democracy in Africa.* Boulder, CO: Lynne Rienner Publishers, 1996.

Putnam, Robert D., with Robert Leonardi and Raffaella Y. Nanetti. *Making Democracy Work, Civic Traditions in Modern Italy.* Princeton, NJ: Princeton University Press, 1993.

West, Cornel. "The New Cultural Politics of Difference." In *Out There: Marginalization and Contemporary Cultures,* ed. Russell Ferguson et al. New York and Cambridge,

MA: The New Museum of Contemporary Arts and MIT Press, 1990.

Zghal, A. "Le concept de société civile et la transition vers le multipartisme." In *Changements politiques au Maghreb,* ed. Michel Camau. Paris: Editions du CNRS, 1991.

CÉLESTIN MONGA

CLEOPATRA VII (69–30 BCE).

The daughter of Ptolemy XII, mother of Ptolemy XV Caesarion by the Roman general and statesman Julius Caesar (100–44 BCE), and mother of twins Kleopatra Selene and Alexander Helios and a younger son, Ptolemy Philadelphus, by the Roman Triumvir (joint ruler) Mark Anthony, Cleopatra VII was ruler of Egypt jointly with her brothers Ptolemy XIII and XIV from 51 BCE and then solely from 44 BCE. Educated in the Alexandrian court and evidently the only Ptolemaic ruler to speak Egyptian, Cleopatra was reputed for her vitality and witty conversation. She understood how to balance the grain surplus of Egypt and its connections to the Nubian gold fields and central African resources with the consumer markets and tortuous politics of the Eastern Mediterranean. Although backed by Rome, she was mindful of her Egyptian responsibilities, identifying herself as the goddess Isis. Her image was carved in several temples, including those at Armant and Dendera. She enacted decrees to protect the land rights of Alexandrians throughout Egypt, and her astute administration maintained the grain supply of Egypt to Rome. After the assassination of Caesar she fought an increasingly desperate political and military campaign against the Roman ruler Octavian (63 BCE–14 CE) with the failing help of Mark Anthony. Her death, apparently by the bite of an asp, ensured that her legendary status is as strong in the twenty-first century as it was in antiquity.

See also **Egypt, Early.**

BIBLIOGRAPHY

Grant, Michael. *Cleopatra.* London: Weidenfeld and Nicolson, 1972.

Kleiner, Diana E. *Cleopatra and Rome.* Cambridge, MA: Harvard University Press, 2005.

Walker, Susan, and Peter Higgs, eds. *Cleopatra of Egypt: From History to Myth.* Princeton, NJ: Princeton University Press, 2001.

PENELOPE WILSON

CLICK LANGUAGES. *See* **Languages: Khoesan and Click.**

CLIMATE.

Africa is the most tropical of continents. Positioned symmetrically astride the equator, almost all of sub-Saharan Africa lies no further than 35° from the equator. This produces north-south climate zones that are almost mirror images. However, within Africa there is a great diversity of climates: from the arid Sahara to glaciers on Mount Kenya to the Mediterranean climate of South Africa.

The climate of sub-Saharan Africa is governed by a number of factors, especially the distribution of solar radiation. On June 21, the sun is directly overhead in the Northern Hemisphere at the tropic of Cancer; on December 21 the sun is directly overhead in the Southern Hemisphere at the tropic of Capricorn. This gives rise to the movement of the Intertropical Convergence Zone (ITCZ), a swath of low atmospheric pressure that is the basis for much of the precipitation, as well as the foundation of wet and dry seasons in sub-Saharan Africa.

Warm, moisture-laden tropical air forms the ITCZ. As the air rises, the northeast and southeast trades take it poleward. As the air cools, it becomes drier and descends at the tropic of Cancer and the tropic of Capricorn. As a result of this global circulation pattern, deserts are usually found in these areas. In Africa, the Sahara straddles the tropic of Cancer, and the Kalahari straddles the tropic of Capricorn.

Bordering the ITCZ are a series of low-pressure systems that produce precipitation; bordering the tropic of Cancer and the tropic of Capricorn are a series of high-pressure systems where precipitation is generally minimal. These systems move as the position of the sun moves. Thus, the ITCZ hovers around the equator at the vernal equinox

(March 21), when the sun is overhead at the equator, and moves north until June 21, the northern equinox. The ITCZ then heads south and crosses the equator again sometime around the autumnal equinox (September 21), and reaches its farthest southern position on December 21, the southern solstice.

This movement is the rough basis for precipitation patterns in Africa. A map of annual precipitation shows this seasonality. Precipitation is greatest along the equator and gradually decreases away from it. The highest mean average precipitation was recorded in Ureka, Equatorial Guinea (410 inches); the lowest was in Wadi Halfa, Sudan (0.02 inches).

The ITCZ's movement determines the length, timing, and number of rainy seasons throughout Africa. Areas within its path have two rainy seasons, governed by its poleward passage during summer and its return toward the equator during late summer and early fall. Thus Nairobi has long rains from April to May and short rains from October to November. The difference in length occurs because the ITCZ tends to move faster toward the equator than poleward. Areas at the northern and southern edges of the ITCZ have only one rainy season. Khartoum in the Sudan and Lusaka in Zambia have just one rainy season. The Sahara and Kalahari are largely outside the influence of the ITCZ, so they receive only sporadic rain.

The ITCZ does not move evenly across Africa. Both mountains and ocean currents play a role in its movement. For instance, the cold Benguela current, which runs north along the Skeleton Coast of Namibia, cools the surrounding air masses and keeps the ITCZ away from the west coast of southern Africa. As a result, precipitation is low. Similarly, precipitation in the east African highlands is greater because mountains such as Kilimanjaro, the Ruwenzori, Aberdares, and Mount Kenya force air masses to rise, cool, and release moisture.

The air masses that meet at the ITCZ are either moist tropical maritime air masses that originate over oceans, or hot and dry tropical continental air masses that originate over land. Because southern Africa is influenced by tropical maritime air masses, it gets more precipitation. In the north, the Sahara and the Sahel (a semiarid region just below the Sahara) are influenced by tropical continental air masses that bring little moisture. Local climate is also influenced by the type of air mass that is prevalent. For much of the year, East Africa is influenced by dry tropical continental air masses. The Congo and Zaire are almost always under the influence of moist tropical maritime air masses.

Precipitation is also strongly influenced by surface winds, particularly a phenomenon known as "continentality." While the winds that meet at the ITCZ are the southeast and northeast trades, surface winds at the equator are generally westerly. These air masses, which blow over the warm water of the South Atlantic, bring moisture that becomes precipitation. As the warm, moist air reaches land, it cools and releases moisture. As the air moves over the continent, it becomes drier and yields less precipitation. For this reason, precipitation is greatest in West Africa and decreases from west to east. There are some exceptions. Mountains cause air masses to rise. As air masses rise, they cool, and release moisture as precipitation. Thus in the east African highlands, precipitation is higher than in surrounding areas.

Because Africa south of the Sahara is almost entirely within the tropics, the mean annual temperature range is small. It is lowest at Barumbu in northern Zaire (2.5° Fahrenheit variance) and greatest in the Sahara (42° variance). Over half the continent experiences a range of less than 10.8 degrees. The mean annual daily temperature range is based on continentality. The range is 10° along much of the coast, but higher in the center of the continent. It is 20° in the Sahara and 15° in the Kalahari Desert.

Even though Africa is almost entirely within the tropics, monsoons affect it in only a limited fashion. The term "monsoon" is based on the Arabic word *mausim*, meaning "fixed season." Monsoons are seasonal airstream reversals caused by pressure changes over ocean and land. They occur to some extent in West Africa. From April to October, the prevailing winds are from the southwest and bring tropical moist air to the coast. From November to March, wind direction changes, and the winds shift to the northeast, bringing dry, continental air.

Precipitation seasonality in Africa creates a series of climate belts; centered on the equator, they are roughly mirror images of each other. For example, at the center of the continent, along the equator, is a tropical wet zone that experiences rainfall throughout the year—as much as 195 inches annually. On either side of this belt is a tropical climate associated with the ITCZ that receives between 39 to 78 inches of precipitation a year, with a dry spell of three to five months. The northern tropical dry belt has a dry season during the winter months, when the ITCZ is far to the south. On either side of this belt is a tropical climate zone with precipitation that ranges from 10 to 39 inches, and a dry spell that can last from five to eight months. This drought-susceptible area includes the Sahel, where famines have occurred in the past. Beyond these belts are areas where rainfall is minimal.

In the north, the Sahel gives way to the Sahara, a subtropical desert climate that is the most extensive type of climate zone on the continent. In the south, because tropical maritime air masses have greater influence on the continent, there are deserts, but precipitation falls in the summer months, as in the Kalahari. Finally, above the Sahara and below the Kalahari are zones of Mediterranea-like climate, where rainfall occurs during the winter months. Precipitation is low, roughly 23 inches annually. These areas are outside the tropics and are influenced by the westerly winds. Interspersed among these broad climatic zones are tropical highland climates such as those found in East Africa, and tropical deserts, like those found in the Horn of Africa.

These zones correspond with vegetation types. Along the equator the vegetation is tropical rainforest, which gives way to moist savanna, dry savanna, the semidesert Sahel, desert, and finally Mediterranean. In some areas vegetation is montane, and in others it is temperate grassland (veld), which is a function of topography in addition to other factors.

This is the overall climatic picture for Africa south of the Sahara. However, climate varies locally, depending upon a number of factors, including the influence of air masses, ocean currents, topography, geography, and the presence of inland lakes.

EQUATORIAL AFRICA

This region comprises the Congo Basin and the southern coast of West Africa as well as Equatorial Guinea, southern Cameroon, and northern Gabon. Due to its position along the equator, as well as the influence of westerly surface winds, which blow across the South Atlantic and bring moist, tropical maritime air, this region receives heavy rain throughout the year. However, ocean currents also play a role in the local climate. The Benguela current, which runs up the coast from Namibia almost to the equator during summer months, cools air masses and reduces rainfall in the Congo Basin; it also affects western Nigeria and Côte d'Ivoire, which are also somewhat drier than their geographical location would warrant. While rain is heavy throughout the year, the seasonal movement of the ITCZ means that along the West African coast there are two periods of low precipitation. The first is in December and January, as the ITCZ reaches its farthest point south. The second is in July and August, when the ITCZ brings rain to the Sahel. Rainy seasons are longer closer to the coast because of the influence of tropical maritime air. West Africa has a limited monsoon, which causes a seasonal reversal of prevailing winds and influences the distribution of precipitation.

WEST AFRICA AND THE SUDAN

This region extends from inland West Africa above the coastal zone to the Ethiopian Highlands and extends from about 20° to 5° north latitude. This zone includes the Sahel, an Arabic word meaning "shore" or "border," a zone roughly 186 miles wide that borders the Sahara.

The ITCZ plays a dominant role in the region's climate, which is characterized by decreasing rainfall and rainy season with increased distance from the equator, as well as a decrease in rainfall from west to east. Rainfall begins in the southern reaches of this area, such as in Wau, Sudan, in March; rainfall begins in July and August for Dakar, when the ITCZ reaches its most northerly position. Rainfall tapers off and ends in the fall, usually around October, but this depends on latitude, with more northerly areas having shorter rainy seasons than those closer to the equator. In June, the ITCZ is far to the north, so southwesterly winds bring tropical air and precipitation to west Africa. The Sahel is influenced by the monsoonal system that affects West Africa. In the dry season, from November to March, the prevailing winds are northeasterly. As they strengthen, they are called *harmattan* winds, a Hausa word meaning "north wind." These dry, cool winds originate in the Sahara.

Ethiopia, in the northern portion of this zone, has one rainy season from late June to early October that is composed of two periods. The short rains called *belg* occur from March to June; the long rains or *krempt* occur thereafter until early October. The Horn of Africa, including Somalia and the Ogaden region, is an anomaly, because despite its equatorial position, it is a desert. Annual precipitation ranges from 12 to 14 inches. This area is a desert due to a number of factors, including the divergence of the monsoonal airstream around the Horn from June to September. Another reason is that the prevailing winds are tropical continental and contain little moisture. Furthermore, they pass over a zone of cold, upwelling water off the coast, which means that the air does not pick up moisture.

SOUTHERN AFRICA

This region extends from 5° to almost 35° south latitude. The climate of this region is somewhat similar to that of West Africa and southern Sudan. From north to south, rainfall in general decreases. In Zimbabwe, the rainy season lasts from mid-November to mid-March. Farther south, in Zambia, the rainy season is shorter, from November to March, and the dry season is longer. The climate of southern Africa, however, is somewhat different, because the Benguela current, which runs up the west coast of southern Africa, cools the air masses as they move toward the continent. The coastal Namib Desert, which lies along this coast, has some two hundred days of fog a year. The Benguela current also hampers the southern movement of the ITCZ along the west coast. Because of this, the ITCZ moves farther south along the east coast of southern Africa but remains far to the north along the west coast. This means that rainfall increases from west to east, a reversal of the pattern found north of the equator.

Because southern Africa is surrounded by the ocean, from April to September it is dominated by high-pressure systems, which bring seasonal drought. But from October to March, the highs weaken and allow tropical maritime air from the east and northeast to bring precipitation. For this reason the Kalahari receives summer rains—more

than the Sahara, even though both are located in zones where dry, hot air descends after rising from the ITCZ.

At the far tip of southern Africa, along the west coast, a Mediterranean climate prevails. This is because this region is outside the tropics and is influenced by westerly winds. Moreover, the Benguela current strips air masses of moisture, so that rainfall occurs only in winter, from April to September in Cape Town. And just as local winds play a role in the climate of the Sahel, so do local winds of Namibia and South Africa. From April to September, hot, dry winds called berg winds blow from the interior of southern Africa toward the coast.

EAST AFRICA

East Africa, comprised of Uganda, Kenya, and Tanzania, straddles the equator. The climate ranges from hot, humid and tropical along the coasts and the shores of Lake Victoria, to a cooler montane zone in the highlands. East Africa receives less rainfall than its position would warrant, especially since much of this region is highland, which should cause an increase in rainfall. Only in the Lake Victoria Basin, the high mountains, and on the islands of Zanzibar and Pemba does precipitation exceed 59 inches. Elsewhere it averages less than 30 inches.

Although rainfall generally increases from east to west, East Africa receives less rainfall because the monsoonal system brings dry, continental air masses to the region for most of the year. When air masses from the southwest monsoon pass over Madagascar, its high mountains strip away moisture. Once these dry air masses reach east Africa, they produce precipitation only after uplifting; the east is low coastline, while the highlands to the west receive more precipitation. Lake Victoria, which is 26,828 square miles in area, generates an almost permanent low-pressure system that produces water vapor and local precipitation. The long rains, which occur as the ITCZ travels north, are from April to May, while the short rains, which occur as the ITCZ moves south, are from October to November. In January, dry northeasterly winds bring dry continental air and little rainfall.

MADAGASCAR

Madagascar's climate is mainly influenced by the surrounding ocean, although the ITCZ has some effect. From December to February, the ITCZ reaches 15° south latitude, placing it over the northern portion of the island. Topographical relief also plays a role in the climate: The prevailing winds across Madagascar are the southeast trades. Because of this, the island's east coast receives most of the precipitation and the west coast is in a rain shadow. There is a dry season on the east coast, which can receive as much as 137 inches of rain a year. Most precipitation occurs during the summer, from January to March, when the ITCZ's influence is most strongly felt. On the west coast, rainfall averages between 15 and 75 inches from north to south. The reason for this variation is the ITCZ, which brings a wet season to the north of the island from December to March.

Cyclones affect the east coast of Madagascar more than any other part of Africa. Cyclones—tropical storms with winds greater than 75 miles per hour—are generated in the southern Indian Ocean between November and April, and January and February. They are formed during periods when sea surface temperatures are high and air over the ocean is unstable.

See also **Desertification, Modern; Ecosystems.**

BIBLIOGRAPHY

Bridges, E. M. "World Geomorphology." In *Africa*, ed. E. M. Bridges. Cambridge, U.K.: Cambridge University Press, 1990.

Buckle, Colin. *Weather and Climate in Africa*. Harlow, U.K.: Longman, 1996.

Griffiths, J. F., ed. *Climates of Africa*. New York: Elsevier, 1972.

Grove, Alfred Thomas. *Africa*, 3rd edition. Oxford and New York: Oxford University Press, 1978.

Lewis, Lawrence A., and L. Berry. *African Environments and Resources*. Boston: Urwin Hyman, 1988.

Leroux, Marcel. *The Meteorology and Climate of Tropical Africa*. London and New York: Springer, 2001.

Nieuwolt, S. *Tropical Climatology*. New York: John Wiley & Sons, 1977.

Stock, Robert F. *Africa South of the Sahara: A Geographical Interpretation*. New York: Guilford Press, 1995.

Tyson, Peter Daughtrey. *The Weather and Climate of Southern Africa*. Oxford and New York: Oxford University Press, 2000.

DAVID SMETHURST

CLITORIDECTOMY. *See* Initiation.

CLOTH. *See* Textiles.

CLOTH MAKING. *See* Textiles.

CLOTHING. *See* Arts; Body Adornment and Clothing.

COASTAL ENVIRONMENTS. *See* Ecosystems: Coastal Environments.

COETZEE, J. M. (1940–). The South African novelist John Maxwell Coetzee was born in Cape Town into a family of both Afrikaans and English South African heritage, with English as his first language. He graduated from the University of Cape Town, where he studied English and mathematics, in 1961. Leaving for England soon after, he worked as a computer programmer and wrote his master's thesis there (awarded by UCT in 1963) on the work of the novelist Ford Madox Ford. From 1965 to 1969, he wrote his doctoral thesis, a linguistic analysis of Samuel Beckett's work, at the University of Texas at Austin. After teaching at the State University of New York at Buffalo, he returned as a lecturer to the University of Cape Town in 1972, becoming Professor of General Literature in 1984. Migrating to Australia in 2002, where he is Honorary Visiting Research Fellow at the University of Adelaide, he holds numerous visiting professorial posts in the United States, notably at the University of Chicago.

Coetzee's work first received international attention with the Booker Prize awarded in 1983 for *Life & Times of Michael K*, though his earlier novels, *Dusklands* (1974), *In the Heart of the Country*

(1977), and *Waiting for the Barbarians* (1980), had already won prizes both within South Africa and beyond, praised for their originality and literary skill. He won a second Booker Prize for *Disgrace* in 1999 and the Nobel Prize in Literature in 2003, sealing his reputation as one of the world's greatest living writers. Among his other novels are *Foe* (1986), *Age of Iron* (1990), *The Master of Petersburg* (1994), *Elizabeth Costello* (2003), and *Slow Man* (2005), the latter his first novel set in Australia. He has also published two autobiographical works, *Boyhood: Scenes from Provincial Life* (1997) and *Youth* (2002)—although these are better described as fictionalized memoirs, written as they are in the third person—and four collections of essays, including *White Writing: On the Culture of Letters in South Africa* (1988) and *Giving Offense: Essays on Censorship* (1996), that demonstrate his deeply thoughtful and scholarly analysis.

Fiercely protective of his own privacy, Coetzee has described himself as believing in "spare prose and a spare, thrifty world." The ethical and philosophical nature of his writing makes it of interest not only to literary scholars but to a much wider readership.

See also **South Africa, Republic of: History and Politics (1850–2006).**

BIBLIOGRAPHY

Attwell, David, ed. *Doubling the Point: Essays and Interviews: J. M. Coetzee.* Cambridge, MA: Harvard University Press, 1992.

Attridge, Derek. *J. M. Coetzee and the Ethics of Reading: Literature in the Event.* Chicago: University of Chicago Press, 2004.

SUE KOSSEW

COLD WAR. During the period from 1945 to 1970, Africa was not a major arena for conflict between the Soviet Union and the United States. The anticolonial struggles were led at least in their initial phases by relatively privileged social strata. Communist parties in Africa were almost nonexistent (except in South Africa and later Sudan, which did have moderately important communist parties). There were some labor unions, student groups, and political parties that developed radical nationalist or even Marxist orientations, and in several instances these played significant roles in the independence movements (this was especially true with regard to the Parti Démocratique de Guinée, under Ahmed Sékou Touré). But in no case did a communist party lead the struggle against colonialism. These facts reduced the value of Africa to the Soviet Union, and the lack of Soviet interest also reduced U.S. interest. For the most part, U.S. interests in Africa were served by the European colonial powers that vigilantly protected their colonies against any prospective ideological threats.

The first major Cold War conflict was the Congo Crisis of 1960 that followed the Congo's decolonization from Belgium. To a large extent the Congo Crisis was an asymmetrical Cold War conflict, in that the interveners were overwhelmingly from the United States and its NATO allies. Belgian-supported mercenaries and mining interests helped engineer the secession of mineral-rich Katanga Province, which functioned as a de facto Belgian puppet state for several years. The political turmoil led to the dispatch of a United Nations peacekeeping force that soon became the largest and most important peacekeeping operation of the entire Cold War period.

Recent documentation shows that the UN peacekeepers were sympathetic to American and European interests in the Congo, and they secretly coordinated their activities with those of the United States. In response, the Soviet Union and its allies made a brief effort to furnish military assistance to the elected Congolese prime minister, Patrice Lumumba. However, the Soviets lacked the long-range transport capability that would have been necessary to match the North American interventions. For the Congolese, these external interventions proved highly destabilizing. Lumumba was assassinated by Belgian military forces and allied mercenary groups (with at least indirect encouragement from the CIA). The accession to power by General Joseph-Desire Mobutu in 1965, with strong U.S. and European support, inaugurated one of the more corrupt and divisive rulers of recent African history.

Overall, the Soviet support for Lumumba, however brief and ineffectual, probably gained the Soviet Union some degree of popular support in Africa, especially among intellectual classes. With regard to the war of ideas, the Soviets enjoyed additional advantages. The Soviet Union itself was (at least in theory) strongly opposed to colonialism. That the Soviets had a record of semicolonial domination of various non-Russian groups within the Soviet Union was generally overlooked at the time. In addition, a new generation of young people throughout Africa became increasingly inclined toward various forms of Marxism and socialism, and these factors also weighed in favor of Soviet influence. These advantages were outweighed, however, by the former colonial powers—that were of course noncommunist—retaining significant economic, cultural, and in some cases military links to their former colonies. In the majority of African states, U.S. and European influence far exceeded Soviet influence throughout the Cold War.

The 1970s brought a new wave of Cold War interventions in Africa. The increased interventionism resulted primarily from fast-paced political change within Africa: Portugal's colonies all achieved independence during this period; in Ethiopia, the monarchy under Haile Selassie was overthrown in a 1974 revolution and replaced by a Marxist-led military government. And the remaining white-ruled states in Southern Africa came under renewed pressure for change. The Soviet Union (and also Cuba) intervened in several of these conflicts. By this period, the Soviet Union possessed enough transport planes and ships to enable large-scale interventions; this was a capability that they had lacked during the Congo Crisis. The United States, on the other hand, was determined to block these perceived Soviet intrusions into what had long been regarded as an American and European sphere of influence. Even the Chinese were now determined to project their influence into African conflicts, and they generally acted in an adversarial fashion vis-à-vis the USSR.

The result was a series of proxy wars throughout the continent during the 1970s. Cuban troops, supplied by the Soviets, fought in the Angolan civil war; the Cubans and Soviets also supported Ethiopia in a complex series of wars on the Horn of Africa. The United States, too, intervened extensively during this period (and in fact it was the United States, not the Soviet Union, that first intervened in Angola in 1974). From the U.S. side, these African interventions never involved large numbers of American troops. Due to the Vietnam debacle and the lack of U.S. public support for overseas adventures, American officials were simply unwilling to accept the political risks of direct military intervention in Africa. Instead, the United States relied on close cooperation with South Africa, France, and Morocco, that intervened on America's behalf. The Central Intelligence Agency was used as an additional interventionist instrument. CIA intervention was coordinated to some extent with that of the Chinese. This was especially true in Angola, where both the United States and Chinese (as well as South African) intelligence services supplied weapons to some of the same factions in the Angolan civil war. These various alternate wars extended well into the 1980s, when the Reagan Doctrine increased further the level of U.S. intervention.

One of the effects of this upsurge of Cold War conflict in Africa was to heighten pressure on the remaining white-ruled states of Southern Africa, Southern Rhodesia (present-day Zimbabwe), Southwest Africa (present-day Namibia), and South Africa. The security of these states was greatly reduced by the political changes that occurred during this period, especially the independence of nearby Angola and Mozambique, both of which furnished bases to African guerrilla groups for operations against the white-ruled states. The Soviets and the Chinese provided limited amounts of aid to several of these groups. These military pressures contributed to the eventual collapse of white rule in Zimbabwe in 1980, and also in Namibia and finally South Africa after the end of the Cold War. The conclusion of the Cold War, after 1989, led to a progressive disengagement by both superpowers. Unfortunately, this disengagement also led to a decline in development assistance, which served to intensify the continent's economic difficulties.

See also **Haile Selassie I; Lumumba, Patrice; Touré, Sékou.**

BIBLIOGRAPHY

Butler, Shannon. "Into the Storm: American Covert Involvement in Angola, 1974–1976." Ph.D. diss. University of Arizona.

De Witte, Ludo. *The Assassination of Lumumba*. London: Verso, 2001.

Gibbs, David N. "The United Nations, International Peacekeeping, and the Question of 'Impartiality':

Revisiting the Congo Operation." *Journal of Modern African Studies* 38, no. 3 (2000): 359–382.

Westad, Odd Arne. *The Global Cold War: Third World Interventions and the Making of Our Times.* New York: Cambridge University Press, 2005.

DAVID N. GIBBS

COLENSO, JOHN WILLIAM (1814–1883).

John William Colenso, born in Saint Austell, England, and educated at Saint John's College, Cambridge, became the first bishop of the Diocese of Natal (1853), where he established the mission station Ekukhanyeni (Place of Light) at Bishopstowe outside Pietermaritzburg. His broad Christian universalism and knowledge of contemporary scientific discovery, together with his awareness of African perceptions of contemporary Christian teaching, soon made him a radical critic of conventional missionary practice. This culminated in his *The Pentateuch and Book of Joshua Critically Examined* (1870), which sought to demonstrate that the Bible was not the literal word of God. The uproar following the book's publication led eventually to Colenso's excommunication.

In 1873 Colenso exposed the injustice with which the authorities in Natal had treated the Hlubi people and their chief, Langalibalele. He did the same for the Zulu people and their king, Cetshwayo kaMpande, when expansionist British policy led to the invasion of the Zulu kingdom in 1879.

Although Colenso's various projects failed in his lifetime, from a twenty-first-century perspective it is possible to see that his biblical criticism was an attempt to place contemporary religious thought on a sounder basis and that his political protest was a courageous exposé of the violence and injustice inherent in imperialism. His daughters, Harriette Emily, Frances Ellen, and Agnes Mary, continued the political struggle for African rights in South Africa.

See also **Cetshwayo; Christianity.**

BIBLIOGRAPHY

Draper, Jonathan A., ed. *Eye of the Storm: Bishop John William Colenso and the Crisis of Biblical Inspiration.* London; New York: T & T Clark International, 2003.

Guy, Jeff. *The Heretic: A Study of the Life of John William Colenso, 1814–1883.* Johannesburg: Raven Press, 1983.

Guy, Jeff. *The View across the River: Harriette Colenso and the Zulu Struggle against Imperialism.* Charlottesville: University Press of Virginia; Oxford: James Currey, 2002.

Rees, Wynn, ed. *Colenso Letters from Natal.* Pietermaritzburg: Shuter and Shooter, 1958.

JEFF GUY

COLONIAL POLICIES AND PRACTICES

This entry includes the following articles:
BELGIAN
BRITISH CENTRAL AFRICA
BRITISH EAST AFRICA
BRITISH WEST AFRICA
EGYPTIAN
FRENCH NORTH AFRICA
FRENCH WEST AND EQUATORIAL AFRICA
GERMAN
ITALIAN
PORTUGUESE
SPANISH

BELGIAN

In most important respects Belgian colonial policy was similar to that of other modern colonial powers, notably Britain and France. Despite significant "philosophical" differences between their respective brands of imperialism, Britain, France, and Belgium (unlike Portugal or Italy) were all advanced industrial powers. In other respects, however, Belgium was a unique colonizer. In contrast to Portugal or Holland (from which Belgium separated in 1830), Belgium lacked a tradition of mercantile colonialism. But unlike other states that achieved their modern form in the nineteenth century (for example, Germany and Italy)—and deliberately embarked upon imperial ventures as a way to affirm their newfound international stature—Belgium was, in some ways, a reluctant, almost inadvertent colonizer. It was, in fact, the only one to have inherited a readymade colonial empire in the form of the Congo Free State: Belgium took it over in 1908, twenty-three years after that singular creation of King Léopold II's (1865–1909) blend of megalomania and rapaciousness had been granted international recognition at the Berlin Conference.

Apart from occasionally—and grudgingly—rescuing Léopold from the financial difficulties he got into on account of his African domains, the Belgian government had little or nothing to do with the administration of the Congo Free State. Because public monies and credit guarantees had been extended to Léopold's Congo, however, Belgium had come, by the turn of the century, to look upon it with the eyes of a mortgage holder. International pressures caused by the disclosure of widespread abuses by Léopold's agents in Africa precipitated a kind of foreclosure, which was euphemized as Léopold's "donation" of the Congo to Belgium. The transfer became effective in 1908, from which date the Congo Free State became known as the Belgian Congo.

The *Charte Coloniale* of 1908, which was to serve until 1960 as the quasi-constitutional statute of the Belgian Congo, was mostly notable for the explicit separation which it carefully established between the Belgian and Congolese treasuries, armed forces, and citizens: thus, only volunteers could serve in the colonial militia (*Force Publique*), and suffrage was denied not only to the Congolese but also to Belgians residing in the colony. Never, over the next fifty years, did Belgium seriously consider extending even nominal Belgian citizenship to the Congolese people, let alone allowing them representation in its parliament. Clearly, assimilation was neither an ideological commitment nor a policy goal. While this position was, in some ways, similar to Britain's, it was not matched by any real attempt to develop in the Congo the limited sort of representative bodies exemplified by the Legislative Councils of British colonial Africa: their nearest equivalent in the Congo, the *Conseil de Gouvernement*, remained until the very end a tame, unelected, all-white advisory body.

Belgian colonial policy was shaped, to a considerable yet unacknowledged degree, by the legacy of the Congo Free State, as well as by a conscious desire to avoid its most notorious abuses, expressed by such measures as phasing out forced labor and giving greater recognition to traditional chiefs. In addition, because of its own bifurcated national identity (French and Flemish), Belgium—unlike every other colonial power—did not or could not project onto the Congolese people a single, unambiguous cultural model, or myth.

The legacy of the Congo Free State was perhaps most apparent in the unusually strong degree of leverage wielded in the Congo by nongovernmental actors, particularly the large capitalist groups and the Catholic Church. Though chartered companies were used by all colonial powers throughout Africa to secure effective occupation during the "scramble," Léopold's relative lack of resources had forced him to rely on this expedient to an extensive degree. He had mitigated the threat that chartered companies might pose to his control by forcing them to take the Congo Free State as a partner. Thus, he paved the way for another characteristic of Belgian colonialism: the prevalence of joint ventures and parastatals (autonomous public agencies operating in areas normally associated with the private sector).

Léopold was also—with some reason—suspicious of the influence that foreign powers might acquire in the Congo through missionaries, and he therefore encouraged the spread of "national" (i.e., Belgian Catholic) orders. Though fears of foreign intrusion had abated by 1908—and despite the constitutional separation of church and state—the Belgian administration continued Léopold's policy, which now came to reflect the dominant role of the Catholic Party in Belgium's own political system. Thus, Catholic missions, entrusted with most of the colony's educational network, and with built-in access to power circles in Belgium, became "established" in all but name, symbiotically tied to Belgian colonialism until the mid-1950s.

The three major actors in the Belgian colonial system—the colonial state apparatus, the Catholic Church, and big business—thus cooperated in what historians have often described as a "Trinity." When working in unison, this Trinity was virtually unopposable. On a number of occasions, however, one of the three actors found itself at odds with the other two, and the result, depending on contextual variables, ranged from vacillation to stalemate, or even (in the late 1950s) complete disarray.

In the matter of "native administration," partly in reaction to the Congo Free State's exploitative disregard of traditional institutions, Belgium inclined toward co-opting African chiefs. The first generation of field officials, trained at the newly created Colonial Institute in Antwerp, was influenced by the concepts of association and indirect rule that had found favor in France and Britain, respectively, and by such models as those offered by Frederick Lugard or Louis-Hubert Lyautey. The Catholic hierarchy, however, objected to any "excessive" dignifying of African traditional rulers whose authority, based on indigenous belief systems, might counteract the influence of Catholic missionaries. The outcome was a compromise in which African chiefs were given official "recognition" (though not civil service status) but little real autonomy. Meanwhile, in order to curb the proliferation of exceedingly small or ethnically heterogeneous "native administration units," Belgium created, alongside the largely traditional *chefferies* which had existed before colonial rule, the hybrid and distinctly nontraditional *secteurs* fashioned by the colonial authorities and headed by appointed "warrant chiefs."

The labor needs of large Belgian firms (especially the Katanga mining industry, owned by the Union Minière, which started production on the eve of World War I) were initially addressed, after the Witwatersrand model, by the recruitment of a rapid turnover, short-term labor force of single males. The disruption of rural communities caused by indiscriminate labor recruitment campaigns in many parts of the Congo drew criticism from missionaries, and also from some field administrators who resented being instructed to assist company recruiters. The mining houses eventually opted for a "manpower stabilization" policy—a novelty at the time—whereby miners were given long-term or renewable contracts, encouraged to build families, provided with housing and other amenities, and increasingly entrusted with skilled jobs. In doing so, the mining firms were able, not coincidentally, to replace their white skilled employees, whose demands were viewed as onerous, by presumably more docile—and nonunionized—Africans. The depression, leading to the stabilization of production (and employment) at reduced levels, contributed to the success of the hiring policy which, as the mining sector achieved unprecedented profits during and after World War II, acquired some features of a paternalistic welfare system.

Indeed, paternalism has often been cited as the single most distinguishing characteristic of postwar Belgian colonial policy. In its simplest or crudest form, this low-grade philosophy postulated the idea that assuring Africans a (relative) degree of well-being would obviate any demands they might otherwise make for meaningful political participation. This "philosophy" was also reflected in the colonial educational system which, under missionary management, emphasized literacy and vocational training but, until the mid-1950s, systematically curbed any form of post-secondary schooling for Africans (apart from seminary training for clergy). The growing number of urbanized Congolese holding midlevel clerical (but not professional) positions was nevertheless a source of concern to Belgium. Its feeble answer was to offer such Africans a diminished form of assimilation represented by a registration procedure and an identification document that certified a "worthy African" on the basis of education, service, or the like. This assimilation carried with it some civil rights, such as exemption from *indigénat* (native status), but no political rights. Indeed, as late as 1955, Belgium had no blueprint for making Africans participants in the Congolese political process, let alone for decolonization.

In 1954, however, general elections in Belgium had brought to power a coalition of the Socialist and Liberal parties, driving the Catholic (Social Christian) Party into the opposition. Domestic church-state conflict (centering mostly on education) soon spilled over to the Congo, where the new minister for Colonial affairs proposed to aggressively develop a network of secular schools, thereby antagonizing Catholic circles. Simultaneously, the Vatican was quietly encouraging all missionaries to disassociate themselves from colonialism. In the Congo, the church moved swiftly to open a Catholic university in Léopoldville (present-day Kinshasa), and some progressive Catholic intellectuals (notably A. A. J. Van Bilsen) openly advocated a commitment to a clear, if gradual, decolonization policy. The message was quickly picked up by a small group of Catholic-educated Africans who, in 1956, published the country's first political manifesto under the imprint of their newly founded review, *Conscience africaine*. Rifts within the Trinity now became apparent to all politically conscious Congolese. The Socialist-Liberal coalition vainly tried to secure nonpartisan consensus for some decolonization plan, but the Catholic Party demurred until, following the 1958 elections, it regained power as the senior partner in a new Catholic-Liberal coalition.

The new cabinet agonized over the scope and terms of decolonization, the need for which had been made even more urgent in 1958 after Charles de Gaulle became president of France with a plan to offer French overseas territories the choice of immediate independence or membership in a "Franco-African" community. Having prolonged its deliberations, the cabinet failed to meet the Africans' widespread expectation that a policy for decolonization would be announced in time to coincide with the fiftieth anniversary celebrations of Belgium's takeover of the Congo. When riots broke out in Léopoldville in January 1959, Belgium realized that it had lost the initiative and that its belated announcement of reforms would now be interpreted as purely reactive. Major concessions to African demands (notably for an acceleration of the decolonization process) were made throughout 1959 until, by December, the government had opted for the startling choice of "immediate decolonization"—for which no adequate foundation had yet been laid. Nevertheless, decolonization was carried out on June 30, 1960.

Belgium's seemingly reckless decision was undoubtedly influenced by the apparent success of de Gaulle's two-stage "gamble" (in 1958 and 1959) that the Africans' emotional drive for independence could be reconciled with the establishment of close cooperative ties with the former colonial power. Belgium's decision may also have been motivated by the calculation that a more gradual decolonization process, occurring at a time when the Congolese economy was undergoing a sharp recession (with slumping copper prices and a $130 million balance of payments deficit in 1957), would inevitably call for subsidies of a magnitude that was bound to be unpopular with the Belgian public, which was disconcerted by the sudden abandonment of a colony that it had been conditioned by official circles to view as an "oasis of peace and prosperity."

Though it failed to ensure a smooth transition from colonialism to neocolonialism (as Britain and France had done, in different ways), Belgium's precipitous political disengagement made the Congo utterly dependent on outside "technical assistance." At the same time, it also left major foreign interests in the Congo essentially intact.

Reappraisals of Belgian colonial policies have emerged slowly and belatedly. Over the next thirty years, public opinion largely forgot the circumstances as well as the sequels of Belgium's botched decolonization policies in the Congo, or in Rwanda and Burundi, preferring instead to focus on the allegedly "positive" aspects of colonial rule, and to ignore the degree to which the colonial legacy was responsible for many of these countries' post-independence problems. The fact that Belgium's influence in Central Africa was now partly supplanted by that of the United States and France also made it easier to shrug off blame for the misdeeds of post-independence regimes.

By the early 1990s, however, the collapse of the Mobutu dictatorship or (in a different way) the escalation of ethnic conflicts in Rwanda and Burundi led to a soul-searching reassessment of colonial policies in general, and more particularly of Belgium's role in the overthrow of the Congo's first (and only) democratically elected government. Following the 1999 publication by Flemish author Ludo De Witte's revealing account of Patrice Lumumba's murder, an extensive parliamentary inquiry eventually led to an admission of Belgium's guilt and to a formal apology by its foreign minister. Reactions to this debate were mixed but nevertheless rekindled interest in the country's colonial record, even among the most tradition-bound circles. Thus, in 2005, the *Musée Royal de l'Afrique centrale* (originally founded by Léopold II) opened a major exhibition offering an "objective" (if somewhat softened) retrospective view of Belgian colonialism.

See also **Colonialism and Imperialism; Congo Independent State; Labor: Industrial and Mining; Lugard, Frederick John Dealtry; Lumumba, Patrice; Mobutu Sese Seko.**

BIBLIOGRAPHY

Anstey, Roger. *King Leopold's Legacy: The Congo under Belgian Rule, 1908–1960.* London: Oxford University Press, 1966.

Brausch, Georges. *Belgian Administration in the Congo.* London: Oxford University Press, 1961.

Bustin, Edouard. *Lunda under Belgian Rule: The Politics of Ethnicity.* Cambridge, MA: Harvard University Press, 1975.

Bustin, Edouard. "Remembrance of Sins Past: Unraveling the Murder of Patrice Lumumba." *Review of African Political Economy* 29, nos. 93–94 (2002).

De Witte, Ludo. *The Assassination of Lumumba*. London and New York: Verso, 2001.

Depelchin, Jacques. *From the Congo Free State to Zaire (1885–1974)*. Dakar, Senegal: CODESRIA, 1992.

Enquête parlementaire visant à déterminer les circonstances exactes de l'assassinat de Patrice Lumumba et l'implication éventuelle des responsables politiques belges dans celui-ci. Rapport fait au nom de la commission d'enquête... Documents Parlementaires: DOC 50 0312/006 and DOC 50 0312/007. 2 vol. Available from http://www.lachambre.be/commissions/LMB/312_6/312_6_volume1.pdf; http://www.lachambre.be/commissions/LMB/312_7/312_7_volume2.pdf;http://www.lachambre.be/commissions/LMB/indexF.html.

La mémoire du Congo: Le temps colonial. Tervuren: Musée Royal de l'Afrique centrale, 2005. Available from http://www.congo2005.be.

Merlier, Michel. *Le Congo de la colonisation belge à l'indépendance*. Paris: Harmattan, 1962.

Nzongola-Ntalaja, Georges. *The Congo from Leopold to Kabila: A People's History*. London and New York: Zed Books, 2002.

Prosser, Gifford, and W. Roger Louis, eds. *The Transfer of Power in Africa: Decolonization, 1940–1960*. New Haven, CT: Yale University Press, 1982.

Young, Crawford. *Politics in the Congo: Decolonization and Independence*. Princeton, NJ: Princeton University Press, 1965.

EDOUARD BUSTIN

BRITISH CENTRAL AFRICA

The term British Central Africa refers to the section of the central east African plateau encompassing present-day Zambia, Malawi, and Zimbabwe. The region was administered as three separate territories—Northern and Southern Rhodesia and Nyasaland—until the creation of the federation in 1953, which had important implications for the manner in which the area was governed and for the nature of African political identities. Initially envisaged as a "second rand," the area attracted a substantial number of white settlers, but its economy came to be based primarily on export agriculture.

EARLY COLONIAL STATE AND ECONOMY

British colonial interest in the region north of the Limpopo River dates to the late 1880s. Confident that the mineral discoveries in South Africa would be replicated further north, Cecil Rhodes, through the British South Africa Company (BSAC), acquired the right to administer the territory, enticing white settlers there during the 1890s with promises of economic rewards. Initial Ndebele resistance was overcome in 1893, while the rebellion of Ndebele and Shona in 1896–1897 was also eventually crushed. Gold mining was slow to develop, however, so the BSAC also turned to farming. Whereas early settler agriculture had floundered at the subsistence level, the white agricultural policy from 1908 involved subsidies, training, and other support for European farmers, including (in 1912) the creation of a Land Bank providing loans for the purchase of farms, livestock, and equipment.

Meanwhile, in 1891 the BSAC established control of the territory north of the Zambezi River (known as Northern Rhodesia after 1911), where African resistance was less pronounced but where, again, the settler economy had inauspicious beginnings. White farmers, based mostly along the newly built railway which ran through the heart of the territory, derived a relatively meager living from agriculture. Such farming became profitable only after the development of Northern Rhodesia's copper industry. The adjacent British Central African Protectorate (called Nyasaland from 1907), which had hosted a strong missionary presence for some years, presented even fewer opportunities for mineral exploitation, but again the BSAC encouraged white settlers to develop plantations, mostly in the Shire Highlands. Although large-scale appropriation of land took place, the settler presence was never as significant here as in the Rhodesias.

From their inception, Northern Rhodesia and Nyasaland were viewed primarily as labor pools for the mines of Southern Rhodesia, and Africans were recruited for that purpose by the Rhodesian Native Labor Bureau; the Witwatersrand Native Labor Association also recruited African labor in Nyasaland for the South African mines. Africans were not always unwilling participants in labor migration, as there were few incentives to stay in Nyasaland, where opportunities for cash-crop production were limited, although some Africans did manage to compete with Europeans in the marketplace. Mostly, however, Africans had to grow crops on white-owned land, where the price for their produce was fixed and Africans often had to provide labor in lieu of rent and taxes. By contrast, the Nyasaland settler economy grew prior to 1914, as white farmers, assisted by new railway links, turned to the cultivation of tobacco and cotton. The increasing impositions of white employers and the hardships of World War I contributed to the brief but intense uprising in Nyasaland in 1915, led by the African clergyman John Chilembwe.

For much of this early period, the expanding mining economy of Southern Rhodesia drove socioeconomic change: the territory absorbed Africans as cheap labor, while the growth of settler farming and attendant land expropriation marginalized African producers. By the 1920s, whites tolerated Africans on settler land only as laborers; if the Africans did not work for wages, high rents and grazing fees forced them to move to reserves. In 1923 the British Colonial Office, having inherited control from the BSAC, granted self-government to the territory's settlers, greatly strengthening the political position of white Rhodesians.

The twin pressures of demand for migrant labor and commercial marginalization had far-reaching consequences for Africans. Both of these forces contributed to rural poverty in many areas. Formerly entrepreneurial peoples, such as the Yao in Nyasaland, were compelled into wage labor in order to pay taxes, while in Southern Rhodesia African farmers were increasingly sidelined, notably by the 1930 Land Apportionment Act, which awarded white settlers 49 million acres compared to 7.5 million acres for Africans. Moreover, African land was comparatively much less fertile and located some distance away from the key market areas. Africans' economic independence was further eroded during the global depression of the 1930s, for while Europeans received government aid, Africans were effectively excluded from the market by the 1934 Maize Control Amendment Act and could scarcely sell their maize profitably.

In Northern Rhodesia the situation was transformed by copper mining, which expanded dramatically in the mid–1920s as a result of new demand from the automobile and electrical industries. The BSAC, which handed administration of the territory to the British government in 1924, granted exclusive mining concessions to large firms, and by the end of the 1920s four new mines were growing rapidly: those at Nkana and Nchanga, owned by the Anglo-American Corporation, and those at Roan Antelope and Mufulira, operated by the

Rhodesian Selection Trust. The growth of the so-called Copperbelt was attended by an expansion of forced labor and the compound system characteristic of much of southern and central Africa. Compounds were built beside mines to house thousands of African workers, and the militaristic organization of labor prevented the growth of worker consciousness and effected racial segregation. Mine owners were able to pay workers a single man's wage without having to provide for families as well, while compounds were controlled by their own police forces; workers who broke their contracts were regarded as having deserted. The copper industry had other important consequences for Northern Rhodesia. It aided the growth of settler farming because of the increased demand for food in the mines, and it led to a greater degree of urbanization than was the case in many other parts of sub-Saharan Africa.

In broader terms of social development, as in many other parts of colonial sub-Saharan Africa, health and education were largely the responsibility of missionaries in central Africa, at least until the interwar years. Thereafter, the three territorial legislatures assumed responsibility for primary and secondary education for Africans. In 1927, for example, Southern Rhodesia created a Department of Native Education; after World War II, this bureau became a branch of the Native Affairs Department with its own director. Education policy achieved only limited success, however; in Southern Rhodesia in 1954, just 65 percent of the African child population was enrolled in school, with half of these students in the two lowest classes. In Northern Rhodesia, the colonial state was responsible for technical education in urban areas, but beyond the towns, responsibility for education remained within the mission compound until the nation became independent. Similarly, in Nyasaland, the state worked largely through missionary organizations, such as the Livingstonia School, to provide education until the early 1960s.

Beginning in the late nineteenth century, missionaries provided health care to Africans in addition to education, for example, at Livingstonia in the mid–1870s. After 1900, the Universities Mission to Central Africa organized medical services for Africans in Nyasaland, and by the 1920s almost every mission station had a hospital and a surgery. In Southern Rhodesia, health care administration was less successful despite missionary efforts; overcrowding in the African-managed hospitals had become commonplace by the 1950s, when there were twenty-one government-run hospitals compared to fifty-three mission hospitals. Here, health care was absorbed into the Native Affairs Department at the beginning of the 1950s. In Northern Rhodesia, a dispersed and sparse population rendered the provision of health care particularly problematic: at the end of the 1930s, more than half of the territory had no medical facilities. Unlike in the other two territories, however, private business offered health care services, with copper-mining companies providing four hospitals serving both Africans and Europeans by the mid–1950s.

AFRICAN RESPONSES

Across the region, the economic system was fed by migrant laborers: primarily single adult males whose movement was strictly controlled through the issuing of passes. Women had even less mobility across the region, at least initially. The white community desired this control because they feared large-scale African settlement in their territories. Coercive though the system was, and as much as it attempted to militate against the exercise of worker muscle, Africans were not passive victims. Throughout central Africa, they developed new methods of resistance and organization. Underground information networks, the forging of passes, and a range of informal industrial activity—from the sabotage of machinery to intentional work slowdowns—all expressed workers' protests, growing in tandem with nationalist movements.

Christian sects also allowed Africans to express their grievances against the injustice of the mining economy: for example, the Jehovah's Witness–based Watchtower movement, originating in northern Nyasaland and exported to the compounds of the Rhodesias, offered spiritual and millenarian solutions to contemporary hardships by equating the Second Coming of Christ with the destruction of colonial rule. Workers were told that they would be saved as "the elect," and ultimately this approach served to unite workers through a collective consciousness. The Mbeni dance society also served to mobilize the nascent African working class through the organization of compound dance teams in competition with one another, transcending ethnicity and contributing to the growth of a working-class consciousness, albeit an uneven and tentative one.

Over time, in the mining areas a settled proletariat emerged that was capable of organized work stoppages, such as the strike at the Shamva mine in 1927 in Southern Rhodesia, or those on the Copperbelt in 1935 and 1940. A wave of strikes in Southern Rhodesia in the late 1940s significantly affected the growth of nationalist protest; more generally, during the 1940s African political movements in central Africa grew in strength, rooted to varying degrees in labor protests. The Nyasaland African Congress, founded in 1944, exercised considerable influence through the one hundred thousand Nyasa migrant laborers in Southern Rhodesia, which in turn boosted Southern Rhodesian nationalist movements; the Northern Rhodesia Congress (1948), which became the Northern Rhodesia African National Congress in 1951, grew in strength alongside the increasingly militant African unions. Strikes in Northern Rhodesia in 1956 caused the authorities to declare a state of emergency, in recognition that the united urban labor movement represented a serious threat to civil order. Urban protest would soon link with rural resistance under the direction of nationalist movements seeking popular support.

THE CENTRAL AFRICAN FEDERATION AND INDEPENDENCE, 1953–1964

In central Africa, the struggle between Africans and Europeans was defined more than anything else by the racial imbalance of the region. Northern and Southern Rhodesia (with fourteen thousand and sixty-five thousand whites compared to 1.5 million and 1.4 million Africans by World War II, respectively) had more in common with Kenya than with Nyasaland (eighteen hundred whites to 1.8 million Africans by 1939); but across the region, white settlers dominated both the government and the economy. London saw these white settlers as indispensable to the region's future development, although only when in partnership with Africans. Until the last moment, however, many settlers could not countenance the transfer of power to Africans. They made limited concessions to nationalists—during the 1940s Africans were given seats in the legislative councils of Northern Rhodesia (1948) and Nyasaland (1949)—but the Africans remained suspicious of British motives, and this distrust was apparently vindicated with the creation of the Central African Federation (CAF) in 1953.

First proposed in the 1920s as the best way to secure the long-term economic and development of the region, the CAF joined the Rhodesias and Nyasaland in a political bloc. Britain envisaged a partnership between Europeans and Africans while also seeking to assure settlers' of their continued dominance; but Africans rejected such multiracialism, and strident nationalism grew during the 1950s. The Nyasaland African and Northern Rhodesia African National Congresses expanded, while in Southern Rhodesia the Youth League and the African National Congress (ANC) were founded in 1955 and 1957, respectively. In fact, African leaders disagreed over the best way to challenge settler dominance: some recommended cooperating with the Federation, while others adopted a more militant stance.

Above all, nationalist movements sought broad-based rural support, and they were able to tap into peasant resentment, which had resulted from the dislocation engendered by migrant labor and the alienation of land to white farmers. The African National Congress in Southern Rhodesia, for example, was greatly boosted by the support of farmers resentful of the Native Land Husbandry Act of 1951, which sought to transform communally-held land into private property and reduce African herds. In Nyasaland, rural unrest escalated during the 1940s and 1950s as a result of aggressive colonial interference in African agricultural practices.

Increasing unrest across the region prompted the colonial governments to begin to consider that the costs of maintaining rule would be unacceptably high; at the same time, however, leading figures were arrested and their movements banned. In 1959, the colonial governments outlawed all African political parties and incarcerated their leaders, including Hastings Banda in Nyasaland and Kenneth Kaunda in Northern Rhodesia. Southern Rhodesia declared a state of emergency and investigated the activities of Joshua Nkomo, Ndabaningi Sithole, and Robert Mugabe. Yet this was also the era of transition to majority rule, now accepted as the only way forward. Following local elections, the Malawi Congress Party under Banda took Nyasaland to independence as Malawi in July 1964, while the United National Independence Party under Kaunda won independence for Zambia in October of the same year.

The CAF became effectively defunct, but in Southern Rhodesia (at this point in history known as Rhodesia) the settler government refused to accept African enfranchisement. The Rhodesian Front government, elected in 1962, made it clear that it would go to any lengths to defend white privilege, and in 1965 Prime Minister Ian Smith made the Unilateral Declaration of Independence. Initially, internal divisions dogged the African movements: the ANC suffered from deep internal cleavages, as did the Zimbabwe African People's Union (ZAPU), formed in 1961. In 1963 ZAPU split, and a large section of its membership founded the Zimbabwe African National Union (ZANU), which believed in a more violent approach to the problem of settler intransigence. Guerrilla war began in 1966, and despite an early lack of success, the Rhodesian guerrillas became better armed, became more experienced, and benefited from the succor provided by both Zambia and Mozambique by the early 1970s. Smith's regime had initially ignored international condemnation, but by the mid–1970s it was crumbling from within; in 1980, elections finally saw the establishment of an African majority government under Mugabe's ZANU, and Rhodesia was renamed Zimbabwe.

See also **Banda, Ngwazi Hastings Kamuzu; Chilembwe, John; Colonialism and Imperialism; Kaunda, Kenneth; Labor: Industrial and Mining; Malawi: History and Politics; Mugabe, Robert; Rhodes, Cecil John; World War I; Zambezi River; Zambia: History and Politics; Zimbabwe: History and Politics.**

BIBLIOGRAPHY

Birmingham, David, and Phyllis M. Martin, eds. *History of Central Africa*. 2 vols. London: Longman, 1983.

Gertzel, C. "East and Central Africa." In *The Cambridge History of Africa*, Vol. 8, ed. M. Crowder. London: Cambridge University Press, 1984.

McCracken, John. *Politics and Christianity in Malawi, 1875–1940: The Impact of the Livingstonia Mission in the Northern Province*. New York: Cambridge University Press, 1977.

McCracken, John. "British Central Africa." In *The Cambridge History of Africa*, Vol. 7, ed. Andrew D. Roberts. New York: Cambridge University Press, 1986.

Palmer, Robin, and Neil Parsons, eds. *The Roots of Rural Poverty in Central and Southern Africa*. Berkeley: University of California Press, 1977.

Phimister, Ian. *An Economic and Social History of Zimbabwe, 1890–1948.* London: Longman, 1988.

Roberts, Andrew D. *A History of Zambia.* London: Heinemann, 1976.

RICHARD REID

BRITISH EAST AFRICA

The histories of Kenya, Uganda, Tanganyika, and Zanzibar (the latter two countries forming present-day Tanzania) were very different, despite the fact that all were ruled by Britain. After 1888 Kenya and Uganda were briefly administered by the Imperial British East Africa Company (IBEAC) until the Foreign Office assumed responsibility in 1893 (Uganda) and 1895 (Kenya). After years of informal control, Britain declared a protectorate over Zanzibar in 1890, but Tanganyika was not taken over until World War I. Precolonial polities varied from sophisticated state structures in Buganda and Bunyoro-Kitara in Bantu southern Uganda, and the Arab sultanate in Zanzibar, to small, acephalous, segmentary lineage societies in Kenya and northern Uganda. Tanganyika's Africans had coalesced into larger communities, although none resembled the elaborate monarchies of southern Uganda.

In both Uganda and Kenya, the imperial government inherited the administrative structure and personnel of the IBEAC and became enmeshed in African rivalries. Of even greater significance was Captain Frederick Lugard's decision to support Buganda's Protestant elite against Catholic, Muslim, and traditionalist challengers during the civil war in the 1890s. The 1900 Uganda Agreement accorded the kingdom considerable autonomy and politically and economically entrenched the new Protestant power structure. Thus, Ganda missionaries carried Christianity, and Ganda "chiefs" the "Pax Britannica," to the stateless peoples of Uganda.

The Protestant oligarchy also took control of large estates, known as *mailo* (square mile). Previously they had governed people; now they owned land. This became important when the British introduced cotton and coffee in Buganda as cash crops in 1904, in order to help meet the $8 million cost of the Uganda railroad and to finance the administration. In contrast to Kenya, the British encouraged African production. By the 1920s Africans accounted for 80 percent of Uganda's export earnings even before European and Asian rubber plantations failed and coffee prices collapsed. The triumph of peasant production, however, left Europeans and Asians controlling the marketing of African-grown crops.

By contrast in Kenya, from Sir Charles N. E. Eliot's period as commissioner from 1900 to 1904, settler interests had predominated. Once Gikuyu and Nandi resistance had been destroyed and the Maasai had been cleared from the central Rift Valley, opening it for European farming, settler interests preoccupied the Nairobi secretariat. Supported by the efforts of Kenya's Agricultural and Veterinary Departments, the settlers prospered throughout the 1920s, and the African "reserves" fell behind. In 1919, the settlers persuaded Governor Northey to authorize the conscription of laborers to work on settler farms; in 1923, they blocked Asian claims for more influence; and in the late 1920s, supported by Secretary of State for the Colonies Leopold Amery, they schemed to secure full internal self-government and "closer union" with Uganda and Tanganyika. Thus, the settlers largely negated the 1923 Devonshire Declaration of African paramountcy.

The Kenyan administration became increasingly cautious in the 1920s, repudiating individual land tenure among the Gikuyu in favor of communal control, and rejecting demands for individual titles from both the chiefs and the educated "new men" of the Gikuyu Central Association. When international commodity prices collapsed in 1927–1929, however, the government expanded peasant production in order to service the colonial state's debts and to subsidize the settlers' survival through the new Agricultural and Land Bank. Despite the 1929 Fazan committee's hostility to individual tenure—which the 1900 *mailo* agreement had introduced in Buganda—and the recommendations of the 1933 Kenya Land Commission, Gikuyu chiefs and members of senior lineages, who controlled the native tribunals, privatized communal land and dispossessed tenants in order to increase cash-crop production.

The administration ignored the problems caused by social differentiation during World War II when Africans, as well as Europeans, were encouraged to maximize output. In 1945, however, prompted by the settlers, who had gained considerable influence during the war, the administration turned against

African commercial farmers and traders and launched a compulsory terracing campaign under the direction of the chiefs. The schemes in Gikuyuland collapsed in 1947–1948, provoking widespread resistance, just as they were to do in Tanganyika's Usambara Mountains and Nyasaland's Shire Valley in the early 1950s. Divided, the Kenya government failed to devise a coherent agricultural development policy, as the conservative Field administration battled with advocates of African individualism (i.e., capitalism) in the Agricultural Department.

The Mau Mau rebellion by dispossessed Gikuyu, which erupted in October 1952, demonstrated the need for action, empowering the Agricultural Department to launch a major campaign to reconstruct Gikuyuland: the Swynnerton Plan. The land of Mau Mau fighters was seized; dispersed plots were consolidated; and individual titles were issued in order to create a conservative yeoman class that would support colonialism. To win Gikuyu support, the British abandoned the settlers, ending their monopoly of cash crops and access to the "White Highlands." The colonial administration now had to turn to moderate nationalists, led by Jomo Kenyatta, whom they had detained in October 1952 as the leader of the Mau Mau movement. Kenyatta, in fact, had always been a moderate, the leader of Gikuyuland's peasant producers and small traders, rather than of its dispossessed. Thus, Kenyatta's government, led by its petite bourgeoisie, proved to be one of Africa's most procapitalist.

The situation in Uganda and Tanganyika was very different. Settlers exerted little influence in either territory. Peasant production had triumphed in Uganda in the 1920s, and Tanganyika's special status as a League of Nations mandate, and the danger in the 1930s of the British returning the territory to Berlin's control, ensured that it attracted few settlers and little investment. African interests, consequently, predominated. Both territories, moreover, adopted indirect rule. The early colonialists' dependence on Ganda allies in Uganda ensured that Buganda enjoyed a special status, and as chiefdoms and "native treasuries" were created in the north, indirect rule spread throughout the protectorate. Tanganyika's first governor, Sir Donald Cameron, who had served as Governor Lugard's chief secretary in Nigeria, after 1925 created a modified system of

"native authorities" and "native treasuries" in Britain's new territory. But when Arthur Creech Jones became secretary of state in the postwar Labour government and "the second colonial occupation" got under way, indirect rule was repudiated as favoring the traditional "tribal" power structure over Western-educated Africans. The 1947 Local Government Dispatch heralded a new era in which chiefs and headmen, even the *kabaka* (king) of Buganda, were challenged by new-style politicians, trained in the politics of "sewage and drains" and social welfare.

In Uganda by this time, the British had become dissatisfied with its Ganda chiefs, who were too autocratic and took too large a portion of the peasantry's crops. Furthermore, they prevented the activist post-1945 colonial administration from intervening in the kingdom's affairs, retarding provision of social services, education, and "agricultural betterment." British concern was intensified by outbreaks of peasant discontent against the chiefs and the colonial Cotton Marketing Board, led by the Bataka movement, which culminated in riots in Kampala in 1945 and 1949. Significantly, the protesters looked to the *kabaka* to restore the traditional moral order and to discipline the chiefs. The protests had little impact in other parts of Uganda. Indeed, migrant laborers from the north and west, who had worked on Ganda cotton and coffee farms, viewed their former employers with as much hatred as Gikuyu share-croppers in Kenya's White Highlands regarded the settlers.

Opposition to European and Asian control over the marketing and processing of cotton, and the monopsony powers of the state marketing boards, united Uganda's peoples. The Uganda government moved swiftly in the early 1950s to redress these grievances, transferring control to African cooperatives. By 1950 Uganda's eight African legislative councilors equaled the number from the other races combined, whereas in Kenya there were eleven Europeans, six Asians, and only four Africans. It was clear that Uganda would follow Britain's West African colonies along the path to African self-government. Consequently, the 1950s were dominated by Ganda attempts to preserve their kingdom's autonomous relationship within the emerging Ugandan state. Thus, the British transferred power in 1962 to a fragile coalition between Milton

Obote's Uganda People's Congress and the Ganda separatist Kabaka Yekka ("the king alone"), the parties of the district-level Protestant establishment outside of Buganda and of Protestant Ganda monarchists, respectively. The agreement was symbolized by the incongruous election of Kabaka Mutesa II as president of the Republic of Uganda in October 1963. Key issues, such as the future of Bunyoro's "lost counties" and of the four semiautonomous monarchies, remained unresolved.

The Mau Mau rebellion in Kenya demonstrated that progress to independence was still disputed in "the white man's country." Further European settlement had been encouraged after 1945. Governor Sir Philip Mitchell might talk of creating a multiracial society, but it was a society in which the white settlers were to provide "the steel frame" for African advance. Following Britain's withdrawal from Palestine in 1948 and from the Suez Canal Zone in 1956, Kenya became even more important as the military base for a rapid deployment force to protect Britain's interests in the Middle East and the Indian Ocean, as well as Africa. The Templar barracks were constructed outside Nairobi as late as 1956. However embarrassing Mau Mau might have been to Britain's international image, it had not destroyed its imperial resolve.

Paradoxically, in the United Nations (UN) Trust Territory of Tanganyika, the "second colonial occupation" was more exploitative than that in Kenya and Uganda; the latter two countries attempted to implement the British social-welfare agenda of Clement Attlee's government. In part, this difference resulted from Britain's determination to develop and prepare the Tanganyika territory for inspection by the UN Trusteeship Council, but more importantly it stemmed from Great Britain's need to minimize expenditures and to find supplies of essential resources in the colonial empire to reconstruct its devastated economy. Thus, $54 million was spent clearing southeastern Tanganyika to produce cooking oil for British housewives in the catastrophic peanut scheme. European settlement was also encouraged and, as in Kenya and Uganda, new land-use rules were introduced, controlling African cultivation with similar results. Africans resisted the new regulations, most notably in the Usambara Mountains and Sukumaland. The 1951 eviction of 3,000 Africans near Mount Kilimanjaro provoked territorywide protests, radicalizing the Tanganyika African Association (which in 1954 became the Tanganyika African National Union [TANU]) and its leader, Julius Nyerere.

Britain's belated attempts to modernize the "native authorities" failed even more clearly in Tanganyika than in Kenya and Uganda. Tanganyika's traditional power structure was too weak to control political events (as in Uganda), but too entrenched and conservative to be modernized like the local native councils in Kenya and transformed into elected African county councils as part of the new political order. They were swept away as continuing rural discontent provided yet more recruits for TANU. In a territory with 8 million Africans and only 17,000 Europeans, by 1958 it was clear that multiracialism had no future. TANU, led by a state bourgeoisie of teachers and administrative clerks, had become Africa's most effective mass nationalist party.

Little changed in Zanzibar between the declaration of the protectorate in 1890 and the end of World War II. The economy, which had been hard hit by the 1930s depression, depended on the export of cloves. The Arab elite, numbering 50,000 in 1960, ruled over 180,000 indigenous Shirazis and 50,000 "Mainlanders," descendants of former slaves, more recent immigrants, and temporary laborers from Tanganyika. The Arab population, financially indebted, had divested many of its commercial interests to the Asian business community. On Pemba, the northern island and center of the clove industry, relations between Shirazi and Arab farmers were good. Most plantations were small, and there were few absentee landlords. On Unguja (Zanzibar), the southern island, plantations were much larger, and many Arab owners lived in Stone Town (a district of Zanzibar City), rarely visited their estates, and employed large numbers of "squatters" and migrant workers.

Following a general strike by dockworkers in 1948, political tension grew. Further riots broke out in 1953 when the Veterinary Department attempted to inoculate cattle against rinderpest and over the expropriation of land to enlarge the airport. Young Arabs, educated in Gamal Abdel Nasser's Egypt, organized the Zanzibar Nationalist Party in 1954–1955 to preempt non-Arab attempts at nationalist mobilization, although these hardly existed. Fearful of Arab control, the Shirazi and Mainlanders responded, launching the Afro-Shirazi Party, which won all six seats in the first elections.

By 1959, however, appeals to Islamic unity and good relations on Pemba enabled Arab political leaders to divide the Pemba Shirazi from those on Unguja and, through the Zanzibar Nationalist Party, narrowly to win preindependence elections in 1961 and 1963.

The British were powerless to control events or to prevent the rapid deterioration of communal relations. The intense political atmosphere and the severe depression in the clove industry in the late 1950s, which encouraged many Arab plantation owners to dispossess their tenants—especially those who had proved politically disloyal—resulted in widespread violence, further exacerbating communal relations. The minuscule British administration, moreover, depended heavily on Arab staff, who provided not only most of the protectorate's agricultural and labor officers, and other technical personnel, but also two-thirds of the district officers. Thus, even more than in Buganda and Tanganyika, the administration in Zanzibar was unable to repudiate its indirect rule allies, who had enabled the British to govern effectively and cheaply for half a century.

Britain left an untested new political order throughout East Africa as it scuttled its empire, ditching its settler, Ganda, and Arab allies in order to reach an accommodation with the new nationalist movements. The outcomes were very different. Kenya, the territory with the most settlers, was well developed, possessing a comparatively sophisticated communications, commercial, and industrial infrastructure and a sizable group of African commercial farmers and traders, who would control the new state. Uganda, although comparatively developed and prosperous, and with a much better cultivation-to-population ratio, was racked by the legacies of indirect rule and the problems of Ganda separatism. The nationalist movement in Tanganyika possessed considerable political legitimacy, and no one tribe dominated in the way that Kenyatta's Gikuyu did in Kenya and the Ganda did economically, if not politically, in Uganda; however, the country was poor and underdeveloped. Zanzibar, ruled by its Arab elite in alliance with wealthy, Islamized Shirazi plantation owners, headed for disaster as the British transferred power to a largely unreformed sultanate, which many of its subjects feared. As a result, the Arab-dominated regime, granted independence on December 9, 1963, was overthrown only four weeks later in a bloody communal revolution that left 5,000 Arabs dead. The end of British rule in East Africa was as disorganized and unplanned as the beginning.

See also **Boundaries, Colonial and Modern; Colonialism and Imperialism; Economic History; Kampala; Kenyatta, Jomo; Lugard, Frederick John Dealtry; Nasser, Gamal Abdel; Nyerere, Julius Kambarage; Obote, Milton.**

BIBLIOGRAPHY

Austen, Ralph A. *Northwest Tanzania under German and British Rule: Colonial Policy and Tribal Politics, 1889–1939.* New Haven, CT: Yale University Press, 1968.

Berman, Bruce. *Control and Crisis in Colonial Kenya.* Athens: Ohio University Press, 1990.

Berman, Bruce, and John Lonsdale. *Unhappy Valley: Conflict in Kenya and Africa.* Athens: Ohio University Press, 1992.

Clough, Marshall S. *Fighting Two Sides: Kenyan Chiefs and Politicians, 1918–1940.* Niwot: University Press of Colorado, 1990.

Iliffe, John. *A Modern History of Tanganyika.* Cambridge, U.K.: Cambridge University Press, 1979.

Ingham, Kenneth. *The Kingdom of Toro in Uganda.* London: Methuen, 1975.

Kiwanuka, M. S. M. Semakula. *From Colonialism to Independence: A Reappraisal of Colonial Policies and African Reactions, 1870–1960.* Nairobi: East African Literature Bureau, 1973.

Lofchie, Michael F. *Zanzibar: Background to Revolution.* Princeton, NJ: Princeton University Press, 1965.

Low, Donald Anthony. *Buganda in Modern History.* Berkeley: University of California Press, 1971.

Low, Donald Anthony. *The Mind of Buganda: Documents of the Modern History of an African Kingdom.* London: Heinemann, 1971.

Low, Donald Anthony, and R. Cranford Pratt. *Buganda and British Overrule, 1900–1955.* New York: Oxford University Press, 1960.

Omara-Otunnu, Amii. *Politics and the Military in Uganda, 1890–1985.* Basingstroke, U.K.: Macmillan in association with St. Anthony's College, 1987.

Pratt, R. Cranford. *The Critical Phase in Tanzania, 1945–68.* Cambridge, U.K.: Cambridge University Press, 1976.

Rosberg, Carl Gustav, and John Nottingham. *The Myth of "Mau Mau": Nationalism in Kenya.* New York: Praeger, 1966.

Sathyamurthy, T. V. *The Political Development of Uganda, 1900–1986*. Aldershot, U.K.: Gower, 1986.

Sheriff, Abdul, and Ed Ferguson, eds. *Zanzibar Under Colonial Rule*. Athens: Ohio University Press, 1991.

Throup, David W. *Economic and Social Origins of Mau Mau*. Athens: Ohio University Press, 1987.

DAVID W. THROUP

BRITISH WEST AFRICA

Most of the 1.25 million square miles of territory that constituted Great Britain's West African empire was acquired during the 1890s, by a combination of diplomacy and military force. But subsequent policies in the four colonies—Nigeria, the Gold Coast (modern Ghana), Sierra Leone, and the Gambia—were heavily influenced by the preexistence of small coastal colonial settlements. During the previous century these had developed as centers where manufactured goods from Europe were exchanged for minerals and raw materials produced by the labor and enterprise of Africans working on their own lands. The new rulers, as well as established trading houses, were thus predisposed to extend their exploitation of African resources by continuing to promote commercial exchanges with peasant societies rather than by taking over the land to establish foreign-owned plantations.

Nineteenth-century practice also left political legacies to the expanded West African empire. As British subjects, African residents in the colonies enjoyed certain civil liberties and political rights that they fought to maintain and extend. Education, imparted by Christian missionaries, had helped to form an elite that retained a limited political influence in London. They continued to voice African grievances and claims in their newspapers, in legislative councils, and in colonial courts.

But these institutions were not allowed to operate directly in the new dependencies, where protectorates became the characteristic form of government. Sometimes these were defined in treaties (not always freely negotiated) with African rulers; sometimes they rested on unilateral declarations by governors. Here the paramount nature of British power was unquestionable. But power was necessarily exercised with the collaboration of African authorities. The British did not have the money or manpower to rule directly.

INDIRECT RULE

Initially, administrative arrangements had to be improvised. In areas without central monarchies, such as southeastern Nigeria, authentic African leaders often avoided contact with the conquerors, who had to impose their own "warrant chiefs." Elsewhere, bargains could be struck with former ruling elites. Frederick D. Lugard, having defeated the rulers of the Sokoto Caliphate in battle and usurped their powers, worked out practical modes of collaboration with them (or their successors). These they proceeded to elaborate into an administrative philosophy known as "indirect rule," which influenced policy throughout the colonial empire.

There was much dispute about the meaning of indirect rule, and great irregularity in its local applications. The term implied not only the preservation of historic institutions but also their gradual transformation; there was no ambiguity about the fact of British rule. When fully applied, indirect rule implied a native authority, constituted with British approval and initially consisting of persons of chiefly status; a native treasury, retaining for local allocation some part of the taxes that the authority collected on behalf of the colonial government; and native courts, with jurisdiction over most civil and many criminal cases. But this full Lugardian model was never applied universally. Many chiefdoms in Sierra Leone, for example, seemed too small and impoverished to adapt in this way. Many in southern Gold Coast proved too resolutely attached to their historic autonomy.

ECONOMIC EXPECTATIONS AND DISAPPOINTMENTS

In 1895 Joseph Chamberlain called the new dependencies "undeveloped estates." But in western Africa much development had already taken place, through the complementary agencies of European merchants and shipping companies and long-established African networks. In colonial centers like Freetown, Cape Coast, and Lagos, liberated Africans and other English-speaking brokers were dealing with Mande or Hausa itinerant traders, exchanging the cheaper products of European industry for cotton, gold dust, palm oil, and groundnuts. These were the foundations on which the new rulers hoped to develop the new imperial estate.

Their own intention was to establish, within the boundaries of each strong government, a new network of railways, feeder roads, and port facilities, capable of exporting the ever-increasing products of African labor. The incentives provided by attractive imports in the markets could be supplemented by imposing direct taxation, payable in cash. But the essence of the West African approach was that the actual producers would be Africans, working freely on their own lands. Although African land law was obscure to foreigners, it was quickly understood that attempts to interfere with it would provoke strong resistance, without necessarily increasing production. Capitalists like Lord Leverhulme argued that plantations could be more efficient, but by the mid-1920s West African governors knew clearly that they were inadmissible. Rights over land were freely granted to foreigners only in limited areas where the exploitation of mineral resources required substantial capital investment.

Given such constraints, development could only take place through the transformation of rural economies. Many African farmers were highly capable of innovating in response to market incentives, as was demonstrated when farmers in the Gold Coast and southern Nigeria adopted new methods of growing cocoa from the 1880s. Others were slower to change, so long as their supply of labor depended on the persistence of domestic slavery (in more or less benign forms). And the transition to free labor proved slow and difficult. Attempts to enforce abolition was liable to alienate the very African notables on whom indirect rule depended; and governors themselves, required to balance budgets without Imperial subsidy, had to condone the use of forced labor on necessary public works.

APPLICATIONS AND MISAPPLICATIONS OF SCIENCE

Colonial officers also based hopes of agricultural improvement on the application of modern scientific methods, encouraged by exemplary practice and exhortation. But the more intelligent agronomists came to appreciate that their own understanding of the African environment was extremely limited, and

that practices commonly condemned as evidence of African "backwardness" could be more appropriate than their own prescriptions. When land was more plentiful than labor, "shifting cultivation" was a practical method of long-term fallowing; bush burning maintained fertility better than green manuring on many soils; inter-cropping provided a form of insurance against the failure of any specific crop. Although some "experts" persisted in trying to enforce their own remedies for perceived problems, staff in the field gradually came to appreciate how relevant the experiences of African peasant communities could be to their own attempts to reconcile development with the long-term conservation of the natural environment.

In western Africa, where there was no pressure on resources from expatriate farmers, it was the exploitation of forests, initially to meet a soaring international demand for rubber, that first raised fears about the side-effects of economic development. As early as the 1880s, Governor C. Alfred Moloney had perceived a need to control the depletion of forest resources in Yorubaland. When professional forestry officers were appointed after 1900 their initial priorities were to establish forest reserves and to prevent local chiefs from authorizing indiscriminate felling. Only gradually did ecologists learn that, for many communities, forests held important resources for agriculture, hunting, apiculture, fuel, and construction, and could be places of refuge, or spiritual significance. But it was wider concerns that eventually raised the profile of environmental policy. From the 1930s colonial governors became increasingly worried about soil erosion and its effects on hydrology, but they lacked the imagination, the motivation, or the funds to approach the perceived crisis in a comprehensive way.

THE LIMITS OF SOCIAL IMPROVEMENT

The makers of colonial policy did not regard "development" as simply a matter of increasing production. Besides their vague sense of a duty to protect supposedly unsophisticated peasants against unscrupulous entrepreneurs, they aspired to improve the lives of their African subjects, notably by promoting medical services and education. But these improvements would have to be financed by taxes raised locally, chiefly by customs duties. During the 1920s favorable terms of trade and the expansion of cocoa allowed the governor of the Gold Coast, Sir Gordon Guggisberg, to take some promising initiatives. Besides developing the port and feeder railway of Takoradi he was able to establish a modern hospital in Accra, and the elite secondary school of Achimota.

Though important tokens of intent, such isolated initiatives made little difference to African lives. Medical understanding of malaria and other tropical diseases improved treatment but made little immediate contribution to prevention; indeed, anxiety to protect the health of European officials led to policies of residential segregation, which aggravated racial grievance. Clinical services, electricity, and piped water were largely confined to administrative centers; only the richest native authorities, like Kano in Nigeria, could afford such services. And, while Achimota did eventually become the seed of a fine university, education at earlier levels was left largely to Christian missionaries, with official support and subsidy—or to African sponsors, like the wealthy Sierra Leonean Abuke Thomas, who endowed an agricultural institute at Mabang.

During the Great Depression of the 1930s, when all public expenditure was cut back, the Colonial Office attempted some serious stock taking; research that they sponsored into such subjects as levels of malnutrition revealed how unreal their hopes of improvement had become. Clearly the needs and aspirations of Africans could not be met without stronger inputs from London. In 1940 the Colonial Development and Welfare Act recognized that those two themes of imperial policy were indivisible, and authorized the U.S. Treasury to subsidize plans to promote them by colonial governments. But the outbreak of war in Europe delayed implementation of more active policies.

THE IMPACT OF INTERNATIONAL CRISES

In West Africa, World War II had both positive and negative consequences, as the beleaguered British government struggled to exploit the resources of the empire. Africans recruited to imperial forces found their experiences broadened—usually disagreeably but often with ultimately liberating effects. Some farmers benefited from increased demand for raw materials, or rice to feed the growing concentrations of laborers and British servicemen in naval ports, or at new airfields. But lessons drawn from hard-won experience were sometimes forgotten. Schemes to grow swamp rice in polders in estuaries north of Freetown ignored local advice from experienced Temne farmers about the danger of salination. In Nigeria, almost 100,000 workers were conscripted to mine tin in deplorable hygienic conditions, and hundreds died.

Intensified exploitation did not end after victory. Britain's perilous finances made it urgent to exploit all opportunities to produce dollar-earning exports in the sterling area. Mineral resources were extracted with increasing vigor; control over colonial exports and imports was tightened within a virtual currency union; there were failed attempts to promote ill-considered technocratic schemes for agrarian development, including an ill-fated Gambia poultry scheme.

But even in wartime planning for reform began, and after 1945 this process was intensified under a Labour government. Colonial rulers now tried to engage wider sections of African society in plans for development and modernization through initiatives described as "nation-building." Provision of education was extended at all levels; voluntary associations, like trade unions and cooperatives, were encouraged, under British supervision; attempts to make the structures of indirect rule more representative gave way to plans for elected local government; more elected members were added to the legislative councils, which gained new responsibilities.

These reforms were not intended to lead to early decolonization; indeed, the Labour government relied more heavily on African resources in its external policies than had any predecessor. The intention was a progressive "substitution of counsel for control"; political authority would be gradually devolved, as economic and social reform built nations that could with confidence be expected to collaborate politically and economically within the British Commonwealth. Such a program would have satisfied the old coastal elite. But wartime experiences, together with the growth of anticolonial pressures from the international community, had prepared the ground for more widely based national movements. The Accra riots of 1948 changed the timescale, and thus the whole context within which the Colonial Office had to envisage a transfer of power.

See also Accra; Cape Coast; Decolonization; Economic History; Freetown; Kano, Alhaji Amina; Lagos; Lugard, Frederick John Dealtry; World War II.

BIBLIOGRAPHY

Anderson, David, and Richard Grove, eds. *Conservation in Africa: People, Policies, and Practice.* Cambridge, U.K.: Cambridge University Press, 1987.

Grove, A. T. "The African Environment, Understood and Misunderstood." In *The British Intellectual Engagement with Africa in the Twentieth Century*, ed. Douglas Rimmer and Anthony Kirk-Greene. Basingstoke: Macmillan, 2000.

Hargreaves, John D. *Decolonization in Africa.* London: Longman, 1988.

Hopkins, Anthony G. *An Economic History of West Africa.* London: Longman, 1973.

Kirk-Greene, Anthony H. M., ed. *The Principles of Native Administration in Nigeria: Selected Documents, 1900–1947.* London: Longman, 1965.

Lovejoy, Paul E., and Jan S. Hogendorn. *Slow Death for Slavery: The Course of Abolition in Northern Nigeria, 1897–1936.* Cambridge, U.K.: Cambridge University Press, 1993.

Phillips, Anne. *The Enigma of Colonialism: British Policy in West Africa.* London: James Currey, 1989.

Richards, Paul. *Indigenous Agricultural Revolution: Ecology and Food Production in West Africa.* London: Hutchison, 1985.

JOHN D. HARGREAVES

EGYPTIAN

Muhammad 'Ali, who ruled Egypt between 1805 and 1848, and his descendants have had a major impact on Egypt. As Ottoman Turkish-speaking outsiders who adopted the country as their own, they were imbued with a vision to transform the country into a respected military and economic power. They financed their costly plans with European loans. Under Khedive Ismail (1863–1879), this heavy borrowing for railways and the Suez Canal, among other projects, led to France and Great Britain imposing a debt administration over Egypt and appointing two European ministers to Ismail's government. He was deposed in 1879 and replaced by a puppet ruler, Tawfiq, who held the position of khedive until 1892.

British naval forces landed at Alexandria in the summer of 1882 in response to a major uprising that same year. The rebellion was led by Ahmed 'Urabi, an officer who demanded a greater role for Arabic-speaking native Egyptian officers in the country's army. The officers' revolt found widespread support in the streets of Cairo, and a cross-section of protesting Egyptians demanded even larger concessions. The slogan "Egypt for Egyptians" was born. Britain and France read the growing outburst of spontaneous protests as a sign that their man Tawfiq would sooner or later be overthrown. To protect their investments and continue collecting on debts owed to them, the British occupied Egypt.

The military occupation was meant to be a temporary measure to restore order: to get the Egyptian troops back to the barracks and scare the ordinary folk off the street. But Britain would ultimately remain in Egypt from 1882 to 1956, when officers led by Colonel Gamal Abdel Nasser overthrew the monarchy of King Farouk in 1952 and nationalized the Suez Canal in 1956. During the seventy years of British rule in Egypt, the authorities cultivated a variety of relationships to manage relations between the British, the Egyptian monarchy, and the public's demands for some form of representative government. British colonial rulers steadily implemented imperial economic policies so that by the start of World War I, Egypt was fully incorporated into the British Empire.

Britain recruited Egyptians for the war effort, mobilized their grain supplies, and used their transportation resources. The Egyptian people suffered the hardships of a war economy for a war that was being fought elsewhere and about which they knew nothing. The postwar period gave rise to renewed Egyptian protests and demands for representation and autonomy. The British granted a very limited independence to the Egyptians in 1922. During the interwar period, struggles continually erupted among members of the Egyptian monarchy, elected representatives in the Egyptian parliament, and the British occupation authorities. The weak and corrupt monarch and the persistent intervention of the British—despite their having declared Egypt "independent"—helped the nationalist movement grow. But the real moment of decolonization came through a secret mobilization in the Egyptian army. Disappointment with the palace and its lack of concern about the war over Palestine in 1947–1948, along with a poorly equipped military force, gave some officers extra impetus to mobilize against the king. Thus in 1952 the so-called free officers movement stormed the palace and sent the king into exile. The British kept an occupying force at the Suez Canal but withdrew its troops after the canal was nationalized by the Egyptians. The British military (with its allies France and Israel) attempted to regain control of the canal in 1956 but failed. This failure signaled the end of Britain's imperial project in Egypt.

See also **Alexandria; 'Ali, Muhammad; Boundaries, Colonial and Modern; Farouk, King of Egypt; Houphouët-Boigny, Félix; Nasser, Gamal Abdel; World War I.**

BIBLIOGRAPHY

Cole, Juan. *Colonialism and Revolution in the Middle East: Social and Cultural Origins of Egypt's Urabi Movement.* Princeton, NJ: Princeton University Press, 1993.

Mitchell, Timothy. *Colonizing Egypt.* Berkeley: University of California Press, 1991.

Tignor, Robert L. *Modernization and British Colonial Rule in Egypt: 1882–1914.* Princeton, NJ: Princeton University Press, 1966.

SHAMIL JEPPIE

FRENCH NORTH AFRICA

French colonial rule in North Africa varied in duration: 132 years in Algeria (1830–1962), 75 years in Tunisia (1881–1956) and 44 years in Morocco (1912–1956) and in legal form. Algeria was juridically absorbed into France forming three departments; Tunisia and Morocco were protectorates.

French colonial rule in the Maghrib also varied in the extent to which colonial rule was contested and in the degree of violence between colonizer and colonized. It took seventeen years of warfare before France in 1847 obtained the surrender of the Algerians led by 'Abd al-Qādir (c.1807–1883). During the last seven years of that time roughly one-third of France's army led by Marshal Bugeaud (1784–1849) fought in Algeria. More time and fighting were needed to "pacify" the Saharan region. The 1870s brought another round of serious armed resistance. There followed a few other outbreaks thereafter. Then, the final phase of the brutal war for independence (1954–1962) was one of the most sustained and violent chapters in the entire history of decolonization.

By contrast, French rule in Tunisia was soon established with only sporadic armed resistance, and the winding down of the Protectorate occasioned only limited violence. In Morocco armed resistance to French rule continued until the early 1930s and reached a peak in the period from 1921 to 1926 when Moroccans from the Rif mountains led by Abd al-Krim al-Khattabi (c. 1882–1963) challenged first the Spanish in their northern protectorate and then the French. The later period of decolonization in the 1950s, while not lacking in violence and resistance, was more nearly like that in Tunisia than the violent struggle for independence in Algeria.

All three countries, however, were distinctive examples of settler colonization. At the peak in the early years of the twentieth century 17 percent of Algeria's population was French or other European stock (Italian and Spanish), and the non-French settlers soon gained French citizenship. A few years later and thereafter until independence in 1962 the proportion of *colons*, as they were called, in Algeria became and remained roughly ten percent of the total population. In Tunisia and Morocco the proportion of European settlers was less but significant, ranging between six and eight percent. By comparison, white settler colonization in Kenya never exceeded one percent of the total population. In all three countries, but especially in Algeria, the presence of these French settlers shaped social, political and economic developments embracing everything from land tenure laws to education to political representation.

Settler colonization began early in Algeria, including state-sponsored colonization promoted by Bugeaud. At the same time, local administration outside the cities was in the hands of special military officers (the *bureaux arabes*). Although harsh and authoritarian this system did at least predispose the individual bureaux arabes officer to co-opt indigenous leadership, respect indigenous customs and, in the process, defend those under their control against the demands of settlers. This paternalist pattern of rule was formalized by Louis Napoleon's policy proclaimed in 1863 when he declared Algeria to be not a "colony" but an "Arab kingdom." Napoleon III was to be as much "emperor of the Arabs as emperor of the French" (Julien 1964, 425).

The would-be "Arab kingdom," never effectively implemented, was overthrown along with Napoleon III, defeated in the 1870 Franco-Prussian War. The Third Republic that replaced it championed settler interests by extending civil administration, passing laws to facilitate settler control of agricultural lands and, in general, imposing a modern bureaucratic structure of government that left little scope for indigenous participation. Indicative of strict control imposed was the *code de l'indigénat*, which restricted the freedom on movement and speech of the native population.

Although complex arrangements offering some limited form of political representation for the Muslim Algerians were established, the deciding power remained in the hands of the minority who were full French citizens. Those few native Algerians coopted in the colonial system were later to earn the sarcastic label of "banu oui-oui" (yes men) by later Algerian nationalists. So thorough was the colonial apparatus that the early stirrings of what became the independence movement are to be found in the work of a few French reformers seeking an ultimate integration of Muslim Algerians into the French body politic matched by a group dubbed the *jeunes algériens* who early in the twentieth century championed the step by step granting of full French citizenship to native Algerians. Modest measures to this end took place immediately after World War I (in which thousands of Algerians served in the French army or the French workforce), failed in the mid-1930s (the Blum-Viollette proposal) and then with an apparent breakthrough after World War II that proved illusory. Soon thereafter the armed resistance to French rule began.

The nature of French rule in Tunisia and Morocco dictated a milder pattern of colonial domination. Because Tunisia and Morocco were protectorates, the indigenous framework of governance was maintained, but controlled at every level by French officials. Thus, in Tunisia alongside the ruling *bey* was the French resident general. The ministry was monitored by the French secretary general. And at the local level the various *qaid*s or *khalifa*s or *shaykh*s were supervised by civil controllers. An equivalent French administrative armature encasing the traditional government from the sultan down to the local *qaid* pertained in Morocco.

Although Tunisia and Morocco never lost their standing as distinctive states and maintained many of the trappings of their distinctive political identity, the French penchant for firm, centralized control plus the influx of settlers insured that the alien rule, less harsh than in Algeria, would be more penetrating that in nonsettler colonies. Indeed, a principal achievement of the French colonial presence in Morocco was to put in place a government effectively ruling the entire country, largely transcending thereby the traditional trope of a Morocco divided into a *blad al makhzan* (land of government) and a *blad al siba* (land of dissidence). A similar result in Tunisia was less dramatic only because that country, smaller and more accessible, had always been more easily governed than Morocco.

The heavy hand of settler colonization was manifest in the early creation of chambers of commerce, agriculture, and industry. These were first established as bodies to represent the settlers. They only later included natives. Even then in Morocco, for example, the native representatives were, until as late as 1947, appointed rather than elected. In a similar way the different institutions created for local or national representation (from city councils to national assemblies) were all characterized by a dominant settler representation or at best in later stages equality of settler and native representation with the Protectorate authority holding the ring.

Still, colonialism in the protectorates offered a lighter touch than that in Algeria. For example, a path-breaking land registration act in Tunisia in 1885 permitted claimants to register their holdings according to either the French law or the existing *shari'a*-based law. The former provided clear title facilitating low-interest development loans. The latter did not. As a result most Tunisian landowners chose the former, but unlike in Algeria (e.g., the notorious 1873 Warnier law that facilitated the breakup of communal lands) an alien, infidel law was not simply imposed.

The protectorates over Tunisia and Morocco came at a time when those influential in French colonial circles viewed the harsh assimilationist (to France) policies in Algeria as a mistake not to be replicated. They looked longingly at what they saw as the less costly and more effective British policy of indirect rule. The first French high officials in Tunisia were of that persuasion. This orientation was even more pronounced in the career of Marshal Lyautey (1854–1934) who served as resident-general in Morocco from 1912 until 1926 (except for a few months service in France during World War I). His celebrated *tache d'huile* (oil spot) doctrine called for conquest with a minimum of violence, penetrating like a bit oil dropped on cloth, with a follow-up effort to co-opt those defeated. He championed working with and through the existing Moroccan state apparatus while respecting Moroccan mores. This extended even into such matters as urban planning where his insistence on imposing an indigenous architecture can be seen in the "neo-Moorish" style characterizing Rabat. He, like others of this persuasion, sought to rein in the demands of settlers.

On balance, the fact that Tunisia and Morocco were protectorates rather than colonies (not to mention outright annexation into France as with Algeria) and were administered by the likes of Lyautey plus the many others influenced by that school of colonial administration, clearly had a liberalizing impact but not so much as to radically modify the persistent settler influence and the French proclivity for direct and hands-on control.

In the field of education the French policy in all three states produced an educational system of a standard equivalent to that in the metropole (the settler population would have settled for nothing less) but available only to a handful of the native population. Alongside this were efforts to foster a hybrid school system, dubbed "Franco-Arabe" (in Tunisia) and epitomized by Lyautey's *Ècoles des fils de notables* (school for sons of notables) in Morocco, but even these had limited enrollments. Only in the last few years before independence were serious efforts made to increase enrollments significantly. Tunisia on the eve of independence had only 26 percent of the primary school age population in school. The figure for Algeria was 14 percent and for Morocco even lower.

Missionaries and missionary education, so important in many African countries, played a role in French North Africa whose limits may best be summed up in the life of Cardinal Lavigerie (1825–1892). Creating the order of the White Fathers, he oversaw during his long years in the Maghrib a bold effort of missionary educational and medical activity among the Muslims. He convinced the Church to appoint him the archbishop of a re-established See of

Carthage (1884) covering all of North Africa, an act surely meant to claim that the once vibrant North African Church of Saint Augustine was destined to return. It was not to be. The church became, however awkwardly, associated with the settler population. Only a handful of Muslim converts resulted. The missionaries, their schools and their hospitals were too few and too categorically resisted by the native population North Africa, did serve, however, as a perceived threat against which North African nationalism could rally. The St. Louis Cathedral built in Carthage honoring the Crusading French king who died there in 1218; the 1930 Eucharistic Congress held with great ceremony in Tunis; and one lone conversion to Christianity of the son of Moroccan notable family in the 1930s—all these incidents fueled the fires of Maghribi nationalism. Even before independence the White Fathers had turned away from proselytism to good works with commendable, but necessarily modest results.

Yet another French activity that misfired was its Berber policy relevant only for Morocco and Algeria where native Berber speakers constitute an estimated 40 and 25 percent, respectively. An informal but influential notion grew up among the French of the good Berber/bad Arab dichotomy, the former being assimilable to France and French ways, the latter not. The classic example of this sentiment in action was the 1930 Berber *dahir* (decree) ruling that Berbers should follow their own customary law rather than laws based on the *shari'a* as in the Arab areas of Morocco. This decree, seen as a crude divide-and-rule tactic, served as a powerful stimulus to Moroccan nationalism. Ironically, if the French had simply abstained from passing a law, which in fact only regularized the existing state of affairs, there would have been no issue for Morocco's fledging nationalists to exploit.

The Berber *dahir* serves as a metaphor for French policies and practices in all North Africa. It was an intensive and penetrating colonialism, bringing to North Africa large numbers of colonial administrators and colonizing settlers. French colonialism was predisposed to direct rather than indirect rule. French colonialism produced impressive changes in the Maghrib's basic economic and cultural infrastructure. It left as a legacy stronger, more centralized governments. It also, as do all forms of colonialism, provoked the ideologies and educated the individuals who led the nationalist movements to independence.

See also 'Abd al-Qādir; Algeria; Carthage; Colonialism and Imperialism; Economic History; Morocco; Plantation Economies and Societies; Postcolonialism; Slave Trades; Tunisia.

BIBLIOGRAPHY

Julien, Charles-Andre. *Histoire de l'Algerie contemporaine.* Paris: Presses Universitaires de France, 1964.

Pennell, C. R. *Morocco since 1830.* New York: New York University Press, 2000.

Perkins, Kenneth J. *A History of Modern Tunisia.* Cambridge, U.K.: Cambridge University Press, 2004.

Ruedy, John. *Modern Algeria: The Origins and Development of a Nation,* 2nd edition. Bloomington: Indiana University Press, 2005.

L. CARL BROWN

FRENCH WEST AND EQUATORIAL AFRICA

At the start of the period of colonial imperialism, around 1880, tropical Africa was almost completely independent (except for the coast of Senegal and the region of Libreville in Gabon). Thirty-five years later, at the beginning of World War I, two federations, AOF (French West Africa) and AEF (French Equatorial Africa), were administered by a homogenous group of colonial civil servants; large French companies had covered the country with a network which, in terms of general form, remained virtually unaltered until the 1960s. Alongside so-called traditional chiefdoms, a French-educated middle class, very small in number, began to prepare to take over and regain their independence.

THE FRENCH COLONIAL IDEA

Although an active minority was convinced by the idea of expansion, metropolitan opinion only adopted the colonial idea reluctantly. Politicians were calculating the cost of a political adventure, while businessmen were afraid of undue state control. The country, caught unawares by how swiftly it had acquired its colonies, lacked the personnel to govern and administer them. Despite this, the advocates of colonization (including Paul Leroy-Beaulieu, who wrote *De la colonisation chez les peuples modernes,* the second [1882] edition of

which was tremendously successful) called for the creation of a specialized colonial system. This was the aim they set out to achieve, from the administrator in the bush to the top of the federal hierarchy: the creation of unified regions, a symbol of the famous French policy of centralization and assimilation.

Formation of the Administration: The Ministry and Officials in the Colonies. West Africa, which was gradually organized around the former Senegalese trading post, served as a model. Equatorial Africa, on the contrary, which was left to the mercy of businessmen, who were often ill informed and lacking adequate capital, showed the damaging effects of a system based upon force. In 1880 the acquisition of the hinterland of Senegal had scarcely begun; in West Africa, confronted by Samori, the military were still in charge; on the Gulf of Bénin, the French settlements of the gold coast and Gabon were restricted to a handful of traders and several fortified half-abandoned stations. In 1881 the Ministry for Trade and the Colonies was established, indicating the hostility that existed between the world of business, which favored peace out of self-interest, and naval officers, who supported an imperious nationalism enacted by force of arms. The Ministry of Colonies was established in 1894.

The *École coloniale* (School of Colonial Administration) opened in 1890. Administrators from this remained in the minority for a long time: in 1907 only 70 out of 489 civil servants in French black Africa were from this school. A symbol of imperial unity, from the beginning this school was intended to produce interchangeable and versatile civil servants, who would be capable of carrying out the widest possible range of tasks (administrative, judicial, etc.) throughout the entire empire, something which explains "the great disadvantages of providing constant encouragement to unite and assimilate to those that should be kept apart or considered separate" (Boutmy 1895, 115).

The "Broussard" (Bushman), Taxation, and Indigenous Politics. This multitasking administrator was the lynchpin that made the whole system work. In charge of a vast area (the "cercle" established by General Léon Faidherbe in Senegal), he had extensive powers (in terms of administration, justice, police) over many thousands of people and was their sole point of contact with higher authority. Known as the Commandant, his first duty was the collection of taxes. There were two reasons why the authorities considered this thankless task exceptionally important: the colonies were poor, but became self-sufficient as time wore on; a tax together with customs duties represented the only way of raising revenue and was introduced everywhere between 1900 and 1910. The aim was to levy payment in cash so as to help with the introduction of a modern economy, but at first payment in kind was accepted: rubber, ivory, or other goods. In Equatorial Africa, the budget deficit prompted the commissaire général Émile Gentil to write an infamous letter to his civil servants on March 19, 1903: "I will not conceal from you that I'll have to base my appreciation on your work according to the taxes you manage to levy from the natives so far (3 francs per head). For you this must be a constant matter of concern" (published in the *Journal official de l'Afrique équatoriale française*). This led to the abuses that were already being carried out in the independent state of Congo: villages terrorized, pillaged by Senegalese militias (*laptots*), there were strokes of the lash for those who resisted, forced carriage of goods overland (*corvées de portage*) to export produce or for military expeditions (for example during the 1920s troops in Chad had to be supplied with 3,000 loads per month of 55 to 65 pounds per person), summary executions, and hostage taking.

The Commandant feared that this would lead to flight and revolts; in 1911 the Gouro in Côte d'Ivoire again refused to pay tax. Extensive attempts at pacification were made, terrorizing the population, who were only disarmed in 1914. In Equatorial Africa, from the Marchand mission and Gentil's troops in 1896 until 1920, there was a constant series of low-level and local uprisings. The instrument of coercion was the *Code de l'indigènat* taken from the colonization of Algeria, which gave the colonial administrator discretionary power over his "subjects." In such circumstances it was difficult to encourage any meaningful indigenous politics among the populace. Nonetheless not all administrators behaved barbarically. Inquisitive individuals anticipated the first anthropologists: Georges Bruel in French Equatorial Africa or Governor Maurice Delafosse, famous for his collection of oral sources

on *Haut-Senegal-Niger* (1912) and his translations of Arabic texts. However, the native inhabitants were generally depicted as large children, lazy and unruly, to be controlled and kept in their place. This contempt led to localized support for Islam, with which the French had already dealt during the conquest of Algeria. The French mindset, with its fondness for order and logic, had little sympathy for the "strange swarms" of the autochthonous religions.

The ideal form of direct government was for the most part to replace those formerly in charge with compliant administrative chiefdoms. The village was the preferred unit of administration and its chiefs were in effect transformed into badly paid civil servants. Tin pot dictators, they were provided with European force in order to fulfill demands that had previously been unheard of (taxes, provision of overland supplies, forced labor), since "there were not two authorities in the region, the French authority and the native authority, there was only one. Only the Commandant of the region was in control, only he was in charge. The native chief was merely a tool, an assistant" (as published in a circular of August 15, 1917; Van Vollenhoven, 207). In 1900 the kingdom of Abomey in Dahomey was overthrown, while in Congo Makoko the king of the Bateke, who had signed a treaty ceding his territory to the French, was almost forgotten. Of course in those places where well-established monarchies existed (such as the Mossi, Abron, and Ani kingdoms in Upper Volta and Côte d'Ivoire), they were still made use of. Wherever possible, local chiefs were chosen from the most important families, but the system itself was open to abuse.

There was one long-standing exception, inherited from the former colonial empire that had been destroyed as a result of the Napoleonic wars. The so-called originaires of the Communes of Senegal (Saint-Louis and Gorée, and later Dakar and Rufisque) had received the right to vote after the French Revolution and elected a deputy to the French parliament. The first black to be elected was Blaise Diagne in 1914. He negotiated French citizenship for them during World War I. The political life of the four Communes on the Senegalese coast was an experience unparalleled elsewhere.

The Federations. As well as having a single civil service, French Africa also had a unified structure. From 1895 in West Africa and from 1908 in Equatorial Africa, colonial governors were themselves subordinate to a governor general. All indirect taxes were paid to the federal government and used to provide comprehensive finance for a policy of public works on a large scale (railways, ports). However, the biggest weakness of these federations consisted in ignoring some quite fundamental ethnic and demographic constraints. In French West Africa, a territory nine times the size of France, with a population of around 12 million, unevenly spread in locations ranging from dense forests to the fringes of the desert, one can easily recognize the sheer vanity of the idea of imposing not just peace, but also French civilization.

In similar fashion to French West Africa, French Equatorial Africa was divided into four territories: Gabon, Congo, Oubangui-Chari, and Chad (together with the mandate over Cameroon after 1918). The aim was to restrict the "Congo scandals" that erupted in 1905 in the Belgian Congo, but had repercussions in the French part as well (the company in Mpoko, near Bangui, was accused of murdering 1,500 natives in 1906). Two later revolts broke out: one by the so-called Awanji hostiles in West Gabon in 1927–1928 against payment of tax and notably another by the Mbaye in Oubangui-Chari. The latter had become desperate because of a combination of factors: the requirement to transport overland supplies, forced recruitment for the construction of the railway between Congo and the ocean (1922–1933), the production and harvesting of rubber and the compulsory cultivation of cotton. Led by a charismatic chief, Karnu, the uprising (or War of Kongo-Wara) was large scale, affecting more than 350,000 people and involving 60,000 fighting men. The revolt spread to the west of Cameroon and to the south of Chad and was only suppressed in 1931. The estimated death toll varies, depending on the source, from 10,000 to 100,000. Nonetheless, a united empire had in the end been created, and had achieved the ideal of producing an identical system across the world, whether in French Indochina, West Africa, or Equatorial Africa.

ECONOMY AND SOCIETY

Contrary to appearances, the natural environment and methods of development of these two federations as colonies was completely different. French West Africa was a mixed bag, but had a less difficult climate and was easier to develop. As well as producing crops, such as rubber and palm nuts, there were other crops cultivated for export which would make the colony relatively wealthy: in Senegal groundnut production increased enormously (from 50,000 tons in 1897 to 240,000 in 1913). Restricted by the impoverished soil and the lack of improvement in methods of cultivation, production was introduced in the Sahel colonies (Upper Volta and Niger). The groundnut accounted for half the total value of exports from French West Africa in 1940. Palm oil and palm products, the key crop on the coast of Bénin, reached record levels in 1911–1912 (12,000 tons of oil and 30,000 tons of almonds in Dahomey, nearly 7,000 tons of each in Côte d'Ivoire). In 1920, the apparent growth in exports was caused by the new mandate over Togo (4,000 tons of oil and 10,000 tons of almonds). After World War I there were also local plantations of coffee and cacao trees.

The long-established French companies on the coast (Maurel et Prom in Senegal, Verdier in Côte d'Ivoire, and Règis which became Mantes et Borelli in Dahomey) remained true to the economic liberalism that had made them their fortune. At the start of the twentieth century their place was taken by several powerful import-export companies: The French West Africa Company (CFAO), the West African Trading Company (SCOA), and the Niger Français company, the latter a British subsidiary. These companies gradually covered French West Africa with a comprehensive network of their plants, which employed large numbers of African staff and dominated business in the federation until after independence.

In contrast with the all-powerful administration of French West Africa, the decline of the same in French Equatorial Africa was almost total. Power was in the hands of large, mean monopolies, organized along the lines of the former chartered companies. Their rights in the trade of ivory, the rubber crop, and wood ended only gradually between 1911 and 1935. A lack of serious investment in infrastructure and the policy of neglect by the public authorities created economic paralysis. Mineral wealth was not exploited before the end of the 1950s, even though diamonds had been discovered in Oubangui-Chari during the 1930s. The same thing applied to the mineral wealth of Gabon, where only mahogany wood was produced. The raw material for plywood, it was first exploited by the Germans at the beginning of the twentieth century. Between the 1920s and the end of the 1950s when it was replaced by plastics, it made the colonists wealthy. The industry, which was very labor intensive, helped to produce an overexploited working class, to the extent that in the 1950s only the private sector called for heavy investment. Hence the colony of the Congo, whose capital Brazzaville was the center of the federation, had been accused by the colony of Gabon of enriching itself at its expense.

From the 1920s political consciousness began to arise in the towns and shanties. A section of the League of Human Rights appeared in Libreville. A Congolese former volunteer who had fought in the Rif War (a war of repression in Morocco in 1925), André Matsoua, attempted to set up in Paris in 1926 an "Amicale des Originaires de l'AOF" (Association of French West African Originaires; a reference to the *Originaires* of the Four Communes of Senegal). In 1930 he was deported by the colonial authorities to Chad where he died in 1942. It was at this point that a messianic cult named Matsouanism began to develop around him among the Lari people (Bakongo). At the same time in Senegal the repression undertaken at the beginning of the century against the Muslim preacher Amadou Bamba had led to the establishment of a powerful marabout cult known as the Mouride.

PROGRESS TOWARD DECOLONIZATION

The postwar hopes, symbolized by the Conference held in Brazzaville in January 1944, ran into numerous difficulties. While the colonial project ran out of steam, disintegrating as a result of ambitious and reactionary colonists and the rapid drying up of the economic revival, a new, occasionally savage, African cultural movement arose to break free from colonial rule. In economic terms, the 1950s saw the introduction of ambitious investment followed by rapid disillusionment. Under the auspices of FIDES (*Fonds d'investissement pour le Développement Économique et social*) [Investment Funds for Economic and Social Development], established in 1947, in 1948 the federations adopted a ten-year plan concentrating on infrastructure and production.

In French Equatorial Africa, priority was given to transport infrastructure: the improvement of waterways and ports. However in 1951, out of 8,300 miles of planned routes, scarcely 214 miles were completed, while the capital of FIDES had been halved. On the eve of independence, the only large transport routes were still the Congo-Oubangui Logone-Chari rivers and, in the south, the Congo-Ocean railroad (317 miles) between Brazzaville and Pointe-Noire, the only ocean outlet for the four colonies. In French West Africa, the federation did not extend the insufficiently profitable Dakar-Niger railroad, instead supporting large-scale construction of ports, first at Dakar between 1903 and 1910, at Abidjan only in the 1950s, and at Cotonou (Dahomey) on the eve of independence.

FIDES failed to provide the federations with significant industrial renewal. While small production units succeeded, such as the breweries, sugar refineries, cigarette factories, and soap factories of Congo and Oubangui, or the tanneries of Chad, the large cement works and paper mills of Gabon were unsuccessful. The cement works at Rufisque in Senegal was the only exception. Hydroelectric plants (Djoue 1949, Boali 1955) remained underused. The only profitable industry was manganese mining in Gabon. In French West Africa, priority was given to homegrown agriculture and oil exports to the oil works of Bordeaux and Marseille. Persistently low salaries and low productivity showed the extent to which the economy continued to be based on a policy of looking outward.

Social change was clearly more extensive in French West Africa, because of the greater level of commercial activity. The Popular Front government there had legalized trade unions in 1936. The next two years saw unprecedented social change, marked by strikes in every sector. The most active trade unions were railworkers and those involving public employees (postal workers and teachers). This movement was crushed violently in 1938 before the outbreak of World War II. It returned with renewed vigor after the war, when two successive general strikes paralyzed railroad traffic in West Africa. This involved RAN (Régie d'Afrique noire). In 1952 the slogan Equal Work for Equal Pay resulted in the enactment of the *Code français du travail* (French Labor Code), a decisive factor in decolonization, since it removed the enormous advantages that the colonists had because of the previous nonapplication of social laws. From this moment the African worker would cost the same as his French counterpart, which meant that business saw no further benefit in colonial rule.

Social change was restricted to a modest improvement in health service provisions, along with the strengthening of the school system (which had been essentially public since the law of 1905 separating church and state). In French Equatorial Africa in 1958, almost 200,000 pupils attended primary schools, both public and private, compared with barely 22,000 in 1938. The increase was ten times higher in French West Africa. The secondary school system remained poor however, with the only African senior school being the famous *École William Ponty* in Senegal, which was a teacher training college. It was here that many of the first independence leaders were educated. There was a grammar school in Saint-Louis in 1940, and another was established after the war, but almost all the pupils were the children of colonists. The first (and only) colonial university was only built at Dakar in the middle of the 1950s.

And yet in response to this dangerous inertia came a major social and economic upheaval: the growth of towns and cities. Starting from the 1930s, caused by the widespread impoverishment of the countryside caused by the Great Depression of the 1930s, and resisted unsuccessfully by the colonial authorities until the late 1950s, this urban allure meant that there was a spectacular expansion of the capitals and a corresponding decline in rural population density (on average 2 inhabitants per square kilometer). Brazzaville went from a population of 25,000 in 1940 to more than 150,000 in 1965; Dakar from 32,500 in 1931 to almost 300,000 in 1960. Places of power, conflict, and encroachment, the cities became critical "places of colonization" (Mbembe 1996), where the colonial administration did not manage to prevent the emergence of an autonomous African culture.

Before 1945, the authorities had constructed their capital cities on a segregated basis, de facto if not de jure (since racial segregation was illegal: the town centers of Dakar and Lomé remained very mixed). On health grounds, urban facilities were restricted to the white part of town, buffer zones separated the districts, everything was laid out so as to give the capitals their distinctive appearance,

which is still visible in the early twenty-first century: a European district on a "plateau," surrounded by the African "villages" of Poto-Poto and Bacongo in Brazzaville, and a semicircular layout in Libreville, where the white town was encircled by the African districts from Montagne Sainte to St. Benoit. This authoritarian urban control was circumscribed after 1945. Land claims, like those by the Lebou at Dakar from 1914 as being the "original inhabitants," or by the Mpongwe chiefs in Libreville (1947–1948), elicited significant financial compensation from the authorities, while they were unable to prevent the increasing presence of impoverished whites in the African districts. Above all, the unequal relationship between the African city and white city, while remaining visible in terms of the urban layout, did not convert into political and cultural subjection. The new status of urban women, the passion for football, intellectual habits and tastes in fashion, and the emergence of an African media are evidence of the dynamic nature of this triumphant and liberating social change, which took place despite consistent attempts at restriction.

Religious belief progressed in the same way. The success of evangelization by missionaries of Catholicism, officially the preeminent religion in French Equatorial Africa, was halted by the vigorous activity of independent churches (Bwiti in Gabon and Matsouanism in the Congo), while Islam remained the dominant religion in Chad and the north of Oubangui. In contrast, in French West Africa, even though a number of black churches developed at a local level (such as Harrism in Côte d'Ivoire), Islam, which was almost the exclusive religion in the Sahel countries, was making appreciable advances south from the 1930s. Despite being opposed by the authorities these beliefs illustrate the ability of local cultures to absorb, convert, and assimilate for their own ends the values imposed by colonization.

World War II played a contrasting role in the development of the two federations. In French Equatorial Africa on August 27, 1940, Félix Éboué, a black born in French Guyana and Governor of Chad, chose to support Général Charles De Gaulle. The Congo, then Oubangui, quickly followed, only Gabon remaining briefly loyal to the Vichy government. When he arrived in Brazzaville on October 24, 1940, De Gaulle made the whole of French Equatorial Africa the main land base for Free French forces. This episode had its effect after the war, in both Africa and Europe. In contrast, after the failed landing of De Gaulle at Dakar in 1940, French West Africa's civil servants continued to support the Vichy regime and only switched sides at the last minute in 1943.

The war served to rekindle colonial antagonisms, however. As a result of the needs of war, forced labor was increased everywhere, resulting in deep dissatisfaction. The Brazzaville conference concerning new French imperial policy, held in January 1944, recommended several reforms: forced labor was officially abolished by the Houphouet-Boigny Law of 1947. The administration of the territories was decentralized and they were given elected assemblies; this prepared the ground for the political battle ahead. Nevertheless, despite being granted the right to vote and the general granting of French citizenship (the Lamine Gueye Law, May 7, 1946), African political representation remained under European control as a result of the dual college electoral system. It was only in 1956 that the *loi-cadre* set up a single college and universal suffrage. Before this date, very few Africans had been on the electoral register: in 1946 there were 110,029 individuals, 2.5 percent of the total population of French Equatorial Africa. In 1953 this number had still only risen to 784,411, 17.8 percent (but women had become the most numerous group following a law of 1951 which allowed women with two children to vote).

As for Europeans, they mostly supported the Gaullist party the Rally of the People of France (Rassemblement du Peuple français), electing conservative deputies to Paris to defend the maintenance of the dual college system. Opposed to these were African parties that were led for the first time by a group of moderate officials. It was only on the coast of French Equatorial Africa, in Oubangui, that Barthélémy Boganda, a defrocked priest from the Lobaye region, continued the tradition of the movements of the 1930s with his Movement for the Social Emancipation of Black Africa (Mouvement pour l'Émancipation Sociale de l'Afrique Noire, MESAN), a radical anti-establishment movement founded in 1952. The radicalization of French West Africa was evident in 1944 with the creation of the African Democratic Rally or RDA (Rassemblement démocratique africain), a powerful opposition party in the federation, which for half a dozen years remained affiliated with the Communist Party. Its various

subsidiaries played a crucial role in the elected assemblies of the various colonies.

During 1955–1956 the bitterness of the political struggles to take control of government, which had been opened up by the *loi-cadre* or Defferre Law of 1956, along with the desire of European parties to find African allies, led to the victory of new men. They were the first generation from the demographic boom of the 1950s, the outcome of a colonial health policy, which had been revised and at the end of the 1930s had introduced basic preventative measures (sleeping sickness was wiped out and vaccination against yellow fever began). In Gabon, Aubame accepted defeat by Léon Mba, a former thorn in the side of the colonial administration, but new protégé of white foresters, a remarkably astute campaigner, who was elected mayor of Libreville in 1956. In 1957, his party the Gabonese Democratic Bloc (Bloc Démocratique gabonais) deservedly won the elections. Only Bartélémy Boganda, who was a charismatic and popular leader, was able to maintain and expand his support in Oubangui-Chari, calling for the creation of a United States of Central Africa. Before independence MESAN was the only truly mass political party in French Equatorial Africa, but the death of Boganda in an air crash on March 28, 1959, led to a period of uncertainty. In Congo, Fulbert Youlou, an ambitious Catholic priest from the Brazzaville region, was elected mayor of the capital in 1956 and head of government in 1958. His maneuverings and the bitterness of the socialist opposition triggered massacres in Brazzaville in February 1959. The slaughter went on for three days (February 16–18). The riots ended with several hundred dead and a brief political alliance between Youlou and his rival.

In French West Africa, political life was marked by rivalry between Félix Houphouët-Boigny, the leader of Côte d'Ivoire, who represented the interests of the small-time Ivorian planters, and the leaders of Senegal, where the Marxist Mamadou Dia was quickly removed following independence by the Socialist Léopold Sédar Senghor, a leading exponent of French culture, despite inventing the idea of *négritude*.

The defining characteristic of the 1950 was the rise in political violence. From 1946, electoral fraud was endemic, with the support of the government, the missions, and individual colonists. Conceiving matters from a tribal perspective, which justified the corruption of "tribal chiefs" or imagined ethnic groups, it led to the creation of new ethnic divisions, which had hitherto been of little political importance. As for election winners, from 1957 onward they adopted a policy of "winner takes all," either banning the opposition or forcing them to join an alliance. The danger of this monopolization of power, a legacy of colonial authority, led to increasingly bitter elections from the beginning of the 1950s: threats, the intimidation of electors, and the use of bands of young supporters. The motley public authorities borrowed from the qualities of *big men* in the precolonial era, from the well-read individual or learned scholar, from the old animist claim for a link between wealth and power, as well as Muslim or Christian rituals or from conflicts between generations. Thus in Senegal the Mouride brotherhood, which had become involved in groundnut production, voted yes in the referendum on the French Community (Communauté française) proposed by General De Gaulle (1958). Or Fulbert Youlou in Congo, taking advantage of rumors that he had magical powers, borrowed from Matsouanism, encouraging ambitious youngsters to vote against the political old guard.

When independence came, there was an orderly transfer of power, except in Cameroon, where the demand for the reunification of French and British territories led to a revolt sparked by the militant trade unionist Ruben Um Nyobe. However, in reality, the continuous reworking of political and cultural identity among the various sections of the population meant that explosive potential still remained everywhere.

See also **Brazzaville; Colonialism and Imperialism; Dakar; Gorée; Houphouët-Boigny, Félix; Human Rights; Libreville; Political Systems: Chieftainships; Saint-Louis; Senghor, Léopold Sédar; Warfare; Warfare: Colonial; World War I; World War II.**

BIBLIOGRAPHY

Akpo-Vaché, Catherine. *L'AOF et la seconde Guerre mondiale: la vie politique.* Paris: Karthala, 1996.

Bernault, Florence. *Démocraties ambigues en Afrique centrale: Congo-Brazzaville, Gabon, 1940–1965.* Paris: Karthala, 1996.

Boutmy, Emile. *Le recrutement des administrateurs coloniaux.* Paris: Colin, 1895.

Cooper, Frederick. *Decolonization and African Society: The Labor Question in French and British Africa.* Cambridge, U.K.: Cambridge University Press, 1996.

Coquery-Vidrovitch, Catherine. *Le Congo [AEF] au temps des grandes compagnies concessionnaires, 1898–1930,* 2nd edition. Paris: EHESS, 2001.

Crowder, Michael. *Senegal: A Study of French Assimilation Policy.* London: Methuen, 1962.

Crowder, Michael. *West Africa under Colonial Rule.* Evanston, IL: Northwestern University Press, 1968.

Cruise O'Brien, Donal. *The Mourides of Senegal: The Political and Economic Organization of an Islamic Brotherhood.* Oxford: Clarendon Press, 1971.

Decalo, Samuel. *Historical Dictionary of Chad,* 2nd edition. Metuchen, NJ: Scarecrow Press, 1987.

Gardinier, David E. *Historical Dictionary of Gabon,* 2nd edition. Metuchen, NJ: Scarecrow Press, 1994.

Gondola, Didier. *Villes miroirs; migrations et identités urbaines: Brazzaville et Kinshasa, 1930–1970.* Paris: L'Harmattan, 1997.

Headrick, Rita. *Colonialism, Health, and Illness in French Equatorial Africa, 1885–1935.* Atlanta, GA: African Studies Association Press, 1994.

Johnson, G. Wesley. *The Emergence of Black Politics in Senegal: The Struggle for Power in the Four Communes, 1900–1920.* Stanford, CA: Stanford University Press, 1971.

Kalck, Pierre. *Historical Dictionary of the Central African Republic.* Metuchen, NJ: Scarecrow Press, 1980.

Kalck, Pierre. *Histoire centrafricaine,* 2nd edition. Paris: L'Harmattan, 1992.

Martin, Phyllis M. *Leisure and Society in Colonial Brazzaville.* Cambridge, U.K.: Cambridge University Press, 1995.

Martin, Phyllis M., and David Birmingham, eds. *History of Central Africa,* Vol. 2. New York: Longman, 1983.

Mbembe, J. Achille. *La naissance du maquis dans le Sud-Cameroun (1920–1960).* Paris: Karthala, 1996.

Sautter, Gilles. *De l'Atlantique au fleuve Congo. Une géographie du sous-peuplement.* 2 vols. Paris: Mouton, 1966.

Thompson, Virginia, and Richard Adloff. *French West Africa.* Stanford, CA: Stanford University Press, 1957.

Thompson, Virginia, and Richard Adloff. *The Emerging States of French Equatorial Africa.* Stanford, CA: Stanford University Press, 1960.

Une âme de chef, le gouverneur général Van Vollenhoven. Paris: Impr. H. Diéval, 1920.

Weinstein, Bryan. *Felix Eboue.* New York: Oxford University Press, 1972.

CATHERINE COQUERY-VIDROVITCH

GERMAN

German colonialism in Africa was short lived. It lasted only thirty years, from April 1884 to 1914, when imperial forces of Great Britain and the Union of South Africa occupied the German colonies.

Thus German colonial rule was limited to the heyday of European imperialism. The colonial movement was influenced by the experience of the mass immigration from Germany and the great economic depression after 1874. During German rule in four African territories—Kamerun and Togo in West Africa, South-West Africa (present-day Namibia), and German East Africa (present-day Tanzania, Rwanda, and Burundi)—very distinct policies developed. South-West Africa was developed as a colony fit for white farm settlement after 1889, when the German control had broken down and only became effective after 1892.

Because of expropriation of land and cattle but also racist settler behavior, the Herero and Nama waged a major war from 1904 to 1907, during which about 80 percent of the Herero and Nama were killed in a deliberate strategy of genocide masterminded by Commander General Lothar von Trotha. After the war South-West Africa became the most repressive of the settler societies in Africa. The German administration enforced ordinances in order to turn the Herero and Nama survivors into forced laborers without the right to own cattle and land and without the right of any tribal organization. After the discovery of copper and diamonds the administration fostered a system of migrant labor recruitment aimed at the Ovambo, who lived in northern Namibia beyond the German police zone.

In West Africa, although both Kamerun and Togo were part of the West African economic system producing tropical export goods from the beginning of the nineteenth century, two rather distinct colonial systems developed. In the small territory of Togo, the precolonial presence of German Bremen-based traders and mission societies formed an alliance that was powerful enough to prevent the introduction of large-scale plantation agriculture and supported peasant-based cash crop production.

Kamerun—despite a variant of indirect rule over the northern emirate of Adamawa, the interests of plantation owners, the distribution of land concessions for speculative use, and a related system of labor recruitment—produced the so-called colonial scandals, which brought colonial policy back into the Reichstag after 1903.

In East Africa, the administration was left to a chartered company, the German East Africa Company. Short of capital, and directed by the overambitious empire builder Karl Peters, it came into conflict with the trading communities of the coast. Clashing interests and German ruthlessness led to the war of 1888 between the coastal communities and the Germans, which was misnamed for propagandistic reasons as the Arab Revolt.

At the turn of the twentieth century the German colonial bureaucracy started to force the southern and central Tanzanian peasantry to work on state farms producing cotton and intervened into the coastal trade and rubber production. This act, combined with an administrative system that used nontraditional foreign African agents for taxation, led to the large-scale Maji-Maji peasant war (1905–1907). The war, which included a German scorched-earth policy, resulted in the loss of about 250,000 African lives, largely as a result of starvation and disease.

In the new period of colonial reform the policy of expanding plantations and state farms was ended by the new governor and the principle of peasant-based cash crop production adopted. This influenced the reform policy in all colonial territories except South-West Africa under colonial secretary Dernburg, a liberal banker.

The adoption of different policies in the four territories indicates that the German colonial system was flexible and ready to adapt to circumstances and distinct colonial interest groups. German colonial rule was characterized by Prussian bureaucratic traditions, which kept white settlers under a certain control, despite the social affinity of many administrators with the settler communities in East Africa and especially in South-West Africa. A rigid style of bureaucratic arrogance with militaristic overtones was not counterbalanced by the judiciary because the legal system was in the hands of the bureaucracy itself.

The German colonial system was greatly influenced by modern scientific thought and method. Systematic research on almost every aspect of the social, geographical, and agricultural structure of the colonial territories was undertaken and applied in experimental farms and research stations.

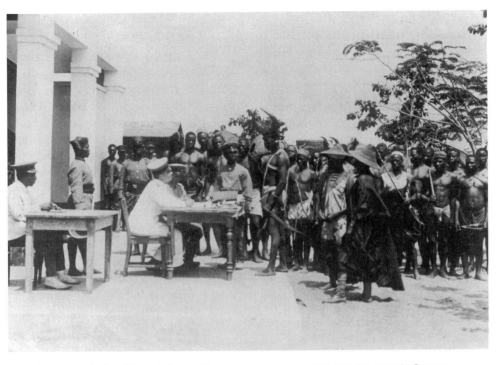

Togolese men in traditional dress. These man were recruited into the army in German-controlled Togoland around 1914. German colonialism in Africa lasted for thirty years, from 1884 to 1914. The Germans eventually withdrew after experiencing bloody wars with the natives and realizing that colonization was of little value to them. THREE LIONS/HULTON ARCHIVE/GETTY IMAGES

Modern medicine—often involving the subjection of the African population to medical experiments—became a prominent feature in the colonial self-image.

German colonial policies resembled the other European colonialisms in Africa. The German administration experimented with all known forms. In certain contexts education policy favored the German language, but in East Africa the development of Swahili was supported. Despite an official Christian, predominantly Protestant, orientation, the colonial administration tolerated Islamic systems of education and administration in Kamerun and in East Africa and the Catholic mission system in Rwanda and Burundi. Even Booker T. Washington, a leader of the early Afro-American movement, was asked for educational advice.

The anticolonial position of the Social Democratic Party, the close links between the Catholic Church and the Zentrum Party, and the free trade traditions in the Left liberal parties led the colonial administration, especially after 1903, to answer growing criticisms about good government, the rights of "natives," and the economic value of reforms. In response, colonial and ultranationalist propaganda organizations like the Pan German League and the Colonial Society attacked humanitarian and Christian arguments for colonial reforms, very often using social Darwinist language.

During World War I, German colonial war aims envisaged a Mittelafrika stretching between Germany's West and East African colonies. The Caprivi Strip of South-West Africa reached the Zambezi in Central Africa. In 1898 and 1914 German-British talks dealt with the Portuguese African colonies as a potential zone of interest.

The memories of German colonialism have long been distorted by German colonial revisionist thoughts, which led to apologetic writings. An enormous amount of fictitious literature on colonies supported this tendency. A critical analysis was delayed due to the fact that the defeated Germany after 1945 did not participate in the debates on decolonization and deep-rooted sympathies with apartheid South Africa prevailed. Although the research of the late 1950s and 1960s and books from West German, British, and American scholars on German colonialism after 1965 offered enough evidence of harsh conditions of the colonial situation and the major wars, their impact was limited by the fact that criticism affecting the "good old times" of the Kaiser Reich was not welcome, in order to isolate the Nazi barbarism from the German past. West Germany's becoming part of western Europe strengthened traditional colonial thinking as part of the assumed "civilizing mission" of the West. So the defense of the German colonial order was left to the traditionalists in German African studies, who largely remained in an early-twentieth-century intellectual mode.

Looking into the wealth of fictions, geographical descriptions, and memoirs that concentrated on colonial and exotic dreams since the late eighteenth century up to the 1930s, scholars in the 1990s have argued that German colonial sentiments were not restricted to the very short period of thirty years. The thinking in the early nineteenth century was more concentrated on Latin America as a potential aim of German mass migration. Scholars argue that the image of the tropical colonial world was rather separated from the realities, which can be shown by the fact that they prevailed although the colonies were not popular between 1884 and 1904.

Another line of scholarly thought concentrates on German radical thinking in fields of radical racial segregation, social hygienic concepts, and biologist race theory. These scholars support the argument that the colonial experiment had an impact on totalitarian and fascist thinking. Some authors even see a direct continuity to the Nazi path of the holocaust and radical colonial policies in eastern Europe during World War I. This line of thought was supported by an intensive debate about the nature of the colonial war in Namibia from 1904 to 1907 as the first genocide in the twentieth century. The broad public debate memorizing the 100th anniversary especially of the Herero War had the impact that in all mayor German newspapers it was accepted that a genocide had occurred. It led to the official apology of the German minister of development aid in Namibia.

A wide conceptual gap can be recognized between research that tends to integrate German colonialism into the general European colonial experiences and images by using the cultural tradition in colonial writings of more than one hundred years, which connects it with general European traditions and those who underline the radicalism of certain aspects of German colonialism, especially its social Darwinist heritage and its application in a genocide and the postwar policies in South-West Africa. This thinking is part of the concept of a German *Sonderweg* (a special German historical development in contrast to western Europe). Although elements of totalitarian thinking and behavior can be identified during the Kaiser Reich and its colonial policies, other aspects—the colonial reform agenda after 1906 and the peasant-orientated policy in Togo and East Africa (Tanzania) after 1907—cannot be overlooked. Similarly, it can be argued that the colonial revisionism was rather isolated in Nazi Germany. Finally a too close connection cannot be established between colonial racism and antisemitism beyond the general tendency of social Darwinist thinking although in the Pan German League both elements were present. Concepts of purity of race informed the ban on mixed marriages in the colonies and influenced the concept of a social hygienic for a "purified" German Volk (people).

See also **Colonialism and Imperialism; Plantation Economies and Societies; World War I; World War II.**

BIBLIOGRAPHY

Berman, Russell. *Enlightenment or Empire: Colonial Discourses in German Culture.* Lincoln: University of Nebraska Press, 1998.

Grosse, Pascal. *Kolonialismus, Eugenik und bürgerliche Gesellschaft in Deutschland, 1850–1918.* New York: Campus Verlag, 2000.

Krüger, Gesine. *Kriegsbewältigung und Geschichtsbewusstsein, Realität, Deutung und Verarbeitung des deutschen Kolonialkrieges in Namibia 1904–1907.* Göttingen: Vandenhoek & Ruprecht, 1999.

Kundrus, Birthe. *Moderne Imperialisten: Das Kaiserreich im Spiegel seiner Kolonien.* Köln: Böhlau, 2003.

Kundrus, Birthe, ed. *Phantasiereiche, Zur Kulturgeschichte des deutschen Kolonialismus.* Frankfurt: Campus, 2003.

Sebald, Peter. *Togo 1884–1914.* Berlin: Akademie Verlag, 1987.

Wildenthal Lora. *German Women for Empire 1884–1945.* Durham, NC: Duke University Press, 2001.

Zantop, Susanne. *Colonial Fantasies: Conquest, Family and Nation in Precolonial Germany 1770–1870.* Durham, NC: Duke University Press, 1997.

HELMUT BLEY

ITALIAN

A late entry in the colonial arena, Italy managed only a short-lived rule over its African possessions south of the Sahara (c. 1890–1941). Italy's colonial effort had weak economic foundations and stumbled over the contrasting ideologies of successive governments in Rome. The two poles of Italy's colonial presence in Africa were the landing of a small force of one thousand men in Massawa (Mitsiwa, in present-day Eritrea) in 1885 and the launching in 1935, fifty years later, of a massive military campaign to fight to the end (including the use of gas) the army of the last independent African monarch, Emperor Haile Sellassie I of Ethiopia. Six years later (5 May 1941), the return of the defeated and exiled emperor to his capital city, Addis Ababa, signaled the end of Italy's colonial empire. It is within this brief and ruptured colonial effort that Italian policies and practices in Africa must be analyzed.

Although Italian colonial policies present remarkable continuity, the rise of fascism to power in 1922 led the way to a more determined and ruthless policy of law and order in the colonies, and to a renewed expansionist and racist mood in fascist colonial rule. Throughout this period it is difficult to speak of a sustained colonial policy in Italy's African possessions. The very shortness of its rule, the absence of a colonial tradition in Italy, and the impact of African resistance, made Italian policies more contingent upon changing local situations than on national directives.

Thus the initial policy of land requisitions and settlements in the Eritrean highlands following the declaration of the colony in 1890 came to a halt after the revolt of Bahta Hagos (1894). The "Adwa complex" named after the site of Menilek II's defeat of a major invading Italian army (1896), gave way to a defensive policy of containment and appeasement with local authorities, which was to last until the late 1920s. In Somalia, an initial harsh military rule over the Benadir coast led to a mass-based revolt among the Bimal of the region, which eventually brought about a more acquiescent policy

of negotiation with local chiefs. In 1936, the proclamation of Italy's colonial Empire was followed by a very crude policy of repression, particularly of Ethiopian resistance, to be belatedly mitigated on the eve of the war.

Coupled with local factors promoting vacillation was the no less important factor of shifting metropolitan politics. The Italian Parliament of the liberal period, and public opinion at large in the country, were far from unanimous in their views on colonial adventures. Italy had from the start a strong anticolonial lobby that included minor but highly vocal spokesmen from the republican and socialist movements, the Catholic Church, and the business sector. Although the Italian government each time gathered a parliamentary majority and swept public opinion along through well-organized (and, during fascism, massive) media campaigns, the lack of a "colonial conscience" among state officials and the public at large weakened colonial policies and their implementation.

Partly as a consequence of this lack of consistent direction and support, Italy had to rely repeatedly on its militaries as the main executors and caretakers of the state's interests in the colonies. Both Eritrea and Somalia were run by the militaries until the 1900s. The War Ministry and the Ministry of Foreign Affairs were initially responsible for administering the colonies, and a Ministry of Colonies was founded only in 1912, after the conquest of Libya. The persistence of war operations throughout the colonial period (up to and including fascism) dictated a pervasive, and ruthless, persisting military presence. This meant that army personnel formulated first colonial policies and applied them according to strict military rules of obedience. Thus "pacification" (i.e., coercion) rather than civilian rule of negotiation and development. Several colonial governors were military men, as were two (out of three) viceroys of Ethiopia. The result was, on the whole, the imposition of a very harsh and hierarchical rule. The Italian presence in sub-Saharan Africa was thus characterized by a continuing dissonance between official state legislation and its actual implementation on the ground. Colonial policies—whether in regard to land settlements or economic production, racial legislation or codified social behavior—often remained mere proclamations separated from social practice. Military improvisation on the ground gave

Italian colonialism a "rugged" nature that lingered long after coherent civilian policies had developed elsewhere in colonial Africa.

Italy's African colonies were never the outlet for population pressures at home that successive Italian governments had hoped they would be, nor were they at any time economically profitable for government or for private investors. Although road infrastructure was greatly improved and land productivity increased, particularly in the 1930s, social investments were poor and public education almost nonexistent. African elites thus learned to grow outside the colonial system. With the end of World War II, Italy lost its colonies, although a ten-year United Nations trusteeship over Somalia allowed it to guide Somalia to independence in 1960.

See also **Addis Ababa; Colonialism and Imperialism; Haile Selassie I; Menelik II; United Nations.**

BIBLIOGRAPHY

Andall, Jacqueline, and Duncan, Derek, eds. *Italian Colonialism: Legacy and Memory*, Oxford-Berne: Peter Lang, 2005.

Del Boca, Angelo. *Gli italiani in Africa orientale.* 4 vols. Bari, Italy: Laterza, 1976–1984.

Goglia, Luigi, and Fabio Grassi. *Il colonialismo italiano da Adua all'impero.* Bari, Italy: Laterza, 1993.

Labanca, Nicola. *Oltremare: Storia dell'espansione coloniale italiana.* Bologna, Italy: Il Mulino, 2002.

Negash, Tekeste. *Italian Colonialism in Eritrea: Policies, Praxis and Impact.* Uppsala, Sweden: University of Uppsala, 1987.

Sbacchi, Alberto. *Legacy of Bitterness. Ethiopia and Fascist Italy, 1935–1941.* Lawrenceville-Asmara: Red Sea Press, 1997.

ALESSANDRO TRIULZI

PORTUGUESE

The Portuguese colonial empire in Africa, like the British and French empires but in sharp contradistinction to the German and Belgian empires, was carved out of territories that had had long commercial relations with the invaders in the centuries before the "scramble" for Africa in the 1880s and the subsequent military imposition of colonial rule during the period of 1890 to 1920. By the time the partition was completed on diplomatic maps,

Portugal had been recognized in Europe, though not as widely on the ground in Africa, as the ruler of five disparate territories: Cape Verde, Portuguese Guinea, São Tomé and Príncipe, Angola, and Mozambique.

The first and oldest Portuguese colony was the Cape Verde archipelago, a group of islands first settled in the 1440s by migrants from Iberia, the Canary Islands, and Senegambia who pioneered systems of tropical planting that were to have a long-standing influence on the European conquest of the world. Slave-grown sugar, indigo-dyed textiles, and intercontinental shipping services were provided by islanders who evolved their own distinctive culture and creolized language. By the twentieth century the islands had a Welsh coaling station for steamers, and local stevedores played cricket. The islands could not, however, support the growing population, and many worked on ships and emigrated to the Caribbean, New England, and, during the great droughts of the 1970s, to Europe. Some of the islanders gained skills in business and became entrepreneurs on the adjacent mainland from which their remote African ancestors had come. Others gained education and literacy and served the Portuguese as clerks, administrators, and even judges in other colonies. The colony in which the presence of emigrants from Cape Verde became most pervasive was Portuguese Guinea, sandwiched between French Guinea and the Casamance, on the islands, rivers, and creeks south of Senegambia.

Guinea-Bissau, so named after the small administrative post that became the twentieth-century colonial and postcolonial capital of the Portuguese mainland territory of West Africa, had been an international trading zone since the fifteenth century and had supplied Europe with ivory and gold and America with slave workers who subsisted on local rice during their Atlantic crossing. When the slave trade dwindled, local farmers took up peanut farming and supplied Portugal with a cheap alternative to olive oil. The colonial trade fell largely into the hands of one of Portugal's families of business tycoons that flourished under the protection of the monetarist dictator António Salazar, a Portuguese disciple of Benito Mussolini's corporatist ideology.

The domestic history of metropolitan Portugal had a profound effect on the colonies. In 1890, when the great powers were tightening their grip on Africa, Portugal seemed to be losing authority in its proclaimed zones of influence. Patriotism became linked to imperialism, and the failure of colonial ventures brought the hitherto stable constitutional monarchy of Queen Victoria's Portuguese Saxe-Coburg cousins into disrepute. A particularly fierce dispute with Britain occurred over the growing of cocoa of the islands of São Tomé and Príncipe, Portugal's third West African colony and one dating back to the 1470s. The cocoa was grown by slaves brought on contract from mainland Africa but in effect held on the plantations for life. When British chocolate manufacturers stopped buying the slave-grown cocoa, the revolutionary atmosphere in Portugal intensified. In 1908 the king was assassinated, and in 1910 the republicans gained power in Lisbon. Because Portugal had by then fallen behind northern Europe in modernizing its farming and diversifying its industry, the new government sought opportunity for its underemployed people in the colonies.

Petty clerks went from Portugal to Africa to take administrative posts previously held by local Africans and itinerant Cape Verdeans, and shopkeepers left home for the colonies to open country stores where they could sell cheap Portuguese wine for colonial peasant produce such as cotton, coffee, and groundnuts. The effect of these settlers on community relations was often harmful, as local people accused the hard-working but privileged diaspora of Portuguese immigrant tradespeople of unfair business practices. Republican colonization had the effect of heightening racial competition and antagonism. Furthermore, the colonists were predominantly male and fathered a mixed-race population that was often painfully caught between hostile white and black neighbors.

The republican era was experienced in rather contrasting ways in Portugal's two large colonies, Angola on the west coast of Central Africa and Mozambique on the east coast. In Angola a relatively strong government was established by a dynamic high commissioner, Norton de Matos, who had been a World War I general and was to become grand master of Portugal's freemasons and, a little ironically, a democratic challenger to the "fascist" dictator António Salazar in the 1940s. He used forced labor to build roads so that colonial maize could be hauled to the transcontinental, eucalyptus-burning railway

that the British built across Angola from copper mines in the southern Belgian Congo to Benguela on the Atlantic coast. He encouraged the investment of Belgian capital in the underutilized land and cheaply coerced labor that could be used to produce both cotton and coffee.

During this era Angola opened diamond mines under the protection of the marketing cartel of South Africa–based DeBeers and allowed local black mine labor to be imprisoned in compounds. Immigrant white fishermen were also given a supply of forced local laborers, which was taken to the desert outpost of the south where fish could be dried for export to the Congo copper mines. The republican state was so preoccupied with restoring Portugal's national finances, after being disastrously forced by Britain into taking part in World War I, that it extracted wealth from Angola without investing significantly in human development. Such educational, medical, and welfare services as were established came mainly from foreign missions, British, French, Swiss, or American, and it was these Christian communities that helped form the political structure of modern society in Angola.

Across the continent in Mozambique, the republican era was rather different. Before 1910 the Portuguese monarchy had recognized its inability to raise the capital necessary to administer and exploit the territories surrounding its old commercial ports on the Indian Ocean coast and had issued charters of colonization to private companies. In the far south the recruitment of labor was granted to a consortium of South African gold mines, the Witwatersrand Native Labor Association (WNLA), and able-bodied men were given the choice of leaving home to work on contract in the deep-level gold mines or staying in Mozambique to be pressed into service in the chain gangs that repaired the colonial roads, as convicts from Europe formerly had been.

To the north of the WNLA recruiting zone, Portugal gave an even more open license to foreign capital, and the Mozambique Company concessionary firm was given a charter that enabled it not only to recruit labor but also to raise taxes and quell rebellions with company police. The company exercised administrative oversight of the railway to Rhodesia and facilitated the harsh recruitment of farm labor for Southern Rhodesia's settlers, who survived in business by paying some of the lowest wages in the colonial world. Women were left behind in the company territory, but their work was also conscripted to help the company make a return on its outlay; they were forced to grow rice as a kind of tax crop for which they received minimal payment. Yet farther north in Mozambique other chartered licenses were issued and private-enterprise colonialism was at its harshest and least supervised. A foraging economy similar to that adopted by the Belgian king Léopold of the Congo developed before tea and sisal plantations were established.

The great turning point in the modern Portuguese empire came in 1930. Four years earlier a clique of conservative Catholic army officers had overthrown the republican government in the hope of stabilizing the finances of the nation, or at least of restoring the well-being of its armed forces. They rapidly found the economy running into yet greater difficulties with the world recession and the closing of both North and South America to emigration, thus ending remittances of migrant earnings. The junta therefore decided to give full powers to a Catholic journalist and economics professor, António Salazar, who would run the country as he saw fit on condition that the pay and status of officers of the armed forces were protected.

Professor Salazar adopted two strategies. The first was to cut drastically all government services and expenses at home and turn the majority of the population of the mother country into idealized peasant paupers without access to schools, clinics, roads, or salaried jobs, while fostering a small semi-privileged elite protected by a disciplined secret police and a network of community informants. The second strategy was to partially retrieve the colonies from the control of foreign capital and use them more efficiently and overtly than before to subsidize the national economy in Europe. During the 1930s and 1940s the strategy saw Portugal sink to an economic level comparable to Albania or the Gold Coast, and its colonies suffered some of the most austere conditions in Africa. Only after World War II did improvement begin as economic planning replaced pre-Keynesian monetarism.

The postwar boom in world commodity prices slowly began to attract Portuguese emigrants to Africa. In Mozambique a few of them became agrarian settlers and opened farms or managed sugar plantations, but the majority went to the towns and worked in the service sectors, notably railways and harbors, that were linked to British Africa. In Angola, by contrast, numbers of settlers went into coffee growing, marketing, and transporting, and the north of the country saw coffee go from being a black peasant crop to being a white plantation crop. The alienation of land, taken by white farmers in northern Angola from black farmers, and the recruitment of seasonal labor in southern Angola, led to ethnic animosity and a neo-ethnic political conflict that had repercussions throughout the twentieth century.

The coffee revenue was partly invested in colonial-style small industry and partly repatriated to Portugal, where construction and manufacturing underwent a minor boom in the 1950s. In 1961, however, a temporary recession brought such distress to African laborers living on the margins of the cash economy that rebellion broke out. Portugal's long-serving dictator was forced to use his hoarded gold reserves to finance an expeditionary army to reconquer northern Angola, and later to quell uprisings in Mozambique and Guinea as well. Salazar did not have the industrial capacity at home, or the assimilated local supporters in the colonies, to turn his military rule in Africa into a neocolonial economic partnership such as France and Britain had achieved. After reconquering the colonies Portugal therefore turned to the noncolonial powers of Africa, the United States, Germany, and Japan, for investment in agriculture, mining, manufacturing, and transport. This strategy brought stability for another ten years. After that, rebellion broke out again with renewed vigor. Only the American-dominated petroleum industry, an economic enclave of northern Angola, survived the long wars of intervention, destabilization, and regional competition.

See also **Angola; Benguela; Cabinda, Angola; Cape Verde; Colonialism and Imperialism; Economic History; Labor: Conscript Forced; Mozambique; Plantation Economies and Societies; Postcolonialism; São Tomé e Príncipe; Slave Trades; Transportation: Railways.**

BIBLIOGRAPHY

Birmingham, David. *A Concise History of Portugal.* Cambridge, U.K.: Cambridge University Press, 1993.

Birmingham, David. *Portugal and Africa*. Athens: Ohio University Press, 2004.

Birmingham, David. *Empire in Africa: Angola and Its Neighbors*. Athens: Ohio University Press, 2006.

Freudenthal, Aida Faria. "Angola." In *O Imperio Africano 1890–1930*, ed. A.H. de Oliveira Marques. Lisbon: Estampa, 2001.

Newitt, Malyn. *A History of Mozambique*. London: Hurst, 1995.

DAVID BIRMINGHAM

SPANISH

The Spanish colonization of Africa became a compensatory outlet for losing the colonies in America. At the end of the nineteenth century, Spanish Africanists started developing an ideology that viewed Africa as a continent representing a geological and "racial" extension of the Iberian Peninsula so its occupation would be legitimized. In this context, mercantile and politic interests for three territories that eventually became a protectorate (north and south of Morocco, 1912–1956) and two colonies (West Sahara, until 1975, and Equatorial Guinea, until 1968) were forged. This doctrine was maintained during different political regimes, but was consolidated under the National-Catholicism of Francisco Franco's regime. The overseas administration, generally controlled by military forces, was oriented to keep the civil order, rather than for socioeconomic exploitation, except in the case of Guinea and the Melilla war of 1909. The situation of the Moroccan and Saharan cases differed from the Guinean experience, since the policies in Guinea consisted of the enforcement of an explicit policy of religious and cultural assimilation.

In the northern zone of the protectorate of Morocco, indirect rule was possible only after 1927, due to existing armed resistance. The system was based upon a paid form of protection by the local authorities and a network of offices that exercised political control and served as a showcase of the so-called civilization. The impact in the socioeconomic area was very limited and, during seasons of famine, part of the peasant population enlisted in the colonial army, due to a lack of employment expectations.

It was precisely during the Spanish Civil War (1936–1939) that the *golpista* faction (in favor of Franco) recruited thousands of Moroccans. In order to justify the Spanish presence, a policy of respect toward Islam was promoted. In practice, however, it was based on the control of religious institutions and authorities, and a shift of strategy in favor of the Muslim brotherhoods, starting in the 1930s, as an opposing force to the nationalist urban reformism.

In the western Saharan territories, the political control of the nomad *qabíla-s* was not enforced until 1934. This was due to multiple factors: the difficulties in supervising populations living in vast desert lands; the effects of local factionalism, and the competition against the French to gain the loyalty of their respective clients. The main consequence was the consolidation of the power of tribes such as the Rgaybât, and the exclusion of others like the Awlâd Dalîm, both divided between the Spanish and French zones of the Sahara. The economic intervention in the zone was minor until the beginning of the exploitation of phosphates in Bu Craa (1963), but the political changes brought with them the transformation of the local systems of shepherding, trade, and military raids.

In the area that is present-day Equatorial Guinea the political and economic colonization developed after 1858 on the Fernando Poo Island (present-day Bioko). The domination strategy was based on military repression, the bribing of chiefs, or the encouragement of division between ethnic groups, mainly the Fang and the rest. The intervention in that territory revolved around a plantation economy (with forced contracts, forced recruits, and mandatory personal assistance) and an influential evangelization and conversion campaign, entrusted mainly to the Claretian missionaries. The other basic institutions of control were the Native Patronage Organization (1904), which was in charge of regulating the life of the Guinean, who were legally considered minors. Other regulations penalized polygamy and changed the family relationship structures (monogamy was a requirement to access to private property and political office) as well as the judicial ones, such as the Courts of the Race (1938).

See also **Colonialism and Imperialism; Economic History; Postcolonialism; Warfare.**

BIBLIOGRAPHY

Castro, Mariano de, and Donato Ndongo. *España en Guinea: Construcción del desencuentro: 1778–1968*. Madrid: Sequitur, 1998.

Felipe, Helena de, and Fernando Rodríguez Mediano, eds. *El Protectorado Español en Marruecos: Gestión colonial e identidades.* Madrid: CSIC, 2002.

López Bargados, Alberto. *Arenas Coloniales: Los Awlād Dalīm ante la colonización franco-española del Sáhara.* Barcelona: Edicions Bellaterra, 2003.

Mateo Dieste, Josep Lluís. *La "hermandad" hispano-marroquí: Política y religión bajo el Protectorado español en Marruecos.* Barcelona: Edicions Bellaterra, 2003.

JOSEP LLUÍS MATEO DIESTE

COLONIAL TRADITIONS AND INVENTIONS.

It is undeniable that, in postcolonial Africa, the importance of tradition as a means of legitimizing social institutions or as a rhetorical resource for designation of specific practices or entire social groups as either modern or traditional has increased rather than decreased. Thus, even in the early twenty-first century in many African countries, customary law is regarded to be legally on par with national and international law. In some post–civil war societies such as Mozambique, the jurisdiction of traditional authorities (chiefs) was expanded, even institutionalized, in order to attenuate political polarization and strengthen community cohesion. Elsewhere, too, chiefs assumed local government duties where central governments were either not willing or not able to provide the staff to perform them. Sometimes the appeal to genuine African political traditions also provided autocratic power elites with a pretense to suppress multiparty democracy and freedom of the press, at least according to the accusations voiced by the political opposition. In any event, tradition, whether characterized as invented or genuine, or as an obstacle to modernization or a robust heritage, is the subject of intense debate not only among historians and social scientists but also politicians, local intellectuals, and people involved in social movements.

THE COLONIAL INVENTION OF TRADITION

The scholarly debate on whether traditions are a product of colonial rule or the result of the *longue durée* of African social institutions was initiated by Terence Ranger's seminal article (1983), published in a volume alongside other case studies dealing mostly with nineteenth-century Europe and analyzing how neotraditions—invented by identifiable actors at identifiable points in time—helped to secure social stability and political domination in rapidly transforming societies. In colonial Africa, Ranger argued, the invention of tradition encompassed both the importation of European neotraditions and new African traditions, particularly those pertaining to tribes, customary law, and traditional religion that disguised innovation behind façades of continuity with ostensibly age-old indigenous beliefs and practices. And while precolonial African societies had once been characterized by competition, fluidity and orally transmitted custom, "loosely defined and infinitely flexible," the colonial constructs of tradition and customary law "became codified and . . . unable . . . to reflect change" (1983, 247–248, 251).

The studies that Ranger's assertions inspired focused at first on the role of invented traditions in cementing colonial authority and patriarchy. Male elders and chiefs used invented tribal traditions, and particularly codified customary law, to maintain control over young men (and their migrant-labor income), women, and immigrants. Chiefs and big men among the Chagga of Kilimanjaro, for instance, transformed precolonial norms and practices into customary law in ways that increased their wealth and power in the newly expanding colonial economy of cash-cropping, as Sally Falk Moore (1986) shows. Other anthropologists and historians analyzed the colonial invention of ethnicity. Emphasizing that many African "tribes" were not relics of a distant past, but rather recent creations, these studies argued that colonial ethnic categories defined group boundaries and cultural attributes much more rigidly than precolonial models of belonging that had been characterized by mobility, overlapping networks, multiple group membership, and the context-dependent drawing of boundaries.

THE DYNAMICS OF CUSTOMARY LAW AND THE LIMITS OF INVENTION

Leroy Vail's influential collection *The Creation of Tribalism in Southern Africa* (1989) marked the beginning of a more nuanced perspective on the colonial creation of tradition. Some contributions drew attention to not only colonial officers and African chiefs, but also broader segments of the population, being able to mobilize newly created traditions in their own interests. Labor migrants, for instance, had vested interests in rural tribes and "traditional" chiefs who would protect their wives and families during their absence, defend their land rights and, most vitally, in the face of urban insecurity, provide a home where to seek refuge during crises. Vail and others also began to examine the complexities of the interactions among, and controversies between, colonial administrators, Christian missionaries, European anthropologists, local educated elites, and chiefs in producing and popularizing a convincing body of tribal traditions and history. It became evident that the effectiveness of such inventions of history and the strategic manipulation of tradition by cultural brokers encountered their limits in the actual experiences and the historical imagination of the African population.

Taking these ideas further, Kristin Mann and Richard Roberts argued that the European capacity to invent and manipulate African traditions was limited, and colonial customary law not as inflexible as Ranger had suggested. Customary law, shaped by both Europeans and Africans, rather became a resource in "struggles over property, labor, power, and authority," and even an instrument "of African resistance, adaptation, and renewal, as well as of European domination" (1991, 3). Colonial rule remained "hegemony on a shoestring," and the colonial "invention" of African traditions "served not so much to define the shape of the colonial social order as to provoke a series of debates over the meaning and application of tradition, which in turn shaped struggles over authority and access to resources" (Berry 1993, 24). In a self-critical article (1993), Ranger himself cast doubt on the usefulness of the term "invention," because it overemphasized the mechanical and authorial, the role of European initiative, and the fictionality and rigidity of the created tradition. He suggested that a concept such as "imagination" may do more justice to the complex long-term process of creating new, and rearranging older, elements of ethnic identification, in which many actors, diverse motives, and a variety of interpretations are involved.

In the early twenty-first century, the discussion is focusing on precisely the limits of invention. Colonial constructions of tradition "were rarely without local historical precedents," and "ethnic concepts, processes, and politics predated the imposition of colonial rule" (Spear 2003, 4, 24–25). Rather than being

created from scratch, "older traditions were continually reinterpreted," and the heritage of the past was reconstituted "to meet the needs of the present." However, as important as it is to understand the longue durée of many African institutions, norms, and identifications, one must not overlook cases in which ethnicity, chieftaincy and other "traditions" venerated by colonial officers played no significant role prior to colonialism. It is necessary, then, to explore both the colonial creation of new traditions by multiple actors with diverse interests and the embeddedness of these new constructs in precolonial modes of social positioning and belonging.

AFRICAN CREATIVITY AND THE MAKING OF CONTINUITY

African engagement with imported institutions and constructs has been remarkably versatile. Studies have shown not only how different African groups appropriated the colonial constructs of "tribe" chiefdom, and customary law, but also how African strategies forced colonial administrators to reshape their political projects. The complexities of the colonial encounter become particularly evident in formerly "stateless" societies where the chieftaincy was introduced.

In northwestern Ghana, for instance, the precolonial political landscape was neither characterized by a strict hierarchy of permanent chiefdoms nor by a purely acephalous type of polity. Beyond local kin groups and earth-shrine areas—ritual congregations united through their sacrifices to the earth deities—locals and powerful outsiders developed networks of alliances and enmities between independent villages, individual strongmen, and, particularly in the nineteenth century, regionally operating Muslim slave-raiders. When British officers later asked for chiefs, it was often the slave-raiders' former mercenaries and the local strongmen who presented themselves as suitable candidates, hoping to benefit from cooperation with the colonial authorities. Symbols and rituals of chiefly office were modeled partly on colonial imports, partly on the paraphernalia of neighboring chiefdoms, and partly on reinterpreted local symbolic repertoires. Defining chiefly hierarchies, establishing the boundaries of new chiefdoms, and recruiting effective chiefs was a matter of trial and error, whereby existing local power structures and the British model of "native states" were gradually made to correspond to each other. However, all colonial attempts of shaping chiefdoms to conform with ethnic boundaries and of uniting the new small chiefdoms under a single "king" failed.

This entire process of the creation of chiefdoms in northwestern Ghana went hand in hand with the construction of new oral traditions and the reinterpretation of existing historical narratives. Colonial officers themselves were divided on the question of whether chieftaincy was a purely colonial innovation or whether the northwest had once been subject to kingdoms later destroyed by Muslim slave-raiders. Local oral traditions insist that the initiative in shaping the chieftaincy came from local actors, and that the colonial masters had only recognized existing power relations. However, opinions differ considerably as to whose power was acknowledged—that of the earth priests, or that of the independent strongmen. The question of what constitutes "authentic" local political tradition, egalitarian and prototypically democratic statelessness, or early forms of chieftaincy, was and is highly controversial and dependent upon competing aspirations for the future. Yet all agree that "chieftaincy has come to stay" and invoke tradition when criticizing the illegitimate machinations of "politics" brought to bear by national power elites in local succession disputes.

If tradition is regarded as not only the unreflected transmission of social practices and knowledge, but first and foremost as the strategic distinction and valuation of particular norms and stocks of knowledge, then strictly speaking no traditions are "invented," and all are "constructed." Colonial traditions are therefore simply a special case, in which external European actors deliberately intervened in the local (re)definition and valuation of past practices and institutions, whereby it is by no means certain that their version effectively became established. Nevertheless, the making of traditions in the colonial context is particularly suited to examine the relations of power that invariably come to play in all (re)constructions of tradition. At the same time, the analyses of historians, anthropologists, and social scientists are themselves enmeshed in these relations of power.

See also **Colonial Policies and Practices; Religion and Ritual; Symbols and Symbolism.**

BIBLIOGRAPHY

Berry, Sara. *No Condition Is Permanent: The Social Dynamics of Agrarian Change in Sub-Saharan Africa.* Madison: University of Wisconsin Press, 1993.

Kratz, Corinne. "We've Always Done It Like This... Except for a Few Details: 'Tradition' and 'Innovation' in Okiek Ceremonies." *Comparative Studies in Society and History* 35 (1993): 30–65.

Lentz, Carola. *Ethnicity and the Making of History in Northern Ghana.* Edinburgh: Edinburgh University Press, 2006.

Mann, Kristin, and Richard Roberts, eds. *Law in Colonial Africa.* London: James Currey, 1991.

Moore, Sally Falk. *Social Facts and Fabrications: "Customary" Law on Kilimanjaro, 1880–1980.* Cambridge, U.K.: Cambridge University Press, 1986.

Ranger, Terence. "The Invention of Tradition in Colonial Africa." In *The Invention of Tradition*, ed. Eric Hobsbawm and Terence Ranger. Cambridge, U.K.: Cambridge University Press, 1983.

Ranger, Terence. "The Invention of Tradition Revisited: The Case of Colonial Africa." In *Legitimacy and the State in Twentieth-Century Africa*, ed. Terence Ranger and Olufemi Vaughan. London: Macmillan, 1993.

Shils, Edward. *Tradition.* Chicago: University of Chicago Press, 1981.

Spear, Thomas. "Neo-Traditionalism and the Limits of Invention in British Colonial Africa." *Journal of African History* 44 (2003): 3–27.

CAROLA LENTZ

COLONIALISM AND IMPERIALISM

This entry includes the following articles:
OVERVIEW
THE AFRICAN EXPERIENCE
CONCESSIONARY COMPANIES

OVERVIEW

The words "colonialism" and "imperialism" cannot be used without invoking their highly politicized pasts. They did not always have negative connotations: European statesmen once proudly proclaimed their imperial reach, insisting that they brought economic progress to the world and relief from backwardness and despotism to Africa. In the 1930s European nations mounted public exhibitions to display the accomplishments of colonization—vivid demonstrations of power, of good works, and of the ability of the colonizing state to integrate diverse but unequal cultures into a harmonious whole. Yet colonialism was also under attack even before European powers consolidated their rule over most of Africa in the early twentieth century. Europe's role as colonizer is often invoked for contradictory purposes: in assertions of Europe's responsibility for extreme forms of inequality and dehumanization and in forms of colonial nostalgia and apology.

Imperialism—the exercise of power by a state beyond its borders—is much older than Europe itself and has taken many forms, from the Romans' conquest of territory around the Mediterranean, to the imperialism of free trade exercised by Great Britain in the early nineteenth century, to the power of large corporations and industrial nations in the early twenty first century. Colonialism—the erection by a state of an apparatus of administrative control over peoples who are defined as distinct—is a specific form of imperialism, and it too has a long history.

Prior to the late nineteenth century, various imperial countries nibbled at the edges of Africa, but rarely did these conquering nations penetrate inland and more rarely still did they try to alter African societies. Before this time, the effects of Europe's economic power—demonstrated through trade in slaves, ivory, gold, and other commodities—were widely though unevenly felt in Africa, influencing but not determining the political and economic structures of coastal and inland communities. Colonialism in the late nineteenth century was self-consciously interventionist. After the Industrial Revolution, the advancement of military technologies and the self-confidence of bourgeois culture gave European elites a sense that their ways of organizing life stood not only for might but also for progress. Africa became an object of reformist imperialism because it could be portrayed as a slavery-ridden continent that was held in check by tyrants and isolated from the beneficial effects of commerce.

This kind of European imperialism soon became the object of critique, for a contradiction lay at its heart. Bourgeois ideology in nineteenth-century Europe derived its power from its claims to universality—to the superiority of the free market, the rationalist heritage of the Enlightenment, the orderly structures of states, and the rightness of self-rule—but colonization necessarily implied the rule of one particular people over another. The late-nineteenth-century conquest of Africa brought forth critics of imperialist violence and exploitation—and some doubts about the wisdom of intervention itself—and by the middle of the twentieth

century, imperialism was being challenged ever more strongly from within and without.

The questioning of imperialism in twentieth-century Europe was sparked in part by Marxism, but Karl Marx himself had a profoundly ambiguous role in this process. He was committed to the idea of progress and saw capitalism as a step toward an eventual socialist world. In his writings on India, he portrayed the British conquest as both a horrific reflection of greed and inhumanity and as an unintentionally progressive step that quashed the backwardness of Hindu culture and opened up the possibility of a capitalist, and later a socialist, future.

The issue of imperialism confronted political theorists with important questions about Europe itself. J. A. Hobson, a British liberal, viewed imperialism as a consequence of underconsumption in metropolitan economies: he argued that by keeping workers' wages as low as possible but investing profits in increased production, capitalists created domestic markets that could not sufficiently absorb their ever-expanding capacity. Capitalists therefore turned to their respective governments to find and protect new markets and maintain privileged access to resources, resulting in competition over the control of foreign territory. Hobson's argument was a plea for improving the standard of living of the English working class in order to stave off deadly wars among rival colonizers.

Vladimir Lenin brought much of Hobson's argument and data back into the Marxist fold, insisting that imperialism did not reflect a remediable flaw of European society but rather an inherent characteristic of a stage of capitalism. He directed much of his polemic against social democratic theories about reform in Europe, which he regarded as part of an imperialist effort to buy off members of the working class with the sweat and blood of conquered peoples abroad. Capitalism in colonies, for Lenin, was not a progressive but a parasitic force. Attached to the Soviet project, Lenin's arguments had a mixed impact, for they were later both mobilized and contradicted by the Soviet Union's shifting foreign policy.

Lenin's argument resonated among—and to a significant extent was radicalized by—many colonial intellectuals in Africa, for it made sense of the exploitation they perceived in colonial economies in the early and mid-twentieth century. For them, colonization was an extractive process, producing superprofits for capitalists in remote wealthy metropoles, misery for local workers, and stagnation for colonial economies. But opponents to colonial rule could also be found in local communities, in regional networks of religious shrines, and in Islamic polities that had consolidated in the eighteenth and nineteenth centuries. Especially in coastal West Africa, Christian, Western-educated elites were marginalized by a European intrusion that claimed to represent values of Christianity and liberal politics. Such elites sometimes tried to find their ways within niches in the colonial system, while merchants and farmers often tried to turn colonial structures to their own interests.

Most people, however, were thwarted by the contradictions of colonial rule itself: the hypocrisy of a politics that professed rationality and individuality but discriminated against individuals on the grounds of race; that spoke in the name of the free market, but acted through arbitrary regulation and monopolies; and that claimed Christian virtues but stunted the development of an autonomous personality. African critics of colonialism, like James Africanus Beale Horton and Edward Wilmot Blyden, emerged even while African states and communities were still trying to stave off or come to grips with the colonizing onslaught. Colonization never went uncontested: it was challenged in a multiplicity of idioms in Europe and in Africa, through different forms of mobilization, via efforts at selective appropriation as well as outright resistance.

Until roughly the 1980s, scholarly writing on colonialism took colonial projects as a given framework, whether evaluated positively or negatively. Colonial enterprises have been praised as innovative, condemned as exploitative, or written off as contributing little to the development of African economies or to capital accumulation in Europe—as a mere "episode" in African history. Much African history written after 1960 was constructed against the traditions of imperial history, both its critical and apologetic strands. Africanists on and off the continent wanted to help build a past usable for an Africa weakened by colonialism, one that would give integrity to Africa's own institutions and cultures and put the contemporary task of nation-building in the context of a longer African history of innovation and adaptation. Precolonial Africa and resistance were worthy subjects for this

nationalist historiography, but what Africans resisted was often treated as obvious—as oppression incarnate—and not worthy of the same kind of culturally attuned analysis received by other aspects of African society.

The fact that economic dependence outlived colonialism's end in the 1960s gave new life to theories of imperialism. In the early 1970s, a West Indian scholar and activist, Walter Rodney, placed colonial rule in the wider context of European economic power, arguing that the "underdevelopment" of Africa began with the slave trade and that the African states and elites that participated in it became addicted to forms of commerce that distorted local economic growth and tied African leaders to a subordinate position in the world economy. Economic dependence had preceded as well as survived colonization.

Rodney's argument remained within the tradition of seeing imperialism in economic terms. Some scholars argue, however, that both the economic causes and effects of imperialism in Africa have been overstated. Far from being a necessary focus of European commercial interests, Africa received very little capital investment from its colonizers, and investors concentrated on just a few places and commodities. Scholars have also explained British involvement in Africa as a necessary side effect of its strategic interests in India, in the Suez Canal, and in Egypt—the vital communications line of the Empire. Britain's attitude, in this analysis, was strictly defensive: to keep other colonizers away from the Nile and retain trading areas established earlier. Even so, Britain did end up with some of the choicest territory.

If Great Britain consolidated its advantages from an earlier imperialism of free trade by claiming territory in Africa, other European states regarded Africa as a resource useful for catching up to the British. France, Germany, Belgium, Italy, and Portugal may have followed fantasies of future economic potential—and fears of being preempted by others—more than current interests. Portugal, relatively poor among European countries, was perhaps the most economic of imperialists; achieving state control over resources in African colonies was the only way for its firms to compete. Several historians have added that the causes of imperialism should not be sought exclusively in Europe but also in Africa itself, since the conflicts between Africans and Europeans gave rise to tensions and insecurities that limited advancing trade frontiers and brought about a radical European intervention to redefine the terms of interaction in the colonizers' favor.

Economic interests, from another perspective, were mediated by the perceptions of publics and elites. In Europe at the end of the nineteenth century, governments were beginning to face the social dislocations of industrialization; consequently, organizing the seemingly chaotic communities— abroad as well as at home—now made political sense. Crucial to making intervention plausible was imperial propaganda, especially after reports of David Livingstone's voyages of the early 1860s contrasted commerce, Christianity, and civilization in Europe with slavery, tyranny, and insecurity in Africa.

As soon as any European power moved into a part of Africa, others were likely to follow for fear of losing future opportunities. In that way, tentative, low-cost initiatives in the 1870s evolved into the "scramble" for Africa. Yet in spite of the rivalries, a collective cultural arrogance shared by European colonizers asserted itself. At the Berlin Conference of 1884 and again at the Brussels Conference of 1889–1890, these European powers set out rules for claiming territory in Africa and agreed on the duties of a colonizing power: preventing Africans from trading in slaves, arms, or liquor. Africans were perceived as disorderly and incapable of self-control or economic progress, and Europeans were viewed as responsible and disciplined.

But if European states arrogated to themselves the right to alter the economic and political lives of Africans, the extent to which the colonizers could actually determine the direction of change was much less clear. Despite its lesser power, wealth, and global influence, Africa had a critical role in shaping its encounter with Europe. Africa, in fact, remains one of the most important examples worldwide of the limits of the forced imposition of European culture and capitalism. Studies of both western and eastern Africa, for instance, show the failure of early British efforts to implement antislavery ideology in order to turn African slaveowners into capitalist landlords and slaves into workers. The colonial state was unable to produce the social or economic forms it sought. Instead,

slaves and slaveowners forged new forms of production by reconstituting less oppressive but still unequal relationships. Some ex-slaves also found niches for themselves in the colonial cash economy, where they could minimize dependence on both their employers and their former masters.

The most successful effort at forcing Africans into a subordinate role in a capitalist economy occurred in South Africa. Oppression there depended not only on the program of racial engineering of the 1890s and 1900s, but also on the presence of a settler population from an earlier period—before the discovery of diamonds in the 1860s and gold in the 1880s gave a new impetus to British involvement. White Europeans' presence in the country allowed them to form a class of capitalists and managers who were conscious of their racial distinctiveness, as well as a bureaucracy that could control the movement of Africans between wage-labor jobs and increasingly miserable lives in rural "reserves." Colonialism became internalized, and a white-run Union of South Africa became independent in 1910. Although the Rhodesias, Kenya, Côte d'Ivoire, and Mozambique also had European settler communities, these nations did not achieve South Africa's version of white domination and capitalist development. In nineteenth-century Algeria, France built a colonial society similar to South Africa on a territory considered an integral part of France itself. European immigrants from around the Mediterranean as well as from France were defined as French citizens, in contrast to the majority Muslim resident population of Algeria, who were deemed "subjects" and denied the rights of citizens.

Some of the economic successes of colonial regimes in Africa came about more through African than European agency. For example, the vast expansion of cocoa production in the Gold Coast at the turn of the twentieth century, in Nigeria starting in the 1920s, and in Côte d'Ivoire beginning in the 1940s took place in the absence of colonial initiatives to develop this natural resource. Colonizers generally had difficulty inducing Africans to produce cash crops. Africans also were reluctant to sell their labor except in small units of time, a tactic designed to straddle a village economy with few cash resources and a wage-labor economy that offered minimal wages and security. This reluctance was probably more important than colonial strategies in forcing wage labor into a largely migrant mold. Most

Africans worked for European employers for only a year or two. Rural resources not only kept urban and industrial wages low, but also made recruitment insecure and reduced employers' control over the production process.

The geography of economic colonialism was therefore highly uneven. Islands of cash-crop production, wage-labor agriculture, and mining were surrounded by vast labor catchment areas in which coercion and lack of economic alternatives were necessary if Europeans were to recruit any laborers at all. These spatial limitations of colonial rule also held true politically. The conquerors could concentrate military force to defeat African armies or "pacify" villages, but the routinization of power often demanded alliances with local authority figures, be they lineage heads or recently defeated kings. Any supposed distinction between British "indirect rule" and French "association" was less significant than the political realities on the ground, in which sparse colonial personnel relied consistently on collaborators among their supposed African "subjects."

In recent years, the study of colonialism has largely moved away from the questions of political economy that were raised in the 1970s toward a focus on European projects of cultural transformation and their complex effects: the "colonization of the mind," as it is sometimes termed. Literary as well as historical scholarship has pointed out that European national or continental self-representations depended on ascribing "otherness" to non-European populations. An Africa of tribes and tradition was set against a Europe of technology and progress that was coupled with a version of Christianity linked to the individual seeking salvation and its earthly benefits. European missionaries played a profoundly influential role in education, especially when compared to the feeble efforts of colonial states until near the end of the colonial era, even in the case of the secular Republican French government.

Such analyses demonstrate how deeply colonialism was woven into what it meant to be European and help to explain competing visions and tensions among colonizers. From the European side, it was not always clear whether the idea of civilization was meant to be a project for raising Africans in a European image or a standard that Africans could never truly meet and which therefore legitimated the colonial hierarchy. From the African side, the

question is what Africans actually thought about the symbolic structure of colonial power or European civilization. The cultural edifice of the West could be taken apart brick by brick by Africans and parts of it could be used to shape quite different cultural visions of their own. The growth of messianic Christian cults, which turned the missionaries' message of deliverance upside down, was only one example of this process. For young people, education and wage labor could be used as a means to subvert patriarchal authority within African communities and maneuver among different secular and religious institutions in colonial society. Literacy in a European language could be a means to record and pass on indigenous conceptions of history and a tool to make claims on European and African authorities. As studies of cultural and social change have deepened, a scholarly trend that began with the duality of European modernity and African tradition has had to confront the artificiality of such dichotomies and acknowledge the complex bricolages that Africans actually assembled out of various practices and beliefs.

An historical perspective on the colonial experience that focuses on the interaction of Africans and Europeans points to a schematic but useful periodization. The early colonial period, around 1900, witnessed attempts at systematically imposed change as well as crude and violent forms of appropriation—most notoriously in King Léopold's Congo and Portuguese Angola—but both methods underestimated the ability of Africans to flee, resist, or selectively assimilate. By World War I, European powers had served notice on one another that their worst excesses were giving imperialism a bad name around the world and endangering order in the colonies, but they had also discovered that African society was not going to be remade easily. In the interwar period, Great Britain, most notably, had the temerity to assert that its failures were actually a deliberate strategy of indirect rule—to conserve African social and cultural forms while slowly purging them of their unacceptable features (such as witchcraft) and adapting them to export economies. The Africa being conserved, of course, was more the product of the previous two decades than that of timeless tradition.

During the Great Depression of the 1930s, the mediocrity of Africa's colonial transformation allowed officials to diffuse the problems of lowered earnings and reduced employment in the cities into the surrounding countryside. The midcentury colonial crisis began with a partial economic recovery in the late 1930s and it exploded during and after World War II. By then, France and Great Britain, especially, saw a heightened need for the resources of their empires to rebuild their domestic economies. They faced challenges, however, not only from opposition movements within Africa and the West Indies but also from their war allies, who saw "self-determination" as a primary aim of the war: to demonstrate that colonized people could find progress under a European aegis.

In response to this imperative, Great Britain and France began "development" drives in 1940 and 1946, respectively. These drives also countered mounting protests from African wage laborers, who found that development within the confines of the narrow colonial infrastructure resulted in escalating prices and little prospect for improvement in their lives. A wave of strikes, beginning in 1935 in British Africa and in 1946 in French Africa, was countered by government attempts to move from migrancy to "stabilization" and to invoke the experience of managing class conflict in Europe to incorporate Africans into the social order in a more controllable way. Doing so meant making a discursive as well as an economic break with the past, starting to think of Africans as potentially modern people. Meanwhile, the attempts to impose a scientific and dynamic vision of agriculture—such as projects to reduce soil erosion—through characteristically coercive colonial methods mobilized opposition in many rural areas. Only after World War II did images of backward Africa and progressive Europe became a program for action rather than a representation of hierarchy—and such a conception soon proved to be costly.

Once again, colonial intervention generated conflict without leading to the breakthrough in economic structure promised by the top-down conception of development. Whether nationalist efforts were strong enough to overthrow colonial rule by themselves is unclear, but social movements of a variety of sorts—from labor unions to anti-conservation movements to consumer revolts—were escalating and coalescing into coherent anticolonial forces, sometimes in conflict with one another. Unable to gain control of Africa, European powers began to think more seriously about the Africa that actually existed. Its potential had to be compared with the alternative possibilities of making additional investments in a Europe that was moving toward closer commercial integration. By the mid–1950s, as France and Great Britain calculated that the costs of colonial rule outweighed the benefits, the possibility of negotiating a disengagement and a positive postcolonial relationship with African elites began to seem more attractive than the political risks and socioeconomic uncertainties of continued colonial rule.

Decolonization meant both a devolution of political power and an abdication of responsibility for the consequences of what Europe had unleashed. Belgium joined the exodus in 1960, leaving the Congo to an ill-prepared future that proved predictably traumatic. Portugal intensified its efforts to extract resources from its empire, exacerbating local resistance and inviting international opprobrium throughout the 1960s. Settler colonists in Zimbabwe held out even longer, until 1980, while white-ruled South Africa became a public pariah (although often a private partner) of Western states until its ability to maintain order at home and connections abroad collapsed in the 1980s and early 1990s.

What followed colonial rule, some scholars say, was not true independence but neocolonialism. The trouble with this concept is that it offers a simple answer where a good question is in order: how is power exercised over formally sovereign states? Relatively weak African states confronted this question in a changing world: the "advanced" as well as the "postcolonial" state was at issue, as was the significance in international politics of multinational corporations and international organizations, such as the World Bank and the International Monetary Fund. But in Africa sovereignty changed the way in which states articulated their missions and the way in which leaders defined their relationship to followers. The once-colonial idea of development became a concept adopted by newly independent nations, with financial and investment policies directed toward national ends.

In African countries, social groups linked to those in power obtained privileged access to resources, often international investments. Colonial and postcolonial development shared a statist orientation and a tendency to claim superior knowledge to be used for the benefit of a peasantry whose ideas were not solicited. Both versions initially achieved positive results, in the form of longer life spans, improved literacy, and the opening up of opportunities to a larger portion of the population, but the development process did not provide the economic strength or autonomy to help Africa through the world economic crisis of the 1970s and 1980s, when much of the former gains were erased. But the burst of citizen activism in colonial Africa in the 1940s and 1950s (and in the 1970s through 1990s in southern Africa), combined with the longer-term ability of Africans to refashion or hold at arms length the changes imposed on them, should continue to serve as reminders that structures of power can indeed be pried apart.

See also **Africa, History of the Name; Blyden, Edward Wilmot; Colonial Policies and Practices; Decolonization; History of Africa; Horton, James Africanus Beale; International Monetary Fund; Livingstone, David; World Bank; World War I; World War II.**

BIBLIOGRAPHY

Aveneri, Schlomo, ed. *Karl Marx on Colonialism and Modernization.* Garden City, NY: Doubleday, 1968.

Boahen, A. Adu, ed. *UNESCO General History of Africa: Africa under Colonial Domination.* Berkeley: University of California Press, 1985.

Cain, P. J., and A. G. Hopkins. *British Imperialism, 1688–2000,* 2nd edition. London: Longman, 2003.

Comaroff, Jean, and John Comaroff. *From Revelation to Revolution.* 2 vols. Chicago: University of Chicago Press, 1997.

Conklin, Alice. *A Mission to Civilize: The Republican Idea of Empire in France and West Africa, 1895–1930.* Stanford, CA: Stanford University Press, 1997.

Cooper, Frederick. *Colonialism in Question: Theory, Knowledge, History.* Berkeley: University of California Press, 1997.

Cooper, Frederick. *Africa since 1940: The Past of the Present.* Cambridge, U.K.: Cambridge University Press, 2002.

Hobson, J. A. *Imperialism: A Study.* New York: Garden Press, 1975.

Lenin, V. I. *Imperialism: The Highest Stage of Capitalism.* New York: International Publishers, 1969.

Marseille, Jacques. *Empire colonial et capitalisme français: Histoire d'un divorce.* Paris: Albin Michel, 1984.

Mazrui, Ali, ed. *UNESCO General History of Africa: Africa since 1935.* Berkeley: University of California Press, 1993.

McKittrick, Meredith. *To Dwell Secure: Generation, Christianity, and Colonialism in Ovamboland.* Portsmouth, NH: Heinemann, 2002.

Robinson, Ronald, and John Gallagher. *Africa and the Victorians: The Climax of Imperialism in the Dark Continent.* New York: St. Martin's Press, 1961.

Rodney, Walter. *How Europe Underdeveloped Africa.* London: Bogle-L'Ouverture, 1972.

Said, Edward W. *Culture and Imperialism.* New York: Knopf, 1993.

Stora, Benjamin. *Algeria 1830–2000: A Short History.* Trans. by Jane Marie Todd. Ithaca, NY: Cornell University Press, 2001.

Thomas, Lynn. *Politics of the Womb: Women, Reproduction, and the State in Kenya.* Berkeley: University of California Press, 2003.

FREDERICK COOPER

THE AFRICAN EXPERIENCE

Colonial rule in Africa was a culmination of the late-nineteenth-century European invasion, partition, and conquest of the continent. The manner in which these imperialist aggressions unfolded, and the experience of African societies under the system instituted by the conquerors for the consummation of their objectives, are the concern of this essay.

THE NATURE OF IMPERIALISM

Shorn of its Hobsonian and Marxist-Leninist theorizings, imperialism is essentially about the establishment of dominion or rule (imperium), usually, but not necessarily, by an alien power over peoples of another stock, for the purposes of expanding the commerce and other economic interests of the imperial power; for the promotion of its political and strategic interests; or sometimes solely for the sake of prestige. Imperialism is thus generally exploitative and aggressive. Ancient imperial powers like Egypt, Assyria, and Rome not only erected boastful memorials to their conquests, they paraded the loot and imposts exacted from subject peoples. The deeds of European empire builders and proconsuls in Africa were little different, no matter the claims of the "civilizing mission" myth.

European imperialism in Africa evolved in two major phases. The first, more aggressive and violent, began with the European "scramble" for African territory and ended with the continent's partition and conquest. The second phase saw the institution of imperialism into a system—colonialism—by which the continent was organized and administered for maximum economic exploitation. It is significant that these events occurred before Africa had had time to recover from the ravages of what was arguably the most tragic episode in human history, the slave trade. For Africa, colonialism was thus, in a sense, a continuation of the slave trade in other ways—the exploitation of the black peoples in situ.

Imperialism in the colonial phase was, however, not entirely without some benefits, such as new infrastructures or, in some localities, new economic opportunities. But it would be an exaggeration to conclude that these palliatives transformed an essentially economic venture into a philanthropic enterprise. In this regard, it is instructive to note that a century or so prior to the 1880s, Africa had witnessed a genuine European philanthropic initiative directed at repairing the ravages of the slave trade. Under the inspiration and leadership of the British antislavery and evangelical movements, and with substantial support from government circles, it was decided to bring Christian civilization to Africa. A colony for freed slaves was founded in Sierra Leone in 1787, and in 1841 an elaborate expedition sponsored by the British government was dispatched to establish a Christian agricultural community on the Niger (in modern Nigeria). Meanwhile, a crusade of sorts by Christian missionaries from all over Europe was making its way to different parts of the African continent to convert the people and propagate Western culture.

The potentials of these humanitarian projects for meaningful change in Africa can be gauged from the results that were becoming manifest along the western African coast by the 1850s. A Western-educated elite was gradually emerging, its members assuming positions of responsibility and eminence in the church, in business, in the professions, and from the 1880s, in the governance of European colonies like the Gold Coast and Lagos. It was at this point, when Africans were starting to adopt and adapt European civilization, and to play a role in the "civilizing" programs designed by the West, that a change in European policy began.

Where Africans had hitherto been accepted as human beings—"benighted" but capable of being civilized—they were now regarded as subhuman, fit only to be conquered and despoiled. This new attitude soon infected even the European missionaries, who henceforth, quite unjustly and on account of racial arrogance, denied otherwise qualified Africans leadership positions in the church. By and large, humanitarianism thereafter became a cover for predatory aggression.

PATTERNS OF EUROPEAN IMPERIAL EXPANSION

Four major factors influenced the pattern of European expansion in Africa before the "scramble": European traders, Christian missionaries, British antislavery patrols off the coasts of Africa, and the situation within the African states. Following the late-fifteenth-century initial Portuguese contact, the first European settlements in Africa were established by traders. These included Saint-Louis in Senegal, Bathurst (Banjul) in present-day Gambia, and the famous Gold Coast forts of Cape Coast and Elmina. The relationship between the traders and their African hosts was regulated by treaties, and in the course of time the Europeans, like the Muslim traders in the medieval Sudan, began to exert some measure of cultural influence on neighboring communities. This was particularly marked in the Gold Coast, where in 1844 Governor George Maclean negotiated a number of "bonds" empowering the British to participate in the administration of justice in the Fante states.

The traders generally preferred to be independent of their home governments. Nevertheless, they naturally turned to the latter whenever their security was threatened. Hence there was the occasional gunboat to overawe menacing African neighbors. This practice, as well as the conclusion of treaties of "commerce and friendship," sometimes with extraterritorial clauses, became common from the 1820s. Similarly, with the commencement of British antislavery naval patrols, a new phase in Afro-European relations came into being. Britain, followed by France and Germany, appointed consuls at strategic points along the coast, or wherever, as in Zanzibar and the bights of Bénin and Biafra, commercial interests or political considerations dictated such a course. The "informal empire" of the trader was thus being reinforced by the influence of the consul supported by military muscle. It was this combination that brought about the deposition of King Kosoko of Lagos in 1851. Across the continent in the Sultanate of Zanzibar, British consuls and political agents had similarly succeeded in converting that state into a quasi-protectorate of their government by the 1860s.

Although European settlement in coastal Africa was pioneered by traders, it was Christian missions that extended imperial influence inland before the "scramble." As outposts of European civilization the mission stations were, according to Sir Harry Hamilton Johnston, a British imperialist agent, "essay[s] in colonization." The missionaries mediated the disputes of host communities and acted as intermediaries between them and the advancing imperialist agencies. Yet neither this nor Christian charity prevented them from sometimes communicating vital intelligence to the invading European armies or inviting military expeditions against states that resisted Christian proselytizing. The Christian missions were, above all, a disruptive force, partly because of their iconoclastic attitude to African culture and partly because their converts usually renounced the authority of their chiefs while advocating the institution of European rule, which they expected to advance the spread of the Gospel and facilitate the development of commerce and Western civilization.

Remarkably, African rulers developed no common policy toward European incursion, even though many of them had a network of diplomatic ties. While empires like Asante and Bénin tried to regulate or ban contact with Europeans, most coastal states had become too dependent on overseas trade to contemplate this course. Moreover, interstate and local tensions enabled the Europeans to recruit African allies.

Thus, until the late 1870s, the trader, the consul, and the missionary were the main agencies of European expansion. It is important to add that for the most part, their activities lacked the brazen aggressiveness that characterized the advent of the "scramble." It is not easy to explain the change, but in addition to traders and missionaries, Africa was now attracting other kinds of Europeans: merchant adventurers, railway engineers, entrepreneurs, and soldiers—ruthless and, for the most part, unscrupulous men who had little sympathy

with the earlier humanitarian dream of re-creating European culture in Africa. Convinced that the era of free trade was at the end, they urged their governments to secure colonies that would serve as sources of raw materials as well as markets for manufactured goods. Meanwhile, the policy makers in Europe, who had hitherto been reluctant to commit themselves to imperial expansion, were now becoming more responsive to the advocates of colonial possessions at home as well as apostles of empire in Africa itself.

The international European rivalry that heralded the "scramble" started in western Africa as a duel between the French and the British, first for control of the Niger Basin and subsequently for the acquisition of the coastal territories between present-day Sierra Leone and Bénin. By 1882 France had succeeded in linking its bases in the Senegal and Upper Niger Valleys, and George Taubman Goldie, the British proprietor of the Royal Niger Company, had in 1884 bought out his French rivals and secured the Lower Niger for Britain.

Almost simultaneously, a four-way conflict involving King Léopold of Belgium, France, Britain, and Portugal was raging over the Congo Basin. While King Léopold and France established posts on opposite banks of the river, Britain and Portugal struck a pact in 1884 reasserting the latter's historic claim to the mouth of the river. Meanwhile Otto von Bismarck, the German chancellor, had joined the race for African colonies by staking claims to territories in eastern Africa, southwestern Africa, Togo, and Cameroon.

The "scramble" was now in full swing. Apart from the diplomatic wrangles, alliances, and intrigues which it generated among the European powers, Africa was invaded by adventurers of all sorts intent on inducing rulers to sign treaties purporting to cede their countries to this or that European power. The Berlin Conference of November 1884 to February 1885 eventually drew up rules regulating the procedure for annexing the territories covered by the treaties and other claims while avoiding intra-European conflict. Except for the recognition by the powers of a new and "sovereign" state (albeit under King Léopold II of Belgium), in the Congo Basin, the actual partitioning began after the conference, through bilateral agreements which took several years to negotiate. Only Emperor Menilek II of Ethiopia, of all African rulers, participated in the partitioning even though he was not invited to the congress. He won this signal distinction by his defeat of the invading Italian forces at Adwa in 1896, thereby saving his country and thereafter embarking on expansionist moves of his own, on the basis of which he concluded boundary agreements with Britain, France, and Italy between 1897 and 1908. In western Africa, the British and the French settled the boundaries of their respective colonies in two phases: 1887 to 1889, and 1892 to 1895. And in eastern Africa, the sultan of Zanzibar's dominions along with the other polities were partitioned between Britain and Germany in the years 1886 to 1890.

Meanwhile, from the late 1870s, the tempo of advancing European imperialism had begun to cause disquiet among African peoples. From the Senegal to the Upper and Lower Niger Basins, as well as in the Congo and east-central Africa, there were apprehensions that the Europeans were out to seize the land. The local conflicts and armed skirmishes that thus developed were subsequently transformed into full-scale wars as European armies invaded Africa to make good their territorial claims in conformity with the Berlin Conference principle of "effective occupation." Although the African forces enjoyed numerical advantage, the outcome of the protracted wars was generally decided by the piecemeal nature of the campaigns; the fact that interstate rivalries enabled European armies to secure African allies; and the superiority of European weapons such as the Gatling and Maxim guns. That African armies gave good accounts of themselves is evident from victories by the Zulu (1879), the Hehe (1891), and the Ethiopians (1896) over European forces. But the ferocity and heroism of the resistance were no match for the ruthlessness and brutality of the invading forces. By the eve of World War I the whole of the continent except Ethiopia and Liberia had been overrun. But even as the conquest was in progress, European imperialism was moving into its next phase—colonialism.

THE COLONIAL ORDER

Pro-imperialism treatises usually represent colonialism as a crusade armed with a blueprint for the development of Africa. In reality the system was designed to promote imperial interests and maintain a level of colonial law and order conducive to maximum economic exploitation. But partly as an afterthought, and by way of rationalizing their activities, the imperial rulers began to advertise colonialism as a humanitarian mission. Yet, the main instrument for securing African acquiescence in the new order was force. Colonial armies and constabularies were organized, into which such Africans as the Zulu, the Somali, and the Hausa (martial races, according to colonial myth) were recruited.

The new order was anchored on two institutions: the colonial economy and the colonial state. The latter was often an amalgam of two or more indigenous polities, its borders sometimes splitting peoples who had hitherto been political and cultural units between different European colonial administrations. Thus, whereas the traditional African state was more or less a community with reciprocal interests, the colonial state at its inception was usually an artificial entity put together for administrative convenience. An important feature of the new state was the urban center, which, for peoples with dispersed settlement patterns like the Igbo (Ibo) and the Gikuyu, was an innovation. The towns eventually became administrative as well as business headquarters.

The administration of the colonial state consisted of two tiers of government, central and local. The former was composed of white officials who exercised somewhat summary legislative, executive, and judicial functions without any real division of powers. Thus the governor was the chief executive as well as the principal lawmaker who could issue decrees and proclamations. Outside the urban centers political officers in fact functioned as magistrates and judges besides their administrative functions, and professional law officers in the judiciary acted more or less as civil servants. The local governments, which supposedly were controlled by traditional authorities, were in reality an expedient device for solving the problems of expense and personnel. Whereas the French and, to a lesser extent, the Belgians virtually reduced African kings and chiefs to petty officials, the British usually increased their powers under a system known as indirect rule, by which the chiefs were made responsible to British officials in the exercise of "traditional" powers defined by the British overlords. Far from strengthening traditional institutions, indirect rule led to their perversion by freeing chiefs from customary restraints and making them instruments of colonial autocracy.

The system of dual administration—the colonial overlying the neotraditional—might have been expected to lead to mutual interaction and the adaptation from this of a modern African system of government. But such interaction could not take place. The colonial administrations were dominated by white officials, and it was only reluctantly that educated Africans, after World War II, were nominated, and later elected, to serve in them. But the same educated elite was, by and large, deliberately excluded from participation in the neotraditional councils and other institutions of indirect rule. The colonial system succeeded in maintaining a modicum of stability without promoting the development of indigenous political institutions or providing any real training for Africans in the Western system. Predictably, when at independence the educated elite had to assume power, it chose to take over the colonial states in preference to both the precolonial political institutions and their neotraditional versions.

The colonial economy was another pivotal institution and, in many ways, the raison d'être of European imperialism in Africa. Well before the nineteenth century, Africa had developed a system of regional trading networks based on products from local industries and agriculture, as well as foreign goods. The European economy became increasingly buoyant, thanks to the scientific and industrial revolutions, plus centuries of overseas trade.

Nevertheless, until colonialism, Africa was Europe's trading partner, not its economic appendage. The colonial economic institution was designed to change all that. The first step was to wrest the control of trade from middlemen, like the Swahili states of the eastern African coast, and powerful magnates, like Ja Ja, king of the Niger Delta state of Opobo. Many of the wars resisting European penetration in the Lower Niger, in eastern Africa, and in the Congo Basin were precipitated by European measures to take control of trade.

A fundamental point in the emergent colonial economy was its export-import reorientation. The decline of regional trading networks, which was facilitated by the new colonial boundaries, as well

as the smothering of local industries through the flooding of African markets with European goods, contributed to this development. Encouragement was, however, given to the growth of cash crops like cocoa, peanuts, coffee, tea, and cotton, organized so as to ensure that a colony specialized in one major crop, such as cocoa in the Gold Coast and Côte d'Ivoire, peanuts in Senegal and the Gambia, and cotton in Uganda. Even in those areas, there were European firms or prosperous merchants and produce buyers who stood between the African producer and the world market, and skimmed off most of the profit.

The preferential treatment reserved for white farmers in settler colonies like Kenya and Southern Rhodesia, not to mention South Africa, is another feature of colonial economic policy. On the excuse that settlers were expected to become the base of economic life in these colonies, the best lands were alienated to them at giveaway prices, while special laws were enacted and taxes instituted to force Africans to leave their plots and seek wage labor on white farms. Paradoxically, even where, as in Kenya, peasant production was doing well in terms of export promotion, the colonial authorities used administrative measures to impose restrictions on African farmers so as to boost white production. In the Belgian Congo, African produce was purchased by white farmers and resold at handsome profits.

A notable feature of the colonial economic system was that its development strategies served, particularly in retrospect, to consolidate imperial rule, to subordinate the African economy to that of the imperial power, and to make European businesses, rather than African communities, the main beneficiaries of the exploitation of African resources. Thus, with the introduction of money and the establishment of banking institutions, these banks' funds, including savings deposited by Africans, were invested in the colonizing countries. Banking laws often discouraged the granting of loans to African entrepreneurs. Similarly, the development of transport infrastructures (railways, ports, and road networks) was geared to the exploitation of minerals and the movement of cash crops for export. In this regard, in places like western Africa, where individual entrepreneurs and motor transport companies were able to participate in road transport, trucks became more effective than railways in stimulating African production and economic activities generally.

Although the new economic dispensation and the colonial state represented the most obvious manifestations of colonialism, Christianity and Western education were also important cultural components of European imperialism in Africa. Of course, neither evangelization nor the spread of education per se was the concern of the imperial rulers. But the advance of European power stimulated a rapid expansion of Christianity after an initial cultural resistance. Christianity, in turn, promoted the educational program (usually with some support from the colonial authorities) which nurtured a new class of Africans—Christian ministers, teachers, and clerks—who sought accommodation with colonial rule. Although it was from this same class that the grave diggers of colonialism later emerged, some of its members, especially Christian ministers, believed that Europe was executing a divine mission to free the African continent from "paganism" and "darkness." In the French, Belgian, and Portuguese colonies, ambitious educated Africans assiduously pursued the qualifications laid down for "assimilation," while their counterparts in the British colonies celebrated Empire Day (24 May) by singing "Rule, Brittania."

By the 1930s the colonial state had achieved a measure of stability except for occasional insurrections against official abuses. The economic infrastructures, whatever their limitations for transforming the age-old system of production in Africa, had secured to the colonial powers' industries a regular supply of raw materials as well as a stable market. Above all, Africans had come to accept colonial rule as a fact of life, such that the most fervent nationalists merely pleaded for a role for Africans within colonial administrations. The traditional rulers, descendants of the intrepid kings who had led their people in resistance against colonial conquest, were now loyal subjects of their imperial masters. Certainly the European powers had every cause to be elated at the success and prospects of the imperial venture in Africa.

AFRICAN SOCIETIES AND THE COLONIAL IMPACT

In spite of this euphoria of the imperial conqueror, the impact of colonialism on Africa, in terms of what development it generated and the extent to which it was a landmark in the continent's history, remains a widely debated issue. Scholarly attention has been devoted to the strategies or initiatives by which African peoples survived imperial rule, and the fact that many African institutions managed, in spite of colonial constraints, to survive until independence and after. There is no gainsaying the fact that these studies have enabled scholars to have a better understanding of the colonial situation as well as the nature of the impact of imperial rule on African societies. Nevertheless, it is necessary to look more closely at the context in which African strategies and initiatives for surviving colonialism operated and the extent to which these somewhat circumscribed circumstances influenced the nature and quality of the initiatives.

Similarly, while it is true that African institutions survived European rule, greater attention needs to be paid to the form in which they have done so. In other words, if Africa had been free (as Japan was at the time it chose to borrow certain aspects of Western civilization), what would it have opted for in such areas as ethos, material production, and sociopolitical institutions? Issues like these can illuminate the limitations of the choices open to African societies under colonialism, as well as the gravity of the problems arising from the foisting on African peoples of institutions not designed for their best interests.

The economy is one important area in which the validity of the above views can be tested. The main problems of production before the colonial era were labor, technology in the form of tools and techniques, land, and transport and related infrastructure. The problems of land and labor were interrelated. Because land was accessible to all, there was no labor market outside of the slave system. At the same time, there was little incentive for innovations in land use, not to mention developments in crafts, techniques, and tools. African peoples were all too conscious of these problems, hence such appeals as that of the Mani Kongo to the Portuguese in the early sixteenth century and that of the chiefs of Old Calabar to Captain William Owen of the British Navy in 1828 for artisans, tools, and machines.

The solutions prescribed by colonialism for these problems are implicit in the economic system instituted by the imperial rulers. The interrelated problem of land and labor was tackled by depriving the peoples of eastern, central, and southern Africa of much of their land, which was alienated to European settlers. Where this was not enough to guarantee cheap labor for white farms, company plantations, and the mines, taxes were instituted as an incentive to wage labor or, whenever necessary, labor was conscripted.

It must be conceded that conditions in other parts of the continent, and indeed in certain areas of the settler colonies, were not as bleak for the average African as described above. In addition, mention ought to be made of signal innovations within the economy, such as the introduction of cash-crop farming, the development of transport facilities, and the promotion of Western education, albeit largely through the efforts of the Christian missions. In other words, the colonial economic system created new opportunities that produced some affluent individuals who, especially in the cash-crop areas, could afford modern tin-roofed buildings or become owners of trucks. There was also a new class of businessmen with some basic education who became agents of the commerical companies owned by Europeans. Nevertheless, living conditions for the new class of wage earners were often hard. They were even worse for the mass of the people tilling the land with the same old tools, who were obliged to pay colonial tributes euphemistically referred to as taxes.

The overall economy was characterized by the concentration of "development" in a few urban centers at the expense of the rural areas, which, in addition, lost their many promising sons and daughters to the cities and towns through migration in search of education or better opportunities. Many traditional local industries became moribund, and no amount of African initiative could change the orientation and structure of an economy dependent on outside forces or arrest the extraction of the wealth of the African continent by the giant European companies. Indeed, the legacy of the colonial economy is one of the major factors in the late-twentieth-century predicament in Africa.

As pointed out earlier, there was considerable disruption of sociopolitical institutions during the colonial era. For example, many of the polities and kingdoms were destroyed, split up, or merged in the process of creating the colonial states. Owing to the divide-and-rule policy of colonial

administrations, there was little desire to integrate the often disparate ethnic, linguistic, and religious groups in these states into coherent units. Nor was there much enthusiasm, since colonial rule was expected to endure almost indefinitely, to provide training in the running of Western political institutions. African societies responded to the disruption of their sociopolitical institutions in different ways. For example, even in the French and Belgian colonies, where the kingdoms were destroyed or split into convenient administrative units, the people kept some of the institutions going by continuing to provide for the maintenance of their kings and chiefs. Similarly, organizations designed for the vitality of social units like clans, lineages, age groups, and the like continued to thrive, especially outside the new urban areas. But perhaps the most crucial impact of colonialism in this area is that it progressively destroyed the social control and judicial functions of esoteric societies and cults, without establishing viable Western alternatives. By the same token, wherever indirect rule was instituted, colonialism served to reinforce existing autocratic tendencies in governance and to introduce them even where they were alien to the indigenous political culture. The manipulations to which the chieftaincy institution was subjected in the colonial period thus began a trend in which traditional rulers became a reactionary and corruptive force in society rather than guardians of communal morality and values.

The nature of the overall cultural impact of colonialism may be evaluated in the field of Western education. By the time colonial rule officially came to an end, Western culture was barely skin deep. In the early twenty-first century basic values derived from Western ideas of individual rights, accountability, and the responsibility of rulers to the governed remain remote from realization in political life. Moreover, the African worldview continues to be defined by the magical and preternatural ethos of African science. Hence diviners and soothsayers enjoy the patronage of the educated elite, and African gods, in spite of revivalist Christianity and Islam, continue to attract followers. Nevertheless, these survivals of authentic African culture do not prevent African models of development from being based on the pattern established by colonialism. Hence, educational policies are often divorced from African values, and research is seldom undertaken in areas such as traditional medicine or the African approach to the mastery of natural forces.

It is in the area of ethos that colonialism may have exerted the greatest negative impact on African societies. Most Africans tended to see the colonial state as an institution for exploitation and plunder. Unlike the traditional polities and communities, it conferred no benefits, rendered no services, and therefore deserved no loyalty. People were therefore not expected to expend much energy in its service, since, according to a Yoruba saying, "*a kii se ise oba Iaagùn*" (one need not dissipate sweat in the service of the king [i.e., the imperial government]). The state was fair game for looters and cheats. And since people today see little distinction between the colonial state and its rulers, on the one hand, and the emergent nation-state and its African overlords, on the other, the attitudes to the former have been transferred to the latter. This is perhaps one important explanation of the incidence of corruption in public life in contemporary Africa, where private morality does not apply in the domain of public office.

In sum, in assessing the overall impact of colonialism, it is vital to see beyond its superstructures, which were created for its own sustenance. After all, Europe went into Africa in pursuit of its own interests, even if the apologists of imperialism maintain that a continent could be invaded, subjugated, and exploited for its own good, or that foreign powers could have a "mandate," as Frederick Lugard claims, to take possession of the resources of other people's land, on the pretext of making them available to humanity. The much-vaunted claim that European rule established peace in Africa has proved rather exaggerated—this much has become obvious with the collapse, since independence, of the fragile structures bequeathed by colonialism. As for the advances Africa is supposed to have made under colonial tutelage, one might observe, with perhaps no more than a touch of overstatement, that the African went into colonialism with the hoe and the machete of his own manufacture, and came out using the same tools, which he now had to import.

See also **Banjul; Cape Coast; Christianity; Colonial Policies and Practices; Education, School; Government;** **History and the Study of Africa; History of Africa; Ja Ja, King; Lugard, Frederick John Dealtry; Menelik II; Postcolonialism; Saint-Louis; Slave Trades; Zanzibar Sultanate.**

BIBLIOGRAPHY

Ajayi, J. F. Ade. "The Continuity of African Institutions under Colonialism." In *Emerging Themes of African History*, ed. Terence O. Ranger. London: Heinemann Educational, 1968.

Ajayi, J. F. Ade. "Colonialism: An Episode in African History." In *Colonialism in Africa, 1870–1960*, Vol. 1, ed. Lewis H. Gann and Peter Duignan. London: Cambridge University Press, 1969.

Boahen, A. Adu, ed. *Africa under Colonial Domination, 1880–1935. UNESCO General History of Africa*, Vol. 7. Berkeley: University of California Press, 1985.

Crowder, Michael. *Colonial West Africa.* London: F. Cass, 1978.

Gann, Lewis H., and Peter Duignan. *Burden of Empire: An Appraisal of Western Colonialism in Africa South of the Sahara.* New York: Praeger, 1967.

Gann, Lewis H., and Peter Duignan. *Colonialism in Africa, 1870–1960.* 5 vols. London: Cambridge University Press, 1969–1975. See Vol. 1: *The History and Politics of Colonialism, 1870–1914*, and Vol. 4: *The Economics of Colonialism*.

Hargreaves, J. D. *Prelude to the Partition of West Africa.* London: Macmillan, 1963.

Hargreaves, J. D. *West Africa Partitioned*, Vol. 1: *The Loaded Pause, 1885–1889.* Madison: University of Wisconsin Press, 1974.

Lugard, Frederick Dealtry. *The Dual Mandate in British Tropical Africa*, 5th edition. Hamden, CT: Archon Books, 1965.

Owen, Roger, and Bob Sutcliffe, eds. *Studies in the Theory of Imperialism.* London: Longman, 1972.

Pakenham, Thomas. *The Scramble for Africa, 1876–1912.* New York: Longman, 1991.

Perham, Margery. *The Colonial Reckoning.* New York: Knopf, 1962.

Roberts, Andrew, ed. *The Colonial Moment in Africa: Essays on the Movement of Minds and Materials, 1900–1940.* Cambridge, U.K. Cambridge University Press, 1990.

G. A. Akinola

CONCESSIONARY COMPANIES

During the three centuries from the foundation of the *Compagnie des Indes* in 1664 to the demise of the Mozambique Company (1941), the European presence in Africa underwent major changes. So did the companies that were granted concessions on that continent.

Before the colonial era, European states relied on private companies for the organization of trade, mainly the slave trade. This system was in itself a continuation of the economic structure prevailing within Europe and between Europe and other parts of the world. The concession, or permission to trade, was given for a fixed quantity of products or for a defined spatial zone over which large powers were granted.

When the legal slave trade ended following the Congress of Vienna in 1815, most companies could not find lucrative products to maintain their profits, and they disappeared. But with the renewed interest in Africa in the second half of the nineteenth century, the concessionary company gained a second life in another form.

CHARTERED COMPANIES

Reluctant to take charge of large areas, some countries resorted to the old system of chartered companies to assert their presence by delegating to private companies administrative powers such as collecting taxes or customs dues, organizing labor, repressing potential uprisings by military means, and creating trading monopolies.

This was specifically but briefly the case for Germany under Wilhelm I (1797–1888). Placing the emphasis on building national unity, Chancellor Otto von Bismarck (1815–1898) did not want to embark on colonial adventures. In the mid-1870s, industrialization and economic growth led some entrepreneurs to look for foreign markets. Private firms developed commercial relationships with Africa, mainly the southwestern part of the continent and the mainland of the Zanzibar sultanate. Later, these firms sought official recognition. At the moment that Germany and France were organizing the Berlin Conference, the explorer Gustav Nachtigal (1834–1885) was given the power by Bismarck to grant concessionary status to two German trading companies: Karl Peters's (1856–1918) German East Africa Company (1885–1890) and Adolf Lüderitz's (1834–1886) German Colonization Company for southwest Africa (1885–1889). However, lack of capital, disappointment over mineral discoveries, and the resistance of the populations quickly pushed the

German government to take over, as early as 1889 for southwest Africa and in 1890 for East Africa. In both cases, German colonization started with the use of repression, especially against the Herero and Nama in present-day Namibia.

In Togo and Cameroon, no trading company was ready to offer a substitute for colonization, but private capital played an active role through the foundation of plantations. This constituted another form of revived chartered companies, such as the South-Kamerun Association (27,792 square miles) or the Nord-West Kamerun Association (30,880 square miles).

Great Britain also provided leading trading entrepreneurs whose chartered companies enforced British presence on the coveted continent. This was the case of George Taubman Goldie (1846–1925), who was granted a charter in 1886. Trading along the Niger River from the 1870s, Goldie absorbed rival firms to form the United African Company in 1879, which became the National African Company in 1882, later known as the Royal Niger Company, which was officially responsible for controlling trade and navigation on the Niger. It had to face both the resistance of several African states and the ambition of France. This made it impossible to organize efficient commercial networks. In 1900 Great Britain took over, giving substantial financial compensation to the company. This territory became the Northern Nigeria Protectorate, whose first high commissioner was Frederick Lugard.

Southern Africa experienced the same process, motivated there by mining interests. In 1889 Cecil Rhodes, who had already built a huge fortune on diamond and gold mining in South Africa, obtained a charter for the British South Africa Company (BSA) over a vast territory, stretching from Transvaal to Congo and from Angola to Mozambique. In reality, though, he had to limit his actual authority to a more realistic zone, centered on Matabeleland and Mashonaland. Competition between white settlers and local peasants, whose economy was based on cattle breeding, quickly led to violence. The revolt of the Ndebele in 1895, temporarily united with the Shona, was followed by the creation of reservations. This region became the heart of Cecil Rhodes's empire.

Even confined to a smaller territory, the BSA represented an important financial interest.

The company retained its administrative powers until the 1920s when they were considered a severe burden. The company was anxious to give them up and be compensated for them, and the settlers were eager to acquire political rights. In 1923 the European population of Southern Rhodesia obtained internal self-government and Northern Rhodesia came under the Colonial Office in 1924. The company's mineral rights were confirmed in Northern Rhodesia. The BSA was by far the most successful chartered company in Africa, thanks mainly to a flourishing mining industry (copper, gold, asbestos) and a prosperous settler community.

To the northeast, William Mackinnon (1823–1893) obtained a charter for his Imperial British East Africa Company in 1888. This company, ill-organized and without much capital, had little commercial success but secured British sovereignty over Uganda and what became Kenya Colony and Protectorate. It disappeared in 1895, and the whole territory became a British protectorate.

These companies had shortcomings and ultimately failed. However, they served as a convenient transition stage between old colonial methods and the modernized version of imperialism.

CONCESSION COMPANIES

Granting vast concessions of land to a few companies would have incurred the opposition of trading firms already active in western Africa. But Central Africa was still little exploited. Faced with large territories and limited financial and administrative means, Léopold II of Belgium (1865–1909) was the first to resort to private companies to help exploit the resources of his vast Congo Free State.

Léopold II was officially given authority over an ill-defined but large territory at the Berlin Conference. As early as 1887 he recognized the *Compagnie du Congo pour le Commerce et l'Industrie* that was given large pieces of land in return for the construction of the Matadi-Leopoldville Railway (1890–1898). Wild rubber and mining prospects (first discovered in 1892) led to the creation of several other companies such as the Katanga Company (1891) and the *Société Anversoise*. Léopold II himself invested much capital in these ventures; his financial difficulties led to a cession of his personal holdings to Belgium in 1908. With the Congo Reform Association and the stubbornness of Edmund D. Morel (1873–1924), a campaign was launched in 1907 against red rubber; exposing the brutal conditions under which this product was extorted from local producers. As a result, freedom of trade was reestablished, forced labor was officially forbidden, and a monetary tax was imposed.

The economic system was still based on the same big private companies in the Belgian Congo, but their administrative powers were strictly limited to the mining zone. The most successful company was the *Union Minière du Haut-Katanga*, which had a paternalist policy providing for most of the needs of its employees.

The example of the apparently successful policy chosen by Léopold II greatly influenced France, which had to deal with a similar ecological and economic environment. Laborious discussions took place in the Chamber of Deputies from 1887 to 1895 on the policies of delegating administrative powers to big companies versus direct takeover. The former was adopted for Central Africa. Relying on private companies was a way of trying to solve the problem of low density, scarce customs duties, and vast territories while attracting capital in a hostile region. About 270,200 (out of 347,400) square miles were divided in 1899 among forty concession companies: For a limited investment and with few constraints, they could exploit the resources of a large area, mainly rubber, while being responsible for collecting the taxes and building the minimal equipment. The companies quickly abused their rights and escaped any kind of control. The main problem was manpower, so they used any means to extort rubber: taxes in goods, forced labor, and imprisonment of women and children. This resulted in a true looting economy, of which Ubangi-Chari is the best example.

Although Pierre P. F. C. Savorgnan de Brazza was initially in favor of this system as a means to develop the country, he was appalled by the way the companies misused their power; in 1905 he was sent on an inspection mission, following a campaign of protest in France. He denounced the brutality and inefficiency, but his death on the way home and the official hushing up of the scandal did not result in a reform of the concession system. It more or less died or evolved because of its own shortcomings: Although some companies had high profit rates before World War I (25 to 35% for some from 1905 to 1911), their lack of investment and the end of wild rubber put a stop to this system. Except for a few companies that could rely on other products, either ores or wood—such as the *Compagnie Forestière Sangha-Oubangi* as late as 1935—most of them disappeared. Central African societies had meanwhile greatly suffered through famines, high mortality rates, social and economic disorganization, displaced people, and diffusion of severe and new illnesses.

The remaining companies, in French Equatorial Africa (a federation instituted in 1910) and in the Belgian Congo, lost their administrative prerogatives and became mere capitalist enterprises. They took advantage of the colonial system that gave them a monopoly situation, a profitable tariff system, and easy access to labor.

PORTUGUESE AFRICA

As a heritage of the first colonial era, Portugal exerted nominal control over large territories without having the means to exploit them. Therefore, it relied on foreign capital (mainly British) and companies to build railways, organize plantations, and exploit mines. Six companies concentrated more than half the capital invested mainly in Mozambique: the Niassa, Mozambique, and Zambesia Companies; the Moçamedes Company; the Benguela Railway; and the Mozambique Sugar Company (which later became the Sena Sugar Estates). They lasted much longer without having proved more efficient than in German or British colonies, where they had long disappeared. The Niassa Company, founded in 1894, was abolished in 1928 without having fulfilled its contract to build the railway. The Mozambique Company (1891) was the most successful and also the last to dissolve in 1941: Its large administrative authority was effectively a state within a state, preventing Mozambique from acting as a single colony, but except for the railway, the company invested little money.

Two kinds of concessions can be distinguished. Some were granted for a specific commercial investment (public works, industrial, or agricultural enterprises). These companies had quasi-governmental functions: They could control labor supplies, organize white settlers, or even be responsible for health measures. Left with almost no external control, they formed autonomous enclaves.

The other type of concession was defined in terms of a certain area of land, over which the company exercised administrative tasks while receiving wide economic privileges. Companies could vary greatly in size and economic importance, but the main purpose when they were granted (1888 to 1894) was to provide a façade of occupation and give Portugal nominal claims over large territories.

The Moçamedes Company was the only one in Angola to be granted a charter with limited powers: no control over taxation or customs dues, and no authority over coastal ports. First French-owned, then taken over by Rhodes, and finally French again, it lasted from 1894 to 1923, having succeeded only in establishing cotton plantations and cattle ranches.

Some enterprises, not given a charter, exercised similar powers. The best example is the *Companhia de Diamantes de Angola* (DIAMANG), whose zone first covered two-thirds of Angola. Though not officially responsible for administration, it acted as the government of the Lunda district where diamonds were found. Its large profits were partially invested in building a communications network and industrial infrastructures related to mining in this remote part of Angola. The company also became the main banker for the Angolan government in the 1920s and 1930s, and received official help for recruiting its annual ten thousand laborers.

The concession system drew more and more criticism: It submitted Portuguese Africa to the rule of foreign capital and showed little results, except for the Sena Sugar Company and DIAMANG, and deprived the administration of its legitimate sources of revenue. Most of the profits made by the companies came from taxation and the sale of contract laborers.

Though the last of the concession companies disappeared in 1941, it was clear at the end of the nineteenth century that they were not the proper instruments to exploit efficiently, and ultimately to develop, African colonies. They nevertheless served their initial purpose: to give the means to lay claim to vast territories not yet controlled, in response to the rules established by the Berlin Conference. In time, they all gave way to purely capitalist enterprises, although strict separation between private interests and public legal procedures was not established at once, for example, for labor supply.

See also **Colonial Policies and Practices; Congo Independent State; Rhodes, Cecil John.**

BIBLIOGRAPHY

Cain, P. J., and A. G. Hopkins. *British Imperialism: Innovation and Expansion, 1688–1914.* London: Longman, 1993.

Clarence-Smith, William G. *Slaves, Peasants, and Capitalists in Southern Angola, 1840–1926.* Cambridge, U.K.: Cambridge University Press, 1979.

Cooper, Frederick. *Decolonization and African Society: The Labor Question in French and British Africa.* Cambridge, U.K.: Cambridge University Press, 1996.

Coquery-Vidrovitch, Catherine. *Le Congo au temps des grandes compagnies concessionnaires, 1898–1930,* 2 vols. Paris: Editions de l'EHESS, 2001.

Flint, John E. *Sir George Goldie and the Making of Nigeria.* London: Oxford University Press, 1960.

Galbraith, John S. *Mackinnon and East Africa, 1878–1895; A Study in the "New Imperialism."* Cambridge, U.K.: Cambridge University Press, 1972.

Gründer, Horst. *Geschichte der deutschen Kolonien.* Paderborn, Germany: Schöningh, 1985.

Hochschild, Adam King. *Leopold's Ghost.* Boston and New York: Mariner Books/Houghton Mifflin, 1998.

Merlier, Michel. *Le Congo, de la colonisation belge à l'indépendence.* Paris: F. Maspero, 1962.

Newitt, Malyn D. D. *Portugal in Africa: The Last Hundred Years.* London: Longman, 1981.

Rotberg, Robert I. *The Founder: Cecil Rhodes and the Pursuit of Power.* New York: Oxford University Press, 1988.

ODILE GOERG

COLOR TERMS. *See* **Symbols and Symbolism.**

COMMERCIALIZATION. *See* **Capitalism and Commercialization; Trade, National and International Systems.**

COMMUNALISM. *See* **Civil Society.**

COMMUNICATIONS

This entry includes the following articles:
ELECTRONIC
ORAL

ELECTRONIC

Although access to and use of the Internet has grown exponentially in Africa as elsewhere since the mid-1990s, the continent is still the least wired major region in the world. In 2006, Africa had 14.1 percent of the world's population but only 2.3 percent of the world's Internet usage capability. However, Africa and the Middle East are the fastest growing in the world in terms of Internet use. Between 2000–2005, Internet use expanded by 423.9 percent and 454.2 percent, respectively.

While the digital divide negatively affects Africa as a whole, there is an even greater divide within countries in terms of access to electronic communications. Personal computers are still prohibitively expensive for most households, and public access points such as Internet cafes or community telecenters usually are situated in urban or peri-urban areas. Consequently, the vast majority of the rural population still does not have access. Typical information communications technology (ICT) users tend to be young, male, and relatively well educated. Women and girls, even in urban areas, are generally less frequent users.

In an effort to extend coverage to rural areas, a number of African countries have established Universal Access Funds aimed at supporting the development of communications infrastructure in rural areas. Rural communications centers, or telecenters, can provide services to local populations, and increasingly private individuals or groups are setting them up as sources of income. Governments, donors, and the private sector are putting emphasis on the further development of telecenters, cybercafes, and community phone services that offer low cost access to telephone, computers, computer training, and a range of related communications services.

The Millennium Development Goals (MDGs) adopted by the United Nations in September 2000 identified ICTs as critical tools in the eradication of absolute poverty and in the improvement of health, education, and agriculture. Consequently there has been substantial effort by national governments, UN agencies, international donors, and NGOs to improve connectivity in Africa. Nonetheless, there remain many obstacles to the widespread use of information communications technologies. These include restrictive regulatory frameworks, antiquated infrastructure, limited landline coverage, lack of stable electricity supplies, and the high cost of connectivity, in addition to general poverty, illiteracy, and lack of exposure to ICTs.

From the late 1990s, the widespread introduction of mobile telephones has had a dramatic impact in Africa. Currently more than 70 percent of telephone subscribers use mobile networks. Accordingly, efforts are underway to develop mobile and wireless broadband networks, rather than using inadequate landline systems for phone and Internet connectivity. To further enhance coverage, many African public and private sector organizations are using Small Aperture Terminal (VSAT) technology to deliver business, educational, and health services, but there continue to be problems with economy of scale and regulatory impediments in some countries.

The New Partnership for Africa's Development (NEPAD) has made the promotion of ICTs a priority, with special emphasis on e-governance and e-democracy; ICT applications for health and education; ICT infrastructure development; ICT-based entrepreneurship and private sector development; ICTs in agriculture and environmental management; and the fostering of a conducive regulatory environment. NEPAD currently is promoting the development of a broadband terrestrial fiber-optic network that aims to connect all fifty-four African countries to a broadband terrestrial optic-optic network. This would provide abundant bandwidth, easier connectivity, and reduced costs.

ICTs already are being used in many different countries to work toward sustainable development. For example, Uganda has a low bandwidth information network for health workers. In Kenya and Senegal, smallholder farmers and fishers are getting market access and credit and price information on Internet and mobile telephone connections, and in Francophone Africa, efforts are underway to measure the digital gender gap and improve women's access to ICTs. South Africa has been particularly active in promoting the use of ICTs and is moving ahead with a number of e-governance initiatives.

Lack of effective ICT policy continues to hamper the further development of the sector. Few African countries have articulated policies on the overall development of the ICT sector, although many have elaborated policies specifically to reform the telecommunications sector. Increased competition is leading to a reduction in prices, greater availability of lines, and, in consequence, increased connectivity, not only in urban centers but also in rural districts.

See also **Literacy; Media.**

BIBLIOGRAPHY

Baskaran, Angathevar, and Muchie, Mammo. *Bridging the Digital Divide. Innovation Systems for ICT in Brazil, China, India, Thailand and Southern Africa.* London: Adonis and Abbey, 2006.

Information and Communication Technologies. "Acacia Initiative." Available from http://www.idrc.ca/acacia/.

New Partnership for Africa's Development (NEPAD) "e-Africa Commission." Available from http://www.eafricacommission.org/.

EVA RATHGEBER

ORAL

Communication is a social activity that requires coordinated efforts of two or three individuals who occupy positions of sender(s) and receiver(s) of a speech event. It takes place when a response has been elicited, through verbal or nonverbal symbols, showing involvement of the receiver. Compared to the written form, oral communication is the one made possible through speech in face-to-face interactions. It is the effective composition, presentation and interpretation of entertainment, information, ideas, and values to a specific audience.

Jack Goody (b. c. 1918), a British anthropologist, attempted to establish a relationship between means of communication and modes of thought, suggesting in the process that individuals who significantly depend on oral communication have different thought processes from those who are literate. According to him, writing gave humans the scope of critical activity and hence of rationality and logic. The weakness of this approach has been well argued by other anthropologists. Moreover, it is not productive to think of orality in a negative fashion by contrasting it with literacy, because both communication types have much in common. Instead, it may be more useful to examine the features of the two modes of communication and to determine their points of convergence and/or divergence. Indeed, the use of oral communication is, as literacy and other information technologies, dependent on social and cultural conventions as well as speech. Oral communication is an earlier form of information technology namely, the acquisition, processing, storage, and dissemination of information by word of mouth.

The first type of communication in which individuals are socialized in the world is oral, and it is therefore primary. Later in life they attain a secondary discourse through social institutions that are located outside the family. This secondary discourse, which is more specialized and detached, is found in both oral and literate cultures. In oral cultures, it manifests itself in, for example, traditional legal discourse, ritual speech, praise poetry, folk tales, and so on, and is acquired through apprenticeship and experiential learning.

As a primary discourse, oral communication is a tool for person-to-person interaction and information sharing. At another level, oral communication is a conveyor of detached individual and community thoughts, aspirations, histories, and philosophies captured in literary narratives, riddles, proverbs, poems, and songs. By using a wide range of artistic devices including voice, improvisation, body movement, repetition, parallelism, contextualization, ideophones, digression, imagery, allusion, parody, and symbolism, the oral artist reaches out to an audience, both entertaining and educating it at the same time. Oral media may be used to preserve the status quo or to challenge it and may deal with concrete particular ties or abstract concepts.

In oral communication, knowledge and experiences are passed verbally from one generation to another. In many parts of Africa, poetry was and still is spoken, and in precolonial Africa established poets could be found at the royal courts of monarchical communities. For instance, among the Mandinka of western Africa, the *griot* was traditionally a court poet. He sang the king's praises and recorded important historical moments in song. He also reminded the ruler of the "established standards of rulership in his people's history" (Okpewho 1988). Among the Ashanti, this

function was undertaken by *kwadwumfo* (minstrels); among the Rwanda it was *umusizi* (poet); and the Xhosa it was *imbongi* (male praise singers) and *iitsomi* (female poets). Poetry was also found in the restricted context of ritual, involving religious and mystical moments, such as at initiation. Poets of this type were formally trained through apprenticeship. Among the LoDagaa of Ghana, the *bo netuuri* poets performed at the Bagre initiation ceremonies. There is also the freelance entertainer at weddings and other merrymaking ceremonies, and the professional mourner who performs with the *nyatiti* (harp) among the Luo of Kenya.

In ritual practice, spiritual hegemony is transmitted, through initiates, in esoteric tongues hardly decipherable by common people. The *somas* and *donso*, traditional healers of West Africa, use oral sacred language to commune with the spirit world. They function as custodians of past knowledge and guardians of social cohesion and order. Statuettes, masks, and other items of African art are important accompaniments to sacred language and indigenous religious rites. The incantations are supposed to have divine power, allowing communication with the spiritual domain. In addition, the chant, sometimes referred to as recitation, is a common form of oral performance in most of Africa. Unlike the speaking voice, the chanting voice has a higher degree of stress in order to achieve a higher level of emotional intensity than in ordinary speech.

Another sphere in which oral communication manifests itself is in oral poetry. This may be simple or intellectually complex, as in Ifa divination poetry among the Yoruba, and *gicandi* poetry among the Gikuyu. Gicandi poetry is a competitive, yet cooperative riddlelike dialogue poem and poetic exchange performed by roving poets in central Kenya, just as the *griots* of West Africa. The roving poet captured particularized individual experiences and community knowledge, and transmitted both orally. He was the custodian of the memory, history, and literary creativity of his people and he was fed and protected by the community. He performed in funerals, initiations, marriage ceremonies, and other social events. Whereas some of these compositions are a consequence of memorizations, others are the result of spontaneous creativity following the requirements of the specific oral genre.

In the contemporary world that has seen technological advances, urbanization, and limitations of time and space for interaction between young and old, oral communication is now mediated and relies less on memory. By fixing vocal sound on tape or compact disc, technology gives oral communication reiteration but denies it variation because it is significantly fixed. The radio, cassette, and television have become important channels for the oral communicator. In this mediated communication, the oral narrator's presence is limited and interaction is mainly unidirectional because audience members are not given an opportunity to respond. In essence, oral communication lives side by side with other forms of expression mediated by technology.

See also **Literature: Epics and Epic Poetry.**

BIBLIOGRAPHY

Barber, Karin, ed. *Readings in African Popular Culture.* Bloomington: Indiana University Press, 1997.

Finnegan, Ruth. *Literacy and Orality.* New York: Blackwell, 1988.

Goody, Jack. *The Domestication of the Savage Mind.* New York: Cambridge University Press, 1977.

Gumpez, John J. *Discourse Strategies.* New York: Cambridge University Press, 1982.

Njogu, Kimani. *Reading Poetry as Dialogue: An East African Literary Tradition.* Nairobi, Kenya: Jomo Kenyatta Foundation, 2004.

Okpewho, Isidora. *African Oral Literature: Backgrounds, Characters, and Continuity.* Bloomington: Indiana University Press, 1992.

Street, Brian. *Literacy in Theory and Practice.* New York: Cambridge University Press, 1984.

Zumthor, Paul. *Oral Poetry: An Introduction.* Minneapolis: University of Minnesota Press, 1990.

KIMANI NJOGU

COMORO ISLANDS

This entry includes the following articles:
GEOGRAPHY AND ECONOMY
SOCIETY AND CULTURES
HISTORY AND POLITICS

GEOGRAPHY AND ECONOMY

The archipelago of the Comoro Islands is a day's sail from the east African coast. This group of four islands has a total area of 785 square miles. Located between 11° and 13° south latitude, approximately halfway between Mozambique and Madagascar, the islands have a tropical, maritime climate moderated by Indian Ocean monsoons. From October to April the winds are primarily from the north and bring moist, warm air to the region. During this period there is abundant rainfall, with the heaviest amounts falling between December and April. As much as 15 inches have been recorded in one month.

Temperatures along the coasts average between 75 and 79° Fahrenheit. From May to September the winds are cooler and drier, blowing from high-pressure centers in southern Africa. Average temperatures during this period drop to as low as 66° Fahrenheit. For centuries sailors used these Indian Ocean winds to establish trade routes between Asia and Africa. The Comoros were an important link in this trade and merchants on the islands became quite wealthy. After the introduction of deep-draft and steam-powered vessels, however, the islands' involvement in trade diminished until they eventually became poor dependencies of France. In the present day, three of the islands, Ngazidja, Nzwani, and Mwali, comprise the Union of the Comoros, while the fourth island, Mayotte (also known as Maore or Mahoré), is a French administrative territory.

The archipelago was created from volcanic activity along a fissure in the earth that runs southeast-northwest between Madagascar and the African coast. This activity produced each island at different times, resulting in distinctive, individual physical characteristics. The oldest island, Mayotte, is closest to Madagascar and is relatively flat, with slow-moving streams and an extensive barrier coral reef. It has a size of 144 square miles, including Pamanzi, an islet on the eastern coast that was the chief French administrative site for the Comoros until 1962.

The administrative center was then moved to Moroni, on the island of Ngazidja, the closest island to Africa and the youngest in the archipelago and the only one with ongoing volcanic activity. Moroni, the capital and a major seaport of the Union of the Comoros, is located on Ngazidja's western shore at the base of the massive volcano, Karthala. This volcano dominates the entire southern third of the island's 396 square miles, rising 7,790 feet above sea level with one of the largest

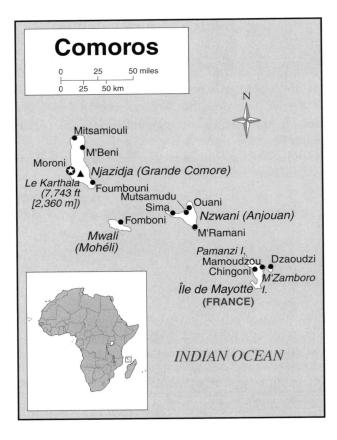

sea through sandy beaches. Its capital city, Mutsamudu, is located on a large bay off the island's northwestern shore. Mutsamudu is the Union of the Comoros' second important seaport.

For centuries, Comorians have been involved in the vast and profitable Indian Ocean maritime trade—either traveling to distant ports with commercial goods or providing provisions for ships stopping in the islands. But, whereas in the past much wealth was brought to the islanders by the trade, today the islands are among the poorest countries in the world. The estimated average income per person is less than $500 per year. The Union of the Comoros also has a very large negative trade balance, with an estimated external debt that exceeded $230 million in 2004. Building materials, petroleum, manufactured goods, and some foodstuffs are imported, while vanilla, cloves, copra, and essential plant oils such as ylang-ylang have been major exports. Since the mid-1980s there has been a decline in per capita gross domestic product. The islands have limited resources and a high population density, making them largely dependent upon external aid. The entire union depends greatly upon France (which historically has been its major trading partner); Mayotte is supported by France entirely. Its currency, the Comorian franc (KMF) has been pegged to the Euro since 1999. The exchange rate in November 2006 was 492.19 KMF = 1 Euro.

The majority of the population depends upon local agriculture, fishing, and animal husbandry. A variety of root, grain, and tree crops are grown, and sheep, goats, and cattle are maintained in small quantities. The sea provides a large variety and quantity of fish. Although the soil has been very fertile and there has been high productivity of foodstuffs, the large population increase that occurred in the last half of the twentieth century put so much pressure on the land that it has become questionable whether it can continue to support the number of people dependent upon it.

The islands' beautiful beaches, coral reefs, marine life, climate, and the hospitality of the people make them a potential tourist haven. This industry has not been well developed, however. While there are some hotels, and tourists have visited the islands over the years, the political turmoil and undeveloped

craters of any active volcano in the world. There have been more than a dozen major eruptions since the middle of the nineteenth century, including one in 1977. The many fresh lava flows over the island have left the surface very permeable and rainwater seeps through it, leaving Ngazidja, except momentarily after a heavy rainfall, with no streams or rivers. Until the 1970s, islanders collected freshwater in large cisterns or from seaside springs, where freshwater rests upon salt water. Since independence, deep wells have been drilled and freshwater is now pumped to inhabitants. (All the other islands have fresh running water sources.)

Mwali, 45 miles south-southeast of Ngazidja, is the smallest of the four islands, with an area of only 81 square miles. Its prominent topographic feature is a mountainous ridge forming a backbone along the middle of the island and rising 2,607 feet above sea level. Twenty-four miles east of Mwali and 43 miles northwest of Mayotte is Nzwani, a triangular-shaped island with a land area of 164 square feet and a central peak that rises 5,200 feet above sea level. It has several swift streams that cascade down waterfalls to enter the

Boats waiting for repair lie at low tide at the docks in Moroni, December 2003. Due to the economic stagnation of the islands at the time, only temporary repairs could be accommodated. Political unrest on the islands between President Azali Azzoumani and opposition parties came to a head in November. MARCO LONGARI/AFP/GETTY IMAGES

infrastructure have been a severe challenge to the development of a major tourist industry.

See also **Aid and Development; Economic History; Geography and the Study of Africa.**

BIBLIOGRAPHY

Battistini, René, and Pierre Vérin. *Géographie des Comores.* Paris: Nathan, 1984.

MARTIN OTTENHEIMER
HARRIET JOSEPH OTTENHEIMER

SOCIETY AND CULTURES

The estimated population of the Comoro Islands for the first decade of the twenty-first century is over 700,000 individuals. Population density is high with an estimate of more than 955 persons per square mile. The most densely populated island is Nzwani. Mwali is the least densely populated island. Over one-fourth of the population lives in urban centers along the coasts. The population would be much greater were it not for a high rate of emigration. Approximately 75,000 Comorians reside in France. The average total fertility rate is 5 percent and the average annual population growth rate for 1980–2000 was 2.98 percent. Life expectancy at birth is 62.2 years for females and 59.4 years for males.

The Comoros have been a multicultural melting pot for centuries. A wide number of ethnic and cultural groups, including east Africans, Arabs, Malagasy, Indians, and Europeans have contributed to the overall cultural mix through the ancient trading networks. Many Comorians trace their ancestry to Arabia or Persia, and the cultural and linguistic contributions from these regions are significant. According to one local legend, Jews were also among the early settlers of the Comoros, and there are some intriguing cultural and linguistic indications that this might, in fact, be so. Early east African immigrants brought Bantu cultural and linguistic traditions that are still evident in the early twenty-first century, and Malagasy immigrants arriving in the nineteenth brought Malayo-Polynesian cultural and linguistic contributions. In the nineteenth century, American whaling ships provisioning in the Comoros, left interesting linguistic traces. Beginning with the colonial period at the end of the nineteenth century, a few French also settled in the Comoros and contributed to the cultural mix. In modern times,

Comorian Zanzibaris and Comorian Malagasy (locally known as Sabenas) returned to resettle in the Comoros as a result of anti-Comorian violence in those two places. All of these groups have added to the rich linguistic and cultural mix that is typified by modern Comorian life.

One of the central features of traditional social life in the Comoros is marriage. A man may legally have up to four wives at the same time and while each wife is expected to be treated equally by the husband, only one will be married in a grand marriage—a large, public ceremony lasting as long as seven days. The grand marriage is characterized by many public activities involving large sums of money. In Nzwani, for example, it is the first marriage for both the man and the woman. The marriage is arranged by the couple's parents, and given social recognition by numerous public dances, feasts, and entertainments. The bride, furthermore, is given jewelry and other gifts that, at times, may be valued well over $10,000.

In contrast, subsequent marriages are primarily simple, private affairs. The choice of a spouse in subsequent marriages of a man or woman is made by the individuals themselves and their marriage is given legal standing by a judge who pronounces them husband and wife in front of a witness. In either case, whether married in a large, public ceremony or a quiet, private one, the husband typically joins the household of his wife which may be in a part of a house she shares with her mother. This arrangement, combining polygyny—the marriage of two or more women to the same man—and matrilocality—the married couple residing with the bride's mother—is unusual. The Comoros is one of the few locations in the world in which this combination is practiced.

The majority of people in the islands are Sunni Muslims with a minority of Christians living primarily on the island of Mayotte. Within the Islamic religion, there are followers of different Sufi orders (*tariqat*; also *tariqa*) including the Qadiri, Shadhili, and Rifai movements. There are also practices, such as the ritual propitiation of animal spirits, which can be traced to traditional African religions. European, Arabian, and African cultural influences are expressed in the different ritual calendars used by Comorians. There is a solar calendar in use for political, economic, and daily life that also determines the cycle of Christian rituals. A lunar calendar determines the cycle of

Islamic rituals and there is also a mathematical calendar based upon a 365-day year that is used to determine the time of traditional ritual behavior. The traditional calendar year is divided into four periods: three 100-day periods each divided into "weeks" of ten days and a final period of 65 days. The final period has special ritual significance and is a time when, for example, fishermen following the traditional calendar will not attempt to catch fish.

The Comoros's history is marked by social differences and rivalries based on both inter- and intra-island loyalties. Each island in the past was ruled by one or more sultans, and although there was much cooperation, there was also occasional conflict. Each sultan ruled over an urban center and the region surrounding it, which meant that in Nzwani, for example, there was a sultan with a palace in Mutsamudu on the western shore of the island and a sultan with a palace in Domoni on the eastern shore of the island. In Ngazidja there were said to have been as many as twelve sultanates and, while each one was independent, all recognized a principal sultan who mediated among the twelve. European colonists generally found it to their advantage to encourage rivalries among and between the various sultans, as they worked to gain dominion over the entire archipelago. These ancient rivalries continue today in different forms and are expressed in inter-community and interisland competitions. In island politics, individuals tend to vote for their town's candidate and sports fans root for their own town's soccer team. Furthermore, people in each area of an island have their own favorite musical groups.

Distinctions in social status also add to the differences among peoples of the islands. As a rule, people along the coast tend to have greater access to resources, wear more expensive clothing, have more extravagant marriage ceremonies, reside in more substantial dwellings, and live in larger communities than do the people living inland. These differences are due, in part, to historical factors. Internal, mountain communities on the islands served as refuges for escaped slaves with limited access to resources and who were primarily concerned with subsistence agriculture. Their descendants are involved in a subsistence economy or work as laborers. In contrast, coastal communities were the homes of landowners with cash crops and merchants involved in lucrative, external trade. Their

Union des Comores (Comoros Union, formerly Islamic Federal Republic of the Comoros)

Population:	711,417 (2007 est.)
Area:	2,034 sq. km (785 sq. mi.)
Official languages:	French and Arabic
Languages:	Arabic, French, Comoran (blend of Arabic and Swahili)
National currency:	Comorian franc
Principal religions:	Sunni Muslim 98%, Roman Catholic 2%
Capital:	Moroni (est. pop. 30,000 in 2006)
Principal islands:	Ngazidja (Grand Comore), Mayotte (Mahoré). Mayotte is claimed by the Comoros but prefers the status of overseas department of France. Nzwani (Anjouan) and Mwali (Mohéli) claimed independence from Comores in 1997.
Principal geographical features:	Mount Kartala (active volcano) on Ngazidja
Economy:	*GDP per capita:* US$600 (2005)
Principal products and exports:	*Agricultural:* vanilla, cloves, perfume essences, copra, coconuts, bananas, cassava (tapioca) *Manufacturing:* perfume distilling
Government:	Independence from France, 1975. Constitution, 1978. New constitution, 1996. New constitution, 2001. President elected for 6-year term by universal suffrage. 33-member Assemblée Fédérale elected for 5-year terms by universal suffrage. President appoints prime minister and cabinet. 3 islands and 4 municipalities.
Heads of state since independence:	1975: President Ahmed Abdallah Abderemane 1975–1976: Prince Said Mohammed Jaffar, chairman of the National Executive Council 1976–1978: President Ali Soilih 1978–1989: President Ahmed Abdallah Abderemane 1990–1995: President Said Mohamed Djohar 1996–1998: President Mohamed Taki Abdulkarim 1998–1999: President Tadijiddine Ben Said Massounde 1999–2006: President Azali 2006–: President Ahmed Abdallah Mohamed Sambi
Armed forces:	President is commander in chief. *Total forces:* 500, serving under French officers
Transportation:	No railroads. One deep-water harbor on Anjouan. *Roads:* 880 km (547 mi.), 76% paved *Airline:* Air Comores *Airports:* Each island has a small airport. The largest, with international facilities, is on Grand Comore, at Hahaya.
Media:	weekly: *Al-Watwan* (government-owned). Radio service is provided through government-owned Radio Comores-Inter. Comoros National TV is the only television station.
Literacy and education:	*Total literacy rate:* 56.5% (2005). Education is free, universal, and compulsory from ages 7–15. All children attend Qu'ranic schools. 1 teacher-training college, 1 agricultural school.

descendants are the businesspeople of today. Social differences and historical backgrounds are also reflected in language usage. There are significant linguistic differences between speakers from different islands and even between peoples from different areas of a single island.

See also **Islam; Marriage Systems; Time Reckoning and Calendars.**

BIBLIOGRAPHY

Blanchy-Daurel, Sophie. *La vie quotidienne: À Mayotte (Archipel des Comores)*. Paris: L'Harmattan, 1990.

Lambek, Michael. *Human Spirits: A Cultural Account of Trance in Mayotte*. Cambridge, U.K.: Cambridge University Press, 1981.

Ottenheimer, Harriet, and Martin Otteneheimer. *Music of the Comoro Islands: Domoni*. Washington, DC: Smithsonian/Folkways, 1992.

Ottenheimer, Martin. *Marriage in Domoni*. Prospect Heights, IL: Sheffield Press, 1994.

MARTIN OTTENHEIMER
HARRIET JOSEPH OTTENHEIMER

HISTORY AND POLITICS

The Comoro Islands played an important role in the history of the western Indian Ocean. Archaeological and historical research undertaken during the second half of the twentieth century showed that they have been inhabited for over 1,000 years and played a significant part in the region's social, economic, and religious developments. Inhabited by populations migrated from southern Arabia, Madagascar, and eastern Africa, they were also settled by the Shirazi, a fabled group of migrants to the Swahili world sometime between the tenth and twelfth centuries. They were a major maritime commerce center in the eastern Indian Ocean during the fifteenth century and a favorite stopover for many European and American seafarers including pirates, whalers, and merchantmen during the seventeenth and eighteenth. As late as the middle of the twentieth century, large Indian sailing vessels carrying diverse cargoes could still be seen in Comorian ports.

For most of their past, the islands did not come under the control of any single political unity. Instead, their history is replete with conflicts between independent communities, regions, and islands. Not until the colonial period did a single political entity emerge that brought a semblance of unity to the archipelago. In 1885, the three major western European powers, France, Great Britain, and Germany, signed an agreement in Berlin that gave France control of the islands. Earlier, in 1843, Mayotte had been established as a French protectorate and by 1909 all of the Comoro Islands came under French protection. In 1912 France declared the Comoros a colony and placed them under the administrative authority of a commissioner in Madagascar.

They remained attached to Madagascar until World War II, when a small British force liberated the islands giving the islands limited autonomy and representation in the French Parliament. They were eventually granted complete internal administrative autonomy in 1961 under a resident French high commissioner. A local government was constituted in which an elected body, the Chamber of Deputies, selected a government council serving under a president.

In 1958 the Comoros were given the opportunity to become independent but voted to remain a French territory. By the 1970s public opinion had changed and most inhabitants wanted independence. In 1974 France agreed to independence subject to a referendum. The vote showed that a large majority of all voters favored independence, but the majority on the island of Mayotte did not. The French parliament then declared in early 1975 that decisions about independence would be ratified island by island, angering many Comorians. In July 1975 the government council unilaterally declared the islands' independence. The country was admitted to the United Nations but France did not recognize the islands' sovereignty over Mayotte. In the early twenty-first century the Mayotte is still claimed by the government of the Comoros but remains a territory of France.

After independence, the Comoros internal factional conflicts and external interference brought about considerable political instability. The newly independent's first president was removed from office in 1975 with the help of foreign mercenaries reported to have been under the leadership of Bob Denard, a well-known French veteran. Denard was subsequently involved in three other coups that took place in 1978, 1989, and 1995. The election of a popular president in May 2006 has brought the promise of stability and the hope that it will last for the foreseeable future.

The Comoro Islands' first constitution was passed by referendum in 1978, and amended in 1982, 1985, 1989, and 1992. In 1996 a new constitution was put into place. It proclaimed that the government of the nation draws its inspiration from Islam and recognized universal suffrage for all citizens over the age of eighteen. In 2001 after the islands of Nzwani and Mwali demanded autonomy from the federal administration, a constitution was ratified that established a new government—the Union of the Comoros—with executive, legislative, and judicial branches.

The Union's executive branch is headed by a presidential council composed of a president and two vice presidents, each from a separate island, elected by a majority of the members of the unicameral legislative body for four years. The presidential position rotates among the three islands. The first president, Colonel Assoumani Azzali, was from Ngazidja; in May 2006 Ahmed Abdallah Mohamed Sambi from the island of Nzwani was elected president. In 2010 the presidental candidates will be from the island of Mwali.

The legislative branch is known as the Union Assembly, a unicameral body of thirty members. Members serve five-year terms. Fifteen assembly seats are selected by universal suffrage while the remaining fifteen are selected by the assemblies of the three islands. Each island selects five representatives.

Independent from both the executive and legislative branches, the Supreme Court is the highest in the country. It is composed of seven members: one named by the president of the Union, two named by the vice presidents, one named by the president of the assembly, and three by the presidents from each of the islands. The term of service is six years with a member permitted to serve a maximum of two terms.

See also **Political Systems; Postcolonialism.**

BIBLIOGRAPHY

Ibrahime, Mahmoud. État français et colons aux Comores (1912–1946). Paris: L'Harmattan, 1997.

Martin, Jean. *Comores: Quatre Îles entre pirates et planteurs.* Paris: L'Harmattan, 1983.

Ottenheimer, Martin, and Harriet Ottenheimer. *Historical Dictionary of the Comoro Islands.* Metuchen, NJ: Scarecrow Press, 1994.

Vérin, Emmanuel, and Pierre Verin. *Histoire de la revolution comorienne.* Paris: L'Harmattan, 1999.

MARTIN OTTENHEIMER
HARRIET JOSEPH OTTENHEIMER

CONAKRY. The Republic of Guinea's capital, Conakry is located on a long and narrow peninsula on West Africa's coastline and has an estimated population of 2 million people, according to 2007 statistics. Sparsely populated by ethnic Susu and Baga inhabitants at the time of French military conquest in 1880, the area with its deepwater port soon became the political and commercial center of the French Guinea colony. In the 1890s a massive program of urban planning transformed a landscape of tropical forest into an urban grid of wide boulevards and avenues, replete with monumental administrative buildings and a significant economic infrastructure (international port and the terminus of Conakry-Niger railway). By 1910 the new town's population had grown to 10,000 inhabitants as newcomers from the interior, mainly the Fula and other Susu, joined immigrant Lebanese traders in settling the burgeoning segregated African quarters. Spared yellow fever and bubonic plague that decimated other French colonial coastal cities, Conakry was known as "the pearl of West Africa."

During the post–World War II era the city grew rapidly in area and population (100,000 by 1958) as increased bauxite mining and public works investment created employment as well as a secondary school, a modern hospital, and a new market center. In 1957 Sékou Touré became the first elected mayor of the city and used his municipal powers to spur anticolonial activities that ultimately led to Guinea's independence in September 1958. Over the subsequent postcolonial period, especially with the economic liberalization since 1984, the city has continued to attract rural migrants (20% of the country's total population). The absence of effective urban planning has created chaotic and high-density growth in Conakry's suburbs and deteriorating public health, as witnessed by successive cholera outbreaks since the late twentieth century.

See also **Guinea; Touré, Sékou.**

BIBLIOGRAPHY

Dollfus, Olivier. "Conakry en 1951–52, étude humaine et économique." *Études guinéennes* 10–11 (1952): 3–111.

Goerg, Odile. *Pouvoir colonial, municipalités et espaces urbains: Conakry et Freetown, des années 1880 à 1914.* 2 vols. Paris: L'Harmattan, 1997.

Goerg, Odile. "From Hill Station (Freetown to Downtown Conakry (1st Ward)): Comparing French and British Approaches to Segregation in Colonial Cities at the Beginning of the Twentieth Century." *Canadian Journal of African Studies* 32, no. 1 (1998): 1–30.

Goerg, Odile. "Chietainships between Past and Present: From City to Suburb and Back in Colonial Conakry, 1890s–1950s." *Africa Today* 52, no. 4 (2006): 3–27.

CHRISTOPHER HAYDEN

CONCESSIONARY COMPANIES. *See* Colonial Policies and Practices; Colonialism and Imperialism: Concessionary Companies.

CONFLICT AND CONFLICT RESOLUTION. *See* Civil Society; Warfare.

CONGO, BRAZZAVILLE. *See* Brazzaville; Congo, Republic of.

CONGO, DEMOCRATIC REPUBLIC OF THE

This entry includes the following articles:
GEOGRAPHY AND ECONOMY
SOCIETY AND CULTURES
HISTORY AND POLITICS

GEOGRAPHY AND ECONOMY

The 905,328 square miles of Democratic Republic of the Congo (also called Congo-Kinshasa) provide a solid basis for its industrialization. Crossed by the equator, this rich and diverse area has attracted the German Orbital Transport and Rockets, Incorporated (OTRAG) rocket-launching project. The country takes up almost the whole of the hydrographic basin of the Congo River.

With a length of 2,718 miles and an annual average regular flow of 158,136 cubic feet per second, the river crosses the Congo in an enormous loop, acting as a waterway toward the center, a sea route to the west, and a source of energy everywhere (for example, the Inga Dam in Bas-Congo, and Nzilo Dam in Katanga). The Congo River is one of the largest reserves of drinking water in the world—reserves sought after by the desert countries of Asia and Africa.

Congo-Kinshasa's central region is a forest basin with an average height of 1,312 feet. Its high temperatures throughout the year (77 degrees Fahrenheit) and its plentiful network of rivers and lakes make it ideal for small-scale farming and industrial agriculture (such as rice, palm oil, coffee, and latex). Its rich fauna includes rhinoceros, elephants, and carnivores such as savage cats and leopards.

The plateaus surrounding the basin are covered in gallery forests and wooded savannas that become more grassy to the south as they move farther away from the equator. Replete with herbivorous mammals, they are suitable for agriculture, fishing, and cattle rearing (Katanga, Bas-Congo, and Bandundu). Its subsoil is rich in minerals: copper, cobalt, manganese, cadmium, silver, and pitchblende in Haut-Katanga; gold in the Kilo-Moto belt in Haut-Uéle; diamonds and iron at Kasaï; and germanium and lead in Bas-Congo. The Atlantic coastline is rich in hydrocarbons and fish. There are also abundant resources in the external territory of the Moanda Long Lease (the maritime region of Moanda that was separated from the rest of the Congo due to its minerals and energy resources and put under Western colonial mandate for a century, much like Hong Kong).

The eastern region has tin and colombo tantalite. Its temperate climate, averaging 68 degrees Fahrenheit, is suitable for the cultivation of potatoes and wheat, and the breeding of cattle and chickens. High mountains (Mount Rwenzori with a peak of 16,795 feet, Mount Mitumba, and the Virunga Volcanoes) encircle vast lakes rich in fish, including Lake Tanganyika (21,748 square feet, the largest in Africa) and Lake Kivu (which holds high concentrations of methane gas and carbon dioxide).

The so-called war of liberation has resulted in the waste of natural resources such as water, land, woods, and especially wildlife. Numerous animals, such as the okapi (a ruminant mammal related to the giraffe), are in danger of extinction, and the forests, the home of animals and the pygmies, have been destroyed. The national parks, such as Virunga, Kahuzi-Biega, and Upemba, have not been spared, either.

There is an absence of industrialization to find the right balance between preserving what nature has provided and using it in order to increase economic prosperity and self-sufficiency in energy.

A LOOTED AND INFORMALIZED ECONOMY

The development of the Congo Free State (EIC) (1885–1908), then the Belgian Congo (1908–1960), had equipped the country with industries based upon agriculture and mineral extraction; industries related to food, such as sugar refining and brewing; a textile industry; and an industry related to construction (cement works). However, by failing to make the fundamental aspirations of the Congolese people their central objective, governments of Congo-Kinshasa have been unable to transform the country into a modern power.

Despite this starting base, the economy of the Congo has gone backward, especially after the 1973 nationalization: incomes were devastated, credit was not available, and banks were ruined.

The impoverished populace was unable to transform their trade unions into pressure groups and hence to give a voice to public opinion. The overall size of the economy reverted to its 1958 level, whereas the population had tripled.

UNPRODUCTIVE CONSUMPTION

Per capita consumption has continued to decline. The annual Gross National Income (GNI) per head is US$82.60, or $6.80 per month, and is spent on imported goods from countries with high GNIs such as Japan ($22,360) and the United States ($21,790). This has led to mass unemployment, wheeling and dealing (the black market), the collapse of the tax base, unofficial transactions, smuggling, lack of investment, corruption, but above all a stagnation of production. The rate of GDP growth went from 6.6 percent in 1990 to −14 percent in 1999, 3 percent in 2002, and 5.6 percent in 2003. This official increase in GDP has not yet been noticeable in everyday life, however.

The disappearance of the large companies—Société Minière de Bakwanga (Mining Company of Bakwanga; MIBA) in Kasaï, Plantations Lever au Congo (Lever Plantation in Congo; P.L.C.) in Bandundu and the Equator Province, Société de Développement Industriel et Minier au Zaïre (Industrial and Mining Development Company in Zaire; SODIMIZA), Société Minière de Tenke-Fungurume (Tenke-Fungurume; SMTF), Générale des Carrières et des Mines (National Mining and Quarrying Company; GECAMINES) in Katanga, among others—has led to the dominance of the informal sector, namely illegal activity, a permanent and increasing source of trouble. These numerous independent and short-lived small businesses exist with the sole aim of selling something in order to survive.

DECREASE IN EMPLOYMENT
Whereas in 1958 the 1,102,270 people in the workforce made up 8 percent of the total population, the 850,000-strong workforce in 1997 represented 1.63 percent of the population. In the early twentieth century, the 450,000 workers amount to 0.75 percent. The government and private insurance does not cover unemployment. Service industries predominate the Congolese workplace; the Agence Nationale de Promotion des Investissements (National Agency for the Promotion of Investments; ANAPI) reported that 82.9 percent of the estimated 50,000 employees for the period 2002–2005 fell into this category.

The thirteen Congolese banks no longer offer credit to their 35,000 customers. The national tax system, with 900 different indirect taxes, discourages investment and hence employment. Only a hundred businesses are able to pay taxes of US$100,000. From 2002 to 2005, ANAPI had only raised US$5,316,029,115 via 314 projects, all based in Kinshasa, Bas-Congo, and Katanga.

AN INCREASE IN INEQUALITY
The rural sector is in utter disarray. Farmers have swelled the ranks of the unemployed in the cities. Outdated equipment, ineffective and insufficient

fertilizer (less than 1 pound per acre), and a lack of state support have affected agricultural food production, which, in the early twenty-first century, makes up just 3 percent of the national budget. Ill-considered exploitation of wood, along with the use of firewood (85,016,786 cubic yards), without a policy of replanting, has resulted in deforestation, with 299,545 acres per year being lost.

The Human Development Index for Congo was estimated at 0.393 for 2003. In other words, half the population does not live long, is illiterate or receives little education, and has insufficient finances to cover their expenses. The increase of inequality between rich and poor is around 18.9 percent.

Congo-Kinshasa, one of the Heavily Indebted Poor Countries (HIPC), is among the ten poorest countries in the world, and lacks the means to develop its routes and methods of communication, its agriculture, food hygiene, and its banking and housing systems. The economy has become regionalized, as can be seen from the dams at Katende in Kasaï and Kakobola in Kwilu, and from the sixty private higher education and university establishments registered on June 21, 2006.

See also **Congo River; Debt and Credit; Ecosystems; Forestry; Labor: Trades Unions and Associations; Metals and Minerals.**

BIBLIOGRAPHY

Ajayi, Ade J. F., and Michael Crowder. *Historical Atlas of Africa*. London: Longman Group UK Limited, 1985.

Bellamy, Carol, ed. *La situation des enfants dans le monde. 2004*. UNICEF, 2004.

Hochschild, Adam. *King Leopold's Ghost: A Story of Greed, Terror, and Heroism in Colonial Africa*. Boston: Houghton Mifflin, 1998.

Malingumu, Syosyo Crispin. "Le paradoxe congolais de la croissance dans la pauvreté." *Le Potentiel* 3242, no. 9 (2004).

Ndaywel è Nziem, Isidore. *Histoire générale du Congo. De l'héritage ancien à la République Démocratique*. Brussels, Belgium: Duculot, 1998.

SINDANI KIANGU

SOCIETY AND CULTURES

The modern society and local cultures of the vast Democratic Republic of the Congo (formerly

Zaïre) derive from a deep common heritage in the Bantu-speaking fishing and farming communities who entered the region some three millennia ago. The still-earlier inhabitants whom they encountered in the heavily forested parts of the region became known abroad for their diminutive stature as pygmies (referring to the small people of classical Greek mythology). From them the Bantu communities learned the spiritualized secrets of the land, and they retain an enduring respect for these first, and by Bantu cultural theory, undisplaceable and hence indispensable, occupants even in the early twenty-first century. The autochthonous forest dwellers lived in close trading relationships with the farmers in their clearings and riverine villages and everywhere adopted their Bantu languages. Until recent centuries their small foraging bands remained an important presence, and recourse in the event of agricultural failure, for the farmers.

Linguistic and cultural differentiation, and eventually ethnic identification of political communities, has also continued within this vast Bantu world until the present. Underlying linguistic distinctions among them derive from two separate slow waves of settlement, the first and much earlier one from the north into and throughout the forested region, and the second much later one from the east through the open savanna woodlands to the south. Adaptations of species of bananas (originally from southeast Asia) enabled the forest dwellers to grow in numbers and to differentiate their growing communities according to their specialized techniques of living in the many micro-environments in the forest. Many living near the copious waters carrying off the high rainfall of this equatorial region specialized in fishing. From their dugout canoes and other technologies of fishing local community leaders (in the literature frequently termed big men, or chiefs) developed trading connections that brought them rare exotic goods, which they distributed among neighbors for women as wives, to male clients, and to acquire captive strangers as slaves.

The communities they assembled they operated primarily as trading corporations and as work teams of men trained for large-scale fishing (with nets and weirs, also embankments channeling the waters they fished) as well as for defense or, in at least some cases, also aggression. Large villages,

formed by alliances of big men and their retinues, muted the competitiveness of this essentially commercial environment by assimilating the leading traders into elaborately ranked secret societies. In these elite groups, ambitious newcomers paid heavily to advance through the ranks, and the top-ranking senior members invested the income in whatever ceremonies or improvements they considered to promote the welfare of the community as a whole. The resulting constant movements of men throughout the region diminished the political significance of regional differentiation, so that the many Mongo languages of the inhabitants of the central forest in the early twenty-first century are distinguished only relatively vaguely. The Lingala-speakers of the lower reaches of the main Congo stream prospered greatly, by absorbing many local people, with development of the Atlantic-oriented trades in slaves, ivory, and wild rubber in the nineteenth century. In the early twenty-first century, Lingala is one of the principal languages of the northwestern parts of the country. The autochthones contributed to these trades both by specializing in providing products of the forests and, involuntarily, also as captives sent down the river as slaves. In modern times, only small pockets of these people remain in the most remote forests of Ituri in the northeast and on the watersheds on the west side of the river in present-day Gabon and Republic of the Congo.

Cereal-cultivating farmers from the east settled the more open woodlands to the south, forming one major cluster of linguistically related Chiluba-speaking (Luba) communities on the upper Congo (Lualaba) River and to the west. The parent immigrants owed their evident success in fostering so many modern cultural and linguistic heirs to the rich lands of the river valleys and their resources of salt and—particularly—copper in the vicinity of the modern Copperbelt along the southern border (with Zambia) of the Democratic Republic of the Congo. The need to specialize in the resources of local environmental niches led communities here to settle definitively and to define stronger ethnic distinctions than among their counterparts along the rivers of the forest. By distinguishing themselves thus from neighbors, whose complementing special products and abilities they needed, ethnicity, as elsewhere, was integrative rather than isolating and hostile, except incidentally. The prestige of trading chiefs who also formed networks facilitating broad circulation of the groups' distinctive products, as well as innumerable ideas and fashions, attracted neighbors to their compounds, and the languages spoken in them, and to a political culture that linked the matrilineal communities of the region (children belonged to their mother's lineages and answered to the authority of their mothers' brothers) through an idiom of permanent patrifilial (father-to-son) ties. Oral traditions in the region later recalled these integrative phases, probably culminating between the tenth and thirteenth centuries, as an ancient Luba empire.

Speakers of Lunda-Chokwe languages living to the southwest in valleys of the rivers flowing through the drier plains there adapted this Luba political technique—called positional succession (that is, from the matrilineal communities to the political titles) and perpetual kinship (the ideally stable father-to-son political relationships thus formed among otherwise unrelated lineages)—to profit from the disruptions of Atlantic slaving in the seventeenth century. A highly successful sequence of warlords, bearing the title of *mwaant yaav*, led raids against the dense Luba populations to the north and dispatched raiding and trading agents to the west in a trading diaspora known later as the Lunda (phonetically Ruund) empire. The Lunda chiefs were major sources of captives sent west toward the Atlantic until the late nineteenth century, and the descendants of the communities they formed retain this general ethnic identity into the early twenty-first century. In the far southwest (present-day central and eastern Angola), so-called Chokwe (Tshokué, Quiôco) refugees from the slaving grew dramatically in numbers from hunting ivory and gathering wax and wild rubber after 1850, and their modern descendants live along the border of Democratic Republic of the Congo with Angola.

To the far west, centered on the lower courses of the Kasai, Kwango, and Congo Rivers flowing from the sandy plains of modern Angola and extending north into southern Gabon, the Atlantic coastlands were settled from the north by speakers of the language ancestral to the numerous dialects of modern Kikongo (Kongo), and its eastern extension as the trade language Kituba. The trading chiefs who integrated this region (holding titles of *mani*, or lord/master, a Bantu term also common

far to the east), probably around the twelfth or thirteenth century, prospered as mediators between the marine salt and seashells (*nzimbu*, used as currency) of the Atlantic, copper from the coastal range of mountains, and raffia-fiber textiles woven from palms found on the fringes of the forests to the north and east. These resources allowed them to recruit local matrilineal cultivators as clients and to integrate them around the Kikongo language of their chiefly compounds. The political systems they devised to regularize these connections seem to have involved authorization of particular members of these networks, by councils of representatives from the other communities involved, to deal externally on behalf of the group; these county seats were termed *mbanza*. The internal authority of these chiefs is much less clear but was probably limited or nonexistent.

Portuguese mariners, as they approached the mouth of the Congo River at the end of the fifteenth century, encountered one such federative political center at Loango along the coasts to the north (in present-day Democratic Republic of the Congo), and south of the river they were conducted to the inland *mbanza* of a *mani* with the title of Kongo (now in northern Angola). Portuguese hopes of finding precious metals, and soon their need for slaves, led them to depict this trading chief as a king worthy of papal legal recognition in Europe (and by extension, also its Christian monarchs) as possessor of landed domains and thus capable of authorizing exclusive commercial and diplomatic collaboration with themselves. This initial legal fiction of a kingdom of Kongo acquired a substantive dimension when the Portuguese maneuvered a Christian convert into the succession to the *mani* Kongo title in 1506; the entire literature on the subsequent history of the region takes this claim to monarchy literally.

The actual politics of this kingdom of Kongo remained rather more local and, as the slave trade grew in the seventeenth century, were increasingly dominated by a new generation of trading chiefs who brokered the caravans of captives moving from Lunda regions toward the Atlantic. The Kituba extension of the Kongo language is the residue of nineteenth-century trading agents of these chiefs working inland in search of ivory and wild rubber, and settling with the slaves they kept as their profits.

The modern inhabitants of the region do not think of themselves in terms of a Kongo monarchy and in fact descend from the members of diverse inland communities brought there in captivity.

The advent of colonial rule in the form of the Congo Independent State, the personal fiefdom of the Belgian king Léopold (1885–1908), was terrifyingly disruptive, even of populations already disturbed by slaving from the Atlantic and also by warlords such as Ahmed bin Mohamed bin Juma el Marijibi (1837-1905, fabled as Tippu Tip) who commandeered whole populations along the upper Congo River. This Arab (in fact Swahili) intrusion left the coastal Swahili language as the major second language of trade and colonial administration throughout the eastern portions of the eventual colony, as it remains in the early twenty-first century. In the shorter run, it left residents there highly vulnerable to European companies chartered by Léopold to commandeer them by methods no less brutal to extract the region's considerable resources of ivory, rubber, gold, and other minerals. Little of the early nineteenth-century cultures remained among the survivors.

Nonetheless, the appeal of the idea of kingdoms, both to the colonial-era successors of the title-holders of the Luba and Lunda regions and to nationalist-era politicians of the 1950s and 1960s, has embedded this monarchical image in the modern political culture of Democratic Republic of the Congo, and—with few exceptions—in the ethnographic and historical literature on the region. These figures, or figments of the European imagination, therefore also became the pivots of ethnic definition promoted by colonial-era ethnographers and were given a particular urgency by Belgian colonial policies promoting traditional law in highly local native jurisdictions (*organisation coutumière des jurisdictions indigènes*). Belgian rule saw no future for its Congo subjects other than in rural villages raising men available (for lack of other opportunities) for recruitment for European mining and agricultural enterprises. Belgian national politics, split between Catholic Walloons and Calvinist Flemings, played out in the Christian religious culture of the colony and did little to unify its residents. A few American Protestant missions built small communities of converts in scattered parts of the country and managed to educate a few young men; from the

ranks of these graduates emerged prominent members of the cadre of nationalists in the 1950s. The best known African adaptation of mission Christianity was the 1920s millennial revival in the lower Kongo area led by Simon Kimbangu (the *Église de Jesus Christ sur Terre par le Prophète Simon Kimbangu*, or The Church of Christ on Earth by the Prophet Simon Kimbangu); though suppressed by colonial authorities as subversive, the church survived and with independence has thrived, claiming some five million believers, though active participants may be far fewer.

Excellent ethnographies and exhibitions going back to the beginning of the colonial period have made the plastic arts of the peoples of Democratic Republic of the Congo virtually paradigmatic of African carving in Western culture. Carvings in the rich woods of the region, masks of the secret societies, representations of political authority, and also consummately decorated products of the commercial era of the nineteenth century represent not so much tradition as they capture and interpret the ongoing moments in the histories of communities there. The stylized representations of human figures may reflect the humanistic overtones of the region's developed commercialism, as in Renaissance Italy and elsewhere in Africa. Diviners assemble baskets of carved objects to discern truth in their patterns. Smiths created spectacularly wrought iron and copper scepters, spears, and knives for men in authority. Geometric designs on pottery, on matting, and in the raffia cloths of the Kongo region are both aesthetic and meaningful. Woven and tied styling of women's hair, as well as elaborate scarification, body painting (often with white clay), and tooth filing and other mutilations adorned and presented people's social and personal identities as richly as clothing performs these functions in less hot and humid climates.

The relative formlessness of ethnicity in the country, or the artificiality of the categories recognized by the Belgians, combined with the very small number of educated politicians with significant name recognition among most of the new country's voters, released a torrent of ethnic politics with independence in 1960. The politicians first formed parties around the six districts inherited from the Belgians, reflecting even the underlying linguistic affinities of

République démocratique du Congo (Democratic Republic of Congo or Congo Kinshasa, formerly Zaire)

Population:	65,751,512 (2007 est.)
Area:	2,344,789 sq. km (905,328 sq. mi.)
Official language:	French
Languages:	French, Kongo, Lingala, Swahili, Tshiluba
National currency:	new zaire
Principal religions:	Roman Catholic 50%, Protestant 20%, other syncretic sects and traditional beliefs 10%, Kimbanguist 10%, Muslim 10%
Capital:	Kinshasa (est. pop. 6,500,000 in 2006)
Other urban centers:	Bandundu, Bukavu, Goma, Kananga, Kindu, Kisangani, Lubumbashi, Matadi, Mbandaka, Mbuji-Mayi
Annual rainfall:	varies from 800–1,500 mm (32–59 in.) in south to 2,000–3,000 mm (79–118 in.) in central Basin rainforest
Principal geographical features:	*Mountains:* Ngoma Range, Virunga Range, Ruwenzori Range, Blue Mountains, Kundelunga Range, Marungu Range *Lakes:* Tanganyika, Mobutu (Albert), Kivu, Edouard (Edward), Moero (Mweru) Mai-Ndombe, Ntomba, Upemba, Kabamba, Nzilo *Rivers:* Zaire (Congo), Uele, Sankuru, Kwango, Lualaba, Kasai, Lomani
Economy:	*GDP per capita:* US$700 (2006)
Principal products and exports:	*Agricultural:* coffee, sugar, palm oil, tea, quinine, cassava (tapioca), bananas, root crops, corn, fruits *Manufacturing:* mineral processing, consumer products (including textiles, footwear, cigarettes, processed foods and beverages), cement, wood processing *Mining:* copper, diamonds, zinc
Government:	Independence from Belgium, 1960. Constitution, 1960. New constitution approved in 1967, amended in 1974, 1978, 1990. Transitional constitutions until new constitution adopted in 2005. Bicameral legislature consists of a National Assembly (500 seats, 5-year terms) and a Senate (108 seats, 5-year terms). According to the new constitution, the 10 provinces will be divided into 26 new provinces.
Heads of state since independence:	1960: Prime Minister Patrice Lumumba 1960–1965: President Joseph Kasavubu 1965–1997: President Mobutu Sese Seko (formerly Joseph Désiré Mobutu) 1997–2001: Laurent Desiré Kabila (assassinated) 2001–: President Joseph Kabila
Armed forces:	President is commander in chief.
Transportation:	*Rail:* 5,138 km (3,193 mi.), but track has been ravaged by neglect and war. *Waterways:* 15,000 km (9,300 mi.) on Zaire river, tributaries, and lakes *Ports:* Boma, Bukavu, Bumba, Kalemie, Kindu, Kinshasa, Kisangani, Matadi, Mbandaka *Roads:* 153,497 km (95,379 mi.), 2% paved *National airline:* Air Zaire *Airports:* International facilities at Kinshasa, Lubumbashi, Kisangani, Goma, and Gbadolite. More than 200 smaller airport and airstrips.
Media:	Profusion of daily newspapers (all in French) including *Elima, Salongo, Boyoma, Majumbe.* Many weekly, monthly, and quarterly periodicals. Publishers include the Centre Protestant d'Éditions et de Diffusion and Presses Universitaires du Zaire. 14 radio broadcast stations. 4 television stations.
Literacy and education:	*Total literacy rate:* 65.5% (2006). Education is universal and compulsory for ages 6–12. Postsecondary education provided by Université Ambakart Université Nationale de Kinshasa, Université de Kisangani, Université de Lumbu Lubumbashi, and other institutions.

its citizens only roughly. The southern district of Katanga seceded almost immediately, less out of ethnic particularism than through the machinations of mining interests linked to South Africa. With defeat of the Katanga rebellion and reintegration of the country by 1963, the country reintegrated around local networks claiming ethnic distinctions worthy of political recognition in an unavoidably plural environment of potentially effective civic communities. After a few years of fragmentation into ever-smaller *ad hoc* groupings, the military strongman Joseph-Désiré Mobutu seized control and became one of

independent Africa's wealthiest, most long-lived, and exceedingly authoritarian rulers (1965–1997), a modern monarch more powerful than many of the reputed kings of the past.

Mobutu consolidated his authority through what he called Bantu African *authenticité*, but his authenticity (beyond his renaming himself Mobutu Sese Seko [Nkuku Ngbendu wa Za Banga]) in practice amounted to utter abandonment of the country, particularly its vast rural populations. They have subsequently had to linger in a twilight of living from their own resources in the midst of repeated episodes of turmoil, including—in the east since the mid-1990s—huge influxes of refugees from the genocidal conflicts in neighboring Rwanda, and in the southwest from the thirty-years-war in independent Angola. Mobutu renamed the Belgian colonial capital of Léopoldville as Kinshasa, as the city grew from 150,000 residents under the Belgians (1950 est.) to 450,000 at independence in 1960; the city had more than 6 million residents in 2005. Unlike the nation's other principal towns, Lubumbashi (née Elisabethville, in the far south) and Kisangani (in the northeast, formerly Stanleyville after its explorer-founder, and the setting of V. Naipaul's celebrated *A Bend in the River*), both ravaged by wars and poverty, Kinshasa has given birth to a vibrant urban culture, producing some of the continent's best-known musicians and a distinctive style of highlife.

See also **Bantu, Eastern, Southern, and Western, History of (1000 BCE to 1500); Body Adornment and Clothing; Ceramics; Congo River; Kimbangu, Simon; Kinshasa; Kongo, Angola, and Western Forests, History of (1500 to 1880); Kisangani; Linguistics, Historical; Linguistics and the Study of Africa; Lubumbashi; Mobutu Sese Seko; Secret Societies; Tippu Tip.**

BIBLIOGRAPHY

Biebuyck, Daniel P. *Lega Culture; Art, Initiation, and Moral Philosophy among a Central African People.* Berkeley: University of California Press, 1973.

Biebuyck, Daniel P. *The Arts of Zaire.* Berkeley: University of California Press, 1985.

Harms, Robert W. *River of Wealth, River of Sorrow: The Central Zaire Basin in the Era of the Slave and Ivory Trade, 1500–1891.* New Haven, Connecticut: Yale University Press, 1981.

Hochschild, Adam. *King Leopold's Ghost: A Story of Greed, Terror, and Heroism in Colonial Africa.* Boston: Houghton Mifflin, 1998.

Hunt, Nancy Rose. *A Colonial Lexicon of Birth Ritual, Medicalization, and Mobility in the Congo.* Durham, North Carolina: Duke University Press, 1999.

Klieman, Kairn A. *'The Pygmies Were Our Compass": Bantu and Batwa in the History of West Central Africa, Early Times to c. 1900 C.E.* Portsmouth, New Hampshire: Heinemann, 2003.

MacGaffey, Wyatt. *Kongo Political Culture: The Conceptual Challenge of the Particular.* Bloomington: Indiana University Press, 2000.

Martin, Marie-Louise. *Kimbangu: An African Prophet and His Church.* Oxford: Blackwell, 1975.

Miller, Joseph C. "Cokwe Trade and Conquest." In *Pre-Colonial African Trade*, eds. Richard Gray and David Birmingham. London: Oxford University Press, 1970.

Naipaul, Vidiadhar Surajprasad. *A Bend in the River.* New York: Knopf; distributed by Random House, 1979. (4th ed., by Paul B. Armstrong. New York: W. W. Norton, 2006.)

Northrup, David. *Beyond the Bend in the River: African Labor in Eastern Zaire, 1865–1940.* Athens: Ohio University Center for International Studies, 1988.

Nzongola-Ntalaja, Georges. *The Congo from Leopold to Kabila: A People's History.* London: Zed Books, 2002.

Reefe, Thomas Q. *The Rainbow and the Kings: A History of the Luba Empire to 1891.* Berkeley: University of California Press, 1981.

Schildkrout, Enid, and Curtis A. Keim, eds. *The Scramble for Art in Central Africa.* New York: Cambridge University Press, 1998.

Strother, Z. S. *Inventing Masks: Agency and History in the Art of the Central Pende.* Chicago: University of Chicago Press, 1998.

Thornton, John K. *The Kingdom of Kongo: Civil War and Transition, 1641–1718.* Madison: University of Wisconsin Press, 1983.

Vansina, Jan. *The Children of Woot: A History of the Kuba Peoples.* Madison: University of Wisconsin Press, 1978.

Vansina, Jan. *Paths in the Rainforests: Toward a History of Political Tradition in Equatorial Africa.* Madison: University of Wisconsin Press, 1990.

Young, Crawford, and Thomas Turner. *The Rise and Decline of the Zairian State.* Madison: University of Wisconsin Press, 1985.

JOSEPH C. MILLER

HISTORY AND POLITICS

The Democratic Republic of the Congo is the successor to the Congo Free State, which was a private colony of Léopold II, king of the Belgians (1835–1909). He established monopolies over ivory and wild rubber and imposed a system of taxes in kind. As villages failed to meet their quotas, many Congolese were killed. An international campaign against the atrocities of red rubber was largely responsible for the Congo Free State being transformed into an orthodox colony, Belgian Congo.

The colonial trinity created under the Free State—the State, the companies, and the Church—

continued to rule. Belgian private interests controlled the companies despite substantial state and foreign holdings. Mineral resources—copper in Katanga, diamonds in Kasai, gold in Orientale—were extracted and refined through monopolistic capitalism. Designated districts supplied labor and food to the mines. Elsewhere, an industrial crop, for example cotton, was imposed. The Catholic Church provided schools and other social services in Congo. Its monopoly was not shaken until the 1950s, when an anticlerical government came to power in Belgium.

Congolese movements for self-rule passed through five partially overlapping stages: primary resistance, millenarian movements, urban violence, prepolitical modern associations, and political parties.

Armed opposition to the establishment of colonial occupation was most frequent where the Free State met well-structured traditional states in areas remote from the colonizer's initial operating bases, such as the Zande. The Boa and the Mbuja, segmentary groups living in the forest, revolted against rubber and ivory collection. The line between primary resistance and revolt remains unclear.

Millenarianism used imported, Christian, and local Congolese beliefs and practices. It appeared when no secular remedy to the frustrations introduced by the colonial situation seemed available. The most important were Kimbanguism and Kitawala. By providing a channel for the externalization of radical hostility to colonialism, the millennial movements created a predisposition toward subsequent diffusion of explicitly nationalist ideas.

Two major riots grew out of workers' demonstrations and are attributed to the dissatisfaction of wage earners with the colonial situation. The most important urban riot took place in Leopoldville in 1959. Belgian postponement of a meeting of the Kongo ethnic party *Association des Bakongo* (ABAKO) set off an explosion: a mob vented its fury on Portuguese shops and on visible symbols of the colonial system, including social centers and Catholic missions.

The prepolitical modern associations initially defended the interests of the petty bourgeoisie. However, members became frustrated with the associations efforts to improve the members' status. As news trickled in of progress toward emancipation elsewhere in the continent, the petty bourgeois turned to anticolonialsm.

INDEPENDENT CONGO

Patrice Lumumba's Congolese National Movement (MNC-Lumumba) did better than any other party in pre-independence elections, winning 33 seats in the 137-seat lower house of parliament. Congo attained independence on June 30, 1960, with Lumumba as prime minister and his rival Joseph Kasavubu of ABAKO as president. A week later, the army mutinied and Katanga seceded. Belgium sent troops to protect its nationals, and Kasavubu and Lumumba invited in the United Nations to defend their country against Belgium. Both Belgium and the United States began plotting against Lumumba. The Americans adopted the Belgian characterization of Lumumba as Communist and acted in terms of Cold War logic. Within a few months, Joseph-Désiré Mobutu, named army chief of staff by Lumumba after the mutiny, ousted him from power.

The United Nations ended the Katanga secession in 1962. The Belgians apparently intended to reconstitute a loose federal structure, within which Katanga would enjoy substantial autonomy. Their plans suffered a setback when Katanga's Moïse Tshombe was unable to consolidate power in Kinshasa during a brief term as prime minister of the central government. The Americans failed to create a strong anti-Lumumbist regime in Kinshasa but exercised indirect rule via the Binza group (including Mobutu) that controlled the ministries of foreign affairs, finance, and other key posts.

Excluded from power, some Lumumbists launched insurgencies. Pierre Mulele (d. 1968) pursued a Maoist strategy of political education and guerrilla warfare in his home area in Kwilu (Bandundu). His men were unable to occupy any of the main towns or to break out of their ethnic base.

The rebellion in the east controlled half the country. It began in South Kivu and spread into North Katanga (home of Laurent Kabila) and Maniema (home of Gaston Soumialot, b. 1922). The fighters of the People's Liberation Army (APL) relied heavily on magical protection, Mai Mulele or Mai Lumumba. Rather than working in the countryside in Maoist manner, they moved from town to town in trucks, and their strategy nearly worked. Toward the end they fell victim to the same sort of ethnic closure that plagued Mulele.

Belgium organized a response to the rebellions, putting white mercenaries as the spearhead of a force comprising former Katanga gendarmes and regular Congo army troops. That force was nearing Kisangani when the Americans dropped Belgian paratroops in the town, decapitating the Lumumbists' People's Republic of the Congo.

In November 1965, before victory was complete, President Kasavubu promised to dismiss the mercenaries. That triggered Mobutu's second coup d'état. Assuming the presidency, Mobutu stayed there for thirty-two years until ousted by Kabila in 1997. Mobutu distanced himself from Belgium while retaining American protection.

In the cultural domain, Mobutu promoted the doctrine of authenticity, meaning that Congo (renamed Zaire) would be true to itself. This generated conflict with the Catholic Church. Mobutu nationalized the universities, thereby depriving the Church of its control of the country's leading institution of higher education, Lovanium University. His People's Revolutionary Movement (MPR) was declared a religion and Mobutu its Messiah.

In the economic sphere, Mobutu attacked the Belgian-dominated corporations and attempted to form a new Zairian capitalist class led by him. His efforts were somewhat successful in the short term, but catastrophic in the long term, leaving the country more dependent on international capitalism than before. He reopened the *contentieux belgo-congolais* (disputes concerning assets and debts of the colonial state) that had supposedly been settled by Tshombe during his brief tenure at the head of the central government. Mobutu attempted to nationalize the Union Minière du Haut-Katanga (UMHK), the most important single Belgian firm, first by obliging the company to relocate its corporate headquarters. When the company refused, Mobutu created a Congolese corporation, the Générale des Carrières et de Mines (General Company of Quarries and Mines), or *Gécamines*. This company managed the holdings of the former UMHK within Congo but was unable to find an alternative to downstream refining and marketing in Belgium. Subsequently, a second state enterprise, Société de Commercialisation des Minerais (SOZACOM), was entrusted with marketing the production of Gécamines and other Zairian producers. As it became a new source of

embezzlement and kickbacks, SOZACOM was liquidated, under pressure from the IMF and the World Bank.

Mobutu's government initially was popular. His moves against the politicians were supported. Nationalization of the universities was popular with professors and students. Authenticity, before it degenerated into a cult of the personality, resonated with many Congolese. Economic conditions were good from 1968 to 1974, thanks to the restoration of order and the high price of copper.

Starting in 1974, there was a series of self-inflicted disasters. Zairianization of the economy damaged the system of distribution of consumer goods, and made the term *acquéreur* (one who had acquired a foreign-owned business) into a term of opprobrium.

Mobutu intervened unsuccessfully in the Angolan war, earning the enmity of the victorious People Movement for the Liberation of Angola (MPLA). In 1977 and 1978, small units of the Congolese National Liberation Front (FLNC) invaded Katanga from Angola, and Mobutu had to seek foreign help. Repeated efforts to rebuild the army or to add new security forces were undermined by nepotism and corruption.

The Catholic Church constituted one of the main forces of opposition to Mobutu's dictatorship. The Church offered its own version of authenticity, speaking of "the God of our ancestors," thereby renewing the support of the faithful. The Protestants and the Kimbanguists, granted formal equality with the Catholics, tended to support Mobutu.

Despite the contradiction between conservative bishops and more radical young priests and lay members of catholic organizations, the Church offered an alternative vision of Congolese society. This could be seen in 1992, when thousands of Catholics and other Christians marched for a reopening of the Sovereign National Conference (CNS), closed by Mobutu. Security forces killed over thirty demonstrators.

The broadly based democracy movement of the early 1990s showed how greatly Congolese wanted change. The skilful maneuvering of Mobutu and allies and the ineptitude of opposition politicians both contributed to the failure.

The wars of 1996–1997 and 1998–2002 have been interpreted as invasions and as civil wars. They were a lethal combination of the two. Rwanda and Uganda recruited Laurent-Désiré Kabila as a front man for their invasion of Congo in 1996. Kabila was supposed to be weak enough to obey his backers yet strong enough to secure their common borders. To survive as president in the face of Congolese hostility to the Rwandans and Ugandans, Kabila broke with them and sought backing from his home province of Katanga.

To rid themselves of Kabila, Rwanda and Uganda invaded Congo a second time, again using Congolese as a screen. The war soon degenerated into a war of partition and pillage in which rival warlords exploited minerals and other wealth of their fragment of the national territory. International efforts to promote a negotiated settlement dragged on, as each side preferred to continue fighting, talking, and pillaging, rather than make meaningful concessions. The assassination of Laurent Kabila in 2001, and the designation of Joseph Kabila as his successor, opened the door to progress. A ceasefire was signed in 2002 and a transitional government took power in 2003.

The Rwanda-supported Congolese Democratic Rally (RCD) proved spectacularly unpopular. Throughout the RCD zone, local resistance groups sprang up, often under the name Mai Mai. They enjoyed broad popular support that earned them a place in the transitional government, along with the other belligerents. Another rebel group, the Congo Liberation Movement (MLC) led by Jean-Pierre Bemba (b. 1962) and supported by Uganda, enjoyed some popular support, especially in Equateur Province.

Presidential voting in 2006 led to the election of President Joseph Kabila, but confirmed his lack of popular support in the Lingala-speaking west, including Kinshasa, where Bemba of the MLC won strong support. Parties linked to the Mai Mai insurgency strongly supported Kabila.

The Democratic Republic struggled to overcome the legacies of abuse and neglect under Mobutu, and the atrocities and pillage of the wars since 1996. On the crucial question of management of the economy, and the need to reconcile development with self-sufficiency, the young president faced critical choices. His father, Laurent Kabila, preached liberation-movement Marxism. Joseph, on the other hand, appeared content to cultivate American and European governments and investors.

The Democratic Republic of the Congo of the early twenty-first century is not the Congo Free State. The Mobutu regime united the people as never before. To some extent, this was the effect of regime education and propaganda. Mobutu also united the people against him. The wars of 1996–97 and 1998–2003 reinforced Congolese national sentiment. The presidential runoff election of 2006 pitted two candidates both claiming to be more nationalist than the other.

In the early twenty-first century, many millions of Congolese are Catholics and there is even a Congolese cardinal. Protestant denominations claim millions more adherents. The Kimbanguist Church long ago broke out of its ethnic limits and today is found in every corner of the republic. New prophetic movements, more or less Christian, compete with the established churches for followers, promising not just heavenly salvation but success here and now.

New sorts of civil society organizations play major roles in the struggles against injustice and for democracy. These include organizations defending human rights, women's rights, and the rights of journalists.

See also **Civil Society; Cold War; Human Rights; Kabila, Laurent Desiré, and Joseph; Kinshasa; Lumumba, Patrice; Metals and Minerals; Socialism and Postsocialisms; Tshombe, Moïse Kapenda; United Nations; Warfare: Internal Revolts; Women: Women and the Law.**

BIBLIOGRAPHY

De Witte, Ludo. *The Assassination of Lumumba*. London: Verso, 2001.

Emizet, Kisangani, and Léonce Ndikumana. "The Economics of Civil War: The Case of the Democratic Republic of Congo." *Understanding Civil War: Evidence and Analysis*. Washington, DC: World Bank and Oxford University Press, 2005.

Kalb, Madeleine G. *Congo Cables: The Cold War in Africa from Eisenhower to Kennedy*. New York: Macmillan, 1982.

MacGaffey, Wyatt. *Modern Kongo Prophets: Religion in a Plural Society*. Bloomington: Indiana University Press, 1983.

Nzongola-Ntalaja, Georges. *The Congo from Leopold to Kabila. A People's History*. London: Zed Books, 2002.

Turner, Thomas. *The Congo Wars. Conflict, Myth and Reality.* London: Zed Books, 2007.

Young, Crawford. *Politics in the Congo: Decolonization and Independence.* Princeton, New Jersey: Princeton University Press, 1965.

THOMAS E. TURNER

CONGO, REPUBLIC OF

This entry includes the following articles:
GEOGRAPHY AND ECONOMY
SOCIETY AND CULTURES
HISTORY AND POLITICS

GEOGRAPHY AND ECONOMY

The Republic of Congo (henceforth Congo) is situated astride the Equator between 4 degrees north latitude and 5 degrees south latitude, covering an irregularly shaped area of 132,000 square miles, which extends 662 miles north-northeast to south-southwest and 250 miles east-southeast to west-northwest. It borders Gabon to the west, Cameroon and the Central African Republic to the north, and Angola's Cabinda enclave to the southwest. It has a short Atlantic coast and, to the south and east, is bounded by the Congo River and its tributary, the Oubangui River. These rivers form much of the boundary with the Democratic Republic of the Congo (formerly Zaire).

Congo is divided into four topographical regions: the region close to the Atlantic coast is a low, treeless plain that rises inland to the Mayombe Mountains, a largely forested region running parallel to the coast and achieving elevations of up to 2,625 feet. Farther inland, positioned south-centrally and between the Chaillu Massif and the Mayombe Mountains, the Niari Valley has lower elevation and fertile soils, which has facilitated agricultural development in the country. Extending from the northern suburbs of Brazzaville, Congo's capital since 1903, are the drier central highlands to the north known as the Téké Plateau, a series of low hills and rolling plains. Finally, the Congo Basin, the largest of the country's regions, is mainly composed of impassable floodplains in its lower section and dry savanna in the upper section.

Congo has a tropical climate that is generally characterized by high temperatures, high rainfall, and high humidity (roughly 80%), though it is somewhat cooler and drier along the coast than elsewhere in the country. More clearly pronounced in the north, Congo experiences two dry and two rainy seasons every year, with the rainy season in the north roughly corresponding to the dry season in the south, and vice versa. North of the equator the rainy season lasts from April until late October, and the dry season lasts from early November until March. Average temperatures range from 68 degrees Fahrenheit (dry season) to 77 degrees Fahrenheit (rainy season) and average rainfall is around 60 inches. The Congo Basin, at 98 inches or more, experiences the highest levels of rainfall in Congo.

The Republic of Congo boasts a small population (3.8 million, 2007 estimate) belonging to more than 70 ethnic groups and averaging about nineteen inhabitants per square mile. Much of it is concentrated in the more urbanized southwestern regions of the country, leaving the vast northern reaches nearly uninhabited. Approximately half of Congo's population lives in either Brazzaville (1.2 million) or coastal Pointe Noire (600,000), as well as along the railway link that connects the two, and that constitutes the backbone of the country.

Earlier impeded by French colonial neglect and abandonment, Congo's economic policy since independence in 1960 has been characterized by frequent ideological transformations. Following independence, successive governments pursued Marxist-based policies of nearly exclusive state participation in the economy, with private sector involvement limited to few economic activities such as mining and transport. From 1977, this was modified under the presidency of Joachim Yhombi-Opango (b. 1939) to allow for more private investment and a mixed economy. This policy was expanded under the leadership of Denis Sassou-Nguesso, who privatized, semi-privatized, or closed much of Congo's state-run industry, terminated the state monopoly, and liberalized investment from the early 1980s. Pressured to restructure by the World Bank and other international institutions, it was only with the 1994 devaluation of the CFA franc that full economic restructuring was initiated. However, as of 2007, many of the resulting policies still await full implementation, partially as a result of the civil war that broke out in Brazzaville in from 1993–1994 and fighting that

resumed in early June 1997 and continued until mid-October of the same year. The post-conflict period has been traumatic and economic recovery has been slow, despite continued intervention by international institutions.

With a total gross domestic product (GDP) of US$5.1 billion, the Congolese economy depends primarily on the oil sector, which, as of 2005, accounts for about 90 percent of total export earnings and 50 percent of the country's GDP. Agriculture, contributing 11 percent of Congo's GDP, consists mostly of low-yield, subsistence-type activities. There is an important gender aspect in that women, including elderly women as well as children, are the primary urban and rural market producers and sellers of various forest products and foodstuffs, including the collection of certain edible insects such as caterpillars. Men rarely engage in this type of informal subsistence livelihood activity. Cassava is grown as the main food crop (though food security remains a problem), and tobacco and sugar are grown for export purposes. The forestry sector and timber production provide another noteworthy economic exporting activity. Finally, mining (zinc, lead, copper, and others) and manufacturing (cement, cigarettes, and food processing) also play a part in the country's economy.

Although recent economic indicators have been relatively hopeful, continued economic recovery and the reduction of widespread poverty in Congo will largely depend on internal political stability and the country's ability to face challenges such as debt management and infrastructure development (such as increasing road networks in the north and improving the country's efficiency to generate hydroelectric power).

See also **Brazzaville; Decolonization; World Bank.**

BIBLIOGRAPHY

Allen, Christopher; Michael S. Radu; Keith Somerville; and Joan Baxter. *Benin, the Congo, Burkina Faso: Economics, Politics and Society.* London: Pinter, 1989.

Decalo, Samuel; Virginia Thompson; and Richard Adloff. *Historical Dictionary of Congo,* 3rd edition. Lanham, MD: Scarecrow Press, 1996.

Fegley, Randall. *The Congo.* Oxford: Clio Press, 1993.

Gouemo, Régis. *Le Congo-Brazzaville: De l'état postcolonial à l'état multinational.* Paris: Harmattan, 2004.

Ndoye, Ousseynou, and Julius Chupezi Tieguhong. "Forest Resources and Rural Livelihoods: The Conflict between Timber and Non-timber Forest Products in the Congo Basin." *Scandinavian Journal of Forest Research,* Volume 19, Supplement 4, August 2004: 36–44.

Vantomme, Paul; Daniela Göhler; and Francois N'Dekere-Ziangba. *Contribution of Forest Insects to Food Security and Forest Conservation: The Example of Caterpillars in Central Africa,* ODI Wildlife Policy Briefing, Number 3, January 2004.

Zika, Jean-Roger. *Démocratisme et misère politique en afrique: Le cas du Congo-Brazzaville.* Paris: Harmattan, 2002.

ALEC THORNTON

SOCIETY AND CULTURES

Compared to neighboring Cameroon, the Central African Republic, and the Democratic Republic of the Congo (DRC), which have larger populations, Congo offers a striking ethnic diversity. An estimated 3.8 million Congolese inhabit 132,000 square miles of land, an average density of about 29 people per square mile. The average annual population growth rate is 3.5 percent. Almost 80 percent of the population lives in the south, especially in the vicinity of Brazzaville, the capital, and Pointe-Noire, Congo's only coastal city and main industrial agglomeration. The remaining 20 percent populates the northwestern two-thirds of the country, which suffers from a lack of communications and other services.

Of all the various ethnic groups that inhabit the country, only the Binga Pygmies—around 20,000 nomadic peoples scattered in small communities deep in the heart of the rain forest—do not belong to the vast Bantu-speaking group of tropical Africa. There are three principal ethnic groups: the Kongo, the Téké, and the Mbochi. These three groups are further divided into some seventy-five distinct subgroups. The Vili, Kongo, Lari, Yombe, Sundi, and Dondo are among the major subgroups of the Kongo and account for 53 percent of the country's total population. They inhabit the area between Brazzaville and the Atlantic coast in the administrative regions of Pool and Niari. They are also to be found in southwestern DRC and northwestern Angola from where they migrated in successive waves to Congo after the collapse of the Kingdom of Kongo in the late seventeenth century.

As the Kongo groups migrated northward they encountered the Téké group, whose demographic extension went as far south as Kinkala and Boko, now occupied by the Kongo. By the late nineteenth century, the Kongo had driven back the Téké (whose control of the region was already contested) beyond the Djoué River, upstream from the Malebo Pool. During the colonial period, the emerging Lari and Sundi elites quickly positioned themselves as auxiliary work forces in the various colonial services, as skilled workers in the growing urban private sectors, and as the first native priests in the Catholic missions. From the 1930s onward, the colonial crackdown on messianic movements that arose among Lari populations of the Pool region contributed to the emergence of an urban and ethnic identity of the Lari group.

In the early twenty-first century, the Téké people are concentrated in the Central Highlands, where they probably settled before the fifteenth century, migrating eastward along the Alima River. The French colonial presence and policies greatly upset their economy, mainly based on inter-regional trade, and adversely disrupted their social institutions. Rather than being absorbed into the colonial economy, many Téké groups withdrew from the Brazzaville area in what can be qualified as "avoidance protest" against colonial upheaval. In 1933 they accounted for only 3 percent of the African population of Brazzaville. Due to low fertility rates and the lack of suitable land for agricultural activities in the dry and sandy Téké Plateau, their proportion has declined considerably to only 13 percent in the 1990s. The Mbochi migrated from the west bank of the Congo River and occupied the fluvial basins surrounding the Mossaka, Sangha, Likouala, and Congo Rivers. Their primary occupations include fishing, trading, boatbuilding, and hunting. They are presently located in the Cuvette and Likouala regions and account for 12 percent of the total population of Congo. The remaining ethnic groups include the Kota (10%), the Boubangui (4%), the Maka (4%), and the Mbeti (3%).

Apart from the north-south ethnic cleavages, exacerbated by the colonial authorities and resurfacing during the northern military regimes of Joachim Yhombi-Opango (1977–1979) and Denis Sassou-Nguesso (1979–1992, and 1997 to the present) that expanded employment opportunities for northerners in the south, there also has been a massive rural-urban migration that made Congo one of the continent's most urbanized countries. At least two-thirds of the population live in Brazzaville and Pointe-Noire, the two terminals of the Congo-Océan railroad, and along the rail line in towns that developed primarily as railway stations. Nearly one-third of the population, and 68 percent of the urban population, live in Brazzaville alone.

European presence heightened incipient ethnic disparities among Congo's various regional groups. On the eve of independence, these disparities turned into ethnic allegiances and ethnopolitical rivalries. Concentration of the Congo's various ethnic groups in Brazzaville did not eliminate regional tensions, for the immigrants tend to cluster in geographically and socially homogenous neighborhoods. Thus,

most Kongo people live in Bacongo, one of the most ancient and populous Brazzaville neighborhoods. The French created this neighborhood in 1909 for Kongo workers who, because of strong family and community networks, succeeded in outnumbering any regional group in the migratory flows to the city. In the more recently built neighborhoods of Talangai live the new Mbochi immigrants, while Poto-Poto, developed in 1911, remains by far the most integrated part of the city, although its streets bear the names of the many ethnic groups that were established there by the colonial municipal administration.

As during the decolonization period, when political parties were created, ethnicity and regionalism continue to polarize political life in Congo, with every ethnic group closing ranks behind an ethnic or regional candidate. Of all the many political parties that were formed in anticipation of the National Conference of February–May 1991, only a few survived as major political fixtures because they succeeded in appealing to voters only by generating ethnic or regional solidarities. Pascal Lissouba, elected president in August 1992, formed an ethno-political coalition of three regions (Niari, Bouenza, Lekoumou) known as Nibolek that propelled him to power, while Bernard Kolélas failed to acquire a majority of the votes of the Kongo people, who were divided by the unexpected candidacy of André Milongo, another prominent Kongo figure. Most Mbochi and related groups voted for the incumbent, Sassou-Nguesso, whose defeat announced the end of the long military rule of the northerners.

However, the Congolese ethnopolitical landscape has recently manifested a certain ambivalence. Though political leaders continue to play the ethnic card as they jockey for political leadership, they have not been too reluctant to adopt a realpolitik approach by entering into pragmatic political alliances across traditional ethnic lines and personal enmities, as seen with Kolélas and Sassou-Nguesso. It is uncertain to what these political alliances and patterns will lead the country. Most Congolese still strongly favor ethnic solidarities over national identity. They continue to view transition to democracy along regional lines and as a result of ethnic pressure as well as military supremacy rather than as the outcome of free and fair elections.

As a result, Congo's foray into a more democratic path was short lived after Sassou-Nguesso

---

République du Congo (Republic of the Congo or Congo Brazzaville)

Population:	3,800,610 (2007 est.)
Area:	342,000 sq. km (132,000 sq. mi.)
Official language:	French
Languages:	French, Kongo, Lingala, Teke
National currency:	CFA franc
Principal religions:	Christian 50%, animist 48%, Muslim 2%
Capital:	Brazzaville (est. pop. 800,000 in 2006)
Other urban centers:	Pointe Noire, Dolisie
Annual rainfall:	varies by region, averaging 1,520 mm (60 in.)
Principal geographical features:	*Mountains:* Chaillu Massif, Mayombe Mountains, Téké Plateau *Rivers:* Congo, Sangha, Oubangui, Motaba, Likouala, Alima, Louesse, Niari, Kouilou
Economy:	*GDP per capita:* US$700 (2003)
Principal products and exports:	*Agricultural:* manioc, sugar, rice, corn, peanuts, vegetables, coffee, cocoa, forest products *Manufacturing:* petroleum refining, food processing, lumber and plywood, textiles, cement *Mining:* oil, potash, lead, zinc, copper, uranium, phosphates, natural gas
Government:	Independence from France, 1960. Five constitutions between independence and 1979. Military dictatorship, officially declared multiparty in 1991. Under new constitution of 2002, president elected for 7-year term by universal suffrage. Bicameral legislature of Senate and National Assembly elected by universal suffrage for 5-year terms. President appoints prime minister and Council of Ministers. For purposes of local government there is 1 commune (Brazzaville) and there are 9 regions headed by commissioners, subdivided into districts, which consist of villages and communes.
Heads of state since independence:	1960–1963: President Abbé Fulbert Youlou 1963–1968: President Alphonse Massemba-Débat 1968–1977: President Major Marien Ngouabi 1977: Military junta 1977–1979: Colonel Joachim Yhombi-Opango, chairman of the Provisional Military Committee 1979–1992: President Colonel Denis Sassou-Nguesso 1992–1997: President Pascal Lissouba 1997–: President Denis Sassou-Nguesso
Armed forces:	Headed by the president. Voluntary enlistment, minimum age 18. *Army:* 8,000 *Navy:* 300 *Air force:* 200 *Paramilitary:* 6,700
Transportation:	*Rail:* 894 km (556 mi.), state-controlled, through the Chemin de Fer Congo-Océan. *Waterways:* Inland rivers used for local traffic; trade to the interior on the Congo and Oubangui. *Ports:* River: Brazzaville, Ouesso, Mossaka. Seaport: Pointe-Noire *Roads:* 17,289 km (10,743 mi.), 10% paved *National airline:* Lina-Congo; Congo has 6% interest in Air Afrique. *Airports:* International facilities at Brazzaville and Pointe Noire. 32 other airports and airstrips throughout the country.
Media:	3 daily newspapers: ACI, *L'Eveil de Pointe Noire*, *Mweti*. All state-owned. 21 periodicals. Four active publishing houses. Radiodiffusion Télévision Nationale Congolaise provides radio service, with television broadcasting only in Brazzaville and its environs.
Literacy and education:	*Total literacy rate:* 83.8% (2003). Education is free, compulsory, and universal for ages 6–16. 36 technical and vocational schools. Higher education provided by Université Marien Ngouabi and several technical and vocational schools.

---

came back to power in October 1997 following a civil war that took on a genocidal course and claimed the lives of tens of thousands of southerner civilians. This occurred against the backdrop of France's fierce resolve to preserve her access to Congo's rich oil reserves. Through her oil company, Elf-Aquitaine, and one its subsidiaries, Elf-Congo, France orchestrated Sassou-Nguesso's comeback by funneling financial support and military equipment to her protégé. France went as far as to enlist the help of Angolan and Chadian troops to rescue a beleaguered Sassou-Nguesso and overthrow the democratically elected government of president Pascal Lissouba. Since then, and despite peace accords signed between the government and the military opposition (Kolélas' Ninja militias) in March 2003 and the return of the Pool's displaced population, the political situation in Congo remains volatile while economic conditions have worsened for the vast majority of the population.

See also **Brazzaville; Decolonization; Government: Military; Pointe-Noire; Sassou-Nguesso, Denis.**

BIBLIOGRAPHY

Bernault, Florence. *Démocraties ambiguës en Afrique centrale: Congo-Brazzaville, Gabon, 1940–1965.* Paris Éditions Karthala, 1996.

Decalo, Samuel; Virginia Thompson; and Richard Adloff. *Historical Dictionary of Congo.* Lanham, MD: Scarecrow Press, 1996.

Gondola, Ch. Didier. *Villes miroirs: Migrations et identités urbaines à Kinshasa et Brazzaville, 1930–1970.* Paris: l'Harmattan, 1997.

Martin, Phyllis. *Leisure and Society in Colonial Brazzaville.* New York: Cambridge University Press, 1995.

CH. DIDIER GONDOLA

HISTORY AND POLITICS

Following the explorations of Diego Cão in the 1480s, the Portuguese established a strong European presence on the African coast near the mouth of the Congo River and remained the dominant European influence there through the seventeenth century. By the 1780s, however, the French had displaced the Portuguese as the major European influence, establishing some seventy French trading firms north of the Congo. French missionary and trading stations were in place on the Gabon coast in the 1830s, and in 1875 France dispatched Pierre Savorgnan de Brazza to consolidate its influence in the area. De Brazza made three missions to the Gabon-Congo region between 1875 and 1885. During the second of these missions he negotiated a treaty with the *makoko* (king) of the Téké providing for a French protectorate; on the third mission he established numerous posts, effectively occupying the territory. Later, the borders of Congo were clarified by treaties with Portugal (1885) and the Congo Free State (1887 and 1892). Brazzaville, Congo's capital, later served as administrative capital of French Equatorial Africa (Afrique Équatoriale Française, or the AEF).

De Brazza, who was named commissioner of French Congo in 1886, resisted attempts by colonial authorities to open Congo to commercial exploitation. As a result, de Brazza was dismissed in 1898, and France set up a concessionary system under which French companies were given monopolies over Congolese tracts in return for fees and tax payments. These companies enjoyed de facto power to extract Congo's resources at a minimum cost, which led to numerous abuses, including the deaths of thousands of African workers. Reports of these abuses led to halting reforms; although the concessionary system was moribund by 1920, the last company survived until 1935. The most important developmental project of the interwar period was the Congo-Océan railway, completed in 1934 at the cost of fifteen thousand to twenty thousand African lives.

At the beginning of World War II, local forces loyal to Charles de Gaulle's Free French seized control of the AEF, including Congo, and fought for the Allies. In return, France promised socioeconomic reforms and limited self-rule for French colonies at the Brazzaville Conference in January 1944. This political opening led to the formation of two important parties in 1946: the Congolese Progressive Party (Parti Progressiste Congolais, or PPC), led by Jean-Félix Tchicaya and supported by the coastal Vili, and the African Socialist Movement (Mouvement Socialiste Africain, or MSA), founded by Jacques Opangault and supported by the northern Mbochi. The former was linked to Félix Houphouët-Boigny's Rassemblement Démocratique Africain and the latter to the French socialist party. Meanwhile, the political attention of the numerous Lari, who occupied Brazzaville and the Malebo Pool (the region of the Congo that includes Brazzaville), was transfixed by a movement called Matswanism. Inspired by a charismatic civil servant, André Matswa, the movement combined a spiritual belief in Matswa's divinity with anticolonial resistance. The political ambition of the Lari gained expression in a political party in 1956, when Fulbert Youlou founded the Democratic Union for the Defense of African Interests (Union Démocratique pour la Défense des Intérêts Africains, or UDDIA).

Congo's moderate postwar leaders generally accepted the pace of reform set by France. In the territorial elections of May 1957, the UDDIA and MSA split the vote evenly, establishing Youlou and Opangault as the country's leading politicians. In 1958, both leaders campaigned for association with France, which was approved overwhelmingly. The defeated PPC then joined the MSA in opposition to a UDDIA–dominated government. The following year new elections gave the UDDIA an overwhelming majority, and Youlou became prime minister. After independence in 1960, Youlou served as president for three more years. His regime could best be described as conservative, francophile, and unitarist, insofar as Youlou attempted to co-opt Mbochi and Vili rivals while undermining their local bases. In April 1963 Youlou sought to further consolidate this power by declaring the establishment of a one-party state in Congo. This usurpation, however, along with a stagnant economy and pro-Katanga foreign policy, incensed Congo's radical youth. As a result, Youlou was overthrown in August 1963 during three days of riots, later celebrated as *les trois glorieuses*.

Congo's next regime was headed by Alphonse Massemba-Débat, a Mukongo, former Assembly president, and moderate socialist. In 1964, radical legislators created a single new party: the National Movement of the Revolution (Mouvement National de la Révolution, or MNR). The MNR proved to be the first of several mass organizations designed to promote revolutionary unity. Yet Massemba's technocratic regime satisfied neither remaining Youlouists nor the young radicals, and a military coup in August 1968 led to his displacement by a revolutionary council. A young northern officer, Captain Marien Ngouabi, emerged as the leader of these forces, becoming president in 1969.

Under Ngouabi's leadership, the country was renamed the People's Republic of Congo and gained a new, ostensibly Marxist-Leninist party, the Congolese Workers' Party (Parti Congolais du Travail, or PCT) in 1969. These steps, however, were as much a product of Ngouabi's desire to consolidate power and assuage the left as they were an expression of ideological conviction. Over the following years Ngouabi used the pretext of several coup attempts, real and invented, to consolidate his power. Meanwhile, he used new mass, PCT–created organizations to tame his social critics.

Despite his charisma, Ngouabi alienated many moderates, southerners, and others, and he was assassinated in March 1977. He was succeeded by General Joachim Yhombi-Opango, another northern officer. Although Yhombi was far less captivated by Marxism than Ngouabi, his views had little impact on policy as he was forced from power in an intraparty coup in February 1979.

Yhombi's successor was Denis Sassou-Nguesso, a Mbochi colonel with strong Marxist credentials. With greater success than Ngouabi, Sassou co-opted social forces through corporatist party organs and eliminated potential rivals through periodic purges. His regime also continued the expansion of the state sector begun in 1963 to reward loyalists. Despite his political skills, Sassou steadily lost influence as declining oil prices devastated Congo's economy during the 1990s.

With global pressures for democratization rising, Sassou reluctantly allowed a "sovereign national conference" to convene in early 1991. The conference effectively stripped him of power, established an interim regime, scheduled elections, and created a new constitution. Pascal Lissouba, a former Massemba prime minister and United Nations Education, Scientific and Cultural Organization (UNESCO) official, was elected president in August 1992. His party, the Pan-African Union for Social Democracy (Union Panafricaine pour la Démocratie Sociale, or UPADS), won a plurality that year and went into coalition with the PCT. When the PCT abandoned the coalition, however, Lissouba dissolved the Assembly and organized new elections in 1993, which the UPADS won decisively. In 1993–1994 Congo experienced serious ethnic violence as Sassou and Bernard Kolélas, head of the chiefly Bakongo Congolese Movement for Democracy and Comprehensive Development (Mouvement Congolais pour la Démocratie et le Développement Intégral, or MCDDI), organized militias to resist Lissouba's regime. Since a series of agreements were reached in 1994, civil peace slowly returned to Congo.

Congo's experiment with competitive, democratic politics ended in June 1997 when full-scale civil war erupted. The trigger for the war was Lissouba's effort to disarm Sassou's militia weeks before a scheduled presidential election featuring the two political figures. With the help of French military hardware and intervening Angolans, Sassou eventually prevailed in the war after five months of combat. His regime subsequently fought an even more murderous war to seize definitive control of the southern regions between December 1998 and November 1999. Low-grade rebellion by Lari elements in the Pool region continued into the early 2000s. In 2001 the Congolese approved a new constitution giving the president wider powers and longer terms in office. Early the following year, Sassou gained a new presidential mandate and his political coalition won a large majority in parliament under this new regime, though it was clear that the elections were far from free or competitive. The Sassou II regime faced daunting challenges as the country's oil production began to decline.

See also **Houphouët-Boigny, Félix; Sessou-Nguesso, Denis; World War II.**

BIBLIOGRAPHY

Bazenguissa-Ganga, Rémy. *Les voies du politique au Congo: Essai de sociologie historique* [The Ways of Politics in Congo: An Essay of Historical Sociology]. Paris: Karthala, 1997.

Clark, John F. "The Neo-Colonial Context of the Democratic Experiment of Congo-Brazzaville." *African Affairs* 101, no. 403 (April 2002): 171–192.

Clark, John F. "The Collapse of the Democratic Experiment in the Republic of Congo: A Thick Description." In *The Fate of Africa's Democratic Experiments*, ed. Leonardo Villalon and Peter VonDoepp. Bloomington: Indiana University, 2005.

Coquery-Vidrovitch, Catherine. *Le Congo au temps des grandes compagnies concessionaires, 1898–1930* [Congo in the time of the Great Concessionary Companies, 1898–1930]. Paris: Mouton, 1972.

Englebert, Pierre, and James Ron. "Primary Commodities and War: Congo-Brazzaville's Ambivalent Resource Curse." *Comparative Politics* 36 (October 2004): 61–81.

Gauze, René. *The Politics of Congo-Brazzaville*, trans. and ed. Virginia Thompson and Richard Adloff. Stanford, CA: Hoover Institution Press, 1973.

Radu, Michael S., and Keith Somerville. "People's Republic of Congo." In *Benin, the Congo, Burkina Faso: Economics, Politics, and Society*, ed. Chris Allen, et al. London: Pinter, 1989.

JOHN F. CLARK

CONGO FREE STATE. *See* **Congo Independent State.**

CONGO INDEPENDENT STATE.

The first European explorations inside the African continent caught the interest of Léopold II, king of the Belgians. In 1876 the Brussels Geographical Conference, which the king convened, led to the establishment of the overtly scientific and humanitarian African International Association. Through the guise of the Association, Léopold financed expeditions by Henry Morton Stanley and others, who began making treaties with local dignitaries and setting up occupation posts along the Congo River and in the east. Through skilful diplomatic maneuvering, which included the guarantee to the European nations then competing for colonies in Africa that the immense territory of the Congo Basin would be open freely to trade, Léopold convinced one power after another to recognize, in 1884 and 1885, what had now become known as the International Congo Association. In April 1885, the Belgian Parliament authorized the king to rule over the Congo Independent State (or Congo Free State; État Indépendant du Congo) in a personal capacity. Léopold did so until 1908 when, following international protest against atrocities in the regions where wild rubber was found, a reluctant Belgium took over the administration of what then (and only then) became the Belgian Congo.

The Africans in the territory reacted to the introduction of European rule in ways that reflected local political and social circumstances. Some groups, such as the Chokwe, fought for their independence. Others welcomed government authority in order to free themselves from subjugation by a neighboring group or from slave raiders, but reverses in alliances occurred frequently. In 1887, the notorious east African slaver Tippu Tip accepted a governorship, which delayed European confrontation with Swahili leaders for another five years. Many groups had mistaken the first European agents for favorable trading partners. Taxation and labor demands, however, soon caused them to change their views.

In 1885, the State proclaimed its ownership of all land not directly occupied by Africans. These "vacant lands" were to be exploited either directly by the state or through concessionary companies. The Compagnie du Katanga, created in 1891 to offset British claims, was in charge of the administration of the southeastern region, whose full mineral wealth had yet to be realized. Concessions were granted for the exploitation of the country's natural resources, but also for the establishment of a system of communication. The construction of the Matadi–Léopoldville railway, set as a priority, was completed in 1898 with west African, Chinese, and other semi-skilled labor, as well as many thousands of local workers. Although the Force Publique (company police) was enlisting levies, and copper and gold mines were beginning to recruit workers, porterage remained the main reason for "contract" (forced) labor in this period: porters carried loads wherever river steamers could not go.

Pressure for revenue was exceptional because the Congo Independent State was a personal venture and Léopold's wealth could not cover the unexpectedly high administrative and investment costs of a country that was not yet self-sustaining. Those escaping displacement were made to contribute to the nascent economy under the guise of taxation: villages had to bring local resources, including food supplies, to the nearest European post. Rubber was abundant in the north and central regions; the ABIR and Anversoise concessionary companies and the king's private Domaine de la Couronne, created by a secret decree in 1896, achieved explosive growth in rubber exportation (100 metric tons in 1890; 6,000 at its peak in 1901) by enforcing increasingly inhumane collection requirements. The atrocities against workers involved in this industry earned the collection system the label "red rubber," coined by the Englishman E. D. Morel apparently to connote the blood shed in collecting it. The journalist Adam Hochschild recently brought back this episode to the fore of Anglo-American and Belgian consciousness, though not without attracting the ire of some historians in Belgium.

The rubber-collection system led to countless revolts among the afflicted Africans, the most enduring by the Budja (1903–1905), as well as continual acts of resistance; the assassination of African supervisors was commonplace. In other parts of the country, the burden of the impositions of Léopold's European business collaborators, although comparatively less abusive, was resisted too. Rural uprisings were frequent; individuals, or often entire villages, took flight. There were two army mutinies in Luluabourg (1895 and 1897).

Societies suffered from the political upheaval, forced labor, and population displacement; mortality was high. The spread of disease, such as sleeping sickness, added to the devastation. Even so, some Africans, including freed slaves, turned the political and social upheaval to their personal advantage. Léopold's understaffed police and administration depended for their survival on mercenary soldiers, notably Hausa from Nigeria, as well as on local collaborators. These interpreters, *kapitas* (headmen), appointed "chiefs," catechists, and teachers were emerging as middlemen between the State and its subjugated populations. Their education was already in the hands of the missionaries, with (Belgian) Catholics enjoying state subsidies denied to (foreign) Protestants (including British Baptists and American Presbyterians). By 1908 the missionaries, generally using African languages, had taught close to one hundred thousand children. There were by then three thousand whites in the Congo, just over half of them Belgians, most of whom were working for the state or for private companies. The colony that Belgium inherited that year possessed an administrative structure in need of partial reform; an economic infrastructure to be built on; and a social makeup determinant of future practices—for example, those related to language use in the colony.

See also **Colonial Policies and Practices: Belgian; Colonialism and Imperialism; Immigration and Immigrant Groups: Chinese; Kinshasa; Stanley, Henry Morton; Tippu Tip.**

BIBLIOGRAPHY

Hochschild, Adam. *King Leopold's Ghost: A Study of Greed, Terror and Heroism in Colonial Africa.* Boston: Houghton Mifflin, 1998.

MacGaffey, Wyatt. "Ethnography and the Closing of the Frontier in Lower Congo, 1885–1921." *Africa* 56, no. 3 (1986): 263–279.

Nzongola-Ntalaja, Georges. *The Congo from Leopold to Kabila: A People's History.* London and New York: Zed Books, 2000.

Samarin, William J. *The Black Man's Burden: African Colonial Labor on the Congo and Ubangi Rivers, 1890–1900.* Boulder, CO: Westview Press, 1989.

Slade, Ruth. *King Leopold's Congo: Aspects of the Development of Race Relations in the Congo Independent State.* London and New York: Oxford University Press, 1962.

Stengers, Jean. *Congo, mythes et réalités: 100 ans d'histoire.* Paris: Duculot, 1989.

MARIE-BÉNÉDICTE DEMBOUR

CONGO RIVER.

Flowing at the rate of 10 million gallons of water per second, the Congo is the second most powerful river in the world after the Amazon. It crosses the equator twice while inscribing an arc through the *cuvette centrale*, a vast, basin-like depression in the equatorial African plateau. On this journey it receives tributaries such as the Aruwimi, the Ubangi, and the Sangha from catchment basins north of the equator; tributaries from the south include the Lomami, the Tshuapa, the Lulonga, and the Kasai. Because the cycle of rainy and dry seasons north of the equator is the opposite of that to the south, the river maintains a strong flow all year long and avoids extreme fluctuations that might otherwise result from the alternation of seasons. With a length of 4,670 kilometers from its source to its mouth, the Congo is the second longest river in Africa, after the Nile, which is 6,690 kilometers long. The Congo is longer than the Niger, at 4,200 kilometers long, and the Zambezi, at 2,700. The river system as a whole contains more than 14,000 kilometers of navigable waterways.

At its source, the river is called the Lualaba. It rises in the savannas of the Democratic Republic of the Congo's Katanga Province and flows northward for 2,100 kilometers to Wagenia Falls, near Kisangani, in the heart of the rain forest. There it takes the name Congo and begins its lazy westward curve through the rain forest. Along this stretch its waters are dotted with innumerable islands, and it broadens at places to a width of 15 kilometers. As it flows through the lowland rain forest, the banks are seldom clearly delineated, and during periods of high water the river spills over into floodplains that stretch as far as 20 kilometers inland. There are also choke points: the river narrows to 2,300 meters at Liranga, 1,400 meters at Lukolela, and 1.5 kilometers at Bolobo.

At Tchumbiri, the Congo River leaves the swampy flatlands of the *cuvette central* and begins to cut its way through the Bateke plateau and the Crystal Mountains to reach the ocean. Its width narrows to less than 1,000 meters, the riverbanks become steep, and islands and sandbanks disappear. At Kinshasa, the river broadens again to form Malebo Pool, 35 kilometers long and 23 kilometers wide, before plunging over Ntamo Falls,

the first of thirty-two cataracts between Kinshasa and Matadi at its mouth at the Atlantic Ocean. Along this stretch of some 350 kilometers, the river plunges nearly 300 meters, creating the largest reserve of water power found anywhere in the world. At Matadi, the river widens into an estuary that is accessible to oceangoing ships for the final 150 kilometers to the Atlantic Ocean. So powerful is the river at this point that its brown waters surge nearly 150 kilometers out to sea, and it has carved a 1,200-meter canyon in the ocean floor.

The cataracts along the lower river played an important role in keeping Europeans out of the Congo basin during the era of the slave trade. Although their ships regularly sailed up the Congo estuary, the Europeans never reached the country beyond the rapids, and they remained ignorant of the upper river. As late as the nineteenth century, European geographers speculated that the Congo estuary was really the mouth of the Niger, almost 2,000 kilometers to the northwest. Throughout this period an active commerce along the upper Congo was controlled by networks of indigenous fishermen-traders such as the Tio, the Bobangi, the Boloki, and the Ngombe, who used dugout canoes that were sometimes over twenty meters long and held up to sixty to seventy paddlers. Such groups sought to monopolize the trade along stretches of the upper river by controlling the choke points at Lukolela, Bolobo, and Tchumbiri and the towns at Stanley Pool. Goods traveled long distances, passing from network to network. By the late eighteenth century, European merchants on the Atlantic coast were purchasing slaves from as far away as the lower Ubangi; a century later, European muskets were being used at Upoto, over 1,700 kilometers upstream from the mouth of the river.

Control of the Congo River played a central role in the establishment of Belgian and French colonies in equatorial Africa. The colonial scramble in the area was initiated by the voyage of Henry Morton Stanley, who entered the river basin from East Africa and then followed the Congo downstream to its mouth. A main focus of early colonial efforts was to transport steamboats, piece by piece on the heads of African porters, from the estuary to Stanley Pool, where the vessels were assembled, launched on the river, and used to control commerce and impose colonial rule along the upper Congo. A second focus of both the Belgians and the French was to bypass the rapids and facilitate the transfer of goods and personnel between the coast and the steamboat networks by building railroads using conscripted labor working under notoriously brutal conditions. It is not surprising that the capital cities of the two colonies—Leopoldville and Brazzaville—faced each other across Stanley Pool, within hearing distance of the rapids, as do the modern capitals, Kinshasa and Brazzaville.

After the initial shock of colonization, African fishermen and traders began to reassert their control of the river by becoming crew members on steamboats or carrying on trade in dugout canoes, often traveling at night to avoid colonial river patrols. In the 1950s a Belgian report estimated that over 90 percent of the trade in fish escaped colonial control. After independence in 1960, when Africans gained permission to travel on the large riverboats, many people became riverboat-based traders. The riverboats with their numerous accompanying barges became floating marketplaces and were even described as floating cities. Today the Congo River system remains the main artery of transportation that links Kinshasa and Brazzaville to Kisangani (on the Upper Congo), Bangui (on the Ubangi), and Ilebo (on the Kasai).

The government of the Democratic Republic of the Congo built two dams, Inga I and Inga II, across the lower Congo in order to harness some of the water power of the river's rapids. The dams provide more electricity than the country is able to consume. In 2005 Eskom, a South African company, announced plans to invest fifty billion dollars to create Inga III, which would generate twice the power of China's Three Gorges dam and would be the cornerstone of a pan-African power grid that could supply the bulk of Africa's needs. Because little industrial activity has developed along the banks of the Congo, it remains one of the least polluted among the world's major rivers.

See also **Brazzaville; Congo, Democratic Republic of the: Society and Cultures; Ecosystems; Wildlife: National Parks.**

BIBLIOGRAPHY

Caputo, Robert. "Lifeline for a Nation: Zaire River." *National Geographic* 180, no. 5 (November 1991): 5–35.

Devroey, Egide J. *Le basin hydrographique congolais.* Brussels: Institut Royal Colonial Belge, Section des sciences techniques, *Mémoires*, vol. 3, no. 3, 1941.

Forbath, Peter. *The River Congo.* New York: Harper and Row, 1977.

Harms, Robert. *River of Wealth, River of Sorrow: The Central Zaire Basin in the Era of the Slave and Ivory Trade, 1500–1891.* New Haven, CT: Yale University Press, 1981.

ROBERT HARMS

CONSERVATION. *See* Ecosystems; Wildlife.

CONSTITUTIONS. *See* Law.

COPTIC CHURCH. *See* Christianity: Coptic Church and Society.

CORREIA, MÃE AURÉLIA. A wealthy trader and power broker in the Guinea-Bissau region from the 1820s through the 1840s, Mãe Aurélia Correia was titled "Queen of Orango" (the largest island of the Bissagos archipelago) by Portuguese and Luso-Africans. Mãe Aurélia's dates of birth and death and her parents and kinship affiliations are uncertain; indisputable are her business acumen and unrivaled influence among Bijago, Papel, and other societies which enabled her and her husband to dominate trade and politics in the regions of the Geba and Grande Rivers and the Bissagos archipelago in the middle third of the nineteenth century. The paucity of information about her reflects the inadequacy of Portuguese record keeping and the reticence of slave traders concerning their business affairs.

Mãe Aurélia exemplifies many African and Eurafrican women traders and commercial intermediaries in western Africa from the seventeenth to the nineteenth centuries. They were known as *nharas* in the Guinea-Bissau region (Casamance River to Grande River), *signares* in Senegal, and *senoras* along the Gambia River, the titles deriving from the Portuguese *senhora* and signifying women of wealth and influence. The most successful of these women, exemplified by Mãe Aurélia and her sister (or aunt) and close business associate Mãe Julia da Silva Cardoso, maintained trading vessels, numerous domestic slaves including seamen and skilled artisans, and European-style dwellings, and accumulated large quantities of gold and silver jewelry and expensive garments. *Mãe* (mother, in Portuguese), a term of respect, and *aurélia* (gold) suggest the translation "Golden Mama," with every connotation of prestige and authority.

Mãe Aurélia's husband, Caetano José Nozolini (1800–1850), a Cape Verdean army officer from the island of Fogo, was dispatched to Guinea around 1825. His leadership qualities must have persuaded Mãe Aurélia of his suitability as a partner, for successful *nharas* were astute in selecting spouses who could be of greatest advantage in their commercial affairs. Mãe Aurélia shared with Nozolini her commercial networks and influence with African traders and elites, and also her retinue of relatives, domestic slaves, and *grumetes* (African seamen and other skilled employees). Success derived from the number and capabilities of people that traders could mobilize, for the Guinea-Bissau region was rife with warfare, pillaging, and slaving. The Portuguese *praça* (fortress) at Bissau and its dependent presidios were in shambles, garrisoned by diseased and dissolute rabble recruited from the dregs of Portuguese regiments and militia groups in the Cape Verde Islands. Mãe Aurélia and Nozolini contributed importantly in the suppression of a mutiny by the Bissau garrison in 1826 and helped to subdue later uprisings by soldiers and inhabitants of Bissau.

Together, Mãe Aurélia and Nozolini dominated trade in slaves and other commodities from the Geba to the Nunez Rivers and the islands of the Bissagos archipelago. They enraged and frustrated the officers of the British Navy by their stratagems, including their subterfuge of shipping slaves to the Cape Verde Islands accompanied by spurious documents attesting that the slaves were members of their extended family. Feared for their ruthlessness, their intimidation of rivals extended to the murder of a Senegal-based French trader in 1835. Colonial officials, bereft of resources, were forced to depend on Mãe Aurélia and Nozolini and other Luso-African and Cape Verdean traders to maintain a semblance of Portuguese authority in Guinea. When the inhabitants of Bissau laid siege to the *praça* in 1842, the governor of the colony of Cabo Verde e Guine counseled the commander of the relief force to seek the assistance of Mãe Aurélia, whom he characterized as administrator of the trading firm of Caetano José Nozolini and a person greatly respected by the Africans.

During the 1830s Mãe Aurélia and Nozolini used slaves to develop peanut plantations along the western shore of the fertile island of Bolama. Bolama's relatively accessible location provided the officers of the British antislavery squadron long-awaited opportunities to strike at them, sporadically raiding their premises and taking hundreds of slaves to Freetown, Sierra Leone, for liberation.

Of Mãe Aurélia and Nozolini's children, a son and three daughters survived past infancy. Their careers mirrored changing circumstances but attest to the family's continuing prominence. Caetano Nozolini, Jr., was educated in France and continued the family business after his father's death in 1850. Eugénia married Dr. António Joaquim Ferreira, who administered the Bissau hospital and also engaged in commerce. Following his death in 1853 or 1854, Eugénia managed a trading establishment and rice and peanut plantations at Ametite on Ilha Wam in the Bissagos archipelago. Leopoldina married Adolphe Demay, a Franco-African trader from Gorée who settled at Bissau in the late 1840s and carried on a thriving commerce in the following decades. Gertrudes Aurélia married Dr. José Fernandes da Silva Leão, also associated with the family business interests.

See also **Slave Trades; Women: Women and Trade.**

BIBLIOGRAPHY

Bowman, Joye. *Ominous Transition: Commerce and Colonial Expansion in the Senegambia and Guinea, 1857–1919.* Brookfield, VT: Avebury Press, 1997.

Brooks, George E. "A Nhara of the Guinea-Bissau Region: Mãe Aurélia Correia." In *Women and Slavery in Africa*, ed. Claire C. Robertson and Martin A. Klein. Madison: University of Wisconsin Press, 1983.

Havik, Philip J. "Women and Trade in the Guinea Bissau Region: The Role of African and Luso-African Women in Trade Networks from the Early Sixteenth to the Mid-Nineteenth Century." *Studia* 52 (1994): 83–120.

GEORGE E. BROOKS

COSMOLOGY. *See* **Myth and Cosmology.**

CÔTE D'IVOIRE

This entry includes the following articles:
GEOGRAPHY AND ECONOMY
SOCIETY AND CULTURES
HISTORY AND POLITICS

GEOGRAPHY AND ECONOMY

The Côte d'Ivoire is located on the Gulf of Guinea in West Africa. It is bordered by Mali and Burkina Faso in the north, Guinea in the northwest, Liberia in the southwest, and Ghana in the east. It has a total area of 124,502 square miles, and a population estimated in 2007 at 18 million. Lying between 5 and 10 degrees north of the equator, it has a climate that is warm, humid, and marked by distinct seasonal variations in rainfall.

A former French colony, Côte d'Ivoire, similar to most African countries, is a highly fragmented society culturally. There are more than sixty ethnic groups in the country. Based on ethnic, cultural, historical, linguistic, and geographic commonalities, these groups are often compacted into five major areas of identities. These are the Kru in the southwest; the Akan in the east, center, and southeast; the Mande in the northwest and west; the Voltaic (the main groups being the Senoufos/Lobi) in the north-center and northeast. Among the five major areas of ethnic identities, the Akan is by far the largest with 42.1 percent of the population. This is followed by the Mandes with 26.5 percent, the Voltaic with 17.6 percent, and the Kru with 11 percent. Within each of these areas of cultural identities, particular groups stand out in terms of size. The Baoules in the Akan group comprise the largest ethnic group with between 15 to 20 percent of the country's population. Similarly, the Senoufos in the north-center and northeast dominate their group and constitute a 10 to 15 percent ratio of the national population, whereas in the Krou group, the Betes constitute the largest subgroup with between 10 to 15 percent of the national population. This is the same ratio of the national population that the Malinkes in the northwest constitute. Migration has further intensified the pluralistic

character of the population, as has religion. Over five million migrants from other African countries were living in Côte d'Ivoire in 2006. More than 33 percent of that number came from Burkina Faso, and the rest came from neighboring countries. Figures for 2001 showed Côte d'Ivoire split between a Muslim population of 35 to 40 percent, a Christian population of between 20 to 30 percent, and a population of 30 to 45 percent following traditional beliefs.

In 2005 Côte d'Ivoire's gross domestic production (GDP) was 16.1 billion U.S. dollars (valued as of 2007). The labor force was estimated to be 6.95 million, 68 percent of which was engaged in agriculture, forestry, or raising livestock. The rest were wage earners in agriculture, government, industry, and commerce.

LANDFORMS

From the low-lying areas along the Atlantic Ocean, the landscape slopes gently upward to the interior, with few areas of bold relief, to elevations close to 1,640 feet in the north. The highest peaks reach over 2,593 feet in the northwest and along the western border. Four drainage basins that run north-south are formed by the country's four main rivers: the Cavally, the Sassandra, the Bandama, and the Comoe (Komoe). Heavy surf and tidal lagoons characterize the 320 mile-long coastline, although there are no natural bays or anchorages.

The geologic structure of Côte d'Ivoire consists mainly of Precambrian gneisses and granites, with more recent formations of Tertiary shales, limestones, and sandstones in the coastal zone. Principal mineral deposits include gold, diamonds, bauxite, and manganese. Of the many soil types in the country, most are lateritic, low in silica and plant nutrients but high in iron and aluminum oxides. The soils in the south are generally more nutrient-rich and fertile.

CLIMATE

The climate of Côte d'Ivoire is conditioned by long-term regional patterns of dry and wet periods. From the early 1600s, the regional climate has been relatively dry, with short wet interludes in the 1890s and from 1930 to 1960. Since 1960, the region has been characterized by sporadic drought conditions. Humidity averages 80 percent in the south and 65 percent in the north, and it increases during the rainy

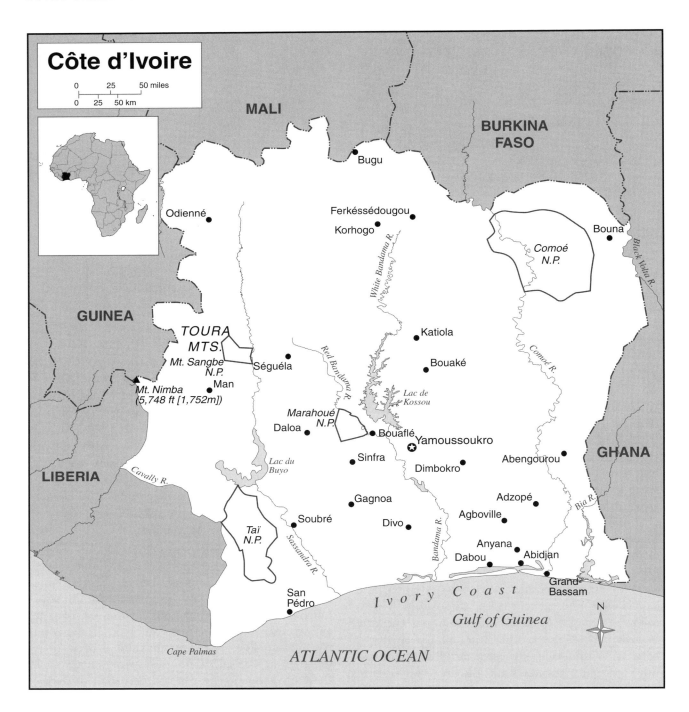

season. Temperatures are warm throughout the year, ranging between 70 and 90 degrees Fahrenheit.

Precipitation patterns in Côte d'Ivoire are related directly to the Intertropical Convergence Zone (ITCZ), which produces two rainy seasons in the south as the frontal system moves in an annual north-south cycle. The first, long rainy season occurs from May to September and the second, shorter

season occurs between October and November. During the long rainy season in the south rainfall reaches 77 inches annually. In the north, there is one short wet season from June to October. Partly because of the shortness of the season and also because the rains are not as heavy in the north as in the south, annual rainfall is only around 43 inches. The dry season takes place from December to April. During this period the average temperature is around

77 to 86 degrees Fahrenheit. Also, between December and February, arid winds from the Sahara (called *harmattan*) blow through the country and carry significant amounts of desert dust that diminish sunshine and reduce both temperature and humidity.

VEGETATION AND WILDLIFE

Côte d'Ivoire has three main vegetation belts that cut across the country from its eastern to its western borders: a southern tropical forest zone and a northern savanna woodland zone, divided by a transitional zone of forest-savanna mosaic. The southern third of the country is characterized by heavy tropical forest, once rich in valuable varieties of tropical hardwoods such as mahogany, iroko, and sapelle. Timber exploitation for exports and a thriving timber industry has led to massive deforestation and degradation of the forest vegetation during the decades after independence in 1960. The forest contains both evergreen and deciduous species, as well as large stands of coconut and oil palms near the coast. The savanna woodland region found in northern Côte d'Ivoire is marked by scattered single trees and clumps of trees, continuous stretches of low grasses and shrubs, and strips of heavier timber along water and drainage courses.

The fauna of Côte d'Ivoire is characteristic of the Ethiopian zoogeographic region but is considerably less rich and varied in species than parts of eastern and southern Africa. Diminishing populations of elephant, hippopotamus, red buffalo, antelope, wild hog, leopard, monkey, and chimpanzee dwell in the forest zone. The savanna woodland houses populations of savanna buffalo, gazelle, waterbuck, and hyena. The country maintains two wildlife parks, the Komoe National Park in the north, and Maraoue National Park in the central forest. Numerous species of birds, insects, and reptiles are also found throughout the country. Both inland and marine fisheries are rich with nutritionally and economically valuable species, although poor management has resulted in recent catch declines and ecosystem degradation.

AGRICULTURE

Farming in Côte d'Ivoire prior to the territory's contact with Europeans was based on a rotational system known as shifting cultivation. This practice involved cultivating a patch of land for a number of years, leaving it fallow for a few more years, and then returning to it after it has regained its fertility. Agricultural products prior to contact with Europeans was also mainly for subsistence. Crops included yams, cocoyams, manioc, plantain, and rice in the south; and millet, sorghum, maize, and groundnuts in the north. In addition, palm oil and shea and kola nuts were usually collected from the wild. Agricultural commerce was insignificant, although some kola nuts, oil, and fish were traded along the Sahelian routes. Land tenure systems involved communal land and labor arrangements, and cultivation was performed manually, without the use of draft animals.

During the colonial period, the French promoted export crops such as cocoa, coffee, rubber, bananas, citrus fruits, palm oil, cotton, tobacco, and pineapple. Colonial land reform allowed for individual and corporate ownership of land, in addition to long-term leasehold of agricultural concessions. A plantation system also emerged, but a chronic shortage of agricultural labor limited the ability of Europeans to run large-scale operations. Instead, most cocoa and coffee is grown on approximately 600,000 locally owned family plantations, which average in size from seven to ten acres.

Since independence from France in 1960, Ivorian economic growth has been based mainly on agriculture, with annual real growth of 7 percent between 1960 and 1990. Côte d'Ivoire is the world's leading producer of cocoa and ranks fifth in coffee production. Among African countries, Côte d'Ivoire is a high-ranking producer of palm oil, rubber, cotton, bananas, and pineapples. Sustained exports of timber, accounting for approximately 8 percent of total exports in recent years, have also contributed to its economy. Côte d'Ivoire ranks among the top five tropical hardwood exporters, although timber exports have, as of the early twenty-first century, declined by nearly 40 percent since 1979. An outcome of the massive exploitation of the country's forests for timber and the expansion of cash crop agriculture over the years since independence is extensive deforestation and ecosystem degradation, which ranks amongst some of the worst in the world.

Pastoralism is widely practiced in northern Côte d'Ivoire by Fulani herders from Mali and Burkina Faso. In the early 1970s, Fulani immigration was encouraged by the Ivorian government to reduce dependence on imported meat. However, the Fulani cattle herds have damaged the crops of the indigenous Senufo farmers of the northern region, particularly cotton and rice crops. These land-tenure conflicts led to violent clashes between the Fulani and Senufo during the early 1980s, culminating in the killing of over eighty Fulani herders in the Korhogo district in 1986. These tensions have continued to be a problem due to greater liberalization of the political system that began in the 1990s.

INDUSTRY AND MINING

Development of Côte d'Ivoire's industrial sector since independence has been built on import substitution, agricultural processing, energy, and construction. Half of manufacturing employment is in agricultural processing. The next largest sector is textile manufacturing and the apparel industry, which employs 17 percent of manufacturing labor and depends on domestically grown cotton. Manufacturing enterprises were transferred from the hands of foreign investors to the Ivorian state, which controls about half of all equity in manufacturing.

Oil was discovered in the 1970s and its production began in 1980. However, the small reserves plus declining world prices for crude oil during the 1980s diminished the country's hopes for a thriving oil economy. The rise in crude oil prices in the early 1990s and further increases in 2003 was a welcome development. The total proven oil reserve that was estimated at 220 million barrels in 2005 and a daily production estimate of 33,000 barrels per day in the same year were too small to make oil production the engine of the Ivorian economy, however. Côte d'Ivoire also has an oil refinery, which has been showing negligible profits since 1985. In attempts to reduce Côte d'Ivoire's reliance on cocoa, coffee, and timber, the government embarked on diversifying the country's agricultural products. Bananas, pineapple, cotton, rubber, palm oil, and sugar were promoted. It also began developing the mining sector and the extraction of diamonds, gold, iron ore, nickel, and manganese. However, these deposits are relatively small and low-grade.

ECONOMIC RESTRUCTURING

In 1976 and 1977, a frost damaged Brazil's coffee crop and resulted in a worldwide price boom for coffee beans. The sudden influx of foreign exchange in Côte d'Ivoire's coffee market led to some loss of control over public expenditure, and by the time the agricultural terms of trade returned to normal levels, Côte d'Ivoire had accumulated considerable foreign debt. Oil crises during the 1970s deepened Côte d'Ivoire's debt problems, precipitating the adoption of structural adjustment reforms beginning in 1981.

By 1986, the World Bank saw Côte d'Ivoire as a structural adjustment success story. When the world market prices for cocoa and coffee collapsed in 1986, though, Côte d'Ivoire's economy contracted. The Ivorian government was forced to embark on a second, more draconian phase of structural adjustment, in which coffee and cocoa prices were cut by 50 percent and 45 percent, respectively; civil servants' salaries were reduced by 15 to 40 percent; a 10 percent tax was placed on private-sector incomes; prices were cut on a variety of items, including rice, sugar, medicine, electricity, fuel, and water; and government expenditure was reduced by 25 percent. By 1993, external debt was over U.S. 17 billion dollars, whereas exports earnings were less than U.S. 3 billion dollars

Since 1994, improved prices for cocoa and coffee, as well as the intensification of nontraditional agricultural exports, have contributed to a slow economic comeback for Côte d'Ivoire. Despite the 50 percent devaluation of the CFA franc in 1994, the country adhered to its structural adjustment program. This resulted in budget surpluses, an increase in public investment, and real growth of over 6 percent between 1994 and 1998. Inflation also fell significantly to a low of 0.7 percent in 1999 from a high of 13.6 percent in 1995.

Economic recovery again suffered a major setback due to a combination of massive government corruption, falling commodity prices, mismanagement of public funds, and the first successful military coup d'etat in the country's history. It overthrew the civilian government of Henri Konan Bedie and brought the coup leader, General Guei to power in December 1999. The economic impact of the 1999 coup was particularly devastating. It contributed to a decline in private foreign investments, capital flight and perhaps most importantly, most non-humanitarian foreign assistance. The result was a further economic decline of 2.3 percent in 2000. And just as that economic situation was being dealt with, another political crisis—a failed coup on September 19, 2002, followed by a brief civil war—exacerbated an already difficult situation. The business and economic outlook that had begun improving in 2002 further declined. It is estimated that the government will lose between 10 and 20 percent of its cocoa harvests because the rebels smuggle cocoa in the areas they control to sell in neighboring countries to finance their operations.

Even though a ceasefire was negotiated and signed between the rebel groups known as the Patriotic Movement of Côte d'Ivoire (MPCI) and government forces in mid-October of 2002, the rebels controlled the northern part of the country and the government controlled the south. The emergence of two other groups in the west of the country—the Ivorian Popular Movement for the Greater West (MPIGO) and the Movement for Justice and Peace (MJP)—allied to the MPCI enhanced the rebel cause even more. The new rebel groups merged with the MPCI into the New Forces. Although the ceasefire has held since its inception (monitored by French troops and troops from the Economic Community of West African States), the country remains partitioned into two parts between the New Forces in the north and the government of President Laurent Gbagbo that came to power after the presidential elections of October 2000 in the south.

The conflict and failure of various peace accords between the two sides, beginning with the January 2003 French-sponsored Linas-Marcoussis Accord, has continued to destabilize the economy. Domestic productivity fell by 3.8 percent in 2003, rose slightly by 1.6 percent in 2004, and rose another 1 percent in 2005.

See also **Climate; Debt and Credit; Ecosystems; Labor: Industrial and Mining; Land: Tenure; Plants; World Bank.**

BIBLIOGRAPHY

Campbell, Bonnie. "The Fiscal Crisis of the State: The Case of Ivory Coast." In *Contradictions of Accumulation in Africa*, eds. Henry Bernstein and Bonnie Campbell. Beverly Hills, California: Sage Publication, 1985.

Dian, Boni. *L'économie de plantation en Côte d'Ivoire forestière*. Abidjan, Côte d'Ivoire: Nouvelles Editions africaines, 1985.

Grootaert, Christiaan. *Analyzing Poverty and Policy Reform: The Experience of Côte d'Ivoire*. Aldershot, U.K.: Avebury, 1996.

Handloff, Robert E. *Côte d'Ivoire: A Country Study*, 3rd edition. Washington, DC: Federal Research Division, 1991.

Hayward, Derek, and Julius S. Oguntoyimbo. *The Climatology of West Africa*. Totowa, New Jersey: Barnes & Noble, 1987.

Kanbur, S. M. Ravi. *Poverty and the Social Dimensions of Structural Adjustment in Côte d'Ivoire*. Washington, DC: World Bank, 1990.

Mundt, Robert J. "Côte d'Ivoire: Continuity and Change in a Semi-Democracy." In *Political Reform in Francophone Africa*, eds. John F. Clark and David E. Gardinier. Boulder, Colorado: Westview Press, 1997.

Tesi, Moses K. "Côte d'Ivoire." In *Governments of the World*, ed. Neal Tate. Detroit, Michigan: Macmillan Reference, 2006.

U.S. Department of State. *Background Note: Côte d'Ivoire*. Washington, DC: Bureau of African Affairs, 2006.

World Bank. *Document 284, Côte d'Ivoire: Strengthening Public Expenditure Management and Controls, Report No. 2714*. Washington, DC: World Bank, 2003.

World Bank. *Document 287, Côte d'Ivoire, Export Promotion and Diversification Project, Report No. 27309*. Washington, DC: World Bank, 2003.

World Bank. *Document No. 292, Côte d'Ivoire: Economic Recovery Credit Project, Report No. 28818*. Washington, DC: World Bank, 2004.

World Bank. *World Development Indicators Database*. Washington, DC: World Bank, 2006.

BARBARA LOUISE ENDEMAÑO WALKER
REVISED BY MOSES KANGMIEVE TESI

SOCIETY AND CULTURES

With an area of 124,502 square miles, Côte d'Ivoire (also called the Ivory Coast) borders Liberia, Guinea, Mali, Burkina Faso, Ghana, and the Atlantic Ocean. In 2007, Côte d'Ivoire's total population was estimated to be 18 million inhabitants, who speak approximately sixty African languages (with Dyula the most widely spoken), belonging to five main language groups (Akan, Mande, Kru, Gur or Voltaic, and Lagoon).

Three major religious traditions are present: practitioners of traditional African religions, 30–45 percent; Muslims, 35–40 percent, and Christians, 20–30 percent. The majority of foreigners (migrant workers) are Muslim (70%) and Christian (20%). However, these figures are approximations, as there is much syncretism in religious practice, and mutual tolerance that seems to be fading away due to the political developments in this country.

The 1998 data structure the country's population as follows: 23 percent Baule; 18 percent Bete; 15 percent Senufo; 11 percent Malinke; and 33 percent other. (These figures, like the following observations, are approximations, given demographic vagaries, migrations, and ethnic intermarriages.) The Akan peoples (42%), including the Baule, Anyi, and Abron, are largely located in the central region and along the eastern coast of the Côte d'Ivoire (and in neighboring countries, especially Ghana). The Mande group includes two subgroups: the northern Mande (the Dyula, Bamana, and Malinke, 17%) and the southern Mande (the Wan, Beng, Mwan, Guro, Dan, Gban, and Tura, 10%). Originally from Liberia, Guinea, and Mali, most of them are located in the center-west of the country. In the west live Kru speakers (including the Guere, Wobe, Kodia, Grebo, Oubi, Neyo, Bakwe, Bete, and Niaboua, 11%), who came from Liberia, the Gambia, and Guinea. In the north (along the borders with Mali and Burkina Faso) is the Gur or Voltaic group (18%), comprising primarily the Senufo, Kulango, Lobi, and smaller groups (Gouin, Site, Degha, Samogho, and Gonja). The Lagoon peoples, Abe, Abidji, Abure, Mbato, Avikam, Nzima, Ebrie, Jackjack, Eotiole; Adjukru, and Alladian, are named for their location next to the coastal lagoon and the Atlantic Ocean.

A significant number of immigrants are from other African nations, as well as from Asia and Europe. While he was president, Felix Houphouët-Boigny encouraged such immigration to further strengthen the economy. From Africa these include people from Nigeria, Burkina Faso, Bénin, Togo, Senegal, Mali, Guinea, Ghana, Mauritania, Niger, Morocco, Liberia, and Ethiopia. Meanwhile, the civil wars in the Democratic Republic of the Congo, Liberia, Sierra Leone, and elsewhere on the continent had opened the doors to new immigrants. From outside Africa, there has been an important presence of people from Lebanon, Vietnam, Korea, France, and the Philippines, as well as elsewhere. However, there has been a population shift due to the civil war that began in September 2002. Many people have been displaced and have sought refuge in the south, especially Abidjan. As for the foreigners, some have returned to their home country temporarily or permanently, while others have relocated to other African countries deemed safer.

Religion can be classified into three basic groups: animism, Christianity, and Islam. In fact, animist groups are fairly heterogeneous, with assorted ancestors, gods, and spirits of the earth, forest, and sky being identified, sometimes alongside a high god. As for the major world religions, many Ivoirians add the Christian or Muslim god and associated religious practices to their old customs and pantheons, rather than converting fully. Committed converts to Christianity or Islam tend to be clustered in the cities rather than the rural areas. Various forms of Christianity, from Roman Catholicism to the independent churches of William Wade Harris and Albert Atcho, have gained a significant following among the Akan and Lagoon peoples, while Islam finds followers among Mande- and Gur-speaking peoples. Immigrants normally retain their original beliefs and practices, although some are affected by their new environment and may opt to join a new religious tradition.

Several elements can explain the initial relative success that Côte d'Ivoire has had in achieving unity among its heterogeneous population, including cultural, political, and economic factors. A major concern of the government after independence in 1960 was to foster regular consciousness of, and interaction among, the many peoples of the country. For example, teachers in the public schools were normally sent to areas other than their native ones. The national television stations regularly aired programs highlighting traditional dances and folk practices, and the national radio stations regularly broadcast programs in local languages, exposing much of the population to a spectrum of cultural traditions. Unfortunately, the subsequent leaders failed to maintain that unity as well as hold the country together. As a result, ethnic and religious rivalries have sparked fear, distrust, and suspicion among the people throughout the country.

On the economic front, significant components of the Ivoirian population remain divided by occupation. Agriculture constitutes the most important occupation for people all over the country. The Akan mostly cultivate cocoa, coffee, rice, pineapple, bananas, and rubber trees while

République de Côte d'Ivoire (Cote d'Ivoire)

Population:	18,013,409 (2007 est.)
Area:	322,463 sq. km (124,502 sq. mi.)
Official language:	French
National currency:	CFA franc
Principal religions:	indigenous 30%–45%, Muslim 35%–40%, and Christian (Catholic, Protestant and other denominations) 20%–30%
Capital:	Yamoussoukro (est. pop. 200,659 in 2005), although Abidjan is the administrative center
Other urban centers:	Daloa, Gagnoa, Korhogo, Man, San Pedro, Bouaké
Annual rainfall:	varies from 1,270–2,413 mm (50–94 in.) on coast to 1,270–1,524 mm (50–60 in.) in the north
Principal geographical features:	*Rivers:* Comoé, Bandama, Sassandra, Cavally *Lakes:* Koussou, Buyo, Ayamé
Economy:	*GDP per capita:* US$1,600 (2006)
Principal products and exports:	*Agricultural:* coffee, cocoa beans, bananas, palm kernels, corn, rice, manioc (tapioca), sweet potatoes, sugar, cotton, rubber, timber *Manufacturing:* foodstuffs, beverages, wood products, oil refining, truck and bus assembly, textiles, fertilizer, building materials, electricity, ship construction and repair *Mining:* petroleum, natural gas, gold, diamonds, nickel
Government:	Independence from France, 1960. Constitution adopted in 1960, amended in 1990. Military coup in 1999; country divided by civil war in 2002. According to 2002 constitution, president is elected for 5-year term by direct universal suffrage. 175-seat unicameral Assemblée Nationale elected for 5-year terms by universal suffrage. President appoints prime minister, who appoints Council of Ministers. For administrative purposes, the country is divided into 19 regions and 58 departments
Heads of state since independence:	1960–1993: President Félix Houphouët-Boigny 1993–2000: President Henri Konan Bédié 2000: General Robert Guei 2000–: President Laurent Gbagbo
Armed forces:	President is commander in chief. The 20,000-man Ivoirian armed forces (now called the Ivorian Defense and Security Forces, or FDS) include an army, navy, air force, gendarmerie, and specialized forces.
Transportation:	*Rail:* 660 km (410 mi.) *Ports:* Abidjan, Aboisso, Dabou, San Pedro *Roads:* 80,000 km (49,710 mi.), 9% paved *National airline:* Air Ivoire (60% government owned); Côte d'Ivoire owns 7% share of Air Afrique. *Airports:* International facilities at Abidjan, Yamoussoukro, and Bouaké. 32 other airports and airstrips throughout the country.
Media:	*Newspapers: Fraternité Matin, Soir Info, Le Jour Plus, L'Inter, Notre Voie.* There are several independent newspapers, mostly from a broad range of political-oppositional perspectives. Active book publishing sector, including warehouses maintained by several French publishers in Abidjan; also Centre d'Edition et de Diffusion Africaines (school texts), University of Abidjan Press, Institute Africaine pour la Développement Economique et Social. Radiodiffusion Télévision Ivoirienne provides radio and television broadcasting. Film production overseen by the Société Ivoirienne de Cinéma.
Literacy and education:	*Total literacy rate:* 51% (2006). Education is free but noncompulsory at all levels. Postsecondary education provided through Université Nationale de Côte d'Ivoire and several technical, vocational, and agricultural schools.

Senufo farmers specialize in rice, sugarcane, millet, mangoes, and cotton. As for Bete farmers they grow rice, coffee, and cocoa whereas other farmers tend to have small plots growing a variety of the above crops. Commerce is largely controlled by Dyula and Malinke traders, with men dominating large-scale trade and women prominent in small-scale trade. The transportation sector has been led predominantly by Dyula, as well as Kulango, Baule, Anyi, and Bete men, while forestry has largely been left to the Lebanese, European businessmen, and the political elite.

Foreign immigrants such as Lebanese also own restaurants and imported-goods shops; Nigerians market food and household goods shops while the Senegalese and Moroccans own imported technology and clothing shops. Shipping is the domain of Europeans while Ghanaians dominate the fishing industry. This immigrant-friendly approach to development yielded important results: Côte d'Ivoire was not only regarded as a mirror of the West and Francophone Africa, but also a symbol and model of economic success on the continent.

On the political front, Côte d'Ivoire has been run largely by Baule, Bete and Dyula leaders, although French interests have also been important in the postcolonial period. Félix Houphouët-Boigny, a Baule from Yamoussoukro, was the country's first president, and he remained in that position until his death on December 7, 1993, at the age of eighty-eight. To realize one of his important dreams—maintaining Baule control of Côte d'Ivoire—he intentionally manipulated the constitution to ensure that a Baule, Henri Konan Bédié, succeeded him in office upon his death. Even before his death, however, Côte d'Ivoire was faced with serious economic and political challenges. Economically, the majority of the people remained unhappy with the dramatic impacts of structural adjustment programs imposed by the foreign financiers (mainly the International Monetary Fund and the World Bank). Politically, the government was forced to embrace multiparty elections for the first time after thirty years of single party system. Tensions grew even greater with the ascension of Alassane Dramane Ouattara (an alleged Burkinabe), as the country's first prime minister.

Immediately upon Houphouët-Boigny's death, the battle for the succession between the various contenders began. The principle contenders were Allasane Ouattara (the prime minister) and Henri Konan Bédié (the president of the National Assembly). A number of painful events followed, which divided the country along ethnic and religious lines. In December 1999, General Robert Guei led a military coup that ousted President-elect Konan Bedie from power, and three years later, in September 2002, civil war erupted between President Gbagbo's regime and three rebels groups: Patriotic Movement of Côte d'Ivoire (MPCI), Movement for Justice and Peace (MJP), and Far West Côte d'Ivoire People's Movement (MPIGO)

See also **Agriculture; Colonialism and Imperialism; Harris, William Wadé; Houphouët-Boigny, Félix; International Monetary Fund; World Bank.**

BIBLIOGRAPHY

Amin, Samir. "Capitalism and Development in the Ivory Coast." In *African Politics and Society*, ed. Irving L. Markovitz. New York: Free Press, 1970.

Amondji, Marcel. *Félix Houphouët-Boigny et la Côte d'Ivoire.* Paris: Karthala, 1984.

Baulin, Jacques. *La politique africaine d'Houphouët-Boigny.* Paris: Eurafor-Press, 1980.

Baulin, Jacques. *La politique intérieure d'Houphouët-Boigny.* Paris: Eurafor-Press, 1982.

Coulibaby, Mamadou. *Houphouet-Boigny: 20 ans de sagesse, 50 ans de travail.* Abidjan: Societe Ivoirienne d'Imprimerie (S.I.I.), 1975.

Hecht, Robert M. "The Ivory Coast Economic 'Miracle': What Benefits for Peasant Farmers?" *Journal of Modern African Studies* 21 (March 1983): 25–53.

Loucou, Jean-Noel. *Histoire de la Côte d'Ivoire*, Vol. 1: *La formation des peuples.* Abidjan: Côte d'Ivoire, 1984.

Mundt, Robert. *Historical Dictionary of Ivory Coast (Côte d'Ivoire): African Historical Dictionary*, Vol. 41. Metuchen, NJ: Scarecrow Press, 1987.

Rapley, John. "Côte d'Ivoire." In *Encyclopedia of Twentieth-Century African History*, ed. Paul Tiyambe Zeleza and Dickson Eyoh. New York: Routledge, 2003.

World Bank. *Ivory Coast: The Challenge of Success.* Baltimore, MD: Johns Hopkins University Press, 1978.

BERTIN K. KOUADIO

HISTORY AND POLITICS

Côte d'Ivoire acquired its independence from France reluctantly. France more or less unilaterally accorded the country independence, although its leaders had sought to enter into a commonwealth arrangement with other French-speaking West African territories rather than gain full sovereignty. Led by Félix Houphouët-Boigny, Côte d'Ivoire attempted to push for a community structure with ultimate sovereignty resting with France. Other French-speaking African leaders did not share Houphouët-Boigny's objective, however, and neither did many Ivorians. The United Nations recognized Côte d'Ivoire as an independent republic on December 7, 1960. Soon thereafter, citizens of the new republic elected Félix Houphouët-Boigny its first president. He would keep this job until his death in November 1993.

Born into a chiefly Baoulé family in Yamoussoukro, probably in 1905 (the actual year is unknown), he rose to prominence in the late 1930s with the creation of the Syndicat Agricole Africain (SAA), the country's first African-led rural union. Elected as Côte d'Ivoire's deputy to the French Constituent Assembly in 1945, he persuaded the

French National Assembly to abolish the hated forced labor law. With this success, he, along with other prominent members of SAA, launched the country's first independent political party, the Parti Démocratique de la Côte d'Ivoire (PDCI), which became part of a larger federation of parties in French-speaking West Africa (Rassemblement Démocratique Africain). While the PDCI–RDA initially positioned itself on the left with the support of the French communist party, in 1950 Houphouët-Boigny broke with the communists and became one of France's staunchest supporters in West Africa.

THE CONSTITUTION

The framers of the Ivorian constitution wanted primarily to endow the country with a set of legal institutions that would ensure national unity in an ethnically and regionally diverse nation. In this respect, the constitution of 1959 was designed to limit what the framers viewed as the inherent divisiveness of a parliamentary form of government. Thus, the emphasis was placed on a strong executive.

Following the French Fifth Republic constitution, the framers of the Ivorian constitution sought to limit the range of legislative powers. By clearly defining the areas of legislative authority, the National Assembly could set forth broad guidelines within its domain. The National Assembly consisted of 147 deputies who nominally represented the often ethnically defined districts from which they were elected. The deputies generally let the president initiate specific legislative proposals. Since the legislative process was actually in the hands of the executive, the National Assembly was more of an echo chamber for presidential wishes than an autonomous legislative body.

THE PRESIDENCY

The most important institution of government in Côte d'Ivoire is the presidency. The constitution that was finally adopted in 1960 gave the president preeminence over the legislative and judiciary branches. The president is elected for five years by direct universal suffrage, and he is able to renew his mandate an unlimited number of times. In 1960 Félix Houphouët-Boigny was elected president. In subsequent elections, Houphouët-Boigny was reelected with more than 90 percent of the popular vote.

Houphouët-Boigny came to dominate the country's political system. He used the broad powers provided to him by the constitution to push through legislation without any significant opposition. Thus, there was no real separation of powers between the various branches of government. Power and decision-making were in the hands of the president and the ministers that he had personally selected. Yet, probably more than any other postcolonial African leader, Houphouët-Boigny continued to seek legitimacy from the public of his personalization of power.

Unlike Sékou Touré in Guinea and Kwame Nkrumah in Ghana, both of whom developed their own ideological systems as guides for their constituents in a broader pan-African context, Houphouët-Boigny never explicitly set out to expose his thoughts. He refused to have his thoughts published and disseminated to the masses and publicly disavowed any official cult of personality. Nevertheless, Houphouët-Boigny cultivated a highly personalized image of himself as the father of the Ivorian nation. He reinforced the country's close identification with his person by holding periodic national dialogues. On these occasions, the president invited the nation's major professional groups together and listened to their complaints about the government, social issues, and economic concerns.

THE NATIONAL ASSEMBLY

In the 1980s, the limited political role of the National Assembly changed somewhat. The National Assembly gained more power and influence in decision-making. Under the new electoral rules, 175 deputies, instead of 147, were elected to the assembly. Before the elections, the government had introduced a degree of competition in the selection of party leaders. The members elected in 1980 were more interested in serving their constituency than the hand-picked deputies had been. While the national assembly has not become a real legislative body, it now played a much more important role in reviewing legislation submitted to it by the president than had previously been the case.

SOCIOECONOMIC CONTEXT

More than sixty ethnic groups inhabit the country. There are seven dominant groups: the Akan, mainly in the southeast; the Kru, in the southwest;

the Lagoon and Kwa along the littoral; the Mande, mostly in the northeast and the Senufo throughout the north; and the Lobi in the central regions. Because of the country's economic expansion in the 1960s and 1970s, a large number of non-Ivorian Africans also live in the country, particularly immigrants from Burkina Faso, Mali, and Guinea, as well as smaller numbers of French and Lebanese.

Most of the African immigrants migrated to work in the cocoa and coffee fields in the forest zone in the south; others, however, worked in urban areas as taxi drivers, day laborers, and domestics. In the countryside, the workers were essential to the economic success of the cocoa industry. Without them, Côte d'Ivoire would not have become the world's leading cocoa exporter.

Cocoa, coffee, and timber are the structural underpinnings of the Ivorian economy and postcolonial state. These three commodities became the main source of income for the state. For cocoa and coffee exports, the state absorbed into its budget the profitable difference between the lower prices paid to rural producers set by the government and higher world prices for the commodities. For the peasantry, the price was fixed in early 1960s with little variation. Much of the surplus acquired by the state was used in the development of the country's infrastructure and the development and expansion of state-owned enterprises.

POLITICAL CRISIS AND INSTITUTIONAL REFORMS

After two decades of rapid economic expansion due largely to exports of cocoa and timber, the economy entered a prolonged crisis. The crisis was precipitated by a sharp drop in cocoa prices in the late 1970s and an increasingly burdensome foreign debt that the country had accumulated during the period of rapid economic growth. In the 1980s, as the economic crisis deepened, the International Monetary Fund (IMF), the World Bank, and popular forces demanded economic and political reforms. Reluctantly, President Houphouët-Boigny introduced a number of changes in the early 1990s. First, he introduced new electoral rules intended to open the political process to the opposition and allow for some degree of democratization. Second, he attempted to decentralize decision-making further by creating municipal governments. Before 1980, there had been only two municipalities,

Abidjan and Bouaké. Afterwards, there were over one hundred recognized municipal governments. Finally, in 1990 President Houphouët-Boigny appointed Alassane Ouattara as prime minister to manage the day-to-day affairs of the country. Ouattara, an economic specialist at the IMF, was brought in to restructure the economy.

Despite the efforts on the part of the Houphouët-Boigny regime to shore up its legitimacy by introducing institutional reforms, the economic situation in the country continued to deteriorate. In the early part of the 1990s, the international donor community forced the government to take drastic steps to manage its huge external debt. In the spring of 1990, the government announced a series of draconian economic measures, all at the expense of the voters accommodated by the preceding political reforms. First, the price paid to cocoa producers would be reduced from 400 French West African francs (4 French francs [FF]) to 200 French West African francs (2 FF); thus, for the first time in twenty years, the price paid to rural producers had been changed. Second, a major reform of the public sector would begin, with the main objective of reducing its bloated numbers. Third, under pressure from the World Bank and the IMF, the process of privatization of the public sector firms would be accelerated. Finally, public and private sector employees would be required to take a cut in pay.

These reforms provoked a social and political reaction. People affected by the budget cuts took to the streets. Faced with a social crisis bordering on open rebellion, President Houphouët-Boigny made a number of concessions to the protesters. The austerity program would not be implemented. Multiparty elections would be permitted during the upcoming presidential election in the fall of 1990, and the government would recognize the principle of freedom of political association. Houphouët-Boigny won reelection. By this time, however, he was nearly ninety years old. He would survive in office for only more three years. Following his death, Henri Konan Bedié, the president of the National Assembly, replaced him. The succession process had been prepared with a 1990 revision of the constitution, which stipulated that in case of death of the president, the president of the National Assembly would assume his office until the next scheduled elections.

THE PRESIDENCY OF HENRI KONAN BEDIÉ

As successor, Konan Bedié had to not only continue the changes introduced under Houphouët-Boigny, but also establish his own political authority as president. He adopted a hard line against the country's opposition forces, which were led by Ouattara and Laurent Gbagbo. Ouattara led the Rassemblement des républicains (RDR), concentrated largely in the north, and Ggabo headed the Ivorian Popular Front (FPI), largely concentrated in the center-west and in Abidjan. During the 1995 elections, the opposition boycotted the elections, and Bedié was elected with the unlikely total of 98 percent of the vote. He then set about to change the constitution in order to reinforce the powers of the president and to prevent the former prime minister, Alassane Ouattara, from running against him. He relied on the strident and dangerous strategy of dividing the country into native and non-native Ivorians. For example, he claimed that Ouattara was not an Ivorian since his father was supposedly from neighboring Burkina Faso.

Bedié's government forced through a change in the country's laws concerning foreigners, essentially taking away the rights of outsiders to participate in elections and to own property. Bedie's shift toward a more restrictive position on citizenship initially appears paradoxical. The PDCI had relied on the exploitation of foreigners in elections in the past and had even benefited from their votes in the 1993 election. Yet, Bedié's regime promoted the concept of *Ivoiritié*, and it restricted the rights of foreign workers in the country. Northern Ivorians viewed the anti-immigrant campaign, directly mostly at Muslims from Burkina Faso and Mali, as an attack on them. *Ivoirité* was viewed as a strategy by ethnic groups in the south—notably the Bedie ethnic community, the Baoulé—to monopolize power by defining Northerners as non-Ivorian. Efforts to deny Ouattara citizenship were also interpreted in this way.

Bedié's ethnic strategy of *Ivoirité* failed to keep him in power, however. On December 24, 1999, for the first time, the military seized power from a civilian-elected government. Over the next two years, Côte d'Ivoire experienced a succession of crises: the ousting of the military leader of the December 1999 coup, Robert Guei; the election of Laurent Gbagbo as president; acts of ethnic cleansing by the military against northerners, and a failed attempt at national reconciliation between the country's different ethnic and religious groups. In September 2002, a bloody mutiny within the military resulted in the death of the former military ruler Guei and hundreds of other Ivorians, precipitating a civil war.

LAURENT GBAGBO'S DIVIDED HOUSE

The 2006 president of Côte d'Ivoire presided over a divided country embroiled in a stalemated civil war resulting from the intensification of ethnic identities over the preceding decade. Following the murder of General Guei and the mutiny by northern military officers, violence erupted between the north and the south. The prospects of a long and bloody civil war appeared imminent; the conflict did not materialize, however, because France intervened. French troops inserted themselves between the north, led by mutinied officers, and the south, led by the remains of the country's military. Violent skirmishes erupted, mostly in the western part of the country. Over the previous two years, France and other international parties had undertaken initiatives to bring the conflict to an end. The peace agreements negotiated before 2006 were not respected, however. All parties eventually agreed to a new reconciliation agreement spearheaded by President Thabo Mbeki of South Africa. Under this agreement, forces in the north were supposed to lay down their arms and reintegrate into the military. Open presidential elections scheduled to take place in October 2006 promised to determine decisively whether the country would take the road towards reconciliation and stability or sink into a prolonged civil war.

See also **Colonial Policies and Practices; Gbagbo, Laurent Koudou; Houphouët-Boigny, Félix; International Monetary Fund; Mbeki, Thabo; Touré, Sékou; United Nations; World Bank.**

BIBLIOGRAPHY

Baulin, Jacques. *La Politique Interieur d'Houphouët-Boigny*. Paris: Eurafor Press, 1982.

Chappell, David A. "The Nation as Frontier: Ethnicity and Clientelism in Ivorian History." *The International Journal of African Historical Studies* 22 (1989): 686–689.

Crook, Richard C. "Winning Coalitions and Ethno-Regional Politics: The Failure of the Opposition in the 1990 and 1995 Elections in Côte d' Ivoire." *African Affairs* 96 (1997): 215–242.

Laporte, Myrielle. *La pensée sociale de Felix Houphouët-Boigny, Le président de la Republique de la Côte d' Ivoire*. Bordeaux: Centre d'Etudes d'Afrique Noire, 1970.

Médard, J. F. "La regulation socio-politique." In *Etat et Bourgeoisie en Côte d' Ivoire*, eds. Y. A. Faure and J. F. Médard. Paris: Karthala, 1982.

Toungara, Jean-Maddox. "The Apotheosis of Côte d' Ivoire's Nana Houphouët-Boigny." *Journal of Modern African Studies* 28, no.1 (1990).

Woods, Dwayne. "Ethno-Regional Demands, Symbolic and Redistributive Politics: Sugar Complexes in the North of the Ivory Coast." *Journal of Ethnic and Racial Studies* 12 (1990): 470–488.

Woods, Dwayne. "The Politicization of Teachers' Associations in the Côte d' Ivoire." *African Studies Review* 39 (1996): 113–129.

Woods, Dwayne. "The Tragedy of the Cocoa Pod: Rent-Seeking, Ethnic, and Land Conflicts in Ivory Coast." *Journal of Modern African Studies* 41, no. 4 (2003): 641–645.

Zolberg, Aristide. *One-Party Government in the Ivory Coast.* Princeton, NJ: Princeton University Press, 1964.

DWAYNE WOODS

CREDIT, PERSONAL. *See* **Debt and Credit: Entrustment.**

CREOLE LANGUAGES. *See* **Languages: Creoles and Pidgins.**

CREOLES.

Creoles are a highly diverse set of ethnic groups and cultures that have emerged as a result of contact between peoples brought by slave trade and slavery throughout the world. Between the sixteenth and eighteenth centuries, the term "Creole" (from the Latin *creare*, to raise) designated—in the African context—any person who was native-born and raised but of foreign or non-African ancestry. Over time, the term has been broadened to refer to any peoples with some mix of African and non-African racial, cultural, or linguistic heritage. This broader definition is more appropriate than the narrow, linguistic definition of Creoles as those who speak a Creole language as a mother tongue, since Creole languages may disappear even when a Creole population remains.

Creole populations are found on islands where there was slavery, in the south of the United States, in some Latin American societies and on many coasts of Africa, since it was there that African populations first came into contact with European, American, and Arab settlers, merchants, soldiers, missionaries, convicts, and administrators. The importance of contacts between highly diverse cultures in the genesis of Creole populations makes this a useful criterion for distinguishing six major Creole groups.

PORTUGUESE CREOLES

Portuguese Creoles, or Luso-Africans, also known as *filhos da terra* (native born), emerged during the late fifteenth century as a result of Portuguese settlement and trade in three distinct loci: the Cape Verde—Upper Guinea Coast; the Bight of Bénin—Angola; and the Zambezi River—Mozambique Coast. A scarcity of human and financial resources made miscegenation with local populations a tactical necessity for Portuguese and Afro-Portuguese trade intermediaries, known as *lançados* in the Upper Guinea Coast, *pombeiros* in Angola, and *prazeros* in Mozambique. By speaking Portuguese or Portuguese-based Creoles, creating markets for Portuguese goods and new foods, such as maize and manioc, ostensibly following Roman Catholicism, propounding Western-style education, wearing European dress, and other practices, the mixed or mestizo offspring of these unions formed the nuclei of Creole communities. Creole intermediaries served as brokers of Portuguese culture and commerce, even though some of the original settlers were actually Spanish, French, Italian, Jewish, and German by origin, and even when many Creole traders were, for long periods, outside of the crown's control.

In Cape Verde, education, cultural proximity to the Portuguese, and physical resistance to tropical diseases made the Creole offspring of Europeans and slaves from Senegambia, Guinea, and the Gold Coast (present-day Ghana) ideal employees in Portuguese firms and administration throughout Portugal's African colonies.

Of the Creole settlements scattered in ports and urban centers along the Upper Guinea Coast from the Senegal River to Sierra Leone, only those in Guinea-Bissau, which were administered from Cape Verde, were substantial enough to justify

528

Portuguese claims when the coast was partitioned among colonial powers between 1870 and 1890. Although some Creoles of Cape Verde and Guinea-Bissau opposed independence from Portugal, most of the Creole elite were catalysts behind the armed struggle for independence and dominated the state apparatus in Guinea-Bissau until a coup in 1980.

The populations of São Tomé, Príncipe, and Annobón are mostly descended from slaves from Angola, Kongo, and coastal chiefdoms along the Bight of Bénin, and from traders, Jews, and convicts from Spain and Portugal. Beginning in 1515, a series of royal decrees emancipated sections of the African population, who assimilated to Portuguese culture and quickly gained economic influence. The culture, language, and ethnic identification of these Creoles are substantially more "African" than their Cape Verdean counterparts, since they experienced only limited Portuguese influence between the late sixteenth century and the mid-nineteenth century, following the exodus of Portuguese settlers due to slave revolts.

In Angola, Creole populations are concentrated in coastal urban centers from Cabinda to Namibe (formerly Moçâmedes), where *pombeiros* of mestizo, Brazilian, and African descent traded and had their greatest influence in the late eighteenth and early nineteenth centuries. Important pro-independence activists, Angolan Creoles continue to dominate the major political party and to exert considerable influence on national, political, and economic affairs.

The *prazeros*, who operated crown-granted land and trade concessions for a limited period, or *prazo*, along the Zambezi River in Mozambique, were entrepreneurs of Portuguese, Indian, and African origin who intermarried with local women to trade and obtain land. Although an important Portuguese influence in the second half of the seventeenth century, Creole *prazeros* and their culture were effectively eliminated by a series of wars between 1830 and 1911, as the Portuguese established control over the interior of Mozambique.

BLACK AMERICAN CREOLES
Black American settlers formed the nucleus of the Creole populations of Sierra Leone, Liberia, and scattered populations along the Gold Coast. Sierra Leonean Creoles, about forty-five thousand in 1980, are the descendants of "recaptives," slaves emancipated from slave ships by the British navy in the early 1800s. These were heavily influenced by free black Americans from Jamaica and Nova Scotia who had settled in the same area in 1792. Under colonial rule, Creoles held the status of British subjects and were concentrated in Freetown and neighboring agricultural villages, which were administered separately from the rest of the Sierra Leone colony. In the late nineteenth century they occupied many senior civil service posts, but by the twentieth century "race" increasingly became the basis for opportunities in the British Empire, and Creoles were relegated to subordinate positions and allowed only limited political representation. Compared with other ethnic groups, however, Creoles dominated political and social affairs in the country. As well-educated, Western-oriented elites, Sierra Leone Creoles were employed as civil servants, missionaries, and other professionals, and as merchants and entrepreneurs for European commercial enterprises throughout coastal west Africa, where they were instrumental in disseminating Christianity, education, Pan-Africanism, and Western ideas throughout the nineteenth century.

In Liberia, the descendants of over sixteen thousand free black Americans from the southern United States and almost six thousand African slaves freed by the British and American navies between 1822 and 1892 form a "nontribal" Creole or Americo-Liberian population that numbered about forty-three thousand in the 1974 census. Concentrated in coastal areas, the Creoles once enjoyed numerous privileges but have been in decline since 1980, when they lost control of the presidency in a coup.

FRENCH CREOLES
French Creoles are found on the islands of Mauritius, Rodrigues, and the Seychelles, as well as in the French territory of Réunion and, in small numbers, in Madagascar. The islands of Mauritius, Réunion, and Seychelles were uninhabited at the time of their colonization, which made them fertile terrains for processes of creolization. Slavery was the matrix of these processes. On these islands, French settlers introduced slaves from East Africa and Madagascar in the eighteenth century. Creolization processes were accelerated and complicated

A Creole woman works in a tobacco field in Arsenal, north of the Mauritian capital, Port-Louis, September 2000. Creoles, a mixed-raced community mostly descendents of African slaves, make up 27 percent of the tiny Indian Ocean island's multiracial society. © AP IMAGES

with the abolition of slavery which, in each island, led to the migration of indentured laborers and traders from India and China, who settled and sometimes intermarried with the island's inhabitants. In Mauritius in the 1980s, a trans-ethnic coalition gave voice for the first time to the *Kreol* population, the descendants of slaves. There have been attempts to make Kreol a national language along with the other national languages, Hindi, Chinese, French, and English.

In the Seychelles most of the population consists of Creoles descended from French, some British settlers, and African slaves freed from Arab dhows by the British navy in the nineteenth century. Small numbers of Chinese, Indians, and Malay immigrants, working mostly as traders and shopkeepers, contributed only minimally to the Creole population. In Réunion, the population is deeply mixed—groups came from Madagascar, Mozambique, South India, South China, Gujarat,

France, and Comoros—and no ethnic group dominates in number. Local power is in the hands of local political parties with representatives of different groups, but there are deep social inequalities inherited from colonial racial hierarchy.

DUTCH CREOLES: COLOUREDS OR CAPE COLOUREDS

The South African Cape "Coloureds" emerged under the Dutch East India Company in the seventeenth and eighteenth centuries through the mixture of free persons of European and Khoesan stock with Asians from Malaysia, Sri Lanka, Indonesia, and India, and African slaves from Madagascar and southern Africa. This largest group of racially mixed South Africans lives mostly near Cape Town, Port Elizabeth, and rural areas of western Cape of Good Hope Province, although smaller migrant populations are also found in Namibia and other southern African countries. A Dutch-based Creole, Afrikaans, is the first language of about 90 percent of the Creole population.

A similar, though smaller Afrikaans-speaking Dutch Creole group are the Basters of Rehoboth or Rehobothers (16,500 in 1970) of Namibia, who are descended from Nama women and Afrikaner trekkers who moved from the Cape Colony in the 1860s.

BRITISH CREOLES

A small population of a few thousand British Creoles, known as Fernandinos, live in the island of Bioko (formerly Fernando Póo) in Equatorial Guinea. Ceded by Portugal to Spain in 1778, Bioko became a refuge for slaves liberated by the British until 1858, when it was transferred to the Spanish and administered from Cuba. Liberated slaves from Sierra Leone and Cuba intermarried with settled immigrants from Cameroon, Ghana, Sierra Leone, and Nigeria in former British West Africa. Their Creole offspring became cocoa planters, and the island of Bioko became the best-developed region of Equatorial Guinea. Fernandinos lost some of their status when the Spanish acquired the island.

ARAB CREOLES

Arab Creoles, mostly of mixed Arab, Malagasy, Melano-Polynesian, and African descent, make up over 90 percent of the 484,000 (1986) inhabitants of the Comoro Islands. The first Melano-Polynesian settlers probably came in the sixth century, followed by immigrants from Africa, Madagascar, Indonesia, Persia, and Arabia around 1600; Portuguese in the early sixteenth century; and Dutch, French, Chinese, and Indians afterward. These recent European and Asian settlers have intermarried with the Creole population to a lesser extent. Creoles practice Islam.

COMMON FEATURES OF CREOLE CULTURE

Many of Africa's islands, with the exception of the Comoros and Bioko, were uninhabited at discovery and are now populated almost exclusively by Creoles. Creole languages predominate on all of the islands and are spoken as national languages in parts of the mainland: Guinea-Bissau, Sierra Leone, Liberia, and South Africa. On islands where their culture and populations dominate, Creoles occupy all levels of the social hierarchy from plantation workers to elites. On the mainland, in contrast, cultural proximity to foreign dominators afforded Creoles economic and political power beyond their meager numbers, contributing to a heightened sense of Creole identity and the formation of political parties. In these places, Creoles eschew agriculture but maximize their ambiguous cultural positions as entrepreneurs, middlemen, and brokers in trade and administration. Many allied themselves to colonial rulers, but some also fought for independence and afterward assumed positions of power. As a rule, most Creoles gradually lost power after independence as political imperatives were transferred to other "more African" ethnic groups of the interior.

Unlike other African ethnic groups, Creoles are more of an achieved than ascribed ethnic status. As a result, Creole groups have easily expanded through various creolization processes. One such process has occurred mostly on the islands, where elements of Creole culture have suffused and come to dominate national popular culture.

A second process has been accretion around a Creole nucleus in urban centers of others seeking "civilized" or "assimilated" status to distinguish themselves from "indigenous" peoples of the mainland interior, with separate status, administration, courts, and other institutions. By adopting the language, dress, technology, residential architecture, culture, and religious practices associated with Creoles, non-Creoles also identify themselves outwardly with this community.

There has been, since the 1990s, a renewed interest in the processes of creolization, notably among artists and writers. Postcolonial theorists have sought to explore the ways in which Creole identities are constituted and performed and what they say about zones of contact and conflict, about transculturality and intercultural creativity. The revision of colonial and postcolonial history has opened up new areas of exploration in cross and transcultural phenomena, with Creole cultures offering a singular experience. Diasporic formations are now often studied as "creolized" processes as well as oceanic formations (as in "The Black Atlantic").

See also **Diasporas; Ethnicity; Freetown; Languages: Creoles and Pidgins.**

BIBLIOGRAPHY

Enwezor, Okwui, et al., eds. *Créolité and Creolization: Documenta 11*. Ostfildern-Ruit: Hatje Cantz, 2003.

Erasmus, Zimitri, ed. *Colored by History, Shaped by Place: New Perspectives on Colored Identities in Cape Town*. Colorado Springs, CO: International Academic Publishers, 2001.

Houbert, Jean. "The Indian Ocean Creole Islands: Geopolitics and Decolonisation." *Journal of Modern African Studies* 30, no. 3 (1992): 465–484.

Isaacman, A. *The Africanization of an European Institution: The Zambezi Prazos, 1750–1902*. Madison: University of Wisconsin Press, 1972.

Jayasuriya, Shihan de Silva, and Richard Pankhurst, eds. *The African Diaspora in the Indian Ocean*. Trenton, NJ: Africa World Press, 2003.

Porter, A. *Creoledom: A Study of the Development of Freetown Society*. London: Oxford University Press, 1963.

Rodney, Walter. *A History of the Upper Guinea Coast, 1545 to 1800*. Oxford: Clarendon Press, 1970.

Smith, Vanessa, ed. *Islands in History and Representation*. Londres: Routledge, 2003.

Uche, Kalu Okoro. "Ebony Kinship: Americo-Liberians, Sierra Leone Creoles, and the Indigenous African Population, 1820–1900." Ph.D. diss. Howard University, 1974.

Vaughan, Megan. *Creating the Creole Island: Slavery in Eighteenth Century*. Durham, NC: Duke University Press, 2005.

Vergès, Françoise. "The Island of Wandering Souls: Processes of Creolization, Politics of Emancipation and the Problematic of Absence on Reunion Island." In *Islands in History and Representation*, ed. Rod Edmond and Vanessa Smith. London: Routledge, 2003.

Wyse, A. J. G. *The Krio of Sierra Leone: An Interpretative History.* London: Hurst, in association with the International African Institute, 1989.

EVE L. CROWLEY

CROPS. *See* Agriculture; Plants.

Reverend Samuel Ajayi Crowther (1806–1891). Crowther, a linguist, was the first African-Anglican bishop in Nigeria. He translated the Bible into the Yoruba language and published a Yoruba grammar book. © STAPLETON COLLECTION/ CORBIS

CROWTHER, SAMUEL AJAYI (1806–1891). Born in Osogun, near Eruwa in Oyo State of Nigeria, Samuel Ajayi Crowther was taken prisoner and enslaved there in early 1821. Traded down the coast to Lagos during the years 1821 and 1822, he was loaded onto a Brazilian schooner on April 7, 1822, rescued at sea the same day by the British antislavery squadron, and taken to Freetown, Sierra Leone. There he was baptized in 1825 and educated by the Christian Missionary Society (CMS). Crowther was taken to London in 1826; the next year he became a foundation student at the CMS's Fourah Bay College in Freetown. He began to study Yoruba, among other languages, and to preach in it. Crowther joined the 1841 Niger Expedition, and was ordained in 1843. He served as a pioneering member of the CMS Yoruba Mission to Badagry in his Yoruba homeland in 1844 and, in 1846, to Abeokuta, where he located his mother.

Crowther was a principal figure in the translation of the Bible into Yoruba, a most remarkable linguistic and literary feat. A well-known traveler, he joined the 1854 Niger Expedition, exploring the Benue River up to Ibi. In 1857 he accompanied another British expedition up to Jebba. Twice, in 1859 and 1871, when the expedition ship ran aground at Jebba, he traveled down to Lagos on foot through Ogbomosho, Oyo, and Ibadan.

Crowther was appointed leader of the Niger Mission in 1857 and subsequently opened mission stations at Akassa, Onitsha, Lokoja, and Idah. In 1864 he was consecrated Bishop of Western Equatorial Africa in Regions beyond the Queen's Dominions with his seat in Lagos; he had no jurisdiction in the Yoruba country where European missionaries operated, but he did supervise Church of England missions in Liberia and Rio Pongas, among other places. He opened another mission in Bonny for the Niger Delta. The Niger Mission was dependent on the operation of the mail steamer that attracted small-scale traders from Freetown and Lagos. The irregular schedule of the steamer made the work of supervising the mission very difficult; problems with the steamer were also why the staff of both the Niger and the Niger Delta missions in the 1860s and 1870s were exclusively Africans (recruited mostly from Freetown), who did not need to go regularly on leaves abroad. The missionaries cooperated with the traders from Freetown and Lagos to open up the Lower Niger Valley to European trade. The mission was hailed among London missionary circles as a great success in the 1870s but, with the rising tide of imperialism, Sir George Goldie and other major British traders came to see African traders as rivals and African missionaries as obstacles.

From the 1850s on, Crowther was the acknowledged leader of the up-and-coming African-educated elite, not only in Nigeria but throughout western Africa. European missionaries, very critical of Crowther's administration, entered the Niger Mission, and in 1890 Crowther was forced to resign. Before he died on New Year's Eve 1891, in Lagos, he made plans to reconstitute the Niger Delta Mission as an autonomous pastorate under his son, Archdeacon Dandeson Crowther. Eventually, in 1898, this pastorate was reconciled with the CMS.

See also **Christianity; Sierra Leone: Society and Cultures.**

BIBLIOGRAPHY

Ajayi, J. F. Ade. *A Patriot to the Core: Samuel Ajayi Crowther.* Ibadan, Nigeria, and St. Heller, Jersey, U.K.: Spectrum Books in association with Safari Books, 2001.

Decorvet, Jeanne. *Samuel Ajayi Crowther: Un père de l'église en Afrique noire.* La Côte-aux-Fées, Switzerland: Neuchâtel, 1992.

Page, Jesse. *The Black Bishop: Samuel Adjai Crowther.* Westport, CT: Greenwood Press, 1979.

J. F. ADE AJAYI

CULTIGENS. *See* **Plants.**

CULTURE, POPULAR. *See* **Popular Culture.**

CUMMINGS-JOHN, CONSTANCE AGATHA (1918–2000). An educator, a politician, and the first black African female mayor of an African capital, Constance Agatha Cummings-John was born into the prominent middle-class Horton family in Freetown, Sierra Leone. Cummings-John's sympathies lay with the grassroots. Through her contacts with prominent Pan-Africanists and black leaders like I.T.A. Wallace-Johnson, George Padmore, Paul Robeson, Jomo Kenyatta, and Nwafor Orizu in Britain and the United States in the 1930s and 1940s, she became an ardent Pan-Africanist, nationalist, prominent educator, and influential leader of women's emancipation in Sierra Leone and West Africa.

In 1938 she was elected the first woman city councilor in Freetown under the political banner of the radical mass-based West African Youth League. After World War II, she spent five years in the United States, returning to Sierra Leone in 1951, where she simultaneously established the Eleanor Roosevelt Preparatory School for Girls, co-founded the Sierra Leone Women's Movement, and became an executive officer in the Sierra Leone People's Party (SLPP). Despite her victory in the general election of 1957, she bowed to pressure to resign her seat in the legislature during a court trial initiated by the opposition party. Nevertheless, her enduring popularity influenced the SLPP to appoint her mayor of Freetown in 1966, a position she held until a military coup d'etat the following year forced her into exile in Britain where she remained a committed to politics and black immigrant welfare activities.

See also **Education, School; Freetown; Kenyatta, Jomo.**

BIBLIOGRAPHY

Cummings-John, Constance A. *Constance Agatha Cummings-John: Memoirs of a Krio Leader*, ed. LaRay Denzer. Ibadan: Sam Bookman for Humanities Research Center, 1995.

Denzer, LaRay. "The Influence of Pan-Africanism in the Political Career of Constance A. Cummings-John." In *Pan-African Biography*, ed. Robert Hill. Los Angeles: African Studies Center, University of California at Los Angeles, 1987.

Denzer, LaRay. "Women in Freetown Politics, 1914–1961: A Preliminary Study." *Africa* 57, no. 4 (1987): 439–456.

LARAY DENZER

CURRENCIES. *See* **Money.**

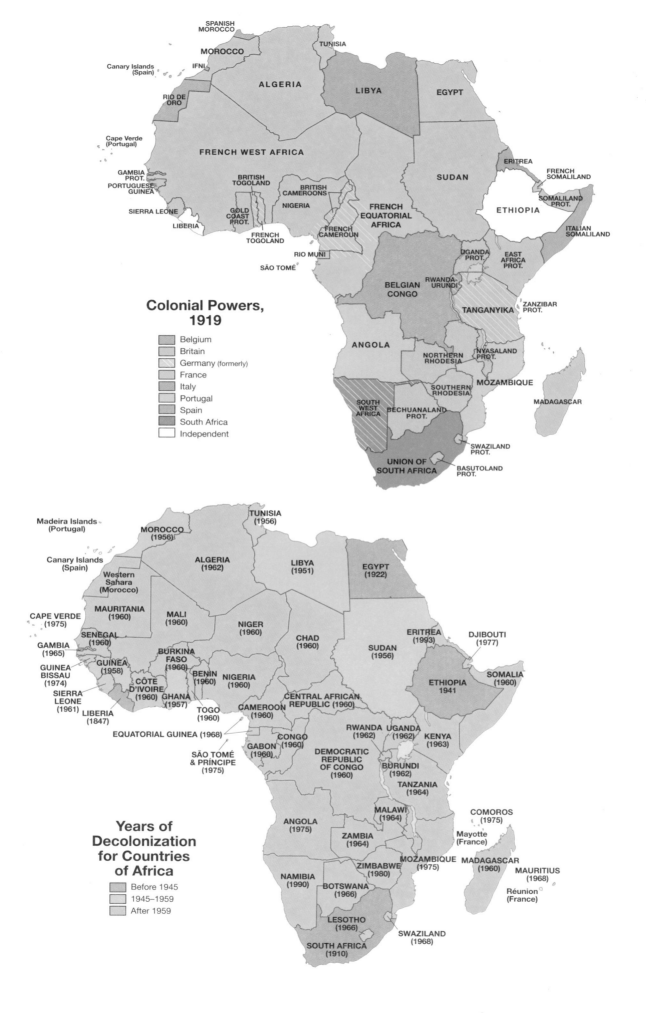

Colonial Powers, 1919

- Belgium
- Britain
- Germany (formerly)
- France
- Italy
- Portugal
- Spain
- South Africa
- Independent

SPANISH MOROCCO
MOROCCO
TUNISIA
Canary Islands (Spain)
IFNI
ALGERIA
LIBYA
EGYPT
RIO DE ORO
Cape Verde (Portugal)
FRENCH WEST AFRICA
SUDAN
ERITREA
FRENCH SOMALILAND
GAMBIA PROT.
PORTUGUESE GUINEA
BRITISH TOGOLAND
BRITISH CAMEROONS
SOMALILAND PROT.
SIERRA LEONE
GOLD COAST PROT.
NIGERIA
FRENCH EQUATORIAL AFRICA
ETHIOPIA
LIBERIA
FRENCH TOGOLAND
FRENCH CAMEROUN
ITALIAN SOMALILAND
RIO MUNI
SÃO TOMÉ
UGANDA PROT.
EAST AFRICA PROT.
BELGIAN CONGO
RWANDA-URUNDI
TANGANYIKA
ZANZIBAR PROT.
ANGOLA
NORTHERN RHODESIA
NYASALAND PROT.
MOZAMBIQUE
MADAGASCAR
SOUTH WEST AFRICA
BECHUANALAND PROT.
SOUTHERN RHODESIA
SWAZILAND PROT.
UNION OF SOUTH AFRICA
BASUTOLAND PROT.

Years of Decolonization for Countries of Africa

- Before 1945
- 1945–1959
- After 1959

Madeira Islands (Portugal)
TUNISIA (1956)
MOROCCO (1956)
Canary Islands (Spain)
ALGERIA (1962)
LIBYA (1951)
EGYPT (1922)
Western Sahara (Morocco)
CAPE VERDE (1975)
MAURITANIA (1960)
MALI (1960)
NIGER (1960)
CHAD (1960)
ERITREA (1993)
DJIBOUTI (1977)
SENEGAL (1960)
SUDAN (1956)
GAMBIA (1965)
BURKINA FASO (1960)
GUINEA BISSAU (1974)
GUINEA (1958)
BENIN (1960)
NIGERIA (1960)
SOMALIA (1960)
SIERRA LEONE (1961)
CÔTE D'IVOIRE (1960)
GHANA (1957)
TOGO (1960)
ETHIOPIA 1941
LIBERIA (1847)
CAMEROON (1960)
CENTRAL AFRICAN REPUBLIC (1960)
EQUATORIAL GUINEA (1968)
CONGO (1960)
GABON (1960)
RWANDA (1962)
UGANDA (1962)
KENYA (1963)
SÃO TOMÉ & PRÍNCIPE (1975)
DEMOCRATIC REPUBLIC OF CONGO (1960)
BURUNDI (1962)
TANZANIA (1964)
COMOROS (1975)
ANGOLA (1975)
MALAWI (1964)
Mayotte (France)
ZAMBIA (1964)
MADAGASCAR (1960)
MAURITIUS (1968)
ZIMBABWE (1980)
MOZAMBIQUE (1975)
Réunion (France)
NAMIBIA (1990)
BOTSWANA (1966)
LESOTHO (1966)
SWAZILAND (1968)
SOUTH AFRICA (1910)